Frommer's 96

FRUGAL TRAVELER'S GUIDES

Europe

FROM $50 A DAY

by
Alice Garrard
Dan Levine
Herbert Bailey Livesey
Nikolaus Lorey
Darwin Porter & Danforth Prince
Patricia Tunison Preston & John J. Preston
Beth Reiber

Macmillan • USA

MACMILLAN TRAVEL

A Simon & Schuster Macmillan Company
1633 Broadway
New York, NY 10019

ISBN 0-02-860635-3
ISSN 0730-1510

Editor: Ron Boudreau
Map Editor: Douglas Stallings
Production Editor: Kathleen Varanese
Design by Michele Laseau
Digital cartography by John Decamillas/Ortelius Design

SPECIAL SALES

Bulk purchases (10+ copies) of Frommer's Travel Guides are available to corporations at special discounts. The Special Sales Department can produce custom editions to be used as premiums and/or for sales promotion to suit individual needs. Existing editions can be produced with custom cover imprints such as corporate logos. For more information write to: Special Sales, Simon & Schuster, 1230 Avenue of the Americas, New York, NY 10020.

Manufactured in the United States of America.

Contents

5 Athens   103

by Dan Levine

12   Edinburgh   375

by Dan Levine

13   Florence   403

by Dan Levine

14 Geneva 443

by Nikolaus Lorey

15 Lisbon 471

by Herbert Bailey Livesey

16   London   506

by Dan Levine

17   Madrid   572

by Herbert Bailey Livesey

18   Munich   625

by Beth Reiber

23   Stockholm   853

by Alice Garrard

24   Venice   904

by Dan Levine

25 Vienna   942

by Beth Reiber

Appendix   995

Index   1019

List of Maps

AN INVITATION TO THE READER

When researching this book, the authors discovered many wonderful places—hotels, restaurants, shops, and more. We're sure you'll find others. Please tell us about them so we can share the information with your fellow travelers in upcoming editions. If you were disappointed with a recommendation, we'd love to know that, too. Please write to:

Author (see byline on each chapter)
Frommer's Europe from $50 a Day '96
c/o Macmillan Travel
1633 Broadway
New York, NY 10019

AN ADDITIONAL NOTE

Please be advised that travel information is subject to change at any time—and this is especially true of prices. We therefore suggest that you write or call ahead for confirmation when making travel plans. The authors, editors, and publisher cannot be held responsible for the experiences of readers while traveling. Your safety is important to us, however, so we encourage you to stay alert and be aware of your surroundings. Keep a close eye on cameras, purses, and wallets, all favorite targets of thieves and pickpockets.

WHAT THE SYMBOLS MEAN

✪ Frommer's Favorites

Hotels, restaurants, attractions, and entertainment you should not miss.

⑤ Super-Special Values

Hotels and restaurants that offer great value for your money.

The following symbols refer to the standard amenities available in all rooms:

A/C	air conditioning
TEL	telephone
TV	television
MINIBAR	refrigerator stocked with beverages and snacks

The following abbreviations are used for credit and charge cards:

AE	American Express	EU	Eurocard
CB	Carte Blanche	JCB	Japan Credit Bank
DC	Diners Club	MC	MasterCard
DISC	Discover	V	Visa
ER	enRoute		

Before Leaving Home

by Alice Garrard

Americans have long harbored a love affair with Europe, so much so that 7.5 million of them cross the Atlantic every year to explore its countries, tracing their roots and soaking up the incomparable culture and architecture. What's different these days is that besides discovering the Old World, you'll encounter the New Europe.

Like it or not, the familiar Old World is becoming a more viable political as well as economic entity, with 370 million inhabitants living in 15 countries of the European Union (formerly the European Community)—Portugal, Spain, France, Italy, Greece, Luxembourg, Belgium, the Netherlands, Germany, Austria, Denmark, Britain, Ireland, Finland, and Sweden. (Norway rejected EU membership by referendum in November 1994, as it had in 1972, but it remains integrated in Europe's life and economy.)

With the Common Market quickly metamorphosing into a Single Market, change is afoot, and travelers aren't exempt. Soon you'll no longer have to show your passport at border crossings, except in Great Britain, Ireland, and Denmark; in addition, you'll hear English used more frequently as the lingua franca.

Duty-free shopping still exists—but only until July 1999—so take advantage of it while you can. The value-added tax, which varies from country to country, will become more uniform throughout Europe, at about 15%; of course, you still can get more of this tax refunded (see "Saving Money On . . . Shopping" in Chapter 2).

To make matters even simpler for travelers, there may be a common European currency, probably called the *ecu,* by the year 1999. Think of the time and fees you'll save by skipping currency-exchange windows!

In 1996 European Union members will synchronize their clocks for daylight saving time, setting them one hour ahead on the same day for spring and summer (the last Saturday in March) and setting them one hour back on the same day for autumn and winter (the last Sunday in October).

Yes, times—and certainly prices—have changed since the first edition of this book, *Europe on $5 a Day,* was published in 1957, just as they had changed in 1957 from the days when Arthur Frommer first explored the Continent as a young soldier on leave in the 1940s. This edition, *Europe from $50 a Day,* has been completely revised and redesigned for 1996. However, be assured that it retains the dependable Frommer emphasis: good value for your money. Traveling frugally provides rewarding opportunities for you to mingle with

Europeans on their own turf—in their plazas, pubs, trains, and sometimes homes.

Doing Europe "from $50 a day" means that $50 is the basic amount you'll spend on accommodations and meals *only*; transportation, sightseeing, shopping, evening entertainment, and the like are *not* included. Expect to use about half that amount on accommodations. Obviously, if two of you are traveling together this budget will be easier to achieve—$50 for accommodations and $50 for meals. You can trim travel costs by taking advantage of advance-purchase airfares to Europe, traveling off-season (October through May), planning a relatively short stay (a week to 10 days instead of two weeks or more), and visiting only one country, two at most, per trip.

The first three chapters of this book alert you to travel resources, savings in airfares and rail passes, discounts, and a multitude of possibilities for squeezing the most out of your European holiday. Refer to individual city chapters for specifics, such as when to time your trip, where to stay, what to do, and how to save money once you arrive.

Prices quoted in this guide are obviously subject to change depending on inflation and currency fluctuations. For up-to-date exchange rates, check the business pages of your newspaper, contact a national tourist office, or call an office of Thomas Cook Currency Services (☎ **212/757-6915** in New York, or 071/480-7226 in London).

Bon voyage, feliz viaje, buon viaggio, and happy vagabonding in the new Old World.

1 Sources of Visitor Information

TOURIST OFFICES   Start with the European tourist offices located in the United States (see the Appendix). You're lucky if you live in or very near New York City, because most tourist offices are located there. Some countries also have offices in Chicago, Los Angeles, Beverly Hills, San Francisco, Washington, D.C., or Dallas. If you're in a rush for information, call and ask them to send it right away; otherwise, you may have to wait a couple of weeks for it. Tourist offices are excellent sources of information about weather, currency, destinations, special events, airlines, rail travel, and inexpensive lodgings.

If you're not sure which country or countries you want to visit, you can get a good overview of Europe, thumbnail sketches of each country, and transportation information from the free 60-page *Planning Your Trip to Europe,* with color photos and maps, compiled annually by the 26-nation European Travel Commission. Write to Europe Planner, P.O. Box 1754, New York, NY 10185.

LIBRARIES   Another information source is your public library, where you can find books and magazine articles on your destination(s), as well as literary works by well-known European authors, from Colette to Kazantzakis. For articles, check the *Readers' Guide to Periodical Literature* for the past few years under the name of the countries or cities you plan to visit. You'll find the titles of articles, where and when they were published, and the pages on which they appear.

TRAVEL VIDEOS   Relatively new though growing sources not only of information but of visual inspiration are travel videos. One of these videos shows a country and its people as you'll find them today and can be invaluable in helping travelers choose which regions of a country to visit. One of the best introductions to European travel is still Rick Steves's 80-minute *Europe Through the Back*

Door, filmed on location in 1987. It costs $24.95 (plus $4 shipping) and can be ordered from Small World Productions, P.O. Box 28369, Seattle, WA 98118-1369 (☎ **206/329-7167** for information, or 800/866-7425 to order). The young, congenial, and well-traveled Steves shares tips on everything from crossing the language barrier to using foreign telephones to museum-going as he guides you on a scenic tour through Europe's cities, towns, and landscapes. For specific cities and countries, select one or more of the 18 videos from his ***Travels in Europe with Rick Steves*** series, originally filmed for and aired on public television (check your local TV listings to see if the series is being repeated). Each video contains travel tips, art and cultural history, and out-of-the-way attractions, all presented by Steves in his personable style. The price per video and the contact address are the same as above, though you can also buy a set of the series tapes at a good discount.

Also check local video-rental stores for travel videos. If nothing is available, request a copy of the 800-page 1995–96 edition of the ***Complete Guide to Special Interest Video*** ($19.95) from Video Learning Library, 15838 N. 62nd St., Scottsdale, AZ 85254-1988 (☎ **602/596-9970,** or 800/526-7002). This video guide contains more than 500 travel listings, dozens on Europe alone, as well as such related topics as adventure, birdwatching, fine arts and architecture, language, and railroading. The travel videos run 30 to 90 minutes, are produced by various manufacturers, and may be rented or purchased directly from Video Learning Library.

TRAVEL AGENTS   The services of an agent are free (he or she gets paid through commissions from such travel suppliers as airlines, hotels, cruise lines, and car-rental companies). So take advantage of them to learn about special fares, early-booking discounts, and other special offers in the constantly changing travel business. A good agent can tailor travel plans to the client's objectives, interests, and budget; arrange all manner of international transport, including air, sea, rail, car rental, and motorcoach; help secure travel insurance; and provide information on passport, visa, and exit-tax requirements. For last-minute or complex bookings, an agent may charge for long-distance calls, Telex, fax, or other services made on the client's behalf; ask about this if you think there might be a charge. Also check to see if there are cancellation fees on bookings made through the agency.

Seek out a travel agent much as you would an accountant or financial planner. Ask your friends and co-workers for recommendations. Meet the agent in person and consider the workspace itself, the attitude of the staff, and the agent's willingness to listen to your needs and concerns.

Also look for someone affiliated with at least one of two trade organizations: the **American Society of Travel Agents (ASTA)** or the newer **Association of Retail Travel Agents (ARTA).** ASTA has been around since 1929; its Consumer Affairs Department (☎ **703/739-2782**) handles complaints from consumers about unsatisfactory service by travel agents; ask for Consumer Affairs when you call.

If the letters ctc follow your agent's name, so much the better—it means that he or she is a Certified Travel Counselor, with 18 months of postprofessional training through the **Institute of Certified Travel Agents (ICTA).**

If you're booking a tour, ask the agent if the tour operator is a member of the **United States Tour Operators Association (USTOA),** which has 40 members and a $5-million pool to reimburse consumers if a member company goes bankrupt, leaving travelers high and dry. Also check with your local **Better Business Bureau** to see that the tour operator has a clean record.

Two helpful free booklets that discuss working with travel agents and other consumer travel tips are **"How to Buy Travel,"** available from American Express, and **"Avoiding Travel Problems."** For the latter, send a self-addressed stamped business-size envelope to ASTA World Headquarters, Fulfillment Department, 1101 King St., Alexandria, VA 22314.

CATALOG-ORDER TRAVEL BOOKSTORES   Your investment in this Frommer's budget-oriented guidebook to Europe will repay itself many times over in both the time and the money you'll save. Since the book is comprehensive it also tends to be bulky, so you may want to cut or tear out pertinent chapters to carry with you on your trip or make photocopies of them and leave the book at home. Some travelers take the book, tearing out pages as they go to lighten their load.

If you want more in-depth coverage on a certain city, note that Frommer's publishes individual city as well as country guides for many European destinations—check out the back of this book for a list of titles or visit your nearest bookstore.

Also, get a pocket-size language guide so you'll at least be able to ask directions, understand what you're ordering on a menu, and find the nearest bathroom. Berlitz has an outstanding series, along with its handy *European Menu Reader.*

Most bookstores carry guidebooks and travel phrase books, but if yours doesn't or you prefer a wider selection, as well as maps and travel products, take heart. Around the country are some excellent travel bookstores offering catalogs and mail-order (or phone-order) service: **Book Passage,** 51 Tamal Vista Blvd., Corte Madera, CA 94925 (☎ **415/927-0960,** or 800/321-9785); **The Complete Traveller,** 199 Madison Ave., New York, NY 10016 (☎ **212/685-9007**); **Forsyth Travel Library,** 9154 W. 57th St. (P.O. Box 2975), Shawnee Mission, KS 66201-1375 (☎ **913/384-3440,** or 800/367-7984); **Travel Books & Language Center,** 4931 Cordell Ave., Bethesda, MD 20814 (☎ **301/951-8533,** or 800/220-BOOK); and **The Traveller's Bookstore,** 22 W. 52nd. St., New York, NY 10019 (☎ **212/664-0995,** or 800/755-8728; send $2 for a catalog, free with purchase). All of the above accept major credit and charge cards.

Europe Through the Back Door, P.O. Box C-2009, Edmonds, WA 98020 (☎ **206/771-8303;** fax 206/771-0833), sells offbeat, upbeat books by Rick Steves that make great supplements to *Europe from $50 a Day*; it also has a free resource library for people in the area, arranges tours of Europe, and sells rail passes. **Travels in Europe,** P.O. Box 28369, Seattle, WA 98118-1369 (☎ **206/329-7167,** or 800/866-7425 for orders only; fax 206/329-0269), also sells books by Steves.

For supplemental guides in Canada, contact **Ulysses Bookshop,** 4176 rue St-Denis, Montréal, PQ H2W 2M5 Canada (☎ **514/843-9447;** fax 514/843-9448), or 101 Yorkville Ave., Toronto, ON M5R 1C1 Canada (☎ **416/323-3609**). Their catalog is in English and French.

INTERNATIONAL TRAVEL NEWS   This nonglossy 100-page monthly overseas-travel magazine, also known as *ITN,* features black-and-white photos and a wealth of information for travelers provided by other travelers. Besides candid letters and articles, you'll find updates on news, bargain airfares, tours, hotels, and more. There are also ads for everything from barge cruises in France to day hikes in the Swiss Alps, apartment rentals in London, and foreign-language immersion courses. The classifieds are fun, too—essentially one big information swap. To subscribe, send $16 ($26 outside the U.S.) to *International Travel News,* 520 Calvados Ave., Sacramento, CA 95815 (☎ **800/366-9192** Monday through Friday from 8am to 5pm Pacific time, for credit/charge-card subscriptions only).

CULTURGRAMS   A useful (and little-known) information source is the Culturgram. Each Culturgram, written by a native of the country or an experienced professional who has lived there for more than three years, contains four pages of details on a country's customs, manners, and lifestyle, along with socioeconomic statistics, maps, and addresses of embassies and national tourist offices. Culturgrams are published by the David M. Kennedy Center for International Studies at Brigham Young University in Provo, Utah; they cost $3 each (less if purchased in quantities of six or more) and can be ordered by calling 800/528-6279.

TRAVEL NEWSLETTERS   Worth the subscription investment, these newsletters will whet your appetite for travel and keep you informed about the latest offerings and savings.

Consumer Reports Travel Letter, Subscription Department, P.O. Box 53629, Boulder, CO 80322 (☎ **800/234-1970**), is particularly useful for airfare discounts. It's published monthly, with a yearly subscription price of $39; for two years it's $59.

Travel Companions, P.O. Box 833-F, Amityville, NY 11701 (☎ **516/454-0880;** fax 516/454-0170), is published by Travel Companion Exchange (members receive listings of potential travel buddies; subscribers don't). This newsletter comes out every two months and offers money-saving tips and information on discounts, as well as savings for single travelers. Overnight printing permits it to include many last-minute travel bargains, including summer and holiday hotel discounts and news about airfare wars and discounts that are usually announced on very short notice. A sample copy costs $5; a one-year subscription is $48. Every new subscriber or member receives six back issues, each one containing many European travel tips.

Travel Smart, 40 Beechdale Rd., Dobbs Ferry, NY 10522 (☎ **914/693-8300,** or 800/327-3633), is one of the longest-running travel newsletters. It's filled with ways to save money traveling to and within Europe and elsewhere and can supply useful travel paraphernalia via mail order. This monthly newsletter has an introductory subscription rate of $37; the renewal rate is $44. Write or call for a trial subscription.

TRAVEL ADVISORIES   If you're concerned that travel to a certain country may be dangerous, call the **U.S. Department of State's Citizens Emergency Center** at 202/647-5225 Monday through Friday from 8am to 10pm and Saturday from 9am to 3pm; other times, call 202/647-4000 and ask to speak with the citizens' emergency duty officer. The center can also assist you if a relative has an emergency situation overseas.

The **Travel Advice Unit,** part of the Foreign Office, gives British travelers advice on security and safety when traveling to foreign countries. Call 071/270-4129 Monday through Friday from 9:30am to 4pm.

2 Passports & Other Required Documents

SECURING & RENEWING A U.S. PASSPORT   Passport applications are available from authorized post offices, clerks of court, or passport agencies. You can also request an application by mail—Form DSP-11 for a new passport, Form DSP-82 for a renewal—from **Passport Services,** Office of Correspondence, Department of State, 1111 19th St. NW, Washington, DC 20522-1705. The back of the application gives the addresses of 13 agencies that can process the applications, including those in Boston, Chicago, Honolulu, Houston, Los Angeles, Miami, New Orleans, New York City, Philadelphia, San Francisco, Seattle, Stamford (Conn.), and Washington, D.C.

Note: Lines are long in these agencies, and you can get a passport more quickly and easily from a post office or clerk of court's office (processing usually takes four weeks in either case).

Your passport application must be accompanied by proof of U.S. citizenship: Your old passport, a certified copy of your birth certificate complete with registrar's seal, a report of your birth abroad, or your naturalized citizenship documents. A driver's license, employee identification card, military ID, or student ID with photo is also acceptable.

The application must be accompanied by two identical recent 2- by 2-inch photos, either color or black-and-white with a white background. Look in the Yellow Pages of your telephone book for places that take passport photos and expect them to be expensive (up to $9 for two).

First-time applicants age 18 and older pay $65 ($55 plus a $10 first-time processing fee); for those under 18 the fee is $40 ($30 plus a $10 first-time fee). Parents or guardians may apply for children under 13, presenting two photos for each child. Children 14 and older must apply in person. Anyone 18 years or older who has an expired passport issued no more than 12 years ago may reapply by mail, submitting the old document with new photos and pink renewal form DSP-82. You must send a check or money order for $55; there's no additional processing fee. Passports for adults are valid for 10 years; children's passports, for 5 years.

If your passport is lost or stolen, submit form DSP-64 along with a new application in person to reapply. There's a $10 processing fee.

The booklet **"Your Trip Abroad"** (publication no. 044-000-02335-1) provides general information about passports and is available for $1.25 from the U.S. Government Printing Office, Superintendent of Documents, P.O. Box 371954, Pittsburgh, PA 15250-7954. Call to verify the price and availability (☎ **202/512-1800** Monday through Friday from 8am to 4pm eastern time; fax 202/512-2250).

To hear recorded passport information, to report a lost or stolen passport, or to amend a passport, call 202/647-0518.

VISAS   Most European countries do not require a visa for American or Canadian citizens. Most European Union countries require only an identity card for citizens of other EU members.

The U.S. Department of State's Bureau of Consular Affairs publishes a 20-page booklet called **"Foreign Entry Requirements."** Its information includes each

---

Precaution: Document Your Documents

Before leaving home, make two backup photocopies of each document you plan to carry—your passport (copy the inside page with your photo), airline ticket, driver's license, International Driving Permit, youth-hostel card, prescriptions (in generic, not brand-name, form), and traveler's check numbers. Leave one set of copies with a friend or relative at home and put the other in your luggage separate from the originals (preferably in your carry-on luggage). Should the documents be lost or stolen, you'll have invaluable backup information to replace them or, in some cases, to get out of Europe and back home.

country's entry requirements—from passport to onward or return ticket, to proof of sufficient funds—and usually the phone number of the country's embassy in Washington, D.C. Fees are given in U.S. dollars. The booklet notes if a visa is not required for stays of a certain duration (say, 30 to 90 days). Visa information is subject to change, so check requirements with tourist offices and a travel agent well in advance of your departure.

You may request "Foreign Entry Requirements" by sending your name, address, and 50¢ (coins or check) to the Consumer Information Center, Dept. 371B, Pueblo, CO 81009. The Bureau of Consular Affairs also operates a phone line for up-to-date visa information (☎ **202/663-1225** Monday through Friday from 8:30am to 4pm).

INTERNATIONAL DRIVING PERMITS   Americans planning to drive in Europe may need an International Driving Permit (IDP). Check with the embassy or consulate of the countries you plan on visiting to see which driving requirements are enforced, as well as with your car-rental agency for its regulations. The International Driving Permit can be obtained from any branch of the **American Automobile Association (AAA)**; you don't have to be an AAA member. To be eligible, you must be at least 18 and submit two 2- by 2-inch photos (you can get them taken at many AAA offices), your valid U.S. driver's license, and a $10 fee. If there's no AAA office near you, call or write for an IDP application; then send it, along with a photocopy of the front and back of your driver's license, the two photos signed on the back, and a check for $10 to AAA, 1000 AAA Dr., Mail Stop 28, Heathrow, FL 32746-5080 (☎ **407/444-4240**). The permit will be mailed back to you and is good for one year. It does not replace your own driver's license, however, so bring both of them along.

3 Currency & Credit

When you go abroad, take a mix of traveler's checks, credit and/or charge cards, and cash, preferably 80% of your money in traveler's checks and the rest in cash. Just make sure that you set aside enough cash to pay the country's exit tax and to get home at the end of the trip. That leaves credit and charge cards for splurges or emergencies or as collateral when booking a hotel room or renting a car.

To figure out how much money you'll need to take with you, first add up anything that's been paid in advance, such as airline and Eurailpass tickets, and subtract that from the total budgeted amount. Then estimate the daily cost of lodging, food, entertainment, and local transportation, using the prices in this book as a guide. Multiply that estimate by the number of days you'll be abroad, then add in what you expect to spend for gifts and souvenirs. Err on the generous side; you can use the leftover traveler's checks when you return home.

If you have an automated-teller machine (ATM) bank card, you may be able to use it abroad. Check with your local bank for a directory of international services or call CIRRUS (☎ **800/424-7787**) or Plus (☎ **800/843-7587**). Ask if you'll need a special personal identification number (PIN) for use in Europe and if a commission will be charged for the transaction. And don't get overdrawn!

Most of the time the exchange rate is better overseas for U.S. dollars than at home, so convert only a small amount of money before departing—perhaps $50, including some small bills to use for tipping and transportation when you first arrive. That way you can avoid potentially long lines at the airport's currency-exchange booth, grab a bus into town, and change more money at a downtown bank, where the exchange rate is likely to be better than at the airport or your hotel. (Always ask the fee for changing money before doing so; it may be so high that the rate is no longer equitable, and you'll want to look elsewhere.)

If you keep cash and traveler's checks in a wallet that you carry in your pants, wrap a rubber band or two around the wallet so it won't slip out of your pocket easily. Note that a front pants pocket is safer than a back one. If you carry your wallet in a purse, choose a purse with a zippered closing and keep it zipped at all times, even if you're only removing a pen briefly to sign a traveler's check. Thieves are lightning fast and quite knowledgeable about tourists' habits. Don't get distracted during your travels and become an easy mark.

Should you become separated from your money—because of theft or simply through your own devices—a friend or relative at home can send you more via a **MoneyGram®** (☎ **800/666-3947** in the U.S., 800/933-3278 in Canada), available through many European currency-exchange offices. The transaction is quick; once the money is sent, you go into a MoneyGram® location with identification or a code word if you lost your ID (the name of the family dog, perhaps) and pick it up, usually in the form of traveler's checks. The sender pays the service fee (figure about $40 to send $500).

TRAVELER'S CHECKS   The safest way to travel with money is in the form of traveler's checks. Extra impetus for using them is that you usually get a little more foreign currency for your traveler's checks than you would for the equivalent amount of cash. (It has a lot to do with the vagaries of the banking business.) If you lose the checks or they're stolen, the loss is only temporary. Paying with traveler's checks can be a handy budgeting tool during a trip because you can pace your spending as you see your check stock dwindling; with credit- or charge-card purchases, it's much easier to overspend.

Most traveler's checks have a standard charge, but **Thomas Cook** often offers its checks free through its travel agents, and **American Express** traveler's checks are offered free to members of the American Automobile Association (AAA) and many credit unions. A typical 1% fee is set by the bank; some will waive the fee for their account holders.

If possible, buy some traveler's checks in the currency of the country you're going to visit, such as French or Swiss francs or Deutsch marks, to avoid the 5% or higher fee that foreign banks may charge to change your checks into local currency. American Express traveler's checks can be obtained in Australian or Canadian dollars, British pounds, German marks, Swiss or French francs, and Japanese yen without paying the currency-conversion fee; you pay only a 1% commission. Thomas Cook MasterCard traveler's checks are available in Australian or Canadian dollars, German marks, Dutch guilders, French and Swiss francs, Spanish pesetas, British pounds, and Japanese yen. Visa checks are available in British pounds, French francs, Dutch guilders, German marks, and Spanish pesetas.

Remember that you'll be buying foreign-currency checks at the current exchange rate, which means you won't have to worry about fluctuations of the dollar or the pound. The down side is that you can't take advantage of improving exchange rates as you travel. However, if your trip is relatively short and you intend to keep purchases to a minimum, it won't make much difference anyway.

Another way to avoid an extra banking fee abroad is cashing traveler's checks at their corresponding bank. For example, cash Visa checks at Barclays Bank and Thomas Cook checks at Midland Bank and Thomas Cook offices (the latter two mainly in Britain), which also cash MasterCard checks at no charge. For no fee,

American Express Travel Service offices will change American Express checks into currency or into traveler's checks in a foreign currency.

Purchase traveler's checks in both large and small denominations. Toward the end of your stay, change the small checks so you won't be left with too much local currency. Changing dollars into foreign currency and then back into dollars means you pay an exchange premium twice.

During your trip, divide your traveler's checks up to avoid losing everything in case you're robbed; put some in your luggage and others in your wallet and keep a list of the check numbers in a separate place. Keep a record of the date of purchase of your checks, along with a hot-line number for the credit- or charge-card company to call in case they're lost. Leave a copy of this information and a list of check numbers at home with a friend or relative, as a backup. Check off the numbers as you cash the checks, so you don't accidentally claim theft for checks you've cashed. Since you may be asked to show your passport in order to cash traveler's checks abroad, always keep it with you. For more information, contact American Express (☎ **800/221-7282** 24 hours a day in the U.S., Canada, and the Caribbean), Barclays Bank (for Barclays' Visa traveler's checks; ☎ **800/847-2245**), and Thomas Cook MasterCard (☎ **800/223-7373**). For Visa and MasterCard, check with your bank.

CREDIT & CHARGE CARDS   Credit and charge cards may prove invaluable abroad: You can use them for special purchases or unexpected expenses to avoid dipping into your cash fund; and if you run out of money, the card can provide a cash advance (for which you're usually charged a service fee).

Don't leave home without checking the expiration date of all cards you intend to bring. Travelers have been known to have their cards become extinct mid-trip.

To avoid paying interest on credit- and charge-card charges that come due when you're abroad, send a check to the card company before you leave home to cover what you expect your expenses to be.

Credit cards are increasingly connected to bank cash machines throughout the world, giving you easier access to funds. Check with your credit-card company (call the information number on your latest bill and you'll be directed to the appropriate department).

Reminder: The actual price tag on anything you buy with a credit or charge card is subject to the fluctuations of the dollar and the pound. The purchase is not converted from foreign currency until it's actually received at the card's headquarters, whether you bought it one week or one month earlier. Like it or not, you're dealing with a time lag. If the dollar or the pound is growing stronger abroad, buying on credit works in your favor; if it's weakening, it works against you.

4 Insurance & Assistance

Don't buy travel insurance unless you're positive that you aren't already covered. Check existing policies, as well as with credit- and charge-card companies whose cards you hold. Some of them offer automatic travel accident insurance for you and your family when you purchase air, rail, or sea passage through them. You may also belong to a social or professional organization through which you're covered on trips abroad.

Be aware that there are different types and degrees of coverage. What suits you? How much insurance can you afford? How much risk can you afford? How much peace of mind do you need? What about the event of an act of terrorism? What if a preexisting medical condition flares up? Although it's important to get the coverage you need, there's no reason to overinsure.

Travel *assistance* provides on-site help in the midst of a travel emergency, including emergency transport, contact with an English-speaking surgeon, arrangement for hospital admittance, or an emergency loan for medical expenses. Travel *insurance*, on the other hand, covers some or much of the cost of the emergency, but only after the fact.

Today these types of coverage are increasingly similar, each offering options of the other—great for consumers. Both assistance and insurance are available through travel agents, as well as through insurance companies. Before you sign on the dotted line, check the fine print for what is *not* covered; it's just as important as what is.

The prices given below are for one or two weeks' coverage for an individual (family rates are often available).

INSURANCE FOR U.S. TRAVELERS   The comprehensive travel insurance and assistance package provided by **Access America,** 6600 W. Broad St., Richmond, VA 23230 (☎ **800/284-8300**), includes medical expenses, on-the-spot hospital payments, medical transportation, baggage insurance, trip cancellation/interruption insurance, collision-damage insurance for a car rental, and a 24-hour hotline connecting you to multilingual coordinators who can help in the event of medical, legal, or travel problems. For 9 to 15 days, this package is $111; less-inclusive plans start at $27.

Wallach & Co., 107 W. Federal St. (P.O. Box 480), Middleburg, VA 22117 (☎ **703/687-3166,** or 800/237-6615), offers a policy called HealthCare Abroad. Policyholders who travel for 10 to 20 days pay $3 per day for $100,000 accident/sickness coverage, medical evacuation, and $25,000 accidental death/dismemberment. Optional trip cancellation insurance costs 5¢ per dollar, with a minimum of $25 (for $500) coverage to a maximum of $250 (for $5,000). Ask about family and extended-stay plans.

International SOS Assistance, Eight Neshaminy Interplex, Trevose, PA 19053-6956 (☎ **215/244-1500,** or 800/523-8930), is strictly an assistance company. It offers a pretrip medical referral, a 24-hour hotline, emergency evacuation, medical consultation abroad, hospital admission, return of unattended minors, and return of remains; the cost is $55 for 1 to 14 days. Ask about couple, family-plan, and frequent-traveler rates, as well as optional medical insurance.

Tele-Trip (Mutual of Omaha), Mutual of Omaha Plaza, Omaha, NE 68175 (☎ **800/228-9792**), offers a Travel Assure package including trip cancellation insurance, baggage loss or delay, accident/medical coverage, death/dismemberment, and traveler's assistance. Prices start at $31 for 9 to 15 days; ask about family plans.

Travel Assistance International (Worldwide Assistance Services), 1133 15th St. NW, Suite 400, Washington, DC 20005 (☎ **202/331-1609,** or 800/821-2828), provides unlimited medical evacuation coverage, four medical coverage plans ranging from $15,000 to $90,000, optional baggage loss or delay insurance, trip cancellation/interruption insurance, accidental death/dismemberment insurance, medical referrals, legal assistance, 24-hour emergency message center, and general travel information. Coverage for 9 to 15 days costs $62. Ask about family, yearly, and extended-stay plans.

Travel Guard International, 1145 Clark St., Stevens Point, WI 54481 (☎ **800/826-1300**), offers a comprehensive insurance package including medical coverage, emergency assistance, accidental death insurance, trip cancellation/interruption insurance, and baggage loss or delay insurance; the price is based on 8% of your total trip cost (some limitations apply). Separate extensive medical, trip-cancellation, and baggage coverage is also available.

A Case of Packing

The following checklist should be used as a general packing guide. To avoid overlooking anything, modify the list to suit your needs, then check off items as you pack them.

If you need a particular item that's unavailable where you live—for example, a portable coffee maker, a currency converter, or a sleep sack—you'll find it in *Magellan's Essentials for the Traveler.* Order this free 56-page catalog from Magellan's, P.O. Box 5485, Santa Barbara, CA 93150 (☎ **800/962-4943**).

Accessories (a few strategic ones)
Address book
Air/rail tickets
Air/seasickness pills
Alarm clock
Antidiarrhea medicine
Aspirin
Camera and/or camcorder, batteries, film
Cash ($50 worth of foreign currency, enough dollars to get you to and from the airport)
Credit/charge cards
Documents: trip itinerary, vouchers, receipts, reservations slips, Eurailpass and validation slip, traveler's check numbers, prescriptions
Dresses, skirts
Eyeglasses or contact lenses, with spare set or prescription
Flashlight, batteries
Guidebook(s)
Hat or cap
Insurance or assistance policy
International Driver's Permit
Jacket
Jewelry (nothing too valuable)
Magnifying glass
Maps
Pants, shorts
Passport or identity card (make photocopies)
Phrase book
Plastic bags to hold damp clothes or washcloth
Prescription medicines and prescriptions (in generic, not brand-name, form)
Raincoat or windbreaker
Sewing kit
Shawl (versatile as accessory, wrap, swimsuit cover, bathrobe)
Shirts, blouses, tops, T-shirts
Shoes, sneakers, sandals, slippers
Sleeping sheet (for hostels)
Sleepwear
Socks, pantyhose, tights
Sunscreen
Sunglasses
Sweater
Swimsuit
Swiss army knife (essential for impromptu picnics)
Tie, scarf
Toiletries
Transformer and/or adapter plugs
Traveler's checks
Underwear
Washcloth (European lodgings often don't supply them)
Umbrella (collapsible)

Reminder: Take half as many clothes as you think you'll need and twice as much money.

Travel Insured International, Inc., P.O. Box 280568, East Hartford, CT 06128 (☎ 203/528-7663, or 800/243-3174), offers illness and accident coverage costing from $10 for 6 to 10 days. For lost or damaged luggage, $500 worth of coverage costs $20 for 6 to 10 days. You can also purchase trip-cancellation insurance for $5.50 per $100 of coverage to a limit of $10,000 per person.

INSURANCE FOR U.K. TRAVELERS   Most big travel agents offer their own insurance and will probably try to sell you their package when you book a holiday. Be sure to think before you sign. Britain's Consumers' Association recommends that you insist on seeing the policy and reading the fine print before buying travel insurance.

You should also shop around for better deals. Try **Columbus Travel Insurance Ltd.** (☎ 0171/375-0011) or, for students, **Campus Travel,** 52 Grosvenor Gardens, London SW1W 0AG (☎ 0171/730-3402). If you're unsure about who can give you the best deal, contact the **Association of British Insurers,** 51 Gresham St., London EC2V 7HQ (☎ 0171/600-3333).

A MEDICAL DIRECTORY   If you decide against coverage of any kind, consider **IAMAT (International Association for Medical Assistance to Travelers),** 417 Center St., Lewiston, NY 14092-3633 (☎ 716/754-4883), which publishes an annual directory of English-speaking doctors in more than 130 countries worldwide who offer services to organization members for a standard fee; in 1995 it was $45 for an office visit, $55 for a house call, and $65 for an appointment during holidays or on Sunday. There's no fee to become an IAMAT member, though the organization does accept donations. It'll send a package including the directory and information on climate, food, water, immunization, and tropical diseases.

THEFT COVERAGE   If you're concerned about theft, check your homeowner's, condo, co-op, or renter's insurance policy to see if it includes an off-premises–theft clause. **Allstate** has outstanding, inexpensive off-premises coverage that repays the recipient within a week of report of theft accompanied by an official police report, even if it's in a foreign language. For more information, contact any Allstate agent.

COMPUTER COVERAGE   If you plan to travel with a computer, be aware that it probably is not covered by your homeowner's, renter's, or travel insurance. (Access America does insure computers and other electronic equipment as baggage for up to $1,000.) It's possible to get coverage specifically for the computer through **Safeware,** 2929 N. High St. (P.O. Box 02211), Columbus, OH 43202 (☎ 614/262-0559, or 800/800-1492). Among the hazards covered are theft (the biggest problem for owners of laptop computers), fire, vandalism, natural disasters, accidental damages, and damages resulting from airport x-rays. The policy goes into effect with a phone call.

5   Health Tips

When packing, don't overlook a prescription for any medicine you take on a regular basis. Ask your doctor to give you a generic prescription because European trade names of prescription drugs are different from those in the United States. Some drugs available over-the-counter in the United States may require a doctor's prescription in some European countries—such as antihistamines in Sweden—so pack anything you could possibly need to avoid time-consuming hassles and extra expense.

If you have ongoing or recurring physical maladies, carry a printed medical history with your Social Security number, insurance company, address, current medications with generic names and dosages, and a list of drug allergies. This will be invaluable to a foreign doctor.

The 198-page book *Health Information for the International Traveler* is available for $7 from the U.S. Government Printing Office, Superintendent of Documents, P.O. Box 371954, Pittsburgh, PA 15250-7954 (☎ **202/521-1800** to order with Visa or MasterCard or for more information); specify stock no. 017-023-00194-9.

VEGETARIAN TRAVELERS   Vegetarian restaurants are listed in most of the city chapters in this book; when they're not available, try ethnic restaurants such as Indian, Thai, or Vietnamese, whose menus offer vegetable dishes. Happily, throughout Europe fruit and vegetable markets and delis are plentiful; come prepared with your own travel utensils because most European delis, which have delicious salads, don't provide forks, knives, or spoons with take-out orders.

In the United States   The **Vegetarian Resource Group,** P.O. Box 1463, Baltimore, MD 21203 (☎ **410/366-8343**), can provide information about resources in individual European countries. The organization's *Vegetarian Journal* sometimes publishes travel articles.

For more information on vegetarian-related travel, contact the *Vegetarian Times,* P.O. Box 570, Oak Park, IL 60303 (☎ **708/848-8100**).

In Britain   Established in 1944, the **Vegan Society,** St. Leonards-on-Sea, England (☎ **0424/427393**), publishes the *Vegan Holiday and Restaurant Guide.*

The **Vegetarian Society of the United Kingdom** is at Parkdale, Dunham Road, Altrincham, Cheshire, WA14 4QG England (☎ **061/928-0793**).

Reminder: Travelers from the United States should expect to find many more smokers in Europe than at home. Few restaurants provide no-smoking sections, and if you ask people in restaurants, cafés, or pubs or on elevators or airplanes to refrain from smoking, they're likely to be offended and tell you so.

6 Tips for Special Travelers

FOR TRAVELERS WITH DISABILITIES

One of the toughest parts of travel to an unfamiliar place is not knowing exactly what you're going to find. For travelers with physical disabilities, this can be especially daunting. The more you can learn about the accessibility of a place before arriving, the better equipped you'll be to maneuver and enjoy yourself once you're there.

FOR U.S. TRAVELERS   Information for people with disabilities is provided by **Mobility International USA (MIUSA),** P.O. Box 10767, Eugene, OR 97440 (☎ **503/343-1284** voice and TDD; fax 503/343-6812), a national nonprofit organization whose purpose is to promote international educational exchange and travel for persons with and without disabilities. MIUSA puts out several publications, including *A New Manual for Integrating Persons with Disabilities into International Exchange Programs* and *A World of Options for the 90s: A Guide to International Educational Exchange, Community Service and Travel for Persons with Disabilities,* as well as videos and a quarterly newsletter, *Over the Rainbow.* Membership—costing $25 annually or $35 for those outside the United States— includes the newsletter and MIUSA's information and referral service. A newsletter subscription alone is $15 annually, $25 annually outside the United States.

Directions Unlimited, 720 N. Bedford Rd., Bedford Hills, NY 10507 (☎ **800/533-5343;** fax 914/241-0243), books tours to Europe for disabled travelers, including tours for the blind.

The **Travel Information Service** of MossRehab Hospital, 1200 W. Tabor Rd., Philadelphia, PA 19141-3099 (☎ **215/456-9603** voice, or 215/456-9602 TDD), a center for treatment of the physically disabled, serves as a clearinghouse of information, much of it from firsthand reports, on accessible hotels, restaurants, and attractions abroad. This is a telephone service only.

FOR U.K. TRAVELERS   The **Royal Association for Disability and Rehabilitation (RADAR)** publishes two annual holiday guides for disabled people: "Holidays and Travel Abroad" (£5 in the U.K., £6.50 in Europe, £8.50 in other destinations) and "Holidays in the British Isles" (£7 in the U.K., £10 in Europe, £13 in other destinations). RADAR also provides a number of holiday fact sheets on such subjects as sports and outdoor holidays, insurance, financial arrangements, and accommodations with nursing care for groups or for the elderly. There's a nominal charge for these publications, which are available from RADAR, 12 City Forum, 250 City Rd., London EC1V 8AF England (☎ **0171/250-3222**).

Another good resource is the **Holiday Care Service,** 2 Old Bank Chambers, Station Road, Horley, Surrey RH6 9HW (☎ **01293/774-535;** fax 01293/784-647), a national association that advises on vacations for older people and the disabled. Its Holiday Care Awards recognize those in the tourism industry who provide excellent service for people with disabilities.

Accessible hotels and accommodations inspected by the Holiday Care Service throughout the United Kingdom offer special discounted rates for bookings made through the Holiday Care office. For inquiries and reservations, call the number above.

If you're flying around Europe, the airline and ground staff will help you on and off planes and reserve seats for you with sufficient leg room, but it's essential that you arrange for this assistance in advance by contacting your airline. The **Air Transport Users Councils,** Kingsway House, 103 Kingsway, 5th Floor, London WC2B 6QX (☎ **0171/242-3882**), publishes a free pamphlet called "Care in the Air," which is full of good information. You can also call the RADAR information desk (☎ **0171/637-5400**) with questions.

FOR SINGLE TRAVELERS

Traveling alone can be pure heaven for some; for others, anathema. One drawback is that solo travelers often spend more money since they have no one with whom to share expenses for food, transportation, and lodging. Hotel rooms usually are booked at a double-occupancy rate, but guesthouses and small hotels often keep prices low for single occupants and may even have a few single rooms on the premises. Ask if there's a single supplement before agreeing to stay anywhere; it could be as high as 50%.

Even those who thrive on freedom and solitude sometimes welcome an in-depth exchange with other people (it doesn't always happen when you're on your own). An excellent way to connect with individuals or families in European countries is through home stays or arranged visits of just a few hours' duration. These may be set up through such organizations as **Servas** and **Friends Overseas** (see "Low-Cost Travel with a Difference" in Chapter 2).

Singleworld, 401 Theodore Fremd Ave., Rye, NY 10580 (☎ **914/967-3334,** or 800/223-6490; fax 914/967-7395), is a travel agency/tour operator catering, as its name implies, to single travelers, who pay a $25 yearly fee from the date of their first departure. Trips are organized in two ways: for people in their 20s, 30s, and 40s plus, or for people of all ages. You may book with Singleworld directly or through your travel agent.

For particularly fun-loving gatherings of singles, not to mention a relaxed way to meet Europeans, consider **Club Med,** 40 W. 57th St., New York, NY 10019 (☎ **800/CLUB-MED**), where half the guests are single and single rooms are available at a number of its properties. Or contact **Contiki Holidays,** 300 Plaza Alicante, Suite 900, Garden Grove, CA 92640 (☎ **800/CONTIKI**), the world's largest travel company for 18- to 35-year-olds only.

If you decide to seek out a single traveler similar to you in age and interests to share experiences and expenses, contact **Travel Companion Exchange,** whose membership includes people of all ages (for details, see "For Older Travelers," below). You may also find someone by putting up notices in youth hostels once you get to Europe.

The **Campus Travel Group,** 52 Grosvenor Gardens, London SW1 W0AG England (☎ **0171/730-3402** in Europe, or 0171/730-8111 outside Europe; fax 0171/730-5739), specializes in travel for students and young independent travelers both within Great Britain and throughout Europe by plane, boat, bus, or train. They sell European rail tickets, as well as student and youth charter flights to a variety of European destinations, including Athens, Budapest, and Prague. There are more than 30 Campus Travel branches throughout Britain; the main office (mentioned above) is at the Victoria tube station.

Also in Britain, **Explore** (☎ **0252/344-161**) has a well-justified reputation for offering fascinating offbeat tours. **HF Holidays** (☎ **0181/905-9388**) also runs a range of packages throughout Europe for travelers 18 to 35.

Dedicated independent travelers may want to check out the **Globetrotters Club,** BCM/Roving, London WCIN 3XX, which enables members to exchange information and generally assist one another in traveling as cheaply as possible. The annual membership fee is £9 for British and European residents ($5 U.S. for others), along with a once-only fee of £3 ($5 U.S.) to join. Membership includes a subscription to *Globe* magazine.

FOR WOMEN TRAVELERS

Women 30 and older interested in biking or trekking with other women may contact **Rainbow Adventures,** 15033 Kelly Canyon Rd., Bozeman, MT 59715 (☎ **800/804-8686**). Founded in 1982 by former Peace Corps volunteer/ biologist Susan Eckert, it attracts a mix of women in age, background, and interests and offers hiking and barging trips in Europe.

FOR GAY & LESBIAN TRAVELERS

Those looking for gay and lesbian travel offerings should contact **Islanders/ Kennedy Travels,** 183 W. 10th St., New York, NY 10014 (☎ **212/242-3222**, or 800/988-1181), which can arrange individual trips, tours, or cruises for gay men and lesbians.

For upscale tour programs for men, contact **Hanns Ebensten Travel,** 513 Fleming St., Key West, FL 33040 (☎ **305/294-8174**); for outdoor trips for men, try **Adventure Bound Expeditions,** 711 Walnut St., Boulder, CO 80302 (☎ **303/449-0990;** call collect, if you like).

A great resource is the **International Gay Travel Association (IGTA),** P.O. Box 4974, Key West, FL 33041 (☎ **800/448-8550;** fax 305/296-6633). Founded in 1983, this network of travel industry professionals is dedicated to encouraging and assisting gay and lesbian travel. Leave your name and mailing address on their voice mail and you'll be sent a list of gay/lesbian-friendly travel agents in your area as well as a list of member accommodations in or near whichever European city or cities you specify.

Are You Two Together?—A Gay and Lesbian Travel Guide to Europe, by Lindsy Van Gelder and Pamela Robin Brandt (Random House, $18), published in 1991, describes with warmth and humor the couple's adventures on the road, relates stories of famous European gay men and lesbians, and recommends gay-friendly hotels and restaurants, as well as bookstores, gay centers, and other resources. If the book is not available in your area, you can purchase it with a credit or charge card directly through the publisher by calling 800/733-3000; outside the U.S., write Random House Direct Mail, 400 Hahn Rd., Westminster, MD 21157. For mail orders, add $2 for shipping and handling; by mail or telephone, specify ISBN no. 679-73599-2 to speed the process along.

For suggestions about, or to order, other books or magazines aimed at the gay or lesbian traveler to Europe, contact **A Different Light Bookstore,** 151 W. 19th St., New York, NY 10011 (☎ **212/989-4850,** or 800/343-4002).

FOR OLDER TRAVELERS

The following travel tips, many gleaned from Arthur Frommer himself, a mature traveler with a lot of miles under his seatbelt, are particularly geared to the traveler emeritus:

- Prepare for your trip by reading history and art-appreciation books. Approach a place with mature deliberation rather than youthful impetuousness.
- Pack less and enjoy more.
- Always carry proof of age—your passport, driver's license, Medicare card, or membership card for an organization for seniors—to take advantage of senior discounts.
- If you plan to travel by train but only in one European country, find out if that country offers senior passes. You could save up to 50%.
- When making your airline reservation, ask for the 10% senior discount offered by airlines on most fares and find out if there's an even lower special promotional fare.
- Combat jet lag by going to sleep for a few hours immediately upon arrival. Otherwise, you may become overly tired and unable to sleep later.
- Buy travel insurance before departing on a trip. You can insure yourself, your luggage, and even the price of your trip in the event of cancellation—yours or the tour operator's. (See "Insurance and Assistance," earlier in this chapter.)
- Seek out the undiscovered rather than the heavily touristed. Nothing is duller than contrived nightspots, souvenir shops, and endless tours. Many mature travelers crave good companionship more than crowds, and that's often found in out-of-the-way places not yet on the tourist circuit.

Youth hostels around the world cater to the young and the young at heart and almost all place no maximum-age limitation on membership. The facilities are clean, though generally lacking the private bath that older travelers tend to prefer. Beds are often cots or bunk beds in privacy-lacking dorms, segregated by sex. Hostel management will provide private rooms for couples or families, which can often be reserved in advance. For membership information, see "Saving Money on . . ." in Chapter 2.

Retired travelers have the advantage of being able to stay longer abroad, even on a budget. If you travel off-season, you can take advantage of extended-stay bargains offered by tour operators such as **Sun Holidays,** 7280 W. Palmetto Park Rd., Suite 301, Boca Raton, FL 33433 (☎ **407/367-0105,** or 800/243-2057). In winter 1994 it offered 28 days in a beachfront apartment on Spain's Costa del Sol beginning at $899 per person, including airfare from New York or Boston (airfare also available from Miami, Los Angeles, and other gateways). That's $32.10 per day.

The single traveler can link up with a group or find a travel companion through a travel club. Two companies specializing in travel and tours for older adults are **Grand Circle Travel, Inc.,** 347 Congress St., Boston, MA 02210 (☎ **617/ 350-7500,** or 800/221-2610); and **Saga International Holidays Ltd.,** 222 Berkeley St., Boston, MA 02116 (☎ **800/343-0273**). Call for a brochure and detailed itineraries. The latter offers educational tours through its Road Scholar programs (☎ **800/621-2151**) as well as Smithsonian Odyssey Tours (☎ **800/ 258-5885**) in conjunction with the Smithsonian Institution.

In Britain, coach tours catering to those over 60, with excellent offerings, are available from **Wallace Arnold** (☎ **0181/464-9696**) and **Cosmos Tourama** (☎ **0181/464-3477**).

Two educational organizations for older adults, **Elderhostel** and **Interhostel,** uniquely combine travel with education, with companionship as a natural by-product. For more information about them and their overseas program, see "Low-Cost Travel with a Difference" in Chapter 2.

Partners-in-Travel, 11660 Chenault St., Suite 119, Los Angeles, CA 90049 (☎ **310/476-4869**), publishes a semiannual newsletter including a directory of 500 travel personals. The service is not limited to older travelers, though people over 55 number 50% of the 500 loyal subscribers. The $25 subscription essentially includes four elements: the directory, a counseling service, a listing of over 100 tour operators, and information for the solo traveler. All members and information are updated at mid-year.

For more choices still, consider the **Travel Companion Exchange,** P.O. Box 833-F, Amityville, NY 11701 (☎ **516/454-0880;** fax 516/454-0170), whose 2,500 active members range in age from 18 to 80. New-member kits contain over 1,000 listings, and subsequent editions of the bimonthly newsletter have several hundred listings each. Members can request extended profiles of people who particularly interest them. Membership is $99 for a minimum eight-month period and includes listings and the bimonthly newsletter. Without becoming an exchange member, you can subscribe to its newsletter (without listings) at $48 for one year; both the subscription and membership include six free back issues right away, plus future issues. The newsletter includes 12 to 14 pages of travel tips; information on airfare, hotel, and cruise discounts; and money-saving ideas for single travelers.

Good sources of a wide range of information for travelers 50 and older include the **American Association of Retired Persons (AARP),** 3200 E. Carson St., Lakewood, CA 90712 (☎ **800/424-3410**), which has an $8 membership fee and a Purchase Privilege Program with discounts on lodging, car rentals, and sightseeing; **Mature Outlook,** 6001 N. Clark St., Chicago, IL 60660-9977 (☎ **800/ 336-6330**), for a bimonthly magazine ($9.95 per year) and discounts; and the **National Council of Senior Citizens,** 1331 F St. NW, Washington, DC 20004

(☎ **202/347-8800**), which, for a $12 single or couple's membership, provides a newspaper 11 times per year, travel discounts, and tours (through a travel agency).

Retirement in Europe can be a reality. If you've ever toyed with the idea, contact **International Living,** 105 W. Monument St., Baltimore, MD 21201 (☎ **800/851-7100;** fax 410/223-2619), which publishes a monthly newsletter, with regular columns on real estate, investing, employment, and budget travel (much of it related to Europe). A one-year subscription costs $29 and includes the free report "The Five Best Retirement Destinations in the World."

FOR FAMILIES

Children add joys and a different level of experience to travel. They speak a universal language with other children, as well as adults, and have the ability to draw sometimes reticent local people like a magnet, which would probably not happen were you alone.

Of course, taking kids along means additional, more thorough planning. Check with the child's doctor before leaving and don't forget to pack first-aid supplies, such as a thermometer, Band-Aids, cough drops, and children's aspirin.

Help children prepare by visiting the library to read encyclopedia accounts of the country you'll be visiting, its culture, customs, climate, and people. Make photocopies of a map of the country or of Europe and have the kids color it in; draw special attention to the places you'll be visiting. Buy a tape of traditional music or stories and rent travel videos.

Make a big deal about getting your child's passport; even infants are required to have one, and a child old enough to sign his or her own name should do so on the document. Give a child who is big enough his or her own kid-size backpack to carry.

When traveling with young children, bring along a favorite (packable) toy and book for familiarity and comfort in new places. Bring plenty of disposable diapers, despite the bulkiness. You'll also be able to buy more at most places you visit.

Get to the airport early for check-in and boarding (folks with kids get to go first). If you're traveling with a stroller, figure out ahead of time if it will fit in the overhead compartment (check when you make your reservations). Reserve bulkhead seats if possible for the extra space they afford.

You may order special children's meals (hot dogs, spaghetti, peanut butter and jelly sandwiches), though you have to request them ahead of time. Airlines don't keep baby food on board, but flight attendants will heat up any you've brought with you.

Don't bring a noisy game that will annoy passengers around you or one with myriad pieces that you'll have to look for at the end of the flight.

Throughout the flight (and the trip), keep snacks on hand: raisins, crackers, fruit, water, or juice. Limit your activities so as not to tire out the child or yourself by planning enough "down time" and ample bathroom breaks.

Try to stay in hotels that are child-friendly, with space for kids to play, such as a garden or courtyard. Check in during the afternoon so the child can get accustomed to the new home-away-from-home.

If your child is overly dependent at the beginning of the trip, be supportive. Hold off on any long excursions until he or she feels more outgoing. When you're ready to venture out, do so early in the day, when lines tend to be shorter. If it's hot, be sure the child has a hat with a brim. If you have to wait in line, play "I Spy" or counting games to pass the time. Relax together in the unbeatable European gardens and parks.

Teach children to identify park, museum, or department-store employees by their uniforms or name tags, so they'll know whom to ask for help if they get lost. You can pin a small whistle to a small child's clothing with instructions to blow it in case you get separated.

Buy souvenirs at the end of the day to lessen the chance that they'll break or get lost before you return to the hotel.

Encourage kids to send postcards to friends and family back home, to collect foreign stamps, to keep a journal, and/or to take photos.

When you return home, put together a scrapbook with the child, including postcards, other souvenirs, stamps, and photos.

An outstanding resource for parents is **Travel with Your Children (TWYCH),** 45 W. 18th St., 7th Floor Tower, New York, NY 10011 (☎ **212/206-0688**), which publishes the newsletter *Family Travel Times* for $40 for four issues. Subscription benefits include discounts on other publications and a free individual consultation service. New subscribers receive a free copy of an airline guide comparing approximately 40 carriers for their child-friendliness and services—whether or not they have changing tables, for example, or allow car seats or strollers in cabins, and what their games packets and children's meals are like. A new edition of the guide, which can be ordered separately for $12, was published in 1994.

The useful 32-page *Family Travel Guides Catalogue* gives you the opportunity to order from a selection of recommended books (including half a dozen dealing specifically with family travel to and in Europe), books on how to travel with kids, books on adventure travel and camping with kids, atlases geared to kids 6 to 12, and books filled with games and amusements. In 1995 the company published its own book, *The Family Travel Guide: An Inspiring Collection of Family-Friendly Vacations,* devoting over 100 pages to traveling with kids in Europe, with general information as well as specifics about eight countries. This 410-page book costs $16.95. To receive more information about this book or a copy of the catalog, send $1 for postage and handling or a self-addressed stamped (55¢) business-size envelope to Carousel Press, P.O. Box 6061, Albany, CA 94706-0061 (☎ **510/527-5849**).

Another excellent resource is *Travel with Children* by Maureen Wheeler (Lonely Planet). The book is actually about travel in Asia and other equally far-flung places, but the advice is universally good.

An increasingly popular vacation destination for families is **Club Med,** 40 W. 57th St., New York, NY 10019 (☎ **800/CLUB-MED**), which first opened in 1950 as a tent village in Majorca, Spain. There are now 45 properties throughout Europe, many of which have Mini Clubs for children 2 to 11 years and Baby Clubs for children 4 to 23 months, with supervised activities. Ask about "Kids Free Weeks," available on a property-by-property basis; one kid age 2 to 5 stays free for each paying adult.

Teach your kids a few key words in a foreign language, such as *bonjour, au revoir,* and *merci,* but don't get upset when they pick up more of the language than you do once you arrive.

FOR STUDENT TRAVELERS

The **International Student Identity Card (ISIC)** is available in the United States for $17 ($16 if you pay in person) from the Council on International Educational Exchange (CIEE), 205 E. 42nd St., Dept. ID, New York, NY 10017 (☎ **212/ 661-1414;** fax 212/972-3231). In Britain the card costs £5 and is available from the CIEE office at 28A Poland St., London W1V 3DB (☎ **0171/437-7767**). The card enables students 12 and up to take advantage of reduced student fares on international flights (some are subject to age restrictions), emergency traveler's assistance, and travel insurance (travel insurance is not provided on ISIC and GO25 cards issued in the United Kingdom). The insurance policy has no deductible and pays benefits even if sickness or accident is covered on another policy. Cardholders may be eligible for other student discounts in individual countries. Call 800/GET-AN-ID for one of the 400 U.S. campus CIEE offices or nearest Council Travel Office.

To be eligible for the card, you must be enrolled full-time or part-time in a degree program at an accredited institution. The application must include proof of student status via a letter on school stationery carrying the school seal (a transcript or bursar's receipt is also acceptable), a $16 registration fee (plus $1 postage and handling), and one passport-size photo. The validity of the card runs from September of one year through December of the next. The card comes with a guide listing student offices worldwide. These offices are great contact points in any city, and they can tell you how to get the most mileage out of the card in their country.

For people 12 to 25 who are not students but want to take advantage of these travel benefits, CIEE issues the **GO25: International Youth Travel Card.** Applicants must send proof of age (a copy of your birth certificate, the personal-data page of your passport, or your driver's license), a $16 fee (plus $1 postage and handling), and one passport-size photo. The card, valid one year from the date of issue, comes with the handy "Travel Handbook: International Youth Travel Card Discounts."

Both the ISIC and GO25 cards carry basic accident and sickness insurance coverage, and cardholders have access to a worldwide hotline for help in medical, legal, and financial emergencies.

In Europe, CIEE has offices in Britain, France, Germany, Italy, and Spain. Its European headquarters is at 66 av. des Champs-Elysées, Bâtiment E, 75008 Paris (☎ 1/40-75-95-10).

7 Some Practical Concerns

CAMERAS & FILM   Determine how many rolls you're likely to shoot in a day or a week, then throw in three more for good measure. If this is your first trip with camera equipment, err on the side of abundance and allow yourself at least one roll a day. Film can be twice as expensive in foreign countries as it is in your hometown camera store or drugstore. It generally comes with processing included, though.

To protect film when going through airport x-rays, put it in a lead-laminated pouch, available in several sizes in camera stores. To be extra careful, ask the attendant to handle the film by hand. Put it in a plastic bag, either unopened in its box or completely free of packing, plastic container and all.

If you have film in your camera, pass it around the x-ray machine as well. Officials claim that the machine will not damage low-speed films—ASA 64 or 100, say—but professional photographers claim different, and multiple doses of low-voltage x-rays do fog film.

To identify what's on each roll of film, carry handy stick-on dots on which to jot down the subject matter. Carry a plastic bag to protect your camera if you'll be shooting in dust or rain.

MAIL & MESSAGES   No matter how much you love to travel, there's nothing better than having news from home while you're away. If you plan an extended stay in Europe, arrange for friends and family to write you there.

General Delivery services (called *Poste Restante*) at **main post offices** will generally hold travelers' mail for a limited time, usually alphabetizing it by the first letter of the last name. Ask correspondents to write on the envelope a request to hold until a certain date, one to a few days after you plan to leave, just to make sure.

Some banks or credit/charge-card companies handle mail for their card- or traveler's-check holders, but American embassies and consulates do not. **American Express** will hold letters (not packages) for 30 days for its cardholders or people using its traveler's checks or other travel services. There's also a nominal fee for all travelers who have their letters forwarded. In an emergency, many American Express offices can send a single mailgram or international cable for a traveler.

If you have a friend abroad (or an amenable friend of a friend), leave his or her address and telephone number, along with the dates you expect to visit. You can also leave the name and address of a hotel where you have a reservation; just alert the hotelier to hold your correspondence.

In the case of a medical emergency, your travel-insurance company may serve as a message center for you.

Before you leave home, select one to three places (depending on your length of stay and your movement abroad) where you'd like to receive mail and prepare a list of places and approximate dates when you'll be there to give to your friends.

ELECTRICITY   Electricity in the United States is 110–120 volts, while in Europe it generally is 220–240 volts. This means that your electric razor, hairdryer, or portable computer will burn out if you plug it into a European outlet—if the plug will even fit in the outlet.

Both U.S. and British travelers will need an adapter plug, and U.S. travelers will also require an electrical transformer. The adapter makes it possible to plug your appliance into the wall, while the transformer (often—incorrectly—called a converter) changes the number of volts flowing to that appliance from 220 to 110. If you use an adapter without a transformer with an American-made appliance, you may smell a faint odor that tells you your appliance has just died.

Buy adapters and transformers before you leave home, because they may not be readily available in Europe. In the United States, hardware stores or electronics shops carry them, as well as travel specialty stores.

If you plan to travel with a portable computer, read the instruction manual carefully or call the manufacturer to see if you'll also need to buy a special heavy-duty transformer that allows for longer periods of operation. Without it, you could overheat the computer and damage it permanently.

Specify to the salesperson the countries you plan to visit. In continental Europe, wall outlets usually require two thin round pins. In Britain, outlets require a large plug with three flat prongs, one of them thicker than the other two and perpendicular to them.

Even a dual-voltage (110/220) appliance may need a special adapter. To find out, contact the **Franzus Company,** Dept. B50, Murtha Industrial Park (P.O. Box 142), Beacon Falls, CT 06403 (☎ **203/723-6664,** ext. 22). Send a self-addressed stamped envelope for the company's free pamphlet "Foreign Electricity Is No Deep Dark Secret."

A simple way to meet all your electrical needs, no matter which country you visit, is to invest in the **Franzus Travel-Lite Worldwide Converter/Adapter Set,** complete with a compact case and four international adapter plugs. The best part is the weight, a mere 8 ounces. It's available for $27.50 from the Traveller's Bookstore, 22 W. 52nd St., New York, NY 10019 (☎ **212/664-0995** or 800/ 755-TRAVEL).

Some foreign hotels have 110-volt outlets marked "For Shavers Only" for 15- to 20-watt devices. Don't use them for anything requiring higher wattage or you may find yourself in the dark.

TIME ZONES   Based on U.S. eastern standard time, Britain, Ireland, and Portugal are five hours ahead of New York City; Greece is seven hours ahead of New York. The rest of the countries featured in this book are six hours ahead of New York. For instance, when it's noon in New York, it's 5pm in London and Lisbon; 6pm in Paris, Copenhagen, and Amsterdam; and 7pm in Athens. The European countries observe daylight saving time, but Britain and Ireland start it a little later than continental Europe. The time change does not usually occur on the same day, or necessarily the same month, as in the United States.

If you plan to travel to Ireland or continental Europe from Britain, keep in mind that the time will be the same in Ireland and Portugal, two hours earlier in Greece, and one hour earlier in the other countries featured in this guide.

Enjoying Europe on a Budget

2

by Alice Garrard

On or off the Continent, it's reassuring to have a friend waiting at your destination. It's more fun (not to mention less frustrating and less expensive) when someone is there to draw the maps, show you the ropes, divulge the bargains, and share the magic. Consider this guidebook such a friend, pointing out ways to get the most out of your visit to Europe for less.

This chapter is filled with suggestions on how to save money on everything—from accommodations and dining out to international telephone calls—as well as ideas for alternative low-cost travel. A friend indeed!

1 Saving Money on . . .

ACCOMMODATIONS

Most tourist offices and travel agents provide listings of bed-and-breakfast accommodations, inns, farmhouses, and small hotels where a couple might spend $20 each for a double room and another $10 each for dinner.

Keep prices down by traveling off-season and off the beaten track. And politely negotiate the price of the room, especially if you sense that there are plenty of empty ones—you might find yourself paying 25% less than expected. Negotiate a trade-off: a lower price for a smaller room, one without a TV, or one at the end of a long hallway. Ask for a better rate if you stay several nights. Perhaps there's a weekend special or an off-season rate. If you're a student or an older traveler, ask for a special discount. If you can't get a lower rate on a room, ask to have breakfast or dinner thrown in. Be pleasant, not pushy; if the proprietor is not easily persuaded, try elsewhere or hope for better luck next time.

As alluring as the great cities of the world are, try to get out of them and into the countryside, which, besides being beautiful, is less expensive than the urban areas, just as at home. For instance, in Italy, besides going to Rome and Venice, also head to Siena, Todi, and Pavia—lovely, photogenic, and historic places in miniature. Instead of visiting the Loire Valley this year, discover the Dordogne in southern France. And consider a country that's less expensive overall, not just in lodging. A room is bound to cost less in a place where you can sip a cup of coffee for 85¢ instead of $2.50 or take a two-mile taxi ride for $2.75 instead of $4.55 (the "What Things Cost" box in each city chapter gives a clear idea of just that).

Another possibility is to rent an apartment, a cottage, or a farmhouse—or even a castle, villa, or chalet—through **Europa-Let,** 92 N. Main St., Ashland, OR 97520 (☎ **503/482-5806** or 800/462-4486; fax 503/482-0660), which represents about 50,000 European properties, many off the beaten path. Imagine living for a week in a cottage or farmhouse in France, England, or Scotland for only $350; a family of four is more likely to pay $500 to $750 for a week—still much less expensive (and roomier) than most hotels. Book as early as possible.

Creative travel alternatives where lodging costs nothing or next to nothing include home stays, work camps, home exchanges, and educational vacations (see "Low-Cost Travel with a Difference," below).

YOUTH HOSTELS   One of the least expensive ways to keep a roof over your head and meet other travelers in an informal, relaxed atmosphere is to stay in youth hostels, which are plentiful in Europe and welcome "youth" of all ages for $8 to $15 per night (figure on about $21 in Paris and $11 to $17 throughout Germany). Membership in **Hostelling International / American Youth Hostels** (HI-AYH), an affiliate of the International Youth Hostel Federation (IYHF), costs $25 per year for people 18 to 54, $15 for those 55 and older, and $10 for those 17 and younger. Family memberships cover parents and children 15 and under and cost $35. Kids as young as five or six are generally welcome at youth hostels. Increasingly, hostels in urban centers are eliminating curfews and obligatory chores. Hostelling International is the new trademark name of the IYHF.

The *Guide to Budget Accommodations,* Vol. I: *Europe and the Mediterranean,* costs $10.95 (plus $3 postage and handling) and is distributed by Hostelling International / American Youth Hostels, 733 15th St. NW, Suite 840, Washington, DC 20005 (☎ **202/783-6161** or 800/444-6111). Travelers can now book hostel accommodations worldwide up to six months in advance by calling the above number or the local hostel number; Paris books up fastest.

Check out the reasonably priced IYHF-sponsored hiking, backpacking, cycling, educational, and independent tours available in a number of European countries—all described in the "Discovery Tours" catalog.

In London an IYHA card can be purchased from the **youth hostel store** at 14 Southampton St. (☎ **071/836-8541**) or through **Campus Travel,** 52 Grosvenor Gardens (☎ **0171/730-3402**). Take your passport and some passport-size photos of yourself, plus your membership fee. In England and Wales, the charge is £3 (for those under 18) or £9 (for those over 18). In Scotland, the fee is slightly less: £2.50 for those under 18, £6 for everyone else.

The IYHF puts together ***The Hostelling International Budget Accommodation You Can Trust,*** listing every youth hostel in 43 European countries. It costs £5.95 when purchased at the Southampton Street store in London (add 61p postage if it's being delivered within the U.K.).

If you're traveling in summer, many youth hostels will be full. To avoid disappointment, it's best to book ahead. In London, you can make advance reservations at the membership department at 14 Southampton St. (see above) or the one at 36 Carter Lane (for a £1 fee).

Reminder: Figure on spending about half your daily budget allotment on lodging. You can save a night here and there by taking an overnight train.

DINING

If you're staying in a hotel or an inn, the price of lodging may include dinner or at least breakfast. Bone up on the kinds of meal plans available and decide which best suits your style of travel:

- **EP** (European Plan), a room without meals
- **CP** (Continental Plan), a simple breakfast of coffee and rolls included
- **AP** (American Plan), three meals daily included (sometimes called "full board")
- **MAP** (Modified American Plan), breakfast and dinner included (sometimes called "half board")

The hotel may serve dinner separately, say, $15 for a five-course meal, including tax and tip. That's more than reasonable by American standards, but you may choose to eat less at a café in town for half the price. Likewise, if a hotel breakfast costs $6, why not go down the street and pick up a roll and coffee for $2?

Learn to read wine lists from the bottom up; the price of a carafe of a regional product might be one-tenth what you'd pay for export variety. In some restaurants and with all fixed-price dinners, wine is included with the meal. Besides being cheaper than other choices, a local bistro, taverna, or pub is a place where you can rub elbows with the people who live in the city. Ask local people you meet for recommendations of places they like, not places they think you'd like.

If you love fine food, but not necessarily by candlelight, consider having your big meal of the day at lunch. Outstanding restaurants may serve the same or similar meals for lunch and dinner, though the fixed-price lunch of three or four courses is likely to be half as expensive. In addition, lunch reservations are easier to come by. In Britain and Ireland, indulge in afternoon tea, a popular custom that's not expensive and will cut your appetite for a huge meal later. Wherever you eat, be sure to check the menu to see if a service charge has been added; don't tip twice by accident.

On the other hand, if your day is filled with sightseeing, lunch can be as quick as a chunk of cheese and a loaf of bread eaten on a park bench.

Reminder: Never skip a meal just to save money. You might end up sick or run-down, and that's the one thing you can't afford. It's bad enough to feel ill at home; in a foreign country, especially if you don't speak the language and need an over-the-counter remedy or a doctor, nothing could be worse.

SIGHTSEEING

It has been said that the best things in life are free. Well, some of the best things in sightseeing are too. You can't get much better than a stroll through Paris's Luxembourg Gardens or an afternoon in London's Tate Gallery. Often a city's tourist office will offer a free booklet of walking tours so you can explore the city on foot, and many chapters in this book include walking tours.. Also note that Frommer's publishes walking-tour guides for Paris, London, England's favorite cities, Venice, Berlin, and Spain's favorite cities.

Visit the tourist office and get as much information as you're likely to need to sightsee on your own. Find out if admission to museums is free on a particular day and go then. Keep in mind that many European museums are closed on Monday, so check the schedule before you go.

SHOPPING

DUTY-FREE SHOPS   Duty-free shopping is available in airports, on ferries and cruise ships, in downtown stores, and at international border crossings. Most of us take advantage of the savings by dashing into airport duty-free shops to get rid of any foreign currency left over at the end of a trip abroad. These stores have traditionally gotten the last few guilders, francs, or schilling in the last few minutes.

To take best advantage of duty-free stores, know the comparable at-home price of any item you're thinking about purchasing, don't judge the savings available in any given shop on just one item, and plan duty-free purchases rather than relegating them to spur-of-the-moment spending. If you're saving only a couple of bucks, it's hardly worth it to lug the stuff home.

The limit on duty-free items Americans can bring back into the United States is $400, including 1 liter of alcohol. Beyond the allotted exemption, the next $1,000 worth of goods is taxed at a flat rate of 10%. For more information on regulations, write to the **U.S. Customs Service,** P.O. Box 7407, Washington, DC 20044; request publication no. 512, the free "Know Before You Go" pamphlet.

For British travelers returning from non–European Union (EU) countries, standard allowances for duty-free-shop purchases apply. Standard allowances do not apply to goods bought in EU countries and brought into the United Kingdom unless the purchases have been made in a duty-free shop. (Note that spot checks may be made, however, to make sure that frequent or heavily laden travelers are not bringing in goods they intend to sell to others.) Note that on July 1, 1999, duty-free shopping will be abolished among member countries of the European Union.

VALUE-ADDED TAX (VAT)   First the bad news: European countries tack a value-added tax, usually referred to as the VAT, onto goods and services. Currently, rates vary from country to country—from 15% to 25% among European Union countries—though the goal is to arrive at a more uniform, low-end rate of around 15%. Still, paying that hefty a tax can quickly put a dent in your travel budget.

Now the good news: You can often get back most of the tax on purchases (not services) over a certain designated amount when you leave the country. Regulations vary from country to country, so check for specific information in the "Shopping" section of each city chapter and inquire at tourist offices when you arrive. To take advantage of the refund, shop in participating stores (look for a sign posted out front or in the window), ask the storekeeper for the necessary forms, save all your receipts, and keep the purchases for which you want the refund in their original packages.

Always ask what percentage of the tax will be refunded, if there are additional service charges, if the refund will be given to you at the airport or train station or mailed to you at a later date, and if the refund will be in dollars or foreign currency. If you make the duty-free purchase on your credit or charge card, the refund may show up as a credit on your account.

When leaving the country, allow an extra hour before your departure to process the VAT-refund forms. If the money is to be mailed to you, expect a wait of several weeks to several months. Unless you've made substantial purchases, this may be one foreign experience you'd just as soon pass up. If you're going to travel in a couple of countries, take care of the VAT refund before you leave each country.

MARKETS, AUCTIONS & SALES   Europe offers bargains if you know where to look for them: They're often found in markets, at auctions, and at department-store sales advertised in local newspapers.

Bargaining may be more prevalent in parts of the world other than Europe, but it's still done in Spain, Portugal, and Greece, and in other countries you'll run across flea markets and the occasional opportunity to haggle.

These tips will help ease the process along: Never appear too interested or too anxious; offer only a third of the first quoted price and slowly work your way up from there (remember: the price should never jump up—it should inch up); tantalize with cash and have the exact amount you want to pay in your hand. Finally, don't take bargaining, the vendor, or yourself too seriously. There's no right or wrong approach and ideally it should be fun for both parties involved.

EVENING ENTERTAINMENT

If you're interested in the theater, ballet, or opera, ask at the tourist office if discount or last-minute-sale tickets are available and where to get them, at the theater itself or a special booth. Some theaters sell standing-room or discount seats on the day of the performance, and students and older travelers may qualify for special admission.

Nightclubs tend to be expensive, but you might be able to avoid a cover charge by sitting or standing at the bar rather than taking a table. If you decide to splurge, keep a lid on your alcohol intake; that's where the costs mount up astronomically. If you have arrived during a public holiday or festival, there may be abundant free entertainment, much of it in the streets.

For leads on stretching your entertainment dollar, check "Deals & Discounts" and "After Dark" in each city chapter.

TIPPING

Try to get an idea about tipping before you get to your destination because you may find yourself in a to-tip-or-not-to-tip situation upon arrival. Ask the tourist board, a travel agent, or friends who have traveled to that country. Once there, ask the local tourist office, a tour guide, or local people you meet. If you still don't know if tipping is appropriate, ask the intended recipient—and don't feel embarrassed about it.

Tour guides should be tipped, along with any guides at a church or historic site. Sometimes ushers at theaters, movies, and sporting events are tipped; take your cue from the people around you. Washroom and cloakroom attendants always receive something. Porters in airports and rail stations usually receive about $1 per bag. Taxi drivers receive no tip in some European countries and 5% to 15% in others.

If no service charge has been added to your hotel bill, you might want to leave $1 per day. The owners of bed-and-breakfast establishments usually are not tipped. In a restaurant, a service charge may well be added to the bill—always check. In France, it's *servis compris*; in Germany, *Bedienung*. If the service has been outstanding, leave a few extra coins.

Always remember that tipping is optional, something done in appreciation for good service; when that's not the case, don't tip. When in doubt about how much to tip, err on the side of generosity and leave 15%—and that's 15% of the total *before* tax; never tip on tax.

For specific information on tipping, see the "Fast Facts" section in each city chapter.

TELEPHONE CALLS

LOCAL CALLS   Increasingly in European countries—the United Kingdom, Ireland, Switzerland, and Denmark—local calls are made by using a telephone card, sold in train stations and post offices and at newsstands. This saves fumbling for coins but costs the same. Some public phones take *only* the cards nowadays.

TRANSCONTINENTAL CALLS   If you can avoid it, never pay for a transcontinental call in Europe. By using AT&T's USA Direct, MCI's World Phone, or Sprint Express, you'll be linked directly to an American operator and the call will be billed to your telephone calling card. This is substantially lower than rates for dialing direct from Europe.

Calling-card calls are billed at operator-assisted station-to-station rates, while collect calls are billed at person-to-person rates. Call the billing office of your telephone company (the number should be on your latest bill) to ask about the most economical way to call from your European destinations and to request a free calling card and international number. You may be able to get an international number immediately over the phone.

Avoid making transatlantic calls from European hotels. Charges are higher and hotels add their own surcharge, sometimes as hefty as 150%, which you may be unaware of until you're presented with the bill. If you have to place the call from the hotel, have your party call you right back. In most countries you're charged only for the actual length of the call, so even with a large surcharge your initial call will not be exorbitant.

Finally, if you must pay for the call, make it from the local post office or from a special telephone center to avoid a surcharge. Check at the telephone desk and you'll be assigned a booth in which to place your call. Afterward, you'll be told the amount you owe.

2 Saving Money on Transportation

BY PLANE

For the most part, air transport within Europe remains in the realm of the business traveler, not the budget traveler. The cost is usually so prohibitively high that frugal travelers consider it only as a splurge or when they're in a pinch for time. Some airlines offer **special promotions** as well as 7- and 14-day **advance-purchase fares.** For instance, British Airways offers the Europe Airpass for 3 to 12 flights primarily from the United Kingdom and back (for other inter-European flights, check with British Airways; ☎ **800/AIRWAYS**). Prices vary from $75 to $150 according to flight zones from Great Britain. Air Inter's Le France Pass offers the tour operator unlimited flying for any 7 days during a 30-day period to any destination in France and Corsica for $329, but the pass must be purchased in the United States from a travel agent or from Jet Vacations (☎ **800/JET-0999**). SAS offers its round-trip transatlantic passengers a Visit Scandinavia Pass, where each trip segment (Oslo to Stockholm, say) for up to six segments costs between $70 and $80, depending on how many segments you buy (children's fares are $20 less); the pass is good in Denmark, Norway, and Sweden and must be purchased in the United States. Check all price details with SAS (☎ **800/221-2350**).

Unlike domestic air travel in the States, lower airfares are available throughout Europe on **charter flights** rather than on regularly scheduled ones. Look in local newspapers to find out about them.

The skies over Europe are changing. In 1993 there was an official liberalization of airline regulations throughout the 12 countries of the then European Community (known as the European Union since November 1993, when the Maastricht Treaty was ratified). The changes have not been so drastic as those that occurred after airline deregulation in the United States, but they should result in lower airfares, perhaps a few fare wars, and special deals and discounts for the air traveler. As this occurs, charter travel may diminish and regularly scheduled carriers may take over a larger chunk of the leisure travel market.

BY TRAIN

European trains are less expensive than those in the United States and far more genteel, imparting the essence of everyday life and rhythms in an extensive 100,000-mile rail system. With modern high-speed trains in many countries— including France, Germany, Italy, Sweden, and Switzerland—the train is faster than a plane for short journeys.

The cost of a train ride from London to Edinburgh on BritRail is $150 in first class or $102 in second class; to Brussels, it's $154 or $123. On Rail Europe, Inc., the price from Paris to Amsterdam is $104 in first class, $71 in second class; and from Paris to Madrid, $162 in first class and $109 in second class. On German Rail, Inc., expect to spend $184 in first class and $121 in second class to travel between Berlin and Vienna. All point-to-point tickets are subject to a $3 charge.

The difference in quality between first- and second-class seats on an international express train is small, a matter of one or two inches of extra padding at most. The slower-moving trains, however, may be kind to your budget but not to your sacroiliac. For additional ticket prices and detailed train schedules, see the Appendix.

TRAIN PASSES

Almost all the countries represented in this guide offer individual rail passes or discounts; regional passes, such as BritFrance Railpass, Benelux Tourrail Pass, ScanRail, and European East Pass (for Austria, Hungary, the Czech Republic, and Poland), are also available. Some passes include senior discounts; some can be purchased only in the United States. Most can be booked through travel agents.

If you plan to visit only one European country or region, keep in mind that a country or regional pass will cost less than a Eurailpass.

Since a pass cannot be replaced, even if it's lost or stolen, guard it carefully. And if you're planning a trip of more than two hours' duration, always make a reservation, even if it's not required by the railroad of a particular country. European trains are popular and can fill up quickly, so don't be left standing.

For American travelers, the most extensive (and popular) passes remain Eurail and BritRail, and information about them is provided below, with 1994 prices that are expected to remain unchanged in 1995.

Passes Available Only in North America

Note that for the Eurailpass, Eurail Saverpass, and Eurail Flexipass, children 11 and under travel for half fare and those under 4 travel free.

- **Eurailpass:** 15 days, $522; 21 days, $678; one month, $838; two months, $1,148; three months, $1,468. Accepted in Austria, Belgium, Denmark, Finland, France, Germany, Greece, Hungary, Ireland, Italy, Luxembourg, the Netherlands, Norway, Portugal, Spain, Sweden, and Switzerland. First class only, with access to many ferries, steamers, and buses free or at a discount.

- **Eurail Saverpass:** For two or more people traveling together October through March or for three people traveling together April through September: 15 days, $452 per person; 21 days, $578 per person; one month, $712 per person. Same privileges as the Eurailpass. First class only.
- **Eurail Flexipass:** Any 10 days within one month, $616; any 15 days within one month, $812. Same privileges as Eurailpass. First class only.
- **Eurail Youthpass:** 15 days, $410; one month, $598; two months, $790. For travelers under 26 years old. Same benefits as Eurailpass. Second class only.

The latest available prices below were for 1996, with rate increases expected for 1997.

- **EurailDrive Pass:** Any 7 days (4 for rail, 3 for car) for use within 2 months, $309. Additional rail days are available for $49 per person per day, additional car days for $49 per car per day.
- **BritRail First Pass:** 8 days, $315 in first class, $230 in second class; 15 days, $515 in first class, $335 in second class; one month, $750 in first class, $520 in second class. Children 16 and under ride for half fare.
- **BritRail Flexipass:** Any 4 days within 8 days, $259 in first class, $195 in second class; any 8 days within 15 days, $399 in first class, $270 in second; any 15 days within one month, $590 in first class, $405 in second. Also ask about BritRail/Drive, Senior Citizen Pass, Youth Pass.
- **BritFrance Railpass:** Any 5 days within 15 consecutive days: one month, $359 in first class, $259 in standard class.

Passes Available in the U.K.

Many rail passes are available in the United Kingdom for travel in Britain and Europe. Stop in at the **International Rail Centre,** Victoria Station, London SW1V 1JY (☎ 0171/834-2345), or **Wasteels,** Victoria Station, London SW1V 1JT (☎ 0171/834-7066), adjacent to Platform 2. They can help you find the best option for your trip.

The **InterRail Card** is the most popular rail ticket for U.K. residents, available to travelers under 26. It costs £249, is valid for one month, and entitles you to unlimited second-class travel in 26 European countries. It also gives you a 34% discount on rail travel in Britain and Northern Ireland, plus an up to 50% discount on the rail portion of travel from London to various continental ports. You'll also get a reduction (between 30% and 50%) on most sailings to Europe and a variety of other shipping services around the Mediterranean and Scandinavia.

If you're not a U.K. resident, you can buy an InterRail Card if you've been in Britain for six months.

Recently, an InterRail Card for those over 26 was introduced, costing £269 for a month or £209 for 15 days.

Another good option for travelers under 26, Eurotrain tickets are valid for two months and allow you to choose your own route to a final destination and stop off as many times as you like along the way. Eurotrain "Explorer" tickets are slightly more expensive but allow you to travel to your final destination along one route and back on another. The price includes round-trip ferry crossing as well as round-trip rail travel from London to the port.

Campus Travel, 52 Grosvenor Gardens, London SW1W 0AG (☎ 0171/730-3402), can give you prices and help you book tickets. **Route 26** (☎ 0171/834-6744) provides low train fares for students (or those under 26) to and from

European destinations. Rail cards, covering 3, 5, or 10 days of first- or second-class travel, are also available for individual European countries (but not for Turkey). Investigate the available options at the Rail Centre in Victoria Station in London or at Wasteels.

FOR MORE TRAIN INFORMATION

For more information, see the *Thomas Cook European Rail Timetable* and contact individual tourist offices or **Rail Europe,** P.O. Box 10383, Stamford, CT 06904. You can get Eurailpass information and a copy of the handy *Europe on Track* by contacting **Rail Europe, Inc.,** 2100 Central Ave., Suite 200, Boulder, CO 80301 (☎ **303/443-5100** or 800/4-EURAIL—lines are often busy, and the best times to get through are between 5:30 and 9pm eastern standard time during peak season or at 9am on Saturday morning in summer only); **BritRail Travel International,** 1500 Broadway, 10th Floor, New York, NY 10036-4015 (☎ **212/575-2667**); or **German Rail/DER Tours,** 9501 W. Devon, Rosemont, IL 60018-4832 (☎ **708/692-6300** or 800/782-2424). Be prepared for busy signals.

If what you'd really like to do is take the train most of the time but have the use of a car for a few days, inquire about Rail Europe's **Rail 'N' Drive** programs, in conjunction with Avis and Hertz rental-car companies, or DER Tours' **Rail/ Hertz** programs.

Train Trip Tips

To make your train travels as pleasant as possible, remember a few general rules:

- Hold on to your train ticket after it's been marked or punched by the conductor. Some European railroad stations require that you present your ticket when you leave the station platform at your destination.

- On an overnight trip, inquire about the availability of second-class couchettes, compartments equipped with six lightly padded ledges along the wall, on which you can stretch out full-length to sleep. Plush they're not, but they're dirt cheap and great for those who can't sleep sitting up.

- While you sleep—or even nap—be sure your valuables are in a safe place; you might temporarily attach a small bell to each bag to warn you if someone attempts to take it. If you've left bags on a rack in the front or back of the car, consider securing them to it with a small bicycle chain and lock to deter thieves, who consider trains happy hunting grounds.

- To vary your routine during a long second-class trip, retire to the dining car and order a drink or a snack; there you'll be able to sit in a cushioned chair as long as you like. Take all valuables with you.

- Few European trains have drinking fountains and the dining car may be closed just when you're at your thirstiest, so take a bottle of mineral water with you. As you'll soon discover, the experienced European traveler comes loaded with hampers of food and drink and munches away throughout the trip.

- If you want to leave bags in a train station locker, don't let anyone help you store them in it. A favorite trick among thieves is feigned helpfulness, then pocketing the key to your locker while passing you the key to an empty one.

BY CAR

Budget travel and rental cars don't usually go hand in hand, but if you're traveling in a group of four you're actually better off renting a car (or van). Besides being the cheaper form of transportation, it gives you added mobility to find a budget hotel or a comfortable spot to camp. And you can carry more bags more easily.

In Europe, not only are rental cars pricey but also **gasoline** costs as much as three times more than Americans are accustomed to paying. The price may *look* lower if it's quoted in liters: Just remember that 1 U.S. gallon equals 3³/₄ liters; in Britain, the Imperial gallon is the equivalent of 1.2 U.S. gallons.

You can get a better deal on a rental car by reserving it ahead, even a couple of days. Expect to be given a standard-shift vehicle unless you specifically ask for an automatic. Find out all the charges you're likely to incur from a car-rental company; besides the daily or weekly rental charge, consider a mileage charge, insurance, the cost of the fuel, an extra driver, and possible tax on the total rental bill (17.5% and 18.6% in Britain and France, respectively). In addition, you'll have to pay for parking and tolls along the way. If you already have collision coverage on your automobile insurance, you're most likely covered when behind the wheel of a rental car—check with your insurance agent before renting a car. If you decide on European insurance, be sure it doesn't come with a $1,000 deductible.

A **collision-damage waiver** costs a hefty $10 to $16 per day for an economy car (more for larger models) and can jack up the price of a rental car incredibly. The cost of the insurance, the scope of coverage, and the deductible will depend on the country, the rental company's regulations, and the size of the car. In some countries, collision insurance is required by law.

The good news is that some credit- and charge-card companies (American Express is one) automatically insure their gold-card holders against collision damage at no additional charge when they rent a car using the card as payment. *Note:* You'll lose this coverage if you take the rental-car company's insurance.

Travel Guard International, 1145 Clark St., Stevens Point, WI 54481 (☎ 800/826-1300), offers eight days of coverage for $19 for repairs up to $25,000; after eight days, additional coverage costs $3 per day (note that these prices and coverage may differ in some states).

You may get slightly lower prices from a European rental company. Try to negotiate the best possible deal—there may be a discount for keeping the car longer, for unlimited mileage (or at least some miles thrown in for free), or for a bigger car for a lower price.

Some car-rental companies, including Avis and Hertz, require that you purchase theft protection coverage in Italy. It costs about $10 to $15 per day.

To begin the shopping-around process, contact some of the American car-rental companies with international branches: **Avis** (☎ 800/331-1084); **Budget** (☎ 800/472-3325); **Dollar Rent a Car,** called **Eurodollar** in Europe (☎ 800/800-6000); **Hertz** (☎ 800/654-3001); or **National,** called **Europcar** in Europe (☎ 800/227-3876). You may be able to pick up a car in one country and leave it in another, and if you keep the car a couple of weeks, there may not be a drop-off charge.

Avis's **Know Before You Go** program offers a 24-hour phone service for Americans planning driving trips with Avis in Britain, France, Germany, and Italy. It can supply information on the price of gasoline in dollars, speed limits in miles per hour, banking hours, driver's license requirements, currency-exchange rates, and the country's major holidays and special events. Avis renters may also request a free map of the country they're planning to visit (☎ **800/297-4447**).

Budget, in its **Discover Europe** program, provides useful motoring itineraries for Belgium, France, Germany, the Netherlands, and Luxembourg. Try not to rent at the airport, where overheads are higher and business travelers on expense accounts do business.

Some U.S.–based companies specialize in European car rentals: **Auto-Europe** (☎ **800/223-5555**), **Europe by Car** (☎ **212/581-3040** or 800/223-1516, 800/252-9401 in California), **Foremost Euro-Car, Inc.** (☎ **800/272-3299**), and **Kemwel** (☎ **800/678-0678**).

Once behind the wheel in Europe, be prepared for fast, aggressive driving on the part of locals. Driving on the right is standard, except in Great Britain and Ireland. Roads are marked in kilometers (km), one of which equals 0.62 mile (100km is 62 miles). Self-service gas stations are readily available, and prices tend to be lower off the freeway. American Automobile Association (AAA) members may be able to get reciprocal member privileges from European auto clubs; ask your local chapter for details.

An **International Driving Permit** is required by some European countries, including Italy, Spain, Austria, and Germany. It may also be required by the car-rental agency and is recommended by the AAA if you plan to drive in any non–English-speaking country. It's readily available through any branch of the AAA for $10; although you may never be asked to show it by either a rental-car clerk or a police officer, it doesn't hurt to have one, just in case. Remember: It doesn't take the place of your U.S. license; it simply accompanies it and serves as a translation of it.

Equally important is a good road map. The European ones are well marked and easy to read. Gas stations and local bookstores in Europe sell them. In the United States, contact **Hagstrom Map & Travel Center,** 57 W. 43rd St., New York, NY 10036 (☎ **212/398-1222**); city maps are $7.95 and up, with country and regional maps $9.95 and up. The **AAA** can provide a European planning map for its members. **Michelin Travel Publications,** P.O. Box 19008, Greenville, SC 29602 (☎ **800/423-0485** outside South Carolina), also publishes maps and guidebooks (a catalog and price list are available). Maps can be ordered by mail or by phone with a credit or charge card, as well as through travel bookstores (see "Sources of Visitor Information" in Chapter 1).

Reminder: Never leave bags in the trunk of a car parked out of your field of vision—no matter where you are, no matter how short the stopover.

BY BUS

Bus transportation is readily available throughout Europe; it sometimes is less expensive than train travel (worth checking into if you don't have a rail pass), and it covers a more extensive area. European buses, like the trains, outshine their American counterparts.

Cosmos, a British operator, specializes in economical bus tours of Europe that can be booked through U.S. travel agents. It will match single travelers who want to share a room to avoid paying a supplement. Inquire through your travel agent.

BY RV/CAMPING
TRAVELING BY RV

Recreational touring—called caravanning in Europe—is as popular in Europe as it is in the United States. Campgrounds are open spring through fall and local tourist offices can direct you to local sites. Before you leave home, ask for a map of sites from individual tourist bureaus.

RV rentals can be made from the States. Get details from **Foremost Euro-Car,** 5658 Sepulveda Blvd., Suite 201, Van Nuys, CA 91411 (☎ **800/272-3299;** fax 818/786-1249).

The **Recreation Vehicle Industry Association,** 1896 Preston White Dr. (P.O. Box 2999), Reston, VA 22090-0999 (☎ **703/620-6003** ext. 311 for information), in conjunction with the **American Association of Retired Persons (AARP),** makes available a free guide to RV driver safety; request "Safety & RV: A Moving Experience," Stock Number D-13149, from AARP Fulfillment, 601 E St. NW, Washington, DC 20049.

Book an RV as far in advance as possible to ensure getting the kind you want. Ask the following questions:

- What sizes and configurations are available?
- Which gets the best gas mileage?
- Will the vehicle I choose be acceptable at campgrounds in all the countries I plan to visit?
- Is mileage included in the rental price?
- When is the rental fee to be paid, at pickup or drop-off?
- Is the RV equipped with linens, towels, pots and pans, and other kitchen supplies?
- Will there be an orientation session on the use of the RV for first-time users?
- Is there an emergency telephone number in case of difficulties?
- Will an operator's manual be provided?
- Is there a cancellation policy?
- What is the minimum age for a driver?

While driving the RV, make an allowance for the vehicle's size when turning; the front and rear wheels are much farther apart than those of a car. Allow more time to brake, change lanes, and enter a busy highway, since the RV will take more time to slow down and accelerate.

CAMPING

Tent-camping gear can be rented in Europe (tourist offices can tell you how to go about it), though it's easier to bring your own. Campgrounds are plentiful, more than 100,000 at last count. Campfires are not allowed and facilities are more functional than picturesque. If you have a cookstove, bring fuel as well. You can expect coin-operated showers, a grocery store, and often a little restaurant conducive to socializing with other campers. The charge per night is about $15—figure $5 per tent and $5 per person. Campgrounds are designated "CAMPINGS" on roadside signs and are well marked on maps.

More detailed information is available from the **Family Campers and RVers Association,** 4804 Transit Rd., Building 2, Depew, NY 14043-4906 (☎ **and fax 716/668-6242**). The organization offers its members an International Camping Carnet for $10; membership is $20 for individuals or families. The carnet is good for some discounts and useful when campground personnel ask you to leave some form of ID and you don't want to relinquish your passport. The organization can also provide a list of European sources for renting or buying camping equipment and renting a car or camper.

BY BICYCLE

Reconnoitering Europe (or parts of it) by bike can be a most exhilarating experience, but it takes stamina and planning. At least a month before you leave home, do some test runs of 10 to 50 miles, increasing the distance as you increase your strength. Take a bike-maintenance refresher course. Link up with a local biking group or join outings planned by American Youth Hostels. Plan your trip when the weather is mild but not too hot.

Bring raingear, sunscreen, a helmet, biker's gloves, and a repair kit. Be sure the helmet has reflector bands; you can find them to fit across your chest as well. The bike should have reflectors and a bell for extra safety (for you and pedestrians). A good bike lock is all-important. Ask at your hostel or inn if there's a room where you may lock your bike.

When plotting your route, try to get a good idea of the grade of the roads; find out about headwinds, which can slow you down, and about the availability of lodging along the way.

Bicycle tours are available, though they're usually out of range for budget travelers. If you plan to bike on your own but could use some ideas for itinerary planning, order the catalogs published by the major biking tour operators. The photos are an inspiration in themselves, and if not this year, perhaps another year you'll be able to sign up with a tour.

The best source of information on who's offering what in the way of bike tours is the annual December **Tourfinder** issue of *Bicycle USA* magazine. A copy costs $6 from the League of American Bicyclists, 190 W. Ostend St., Suite 120, Baltimore, MD 21230-3755 (☎ **410/539-3399** or 800/288-BIKE).

REMINDER   If you plan to take your bicycle to Europe, find out the airline's regulations when making reservations. You may be asked to disassemble part of the bike or box it up; some airlines provide boxes, though others do not.

3   Independent vs. Group Travel

The two major lures of package tours are lower cost and no planning. Tour operators buy airline seats, hotel rooms, tables in restaurants, and surface transportation in bulk and pass the savings on to consumers. The independent traveler can essentially create the same itinerary but must rely on more modest hotels and restaurants to keep costs down.

For the latest in what's available, check the ads in the travel section of your newspaper. Tours are most often put together by airlines or charter companies, hotels, or tour operators and sold through travel agents. Before signing up for one, carefully read the fine print and investigate the following:

- **What is the size of the tour?** Decide whether you can handle an experience shared with 40 other people or if your limit is 20. A smaller tour is a better-quality tour.
- **Will the same guide stay with you throughout the tour?** This works better than being passed from guide to guide, city to city.

- **What kind of hotels will be used and where are they located?** Get the names of the hotels and then look them up in guidebooks. If you sense that the hotels provide only minimal essentials, so might the entire tour. If the hotel is not conveniently located, it'll be less expensive, but you may feel isolated or unsafe and you'll spend extra money and time getting to and from attractions and nightspots.
- **If meals are included, how elaborate are they?** Is breakfast continental or buffet? Is the menu for the group limited to a few items?
- **How extensive is the sightseeing?** You may have the chance to get on and off the bus many times to explore a number of attractions, or you may be able to see them only through the bus window. If you like to explore, pick an attraction you're particularly interested in and ask the operator precisely how much time you can expect to spend there. Find out if all admissions are included in the price of the tour.
- **Are the optional activities offered at an additional price?** This usually is the case, so make sure the activities that interest you the most are included in the tour price.
- **What is the refund policy should you cancel?**
- **How is the package price paid?** If a charter flight is involved, make sure that you can pay into an escrow account (ask for the name of the bank) to ensure proper use of the funds or their return in case the operator cancels the trip.
- **How reputable is the tour operator?** Ask for references of people who have participated in tours run by this outfit. Call travel agents and the local Better Business Bureau. The consumer department of the U.S. Tour Operators Association (USTOA), 211 E. 51st St., Suite 12-B, New York, NY 10022 (☎ **212/750-7371**), will provide information on its members, who are insured in case of bankruptcy. Be leery of any outfit that doesn't give you details of the itinerary before demanding payment.

U.K.-BASED TOUR OPERATORS Consider mixing independent travel with a tour once you get to Europe by linking up with a European operator that specializes in low-cost bus tours or minitours and excursions. A number are based in London, among them **Globus Cosmos Tourama,** 177–179 Hammersmith Rd. (☎ **0171/741-8507** in London, or 800/556-5454 in the U.S.); **Trafalgar Tours,** 15 Grosvenor Place (☎ **0171/235-7090** in London; or, for consumer information and brochures, 800/854-0103 in the U.S.); and **Trophy Tours/Frames Rickards,** 11 Herbrand St. (☎ **0171/637-4171** or fax 071/833-3752 in London, or 800/527-2473 in the U.S., 800/762-3904 in Dallas).

4 Low-Cost Travel with a Difference

EDUCATIONAL TRAVEL

Educational travel provides one of the most invigorating ways to learn, allowing for a nice mix of schooling and vagabonding. Request the free booklet "Basic Facts on Study Abroad" from the **Institute of International Education (IIE),** 809 United Nations Plaza, New York, NY 10017 (☎ **212/883-8200**). It can also provide a list of related books, including its *Vacation Study Abroad* ($36.95). The **Council on International Educational Exchange (CIEE),** 205 E. 42nd St., New York, NY 10017 (☎ **212/661-1414** or 800/349-2433 to order books and other publications), offers the free magazine *Student Travels,* as well as the 500-page

Work, Study, Travel Abroad: The Whole World Handbook, edited by Lazaro Hernandez and Max Terry and updated in even-numbered years (St. Martin's Press, $13.95). The book lists over 1,000 study opportunities abroad.

Many people, especially older travelers, register for language courses at the Alliance Française or Eurocentre in Paris; the Goethe Institute in Berlin, Munich, or Düsseldorf; the Istituto Dante Alighieri in Florence; and the Colegio de Estudios Hispanicos in Salamanca (contact the appropriate tourist office for information; see the Appendix). Some travelers choose to stay one or more weeks at the English-language "folk high school" (adult residential college) in Denmark. There are no exams (entrance or otherwise), no tests, no certificates—just learning for the sake of learning. Contact **Den Internationale Højskole (International People's College),** Montebello Alle 1, DK-3000 Helsingør, Denmark (☎ **49-21-33-61;** fax 49-21-21-28). Still others enroll in summer courses at Oxford or Cambridge University in England or Trinity College in Ireland.

Those age 60 and older, and their spouses, "significant others," relatives, or friends age 50 or older, can take advantage of the Elderhostel program abroad and at home. **Elderhostel,** 75 Federal St., Boston MA 02110-1941 (☎ **617/ 426-7788**), sends almost 30,000 people to school abroad every year. Courses last two to four educational weeks, starting at $1,700, including airfare, meals, lodging, daily classroom instruction, and admission fees. Elderhostel also offers, in conjunction with the World Learning, Inc. (see below), educational programs with a home-stay component. Write or call for a free catalog.

Interhostel, University of New Hampshire, 6 Garrison Ave., Durham, NH 03824 (☎ **603/862-1147** or 800/733-9753), offers two-week educational programs for persons 50 and older. The approximately $2,100 to $3,500 price includes tuition, room and board, airfare, and ground transportation. Take Interhostel a step farther—where children, parents, and grandparents travel and learn together in Europe—and you've got **Familyhostel.** For more information, contact the University of New Hampshire (address and telephone above).

The **Folkways Institute,** 14600 SE Aldridge Rd., Portland, OR 97236 (☎ **503/658-6600** or 800/225-4666), has senior studies for people over 55 called ElderFolk courses, with enrollment between 8 and 20 people. They're designed for active people who enjoy in-the-field learning experiences in natural and cultural history. Folkways offers other courses for participants of all ages. The courses last one to three weeks and cost $1,300 to $2,700, including lodging, land transportation, lecture and museum fees, and most meals, but not airfare.

Earthwatch, 680 Mt. Auburn St. (Box 403TR), Watertown, MA 02272 (☎ **617/926-8200** or 800/776-0188 in the U.S., 0865/311-600 in the U.K.), sponsors research expeditions including archeological excavations. It also sponsors about 160 projects in all aspects of biological and ecological research, where participants assist in everything from mapping volcanoes to tracking endangered species. Special skills are welcome yet not necessary. The European expeditions average two weeks and range in price from $800 to $2,500, including food, lodging, local transportation, and equipment, but not airfare. For U.S. citizens, the cost is actually lower if you consider that you may receive a tax deduction for your contribution.

Smithsonian Study Tours and Seminars, from the Smithsonian Institute, 1100 Jefferson Dr. SW, Room 3045, Washington, DC 20560 (☎ **202/ 357-4700**), offers more than 100 European study tours and cruises. Offerings, which vary from year to year, emphasize such topics as culture, history, and natural history and are led by professors. You must be a member of the Smithsonian ($22 per year) to participate; members receive *Smithsonian* magazine and may request the *Smithsonian Traveler* newsletter detailing the trips. Although all ages may participate, the study is geared to adults and about 70% of participants are over 50.

HOME STAYS OR VISITS

Servas (from the Esperanto word meaning "to serve"), represented in the United States by **U.S. Servas, Inc.,** 11 John St., Suite 407, New York, NY 10038-4009 (☎ 212/267-0252), seeks to promote friendship and goodwill through two-night home stays. The organization has 13,000 hosts in 130 countries worldwide. Membership requires an interview to make sure of the traveler's serious intent. Servas travelers include singles, couples, and families; they pay $55 per person per year for membership (children under 18 pay nothing but must be accompanied by an adult) and a refundable $25 deposit for up to five host lists, $25 for each additional five. The directories provide information on hosts, including city of residence, phone number, occupation, year of birth, languages spoken, and interests. The traveler contacts the host and sets up the visit. Travelers may stay with several hosts in the same city or region, and they do not have to reciprocate and become hosts themselves—though many do.

Since 1971, **Friends Overseas,** 68-04 Dartmouth St., Forest Hills, NY 11375, has put American travelers to Denmark, Norway, Sweden, and Finland in touch with Scandinavians who share the same interests and/or background. Participants receive the names and addresses of a number of selected Scandinavian members and you must write to them before your departure; otherwise, they may not have enough advance notice to plan a meeting with you. Some 4,000 Scandinavians—singles, couples, and families—belong to the organization. For more information, send a self-addressed stamped business-size envelope to Friends Overseas at the above address. Those writing from overseas should include the equivalent of $1.50 (U.S.) in return postage or three international postal coupons.

Amateur radio operators can meet their European counterparts by joining the **International Travel Host Exchange,** sponsored by the American Radio Relay League. Members of the exchange list their name, telephone number, address, and languages spoken and state whether they can accommodate overnight visitors or merely show them the local sights (expect plenty of shop talk too). For more information or an application, contact the American Radio Relay League, 225 Main St., Newington, CT 06111 (☎ 203/666-1541).

If you prefer group interaction to one-on-one experiences, **Friendship Force,** 57 Forsyth St. NW, Suite 900, Atlanta, GA 30303 (☎ 404/522-9490), can help. Throughout the year this organization, with which former President Jimmy Carter has been associated, assembles groups of 21 to 42 people and flies them to one- or two-week stays with families in Western or Eastern Europe, followed by an optional one-week organized tour of the country. The emphasis is on personal interaction; no money changes hands between guests and hosts, and the major expense for the traveler is the airfare, usually advance purchase.

In its summer program, **World Learning, Inc.** (founded in 1932 as the Experiment in International Living), Kipling Rd. (P.O. Box 676), Brattleboro, VT 05302 (☎ 802/257-7751 or 800/345-2929 outside Vermont), places students aged 14 to 20 in the homes of foreign families for three to five weeks; they participate in family life (usually there are children their age in the family) as well as get together with other program participants and their group leader at least once a week. Beyond home stays, there are options for community service, intensive language study, ecological adventure, and short tours in 17 different countries. The organization can also arrange home stays for adults.

WORK CAMPS

There's no better or more enjoyable way for someone 16 and older to participate in international cooperation and goodwill than at a work camp. Volunteers from around the world arrange and pay for their own transportation and work in exchange for room and board and the chance to perform a socially significant task. Groups generally number 10 to 20; volunteers generally spend two to three weeks at a camp, work a 5-day, 30-hour week, and receive basic lodgings and communal meals. They may do manual or physical labor or perform a service, such as restoring hiking trails in a national park or working with underprivileged kids or the elderly. Most work camps take place from June through September.

For detailed information, contact **Volunteers for Peace International Workcamps (VFP),** 43 Tiffany Rd., Belmont, VT 05730 (☎ **802/259-2759**). VFP generally requires a minimum age of 18 for participants, although it will accept 16- and 17-year-olds for camps in France, Germany, and Russia. Its directory, published in April, costs $12 postage paid, which includes a newsletter subscription. This cost is deducted from any later registration fee, which is $150 per work camp. You can request a free copy of their newsletter by contacting the above address.

Also contact **SCI International Voluntary Service (SCI/IVS),** Route 2, Box 506, Crozet, VA 22932 (☎ **804/823-1826**), which accepts volunteers 18 and older for its European camps. Its directory, "International Workcamp Listings," is available each April for $5. Applicants pay $80 per project.

The **Council on International Educational Exchange (CIEE),** 205 E. 42nd St., New York, NY 10017 (☎ **212/661-1414**), offers a work-camp program. The minimum age to participate is 18. Its brochure on international work camps is free, but the actual application requires a $165 fee.

HOME EXCHANGES

The **Vacation Exchange Club,** P.O. Box 650, Key West, FL 33041 (☎ **and fax 305/294-1448** or 800/638-3841 in the U.S.), can help you set up a home swap—your house or apartment for a residence in a European country for a mutually determined amount of time. The cost of a listing in the directory, which is published twice a year (in January and February) and updated three times a year (in April, May, and June), is $70 for a two-year membership, which includes a copy of the 10,000-entry directory.

SPECIAL-INTEREST TRAVEL

For the best prices where special-interest travel is concerned, start with trips focusing on your interests organized by local colleges and universities. These are often led by knowledgeable faculty members and offer a variety of options—from architecture to wine tasting.

ADVENTURE TRAVEL

Adventure expeditions offered by tour companies can be expensive. If you're interested in a particular tour, ask these questions about it:

- In what currency are prices quoted?
- What does the fee cover?
- Can you make connecting air arrangements?
- Is insurance available?
- Is the group composed of amateurs as well as professionals?
- Does the leader give formal instruction or only informal interaction?
- If it is a photography tour, will film be processed en route so that images can be criticized?
- What is the ratio of leaders to participants?
- Are supplies and equipment provided?
- Are references available from people who have taken this trip with this leader?

IN THE U.S.   The least expensive of the adventure companies is the **Adventure Center,** 1311 63rd St., Suite 200, Emeryville, CA 94608 (☎ **510/654-1879** or 800/227-8747). Trips are slow-paced and flexible, with accommodations in small hotels or pensions or at camping sites. The active itineraries range from hiking in Tuscany to canoeing the Danube, sailing along the Turkish coast, or a Romanian jaunt focusing on hiking and wildlife. Land-only prices start at $445 for 8- to 22-day trips to European destinations. Request their "Explore" catalog.

Other adventure-travel operators featuring European trips include **Above the Clouds,** P.O. Box 398, Worcester, MA 01602-0398 (☎ **508/799-4499** or 800/233-4499); **Mountain Travel Sobek,** 6420 Fairmount Ave., El Cerrito, CA 94530 (☎ **510/527-8100** or 800/227-2384); and **Overseas Adventure Travel,** 625 Mt. Auburn St., Cambridge, MA 02138 (☎ **617/876-0533** or 800/221-0814).

IN THE U.K.   **Waymark Holidays,** 44 Windsor Rd., Slough SKI 2EJ (☎ **0753/516-477**), and **Sherpa Expeditions,** 131a Heston Rd., Hounslow, Middlesex TW5 0RD (☎ **0181/577-2717**), both cover Europe well. Find out how hard the walks are before making your booking and choose a walk or trek that's suited to your fitness level.

Walking holidays can be cheaper and less rigorous. There are plenty of companies to choose from, but **HF Holidays,** Imperial House, Edgware Rd., Colindale, London NW9 5AL (☎ **0181/905-9388** for a brochure), offers a range of one- to two-week packages in Austria, Britain, Italy, France, Slovenia, and Switzerland.

Cycling tours are a good way to see a country at your own pace. There are many companies that specialize in particular destinations. For instance, **Anglo Dutch Sports** (☎ **0181/650-2347**) offers a series of economical packages in Holland. **Alternative Travel Group Limited,** 69–71 Banbury Rd., Oxford OX2 6PE (☎ **0865/310-555**), runs cycling tours in Italy and France, through scenic countryside and medieval towns. Prices vary depending on whether you want basic or luxury accommodations, with flights and bike rental extra. Other good alternatives are **Bike Tours** (☎ **0225/480-130**) and the **Cyclists' Touring Club** (☎ **0483/417-217**). The CTC has a membership fee of £24 for adults and £12 for children and runs trips to most European countries. (Always remember to check whether the cost of bike rental is included in the total price.)

Getting to Europe

by Alice Garrard

This chapter explores various options for getting to Europe by air and sea for both U.S. and U.K. travelers, treating not only the obvious choices but also some you may not have thought of that can save you money.

1 By Air

BUCKET SHOPS

With the deregulation of air travel from the United States, major scheduled airlines are increasingly making a portion—up to 40%—of their transatlantic seats available to consolidators. These consolidators then distribute the tickets to the public through retail discount travel agencies known as "bucket shops," at reductions of about 20% to 30%.

These sharply reduced fares are now the least-expensive means of traveling to Europe, lower in most instances than charter-flight fares. However, the tickets are restrictive, valid for only a particular date or flight, nontransferable, and nonrefundable except directly from the bucket shop. The best prices are offered off-season rather than during high (summer) season.

Ads for bucket shops are small, usually a single column in width and half a dozen lines deep, most notably in the Sunday travel section of major newspapers. An ad will contain a list of cities and, opposite it, a list of corresponding prices. Short and to the point. **Travac,** 989 Ave. of the Americas, New York, NY 10018 (☎ 212/563-3303, or 800/TRAV-800), offers discounts to most major U.S. and European cities.

Although prices for flights available through bucket shops are low, at times they may be eclipsed by specials offered by the airlines. Watch for these advertised specials.

MORE THAN A BUCKET SHOP If you want to get to Europe within a certain time frame but still have a flexible schedule, consider **Airhitch,** 2472 Broadway, Suite 200, New York, NY (☎ 212/864-2000). This "self-help" organization founded by and for students (but you don't have to be a student to become a member) helps travelers fly to Europe (though not necessarily their preferred city) by taking advantage of last-minute seating availability. However, Airhitch isn't considered a "standby" service since the probability of seat vacancies is known in advance. Participants pay $169 one way if leaving from the East Coast, $269 from the West Coast, or $299 from other U.S. gateways; the first $25 of the payment is nonrefundable and considered the membership fee. In return, participants receive a listing of flights and a voucher that's later exchanged for a boarding pass.

A traveler may return to the United States via Airhitch (same prices as above); baggage requirements are the same as with any regular flight. It's possible to change the dates of a flight or get a refund, but some restrictions apply.

CHARTERS

The second-cheapest way to cross the Atlantic is on a charter flight. Competition from the bucket shops, not to mention competitive commercial airlines, has pared their number somewhat, but there are still plenty to choose from. **Homeric Tours, Inc.** (☎ **212/753-1100,** or 800/223-5570), specializes in charters and tours to Athens and Thessalonia for $499 to $649 round-trip, depending on date, plus a hefty tax. **Sceptre Charters, Inc.** (☎ **718/738-9400,** or 800/221-0924 outside New York State), operates from May through mid-October charters from New York, Boston, and Chicago to Shannon, Ireland, from only $439 round-trip, plus direct charters to Dublin (the only operator to offer direct flights) and to Belfast from only $489 round-trip. **Martinair** (☎ **407/391-1313,** or 800/627-8462) operates weekly charters to Amsterdam from seven major U.S. cities, plus Toronto and Vancouver; round-trip prices are $538 from Toronto, $448 from Florida, and $598 from the West Coast.

Jet Vacations, Inc. (☎ **800/JET-0999**), the well-known subsidiary of Air France, operates charters from eight U.S. gateways to Paris for one-way East Coast prices of $260 to $300, depending on city; from Houston for $349 to $374; and from Los Angeles for $370 to $398.

One of America's oldest charter companies, **Council Charter,** 205 E. 42nd St., New York, NY 10017 (☎ **212/661-0311** or 800/800-8222), offers a combination of charters and scheduled flights to major European cities from a variety of U.S. gateways. The company offers one-way and round-trip fares and allows passengers to fly into one city and out of another. It also offers a $30 cancellation waiver allowing passengers to cancel for any reason up to three hours prior to departure from the States and receive a full refund, minus a $75 fee (valid for only some cities).

For dates, departure cities, and prices for charter transportation between North America and Europe, check the Sunday travel section of a large city newspaper. *Jax Fax,* the monthly magazine of the air-chartering industry, is a comprehensive information source. Browse through your travel agent's latest copy.

Before deciding to take a charter flight, check the restrictions. You may be asked to purchase a tour package, pay far in advance, be amenable if the day of departure or destination is changed, pay a service charge, fly on an airline you're not familiar with (usually not the case), and pay harsh penalties if you cancel but be understanding if the charter doesn't fill up and is canceled up to 10 days before departure (seriously consider cancellation insurance; see "Insurance & Assistance" in Chapter 1). Summer charters fill up more quickly than others and are almost sure to fly.

Also, be sure you have received full information on the prices: Some charter companies have high-season supplements; many pass airport taxes directly on to the traveler. Make sure that the flight you want is available on the days you need.

If the base rate furnished is from an eastern gateway city, the company may run connecting flights either as charters or in conjunction with regularly scheduled airlines from other U.S. cities. These flights will be cheaper than independently booked flights, but you'll pay an "add-on" fee.

REBATORS

In another category are rebators, companies that pass all or part of their commissions on to the consumer; some charge a fee for their services. If you know where you want to go, call and find out the rebator's asking price; unlike travel agents, rebators don't help you make plans, but they do help you carry them out for a discounted price. For instance, **Travel Avenue,** 10 Riverside Plaza, Suite 1404, Chicago, IL 60606 (☎ **312/876-1116,** or 800/333-3335), offers an average 5% (or larger) rebate on airfares of $300 or more, depending on airline and cities booked. There is no cost; the fee is included.

Another rebator, **The Smart Traveller,** 3111 SW 27th Ave. (P.O. Box 330010), Miami, FL 33133 (☎ **305/448-3338,** or 800/448-3338; fax 305/443-3544), discounts international flights 4% to 22%, package tours 7%, and cruises 7% to 40%.

Travel Management International (TMI), 12173 E. Desert Cove, Scottsdale, AZ 85259 (☎ **602/661-8094,** or 800/959-0330; fax 602/661-8095), offers discount tickets on major airlines, though it specializes in cruises and tours to Europe, with many departure points.

GOING AS A COURIER

Travelers who wear two caps, that of airline passenger and that of courier, stand to save a lot of money crossing the Atlantic. The courier company handles the check-in and pickup of packages at each airport, and all you have to do is give up your checked-baggage allowance and make do with carry-on. Expect to meet a courier-service representative at the airport before departure to get the manifest of the checked items; upon arrival, you deliver the baggage-claim tag to a waiting courier agent. The system benefits not only travelers but also companies transporting time-sensitive materials, such as film or documents for banks and insurance firms.

One drawback (besides restricted baggage) is that you have to travel alone, since only one person can take advantage of any given flight. If there are two of you, try to arrange your departures on two consecutive days; the first to arrive can secure the hotel room and learn the lay of the land.

Companies offering frequent courier service to Europe include **Now Voyager Freelance Couriers,** 74 Varick St., Suite 307, New York, NY 10013 (☎ **212/431-1616**), which flies about 18 couriers to Europe per day; **Discount Travel International,** 169 W. 81st St., New York, NY 10024 (☎ 212/362-3636); and **Halbart Express,** 147-05 176th St., Jamaica, NY 11434 (☎ **718/656-8189** between 9am and 3pm Monday through Friday), which makes reservations up to two months in advance of departure.

Most flights depart from New York City, so you may have to tack on the additional cost to get to the gateway city. Prices change all the time, from low to very low. If a company needs emergency courier service and you can fly immediately, you could travel for next to nothing—say, $99 round-trip.

Sample Now Voyager charges for spring 1995 were $285 round-trip from New York to London and $299 round-trip from New York to Copenhagen, Frankfurt,

Madrid, Milan, Paris, Rome, and Stockholm. Sometimes flights are available from Miami and Houston, primarily to London. Now Voyager books flights up to two to three months in advance, but call the 24-hour number for last-minute immediate departure specials.

Foreign destinations are booked round-trip for specific dates. On occasion, the return flights to London have no courier delivery on the day of departure, so checked baggage space is available; call to find out.

For current information about courier travel and courier services, subscribe to *Travel Unlimited,* P.O. Box 1058, Allston, MA 02134, an eight-page typewritten newsletter that's been published monthly since 1986. The cost is $25 per year ($35 outside the U.S.) or $5 per single issue.

"BARGAIN" AIRLINES

An almost equally frugal way to cross the Atlantic is flying aboard an airline that's a relative newcomer to transatlantic routes and may not be identified by consumers with particular European destinations. To attract a little attention, these carriers drop their fares below those of the established competition. Actually, the only thing "cheap" about them is their price structure—not their service, standards, or safety.

Continental Airlines (☎ **800/231-0856**) offered summer 1995 round-trip midweek flights from New York City (Newark International) to London starting at $618. Other Continental gateways include Houston and Denver; other European destinations include Paris, Frankfurt, Madrid, and Munich.

In summer 1995 **Virgin Atlantic Airways** (☎ **800/862-8621**) offered round-trip flights with a Monday through Thursday departure to London from New York City and Boston for $667, from Miami and Orlando for $777, and from Los Angeles for $848.

Tower Air (☎ **718/553-8500,** or 800/34-TOWER in the U.S. outside New York State) offered summer 1995 round-trip fares from New York to Paris starting at $538 and from New York to Amsterdam starting at $498 ($100 to $200 less off-season) with no restrictions.

Icelandair (☎ **800/223-5500**) offered 1995 fares to Luxembourg from $358. For travelers with a flexible summer schedule, its "Three Days Before" fares, which must be booked no *earlier* than three days before departure date, were $598 from New York, $598 from Baltimore-Washington, and $398 from Orlando or Fort Lauderdale with up to a seven-day maximum purchase time. These fares are for Monday through Thursday departures; you pay more for a weekend departure. Icelandair also flies to many other European cities; in addition, it provides bus service from Luxembourg to selected cities in Germany for $12 one way; the train fare to Paris is about $66.

Sometimes cut-rate fares pop up unexpectedly—for instance, when a carrier inaugurates service from a new U.S. gateway. Always keep an eye out for these short-term, one-shot deals.

ADVANCE-PURCHASE FARES

If you can't find an acceptable charter or bucket-shop fare and no "bargain" airline flies from a gateway near you, look into advance-purchase fares, which are offered by every airline and are also known as excursion fares. Note that restrictions always apply. You usually have to purchase the ticket 7 to 14 days before departure and stay in Europe for a certain number of days, usually no fewer than 7 and no more than 21. The ticket may be called "nonrefundable," but

Europe's National Airlines

- **Austria:** Austrian Airlines (800/843-0002)
- **Belgium:** Sabena (800/955-2000)
- **England:** British Airways (800/AIRWAYS)
- **Scotland:** British Airways (800/AIRWAYS)
- **Denmark:** SAS World Airlines (800/221-2350)
- **Sweden:** SAS World Airlines (800/221-2350)
- **France:** Air France (800/AF-PARIS)
- **Germany:** Lufthansa (800/645-3880)
- **Greece:** Olympic Airways (800/223-1226 outside New York State)
- **Hungary:** Malev Hungarian Airlines (800/262-5380)
- **Ireland:** Aer Lingus (800/223-6537)
- **Italy:** Alitalia (800/223-5730)
- **The Netherlands:** KLM Royal Dutch Airlines (800/777-5553)
- **Portugal:** TAP Air Portugal (800/221-7370)
- **Spain:** Iberia (800/772-4642)
- **Switzerland:** Swissair (800/221-4750)

some airlines will let you change the return date for $75 or so; it pays to ask when you book the ticket.

Advance-purchase fares are often higher than those mentioned in previous categories, so it behooves you to search out other possibilities first, including connecting airfare to cities served by charters, bucket shops, "bargain" airlines, or courier services. If you're a student or an older traveler, ask if you qualify for a discount. Airfares are as changeable as the weather, so it pays to call around—to both American and European carriers.

EUROPEAN CARRIERS

When investigating the best fares, don't overlook the European carriers themselves. Most European countries have their own national carrier, which is either partially or totally state-owned (British Airways is an exception). These carriers fly to more destinations within Europe and have more scheduled flights within their own countries. And many of them have long been praised for outstanding service.

You may find that the European carriers offer prices comparable to U.S. airlines, and they do sometimes advertise special bargains. Many European carriers regularly advertise packages including both airfare and hotel, which can represent a great savings.

Check what the European carriers have to offer, especially if you plan to fly within Europe. Some have partnership arrangements with American carriers, such as SAS with Continental. This works particularly well for travelers departing from outside the New York City area. For example, when you board a Continental flight in Denver, you're given a boarding pass for SAS at Newark International Airport and your baggage is checked through to Copenhagen.

FLY/DRIVE TOURS

A good option for the independent-spirited budgeteer is a fly/drive holiday. A tour operator will get you to and from Europe and have a car waiting for you at a price much lower than you could get by paying the airfare and car-rental charges separately. Sometimes these tours include lodging and some food and entertainment.

CIE Tours International (☎ **800/243-8687;** 800/248-6832, 24 hours, for brochure requests only) is the largest tour operator to Ireland. Its 56-page 1995 brochure features over 21 coach tours per week in Ireland, Scotland, and England, with $55 discounts for those 55 or over (on selected tour departures). The company's self-drive "Go-As-You-Please Ireland" vacation is priced from $39 to $52 per person per day (based on seven-night minimum stay) and includes a Ford Fiesta, B&B accommodation at your choice of over 1,000 farmhouses or private homes, and a unique option to upgrade to hotel accommodations from as little as $14 per person. CIE Tours also offers special airfares with Aer Lingus and British Airways.

Similarly, **Aer Lingus** (☎ **212/557-1110,** or 800/223-6537) offers its own "Go as You Please" fly/drive packages including hotel vouchers and the option to stay in farmhouses and country homes. Its "Discover Ireland Vacation" program provides a car, unlimited mileage, and lodging in a B&B, with full Irish breakfast, from $39 per day, or lodging in Best Western hotels from $64 per day.

The **British Airways** (☎ **800/AIRWAYS**) "London Plus Holiday Collection" offers a wide variety of destinations—in Britain, Ireland, or Europe—and lets travelers create the vacation best suited to their interests and budget, with discounted hotel and rental-car rates (using Hertz), as well as tickets to over 30 London theater productions.

SAS World Airlines (☎ **800/221-2350**) offers a rental car for $69 for three days for travel in Scandinavia only, to those who book a flight seven days in advance; the price is based on two people traveling together.

REMINDER

To lodge a complaint about a commercial airline, be it a U.S. or a foreign carrier, go first to the airline's consumer-relations representative. To get the name and phone number of that person or to complain further if you're dissatisfied with the response, contact the **Department of Transportation's Office of Consumer Affairs,** C-75, Washington, DC 20590 (☎ **202/366-2220**).

2 By Sea

CRUISE LINES

The best value for your travel dollar to Europe is going by air. Still, if your big dream—undeniably, a romantic one—is to make a transatlantic crossing once in your lifetime, by all means pursue it.

Only one cruise ship plies the Atlantic with regularity anymore—the *Queen Elizabeth 2,* from June 1 to October 8—and it's not cheap, with prices starting at $2,495. When you consider that round-trip airfares to Europe are in the $500 to $600 ballpark and the ship provides your lodging and three meals a day, it's not the splurge it might initially seem. For more information, contact **Cunard,** 555 Fifth Ave., New York, NY 10017 (☎ **800/221-4770**).

Start your research by studying your travel agent's or librarian's copy of the bimonthly *Official Steamship Guide,* which has a transatlantic section listing ships and passenger freighters, date of departure, port of embarkation, ports of call, port of debarkation, length of cruise, lowest available price, and telephone number. The guide also includes information on barge, canal, and river cruises.

FREIGHTERS

Cruise liners cross the Atlantic in about 5 days, while it takes a freighter 8 to 10 days. Freighters carry no more than 12 passengers (otherwise they'd be required to have a doctor on board), charge less than cruise lines (though more than airlines), and provide unbeatable service. Plus you'll have the run of the ship and form a fast camaraderie with the other passengers and the crew. On the other hand, you may find yourself at the mercy of erratic sailing schedules (some passengers have waited a week in port for their freighter to leave).

By freighter tradition, passengers pay for a fixed number of days; if the trip comes in early, they might receive a refund; if it takes longer, and it often does, they may get the extra days for free. Tipping is expected, as it is on cruise ships. On a freighter you pay about half the daily cost of a passenger liner—about $100 per day. Some budget-style ships and originating foreign freighters charge less.

The **Mediterranean Shipping Company,** c/o Sea the Difference, 420 Fifth Ave., 8th Floor, New York, NY 10018-2702 (☎ **212/354-4409** or 800/666-9333), offers one-way trips year round from Boston, calling at New York City, Baltimore, Portsmouth (Va.), Antwerp, Bremerhaven, Hamburg, Felixstowe (England), and Le Havre, starting at $1,800 from Boston or New York, at $1,600 from Baltimore and Portsmouth (Va.). The round-trip fare is $3,200 for 28 days. The company also offers weekly departures from Houston, Miami, New Orleans, Wilmington, and Charleston to Antwerp, Bremerhaven, and Felixstowe, starting at $1,600 to $2,300 one way; round-trip passage is $3,800 for 35 days.

The **Mediterranean Great Lakes Line,** c/o Freighter World Cruises, 180 S. Lake Ave., Suite 335, Pasadena, CA 91101 (☎ **818/449-3106**), has an approximately 20-day round-trip that sails from Montréal down the St. Lawrence River and on to Liverpool and Le Havre. The round-trip fare per person is $2,016 for a double-occupancy room and $1,953 for a single-occupancy room. A one-way fare is available for $1,100.

Mineral Shipping, c/o Freighter World Cruises (see address and telephone number above), offers more basic accommodations and amenities on monthly sailings from Savannah, Ga., to two Dutch ports for a two- to four-day stay in each, then returning to an East Coast U.S. port. Prices start at $1,160 one way and $2,520 round trip for 32 to 40 days. Rates for a vehicle accompanying a passenger, one way in either direction, are as following: motorbike, $330; auto, from $650; van, from $850.

Even "cheap" freighters like those above charge considerably more than airlines, though they do provide a memorable experience. Waiting lists for freighter travel range from two weeks to four months to a year, but last-minute berths are fairly easy to come by. People who are retired or on sabbatical are prime candidates for this type of vagabonding. Most lines have a maximum age of 75-plus.

A directory called *Ford's Freighter Travel* does a thorough job of listing freighters and their itineraries by departure point (with additional sections on river and canal travel), as well as travel agencies specializing in freighter travel. The cost of the directory, published twice yearly, is $14.95 for one issue and $20 for two in any given year. Contact Ford's Travel Guides, 19448 Londelius St., Northridge, CA 91324 (☎ **818/701-7414**).

Those who subscribe to *TravLtips,* P.O. Box 580188, Flushing, NY 11358 (☎ 718/939-2400 or 800/872-8584), receive the magazine six times a year, along with discounts on specific cruises. *TravLtips* carries first-person accounts of freighter trips worldwide and a listing of reliable freighter cruise lines, including half a dozen or more that are Europe-bound. Reservations may be made directly through *TravLtips* at no extra charge. The price is $15 per year in the United States, $20 (Canadian) per year in Canada. People from other countries should inquire at the number above.

3 For U.K. Travelers

BY PLANE

You can fly to European destinations from 18 British airports (different destinations are served by different airports). Journey times vary from 30 minutes to Ostend in Belgium to five hours to the Canary Islands or Turkey.

There are no hard-and-fast rules about where to get the best deals for European flights from the United Kingdom, but bear the following points in mind:

- Daily newspapers often carry advertisements for companies offering cheap flights. London's *Evening Standard* has a daily travel section, and the Sunday editions of almost any newspaper will run many ads. Highly recommended companies include **Trailfinders** (☎ 0171/938-3366) and **Platinum Travel** (☎ 0171/937-5122).
- Around Victoria and Earls Court in London are many bucket shops offering low fares. Make sure the company you deal with is a member of the IATA, ABTA, or ATOL. These umbrella organizations will help you out if anything goes wrong.
- **CEEFAX,** a British television information service included on many home and hotel TVs, runs details of package holidays and flights to Europe and beyond. Just switch to your CEEFAX channel and you'll find a menu of listings that includes travel information.

BY TRAIN & FERRY

For information about traveling to the Continent by train and ferry, call **British Rail International** (☎ 0171/834-2345). Credit- and charge-card bookings may be made by calling 0171/828-0892, or you can make reservations in person at the office in Victoria Station, London SW1V 1JZ.

BY COACH & FERRY

If you want to take your time, coach travel is a relaxing way to see Europe. Many package trips around Europe or individual countries are available. **Cosmos Tourama** (☎ 0181/464-3477) provides a wide range of trips all over Europe, from 3 to 22 nights.

Eurolines, 52 Grosvenor Gardens, London SW1W 0AU (☎ 0171/730-0202), offers a range of budget coach trips around Europe, all including the cost of the ferry.

The U.K. ferry company **Sally Line** (☎ 0181/858-1127) runs a cheap coach/ferry service from Liverpool Street to Copenhagen between April and November.

If you're looking for a cheap camping/coach tour, try **Contiki Concept** (☎ 0181/290-6422). Tours range from 7 to 33 days and allow you to see much of Europe with a minimum of effort.

By Car & Ferry

Taking your car abroad gives you maximum flexibility to travel at your own pace and to set your own itinerary. You can make ferry/drive reservations with any good travel agent. There are many options, so shop around for the best deals.

Brittany Ferries is the U.K.'s largest ferry/drive company, sailing from the south coast of England to five destinations in France and Spain. Sailings depart from Portsmouth to St-Malo and Caen (☎ **0705/827-701**); from Poole to Cherbourg (☎ **0705/82770**); and from Plymouth to Roscoff and Santander, Spain (☎ **0752/221-321**). Brittany also runs ferries from Cork in Northern Ireland to Roscoff and St-Malo (☎ **0752/269-926** for a brochure). Ask about standard tickets, which allow you to take "as many people as you can get into your car," according to Brittany Ferries. In some cases, these prices will be lower.

Stena Sealink Lines (☎ **0233/647-047**) runs ferries from Dover to Calais, Southampton to Cherbourg, Newhaven to Dieppe, Harwich to the Hook of Holland, and the west coast of England to Ireland.

P&O Ferries (☎ **0181/575-8555**) sails from Portsmouth to Cherbourg and Le Havre in France and to Bilbao, Spain; from Dover to Calais, France, and Ostend, Belgium; and from Felixstowe to Zeebrugge, Belgium. Their fares are excellent.

Scandinavian Seaways (☎ **0171/409-6060**) allows you to travel farther afield—to Germany, Sweden, Finland, Denmark, and Norway. Ask about Flag Days, when fares are reduced, and about discounts for students who show valid identification.

With any ferry trip you can buy "open jaw" tickets allowing you to depart from and return to different ports in the United Kingdom, so long as you travel both ways with the same ferry company.

By Hovercraft

Traveling by Hovercraft or SeaCat cuts your journey time from the United Kingdom to the Continent. A Hovercraft trip is definitely a fun adventure, as the vessel is technically "flying" off the water. The SeaCat (or catamaran) is a recent addition to the U.K.'s sailing fleet, and its Channel crossing requires only a fraction of the time a ferry would take.

You can travel from Dover to Calais in 35 minutes on the Hovercraft, in 50 minutes by SeaCat. Catamaran service runs between Folkestone and Boulogne, taking only 55 minutes (this is the cheaper of the two routes). Standby sailings at reduced rates are available. SeaCats also travel to the Isle of Wight, Belfast, and the Isle of Man. For more details, call 0304/240-101 for Dover sailings or 0303/221-281 for Folkestone crossings.

Via the Channel Tunnel

The "Chunnel" opened for passenger service in fall 1994, with three-hour non-stop Eurostar service between London and Paris and $3^{1}/_{4}$-hour nonstop service between London and Brussels. In 1996, overnight service will commence, linking middle, northern, and southwestern England, Scotland, and south Wales with Paris and Brussels.

At the time of this writing, six trains make the trip between London and Paris Saturday through Thursday, with seven trains on Friday (15 daily departures are planned eventually). Special discounts are available for BritRail, BritFrance, and Flexipass holders.

Similar to airfare pricing, tickets for Eurostar service are discounted when a Saturday-night stopover or a 14-day advance purchase is involved (combine the two to get the lowest fare; in summer 1995 it was $62.50 one way between London and Brussels and $67 between London and Paris, standard class). Availability is limited but the price is certainly right. Also available are packages including rail travel, hotel accommodations, and a city tour.

For cars and their passengers only, there's 35-minute Le Shuttle service between Folkestone, England, and Calais, France. The trains carry 180 cars, and in the peak summer season shuttle service runs every 15 minutes. Reservations are not necessary.

You can get up-to-the-minute information and prices on Eurostar service by calling **BritRail** (☎ 800/677-8585) or **Rail Europe** (☎ 800/94-CHUNNEL); for information on **Le Shuttle** service, call 215/741-5153.

4 Travel Clubs

Members of travel clubs are doubly fortunate: Their lifestyle permits them to pick up and travel at the last (or next-to-last) minute and through their club they can choose from bookings all over the world. The offerings are usually within a few weeks of departure, when remaining seats, rooms, or berths need to be filled, and the discounts are impressive—from 20% to 40%.

Bookings are done entirely by telephone, so you might find yourself on hold for five minutes or so, waiting your turn. The closer it gets to departure time, the better the discount will be.

Membership fees range from nothing to $60. When deciding which travel club to join, consider the following:

- What kinds of travel are available?
- How are members notified of offerings?
- Is there a newsletter?
- Is there a toll-free hotline?
- How often are the offerings updated?
- How difficult is it to get through on the hotline?
- Is there a service charge for overnight delivery of a ticket?
- Can a ticket be left at the airport for immediate pickup and use? Is there a charge?
- May a companion who's not a club member travel at the same rate? How about more than one other person?
- How soon and how far into the future can a member book a trip?
- What is the method of payment?
- What are the primary gateways?
- Are car-rental discounts offered?
- Is it possible to register for a particular destination or cruise and be notified when it's available? Is there an extra charge?
- What is the cancellation policy?

Travel clubs nationwide include the following:

Last Minute Travel, 1249 Boylston St., 1st Floor, Boston, MA 02215-3410 (☎ **617/267-9800** or 800/LAST-MIN), has no membership fee. Members of **Moment's Notice,** 163 Amsterdam Ave., Suite 137, New York, NY 10023 (☎ **212/486-0500**), have access to a hotline, but it's not toll free. The annual fee is $25.

For $49 per year you can become a member of **Travelers Advantage,** 3033 S. Parker Rd., Suite 900, Aurora, CO 80014 (☎ **800/548-1116** 24 hours). Besides special discounts, members receive a 5% cash-back bonus on air, hotel, and car rentals booked through the club's reservations system. Members must be MasterCard or Visa cardholders.

Annual membership for **Vacations to Go,** 1502 Augusta, Suite 415, Houston, TX 77057 (☎ **713/974-2121** or 800/338-4962 outside Texas), is $19.95, or $50 for three years; it includes four issues of *Cruises & Tours* magazine, plus discounts on car or RV rentals and airline tickets. They specialize in cruises.

Worldwide Discount Travel Club, 1674 Meridian Ave., Miami Beach, FL 33139 (☎ **305/534-2082**), offers a toll-free number to members, who receive every 25 days a travelog with 400 listings. Individual membership is $40 per year; families pay $50.

Encore Marketing International, 4501 Forbes Blvd., Lanham, MD 20706 (☎ **301/459-8020** or 800/638-8976), operates three specialty discounting organizations: Short Notice provides last-minute discounts on tour packages and organized trips (annual membership $36); Encore offers additional free nights or up to 50% discounts at about 700 European hotels, as well as discounts on car rentals, airfares, leisure activities, and dining, plus special offerings on vacation packages and cruises (annual membership $49); and Villas of the World provides 20%- to 25%-per-night discounts on villas, condos, and resorts (one year $60).

Reminder: Airfares and other travel costs reach their peak during tourist season: In Europe, that's June through September. Fortunately, travel clubs offer the most discounts for Europe at the same time. Those who can leave on short notice pay a fraction of the normal fares.

4 Amsterdam

by Nikolaus Lorey

"In Rotterdam they work, in The Hague they rule, but in Amsterdam they live." This old saying was shared with me by a Dutch doctor I met on a train in the Netherlands, and you'll find that it's true. Amsterdammers have a zest for life that's evident in their bustling nightlife, their numerous museums, and their thousands of restaurants serving foods from all over the world. In summer Amsterdam's sidewalks and squares fill with tables and chairs as café-sitters enjoy the warm air while sipping a Heineken or a coffee. In winter they strap on their skates and race down the frozen canals (if it gets cold enough—which is rare). And at any time of year these health-conscious people take to the streets and bridges on their bicycles. You'll find it impossible to visit Amsterdam without falling under its spell and joining Amsterdammers as they enjoy their lively city.

Amsterdam is also a city that takes pride in its history. Not only are there dozens of museums, but also the entire city center is one large historic district of restored buildings, most dating from Amsterdam's golden age in the 17th century. At that time Amsterdam was the world's most prosperous port, and the wealthy merchants built a beautiful city of elegant canal mansions that are preserved for all to enjoy. The preservation process continues today as young and energetic Amsterdammers restore the Jordaan neighborhood.

However, like all great cities, Amsterdam has its dark side. The streets and canals could be cleaner, there's a growing drug problem, and the Red Light District, long a sightseeing attraction, is no longer safe for strolling. However, Amsterdam is an exciting cosmopolitan city where you'll find plenty to see and do while staying within your budget.

1 Amsterdam Deals & Discounts

BUDGET BESTS Amsterdam's best deal by far is simply strolling along the shady canals with their bridges and beautiful 17th-century houses. Few cities in the world have so many buildings of this vintage still standing. While strolling, you'll likely see many street performers, from marionettes to five-piece rock n' roll bands. The entertainment costs as much as you wish to toss into the hat.

What's Special About Amsterdam

Canals
- Attracive old homes lining the city's five main canals.
- Canal tours, canal buses, canal taxis, and canal bikes.

Museums
- The Rijksmuseum, the Vincent van Gogh Museum, the Amsterdam Historisch Museum, and the Tropenmuseum.

Monuments
- *Homomonument*—in memory of those gays and lesbians killed during World War II.
- The Dockworker—a moving memorial to the February Strike against the deportation of Jews in World War II.

The Netherlands
- Windmills, tulips, and people in wooden shoes within an hour or so of Amsterdam.

Bicycles
- The best way to get around Amsterdam.
- Reasonable rates at rental shops.

Patates Frites (French Fries)
- Better than the much-acclaimed Brussels fries (if you're visiting both cities, you can make your own taste comparison).

Nightclubs
- Melkweg and Paradiso—still going strong after all these years.
- Lectures, classes, food, galleries, film presentations, and live concerts.

Concertgebouw
- The center of Amsterdam's classical music scene, a concert hall with one of the world's best acoustics and performances almost every night.

SPECIAL DISCOUNT OPPORTUNITIES   One of the best all-around discounts in Amsterdam is the **National Museum Card** (described below). To purchase one of these cards you'll need a passport-size photo to attach to it. Note that the Anne Frankhuis, one of Amsterdam's most popular museums, does not honor this card.

For Students   If you're under 26 and not necessarily a student, you can purchase a **Cultureel Jongeren Passport (CJP)** or Cultural Youth Passport, entitling you to free admission to many of the city's museums, as well as to discounts on theater performances, concerts, and other events. The cost is only Dfl 15 ($8.80) and the passport is good for one year. You can get your CJP at the Amsterdam Tourist Information Offices at Centraal Station and on Leidseplein. Be sure to bring your passport and a passport-size photo of yourself.

If you're under 19, you can also get a **National Museum Card,** good for one year, for only Dfl 15 ($8.80). The National Museum Card allows you free admission to most of Amsterdam's major museums.

For Senior Citizens   Almost all Amsterdam museums have reduced admission for senior citizens, and there's also a senior citizens' **National Museum Card,** available for Dfl 25 ($14.70).

For Everyone   The **National Museum Card** gives free admission to more than 350 museums all over Holland for one year. The normal adult rate for the card is Dfl 40 ($23.50). If you plan to visit more than five or six museums in Amsterdam, you'll save money by purchasing this card. Museum Cards are available from museum ticket windows and at the Tourist Information Office in front of Centraal Station.

For getting around town on the public transit system—which includes trams, buses, and a subway system—buy either the *dagkaart* **(day card)** for Dfl 11 ($6.45) or a 15-strip *strippenkaart* for Dfl 12 ($7.05). The dagkaart is good for one day's unlimited travel in the city, and the strippenkaart is good for as many as seven trips with no time limit. A dagkaart is available from bus and tram drivers and in Metro stations; the strippenkaart is available in tobacco shops, at the ticket office in front of Centraal Station, and at post offices.

WORTH THE EXTRA MONEY   Amsterdam is a city of canals—in fact, there are more here than in Venice. It would be a shame to visit this watery city without staying in a hotel overlooking one of the canals, especially since these **canal-house hotels** are generally in 300-year-old buildings. So if you really want to experience Amsterdam, splurge a bit, even if it's only for one night, and stay at one of the canal-house hotels recommended later in this chapter.

The other Amsterdam splurge you won't want to miss is an **Indonesian rijsttafel dinner.** This dining extravaganza includes 15 to 20 different courses and will cost you between Dfl 40 and 60 ($23.50 and $35.30).

2 Pretrip Preparations

REQUIRED DOCUMENTS   Citizens of the United States, Canada, the United Kingdom, Australia, and New Zealand need only a valid passport for a visit to the Netherlands for stays of less than three months.

TIMING YOUR TRIP   You'll see from the chart below that Amsterdam gets plenty of rain all year. Although July and August receive the most rainfall, they also receive plenty of sunshine, making summer the best time of year for sidewalk café-sitting. In addition, many excursions from Amsterdam operate only during summer; this is when the Alkmaar Cheese Market and the Zuiderzee Museum in Enkhuizen are both open.

Amsterdam's Average Daytime Temperature & Days of Rain

	Jan	Feb	Mar	Apr	May	June	July	Aug	Sept	Oct	Nov	Dec
Temp. (°F)	36	36	41	46	54	59	62	62	58	51	44	38
Days of Rain	21	17	19	20	19	17	20	20	19	20	22	23

Special Events   The most popular time of year to visit the Netherlands is the **bulb-flowering season.** From the end of March to mid-May the bulb fields— tulips, hyacinths, daffodils, and crocuses—are in full bloom. There are plenty of excursions available from Amsterdam to view the colorful fields, and at the end of April each year there's a **Flower Parade** from Haarlem to Noorwijk.

What Things Cost in Amsterdam	U.S.$
Taxi from the airport to the city center	35.30
Metro from Centraal Station to Waterlooplein	1.75
Local telephone call	.15
Double room at the Amsterdam Hilton (deluxe)	370.60
Double room at the Hotel Seven Bridges (moderate)	76.45
Double room at the Hotel Pax (budget)	47.05
Lunch for one at Sama Sebo (moderate)	14.70
Lunch for one at Broodje van Kootje (budget)	5.90
Dinner for one, without wine, at the Five Flies (deluxe)	32.35
Dinner for one, without wine at Haesje Claes (moderate)	14.70
Dinner for one, without beverage, at the Egg Cream (budget)	9.40
Glass of beer	2.05
Coca-Cola in a restaurant	2.05
Cup of coffee	1.45
Roll of ASA 100 color film, 36 exposures	8.25
Admission to the Rijksmuseum	7.35
Movie ticket	6.45
Theater ticket to the Concertgebouw	8.82–111.75

April 30 is **Queen's Day,** when Amsterdam takes to the streets for a day of merry-making with performances, exhibits, parades, and markets.

Throughout June, Amsterdam celebrates the **Holland Festival** with cultural and musical events all over the city.

BACKGROUND READING   Anyone interested in the Holocaust and World War II will want to read *Anne Frank: The Diary of a Young Girl* (Washington Square Press). Written by a 14-year-old Jewish girl while her family was in hiding in an attic from the Germans during World War II, the diary provides a feel for life in occupied Amsterdam. Once you arrive, you can visit the house where Anne and her family lived until they were discovered. Another fascinating war diary is *An Interrupted Life* (Pocket Books) by Etty Hillesum, a young Jewish woman who lived in Amsterdam until she was taken to Auschwitz, where she died.

For those interested in history, Simon Schama's *The Embarrassment of Riches* (Knopf) is an extremely accessible examination of golden age Amsterdam.

Novels set in and around Amsterdam include Janwillem van de Wetering's *Corpse on the Dike* and *Hard Rain* (Ballantine), both enjoyable, offbeat detective stories.

3 Amsterdam Specifics

ARRIVING
FROM THE AIRPORT   If you fly into Amsterdam, you'll arrive at the efficient **Schiphol Airport,** where the runways are 16 feet below sea level, on the floor of what was once a large lake. For many years Schiphol has been voted the best airport in Europe, in part because of its massive duty-free shopping center.

Making Schiphol even more convenient is the train connecting the airport with Amsterdam's Centraal Station. Leaving directly from the air terminal, this train costs Dfl 6 ($3.50) one way in second class. It's also possible to catch trains to other European cities directly from the airport.

FROM THE TRAIN STATION Whether you fly into Amsterdam or take a train from another city in Europe, you'll find yourself at Amsterdam's massive **Centraal Station,** built a little over 100 years ago on an artificial island. Inside the terminal you'll find a currency-exchange counter and a railway information center. Directly in front of the station is the Amsterdam Tourist Information Office, a Metro station, and a ticket office where you can purchase a strippenkaart or dagkaart for use on the trams and buses. These cards are less expensive here than when bought from tram and bus drivers. Many tram and bus stops are also located in front of Centraal Station.

VISITOR INFORMATION

The **Amsterdam Tourist Information Office,** Stationsplein 10 (☎ **06/340-34-066**), is directly in front of Centraal Station in a small white building that also contains a coffee shop and boat dock. Hours vary with the season, but throughout the year the office is open daily. Here you can get maps and information about the city, as well as reserve hotels and tours; there's also a window for buying theater and concert tickets. Another information center at Leidsestraat 16 is open Monday through Saturday.

Be sure to pick up a copy of *What's On in Amsterdam* for Dfl 3.50 ($2.05). This small magazine is full of information about the month's art exhibitions, concerts, and theater performances, and lists popular bars, discos, and restaurants.

Another great information source for the young and the budget-conscious is the free **"Use-It"** youth information guide, available at the Tourist Information Office at the Arena, s'Gravesandestraat 51. Aimed specifically at students and young travelers, this booklet is crammed with great information for everyone.

For additional information on cultural events or to make reservations, stop by the **Amsterdam Uit Buro (AUB),** on Leidseplein, open Monday through Saturday from 10am to 6pm.

CITY LAYOUT

When you step out of the Centraal Station main entrance you're facing the center of Amsterdam. Using this point as a reference, you'll see that the city is laid out along five concentric semicircles of canals called **Singel, Herengracht, Keizersgracht, Prinsengracht,** and the outermost, **Singelgracht** (*gracht* means "canal"). It was along these canals that wealthy 17th-century merchants built their elegant homes, which are still standing. The largest and most stately of the canal houses are along Herengracht. Within these canals are many smaller canals radiating out from the center. The area within Singelgracht is known as the Old City.

Damrak is a very busy tourist street that leads from Centraal Station to **Dam Square,** location of the former dam on the Amstel River that gave Amsterdam its name. To the left of Damrak is Amsterdam's famous **Red Light District,** where government-licensed prostitutes sit in their windows with red lights glowing, waiting for customers. One block to the right of Damrak is **Nieuwendijk** (which becomes **Kalverstraat** when it crosses Dam Square), a pedestrians-only shopping street. If you follow Kalverstraat to the end, you'll find yourself at **Muntplein** (*plein*

The Dutch Guilder

For American Readers At this writing, $1 was approximately Dfl 1.70 (or Dfl 1 =59¢), and this was the rate of exchange used to calculate the dollar values given in this chapter (rounded to the nearest nickle).

For British Readers At this writing, £1 was approximately Dfl 2.70 (or Dfl 1 = 37p), and this was the rate of exchange used to calculate the pound values in the table below.

Note: The rates given here fluctuate from time to time and may not be the same when you travel to Holland. This table should be used only as a guide.

Dfl	U.S.$	U.K.£	Dfl	U.S.$	U.K.£
.25	.15	.09	30	17.64	11.11
.50	.29	.18	35	20.58	12.96
.75	.44	.27	40	23.52	14.81
1	.59	.37	45	26.47	16.66
2	1.17	.74	50	29.41	18.51
3	1.76	.11	60	35.29	22.22
4	2.35	1.48	70	41.17	25.92
5	2.94	1.85	80	47.05	29.62
6	3.53	2.22	90	52.94	33.33
7	4.11	2.59	100	58.82	37.03
8	4.70	2.96	125	73.52	46.29
9	5.29	3.33	150	88.23	55.55
10	5.88	3.70	175	102.94	64.81
15	8.82	5.55	200	117.65	74.07
20	11.76	7.40	250	147.05	92.59
25	14.70	9.25	500	176.47	111.11

means "square") beside the old Mint Tower. Cross the Singel and continue in the same direction and you'll reach **Rembrandtplein,** one of Amsterdam's main evening entertainment areas.

The other main nightlife area is **Leidseplein,** on the last of Amsterdam's concentric canals, Singelgracht (not to be confused with Singel, which is the first of the concentric canals). Leidseplein is at the end of **Leidsestraat,** another pedestrian shopping street that leads from Singel to Singelgracht. Leidsestraat is reached from Kalverstraat by **Heiligeweg,** another short pedestrian shopping street.

Museumplein, where you'll find Amsterdam's three most famous museums—the Rijksmuseum, the Vincent van Gogh Museum, and the Stedelijk Museum of Modern Art—is a five-minute walk along Singelgracht from Leidseplein.

One other area worth mentioning is the **Jordaan,** a quickly developing old neighborhood now filled with inexpensive restaurants, unusual shops, and small galleries. You'll find the Jordaan between Prinsengracht and Singelgracht in the area bounded by Rozengracht and Brouwersgracht. To reach this area, turn right off Damrak at any point between Centraal Station and Dam Square. When you cross Prinsengracht, you're in the Jordaan.

GETTING AROUND

Amsterdam offers many options for getting around the city. Trams and buses are generally the most convenient and bicycles are certainly the most fun.

BY SUBWAY   Amsterdam's subway system, called the **Metro,** unfortunately doesn't serve most areas tourists want to visit. You can, however, use it to reach Waterlooplein or the Amstel Station from Centraal Station. Both these stops are within Zone 1 and require two boxes on a strippenkaart (see below).

BY BUS & TRAM   Sixteen tram lines and 30 bus lines serve Amsterdam. The buses and trams are the most convenient means of getting around the city, although they can be slow during rush hours. Tram nos. 1, 2, 4, 5, 9, 13, 16, 17, 24, and 25 and bus nos. 18, 21, 32, 33, 34, 35, 39, and 67 all originate at Centraal Station.

Now comes the confusing part: How do you pay for your ride? A **single ticket** is Dfl 3 ($1.75), but the best idea is to buy a **strippenkaart** for Dfl 11 ($6.45) at a tobacco shop, a newsstand, a post office, or the Centraal Station public transportation ticket office, opposite the station's main entrance. Before boarding a bus or tram, consult the map posted at every stop to determine how many zones you'll be traversing. Fold your strippenkaart so that one more box than the number of zones you're traveling through is facing up and stick this end into the yellow box near the door as you enter. The machine will stamp your card. If you're traveling through one, two, or three zones, your card is good for one hour and as many transfers as you need. On buses, have the driver stamp your card. If you don't have a strippenkaart, you can buy 2-, 3-, and 10-strip cards from the driver, but this is a more-expensive option than buying the strippenkaart ahead of time.

Want a less complicated solution? For Dfl 12 ($7.05), a **dagkart** is available from bus and tram drivers, good for 24 hours and as many rides across as many zones as you like. Be sure to get it stamped the first time you use it. There are also tickets good for two to nine days, ranging from Dfl 16 to 42.25 ($9.40 to $24.85).

Should you be considering not paying the fare, keep in mind that inspectors, sometimes undercover, may demand to see your ticket at any time. If you haven't paid the proper fare, you'll be fined Dfl 60 ($35.30). They won't accept the fact that you're a tourist as an excuse for not paying.

ON FOOT   When looking at a map of Amsterdam, you might think that the city is too large to explore on foot. This simply isn't true. In fact, it's possible to see almost every important sight in the city on a four-hour walking tour. One important thing to remember when strolling around town is that cars and bicycles have the right of way when turning. Don't step in front of one thinking that it's going to stop for you.

BY BICYCLE   Of the approximately 700,000 Amsterdammers, around 550,000 own bicycles. You'll see children barely old enough to walk, their great-grandparents, even businesswomen in high heels pedaling around the city in any weather. A bicycle is one of the best ways of getting around in this flat city where too many cars clog the narrow streets. There are two things to remember, though: Watch out for unpredictable drivers, and always lock your bike—theft is a common problem.

Bikes can be rented all over Amsterdam, but the following shops offer good rates: **Take a Bike,** in the basement of Centraal Station, to the right of the main entrance as you face the station (☎ **020/624-83-91**), charges only Dfl 8 ($4.70) per day plus a passport and a Dfl 200 ($117.65) deposit. **MacBike,** Nieuwe Uilenburgerstraat 116 (☎ **020/620-09-85**) or Marnixstraat 220 (☎ **020/ 626-69-64**), charges Dfl 11 ($6.45) per day plus a passport and a Dfl-50 ($29.40) deposit.

Even more fun than cycling around the city is touring the countryside. Ask at the Tourist Information Office in front of Centraal Station for brochures outlining cycling routes, then head off on your own. A tour is offered by **Yellow Bike Guided Tours,** Nieuwezijds Voorburgwal 66 (☎ **020/620-69-40**) for Dfl 42.50 ($25). This company also offers bicycle tours of Amsterdam for Dfl 29 ($17.05).

Amsterdam has one other pedal-powered means of transportation—**canal bikes.** These are small pedal boats for two to four people that are available on Leidseplein, near the Rijksmuseum, on Prinsengracht near the Anne Frankhuis, and on Keizersgracht near Leidsestraat. Canal bikes are available daily from 9am to 7pm in spring and autumn and until 11pm in summer. Rates are Dfl 20.50 ($12.05) per hour for a two-person boat and Dfl 31.50 ($18.50) per hour for a four-person boat. There's also a Dfl-50 ($29.40) refundable deposit.

BY TAXI   You can get a taxi in front of any major hotel or at Leidseplein, Rembrandtplein, or Centraal Station. To phone for a cab, call 677-77-77. Rates start at Dfl 5.60 ($3.30) and increase by Dfl 2.80 ($1.65) per kilometer.

BY CAR   A car is a good way to see the nearby countryside, and in Holland everything is nearby. On a day trip from Amsterdam it's possible to visit almost any area of the country. All the major car-rental agencies have offices in Amsterdam, and a number of smaller companies offer rates as low as Dfl 45 to 65 ($26.50 to $38.25) per day for very economical subcompacts. These rates do not, however, include the mileage cost, insurance, or the 17.5% tax. Expect your total bill to come to around Dfl 180 ($105.90) per day. Try **Diks,** van Ostadestraat 278–280 (☎ **020/662-33-66**), or **Kaspers en Lotte,** van Ostadestraat 232–234 (☎ **020/ 671-70-66**).

BY BOAT   One last means of getting around in Amsterdam is by boat. The best option for tourists is the **Museumboat** (☎ **020/622-21-81**), which stops near virtually all of Amsterdam's museums and attractions. The boats leave from behind the Tourist Information Office in front of Centraal Station every 30 minutes daily between 10am and 5pm. Tickets are available at the Lovers Canal Cruises counter near the dock. A day ticket costs Dfl 19 ($11.15) for adults and Dfl 15 ($8.80) for senior citizens or children 13 and under. This ticket also allows you half-price admission at most of the museums. There's also a combination ticket for Dfl 35 ($20.60), which includes free admission to three museums. However, this is a bargain only if you choose to visit three of the most expensive museums, such as the Rijksmuseum, the Vincent van Gogh Museum, or Anne Frankhuis. There are English-speaking guides on the boats.

There are also **water taxis,** but these are quite expensive. If you feel like a splurge, call 020/622-21-81.

The **Canal Bus** (☎ **020/623-98-86**), a boat operating on a fixed route, stops at the Rijksmuseum, Leidseplein, Leidesestraat/Keizersgracht, Westerkerk/Anne Frankhuis, Centraal Station, and City Hall/Rembrandthuis. A ticket costs Dfl 15 ($8.80) and is good all day.

FAST FACTS: Amsterdam

Babysitters A student babysitting service, Kriterion, Roetersstraat 170 (☎ **020/624-58-48**), takes calls daily from 5:30 to 7pm. Sitters are students who are at least 18 years old.

Banks Two convenient banks are ABN–Amro Bank, Rokin 82 (☎ **020/624-25-90**), open Monday through Friday from 9am to 4 pm; and ABN–Amro Bank, Rokin 16 (☎ **020/520-66-66**), open Monday through Friday from 9am to 5 pm.

Business Hours Most **banks** are open Monday through Friday from 9am to 4 or 5pm, occasionally later on late-night shopping evenings. **Shops** are generally open Monday through Friday from 8:30 or 9am to 5:30 or 6pm and Saturday from 8:30 or 9am to 4 or 5pm. Almost all shops are closed Sunday, and many don't open until 11:30am Monday and stay open until 9pm Thursday or Friday.

Consulates The Hague is the seat of government of the Netherlands, and that's where all embassies are located. But there are a few consulates in Amsterdam, including those of the **United States,** Museumplein 19 (☎ **020/664-56-61**), open Monday through Friday from 8:30am to noon and 1:30 to 3:30 pm; and the **United Kingdom,** Konigslaan 44 (☎ **020/676-43-43**), open Monday through Friday from 9am to noon and 2 to 4pm.

Currency The Netherlands **guilder** (abbreviated **f.** or **Dfl** for florin or Dutch florin, which was the old name of the currency) is the basic monetary unit. The guilder is divided into 100 cents and there are coins of 5, 10, and 25 cents, as well as 1, 2.50, and 5 guilders. Paper-note denominations include 5, 10, 25, 50, 100, 250, and 1,000 guilders.

When changing money, be absolutely sure to ask the exchange rate and the service charge. Rarely will a currency-exchange office give you the official rate, so shop around. Banks are usually best, followed by windows in train stations and tourist offices. American Express and Thomas Cook also offer good rates, and can be found at several locations in Amsterdam.

Emergencies For 24-hour doctor and dentist referrals, call 06/350-32-042 or 020/624-57-93. For police emergencies, call 622-22-22. For an ambulance or in case of a fire, call 06-11. Before and after regular pharmacy hours (Monday through Friday from 9am to 5:30 pm), call 06/350-32-042 for information on where you can get a prescription filled.

Eyeglasses If you need to have your glasses repaired or replaced, contact Pearle Express, Kalverstraat 108 (☎ **020/623-64-29**), or FA J. M. Schmidt, Rokin 72 (☎ **020/623-19-81**).

Holidays Public holidays in Amsterdam include New Year's Day, Good Friday, Easter Monday, Queen's Day (Apr 30), Ascension Day, Whit Sunday and Monday, Christmas Day, and Boxing Day (Dec 26).

Hospitals The following hospitals have a first-aid department: Academisch Medisch Centrum, Meibergdreef 9 (☎ **020/566-33-33** or 566-91-11), and Onze Lieve Vrouwe Gasthuis, Oosterparkstraat 179 1e (☎ **020/599-91-11**).

Information The Amsterdam Tourist Information Office is directly in front of Centraal Station in a small white building that also contains a coffee shop and boat dock. See "Visitor Information" under "Amsterdam Specifics," earlier in this chapter.

Laundry/Dry Cleaning When it's time to clean up those travel-weary clothes, head to a *wasserette*. Most are open daily from 7 or 8am to 8 or 9pm. Convenient locations include the following: Ferdinand Bolstraat 9, near the Heineken brewery, where 6 kilos (13¹/₄ lb.) costs Dfl 11 ($6.45); Rozengracht 59, on the edge of the Jordaan area, where you can do 7.5 kilos (16¹/₂ lb.) for Dfl 12.50 ($7.35).

Get your dry cleaning done at the Clean Center, Elandsgracht 59–61 (☎ **020/ 625-07-31**), or at Ferdinand Bolstraat 9 (☎ **020/662-71-67**), near the Heineken brewery. Klardinette, Rozengracht 23 (☎ **020/627-82-71**), is another convenient choice.

Lost & Found There's a general lost-and-found office at Waterlooplein 11 (☎ **020/559-80-05**), open Monday through Friday from 9am to 2pm. For items lost on a tram, a bus, or the Metro, go to the GVB head office at Prins Hendrikkade 108–114 (☎ **020/551-44-08**). It's open Monday through Friday from 9am to 4pm. For items lost on trains, check at Stationsplein 1 (☎ **020/ 557-85-44**) between 7am and 10 pm.

Mail The PTT–Main Post Office, located at Singel 250, at the corner of Raadhuisstraat, is open Monday through Friday from 9am to 6pm (on Thursday to 8pm) and Saturday from 9am to 3pm. Branch offices are open Monday through Friday from 9am to 5pm. A letter to the United States will cost Dfl 1.60 (95¢) and a postcard, Dfl 1 (60¢).

Newspapers You'll find plenty of English-language newspapers, magazines, and books at W. H. Smith, Kalverstraat 152 (☎ **020/638-38-21**), open Monday from 11am to 6pm, Tuesday and Saturday from 10am to 6pm, Wednesday and Sunday from 11am to 5pm, and Thursday from 9am to 9pm.

Photographic Needs You'll find one-hour photo processing all along Damrak, Leidsestraat, Nieuwendijk, and Kalverstraat. Swank Shot Studios, Spui 4 (☎ **020/624-40-00**), is a convenient camera store.

Police For police emergencies, dial 622-22-22.

Radio/TV There are 16 cable TV stations in Amsterdam, including three British and one American. There are only a few local radio stations, but the programming is fairly diverse.

Religious Services Churches with services in English include St. John and St. Ursula, Begijnhof 30 (☎ **020/623-35-65**); the English Reformed Presbyterian/ Church of Scotland, Begijnhof 48 (☎ **020/662-49-65**); and the Anglican Church, Groenburgwal 42 (☎ **020/624-88-77**).

Shoe Repair Get shoes repaired at Schoenreparatie 2000, Kerkstraat 72 (☎ **020/623-51-37**), open Monday through Friday during regular business hours. Other shoe-repair shops can be found at Kalverstraat 4 and Spui 5.

Tax Look for the HOLLAND TAX-FREE SHOPPING sign in shop windows around Amsterdam. These shops will provide you with the form you need for recovering the VAT (value-added tax) when you leave the country. Refunds are available only when you spend more than Dfl 300 ($176.45) in a store. For more information, see "Shopping," later in this chapter.

Telephone A **local phone call** costs Dfl .050 (30¢) for three minutes. Telephone instructions are in English, and machines accept 25-cent and Dfl-1 coins. For **international phone calls,** there's the Telecenter at Raadhuisstraat 46–50, near Westerkirk (☎ 020/484-36-54), open daily from 8am to 2am. A three-minute call to the United States costs Dfl 9 ($5.30). You can reach an AT&T operator by dialing 06 (wait for the tone), then 022-9111. The center also sells **phone cards:** 20 unit-cards cost Dfl 5 ($2.85), 45-unit cards cost Dfl 10 ($5.80), and 115-unit cards cost Dfl 25 ($14.70). **Faxes** can be sent overseas for Dfl 3.50 ($2.05) per page to the United States, and for Dfl 7.50 ($4.40) per page to Australia, plus a surcharge of Dfl 5 ($2.95). The center also receives faxes at 020/626-38-71 and 020/626-53-26. Another phone center is at Leidsestraat 101.

Tipping In almost all restaurants, a service charge is included in the price of the meals, so it's not necessary to leave any tip. However, if service is exceptionally good, you may want to leave a small tip, depending on the price of the meal. Taxi fares include a service charge, but drivers expect a small tip as well.

4 Accommodations

Be prepared to climb hard-to-navigate stairways if you want to save money on lodging in Amsterdam. Narrow and steep as ladders, Amsterdam's stairways were designed to conserve space in the narrow houses along the canals. Today they're an anomaly that'll make your stay even more memorable. There was a time when the canal-house hotels of Amsterdam were quite cheap, but those days are gone. Most canal-house hotels have raised their rates beyond the budget range, but you'll still find a few listed here. Even if you don't stay in a canal house, you'll most likely stay in a building built 250 to 350 years ago during Amsterdam's golden age. If you have difficulty climbing stairs, ask for a room on a low floor.

In most cases a large Dutch breakfast is included in the rate for a night. These hearty repasts usually include ham, cheese, a boiled egg, several types of bread, butter, milk, and sometimes chocolate sprinkles, which are very popular.

DOUBLES FOR LESS THAN DFL 120 ($70.80)
NEAR DAM SQUARE & CENTRAAL STATION

Hotel Pax

Raadhuisstraat 37, Amsterdam 1016 DC. ☎ **020/624-97-35.** 8 rms, none with bath. Dfl 50 ($29.40) single; Dfl 80 ($47.05) double. AE, MC, V. Tram 13, 14, or 17 to Westermarkt.

Most rooms here are large, and all are simply furnished and clean; two of them have small balconies overlooking the street. Room 19, with four beds and plenty of space, is particularly well suited to students or young people traveling together. Mr. Veldhuizen has been in business for nearly 30 years. Breakfast is not included here.

Hotel de Westertoren

Raadhuisstraat 35B, Amsterdam 1016 DC. ☎ **020/624-46-39.** 8 rms, 4 with shower only. Dfl 60 ($35.30) single without bath; Dfl 95 ($55.90) double without bath, Dfl 105 ($61.80) double with shower only. Rates include full Dutch breakfast. AE, DC, EURO, MC, V. Tram 13, 14, or 17 to Westermarkt.

Getting the Best Deal on Accommodations

- Stick to hotels listed in this book or recommended by the Amsterdam Tourist Information Office in front of the train station. Politely decline the offers of young men and women in the train stations who'll want to take you to a hotel.
- Hotels near the Jordaan and Leidseplein offer great deals.
- Note that discounts are often offered in winter. Even if the rates have not been lowered, it's often possible to get a few guilders off the quoted price.
- Advance reservations are extremely important in summer, when Amsterdam is the youth vacation capital of Europe.

Perhaps the best of the hotels on this block is the recently renovated Westertoren. The two rooms in the front with balconies are attractive but tend to be a bit noisy; the quieter rooms in the back are large and bright. The breakfast is served in the rooms, and proprietors Tony and Chris van der Veen, who speak English, will share a wealth of information about the city.

NEAR THE RIJKSMUSEUM & LEIDSEPLEIN

Euphemia Budget Hotel

Fokke Simonszstraat 1, Amsterdam 1017 TD. ☎ **020/622-90-45.** 26 rms, 1 with bath. TV. Dfl 95 ($55.90) double without bath, Dfl 120 ($70.60) double with bath; Dfl 140 ($82.35) triple or quad without bath. Breakfast Dfl 6.50 ($3.80) extra. AE, DC, EURO, MC, V. Tram 16, 24, or 25 to Prinsengracht.

Five minutes' walk from the Rijksmuseum, the Euphemia is popular with students and young travelers. Though a bit frayed around the edges, this is still a clean and inexpensive place to stay, with ground-floor rooms that are wheelchair accessible. In addition to the color TV in most rooms, there's a TV and VCR in the breakfast room; you can even rent videos from the hotel. Inexpensive snacks are sold during the afternoon and evening.

Hotel Asterisk

Den Texstraat 14–16, Amsterdam 1017 ZA. ☎ **020/624-17-68.** Fax 020/638-27-90. 29 rms, 22 with bath. TEL. Dfl 65 ($38.25) single without bath, Dfl 80($47.05) single with bath; Dfl 115 ($67.65) double without bath, Dfl 160 ($94.10) double with bath; Dfl 180 ($105.90) triple with bath. Rates include full breakfast. EURO, MC, V. Tram 16, 24, or 25 to Weteringcircuit.

This is the nicer of the Texstraat options. All the rooms come with new carpets and furniture, and a buffet Dutch breakfast, with at least five types of bread as well as meats and cheeses, is served every morning in the bright breakfast room; over the years visitors from all over the world have tacked pieces of their own money on the wall. There are a few rooms on the ground floor, an elevator, and babysitters available, making this a good choice for older travelers and families alike.

Hotel Bema

Concertgebouwplein 19b, Amsterdam 1071 LM. ☎ **020/679-13-96.** Fax 020/662-36-88. 7 rms, 4 with shower. Dfl 60 ($35.30) single without bath; Dfl 85 ($50) double without bath, Dfl 105 ($61.75) double with shower only; Dfl 125 ($73.50) triple without bath, Dfl 140

($82.35) triple with shower only; Dfl 175 ($102.95) quad without bath. Rates include full breakfast. V. Tram 5 or 16 to Concertgebouwplein.

American ownership/management and an enviable location directly across from the Concertgebouw make this a popular budget choice in Amsterdam, albeit with younger visitors. The rooms are large, although a bit worn, and many still show the building's original ornate plasterwork. Breakfast is served in the rooms.

Hotel Casa-Cara

Emmastraat 24, Amsterdam 1075 HV. ☎ **020/662-31-35.** Fax 020/676-81-19. 9 rms, 6 with bath. TEL. Dfl 55 ($32.35) single without bath, Dfl 85 ($50) single with bath; Dfl 75 ($44.10) double without bath, Dfl 100 ($58.80) double with bath; Dfl 130 ($76.45) triple with bath; Dfl 160 ($94.10) quad with bath. Rates include full breakfast. No credit cards. Tram 2 or 16 to Emmastraat.

Though it's a 10-minute walk from the Rijksmuseum, the Casa-Cara is another good choice. A marble floor in the entry hall and black contemporary furniture in the breakfast room lend an air of sophistication to the hotel. The guest rooms are spacious and clean, with large windows and high ceilings.

Hotel de Leydsche Hof

Leidsegracht 14, Amsterdam 1016 CK. ☎ **020/623-21-48.** 10 rms, 4 with shower only. Dfl 85 ($50) double without bath, Dfl 95 ($55.90) double with shower only; Dfl 135 ($79.40) triple with shower only; Dfl 170 ($100) quad with shower only. No credit cards. Tram 1, 2, or 5 to Keizersgracht.

Built in 1665 and overlooking Leidsegracht, this home has long been an excellent budget hotel. Rooms vary in size, the larger ones with high ceilings and big windows. Many rooms have wood paneling that makes them look a bit like saunas, but original plasterwork and old (unused) fireplaces in some rooms hint at the building's past. If you need a firm mattress, you might want to look elsewhere. The most interesting feature of the hotel is its intricately carved stairway railing. Breakfast is not included here.

✪ Hotel Impala

Leidsekade 77, Amsterdam 1017 PM. ☎ **020/623-47-06.** Fax 020/638-92-74. 14 rms, 6 with bath. Dfl 75 ($44.10) single; Dfl 120 ($70.60) double; Dfl 155 ($91.20) triple; Dfl 180 ($105.90) quad; Dfl 220 ($129.40) quint. Rates include full Dutch breakfast. EURO, MC, V. Tram 1, 2, or 5 to Leidseplein.

Around the corner from Leidseplein, the Impala overlooks the junction of two canals. The singles and doubles here are small, but the triples and quads are large, and one is particularly popular for its bay window overlooking the canals. The hotel was renovated in 1994, and the rooms are clean and pleasant. The breakfast is served in a large asymmetrical breakfast room with a hardwood floor and an unusual modern wall tapestry. The hotel has always been under the same family management, and their first guest 35 years ago gave them the inspiration for the name: He was from South Africa and wore a pin in the shape of an impala, the red antelope.

Hotel Kap

Den Texstraat 5B, Amsterdam 1017 XW. ☎ **020/624-59-08.** 17 rms, 1 with shower only, 4 with shower and toilet. Dfl 60 ($35.30) single without bath; Dfl 90 ($52.95) double without bath, Dfl 110 ($64.70) double with shower only, Dfl 130 ($76.50) double with shower and toilet; Dfl 145 ($85.30) triple without bath, Dfl 175 ($102.95) triple with shower and toilet; Dfl 180 ($105.90) quad without bath; Dfl 245 ($144.10) quint with shower and toilet. Rates include full Dutch breakfast. AE, DC, MC, V. Tram 16, 24, or 25 to Weteringcircuit.

Across from the Asterisk (above), this hotel has several large family rooms as well as smaller rooms. Simply furnished and decorated, the rooms are clean and comfortable. A dark wooden table and chairs fill the breakfast room.

Hotel Museumzicht

Jan Luykenstraat 22, Amsterdam 1071 CN. ☎ **020/671-29-54.** 14 rms, 3 with bath. Dfl 65 ($37.75) single without bath; Dfl 105 ($61.75) double without bath, Dfl 140 ($82.35) double with bath; Dfl 150 ($88.25) triple without bath, Dfl 165 ($97.05) triple with bath. Rates include full breakfast. EURO, MC, V. Tram 2 or 5 to Hobbemastraat.

This hotel is ideal for museum-goers since it's right across from the back of the Rijksmuseum. The breakfast room commands an excellent view of the museum with its numerous stained-glass windows. Robin de Jong, the proprietor, has filled the guest rooms with an eclectic collection of furniture, from 1930s English wicker to 1950s modern.

Hotel P. C. Hooft

P. C. Hoofstraat 63, Amsterdam 1071 BN. ☎ **020/662-71-07.** 16 rms, 3 with shower only. TV. Dfl 65 ($38.25) single with shower only; Dfl 95 ($55.90) double without bath, Dfl 105 ($58.80) double with shower only. Rates include full breakfast. MC, V. Tram 1, 2, or 5 to Leidseplein.

Imagine staying on Amsterdam's most upscale shopping street, amid the chic boutiques and classy restaurants, for no more than you'd pay in any other budget hotel in town. That's what you get at the P. C. Hooft, although you'll have to climb quite a few stairs to enjoy your stay. Most of the rooms here have been recently updated with contemporary furnishings and new carpets, and there are plans to add full baths to some. The breakfast room is painted wild shades of orange and blue that are guaranteed to wake you up in the morning.

✪ Hotel Wynnobel

Vossiusstraat 9, Amsterdam 1071 AB. ☎ **020/662-22-98.** 12 rms, none with bath. Dfl 70–75 ($44.15–$44.10) single; Dfl 95–110 ($55.90–$64.70) double; Dfl 150 ($88.20) triple; Dfl 200 ($117.65) quad. Rates include full Dutch breakfast. No credit cards. Tram 1, 2, or 5 to Leidseplein; then cross the canal, turn left, and watch for the street on the far side of the Vondelpark entrance.

The Wynnobel is around the corner from the chic boutiques of P. C. Hoofstraat and a few minutes' walk from the Rijksmuseum. It overlooks part of Vondelpark and is run by friendly Pierre Wynnobel and his wife, who sees to it that the hotel is kept clean. The large rooms are furnished with old or antique furniture, and a large breakfast is served in your room. A beautiful central stairway winds around to the four floors, and the first floor is only a short climb. A stay here is always pleasant.

Van Ostade Bicycle Hotel

Van Ostadestraat 123, Amsterdam 1072 SV. ☎ **020/679-34-52.** Fax 020/671-52-13. 15 rms, 3 with shower only. Dfl 60 ($35.30) single without bath; Dfl 90 ($52.95) double without bath, Dfl 115 ($67.65) double with shower only. Rates include breakfast. No credit cards. Tram 24 or 25 to Ceintuurbaan (the ninth stop).

The young owners of this budget hotel have hit on an interesting idea: They cater to visitors who wish to explore Amsterdam on bicycles. Their guests can rent bicycles for only Dfl 8 ($4.70) per day and a deposit is not required. They're also helpful in planning bicycling routes. The recently renovated guest rooms feature new carpets and comfortable modern furnishings; some have kitchenettes and small balconies, and there are large rooms for families. The hotel is a few blocks from the popular Albert Cuypstraat Market. An old bike hangs on the facade, and there are always bikes parked in front. For long stays, two doubles with kitchenettes in an annex near Rembrandtplein can be rented to "selected tourists." The atmosphere is friendly and easygoing.

IN & NEAR THE JORDAAN

Hotel de Bloiende Ramenas

Haarlemmerdijk 61, Amsterdam 1013 KB. ☎ **020/624-60-30.** Fax 020/420-22-6l. 10 rms, none with bath. Dfl 45 ($26.50) per person. No credit cards. Bus 11 or 18 to Oranjestraat (third stop from Centraal Station).

On a street lined with all sorts of shops on the edge of the Jordaan, this hotel (no elevator) is a good choice for readers traveling in small groups. Most of the spacious rooms have up to five beds. The hotel is on three floors in a 17th-century building, with a street-level coffee shop and bar. The hotel, whose name means the "Blooming Radish," has been open for more than 100 years and radiates a kind of austere charm. Don't expect more than average comfort, but the location and price are excellent.

DOUBLES FOR LESS THAN DFL 135 ($79.40)
NEAR REMBRANDTPLEIN

Hotel Adolesce

Nieuwe Kiezersgracht 26, Amsterdam 1018 DS. ☎ **020/626-39-59.** Fax 020/627-42-49. 23 rms, 11 with bath. Dfl 130 ($76.45) double without bath, Dfl 160 ($94.10) double with bath; Dfl 170 ($100) triple without bath; Dfl 190 ($111.75) quad without bath. Rates include full breakfast. MC, V. Closed Nov–Mar. Metro: Waterlooplein.

Quilts and parrots are the themes at this hotel. You'll find live parrots in the lobby and parrot prints decorating the rooms and halls. Likewise, old quilts are displayed throughout. All guest rooms are outfitted with new furnishings. The breakfast room, which includes a small bar, a patio garden, and a TV lounge, is in the basement but made bright with large skylights. This six-story building has steep stairs and no elevator, but a few rooms are on the ground floor, including two off the back patio.

Hotel Barbacan

Plantage Muidergracht 89, Amsterdam 1018 TN. ☎ **020/623-62-41.** Fax 020/627-20-41. 20 rms, 13 with bath. TV TEL. Dfl 60–115 ($35.30–$67.65) single without bath; Dfl 115 ($67.65) double without bath, Dfl 130–170 ($76.45–$100) double with bath. Rates include full breakfast. EURO, MC, V. Tram 9 to Artis Zoo.

You can't miss the Barbacan—it's the building with all the flags out front. Inside you'll find a collection of police memorabilia and a lobby gift shop. The rooms are clean, modern, and quiet, with new carpets and contemporary furnishings. There are even safes in all rooms.

Hotel Keizershof

Keizersgracht 618, Amsterdam 1017 ER. ☎ **020/622-28-55.** Fax 020/624-84-12. 6 rms, 2 with shower only. Dfl 75 ($44.10) single without bath; Dfl 110 ($65) double without bath, Dfl 130 ($76.45) double with shower only, Dfl 140 ($82.35) double with shower and toilet. Rates include full Dutch breakfast. No credit cards. Tram 16, 24, and 25 to Keizersgracht.

This hotel, in a large old canal house, is run by the genial Mrs. de Vries and her son, Ernest. The rooms are named after movie stars, and there are several other special touches that make a stay here memorable. You enter through a street-level door, and to reach the upper floors you must climb a wooden spiral staircase built from a ship's mast. The ceilings of most rooms have exposed beams. Breakfast is served in the ground-floor breakfast room.

✪ Hotel Prinsenhof

Prinsengracht 810, Amsterdam 1017 SL. ☎ **020/623-17-72** or 627-65-67. Fax 020/638-33-68. 10 rms, 2 with bath. Dfl 85 ($50) single without bath; Dfl 120–125 ($70.60–$73.50) double without bath, Dfl 160–165 ($94.10–$97.05) double with bath; Dfl 180 ($105.90) triple without bath, Dfl 215 ($126.45) triple with bath; Dfl 295 ($l73.50) quad with bath. Rates include full breakfast. No credit cards. Tram 4 to Prinsengracht.

One of the best deals in Amsterdam, the Prinsenhof is not far from the Amstel River in a renovated canal house. Most rooms are quite large, with beamed ceilings, and the front rooms look out onto Prinsengracht, where colorful small boats are docked. The large breakfast is served in a very attractive blue-and-white dining room. The friendly proprietor, Mr. André van Houten, takes pride in the quality of his hotel and will make you feel at home. A pully will haul your bags to the upper floors.

✪ Hotel Seven Bridges

Reguliersgracht 31, Amsterdam 1017 LK. ☎ **020/623-13-29.** 11 rms, 6 with bath. Dfl 100 ($58.80) single without bath, Dfl 160 ($94.10) single with bath; Dfl 130 ($76.45) double without bath, Dfl 180 ($105.90) double with bath. Rates include full Dutch breakfast. No credit cards. Tram 16, 24, or 25 to Keizersgracht.

This may be the best hotel value in all Amsterdam. If you're going to splurge for a room with an attached bath, this is the place to do it. Each of the huge rooms is unique, with antique furnishings, plush carpets, and reproductions of modern art on the walls; one room even has a bath with a skylight and wooden walls similar to those in a sauna. The front rooms overlook a small canal and the rear rooms overlook a garden. Your large breakfast will be served in your room at the time you request. Proprietors Pierre Keulers and Gunter Glaner are extremely helpful. An added bonus is that the hotel is only two blocks from busy Rembrandtplein.

In & NEAR THE JORDAAN

Hotel Acacia

Lindengracht 251, Amsterdam 1015 KH. ☎ **020/622-14-60.** Fax 020/638-07-48. 14 rms, 2 studios, 1 houseboat, all with bath. Dfl 95 ($55.90) single; Dfl 125 ($73.50) double; Dfl 160 ($94.10) triple; Dfl 210 ($123.50) quad; Dfl 150 ($88.25) studio; Dfl 150 ($88.25) houseboat for one, Dfl 230 ($135.30) houseboat for four. Rates include full breakfast. EURO, MC, V (add 5% to rates). Bus 18 to Nieuwe Willems Straat.

This unusual triangular corner building faces a picturesque small canal. The young Dutch owners, Hans and Marlene van Vliet, are proud of their hotel. All rooms are furnished with modern beds, small tables, and chairs, as well as attractive new carpets. The large front-corner rooms sleep as many as five and have windows on three sides. On the ground floor is a cozy Old Dutch–style breakfast room where a full breakfast is served at long wooden tables. There are also a couple of studio doubles here with tiny kitchenettes, plus a spacious houseboat moored in the canal across the street.

✪ Hotel van Onna

Bloemgracht 102–104 and 108, Amsterdam 1015 TN. ☎ **020/626-58-01.** 39 rms, 21 with bath. Dfl 60 ($35.30) per person in a room without bath; Dfl 65 ($38.25) per person in a room with bath. Rates include full breakfast. No credit cards. Tram 13, 14, or 17 to Westermarkt.

Consisting of three canal houses (two old and one new), this hotel has grown over the years, but its genial owner, Loek van Onna, continues to keep his prices reasonable. Mr. van Onna has lived here since he was a boy and will gladly tell you of the building's history. Accommodations in the three buildings vary considerably, with the best rooms in the new building (1993). However, the oldest and simplest rooms also have a great deal of charm. Whichever building you wind up in, ask for a room in front overlooking the canal.

NEAR THE RIJKSMUSEUM & LEIDSEPLEIN

Hans Brinker Hotel

Kerkstraat 136–138 (a few blocks from Leidseplein), Amsterdam 1017 GR. ☎ **020/ 622-06-87.** Fax 020/622-06-87. 115 rms, all with bath. Dfl 75 ($44.10) single; Dfl 120 ($70.60) double; Dfl 180 ($105.90) triple; Dfl 200 ($117.65) quad; Dfl 39.50 ($22.35) per person in a dorm. AE, EURO, MC, V. Tram 1, 2, or 5 to Leidseplein.

The Hans Brinker was completely renovated in 1992 and 1993, and the rooms have new carpeting and contemporary furnishings. Lockers in every room are a holdover from the hotel's days as a youth hostel–type accommodation. There are still a few dorm rooms here with 6 to 12 beds, but they're expensive compared to other dorm rooms around town. However, the regular rooms with private baths are a good deal.

Hotel Linda

Stadhouderskade 131, Amsterdam 1074 AW. ☎ **020/662-56-68.** 17 rms, 5 with shower only, 5 with bath. Dfl 105 ($61.75) double without bath, Dfl 130 ($76.45) double with shower only, Dfl 180 ($105.90) double with bath. Rates include full Dutch breakfast. Closed Nov–Jan. No credit cards. Tram 4, 16, 24, or 25 to Stadhouderskade.

The Linda is an elegant moderately priced hostelry overlooking a wide canal. The front door's huge old-fashioned key for a handle makes it impossible to miss. Inside there are Persian carpets on the floors, a marble entrance, and stained-glass doors. The rooms are well furnished, and a delicious breakfast is served each morning.

⑤ Kooyk Hotel

Leidsekade 82, Amsterdam 1017 PM. ☎ **020/623-02-95** or 622-67-36. Fax 020/ 638-83-37. 19 rms, none with bath. Dfl 75 ($44.10) single; Dfl 110 ($64.70) double; Dfl 140 ($82.35) triple; Dfl 175 ($105.90) quad. Rates include full Dutch breakfast. MC, V (add 4% to rates). Tram 1,2, or 5 to Leidseplein.

Most rooms at the Kooyk contain TVs, and all have been refurnished and redecorated; several are wheelchair accessible. A huge four-bed room in front overlooks Singelgracht. Reproductions of Dutch paintings, old photographs of Amsterdam, and photos of American movie stars hang on the breakfast room's walls.

SUPER-BUDGET CHOICES
STUDENT HOTELS & YOUTH HOSTELS

If you plan to stay in a hostel or student hotel in summer, it's imperative that you look for a room early in the day—by late afternoon, hostels are usually full. Try to avoid arriving in Amsterdam after dark since this will make finding a place to stay very difficult.

Arena Budget Hotel

s'Gravesandestraat 51, Amsterdam 1092 AA. ☎ **020/694-74-44.** Fax 020/663-26-49. 38 rms, all with shower only, plus 520 dorm beds. Dfl 90 ($52.95) double; Dfl 125 ($73.50) triple with shower; Dfl 20–32.50 ($11.75–$19.10) per person in a dorm. No credit cards. Metro: Weesperplein. Tram 14 or 9 to Tropenmuseum.

In a massive red-brick house built in 1890 as a hospital, the hotel is today not only a place to sleep but also a cultural center. The large dorms have 60 beds in each; 8 smaller dorms have 6 to 8 bunk beds each. There are also 34 doubles, four triples, and one apartment with 6 beds. The hotel features an information center, a concert hall, and a TV/video lounge, as well as a restaurant and a garden. Bike rentals are offered. In summer, pop concerts, dance parties, and film showings liven up the atmosphere. This is no doubt the happiest hostel in town!

Bob's Youth Hostel

Nieuwezijds Voorburgwal 92, Amsterdam 1012 SG. ☎ **020/623-00-63.** 6 apts, all with bath, plus 200 dorm beds. Dfl 125 ($73.50) apt for two to four; Dfl 25 ($14.70) per person for a dorm bed, plus a refundable deposit of Dfl 25 ($14.70) for locker key. Rates include breakfast and showers. Dinner (summer only) Dfl 8 ($4.70) extra. No credit cards. Tram 1, 2, 5, 13, or 17 from Centraal Station to the second stop.

Conveniently located halfway between Centraal Station and Dam Square, this hostel is open all year. Guests are accommodated in dorms with 4 to 16 bunk beds. Sheets and blankets are furnished, and there's a 3am curfew. Reception and the breakfast room are a few steps below street level. The atmosphere is international; 50% of the customers are from English-speaking countries. Users of alcohol and drugs are definitely barred. In 1995 Bob's opened an annex around the corner, at Spui 47, renting six modern apartments with fully equipped kitchenettes and color TV for two to four guests—one of the best deals in town.

Eben Haezer

Bloemstraat 179, Amsterdam 1016 LA. ☎ **020/624-47-17.** 114 dorm beds. Dfl 16 ($9.40) per person in a dorm, plus a refundable deposit of Dfl 10 ($5.90). Rates include full breakfast. No credit cards. Tram 13 or 17 to Marnixstraat.

The nicer of the two Christian Youth Hostels, the Eben Haezer is located on the edge of the Jordaan area, a 10-minute walk from Dam Square. The beds are bright-red bunk beds in large dormitories with huge windows. There's a midnight curfew Sunday through Thursday night (1am on Friday and Saturday), and the dorms are closed for cleaning every day between 10am and 2pm. New showers, central heating, a small lounge, a large dining hall serving three meals a day, and a peaceful patio all add up to a great deal if you don't mind sleeping in a dorm.

International Budget Hostel

Leidsegracht 76, Amsterdam 1016 CR. ☎ **020/624-27-84.** 52 beds. Dfl 90–110 ($52.95–$64.70) double with bath; Dfl 28–35 ($16.45–$20.60) per person in a dorm. Breakfast Dfl 5 ($2.95) extra. AE, DC, MC, V. Tram 1, 2, or 5 to Leidseplein.

The rooms here are basic and most are shared four-bed rooms, but a few are single and double rooms that come with their own TVs. There's also a lounge with several large sofas, a TV, a VCR and videotapes for rent, and a breakfast room. This hotel is popular with students and housed in a restored former canal warehouse with large shutters and windows facing Leidsegracht.

The Shelter

Barndesteeg 21, Amsterdam 1012 BV. ☎ **020/625-32-30.** Fax 020/623-22-82. 166 dorm beds. Dfl 15 ($8.80) per person in a dorm, plus a refundable deposit of Dfl 10 ($5.90) for a locker key. Rates include full breakfast. No credit cards. Metro: Nieuwmarkt.

The other Christian Youth Hostel is in the heart of the Red Light District, only a block from the Nieuwmarkt. The management here is very friendly, and they accept people between 15 and 35. Large dormitories filled with bunk beds can accommodate up to 166 visitors. No alcohol is allowed on the premises, and there's a midnight curfew Sunday through Thursday night, at 1am on Friday and Saturday. There's a garden with a large fish pond, a recreation room, and a restaurant where lunch and dinner are served. Note that the Shelter's location may make some people uncomfortable; unaccompanied women, especially, may be bothered at night.

Stadsdoelen

Kloveniersburgwal 97, Amsterdam 1011 KB. ☎ **020/624-68-32.** 190 dorm beds. Dfl 25 ($14.70) per person for IYHF members, Dfl 5 ($2.95) extra for nonmembers for the first six nights. Rates include full breakfast. No credit cards. Closed Jan–Feb. Metro: Nieuwmarkt.

This official youth hostel is on a canal at the edge of the Red Light District, and for that reason unaccompanied women may be uncomfortable staying here. Note that you can avoid walking through the district by taking tram no. 16, 24, or 25 from Centraal Station to Muntplein (fourth stop) and walking up Nieuwe Doelenstraat (past the Hotel Europe) to the end of the street, which leads directly to the hostel. Besides the standard dorm accommodations, there are large lockers, a self-catering kitchen, and two washing machines with a dryer.

✪ Vondelpark

Zandpad 5, Amsterdam 1054 GA. ☎ **020/683-17-44.** Fax 020/616-65-91. 300 beds. Dfl 75 ($44.10) double; Dfl 140 ($82.35) quad; Dfl 30 ($17.65) in a dorm for IYHF members, Dfl 5 ($2.95) extra for nonmembers for the first six nights. Rates include full breakfast. No credit cards. Tram 1, 2, or 5 to Leidseplein.

The hostel is housed in an imposing old school building, with its own entrance gate from Vondelpark. Dorms are outfitted with six to eight double-decker bunk beds. The new furnishings and carpets and the cleanliness make this an exceptional deal. There are a few double and quad rooms available. Other amenities include sturdy lockers for only $1.75 per day (refunded), a self-service kitchen, a bar at night with a small dance floor, a no-smoking reading room, and a covered bicycle shed. The hostel has a second building under construction, scheduled to open in 1997 with 485 beds.

ROOMS IN PRIVATE HOMES

Bed & Breakfast

Vossiusstraat 26, Amsterdam 1071 AE. ☎ **020/671-60-09.** 2 rms, both with shower. Dfl 50 ($29.40) per person. Rates include full breakfast. No credit cards. Tram 1, 2, or 5 to Hobbemastraat (one stop after Leidseplein).

This place is unique, with an atmosphere like that of a Charles Dickens novel. Mr. Knoppers and Mr. Vos, the English-speaking owners since 1974, are in their 70s. Both are hatters, and you'll pass their workroom when walking up the one flight to your room. The rooms are basically furnished but spacious and clean; one faces a canal. Breakfast is served in a large living room decorated with plants, books, and hats of all kinds. Readers looking for an out-of-the-ordinary place to stay will love this private home. Their handmade hats, by the way, range from Dfl 250 ($147) for a straw hat to Dfl 1,000 ($588) for a mink hat. One of their clients is a lady-in-waiting to Queen Beatrix.

Charlotte Geisel

Burgemeester Rendorpstraat 34, Amsterdam 1064 EP. ☎ **020/611-51-89** or 610-53-70. 3 rms. Dfl 35 ($20.60) double. Rates include full breakfast and showers. No credit cards. Take tram no. 13, then see the directions below.

This cozy home is in a quiet neighborhood in the Slotermeer district on the western outskirts of Amsterdam. There's ample parking space, and a color TV and a refrigerator are available for guest use. Frau Geisel was in the merchant marine and has traveled all over the world. She speaks good English and is eager to please her guests. Her home is recommended to all age groups.

To get here, take tram no. 13 from Centraal Station to Burgemeester Rendorpstraat, a 25-minute ride; when you get off, walk on the side of the street with the small houses (don't cross the street to the apartment blocks) and you'll be at Frau Geisel's place in two minutes. If you arrive at Schiphol Airport, call her and she'll explain how to reach her home without first going into the city.

Mrs. J. Sloof
Willem de Zwijgerlaan 353, Apt. 2, Amsterdam 1055 RG. ☎ **020/684-11-66.** 4 rms. Dfl 40 ($23.50) per person. Rates include full breakfast. No credit cards. Minimum stay two nights. Bus 2l from Centraal Station to Charlotte Bourbonstraat.

Mrs. Sloof rents two single and two double rooms to tourists, most of whom are English-speaking. You have to walk up a steep flight of stairs to reach her apartment, located in a row of modern residential buildings about 2½ miles west of Centraal Station, a 15-minute trip—it's worth the effort to stay at this pleasant accommodation. The clean rooms have modern furniture, there's plenty of hot water, and the morning coffee is among the best you'll ever taste. Mrs. Sloof is a motherly type, always ready to help, advise, and even listen to your personal problems.

WORTH THE EXTRA MONEY

The Amstel Botel
Oosterdokskade 2–4, Amsterdam 1011 AE. ☎ **020/626-42-47.** Fax 020/639-19-52. 176 cabins, all with bath (shower only). TV TEL. Dfl 130 ($76.45) single; Dfl 160 ($94.10) double; Dfl 210 ($123.50) triple. Rates include buffet breakfast. AE, DC, EURO, MC, V. Free parking.

This is a boat-hotel, moored 250 yards off Centraal Station, with 352 beds in 176 cabins on four decks, connected by an elevator. The boat was built in 1993 as a hotel and has never sailed on the open sea. There's no curfew here. The Amstel is the only floating hotel in Amsterdam, and it has become quite popular since its opening, largely because of its central location and reasonable rates. To find the botel, leave Centraal Station and turn left, passing the bike rental—it's painted white and directly in front of you.

✪ COK City Hotel
Nieuwezijds Voorburgwal 50, Amsterdam 1012 SC. ☎ **020/422-00-11.** Fax 020/422-04-57. 106 rms, all with bath. TV TEL. Dfl 170 ($100) single; Dfl 220 ($129.40) double; Dfl 260 ($152.95) triple. Rates include buffet breakfast. AE, DC, EURO, MC, V. Tram 1, 2, 5, 13, or 17 (first stop from Centraal Station).

This hotel, new in 1994, is a five-minute walk from Centraal Station and Dam Square. The brightly colored rooms (with lilac dominating) have modern shapes and are equipped with trouser presses, hairdryers, and safes. Ironing boards are available on every floor, as well as food, beverage, and ice-cube dispensers. Breakfast includes eggs any style, cereals, fruit, and more. Shops on the ground floor stay open 24 hours. This hotel offers five-star comfort for three-star rates.

✪ Hotel Agora
Singel 462, Amsterdam 1017 AW. ☎ **020/627-22-00.** Fax 020/627-22-02. 15 rms, 12 with bath. TV TEL. Dfl 115 ($67.65) single without bath, Dfl 150 ($88.25) single with bath;

Dfl 125 ($73.52) double without bath, Dfl 170 ($100) double with bath; Dfl 240 ($141.20) triple with bath; Dfl 275 ($161.75) quad with bath. Rates include full Dutch breakfast. AE, DC, EURO, MC, V. Tram 1, 2, or 5 to Spui.

Two houses built in 1735 have been fully restored to create this fine hotel, only steps away from the floating flower market. Three rooms fall within our budget and the 12 others (with bath) are worth the extra money. All rooms are carpeted and attractively furnished with new beds and a few antiques. The large family room has three windows overlooking the Singel canal. The hotel is efficiently run and well maintained by a friendly couple, Yvo Muthert and Els Bruijnse. Breakfast is served on marble-top tables in the ground-floor breakfast room.

Hotel Amsterdam Wiechmann

Prinsengracht 328–332, Amsterdam 1016 HX. ☎ **020/626-33-21.** Fax 020/626-89-62. 38 rms, all with bath. TV TEL. Dfl 150–225 ($88.25–$132.35) double; Dfl 300 ($176.45) triple or quad. Rates include full buffet breakfast. No credit cards. Tram 1, 2, or 5 to Prinsengracht.

This hotel, constructed from three canal houses, offers attractively furnished and recently redecorated rooms. It's owned/operated by American Ted Boddy and his English-speaking Dutch wife, who are extremely knowledgeable about Amsterdam and the rest of Holland. The buffet breakfast here includes cereal, juice, meat, eggs, cheese, breads, honey cakes, and, of course, plenty of Dutch butter.

ROOMS FOR LONGER STAYS

The **Amsterdam Home Agency,** Amstel 176a, Amsterdam 1017 AE (☎ **020/ 626-25-77;** fax 020/626-29-87), rents about 30 apartments and six houseboats for shorter and longer stays, either per night, per week, or longer. Rates range from Dfl 125 ($73.25) for a studio per day to Dfl 2,000 ($1,180) for a three-bedroom houseboat per week. Linen, towels, and cleaning are included. Ask for the owner, Willemina Visser, in her office near Rembrandt Square, open daily from 10am to 6pm.

5 Dining

Amsterdammers love to eat. Not only are there plenty of traditional Dutch restaurants, but also there are dozens of ethnic restaurants serving everything from Argentine to Tunisian food. Two great areas for discovering new restaurants are around Leidseplein and in the Jordaan.

Indonesian food is extremely popular in Amsterdam. Even if you're on a tight budget, try to have at least one *rijsttafel* dinner, a traditional "rice table" banquet of as many as 20 succulent and spicy foods served in tiny bowls. Pick and choose from among the bowls and add your choice to the pile of rice on your plate. It's almost impossible to eat all the food that's set on your table, but give it a shot—it's delicious. For an abbreviated version of rijsttafel served on one plate, try *nasi rames*. At lunch, the standard Indonesian fare is *nasi goreng* (fried rice with meat and vegetables) or *bami goreng* (fried noodles prepared in the same way).

Amsterdam's favorite lunch is a *broodje*, a small sandwich made with a soft roll or French bread and filled with meat or fish. You'll find these tasty and inexpensive sandwiches in restaurants and at street stands throughout Amsterdam. An especially popular street food is *broodje haring,* raw herring and onions in a soft bun for around Dfl 4 ($2.35). The traditional method for eating herring is to tip your head back and lower the fish head-first into your mouth.

Getting the Best Deal on Dining

- Save money by grabbing a quick lunch from an Automat.
- For lunch, try those Dutch favorites, *broodjes* and *uitsmijters*, both tasty and inexpensive.
- Dutch cheese is wonderful and makes an ideal picnic food.
- A cone of hot fries can be a filling and inexpensive snack.
- Tourist menus usually offer three-course fixed-price meals that allow you to eat in a restaurant otherwise out of your range.

Another traditional Dutch lunch is *uitsmijters* (pronounced *out*-smayters): two pieces of toast topped with ham or cheese and two fried eggs, often served with a small salad.

If you want to experience Amsterdam conviviality at its finest, head to one of the city's hundreds of brown cafés. A brown café is a local bar that gets its name from the interior's predominantly brown coloring. Why are the interiors of these cafés brown? Hundreds of years of thick tobacco smoke have stained the walls and furniture—and continue to do so today.

If you have a sweet tooth, be sure to try some traditional Dutch desserts, such as *poffertjes* (miniature pancakes), *oliebollen* (literally oily balls, a bit like powdered sugar–covered doughnut holes), or pancakes. All these come with various fillings or toppings, many of which contain a liqueur of some sort. Traditional pofferje restaurants are garish affairs that look as though they've run away from the circus. You'll find one on the Nieuwendijk pedestrian shopping street and another on the Weteringcircuit not far from Leidseplein.

As in most European cities, you'll find that the best meal bargains are the offerings of the most recent immigrants. In Amsterdam's case it's Turkish snack bars and Surinamese fast-food restaurants that offer the cheapest meals in town. The former specialize in *shwarma* and *falafel* and can be found around Leidseplein and Rembrandtplein; the latter are known for their *chicken roti* and can be found in the vicinity of Albert Cuypstraat, the site of a popular daily market. Dfl 6 to 8 ($3.50 to $4.70) will get you a filling meal in either type of restaurant.

MEALS FOR LESS THAN DFL 16 ($9.40)
NEAR DAM SQUARE & CENTRAAL STATION

The Atrium
Oudezijds Achterburgwal 237. ☎ **020/525-39-99.** Dfl 7–9 ($4.10–$5.30). Mon–Fri 9am–2pm and 5–9pm. DUTCH.

This spectacular facility is the self-service restaurant on the grounds of Amsterdam's old university. A courtyard between four restored buildings has been covered over with a glass roof that lets in plenty of light all year. To reach the food lines, walk up the stairs just inside the door and across the pedestrian bridge.

Another university cafeteria, **Agora,** is at Roeterstraat 11–13, near Waterlooplein. The hours and prices are similar. This latter establishment also houses a more-upscale dining room and a café.

Cafe de Pilserlj

Gravenstraat 10. ☎ **020/625-00-14.** Dfl 10–25 ($5.90–$14.70). No credit cards. Mon–Fri noon–midnight, Sat noon–8:30pm. DUTCH.

This high-ceilinged café/bar may look as though it has been here forever, but not too long ago it was a stationery store. Inside you'll find tables in front and back, with hanging plants adding a bit of color to the dark interior. Old jazz recordings are a favorite with the bartender. Located behind the Nieuwekerk and only steps from the Nieuwendijk pedestrian shopping street, this atmospheric café is an excellent place to try a traditional Dutch lunch of uitsmijters.

Calypso Sandwich Shop

Zoutsteeg 3–5. ☎ 020/626-33-88. Dfl 5–12 ($2.95–$7.05). No credit cards. Sun–Wed and Fri 8am–7pm, Sat 8am–5pm. DUTCH (BROODJES).

If you're looking for an inexpensive place for a quick broodje or two while strolling along Nieuwendijk, duck into one of the many little alleys that lead toward Damrak—there are at least two or three sandwich shops on most alleys. This is one of the nicest, with 30 seats inside. It serves a wide selection of broodjes, uitsmijters, and croquettes.

Egg Cream

St. Jacobsstraat 19. ☎ **020/623-05-75.** Dfl 6–16 ($3.50–$9.40); daily special Dfl 12 ($7.05) at lunch, Dfl 17 ($10) at dinner. No credit cards. Wed–Mon 11am–8pm. VEGETARIAN.

This 40-seat restaurant down a nondescript alleyway near the Centraal Station end of Nieuwendijk is a holdover from Amsterdam's hippie heyday, and it still attracts a young crowd. Lots of varnished wood and a notice board advertising everything from meditation classes to apartments for rent give it the feel of a university hangout. Simple surroundings and basic vegetarian meals at extremely low prices are this place's main attractions.

Hema Department Store

Nieuwendijk 174. ☎ **020/623-41-76.** Dfl 7–15 ($4.10–$8.80). No credit cards. Mon 11am–6pm, Tues–Wed and Fri 9:30am–6pm, Thurs 9:30am–9pm, Sat 9am–6pm. DUTCH.

This second-floor cafeteria is just what you'd expect from a discount department store. Still, the prices are low and the food is quite acceptable, especially such Dutch specialties as pea soup with bread and bacon. The steak dinner with mushrooms, potatoes, and green beans is a real bargain.

Keuken Van 1870

Spuistraat 4. ☎ **020/624-89-65.** Dfl 10–20 ($5.90–$11.75). AE, DC. Mon–Fri 11am–8pm, Sat–Sun 4–9pm. DUTCH.

In business for more than 120 years, this restaurant is one of Amsterdam's cheapest. At one time the place was primarily for feeding the poor, but today it's frequented by working people, students, and shoppers from Nieuwendijk two blocks away, all of whom line up for the inexpensive self-service meals. The spotless large dining area seats more than 100.

✪ Nordsee

Kalverstraat 122. ☎ **020/623-73-37.** Dfl 5–9 ($2.95–$5.30). No credit cards. Mon–Sat 9:30am–6:30pm, Sun noon–4:30pm. DUTCH/SEAFOOD.

If you're walking down crowded Kalverstraat and your eyes are suddenly drawn to a most colorful sandwich display, you've undoubtedly stumbled on the Nordsee. The herring, mackerel, shrimp, tuna, and crab are delicious.

The Station

On Platform 1 in Centraal Station. ☎ **020/627-33-06.** Dfl 6–20 ($3.50–$11.75); daily specials Dfl 15.50–17.50 ($9.10–$10.30). No credit cards. Mon–Sat 7am–10pm, Sun 8am–10pm. DUTCH.

This clean cafeteria offers a wide choice of hot meals, sandwiches, salads, and pastries. The selection of meals is unusually varied, with half a dozen types of salads as well as specials that change daily and monthly. You can even have wine with your meal. The carpeting keeps this large eating hall quiet—you'd hardly know you were in a train station.

NEAR THE RIJKSMUSEUM & LEIDSEPLEIN

Bojo

Lange Leidsedwarsstraat 51. ☎ **020/622-74-34.** Main courses Dfl 12–18 ($7.05–$10.60). No credit cards. Sun–Thurs 5pm–2am, Fri–Sat 5pm–3:30am. INDONESIAN.

Not only is this excellent Indonesian restaurant inexpensive and conveniently located near Leidseplein, but also it's open all night on weekends. So if hunger strikes after a late night on the town, drop in for a flavorful longtong rames special (served with chewy rice cakes). If it looks too crowded when you stop by, be sure to check the adjoining dining room, which has its own separate entrance.

Brooje Van Kootje

Leidseplein 20. ☎ **020/623-20-36.** Dfl 4–10 ($2.35–$5.90). No credit cards. Sun–Thurs 9:30am–1am, Fri–Sat 9:30am–3am. DUTCH (BROODJES).

This is basically a Dutch-style fast-food restaurant. Brightly lit, with only a few tables, Broodje van Kootje is popular with Amsterdammers on the go. If you can't stomach the idea of eating a raw herring from a street vendor, maybe it'll seem more palatable here. A specialty is the creamy croquette broodje.

There's another, equally popular location at Spui 28 (☎ **020/623-74-51**).

The Hot Potato

Leidsestraat 44 (near the corner of Keizersgracht). ☎ **020/623-23-01.** Baked potato platters Dfl 2.75–7.50 ($1.60–$4.40); hot dogs Dfl 4.50 ($2.65). Mon–Fri 8:30am–1pm, Sat 9am–1:30pm, Sun 10am–10pm. DUTCH/AMERICAN.

This restaurant serves up 30 varieties of baked potato platters, ranging from one with butter or cream to a deluxe spud prepared with crabmeat. It's a tiny place, with only stools (no chairs), but it's a good value—especially for those fed up with chips and burgers.

IN & NEAR THE JORDAAN

Moeder's Pot

Vinkenstraat 119. ☎ **020/623-76-43.** Dfl 10–25 ($5.90–$14.70). Mon–Fri 5–10pm, Sat 5–9:30pm. DUTCH.

This restaurant close to Haarlemer Square is small, but the meals it serves are huge. The daily specials of typical Dutch food are a particularly good deal. Moeder's Pot, managed since 1970 by the friendly Mr. Cor, has been around for years and is a popular neighborhood hangout. You'll find this place especially convenient if you're staying at the Hotel Acacia or Hotel de Bloiende Ramenas.

✪ Pancake Bakery

Prinsengracht 191. ☎ **020/625-13-33.** Pancakes Dfl 8–20 ($4.70–$11.75). Daily noon–9:30pm. PANCAKES.

In the basement of a 17th-century canal warehouse is this long, narrow restaurant serving some of the most delicious and unusual pancakes you'll ever taste. There are several dozen varieties on the menu, almost any of which is a full meal. Choices include such concoctions as salami and cheese, cheese and ginger, chestnuts with whipped cream, and advokaat (a Dutch egg nog–like cocktail). In summer a few tables are placed in front of the restaurant overlooking the canal. This place near the Anne Frankhuis is popular with tourists.

MEALS FOR LESS THAN DFL 35 ($20.60)
NEAR DAM SQUARE & CENTRAAL STATION

David & Goliath

Kalverstraat 92. ☎ **020/623-67-36.** Dfl 9–30 ($5.30–$17.60); tourist menu Dfl 25 ($14.70). No credit cards. Daily 10am–5pm (to 6pm in summer). DUTCH.

At the entrance to the Amsterdam Historisch Museum and affiliated with the museum, David & Goliath is popular with well-to-do older Amsterdammers. The meals are well-prepared Dutch standards, such as broodjes, uitsmijters, and solid meat-and-potatoes hot meals, but the real reason to eat here is the decor. A "life-size" wooden statue of David and Goliath, carved in 1650 for a local amusement garden, stands in one corner of the high-ceilinged dining room. The immense ogre watching over diners is an Amsterdam artwork not to be missed.

✪ Haesje Claes

Spuistraat 273–275. ☎ **020/624-99-98.** Dfl 15–42 ($8.80–$24.70); tourist menu Dfl 32 ($14.70). AE, DC, EURO, MC, V. Daily noon–midnight. DUTCH.

Dark-wood paneling, low-beamed ceilings, and stained-glass windows create just the right atmosphere for the traditional Dutch food. The meals are hearty and the portions large enough to satisfy even the hungriest person. The 250-seat restaurant is popular with everyone from executives to shoppers from nearby Kalverstraat, who fill the small tables in the two dining rooms. They come for the delicious food and reasonable prices.

NEAR THE RIJKSMUSEUM & LEIDSEPLEIN

De Blauwe Hollander

Leidsekruisstraat 28. ☎ **020/623-30-14.** Dfl 17–40 ($10–$23.50); tourist meals Dfl 24 ($14.10). No credit cards. Daily 5–10pm. DUTCH.

The atmosphere here is casual and relaxed, and it's popular with the younger set who are on their way out for a night of bar-hopping around nearby Leidseplein. Along the front window is a long table piled with magazines in several languages for guests to read over tea, coffee, or a beer or while you wait for your meal. Best of all, the special tourist meals might include pea soup, ribs, bacon, black bread and butter, or meatballs, potatoes, and a salad or vegetable.

✪ De Boemerang

Weteringschans 171. ☎ **020/623-42-51.** Dfl 17.50–38 ($10.30–$22.35). AE, EURO, V. Mon–Fri noon–9pm, Sat–Sun 4–9pm. MUSSELS/STEAK.

If you like mussels, this legendary restaurant, which opened in 1915, is the place to go in Amsterdam. The decor is old and eclectic—notice the 500 paper banknotes hanging from the ceiling behind the counter and the largest copper tea-kettle I've ever seen above the main door. The selection on the jukebox is 40 years old (corresponding to the term of the current owner), but you don't come here for the atmosphere—you come for the most succulent mussels you've ever tasted, served in huge pots in a quantity that's almost impossible to finish. Choose from among a number of dipping sauces, all delicious. It's a favorite eatery of various airline pilots and staff, which is an additional recommendation. (By the way, the owner named the place after a boomerang, in hopes that his customers would return just as the Australian hunting weapon does.)

Ristorante Mirafiori

Hobbemastraat 2. ☎ **020/662-30-13.** Pasta Dfl 12–40 ($7.05–$23.50), dinner (with wine) Dfl 90 ($52.90). AE, MC, V. Wed–Mon noon–3pm and 5pm–midnight. Tram 2 or 5 to Hobbemastraat. ITALIAN.

Founded in 1941 by the same family that runs it today, this typical Italian eatery has seen many famous guests—the late Sammy Davis, Jr., Liza Minnelli, and Eddie Murphy have eaten here. Though a full meal in this excellent restaurant may be pricy, if you order just soup and pasta and a glass of wine, your bill, including tip, shouldn't be more than Dfl 30 ($17.65).

✪ Sama Sebo

P. C. Hoofstraat 27. ☎ **020/662-81-46.** Dfl 25–45 ($14.70–$26.50); nasi rames or bami rames lunch Dfl 22.50 ($13.25); rijsttafel Dfl 45 ($26.50). AE, DC, EURO, MC, V. Mon–Fri noon–3pm and 6–10pm, Sat to 11pm. INDONESIAN.

Sama Sebo serves the best bami goreng and nasi goreng in Amsterdam (only at lunch). A meal here is a worthwhile splurge. When you order either of the two lunch specials, you get a heaping mound of food that's really a nasi rames or bami rames (one-plate rijsttafel). The restaurant has two sections—the main dining room with its Indonesian motif and the bar area for more casual dining.

NEAR REMBRANDTPLEIN

Eethuisje Cantharel

Kerkstraat 377 (off Utrechtsestraat). ☎ **020/626-64-00.** Reservations recommended in the evening. Dfl 14.50–25.95 ($8.50–$15.25); daily specials Dfl 13–19 ($7.65–$11.20). AE, EURO, MC, V. Tues–Sat 5–10pm. DUTCH.

Small and dark, this restaurant is a classic Dutch eatery that's been serving up hearty meals for years. Meat and potatoes are the order of the day, but the choices can be surprising—from liver and onions to schnitzel paprikasaus, marinated spareribs to chicken Cordon Bleu. You'll find Eethuisje Cantharel across from the old wooden church (one of the only wooden buildings left in Amsterdam).

IN & NEAR THE JORDAAN

De Bolhoed Restaurant

Prinsengracht 60–62. ☎ **020/626-18-03.** Dfl 15–30 ($8.80–$17.65). No credit cards. Daily noon–10pm. VEGETARIAN/HEALTH FOOD.

You may be hesitant to enter this restaurant when you see how badly it's leaning (a common problem in a city built on wooden pilings), but the owner assured me that the building had been that way for hundreds of years. High ceilings, large windows, and blond hardwood floors give this place a bright and airy feel. Live piano music is often offered in the evenings.

Cafe de Jaren

Nieuwe Doelenstraat 20–22. ☎ **020/625-57-71.** Dfl 15–25 ($8.80–$14.70); dinner menu Dfl 28 ($16.50). No credit cards. Daily 10am–1am. Tram 9 or 14 to Muntplein. DUTCH/CONTINENTAL.

This is one of Amsterdam's largest café/restaurants, with 300 seats in the spacious high-ceilinged dining rooms, plus 150 more on an outside terrace. Anyone who likes picturesque surroundings will like this place. Many students eat lunch here (it's near the university). Supposedly Rembrandt live and worked in this house more than 300 years ago.

Padi

Haarlemmerdijk 50. ☎ **020/625-12-80.** Dfl 12–20 ($7.05–$11.75); rijsttafel Dfl 29 ($17.05); nasi rames Dfl 18 ($10.60). No credit cards. Daily 5–10pm. INDONESIAN.

This small Indonesian restaurant near the Jordaan is especially convenient if you're staying at the Hotel Schroder. Match-stick blinds and tree trunks against the walls, basket lampshades, and lots of potted plants give it a suitably tropical decor. The 11-dish rijsttafel is a good deal, as is the nasi rames, the less spectacular version of rijsttafel.

Speciaal

Nieuwe Leliestraat 142. ☎ **020/642-97-06.** Dfl 20–55 ($11.75–$32.35); rijsttafel Dfl 41.50 ($24.40). AE, EURO, MC, V. Daily 5:30–11pm. INDONESIAN.

For an Indonesian meal in the Jordaan, try this tiny restaurant. The woven-bamboo walls are hung with framed batiks and photos of Indonesia; the tablecloths are also batik. Besides the standard Indonesian dishes, they have some unusual offerings for those already familiar with Indonesian food.

SUPER-BUDGET MEALS

For the cheapest food in Amsterdam, stop by one of the city's many snack bars, known as *automatiek,* which are reminiscent of the Automats that long ago disappeared from the American scene. Walls of little glass boxes display croquettes, broodjes, and other snacks. Just drop your coins in the slot and take your pick. Croquettes are Dfl 1.50 (90¢), and broodjes, Dfl 2.50 ($1.50). These snack bars also sell delicious fries. For Dfl 3 ($1.75) you get a large container or cone of fries with your choice of ketchup or the Dutch mayonnaiselike sauce that's traditionally served on fries here.

Febo, the best known of the automatieks, can be found at Kalverstraat 142, Leidsestraat 94, Nieuwendijk 220, and Reguliersbreestraat 38.

PICNICKING

You can pick up almost anything you might want for a picnic, from cold cuts to a bottle of wine, at the **Mignon supermarket,** Leidsestraat 74, open Monday through Saturday from 9am to 6:30pm. Then head over to the **Vondelpark,** only a 15-minute walk away. If it's summer, you might even catch a free concert at the outdoor theater.

6 Attractions

SIGHTSEEING SUGGESTIONS

If You Have 1 Day

The first thing you should do in Amsterdam is take a boat tour of the canals. Then head to the Rijksmuseum and see several Rembrandts and the museum's large collection of paintings by such 17th-century Dutch masters as Vermeer, Jan Steen, and Frans Hals. After lunch, visit the Vincent van Gogh Museum and finish your day with a visit to the Museum Het Rembrandthuis; not only will you get a look at virtually all the prints that Rembrandt made, but also you'll get to see inside the restored 17th-century house where he once lived.

If You Have 2 Days

For your first day, follow the itinerary above. On your second day, visit the famous Anne Frankhuis, where the Jewish Frank family hid from the Nazis during World War II. After visiting the museum, stroll around the Jordaan area, an old section of Amsterdam that has been restored only in the past few years. Have lunch at one of the many restaurants in the Jordaan, then head for the Amsterdam Historical Museum on Kalverstraat. This excellent museum covers several hundred years of local Amsterdam history. When you leave, be sure to take a stroll around the Begijnhof, a peaceful courtyard surrounded by old houses. Since you're on Lakverstraat, Amsterdam's busiest pedestrian shopping street, you might want to get in a bit of shopping.

If You Have 3 Days

After your canal tour, spend the rest of your first day on Museumplein. Visit the Rijksmuseum, the Vincent van Gogh Museum, and the Stedelijk Museum of Modern Art.

On Day 2, visit the Museum Het Rembrandthuis and the Jewish Historisch Museum, only a few blocks away. While you're in this area, you can stroll around the Waterlooplein flea market. If you're interested, this would be a good time, and much safer than at night, to stroll through Amsterdam's famous Red Light District, where the women sit in their windows. Take precautions if you visit the Red Light District—night or day. In the afternoon, visit the Amsterdam Historisch Museum and the Begijnhof.

❓ Did You Know?

- About half the area of the Netherlands is below sea level; only the dikes stop the country from being swallowed by the sea.
- There are close to 200 canals and more than 1,200 bridges in Amsterdam.
- There are 600,000 flower bulbs in Amsterdam's public parks and gardens.
- The word *yacht* comes from the old Dutch *jaght*; the first yacht race ever— between the English and the Dutch—took place in 1662 on the Thames.
- Amsterdam boasts 2,400 houseboats.
- KLM, Royal Dutch Airlines, is the world's oldest airline—service was initiated between Amsterdam and London in 1920.
- There are 206 van Gogh paintings in Amsterdam.
- The Pilgrims, though they were English, lived in Holland for 11 years before sailing for America.
- There are more than 12 million bicycles in the Netherlands.
- Two-thirds of the cut flowers sold in the world come from the Netherlands.
- Though Amsterdam is the official capital of the Netherlands, the seat of government is The Hague.

On your third day, visit the nearby museum village of Zaanse Schans in the morning. Working windmills and Dutch artisans are two of the attractions in this beautiful little village only 20 minutes from the city. In the afternoon, visit the Anne Frankhuis and tour the Jordaan.

If You Have 5 Days

Spend your first three days as suggested above. On your fourth day, get up early and take the bus to the flower auction in Aalsmeer, the largest flower auction in the world. Back in town, visit the Tropenmuseum, Amsterdam's museum of the tropics. To continue your exotic journey, visit the Albert Cuypstraat open-air market next. This market is lined with vendors selling all manner of goods, from fresh fish to Japanese electronics. You might even be able to catch a tour of the Heineken Brewery if you time things well.

On Day 5, try an all-day excursion to Enkhuizen's Zuiderzee Museum, a restored village featuring more than 100 houses and other buildings from around the former Zuiderzee. An alternative to this is a trip to Rotterdam and The Hague, with a visit to the miniature village of Madurodam.

TOP ATTRACTIONS

The Netherlands calls itself "Museum Land," and Amsterdam, with 42 museums, is its de facto capital. These museums range from the grandiose 200-plus-room Rijksmuseum to the fascinating little Amstelkring, also known as "Our Lord in the Attic." Even if you plan to visit only the first six museums listed below, you should purchase a **Museumkaart (museum card),** entitling you to free admission to more

---

Special & Free Events

In keeping with Amsterdammers' enthusiasm about life, every day is filled with special events. Some of Amsterdam's best freebies are its **street performers.** You'll find them primarily in front of Centraal Station during the day and on Leidseplein and Rembrandtplein in the evening.

April 30 is **Queen's Day** and the city crowds the streets to enjoy performances, parades, markets, and general merrymaking.

The single most important annual event in the Netherlands is the **flowering of the bulb fields** each spring from March to mid-May. Two-thirds of all the cut flowers sold in the world come from the Netherlands. The best flower-viewing areas are between Haarlem and Leiden and between Haarlem and Den Helder. The highlight of the bulb season is the annual **flower parade** from Haarlem to Noorwijk in late April. There's another flower parade from Aalsmeer (home of the world's largest flower auction) to Amsterdam on the first Saturday in September.

In June, July, and August **open-air concerts** are held in Vondelpark. Check at the Tourist Information Office for times and dates. In June the city hosts the **Holland Festival,** an extravaganza of music, dance, and other cultural offerings that take place all over the city and feature a different theme each year. In September, the **Jordaan Festival** showcases this old neighborhood where small inexpensive restaurants, secondhand shops, and unusual boutiques and galleries are found.

than 350 museums all over the Netherlands, including many others in Amsterdam. The pass costs Dfl 45 ($26.50) for adults, Dfl 15 ($8.80) for those under 18, and Dfl 32.50 ($19.10) for those over 65. When purchasing a Museumkaart you must have a passport-size photo, which you can get in the photo booths at Centraal Station. Note that the Anne Frankhuis does not accept the Museumkaart.

✪ Rijksmuseum

Stadhouderskade 42. ☎ **020/673-21-21.** Admission Dfl 12.50 ($7.35) adults, Dfl 5 ($2.95) senior citizens and children 6–18, free for children 5 and under. Tues–Sat 10am–5pm, Sun 1–5pm. Closed Jan 1. Tram 2, 5, or 16 to Museumplein.

This is the Netherlands' largest and most important collection of art, focusing, of course, on the Dutch masters—Rembrandt, Vermeer, Frans Hals, Jan Steen, and others. In addition, there are large collections of sculpture and applied arts, Asian art, prints and drawings, and Dutch antiquities.

The museum was founded in 1798 as the National Art Gallery located in The Hague. The steady growth of the collection of paintings and prints necessitated several moves: In 1808 King Louis Napoléon had it moved to the Royal Palace in Amsterdam and renamed the Royal Museum (the name Rijksmuseum—State Museum—dates from 1815). Then in 1816 it was moved to a large patrician residence called the Trippenhuis. However, that building soon proved too small and another was sought.

After years of negotiations, architect P. J. H. Cuypers designed the core of the present museum and this monumental neo-gothic building opened in 1885. Since then, many additions have been made to the collections and the building so that the museum now encompasses five collecting departments: Painting, Print Room, Sculpture and Decorative Arts, Dutch History, and Asiatic Art.

Although the museum has literally hundreds of rooms full of art, first-time visitors invariably head for *The Night Watch,* Rembrandt's most famous masterpiece. Painted in 1642 and, since 1947, correctly titled *The Shooting Company of Captain Frans Banning Cocq and Lieutenant Willem van Ruytenbuch,* this large canvas was commissioned as a group portrait to hang in a guild hall. In the two small rooms directly preceding *The Night Watch* room are several of Rembrandt's most beautiful paintings, including *The Jewish Bride* and *Self-portrait as the Apostle Paul.* Rembrandt was a master of chiaroscuro (light and shadow), and these paintings from late in his life are some of his finest. In the rooms to the left are more works by Rembrandt and other 17th-century Dutch masters.

✪ Vincent van Gogh Museum

Paulus Potterstraat 7. ☎ **020/570-52-00.** Admission Dfl 12.50 ($7.35) adults, Dfl 5 ($2.95) senior citizens and children 17 and under. Recorded audio tours, Dfl 5–6.50 ($2.95–$3.80) extra. Daily 10am–5pm (ticket office closes at 4pm). Closed Jan 1. Tram 2, 5, or 16 to Museumplein.

This modern museum houses the world's largest collection of works—200 paintings and 500 drawings—of the 19th century's most important Dutch artist. It gives both a chronological and a thematic presentation of van Gogh's Dutch and French periods, plus includes his private collection of Japanese prints, magazine illustrations, and books. The museum also displays works by contemporaries who both influenced him and in turn were influenced by him; the periods before he was born and after his death are also represented. As you view the paintings, you'll see van Gogh's early, gloomy style slowly change to one of vibrant colors and see his brushstrokes getting bolder as he developed his unique style.

The Rijksmuseum

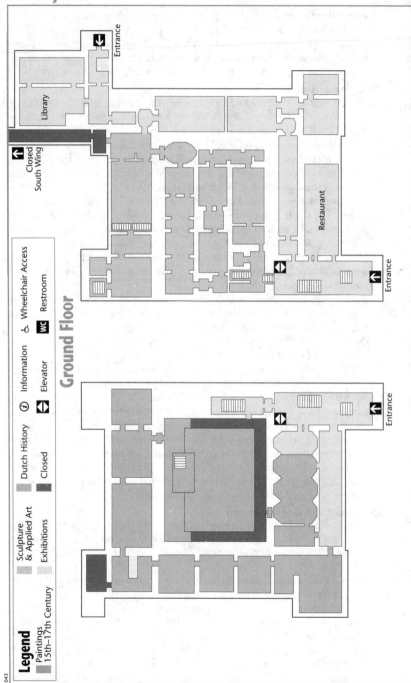

Ground Floor

Legend

Paintings
15th–17th Century

**Sculpture
& Applied Art**

Exhibitions

Dutch History

Closed

ⓘ Information

🛗 Elevator

♿ Wheelchair Access

WC Restroom

Library

Closed
South Wing

Restaurant

Entrance

Entrance

Entrance

1043

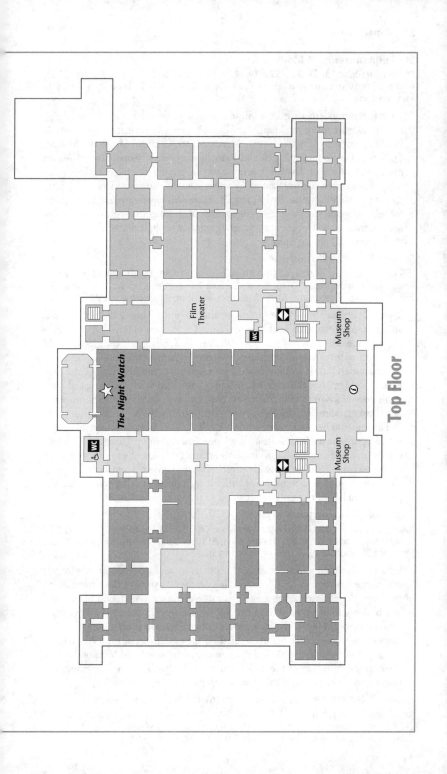

The Night Watch

Film
Theater

Museum
Shop

Museum
Shop

Top Floor

Stedelijk Museum of Modern Art

Paulus Potterstraat 13. ☎ **020/573-29-11.** Admission Dfl 8 ($4.70) adults, Dfl 4 ($2.35) senior citizens and children. Daily 11am–5pm. Closed Jan 1. Tram 2, 5, or 16 to Museumplein.

Focusing on modern art from 1850 to the present, the Stedelijk is Amsterdam's most innovative major museum. Virtually all its extensive permanent collection—including works by Chagall, Picasso, Monet, Manet, Cézanne, Mondrian, Matisse, Dubuffet, De Kooning, Appel, and Rauschenberg, among many others—is on display every summer. In winter, many works are put into storage to make way for temporary exhibits and installations by artists from the current art scene. The most recent trends in European and American art are well represented, so be prepared for exhibitions of today's cutting-edge artists. In addition to the paintings, sculptures, drawings, and engravings, there are exhibits of applied arts, videos, industrial design, and photography.

Museum Het Rembrandthuis

Jodenbreestraat 4–6. ☎ **020/624-94-86.** Admission Dfl 7.50 ($4.40) adults, Dfl 5 ($2.95) senior citizens and children 10–15, free for children 9 and under. Mon–Sat 10am–5pm, Sun and hols 1–5pm. Closed Jan 1. Metro: Waterlooplein. Tram 9 to Waterlooplein.

When Rembrandt van Rijn moved into this three-story house in 1639, he was already a well-established wealthy artist. However, the cost of buying and furnishing the house led to his financial downfall in 1656. When Rembrandt was declared insolvent, an inventory of the house's contents listed more than 300 paintings by Rembrandt and some by his teacher, Pieter Lasteman, and his friends Peter Paul Rubens and Jan Lievens. In 1640 Rembrandt was forced to sell the house and most of his possessions to meet his debts. He remained here until 1660, then moved to much less grandiose accommodations on Rozengracht, in the Jordaan.

The museum houses a nearly complete collection of Rembrandt's etchings. Of the 280 prints he made, 250 are on display here, along with paintings by his teachers and pupils. Rembrandt's prints show amazing detail, and you can see his use of shadows and lights for dramatic effect. Wizened patriarchs, emaciated beggars, children at play, and Rembrandt himself in numerous self-portraits are the subjects you'll long remember after a visit to the Rembrandthuis.

Amsterdam Historisch Museum

Kalverstraat 92. ☎ **020/523-18-22.** Admission Dfl 7.50 ($4.40) adults, Dfl 3.75 ($2.20) senior citizens and children 16 and under. Mon–Fri 10am–5pm, Sat–Sun 11am–5pm. Closed Jan 1, Apr 30, and Dec 25. Tram 1, 2, 4, or 5 to Spui.

Of all Amsterdam's many museums, none is so well designed as this former orphanage now housing exhibits covering nearly 700 years of the city's history. Items in the collection range from a pair of old leather shoes found in the mud of a building foundation to huge canvases depicting 17th-century Civic Guards. The museum halls are laid out so visitors can go chronologically through the history of Amsterdam, with the main focus on the golden age of the 17th century. During this age Amsterdam was the richest city in the world, and some of the most interesting exhibits are of the trades that made Amsterdam rich. Everything you might want to know about this fascinating city is housed here.

Joods Historisch Museum (Jewish Historical Museum)

Jonas Daniel Meijerplein 2–4. ☎ **020/626-99-45.** Admission Dfl 7 ($4.10) adults, Dfl 3.50 ($2.05) senior citizens and children 10–16, free for children 9 and under. Daily 11am–5pm. Closed Yom Kippur. Metro: Waterlooplein. Tram 9 to Waterlooplein.

The Jewish Historical Museum is housed in four restored 17th- and 18th-century synagogues. The neighborhood surrounding the museum was the Jewish quarter of Amsterdam for 300 years until the Nazi occupation during World War II emptied the city of its Jewish population. The oldest of the museum's four synagogues, built in 1670, is the oldest public synagogue in Western Europe; the newest of the four was built in 1752. Inside are exhibits covering the history of Jews in the Netherlands, including their persecution throughout Europe under Hitler. Jewish religious artifacts are a major focus.

✪ Museum Amstelkring ("Our Lord in the Attic")

Oudezijds Voorburgwal 40. ☎ **020/624-66-04.** Admission Dfl 5 ($2.95) adults, Dfl 3.50 ($2.05) senior citizens, students, and children. Mon–Sat 11am–5pm, Sun 1–5pm. Closed Jan 1. From Centraal Station, cross the bridge and the wide avenue, then cross to the far side of Damrak and head down the narrow Nieuwebrugsteeg; turn right at the end of the street and follow the canal for half a block.

Although Amsterdam has been known as a tolerant city for many centuries, just after the Protestant Reformation Roman Catholics fell into disfavor. Forced to worship in secret, they devised ingenious ways of gathering for Sunday services. In an otherwise ordinary-looking 17th-century canal house in the middle of Amsterdam's Red Light District is the most amazing of these clandestine churches, known to the general public as "Our Lord in the Attic." The three houses comprising this museum were built in the 1660s by a wealthy Catholic merchant specifically to house a church. Today the buildings are furnished much as they would have been in the mid-18th century. Nothing prepares you for the minicathedral you come upon so unexpectedly when you climb the last flight of stairs into the attic. A large baroque altar, religious statuary, pews to seat 150, an 18th-century organ, and an upper gallery complete this miniature church.

Tropenmuseum

Linnaeusstraat 2. ☎ **020/568-82-00.** Admission Dfl 10 ($5.90) adults, Dfl 5 ($2.95) for senior citizens and children 6–17, free for children 5 and under. Mon–Fri 10am–5pm, Sat–Sun and hols noon–5pm. Closed Jan 1, Apr 30, May 5, and Dec 25. Tram 9 from Centraal Station to Limaestraat.

One of Amsterdam's finest and most unusual museums is dedicated to presenting the tropics to people living in a far different climate. On the three floors surrounding the spacious main hall are numerous life-size tableaux depicting life in tropical countries. Although there are displays of beautiful handcrafts and antiquities from these regions, the museum's main focus is the life of the people today. There are hovels from the ghettoes of Calcutta and Bombay, as well as mud-walled houses from the villages of rural India. Bamboo huts from Southeast Asia and crowded little shops no bigger than closets show you how people today live in such areas as Southeast Asia, Latin America, and Africa. Sound effects play over hidden speakers: Dogs bark, children scream, car horns blare, frogs croak, and vendors call out their wares. In the main hall and in separate exhibition halls, the museum organizes temporary exhibitions, events, and dance and music workshops. In the Children's Museum, youngsters 6 to 12 can explore and participate in all sorts of activities.

Anne Frankhuis

Prinsengracht 263–265. ☎ **020/556-71-00.** Admission Dfl 8 ($4.15) adults, Dfl 4 ($2.35) students 10–17, free for children 9 and under. Sept–May, Mon–Sat 9am–5pm, Sun 10am–5pm; June–Aug, closes at 7pm. Closed Jan 1, Yom Kippur, and Dec. 25. Tram 13 or 17 to Westermarkt.

Central Amsterdam

Lindengracht

Lijnbaansgracht

Westerstraat

1

Nassaukade

Singelgracht

Marnixstraat

Anjeliersstraat

Egelantiersstraat

Egelantiersgracht

Herengracht

Singel

Bloemgracht

2

3

Raadhuisstr.

Dam
Square 4

Prinsengracht

Keizersgracht

7

5

Rozengracht

Rozenstraat

Reestraat Hartenstraat

Laurierstraat

Spuistraat

N.Z. Voorburgwal

Lijnbaansgracht

Lauriergracht

Elandsstraat

Berenstraat Wolvenstraat

Marnixstraat

Elandsgracht

Runstraat Huidenstraat

9

Nassaukade

Looiersgracht

Spui

10

Muntplein

11

Leidsegracht

Herengracht

Leidsestraat

Keizersgracht

Singelgracht

Kerkstraat

Prinsengracht

Overtoom

Nieuwe Spiegelstraat

Leidseplein

14

Vondelstraat

Stadhouderskade

Vondelpark

Vossiusstraat

Constantijn Huygenstraat

P. C. Hooftstraat

Jan Luykenstraat

Museumstraat

15

16

Hobbemakade

17

Museumplein

Today there are more than 13 million copies in 50 languages of *The Diary of Anne Frank*, written by a teenage Jewish girl during her two years of hiding in this building. On July 6, 1942, the Franks and another Jewish family went into hiding to avoid being deported to German concentration camps. Anne, the youngest Frank daughter, had been given a diary for her 13th birthday in 1942. With the eyes of a child and the writing skills of a girl who hoped one day to be a writer, she chronicled their almost-silent life in hiding, the continued persecution of Jews by Hitler, and the progress of the war. On August 4, 1944, the two families were discovered by the German police and deported on the last transport from the Netherlands to Auschwitz. Only Mr. Frank survived the concentration camps, and when he returned to Amsterdam a former employee gave him Anne's diary, which had been left behind when the police arrested the family.

Although the rooms here contain no furniture, the exhibits, including a year-by-year chronology of Anne's life, fill in the missing details. The museum is operated by the Anne Frank Foundation, an organization founded to eliminate anti-Semitism, fascism, and neo-Naziism and continue Anne Frank's struggle for a better world.

MORE ATTRACTIONS

The Begijnhof

Spui. Admission free. Daily. Tram 1, 2, or 5 to Spui.

Only steps from Amsterdam's busiest pedestrian shopping street is the city's most tranquil spot. Hidden behind a nondescript facade is a courtyard ringed with old restored almshouses. Since the 14th century the Begijnhof has been home to poor widows and lay nuns of the order of the Beguines (Begijns in Dutch; *Begijnhof* means Beguine Court). The oldest and one of the last remaining wooden houses in Amsterdam is here at no. 34, built in 1475. In the center of the courtyard are a clandestine Roman Catholic church and an English Presbyterian church.

Museum Willet-Holthuysen

Herengracht 605. ☎ **020/523-18-70.** Admission Dfl 5 ($2.95) adults, Dfl 2.50 ($1.50) senior citizens and children 16 and under. Mon–Fri 10am–5pm, Sat–Sun 11am–5pm. Tram 4 to Herengracht.

For a glimpse of what life was like for Amsterdam's wealthy merchants during the 18th and 19th centuries, pay a visit to this elegant canal-house museum. Each room is furnished much as it would have been 200 years ago. In addition, there's an extensive collection of ceramics, china, glass, and silver. Of particular interest are the large old kitchen and the formal garden in back.

Nieuwe Kerk

Dam Square. ☎ **020/638-69-09.** Admission varies. Daily 11am–5pm. To get here, walk down Damrak from Centraal Station.

This church across from the Royal Palace is new in name only. Construction on this late gothic structure was begun about 1400, but much of the interior, including the organ, dates from the 17th century. Since 1815 all Dutch kings and queens have been crowned here. Today the church is used primarily as a cultural center where special art exhibits are held. Regular performances on the church's huge organ are held in summer.

Oude Kerk

Oudekerksplein 1. ☎ **020/624-91-83.** Admission Dfl 5 ($2.95) adults, Dfl 3.50 ($2.05) students and seniors. Daily 1–5pm. Walk three blocks from Damrak to the middle of the Red Light District.

This gothic church dating from the 13th century is the oldest in the city. Its many stained-glass windows are particularly beautiful. Inside are monumental tombs, including that of Rembrandt's wife, Saskia van Uylenburg. The organ, built in 1724, is played regularly in summer; many connoisseurs believe that it has the best tone of any organ in the world. During the summer you can climb the 230-foot-high tower for an excellent view of Old Amsterdam.

Koninklijk Paleis (Royal Palace)

Dam Square. ☎ **020/624-86-98.** Admission Dfl 5 ($2.95) adults, Dfl 3 ($1.75) senior citizens and children 13–18, Dfl 1.50 (90¢) children 12 and under. Early June to late Aug, daily 12:30–5pm; Sept–May, only by guided tour Wed–Thurs at 1 and 4pm. To get here, walk down Damrak from Centraal Station.

Built in the 17th century on top of 13,659 wooden pilings to prevent it from sinking into the soft Amsterdam soil, the Royal Palace was originally the Town Hall. At the time it was built, the building was referred to as the Eighth Wonder of the World because of its immense size (it was the largest town hall ever built) and the fact that it used so many pilings to support it. In 1808 the building was converted into a palace. The dazzling interior is filled with sculptures, frescoes, and furniture. In summer (occasionally in other months as well) conducted tours are given.

Theater Institute Netherlands

Herengracht 168. ☎ **020/623-51-04.** Admission Dfl 5 ($2.95) adults, Dfl 3 ($1.75) seniors and children 4–9, free for children 3 and under. Tues–Sun 11am–5pm. Tram 13, 14, or 17 to Dam Square.

Splendid marble corridors, wall and ceiling frescoes, and ornate plasterwork make this patrician canal house one of the most beautiful in the city. Richly ornamented roof gables of different styles were a sign of wealth during Amsterdam's golden age, and crowning this building is the oldest extant example of an ornate neck gable. Although it's worth visiting this museum simply to see how the wealthy once lived, there are also many interesting exhibits pertaining to theater in the Netherlands over the centuries. Be sure to press the buttons of the miniature stage sets. You'll see how waves once rolled across the stage and other equally dramatic effects.

Westerkerk

Prinsengracht 279. ☎ **020/624-77-66.** Admission: Church, free; tower, Dfl 3 ($1.75); concerts, Dfl 15 ($8.80) adults, Dfl 10 ($5.80) seniors and students. May 15–Sept 15, Mon–Sat 10am–4pm. Closed Sept 16–May 14. Tram 13 or 17 to Westermarkt.

Built between 1620 and 1630, this church is a masterpiece of Dutch Renaissance style. At the top of the 275-foot-high tower is a giant replica of the imperial crown of Maximilian of Austria. Somewhere in this church (no one knows exactly where) is Rembrandt's grave. During summer regular organ concerts are played on a 300-year-old instrument. Also in summer you can climb the tower.

Artis Zoo

Plantage Kerklaan 40. ☎ **020/523-34-00.** Admission (including zoo, children's farm, planetarium, and zoological museum) Dfl 19 ($11.20) adults, Dfl 12.50 ($7.35) children 10 and under. Daily 9am–5pm.

Museumplein Area & Amsterdam South

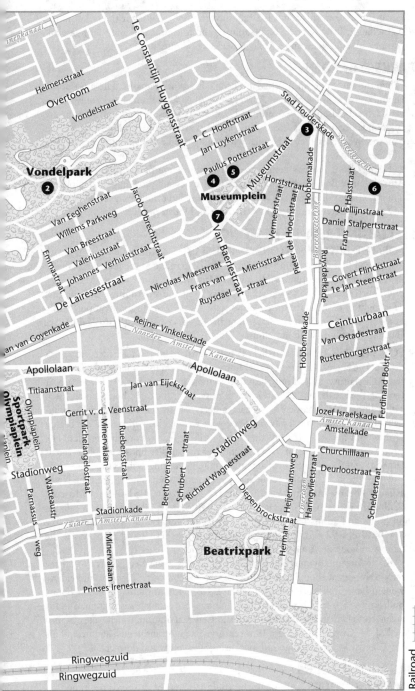

Railroad ┼┼┼┼┼┼

Great for all ages, this zoo was established in 1838, making it the oldest in the Netherlands. It houses over 6,000 animals and features a children's farm, a planetarium, an aquarium, and a geological/zoological museum.

PARKS & GARDENS

When the sun shines in Amsterdam, people head for the parks. The most popular and conveniently located of Amsterdam's 20 parks is **Vondelpark,** only a short walk from Leidseplein. Covering 122 acres, its lakes, ponds, and streams are surrounded by meadows, trees, and colorful flowers. This park, open daily from 8am to sunset, is extremely popular with young people from all over the world in summer.

Farther from the city center are many more large parks, such as the huge **Amsterdamse Bos,** covering more than 2,000 acres and providing hiking, biking, and horseback-riding trails, as well as picnic areas and campgrounds. Closer to the city center are **Rembrandtpark, Artis Zoo,** and **Oosterpark.**

SPECIAL-INTEREST SIGHTSEEING

FOR THE JEWISH HISTORY ENTHUSIAST   Anyone interested in Jewish history will find Amsterdam fascinating. The centerpiece of the Jewish experience in Amsterdam is the **Jewish Historical Museum,** at Jonas Daniel Meyerplein 2–4 (☎ **020/626-99-45**), directly across from the **Portuguese Synagogue.** The plight of the Jews in Amsterdam during World War II is brought poignantly home at **Anne Frankhuis,** Prinsengracht 263–265 (☎ **020/556-71-00**). See above for details on both museums.

FOR THE ARCHITECTURE LOVER   Amsterdam is an architecture lover's dream. The fascinating narrow **canal houses** and warehouses built primarily during the 17th century are not only beautiful to look at (and best viewed from a boat cruising the canals) but also great places to stay. All the canal-house hotels listed earlier under "Accommodations" feature steep narrow stairways and other original period touches. You'll have to crane your neck a bit to appreciate the beauty of these old houses fully since their most striking features are their gables. The largest canal houses are on Herengracht, but the smaller houses on other canals (especially in the Jordaan area) are much more interesting architecturally.

To see the inside of some restored canal houses other than hotels, visit the **Netherlands Theater Institute,** Herengracht 168 (☎ **020/623-51-04**); the **Museum Willet-Holthuysen,** Herengracht 605 (☎ **020/523-18-70**) (see above for details on hours and admission fees); or the **Museum van Loon,** Keizersgracht 672 (☎ **020/624-52-55**). An interesting contrast to these grand mansions is the narrowest house in Amsterdam (only a yard wide) at Singel 7.

An architecturally interesting spot off the canals is the **Begijnhof,** just off the busy Kalverstraat shopping area. In this peaceful courtyard, lay nuns and elderly women have lived since the 14th century. No. 34 is Amsterdam's oldest home, built in 1475 (see "More Attractions," above, for details). Also fascinating for architecture fans are the **Rijksmuseum** and **Centraal Station,** which were designed by P. J. H. Cuypers in the late 19th century. The most influential architect of his time, he worked in a neo-gothic style, using steep roofs and dormers.

ORGANIZED TOURS

WALKING TOURS   Although you could see most of Amsterdam's important sights in a single long walking tour, it's best to break the city up into smaller tours.

Amsterdam East

Hollandse Schouwburg **6**

Hortus Botanicus **5**

Joods Historisch Museum **4**

Museum Het Rembrandthuis **2**

Natura Artis Magistra (Amsterdam Zoo) **7**

Netherlands Maritime Museum **1**

Portuguese Synagogue **3**

Tropenmuseum **8**

Luckily, the Tourist Information Office has done the work for you. For only Dfl 3.50 ($2.05) you can buy a brochure outlining one of six different walking tours, including "Voyage of Discovery Through Amsterdam," "A Walk Through Jewish Amsterdam," "A Walk Through the Jordaan," and "A Walk Through Maritime Amsterdam."

BUS TOURS For a much-faster tour that covers much of the same ground as the walking tours, try one of the three-hour guided bus tours offered by **NZH Travel,** Damrak between Centraal Station and the Victoria Hotel (☎ **020/625-07-72**), or **Lindbergh Excursions,** Damrak 26 (☎ **020/622-27-66**). In addition to pointing out the major sights of Amsterdam, tours include a visit to a diamond cutter. Tours cost Dfl 27 to 38 ($15.90 to $22.35).

BOAT TOURS Gazing up from a boat on a canal is absolutely the best way to view the old houses and warehouses of Amsterdam. If you have to choose between a walking tour, a bus tour, and a boat tour, definitely take a boat. This is a city built on the shipping trade, so it's only fitting that you should see it from the water, just as the merchants of the 17th century's golden age saw their city. Not only will you get a sense of Amsterdam as a city of canals, but also you'll see the city's international harbor.

The city is filled with canal-boat docks, all of which have signs stating the time of the next tour. Tours last 1 1/2 hours and cost Dfl 10 to 15 ($5.90 to $8.80). The greatest concentration of canal-boat operators is along Damrak, a block from Centraal Station. Since the tours are all basically the same, simply pick the one that's most convenient for you.

A BREWERY TOUR   The **Heineken Brewery Museum,** Stadhouderskade 78 (☎ **020/523-96-66**), is a short walk along Singelgracht canal from the Rijksmuseum. Tours are held Monday through Friday at 9:30 and 11am (also at 1 and 2:30pm from June 1 to September 15), and the only charge is a Dfl 2 ($1.20) donation given to several different charities. Heineken opened its first Amsterdam brewery in 1864, and over the years it expanded as its beer gained popularity. The guides take you on a "history of beer" tour, explaining the brewing process (highlighting the Heineken story) and show you the characteristic copper brew house, the horse stables, and many other facilities traditionally used in beer brewing. After watching a film on the company's history, you'll be invited to sample the beer, served with snacks, in a large room overlooking the city.

DIAMOND FACTORY TOURS   For more than 400 years Amsterdam has been associated with diamonds, and while you're here be sure to take a tour of a diamond-cutting and -polishing facility. Tours are offered daily at many of the city's largest companies. The tours show you how the rough stones are cut and then polished, a process that reduces 50% of every stone to diamond dust. There's no pressure to buy stones or jewelry when you're taken to the company's showroom as part of the tour. Here your guide will show you the different cuts and how to determine the quality of a diamond. Diamond cutting is a very specialized skill and to this day it is still done by hand.

Diamond factories offering free individual and small-group tours include the **Amsterdam Diamond Center,** Rokin 1 (☎ **020/624-57-87**), just off Dam Square, down Damrak from Centraal Station, open daily from 10am to 5:30pm (on Thursday to 8:30pm); **Coster Diamonds,** Paulus Potterstraat 2–6 (☎ **020/676-22-22**), reachable by tram no. 1, 2, or 5 to Museumplein, open daily from 9am to 5pm; and **Van Moppes Diamonds,** Albert Cuypstraat 2–6 (☎ **020/676-12-42**), near the Albert Cuypstraat stop on tram no. 16, 24, or 25, and open daily from 9am to 5pm.

7 Shopping

Strolling Amsterdam's streets, you could easily get the impression that the city is one giant outdoor shopping mall. Everywhere you look are stores ranging in price and variety from the Jordaan's used-clothing shops and bookstores to P. C. Hoofstraat's designer boutiques. Unfortunately, most stores offer little in the way of bargains. However, many typically Dutch souvenirs and gift items might appeal to you and can be real bargains if you shop around.

The **main shopping areas** include Nieuwendijk and Kalverstraat. On these streets you'll find inexpensive clothing stores, plus many souvenir shops—recommendable is Delftware, Nieuwendijk 24 (☎ **020/627-39-74**), open daily from 10am to 6pm, with friendly owners who accept all credit cards. Amsterdam's upscale shopping area is P. C. Hoofstraat, near Museumplein, a street lined with designer boutiques and expensive restaurants. For secondhand goods, wander the streets of the Jordaan, and for pricey antiques, try Nieuwe Spiegelstraat, which leads to the Rijksmuseum.

Magna Plaza, a three-story shopping mall, opened recently in the former Central Post Office building at the corner of Nieuwezijds Voorburgwal and Raadhuisstraat, a one-minute walk from Dam Square. It's open Monday through Saturday from 11am to 9pm (on Thursday to 9pm). Here you can find almost everything there is to buy in Amsterdam—except food.

You'll find paperbacks by the thousand at **W. H. Smith,** Kalverstraat 152, at the corner of Spui (☎ **020/638-38-21**), open daily from 11am to 5pm. British travelers will find a taste of home at **Marks & Spencer,** Kalverstraat 66 (☎ **020/ 620-00-06**), open Monday through Friday from 10am to 6pm and Saturday from 9:30am to 6pm.

The **Bijenkorf** and **C&A,** two of Amsterdam's largest department stores, face each other on Damrak near Dam Square.

Most shops that deal with tourists will be happy to **ship your purchases home** for an additional charge. If you want to ship something yourself, go to the Main Post Office, where there's a special counter selling boxes and packing materials. They'll also provide you with the necessary Customs forms to fill out.

Watch for the TAX FREE FOR TOURISTS signs in shop windows. These stores will provide you with a form for claiming a **refund of the VAT** (value-added tax). This refund amounts to 17.5% of the total cost of purchases in Amsterdam and throughout the Netherlands. However, before you can get a refund, you'll have to make a purchase of at least Dfl 300 ($176.45) in any participating store. When you're leaving the country by air, you must present the form and the goods to Customs. After Customs has stamped your form, you put it in an envelope and mail it directly from Customs. Your refund will be mailed to you within 10 days. You can also claim an immediate cash refund at any Grens Wissel Kontor (GWK) office, located in Schiphol Airport and at all major border crossings into Germany and Belgium.

MARKETS   Amsterdam's two most famous markets are the **Waterlooplein flea market** and the **Albert Cuypstraat open-air market.** Both generally sell the same sorts of goods, but you can still find a few antiques and near antiques on Waterlooplein. The flea market surrounds the modern Muziektheater building. Most of what's offered here these days is used and cheap clothing. On Albert Cuypstraat you'll find more cheap clothing than you'd ever want to look at, plus fresh fish, Asian vegetables, fresh-cut flowers, electronics, cosmetics, and all the assorted people who buy and sell such an array of products. Both markets are open Monday through Saturday from 9am to 5pm.

Other Amsterdam markets include the **Sunday Antiques Market,** by the Weigh House on Nieuwmarkt, which is open May to October from 10am to 4pm. The **Floating Flower Market** is along Singel between Muntplein and Leidsestraat, open Monday through Saturday from 9am to 5pm. There's a **flea market** on Noordermarkt in the Jordaan on Monday morning and a **farmer's market** on Saturday from 10am to 3pm. The **Book Market** on Oudemanhuispoort, between Oudezijds Voorburgwal and Klovveniersburgwal on the edge of the Red Light District, is held Monday through Saturday from 10am to 4pm; another is held on the Spui on Friday from 10am to 6pm. On Sunday from 10am to 5pm there's an **art market** on the Spui.

8 Amsterdam After Dark

Since Leidseplein and Rembrandtplein are Amsterdam's nightlife centers, you'll find dozens of bars, nightclubs, cafés, discos, and movie theaters around these two squares. However, more cultured evening entertainments are to be found in various parts of the city.

For listings of the week's performances in the many theaters and concert halls, consult *What's On in Amsterdam*, a magazine available for Dfl 4 ($2.35) at the Tourist Information Office in front of Centraal Station or at the AUB reservation office on Leidseplein. At these locations you can also make reservations and buy tickets for shows at many venues in Amsterdam.

THE PERFORMING ARTS
THEATER

Théâtre Carré

Amstel 115–125. ☎ **020/622-52-25.** Tickets Dfl 25–90 ($14.70–$52.95). Metro: Weesperplein.

The Carré, a huge old domed theater on the Amstel River near the Skinny Bridge, occasionally presents touring plays from New York's Broadway or London's West End. The box office is open Monday through Saturday from 10am to 7pm and Sunday from 1 to 7pm.

CLASSICAL MUSIC

Beurs van Berlage

Damrak 243. ☎ **020/627-04-66.** Tickets Dfl 10–50 ($5.90–$19.40). Tram 1, 2, 4, 5, 9, 16, or 24.

This impressive building on Damrak was once the Amsterdam stock exchange, but a few years ago it was converted into two concert halls that host frequent symphony performances. The box office is open Tuesday through Friday from 12:30 to 6pm and Saturday from noon to 5pm.

Concertgebouw

Concertgebouwplein 2–6. ☎ **020/573-05-73.** Tickets Dfl 15–190 ($8.80–$111.75). Tram 2, 3, 5, 12, or 16.

This world-famous concert hall, with its ornate Greek revival facade, is said to have one of the best acoustics of any hall in the world. Performances, including those by the renowned **Royal Concertgebouw Orchestra,** are held almost every night in the building's two halls. There are free lunchtime concerts on Wednesday at 12:30pm. The box office is open daily from 10am to 7pm.

OPERA & DANCE

Het Muziektheater

Amstel 3. ☎ **020/625-54-55.** Tickets Dfl 20–100 ($11.75–$58.80). Tram 9 or 14.

This ultramodern 1,600-seat hall caused quite a stir when it was built, for Amsterdammers thought the architecture clashed with the neighborhood. The innovative **Netherlands Opera** and the famed **Netherlands Dance Theater** perform here. The box office is open Monday through Saturday from 10am to 8pm and Sunday from 11:30am to 6pm.

Stadsschouwburg

Leidseplein 26. ☎ **020/523-77-00.** Tickets Dfl 15–75 ($8.80–$44.10). Tram 1, 2, or 5.

Amsterdam's former opera and ballet theater, built in 1894, is neoclassical with Dutch Renaissance features. Performances include plays in Dutch and English, plus music and dance performances by international companies. The box office is open daily from 10am to 6pm.

ROCK & JAZZ

Listed here are some of Amsterdam's biggest and most popular clubs, booking up-and-coming acts and always charging admission. However, plenty of smaller clubs showcase local bands and charge no admission. Among these, check out the **Bamboo Bar,** Lange Leidsedwarstraat 64 (☎ **020/624-39-93**), and the **Café Alto,** Korte Leidsedwarstraat 115 (☎ **020/626-32-49**), for nightly live jazz; and **Korsakoff,** Lijnbaansgracht 162 (☎ **020/625-78-54**), for Wednesday night alternative rock. All three clubs are near Leidseplein.

Akhnaton

Nieuwezijds Kolk 25. ☎ **020/624-33-96.** Cover Dfl 5–15 ($2.90–$8.80). Tram 1, 2, 5, 13, or 17.

The world beat-music scene is very much alive in cosmopolitan Amsterdam, and Akhnaton is the city's most popular club for ethnic rhythms. During any given week there might be a night of Latin dance music, Arabic pop, African drumming, and Javanese gamelan music. Open Wednesday through Sunday from 9pm to 3am.

Bimhuis

Oude Schans 73–77. ☎ **020/623-13-61.** Cover Dfl 15–25 ($8.80–$14.70). Metro: Waterlooplein.

Housed in an old canalside warehouse, Bimhuis is Amsterdam's premier jazz club. Music workshops are held on Monday and Tuesday; on Wednesday the Dutch Jazz Orchestra performs. During the rest of the week jazz musicians from all over Europe perform. Food is served. Open Monday through Saturday from 8pm to 3am.

Melkweg

Lijnbaangracht 234a (just off Leidseplein behind the Stadsschouwburg). ☎ **020/ 624-17-77.** Cover Dfl 7.50–35 ($4.40–$20.58). Tram 1, 2, or 5.

This is the most popular of the four clubs these days, with activities starting at 8pm and continuing until the early hours. You can see films, dance to recorded music, hang out in the café, view the changing art exhibits, hear a live band, or watch art videos. A bookshop, a restaurant, and a café are also here. Open Wednesday through Sunday from 2pm to midnight.

Paradiso

Weteringschans 6–8 (near Leidseplein). ☎ **020/626-45-21.** Cover Dfl 10–35 ($5.80–$20.60) plus Dfl 4 ($2.35) monthly membership. Tram 1, 2, or 5.

This club has changed its image considerably since it first opened. It's now more a venue for political forums and lectures, in addition to frequent rock, pop, and jazz concerts. Open from Wednesday through Saturday from 8pm to 2am.

THE CASINO

Amsterdam's only casino opened in 1994: **Casino 2000,** Max Euweplein 6 (☎ **020/620-10-06**), facing a canal near Leidseplein. You can play roulette, baccarat, black jack, big wheel, and banco. In another part of the building you'll find 300 slot machines. Its open daily from 2pm to 2am; admission is Dfl 5 ($2.95).

FILMS

Amsterdam always offers a good selection of the best films from all over the world, and foreign films are shown in their original language with Dutch subtitles. In front of each theater is a list of all the films playing that week. The greatest concentration of theaters is on Leidseplein. Tickets cost around Dfl 13 ($7.65). You can save money by going to a matinee Monday through Thursday, when tickets are only Dfl 10 ($5.80). Keep in mind that there are 15 to 30 minutes of commercials and previews before the film starts. The posted times are when the commercials, not the film, begin.

If you see only one movie while in Amsterdam, try to see it at the **Tuschinski Theater,** Reguliersbreestraat 26–28 (☎ **020/626-26-33**), just off Rembrandtplein, a beautiful art deco movie palace built in 1921.

BARS & BROWN CAFES

Particularly old and traditional bars, the sort that might've appeared in a Rembrandt painting, often earn the appellation of brown café. The name is said to have been derived as much from the preponderance of wood furnishings as from the browning of the walls from years of dense tobacco smoke. To experience Amsterdam conviviality at its finest, head to one of these brown cafés (be prepared for thick smog when you walk through the doors). Here you'll encounter a warm and friendly atmosphere where you can sit and sip a glass of beer or a mixed drink and even get a cheap meal.

There are countless bars in Amsterdam, most around Leidseplein and Rembrantplein. They don't start to get busy until at least 10pm, although they usually open at noon and stay open all day. In both the cafés and the bars the most popular drink is draft Heineken served in small glasses with two fingers of head on top for around Dfl 3.50 ($2.05). Also popular is *genever* (Dutch gin) available in *jonge* (young) and *oude* (old) varieties—oude is quite a bit stronger in taste and alcoholic content. Genever shots start at Dfl 3.50 ($2.05) as well.

Most cafés and bars are open Friday and Saturday from noon to 2am and Sunday through Thursday from noon to 1am. On Sunday from about 6pm on, you'll find live traditional Dutch music in several bars on the Rembrandtplein.

Cafe Papeneiland

Prinsengracht 2 (on the corner of Prinsengracht and Brouwersgracht). ☎ **020/624-19-89.** Bus: Haarlemmer Houttuinen.

Papeneiland is the oldest café in Amsterdam: Since 1600 or thereabouts, folks have been dropping by for shots of genever and glasses of beer. The walls near the huge front windows are covered with blue-and-white tiles, and there's an old woodstove. If you have a feeling of déjà vu while here, it's probably because you saw the same view in a painting in the Amsterdam Historisch Museum.

De Drie Fleschjes

Gravenstraat 18 (between the Nieuwe Kerk and Nieuwendijk). ☎ **020/624-84-43.** Tram 13 or 17.

Originally a tasting house where people could try liqueurs distilled and aged on the premises, De Drie Fleschjes has been in business for more than 300 years. One wall of this bar is lined with old wood aging barrels. De Drie Fleschjes is popular with businesspeople and journalists, who stop by to sample the wide variety of oude and jonge genevers. Open Monday through Saturday from noon to 8:30pm.

✪ Hoppe

Spui 18–20. ☎ **020/624-07-56** or 623-78-49. Tram 1, 2, or 5.

Although you'll see signs for Hoppe genever in front of most cafés, there's only one Cafe Hoppe—one of Amsterdam's oldest, most traditional, and most popular brown cafés. The dark walls, low ceilings, and old wooden furniture have literally remained unchanged since the café opened in 1670. If you want to feel as though you stepped into a Breughel painting, this is the place for you.

De Kroon Royal Cafe

Rembrandtplein 15. ☎ **020/625-20-11.** Tram 4, 9, or 14.

The concept of the "Grand Café" has recently taken Amsterdam by storm. New Amsterdammers, tired of cramped and crowded brown cafés, have been flocking to these new large cafés. De Kroon is one of the best. On the second floor of a building overlooking Rembrantplein, it features such unusual decor as old display cabinets of stuffed animals and human anatomy models. Whether you're in jeans or theater attire, you'll feel comfortable here.

De Twee Zwaantjes

Prinsengracht 114. ☎ **020/625-27-29.**

In the Jordaan, this small brown café is very popular with neighborhood locals and tourists alike for its weekend sing-alongs. Late in the evening the musical instruments begin to show up, and once everyone has had enough Heineken and genever, the old music begins. You're welcome to join in and learn a few traditional Amsterdam favorites while the accordion wheezes away.

DISCOS

You'll find dozens of large and small discos clustered around Leidseplein and Rembrandtplein. They tend to rise and fall in popularity, so ask someone in a café what the current favorite is and check it out.

Escape

Rembrandtplein 11. ☎ **020/622-35-42.** Cover Dfl 12.50 ($7.35), free for students Thurs. Tram 4, 9, or 14.

This disco is large and popular. Here you have a choice of several dance floors, all with plenty of flashing lights and a great sound system. Thursday is free to students with an ID. A small glass of Heineken costs Dfl 4 ($2.35); mixed drinks begin at Dfl 10 ($5.90). Open Thursday from 10pm to 4am and Friday and Saturday from 10pm to 5am.

Roxy

Singel 465–467. ☎ **020/620-03-54.** Cover Dfl 7.50 ($3.95) Sun–Wed, Dfl 12.50 ($6.55) Thurs–Sat. Tram 1, 2, 5, or 11.

The Roxy, a huge multilevel disco created from an old movie theater near the flower market, has for many years been the place to go dancing. Inside there's room for more than 600, and the place stays packed on weekends. A small glass of Heineken costs Dfl 4 ($2.35) and mixed drinks start at Dfl 9 ($5.30). Open Wednesday, Thursday, and Sunday from 11pm to 4am and Friday and Saturday from 11pm to 5am.

9 Networks & Resources

STUDENTS   Student activities in Amsterdam don't revolve around a university because the city's main university has relocated many miles outside central Amsterdam and is no longer convenient to the bars, cafés, discos, theaters, and other places young people frequent. However, classes are still held in various buildings around the city, and you'll find students gathering at two student restaurants within the city: **The Atrium,** Grimburgwal 237 on the Voorburgwal canal, is open daily from noon to 7pm; **The Agora** is a short walk from Waterlooplein at Roeterstraat 11–13, open daily from noon to 7:30pm, with a café that stays open until 1am.

For information about cultural events in Amsterdam, visit the **AUB,** on Leidseplein at Marnixstraat. If you're under 26 you can pick up a CJP (Cultural Youth Pass) here for Dfl 20 ($11.75). The CJP is good for free admission to most of the city's museums and for discounts on most cultural events. The AUB is open Monday through Saturday from 10am to 6pm (on Thursday until 9pm). If you're young and in trouble or just want someone to talk to, contact the **JAC (Youth Advice Center),** Amstel 30 (☎ **020/624-29-49**), along the river near Rembrandtplein.

GAY MEN & LESBIANS   Amsterdam bills itself as the gay capital of Europe, so there are dozens of gay and lesbian bars and discos all over the city, with a concentration near Rembrandtplein. To find out more about the gay and lesbian scenes, stop by **COC,** Rozenstraat 14 (☎ **020/623-40-79**), two blocks off Westerkirk. It houses a coffeeshop that's open Tuesday to Sunday from 1 to 5pm and 8pm to midnight. Every Friday the disco is for men and women; Saturdays are for women only.

You can also call the **Gay and Lesbian Switchboard** (☎ **020/623-65-65**), open daily from 10am to 10pm to provide information and advice.

The **"Use-It" guide,** available at the Tourist Information Office in front of Centraal Station, also has listings of popular gay and lesbian bars, discos, baths, and bookstores; *The Best Gay Guide,* available at the W. H. Smith bookstore on Kalverstraat, provides a thorough introduction to the city's gay life.

WOMEN   There are several women's centers around the city, including **Vrouwenhuis,** Nieuwe Herengracht 95 (☎ **020/624-47-04**), near Waterlooplein, open Monday through Friday from 10am to 4pm (closed in summer).

At the **Vrouwencentrum de Pijp,** Karel du Jardinstraat 52 (☎ **020/679-57-22**), a women's library is open Tuesday to Saturday from 2 to 5pm, Thursday to 8pm.

Saarein, Elandstraat 119 (☎ **020/623-49-01**), near Leidseplein, is a women-only bar, open Monday from 8pm to 1am, Tuesday through Thursday and Sunday from 3pm to 1am, and Friday and Saturday from 3pm to 2am.

Xantippe, Prinsengracht 290 (☎ **020/623-58-54**), is a women's bookstore selling more than 8,000 titles in five languages, including English, open Monday from 1 to 6pm, Tuesday through Friday from 10am to 6pm, and Saturday from 10am to 5pm.

For more information, check in the "Use-It" guide available at the Tourist Information Office in front of Centraal Station.

10 Easy Excursions

If Amsterdam is your only stop in the Netherlands, try to make at least one excursion into the countryside. Dikes, windmills, and some of Holland's quaintest villages await you just beyond the city limits.

ZAANSE SCHANS   If you have time for only one excursion, make this the one. Zaanse Schans is a beautiful little village on the banks of the river Zaan 15 miles north of Amsterdam. Along the riverbank are six windmills, two of which are still operating and can be visited. Surrounding the village are pastures where cows graze, and the nearby cocoa factory fills the air with the smell of chocolate.

Zaanse Schans is open daily from April to November 1, on weekends only during the rest of the year. The best way to get here is by train from Amsterdam's Centraal Station. There are departures every 30 minutes, and the trip takes 15 minutes. Take a train bound for Alkmaar that makes local stops, and get off at the Koog-Zaandijk station. From the station, follow the signs. It's about an eight-minute walk. The round-trip fare is Dfl 9.20 ($5.40). A railway excursion ticket, available for Dfl 23.50 ($12.35), includes round-trip rail fare, a 45-minute cruise on the River Zaan, coffee and a pancake in the De Krai pancake restaurant, and admission to the Zaandam Clockwork Museum.

For information, phone 075/16-82-18.

ENKHUIZEN   If you have more time, you should visit the **Zuiderzee Museum** in Enkhuizen. The famous Zuiderzee was once a very tempestuous sea, until ingenious Dutch engineers closed it off from the open sea in 1932, forming the freshwater IJsselmeer. This museum preserves the history of the Zuiderzee in 130 typical houses, shops, and workshops from the many fishing villages that once dotted this coastline. Several former warehouses house an indoor museum displaying model ships, costumes, pottery, paintings, and furniture from the Zuiderzee fishing villages.

The Zuiderzee Museum is open daily from 10am to 5pm between April and October. Admission, including the cost of the boat to the museum, is Dfl 20 ($11.75) for adults, Dfl 15 ($8.80) for seniors and children 6 to 17, and free for children 5 and under. Trains leave Amsterdam's Centraal Station every hour for Enkhuizen, and the trip takes about an hour. The round-trip fare is Dfl 27.50 ($16.20). There's also a Dfl-29 ($17.05) railway excursion ticket that includes the train fare, museum ferry, and museum admission.

AALSMEER FLOWER AUCTION   The Netherlands is the world's largest exporter of cut flowers, and nearly 50% of the flowers that leave the country are sold at this massive auction house. Nothing could adequately prepare you for the sight of these acres of cut flowers stacked three tiers high on constantly moving carts. In six auction halls, hundreds of buyers from all over the world compete for the best flowers at the lowest prices. The Flower Auction is open Monday through Friday from 7:30 to 11am. Admission is Dfl 8 ($4.70).

To reach the Flower Auction in Aalsmeer, take bus no. 172 from in front of the Victoria Hotel across the square from Centraal Station. The trip will take five strips on your strippenkart.

ALKMAAR   One of the most popular summer excursions is to the **open-air cheese market** in Alkmaar. Held every Friday morning between mid-April and September from 10am to noon, the cheese market attracts thousands of picture-taking visitors to this historic old town. Huge piles of yellow cheese cover the paving stones of Alkmaar's main square while men in white suits and red, yellow, green, or blue hats rush about carrying wooden platforms stacked with still more rounds of cheese. When the auction is over, be sure to take time to explore the town.

Trains leave regularly from Amsterdam's Centraal Station for the 45-minute trip to Alkmaar. A round-trip ticket is Dfl 19.50 ($11.50).

GUIDED TOURS AROUND HOLLAND   There are more than 20 organized tours available from Amsterdam, ranging in length from a few hours to a few days. **Lindbergh Excursions,** Damrak 26 (☎ **020/622-27-66**), and **NZH Travel Excursions** (☎ **020/625-07-72**), which has its office across from Centraal Station and in front of the Victoria Hotel, offer the lowest rates on bus tours. Stop by their offices and pick up their brochures.

Some of their more popular tours are to **Marken and Volendam,** two Zuiderzee fishing villages. In summer this trip, costing around Dfl 40 ($23.50), can be done by boat and bus. Another interesting tour is the all-day trip **around the former Zuiderzee.** This tour allows you to see the amazing Afsluitdijk, the Enclosure Dike that turned the Zuiderzee from a stormy sea into a placid lake. Expect to pay around Dfl 62 ($36.50).

Athens 5

by Dan Levine

When you arrive in Athens you'll be immediately confronted with colorless concrete buildings, congested streets, and sometimes stifling smog—not the romantic wonderland you dreamed about when you planned your trip to the city of gods. Then suddenly you'll catch a glimpse of the Acropolis, your heart will skip a beat, and in a magic moment you'll be right where you had imagined. Climbing toward the Parthenon, you won't be able to help envisioning yourself walking in the footsteps of Socrates and Aristophanes. And if you've never been interested in the history of Western civilization, you'll find yourself asking questions, reading brochures, and even buying books about early times.

While Athens may not be beautiful physically, it does have worthy attractions. The city is packed with some of the most boisterous, friendly, and fun people in the world, and few cities can boast livelier restaurants or more energetic nightclubs. Athens's good food and relatively inexpensive accommodations will also be welcomed by budget travelers. Seldom does Europe offer such abundance without putting a strain on your wallet.

1 Athens Deals & Discounts

BUDGET BESTS   From hotels and restaurants to sights and transportation, the entire city of Athens is a great value for travelers. The meticulous budgeteer could live for far less than $50 a day here, and those who spend their full allotment will live quite comfortably.

SPECIAL DISCOUNTS   For Students   If you hold an **International Student Identification Card** (ISIC) you can realize a substantial discount on museum fees—usually 50%. If you're under 26, student or not, you can purchase rail, coach, airline, and ship tickets for up to 40% below the official prices by visiting the **Transalpino Travel Office,** 28 Nikis St. (☎ 322-0503), two blocks from Syntagma Square. It's open June 15 through October, Monday through Friday from 8am to 7pm and Saturday from 8:30am to 1pm; the rest of the year, Monday through Friday from 9am to 5pm and Saturday from 8:30am to 1pm.

For Seniors   Most museums grant 30% to 50% ticket discounts to senior citizens—women over 60 and men over 65.

What's Special About Athens

Ancient Monuments
- The Acropolis, the West's most fantastic architectural remnant of ancient times.
- Ancient Agora, Socrates' old stomping ground and the marketplace of ancient Athens.
- Delphi, the Ancient's center of the universe is just three hours from Athens.

Museums
- National Archaeological Museum, a vast warehouse of history and the best ancient Greek relics anywhere.

Natural Landmarks & Neighborhoods
- Lycabettus Hill, offering a bird's-eye view over all of Athens.
- Plaka, laid-out in ancient times, this tangle of pedestrian streets is still the best for strolling, shopping, and eating.

Shopping
- The Flea Market, filled with small stores and tourist trinkets, it's both fun and affordable.

2 Pretrip Preparations

REQUIRED DOCUMENTS   Citizens of the United States, Canada, New Zealand, and Australia need no visas, just a valid passport, for stays up to three months. U.K. citizens need only an identity card.

TIMING YOUR TRIP   March through May is pleasant and mild, while June to October can be dry and hot. Even during summer there's relief in the afternoons and evenings when cool breezes usually blow in from the sea. December through February are colder than you might imagine—and wet and windy. too.

Athens's Average Daytime Temperature & Days of Rain

	Jan	Feb	Mar	Apr	May	June	July	Aug	Sept	Oct	Nov	Dec
Temp. (°F)	52	54	58	65	74	86	92	92	82	72	63	56
Days of Rain	14	12	11	9	8	5	2	3	4	9	12	14

Special Events   The annual **Athens Festival,** held from mid-July to mid-September, is the city's main festival of the arts. The ancient Odeon of Herodes Atticus, built in A.D. 161, is the unique setting for both the well- and lesser-known orchestras, ballet companies, singers, and dancers performing here. Seats cost 1,000 to 6,000 Dr ($4.15 to $25). For ticket and schedule information, contact the Odeon at 4 Stadiou St. (☎ **01/322-1459**).

BACKGROUND READING   *The Iliad* and *The Odyssey* (Penguin) are obvious Greek travel companions. Plato and Aristotle are also good reads, though not light beach materials.

Recommended histories include Chester G. Starr's *Origins of Greek Civilization 1100–650 B.C.* (Norton), an enjoyable read chronicling the classical city-state. *Democracy and Participation in Athens* (Cambridge University Press) by

What Things Cost in Athens	U.S.$
Taxi from the airport to Syntagma Square	8.90
Taxi from Larissis train station to hotel	3.50
Public transportation (bus or metro)	.55
Local telephone call	.04
Double room at the Grande Bretagne (deluxe)	302.50
Double room at the Hotel Dorian Inn (moderate)	103.15
Double room at Hotel Tempi (budget)	30.25
Continental breakfast	4.00
Meal for one, without beverage, at Gerofinikas (deluxe)	50.00
Meal for one, without beverage, at Nea-Olympia (moderate)	9.10
Meal for one, without beverage, at Taverna Bairaktaris (budget)	6.05
Half a liter of beer	1.50
Half a liter of retsina (wine)	.90
Coca-Cola in a restaurant	.80
Cup of coffee in a restaurant with table service	.70
Roll of ASA 100 color film, 36 exposures	4.95
Admission to the Acropolis	6.25
Movie ticket	4.15

R. K. Sinclair is a detailed look at citizenry and social history of ancient Greece. *Greece and the Hellenistic World* (Oxford University Press), edited by John Boardman et al., is a hefty paperback outlining over 800 years of history for lay readers.

For a more detailed guide to the city, see *Frommer's Athens* (Macmillan Travel).

3 Athens Specifics

ARRIVING

FROM THE AIRPORT   Nearly all visitors to Athens arrive by plane at one of two airports. All domestic and international flights of the national airline, Olympic, arrive at **Hellinikon (or West) Airport** (☎ **01/969-9466**), 7 miles southeast of the city. Several banks in the arrivals area are open daily from 7am to 11pm, and a Greek Tourist Office offers city maps and other information on an erratic schedule. A blue express bus connects the airport with downtown Athens every 20 to 30 minutes from 6am to midnight for only 170 Dr (75¢) and hourly after midnight for 220 Dr ($1). The bus stops at Amalias Avenue near Syntagma Square and at Stadiou Street near Omonia Square; during summer the bus also adds stops at the train and bus stations. Hard-core budgeteers may wish to take local bus no. 122 or 133 into town for only 120 Dr (55¢).

If you're flying any carrier other than Olympic, you'll arrive and depart from **East Airport** (☎ **01/969-9111**), about 8 miles from the city center. As at the other airport, you'll find at least one bank here open from 7am to 11pm daily. You can get information from the Greek Tourist Office window, to your left after exiting Customs. The express bus downtown runs on the same schedule with the same stops as at the West Airport, for the same price. Local bus no. 121 also makes the journey.

Taxis from either airport to town should cost no more than 2,000 Dr ($8.90)—but read the warnings in "By Taxi" under "Getting Around," below, before entering. To get between the two airports, take yellow bus no. 19 for 200 Dr (90¢). This bus also goes to the port at Piraeus, so make sure you ask if it's going in the right direction.

FROM THE TRAIN STATION   There are two train stations, located a few blocks from each other, about a mile northwest of Omonia Square. The main station, **Larissis,** services northern Greece (Larissa, Saloniki, and Volos) and provides connections to Vienna, Zurich, and Paris. Here you'll find a currency-exchange office open daily from 8am to 9:15pm with high commission rates, plus a luggage-storage office charging 250 Dr ($1.05) per bag per day, open from 6:30am to 9:30pm. The **Peloponnese station,** just to the south, services trains to and from the Peloponnese (Corinth, Patras, and Olympia).

Yellow trolleybus no. 1 connects the stations with Syntagma Square; a taxi into town should cost about 500 Dr ($2.10).

FROM THE HARBOR   Athens's main seaport, Piraeus, 7 miles southwest of town, is a 15-minute subway ride from Omonia and Monastiraki Squares. Ships from European and overseas harbors arrive and depart here, and in summer the city's best discos are located by this seashore. The subway runs from about 5am to midnight and costs 75 to 100 Dr (35¢ to 45¢), depending on how far you go.

VISITOR INFORMATION

The **Tourist Information Office,** 2 Karageorgi St. (☎ **322-3111**), at the northwest corner of Syntagma Square, staffs a walk-up window outside the National Bank of Greece. Look for the modern 10-story building next to the Lufthansa office. Information about Athens, free city maps, hotel lists, and other general information booklets are available in English. The office is usually open in summer, Monday through Thursday from 8am to 2pm and 3:30 to 8pm, Friday from 8am to 1:30pm and 3 to 8pm, Saturday from 9am to 3pm, and Sunday from 9am to 2pm; from November to the end of Easter, hours are Monday through Thursday from 8am to 2pm and 3:30 to 6:30pm, Friday from 8am to 1:30pm and 3:30 to 6:30pm, Saturday from 9am to 2pm, and Sunday from 9am to 1pm.

Inside the bank, the Hellenic Chamber of Hotels books hotel rooms in all price categories (see "Accommodations," later in this chapter, for details).

CITY LAYOUT

Athens has two hearts, both somewhat diseased. Syntagma (Constitution) Square, now construction site for a future subway station, is home to the Parliament building dozens of airline offices, as well as McDonald's and Kenny Roger's Roasters fast-food restaurants. Omonia Square, about a mile away, is an even larger, busier, and grimier traffic circle ringed with gray office buildings and full of out-of-work immigrants and porno magazine sellers. Approximately a mile apart, these two squares are connected by two parallel avenues, Stadiou Street and Panepistimiou Street. From Syntagma Square, Mitropoleos Street leads, slightly downhill, to Monastiraki Square, near the flea market and the Plaka district. From Monastiraki Square, mile-long

The Greek Drachma

For American Readers   At this writing $1 = approximately 225 Dr (or 1 Dr = 0.4¢), and this was the rate of exchange used to calculate the dollar values given in this chapter (rounded to the nearest nickel).

For British Readers   At this writing, £1 = approximately 340 Dr (or 1 Dr = 0.29p), and this was the rate of exchange used to calculate the pound values in the table below.

Note: The rates given here fluctuate from time to time and may not be the same when you travel to Greece. Therefore this table should be used only as a guide:

Dr	U.S.$	U.K.£	Dr	U.S.$	U.K.£
5	.02	.01	1,500	6.67	4.41
10	.04	.03	2,000	8.89	5.88
15	.07	.04	2,500	11.11	7.35
20	.09	.06	3,000	13.33	8.82
25	.11	.07	3,500	15.55	10.29
50	.22	.15	4,000	17.78	11.76
75	.33	.22	4,500	20.00	13.25
100	.44	.29	5,000	22.22	14.70
150	.67	.44	6,000	26.67	17.65
200	.89	.59	7,000	31.11	20.59
250	1.11	.74	8,000	35.55	23.53
300	1.33	.88	9,000	40.00	26.47
400	1.78	1.18	10,000	44.44	29.41
500	2.22	1.47	12,500	55.55	36.76
750	3.33	2.20	15,000	66.67	44.12
1,000	4.44	2.94	17,500	77.78	51.47

Athinas Street leads to Omonia Square. In the triangle formed by these three squares—Syntagma, Omonia, and Monastiraki—lies Athens's inner city, its shopping area, the central market, the main department stores, the post offices, banks, and many of the hotels, pensions, tavernas, and restaurants listed in this chapter.

Two helpful landmarks for orientation—the Acropolis and Lycabettus Hill (the latter with the small white church and the Greek flag on top)—are both visible from most parts of the city.

In general, finding your way around Athens is relatively easy, despite signs that look "Greek" to you. An exception is Plaka, with its small winding streets at the foot of the Acropolis, a labyrinth that'll challenge even the best navigators. Most maps don't include all of Plaka's streets, so if you're concerned about getting lost, invest in the pricey German-published Falk-plan (available at Syntagma Square newsstands), which costs 2,000 Dr ($8.90).

GETTING AROUND

BY BUS, TROLLEYBUS & SUBWAY   In general, the orange trolleybuses (directly connected to electric lines above) serve areas in the center of the city, while the blue buses go to more remote areas. Tickets cost 75 Dr (35¢) for both and must be purchased in advance, either from any news kiosk or from special bus ticket kiosks located at main stations. When you board, cancel the ticket in an automatic machine. Buses run all the time but with limited night service. You probably won't use the bus too often, as many sights of interest can be reached by foot.

The subway is useful primarily as a link with Piraeus, the seaport of Athens. The line originates in suburban Kiffisia and passes through Athens, stopping at Victoria, Omonia, and Monastiraki before going on to Piraeus. The subway costs 75 to 100 Dr (30¢ to 40¢), depending on how far you go, and runs about every 10 minutes from 5am to midnight.

BY TAXI   Theoretically, taxis are inexpensive in Athens. But many travelers have complained of special "tourist prices," facilitated by an illegally fast meter or unheard-of "supplements" to the fare; upon your arrival, some drivers may also try to steer you away from your hotel to their "favorite," where they receive a kickback.

As of this writing, the minimum fare is 300 Dr ($1.25), the typical fare for a short hop in central Athens. Various additional charges include a luggage fee of 40 Dr (15¢) per 22-lb. bag and an extra 100 to 200 Dr (40¢ to 90¢) for stops at transportation centers such as the airport or train station. Of course, these rates could change by the time you arrive, so the best thing to do is ask locals what the fare should be before you enter a taxi. If you have a problem or dispute, threaten to calling the **Tourist Police** (☎ 171), a surprisingly effective negotiating tool.

You may see locals shouting at the windows or running alongside taxis trying to get in a word with the driver. What's going on? Taxis can pick up several passengers at the same time, and these people are trying to see if the taxi is going their way. If you're picked up halfway through another passenger's ride, note the amount on the meter as you board and subtract it from the final fare (200 Dr/90¢ minimum). If a taxi flashes its lights, it's available for hire.

There are several radio taxi companies in town, including **Aris** (☎ **346-7102**), **Express** (☎ **993-4812**), and **Parthenon** (☎ **581-4711**).

ON FOOT   Like so many other European cities, Athens is creating pedestrian zones, mostly in major shopping areas, making window-shopping and strolling a pleasure. In 1995, the city closed the majority of Plaka to traffic for a three-month trial. Let's hope it becomes permanent.

Most sightseeing in Athens can be done on foot. When crossing a street, keep in mind that in Athens a red traffic light does not necessarily mean that cars will stop.

BY CAR & MOPED   Not far from Syntagma Square, **Avis,** 48 Amalias St. (☎ **322-4951**), charges about 73,100 Dr ($324.90) per week with unlimited mileage, not including about 1,600 Dr ($7.15) for daily insurance, plus 16% tax. Similar prices are offered by **Budget,** 8 Syngrou Ave. (☎ **921-4711**); and **Euro-dollar,** 29 Syngrou Ave. (☎ **922-9672**). **Athens Cars,** 10 Filellimon St. (☎ **323-3783**), is usually cheaper, charging about 70,000 Dr ($311.15), not including insurance and tax. Off season rates are lower.

Mopeds can be rented from **Meintanis,** 4 Dionisiou Aeropagitou in Plaka, at the foot of the Acropolis near the intersection with Amalias Street (☎ **323-2346**), for about 3,600 Dr ($16) per day or 22,500 Dr ($100) per week, depending on the time of year. They require a deposit of 10,000 Dr ($41.65) or a credit or charge card. They're open Monday through Saturday from 9am to 8pm and Sunday from 11am to 3pm.

Street parking is a problem in Athens. Ask at your hotel for the nearest parking place, which will cost up to 1,000 Dr ($4.45) per day.

FAST FACTS: Athens

Banks   Banks are generally open Monday through Thursday from 8am to 2pm and Friday from 8am to 1:30pm. All banks have currency-exchange counters. The **American Express** office, 31 Panepistimiou St. (☎ **323-4781**), offers currency-exchange and other services Monday through Friday from 8:30am to 4pm and Saturday from 8:30am to 1:30pm. Avoid changing money on Sunday and holidays; the exchange rates offered by illegal street agents are outrageous.

Business Hours   In winter, shops are generally open Monday and Wednesday from 9am to 5pm; Tuesday, Thursday, and Friday from 10am to 7pm; and Saturday from 8:30am to 3:30pm. In summer, shops are generally open Monday, Wednesday, and Saturday from 8am to 3pm; and Tuesday, Thursday, and Friday from 8am to 1:30pm and 5:30 to 10pm. Note that many shops geared to tourists keep especially long hours, and some shops close for "siesta" from about 2 to 5pm. Most food stores and the central market are open Monday and Wednesday from 9am to 4:30pm, Tuesday from 9am to 6pm, Thursday from 9:30am to 6:30pm, Friday from 9:30am to 7pm, and Saturday from 8:30am to 4:30pm. Many small shops, such as groceries and bakeries, are open on Sunday, too.

Currency   The drachma (Dr) is the Greek national currency. Coins are issued in 1, 2, 5, 10, 20, 50 and 100 Dr; bills are denominated in 50, 100, 500, 1,000, and 5,000 Dr.

Embassies   **United States,** 91 Vas. Sofias Ave. (☎ **721-2951**), **Canada,** 4 Ioannou Genadiou St. (☎ **723-9511** or 725-4011), the **United Kingdom,** 1 Ploutarchou St. (☎ **723-6211**); **Australia,** 37 D. Soutsou Ave. (☎ **644-7303**); and **New Zealand,** 15 Tsoha St. (☎ **641-0311**).

Emergencies   In an **emergency,** dial **100** for the police and **171** for the very effective **Tourist Police.** Dial **199** to report a **fire** and **166** for an **ambulance and hospital.** If you need an English-speaking doctor or dentist, call your embassy for advice.

A centrally located **pharmacy** is at 2 Ermou St. (☎ **322-3339**), half a block from Syntagma Square. It's open Monday and Wednesday from 8am to 2:30pm and Tuesday, Thursday, and Friday from 8am to 2:30pm and 5 to 8pm. At other times, consult the list of pharmacies open on Saturday and Sunday posted on the door, or dial 107 for the address of an open pharmacy.

Holidays   Public holidays in Athens include New Year's Day (January 1), Epiphany (January 6), Ash Wednesday, Independence Day (March 25), Good Friday, Greek Orthodox Easter Sunday and Monday (usually one week after Catholics and Protestants celebrate Easter), Labor Day (May 1), Assumption Day (August 15), National Day (October 28), and Christmas (December 25–26).

Information   The main Tourist Information Office is at 2 Karageorgi St., in Syntagma Square. See "Athens Specifics," above, for details.

Laundry   The laundry at 10 Angelou Geronda St., off Kidathineon Street, in Plaka, is open daily from 8:30am to 7pm. It charges 1,300 Dr ($5.75) for wash, dry, and soap. Another self-service laundry is **Maytag Launderette,** at 46 Didotou

St., near Omonia Square, three blocks off Akadimias Street (☎ **361-0661**), which charges 1,500 Dr. ($6.70) for you to wash and dry 5 kilos (11 lb.) or 1,700 Dr ($7.55) if they do the work. It's open Monday through Saturday from 8am to 9pm.

Libraries   The best libraries for English speakers are the **American Library,** 22 Massalias St. (☎ **363-7740**), in Kolonaki; and the **British Council Library,** Kolonaki Sq. (☎ **363-3211**).

Lost & Found   If you lose something on the street or on public transportation, contact the **Police Lost and Found Office,** 173 Leoforos Alexandras St. (☎ **770-5771** or 644-5940), open Monday through Saturday from 9am to 3pm. If you lost it on a bus or train, call **642-1616.** Lost passports and other documents are returned by the police to the appropriate embassy, so check there, too.

Mail   The main **post office,** on Syntagma Square (☎ **323-7573**), is open Monday through Friday from 7:30am to 8pm and Saturday and Sunday from 9am to 2pm. There's also a little mobile post office on Monastiraki Square, open Monday through Saturday from 8am to 6pm and Sunday from 8am to 5pm.

Friends and family can write to you in Athens care of **American Express,** 31 Panepistimiou St., Athens 10225 (☎ **01/323-4781**). If you have an American Express card or traveler's checks, the service is free; otherwise, each collection costs a steep 400 Dr ($1.80). It's open Monday through Friday from 8:30am to 4pm and Saturday from 8:30am to 1:30pm.

The **parcel post office** (for packages over 1 kilo, 2.2 lb.), 4 Stadiou St., inside the arcade (☎ **322-8940**), is open Monday through Friday from 7:30am to 8pm. Note that they sell four sizes of boxes there as well.

Newspapers/Magazines   There's no shortage of English-language news. Most central-Athens newsstands carry the local daily **Athens News,** along with the **International Herald Tribune** and **USA Today.** Local weeklies include the **Greek News** and **Greece's Weekly,** both good for in-depth local news and entertainment listings. **Athenscope,** a weekly magazine costing 300 Dr ($1.30), is a fairly comprehensive guide to arts and entertainment.

Police   In an **emergency,** dial **100.** For help dealing with an irate taxi, hotel, or restaurant owner, call the **Tourist Police** (☎ **171**)—feared and powerful advocates for visitors.

Radio/TV   There are six Greek TV stations in Athens. In addition, a staggering array of foreign-language channels include transmissions from Italy, France, Germany, and even Russia. **CNN** broadcasts in English around the clock on Channel 14, and American movies on Greek television are usually with the original soundtrack and Greek subtitles.

Tax   Value-added tax (VAT) is included in the ticket price of all goods and services in Athens, ranging from 13% to 36% on certain luxury items.

Telephone   At just 10 Dr (4¢), local telephone calls in Athens are the cheapest in western Europe. Most of the city's public telephones only accept **telephone cards,** available at newsstands, hotels, and post offices available in three denominations: 500 Dr ($2.20), 1,000 Dr ($4.40), and 2,000 Dr ($8.90). There are still some coin-operated pay phones around, but they're frequently broken. Most newspaper stands also have telephones for public use—they cost the same as pay phones.

You can also place international telephone calls at the **Overseas Telephone Exchange** (O.T.E.), 15 Stadiou St. (☎ **322-1002**), three blocks from the Syntagma Square. The office is open Monday through Friday from 7am to midnight and Saturday, Sunday, and holidays from 8am to midnight. North Americans can phone home directly by contacting an **MCI** (☎ toll free **00-800-1211**) or **AT&T** (☎ toll free **00-800-1311**) operator. Both companies allow collect calls or will bill your telephone charge card.

Tipping   Restaurants already include a service charge in the bill, but many locals round up tabs larger than 1,000 Dr ($4.45) to the nearest 100 Dr (45¢). You should also round off a taxi fare by adding some extra drachmas.

4 Accommodations

Good news will be awaiting you on your arrival at one of Athens's budget hotels: the lowest prices of any capital in the European Community. Don't expect too much comfort for these incredible rates, though. Most rooms are plain, free of decoration and furnished with beds and bureaus from the 1950s and 1960s.

Since many budget hotels feel similar inside, location is usually the most important consideration. Without a doubt, Plaka is best, with its twisting lanes and small houses at the foot of the Acropolis. Next, try hotels adjacent to Plaka: between Monastiraki Square and Omonia Square or between Monastiraki Square and Syntagma Square. Worst and cheapest are the hotels near Omonia Square. These accommodations are only about 15 to 20 minutes away from Plaka on foot, but Omonia Square has degenerated into an exceptionally seedy hang-out for derelicts and refugees from neighboring war-torn countries. You'll occasionally find a good budget pick outside these areas; several are listed below.

If you arrive without a reservation, either contact one of the hotels listed below or visit the service window of the **Hellenic Chamber of Hotels,** inside the National Bank of Greece on Syntagma Square at 2 Karageorgi St. (☎ **01/323-7193**). This for-profit agency can reserve you a room on the spot, based on price and other specifics, for which you pay a deposit of a third or half the cost of your stay; no additional charges are levied (they take a commission from the hotel). Note that they deal with many of the budget hotels in this chapter, but not the smallest ones. They can also make reservations for hotels elsewhere in Greece. The office is open Monday through Saturday from 10am to 4pm in low season, from 8:30am to 8pm in high season. To write ahead for a reservation, the mailing address is 24 Stadiou St., Athens 10564 (fax 01/322-5449).

One final piece of advice: Since many budget hotels are on small side streets that can be difficult at first or are 5 to 15 minutes on foot from the main public transportation hubs of Omonia or Syntagma Square, you might consider taking a taxi to your hotel if you have a lot of luggage when you first arrive. A short hop within the center from Syntagma or Omonia Square often costs as little as 500 Dr ($2.20).

DOUBLES FOR LESS THAN 8,000 DR ($35.55)
IN PLAKA

Dioskouros Hotel

6 Pittakou St., Athens 10558. ☎ **01/324-8165** or 324-6582. 14 rms, none with bath. June–Oct 15, 6,500 Dr ($28.90) single; 7,300 Dr ($32.45) double; 8,000 Dr ($35.55) triple. Oct 16–May 1, prices drop about 30%. No credit cards. To get here from Syntagma Square, walk south on the large Boulevard Leof. Amalias past seven streets to your right (many of them

---

Getting the Best Deal on Accommodations

- Seek out hotels near Plaka, the most charming area of town.
- Note that the service window of the Hellenic Chamber of Hotels will reserve rooms without charging the usual commission fee.
- Remember that hotel rates are usually negotiable—always ask whether they have something cheaper.

---

rather small lanes), and on the eighth, turn down Thalou and take the first right to find Pittakou (which, incidentally, is not indicated on most maps).

At the Dioskouros you'll find a quiet ambience, as most rooms face an interior courtyard or garden. The rooms have wooden floors and high ceilings and are free from pesky wall art and other "artistic" features. The rooms may not be spotless, but that doesn't deter Eurailers and other primarily student-age travelers who usually come in small groups.

Guest House Kouros

11 Kodrou St., Athens 10558. ☎ 01/322-7431. 10 rms, none with bath. 5,300 Dr ($23.55) single; 8,000 Dr ($35.55) double. No credit cards.

On a narrow, pretty pedestrian street in the heart of Plaka, this 200-year-old house has 10 basic rooms and three balconies, the uppermost of which has a nice view over the quiet neighborhood. Some rooms have molded ceilings—a nice touch in such a modest hotel. The front rooms are best, as they let in lots of light.

BETWEEN MONASTIRAKI & OMONIA SQUARES

Hotel Hermion

66c Ermou St. (near Monastiraki Square), Athens 10551. ☎ **01/321-2753.** 29 rms, none with bath. May–Oct 5,300 Dr ($23.55) single; 7,600 Dr ($33.75) double; 9,000 Dr ($40) triple. Nov–Apr, 4,000 Dr ($17.75) single; 5,600 Dr ($24.90) double; 7,500 Dr ($33.35) triple. No credit cards. Walk 10 minutes down Ermou from Syntagma Square.

The rooms in this old building take you through a budget-hotel time warp, for they've changed little over recent decades. Some rooms have so many tiny cracks in the paint that the dim lighting makes it appear as if there's a pattern on the walls. The hotel does have a few virtues, though: Those who walk up to the fourth floor may be rewarded with a view of the Acropolis, and owner Yeorgo Mouroulis speaks perfect English, complete with an American twang.

ⓢ Hotel Tempi

29 Eolou St. (next to Monastiraki Square), Athens 10551. ☎ **01/321-3175.** Fax 01/325-4179. 24 rms, 8 with shower. 4,200 Dr ($18.65) single without shower, 5,500 Dr ($24.45) single with shower; 6,800 Dr ($30.25) double without shower, 7,800 Dr ($34.65) double with shower; 9,000 Dr ($40) triple without shower. Breakfast 1,000 Dr ($4.45) extra. AE, MC, V. Subway: Monastiraki.

In Plaka, this three-story house (no elevator) has simply furnished rooms with firm beds, high ceilings, and hot showers (sometimes). Managed by Yannis and Katerina, a friendly, helpful, English-speaking husband and wife, the hotel is the best-value choice in all of Athens. It's quiet, on a pedestrian-only street, and ten rooms have balconies from which—if you lean—you can see the Acropolis. There's a rooftop lounge, laundry facilities, free luggage storage, and a book exchange that includes a number of travel guides.

NEAR OMONIA SQUARE

Athens House Hotel

4 Aristotelous St., Athens 10432. ☎ **01/524-0539.** 14 rms, none with bath. May–Sept, 4,000 Dr ($17.80) single; 8,700 Dr ($38.65) double; 10,200 Dr ($45.35) triple. Breakfast 900 Dr ($4) extra. No credit cards. To get here from Omonia Square, walk north up Septemvriou Street, take the third left down Chalkokondyl, and then take the first right onto Aristotelous Street. The hotel will be immediately on your right.

This pension is on the fifth floor of an old apartment building. There's elevator access to the rooms, which are basic but clean, with one or two prints on the aging painted walls. The main attraction here is very low rates.

ELESWHERE AROUND TOWN

Pension Marble House

35 Zinni St., Athens 11741. ☎ **01/923-4058.** 15 rms, 9 with shower. Summer, 4,600 Dr ($20.45) single without shower, 5,600 Dr ($24.85) single with shower; 6,800 Dr ($30.25) double without shower, 7,800 Dr ($34.65) double with shower. Winter, rates are 15%–20% less. Breakfast 700 Dr ($3.10) extra. No credit cards. Bus 1 or 5 from Syntagma Square.

There's marble nearly everywhere in this small hotel—on the floors, stairs, and walls. In fact, the only place marble is missing is in the baths, where you'd expect it most. The guest rooms are clean, with wood-frame beds, stone floors, baby-blue walls, and balconies overlooking the quiet though unexceptional neighborhood. There's a small English-language book exchange. You'll find the hotel at the back left-hand corner of a dead-end lane that begins at no. 35 Zinni, not far from the Olympic Airways terminal on Syngrou Avenue. Pension Marble has no elevator.

DOUBLES FOR LESS THAN 11,500 DR ($51.15)
IN PLAKA

Adams Hotel

Herefontos and Thalou Sts., Athens 10558. ☎ **01/322-5381** or 324-6582. 15 rms, some with bath. 7,900 Dr ($35.15) single without bath, 8,800 Dr ($39.15) single with bath; 9,500 Dr ($42.25) double without bath, 10,400 Dr ($46.25) double with bath. Breakfast 800 Dr ($3.55) extra. No credit cards. To get here, from Syntagma Square, walk south on the large Boulevard Leof. Amalias past seven streets to your right (many of them rather small lanes), and on the eighth, turn down Thalou and continue straight to the hotel.

Good views of the Acropolis and the city can be had from almost every room here. All have balconies, and some (most notably Room 303) have large terraces. Rooms without attached baths have private baths in the hallway. There's a big bar in the lobby lounge, where English is spoken fluently. The only drawback is the 2am curfew.

✪ Hotel Adonis

3 Kodrou St. (a few short blocks off Syntagma Square), Athens 10558. ☎ 01/324-9737. Fax 01/323-1602. 26 rms, 24 with bath. 8,200 Dr ($36.45) single without bath, 9,500 Dr ($42.25) single with bath; 10,100 Dr ($44.85) double without bath, 12,000 Dr ($53.35) double with bath. 10% discount for stays longer than two nights. Breakfast 700 Dr ($3.10) extra. No credit cards.

The Adonis features well-maintained rooms, small balconies, and clean baths in an appealing location. Though you might not have chosen the tan-and-brown wallpaper for your home, you'll certainly appreciate the view from the lovely roof-top garden overlooking both the Acropolis and Lycabettus Hill. You'll see a group of flags flying out front.

Byron Hotel

19 Vironos St. (on a quiet Plaka backstreet), Athens 10558. ☎ **01/323-0327.** Fax 01/ 322-0276. 20 rms, all with bath. 11,500 Dr ($51.15) single with bath; 13,300 Dr ($59.15) double with bath. Breakfast 1,000 Dr ($4.45) extra. No credit cards. To get here, from Syntagma Square, walk south on the large Boulevard Leof. Amalias, turn right on Areopagitou, and right again on Vironos Street. The hotel will be on your right.

One of the finest budget hotels in Athens, this small hostelry is everything a value-priced place should be—clean, friendly, cozy, and full of character. There's no el-evator and the four floors of rooms are located up steep stairs. But those who make the climb to the top are rewarded with views of the Acropolis and nearby rooftops.

BETWEEN OMONIA & MONASTIRAKI SQUARES

Carolina Hotel

55 Kolokotroni St., Athens 10560. ☎ 01/322-0837, 322-0838, or 322-8148. 31 rms, 4 with private shower across the hall, 16 with shower. July–Oct, 6,700 Dr ($29.75) single without shower, 7,700 Dr ($34.25) single with shower; 9,000 Dr ($40) double without shower, 10,400 Dr ($46.25) double with shower. Apr–June, 5,300 Dr ($23.55) single without shower, 6,700 Dr ($29.75) single with shower; 7,700 Dr ($34.25) double without shower, 9,000 Dr ($40) double with shower. Nov–Mar, lower rates available. No credit cards.

The three-story Carolina (with elevator) is a good budget standby offering clean rooms with balconies and plenty of quiet. The ground floor has a snack bar/lounge. There's a storeroom where you can leave your luggage while you explore nearby islands. Co-owner George Papagiannoulas (who runs the place with his brother) worked in Australia for 10 years and speaks English well. Kolokotroni Street runs between Stadiou and Eolou.

Hotel Alkistis

18 Platia Theatrou (halfway between Omonia and Syntagma Squares, between Menandrou and Sokratous Streets), Athens 10552. ☎ **01/321-9811.** 128 rms, all with bath. 6,700 Dr ($29.75) single; 10,000 Dr ($44.45) double. Rates include continental breakfast. AE, DC, MC, V. Closed Nov–Jan.

This is one of the largest hotels in town, so you can almost always find a room here. Two elevators service the 10 floors of comfortable rooms containing electric fans and small aging baths with showers. Most have medium-size terraces.

Hotel Attalos

29 Athinas St., Athens 10554. ☎ **01/321-2801.** 80 rms, all with bath. Apr–Oct 7,900 Dr ($35.15) single; 11,300 Dr ($50.25) double; 13,500 Dr ($60) triple. Nov–Mar, 6,700 Dr ($29.75) single; 8,500 Dr ($37.75) double; 8,600 Dr ($38.25) triple. Breakfast 1,000 Dr ($4.45) extra. V. From Syntagma Square, walk down Ermou and turn right after the second traffic light.

The Attalos is a modern six-story building (with elevator) offering unusually well-furnished rooms. Each has a print and a mirror, and attention is obviously paid to details. Twelve rooms in back have large balconies with views of the Acropo-lis, and everyone can enjoy the view from the hotel's spectacular roof garden, which has the most stunning vista in town. The receptionist speaks perfect English.

Hotel Neon-Kronos

12 Agion Asomaton St., Athens 10553. ☎ **01/325-1106,** 325-1107, or 325-1108. 54 rms, all with bath. July–Oct, 8,300 Dr ($36.90) single; 11,500 Dr ($51.15) double. Mar 16–June and Nov–Dec, 7,300 Dr ($32.45) single; 9,300 Dr ($41.35) double. Jan–Mar 15, 5,200 Dr ($23.15) single; 6,900 Dr ($30.65) double. 10% supplement for stays of only one night. Rates include breakfast. V. Subway: Thission. Bus 25, 26, 27, or 28 from Syntagma Square to Thission. Located on a side street of Ermou Street.

Another good choice when the pickings get slim, the Neon-Kronos (with elevator) offers simple rooms without decoration but with balconies, baths, and excellent rates.

BETWEEN SYNTAGMA & MONASTIRAKI SQUARES

Hotel Imperial

46 Mitropoleos St., Athens 10563. ☎ **01/322-7617.** 25 rms, 22 with bath. 6,500 Dr ($28.85) single without bath, 7,300 Dr ($32.45) single with bath; 8,700 Dr ($38.65) double with bath. MC, V.

Ideally located almost in front of the Athens cathedral, on one of the main roads connecting Syntagma and Monastiraki Squares, the Imperial has small but cozily furnished rooms with aging patterned wallpaper. The hotel's services and facilities leave something to be desired, and without its premier location and spectacular views of the Acropolis and church below, Imperial would be wildly overpriced. Compared to many others it's still relatively cheap. Some rooms have balconies, and there's a small library of English-language books downstairs.

NEAR OMONIA SQUARE

Hotel Achillion

32 Agiou Constantinou, Athens 10437. ☎ **01/523-0971,** 522-5618, or 522-1918. 51 rms, all with bath; 5 apts. Mar 15–Oct, 7,900 Dr ($35.15) single; 9,700 Dr ($43.15) double; 19,000 Dr ($84.45) apt. Nov–Mar 14, 6,500 Dr ($28.85) single; 7,700 Dr ($34.25) double; 15,300 Dr ($68) apt. Breakfast 800 Dr ($3.55) extra. No credit cards. Agiou Constantinou begins on the west side of Omonia Square (look for the 10-story Hotel Mirage on the square and take the street that begins a few storefronts to the left).

This modern seven-story building has a restaurant, a TV lounge, and a small bar behind the marble-floored reception area. The hotel caters primarily to groups from Eastern Europe and Russia, and the entrance area is decorated with city flags from these countries. The apartments are especially recommended; they hold up to four persons, and most have large bathtubs.

Hotel Epidauros

14 Koumoundouru St., Athens 10437. ☎ **01/523-0421.** 50 rms, 36 with bath. 9,000 Dr ($40) single without bath, 10,900 Dr ($48.45) single with bath; 11,700 Dr ($52) double without bath, 13,600 Dr ($60.45) double with bath. Breakfast 700 Dr ($3.15) extra. No credit cards. From Omonia Square, walk down Agiou Constantinou for four blocks and then turn left onto Koumoundouru Street.

Here all rooms come with light-brown wallpaper, two prints on the wall, and a small desk, and most have a tiny bath and small balcony. The seven-story building has two elevators and a small bar at the back of the lobby. Note that rates here are extremely negotiable during off-season.

Hotel Pythagorion

28 Agiou Constantinou St. (three blocks from Omonia Square), Athens 10437. ☎ **01/524-2811** or 524-2814. Fax 01/524-5581. 56 rms, all with bath. A/C. Apr–June 15, 8,900 Dr ($39.55) single; 11,400 Dr ($50.65) double. June 16–Sept, 9,400 Dr ($41.75) single; 12,800 Dr ($56.85) double. Oct–Mar, 4,800 Dr ($21.35) single; 7,900 Dr ($35.15) double. Triples about 2,000 Dr ($8.90) more than doubles, year-round. DC.

This hotel accommodates large groups of (mostly) European travelers but has good rates and is far enough away from Omonia to feel safe. The rooms in this modern seven-story building are all spacious and simply furnished, with soundproof windows; some have large terraces. The hotel staff speaks English.

SUPER-BUDGET CHOICES
HOTELS
Athens Youth Hostel

57 Kypselis St. (four blocks behind the National Archeological Museum), Athens 11361.
☎ **01/822-5860.** 180 beds. 1,400 Dr ($6.25) per person with the IYHF membership card,
1,900 Dr ($8.45) per person without one. You can buy an IYHF card here for 2,100 Dr
($8.75). No credit cards. Bus 2, 4, or 9 from Syntagma Square to one stop after "Museum";
then turn right.

This spacious three-story house is the only official youth hostel in Athens. Each
dorm room has 6 to 12 bunk beds, and the first and second floors are segregated
by sex. Facilities include a laundry room, free showers, and a cafeteria in the basement seating 70. The hostel is closed between 10:30am and 1:30pm, and there's
a midnight curfew.

Pension Argo

25 Victor Hugo (Victoros Ougo) St. (between Larissis Station and Omonia Square), Athens
10437. ☎ **01/522-5939.** 18 rms, 4 with bath. May 15–Oct 15, 4,500 Dr ($20) single with-
out bath; 5,600 Dr ($24.85) double without bath, 6,800 Dr ($30.25) double with shower
only; 7,200 Dr ($32) triple without bath; 2,000 Dr ($8.90) per person quad without bath.
Oct 16–May 14, 3,300 Dr ($14.65) single without bath; 4,100 Dr ($15.25) double without
bath; 5,500 Dr ($24,45) triple without bath; 1,700 Dr ($7.55) per person quad without bath.
Rooms with bath 300 Dr ($1.25) extra; breakfast 700 Dr ($3.10) extra. No credit cards.
If you take the bus from the airport, get off at Karaiskaki Square and the pension will be only
two blocks away.

In a rather shabby building, the Argo is acceptable as a spartan money-saver.
Facilities include free showers and a self-serve laundry in the basement—1,000 Dr
($4.45) for 5 kilos (11 lb.). There's no elevator to the three floors. Kostas, the
co-owner, speaks English well.

⑤ Student and Travelers Inn

16 Kidathineon St. (a 10-minute walk from Syntagma Square), Athens 10558. ☎ **01/324-
4808.** 35 rms, none with bath. 3,300 Dr ($14.65) single; 5,600 Dr ($24.90) double; 2,600
Dr ($11.55) per person triple. Breakfast 700 Dr ($3.10) extra. No credit cards. From Syntagma
Square, walk south down Filellinon Street for three blocks and turn right on Kidathineon.

My top super-budget choice in Athens is the Student and Travelers Inn, mostly
because of its enviable location in the heart of Plaka. In addition, it offers an
appealing back garden covered by a trellis for morning breakfast and afternoon
relaxation. Almost all the basic but clean rooms have balconies, and the place even
has an elevator. To top off this budget find, lively owner Spiros Mavromates speaks
perfect English—the result of living 25 years in New York City.

WORTH THE EXTRA MONEY
Hotel Dorian Inn

17 Pireos St. (three blocks from Omonia Square), Athens 10552. ☎ **01/523-9782** or
523-9784. 146 rms, all with bath. Apr–Oct, 15,300 Dr ($68) single; 23,200 Dr ($103.15)
double; 27,800 Dr ($123.55) triple. Nov–Mar, 9,500 Dr ($42.25) single; 14,400 Dr ($64)
double; 17,300 Dr ($76.85) triple. Rates include full breakfast. AE, DC, EC, MC, V.

This 12-story hotel (with elevator) has spacious, well-furnished rooms, all of which
have a pleasant sitting area with a writing desk. Ceiling-to-floor windows let in lots
of light, but the rooms themselves (some with balcony) are slightly worn. The
Dorian Inn is one of the very few hotels in Athens with its own private pool, free
to guests. There are two bars, plus a restaurant serving three meals daily.

5 Dining

Happily, Athens is a city of many inexpensive restaurants. You'll find the most charming ones in the heart of Plaka, many featuring traditional Greek ambience inside and seating outside as well. Unfortunately, these restaurants tend to attract many tourists, and several close for the winter. The budget restaurants near Syntagma and Omonia Squares I've listed here often cook up just as good food, but in simpler settings that often recall the 1950s or early 1960s in decor.

Most places have menus printed in both Greek and English. When in doubt, ask for moussaka, a staple served in all tavernas (smaller and unpretentious restaurants) and 95% of the cafeterias and restaurants. Moussaka consists of baked ground meat topped with spicy vegetables and sometimes a layer of dough or mashed potatoes. Another staple is dolmothakia (rice and meat wrapped in grape, or sometimes cabbage, leaves). For a snack, ask for souvlaki (roasted and spitted chunks of lamb spiced with oregano). A popular Greek table wine is retsina, a white wine flavored with pine resin—if you don't like its taste, ask for aresinato (wine without resin). The Greek before-meal drink is ouzo, about 200 to 300 Dr (90¢ to $1.35) a shot, taken either straight or with water, which turns it cloudy white.

Coffee shops are abundant. By far the largest concentration of them is on Syntagma and Kolonaki Squares, with seating for over 1,000. On summer evenings all the seats are occupied by Athenians and tourists alike. In addition to coffee, you can usually get soft drinks, sandwiches, ice cream, and beer. Expect to pay about 800 Dr ($3.55) for a coffee with milk; if you stand up you'll pay considerably less.

MEALS FOR LESS THAN 1,100 DR ($4.90)
IN PLAKA

Platanos Restaurant

4 Diogenes St. ☎ **01/322-0666**. 900–2,000 Dr ($4–$8.90). No credit cards. Mon–Sat noon–4:30pm and 8pm–midnight. GREEK.

Its location on a lovely, quiet pedestrian square makes this one of my favorite romantic spots in Plaka. Established in 1932, it has seen several nips and tucks since then, maintaining a pleasant ambience of paintings, photos, and certificates on the walls beneath the modern wooden ceiling. If it's a nice day, try to sit at a table on the square in front. Platanos is famous for its Greek specialties and large list of white, red, and rosé wines.

Restaurant Eden

12 Lissiou St. ☎ **01/324-8858**. 1,300–2,000 Dr ($5.75–$8.90). No credit cards. Daily noon–midnight. VEGETARIAN.

One of the few solely vegetarian restaurants in Greece, this place serves up good low-cost food in an attractive contemporary decor that includes 1920s-style prints and mirrors, hanging wrought-iron lamps, and views of a pretty Plaka street. Greeks and tourists alike gather here to sample a large variety of delicious dishes, such as minestrone soup, soy moussaka, mushroom pie, salads, juices, and desserts. Owner Theodore Kamperidis lived on Cape Cod for eight years and speaks good English, as does much of the staff.

Thanasis

69 Mitropoleos St. ☎ **01/324-4705**. 400–1,200 Dr ($1.75–$5.35). No credit cards. Daily 8:30am–1 or 2am. GREEK.

Getting the Best Deal on Dining

- Try restaurants in the heart of Plaka and near Syntagma and Omonia Squares.
- There are inexpensive coffee shops on Syntagma Square.
- Moussaka makes a filling, tasty meal.

It's not easy to make the best souvlaki in all of Athens, but that's exactly what they do in this specialized "souvlakiteria" at the northeast corner of Monastiraki Square. Each lamb sandwich is individually roasted on open coals and served either wrapped "to go" or on a plate with pita bread at one of two dozen wooden tables. Packed with locals who don't seem to mind the brusque service or the blaring TVs, Thanasis is truly an Athenian institution.

NEAR THE SYNTAGMA SQUARE

Diros Restaurant

10 Xenophonos St. (two blocks from Syntagma Square). ☎ **01/323-2392.** 1,300–4,600 Dr ($5.75–$20.45). AE, DC, V. Daily noon–midnight. GREEK.

Many demanding Greek regulars frequent this air-conditioned restaurant, so you can count on getting good, simple, home-cooked food. Menu items include avgolemono (rice, egg, and lemon soup), bean soup, a large selection of spaghetti dishes, and roast chicken with french fries. There's seating for 50 both inside and out, and the waiter and manager speak some English. The plain decor, imitation wood paneling and bright light, suggests an upscale cafeteria.

Wendy's

4 Stadiou St.(at Syntagma Sq.). ☎ **01/323-9322.** Salad bar 1,000–1,700 Dr ($4.45–$7.55); burgers 700–1,300 Dr ($3.10–$5.75). No credit cards. Sun–Thurs 6am–3am, Fri–Sat 7am–4am. AMERICAN FAST FOOD.

Clean, loud, and neon-lit, this American fast-food restaurant looks like its other franchises around the world—except this one's packed almost around the clock. Opened in 1991, Wendy's gets mention here for its small but well-maintained salad bar, perhaps the only one in all of Greece, a welcome respite from the heavy, meaty fare served most everywhere else. Baked potatoes and burgers are also sold.

William of Orange

4 Apolonos St. ☎ **01/323-8743.** 800–2,000 Dr ($3.55–$8.90). No credit cards. Daily 8am–11pm. Closed Sun in winter. GREEK.

Whether you choose to sit on the carpeted sidewalk patio or in the air-conditioned interior, you'll be treated to traditional Greek specialties like souvlaki and various spinach dishes in a New York–style coffee-shop setting. Hamburgers, spaghetti, and other more tourist-accessible foods are also available and often prepared by William himself.

NEAR OMONIA SQUARE

Fontana Café

20 Omonia Sq. ☎ **01/522-4349.** 800–2,000 Dr ($3.55–$8.90). No credit cards. Summer, daily 5:30am–3am; winter, daily 6:30am–midnight. GREEK.

With three floors overlooking the principal transportation hub,Fontana offers a welcome touch of serenity in one of Athens's busiest areas. Good breakfasts are served here, as are a number of toasted sandwiches and other snacks. The café is popular with locals who relax all day over a cup of coffee and a sweet piece of baklava.

MEALS FOR LESS THAN 2,300 DR ($10.25)
IN PLAKA

Piccolino Restaurant
26 Sotiros St. (a few blocks from Syntagma Square, at the corner of Kidathineon Street). ☎ 01/324-9745. 1,300–2,500 Dr ($5.75–$11.15). No credit cards. Daily 6pm–3am. ITALIAN/GREEK.

In the Plaka district, Piccolino is especially popular with students and young people. Dishes include generous portions of spaghetti carbonara, macaroni and cheese, pastitsio (fried noodles), octopus with french fries, mussels stewed in white wine, fish and chips, and 10 varieties of pizza baked in a traditional wood-fired oven.

Taverna Attalos
16 Erechttheos St. ☎ 01/325-0353. 1,500–4,500 Dr ($6.65–$20). No credit cards. Apr–Oct, daily 10am–1:30am. Nov–Mar, Thurs–Sun 11am–1:30am. GREEK.

For the pure loveliness of the view you'll be hard-pressed to find a better choice than the Attalos, where a roof garden with a trellis overlooks the Acropolis in the distance. The food is acceptable, and the romantic view exceptional. It's on a small street at the foot of the Acropolis, roughly between the Athens cathedral and the Acropolis.

Taverna Poulakis
6 Panos St. ☎ 01/321-3222. Meals for less than 3,200 ($14.25). No credit cards. Daily noon–midnight. GREEK.

Next to the Roman Agora in Plaka, at the foot of the Acropolis, you'll be served home-cooked Greek food you can select at the counter. The menu includes dolmades (cabbage leaves stuffed with ground meat), pastitsio (macaroni stew), and farmer's salad with feta cheese. This typical taverna has seating for 20 inside and 100 outside.

Trattoria Restaurant
4 Farmaki St. ☎ 01/324-5474. 1,200–3,200 Dr ($5.35–$14.25). AE, V. Daily 10am–midnight. ITALIAN.

For a change of pace from Greek food, you may enjoy the selection of spaghetti, soups, and eight varieties of pizza at this restaurant in the heart of Plaka. Paintings of Venice and other Italian scenes adorn the interior walls, and outside tables spill onto an attractive, though much-touristed, pedestrian square. You'll find the square just off Kidathineon Street in Plaka.

NEAR SYNTAGMA SQUARE

Apotsos
10 Panepistimiou St. ☎ 01/363-7646. 1,900–3,900 Dr ($8.45–$17.35). AE, DC, MC, V. Mon–Sat 11am–2:30pm and 7–11:30pm. GREEK.

A favorite haunt of journalists, Apotsos is both cheap and good. The restaurant's specialties include grilled chicken, rolled pork, roasted lamb, and a huge selection of traditional appetizers. It's in the arcade, one block from Syntagma Square, near some of the city's largest playhouses.

Delfi Restaurant

13 Nikis St. ☎ **01/323-4869.** 1,200–3,900 Dr ($5.35–$17.35). AE, DC, MC, V. Mon–Sat 11am–11 or 11:30pm. GREEK.

Waiters in green jackets and black ties (some of whom speak English) serve tasty dishes in this restaurant popular with businesspeople. The L-shaped eatery is styled with attractive wood paneling on some walls and stretches of imitation red brick on others. Taped music plays in the background.

Golden Flower

30 Nikis St. ☎ **01/323-0113.** 2,000–3,900 Dr ($8.90–$17.35); complete meal for two 6,800 Dr ($30.25). Mon–Fri noon–3:30pm; daily 7pm–midnight. CHINESE.

At the Golden Flower, one of the few Cantonese restaurants in central Athens, the Chinese cooks and staff serve up some tasty dishes to eat in or take out. The decor includes all the Chinese-restaurant classics: hanging red lamps, dragons on the ceilings, a red archway separating the two sides of the restaurant, and many other small decorations. Chinese pop music plays in the background.

Restaurant Corfu

6 Kriezotou St. ☎ **01/361-3011.** 2,000–3,200 Dr ($8.90–$14.25). Reservations recommended. AE, DC, V. Mon–Fri noon–midnight, Sat noon–5pm. GREEK/FISH.

Everyone from top government officials from the nearby Parliament to local workers favors this restaurant near Syntagma Square. Some clients have been coming here for 25 years, and to cater to their conservative regulars the management has left the decor much as it was when the place opened in 1964. Waiters in white jackets and black ties provide an elegant touch, and several areas provide romantic corners.

Restaurant Kentrikon

3 Kolokotroni St. ☎ **301/23-2482.** 1,300–3,900 Dr ($5.75–$17.35). No credit cards. Sun–Fri noon–6pm. GREEK.

The decor here will march you back to the early 1960s with its large open dining room with wood panels covered by prints of ancient Athens on the walls and glass balls hanging above for lights. Since the restaurant is open for lunch only, it caters mostly to local workers and businesspeople.

NEAR OMONIA SQUARE

Neon

1 Dorou St., Omonia Sq. ☎ **01/523-6409.** 800–2,000 Dr ($3.55–$8.90). No credit cards. Daily 7am–2am. GREEK/CONTINENTAL.

In 1924, when Neon first opened in the oldest building on Omonia Square, Athens lacked a proper water-supply system, so the water served in cafés and restaurants was unfiltered and cloudy. Neon's innovative owners built a sand-filter purifying system that quickly made their café Athenians' meeting place of choice. Recently reopened after a serious fire, the café has been totally redesigned around a cafeteria-style kitchen. The food is surprisingly good and the variety might be the largest in Athens. Three or four international and Greek specialties like lasagne, moussaka, and baked chicken are always served, along with sandwiches, soups, croissants, a salad bar, and a large selection of cakes and pastries. Although there are dozens of tables on two levels, it's often difficult to find an empty seat, not to mention one that's not surrounded by smokers. Still, Neon's bright, clean restaurant is a welcome oasis in an otherwise seedy neighborhood.

Other equally recommendable Neon restaurants are at 6 Skoufa St. (☎ **01/ 364-6233**), in Kolonaki; and 3 Amalias St. (☎ **01/322-8155**), on Syntagma Square.

Restaurant Nea-Olympia

3 Emanuel Benaki St (off Stadiou Street, two blocks off Omonia Sq.). ☎ **01/321-7972.** 1,300–3,200 Dr ($5.75–$14.25). No credit cards. Mon–Fri 11am–midnight, Sat 11am–4pm. INTERNATIONAL.

This is one of the largest restaurants in town, with a slightly more attractive decor than some of the area's other budget picks. Glass windows overlook the street and Greek prints adorn the shiny blond-wood walls. Daily specials are posted at each table in Greek, so make sure to ask the waiter for a translation; the regular menu is in English.

IN KOLONAKI

Grand Café

19 Sina St., Kolonaki. ☎ **01/645-0776.** 800–2,000 Dr ($3.55–$8.90). No credit cards. Mon–Sat 10am–2am, Sun 6pm–2am. The Grand Café is located in Athens's Kolonaki area. Exit Syntagma Square on Stadiou Street and, after one block, turn right onto Voukourestiou Street. Continue uphill for six blocks and turn left onto Skoufa Street. The café is about five blocks ahead on your right, on the corner of Sina Street. INTERNATIONAL.

One of Kolonaki's most stylish cafés is also one of the newest. Occupying the second and third floors of a pretty white corner building, the contemporary café features high ceilings, well-stocked bars, and good-looking yet uncomfortable furniture that epitomizes form over function. Drinks, hot and cold, are the menu's main feature, but competently prepared sandwiches and omelets are also served.

Taverna Dimokritos

23 Dimokritou St., Kolonaki. ☎ **01/361-3588** or 361-9293. Main courses 1,300–2,200 Dr ($5.75–$9.85). No credit cards. Mon–Sat 1–5pm and 8pm–1am. Taverna Dimokritos is in Athens's Kolonaki area. Exit Syntagma Square on Stadiou Street and, after one block, turn right onto Voukourestiou Street. Continue uphill for six blocks and turn left onto Skoufa Street. After one block, turn right onto Dimokritou Street. The restaurant is on your left, up a short flight of stairs, and is marked only by the word TAVERNA on its doors. GREEK.

Overlooking a small park, facing Skoufa Street, this two-room traditional Greek taverna serves some of the finest food to a dedicated clientele. The large menu, in both Greek and English, features grilled veal, rabbit, fish, and lamb, though many knowledgeable locals swear by the swordfish souvlaki. A variety of Greek salads, in a case by the entrance, welcome you to a spotless, pretty interior.

ELSEWHERE AROUND TOWN

Restaurant Costoyanis

37 Zaimi St. ☎ **01/822-0624.** 1,300–3,200 Dr ($5.75–$14.25). No credit cards. Mon–Sat 8am–2am. Trolleybus 3 or 5 to the National Archaeological Museum. GREEK.

As you enter the Costoyanis you'll see an impressive display of fish and other foods, and you can choose the items you'd like to sample. You can also order from the menu while seated in the attractive dining room with wooden ceiling beams and a long array of windows covered by curtains to one side. This well-known gourmet restaurant is located a few blocks behind the National Archaeological Museum.

PICNICKING

The best place to buy picnic supplies is the **Central Market** on Athinas Street, between Monastiraki and Omonia Squares. The market, one of the best in Europe, is open Monday and Wednesday from 9am to 4:30pm, Tuesday from 9am to 6pm, Thursday from 9:30am to 6:30pm, Friday from 9:30am to 7pm, and Saturday from 8:30am to 4:30pm. Another option is the food store in the basement of the Minion Department Store, 28 Oktovriou St. near Omonia Square, open Monday and Wednesday from 9am to 5pm; Tuesday, Thursday, and Friday from 10am to 7pm; and Saturday from 8:30am to 3:30pm. On Sunday many grocery stores, fruit stores, and bakeries around Plaka are open.

The best place for a picnic is Athens's **National Garden,** near Syntagma Square. It's the largest public park in the city, with trees, lawns, ponds, and even a few peacocks. On warmer days, it's great to picnic atop breezy Lycabettus Hill, the tallest peak in central Athens (take the funicular from Chersonos Street).

6 Attractions

SIGHTSEEING SUGGESTIONS

If You Have 1 Day

Head right up the mighty Acropolis to visit the Parthenon. Afterward, explore Plaka, down below, Athens's most charming neighborhood. Visit the ancient Agora nearby, and consider lunch or dinner in one of Plaka's romantic restaurants.

If You Have 2 Days

It's worth spending three or four hours of your second day at the National Archaeological Museum. If you're not too tired, take the funicular to the top of the 1,000-foot Lycabettus Hill for a marvelous view of Athens, Piraeus, and beyond. Also consider another museum or two, listed below.

If You Have 3 Days or More

Visit more of the museums listed below or consider a day trip to one of the great sights of antiquity, such as Delphi, Corinth, Mycenae, or Epidaurus (see "Easy Excursions," at the end of this chapter, for details). Or take a day-long excursion by boat to the three islands of Aegina, Poros, and Hydra in the nearby Saronic Gulf.

TOP ATTRACTIONS

The Acropolis

Above Plaka. ☎ **321-0219.** Admission 1,500 Dr ($6.70) adults, 800 Dr ($3.55) students and youths 12–16, free for children under 12. If you bring a video camera, there's an extra 1,000 Dr ($4.45) charge. Apr–Oct, Mon 11:30am–7pm, Tues–Fri 8am–7pm, Sat–Sun 8:30am–2:30pm; Nov–Mar, Mon–Fri 8am–5:45pm, Sat–Sun 8:30am–2:45pm. Subway: Thission. Bus 5 or 9 from Syntagma Square to Makrigiani; then a 15-minute walk uphill.

Originally the residence/fortress of the king from as far back as the 13th century B.C., the Acropolis ("high point of the city") gradually grew into a religious sanctuary. A visit to the remaining 5th-century B.C. temples built during Athens's golden age is breathtaking—both in the discovery of such well-preserved antiquity and in the rigorous climb up the mighty hill at Athens's center.

Crowning the Acropolis is the beautifully proportioned Doric Parthenon, built of Pentellic marble under Pericles, the Athenian leader, between 447 and 432 B.C.

The Plaka

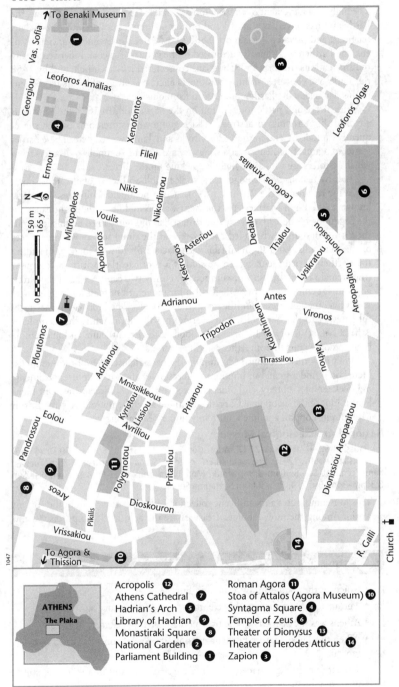

↑ To Benaki Museum

Vas. Sofia

Georgiou

Leoforos Amalias

Xenofontos

Ermou

Filell

Nikis

Nikodimou

Mitropoleos

Voulis

Apollonos

Kekropos

Asteriou

Dedalou

Thalou

Leoforos Amalias

Dionissiou

Lysikratou

Leoforos Olgas

Areopagitou

Adrianou

Antes

Vironos

Tripodon

Kriathineou

Thrassilou

Vakhou

Ploutonos

Adrianou

Mnissikleous

Pritanou

Dionissiou Areopagitou

Eolou

Kyristou

Lissiou

Avriliou

Polygnotou

Pritaniou

Pandrossou

Areos

Pikilis

Dioskouron

Vrissakiou

To Agora &
↓ Thission

R. Galli

Church

150 m
165 y
0

N

1047

ATHENS
The Plaka

Acropolis **12**
Athens Cathedral **7**
Hadrian's Arch **5**
Library of Hadrian **9**
Monastiraki Square **8**
National Garden **2**
Parliament Building **1**

Roman Agora **11**
Stoa of Attalos (Agora Museum) **10**
Syntagma Square **4**
Temple of Zeus **6**
Theater of Dionysus **13**
Theater of Herodes Atticus **14**
Zapion **3**

The highest achievement of classical form with its massive, powerful columns, the Parthenon has served as a model and prototype for Western architecture—civic, religious, and private—for almost 2,500 years. After the decline of ancient Athens, the Parthenon, originally dedicated to the goddess Athena, underwent many transformations. In A.D. 450 Christians consecrated it as a church, and by 1458 the Turks had converted it into a mosque (a circular staircase of a minaret remains to this day inside the Parthenon, unseen from outside).

Years of use and battle took its toll on the Parthenon. In 1687 the Venetians attacked the Acropolis to destroy Turkish gunpowder storerooms (which subsequently exploded), and in the 1820s Greeks and Turks warred here. These battles scattered temple fragments over a wide area around the Acropolis—disasters from which restorers are still, quite literally, picking up the pieces.

Theft by zealous archaeologists also took its toll on the Acropolis, most notably in the removal of the Parthenon's spectacular pediment sculptures, popularly known as the Elgin Marbles. Yet this heist was no middle-of-the-night caper. In the beginning of the 19th century, the British Earl of Elgin gained permission from the Ottoman Turks (who ruled over Greece at the time) to remove large pieces of the Acropolis. Lord Elgin and his men hacked off tons of marble, including the Parthenon pediment, which he sold at a profit to the British government (they remain in the British Museum today). Nearly two centuries later, the Greek government continues to press the British for the return of these antiquities.

Several other temples adorn the top of the Acropolis. The Propylaea is the graceful gateway to the Acropolis, and overlooking the approach is the Temple of Athena Nike (Victory). Also on the Acropolis is the Erechtheum, an Ionic temple built to house cults to both Athena and Poseidon.

Don't miss the Acropolis Museum, on the back right corner of the Acropolis. Here you'll find a small but important collection of ancient sculpture, pediments of Greek temples, pottery, and other artifacts from several different eras. One highlight is four of the six original Caryatids from the Erechtheum (one is in the British Museum in London and one is currently under restoration).

National Archaeological Museum

44 Patission St. ☎ **01/821-7717.** Admission 1,500 Dr ($6.70) adults, 800 Dr ($3.55) students and youths 12–16, free for children under 12. Summer, Mon 12:30–7pm, Tues–Fri 8am–7pm, Sat–Sun 8:30am–3pm; winter, Mon 11am–5pm, Tues–Fri 8am–5pm, Sat–Sun 8:30am–3pm. Bus 2, 4, 5, or 9 from Syntagma Square.

This museum houses a magnificent collection of Greek artifacts from the ancient world. Among the most-fabulous treasures are the gold masks, cups, dishes, and

---

❷ Did You Know?

- Athens is the southernmost capital in Europe.
- The ancient Olympiad originated around the 13th century B.C.
- Athens was the host city of the first modern Olympic Games, in 1896.
- When the Turks captured Athens in 1456, the Parthenon was turned into a mosque.
- The city's horseshoe-shaped white marble stadium, built in A.D. 143, is still used for athletic events.

jewelry unearthed in Mycenae by Schliemann in the 19th century. Also displayed are sculptures found on the Greek islands, including a Zeus, an Apollo, a Hygeia, a jockey, and many hand-painted vases. Recent additions to the collection include remarkably well preserved 3,500-year-old frescoes found on Santorini.

Ancient Agora

Between the Acropolis and Monastiraki Sq. in Plaka. ☎ **01/321-0185.** Admission 800 Dr ($3.55) adults, 400 Dr ($1.80) students and youth 12–16, free for children under 12. Tues–Sun 8:30am–3pm. Subway: Thission.

A visit to Athens's ancient agora (marketplace and city center) comprises the Temple of Hephaestus, overlooking the agora from the west, and the Stoa of Attalos, on the east side. The Temple of Hephaestus, built in the first half of the 5th century B.C., is one of the best-preserved ancient buildings in Greece. The Stoa of Attalos, a long open colonnade designed to offer shelter from all kinds of weather while providing a place for informal discussion, was rebuilt to serve as a museum. The Stoa of Attalos is the setting for many of Plato's Dialogues.

The museum can be entered from either Thission Sq. or 24 Andrianou St.

MORE ATTRACTIONS

Athens Cathedral

Mitropoleos St., between Syntagma and Monastiraki Sqs. Admission free. Daily 6am–1pm and 4–7pm. Walk five minutes downhill from Syntagma Square.

A big but architecturally disappointing Byzantine-style cathedral, Athens's Greek Orthodox headquarters features a modern stone facade and is decorated with silver votive offerings. The smaller cathedral in its shadow, built in the 13th century, is a gem from the Byzantine era. Its facade of white marble and red brick and its cupolas are an eye-catching sight amid the modern apartment buildings.

Benaki Museum

1 Koumbari St. ☎ **01/361-1617.** Admission 400 Dr ($1.80) adults, 200 Dr (90¢) students and youths 12–16, free for children under 12. Wed–Mon 8:30am–2pm. Trolleybus 3; or a five-minute walk from Syntagma Square.

In addition to an important collection of Greek folk art, costumes, jewelry, and pottery, the museum contains relics from the country's 1821 War of Independence, including Lord Byron's writing desk and pen. The Benaki, in a beautiful neoclassical mansion at the corner of Vass. Sofias Avenue recently reopened after an extensive restoration.

Byzantine Museum

22 Vassilissis Sofias Ave. ☎ **01/723-1570.** Admission 1,000 Dr ($4.45) adults, 500 Dr ($2.25) students and youths 12–16, free for children under 12. Summer, Tues–Fri 8am–7pm, Sat–Sun 8:30am–3pm; winter, Tues–Sun 8:30am–3pm. Trolleybus 3; or a 10-minute walk from Syntagma Square.

Housed in a former ducal residence, this museum is devoted entirely to the art and history of Byzantium. The region's most-important collection of icons and religious art is exhibited on three courtyarded floors along with sculptures, altars, mosaics, bishops' garments, bibles, and a small-scale reconstruction of an early Christian basilica.

Cemetery of Keramikos

148 Ermou St., near Monastiraki Sq. in Plaka. ☎ **01/346-3552.** Admission 500 Dr ($2.25) adults, 250 Dr ($1.10) students and youths 12–16, free for children under 12. Tues–Sun 8:30am–3pm.

Athens

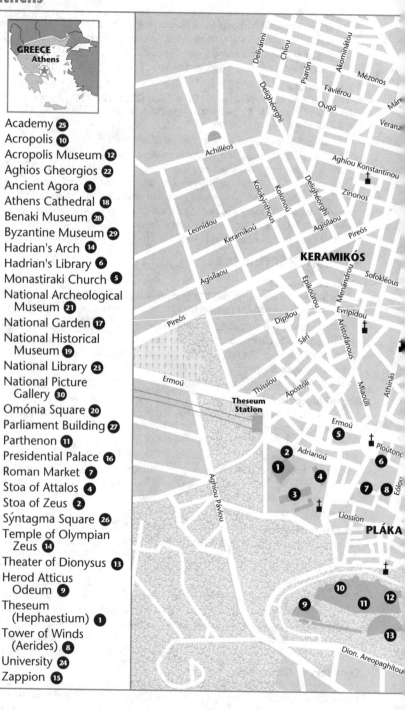

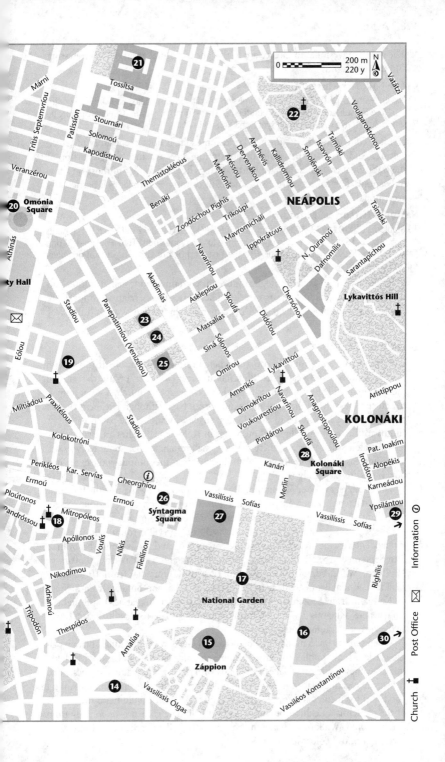

Church ✝■ Post Office ⊠ Information ⓘ

The oldest gravestones in Greece are in this ancient burial ground. An interesting and unusual sight.

Greek Folk Art Museum

17 Kidathineon St. ☎ **01/321-3018.** Admission 400 Dr ($1.80) adults, 200 Dr (90¢) youths 12–16, free for students and children under 12. Tues–Sun 10am–2pm. Directions: Walk up Filellinon Street, five minutes from Syntagma Square in Plaka.

Is it just coincidence that a former Turkish mosque is now a repository of Greek culture? And what are they really demonstrating anyway, since a large portion of the traditional costumes, jewelry, and paintings here are similar to those on show in Istanbul? The collection of 18th- and 19th-century embroideries is particularly exceptional.

National Historical Museum

13 Stadiou St. ☎ **01/323-7617.** Admission 500 Dr ($2.25) adults, 250 Dr ($1.10) students and youths 12–16, free for children under 12; free for everyone Thurs. Tues–Fri 9am–1:30pm, Sat–Sun 9am–12:30pm. Bus 1, 2, or 4 to the first stop before Omonia Square; or a five-minute walk from Syntagma Square.

The country's primary ethnological museum contains traditional costumes and the personal effects of famous Greeks. There are objects relating to local life from the Byzantine era, the Turkish occupation, the Balkan War, and the War of Independence.

A HILL & A GARDEN

You can see two hills from almost everywhere in Athens: **Acropolis** (the one with the Parthenon), and **Lycabettus,** Plutarchou Street (☎ 722-70650), the taller of the two. Plant-filled Lycabettus is topped by St. George's Church, a squat domed structure always flying the blue-and-white Greek flag. Although Lycabettus looks high, you don't have to be in top physical shape to walk up the paved path that climbs to the top from Ploutarchou Street in Kolonaki. Benches are placed strategically along the route, and there's even a small restaurant/bar about halfway up. Views increase exponentially with altitude, and from the summit you can see just how huge this city really is.

The climb takes about 30 minutes. If you're not up for a walk, ride the funicular (called a teleferik), which goes through a tunnel from Kolonaki's Chersonos Street to the top of the hill in about 3 minutes. It runs every 10 minutes. Admission to Lycabettus Hill is free; the funicular costs 300 Dr ($1.25) round-trip (walking is free). The viewing area in front of St. George's is open daily 24 hours. From June 7 to September 15, the funicular runs on Monday and Tuesday from 9:30am to 12:45am, Wednesday from 8:45am to 12:45am, Thursday from 10:30am to 12:45am, Friday from 9:30am to 12:45am, Saturday and Sunday from 8:45am to 12:45am; from September 16 to June 6, it stops running at 12:15am nightly. To get here, take bus 3, 7, or 13 from Syntagma Square to Vassilissis Sofia Ave. at the corner of Plutarchou Street.

When Greece was a monarchy, the **National Garden** was the king's private palace garden. Now public, the area combines a park, garden, and zoo with shady trees, benches, a café, small lakes and ponds with ducks, swans, and a few peacocks. A favorite meeting place for young and old Athenians on hot summer days, it's a good spot for picnics and for jogging. The huge palacelike building in the middle of the garden is an exhibition and reception hall. The garden is open daily from 7am to 10pm. Walk from Syntagma Square to the yellow Parliament House, then turn right onto Leoforos Amalias Street.

7 Shopping

Athens is a great place to buy unique and inexpensive gifts and has a good variety of offbeat clothes and crafts shops. The most unique items, at the best prices, are sold in and around the **Flea Market,** a daily spectacle starting at Plaka's Monastiraki Square. It's best on Sunday, when it's packed with locals. Other days are good, too, offering the usual tourist-oriented trinkets, statues, jewelry, sandals, and various handmade goods. Poke around some of the nearby side streets for antiques and other finds.

Inexpensive to mid-price fashions can be found on the many streets within the Omonia Square/Syntagma Square/Monastiraki Square triangle. For top-of-the-line goods, wander around the smaller streets near Kolonaki Square, between Syntagma Square and Lycabettus Hill.

Compendium, 28 Nikis St. (☎ **01/322-1248**), is Athens's best English-language bookstore, selling both new and used fiction and nonfiction, as well as newspapers, magazines, and maps. The shop is close to Syntagma Square. In winter it's usually open Monday and Wednesday from 9am to 5pm; Tuesday, Thursday, and Friday from 10am to 7pm; and Saturday from 9am to 3:30pm. In summer, hours are Monday and Wednesday from 9am to 3pm; Tuesday, Thursday, and Friday from 9am to 1:30pm and 5:30 to 8:30pm; and Saturday from 9am to 3:30pm.

8 Athens After Dark

When it comes to nightlife, Greeks may be the world's best partiers. An evening's activities usually start with dinner around 9pm, an extremely leisurely event that often seems to be more about socializing than eating. When midnight rolls around and the last glass of ouzo is emptied, revelers seek out a bouzoukieria for some traditional entertainment or head to a dance club, bar, or café. Travelers in their 20s will find their Greek compatriots hanging around the cafés in Kolonaki Square, where it's sometimes hard to find an empty seat among hundreds of chairs. Cafés on Syntagma and Monastiraki Squares also front busy street scenes and are good places to idle an evening away.

Check the daily *Athens News,* sold at most major newsstands, for current cultural and entertainment events, including films, lectures, theater, music, and dance. The weekly *Athenscope* is even better, filled with a good list of happening nightspots.

THE PERFORMING ARTS

Athens Opera House
59 Acadimias St. ☎ **01/360-0180.** Tickets, 700–2,000 Dr ($3.10–$8.90).

The capital's primary stage for traditional and contemporary opera and theater sponsors productions from mid-November to late April. Ballets and chamber-orchestra concerts are also held here. Check Athenscope to see what's on. The box office is open Monday through Saturday from 9am to 1pm and 5 to 7pm, Sunday from 10am to 1pm and 5 to 7pm.

Megaron Concert Hall
89 Vassilissis Sofias. ☎ **01/728-2333.** Admission 1,000–30,000 Dr ($4.45–$133.35).

This recently completed, skillfully planned concert hall hosts a wide range of classical music programs that include quartets, operas in concert, symphonies, and recitals. The Megaron is near the American Embassy. Check the listings magazines to see what's on. The box office is open Monday through Friday from 10am to 6pm and Saturday from 10am to 2pm.

Hellenic American Union Auditorium

22 Massalias St. ☎ **01/362-9886.** Admission free–3,000 Dr ($13.35).

English-language theater and American-oriented music are regularly performed here for local and expatriate audiences. Arrive early and check out the art show or photo exhibition at the adjacent art gallery. The Union is in the fashionable Kolonaki section of town. The box office is open Monday and Wednesday from 9am to 5pm; Tuesday, Thursday, and Friday from 10am to 7pm; and Saturday from 8:30am to 3:30pm.

Aliki Theater

4 Amerikis St. ☎ **01/324-4145** or 324-4395. Admission 3,000–13,000 Dr ($13.35–$57.75).

One of the most popular Greek-language theaters, the Aliki stages national and international plays and musicals, as well as occasional dance and music performances throughout the year. Curious to see *The Sound of Music* in Greek? The box office is open daily from 10am to 10pm.

LIVE MUSIC

Walk the streets of Plaka on any night and you can literally pass a dozen or more tavernas offering live music. **Nefeli,** 24 Panos St. (☎ 321-2475); **Diogenis,** 3 Selev St. (☎ 324-7933); and **Stamatopoulou,** 26 Lysiou St. (☎ 322-8722), are three of the most reliable. For an even more authentic Greek experience, visit one of the establishments listed below.

Memphis

5 Ventiri St. ☎ **01/722-4104.** Cover 500–2,000 Dr ($2.25–$8.90).

Want to check out the local rock and blues scene? Athenian popsters play here, along with small doses of metal. The club is open Tuesday through Friday from 10:30pm to 2:30am.

Rebetiki Isotoria

181 Ippocratous St. ☎ **01/642-4937.** Cover 1,700–3,300 Dr ($7.55–$14.65).

Housed in a neoclassical building, this down-scale smoke-filled room features old-style bouzouki music, played to a mixed crowd of older regulars and younger students and intellectuals. The music usually starts at 11pm, but arrive earlier to get a seat.

Taverna Mostrou

22 Mnisikleos St. ☎ **01/322-5337.** Cover 4,000 Dr ($17.80).

This is one of the largest, oldest, and best-known clubs for traditional Greek music and dancing. Shows here begin about 11pm and usually last until 2am. The entrance cost includes a fixed-menu supper. À la carte is available but expensive.

Zoom

37 Kidathineon St. ☎ **01/322-5920.** Cover 1,500–2,000 Dr ($6.70–$8.90).

In the heart of Plaka, Zoom is the place to go to hear the best of Greek pop music. Performers, who are likely to have current hit albums, are showered with carnations by adoring audience members.

DANCE CLUBS

Alarm

9 Spiliotopoulou St. ☎ **01/771-1315.** Cover 2,000–3,000 Dr ($8.90–$13.35).

A converted cinema is now the setting for live local music played to a fashion-unconscious young crowd. Bands usually start around midnight.

Autokinisis

7 Kifisias Ave., Plothei. ☎ **01/681-2360.** Cover 2,500 Dr ($11.10) Fri and Sat.

Athens's trendy 20-something crowd packs shoulder-to-shoulder into this New York–style dance club. There's no dance floor per se; rather, the entire club hops to the beat. The place really goes wild around 2am, when new American sound gives way to traditional Greek music. Closed on Sunday and Monday.

Boose

57 Kolokotroni St. ☎ **01/324-0944.** Cover 2,000 Dr ($8.90).

Hidden on a backstreet on the outskirts of Plaka, this second-floor club blasts danceable rock music to a hip student crowd. There's art on every wall, jelled stage lights, and two bars.

Delirious

4 Orminiou St. ☎ **01/729-0165.**

So it's 3am and you still want to dance? Techno, House, and pop spin in this small club with a good wooden dance floor that surrounds the bar. It's near the Hilton Hotel and stays open nightly until about 6am.

FILMS

Movies are popular in Athens, and shows during the evenings are often sold out. Films are usually screened in their original language and tickets cost 1,000 Dr ($4.45). Most of the downtown movie houses are near Omonia Square, on Stadiou or Patisson streets. Check the local daily newspaper, *Athens News,* for shows and schedules.

9 Easy Excursions

Located as it is right in the center of the country, Athens makes a perfect launching pad for explorations throughout Greece. Ferries leave from Athens's port, Piraeus, for myriad idyllic islands, and Olympic Airways's domestic flights to the islands and other destinations in Greece are refreshingly moderate in price. For a list of ferry or long-distance bus routes and times, drop by the information window of the National Tourist Organization of Greece, in Syntagma Square. For flight schedules, try any Olympic Airways office.

✪ **DELPHI**   Everyone's favorite excursion is to Delphi, three hours from Athens by bus. The bus to Delphi leaves from the station at 260 Lission St. (take bus no. 24 from Amalias Street in front of the National Gardens to the bus station).

Famous in antiquity for its oracle, which made divine prophecies, Delphi has attracted pilgrims for several millennia and was consulted by many of the greatest figures in ancient history. Inscriptions on the temple pediments advised visitors "Know thyself" and "Nothing in excess." Today Delphi is one of Greece's most exciting ancient sites.

The main archaeological site is a 10- to 15-minute walk from the bus stop, from which two roads slope upward at a fork in the highway. Walk up the road on the right, straight through town and beyond. After you exit the small town you'll pass the museum on your left, and soon after you'll arrive at the ruins. The lovely Temple of Athena Pronaia is about another 10 minutes farther down the road.

You'll pass the tourist office, in the center of town at Pavlou and 44 Frederikis St. (☎ **0265/82-900**), where you can pick up a pamphlet on Delphi with a map of the ruins, as well as bus and other information. The tourist office is open April to September, daily from 8am to 9pm; and October to March, Monday through Saturday from 8am to 8pm and Sunday from 10am to 3pm.

The Archaeological Sight　　After passing along the **Sacred Way,** with important civic religious buildings, you'll arrive at the **Temple of Apollo,** site of the ancient oracle of Delphi. Six columns remain, only one at its original height. The setting is stunning, with a valley in front and tall rocky mountains rising immediately behind, with more in the distance. Behind the Temple of Apollo is the well-preserved theater, with complete tiers of seating. A short hike up the hill from the main site brings you to an impressive, long oval stadium with seating still intact. Admission is 1,500 Dr ($6.70).

Summer hours are Monday to Saturday from 8am to 7pm and Sunday from 8:30am to 3pm; the rest of the year, hours are Monday from 7:30am to 5pm, Tuesday to Friday from 7:30am to 5:30pm, and Saturday and Sunday from 8:30am to 3pm.

Delphi Museum　　After your visit to the archaeological site, you can go to the Delphi Museum (☎ **0265/82-1313**) to examine some of the fine architectural detail of the **Sanctuary of Delphi** from the 6th century B.C., including various friezes, sculptures, votive offerings, and more. Admission is 1,500 Dr ($6.70). Summer hours are Monday from noon to 7pm, Tuesday to Saturday from 8am to 7pm, and Sunday from 8:30am to 3pm; the rest of the year, hours are Monday from 11am to 5pm, Tuesday to Friday from 7:30am to 5:30pm, and Saturday and Sunday from 8:30am to 3pm.

OTHER DAY TRIPS　　Delphi is just the beginning of the rich antiquity that can be explored around Athens. Other famous sites include **Corinth,** with its mostly A.D. 1st century ruins of a powerful Greek city; **Mycenae,** the city of Agamemnon, with ruins of the royal citadel and "beehive" tombs dating from 1200 B.C.; and **Epidaurus,** home to the best-preserved ancient theater in Greece, with seating for 14,000. Buses serve all these destinations; ask the tourist office for the latest schedule (note that buses leave from two different stations in Athens).

Barcelona 6

by Herbert Bailey Livesey

Although the glow of the 1992 Olympic Games has cooled somewhat, Barcelona can still savor the multitude of improvements made
to its infrastructure for that watershed event. The accolades the city
enjoyed for its handling of the Games stoked community spirit, and
Barcelona continues to show itself comfortable with both its heritage
and the approach of another millennium.

In part, Barcelona's topography was its destiny: Unlike cities that
sprawl unimpended across flat plains (like Madrid or Chicago),
Barcelona is cradled in a great half bowl, open to the Mediterranean
on one side but contained by a brooding hill called Montjuïc at the
harbor's southwest edge and backed up to the north by a massif
dominated by Tibidabo's peak. Apart from church steeples and a few
misguided efforts at skyscraper modernity, most of human-made
Barcelona tops out at under eight stories. It rises gently from the sea
and climbs its slopes and elevations with admirable respect for the
land in which it's embraced.

Several times during its 2,000-plus-year history Barcelona has
seized the moment and squeezed the most from it. In 1888 and 1929
it hosted World Exhibitions, which, like the 1992 Olympic Games,
altered the face of the city forever. After the last huge effort, Spain's
most energized city is better than ever, respecting and recycling its
past while accommodating its present and future.

In A.D. 874 Barcelona was nicknamed "La Ciudad Condal" for
the counts who'd negotiated its independence. In the 13th and 14th
centuries it was the capital of the Kingdom of Catalonia and Aragón,
whose colonial influence extended into southern France, down to
Valencia, and on to Sicily and Greece. In 1259 it promulgated the
first code of European martimite law, on which other Mediterranean
states modeled theirs. This is still the Mediterranean's third-largest
port—and, arguably, its Queen City. Long Spain's most progressive
and "European" city, Barcelona was the country's first industrial
force, beginning in the mid-19th century.

From the gothic cathedral to Gaudí's Sagrada Família to Ricardo
Bofill's new National Theater, Barcelona demonstrates a flair for eye-
catching architecture. And with parlays like Picasso to Miró to
Tàpies, the city has fostered more than its share of artistic genius.

Now eager to be a key player within Spain, the European Union,
and the world beyond, Barcelona has everything going for it—good

What's Special About Barcelona

Architectural Highlights
- Gaudí's La Sagrada Família, an immense modernist cathedral crawling its way to completion.
- Palau de la Música Catalana, an outstanding example of modernism and one of the Europe's finest concert halls.

Top Attractions
- Les Rambles, a bumptious pedestrian boulevard (made up of five individual boulevards) that never fails to entertain, from early morning until far into the night.
- The gothic cathedral, noted for its cloisters, *Cristo de Lepanto*, and tomb of Santa Eulàlia, one of the city's patron saints.

Museums
- Museu Picasso, home to an enlightening collection of the master's works.
- Fundació Joan Miró, with more than 10,000 works by the important Catalan artist.

Scenic Vistas
- From the top of Montjuïc.
- From the top of Mount Tibidabo.
- From the Transbordador del Puerto.
- From Parc Güell.
- From the cafeteria atop El Corte Inglés department store.

A Park
- Parc de la Ciutadella, home to the zoo, the Museu d'Art Modern, and many sculptures and fountains.

A Neighborhood
- Barri Gòtic, a maze of medieval streets with a growing numbers of shops and cafés.

Transportation
- *Tramvía blau,* running past the stately, often eccentric, modernist mansions of Avinguda Tibidabo.

An Excursion
- Montserrat Monastery, a popular pilgrimage destination and home of the Black Virgin.

looks, good business sense, an appreciation for all forms of culture, and an unerring eye for style.

1 Barcelona Deals & Discounts

BUDGET BESTS At lunch—and in some restaurants, dinner—the three-course *menu del día* is usually a bargain. Make that the main meal and stick to snacks, sandwiches, pizza, or *tapas* (assorted hors d'oeuvre–size snacks) at other times.

January, February, and July are sale months, when signs on almost every type of store shriek ¡REBAIXES! (Catalan) or ¡REBAJAS! (Spanish). Toward the end of these months prices hit rock-bottom.

SPECIAL DISCOUNTS Ask about the "Barcelona Amigo" promotions offered by Iberia (☎ **800/772-4642**). British travelers will also want to check British Airways for special promotions or charters.

For Students Students with appropriate ID enjoy reduced or free admission to most of the city's museums and monuments.

The **"Youth Card"** issued by the Generalitat de Catalunya makes it easy and cheap for young people to get the most out of their stay. The "Youth Card" guide lists almost 8,000 establishments offering discounts. For information, contact the Direcció General de Joventut, Generalitat de Catalunya, Viladomat 319, 08029 Barcelona (☎ **3/322-90-61**), open Monday through Friday from 3:30 to 7:30pm.

Two other establishments also offer special services and discounts to young travelers: The **Youth Travel Office** (Oficina de Turisme Juvenil—TIVE), Calabrina 147, 08001 Barcelona (☎ **3/483-83-83**), is open in winter Monday through Friday from 9am to 1pm and 4 to 5:30pm and in summer Monday through Friday from 9am to 2pm; and **Information Service and Youth Activities (SIPAJ)**, Rambla de Catalunya 5-Pral., 08007 Barcelona (☎ **3/301-40-46**), open Monday through Friday from 5 to 9pm.

For Everyone The **"Barcelona-Unica" package** offers weekend stays in three- to five-star hotels at discount prices of $29 to $50 per person per night in a double room. Breakfast is included, as are a basket of fruit and the morning newspaper. At check-in, a BIP (Barcelona Important Person) card is issued entitling the bearer to discounts on tours, meals, shopping, nightclubs, casinos, car rentals, concerts, and museum admissions. For further information and reservations, contact the Asociació Barcelona Turística, Copérnic 37, 3-2, 08021 Barcelona (☎ **3/414-4540**; fax 3/414-66-87).

WORTH THE EXTRA MONEY Performances at the Palau de la Música Catalana are definitely worth spending a few more pesetas for. Sampling Catalunya's fine *cavas* (champagnes) in a sophisticated *xampanyeria* or nursing a pricey beer in one of the city's celebrated designer bars makes for a splurge that won't be regretted.

2 Pretrip Preparations

REQUIRED DOCUMENTS Citizens of the United States and Canada need only a valid passport for stays of up to three months. A British subject entering from Britain needs only an identity card.

TIMING YOUR TRIP Temperatures here are mild most of the year but the humidity is high, so the July and August heat can be oppressive. Rain is most likely to fall in spring and autumn, though these are still the best times to go. Snowfalls are rare and nearly always melt quickly.

Barcelona's Average Daytime Temperature

	Jan	Feb	Mar	Apr	May	June	July	Aug	Sept	Oct	Nov	Dec
Temp. (°F)	49	51	54	59	64	72	76	76	72	64	57	51

Special Events Locals gather regularly to **dance the sardana,** a sedate, precisely choreographed Catalan folk dance. Watch them in front of the cathedral on Saturday at 6:30pm and Sunday at noon, at Plaça Sant Jaume on Sunday and holidays at 7pm in summer and 6:30pm in winter, at Plaça Sant Felip Neri the first Saturday of the month at 6pm, and at Plaça Sagrada Família on Sunday at noon.

What Things Cost in Barcelona	U.S.$
Taxi from the airport to the Hotel R. Regencia Colón	22.70
Metro fare	.95
Local telephone call	.10
Double room at the Hotel Claris (deluxe)	226.90
Double room at the Hotel R. Regencia Colón (moderate)	104.00
Double room at the Hostal-Residencia Windsor (budget)	46.45
Continental breakfast	3.05
Lunch for one, without wine, at La Poma (moderate)	12.50
Lunch for one, without wine, at Self Naturista (budget)	5.70
Dinner for one, without wine, at Neichel (deluxe)	70.00
Dinner for one, without wine, at Set Portes (moderate)	18.50
Dinner for one, without wine, at Pitarra Restaurant (budget)	10.85
Small beer (una caña)	.70–1.30
Coca-Cola in a restaurant	1.25
Cup of coffee	.65
Roll of ASA 100 color film, 36 exposures	2.95
Admission to Museu Picasso	3.85
Movie ticket	4.45
Theater ticket	7.50 and up

The night of June 23 Barcelona celebrates the **Verbena de Sant Joan** with bonfires in the streets and plazas. It's customary to eat *coca,* a special sweet made from fruit and pine nuts, and festivities held on Montjuïc culminate in an impressive fireworks display.

During the week of September 24 are the celebrations of the **fiestas de la Mercé,** Barcelona's most important popular festival. Concerts and theatrical performances animate Plaças Sant Jaume, de la Seu, del Rei, Sot del Migdia, Escorxador, and Reial, and giants, devils, dragons, and other fantastic creatures parade through the Old Town. At the end of it all is a music pageant and fireworks. The days-long pre-Lenten Carnaval has grown in importance in recent years, with elaborately custumed citizens partying all night in the streets and nightspots.

During November the **Festival Internacional de Jazz de Barcelona** takes place in the Palau de la Música Catalana.

BACKGROUND READING   For insight into Catalunya's role in the Spanish Civil War, read George Orwell's *Homage to Catalonia.* The definitive study of that tragedy is Hugh Thomas's *The Spanish Civil War,* which discusses in depth the progress of the conflict in Barcelona. For general insight into Spain, pick up Nikos Kazantzakis's *Spain* or the book of the same name by Jan Morris. Robert Hughes, an art critic for *Time* magazine, wrote his engrossing *Barcelona* in anticipation of the 1992 Summer Olympics. See also "Background Reading" under "Pretrip Preparations" in Chapter 17 on Madrid.

3 Barcelona Specifics

ARRIVING

FROM THE AIRPORT   Newly expanded **El Prat Airport** is about eight miles from the center city. A train runs between the airport and the Estació Sants every 30 minutes from 6am to 10:15pm, taking about 20 minutes to Estació Sants and continuing to the more central Praça de Catalunya; it costs 250 ptas. ($1.95). A convenient, comfortable bus runs between the airport and Plaça de Catalunya (with intermediate stops) Monday through Friday every 15 minutes between 6:30am and 11pm and Saturday, Sunday, and holidays every 30 minutes between 6:45am and 10:45pm. The trip takes 15 to 30 minutes and costs 400 ptas. ($3.10). A taxi into town costs 2,000 to 2,500 ptas. ($15.40 to $19.25).

FROM THE TRAIN STATION   Most national and international trains arrive at the Estació Sants, Estació de França, or Passeig de Gràcia station, all centrally located and linked to the municipal Metro network.

VISITOR INFORMATION

The following **tourist offices** offer basic maps, materials, and timely information on exhibitions and other cultural events: Estació Sants, open Monday through Friday from 8am to 8pm and Saturday, Sunday, and holidays from 8am to 2pm; Ajuntament de Barcelona (in Plaça Sant Jaume), open June 24 to September 30, Monday through Friday from 9am to 8pm and Saturday from 8:30am to 2:30pm. The airport information office is open Monday through Saturday from 9:30am to 8pm and Sunday and holidays from 9:30am to 3pm.

For information on Barcelona, Catalunya, and the rest of Spain, inquire at the **Oficina de Informació Turística,** Gran Vía C.C. 658 (☎ **93/301-74-43**), open Monday through Friday from 9am to 7pm and Saturday from 9am to 2pm. If you want to phone for information, this last office is the best bet.

During summer, uniformed **"roving hosts"** in the principal tourism areas offer assistance in various languages.

For **24-hour information** on what's happening in Barcelona, dial 010 on Monday through Friday from 7am to 11pm and Saturday from 9am to 2pm.

Barcelona is in the process of providing multilingual telephone lines for information on all matters of tourist interest. For the numbers, pick up the brochure **"Facil parlar"** at any tourist office.

CITY LAYOUT

Barcelona took shape under the Romans and later expanded from a walled medieval core at the water's edge. Between the harbor and the ordered grid of the 19th-century Eixample district lies the **Ciutat Vella (Old Town)**, bordered by the Parc de la Ciutadella to the northeast and the fortress-topped hill of Montjuïc to the southwest. Its focal point is the **Barri Gòtic.**

To the east is the **Barri de la Ribera,** focal point of Barcelona's 13th- and 14th-century colonial and commercial expansion. Below the Parc de la Ciutadella and enclosing the east end of the harbor is **Barceloneta,** originally home to the city's mariners and fishermen and now known primarily for its concentration of seafood restaurants. It connects to the southwestern edge of the **Vila Olímpica,** the Olympic Village that's now, in effect, an urbanized satellite of the central city.

The Spanish Peseta

For American Readers   At this writing $1 = approximately 130 ptas. (or 1 pta. = .8¢), and this was the rate of exchange used to calculate dollar values given in this chapter (rounded to the nearest nickel).

For British Readers   At this writing £1 = approximately 204 ptas. (or 1 pta. = .49p), and this was the rate of exchange used to calculate the pound values in the table below.

Note: The rates given here fluctuate from time to time and may not be the same when you travel to Spain. Therefore this table should be used only as a guide:

Ptas.	U.S.$	U.K.£	Ptas.	U.S.$	U.K.£
5	.04	.02	1,000	7.69	4.90
10	.08	.05	1,500	11.54	7.35
15	.12	.07	2,000	15.38	9.80
20	.15	.10	2,500	19.23	12.25
25	.19	.12	3,000	23.08	14.70
30	.23	.15	4,000	30.77	19.60
40	.31	.20	5,000	38.46	24.51
50	.38	.25	6,000	46.15	29.41
75	.58	.37	7,000	53.85	34.31
100	.77	.49	8,000	61.54	39.21
150	1.15	.74	9,000	69.23	44.12
200	1.54	.98	10,000	76.92	49.02
250	1.92	1.23	11,000	84.62	53.92
500	3.85	2.45	12,000	92.31	58.82

At the Barri Gòtic's western edge, bisecting the Old Town, is **Les Rambles**; this boulevard is actually composed of five sections, each a separate Rambla. On the other side, down by the port, is the notorious **Barri Xinés**, a potentially danger-ous neighborhood best avoided at night. Above the Barri Xinés, roughly north of the street called Nou de la Rambla, is a residential district called **El Raval,** currently enjoying a measure of rejuvenation.

To the north of Plaça Catalunya is the **Eixample,** a grid of wide streets that's the product of Barcelona's growing industrial prosperity in the late 19th century. North of the Eixample are **Gràcia,** an area of small squares and lively bars and restaurants that was once a separate village, and **Tibidabo,** Barcelona's tallest mountain.

GETTING AROUND

The city is accessible by Metro (subway), bus, funicular, cable car, taxi, or train or on foot. Given the city's persistent traffic congestion, the Metro and walking are quickest. Note that public transport fares are slightly higher on weekends and holidays. Call 93/412-00-00 Monday through Friday from 7:30am to 8:30pm and Saturday from 8am to 2pm for general public-transportation information.

Barcelona Metro

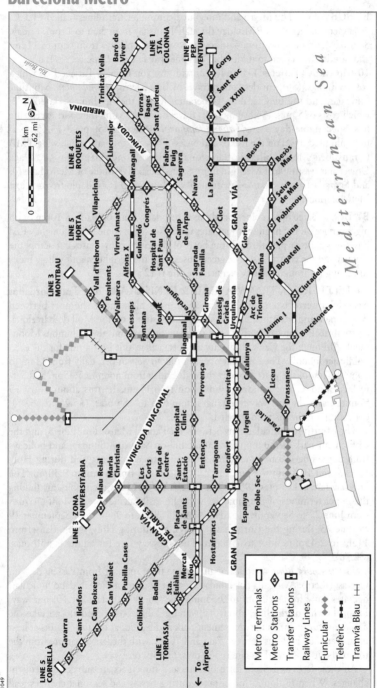

BY SUBWAY   The Metro and integrated commuter train lines (called FF.CC. de la Generalitat) operate Monday through Thursday from 5am to 11pm; Friday, Saturday, and holidays from 5am to 1am; weekday holidays from 6am to 11pm; and Sunday from 6am to midnight. The one-way fare is 125 ptas. (95¢), but two **10-trip cards (Tarjetas T-1 and T-2)** will save you money. Tarjeta T-1, which costs 650 ptas. ($5), entitles you to travel by bus, Metro, *tramvía blau,* Montjuïc funicular, and the FF.CC. de la Generalitat within the city limits; Tarjeta T-2, which costs 625 ptas. ($4.80), permits travel on all the same transport except the bus. **Special one-day passes (*abono temporales*),** costing 450 ptas. ($3.45), permit unlimited travel on the Metro and buses. These are sold at the following TMB (Transports Metropolita de Barcelona) offices: Ronda Sant Pau 41; Plaça Universitat (vestibule of Metro station); Sants-Estació (vestibule of Metro Line 5); and Sagrada Família station (vestibule). A Metro map is available free at most Metro stations.

BY BUS   Barcelona's color-coded buses run daily from 6:30am to 10pm, with night service on the main thoroughfares until 4am (or in some cases all night). Red buses originate or pass through the heart of the city; yellow buses cut across the city beyond the central districts; green buses serve the periphery; and yellow buses run at night through the city center. The fare is 125 ptas. (95¢).

BY TELEFÉRICO, TRAMVÍA BLAU & FUNICULAR   The **Transbordador Aeri del Puerto** is an aerial cable car running high above the port between Barceloneta and Montjuïc hill; an intermediate stop is on the Moll de Barcelona, a jetty thrusting into the harbor from the plaza that contains the Columbus Monument. Although the views of the city are spectacular, this isn't a ride for the even mildly acrophobic. The cable car operates July to September, daily from 11am to 9pm; the rest of the year, Monday through Friday from noon to 5:45pm and Saturday, Sunday, and holidays from noon to 6:15pm. It runs about every 15 minutes, and the one-way fare ranges from 685 to 785 ptas. ($5.25 to $6.05), depending on the distance traveled.

The **Montjuïc funicular** runs between the Parallel Metro stop (Line 3) and the amusement park at the top of Montjuïc hill on Saturday, Sunday, and holidays from September 30 to June, during the Christmas holidays, and during Holy Week, from 10:45am to 8pm; and daily in summer from 11am to 9:30pm. The one-way fare is 125 ptas. (95¢). The **Teleférico de Montjuïc** (cable car) linking the upper terminus of the funicular with the castle at the top of Montjuïc runs from June 22 to September 15, daily from 11:30am to 9pm; from September 29 to June 23, during the Christmas holidays, and during Holy Week, daily from 11am to 2:45pm and 4 to 7:30pm. The one-way fare for adults is 350 ptas. ($2.70).

The *tramvía blau,* a replica of an antique tram running from Passeig de Sant Gervasi (*M*etro: Avinguda del Tibidabo) to the bottom of the Tibidabo funicular, operates daily from 7:05am to 9:55pm. The fare is 150 ptas. ($1.15) one way. From the end of the line, about halfway up Tibidabo hill, riders can take the **Tibidabo funicular** to the amusement park and basilica at the top. It runs at least once every half an hour between 7am and 10pm, with the last departure from the top at about 9:55pm. The fare is 300 ptas. ($2.30) one way.

All these fares and times for cable cars and funiculars are subject to frequent changes. When in doubt, for instance during fiestas and seasonal changes, call 93/412-00-00.

ON FOOT   Barcelona's Ciutat Vella can easily be covered on foot, as can much of the Eixample.

BY TAXI   Most Barcelona taxis are black and yellow. When available, they display a sign reading LIBRE (Spanish) or LLIURE (Catalan) and/or an illuminated green roof light. The initial charge is 275 ptas. ($2.10); each additional kilometer is 93 ptas. (70¢). This jumps to 107 ptas. (80¢) after 10pm and on Saturday, Sunday, and holidays. Among a number of legitimate supplemental charges are 400 ptas. ($3.10) to and from the airport, plus 125 ptas. (95¢) for each large bag.

Taxi stands are abundant and cabs can be hailed on the street or called at 357-77-55, 358-11-11, or 300-38-11.

BY CAR   Having a car in Barcelona is a burden, and renting one is expensive. If one is nonetheless a necessity, an airline fly/drive package may be the most economical solution. Otherwise, shop for the best deal among the following agencies with in-town and airport offices: **Atesa,** Carrer de Balmes 141 (☎ **93/237-81-40** or 93/302-28-32 at the airport); **Avis,** Carrer de Aragó 235 (☎ **93/215-84-30** or 93/379-40-26 at the airport); **Europcar,** Carrer de Consell de Cent 363 (☎ **93/317-58-76** or 93/379-92-051 at the airport); and **Hertz,** Estació Sants (☎ **93/490-86-62** or 93/370-58-11 at the airport).

FAST FACTS: Barcelona

Addresses   In Spain, street numbers follow street names and the ° sign indicates the floor. *Dcha.* or *izqda.* following the floor means *derecha* (right) or *izquerda* (left). *Baja* refers to the ground floor, and the Spanish first floor (1°) is the American second.

Banks   Money and traveler's checks can be changed at any bank advertising *cambio*; a commission is always charged, which makes cashing small amounts expensive. When banks are closed (see "Business Hours," below), money can be changed at the Estació Sants daily from 8am to 10pm or at the airport daily from 7am to 11pm.

Only in a pinch, there are Chequepoint offices at Les Rambles 15, 64, and 130, as well as other locations, where money or traveler's checks can be changed daily from 9am to midnight. They don't charge a commission, but their exchange rate is significantly lower than the banks' prevailing rate. There are also exchange machines at Banco Santander, on Plaça San Jaume (at the corner of C. Fernando) and at Plaça de Gràcia 5.

Automated-teller machines (ATMs) can be found throughout the city, especially in tourist and commercial areas. They permit users to obtain cash advances with their credit cards; however, more important, they provide access to checking and savings accounts through the CIRRUS and Plus networks. A four-digit Personal Identification Number (PIN) is required. Some Stateside banks charge excessive fees for this service, so that issue should be addressed before you leave for Spain.

Business Hours   Hours at **banks** vary, though are usually Monday through Friday from 9am to 2pm and Saturday from 9am to 1pm (closed Saturday June to September). Typical **office** hours are Monday through Friday from 9am to 1:30pm and 4 to 7pm, but some offices have special summer hours from 8am to 3pm. **Shop** hours vary widely—the norm is from 10am to 1:30pm and 5 to 8pm.

Consulates   The Consulate of the **United States,** Passeig Reina Elisenda 23
(☎ **93/280-22-27**), is open Monday through Friday from 9am to 12:30pm and
3 to 5pm. The Consulate of **Canada,** Vía Augusta 125 (☎ **93/209-06-34**), is
open Monday through Friday from 9am to 1pm. The Consulate of the **United
Kingdom,** at Avinguda Diagonal 477 (☎ **93/419-90-44**), is open Monday
through Friday from 9:30am to 1:30pm and 4 to 5pm.

Currency   The unit of currency is the Spanish **peseta (pta.),** with coins of 1,
5, 10, 25, 50, 100, 200, and 500 ptas. Be aware that the 500-peseta coin is easily
confused with the 100-peseta coin. Notes are issued in 500- (rare nowadays),
1,000-, 2,000-, 5,000-, and 10,000-pta. denominations.

Doctors   Call 061 for a doctor. If hospital attention is required, possibilities
are Hospital Clínic i Provincial, Casanova 143 (☎ **93/454-70-00**), or Hospital
Creu Roja de Barcelona, Dos de Maig 301 (☎ **93/433-15-51**).

Emergencies   In a **medical emergency,** call 061. For the **police,** call 091 or
092. In the event of **fire,** call 080.

Holidays   For local holidays, see "Timing Your Trip" under "Pretrip Preparations,"
earlier in this chapter. Others include New Year's Day (Jan 1), January 6 (Epiph-
any), Good Friday, Easter Monday, May 1 (Pentacost), June 24 (St. John's Day),
August 15 (Feast of the Assumption), September 11,October 12 (Fiesta of the
Hispanic Nations), November 1 (All Saints Day), December 6 (Constitution
Day), December 8 (Immaculate Conception), and December 25–26 (Christmas).

Hospitals   See "Doctors," above.

Information   See "Visitor Information" under "Barcelona Specifics," earlier in
this chapter.

Language   Catalan, the indigenous language of Catalunya, is the official language of the region, and most signs appear either solely in Catalan or in both
Catalan and Spanish. Catalan is a discrete language, not a dialect, and is related
to *langue d'oc* and *provençal,* spoken across the Pyrenees in southern France. To
the casual ear, spoken Catalan sounds like a mix of French and Spanish.

Laundry/Dry Cleaning   Hotel laundry costs are prohibitively expensive
and Laundromats are rare. One alternative is Joaquín Costa, Prop del Carrer del
Carme 16 (☎ **93/442-59-82**), offering self-service laundry facilities Monday
through Saturday from 8am to 8pm. They'll do 3 kilos (6¹/₂ lb.) of laundry for
700 ptas. ($5.40); 6 kilos (13¹/₂ lb.) for 1,000 ptas. ($7.70),or 10 kilos (22 lbs.)
for 1,260 ptas. ($9.70). Bugaderia Lava-Super, Enric Granados 94 (☎ **93/237-
23-16**), is open Monday through Friday from 8:30am to 8pm and offers to do
laundry for 1,400 ptas. ($10.75) for 6 kilos (13¹/₂ lb.), washed and dried.
    Take dry cleaning to Tintorería Ungria, Enrique Granados 99–101
(☎ **93/218-10-54**), open Monday through Friday from 8:30am to 2pm and
3:30 to 8pm and Saturday from 9am to 1pm.

Lost & Found   Dial 317-38-79 for a lost item. If it was lost on public transportation, contact the Metro office in Plaça Catalunya, across from Carrer Bergara
(☎ 93/318-52-93).

Mail   Post offices are generally open Monday through Friday from 9am to 2pm.
The central post office in Plaça Antoni López (☎ **93/318-38-31**) is open
Monday through Friday from 8am to 9pm and Saturday from 8am to 2pm.
Letters and postcards to the United States cost 95 ptas. (75¢).

Newspapers   Barcelona's leading dailies are *La Vanguardia* and *El Periódico*. The national *El País,* Spain's leading daily, prints a Barcelona edition. Foreign-language newspapers, including the *International Herald Tribune* and *USA Today,* are readily available at newsstands along Les Rambles and throughout the Eixample.

Photographic Needs   Panorama, Plaça de Gràcia 4 (☎ **93/318-37-00**), is open Monday through Saturday from 9am to 8pm to satisfy most photographic needs, including processing.

Police   In an emergency, call 091 or 092. The police station at Les Rambles 43 (☎ **93/301-90-60**), offers 24-hour service. Also seen in tourist areas are small, roving trailers marked OFICINA DE DENUNCIAS that can provide assistance or accept crime reports.

Radio/TV   Private TV stations have just come to Spain and offerings in Catalan, Spanish, and other languages are growing by the day. Hotels with satellite-fed television usually carry two or three English-language channels, often including CNN or Britain's Sky News.

Religious Services   Most of Barcelona's churches are Roman Catholic. Masses are generally held between 7am and 2pm and between 7 and 9pm on Sunday and holidays and between 7 and 9pm on Saturday. Mass in English is held at 10:30am on the first and third Sunday of the month at Paroisse Française, Anglí 15 (☎ **93/204-49-62**), and Anglican Mass in English is celebrated every Sunday at 11am and every Wednesday at 11:30am at St. George's Church, Sant Joan de la Salle 41 (☎ **93/417-88-67**).

Shoe Repair   For a quick fix, go to Rápido López, Plazueleta de Montcada 5, open Monday through Friday from 9am to 1pm and 4:30 to 8pm and Saturday from 9am to 1pm.

Tax   For information on the value-added tax (VAT), known as IVA in Spain, see "Shopping," later in this chapter. It used to run as high as 15% for luxury hotels, restaurants, and purchases but was dropped to 7% in January 1995.

Taxis   See "Getting Around" under "Barcelona Specifics," earlier in this chapter.

Telephone   Barcelona's **area code** is 93 when calling from elsewhere in Spain, 3 when calling from outside Spain.

If you're calling long distance from a hotel or hostal, expect a hefty surcharge. Most **public phone** *cabinas* provide clear instructions in English. Place at least 25 pesetas' worth of coins in the rack at the top for a local call—they'll roll in as required.

To make an **international call,** dial 07, wait for the tone, and dial the area code and number. Note, however, that an international call from a phone booth requires stacks and stacks of heavy 100-peseta coins.

As an alternative, purchase **phone cards** worth 1,000 or 2,000 ptas. ($7.70 or $15.40) and use them to make international calls from specially equipped booths, which are clearly identified. Phone cards are available in *estancos* (tobacco shops), at the post office, and at other authorized outlets. Some phones are also equipped to take American Express and Diners Club cards. Or you can make calls and pay for them after completion at the currency-exchange booth at Les Rambles 88, Monday through Saturday from 10am to 11pm and Sunday from 10am to 1:30pm. Contact MCI (☎ **900/99-00-14**) or AT&T (☎ **900/99-00-11**) directly from any phone.

Tipping   While tipping for certain services is customary, large amounts are not expected. A bellhop should get 100 ptas. (75¢) per bag. Taxi drivers usually get 10%. Virtually all restaurants include a service charge in the bill, so a 5% to 10% tip usually suffices. Ushers in cinemas and theaters and at the bullring get 50 to 75 ptas. (40¢ to 60¢). At bars and cafeterias, tip 10 to 100 ptas. (10¢ to 75¢) depending on the amount of the bill. The percentage left as a tip decreases as the amount of the bill increases.

Useful Telephone Numbers   Airport information: 93/478-50-00. RENFE (Spanish railways) information: 93/490-02-02.

4 Accommodations

Budget accommodations have never been abundant in Barcelona, and the 1992 Olympic Games helped lessen their number since many hostelries upgraded their facilities to capitalize on the flood of visitors. A few budget-conscious hostals were opened at that time, however, and while renovations enhanced the facilities of some old reliables, they didn't necessarily propel them out of their relatively low-priced categories. Most of these inexpensive digs are in the Old Town, with a few scattered throughout the Eixample. Rooms without a shower or bath will usually at least have washbasins.

   Note: Unless otherwise indicated, rates below do not include breakfast or VAT. And remember that Barcelona's telephone area code is 93 when calling from elsewhere in Spain, 3 when calling from outside Spain.

DOUBLES FOR LESS THAN 5,000 PTAS. ($38.45)

Hostal Layetana

Plaça Ramón Berenguer el Gran 2, 08002 Barcelona. ☎ **3/319-20-12.** 20 rms, 14 with bath. 1,900 ptas. ($14.60) single without bath; 3,200 ptas. ($24.60) double without bath, 4,700 ptas. ($35.15) double with bath. No credit cards. Metro: Jaume I.

   Several flights up, this hostal faces a small park next to an imposing section of the old Roman wall. Its rooms are somewhat more spacious than the rooms at other hotels in this price category, and all have sinks. Beer and soft drinks are available in the TV lounge. Breakfast isn't served, but an acceptable café is on the ground floor. The amiable manager speaks some English.

Hostal Residencia Call

Arc de Sant Ramón del Call 4 (just off Carrer Call), 08002 Barcelona. ☎ **3/302-11-23.** Fax 3/318-19-78. 25 rms, all with bath. TEL. 2,500 ptas. ($19.25) single; 3,500 ptas. ($27.70) double; 5,000 ptas. ($38.45) triple. MC, V. Metro: Liceu.

   This newly renovated hostal, in what used to be the Jewish quarter, combines basic comfort and function with a central location that's ideal for exploring the Old City. The cathedral and Les Rambles are only minutes away.

Hostal R. Ramos

Carrer Hospital 36, 08001 Barcelona. ☎ **3/302-04-30.** 15 rms, all with bath.TEL. 3,150 ptas. ($24.25) single; 4,725 ptas. ($36.35) double; 5,880 ptas. ($45.25) triple. AE, MC, V. Metro: Liceu.

   At a quiet remove from the nearby Rambles, this one-flight-up hostal offers small rooms (13 doubles, 2 triples) with truncated tubs in the bath. The framed chromos on the walls and floral carpets in the halls will make you feel as if you're

---

Getting the Best Deal on Accommodations

- Some accommodations choices offer rate reductions if you pay in cash instead of with a credit or charge card.
- Long-term discounts may be available if you plan to stay more than a week.
- Don't forget to bargain—especially off-season.
- Ask if there's a surcharge for local or long-distance telephone calls. Usually there is, and it can be as high as 40%. Make calls at the nearest telephone office instead.
- Also ask if service is included or will be added to the final bill. Likewise, inquire if all taxes are included or will be billed extra.

---

visiting a Spanish family. There's always someone around to ring the street door open, even at 3am. No breakfast is served.

✪ Pension Arosa

Portal de l'Angel 14, 08002 Barcelona. ☎ **3/317-36-87.** 7 rms, 3 with bath. 2,100 ptas. ($16.15) single without bath; 4,200 ptas. ($32.30) double with bath. Rates include VAT. No credit cards. Metro: Catalunya.

All is clean, comfortable, and quiet at this intimate pension between the Barri Gòtic and the Eixample. The street-level entrance is beside a watch shop on an active shopping street near the Plaça de Catalunya, while the pension is a couple of flights up (no elevator). All rooms have settees in addition to various combinations of single and double beds; no. 7 is the largest.

Pension Dalí

Carrer de Boquería 12, 08002 Barcelona. ☎ and fax **3/318-55-80.** 60 rms, 22 with bath. 1,700 ptas. ($13.10) single without bath, 2,500 ptas. ($19.25) single with bath; 2,700 ptas. ($20.80) double without bath, 3,700 ptas. ($28.45) double with bath. MC, V. Metro: Liceu.

The heavily sculptured doorframe (check out the man in the top hat on the right) is the best decorative feature of this otherwise bland *modernista* building just off Les Rambles. However, this pension is unusually large, so rooms are often available when other places are full. In the warmer months you'll find many groups staying here, particularly students. Other times, a little bargaining will get you a discount. The varying room configurations and sizes make it wise to check yours before accepting.

Pension Mont-Thabor

Les Rambles 86, 1a, 08002 Barcelona. ☎ **3/317-66-66.** 8 rms, 5 with sink and tub, 3 with bath. 2,100 ptas. ($16.15) single without bath; 4,600 ptas. ($35.40) double with sink and tub, 4,900 ptas. ($37.70) double with bath. No credit cards. Metro: Liceu.

Though there are no frills at this solid, pleasant, cheap lodging in the heart of Les Rambles, all is clean and cozy. There's no elevator for the three floors. Some rooms have balconies.

DOUBLES FOR LESS THAN 7,000 PTAS. ($53.85)

Hostal-Residencia Ciudad Condal

Carrer Mallorca 255, 08008 Barcelona. ☎ **3/487-04-59.** 11 rms, all with bath. TEL. 3,500 ptas. ($26.90) or 4,000 ptas. ($30.75) single; 5,500 ptas. ($42.30) double; 7,500 ptas. ($57.70) triple. MC, V. Metro: Passeig de Gràcia or Diagonal.

A sparkling-clean choice in an excellent part of town, the Ciudad Condal is installed in a late 19th-century modernist structure. Although the furnishings are basic, the overall feel of the place is welcoming. Rooms facing the street have pretty balconies; interior rooms face a lovely garden rather than the usual airshaft. This hostal is two elevatorless flights up, however.

Hostal-Residencia Oliva

Passeig de Gràcia 32, 08007 Barcelona. ☎ **3/488-01-62.** 16 rms, 5 with bath. 2,775 ptas. ($21.35) single without bath; 5,000 ptas. ($38.40) double without bath, 6,125 ptas. ($47.10) double with bath. Rates include breakfast. No credit cards. Metro: Passeig de Gràcia.

The Oliva is in a fine Eixample building above a tony clothing store, with a beautiful vintage elevator. This hostel boasts comely, high-ceilinged rooms with tile floors, lace curtains, and sinks; some are cramped, though.

Hostal-Residencia Windsor

Rambla de Catalunya 84, 08008 Barcelona. ☎ **3/215-11-98.** 15 rms, all with shower and toilet. 3,100 ptas. ($23.85) single without bath, 3,900 ptas. ($30.00) single with bath; 5,400 ptas. ($41.55) double without bath, 6,000 ptas. ($46.15) double with bath. No credit cards. Metro: Passeig de Gràcia or Provença.

The carpeted rooms here are small though quiet and comfortable; some have balconies. As befits this upscale neighborhood, the hostel's lobby, halls, and TV room are elegantly outfitted; all areas have recently been repainted. Rooms without a bath share a bath with just one other room. There's an elevator, but the hostel is only one flight up.

Hotel Inglés

Carrer de Boquería 17, 08002 Barcelona. ☎ **3/317-37-70.** Fax 3/302-78-70. 28 rms, all with bath. TEL. 3,825 ptas. ($29.40) single; 6,375 ptas. ($49.05) double. AE, MC, V. Metro: Liceu.

Tucked in a narrow, busy side street off Les Rambles, this four-floor hotel (with elevator) offers rooms that are surprisingly quiet, especially those in back. The furnishings are utilitarian, the floors vinyl tile, and the baths marble, with hand-held showerheads. English is spoken. Next to the lobby is a bar/restaurant with several special fixed-price meals, including a paella for only 850 ptas. ($6.55).

Hotel Jardi

Plaça Sant Joseo Oriol 1, 08002 Barcelona. ☎ **3/301-59-00** or 3/301-59-58. Fax 3/318-36-64. 38 rms, all with bath. 3,800 ptas. ($29.25) single; 5,000 ptas. ($38.45) or 6,000 ptas. ($46.15) double. MC, V. Metro: Liceu.

The Jardi overlooks the enchanting plazas that embrace the 14th-century Santa María del Pi church and is only a block from the middle of Les Rambles. Down below is a favorite bar of the district's artists and students. Rooms, varying in size and configuration, are routinely furnished. Some doubles have been renovated, and they go for the higher rate; ask to see your room first. Breakfast is available, but a cheaper one can be had at bars on or near the plaza.

Hotel Mare Nostrum

Carrer Sant Pau 2 08001 Barcelona. ☎ and fax **3/318-53-40** or 3/412-30-69. 30 rooms, 21 with bath. A/C TV TEL. 2,500 ptas. ($19.25) single without bath, 3,500 ptas. ($26.90) single with bath; 4,000 ptas ($30.75) double without bath, 6,000 ptas. ($46.15) double with bath. AE, DC, MC, V. Metro: Liceu.

For the 1992 Olympics, this old building directly on Les Rambles was stripped down and spruced up with comforts not often found at this price level. Though the air conditioning isn't essential much of the year, it's a relief in a humid

Barcelona July. The most attractive room is the breakfast salon, with a wide window displaying the full pageant of Les Rambles. Many rooms have balconies; five have double beds, not easy to find. There's a laundry service, also rare at this level. Apart from a slightly haphazard quality, this represents good value.

Hotel Residencia Neutral

Rambla de Catalunya 42, 08007 Barcelona. ☎ 3/487-63-90. 28 rms, all with bath. TEL. 2,730 ptas. ($21.00) single; 5,100 ptas. ($39.25) double; 6,850 ptas. ($46.55) triple. No credit cards. Metro: Passeig de Gràcia.

A budget choice in a luxury area, the Neutral has an entrance that's one flight up. Colorful antique floor tiling helps brighten the high-ceilinged rooms furnished with assorted odds and ends. The rooms are small, but the breakfast room, with an impressive coffered ceiling, and the adjacent TV room are spacious.

Hotel Rey Don Jaime I

Carrer Jaume I 11, 08002 Barcelona. ☎ and fax 3/310-62-08. 30 rms, all with bath. 3,500 ptas. ($26.90) single; 5,000 ptas. ($38.45) double. Additional person 1,000 ptas. ($7.70) extra. No credit cards. Metro: Jaume I.

A solid choice off the main plaza of the Barri Gòtic, this hotel (no elevator) has three floors of recently renovated rooms with small balconies. Since the hotel is on a busy street, the rooms in the back are quieter.

DOUBLES FOR LESS THAN 10,000 PTAS. ($76.90)

✪ Hotel Cataluña

Carrer de Santa Anna 24, 08002 Barcelona. ☎ 3/301-91-50. Fax 3/302-78-70. 50 rms, all with bath. TV TEL. 4,495 ptas. ($34.60) single; 7,490 ptas. ($57.60) double. AE, DC, MC, V. Rates include breakfast. Metro: Plaça Catalunya.

About a block east of the upper Rambles, this spotless budget choice is even more desirable than before since it has undertaken renovations *and* reduced its rates. New bathrooms were also added. The 50 rooms (including 16 singles) are simply furnished but well maintained. Next to the handy streetside lobby is the café where breakfast is served. If the Cataluña is full, the Cortés across the street (below) is quite similar.

Hotel Continental

Les Rambles 138, 2a, 08002 Barcelona. ☎ 3/301-25-70. Fax 3/302-73-60. 35 rms, all with bath. A/C TV TEL. 6,150–6,6950 ptas. ($47.30–$53.40) single; 8,300–8,650 ptas. ($63.85–$66.55) double; 12,285 ptas. ($94.50) triple. Rates include breakfast. AE, DC, MC, V. Metro: Liceu or Plaça Catalunya.

Try not to be put off by the unpromising entrance or the lobby with its clanging colors and patterns. This is now a three-star hotel that delivers considerable value for its price range. The two floors of rooms have new baths, air conditioning, ceiling fans, TVs with English channels, and refrigerators (unstocked)—as well as a certain goofy charm. Nine have balconies. The windows are double-paned, reducing street noise to a murmur. The cozy salon off the reception area is a gathering place where drinks and an ample buffet breakfast are offered. Rooms overlooking Les Rambles are more expensive, while some of those in back are cheaper than indicated above. Some of the staff speak English.

Hotel Cortés

Carrer de Santa Anna 25, 08002 Barcelona. ☎ 3/317-91-12. Fax 3/302-78-70. 46 rms, all with bath. TV TEL. 4,495 ptas. ($34.60) single; 7,490 ptas. ($57.60) double. Rates include breakfast. AE, DC, MC, V. Metro: Plaça Catalunya.

Across from the Cataluña (above) and under the same ownership, the Cortés is popular with American students on youth tours. The ground-floor lobby is inviting, with an adjoining café/restaurant. The rooms are clean, with modern tile baths, and have recently been renovated.

✪ Hotel España

Carrer Sant Pau 9–11, 08002 Barcelona. ☎ 3/318-17-58. 84 rms, 62 with bath. TEL. 4,350 ptas. ($33.54) single; 8,260 ptas. ($63.54) double. AE, MC, V. Metro: Liceu.

Since seeing the inside of a *modernista* building (most of which are still in private hands) is rare, you should feel it an honor to pass an hour or two in one of the dining rooms here. This 1904 hotel was designed by Domènech i Montaner, a coequal of Antoni Gaudí. A mural in one dining room was painted by Ramón Casas, one of the most prominent artists of his time, and the fantastical limestone fireplace in another was carved by Eusebi Arnau, who did the proscenium sculptures in Domènech's Palau de la Música. It's difficult to maintain a landmark at these prices, though, so the facilities look a bit worn. The rooms are of varying sizes, with clean tile baths, ceiling fans, and safes. Fixed-price meals in those eye-filling dining rooms go for only 1,000 ptas ($7.70).

Hotel Residencia Internacional

Les Rambles 78–80, 08002 Barcelona. ☎ 3/302-25-66. Fax 3/317-61-90. 60 rms, all with bath. TEL. 5,180 ptas. ($39.85) single; 6,600 ptas. ($50.80) double. AE, DC, MC, V. Metro: Liceu.

This is one of the ubiquitous HUSA chain, situated across from the opera house. All the functional rooms are of good size, with ample baths. Some sleep three or four, at a substantial saving over two separate rooms. The large, friendly breakfast room overlooks Les Rambles where, in summer, the hotel also runs an alfresco café.

Hotel Residencia Meson Castilla

Carrer Valdoncella 5, 08001 Barcelona. ☎ 3/318-21-82. Fax 3/412-4020. 56 rms, all with bath. TEL. 6,500 ptas. ($50) single; 9,250 ptas. ($71.15) double. AE, MC, V. Metro: Universitat.

If you appear at the door here looking harmless, the person at the desk will buzz the door open, which can be both reassuring and unsettling; however, the hotel is on a busy, largely residential square not far from the Plaça de Catalunya. The rooms and the restaurant are old-fashioned in decor, with lots of inept paintings and knotty paneling. TVs are available on request.

✪ Hotel San Agustin

Plaça Sant Agustí 3, 08001 Barcelona. ☎ 3/318-16-58. Fax 3/317-29-28. 77 rms, all with bath; 3 suites. A/C TV TEL. 5,800 ptas. ($44.60) single; 8,000 ptas. ($61.55) double; 10,100 ptas. ($77.70) triple; 13,900 ptas. ($106.90) two-room suite. Rates include breakfast. AE, MC, V. Metro: Liceu.

This may well be Barcelona's top-value hotel. A block west of Les Rambles, on a square shaded by a grove of plane trees, this building was built as a convent in 1740 and was converted to a hotel in 1840—making it the city's oldest, according to the management. The attractive lobby makes effective use of ancient stone-and-brick arches and a bank of windows overlooking the plaza. Some ceilings soar far overhead, while hand-hewn wood beams in other sections are consistent head-knockers. Each room renovated for the Olympics contains air conditioning, a radio, a minibar, and a TV with satellite channels. The baths are sheathed in marble, and some have hairdryers. Particularly good for families are the two-room suites with two baths. The brand-new attic rooms are very desirable: Ask for Rooms 401 to 408. The commendable restaurant offers three-course fixed-price lunch and dinner menus. Some staff members speak English. This is now a three-star hotel.

SUPER-BUDGET CHOICES
A YOUTH HOSTEL

Alberg Mare de Déu de Montserrat

Passeig Mare de Déu del Coll 41–51, 08023 Barcelona. Fax 3/213-86-33. 160 beds. 1,000 ptas. ($7.70) per person under 26 with youth-hostel card, 1,500 ptas. ($11.55) per person over 26 with youth-hostel card. Surcharge of 325 ptas. ($2.50) per night for six nights for those without youth-hostel card (applies toward purchase of card). Rates include breakfast. No credit cards. Metro: Vallcarca. Bus 25 or 28.

This hostel, with a colorfully Moorish lobby, occupies a former modernist mansion in a northern area of the city. You can find great views here and there. The hostel closes at midnight but opens its doors for night owls at 1am and 2am.

CAMPING

Campgrounds are rated luxury, first, second, and third class. All have the following facilities and basic services: drinking water, wash basins, showers, toilets, sinks, wash-houses, electricity, daily rubbish collection, fences, around-the-clock surveillance, medical assistance, a small pharmacy, safekeeping for valuables, and fire extinguishers. Most campgrounds offer special rates outside the peak season—June, July, and August—and discounts for children 9 and under.

For camping information and reservations, contact the **Asociación de Campings de Barcelona,** Central de Reservas (☎ **3/412-59-55;** fax 3/302-13-36).

LONG-TERM STAYS

Students can stay in any of these dormitory facilities open all year: **Residencia Universitaria "Athenea"** (women only, except summer), Baró de la Barre 5–7, 08023 Barcelona (☎ **3/210-72-53**); **Colegio Mayor "Bonaigua"** (women only), Jiménez i Iglesias 3, 08034 Barcelona (☎ **3/204-91-08**); **Residencia "Bonanova"** (men only), Camp 75, Bajos, 08022 Barcelona (☎ **3/417-52-21**); **Colegio Mayor C. D. "Influencia Católica"** (mixed), Santaló 27, 08021 Barcelona (☎ **3/209-04-00**); **Colegio Mayor Ramón Llull** (mixed), Comte d'Urgell 187, 08036 Barcelona (☎ **3/430-84-00**); and **Colegio Mayor Sant Raímon de Penyafort** (mixed), Avinguda Diagonal 643, 08028 Barcelona (☎ **3/330-87-11**).

WORTH THE EXTRA MONEY

Hotel R. Regencia Colón

Sangristans 13–17, 08002 Barcelona. ☎ **3/318-98-58.** Fax 3/317-28-22. 55 rms, all with bath. A/C MINIBAR TV TEL. 7,900 ptas. ($60.75) single; 13,500 ptas. ($103.85) double. AE, DC, MC, V. Metro: Urquinaona or Jaume I.

With the cathedral only a block away, this is a great location for exploring the Gothic Quarter. The lobby is soothingly understated, and the cheerful, sound-insulated rooms were fully redecorated for the Olympics. For reservations, contact Marketing Ahead, 433 Fifth Ave., New York, NY 10016 (☎ **212/686-9213**).

5 Dining

Eating well in Barcelona is easy. Eating inexpensively is a bit more challenging. The city's restaurants offer a wealth of dishes primarily Mediterranean in their basic ingredients—olive oil, almonds, garlic, aromatic herbs, and tomatoes. Sausages like the traditional *butifarra,* succulent roasts, robust game, delicate seafood, savory rice dishes and stews, and myriad renditions of mushrooms are the mainstays of the Catalan repertoire, often in such unusual combinations as fruit with poultry or shellfish with game. The highest concentrations of low-priced eateries are in Ciutat Vella.

Note: More and more restaurants are charging a "cover." Allegedly for bread and such, it's really just a way to boost the bill.

MEALS FOR LESS THAN 1,500 PTAS. ($11.55)

Cerveseria d'Dor

Consell de Cent 339. ☎ **93/216-02-41.** Under 1,500 ptas. ($11.50). AE, V. Mon–Sat 8am–1am. Metro: Passeig de Gràcia. SPANISH.

This reliable tapas bar/café has a long list of combination plates, filling one-dish meals usually costing under 1,000 ptas. ($7.70). Among the tastier tidbits lined up along the bar are crispy nuggets of creamy potatoes, zippy pork brochettes called pinxos morunos and empanadillas, slabs of chicken or tuna pie. German beers are featured, several on draft.

The Chicago Pizza Pie Factory

Carrer Provença 300. ☎ **93/215-94-15.** Pizzas 1,615–4,200 ptas. ($12.40–$32.30); main dishes under 1,350 ptas. ($10.40). AE, MC, V. Sun–Thurs 1pm–midnight, Fri–Sat 1pm–1:30am. Metro: Passeig de Gràcia. AMERICAN.

Here you'll find pizzas, of course, of both deep-dish and thin-crust varieties, but also salads, chili con carne, and fried chicken. Not exactly home, despite the Windy City street signs and team pennants, it's close enough to keep the place jumping with young Spaniards and Americans until well past midnight. From 6 to 9pm cocktails are two for one.

La Cuina

Sombrerers 13. No phone. Under 1,500 ptas. ($11.50). MC, V. Tues–Sun noon–4pm and 8–11pm. Metro: Jaume I. CATALAN/SPANISH.

Hard against the Santa María del Mar Church and only a short walk from the Picasso Museum, this neighborhood favorite has managed to avoid discovery by the tourist hordes. Prices remain low—the three-course *menu del día* is only 900 ptas. ($6.90). Upgrade to a better cut of meat or fish main course for only 350 ptas. ($2.70) more. The warming and substantial offerings include white beans with butifarra sausage.

La Finestra

Carrer de les Moles 25. ☎ **93/317-58-66.** *Menu del día* 1,100 ptas. ($8.45). No credit cards. Mon–Fri 8am–5pm. Metro: Plaça de Catalunya. CATALAN.

Tucked away on a narrow street two blocks east of Les Rambles, this attractive eatery is a large room adorned with tiles and flowers. It offers primarily fixed-price menus and daily specials at reasonable prices. Examples are smoked salmon on toast for 675 ptas ($5.20), beefsteak with garniture for 750 ptas ($5.80), and grilled jumbo shrimp for 1,200 ptas ($9.25). The choice of full breakfasts is another draw.

Getting the Best Deal on Dining

- Take advantage of the three-course *menu del día* offered at lunch in most restaurants and at dinner in some.

- Try eating or drinking standing up. Many establishments have two prices: *mesa* (table) and *barra* (bar).

✪ Govinda

Plaça Vila de Madrid 4–5 (off Carrer Canuda, near the top of Les Rambles). ☎ 93/ 318-77-29. Pizzas 760–1,050 ptas. ($5.85–$8.10); Indian dishes 1,000–1,155 ptas. ($7.70–$8.90); *menu del día* 1,155 ptas. ($8.90). AE, DC, MC, V. Tues–Sat 1–4pm and 8:30–11:45pm, Sun 1–4pm. Closed most of Aug. Metro: Plaça Catalunya. INDIAN/ VEGETARIAN.

Though largely Indian and completely vegetarian, the menu here holds some surprises—like pizzas, crêpes, and a conventional Spanish *menu del día* (available only at midday). The house specialty is thali, an array of various Indian dishes constituting a meal. Other choices are samosas, pakoras, and sapnam curry.

El Niagara

Carrer de los Moles 21 (off Carrer Comtal). ☎ 93/301-42-17. *Menus del día* 1,000 and 1,100 ptas. ($7.15 and $7.85). No credit cards. Mon–Fri 8am–5pm. Metro: Plaça de Catalunya. SPANISH.

Three-course *menus del día* are one possibility at this pleasant restaurant, where a medieval facade gives way to a contemporary interior decor. Others are the 10 *platos combinados,* Spanish versions of North American diner specials. They range from a roasted quarter chicken with salad, potatoes, and a fried egg for 725 ptas. ($5.60) to a steak with vegetables at 1,490 ptas. ($11.45). They also specialize in hearty salads.

Nuria

Les Rambles 133. ☎ 93/302-38-47. Under 1,500 ptas. ($11.50). MC, V. Daily 8am–1am. Metro: Plaça de Catalunya. SPANISH.

Never hard to find since its facade is forever plastered with signs, Nuria does its best to fulfill every need for sustenance or refreshment. Sandwiches, combination plates, tapas, pastries, and full meals are available most of the day and night. Typical choices for the three-course *menu del día*—at only 1,100 ptas. ($8.45)—are mixed vegetables or ravioli followed by grilled rabbit or roasted quarter-chicken, with dessert and wine or beer.

✪ Pinotxo

In La Boquería Market. ☎ 93/317-17-31. Under 1,500 ptas. ($11.50). No credit cards. Mon–Thurs 6am–5pm, Fri–Sat 6am–8pm. Closed hols and 20 days in Aug. Metro: Liceu. SPANISH.

To get to this Barcelona institution, enter the market and take a right. The sign for the place reads only BAR KIOSCO with a picture of Pinocchio (Pinotxo in Catalan, Pinocho in Spanish). There's no menu. The owner, Juanito, will gladly tender samples of what's cooking on the stove. Cold offerings include three fresh oysters with a glass of cava, the Catalan sparkling wine, for 550 ptas. ($4.25). It's a good place for breakfast too. As there are only eight stools, lingering too long is impolite.

✪ Pitarra

Carrer d'Avinyó 56. ☎ **93/301-16-47.** Main courses 700–1,975 ptas. ($5.40–$15.20); *menu del día* 1,075 ptas. ($8.30). AE, DC, MC, V. Mon–Sat 1–4pm and 8:30–11pm. Closed Aug. Metro: Liceu or Jaume I. CATALAN.

Pitarra occupies the former home and watch shop of the prolific and much hon-ored Catalan playwright/poet Federic Soler Hubert (pseudonym "Pitarra"). The atmosphere is friendly, the service attentive, and the food hearty. Look for the game dishes in winter. This newly renovated eatery offers good value. Given its location, however, deep in the Gothic Quarter, it might be best to use it for lunch rather than dinner.

✪ La Pizza Nostra

Carrer Montcada 29. ☎ **93/319-90-58.** Pizzas 835–1,365 ptas. ($6.40–$10.50); pastas 1,000–1,340 ptas. ($7.70–$10.30); *menu del día* 1,300 ptas. ($10.00). MC, V. Tues–Sun 10am–midnight. Metro: Jaume I. ITALIAN.

Within the walls of a medieval mansion on the same block as the Picasso Museum you can enjoy some of the best pizza in town, served up with all manner of exotic toppings. Salads are also available.

Qu Qu (Quasi Queviures)

Passeig de Gràcia 24. ☎ **93/317-45-12.** Under 1,500 ptas. ($11.55). AE, MC, V. Daily 8:30am–1am. Metro: Passeig de Gràcia. SPANISH.

This is one of the new breed of updated tapas bars showing up in Barcelona's better quarters (see Tapa Tapa, below). On the left is a take-out counter for meats, sal-ads, and pastas; on the right, a bar for the consumption of the truly delectable tapas; in the back, a sit-down section for light meals. Try the torradas, Catalan bread rubbed with tomatoes, drizzled with oil, and layered with a variety of toppings like air-cured ham or chopped asparagus with garlic. Funky jazz and alternative rock on the stereo proclaim that this isn't your grandparents' tapas joint.

✪ Self Naturista

Carrer de Santa Anna 11–15. ☎ **93/318-23-88.** Main courses 260–590 ptas. ($2–$4.55); *menu del día* 810 ptas. ($6.25). No credit cards. Mon–Sat 11:30am–10pm. Closed hols. Metro: Plaça Catalunya. VEGETARIAN.

Off the upper Rambles, this crisp self-service vegetarian restaurant is as good as it gets in quality and price. The munificent selection of salads, main courses, and desserts varies daily, and there's a healthy choice of fresh fruit juices. Seating is McDonald's style in a large dining room with a window on the street.

Tapa Tapa

Passeig de Gràcia 44. ☎ **93/488-33-69.** Tapas 180–1,000 ptas. ($1.40–$7.70); casseroles 290–995 ptas. ($2.25–$7.65). AE, MC, V. Mon–Fri 8am–1am, Sat 9am–2am, Sun 11am–2am. Metro: Plaça Catalunya. TAPAS.

Slick, gleaming, and contemporary, this popular tapas emporium sets the pace for a new breed of restaurant. With its sidewalk tables, twin long bars open to the street, and large elevated dining room, this place is perfect for all conventional meals and snacks. They claim 80 different tapas, with daily specials. Food and drink costs more at the tables than at the bar.

El Turia

Carrer Petxina 7. ☎ **93/317-95-09.** Main courses 500–1,400 ptas. ($3.85–$10.80); *menu del día* 850 ptas. ($6.55). MC, V. Mon–Sat 1–4pm and 8:30–11pm. Closed Aug 16–Sept 15, and for dinner on hols. Metro: Liceu. SPANISH.

Especially lively at lunch, this restaurant is frequented by actors, writers, and other arts professionals who live and work nearby. The fare is simple and uneven, featuring grilled meats. Find it down the lightly used street just below La Boquería.

Xarcuteria L. Simó

Passeig de Gràcia 46 (opposite the modernist "Block of Discord"). ☎ **93/216-03-39.** Under 1,500 ptas. ($11.50). No credit cards. Daily 8am–9pm. Metro: Passeig de Gràcia. CATALAN/SPANISH.

Keep this place in mind for a sandwich lunch at the rear bar or for assembling a picnic from the take-out section in front. A glass case to the left is filled with cheeses, smoked fishes, pâtés, and various salads.

MEALS FOR LESS THAN 2,500 PTAS. ($19.25)

Egipte

Carrer Jerusalem 3. ☎ **93/317-74-08.** Main courses 1,025–1,655 ptas. ($7.90–$12.75); *menu del día* 935 ptas. ($7.20). AE, DC, MC, V. Mon–Sat 1–4pm and 8pm–midnight. Closed hols. Metro: Liceu. CATALAN/SPANISH.

Not to be confused with the bar down the street or the more expensive restaurant on Les Rambles, this Egipte has nothing to do with the Middle East. Its food is strictly Spanish, with a few idiosyncratic touches—a cherry on the mashed potatoes for one. The bilevel space fills to the walls most nights, with not only bargain-seekers but also businesspeople and suburbanites who love its comfort food. Among the favorites are gazpacho, chicken with mustard-herb sauce, and veal scallops with mushrooms.

Moka

Les Rambles 126. ☎ **93/302-68-86.** Main courses 785–2,400 ptas. ($6–$18.45); *menu del día* 1,300–1,680 ptas. ($10–$12.90). V. Daily 8am–1:30am. Metro: Plaça Catalunya. INTERNATIONAL.

This airy, bright place next to the Hotel Rivoli Rambla features salads and pastas, but the best deals are the combination plates. The top choice for variety and price is the 1,200-pta. ($9.25) Catalan combo, with a dozen typical items crowding the plate. Otherwise, main courses cover the usual range of fish and meats.

La Poma

In the Royal Hotel, Les Rambles 117. ☎ **93/301-94-00.** Main courses 1,000–2,300 ptas. ($7.70–$17.70); *menu del día* 1,500 ptas. ($11.55). MC, V. Downstairs, daily 9am–1am. Upstairs, daily 1–4pm and 8–11pm. Metro: Plaça Catalunya. INTERNATIONAL.

This bilevel hotel restaurant facing Les Rambles features salads, pizzas, and pastas downstairs and somewhat more formal Catalan and Spanish meals upstairs. It's convenient and lively rather than a gastronomic experience.

Les Quinze Nits

Plaça Reial 6. ☎ **93/317-30-75.** Main courses 900–2,200 ptas. ($6.90–$16.90); fixed-price meal 950 ptas. ($7.30). AE, MC, V. Daily 1–3:45pm and 6:30–11:45pm. Metro: Liceu. SPANISH/CATALAN.

If you choose recklessly from the à la carte menu, a meal can sail past budget parameters, so stick with the fixed-price deals, as most people do. The large front room overlooks the plaza, with tables outside most of the year. A smaller, quieter room in back suits couples who don't have a need to be seen (this place attracts chic nightbirds). An earnest, if not always precise, young staff swiftly brings on such edibles as spinach-filled canneloni under a blanket of melted cheese and tender beef filet with shoestring potatoes. Good bread, passable house wines.

THE CHAINS

Burger King has two outposts: Les Rambles 135, near Plaça Catalunya (☎ **93/302-54-29**), and Passeig de Gràcia 4, on the opposite side of Plaça Catalunya (☎ **93/317-18-57**), both open Sunday through Thursday from 10am to 12:30am, Friday from 10am to 1:30am, and Saturday from noon to 1:30am.

Kentucky Fried Chicken, Les Rambles 60, offers three pieces of chicken for 560 ptas. ($4.30) and combination platters for 580 to 730 ptas. ($3.85 to $5.60). It's open Sunday through Thursday from 11am to midnight and Friday and Saturday from 11am to 1am.

McDonald's, offering hamburgers for 160 to 370 ptas. ($1.25 to $2.85), has several Barcelona outposts. The three most central are Carrer de Pelai 62, near Plaça Catalunya (☎ **93/318-29-90**); Les Rambles 62; and Portal de l'Angel 36. All are open Monday through Thursday from 10am to midnight and Friday and Saturday from 11am to midnight,

Pizza Hut has numerous branches, including those at Avinguda Diagonal 646 (☎ **93/280-19-14**); Urgel 239 (☎ **93/410-62-20**); Passeig de Gràcia 125–127 (☎ **93/238-30-05**); Rambla de Catalunya 91–93 (☎ **93/487-31-08**); and Avinguda Paralelo 87 (☎ **93/241-73-04**).

Pans & Company is a chain of sandwich restaurants with outposts throughout the city that are open Monday through Saturday from 9am to midnight and Sunday from 10am to midnight. You can eat well here, with good, crispy bread, for under 1,000 ptas. ($7.70). Similar domestic fast-food operations are **Bocatta** and **Pokin's.**

PICNICKING

Found in almost every neighborhood, *xarcuterias* (*charcuterias* in Spanish) specialize in sausages, meats, and cheeses and usually have bottles of wine and stocks of canned goodies that complement a picnic. One of the most atmospheric is **La Pineda**, at Carrer del Pi 16, near the Plaça del Pi; **L. Simó,** described above, also offers prepared salads. Or you can stock up on everything at the incomparable **La Boquería market** on Les Rambles.

Wherever you load up on supplies, head for the **Parc de la Ciutadella** or the **park at the Montjuïc end of the Transbordador del Puerto**.

WORTH THE EXTRA MONEY

Set Portes (Siete Puertas)

Passeig Isabel II 14. ☎ **93/319-29-50.** Reservations required on weekends. Main courses 900–2,900 ptas. ($6.90–$22.30). Daily 1pm–1am. Metro: Barceloneta. CATALAN/SPANISH.

This is Barcelona's oldest restaurant, with over 150 years behind it, and still one of the most popular. These "seven doors" open onto as many rooms, with smaller salons on the second floor. Cloth-covered hanging lamps provide a peachy glow for the crowd of businesspeople, trendies, families, and tourists, served by an efficient and attentive staff. House specialties are rice dishes, including paella, and the Catalan combinations of fruit with seafood or meats. Careful selection (avoiding the costly shellfish and crustaceans) can keep your meal cost near budget levels. Most nights, a piano player enhances the jolly mood.

6 Attractions

SIGHTSEEING SUGGESTIONS

Even if you don't have time to visit a single museum or monument, take a stroll along Les Rambles. The spectacle is real street theater.

If You Have 1 Day

In the morning, stroll along Les Rambles, where Spain's *paseo* (*passeig* in Catalan) tradition runs from the seedy to the sublime, and take in the Columbus Monument and the eye-filling La Boquería market. In the afternoon, head for the Museu Picasso and the cathedral.

If You Have 2 Days

Spend the first day as suggested above. On the morning of the second, visit La Sagrada Família and stroll along Passeig de Gràcia to see some of the masterpieces of modernist architecture. In the afternoon, head for Montjuïc and visit the fortress overlooking the city and harbor, the Museu d'Art de Catalunya (if it's finally reopened after its long restoration), the Fundació Joan Miró, and the Poble Espanyol.

If You Have 3 Days

Spend the first two days as indicated above. On the third morning, head north to the Museu-Monestir de Pedralbes and Museu de Cerámica and spend the afternoon wandering around the Barri Gòtic and visiting the Saló del Tinell, Capilla de Santa Agueda, Museu Frederic Marès, and Museu de l'Historia de la Ciutat.

If You Have 5 Days

Spend the first three days as indicated above. On the fourth day, explore the Ribera barrio, visiting its Santa María del Mar Church and Museu Textil i d'Indumentària (opposite the Museu Picasso). Then stroll through the Parc de la Ciutadella and visit the zoo. Have lunch in Barceloneta and, weather permitting, take to the beach or stroll along the waterfront's Moll de la Fusta and make a trip in *Las Golodrinas*—harbor sightseeing boats.

On the fifth day, tour the Eixample district to see the results of the Catalan *modernisme* movement and pay a visit to Parc Güell in the morning. Then go to the top of Tibidabo Mountain for a late lunch and spend the afternoon enjoying the views and, if you've brought children along, the amusement park.

TOP ATTRACTIONS

All Barcelona's municipal museums are free for those under 18, students with international ID cards, and members of the International Council of Museums (ICOM). Municipal museums are closed January 1 and 6, April 12 and 19, May 1 and 31, June 24, September 11 and 24, October 12, November 1, and December 6, 8, and 25. Nearly all museums are closed on Monday, though many now stay open through the afternoon siesta period, when most stores are closed.

Catedral de Barcelona

Plaça de la Seu. ☎ **93/315-35-55.** Cathedral and cloister, free; Museu de la Catedral, 55 ptas. (40¢). Cathedral, daily 7:45am–1:30pm and 4–7:45pm; museum, daily 11am–1pm. Metro: Jaume I. Bus 16, 17, 19, 22, or 45.

Barcelona

BARCELONA

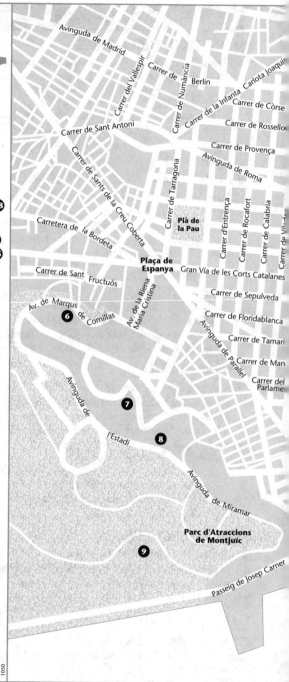

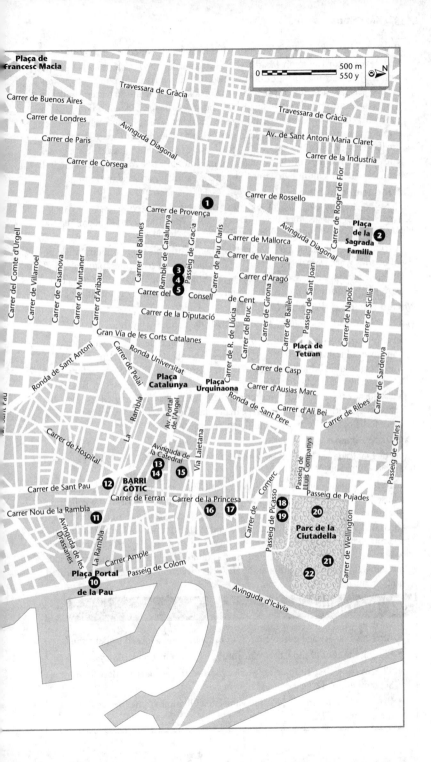

Begun at the end of the 13th century and completed around the mid-15th century (except for the main facade, which dates from the late 19th), this gothic cathedral reflects the splendor of medieval Barcelona. Its main points of interest are the central choir; the crypt of Santa Eulàlia, whose white alabaster sepulcher is of 14th-century Italian craftsmanship; and the *Cristo de Lepanto*, whose twisted torso allegedly dodged a bullet during the naval battle of the same name. A most popular feature is the adjoining cloister, which encloses palm trees, magnolias, medlars, a fountain erupting from a moss-covered rock, and a gaggle of live geese, said to be reminders of the Roman occupation. Try not to miss the cathedral exterior when it's illuminated on a Thursday, Saturday, or Sunday evening.

✪ Fundació Joan Miró

Plaça Neptú, Parc de Montjuïc. ☎ **93/329-19-08.** Admission 500 ptas. ($3.85) adults, 250 ptas. ($1.90) students. Tues–Wed and Fri–Sat 11am–7pm, Thurs 11am–9:30pm, Sun and hols (Mon hols too) 10:30am–2:30pm. Bus 61 from Plaça Espanya.

A tribute to the Catalan lyrical surrealist Joan Miró, this contemporary museum follows his work from 1914 to 1978 and includes many sculptures, paintings, and multimedia tapestries. Even the roof is space for his whimsical sculptures. Temporary exhibitions of other contemporary artists are also held on a regular basis.

Museu Nacional d'Art de Catalunya

Palau Nacional, Parc de Montjuïc. ☎ **93/423-71-99.** Metro: Espanya.

In this building—built for the 1929 World's Fair and newly designed inside by controversial Italian architect Gae Aulenti—is a collection of Catalan art from the romanesque and gothic periods as well as the 16th to the 18th century, along with a smattering of works by such high-caliber non-Catalan artists as El Greco, Velázquez, Zurbarán, and Tintoretto. The museum has been closed for years for restoration, with the reopening repeatedly delayed. Recent plans are for the galleries to be opened as they're completed, but call ahead.

✪ Museu Picasso

Carrer de Montcada 15–19. ☎ **93/319-63-10.** Admission 500 ptas. ($3.85). Tues–Sat and hols 10am–8pm, Sun 10am–3pm. Metro: Jaume I.

Barcelona's most popular attraction, this museum reveals much about the artist whose long, prolific career extended well beyond cubism. Most of the collection of paintings, drawings, engravings, and ceramics relate to the artist's earliest years, when he lived and studied in Barcelona and spent summers in Catalan hilltowns. Visitors expecting to see anything further than hints of Picasso's more famous works may be disappointed. The museum is housed in three adjoining Renaissance mansions that are as interesting as the artworks they contain. A new café has proved quite popular.

❓ Did You Know?

- After his first voyage to the New World, Columbus returned to Barcelona.
- Raising the roof of the Palau Sant Jordi took 12 cranes and 10 days.
- The world's first submarine was immersed in the port of Barcelona on September 23, 1859.
- Barcelona bid for the 1924, 1936, and 1972 Olympic Games before winning the honor in 1992.

✪ La Sagrada Família

Carrer de Mallorca 401. ☎ **93/455-02-47.** Admission: Cathedral, 630 ptas. ($4.85); elevator, 315 ptas. ($2.40). Nov–Feb, daily 9am–6pm; Mar–Apr and Oct, daily 9am–7pm; May and Sept, daily 9am–8pm; June–Aug, daily 9am–9pm. Metro: Sagrada Família. Bus 19, 34, 43, 50, 51, or 54.

An ambitious work in perpetual progress, this modernist rendition of a cathedral will, if finished, be Europe's largest. Work began on the Church of the Holy Family in 1882; two years later architect Antoni Gaudí i Cornet took over and projected a temple of immense proportions—the central dome is slated to be 525 feet high. His vision, as seen in other commissions of his around the city, amounts to a flamboyant surrealism composed of extensive stonecarving and iron and ceramic work. At the pinnacles of the completed towers, for example, are vivid sunbursts of gold and crimson mosaics. Controversy swirls around the cathedral's completion: Since Gaudí died in 1926 leaving no detailed plans, construction has continued by fits and starts, and the style and direction of recent additions aren't to everyone's liking. One of the towers has an elevator that ascends to a magnificent view. The Museu del Templo in the crypt chronicles the cathedral's structural evolution.

MORE ATTRACTIONS

Monument à Colom (Columbus Monument)

Plaça Portal de la Pau. ☎ **93/302-52-24.** Admission 210 ptas. ($1.60) adults, 110 ptas. (85¢) children 4–12 and senior citizens over 60, free for children 3 and under. June 24–Sept 24, daily 9am–9pm; Sept 25–June 23, Tues–Sat 10am–2pm and 3:30–6:30pm, Sun and hols 10am–7pm. Metro: Drassanes.

This waterfront landmark, erected for the 1888 Universal Exhibition, commemorates Columbus's triumphant return after his first expedition to the New World. After sailing into Barcelona, he delivered news of his discoveries to Queen Isabel and King Ferdinand. A 25-foot-high bronze statue of the explorer surmounts the Victorian-era monument. Oddly, it has been positioned so that he's pointing vaguely off to Africa, rather than the New World. Inside the iron column on which he stands is a creaking elevator that ascends to give you a panoramic view.

✪ Fundació Antoni Tàpies

Carrer Aragó 255. ☎ **93/487-03-15.** Admission 400 ptas. ($3.10). Tues–Sun 10am–8pm. Metro: Passeig de Gràcia.

Housed in a *modernista* building designed by Lluís Domènech i Montaner and refurbished by his great-grandson in 1989, this museum continues the Barcelona tradition of honoring prominent native artists. Tàpies is thought by many to be the living heir to Miró and Picasso, and this exhibition space rotates examples of his work, as well as that of younger Catalan artists. The tangle of tubing atop the building is a Tàpies sculpture called *Chair and Cloud.*

Galería Olímpica

Passeig Olímpica. ☎ **93/426-06-60.** Admission 325 ptas. ($2.50). Apr–Sept, Tues–Sat 10am–2pm and 4–8pm, Sun and hols 10am–2pm; Oct–Mar, Tues–Sat 10am–1pm and 4–6pm, Sun and hols 10am–2pm. Metro: Plaça Espanya. Bus 61 from Plaça Espanya.

Located in the Olympic Stadium, this exhibit lets vistors share the medalists' joy, run the last torch relay, stay in the Olympic Village—in short, relive the highlights of the 1992 Summer Olympic Games. Facilities include a photo and video library, a reading room, an auditorium, a gift shop, and a picnic area.

Las Golondrinas

☎ **93/412-59-44.** Admission 350 ptas. ($2.50). Mon–Fri at 11am, 1pm, and 4pm; Sat, Sun, and hols at 11am, 1pm, 4pm, and 6pm (the last until Aug 28). Metro: Drassanes.

Both children and adults enjoy the 30-minute round-trip boat ride from the Portal de la Pau, near the Monument à Colom, to the harbor breakwater and back.

✪ Gran Teatre del Liceu

Les Rambles 61–65. ☎ **93/318-91-22.** Metro: Liceu.

Barcelona's majestic opera house dates from the mid-19th century. A study in Victorian opulence, it features an entrance hall with blue silk walls, a sweeping staircase leading to a salon of mirrors, and one of Europe's largest stages. Destroyed by fire not long after completion, it was rebuilt in under a year. A January 1994 fire caused similar damage, but repairs are taking much longer. Even optimistic estimates set the reopening for 1997.

Museu d'Art Modern

Parc de la Ciutadella. ☎ **93/319-57-28.** Admission 500 ptas. ($3.85). Wed–Sun 9am–9pm. Metro: Arc de Triomf.

This museum focuses on the work of Catalan painters and sculptors who worked during the *modernista* period (ca. 1880–1930), along with some fine examples of furniture and decorative arts.

Museu de Ceramicà

Avinguda Diagonal 686. ☎ **93/280-16-21.** Admission 250 ptas. ($1.90). Tues–Sun 10am–2pm. Bus 61 from Plaça Espanya.

Located in a 1920s palace, the collection here traces the history of Spanish ceramics from the 13th century to the present. Included are a few Moorish pieces and plates executed by Picasso and Miró. This museum is considered one of the most important of its kind in Europe. The building sits on attractive parklike grounds that are worth a visit by themselves.

Museu Marítim

Plaça Portal de la Pau 1. ☎ **93/318-32-45.** Admission 200 ptas. ($1.55). Tues–Sat 9:30am–1pm and 4–7pm, Sun and hols 10am–2pm. Metro: Drassanes.

Installed in the Drassanes, the 14th-century royal shipyards, this museum's superb collection of maritime vessels and artifacts is distinguished by a full-size replica of Don Juan of Austria's galleon, the marvelously baroque flagship of the Spanish and Italian fleet that defeated a naval force of the Ottoman Empire in the 1571 Battle of Lepanto. There are also humbler fishing boats, many intricate ship models, and a map owned by Amerigo Vespucci.

✪ Museu-Monestir de Pedralbes

Baixada del Monestir 9. ☎ **93/203-92-82.** Admission 250 ptas. ($1.90). Tues–Fri and Sun 10am–2pm, Sat 10am–5pm. Closed Good Fri, May 1, June 24, and Dec 25–26. Bus 22 or 64. FF.CC.: Line Sarrià–Reina Elisenda to the Reina Elisenda stop.

This 14th-century monastery boasting beautiful stained-glass windows was founded by Queen Elisenda de Montcada, whose sepulcher is inside the early gothic church. The cloisters provide glimpses of several monk's cells, an apothecary, a kitchen that was in use until recently, a 16th-century infirmary, and St. Michael's Chapel, which features murals from the 14th century. A newly renovated wing houses over 80 medieval paintings and sculptures from the Thyssen-Bornemisza collection, the bulk of which is now housed in its own museum in Madrid.

Museu Textil i d'Indumentària
Carrer de Montcada 12–14. ☎ **93/310-45-16.** Admission 250 ptas. ($1.90). Tues–Sat 10am–5pm, Sun and hols 10am–2pm. Metro: Jaume. Bus 16, 17, or 45.

Occupying two 13th-century gothic palaces opposite the Museu Picasso (above), this museum contains a collection of textiles spanning ancient times to the 20th century. Particularly impressive are the clothing and accessories from the 18th to the 20th century and the lace collection from the 16th. The manufacture of textiles was central to Barcelona's participation in the Industrial Revolution. A pleasant courtyard café invites lingering.

○ Poble Espanyol
Avinguda Marqués de Comillas, Montjuïc. ☎ **93/325-78-66.** Admission 650 ptas. ($5) adults, 300 ptas. ($2.30) children 7–14, free for children 6 and under. Mon 9am–8pm, Tues–Thurs and Sun 9am–2am, Fri–Sat 9am–4pm. Bus 61 from Plaça Espanya or free double-decker Poble Espanyol shuttle.

This consolidated "village" of examples of the varied architectural styles found throughout Spain was conceived and executed for the 1929 World's Fair. After substantial renovations and alterations in operational philosophy, it's now much more than an open-air museum. In fact, it has become almost a village in its own right, with working artisans, many crafts shops, restaurants, and assorted nightclubs and bars, a few of which are much in vogue.

PARKS & GARDENS

The **Parc de la Ciutadella** occupies the former site of a detested citadel, some remnants of which remain. Here, too, are found the Museu d'Art Modern, the Museu de Zoología, the Museu de Geología, the Parliament, the zoo, and an ornate fountain that's in small part the work of young Gaudí.

The **Parc Güell,** in the northern rim of the Gràcia section, was to be an upper-crust development of 60 homes with a full complement of roads, markets, and schools. Financed by Eusebi Güell and designed by Gaudí, the project was aborted after only two houses and a smattering of public areas were built. One of the two houses is now the Casa-Museu Gaudí. Don't miss the park's entrance stairway, the Hall of a Hundred Columns, and the view from the plaza above.

STROLLING AROUND TOWN

MODERNIST BARCELONA   Architecture enthusiasts may want to explore modernist Barcelona. Brochures with suggested itineraries of the most important examples of this turn-of-the-century style, a Catalan version of art nouveau, are available from the tourist information offices (see "Visitor Information" under "Barcelona Specifics," earlier in this chapter).

THE BARRI GÒTIC   This two-hour walk takes in the quarter's most important structures. Begin at **Plaça Nova,** near the cathedral, where there are remnants of the Roman wall. As you walk up the ramp between the cylindrical Roman towers into the Carrer del Bisbe, the first building on your left is the **Casa de l'Ardiaca (Archbishop's House).** Its 18th-century portal opens onto an attractive courtyard with romanesque construction below and gothic above. At the top of the stairway is a patio with a 13th-century mural and a splendid coffered ceiling. The courtyard is open to the public daily from 10am to 1:30pm.

Opposite the Casa de l'Ardiaca on Carrer Santa Llúcia is the romanesque doorway to the **Capilla de Santa Llúcia** (open daily from 8am to 1:30pm and

4 to 7:30pm), a vestige of the 11th-century cathedral that preceded the current one. Walk through the chapel and exit at the far side, then enter the cathedral cloisters (see "Top Attractions," above). After a circuit of the cloisters, enter the cathedral proper and walk through it and out the main entrance.

Turn right, then right again, and proceed up Carrer dels Comtes (look up to see some classic gothic gargoyles); make yet another right along Carrer de la Pietat behind the cathedral. Leading off to the left is Carrer Paradís, where inside the **Centre Excursionista de Catalunya** (no. 10) are surviving columns of the city's largest Roman temple, which honored Augustus. Return to Carrer de la Pietat and continue to the left behind the cathedral.

Turn left on Carrer del Bisbe Irurita and walk to Plaça de Sant Jaume. On the right is the **Palau de la Generalitat,** seat of the regional Catalan government; its main 16th-century Renaissance facade faces the plaza and the **Casa de la Ciutat (City Hall),** whose 19th-century neoclassic facade supersedes a gothic one. To the left off Carrer de la Ciutat runs the narrow Carrer d'Hercules, leading into **Plaça Sant Just.** Notice the 18th-century mansions with the sgraffito decoration and the Sants Just i Pastor Church.

Now turn left onto Carrer Dagueria, cross Carrer Jaume I and Carrer de la Llibretería, and continue along Carrer Frenería. Turn right onto the Baixada de Santa Clara and in a few yards enter the enclosed **Plaça del Rei.** At that corner is the **Palau Reial Major,** the former residence of the comtes (counts) de Barcelona and the kings of Aragón. The staircase with semicircular risers at the opposite corner leads up to (on the left) the **Saló del Tinell,** where Queen Isabel and King Ferdinand are said to have received Columbus upon his return from the New World, and (on the right) the **Capilla de Santa Agata,** built atop the Roman wall and featuring a handsome 15th-century retablo.

Turn right on Carrer del Veguer to the entrance of the **Museu de l'Historia de la Ciutat** (☎ 93/315-11-11), open Monday through Saturday from 10am to 2pm and 4 to 8pm and Sunday and holidays from 10am to 2pm. Admission is 325 ptas. ($2.50). Housed in a 15th-century mansion that was moved here stone by stone from Carrer Mercaders, several blocks away, this museum features below-ground excavations of Roman and Visigothic remains and on its upper floors a gallimaufry of sculptures, weapons, ceramics, household implements, and more—a sort of municipal attic.

Returning to the Baixada de Santa Clara, turn right on Carrer dels Comtes. Alongside the cathedral in Plaça de Sant Iu is the **Museu Frederic Marès** (☎ 93/310-58-00), open Monday through Saturday from 10am to 5pm and Sunday and holidays from 10am to 2pm; admission is 325 ptas. ($2.50). It houses the eclectic collection of antiquities and curios of benefactor Mares, a Catalan sculptor. At the far end of the exterior courtyard is a section of Roman wall.

TOURS

AERIAL TOURS   The Montjuïc cable car, the Transbordador del Puerto, and the Tibidabo funicular are fine ways to survey the city, sea, and surrounding mountains from on high.

BUS TOURS   From June 12 to October 12, look for the bargain **bus no. 100,** called the **Bus Turístic.** A single ticket permits unlimited travel on this special tourist bus, the Montjuïc funicular and cable car, and Tibidabo's *tramvía blau.* Originating at Plaça de Catalunya, bus no. 100 makes a sweep of the entire city,

Barri Gòtic

Plaça Nova ❶

Avinguda Catedral

Plaça de Antoni Maura

Carrer de la Tapineria

Plaça de la Seu ❹

✝ ❷ ❸

❺ ❻

Carrer del Bisbe

Via Laietana

Catedral

Carrer de la Pietat

Sant Honorat

Plaça de Ramón Berenguer el Gran

❼

Plaça del Rei

❿

Palau de la Generalitat

❽

Carrer dels Comtes

❾

Carrer del Paradis

Carrer de la Tapineria

Carrer de

⓫

Carrer de la Llibreteria

Baixada de la Llibreteria

Plaça de Sant Jaume ⓭

Arlet

⓬

JAUME 1 Ⓜ

Carrer de Sant Jaume I

Carrer de la Ciutat

Carrer de

Carrer d'Hércules

Carrer Dagueria

Via Laietana

Church ✝■

Plaça de Sant Just

✝■ ⓮

Plaça de Emili Vilanova

Carrer del Sots-Tinent Navarro

Metro Ⓜ

Palma de Sant Just

Carrer dels Lledó

1051

BARCELONA

Barri Gòtic

passing through the Barri Gòtic, along Les Rambles and Passeig de Gràcia, by La Sagrada Família, along Avinguda del Tibidabo and Avinguda Diagonal, by the Estació Sants, through the Parc de Montjuïc, and along the Passeig de Colom. It makes 15 stops along its 2-hour route, and passengers can get off and reboard as often as they please. This bus runs from June 11 to October 12, daily every 20 minutes from 9am to 9:30pm. An all-day ticket costs 1,000 ptas. ($7.70); a half-day ticket, valid after 2pm, costs 700 ptas. ($5.40); and a ticket good for 2 consecutive days costs 1,500 ptas. ($11.55). Tickets are available on the bus.

Both **Julia Tours** (☎ **93/317-64-54**) and **Pullmantur** (☎ **93/317-12-97**) offer guided bus tours starting at 3,580 ptas. ($26.95).

TOMBBUS links Plaça Reina María Cristina with Plaça Catalunya. This modern vehicle with a comfortable 18-seat interior and a telephone makes 28 stops. Frequency is every five minutes between 8:45am and 21:40pm. The fare is 160 ptas. ($1.25).

TAXI TOUR   Barcelona Taxi Turistic (☎ **93/268-48-67**) offers routes both within the city and beyond. Call for current prices.

7 Shopping

Barcelona's value-added tax, known as IVA in Spain, is now 7% for most items and services. VAT recovery is possible for residents of countries outside the European Union on single purchases of more than 78,800 ptas. ($606).

There are two ways to recover the tax: When leaving from Barcelona's El Prat Airport, present the store's signed and stamped official bill—along with your passport and the article(s) purchased—for endorsement at Spanish Customs before check-in. The Customs official will return the duly signed blue copy of the bill. Present this to the Banco Exterior de España offices inside the airport terminal and they'll refund the tax in the currency of your choice. The other possibility is to mail the blue copy of the bill endorsed by the Customs official to the store and wait for a check to be sent to your home within (one hopes) 60 days.

The **main shopping streets** in the Old Town are Avinguda Portal de l'Angel, Carrer Portaferrissa, Carrer del Pi, Carrer de la Palla, and Carrer Pelai. In the Eixample they are Passeig de Gràcia and Rambla de Catalunya; in the northern reaches of town, Avinguda de la Diagonal, Vía Augusta, Travessera de Gràcia, Carrer de Balmes, and Carrer Muntaner.

The big department stores are **El Cortes Inglés,** Plaça Catalunya 14 (☎ **93/302-12-12**) and Avinguda de la Diagonal 617–619 (☎ **93/419-52-06**), and **Galerías Preciados,** Avinguda Portal de l'Àngel 19–21 (☎ **93/317-00-00**) and Avinguda de la Diagonal 471–473 (☎ **93/322-30-11**). Both are open Monday through Friday from 10am to 8pm and Saturday from 10am to 9pm. They don't close for the afternoon siesta.

Barcelona's strengths are fashion and design, examples of which are nearly always costly. **Vinçon,** Passeig de Gràcia 96 (☎ **93/215-60-50**), carries the latest gadgets and home furnishings. A number of shops offer authentic ceramics from prominent regions of the country, as well as from Morocco. Three worthwhile possibilities are **La Caixa de Frang**, on Carrer Freneria, behind the cathedral; **Itaca**, on Carrer Ferrán, near Plaça Sant Jaume (☎ **93/301-3044**); and **Molsa**, on Plaça Sant Josep Oriol (☎ **93/302-3103**). Several bookstores carry

English-language volumes, but **Come In Bookshop**, Provença 203 (☎ **93/253-1204**), specializes in British and American travel guides, novels, and nonfiction.

MARKETS   La Boquería, officially the Mercat de Sant Josep, is one of Europe's cleanest, most extensive, and most fascinating produce markets. Antiques lovers will enjoy the open-air **Mercat Gòtic de Antigüedades** by the cathedral, held every Thursday from 9am to 8pm (except during August).

8 Barcelona After Dark

Barcelona's nightlife runs from the campy burlesque of El Molino to the bizarre opulence of the Palau de la Música Catalana. For the latest information on concerts and other musical events, call the **Amics de la Música de Barcelona** (☎ **93/302-68-70** Monday through Friday from 10am to 1pm and 3 to 8pm). For information on performances by the **Ballet Contemporáneo de Barcelona,** call 93/322-10-37. For a comprehensive listing of evening activities, pick up a copy of the weekly *Guía del Ocio* or the entertainment guide offered with the Thursday edition of *El País*. For a guide to the gay scene, pick up a map of gay Barcelona at **Sextienda,** Carrer Raurich 11.

Unfortunately, the **Gran Teatre del Liceu,** home to opera and ballet, recently suffered a devastating fire and it's not expected to reopen until 1997 or later.

THE PERFORMING ARTS

Palau de la Música
Catalana, Amadeu Vives 1. ☎ **93/268-10-00** for reservations. Tickets 650–5,250 ptas. ($5–$40.40). Metro: Urquinaona.

This magnificent modernist concert hall is the work of Catalan architect Lluís Domènech i Montaner, a rival of Antoni Gaudí. Its distinctive facade is a tour de force of brick, mosaic, and glass. However, the drama and elegance found within are what truly set it apart from its peers. The interplay of ceramic mosaics, stained glass, and a central skylight build to the stunning crescendo of massive, dramatic carvings framing the stage. Throughout the year a variety of classical and jazz concerts and recitals are held here.

MUSIC CLUBS

At nightfall, the **Poble Espanyol** switches from museum village to entertainment complex, offering everything from jazz to flamenco to discos to designer bars. The latest rage here is the **Torres de Avila** bar, conceived by the white-hot designers Marisol and Arribas and installed in one of the fake fortified towers near the main entrance. On warm nights, head for the open-air roof for a spangled city view. Nurse the drinks, which run about 800 to 1,200 ptas. ($6.15 to $9.25).

Also commendable is **El Tablao de Carmen,** Poble Espanyol, Arcos 9 (☎ **93/325-68-95**). This is the best place in Barcelona to see flamenco, which isn't much of a compliment. The passionate traditional dance of southern Spain is seen to better advantage in Seville, the capital of Andalucia; however, this will do as a substitute if you can't make it to the south. Admission is 7,000 ptas. ($53.85) for dinner and the first show, 4,000 ptas. ($30.75) for the first show and one drink. Dinner begins at 9pm; the first show is at 10:30pm, the second at 1am.

La Cova del Drac
Carrer Vallmajor 33. ☎ **93/200-70-32.** No cover. Metro: Muntaner or La Bonanova.

A reliable venue for top-drawer jazz performers, the Cave of the Dragon is in a less intimidating neighborhood than the Harlem Jazz Club (below), with many other fun spots on nearby blocks. Open daily from 8pm to 3am.

Harlem Jazz Club

Comtessa Sobradiel 8. ☎ **93/310-07-55.** No cover. Metro: Jaume I.

This Barri Gòtic hole-in-the-wall fills with aficionados who come for the music, not the setting. Open Tuesday through Sunday from 7pm to 3am; live performances are Tuesday through Thursday at 10 and 11:30pm, Friday and Saturday at 11pm and midnight, and Sunday at 9:30 and 11pm.

FILMS

Most first-run movies are dubbed into Spanish. The following cinemas often show English-language films: **Arkadin,** Travessa de Gràcia 103 (☎ **93/218-62-42**); **Casablanca I & II,** Passeig de Gràcia 115 (☎ **93/218-43-45**); **Malda,** Carrer del Pi 5 (☎ **93/317-85-29**); and **Verdi,** Verdi 32 (☎ **93/237-05-16**). Look for the legend *v.o. subtitulada* on movie posters, indicating Spanish subtitles.

THE BAR SCENE

In summer, the lower end of Rambla de Catalunya blossoms with outdoor café/bars. The bars of Carrer Santaló, near Plaça de Francesc Macià on the Diagonal, are popular with the younger crowd. Passeig del Born, near the Museu Picasso, has several low-key "bars of the night."

Over in Poblenou, near the Parc de la Ciutadella, the two skyscrapers marking the location of the former Olympic Village also point the way to the site of the latest hot bar scene. The artificial harbor that was the launch point for the Olympic sailing competition is now lined on three sides with over 50 bars and cafés that pound on toward dawn. Among the headliners are **Dreams**, **Up y Down**, **Garatage Club**, and **Zeleste**. It's one of the safest nightlife districts.

The following are standouts among the "designer" bars and the larger disco/bar/restaurants sometimes known as *multispacios*:

Nick Havanna

Rosselló 208. ☎ **93/215-65-91.** Metro: Provença or Diagnal.

This place bills itself, in English, as the "Ultimate Bar." That's a stretch, but it was one of the first designer bars, an inspiration for its many followers. One feature is a bank of video monitors bouncing with MTV-like images. Open Monday through Saturday from 10pm to 4am and Sunday from 7pm to 4am.

Oliver y Hardy

Diagonal 593. ☎ **93/419-31-81.** Metro: María Cristina.

Upscale facilities and prices to match ensure a slightly older crowd here, about 25 to 40. Diners can move from the outdoor terrace to the piano bar and wind up in the disco. Open daily from 8pm to 4am.

Otto Zutz

Lincoln 15. ☎ **93/238-07-22.** Cover 2,000 ($15.40), which includes the first drink. Metro: Plaça Molina.

Conjure an abandoned county jail or perhaps a two-story parking garage—that'll give you a foretaste of this place's general ambience. Go before 2am to avoid the restrictive entrance policy. Open daily from midnight to 4am or later.

Ticktacktoe
Roger de Llúria 40. ☎ **93/318-99-47**. Metro: Urquinaona.

This ultramodern nightspot is part bar, part restaurant, and part billiard hall. Open daily from 8pm to 1:30am.

Universal
Marià Cubí 182–184. ☎ **93/201-46-58**. FF.CC. Generalitat: Gràcia.

Universal's minimal postmodernist decor recalls barely converted warehouses. The crowd is young, the music loud. Performance artists sometimes appear. Open daily from 11pm to 3am.

Velvet
Balmes 161. ☎ **93/217-67-14**. Metro: Diagonal.

Installed in a modernist structure, Velvet has a dance floor and two bars lined with buttocks-shaped bar stools. Don't miss the bathrooms. Open Monday through Thursday from 7:30pm to 4:30am, Friday and Saturday from 7:30pm to 5am, and Sunday from 7pm to 4:30am.

XAMPANYERIAS

These establishments specialize in *cavas,* the sparkling wines of Catalunya made by the *méthode champenoise.*

La Cava del Palau
Verdaguer i Callis 10. ☎ **93/310-09-38**. Metro: Urquinaona.

It stocks over 40 regional cavas, 40 French champagnes, and some 350 appellation wines from Spain, France, and Chile. Champagne connoisseurs will want to try the *brut natures,* the driest and most natural of all cavas. To accompany the libations, there's a selection of cheese, pâtés, and salmon for 1,200 to 2,000 ptas. ($9.25 to $15.40) per *ración* (larger than a tapas portion). A glass of cava averages about 575 ptas. ($4.40). Open Monday through Thursday from 7pm to 2:30am and Friday and Saturday from 7pm to 3:30am, with live piano music starting at 11:30pm.

Xampu Xampany
Gran Vía 702. ☎ **93/265-04-83**. Metro: Girona.

This sleek, spacious enterprise offers a good sound system and highly eclectic music programs to go with a few score *cavas.* Apt accompaniments are the smoked salmon and caviar nibbles. Open daily from 6pm to 1am.

A DANCE CLUB

In addition to discos galore, Barcelona has some classic dance halls. This is an old favorite:

La Paloma
Tigre 27. ☎ **93/301-68-97**. Cover 650 ptas. ($5). Metro: Universitat.

A Barcelona institution since 1903, this campy dance hall has a certain passé elegance, with a decor last in favor during the Eisenhower presidency. The music is always live, performed by a big band, and local tradition calls for Barcelona wedding parties to stop here at some time. Birthday and retirement celebrations are regularly announced between dance numbers. Open Thursday through Sunday and holidays from 6 to 9:30pm and 11:30pm to 3:30am.

9 Easy Excursions

MONTSERRAT MONASTERY   The vast Montserrat Monastery complex, 35 miles northwest of Barcelona, contains a basilica with a venerated Black Virgin, a museum, numerous hotels for pilgrims, restaurants, and a wealth of souvenir shops and food stalls. The monastery—a 19th-century structure that replaced one leveled by Napoleon's army in 1812—is situated at 2,400 feet up Montserrat, a name that refers to the serrated peaks of the range. One of its noted institutions is the Boys' Choir, established in the 13th century; the choir sings at 1 and 7:10pm. Numerous funiculars and paths lead to some 13 hermitages and many shrines scattered across the mountain.

The best way to get here is via bus tour. **Julià,** Ronda Universitat 5 (☎ **93/316-64-54**), and **Pullmantur,** Gran Vía C.C. 635 (☎ **93/317-12-97**), offer half-day bus tours leaving daily all year. The cost is 4,700 ptas. ($36.15).

SITGES   A popular beach destination just 25 miles south of Barcelona, Sitges really swings in summer; by mid-October it goes into hibernation, but its scenic charms and museums are still motive enough for a visit. The **Museu Cau Ferrat,** Fonollars (☎ **93/894-03-64**), is the legacy of wealthy Catalan painter Santiago Rusinyol, a leading light of belle époque Barcelona who lived and worked in his 19th-century house fashioned of two 16th-century fishermen's homes. Although remembered primarily as a painter, Rusinyol was also a novelist, playwright, and journalist. The museum collection includes not only his works but also several pieces by Picasso and El Greco, much ornate wrought iron (a particular Catalan specialty), ceramic tiles, diverse folk art, and archeological artifacts.

Next door is the **Museu Maricel de Mar** (☎ **93/894-03-64**), the legacy of Dr. Pérez Rosales, whose impressive accumulation of furniture, porcelain, lamps, and tapestries draws largely from the medieval, Renaissance, and baroque periods. There are also romanesque frescoes and an entire 14th-century chapel. Both museums are open Tuesday through Sunday from 9:30am to 2pm and 4 to 6pm. Admission to each is 225 ptas. ($1.75).

Trains run daily to Sitges from the Estació Sants; the round-trip fare is 550 ptas. ($3.95).

WINE COUNTRY   The wineries in Sant Sadurní d'Anoia, just 25 miles from Barcelona off the A-2 *autopista* (turnpike), produce Catalunya's estimable cavas. **Freixenet** (☎ **93/891-07-00**) and **Codorniu** (☎ **93/891-01-25**) offer the best tours and tastings. Call for hours.

Trains run daily to Sant Sadurní d'Anoia (the station is right next to Freixenet) from the Estació Sants. The round-trip fare is 550 ptas. ($4.25). A car is all but essential to visit Codorniu, as taxis from the Sant Sadurní d'Anoia train station are unreliable.

That reservation applies as well to a visit to **Vilafranca del Penedès,** about 10 miles beyond Sant Sadurní d'Anoia. This is the center of the Penedés wine district, a worthy rival to the better-known Rioja region, in north-central Spain. It may be instructive to think of Penedés as Spain's Burgundy and of Rioja as its Bordeaux, for the wines they produce share characteristics with those French wine-producing regions. Probably the best-known winery is **Miguel Torres,** Carrer Comercio 22 (☎ **93/890-01-00**), which offers tours and tastings.

Berlin

by Beth Reiber

The history of Berlin in this century—particularly given the events of the past seven years—is certainly a most compelling and riveting story. Just a decade ago, who'd ever have imagined that the Wall would come tumbling down, that Communism would meet with defeat throughout Eastern Europe, and that the two Germanys would reunite, with Berlin as the new capital?

Berlin began as a divided city back in the 13th century, when two settlements were founded on opposite banks of the Spree River. These settlements grew and eventually merged. Berlin served as capital of Prussia under the Hohenzollern kings and then as capital of the German nation. After the turn of this century, Berlin began to challenge Munich as the cultural capital as well, attracting such artists as Max Liebermann, Lovis Corinth, and Max Slevogt. Max Reinhardt came to Berlin to take over as director of the Deutsches Theater, Richard Strauss became conductor at the Royal Opera, and Albert Einstein was director of physics at what later became the Max Planck Institute.

After the German defeat in World War II, Germany and its former capital were carved into four sections: Soviet, American, French, and British. Berlin, buried in the Soviet sector, was divided into East and West, with East Berlin serving as the capital of East Germany. In 1961, after a series of disputes and standoffs, a wall 29 miles long and 13 feet high was erected around West Berlin, in part to stop a mass exodus of East Germans to the West. Three million had already fled, most of them young, draining East Germany of many of its brightest and most educated. How ironic that in 1989 it was another exodus from the East to the West that triggered the Wall's sudden demise.

Today Berlin is changing so rapidly that it's difficult—if not impossible—to keep abreast of the changes. As the focal point of a reunited Germany, Berlin has not escaped the problems that beset the nation, including economic recession and ideological differences between eastern and western Germans. However, Berlin is an exciting city for visitors, with some of the best museums in the world, a thriving nightlife, and a rich cultural legacy.

What's Special About Berlin

Museums

- The famous Pergamon Museum in eastern Berlin, with the Pergamon Altar, the Market Gate, and other architectural wonders of the ancient world.
- The Gemäldegalerie in Dahlem, with 20-some paintings by Rembrandt.
- The Egyptian Museum, with the bust of Nefertiti.
- Museum Haus am Checkpoint Charlie, documenting the history of the Wall.

Nightlife

- Famous opera houses and concert halls, including the Deutsche Oper Berlin and the Philharmonie.
- Cabarets, a Berlin tradition.
- A number of live-music houses, featuring jazz and rock.
- Bars and pubs, open all night.
- Discos and dance halls for all ages.

Shopping

- KaDeWe, the largest department store on the Continent.
- The Ku'damm, one of Europe's most-fashionable streets, and Wilmersdorfer Strasse, a pedestrian lane lined with boutiques and department stores.
- The Europa-Center, a large mall with 70 shops, restaurants, and bars.
- Outdoor and indoor markets, a treasure trove for antiques, junk, and crafts.

1 Berlin Deals & Discounts

BEST BESTS   If you're on a tight budget but love museums, note that most Berlin museums offer free admission on Sunday and public holidays, including the cluster of famous museums in Dahlem and on Museumsinsel (Museum Island).

Another bargain in Berlin is its **theaters, operas, and concerts**, particularly in eastern Berlin. Opera tickets start at around $4, while tickets to the Berlin Philharmonic Orchestra begin at $8.65. Because most theaters are small, the cheaper tickets are perfectly acceptable.

As for dining, your ticket to cheap meals is the *Imbiss*, a streetside food stall or tiny locale serving food for take-out or for dining standing up at chest-high counters. Sausages, Berliner Boulettes, hamburgers, french fries, pizza by the slice, Turkish pizza, döner kebab, and other finger foods are common fare, as well as beer and soft drinks. You can easily dine for less than 7 DM ($4.65). You'll find Imbisse along side streets of the Ku'damm, as well as on Alexanderplatz, Savignyplatz, and many other thoroughfares throughout Berlin.

SPECIAL DISCOUNTS   Students can obtain cheaper admission to most museums by presenting an **International Student Identity Card (ISIC)**. In addition, some theaters and live-music venues offer student reductions.

If you've arrived in Berlin without an ISIC and can show proof of current student status, you can obtain the card at **ARTU,** Hardenbergstrasse 9 (☎ **030/313 04 66**), a travel agency located in the technical university district not far from the train station. It also offers discount plane fares around the world. ARTU is open Monday, Tuesday, Thursday, and Friday from 10am to 6pm; Wednesday from 11am to 6pm; and Saturday from 10am to 1pm.

2 Pretrip Preparations

REQUIRED DOCUMENTS   The only document needed for citizens of the United States, Canada, Australia, and New Zealand is a valid passport, which allows stays of up to three months. Visitors from the United Kingdom need only an identity card.

Students should be sure to bring an International Student Identity Card (ISIC) as well.

TIMING YOUR TRIP   At about the same latitude as Vancouver, Berlin is a tourist destination throughout the year. Its temperature and amount of rainfall, however, can vary widely from year to year. The following may help you plan your trip, though remember it can be much colder or hotter than the average temperatures indicate.

Berlin's Average Daytime Temperature & Rainfall

	Jan	Feb	Mar	Apr	May	June	July	Aug	Sept	Oct	Nov	Dec
Temp. (°F)	30	32	40	48	53	60	64	62	56	49	40	34
Rainfall "	2.2	1.6	1.2	1.6	2.3	2.9	3.2	2.7	2.2	1.6	2.4	1.9

Special Events   Festivals in Berlin revolve around its cultural calendar, beginning with the **International Film Festival** held at the end of February. The biggest event is the **Berlin Festival**, which recognizes excellence in all fields of art and is held from the end of August to October. The **Berlin Jazzfest**, in November, attracts musicians from both Europe and the United States. If you come to Berlin during any of these festivals, you should reserve a room in advance to avoid disappointment or wasting time searching for a hotel. If you come to Berlin any time between December 1 and Christmas Eve, you'll be treated to the colorful **Christmas market,** with more than 150 booths set up around the Kaiser Wilhelm Memorial Church selling ornaments and candies. There are also Christmas markets in Spandau and Karl-Liebneckt Platz.

BACKGROUND READING   In the 1920s Berlin was the third-largest city in the world. Otto Friedrich's *Before the Deluge: A Portrait of Berlin in the 1920s* (Fromm International, 1986) describes this interesting and intriguing chapter in Berlin's history, a time when such well-known people as Dietrich, Einstein, Garbo, Brecht, Gropius, Kandinsky, and Klee all made their homes here. For accounts of Berlin's more recent history, read Norman Gelb's *The Berlin Wall: Kennedy, Khrushchev, and a Showdown in the Heart of Europe* (Touchstone, 1986); *Living with the Wall: West Berlin 1961–1985* (Duke Publishing Co., 1985) by Richard and Anna Merritt; and Jerry Bornstein's *The Wall Came Tumbling Down: The Berlin Wall and the Fall of Communism* (Arch Cape Press, 1990), illustrated with photographs chronicling the demise of the Wall.

Berlin's most recent history, including the socioeconomic problems posed by reunification, is captured in John Borneman's two thought-provoking books, *After the Wall: East Meets West in the New Berlin* (Basic Books, 1991) and *Belonging in the Two Berlins: Kin, State, Nation* (Cambridge University Press, 1992).

If you liked the movie *Cabaret,* you may wish to read Christopher Isherwood's *Goodbye to Berlin* (New Directions, 1954), on which the movie was based.

3   Berlin Specifics

ARRIVING

FROM THE AIRPORT   If you're flying to Berlin on Lufthansa or any of the other airlines serving Berlin from Frankfurt, Western Europe, or the United States, most likely you'll arrive at **Tegel Airport** (☎ **030/41 01-1**), 5 miles from the city center. The best and easiest way to get into town is on city bus no. 109, which departs about every 10 to 15 minutes from outside the arrivals hall. The fare is 3.70 DM ($2.45) one way. The bus travels to Stuttgarter Platz and along Kurfürstendamm, where most of Berlin's hotels are concentrated, to Bahnhof Zoologischer Garten (Berlin's main train station, usually called simply Bahnhof Zoo). The trip by taxi from Tegel Airport to Bahnhof Zoo costs about 30 DM ($20).

Schönefeld Airport (☎ **030/60 91-0**), which once served as East Berlin's major airport, is still the destination for most flights from Eastern Europe, Asia, and Latin America. The easiest way to get from Schönefeld to Bahnhof Zoo and the center of Berlin is via S-Bahn S-9 from Schönefeld Station (a five-minute walk from the airport) to Alexanderplatz, Bahnhof Zoo, and Savignyplatz. The fare is 3.70 DM ($2.45).

Finally, because of Berlin's sudden rise in status to capital of Germany, **Berlin–Templehof Airport** (☎ **030/69 51-0**) has been resurrected for commercial use, serving flights from Amsterdam, Basel, Budapest, Brussels, and several cities in Germany. Transportation from the airport is either bus no. 119, which travels the length of the Ku'damm, or via U-Bahn from the Platz der Luftbrücke station. In either case, the fare is 3.70 DM ($2.45).

FROM THE TRAIN STATION   If you're arriving by train from Western Europe, you'll probably end up at the **Bahnhof Zoologischer Garten,** Berlin's main train station, popularly called Bahnhof Zoo. Travel time from Hamburg is less than five hours, and from Frankfurt, less than eight.

Bahnhof Zoo is in the town center, not far from Kurfürstendamm with its hotels and nightlife. Both the subway and bus system connect the train station to the rest of the city. A post office and money-exchange office are located in the train station. For information on train schedules, call 194 19.

If you're arriving in Berlin from Eastern Europe, you may arrive at **Berlin Hauptbahnhof** or **Berlin-Lichtenberg,** where you'll find S-Bahn connections to take you on to your final destination. S-Bahn S-5 and S-7 will take you to Bahnhof Zoo (make sure you board the S-Bahn traveling the correct direction—otherwise you'll end up going in the opposite direction from Bahnhof Zoo).

VISITOR INFORMATION

Berlin's main **Tourist Information Office (Verkehrsamt Berlin, or VBB)** is located in the Europa-Center, with its entrance on Budapester Strasse (☎ **030/262 60 31**), just a few minutes' walk from Bahnhof Zoo. In addition to stocking maps and brochures about the city, the tourist office will book a room for you for a 5-DM ($3.35) fee. It's open Monday through Saturday from 8am to 10:30pm and Sunday from 9am to 9pm. Other tourist offices are at Tegel Airport (☎ **030/41 01-31 45**) and the Bahnhof Zoo train station (☎ **030/313 90 63**), both open daily from 8am to 11pm and also able to book you a room; at the Hauptbahnhof (☎ **030/279 52 09**), open daily from 8am to 8pm; and at Brandenburg Gate (☎ **030/229 12 58**), open daily from 10am to 6pm.

What Things Cost in Berlin	U.S. $
Taxi from Tegel Airport to Bahnhof Zoo train station	20.00
Underground from Kurfürstendamm to Dahlem	2.45
Local telephone call	.20
Double room at the Bristol Hotel Kempinski (deluxe)	260.00
Double room at the Hotel Tiergarten (moderate)	143.35
Double room at the Pension München (budget)	56.65
Lunch for one at Restaurant Marché Mövenpick (moderate)	10.00
Lunch for one at Ashoka (budget)	6.00
Dinner for one, without wine, at Fioretto (deluxe)	60.00
Dinner for one, without wine, at Hardtke (moderate)	16.00
Dinner for one, without wine, at the Athener Grill (budget)	6.50
Half liter of beer	2.65
Glass of wine	3.30
Coca-Cola in a restaurant	1.80
Cup of coffee	2.35
Roll of ASA 100 color film, 36 exposures	6.00
Admission to Pergamon Museum	2.65
Movie ticket	6.65
Ticket to the Berlin Philharmonic Orchestra	8.65

Your best bet for information on what's happening in Berlin, including concerts, plays, operas, and special events, is *BerlinBerlin* (written in both German and English and published every three months), available at the Verkehrsamt Berlin for 3.50 DM ($2.35). It also has a good city map and a subway map.

Although printed only in German, the most thorough publication of what's happening when and where is *Berlin Programm,* available at the tourist office and at magazine kiosks for 2.80 DM ($1.85). Issued monthly, it also lists museums and their opening hours. Other German publications include city magazines *tip* and *zitty,* which come out on alternate weeks with information on fringe theater, film, rock, folk, and all that's happening on the alternative scene. *Zitty* costs 3.60 DM ($2.40); *tip* costs 4 DM ($2.65).

CITY LAYOUT

One of the most famous streets in Berlin is **Kurfürstendamm,** affectionately called the **Ku'damm.** About 2¹/₂ miles long, it starts at the Kaiser-Wilhelm Gedächtniskirche (Memorial Church), a ruined church that has been left standing as a permanent reminder of the horrors of war. Near the Memorial Church is Bahnhof Zoo (the main train station), a large park called the Tiergarten, and the Europa-Center, a 22-story building with shops, restaurants and bars, and the Berlin Tourist Information Office. Along the Ku'damm are many of the city's smartest boutiques, as well as many of its hotels. Note that the numbering system of buildings runs on one side of the Ku'damm all the way to the end, then jumps to the other side of the street and runs all the way back. For example, across the street

The German Mark

For American Readers   At this writing $1 = approximately 1.50 DM (or 1 DM = 67¢), and this was the rate of exchange used to calculate the dollar values given in this chapter (rounded to the nearest nickel).

For British Readers   At this writing £1 = approximately 2.30 DM (or 1 DM = 43p), and this was the rate of exchange used to calculate the pound values in the table below.

Note: The rates given here fluctuate from time to time and may not be the same when you travel to Germany. Therefore this table should be used only as a guide:

DM	U.S.$	U.K.£	DM	U.S.$	U.K.£
.25	.17	.11	20	13.33	8.70
.50	.33	.22	25	16.67	10.87
.75	.50	.33	30	20.00	13.04
1.00	.67	.43	35	23.33	15.22
2.00	1.33	.87	40	26.67	17.39
3.00	2.00	1.30	45	30.00	19.57
4.00	2.67	1.74	50	33.33	21.74
5.00	3.33	2.17	60	40.00	26.09
6.00	4.00	2.61	70	46.67	30.43
7.00	4.67	3.04	80	53.33	34.78
8.00	5.33	3.48	90	60.00	39.13
9.00	6.00	3.91	100	66.67	43.48
10.00	6.67	4.35	125	83.33	53.35
15.00	10.00	6.52	150	100.00	65.22

from Ku'damm 11 is Ku'damm 230. It's a bit complicated at first, but numbers for each block are posted on street signs.

The Ku'damm has Berlin's most exclusive shops, but **Wilmersdorfer Strasse** is where most of the natives shop. A pedestrian street located near a U-Bahn station of the same name, Wilmersdorfer Strasse boasts several department stores, numerous shops and boutiques, and restaurants. Not far away is Charlottenburg Palace and a cluster of fine museums, including the Egyptian Museum (with the famous bust of Nefertiti) and the Bröhan Museum (with its art nouveau collection). All of this area around the Ku'damm is part of Charlottenburg, western Berlin's most important precinct.

Berlin's other well-known street—and historically much more significant—is **Unter den Linden,** located in a precinct called **Berlin-Mitte.** This was the heart of Old Berlin before World War II, its most fashionable and lively street, and thereafter was part of East Berlin. The Brandenburg Gate is the most readily recognized landmark, and buildings along the tree-lined street have been painstakingly restored. Unter den Linden leads past **Museumsinsel (Museum Island),** which boasts the outstanding Pergamon Museum and a number of other great museums, to the modern, spacious square called **Alexanderplatz,** with its tall television tower.

Nearby is the **Nikolai Quarter,** a reconstructed neighborhood of shops, bars, and restaurants built to resemble Old Berlin.

Berlin's other important museum districts, **Tiergarten** and **Dahlem,** are within easy reach of the city center by subway or bus. Spread along the southwestern edge of the city and accessible by S-Bahn are Berlin's most famous woods, the **Grünewald,** and waterways, the Havel and Wannsee. In the east, the **Spreewald** is a huge refuge of waterways and woods.

By the way, if you're wondering where Berlin's Wall stood before Germany reunited in 1990, it divided the city into eastern and western sectors at the Brandenburg Gate and stretched north and south from there. If you're using an old map, keep in mind that the names of many streets and stations have changed in the eastern part since reunification.

GETTING AROUND

Berlin has an excellent public transport network, including buses, the U-Bahn (underground), and the S-Bahn (inner-city railway). All are run by the **Public Transport Company Berlin-Brandenburg, the BVG** (☎ **030/752 70 20**), which maintains an information booth outside Bahnhof Zoo on Hardenbergplatz. Open daily from 8am to 8pm, it provides information on how to reach destinations and the various ticket options available and also sells tickets.

The best thing about Berlin's transportation system is that you can use one ticket for transfer to all lines. A **single ticket** costs 3.70 DM ($2.45) and is good for up to two hours, allowing transfers, round-trips, or even an interruption of your trip (you could, for example, go to Dahlem for an hour or so and then return to the center with the same ticket). If you're traveling only a short distance (six stops by bus or three stops by subway), you can purchase a **Kurzstreckenkarte** for 2.50 DM ($1.65).

However, if you plan on traveling frequently by bus or subway you're better off buying a **Sammelkarte,** a card with four tickets for 12.50 DM ($8.35). A Sammelkarte with four short-distance tickets costs 8.50 DM ($5.65).

Even more convenient, especially if you're going to be traveling more than four times on public transportation during the day, is the **30-hour ticket** for 15 DM ($10), good for Greater Berlin, including trips to and throughout Potsdam. If there are two of you, you can save even more money with the **30-hour Gruppenkarte (Group Ticket)**, which costs 20 DM ($13.35) and allows two adults and up to three children to travel together throughout Berlin for 30 hours.

If you're going to be in Berlin at least three days and plan on doing a lot of sightseeing, you might consider purchasing a **WelcomeCard,** available at all tourist offices and at the VBB information booth for 29 DM ($19.35). It allows one adult and up to three children unlimited travel in Greater Berlin for three days, as well as 20% to 50% reductions on sightseeing trips, museums, and attractions in Berlin and Potsdam. Keep in mind, however, that children aged 5 and under always travel free on Berlin's public transportation system and that children 6 to 14 receive reductions on both public transportation and at museums and attractions.

Finally, if you're going to be in Berlin for at least a week, of excellent value is the **seven-day ticket** for 40 DM ($26.65), valid for any seven consecutive days you wish to travel.

Tickets are available from automatic machines at U-Bahn and S-Bahn stations, ticket windows, bus drivers, and even at some automatic machines at bus stops (most common at bus stops on the Ku'damm). Once purchased, you must

The U-Bahn & the S-Bahn

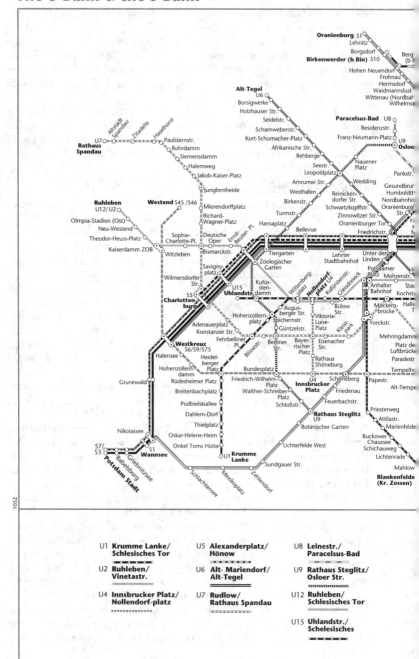

U1 **Krumme Lanke/**
Schlesisches Tor

U2 **Ruhleben/**
Vinetastr.

U4 **Innsbrucker Platz/**
Nollendorf-platz

U5 **Alexanderplatz/**
Hönow

U6 **Alt- Mariendorf/**
Alt-Tegel

U7 **Rudlow/**
Rathaus Spandau

U8 **Leinestr./**
Paracelsus-Bad

U9 **Rathaus Steglitz/**
Osloer Str.

U12 **Ruhleben/**
Schlesisches Tor

U15 **Uhlandstr./**
Schelesisches

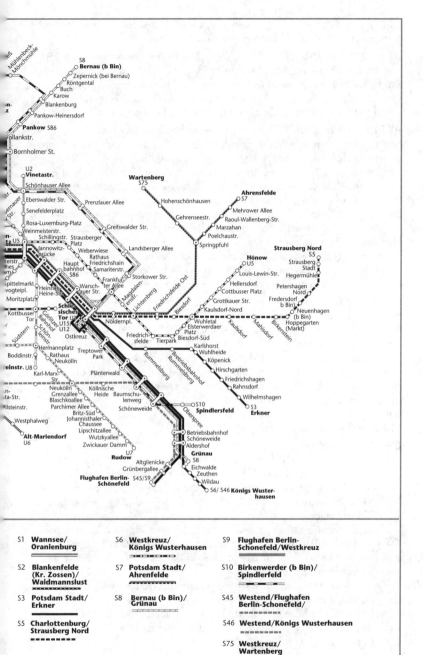

validate your ticket yourself by inserting it into one of the red machines located at the entrance to S- and U-Bahn platforms and on buses.

BY S-BAHN & U-BAHN   The U-Bahn has 10 lines with more than 130 stations. Lines run from about 5am until midnight or 1am (except for lines U-1 and U-9, which run all night on weekends). The S-Bahn stretches throughout Greater Berlin and is useful for trips to Wannsee and even Potsdam. If you have a valid Eurailpass, note that you can use it on Berlin's S-Bahn but not the U-Bahn.

BY BUS   Many of Berlin's buses are double-deckers, affording great views of the city. You can purchase only a single ticket from the bus driver; otherwise, stamp your Sammelkarte or use one of the other ticket options described above. If you're transferring, simply show the driver your ticket. Apart from the normal day services, there are also special night buses (*Nachtbusse,* marked with an N before the route number) that run the entire night. You can pick up the schedule at the BVG office in front of the Bahnhof Zoo station. In summer, special excursion buses marked with a triangle make fast and convenient runs from Theodor-Heuss-Platz to recreation areas at Grünewald, from the Wannsee station to Pfaueninsel, and from the Nikolassee station to Wannsee Beach. Bus no. 100, a double-decker, travels 24 hours a day between Bahnhof Zoo and Alexanderplatz. This interesting ride is a good way to travel between the eastern and western parts of the city.

BY BICYCLE   Riding a bicycle in Berlin can be a hair-raising experience, but there are parts of the city and parks that are pleasant for cycling. **Fahrradstation/ Berlin by Bike,** at Möckernstrasse 92 (☎ 030/216 91 77), offers city/trekking bicycles for rent beginning at 20 DM ($13.35) for one day or 110 DM ($73.35) for a week; students receive a 15% discount. Mountain bikes, racing bikes, and tandems are also available. Maps and recommended cycling routes are dispensed for free and organized bike tours are also offered. The bike shop is open Monday through Friday from 10am to 6pm and Saturday from 10am to 2pm and can be reached via U-Bahn to the Yorckstrasse or Möckernbrücke station or by bus no. 119 to the Katzbachstrasse stop.

BY CAR   Several well-known car-rental agencies have offices in Berlin. **Avis** has a counter at Tegel Airport (☎ **030/410 13 148**), as well as an office near Bahnhof Zoo at Budapester Strasse 41 (☎ **030/261 18 81**), open Monday through Friday from 7am to 6pm and Saturday from 8am to 2pm. Prices here start at 169 DM ($112.65) for one day in an Opel Corsa Swing, including 15% sales tax and unlimited mileage.

Hertz, another big name with similar prices, also has a counter at Tegel Airport (☎ **030/410 13 315**) and at Budapester Strasse 39 (☎ **030/261 10 53**). The downtown office is open Monday through Friday from 7am to 6:30pm and Saturday from 8am to 2pm.

Keep in mind that there are often special promotional fares with rates much lower than those given above, including weekend rates. Hertz, for example, recently offered a special daily rate of 55 DM ($36.65) per day and 333 DM ($222) per week for a Fiat Punto, including sales tax and unlimited mileage.

BY TAXI   You shouldn't have to take a taxi, but if you do, there are several taxi companies with the following telephone numbers: 690 22, 26 10 26, 69 10 01, 21 01 01, or 21 02 02. The meter starts at 4 DM ($2.65), then increases according to a complicated tariff system. A 6-DM ($4) surcharge is added for taxis ordered by phone. Luggage costs an extra 1 to 2 DM (65¢ to $1.35).

FAST FACTS: Berlin

Banks   Banks are open Monday through Friday from 9am to 1 or 3pm, with slightly longer hours one or two days a week, depending on the bank. The **American Express** office is located in the center of town at Uhlandstrasse 173–174 (☎ **030/8845 880**), just off the Ku'damm. It's open Monday through Friday from 9am to 5:30pm and Saturday from 9am to noon. You can have your mail sent here free if you have American Express traveler's checks or its card. Otherwise the service costs 2 DM ($1.35) per inquiry.

If you need to **exchange money** outside bank hours, your best bet is the Deutsche Verkehrs-Bank (☎ **030/881 71 17**), the exchange office at Bahnhof Zoo. It's open Monday through Saturday from 7:30am to 10pm and Sunday and holidays from 8am to 7pm. You'll also find ATMs (called *Geldautomat* in German) open 24 hours throughout the city, including the Deutsche Verkehrs-Bank at Bahnhof Zoo and banks up and down the Ku'damm. You must have a four-digit PIN number, and though transaction fees are high, the exchange rate is better than that offered at banks, making it useful for exchanging large amounts of money.

Business Hours   Downtown **businesses and shops** are open Monday through Friday from 9 or 10am to 6 or 6:30pm and Saturday from 9am to 1 or 2pm. On the first Saturday of the month (called *langer Samstag*), shops remain open until 6pm in winter and 4pm in summer. In addition, some shops and most department stores remain open longer on Thursday, until 8:30pm.

Consulates   The Consulate of the **United States** is in Dahlem at Clayallee 170 (☎ **030/832 40 87**). It's open for Americans who have lost their passports Monday through Friday from 8:30am to noon, while its visa section (☎ **030/819 74 54**) is open Monday through Friday from 8:30 to 10:30am. The Consulate of **Canada** is at Friedrichstrasse 95 (☎ **030/261 11 61**), open Monday through Friday from 1:30 to 3pm. The Consulate of the **United Kingdom** is at Uhlandstrasse 7–8 (☎ **030/309 52 93** or 309 52 92), open Monday through Friday from 9am to noon and 2 to 4pm (visa section, only in the morning). The Consulate of **Australia** is at Markgrafenstrasse 46, Berlin-Mitte (☎ **030/392 21 09** or 392 15 58), open Monday through Friday from 9am to noon and 2 to 4pm.

Currency   The German **Deutsch Mark (DM)** is divided into 100 **Pfennig.** Coins come in 1, 2, 5, 10, and 50 Pfennig, and 1, 2, and 5 DM. Notes are issued in 5, 10, 20, 50, 100, 200, 500, and 1,000 DM.

Dentists/Doctors   The Berlin Tourist Information Office in the Europa-Center has a list of English-speaking doctors and dentists in Berlin. If you need a doctor in the middle of the night or in an emergency, call 31 00 31. Call an emergency dentist at 011 41.

Emergencies   In Berlin, important numbers include 110 for police, 112 for the fire department or an ambulance, and 31 00 31 for an emergency doctor. To find out which pharmacies are open nights, call 011 41.

Holidays   Berlin celebrates New Year's (Jan 1), Good Friday, Easter Sunday and Monday, Ascension Day, Whit Sunday and Monday (variable dates in April and May), Labor Day (May 1), German Reunification Day (Oct 3), Day of Prayer and Repentance (third Wed in Nov), and Christmas (Dec 25–26).

Information   For information regarding Berlin's tourist offices and useful publications on what's going on in the city, see "Visitor Information" under "Berlin Specifics," earlier in this chapter.

Laundry/Dry Cleaning   Ask the staff of your pension or hotel where the most conveniently located self-service laundry is. Otherwise, Wasch Center is near the center of town at Leibnizstrasse 72 (on the corner of Kantstrasse) and at Uhlandstrasse 53 (between Pariser Strasse and Düsseldorfer Strasse). Hours for both locations are daily from 6am to 10pm. A wash cycle with detergent is 7 DM ($4.65), 1 DM (65¢) for a spin, and 1 DM (65¢) for a dryer for 10 minutes.

Lost & Found   Berlin's general lost-property office is at Platz der Luftbrücke 6 (☎ **030/699-0**). For property lost on public transportation services, check the BVG lost and found at Lorenzweg 5, Tempelhof (☎ **030/751 80 21**).

Mail   The post office in Bahnhof Zoo is open Monday through Saturday from 6am to midnight and Sunday and holidays from 8am to midnight for mail, telephone calls, and telegrams. You can have your mail sent here in care of Hauptpostlagernd, Postamt 120, Bahnhof Zoo, D-10623 Berlin 12 (☎ **030/ 313 97 99** for inquiries). Mailboxes in Germany are yellow.

   Airmail letters to North America cost 3 DM ($2) for the first 20 grams, while postcards cost 2 DM ($1.35). If you want to mail a package, you'll have to go to one of the city's larger post offices such as Goethestrasse 2–3 or Marburger Strasse 12–13, which is near the Europa-Center. At these post offices you can buy boxes, complete with string and tape. Boxes come in six sizes and range in price from 2.90 to 5.50 DM ($1.95 to $3.65). Both of these post offices are open Monday through Friday from 8am to 6pm and Saturday from 8am to 1pm.

Newspapers   Europa Presse Center (☎ **030/216 30 03**), on the ground floor of the Europa-Center, sells international newspapers and magazines and is open daily from 9am to 11pm. In addition, the Presse Zentrum in Bahnhof Zoo is open daily from 5am to 10pm.

Police   The emergency number for police is 110.

Radio/TV   Tune in to 90.2 FM (87.6 for cable) for the BBC World Service. Many medium- and upper-range hotels offer cable TV with CNN news broadcasts from the United States, a sports channel in English, Super Channel from the United Kingdom, and MTV, a music-video channel.

Shoe Repair   For quick service on shoe repairs, head for Wertheim department store, Kurfürstendamm 231, or either Karstadt or Hertie department store on Wilmersdorfer Strasse, where you'll find a Mister Minit specializing in repairs.

Tax   Germany's 15% government tax is included in the price at restaurants and hotels, including all the locales listed in this chapter. You can recover part of the 15% value-added tax (VAT) added to most goods—for more information, check "Shopping," later in this chapter.

Taxis   See "Getting Around" under "Berlin Specifics," earlier in this chapter.

Telephone   A **local telephone call** costs 30 Pfennig (20¢) for the first three minutes; restaurants and shops usually charge more for the use of their public telephones, generally 50 Pfennig (35¢). If you want to make an **international call,** look for phone booths with the green INTERNATIONAL sign or go to the post office. The main post office at Bahnhof Zoo is open until midnight. It costs

7.20 DM ($4.80) to make a three-minute long-distance phone call to the United States.

If you're going to make a lot of phone calls or wish to make an international call from a phone booth, you might wish to purchase a **telephone card.** For sale at post offices, they come in values of 12 DM ($8) and 50 DM ($33.35). Simply insert them into the telephone slot. Telephone cards are becoming so popular in Germany that many public telephones no longer accept coins. The 12-DM card gives you approximately 40 minutes of local telephone calls; the 50-DM card is useful for long-distance calls.

The country code for Germany is 49. The area code for all of Berlin is 30 if you're calling from the United States or from countries outside Germany, 030 if you're calling from within Germany. For **information** on telephone numbers in Berlin (those in the east are slowly being changed), call 011 88.

Incidentally, if you come across a number with a dash, the number following the dash is the extension number, which you reach directly simply by dialing the entire number.

Tipping   Since service is already included in hotel and restaurant bills, you're not obliged to tip. However, it's customary to round up restaurant bills to the nearest mark; if a meal costs more than 10 DM ($6.65), most Germans add a 10% tip. For taxi drivers, add a mark. Porters receive 2 DM ($1.35).

4 Accommodations

Most of Berlin's pensions and hotels are clustered along and around the city's main street, Kurfürstendamm, called Ku'damm for short. Even those establishments farther away are not very far, usually within a 5- or 10-minute subway ride to Bahnhof Zoo (Bahnhof Zoologischer Garten, Berlin's main station).

You can save lots of money by taking a room without a private bath, and unlike cheaper accommodations in Munich, you rarely have to pay extra for a shower in Berlin. A pension is usually a small establishment with fewer rooms and lower prices than a hotel, though sometimes there's only a fine line between the two. Continental breakfast is sometimes optional in the lower-priced establishments—therefore, if there are two or more of you who like breakfast, you might be as well off taking a more expensive room offering breakfast in the price.

However, keep in mind that although every effort was made to be accurate, prices for rooms may go up during the lifetime of this edition. Since the fall of the Wall room rates have shot upward, a reflection of the fact that Berlin has become such a popular destination that the demand for rooms has sometimes exceeded the supply. In addition, Berlin real estate has skyrocketed, making it difficult for small pension owners to make ends meet. Be sure to ask about the exact rate when making your reservation. At the most, prices should be no more than 10 to 15 DM ($6.65 to $10) higher than those given below.

Notes: In Germany, floors are counted beginning with the ground floor (the American first floor) and go up to the first floor (the American second) and beyond.

The area code for all of Berlin is 30 if you're calling from the United States or from countries outside Germany, 030 if you're calling from within Germany.

Remember, if the recommendations below are full, the tourist office will find you a room for a 5-DM ($3.35) fee.

Finally, all prices given below include tax and service charge.

Getting the Best Deal on Accommodations

- Try staying in a room without a private bath, which is much cheaper than a room with bath.
- Note that inexpensive lodging can be found in the heart of town.
- Take advantage of winter discounts.
- Ask if breakfast is included in the room rate—if it's buffet style, you can eat as much as you wish.
- Before dialing, check to see if there's a surcharge on local and long-distance telephone calls made from the lodging.

DOUBLES FOR LESS THAN 100 DM ($66.65)
NEAR THE KU'DAMM & BAHNHOF ZOO

⑤ Hotel Crystal

Kantstrasse 144 (off Savignyplatz), 10623 Berlin. ☎ **30/312 90 47** or 312 90 48. Fax 30/ 312 64 65. Telex 184022. 33 rms, 7 with shower only, 21 with tub or shower and toilet. TEL. 70 DM ($46.65) single without shower or toilet, 80 DM ($53.35) single with shower only, 80–120 DM ($53.35–$80) single with tub or shower and toilet; 90 DM ($60) double without shower or toilet, 110 DM ($73.35) twin with shower only, 120 DM ($80) double with shower only, 130–150 DM ($86.65–$100) double with tub or shower and toilet; 170–190 DM ($113.35–$126.65) triple with tub or shower and toilet. Rates include continental breakfast. Cribs available. AE, MC, V. S-Bahn: Savignyplatz; then a one-minute walk. Bus 109 from Tegel Airport to Bleibtreustrasse, or 149 from Bahnhof Zoo to Savignyplatz (two stops).

A five-minute walk from the Ku'damm, this older hotel is housed in an early 1900s building with a striking facade. Yet the interior seems like a relic from the 1950s: old-fashioned, comfortable, and endearingly German. Owners John and Dorothee Schwarzrock (John is American) are real characters—friendly, outgoing, and happy to see American guests. The rooms (with just the basics) are spotless, and TVs are available. All employees speak English. The rooms with baths here are among the cheapest in the city center.

Hotel-Pension Funk

Fasanenstrasse 69, 10719 Berlin. ☎ **30/882 71 93.** Fax 30/88 333 29. 15 rms, 11 with shower only, 1 with shower and toilet. TEL. 60–75 DM ($40–$50) single without shower or toilet, 75 ($50) single with shower only; 100 DM ($66.65) double without shower or toilet, 120–130 DM ($80–$86.65) double with shower only, 150 DM ($100) double with shower and toilet. No credit cards. Rates include breakfast. U-Bahn: Uhlandstrasse. Bus 109 from Tegel Airport or Bahnhof Zoo to Uhlandstrasse (or an eight-minute walk from Bahnhof Zoo).

This clean and orderly pension, once the home of famous silent-film star Asta Nielsen, features a sweeping white marble staircase in the entranceway, tall ceilings, and flowered wallpaper. The guest rooms are large, with French provincial furnishings. Its location is convenient to the Europa-Center, the Ku'damm, and Bahnhof Zoo.

⑤ Pension Cortina

Kantstrasse 140 (just west of Savignyplatz), 10623 Berlin. ☎ **30/313 90 59.** Fax 30/ 312 73 96. 21 rms, 5 with shower. 65–70 DM ($43.35–$46.65) single without shower; 90–100 DM ($60–$66.65) double without shower, 110–130 DM ($73.35–$86.65) double with shower; 120–130 DM ($80–$86.65) triple without shower, 150–165 DM ($100–$110) triple with shower. Rates include continental breakfast. Additional person 40–50 DM ($26.65–$33.35) extra. No credit cards. S-Bahn Savignyplatz. Bus 109 from Tegel Airport or Bahnhof Zoo to Schlüterstrasse.

This building, a five-minute walk from the Ku'damm is 100 years old, but the breakfast room has been remodeled in bright colors and some showers have recently been installed. Run more than 30 years by a Berlin native and her Italian husband, the Cortina offers mostly good-size rooms, each unique (some with phone). Several larger rooms can sleep four or more, including one facing the front that boasts a flower-planted balcony. The reception is up on the first floor.

Pension Fischer

Nürnberger Strasse 24a (near the Europa-Center), 10789 Berlin. ☎ **30/218 68 08.** Fax 30/213 42 25. 10 rms, 8 with shower. 60 DM ($40) single without shower, 70 DM ($46.65) single with shower; 80 DM ($53.35) double without shower, 100 DM ($66.65) double with shower; 130–150 DM ($86.65–$100) triple with shower. Breakfast 8–10 DM ($5.35–$6.65) extra. No credit cards. U-Bahn: Augsburger Strasse; then a one-minute walk. Bus 109 from Tegel Airport to Joachimstaler Strasse (or a seven-minute walk from Bahnhof Zoo).

Each spacious room here has large windows and an old-fashioned tiled stove, the kind that once heated all German homes. There's an automatic machine for coffee or hot chocolate, and the breakfast room is pleasant with plants and flowers and a TV. Reception is on the second floor.

○ Pension München

Güntzelstrasse 62, 10717 Berlin. ☎ **30/857 91 20.** Fax 30/853 27 44. 8 rms, 4 with shower and toilet. 60 DM ($40) single without shower or toilet, 110 DM ($64.70) single with shower and toilet; 85 DM ($56.65) double without shower or toilet, 130 DM ($86.65) double with shower and toilet. Additional person 35 DM ($23.35) extra. Breakfast 9 DM ($6) extra. No credit cards. U-Bahn: Güntzelstrasse.

This third-floor pension (with elevator) is about a 20-minute walk from the Ku'damm or just two stops on the U-Bahn. You'll be able to tell immediately that it's run by an artist: Original artwork by Berlin artists adorns the walls, flowers fill the vases, and everything is tastefully done. Frau Renate Prasse, the charming proprietor, is indeed a sculptor (her work decorates the corridor), and her rooms are bright-white and spotless, with firm beds.

Pension Zimmer des Westens

Tauentzienstrasse 5, 10789 Berlin. ☎ **30/214 11 30.** 8 rms, 1 with shower only, 2 with shower and toilet. 70 DM ($46.65) single with shower only, 85 DM ($56.65) single with shower and toilet; 95 DM ($63.35) double without shower or toilet, 100–110 DM ($66.65–$$73.35) double with shower and toilet. Rates include continental breakfast. Additional bed 40 DM ($26.65) extra. No credit cards. U-Bahn: Wittenbergplatz; then a one-minute walk (or about a seven-minute walk from Bahnhof Zoo).

This clean and pleasant pension is tucked away in an inner courtyard on busy Tauentzienstrasse, up three flights of rickety stairs. This is a good value in a great location, between the Europa-Center and KaDeWe department store.

IN KREUZBERG

○ Hotel Transit

Hagelberger Strasse 53–54, 10965 Berlin. ☎ **30/785 50 51.** Fax 30/785 96 19. 49 rms, all with shower. 80 DM ($53.35) single; 99 DM ($66) double; 150 DM ($100) triple; 170 DM ($113.35) quad; 33 DM ($22) per person in six-bed dorm rooms. Rates include buffet breakfast. AE, MC, V. U-Bahn U-9 from Bahnhof Zoo to Berliner Strasse, then U-7 from Berliner Strasse to Mehringdamm. Bus 119 or 219 from the Ku'damm to Mehringdamm, or 109 from Tegel Airport to Adenauerplatz and then 119 from Adenauerplatz to Mehringdamm.

Under youthful ownership, this great place for young travelers from around the world opened in 1987 in a converted tobacco factory. It's in the inner courtyard of an old brick building, on the fourth floor reached via elevator. The singles and doubles are a bit expensive, but the economical dormitory-style rooms that sleep six are perfect for frugal travelers. All rooms are painted white, a bit stark and factorylike, but all have huge windows, high ceilings, and slick black furniture. The airy breakfast room features a buffet offering as much coffee or tea as you want, and there's also a bar open around the clock with a big-screen cable TV.

⑤ Pension Kreuzberg

Grossbeerenstrasse 64, 10963 Berlin. ☎ **30/251 13 62.** Fax 30/251 06 38. 12 rms, none with bath. 60–65 DM ($40–$43.35) single; 90 DM ($60) double; 120 DM ($80) triple; 160 DM ($106.65) quad. Rates include continental breakfast. No credit cards. U-Bahn U-9 from Bahnhof Zoo to Berliner Strasse, then U-7 from Berliner Strasse to Mehringdamm; then a five-minute walk. Bus 119 or 219 from the Ku'damm to Grossbeerenstrasse, or 109 from Tegel Airport to Adenauerplatz and then 119 from Adenauerplatz to Grossbeerenstrasse.

Housed in a building with character, this 50-year-old pension on the second floor (no elevator) is owned by energetic young people who renovated the place themselves. The breakfast room is cheerful and bright, and the rooms are perfectly acceptable, especially for younger backpackers. This is one of Berlin's best values.

NEAR BAHNHOF CHARLOTTENBURG

✪ Hotel Charlottenburger Hof

Stuttgarter Platz 14, 10627 Berlin. ☎ **30/32 90 70** or 324 48 19. Fax 30/323 37 23. 45 rms, 38 with shower and toilet. TV TEL. 75–80 DM ($50–$53.35) single without shower or toilet; 90–120 DM ($60–$80) single with shower and toilet; 90–110 DM ($60–$73.35) double without shower or toilet, 110–150 DM ($73.35–$100) double with shower and toilet. Discounts available during the winter and for longer stays. Additional bed 40 DM ($26.65) extra. No credit cards. S-Bahn: Charlottenburg. Bus 109 from Tegel Airport or Bahnhof Zoo to Charlottenburg.

This is one of Berlin's most modern budget hotels, complete with laundry facilities and a friendly young staff. The white rooms come with modern furniture and colorful pictures adorning the walls. All rooms have cable TV offering English programs, room safes, and alarm clocks. Breakfast is not included, so you may want to go to the adjoining Café Voltaire, open 24 hours, with its large windows, plants, and artwork, where breakfast costs 5 to 8 DM ($3.35 to $5.35).

DOUBLES FOR LESS THAN 135 DM ($90)
NEAR THE KU'DAMM & BAHNHOF ZOO

Arco

Kurfürstendamm 30, 10719 Berlin. ☎ **30/882 63 88.** Fax 30/881 99 02. 20 rms, 10 with shower only, 6 with shower and toilet. TEL. 110 DM ($73.35) single with shower only, 140 DM ($93.35) single with shower and toilet; 110 DM ($73.35) double without shower or toilet, 140 DM ($93.35) double with shower only, 170 DM ($113.35) with shower and toilet. Rates include continental breakfast. AE, DC, MC, V. U-Bahn: Uhlandstrasse, a one-minute walk. Bus 109 from Tegel Airport to Uhlandstrasse, then a one-minute walk.

Right on the Ku'damm, this third-floor pension would certainly cost more if there were an elevator. The reception and breakfast rooms serve as an art gallery, and the guest rooms are spacious and tastefully decorated. Four of the seven rooms that overlook the Ku'damm have balconies, but those facing the back courtyard are much quieter. If you like being in the center of things, you can't go wrong here.

Galerie 48

Leibnitzstrasse 48, 10629 Berlin. ☎ **30/324 26 58.** Fax 30/324 26 58. 8 rms, 3 with shower only. 85 DM ($56.65) single without shower; 120 DM ($80) double without shower, 130 DM ($86.65) double with shower; 160 DM ($106.65) triple with shower. Rates include continental breakfast. No credit cards. U-Bahn: Adenauerplatz; then a five-minute walk. Bus 109 to Olivaer Platz.

Just north of the Ku'damm, this personable small pension offers clean and cheerful rooms on the first floor. The breakfast room is especially nice, with a long wooden bar that serves as the reception desk. Paintings line the corridor, giving it the feel of an art gallery.

Hotel Alpenland

Carmerstrasse 8 (near Savignyplatz), 10623 Berlin. ☎ **30/312 39 70** or 312 48 98. Fax 30/313 84 44. 40 rms, 10 with shower only, 20 with shower and toilet. 90 DM ($60) single without shower or toilet, 110 DM ($73.35) single with shower only, 140 DM ($93.35) single with shower and toilet; 120 DM ($80) double without shower or toilet, 180–210 DM ($120-$140) double with shower only or shower and toilet. Additional bed 65 DM ($43.35) extra. All rates include continental breakfast. MC, V. S-Bahn: Savignyplatz; then a three-minute walk. Bus 109 to Uhlandstrasse; then a five-minute walk (or a 10-minute walk from Bahnhof Zoo).

North of the Ku'damm and less than a 10-minute walk from Bahnhof Zoo, this simple hotel occupies a 100-year-old building, with rooms spread over four floors (no elevator). Decorated with Scandinavian-style wood furniture, most rooms are equipped with telephones, TVs, room safes, and tiny baths, and those that face toward the back are quieter (though the view is duller). Its one German restaurant serves German food.

✪ Hotel Bogota

Schlüterstrasse 45, 10707 Berlin. ☎ **30/881 50 01.** Fax 30/883 58 87. Telex 0184946. 130 rms, 12 with shower only, 65 with shower and toilet. TEL. 75 DM ($50) single without shower or toilet, 105 DM ($63.35) single with shower only, 135 DM ($90) single with shower and toilet; 120 DM ($80) double without shower or toilet, 160 DM ($106.65) double with shower only, 195 DM ($130) double with shower and toilet. Rates include continental breakfast. Additional bed 40–45 DM ($26.65–$30) extra. AE, DC, MC, V. U-Bahn: Adenauerplatz; then a six-minute walk. Bus 109 from Tegel Airport or Bahnhof Zoo to Bleibtreustrasse.

Just off the Ku'damm, this older hotel is well maintained and has a friendly staff. The century-old building boasts a stairway that wraps itself around an old-fashioned elevator and lobbies on each floor that are reminiscent of another era. Each room is unique, and there's a cozy TV room where you can spend a quiet evening.

Hotel Pension Bialas

Carmerstrasse 16 (off Savignyplatz), 10623 Berlin. ☎ **30/312 50 25** or 312 50 26. Fax 30/312 43 96. Telex 186506. 38 rms, 2 with toilet only, 10 with shower and toilet. 70 DM ($46.65) single without shower or toilet, 85 DM ($56.65) single with toilet only, 105 DM ($70) single with shower and toilet; 105 DM ($70) double without shower or toilet, 165 DM ($110) double with shower and toilet. MC, V. Rates include continental breakfast. Additional person 40–50 DM ($26.65–$33.35) extra. S-Bahn: Savignyplatz. Bus 109 from Tegel Airport to Bahnhof Zoo; then a six-minute walk.

Located on a quiet street, this establishment is a cross between a hotel and a pension. An older building with large, simple rooms spread over four floors (no elevator), the Bialas offers no frills—it's just a place to sleep.

Hotel-Pension Bregenz

Bregenzer Strasse 5, 10707 Berlin. ☎ **30/881 43 07.** Fax 30/882 40 09. 21 rms, 5 with shower only, 12 with shower and toilet. MINIBAR TV TEL. 75–80 DM ($50–$53.35) single without shower or toilet, 120–130 DM ($80–$86.65) single with shower and toilet; 110–120 DM ($73.35–$80) double without shower or toilet, 140–150 DM ($93.35–$100) double with shower only, 170–185 DM ($113.35–$123.35) double with shower and toilet; 200 DM ($133.35) quad with shower only, 230 DM ($153.35) quad with shower and toilet. Rates include continental breakfast. Crib available. MC. U-Bahn: Adenauerplatz; then a five-minute walk. Bus 109 from Tegel Airport or Bahnhof Zoo to Leibnitzstrasse.

On a quiet residential street south of Olivaer Platz and the Ku'damm, this friendly small hotel (with elevator) occupies the fourth floor. The guest rooms are clean and good-size, and the staff will make bookings for the theater and sightseeing tours.

Hotel-Pension Modena

Wielandstrasse 26 (on the western edge of the Ku'damm, near Olivaer Platz), 10707 Berlin. ☎ **30/881 52 94** or 88 57 01-0. Fax 30/881 52 94. 21 rms, 9 with shower only, 5 with shower and toilet. TEL. 75 DM ($50) single without shower or toilet, 90 DM ($60) single with shower only, 110 DM ($73.35) single with shower and toilet; 130 DM ($86.65) double without shower or toilet, 150 DM ($100) double with shower only, 170 DM ($113.35) double with shower and toilet. Rates include continental breakfast. Additional person 50 DM ($33.35) extra. No credit cards. U-Bahn: Adenauerplatz; then a six-minute walk. Bus 109 from Tegel Airport or Bahnhof Zoo to Leibnitzstrasse.

The Modena, on the second floor of a lovely turn-of-the-century building, is a good place to stay in terms of location and price. Managed by Frau Kreutz, this small pension offers spotless rooms, and guests receive upon check-in a key to operate the ancient-looking elevator.

Hotel-Pension Seifert

Uhlandstrasse 162, 10719 Berlin. ☎ **30/884 19 10.** Fax 30/884 19 13 30. 52 rms, 14 with shower only, 20 with shower and toilet. TEL. 80 DM ($53.35) single without shower or toilet, 95 DM ($63.35) single with shower only, 110 DM ($73.35) single with shower and toilet; 115 DM ($76.65) double without shower or toilet, 140 DM ($93.35) double with shower only, 170 DM ($113.35) double with shower and toilet. Rates include continental breakfast. Additional bed 40 DM ($26.65) extra. E, MC, V. U-Bahn: Uhlandstrasse; then a three-minute walk. Bus 109 from Tegel Airport to Uhlandstrasse.

This simple pension (with elevator) is a bit worn around the edges, with old carpeting and wallpaper, but is conveniently located near the Ku'damm. The reception area is up on the second floor, and its rooms are clean and spread over three floors (some have radios). Breakfasts are generous, and the small house bar is open in the evenings.

Hotel West-Pension

Kurfürstendamm 48–49, 10707 Berlin. ☎ **30/881 80 57** or 881 80 58. Fax 30/881 38 92. 33 rms, 8 with shower only, 15 with shower (or tub) and toilet. TEL. 75 DM ($50) single without shower or toilet, 100 DM ($66.65) single with shower only, 110 DM ($73.35) single with shower and toilet; 130 DM ($86.65) double without shower or toilet, 150 DM ($100) double with shower only, 175–220 DM ($116.65–$146.65) double with shower (or tub) and toilet. Additional bed 30 DM ($20) extra. Buffet breakfast 12 DM ($8) extra. MC, V. U-Bahn: Uhlandstrasse; then a three-minute walk. Bus 109 from Tegel Airport or Bahnhof Zoologischer Garten to Bleibtreustrasse.

With a great location right on the Ku'damm, this pension (with elevator) occupies the second floor of a beautiful turn-of-the-century building that boasts an old-world atmosphere. Facilities include a comfortable bar, a pleasant breakfast room, and guest rooms furnished with either antiques or modern pieces. Some of the doubles with tub/shower and toilet face the Ku'damm; the rest face the back and are quieter. Since a variety of rooms is available, specify what you want when making your reservation.

Pension Knesebeck

Knesebeckstrasse 86, 10623 Berlin. ☎ **30/312 72 55.** Fax 30/313 95 07. 12 rms, none with bath. 85–90 DM ($56.65–$60) single; 130 DM ($86.65) double; 160 DM ($106.65) family room. Breakfast 10–20 DM ($6.65–$13.35) extra. AE, MC, V. S-Bahn: Savignyplatz; then a three-minute walk. Bus 109 from Tegel Airport or Bahnhof Zoo to Uhlandstrasse (or a seven-minute walk from Bahnhof Zoo).

Friendly English-speaking Jutta Jorende took over this older pension several years ago, making it more livable and pleasant by adding plants and modern lighting to the breakfast room; 10 rooms face an inner courtyard, making them very quiet. There's also a large family room with four beds and two rooms with phones; TVs are available on request. You can't go wrong here. It's a 10-minute walk north of the Ku'damm, past Savignyplatz.

Pension Nürnberger Eck

Nürnberger Strasse 24a, 10789 Berlin. ☎ **30/218 53 71.** Fax 30/214 15 40. 8 rms, none with bath. 80 DM ($53.35) single; 130 DM ($86.65) double; 165 DM ($110) triple. Rates include continental breakfast. No credit cards. U-Bahn: Augsberger Strasse; then a one-minute walk. Bus 109 from Tegel Airport to Joachimstaler Strasse (or a seven-minute walk from Bahnhof Zoo).

Fresh flowers decorate the hallway of this second-floor pension (with elevator), and the pleasant rooms have comfortable old-style furniture. The huge doors and stucco ceilings are typical of Old Berlin.

Pension Peters

Kantstrasse 146 (just east of Savignyplatz), 10623 Berlin. ☎ **30/312 22 78.** Fax 30/312 33 14. 8 rms, none with bath. 80 DM ($53.35) single; 110 DM ($73.35) double. Rates include continental breakfast. Additional bed 30 DM ($20) extra. AE, DC, MC, V. S-Bahn: Savignyplatz; then a two-minute walk. Bus 109 from Tegel Airport to Uhlandstrasse, or 149 from Bahnhof Zoo to Savignyplatz (two stops).

Recently acquired by the same people who own Pension Viola Nova in the same building (below), this inexpensive pension is within a 10-minute walk of Bahnhof Zoo. It occupies the second floor (no elevator) of an 1890 building, complete with stucco ceilings and double-paneled windows. It offers four single rooms, as well as four doubles that actually have three and four beds, making them perfect for families or small groups. One room has a TV.

Pension Viola Nova

Kantstrasse 146 (east of Savignyplatz), 10623 Berlin. ☎ **30/313 14 57.** Fax 30/312 33 14. 15 rms, 2 with shower only, 4 with shower and toilet. TEL. 85 DM ($56.65) single without shower or toilet, 110 DM ($73.35) single with shower only, 130 DM ($86.65) single with shower and toilet; 110 DM ($73.35) double without shower or toilet, 130 DM ($86.65) double with shower only, 150 DM ($100) double with shower and toilet. Rates include continental breakfast. Additional bed 30 DM ($20) extra. AE, DC, MC, V. S-Bahn: Savignyplatz; then a two-minute walk. Bus 109 from Tegel Airport to Uhlandstrasse, or 149 from Bahnhof Zoo to Savignyplatz (two stops).

About a 5-minute walk from the Ku'damm and a 10-minute walk from Bahnhof Zoo, this updated pension has a cheerful breakfast room and reception area on the ground floor. It offers bright rooms, several of which sleep three to four, with sleek black furniture, modern lighting, and tall stucco ceilings. TVs are provided in some rooms and available for rent in others.

SOUTH OF CITY CENTER

Hotel-Pension Postillon

Gasteiner Strasse 8, 10717 Berlin. ☎ **30/87 52 32**. Fax 30/862 38 59. Telex 182946. 24 rms, 5 with shower only, 4 with shower and toilet. TEL. 70 DM ($46.65) single without shower or toilet, 80 DM ($53.35) single with shower only, 95 DM ($63.35) single with shower and toilet; 120 DM ($80) double without shower or toilet, 140 DM ($93.35) double with shower only, 160 DM ($106.65) double with shower and toilet. Rates include buffet breakfast. Additional bed 45–50 DM ($30–$33.35) extra. No credit cards. U-Bahn U-9 from Bahnhof Zoo to Berliner Strasse and then U-7 from Berliner Strasse to Blissestrasse. Bus 109 from Tegel Airport to Jakob-Kaiser-Platz (first stop) and then U-Bahn U-7 from Jakob-Kaiser-Platz to Blissestrasse.

Although it's about a 20-minute walk from the Ku'damm, Postillon is easily reached by U-Bahn. The building is a bit old and its rooms are simple, but those facing the front have balconies. The pension is owned by English-speaking Herr Bernd Lucht.

SUPER-BUDGET CHOICES

YOUTH HOTELS

Although catering largely to youth groups, most of these hotels will also take individual travelers of any age; most have single and double rooms in addition to multibed dormitory rooms.

Jugendgästehaus Am Zoo

Hardenbergstrasse 9a, 10623 Berlin. ☎ **30/312 94 10.** 85 beds. 50 DM ($33.35) single; 90 DM ($60) double; 35 DM ($23.35) dorm bed. No credit cards. Bus 109 from Tegel Airport to Bahnhof Zoo; then a 10-minute walk.

This no-frills establishment with no curfew is easy to overlook—there's no sign and the building, though recently renovated outside, still looks a bit run-down and neglected inside. However, its prices can't be beat. And neither can its location, a 10-minute walk from Bahnhof Zoo. The reception area is on the fourth floor (the elevator doesn't always work), and the bar is open from 9:30pm to 7am. Athough this hostel is intended for those 27 and younger, people of any age are welcome if there's room (those over 27 pay a 5-DM/$3.35 supplement). Dorm rooms sleep three to eight.

Jugendgästehaus Central

Nikolsburger Strasse 2–4, 10717 Berlin. ☎ **30/87 01 88.** Fax 30/861 34 85. 456 beds. 34 DM ($22.65) dorm bed. Rates include breakfast. Sheets 7 DM ($4.65) extra for stays of one or two nights, free for stays of three nights or longer. No credit cards. U-Bahn: Güntzelstrasse, Spichernstrasse, or Hohenzollernplatz; then a five-minute walk.

This dormitory-style accommodation caters to school groups with multibed rooms, but will accept single travelers if there's room. Note, however, that it's open only to those under 25 or bona-fide students and there's a 1am curfew. The rooms sleep 8 to 12, and you'll need your own towel here. You can make your own box lunch to take with you for an extra 4 DM ($2.65).

Jugendgästehaus Feurigstrasse

Feurigstrasse 63, 10827 Berlin. ☎ **30/781 52 11.** Fax 30/788 30 51. 200 beds. 37 DM ($24.65) dorm bed. Rates include buffet breakfast. Sheets 5 DM ($3.35) extra for stays of one to two nights, free for stays of three nights or longer. No credit cards. U-Bahn: Kleistpark; then about a five-minute walk. Bus 146 from Bahnhof Zoo to Haupt/Dominicusstrasse.

In Schöneberg, this youth hotel (no curfew) caters to school groups but will take individuals if there's room, giving preference to younger people. The rooms sleep 4 to 12. A few singles and doubles are also available.

Studenten-Hotel Berlin

Meininger Strasse 10 (near John F. Kennedy Platz and Rathaus Schöneberg), 10823 Berlin. ☎ **30/784 67 20** or 784 67 30. Fax 30/788 15 23. 50 rms, none with bath. 41 DM ($27.35) per person double; 37 DM ($24.65) dorm bed. Rates include breakfast and sheets. No credit cards. U-Bahn: Schöneberg. Bus 109 from Tegel Airport or Bahnhof Zoo and then 146 from Bahnhof Zoo to JFK Platz.

Although this is called a student hotel, you don't have to be a student to stay here (any age is welcome) and there's no curfew. It has 20 double rooms; the remaining rooms contain four or five beds each. The games room is outfitted with a pool table, soccer game, and pinball machine.

YOUTH HOSTELS

To stay at Berlin's youth hostels, you must have a youth-hostel card, which is available at youth hostels for 36 DM ($24). Alternatively, you can pay an extra 6 DM ($4) per night for a "guest card"; after six nights, your guest card becomes a regular youth-hostel card. There's no age limit (though "seniors," those older than 27, pay more), but keep in mind that the curfew at these places is midnight.

Jugendgästehaus Am Wannsee

Badeweg 1, 14129 Berlin. ☎ **30/803 20 34.** Fax 30/803 59 08. 264 beds. 29 DM ($19.35) per person for "juniors" (age 26 and under), 38 DM ($25.35) per person for "seniors" (age 27 and older). Rates include breakfast and sheets. Dinner 8.50 DM ($5.65) extra. No credit cards. S-Bahn: Nikolassee; then a seven-minute walk.

Berlin's newest youth hostel, this handsome brick building with red trim is on Berlin's outskirts close to Wannsee, a lake popular for swimming and boating in summer. The rooms have four beds each and showers are plentiful.

Jugendgästehaus Berlin

Kluckstrasse 3, 10785 Berlin. ☎ **30/261 10 97.** 364 beds. 29 DM ($19.35) per person for "juniors" (age 26 and under), 38 DM ($25.35) per person for "seniors" (age 27 and older). Rates include breakfast and sheets. Dinner 8.50 DM ($5.65) extra. No credit cards. U-Bahn: Kurfürstenstrasse; then a 12-minute walk. Bus 109 from Tegel Airport to Bahnhof Zoo and then 129 from Bahnhof Zoo to Kluckstrasse.

This is Berlin's most conveniently located hostel. A white-and-black modern building not far from the Kurfürstenstrasse U-Bahn station, it's so popular that between February and November you should write a month in advance to reserve a bed. All rooms have four to six beds, and everyone gets a locker with a key.

Jugendherberge Ernst Reuter

Hermsdorfer Damm 48–50, 13467 Berlin. ☎ **30/404 16 10.** 110 beds. 24 DM ($16) per person for "juniors" (age 26 and under), 31 DM ($20.65) per person for "seniors" (age 27 and older). Rates include breakfast and sheets. Dinner 8.50 DM ($5.65) extra. No credit cards. From Bahnhof Zoo, take U-Bahn U-9 to Leopoldplatz, then U-6 from Leopoldplatz to Tegel (last stop), and then bus 125 to Jugendherberge; from Tegel Airport, take bus no. 128 to Kurt Schumacher Platz, then U-Bahn U-6 to Tegel (last stop), and then bus no. 125 to Jugendherberge.

Surrounded by woods on the far outskirts of Berlin, this youth hostel is about 35 minutes from the city center—if you make good connections. All rooms have eight beds; facilities include table tennis and a TV.

A YOUTH CAMP

Internationales Jugendcamp
Ziekowstrasse 161, 13509 Berlin. ☎ **30/433 86 40.** 9 DM ($6) per person. Rates include showers and sheets. Open July 1 to end of Aug. Take U-Bahn U-6 to Alt-Tegel (last stop); then bus no. 222 to Titusweg stop (four stops).

This youth camp consists of a large tent, with mattresses and sheets provided. Showers are free, and breakfast and dinner are available. Guests must be between 14 and 26 and must leave the premises from 9am to 5pm. In addition, stays are limited to three nights. No written reservations are accepted, so call when you get to Berlin.

WORTH THE EXTRA MONEY

Hotel-Pension Dittberner
Wielandstrasse 26 (off the Ku'damm, near Olivaer Platz), 10707 Berlin. ☎ **30/881 64 85.** Fax 30/885 40 46. 20 rms, 13 with shower only, 7 with tub (or shower) and toilet. TEL. 100 DM ($66.65) single with shower only, 140–175 DM ($93.35–116.65) single with tub (or shower) and toilet; 150–170 DM ($100–$113.35) double with shower only, 160–220 DM ($106.65–$146.65) double with tub (or shower) and toilet. Rates include continental breakfast. No credit cards. U-Bahn: Adenauerplatz; then a six-minute walk. Bus 109 from Tegel Airport or Bahnhof Zoo to Leibnitzstrasse.

This small pension is like a gallery—a Japanese screen and artwork in the small lobby, woodblock prints and posters in the corridors. Little wonder! The owner's husband runs the gallery downstairs. The breakfast room is grandly decorated with thick upholstered chairs, white tablecloths, and fresh flowers on each table. Guests return again and again to this 30-year-old pension. The reception is on the third floor; guests receive a special key for the elevator.

✪ Hotel Tiergarten Berlin
Alt-Moabit 89, 10559 Berlin. ☎ **30/391 30 04** or 399 89 600. Fax 30/393 86 92. 40 rms, all with shower and toilet. MINIBAR TV TEL. 180 DM ($120) single; 215 DM ($143.35) double. Rates include buffet breakfast. Weekend discounts available. Additional person 35 DM ($23.35) extra; children under 10 stay free in parents' room. AE, DC, MC, V. U-Bahn U-9 to Turmstrasse; then a three-minute walk.

This intimate hotel (with elevator) possesses all the makings of a first-rate establishment: polite and efficient staff, turn-of-the-century charm and elegance, and light and airy rooms sporting tall stucco ceilings. The baths are modern and spotless, complete with a magnifying mirror for shaving or applying makeup. Even the breakfast room with its great buffet breakfast is something to write home about. In short, this is the kind of place that appeals to both business and pleasure travelers; it's certainly one of my favorite hotels in Berlin. The small reception area is on the ground floor.

5 Dining

Berlin contains an estimated 6,000 restaurants and bars, a great many of which serve international cuisine—not surprising considering Berlin's large foreign population. Even young Germans are more likely to go out for Greek or Italian food than they are for their own heavier cuisine. What's more, ethnic restaurants are often cheaper than their German counterparts.

You'll find many restaurants clustered along the Ku'damm, as well as on the pedestrians-only Wilmersdorfer Strasse and around Savignyplatz. The cheapest of

Getting the Best Deal on Dining

- Take advantage of the stand-up food stalls (*Imbiss*), many in the area of the Ku'damm.
- Ask about the daily special (*Tageskarte*), which may not be on the menu.
- An especially good value in Berlin are department-store food counters and restaurants.
- Try one of the coffee-shop chains, such as Tschibo, where coffee costs 1.95 DM ($1.30) a cup.
- Ask if there's a charge for an extra piece of bread or if your entree come with side dishes.

these is the *Imbiss,* a stand-up eatery where everything from sausages to fish sandwiches might be offered.

In addition to the restaurants below, several nightspots in "Berlin After Dark," later in this chapter, offer food. In fact, a few of the bars specialize in breakfast for those who stay out all night.

FAVORITE MEALS

Most main dishes served in a German restaurant come with side dishes such as potatoes and/or sauerkraut. One of Berlin's best-known specialties is *Eisbein* (pig's knuckle), usually served with sauerkraut and potatoes or puréed peas. *Kasseler Rippenspeer* is smoked pork chops, created by a butcher in Berlin named Kassel. *Bockwurst,* also created in Berlin, is a super-long sausage, and *Boulette* is a type of meatball. Other foods you might encounter on a menu include *Sauerbraten* (marinated beef in sauce), *Leberkäs* (a Bavarian specialty, a type of meatloaf), and *Schnitzel* (breaded veal cutlet). In any case, since most main dishes in a German restaurant include one or two side dishes, that's all you'll need order. And by all means, try a *Berliner Weisse*—a draft beer with a shot of raspberry.

AFTERNOON COFFEE   Just as the British crave their afternoon tea, the Germans love their afternoon coffee, which naturally requires a slice of cake to accompany it.

If you're a caffeine addict, the cheapest place for a cup of coffee is **Tschibo,** a chain that sells both the beans and the brew, and sometimes small cakes as well. A cup of coffee or an espresso is usually about 1.95 DM ($1.30), which you can drink at one of the stand-up counters. You can find Tschibo shops at Ku'damm 11 (near the Kaiser Wilhelm Memorial Church) and Wilmersdorfer Strasse 117.

Another place for afternoon coffee is one of the department-store restaurants (described below). But if you want to splurge, go to **Café Kranzler,** Kurfürstendamm 18–19 (☎ **030/882 69 11**), one of the few cafés to have survived the ravages of World War II. It's the favored people-watching spot on the Ku'damm, and in summer you can sit outside. Coffee starts at 3.70 DM ($2.45), with cakes costing more. It's open daily from 8am to midnight.

In eastern Berlin, the place to go is the newly renovated **Opernpalais,** Unter den Linden 5 (☎ **030/200 22 69**). One of Berlin's most celebrated cafés, it's part of a palace built in 1733, destroyed during World War II, then rebuilt. On the ground floor is an opulent coffee shop where a breakfast buffet is offered until noon. Coffee here is 3.50 DM ($2.35), but the main attraction is the more than 40 different tortes, prepared daily. In summer there's an outdoor Imbiss selling coffee, drinks, and snacks with outdoor seating.

LOCAL BUDGET BESTS
DEPARTMENT STORES

Hertie

Wilmersdorfer Strasse 118–119. ☎ **030/311 050**. 8.50–15 DM ($5.65–$10). No credit cards. Mon–Wed and Fri 9:30am–5:30pm, Thurs 9:30am–7:30pm, Sat 9am–1:30pm (to 5:30pm the first Sat of the month in winter, to 3:30pm in summer). U-Bahn: Wilmersdorfer Strasse. GERMAN.

Hertie's Le Buffet, a restaurant with waitress service, is on the first floor. Daily it offers several choices of a complete meal for less than 13 DM ($8.65), as well as about 10 other changing dishes, such as fish, sausages, spaghetti, kidney ragoût, or Schnitzel. There's a salad bar.

✪ KaDeWe

Wittenbergplatz. ☎ **030/212 10**. 5–20 DM ($3.35–$13.35). No credit cards. Mon–Wed and Fri 9:30am–6pm, Thurs 9:30am–8pm, Sat 9am–1pm (to 5:30pm the first Sat of the month in winter, to 3:30pm in summer). U-Bahn: U-1, U-2, or U-3 to Wittenbergplatz. INTERNATIONAL.

KaDeWe is short for Kaufhaus des Westens, and on the top floor of this large department store is the biggest food department in continental Europe. It's so amazing that it may be worth coming to Berlin just to see it—sausages galore (the Germans must make more types of sausage than anyone else in the world), cheeses, teas, breads, jams, sweets, vegetables, coffees, spices, wines, salads, meats (including more cuts of pork than I can count), tanks full of live fish, and much more. And in the middle of all these sections are sit-down counters serving a wide variety of food and drink, specializing in such things as salads, pasta, ice cream, potato dishes, coffee, seafood, grilled chicken, and wines. There are many more counters, but I couldn't keep track of them all. At any rate, this place is overwhelming—and you'll find the profusion of food either wonderful or decadent.

Karstadt

Wilmersdorfer Strasse 109–111. ☎ **030/31 891**. 8–15 DM ($5.35–$10). No credit cards. Mon–Wed and Fri 9:30am–6pm, Thurs 9:30am–8pm, Sat 9am–1:30pm (to 5:30pm the first Sat of the month in winter, 3:30pm in summer). U-Bahn: Wilmersdorfer Strasse. GERMAN.

On Berlin's best-known pedestrian shopping lane, this department store's fourth-floor cafeteria, Restaurant-Café, offers several counters with various types of food, including a salad bar, a beverage bar, and a counter devoted solely to vegetables (for those who miss your veggies, this is a true gift from above). Another counter offers German specials ranging from fish and Sauerbraten to Schnitzel and duck, another offers daily pasta specials, and yet another offers desserts. And wonder of wonders, there's even a no-smoking section.

Hertie Bei Wertheim

Kurfürstendamm 231. ☎ **030/88 20 61**. 7–20 DM ($4.65–$13.35). No credit cards. Mon–Wed and Fri 9:30am–6pm, Thurs 9:30am–8pm, Sat 9am–1:30pm (to 5:30pm the first Sat of the month in winter, to 3:30pm in summer). U-Bahn: Kurfürstendamm. GERMAN/SNACKS.

This store's food department is in the basement, with counters serving various types of snacks and meals. Salads, stews, pasta, sandwiches, grilled chicken, wine, beer, and German specialties are just some of the items you can eat here. There are tables where you can sit after you've made your purchase. The Club Culinar counter offers soup and choices of several main dishes, including vegetarian.

MEALS FOR LESS THAN 12 DM ($8)
ON OR NEAR THE KU'DAMM

Ashoka

Grolmanstrasse 51 (just north of Savignyplatz). ☎ **030/313 20 66**. 5–13 DM ($3.35–$8.65). No credit cards. Daily 11am–midnight. S-Bahn: Savignyplatz. INDIAN.

This is a tiny hole-in-the-wall Indian restaurant with an open kitchen that takes up half the place. It's popular with area students, and it features more than a dozen vegetarian dishes alone—the Gemüseplatte Benares, a vegetarian platter, is a great bargain at 10 DM ($6.65). Good for a hot-and-spicy fix, it even has outdoor seating.

Asia-Quick

Lietzenburgerstrasse 96. ☎ **030/882 15 33**. 9–15 DM ($6–$10). No credit cards. Mon–Fri 11:30am–11:30pm, Sat 2pm–1am. U-Bahn: Uhlandstrasse. CHINESE.

This simple place is, as its name implies, quick to serve soups and dishes of fish, pork, beef, chicken, rice, and noodles, as well as vegetarian selections. The meat dishes come with a choice of several sauces, including chop suey and sweet-and-sour. There's a TV in the corner (as in most restaurants in Asia), and you can either eat your food here or take it out. It's a three-minute walk south of the Ku'damm, near Bleibtreustrasse.

Athener Grill

Kurfürstendamm 156 (past Adenauerplatz, on the corner of Albrecht-Achilles-Strasse). ☎ **030/892 10 39**. 7–15 DM ($4.65–$10). AE, DE, MC, V. Sun–Thurs 11am–4am, Fri–Sat 11am–5am. U-Bahn: Adenauerplatz; then a one-minute walk. GREEK/ITALIAN.

If you can't decide whether you want Greek or Italian food, or if you want both, or if you want a meal at 3am, head for the Athener Grill toward the western end of the Ku'damm (look for a modern brick building). Its menu is on the wall—decide what you want, pay the cashier, and then hand your ticket to the cook at the respective counter. Counters are divided into various specialties, with Greek food at one, pizzas and pastas at another, and so on. It has a cheerful interior, and Greek and Italian wines start at 3.20 DM ($2.15).

Avanti

Rankestrasse 2. ☎ **030/883 52 40**. 6.50–17.50 DM ($4.35–$11.65). No credit cards. Daily 11am–2am. U-Bahn: Kurfürstendamm. ITALIAN.

I wouldn't be surprised to hear that there are more self-service Italian cafeterias than any other ethnic restaurant in Berlin (with the possible exception of Turkish Imbisse); they're seemingly on every corner. This one is just off the Ku'damm near the Gedächtniskirche and the Hertie Bei Wertheim department store. It's clean and modern, with contemporary artwork on the walls and an ice-cream/cocktail/espresso bar. Pizzas and pastas are priced under 12 DM ($8), and at the salad bar you can help yourself at 6.50 DM ($4.35) for a small plate. There are also daily specials.

Cafe Hardenberg

Hardenbergstrasse 10. ☎ **030/312 26 44**. Main courses 8–14 DM ($5.35–$9.35). No credit cards. Daily 9am–midnight. U-Bahn: Ernst-Reuter-Platz. GERMAN/INTERNATIONAL.

In the technical university district less than a six-minute walk from Bahnhof Zoo, this café is always packed with students and people who work nearby. The portions of the daily specials (which can range from Schnitzel to spaghetti) are hearty, breakfast is served all day, and the place is decorated with museum posters, plants, and ceiling fans. Classical music can be heard until 4pm, when it's replaced by 20th-century music. In the evening the atmosphere is more like that of a bar—beer and cocktails are served in addition to dinner. In summer you can sit outside.

Einhorn

Wittenbergplatz 5–6. ☎ **030/218 63 47.** 7–11 DM ($4.65–$7.35). No credit cards. Mon–Fri 10am–6pm, Sat 10am–1:30pm. U-Bahn: Wittenbergplatz; then a one-minute walk. VEGETARIAN.

This natural-foods shop, on the opposite end of the square from KaDeWe, sells daily specials of ready-made vegetarian dishes that may include curry risotto with vegetables, spinach canneloni, vegetarian lasagne, stews, salads, and fruit juices. You can eat at its stand-up counter or take your food outside and sit on one of the benches lining the square.

Higher Taste

Kurfürstendamm 157–158. ☎ **030/892 99 17.** 6–10 DM ($4–$6.65). No credit cards. Mon–Fri 11am–6:30pm, Sat 11am–2pm (to 6pm the first Sat of the month). U-Bahn: Adenauerplatz. VEGETARIAN.

Operated by the Hare Krishna organization, this bright, clean, and cheerful vegetarian restaurant/health-food store is on the west end of the Ku'damm (look for its entrance on Albrecht-Achilles-Strasse). Snacks include samosas, pakora, and various breads, while warm dishes usually range from vegetable dishes called sabji to quiche and rice casseroles. A small changing menu offers soup of the day and such specials as polenta with tomato and zucchini and cauliflower sabji with potatoes. Food is available for take-out or for eating at one of the chest-high chairless tables.

Ihre Frisch-Backstübe

Knesebeckstrasse 12 (on the corner of Knesebeckstrasse and Goethestrasse, north of Savignyplatz). ☎ **030/31 90 710.** 4.50–12 DM ($3–$8). No credit cards. Mon–Sat 6am–6:30pm, Sun 1–5pm. U-Bahn Ernst-Reuter-Platz. S-Bahn: Savignyplatz. GERMAN.

This cheerful self-service restaurant offers a wide variety of breads, cakes, pizza by the slice, sandwiches, and a changing menu of warm dishes, which may range from smoked pork chops to Leberkäs. There are tables where you can sit and eat or you can take your food with you. It's a 10-minute walk north of the Ku'damm.

Jimmy's Diner

Pariser Strasse 41 (on the corner of Sächsische Strasse and Pariser Strasse). ☎ **030/882 31 41.** 7–15 DM ($4.65–$10). No credit cards. Mon–Thurs noon–3am, Fri noon–6am, Sat 11am–6am, Sun 11am–3am. AMERICAN/MEXICAN.

Come here for a bit of 1950s Americana. It looks like a diner, with its blood-red furniture and chrome, drive-in speakers hanging above the window, and old advertisements on the wall. Its menu is eclectic, from corn on the cob and Aunt Mary's chicken salad to huge hamburgers with fries, sandwiches, spareribs, spaghetti, tacos, enchiladas, burritos, and chili con carne, most under 12 DM ($7.05). A five-minute walk south of the Ku'damm, this place is popular with the young student crowd.

Karavan

Kurfürstendamm 11. ☎ **030/881 50 05.** 4–10 DM ($2.65–$6.65). No credit cards. Daily 9am–midnight. U-Bahn: Kurfürstendamm or Bahnhof Zoo. TURKISH.

Conveniently located across the plaza from the Kaiser Wilhelm Memorial Church, this is a tiny Turkish take-out establishment where you can sample ethnic food at low prices. I especially recommend the Turkish pizza, which has a thick, soft crust with a thin spread of meat and spices; the kofti burger, a Turkish-style burger; or the Spinat-tasche, a spinach-filled pastry. There are also sandwiches and salads, as well as a changing daily special available for 10 DM ($6.65). Since all the food is visible behind the glass counter, you can just choose and point.

Ⓢ Mensa

Technische Universität, Hardenbergstrasse 34. ☎ **030/3140.** 2.80–9 DM ($1.85–$6); main courses 2.80–4 DM ($1.85–$2.65). No credit cards. Mon–Fri 11:30am–2:30pm. U-Bahn: Ernst-Reuter-Platz. GERMAN.

This student cafeteria serves fixed-price meals and is by far the cheapest place to eat near the Ku'damm. Upstairs you'll find the bustling cafeteria, where non-students pay slightly more than prices charged university students. Main courses, complete with side dishes, may consist of Schnitzel with noodles and vegetables or spaghetti with salad. On the top floor of the same building is a slightly more expensive restaurant, offering daily changing main courses such as an Eintopf (stew), Gulasch, curry rice, turkey breast, or vegetarian ragoût, priced between 3.40 and 9 DM ($2.25 and $6). Side dishes, priced under 1.80 DM ($1.20), include salads, Sauerkraut, and rice. While not an aesthetic place for a meal (it looks like the student establishment it is), you can't beat its prices or its location, just a six-minute walk from Bahnhof Zoo.

Piccola Taormina Tavola Calda

Uhlandstrasse 29. ☎ **030/881 47 10.** 6.50–15 DM ($4.35–$10). No credit cards. Daily 11am–2am. U-Bahn: Uhlandstrasse. ITALIAN.

This is one of the cheapest places in town for Italian pizza, pasta, and risotto. The menu is written on the wall: After deciding what you want, place your order at the counter opposite. These guys—all Italian—are fast and will have your food ready in no time. You can take out your meal—one slice of pizza is only 2 DM ($1.35)—or sit at one of the wooden tables. As for the food, the crowd at this usually packed eatery a three-minute walk south of the Ku'damm speaks for itself. Beer and wine are available.

IN BERLIN-MITTE (EASTERN BERLIN)

For several choices in fast-food dining under one roof, head for **Die Berliner Markthalle,** on Alexanderplatz near the S-Bahn station and Kaufhof department store. McDonald's, Nordsee, Ihre Frisch-Backstube, and other chains have concessions here, open every day from about 10am or even earlier to as late as 8pm or even midnight.

Casino

In the Staatsbibliothek, Unter den Linden 8. ☎ **030/2037 83 10.** Soup or salad 2.50–5.50 DM ($1.65–$3.65); main courses 6–11 DM ($4–$7.35). No credit cards. Mon–Fri 9am–6pm, Sat 10am–4pm. Bus 100 or 157 to the Staatsoper stop. GERMAN.

Casino means "canteen" in German, and the only gamble here is whether you'll be able to find an empty seat during the busy lunch hour. This inexpensive cafeteria in a public library offers a limited chalkboard menu of soups, stews, salads, and daily specials. Offerings may include Schnitzel with fries and a salad, rumpsteak, chicken, or fish. Coffee is a cheap 1.50 DM ($1) per cup. This place is convenient for sightseeing jaunts along Unter den Linden and to Museum Island.

Nordsee

Spandauer Strasse 4 (just off Alexanderplatz). ☎ **030/242 68 81.** 7–13 DM ($4.65–$8.65). No credit cards. Mon–Sat 10am–9pm, Sun 11am–9pm. S-Bahn and U-Bahn: Alexanderplatz. Bus 100 to Spandauer Strasse. FISH.

One of the first chain restaurants to open in what was formerly East Berlin, this Nordsee is bigger than most, offering plenty of tables (including a no-smoking section) and doing a brisk business. Like others in this chain, the menu is behind the self-service counter, illustrated with pictures of fried haddock, fish soup, fish sticks, and half a dozen other choices. There's also salad and fish sandwiches.

Self-Service Terrace of Opernpalais

Unter den Linden 5. ☎ **030/200 22 69.** 3.50–6 DM ($2.35–$4). No credit cards. Summer, daily 11am–midnight; autumn and spring, daily noon–6pm. Closed Jan–Mar. U-Bahn: Französische Strasse. Bus 100 to the Staatsoper stop. GERMAN/SNACKS.

The Opernpalais, on eastern Berlin's famous boulevard not far from Museum Island, is one of the city's best-known restaurants and coffeehouses. Prices inside are well over 12 DM ($8), but outside the café, in a pretty tree-shaded square, is a self-service Imbiss selling Würste (sausages), Boulette, soups, coffee, beer, and other drinks. Eat your purchase at one of the tables beside the Imbiss—but don't wander to the tables on the terraces, as these are reserved for coffeehouse customers.

Zum Nussbaum

Am Nussbaum 3. ☎ **030/0171 33 04182.** 6–15 DM ($4–$10). No credit cards. Daily noon–10pm. S-Bahn and U-Bahn: Alexanderplatz. GERMAN.

In the restored historic Nikolai Quarter just a few minutes' walk from Alexanderplatz, this establishment was modeled after a 1507 bar that was destroyed in World War II. Pleasant and cozy, with wood-paneled walls and tiny rooms, it offers a small menu of German and Berlin specialties, including Würste, Boulette, lentil stew, Berliner Eisbein with Sauerkraut and puréed peas, Sülze (jellied meat) with fried potatoes, Kasseler with potato salad, and Rote Grütze (cooked fruits with vanilla sauce, a North German specialty). Half a liter of beer to wash it all down costs 5 DM ($3.35).

ON WILMERSDORFER STRASSE

These simple restaurants are convenient if you're exploring Berlin's most popular shopping street, Wilmersdorfer Strasse. In addition, be sure to read "Local Budget Bests," above, for area department stores with food service.

Joseph Langer

Wilmersdorfer Strasse 118. ☎ **030/31 67 80.** 2–9 DM ($1.35–$6). No credit cards. Mon–Fri 9am–6:30pm, Sat 8:30am–2pm (to 6pm the first Sat of the month in winter, to 4pm in summer). U-Bahn: Wilmersdorfer Strasse. GERMAN.

This small butcher shop sells inexpensive and simple meals, which you can eat at one of its stand-up tables or take out. Cheapest are the various Wurst, including Weisswurst (a white sausage from Munich) and Bockwurst (a thick sausage). Other dishes include soups, Leberkäs, Eisbein, Schnitzel, Boulette, and smoked pork chops.

Nordsee

Wilmersdorfer Strasse 58. ☎ **030/323 10 44.** 7–11 DM ($4.65–$7.35). No credit cards. Mon–Wed and Fri 9am–7pm, Thurs 9am–8:30pm, Sat 9am–3pm (to 6:30pm the first Sat of the month in winter, to 4:30pm in summer). U-Bahn: Wilmersdorfer Strasse. FISH.

Nordsee is part of a national chain of fast-food fish restaurants, where ordering is made easy with an illustrated menu behind the cashier. Simply go through the cafeteria line and order one of the dozen choices, such as fried haddock, fish soup, or fish sticks. There's also take-out service, with all kinds of fish sandwiches starting at about 3 DM ($2).

Rogacki

Wilmersdorfer Strasse 145–146 (between Bismarckstrasse and Zillestrasse). ☎ **030/341 40 91.** 5–15 DM ($3.35–$10). No credit cards. Mon–Fri 9am–6pm, Sat 8am–2pm. U-Bahn: Bismarckstrasse. GERMAN.

This immensely popular stand-up cafeteria shares quarters with a famous butcher shop selling all kinds of meats, Wurst, fish, stews, salads, cheese, bread, and more, with various buffets offering sausages, Leberkäs, Schnitzel, and more. There's great variety, and prices are about the best in Berlin. It has been around for 60 years and is located about a 7-minute walk north of the Wilmersdorfer Strasse pedestrian section (look for the lighted fish on its facade).

MEALS FOR LESS THAN 23 DM ($15.35)

ON OR NEAR THE KU'DAMM

Chung

Kurfürstendamm 190 (near Schlüterstrasse). ☎ **030/882 15 55.** Main courses 16–30 DM ($10.65–$20); fixed-price lunch 11–15 DM ($7.35–$10). AE, DC, MC, V. Daily 11:30am–11pm. U-Bahn: Uhlandstrasse or Adenauerplatz. CHINESE.

This ornate Chinese restaurant with hanging lanterns and a red-and-black ceiling occupies a prime spot on the Ku'damm. In fact, it extends over half the side-walk, offering a good view of the famous boulevard. Monday through Friday from 11:30am to 3pm the special lunch menu includes an appetizer and a choice of almost two dozen main courses. There's an English menu, so ordering is no problem.

✪ Hardtke

Meinekestrasse 27 a/b. ☎ **030/881 98 27.** Main courses 15–30 DM ($10–$20). No credit cards. Daily 11am–11:30pm. U-Bahn: Uhlandstrasse; then less than a two-minute walk. GERMAN.

Just off the Ku'damm, this typical German eatery has been here more than 40 years and is popular with German visitors to Berlin. It has its own butcher shop, ensuring the freshest cuts; its sausages are excellent. Although you could spend up to 30 DM ($20) here for dinner of Eisbein, Schnitzel, and Schweinebraten on a splurge, you can also dine on sausages for 10.50 DM ($7) until 6pm; afterward the price increases to 15 DM ($10). Either way, you're in for a treat.

Restaurant Marche Mövenpick

Kurfürstendamm 14–15. ☎ **030/882 75 79.** Main dishes 8–15 DM ($4.35–$10). AE, MC, V. Daily 8am–midnight. U-Bahn: Kurfürstendamm; then a one-minute walk. INTERNATIONAL.

This is one of my favorite places on the Ku'damm. A cafeteria, it imitates the neighborhood market, with various stands of fresh meals—most prepared in front of the customers. There's a salad bar (with prices varying according to which size plate you select), a vegetable stand, and counters offering a selection of meat dishes, soups, pastas, salads, daily specials, cakes, ice cream, desserts, and more. Simply grab a tray and walk around to the various counters. It's a good place to load up on veggies; there are also freshly squeezed fruit and vegetable juices. A meal here will run between 10 and 20 DM ($6.65 and $13.35), depending on what you eat.

San Marino

Savignyplatz 12. ☎ **030/313 60 86.** Pizzas and pasta 8–18.50 DM ($5.35–$12.35). AE, MC. Daily 11am–midnight. S-Bahn: Savignyplatz. ITALIAN.

Most of the pizza and pasta dishes, which is all you need order, are priced under 14 DM ($9.35), but if you feel like splurging you can also order the much higher priced steaks and seafood from the English menu. Even better, come Monday through Friday for the three-course fixed-price lunch costing less than 20 DM ($13.35). The restaurant is pleasant, upscale, and artsy; in summer you can sit outside with a view of Savignyplatz.

Taverna Plaka

Joachimstaler Strasse 14. ☎ **030/883 15 57.** Appetizers and salads 6–12 DM ($4–$8); main courses 15–30 DM ($10–$20). No credit cards. Mon–Fri 4pm–1am, Sat–Sun and hols noon–1am. U-Bahn: Kurfürstendamm. GREEK.

Although most dishes here begin at 16 DM ($10.65), I recommend ordering the plentiful 11-DM ($7.35) mesedes Plaka: an appetizer plate with dolmades (stuffed grape leaves), eggplant salad, feta cheese, and a sampling of other Greek delicacies—the waiter didn't blink twice when that's all I ordered. An alternative is the huge Greek salad (choriatiki) for 12 DM ($8). There's also moussaka, fish, souvlaki, and gyros. Greek wines are available. In any case, this first-floor restaurant is decorated in Mykonos white and blue, with flowers and candles on each table. The service is friendly, and the recorded music is cheerfully Greek.

IN BERLIN-MITTE (EASTERN BERLIN)

Oren

Oranienburger Strasse 28. ☎ **030/282 82 28.** Main courses 11–25 DM ($7.35–$16.65). Daily 10am–midnight. No credit cards. S-Bahn: Oranienburger Strasse. KOSHER/ VEGETARIAN.

About a six-minute walk north of Museum Island, next to a towering gold-domed synagogue currently under renovation, this is the former East Berlin's first modern kosher restaurant. Decorated like a 1920s Berlin coffeehouse and catering to an intellectual crowd, it offers excellently prepared food, with an interesting menu that draws inspiration from Asia, the Middle East, and international vegetarian cuisine. Perhaps start with the Russian borscht or falafel with hummus and pita, followed by grilled fish, vegetarian lasagne, or one of the daily specials. The Orient Express is an assortment of Middle Eastern vegetarian food, including hummus, tachina, falafel, tabouleh, eggplant salad, and pita.

T.G.I. Fridays

Karl-Liebknecht-Strasse 5. ☎ **030/2382 79 60.** Main dishes 14–30 DM ($9.35–$20). AE, DC, MC, V. Daily noon–midnight. S-Bahn: Alexanderplatz or Hackescher Markt. Bus 100 to Spandauer Strasse. AMERICAN.

Just like home—and in the heart of former East Berlin. Opened in 1994, this well-known American chain just a stone's throw from Museum Island is one of the city's best places for bar food, cocktails (more than 400 mind-boggling concoctions), and a variety of American cuisine. Buffalo wings, potato skins, spinach-and-artichoke dip, nachos, black-bean soup, fajitas, Mexican pizza, fettuccine Alfredo, baby back ribs, filet mignon, blackened Cajun chicken, burgers, club sandwiches, and salads are some choices on an extensive menu that's sure to attract the homesick in droves. There's also a children's menu, and Monday through Friday from 11am to 5pm a fixed-price lunch is available for less than 12 DM ($8). The staff is enthusiastic, and in summer there's outdoor dining beside the Spree River with a view of the Berliner Dom.

Wienerwald

Rathausstrasse 5 (just off Alexanderplatz). ☎ **030/242 32 91.** Soups and salads 4–12 DM ($2.65–$8); main courses 11–20 DM ($7.35–$13.35). AE, DC, MC, V. Daily 10am–midnight. S-Bahn and U-Bahn: Alexanderplatz. GERMAN.

Wienerwald is a successful chain of restaurants specializing in grilled chicken, so it's not surprising that they've opened a branch here. Its menu includes a variety of chicken dishes (a quarter chicken with a choice of side dish costs less than $6), fish, soups, and a salad bar.

✪ Zur Letzten Instanz

Waisenstrasse 14–16. ☎ **030/242 55 28.** 15–20 DM ($10–$13.35) AE, DC, MC V. Daily noon–midnight. U-Bahn: Klosterstrasse; then about a two-minute walk. GERMAN.

Open since 1621, this tiny restaurant claims to be Berlin's oldest Gaststätte. Its rooms are rustic, with plank floors, wainscoting, and a few antiques here and there. Its menu offers Berlin specialties, including Boulette, Kohlroulade (stuffed cabbage rolls), and Berliner Eisbein, all served with side dishes. In summer a few tables are placed outside. It's located about a five-minute walk from Alexanderplatz, behind the Rathaus.

NEAR CHARLOTTENBURG PALACE

✪ Luisen-Bräu

Luisenplatz 1. ☎ **030/341 93 88.** 9–20 DM ($6–$13.35). No credit cards. Daily 11am–1am. Bus 109, 121, 145, or 204. GERMAN.

Southeast of Charlottenburg Palace on the corner of Spandauer Damm, Luisen-Bräu brews its own beer on the premises (you can see the stainless-steel tanks) and sells German dishes to go along with it. The food, offered buffet style, changes daily but may include Spiessbraten (skewered meat and vegetables), Kasseler Rippenspeer (pork chops), Schweinebraten (pot-roasted pork), Boulette (a meatball), salads, and stews. Dining is at long wooden tables (which includes conversation with neighbors) or, in summer, outside. This place is convenient if you're visiting the palace or the many area museums. And it's a good place for just a beer, served in a tiny mug for 2.60 DM ($1.75).

IN DAHLEM

Luise

Königin-Luise-Strasse 40. ☎ **030/832 84 87.** 7.50–17 DM ($5–$11.35). No credit cards. Daily 10am–11pm. U-Bahn: Dahlem-Dorf; then about a one-minute walk. GERMAN/ INTERNATIONAL.

If you're visiting the many Dahlem museums, try this popular watering hole for people who live in the area (as crowded as it can get on a weekday afternoon, I wonder whether any of them work). It serves snacks and main courses, including spaghetti, Leberkäs with fried egg and potatoes, garlic chicken, Cordon Bleu, tortellini in Gorgonzola sauce, eggplant casserole, and daily specials. The indoors tends to be smoky since every other German smokes, but in fine weather Luise boasts a large outdoor beer garden.

NEAR WILMERSDORFER STRASSE & BAHNHOF CHARLOTTENBURG

Ty Breizh Savoie Rire
Kantstrasse 75. ☎ **030/323 99 32.** Main courses 18.50–27 DM ($12.35–$18). No credit cards. Mon–Fri 5pm–midnight, Sat 6pm–midnight. U-Bahn: Wilmersdorfer Strasse. S-Bahn: Charlottenburg. FRENCH

This simple restaurant resembling a college pizza parlor more than a French establishment is owned by the gregarious Patrick Matteï, who speaks English, Italian, French, German, and Finnish; he works as the chef here and even sings chansons when he has time. His specialties are the appetizer of mushrooms with shrimp and cheese, housemade pâté, cheeses imported from Savoie, and the fish soup. Other dishes include avocado with shrimp, orange duck with pepper sauce, oysters, pork filet, and beef cooked in a burgundy sauce with onions, plus seafood. There are also changing specials, which may include couscous, lamb, duck, mussels, or tripe. A good place for French food on a budget.

STREET EATS

There are a number of food stalls (Imbisse) up and down the Ku'damm and on Alexanderplatz selling Wurst, french fries, Turkish specialties, and beer. Prices are generally under 4 DM ($2.65). In addition, a number of restaurants described above—including Higher Taste, Ihre Frisch-Backstübe, Nordsee, Joseph Langer, Rogacki, Piccola Taormina Tavola Calda, Einhorn, Asia-Quick, Ashoka, and Karavan—sell take-out food at low prices.

PICNICKING

All the **department stores** above have large food departments (especially KaDeWe) and counters serving prepared meats, salads, and take-out food. You can also buy take-out food at the stand-up establishments listed above.

As for a place to consume your purchases, the most convenient green space is the huge **Tiergarten** park just northwest of Bahnhof Zoo.

WORTH THE EXTRA MONEY

✪ Zitadelle
Am Juliusturm, Spandau. ☎ **030/334 21 06.** Reservations recommended. Fixed-price banquet 74.50 DM ($49.65). AE, DC, MC, V. Tues–Sun 7–11pm. U-Bahn: Zitadelle. GERMAN.

Imagine sitting in the bowels of a 700-year-old fortress with stone walls and an open fireplace and then eating fish or skewered grilled meat much as people did centuries ago. The Zitadelle is such a fortress, offering a medieval banquet every evening except Monday with ballad-singing and special entertainment; it's best to make a reservation. Meals include a welcoming drink in a bull's horn, bread, an appetizer, a main dish such as Spiessbraten, and several other dishes. Although Spandau is on the outskirts of Berlin and was its own city until incorporated in 1920, it's easily reached by subway.

6 Attractions

SIGHTSEEING SUGGESTIONS

Berlin is compact, with an efficient public transportation system, so you can see quite a lot of the city in a few days. To help you get the most out of your visit, here are some suggestions to guide you to the most important attractions.

If You Have 1 Day

Berlin's most famous treasures are the Pergamon Altar and the bust of Nefertiti. If you want to see both, head first thing in the morning to the Ägyptisches Museum (closed Friday) in Charlottenburg, where Berlin's legendary beauty—Nefertiti—holds court. Across the street is Schloss Charlottenburg, Berlin's beautiful baroque palace, where you should visit the Historical Rooms, Knobelsdorff Flügel, and the Schinkel Pavilion for a look at how Prussian royalty lived. You can also stroll its lovely gardens.

In the afternoon, head for the Brandenburger Tor (Brandenburg Gate), built in the 1780s as the finishing touch to Unter den Linden, one of Berlin's most famous boulevards. When the Berlin Wall fell, it was here at the gate that many Berliners gathered to rejoice. Take a stroll down Unter den Linden to the Pergamon Museum on Museumsinsel (Museum Island) with its incredible Pergamon Altar.

If you still have the energy for more sightseeing, round out your eastern Berlin experience with a trip to the Museum Haus am Checkpoint Charlie, which opened in 1961 with the sole purpose of documenting the Berlin Wall and the many attempts of East Berliners to escape to the West. Today it's the best place in the city to gain an understanding of what Berlin was like during the decades of division.

Finish off the day with a leisurely evening stroll along the Ku'damm and a meal in a German restaurant.

If You Have 2 Days

Devote the entire first morning to Dahlem, which boasts half a dozen museums (note that most of these are closed Monday). The most significant is the Gemäldegalerie (Picture Gallery), with masterpieces from the 13th to 18th century. Add to it one or two of the museums that most interest you. The Museum für Deutsche Volkskunde (Museum of German Ethnology) has an excellent display of simple furniture and household items used by Germany's middle class, peasants, and farmers. The ethnological museum is one of the world's largest. There are also fine museums displaying Asian art.

In the afternoon, head for Charlottenburg, where in addition to Schloss Charlottenburg and the Ägyptisches Museum, there's the Museum of Greek and Roman Antiquities, the Museum of Pre- and Early History, and the wonderful Bröhan Museum with its art deco and Jugendstil (art nouveau) collection.

On Day 2, go to eastern Berlin, visiting the Brandenburg Gate and Museum Island with the Pergamon Museum and three other worthwhile museums. Finish the afternoon with a walk to Alexanderplatz, once the heart of East Germany's capital, and the nearby Nikolai Quarter, a small neighborhood of restored buildings. At the end of the day, head for the Museum Haus am Checkpoint Charlie with its important collections documenting the history of the Wall.

If You Have 3 Days

Spend Days 1 and 2 as outlined above. On Day 3, include the Nationalgalerie in your morning activities for a look at German and European artists of the 20th century. Spend the rest of the day according to your own special interests: the Käthe-Kollwitz-Museum with its powerful drawings, the Bauhaus-Archiv and the Hansa Quarter for architectural buffs, the Ku'damm and Wilmersdorfer Strasse for shopping.

If You Have 5 Days

Spend Days 1 to 3 as outlined above. In addition, be sure to include a visit to the flea market held every Saturday and Sunday on Strasse des 17. Juni near the Tiergarten. If you're in Berlin on a Tuesday or Friday afternoon, consider visiting the Turkish Market with its colorful stands of fruits, vegetables, and exotic spices and food.

On Day 4, take an excursion to Lake Wannsee or Havel, where you can swim or take a boat trip and spend a relaxing day. On Day 5, visit Potsdam in eastern Germany with its palace and park of Sanssouci.

TOP ATTRACTIONS

Berlin has four major museum centers: **Dahlem,** with its famous Gemäldegalerie and museums of non-European art; **Charlottenburg,** with its palace and museums of ancient art and antiquities; the **Tiergarten,** a newly developed center for European art; and the excellent museums on **Museumsinsel (Museum Island),** formerly of East Berlin. It therefore makes sense to cover Berlin section by section—it saves not only time but also money. Most of the museum clusters, including many of those in Dahlem, several on Museum Island, and those in the Tiergarten, offer their own combination ticket (called *Sammelkarte,* or *Tageskarte*), allowing entrance to several museums in the area at a reduced rate if visited on the same day. If you're on a tight budget, remember that most museums in Berlin are free on Sunday and holidays.

MUSEUMS IN DAHLEM

All museums below are in the section of Berlin called Dahlem, which you can reach by taking U-Bahn U-1 from Wittenbergplatz to the Dahlem-Dorf station; you'll find signs pointing to the museums. Under the same sprawling roof as the Gemäldegalerie are the museums for sculpture, ethnology, and for East Asian,

---

❓ Did You Know?

- By the year 1700, nearly one Berliner in five was of French extraction.
- In the 1920s Berlin boasted 35 theaters, several opera houses, more than 20 concert halls, and as many as 150 daily newspapers.
- More than 30% of Berlin is forests, rivers, and lakes with miles of hiking trails and biking paths.
- Founded in 1841, Berlin's Tiergarten zoo housed more than 12,000 specimens by 1939; only 91 animals survived the war.
- Berlin has more students than any other German city.

Dahlem Museums

TOP FLOOR
(not shown)

UPPER FLOOR

3 Museum für Völkerkunde
   (South Seas)
4 Skulpturengalerie
5 Gemäldegalerie
7 Museum für Völkerkunde
   (Africa)
9 Museum für Islamische Kunst
10 Museum für Ostasiatische
    Kunst
11 Museum für Völkerkunde
    (Southeast Asia)
12 Special exhibitions

GROUND FLOOR

1 Museum für Indische Kunst
2 Museum für Völkerkunde
   (America)
3 Museum für Völkerkunde
   (South Seas)
4 Skulpturengalerie
5 Gemäldegalerie

LOWER FLOOR

A Lecture Room
B Young People's Museum
C Cafeteria
D Museum for the Blind

UPPER FLOOR

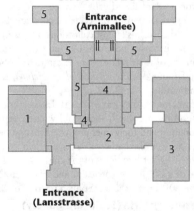

GROUND FLOOR

LOWER FLOOR

Islamic, and Indian arts, and the admission price to all of them is only 4 DM ($2.65), one of Berlin's best bargains. There are entrances to the museum complex at both Arnimallee 23—27 and Lansstrasse 8; look for the sign that says STAATLICHE MUSEEN.

Note: A couple of the Dahlem museums will be moved to new quarters near the Tiergarten by the turn of the century. The Gemäldegalerie will move to the Tiergarten in 1998, followed by the Skulpturengalerie after the end of the century. Tiergarten will thus become the center for European art, while Dahlem will house collections of non-European art; Charlottenburg will continue to be the place to go for ancient and early art.

✪ Gemäldegalarie (Picture Gallery)

Arnimallee 23–27 or Lansstrasse 8. ☎ **030/8301 216.** (Dahlem complex combination ticket) 4 DM ($2.65) adults, 2 DM ($1.35) students and children; free for everyone Sun and hols. Tues–Fri 9am–5pm, Sat–Sun 10am–5pm. U-Bahn: U-1 to Dahlem-Dorf.

Western Berlin's top art museum, this famous collection offers a comprehensive survey of European painting from the 13th to the 18th century. Although 400 major works were destroyed in World War II and the remaining collection was divided between East and West Berlin in the war's aftermath, the gallery still owns more than 1,500 paintings, half of which are on display (more will be shown when it moves into its new Tiergarten home).

Included in the German, Dutch, Italian, French, English, Flemish, and Spanish works are paintings by Dürer, Cranach, Holbein, Gainsborough, Brueghel, Botticelli, Raphael, Rubens, Vermeer, Murillo, and Velázquez, to name only a few. The top attractions of the Dutch section are the 20-some paintings by Rembrandt, one of the world's largest collections by this master. Look for his self-portrait and (my favorite) his portrayal of Hendrickje Stoffels, his common-law wife—the intimacy of their relationship is captured in her face as she gazes at Rembrandt. The famous *Man with the Golden Helmet,* however, is no longer attributed to Rembrandt.

Another of my favorites is Lucas Cranach's *Fountain of Youth* (Der Jungbrunnen), which shows old women being led to the fountain, swimming through it, and then emerging youthful and beautiful. Note that apparently only women need the bath—men regain their youth through relations with younger women! Other highlights of the collection include Botticelli's *Venus,* Dürer's portrait of a Nürnberg patrician, and Hans Holbein's portrait of merchant Georg Gisze. Of course, these are only a fraction of what the museum offers.

Skulpturengalerie (Sculpture Gallery)

Arnimallee 23–27. ☎ **030/8301 252.** (Dahlem complex combination ticket) 4 DM ($2.65) adults, 2 DM ($1.35) students and children; free for everyone Sun and hols. Tues–Fri 9am–5pm, Sat–Sun 10am–5pm. U-Bahn: U-1 to Dahlem-Dorf.

This museum contains European sculptures from the early Christian and Byzantine periods to the end of the 18th century and rates as one of the foremost sculpture collections in Germany. Particularly well represented are works from the Italian Renaissance and German gothic era, including carvings byRiemenschneider, but there are also ivories and bronzes.

Museum für Völkerkunde (Ethnological Museum)

Lansstrasse 8. ☎ **030/8301 226.** (Dahlem complex combination ticket) 4 DM ($2.65) adults, 2 DM ($1.35) students and children; free for everyone Sun and hols. Tues–Fri 9am–5pm, Sat–Sun 10am–5pm. U-Bahn: U-1 to Dahlem-Dorf.

One of the world's largest ethnological museums, it possesses half a million items from around the world, including those from ancient America, Africa, the South Seas, and Asia. Particularly fascinating are the life-size boats and dwellings and facades from various corners of the earth.

Museum für Islamische Kunst (Museum of Islamic Art)

Lansstrasse 8. ☎ **030/8301-1.** (Dahlem complex combination ticket) 4 DM ($2.65) adults, 2 DM ($1.35) students and children; free for everyone Sun and hols. Tues–Fri 9am–5pm, Sat–Sun 10am–5pm. U-Bahn: U-1 to Dahlem-Dorf.

Carpets, sculpture, examples of Arabic script, pottery, glass, jewelry, miniatures, and other applied art from the 8th to the 18th century are on display here, with works of art from all Muslim countries represented.

Museum für Indische Kunst (Museum of Indian Art)

Lansstrasse 8. ☎ **030/8301 361.** (Dahlem complex combination ticket) 4 DM ($2.65) adults, 2 DM ($1.35) students and children; free for everyone Sun and hols. Tues–Fri 9am–5pm, Sat–Sun 10am–5pm. U-Bahn: U-1 to Dahlem-Dorf.

The most significant collection of Indian art in Germany, this museum covers a period of almost 4,000 years with its displays of terra-cotta and stone sculptures, miniatures, bronzes, and frescos from Turfan. Included are items from throughout India and Nepal, Tibet, Burma, Thailand, Indonesia, and other centers of Buddhism.

Museum für Ostasiatische Kunst (Museum of Far Eastern Art)

Lansstrasse 8. ☎ **030/8301 382.** (Dahlem complex combination ticket) 4 DM ($2.65) adults, 2 DM ($1.35) students and children; free for everyone Sun and hols. Tues–Fri 9am–5pm, Sat–Sun 10am–5pm. U-Bahn: U-1 to Dahlem-Dorf.

Displayed here are works from China, Korea, and Japan from 3000 B.C. to the present, including woodcuts, paintings, bronzes, ceramics, lacquerware, and sculptures.

Museum für Deutsche Volkskunde (Museum of German Ethnology)

Im Winkel 6–8. ☎ **030/839 01-01.** Admission 4 DM ($2.65) adults, 2 DM ($1.35) students and children; free for everyone Sun and hols. Tues–Fri 9am–5pm, Sat–Sun 10am–5pm. U-Bahn: U-1 to Dahlem-Dorf; then a five-minute walk (follow the signs).

In Dahlem but not part of the Dahlem complex, this museum is devoted to past generations of middle- and lower-class Germans, including farmers, artisans, and homemakers. It contains a fascinating exhibit of items used in work, leisure time, and religious celebrations, including peasant furniture, clothing, pottery, household items, and utensils for making butter and turning flax into linen. On display are items collected from throughout Germany and Austria. Unfortunately, explanations are in German only, but there's an English pamphlet.

SIGHTS IN CHARLOTTENBURG

To get to the attractions below, take city bus no. 109, 110, 145, or X26 (from the Ku'damm, no. 109 is the most convenient; get off at Luisenplatz). An alternative is to take U-Bahn U-2 to Sophie-Charlotte-Platz, then walk 10 minutes up Schlossstrasse to Spandauer Damm. Most of the museums are on the corner of Schlossstrasse and Spandauer Damm.

If you plan to visit several museums, consider purchasing an 8-DM ($5.35) combination ticket allowing entry to the Egyptian Museum, Museum of Antiquities, Museum of Pre- and Early History, and the Galerie der Romantik. Note that the ticket is valid for only one day. In addition, Charlottenburg Palace has its own combination ticket for the various sights on its grounds.

✪ Charlottenburg Palace

Spandauer Damm. ☎ **030/32 09 11.** Knobelsdorff Flügel, 3 DM ($2) adults, 1.50 DM ($1) students and children; Schinkel Pavilion and Belvedere, each 2.50 DM ($1.65) adults, 1.50 DM ($1) students and children; Mausoleum, 1 DM (65¢) adults, .50 DM (35¢) students and children; Galerie der Romantik, 4 DM ($2.65) adults, 2 DM ($1.35) students and children; combination ticket covering all the above and guided tour, 8 DM ($5.35) adults, 3 DM ($2) children and students. Tues–Fri 9am–5pm, Sat–Sun 10am–5pm. Mausoleum closed Nov–Mar. U-Bahn: U-2 to Sophie-Charlotte-Platz; then a 10-minute walk. Bus 109, 110, 145, or X26 to Luisenplatz.

Charlottenburg Palace was built in 1695 for Sophia Charlotte, wife of the future king of Prussia, Frederick I. Later it was expanded and served as the summer residence of the Prussian kings, the Hohenzollern family. Badly damaged during World War II and since restored, it consists of one main building and several outlying structures. Straight ahead as you enter the main gate is the **Nering-Eosander Building,** which contains the Historical Rooms, once the private quarters of Sophia Charlotte and her husband. Of these, the Porcelain Cabinet is the most striking (and kitschy), filled with about 2,000 pieces of porcelain. Unfortunately, you have to join a guided tour conducted only in German to visit this part of the palace, but it's worth it because upstairs are some rooms you can wander through on your own before or after your tour—these rooms contain a collection of tapestries, goblets, swords, portraits, and other royal possessions, including the royal Hohenzollern insignia and a stunning silver place setting completed in 1914 but never used by the royal family because of the outbreak of World War I.

To the right of the Nering-Eosander Building is the **Knobelsdorff Flügel (New Wing),** where you can wander on your own through more royal quarters, the state dining hall, and the elaborate ballroom, as well as through the Galerie der Romantik with its 19th-century paintings.

Next head for the **Schinkel Pavilion,** located behind the New Wing. This delightful small summerhouse, built in the style of an Italian villa, has cozy rooms, each unique and decorated with period arts and crafts. After strolling through the park (laid out in the French style in 1697 and restored to its baroque form after World War II), visit the **Belvedere,** a former teahouse that now contains 18th- and 19th-century Berlin porcelain. On the west side of the park is the **Mausoleum** with the tombs of King Frederick William III, Queen Louise, and others.

✪ Ägyptisches Museum (Egyptian Museum)

Schlossstrasse 70. ☎ **030/32 09 11.** Admission 4 DM ($2.65) adults, 2 DM ($1.35) students and children; combination ticket, 8 DM ($5.35) adults, 4 DM ($2.65) students; free for everyone Sun and hols. Mon–Thurs 9am–5pm, Sat–Sun 10am–5pm. U-Bahn: U-2 to Sophie-Charlotte-Platz; then a 10-minute walk. Bus 109, 110, 145, or X26 to Luisenplatz.

Across from Charlottenburg Palace is this collection illustrating Egyptian cultural history. Berlin's most famous art object is here, on the first floor in a dark room reserved just for her. Created more than 3,300 years ago, the Queen Nefertiti bust amazingly never left the sculptor's studio but rather served as a model for all other portraits of the queen and was left on a shelf when the ancient city was deserted. The bust was discovered early this century by German archaeologists.

In an adjoining room you can see smaller likenesses of Pharaoh Akhenaton (husband of Nefertiti) and the royal family, including Nefertiti's eldest daughter, Princess Meritaton. Look also for Queen Tiy, Akhenaton's mother. There are

Around Charlottenburg

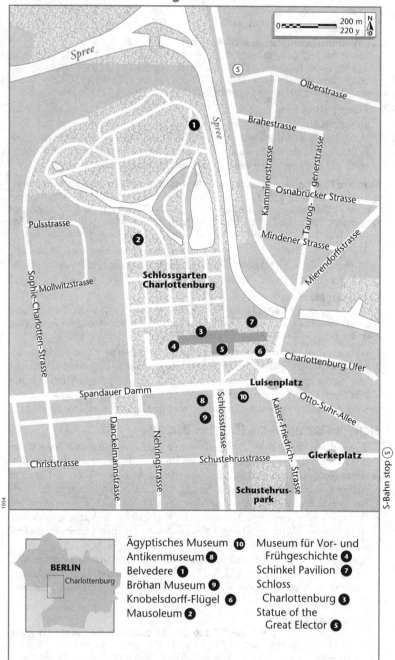

Spree

Olberstrasse

Brahestrasse

Kamminerstrasse

Osnabrücker Strasse

Taurog-
generstrasse

Mindener Strasse

Mierendorffstrasse

Pulsstrasse

Sophie-Charlotten-Strasse

Mollwitzstrasse

**Schlossgarten
Charlottenburg**

Charlottenburg Ufer

Luisenplatz

Spandauer Damm

Schlossstrasse

Otto-Suhr-Allee

Kaiser-Friedrich-Strasse

Danckelmannstrasse

Nehringstrasse

Schustehrusstrasse

Gierkeplatz

Christstrasse

**Schustehrus-
park**

S-Bahn stop Ⓢ

1054

BERLIN

Charlottenburg

Ägyptisches Museum ⑩
Antikenmuseum ⑧
Belvedere ❶
Bröhan Museum ❾
Knobelsdorff-Flügel ❻
Mausoleum ❷

Museum für Vor- und
  Frühgeschichte ❹
Schinkel Pavilion ❼
Schloss
  Charlottenburg ❸
Statue of the
  Great Elector ❺

many other amazing items in this wonderful museum, including the Kalabasha Gate, bronzes, vases, burial objects, and tools used in everyday life.

Antikenmuseum (Museum of Antiquities)

Schlossstrasse 1. ☎ **030/32 09 11.** Admission 4 DM ($2.65) adults, 2 DM ($1.35) students and children; combination ticket, 8 DM ($5.35) adults, 4 DM ($2.65) students; free for everyone Sun and hols. Mon–Thurs 9am–5pm, Sat–Sun 10am–5pm. U-Bahn: U-2 to Sophie-Charlotte-Platz; then a 10-minute walk. Bus 109, 110, 145, or X26 to Luisenplatz.

Directly across from the Egyptian Museum, this museum of Greek and Roman antiquities contains pottery, ivory carvings, glassware, jewelry, and wood and stone sarcophagi, and small marble statuettes. Particularly outstanding are the Attic red-figure vases of the 5th century B.C. and the treasury (in the basement) with its silver and exquisite gold jewelry from about 2000 B.C. to late antiquity.

Museum für vor- und Frühgeschichte (Museum of Pre- and Early History)

Spandauer Damm. ☎ **030/32 09 11.** Admission 4 DM ($2.65) adults, 2 DM ($1.35) students and children; combination ticket, 8 DM ($5.35) adults, 4 DM ($2.65) students; free for everyone Sun and hols. Mon–Thurs 9am–5pm, Sat–Sun 10am–5pm. U-Bahn: U-2 to Sophie-Charlotte-Platz; then a 10-minute walk. Bus 109, 110, 145, or X26 to Luisenplatz.

To the left of Charlottenburg if you're facing the palace, this museum houses archeological finds from the Stone Age, Bronze Age, and late Iron Age, with objects arranged chronologically illustrating life in Europe and the Near East.

✪ Bröhan Museum

Schlossstrasse 1a. ☎ **030/321 40 29.** Admission 4 DM ($2.65) adults, 2 DM ($1.35) students. Tues–Sun 10am–6pm. U-Bahn: U-2 to Sophie-Charlotte-Platz; then a 10-minute walk. Bus 109, 110, 145, or X26 to Luisenplatz.

Next to the Antikenmuseum is the only private museum of the bunch. It specializes in objects dating from 1889 to 1939 of the art nouveau (Jugendstil in German) and art deco periods, with exquisite vases, glass, furniture, silver, paintings, and other works of art arranged in drawing-room fashion. The rooms serve as a welcome change from the antiquities of the surrounding museums. Don't miss it.

SIGHTS IN BERLIN-MITTE (EASTERN BERLIN)

To see the following sights, I suggest you start your tour with a stroll down Unter den Linden (the closest S-Bahn station is Unter den Linden, or take bus no. 100), where you'll see the Brandenburg Gate and pass the Neue Wache, dedicated to victims of war and totalitarianism. Farther down is Museumsinsel with the excellent Pergamon Museum. Alexanderplatz, the concrete modern heart of eastern Berlin, is a five-minute walk farther west on Karl-Liebknecht-Strasse and is where you'll find the TV tower. Nearby is also the Nikolai Quarter, a reconstructed Old Berlin neighborhood.

A *Tageskarte,* or combination ticket valid for one day, in this part of Berlin costs 8 DM ($5.35) for adults and 4 DM ($2.65) for students and children and allows entry into three museums on Museum Island—the Pergamon Museum, Bodemuseum, and Alte Nationalgalerie.

✪ Pergamon Museum

Bodestrasse 1–3, on Museum Island. ☎ **030/203 55-0.** Admission 4 DM ($2.65) adults, 2 DM ($1.35) children; combination ticket, 8 DM ($5.35) adults, 4 DM ($2.65) students; free for everyone Sun and hols. Tues–Sun 9am–5pm. S-Bahn: Hackescher Markt or Friedrichstrasse; then a 10-minute walk. Bus 100 to the Deutsche Staatsoper stop.

Eastern Berlin

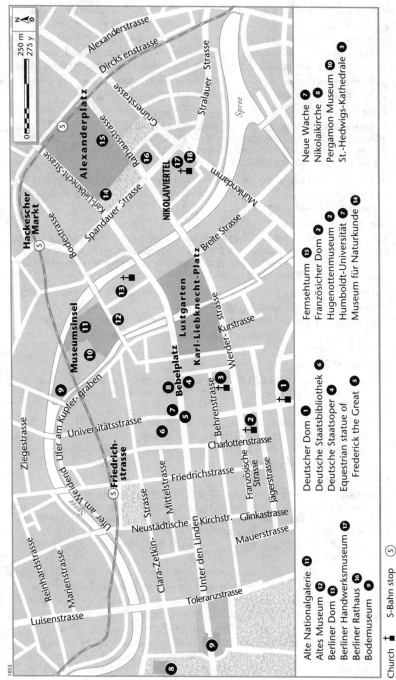

Deutscher Dom **1**
Deutsche Staatsbibliothek **6**
Deutsche Staatsoper **4**
Equestrian statue of
Frederick the Great **5**

Neue Wache **7**
Nikolaikirche **8**
Pergamon Museum **10**
St.-Hedwigs-Kathedrale **3**

Fernsehturm **15**
Französischer Dom **2**
Hugenottenmuseum **2**
Humboldt-Universität **7**
Museum für Naturkunde **14**

Alte Nationalgalerie **11**
Altes Museum **12**
Berliner Dom **13**
Berliner Handwerksmuseum **17**
Berliner Rathaus **16**
Bodemuseum **9**

Church ✝ ■   S-Bahn stop Ⓢ

Entrance to Berlin's most famous museum is via the bridge on Kupfergraben, behind and to the left of Das Alte Museum. It's named after its most prized possession, the Pergamon Altar, a magnificent masterpiece of Hellenistic art of the 2nd century B.C. and certainly one of the wonders of the ancient world. Essentially a museum of architecture, the Pergamon also contains the Market Gate of Milet, as well as the dazzling Babylonian Processional Way leading to the Gate of Ishtar. There's also an Islamic section and an East Asian collection.

Bodemuseum

Bodestrasse 1–3, on Museum Island. ☎ **030/203 55-0.** Admission 4 DM ($2.65) adults, 2 DM ($1.35) children; combination ticket, 8 DM ($5.35) adults, 4 DM ($2.65) students; free for everyone Sun and hols. Tues–Sun 9am–5pm. S-Bahn: Hackescher Markt or Friedrichstrasse; then a 10-minute walk. Bus 100 to the Deutsche Staatsoper stop.

This is several museums in one, housing the Egyptian Museum, the Papyrus Collection, the Early Christian and Byzantine Collection, the sculpture collection, and the Picture Gallery with art from the 13th to the 18th century.

Alte Nationalgalerie

Bodestrasse, on Museum Island. ☎ **030/203 55-0.** Admission 4 DM ($2.65) adults, 2 DM ($1.35) children; combination ticket, 8 DM ($5.35) adults, 4 DM ($2.65) students; free for everyone Sun and hols. Tues–Sun 9am–5pm. S-Bahn: Hackescher Markt or Friedrichstrasse; then a 10-minute walk. Bus 100 to the Deutsche Staatsoper stop.

Looking much like a Corinthian temple, the National Gallery is devoted to 19th-century painting and sculpture, by artists of Germany, France, and other European countries. Of special note are the works by German expressionists, the world's largest collection of Berlin artist Adolph von Menzel, and works by French impressionists.

Das Alte Museum

Museum Island. ☎ **030/203 55-0.** Admission varies according to the exhibit. Tues–Sun 9am–5pm. S-Bahn: Hackescher Markt or Friedrichstrasse; then a 10-minute walk. Bus 100 to the Lustgarden stop.

Resembling a Greek temple and designed by Berlin's greatest architect, Karl Friedrich Schinkel, this is the first museum you see on Museum Island if you approach from Unter den Linden. It offers changing exhibitions, devoted mainly to art and objects of ancient times.

Berliner Dom

In the Lustgarten, on Museum Island. ☎ **030/246 91 35** or 246 91 19. Cathedral, free; crypt, 3 DM ($2) adults, 1.50 DM ($1) students; organ concerts, 8 DM ($5.35) adults, 5 DM ($3.35) students and senior citizens, free for children 13 and under. Cathedral, Mon–Sat 9am–6:30pm, Sun 11:30am–6:30pm; worship service, Sun 10–11:30am (English translation provided); organ concerts, Mon–Sat at 3pm, Sun at 2pm. Bus 100 to the Lustgarten stop.

The most striking and dominating structure on Museum Island, the Berlin Cathedral was constructed at the turn of the century in Italian Renaissance style to serve as the central church for Prussian Protestants and as the court church and primary burial site of the Hohenzollern imperial family. Severely damaged during World War II, it was finally reopened in 1993 after decades of restoration. Of special note are the gilded wall altar of the 12 apostles designed by Schinkel, the impressive Sauer organ with more than 7,000 pipes, and the ornate coffins of King Frederick I and his wife, Sophie Charlotte, designed by Andreas Schlüter. The basement crypt holds more coffins but is not worth the admission fee unless you're a real Hohenzollern fan.

Deutsches Historisches Museum

Unter den Linden 2. ☎ **030/215 02-0.** Admission varies according to the exhibit. Thurs–Tues 10am–6pm. Bus 100 to the Deutsche Staatsoper stop.

This rather austere baroque building was built in the 17th century as an arsenal for the Prussian army. The inner courtyard is famous for its 22 masks of dying soldiers designed by Schlüter. Today it features changing exhibits related to German history.

Brandenburger Tor (Brandenburg Gate)

Unter den Linden. Admission free. Room of Silence, daily 11am–4pm. S-Bahn: Unter den Linden. Bus 100 to the Unter den Linden/Brandenburger Tor stop.

During the decades of the Wall, the Brandenburger Tor stood in a no-man's land, marking the boundary of East and West Berlin and becoming the symbol of a divided Germany. After the November 1989 revolution and the fall of the Wall, it was here that many Berliners gathered to rejoice and dance together on top of the Wall. The Gate was built from 1788 to 1791 by Carl Gotthard Langhans as the grand western entrance onto Unter den Linden. One of the gate's guardhouses serves as a Room of Silence, a place for silence and reflection; the other guardhouse is home to a Berlin tourist office, open daily from 10am to 6pm.

Reichstag (Parliament)

Platz der Republik. ☎ **030/39 77-0.** S-Bahn: Unter den Linden. Bus 100 to the Reichstag stop.

Although technically in western Berlin, the Reichstag is most easily combined with a trip to eastern Berlin. Completed in 1894 in neo-Renaissance style to serve the needs of Bismarck's united Germany, it is now being renovated for future use by Germany's parliament (which is now in Bonn) and is presently closed. In 1995 the Bulgarian-born artist Christo brought international attention to the structure when he wrapped it in a million square feet of aluminum sheeting to dramatize the transformation of post-Wall Germany. Behind the Reichstag are white crosses serving as a simple memorial to East Berliners who died trying to escape to West Berlin— the Wall used to run behind the Reichstag, with the Spree River and a watch tower on the other side.

IN KREUZBERG

○ Museum Haus am Checkpoint Charlie

Friedrichstrasse 44. ☎ **030/251 10 31.** Admission 7.50 DM ($5) adults, 4.50 DM ($3) students. Daily 9am–10pm. U-Bahn: Kochstrasse.

If this is your first trip to Berlin, this museum is a must-see. Near what was once the most frequently used border crossing into East Berlin, Checkpoint Charlie, this important collection documents events that took place around the Berlin Wall, including successful and failed attempts to escape from East Berlin. With displays in English, the museum aptly illustrates these years in Berlin's history with photographs, items used in escape attempts (such as cars with hidden compartments), and newspaper clippings. A block farther north, on the original site of Checkpoint Charlie, is a small open-air museum of sorts, complete with a section of the Wall, a guard tower, and other relics of the Cold War.

MORE ATTRACTIONS

IN THE TIERGARTEN

A combination ticket costing 8 DM ($5.35) for adults and 4 DM ($2.65) for students and children allows entry to the Kunstgewerbe Museum and Neue

Nationalgalerie, as well as the nearby Musikinstrumenten Museum (Museum of Musical Instruments).

Kunstgewerbe Museum (Museum of Applied Arts)

Tiergartenstrasse 6. ☎ **030/266 29 11.** Admission 4 DM ($2.65) adults, 2 DM ($1.35) students and children; combination ticket, 8 DM ($5.35) adults, 4 DM ($2.65) students; free for everyone Sun and hols. Tues–Fri 9am–5pm, Sat–Sun 10am–5pm. U-Bahn: Kurfürstenstrasse; then bus no. 148 or 248. Bus 129 from the Ku'damm.

A three-minute walk from the Neue Nationalgalerie (below), this museum is housed in a modern red-brick building and devoted to European applied arts from the early Middle Ages to the present, including glassware, porcelain, beer steins, tableware, and measuring instruments. The collection of medieval goldsmiths' works is outstanding, as are the displays of Venetian glass, early Meissen porcelain, and art nouveau (Jugendstil) vases and objects. The bottom floor features changing exhibits of contemporary crafts and product design, from typewriters to tea pots or furniture.

Kupferstichkabinett—Sammlung der Zeichnungen und Druckgraphik (Collection of Prints and Drawings)

Matthaikirchplatz 8. ☎ **030/266 20 02.** Admission free. Museum, Tues–Fri 9am–5pm, Sat–Sun 10am–5pm; Studien Saal, Tues–Fri 9am–4pm. U-Bahn: Kurfürstenstrasse; then bus no. 148 or 248. Bus 120 from the Ku'damm.

This museum specializes in prints and drawings from the German masters, including important works by Albrecht Dürer, and more modern works by such artists as Käthe Kollwitz, Schinkel, and Caspar David Friedrich. It's also a repository for architectural sketches from the late 15th century to the present, more than 40,000 photographs ranging from documentary to art, book illustrations, and poster and advertisement art. Works from the extensive collections are shown only on a temporary basis in themed exhibitions; if you wish to view specific prints or drawings, such as works by Dürer, you can do so at the Studien Saal (Study Hall).

Neue Nationalgalerie (New National Gallery)

Potsdamer Strasse 50. ☎ **030/266 26 62.** Admission 4 DM ($2.65) adults, 2 DM ($1.35) students and children; combination ticket, 8 DM ($5.35) adults, 4 DM ($2.65) students; free for everyone Sun and hols; temporary special exhibits, varies. Tues–Fri 9am–5pm, Sat–Sun 10am–5pm. U-Bahn: Kurfürstenstrasse; then bus no. 148 or 248. Bus 129 from the Ku'damm.

This was one of the first museums to open in the new museum area near the Tiergarten. A starkly modern building designed by Mies van der Rohe and set into a vast square surrounded by a sculpture garden, the Nationalgalerie houses art of the 20th century. The ground floor is devoted to changing exhibitions, while the permanent collection in the basement shows works of Munch, Liebermann, Max Slevogt, Emil Nolde, and other members of Die Brücke (The Bridge) group of artists, plus such internationally known artists as Picasso, Ernst, Kokoschka, Dix, Klee, Feininger, and more.

NEAR THE KU'DAMM

Kaiser-Wilhelm Gedächtniskirche (Kaiser Wilhelm Memorial Church)

Breitscheidplatz. ☎ **030/24 50 23.** Admission free. Ruined church, Tues–Sat 10am–4pm; new church, daily 9am–7pm; organ concerts in new church Sat at 6pm. U-Bahn: Bahnhof Zoologischer Garten or Kurfürstendamm.

Around the Tiergarten

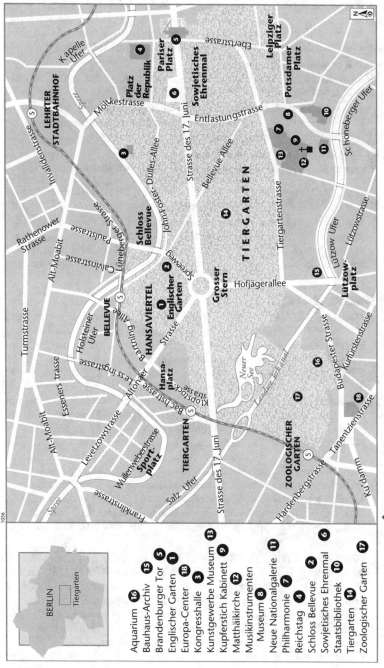

✝ Church   Ⓢ S-Bahn stop

BERLIN
Tiergarten

Completed in 1895, this church was destroyed by bombs during World War II and was left in ruins as a reminder of the horrors of war. Today it contains a small museum with displays related to war and destruction. Beside the ruined church is a new church designed by Prof. Egon Eiermann and finished in 1961.

○ Käthe-Kollwitz-Museum

Fasanenstrasse 24 (just off the Ku'damm). ☎ 030/882 52 10. Admission 6 DM ($4) adults, 3 DM ($2) students. Wed–Mon 11am–6pm. U-Bahn: Uhlandstrasse.

This small but significant museum shows the powerful drawings and sketches of Käthe Kollwitz (1867–1945), a Berliner who managed to capture human emotions both tender and disturbing in her subjects.

○ Zoologischer Garten (Berlin Zoo)

Budapester Strasse 32 and Hardenbergplatz 8. ☎ 030/25 40 10. Combination ticket for both zoo and aquarium, 15 DM ($10) adults, 12 DM ($8) students, 7.50 DM ($5) children; zoo only, 10 DM ($6.65) adults, 8 DM ($5.35) students, 5 DM ($3.35) children. Summer, daily 9am–6:30pm; winter, daily 9am–5pm. S-Bahn or U-Bahn: Bahnhof Zoologischer Garten.

Founded in 1844, the Berlin Zoo is considered one of Europe's best—and it's one of my favorites. Just a short walk from the Ku'damm or Bahnhof Zoo, it's home to more than 11,000 animals of almost 2,000 species and is a beautiful oasis in the middle of the city. The Aquarium contains more than 6,000 fish, reptiles, and amphibians.

SPECIAL-INTEREST SIGHTSEEING

FOR THE ARCHITECTURE LOVER   The **Hansa Quarter** is the result of a 1957 international gathering by 48 leading architects from more than 13 countries—they were asked to design a community of homes, apartments, and shops for Berliners still without adequate housing as the result of World War II. Corbusier's design, however, was too large and therefore built in the western end of the city near the Olympisch Stadion (Olympic Stadium); it's western Berlin's largest housing project, with 530 apartments. The Hansa Quarter is located just north of the Tiergarten park (the nearest U-Bahn station is Hansaplatz).

Another good choice is the **Bauhaus-Archiv,** Klengelhöfer Strasse 13–14 (☎ 030/2540 02-0). The Bauhaus school of design, founded by Walter Gropius in Weimar in 1919 and disbanded in Berlin in 1933, revolutionized the teaching of architecture and industrial design. A few selected works of art by Bauhaus masters and students are on display, including tubular-steel chairs, tea pots, and lamps. There are also special exhibitions. Admission is 4 DM ($2.65) for adults and 2 DM ($1.35) for students; free for everyone on Monday. It's open Wednesday through Monday from 10am to 5pm. Get there by bus no. 100, 109, 129, or 341 to Lützowplatz.

FOR THE VISITING AMERICAN   John F. Kennedy gave his famous "Ich bin ein Berliner" speech in front of the **Schöneberg Rathaus** (☎ 030/7831) on June 26, 1963, just months before he was assassinated. The square in front of the Rathaus is now called John F. Kennedy Platz, and inside the Rathaus tower is a replica of the Liberty Bell, given to Berlin by the American people in 1950 and called the Freedom Bell. There isn't much to see here, but if you're a history buff and don't mind heights, you can climb the steps to the top of the bell tower on Wednesday and Sunday between 10am and 3:30pm (follow the signs ZUM TURM) where you have a good view of the city. It's free. Take the U-Bahn to Rathaus Schöneberg.

ORGANIZED TOURS

BY BUS   Sightseeing tours of Berlin and Potsdam are offered by a number of tour companies, with buses departing from the Ku'damm area. Oldest and largest of these is **Severin + Kuhn,** Kurfürstendamm 216 (☎ **030/883 10 15**), which is open daily from 9am to 6pm. A two-hour tour of Berlin, for example, costs 30 DM ($20), while a four-hour tour with a stop at the Pergamon Museum is 45 DM ($30).

BY BOAT   If you're in Berlin from April to the end of October, you can climb aboard one of the many pleasure boats plying the River Spree and Havel and Wannsee lakes. One of the most popular trips is from Wannsee (near the U-Bahn station) to Glienicker Brücke and back, operated by **Stern und Kreisschiffahrt** (☎ **030/810 00 40**).

Also available are two-, three-, and four-hour boat trips along the Spree River, with departures at several places throughout Berlin. One of the most convenient departure spots is at the Schlossbrücke in Berlin-Mitte (eastern Berlin), next to Museum Island. Operated by the **Berliner Wassertaxi Stadtrundfahrten** (☎ **030/972 61 24**), one-hour excursions through the historic heart of the city depart every half hour daily in summer and every hour or two on weekends in winter, costing 9 DM ($6) for adults and 5 DM ($3.35) for students and children. For more information on boat trips, contact the Berlin Tourist Office.

7 Shopping

If it exists, you can buy it in Berlin. At least, that's what they say. A look inside **KaDeWe,** the largest department store on the Continent, made a believer out of me. Start your shopping spree in the KaDeWe, on Wittenbergplatz—with a merchandise inventory of 250,000 items, it may be as far as you get.

But that would mean you'd miss the **Ku'damm,** just around the corner, the showcase of western Berlin's fashionable and elegant boutiques and art galleries. They may be beyond your budget, but window-shopping and people-watching are free. Another shopping street is the pedestrians-only **Wilmersdorfer Strasse,** where you'll find the Karstadt, Hertie, and Quelle department stores in addition to many smaller boutiques and restaurants.

Typical souvenirs of Berlin are stuffed toy bears (the city mascot), porcelain freedom bells (fashioned after the Freedom Bell hanging in the Schöneberg Rathaus), fragments of the Wall, and the Brandenburg Gate pictured on ashtrays and bowls. If kitsch doesn't appeal to you, Germany is known for kitchen gadgets and cutlery, linens, those luxuriously fluffy Federbetten (feather beds), binoculars and telescopes, cameras, and toys (model trains, tin soldiers, building blocks). If you like porcelain, brands to look for include Rosenthal, antique Meissen, and Berlin's own Staatliche Porzellan Manufaktur (better known as KPM)—assuming, of course, that you have a Swiss bank account.

If you purchase more than 60 DM ($40) worth of goods from any one store and are taking purchases out of the country, you're entitled to **partial recovery of the value-added tax (VAT),** which is 15% in Germany. Most stores will issue a Tax Refund Cheque at the time of the purchase. Fill in the reverse side, and upon leaving the *last* European Union country you visit before heading home, present the Tax Refund Cheque, the receipt from the store, and the purchased articles to Customs. Airports in Berlin, Frankfurt, and other large cities will refund your money immediately. If you're leaving Germany by train, ask the Customs official who comes into your train compartment to stamp your check. You can then mail your Tax Refund Cheque back to the country of purchase in a Tax-Free Envelope provided by the store.

MARKETS

Berlin's best buys are found at the many antiques and flea markets. Some are indoor and held almost daily; others are open just one or two days a week.

Berliner Antik und Flohmarkt (Berlin Antique and Flea Market)

Georgenstrasse, at the Friedrichstrasse S-Bahn station. ☎ **030/208 26 45** or 215 02 129. Wed–Mon 11am–6pm. S-Bahn: Friedrichstrasse.

Under the arches of the elevated track, this relatively new market features dozens of vendors selling antiques and curios, including jewelry, porcelain, glassware, pocketwatches, dolls, silver, canes, books, lamps, and odds and ends. Prices are relatively high, but you may find a bargain. If you get thirsty, drop by Zur Nolle, a pub/restaurant decorated 1920s style.

✪ Grosser Berliner Trödelmarkt mit Kunstmarkt (Market on Strasse des 17. Juni)

Just east of the Tiergarten S-Bahn station. ☎ **030/322 81 99.** Sat–Sun 8am–4pm. S-Bahn: Tiergarten.

I love this market! A staggering selection of silverware, books, china, glass, original artwork, jewelry, clothing, and junk is sold at this weekend market, Berlin's best known. Don't miss it.

Turkish Market

Bank of Maybachufer, Kreuzberg. Tues and Fri noon–6:30pm. U-Bahn: Kottbusser Tor; then about a five-minute walk.

Kreuzberg is home to most of the city's Turkish population, so here you'll find Berlin's most colorful produce market. Spread along the bank of a canal, it offers a taste of the exotic, with both German and Turkish vendors selling vegetables, sheep's-milk cheese, pita bread, beans, rice, spices, and odds and ends. Friday's markets are livelier, with more vendors.

Weihnachtsmarkt

Breitscheidplatz and from Nürnberger Strasse to Joachimstaler Strasse. Dec 1–24, daily 11am–9pm. U-Bahn: Kurfürstendamm, Bahnhof Zoo, or Wittenbergplatz.

Every December from the beginning of the month to Christmas Eve, a Christmas market is held in the inner city radiating out from the Gedächtniskirche onto side streets. Christmas decorations, candles and cookies, sausages, and other goodies are sold from colorful booths. (Other Christmas markets are held in Spandau and Alexanderplatz.)

Winterfeldplatz

In Schöneberg. Wed and Sat dawn–1pm. U-Bahn: Nollendorfplatz.

Berlin's largest weekly market of fruits, vegetables, meat, flowers, clothing, and accessories is a five-minute walk south of the Nollendorfplatz U-Bahn station.

8 Berlin After Dark

Berlin never sleeps. There are no mandatory closing hours for nightclubs, discos, and bars, so you can stay out all night if you want to. In fact, a native Berliner once told me, "The reason everyone comes to Berlin is its nightlife"—and he was serious. I pointed out that people might come also because of the excellent museums, but it appeared to be a possibility he had never considered.

Nightlife in Berlin means everything from far-out bars or cozy wine cellars to world-renowned opera and theater. To find out what's going on in the performing arts, pick up a copy of *Berlin Programm.* The performance arts, rock concerts, experimental theater, and avant-garde happenings are also covered in *Berlin/Berlin* (a quarterly published in both German and English) and *tip* and *zitty,* German city magazines.

THE PERFORMING ARTS

If you don't mind taking a chance on what's available on any given night, the best bargain for last-minute tickets is **Hekticket,** located at Kurfürstendamm 14 and Rathausstrasse 1 on Alexanderplatz (☎ 030/242 67 09). Unsold tickets for that evening's performances are available for more than 80 venues throughout Berlin, including the Deutsche Staatsoper, Komische Oper, classical concerts, pop concerts, and cabaret, most at a discount of up to 50%. Both locations are open Monday from 5 to 7:30pm, Tuesday through Thursday from 4 to 7:30pm, Friday and Saturday from 4 to 8pm, and Sunday from 4 to 7:30pm. If you wish to know whether tickets for a certain performance are still available, you can call before dropping by Hekticket.

Otherwise, if you have your heart set on a specific performance and don't mind paying a commission, convenient ticket box offices can be found at **Centrum,** Meinekestrasse 25 (☎ 030/882 76 11), and in the **Europa-Center,** Tauentzienstrasse 9 (☎ 030/264 11 38).

Tickets for theater and opera, sometimes with student discounts, are also available during box-office hours and about an hour before the performance starts at the venue itself.

If you don't mind the risk, you can wait until the day of performance for "last-minute tickets" for the Deutsche Oper Berlin, when unsold tickets are available for about 50% off regular price.

OPERA

The **Deutsche Oper Berlin**, Bismarckstrasse 35, Charlottenburg (☎ 030/34381 for information, 341 02 49 for tickets), has performances of opera virtually every evening, usually at 7 or 8pm, except when there's ballet. Tickets run 15 to 135 DM ($10 to $90), with a 50% reduction for students and for "last-minute tickets"; unsold tickets are available on the day of performance. The box office is open Monday through Saturday from 11am to 7pm and Sunday from 10am to 2pm. Take the U-Bahn to Deutsche Oper.

The **Deutsche Staatsoper Unter den Linden** (the German State Opera), Unter den Linden 7, Berlin-Mitte (☎ 030/200 47 62 or 200 43 15), has long been one of Berlin's famous opera houses, featuring opera, ballet, and concerts. Tickets go for 6 to 150 DM ($4 to $100), and the box office is open Monday through Saturday from noon to 6pm and Sunday from 2 to 6pm; performances are usually at 7 or 8pm. Take the U-Bahn to Friedrichstrasse or Französische Strasse, or bus no. 100 to the Deutsche Staatsoper stop.

The **Komische Oper** (Comic Opera), Behrenstrasse 55–57, Berlin-Mitte (☎ 030/229 26 03 for information, 229 25 55 for tickets), an innovative opera company in eastern Berlin, serves as an alternative to the grander, more mainstream productions of Berlin's two other opera houses, presenting a varied program of opera, operetta, and ballet. Tickets cost 10 to 75 DM ($6.65 to $50). The box office, at Unter den Linden 41, is open Monday through Saturday from 11am to 7pm and Sunday from 1pm until 90 minutes before the performance begins (usually at 7 or 8pm). Take the S-Bahn to Unter den Linden, the U-Bahn to Französische Strasse, or bus no. 100.

THEATER

Popular productions, musicals, and spirited revues are presented in the turn-of-the-century **Theater des Westens,** Kantstrasse 12 (near the Ku'damm), Charlottenburg (☎ **030/882 28 88**). Tickets cost 18 to 76 DM ($12 to $50.65). The box office is open Tuesday through Saturday from noon to 6pm and Sunday from 2 to 46pm; performances are at 8pm. Take the S-Bahn or the U-Bahn to Bahnhof Zoologischer Garten.

CLASSICAL MUSIC CONCERTS

Performances of the world-renowned Berlin Philharmonic Orchestra and the Berlin Symphonic Orchestra take place at the **Philharmonie,** Matthaikirchstrasse 1 (☎ **030/254 88-132 or 261 43 83**). Tickets begin at 13 DM ($8.65). The box office is open Monday through Friday from 3:30 to 6pm and Saturday, Sunday, and holidays from 11am to 2pm. Performances are usually at 8pm, with a matinee on Sunday. You can get to the hall on bus no. 129, 148, or 248.

CHURCH MUSIC

One of the least expensive places to hear music is at a church. The **Berliner Dom** on Museum Island in Berlin-Mitte features organ concerts Monday through Saturday at 3pm and Sunday at 2pm, with admission of 8 DM ($5.35) for adults and 5 DM ($3.35) for students and senior citizens. In addition, organ, choir, and instrumental classical music concerts are held most weekends, usually on Saturday at 6pm and Sunday at 4pm. Prices for these are generally 12 to 15 DM ($8 to $10).

Berlin's other famous church, the **Kaiser-Wilhelm Gedächtniskirche** on Breitscheidplatz, off the Ku'damm, stages free organ concerts most Saturdays at 6pm, as well as choirs, soloists, and other performances throughout the month.

CABARET

Die Stachelschweine

In the basement of Europa-Center (Tauentzienstrasse at Breitscheidplatz), Charlottenburg. ☎ **030/261 47 95.** Tickets 22–38 DM ($14.65–$25.35). U-Bahn: Bahnhof Zoologischer Garten or Kurfürstendamm.

The "Porcupine" has been around for 40 years. You have to speak German if you want to understand its political commentaries. The box office is open Monday through Friday from 10:30am to 12:30pm, Tuesday through Friday from 4 to 7pm, and Saturday and Sunday from 5 to 6pm. Shows are Monday through Saturday at around 7:30pm.

LIVE-MUSIC HOUSES

A-Trane

Bleibtreustrasse 1 (on the corner of Bleibtreustrasse and Pestalozzistrasse, not far from Savignyplatz), Charlottenburg. ☎ **030/313 25 50.** Cover usually 15 DM ($10), 10 DM ($6.65) for students, and usually free Tues–Wed. S-Bahn: Savignyplatz.

This small but classy venue features live jazz beginning at 10pm Tuesday through Saturday evenings in an intimate setting.

Eierschale an der Gedächtniskirche

Rankestrasse 1 (just off the Ku'damm), Charlottenburg. ☎ **030/882 53 05.** Cover 4 DM ($2.65) when there's live music, which goes toward the first drink. U-Bahn: Kurfürstendamm.

Just off the Ku'damm, across from the Gedächtniskirche, this popular music house offers traditional jazz, blues, oldies, rock 'n' roll, and country and popular music. It's also a good place to come for breakfast, especially on Sunday, when there's live music all day long. It's open Sunday through Thursday from 8am to 2am, and Friday and Saturday from 8am to 4am. Live music begins at 8:30pm. A half liter of beer costs 6.30 DM ($4.20) when there's live music, 4.90 DM ($3.25) when there isn't.

Ewige Lampe

Niebuhrstrasse 11a (entrance on Leibnizstrasse), Charlottenburg. ☎ **030/324 39 18.** Cover 10 DM ($6.65), occasionally more for big names.

This casual jazz bar features bands primarily from the United States, Germany, and Holland and can get pretty crowded. Either buy your ticket in advance or get there early. It's open Wednesday through Sunday from 8pm to 2am, with live music from 9pm.

Quasimodo

Kantstrasse 12a, Charlottenburg. ☎ **030/312 80 86.** Cover 10–25 DM ($6.65–$16.65), depending on the band. U-Bahn: Bahnhof Zoologischer Garten.

Dwarfed by the large Theater des Westens next to it, Quasimodo features contemporary jazz and rock groups. It's open daily from 9pm and concerts usually begin around 10pm.

FILMS

Although there are plenty of cinemas showing the latest movies from Hollywood and German producers (unfortunately, dubbed in German), Berlin's main cinematic attraction lies in its "Off-Ku'damm" cinemas, those that specialize in the classics of film history as well as new German and international productions of independent filmmakers. Check the city magazines for listings of current films being shown in English. (*OF*) means that the film is in the original language, and (*OmU*) means it's in the original language with German subtitles.

The original Off-Ku'damm cinema, **Arsenal,** Welserstrasse 25 (☎ **030/ 218 68 48;** U-Bahn Wittenbergplatz), features extensive retrospectives, film series, and avant-garde films. Tickets cost 10 DM ($6.65). The **Odeon,** Hauptstrassse 116 (☎ **030/781 56 67;** U-Bahn Innsbrucker Platz), specializes in recent English-language releases. Tickets are 10 DM ($6.65).

PUBS & BARS
AROUND THE KU'DAMM & SAVIGNYPLATZ

Aschinger

Kurfürstendamm 26. ☎ **030/882 55 58.** U-Bahn: Kurfürstendamm.

This is one of the most civilized places to go for a beer on the Ku'damm. A basement establishment with vaulted cellar rooms and subdued lighting, it's actually a brewery, featuring everything from its dark and heavy "bock bier" to a more light and thirst-quenching pilsner. German food is available "Imbiss-style"—simply go up to the food counter and choose what looks good. Various Würste, Boulette, Leberkäse, and pork dishes are usually available. Open Sunday through Thursday from 11am to 1am, and Friday and Saturday from 11am to 2am.

Cafe Bleibtreu

Bleibtreustrasse 45. ☎ **030/881 47 56.** S-Bahn: Savignyplatz.

This café/bar has a warm, pleasant feel to it, with plants, ceiling fans, and large front windows. One of the first so-called café/bars to open (in 1972), it's popular with the 30-ish crowd and also serves breakfast until 2pm. Open Sunday through Thursday from 9:30am to 1am, and Friday and Saturday from 9:30am to 2:30am.

Dicke Wirtin

Carmerstrasse 9. ☎ **030/312 49 52.** S-Bahn: Savignyplatz.

Named after the rather large barmaid who used to run the place, this old-style German pub is still popular and is known for its stews. Open daily from noon to 4am.

Hard Rock Café

Meinekestrasse 21 (just south of the Ku'damm). ☎ **030/884 62-0.** U-Bahn: Kurfürstendamm.

Opened in 1992, this worldwide chain features the usual rock n' roll memorabilia, T-shirts for sale, hamburgers, and beer. Be forewarned, however, that the music is loud and the prices are too high for budget travelers. If you must, come for a beer and a T-shirt. Open Monday through Saturday from noon to 2am and Sunday from 11:30am to 2am.

Ku'Dorf

Joachimstaler Strasse 15. ☎ **030/883 66 66.** Cover 5 DM ($3.35). U-Bahn: Kurfürstendamm.

Some 18 different bars are located in this basement "village," which consists of several "lanes" with one tiny bar after the other, each decorated in a different theme. At one end is a disco. Most of the people who come here are tourists, perhaps because the place is so convenient. Open Tuesday through Thursday from 8pm to 1am and Friday and Saturday from 8pm to 5am.

New York

Olivaer Platz 15 (just off the Ku'damm). ☎ **030/883 62 58.** U-Bahn: Adenauerplatz.

This is one of the "in" bars, casual yet trendy, a hangout for people in their 20s and 30s. This is the place to go if you want a drink in the middle of the day, with large windows letting in plenty of sunshine. Breakfasts and American food are specialties. Open Sunday through Thursday from 9:30am to 2am and Friday and Saturday from 9:30am to 4am.

Schwarzes Cafe

Kantstrasse 148. ☎ **030/313 80 38.** S-Bahn: Savignyplatz.

The Black Café is true to its name, with a black interior and unconventional hours. Its specialty is breakfast available anytime and ranging from a continental for 8.50 DM ($5.65) to the works. It also has a large selection of coffees (including concoctions with alcohol), beginning at 3 DM ($2). Open daily around the clock, except Tuesday from 3am to noon.

Wirtshaus Zum Löwen

Hardenbergstrasse 29 (across from Gedächtniskirche, toward Bahnhof Zoo). ☎ **030/ 262 10 20.** U-Bahn: Bahnhof Zoologischer Garten or Kurfürstendamm.

This beer hall is reminiscent of those in Munich and even serves Bavarian beer— Löwenbräu. There's outdoor seating in summer, but even the interior is ingeniously constructed to resemble a beer garden. Live music begins at 7pm, and though there's no cover charge, prices for beer are higher in the evening— a half liter is 5.90 DM ($3.95) during the day, 6.90 DM ($4.60) at night. Hearty platters of German food are served for 10 to 20 DM ($6.65 to $13.35). Open Sunday through Thursday from 10am to midnight and Friday and Saturday from 10am to 2am.

Zwiebelfisch

Savignyplatz 7–8. ☎ **030/31 73 63.** S-Bahn: Savignyplatz.

This is one of Berlin's oldest new bars, which means it's been around for about 20 years and still enjoys great popularity. It's open daily from noon to 6am, and because it stays open later than other bars in the area, it's where everyone ends up and can be packed at 4am.

IN KREUZBERG

○ Leydicke

Mansteinstrasse 4. ☎ **030/216 29 73.** S-Bahn and U-Bahn: Yorckstrasse; then a five-minute walk. Bus 119 from the Ku'damm to the Mansteinstrasse stop.

Opened in 1877, this bar claims to be Berlin's oldest. It certainly looks like a likely contender, with its dark wainscoting, decorated ceiling, and long bar. Note the bottles of wine behind the counter—Leydicke even sells its own wine and liqueur, produced in Berlin using grapes and fruit imported from western Berlin. The bottles you see are for sale, certainly a unique souvenir of Berlin. Open Monday through Friday from 5pm to midnight, Saturday from 2pm to midnight, and Sunday from 6pm to midnight.

Madonna

Wiener Strasse 22. ☎ **030/611 69 43.** U-Bahn: Görlitzer Bahnhof. Bus 129.

Kreuzberg has long been the center of Berlin's avant-garde and alternative scene (though in recent years Oranienburger Strasse in Berlin-Mitte has stolen the spotlight). This establishment is one of Kreuzberg's best-known bars, and it seems that anyone familiar with Berlin's bar scene has either been here or heard of it. Although singer Madonna may first come to mind, its namesake is the other Madonna, present in several religious and sacrilegious statues decorating the place, along with fake stained-glass windows. If you want to dress like everyone else here, wear denim or leather. Open Sunday through Thursday from noon to 3am and Friday and Saturday from noon to 4am.

Morena

Wiener Strasse 60. ☎ **030/611 47 16.** U-Bahn: Görlitzer Bahnhof. Bus 129.

This seems to be the watering hole for Kreuzberg's hippest avant-garde, where hairstyles range from dredlocks to bleached long hair to no hair, and nose studs are so common they're almost passé. Across from Madonna (above), this place is crowded even during the day, especially in nice weather, when you can sit outside. Open daily from 9am to 3am.

In Berlin-Mitte (Eastern Berlin)

Georg Brau

Spreeufer 4 (not far from Alexanderplatz). ☎ **030/242 42 44** or 242 34 15. U-Bahn: Alexanderplatz or Klosterstrasse.

On the banks of the Spree in the heart of the renovated Nikolai Quarter, this brewery features spacious indoor seating and outdoor tables beside the river. As with most microbreweries, beer is served only in small fifth-liter glasses to keep it at its freshest. If that's too much of a bother, for 28.20 DM ($18.80) you can order the 1-meter-long "Georg-Pils," a board with 12 small glasses of beer. Live music and beer at half price are featured every Saturday and Sunday from 10am to 1pm. Open in summer, daily from 10am to midnight; winter, Monday through Friday from noon to midnight and Saturday and Sunday from 10am to midnight.

Tacheles

Oranienburger Strasse 53–54. ☎ **030/282 31 30.** S-Bahn: Oranienburger Strasse.

This place has such an alternative identity that for several years it didn't have a telephone or a sign outside and didn't seem likely to make it through another year. No wonder: The building itself is a bombed-out department store, famous for its extraordinary state of disrepair and taken over in 1990 by squatting artists who've slowly transformed it into studio/gallery/living space. On the ground floor is a café where characters from *Star Wars* would feel right at home. It's open daily from 10am to about 4am or later.

Zum Nussbaum

Am Nussbaum 3.☎ **030/242 30 95.** S-Bahn and U-Bahn: Alexanderplatz.

This is my favorite bar in the Nikolai Quarter—small, cozy, and comfortable, modeled after a bar built in 1507 but destroyed in World War II. There are a few tables outside, where you have a view of the Nikolai Church. Open daily from noon to 2am.

DISCOS & DANCE CLUBS

Big Eden

Kurfürstendamm 202, Charlottenburg. ☎ **030/882 61 20.** Cover 10 DM ($6.65) Fri–Sat, which includes a ticket good for 2 DM ($1.35) worth of drinks; unaccompanied women admitted free. U-Bahn: Uhlandstrasse.

Opened in 1968, this place has a strict front-door policy that won't admit anyone who even looks like he or she is drunk. It attracts young people of every nationality and features a large dance floor, pool tables, and video games. Beer costs 5 DM ($3.35) until 10pm, 8 DM ($5.35) and up thereafter. Open Sunday through Thursday from 8pm to 4am and Friday and Saturday from 8pm to 6am.

Cafe Keese

Bismarckstrasse 108, Charlottenburg. ☎ **030/312 91 11.** Drink minimum 8 DM ($5.35) Sun–Thurs, 16 DM ($10.65) Fri–Sat and hols. U-Bahn: Ernst-Reuter-Platz.

About a 15-minute walk from the Ku'damm (close to the Ernst Reuter U-Bahn station), this large dance hall is popular with the middle-aged, and here it's always the women who ask the men to dance (except for the hourly "Men's Choice," when the green light goes on). This Cafe Keese opened in 1966, a sister to one that has been in operation in Hamburg since 1948, and both claim that in the past 40 years more than 95,000 couples have met on their dance floors and married. Who knows, maybe this will be your night. No jeans or tennis shoes are allowed; most men are in coat and tie, and women are dressed up. If you're over 30, you'll probably get a kick out of this place. A live band plays most evenings. A third of a liter of beer costs 8 DM ($5.35). Open Monday through Thursday from 8pm to 3am, Friday and Saturday from 8pm to 4am, and Sunday from 4pm to 1am.

✪ Clärchen's Ballhaus

Augustrasse 24–25, Berlin-Mitte. ☎ **030/282 92 95.** Cover 4.60 DM ($3.05) Tues, 6.40 DM ($4.25) Wed and Fri–Sat. S-Bahn Oranienburger Strasse. U-Bahn: Rosenthaler Platz.

This dance hall is a relic of a more innocent age, when such establishments dotted the city. Now it's one-of-a-kind, founded by Clärchen in 1913 and presently run by her grandson. Much more casual and modestly appointed than the Cafe Keese (above), it's popular with the middle and older generations, both married and single. A live band serenades those on the dance floor, and on Wednesday it's the women who do the asking. Open Tuesday, Wednesday, Friday, and Saturday from 7:30pm (closing varies according to the crowd).

Far Out

Kurfürstendamm 156. ☎ **030/32 00 07 24.** Cover 6 DM ($4) Tues–Thurs and Sun, 10 DM ($6.65) Fri–Sat. U-Bahn: Adenauerplatz.

Catering to a slightly older and more sophisticated crowd than the Big Eden, this disco is modern, spacious, clean and laid-back, featuring rock 'n' roll from the 1970s and 1980s. Wonder of wonders, it features a no-smoking night Tuesday evenings. If you want to see it at its roaring best, don't even think about showing up before midnight. It's located toward the western end of the Ku'damm, on the side street between the Ciao Ciao restaurant and the Schaubühne am Lehniner Platz theater. Open Tuesday through Thursday and Sunday from 10pm to 4am, and Friday and Saturday from 10pm to 6am.

Metropole

Nollendorfplatz 5. ☎ **030/216 41 22.** Cover 12 DM ($8), 3 DM ($2) of which goes toward the first drink. U-Bahn: Nollendorfplatz.

It's hard to miss this place—a colossal, striking building converted from a former theater. Very popular, on weekends it features a giant-size disco with all kinds of technical gags, including a laser show. There are also live concerts through the week. Open for dancing Friday and Saturday from 9pm to 6am.

9 An Easy Excursion

POTSDAM Located only 15 miles southwest of Berlin, Potsdam was once Germany's most important town, serving as both a garrison and as the residence of Prussia's kings and royal families throughout the 18th and 19th centuries. Its most famous resident was Frederick the Great, who succeeded in uniting Germany under his rule, and who built himself a delightful rococo palace in Potsdam called Sanssouci ("without care"). Frederick the Great retreated to Sanssouci as a place for quiet meditation, away from the rigors of war and government.

Today **Sanssouci** (☎ **03733/23 931** or 22 051) is Potsdam's most famous attraction and is open only for guided tours throughout the year. These tours, in

German only, last 40 minutes, depart every 20 minutes, and cost 8 DM ($5.35) for adults, 4 DM ($2.65) for students. The palace is open daily: April to September from 9am to 5pm; in February, March, and October from 9am to 4pm; and November to January from 9am to 3pm. Note that it's closed the first and third Monday of every month.

Other places of interest in Potsdam include **Sanssouci Park;** the **Neues Palais,** built after the Seven Years' War as a show of Prussian strength; and **Cecilienhof,** headquarters of the Potsdam Conference in 1945 where Truman, Stalin, and Churchill met to discuss the disarmament and future of a divided Germany.

To reach Potsdam, take S-Bahn 3 or 7 directly from Berlin to the Potsdam-Stadt station. You can walk to Sanssouci palace from the Potsdam-Stadt station in about an hour; otherwise, take tram no. 91 or 96 to Luisenplatz, from which it's a 10-minute walk.

Brussels 8

by Nikolaus Lorey

As capital of the European Union (EU), Brussels is no longer the staid old city that travelers brushed off as devoid of nightlife or excitement. From the narrow cobblestone streets of the "low town" to the wide boulevards of the "upper town," you can sense excitement in the air as Brussels takes its place among Europe's most important cities.

With buildings dating from the early 15th century, the Grand' Place, which Victor Hugo called "the most beautiful square in the world," is the heart of Brussels. Even more tempting are the cafés: At the turn of the century Brussels was at the forefront of art nouveau design, and many of its most popular cafés date from this period.

Sitting at a small table in one of these cafés, you may wonder about the language you overhear: Is it French or Dutch? In Brussels the population is made up of French-speaking Walloons (80%) and Dutch-speaking Flemish (20%). You'll find every sign in both languages, which can be a bit confusing. However, it's partly because Brussels is at the heart of Europe, a mixing pot of Germanic people from the north and Latin people from the south, that it was chosen to be the Continent's capital. This mixing of cultures gives Brussels much of its vibrancy, and it can only become more exciting and cosmopolitan in the upcoming years.

1 Brussels Deals & Discounts

BUDGET BESTS Brussels's great masterpiece, the **Grand' Place,** can be enjoyed for free, and you can see a wide variety of events there—from the summer "sound and light" shows to the Sunday bird market—without ever reaching for your wallet.

Brussels's many **markets** are a source of free amusement, as are its **state museums,** such as the Musée Royaux des Beaux-Arts and the Musée Instrumental.

Belgium's **cafés** are a bargain, for they allow you to spend hours lingering over just one drink. And Belgium's excellent beers are moderately priced and widely available. Further, the superb **Belgian frites** (which we mistakenly call "french fries") sold on the street cost only about 50F to 65F ($1.60 to $2.10).

The **Cinema Museum** screens movie classics for 80F ($2.60) per showing.

What's Special About Brussels

Grand' Place
- The heart of Brussels and one of the most beautiful squares in Europe.
- The daily flower market and the Sunday bird market.
- Cafés and restaurants, where you can sip beer by a fire.

Cafés
- Sip delicious Belgian beer or an elegantly served cup of hot chocolate.
- Art nouveau and art deco surroundings.

Art Nouveau
- The Horta Museum and the Belgian Comic Strip Museum building, among others.
- Tours given by ARAU Tourville.

Musée d'Art Moderne
- The extensive collection of surrealist paintings by René Magritte.

Comic Books
- The Belgian Comic Strip Museum, a comic-book museum.
- The irresistible hardcover adventures of Tintin, Asterix, and other comic-book heroes.
- Comic-book stores all over the city.

Patats Frites (French Fries)
- Traditionally served in paper cones and smothered with mayonnaise.

Beer
- Many flavored with fruit, tasting a bit like sweet sparkling wine—order as many types as you can.

Bruparck
- Nearly 30 movie theaters, a water amusement park, a restaurant-and-café complex, a miniature Europe, a planetarium, and the fantastic Atomium.

SPECIAL DISCOUNTS   **Students** can enjoy half-price tickets to many cultural events, as well as discounts on train and plane fares and certain tours. Select cultural arenas, cinemas, and some museums offer **senior discounts.**

Every Friday through Sunday night throughout the year, and daily in July and August, many first-class hotels rent their rooms at half price in order to fill vacancies when business travelers are away. **Anyone** can book these discounts through the Brussels Tourist Office.

If you plan to visit many of Brussels's attractions that charge admission (most museums are free), then you might want to purchase a **Tourist Passport.** This "passport" includes a Brussels restaurant guide; a 24-hour bus, tram, and subway pass and transit system map; and discounts at several of the city's top attractions, including the Atomium, Mini-Europe, the Belgian Comic Strip Museum, the Horta Museum, and Autoworld. The cost of this passport is 280F ($9.05), and since the transit pass alone is worth 200F, if you go to only a couple of the discounted attractions, you'll have saved money on the deal.

What Things Cost in Brussels	U.S. $
Taxi from the airport to the city center	32.25
Underground from train station to outlying neighborhood	1.60
Local telephone call	.30
Double room at the Hotel Amigo (deluxe)	225.00
Double room at the Hôtel La Madeleine (moderate)	96.75
Double room at the Hôtel Pacific (budget)	46.75
Lunch for one at Falstaff (moderate)	16.10
Lunch for one at King Sandwich (budget)	4.50
Dinner for one, without wine, at Villa Lorraine (deluxe)	96.75
Dinner for one, without wine, at Restaurant Falstaff (moderate)	20.96
Dinner for one, without wine, at Restaurant Istanbul (budget)	13.85
Glass of beer	2.25
Coca-Cola in a café	1.60
Cup of coffee in a café	1.45
Roll of ASA 100 color film, 36 exposures	6.20
Admission to the Museum of Lace	2.60
Movie ticket	7.10
Opera ticket	9.65–96.75

2 Pretrip Preparations

REQUIRED DOCUMENTS   Americans, Canadians, Australians, and New Zealanders need just a valid passport to enter Belgium. U.K. travelers need only an identity card.

TIMING YOUR TRIP   May to September is the best time of year to visit as the weather grows warm and the city more lively. However, since it never becomes overly cold in winter, you might consider an off-season visit as well.

Brussels's Average Daytime Temperature & Days of Rain

	Jan	Feb	Mar	Apr	May	June	July	Aug	Sept	Oct	Nov	Dec
Temp. (°F)	35	38	43	49	56	61	63	63	60	52	43	37
Days of Rain	19	16	18	17	15	15	17	16	15	17	18	20

Special Events   July and August are especially active months in Brussels. On the first Thursday in July you can watch the **Ommegang** in the Grand' Place, a parade of noble families dressed in historic costumes around the square; July 21, **National Day,** is marked by various celebrations, including fireworks; July 21 to August 20 brings the bustling **Brussels Fair** near Gare du Midi; on August 9 the Bruxellois celebrate the raising of the **"Meiboom,"** a tradition marked by planting a tree at the intersection of rue des Sables and rue du Marais, as bands and various other activities celebrate the event.

For the most up-to-date information on this year's special events, contact the **Belgian National Tourist Office,** 745 Fifth Ave., New York, NY 10151 (☎ **212/ 758-8130**).

BACKGROUND READING Mystery lovers will enjoy the novels of Georges Simenon, whose Inspector Jules Maigret has often walked the streets of Brussels in his quest to solve crime.

For many Belgians, comic-book figure Tintin by Hergé is a "national hero" whose exploits show off Belgian characteristics of calculated savvy rather than rash action or brute force to solve problems.

History lovers may consider reading about 16th-century Belgium, when Brussels was at its heyday, or brush up on accounts of the Battle of Waterloo.

3 Brussels Specifics

ARRIVING

FROM THE AIRPORT Brussels's completely renovated **National Airport** at Zaventem is just under 8 miles from the city center. A convenient 20-minute shuttle-train service connects first with Gare du Nord and then with Gare Centrale every 30 minutes from 5:43am to 11:18pm. Second-class tickets cost 85F ($2.75), 55F ($1.75) for children 6 to 12; first-class tickets are 125F ($4.05) for adults, 85F ($2.75) for children. Buy your tickets at the tourist office in the airport baggage-collection hall or at the ticket window near the entrance to the train platforms. A taxi will cost you about 1,000F ($32.25).

Several windows at the airport offer money exchange, and a National Tourist and Information Office (☎ **02/722-30-00**), open daily from 7am to 10:15pm, provides information, maps, and brochures, as well as hotel reservations.

FROM THE TRAIN STATION Brussels has three major train stations (as well as several smaller ones), but you should try to arrive at **Gare Centrale (Central Station),** as it's centrally located and in the best neighborhood. Trains leave from Gare Centrale back to the airport three times per hour starting at 5:39am and continuing until 11:14pm.

If you're staying in the area near the Grand' Place, your hotel may be within walking distance of Gare Centrale. To reach the Grand' Place from the station, head toward the tower of the Town Hall, a few blocks away.

If you're going elsewhere in town, you can connect to the Métro. When you arrive at Gare Centrale, climb the stairs to the main hall and look for signs to the Métro (a white "M" on a blue background).

To catch the Métro from the Gare du Nord (North Station), go to the area adjacent to the central ticket hallways. If you prefer to walk into town (a 20-minute stroll), follow the sign reading CENTRE, which leads you through a block-long elevated pedestrian walkway and then points you toward town.

Because one of Brussels's worst neighborhoods surrounds the **Gare du Midi (South Station),** it's usually best to arrive at one of the other stations. Yet you may find it useful to get off here to catch a direct Métro to the east side of town (called "upper Brussels"), site of several budget hotels. You catch the Métro from the exit of the station; ask to make sure you're heading the right way. Part of the station was modernized in 1995 to include the terminal for the Eurostar Chunnel train that connects with London ($3^{1}/_{2}$ hours).

The Belgian Franc

For American Readers   At this writing $1 = approximately 31 francs (or 1 franc = 3.2¢, and this was the rate of exchange used to calculate the dollar values given in this chapter (rounded to the nearest nickel).

For British Readers   At this writing £1 = approximately 49 francs (or 1 franc = 2.04p), and this was the rate of exchange used to calculate the pound values in the table below.

Note: The rates given here fluctuate from time to time and may not be the same when you travel to Belgium. Therefore this table should be used only as a guide:

Francs	U.S.$	U.K.£	Francs	U.S.$	U.K.£
1	.03	.02	150	4.83	3.06
5	.16	.10	200	6.45	4.08
10	.32	.20	250	8.06	5.10
15	.48	.31	500	16.13	10.20
20	.65	.41	750	24.19	15.31
25	.81	.51	1,000	32.26	20.41
30	.97	.61	1,250	40.32	25.51
35	1.13	.71	1,500	48.39	30.6l
40	1.29	.82	1,750	56.45	35.71
45	1.45	.92	2,000	64.52	40.82
50	1.61	1.02	2,250	72.58	45.92
75	2.42	1.53	2,500	80.65	51.02
100	3.23	2.04	2,750	88.71	56.12

VISITOR INFORMATION

TIB (Tourist Information Brussels), on the ground floor of the Hôtel de Ville de Bruxelles (Town Hall), Grand' Place (☎ **02/513-89-40**), in addition to answering questions of all sorts about Brussels, also gives out the entertainment guide *What's On* and sells the *Brussels Guide and Map* for 70F ($2.25). Its staff can reserve you a room (see "Accommodations," later in this chapter) or reserve concert and theater tickets for a 25F (80¢) fee. In addition, you can buy tram, Métro, and bus tickets here. It's open daily from 9am to 6pm; in October and November, Sunday hours are 10am to 2pm, and December through February it's closed Sunday.

The **Tourist Information Office,** rue Marché-aux-Herbes 63, 1000 Bruxelles (☎ **02/504-03-90**), reserves hotel rooms in Brussels as well as in the rest of Belgium without a fee, though it does require a deposit. As opposed to the office above, this one specializes in all of Belgium, so it's the place to come before planning side trips. It stocks a wide variety of brochures. Just one block from the Grand' Place, the office is open June to September, daily from 9am to 7pm; in April, May, and October, daily from 9am to 6pm; and November to March, Monday through Saturday from 9am to 6pm and Sunday from 1 to 5pm.

Finally, the **Hotel Reservation Service** (☎ **and fax 02/534-70-40**), in the Central Station, will reserve rooms in one- to five-star hotels for a flat fee of 85F ($2.75) per party (it charges 85F/$2.75 even if you book three or more rooms) in Brussels, 185F ($5.95) in other European countries. Open daily from 9am to 9pm in summer and 10am to 8pm in winter, it's a private firm staffed with English-speaking hostesses. I'm told they'll find a room even on days when Brussels is "sold out."

CITY LAYOUT

Brussels is not laid out in an organized grid, so a brief assessment of its major streets and landmarks may come in handy.

The small cobblestone streets in the center of the city are clustered around the magnificent **Grand' Place.** Two of the most traveled lanes nearby are the restaurant-lined **rue des Bouchers** and **petite rue des Bouchers.** Just a block from the Grand' Place you'll see the classical colonnaded **Bourse,** Belgium's most important stock exchange; there's also a major Métro stop on this square, which takes its name from the stock exchange. A few blocks north you'll reach another important landmark, the National Opera on **place de la Monnaie** (named after the mint that once stood on the square). Brussels's busiest shopping street, **rue Neuve,** starts from this square and runs north for several blocks.

Brussels's uptown, although located to the southeast of the center, is literally atop a hill. Here you'll find Brussels's second great square, **place du Grand-Sablon,** as well as the Royal Museums of Fine Arts and the Royal Palace. A few blocks to the south you'll see an easy point of reference in the huge white Palace of Justice lined with dozens of classical columns. It's just a few blocks from the start of **avenue Louise,** site of Brussels's ritziest stores.

To make navigating challenging, maps list street names in both French and Dutch. For consistency and ease, I've used the French names in this chapter, and in mailing addresses I've used the French name of the town itself—Bruxelles.

GETTING AROUND

BY METRO   Brussels's pleasant Métro system consists of three major lines in the center, spruced up with art and music in many stations. There are stops at the three major train stations; other important stations include Bourse, the stock exchange; De Brouckere, near the Opera House and the start of the rue Neuve pedestrian street; Rogier, at the other end of rue Neuve; and place Louise, near the Palace of Justice and avenue Louise.

Rides cost 50F ($1.60) and allow transfers onto all modes of transportation for one hour. You can also buy a five-ticket card for 230F ($7.40), a 10-journey card for 305F ($9.85), or a pass for 220F ($7.10). The Métro runs daily from 6am to midnight. Signs showing a white "M" surrounded by blue indicate the stations. Keep an eye on your wallet or bag.

BY BUS & TRAM   A web of buses and trams service areas where the Métro doesn't go. If the stop says SUR DEMANDE, you must flag down the bus. Fares are the same as on the Métro. Make sure to watch your wallet or bag.

ON FOOT   You'll find no better way to explore the historic core of the town than on foot, especially around the Grand' Place. You'll also enjoy strolling uptown around place du Grand-Sablon.

BY BICYCLE   Because of the many hills in Brussels and its aggressive car drivers, few locals get around by bicycle.

BY TAXI   The fare starts at 100F ($3.20) and then increases rapidly by 40F ($1.30) per kilometer inside the city or 80F ($2.60) outside the city limits. A typical fare from one point to another in the center costs 225F to 300F ($7.25 to $9.70).

BY CAR   Brussels's proximity to the rest of the country, as well as to France, Germany, and Holland, make a car an attractive transportation option for continuing on from here. All the top American firms rent in Belgium—including Hertz, Avis, and Budget. Note that car rentals are taxed 20.5% in Belgium. The smallest car at **ABC Rent a Car,** rue d'Anderlecht 133 (☎ **02/513-19-54**), rents for 1,600F ($51.60) per day, with unlimited mileage and VAT included.

FAST FACTS: Brussels

Baby-sitters   If you need a baby-sitter, contact ULB babysitting service, av. Paul Héger 22, Préfab 4 (☎ **02/650-21-71**). They charge about 250F ($8.05) per hour.

Banks   There are several banks in the area around the Grand' Place and the Bourse, including Crédit Générale Bank, Grand' Place 5 (☎ **02/516-12-11**), open Monday through Friday from 8:45am to 4:30pm; and Kredietbank, Grand' Place 17 (☎ **02/517-41-11**), open Monday through Thursday from 9am to 4:30pm and Friday from 9am to 5:15pm.

Business Hours   Most **stores** are open Monday through Saturday from 10am to 6 or 7pm; some larger stores stay open on Friday until 8 or 9pm. **Post offices** are open Monday through Friday from 9am to 5pm. **Banks** generally are open Monday through Thursday from 9am to 4:30pm and Friday from 9am to 5pm.

Consulates   If you should need to contact your home government, Brussels has consulates of a number of countries, including the **United States,** bd. du Régent 25 (☎ **02/513-38-30**); **Canada,** av. Tervueren 2 (☎ **02/735-60-40**); the **United Kingdom,** rue Arlon 85 (☎ **02/287-62-11**); **Australia,** rue Guimard 6 (☎ **02/231-05-00**); **New Zealand,** bd. du Régent 47 (☎ **02/512-10-40**); and **Ireland,** rue Luxembourg 19 (☎ **02/513-66-33**).

Currency   The Belgian currency is the **Belgian franc (F),** made up of 100 centimes. Coins come in 50 centimes and 1, 5, 10, 20, and 50 francs; bills are denominated in 100, 500, 1,000, and 5,000 francs.

Currency Exchange   Banks charge a 150F ($4.85) commission on traveler's checks and none on cash. Currency-exchange offices charge a lower commission (or none at all) but give a lower rate per dollar. If you're changing a small amount you may save at an exchange office, but for several hundred dollars or more you'll do best at a bank. Remember to shop around, as exchange rates and commissions differ widely.

Emergencies   If you need a doctor, dial 479-1818 or 648-8000. If you need a dentist, dial 426-1026 or 428-5888 (evenings and weekends only). For the police, dial 100 or 101. For an ambulance or in case of a fire, dial 100.

Eyeglasses   There are several opticians in and near the City 2 shopping mall on Rue Neuve at boulevard du Jardin Botanique.

Holidays In Brussels the following are official holidays: New Year's Day (Jan 1), Easter Monday, Labor Day (May 1), Ascension (sixth Thurs after Easter), Whit Monday (seventh Mon after Easter), National Day (July 21), Assumption (Aug 15), All Saints' Day (Nov 1), Armistice Day (Nov 11), and Christmas (Dec 25).

Hospitals If you need a hospital, contact Cliniques Universitaires St-Luc, av. Hippocrate 10 (☎ **02/764-11-11**), or Clinique St-Michel, rue de Linthou T 19 (☎ **02/739-07-11**).

Information See "Visitor Information" under "Brussels Specifics," earlier in this chapter.

Laundry/Dry Cleaning Self-service laundries can be found throughout Brussels. Ipsomat, rue de Flandre 51, a block from place Ste-Catherine (just two blocks from the Bourse), charges 110F ($3.55) for 5 kilos (11 lb.); it's open daily from 7am to 10pm. Ipsomat also has a branch at chausée de Wavre 123, on the other side of town, open daily from 7am to 10pm. Lav-o-Net, rue Antoine-Dansaert 155, charges 120F ($3.85) to wash 6 kilos (13¹/₄ lb.); it's open daily from 7am to 10pm.

The chain of stores called 5 à Sec offer some of the city's best-priced dry cleaning in one-day service. There's one on rue du Marché-aux-Herbes, off the Grand' Place, open Monday through Friday only from 7:30am to 6pm. You'll find another branch at chaussée de Charleroi 37, in the place Louise area, open Monday through Friday from 7:30am to 6pm and Saturday from 7:30am to 1pm.

Lost & Found If you lost something on a plane, call Brussels International Airport (☎ **02/723-60-11**); in the airport, call 02/722-39-40; on the Métro or a tram, call 02/515-23-94; on a train, call 02/219-26-40 immediately (or after a week, 02/224-61-12); on the highway, call 02/517-96-75.

Mail A conveniently located post office is at Gare Centrale, open Monday through Friday from 9am to 6pm. Postage for a postcard to the United States, Canada, or Australia is 38F ($1.22), and for a letter, 42F ($1.35); postcards and letters to Great Britain and the rest of Europe are 16F (51¢ or 32p).

You can receive mail at **American Express,** place Louise 2, 1050 Bruxelles (☎ **02/512-17-40**). If you're not an American Express client, a small fee will be imposed. There's an American Express cash machine outside the office. The American Express office is open Monday through Friday from 9am to 5pm and Saturday from 9:30am to noon.

Newspapers You'll find plenty of English-language newspapers, magazines, and books at W. H. Smith, bd. Adolphe-Max 75 (☎ **02/219-27-08**), open Monday and Wednesday through Saturday from 9am to 6:30pm and Tuesday from 10am to 6:30pm.

Photographic Needs Try Technaphot, bd. Anspach 23 (☎ **02/217-68-00**), open Monday through Friday from 9am to 6:30pm and Saturday from 10am to 6:30pm. There are also one-hour photo-processing centers along rue Neuve and in City 2.

Police In an emergency, dial 100 or 101 to reach the police.

Radio/TV There are several local radio and TV stations, as well as the BBC.

Religious Services Call Bruxelles-Accueil, rue de Tabora 6 (☎ **02/511-27-15** or 511-81-78), Monday through Saturday between 10am and 6pm for timetables of religious services at churches all over Brussels.

Tax   There is a value-added tax (VAT)—called TVA in Belgium—of 20.5% on all goods and services. You can get a tax refund for purchases once you leave Belgium by asking the shopkeeper to give you a tax-free form. At the border or airport, show the Customs officials your purchase and receipt and they'll stamp the form. Then you can mail this form back to the Belgian Tax Bureau (the address is on the form) or, if you're leaving via the airport, bring it directly to the "Best Change" office, which charges a small commission but gives you an on-the-spot refund.

Taxis   For a radio taxi, call 349-49-49.

Telephone   A **local phone call** costs 10F (30¢) for three minutes. To make **international calls,** walk one block north of Gare Centrale to bd. de l'Impératrice 17 (☎ **02/540-61-11**) to the large PTT telegraph, telephone, and Telex office, open from 8am to 10pm daily. It costs 180F ($5.80) for a three-minute call to the United States or 150F ($4.85) with a **PTT telecard,** which is available at PTT or Telecom offices. PTT telecards cost 200F, 600F, and 1,000F ($6.45, $19.35, and $32.25) and can be used in all phone booths in the city. You can also make international calls from the PTT office at the airport. In addition, you can dial an American operator using **AT&T's "USA Direct"** service, which allows collect and credit- and charge-card calls at the local number: 11-0010.

Tipping   The prices on restaurant menus already include a service charge of 16%, along with a value-added tax (called TVA in Belgium) of 20.5% (you'll see a little note on the menu reading " *T.V.A. et service compris*"), so it's not necessary to tip. It's acceptable to round up if you want to. Service is included in your hotel bill as well.

4   Accommodations

You shouldn't have much trouble finding lodgings within your budget, thanks to the city's many family hotels in old town houses. Although some of these feature charming vintage furniture, most offer modest comfort in a friendly atmosphere, usually with an English-speaking staff. It's best to arrive during the day, since some receptions close once the owner has gone to bed.

You'll find a few budget offerings in the Grand' Place area, the most charming part of Brussels, and more in the area around avenue Louise.

Some of the best youth hostels in Europe are in Brussels, offering another viable option.

If you arrive without a reservation, you might want to stop by **Tourist Information Brussels** or the **Hotel Reservation Service** (see "Visitor Information" under "Brussels Specifics," earlier in this chapter).

You can also write ahead to **Belgium Tourist Reservations,** bd. Anspach 111, B-1000 Bruxelles (☎ **02/513-74-84**).

DOUBLES FOR LESS THAN 1,750F ($56.45)
NEAR THE GRAND' PLACE

Hôtel Pacific

Rue Antoine-Dansaert 57 (a five-minute walk from the Grand' Place and two blocks from the Bourse), 1000 Bruxelles. ☎ **02/511-84-59.** 18 rms, 2 with shower only. 950F ($30.65) single without bath; 1,450–1,550 ($46.75–$50) double without bath, 1,950 ($62.90) double with shower only. Rates include breakfast. Showers 100F ($3.20) extra for those in rooms without shower. No credit cards. Métro: Bourse.

> # Getting the Best Deal on Accommodations
>
> • Try hotels in the residential neighborhood along avenue Louise.
> • Youth hostels are excellent bargains and offer quite a few singles and doubles for those who don't want to sleep in a dorm.
> • Also a good bargain are hotels within a block or two of the Grand' Place.

A good value in an unbeatable location, the Pacific has a soft-spoken friendly owner, Paul Pauwels (unfortunately, he usually enforces a midnight curfew). Most rooms are large, though with plumbing dating from 80 years ago; the front rooms also have small balconies. Breakfast is served at street level in a fin-de-siècle room decorated with a zebra skin, copper pots, a Buddhist prayer wheel, and a Canadian World War II steel helmet. Recently monks from the Dalai Lama's entourage stayed here and left mystical signs and symbols in some rooms. This is Brussels's only hotel boasting a (simplified) version of Foucault's pendulum, which visibly marks the earth's rotation in space. And twice a week guests are invited to attend a free one-hour slow-motion gymnastic session, half yoga and half tai chi chuan. Everything at the Pacific is peaceful and low-key—highly recommended to those who prefer atmosphere to comfort.

Pension des Eperonniers

Rue des Eperonniers 1, 1000 Bruxelles. ☎ **02/513-53-66.** 26 rms, 14 with shower or toilet only, 9 with bath. 1,100F ($35.50) single without bath, 1,300F–1,500F ($41.95–$48.40) single with shower or toilet only, 1,600F ($51.60) single with bath; 1,650F ($53.20) double without bath, 1,750F–1,900F ($56.45–$61.30) double with shower or toilet only, 2,000F ($64.50) double with bath. Rates include breakfast. MC, V. Métro: Gare Centrale.

It's almost impossible to stay close to the Grand' Place at any price, so this budget accommodation is a welcome surprise. However, don't expect much character, though most of the rooms are fairly large and have been recently renovated. Colorful floral curtains and bedspreads lend a vaguely Asian feel, and a few rooms have pieces of almost-antique furniture. You'll find the reception desk up a flight of stairs from the street.

SOUTH OF GARE DU NORD

Hôtel-Residence Albert

Rue Royale-Ste-Marie 27–29, 1030 Bruxelles. ☎ **02/217-93-91.** Fax 02/219-20-17. 22 rms, 12 with shower only, 10 with bath; 22 apts. TEL. 1,600F ($51.60) single with shower only, 1,750F ($56.45) single with bath; 1,700F ($54.85) double with shower only, 2,200F ($70.95) double with bath; 2,100F–2,750F ($67.75–$88.70) apt. No credit cards. From Gare du Nord, walk five minutes uphill on rue Dupont.

The rooms here are free of decoration and have tiny writing desks; some furnishings are fairly new. The private baths are separated only by a curtain, and rooms with shower have only a free-standing unit in the room. The apartments are suitable for one or two guests. For maximum quiet, ask for the rooms in the back away from the busy street. There's a bar on the premises.

Hôtel Sabina

Rue du Nord 78 (off place des Barricades), 1000 Bruxelles. ☎ **02/218-26-37.** Fax 02/219-32-39. 24 rms, 2 with shower only, 22 with bath. TV TEL. 1,600F ($51.60) single; 1,700F ($54.85) double. Rates include breakfast. EURO, MC, V. Métro: Madou.

Though some of the beds are a bit old, each room here comes with a writing desk and remote-control color TV. Most have baths that are no larger than a closet (though hairdryers are supplied). The breakfast room contains a large fireplace, a wood-beamed ceiling, and a TV to the side. Because this hotel is popular with EU business travelers, reserve in advance for a weeknight stay.

IN THE AVENUE LOUISE AREA

Hôtel Berckmans

Rue Berckmans 12, 1060 Bruxelles. ☎ 02/537-89-48. 23 rms, 15 with shower only, 6 with bath. TEL. 750F ($24.20) single without bath, 1,100F ($35.50) single with shower only, 1,700F ($54.85) single with bath; 1,300F ($41.95) double without bath, 1,700F ($54.83) double with shower only, 1,800F ($58.05) double with bath. Rates include breakfast. ACCESS, AE, DC, EURO, MC, V. Métro: Place Louise. Bus 60.

Despite the upscale tone of the avenue Louise district, it's still possible to get an inexpensive room in the area. The Hôtel Berckmans is comfortable. Rooms vary in size, and those with private bath have the facilities behind a curtain rather than in a separate room. Some rooms have TVs, which adds to the price.

○ Hôtel de Boeck

Rue Veydt 40 (a 10-minute walk from place Louise), 1050 Brussels. ☎ 02/537-40-33. Fax 02/534-40-37. 35 rms, all with bath. 1,400F–2,500F ($45.15–$80.65) single; 1,650F–2,900F ($53.20–$93.55) double. Rates include buffet breakfast. Additional bed 675F ($2l.75) per person extra. AE, DC, EURO, MC, V. Métro: Place Louise.

This hotel offers unusually spacious, quiet, and adequately furnished rooms. Price differences depend on whether you arrive on a weekend, make a longer stay, or book a room with color TV and/or direct-dial phone, so call first to find out what the best deal is. Fourteen rooms, ideal for small groups, can be used as quads or even quints. Since 1970 the owner has been Londoner Eric Gibbs, who's helpful and friendly. The hotel is behind the Holiday Inn, and street parking is possible.

DOUBLES FOR LESS THAN 2,000F ($64.50)
SOUTH OF GARD DU NORD

Hôtel Barry

Place Anneessens 25 (halfway between the Bourse and Gare du Midi), 1000 Bruxelles. ☎ 02/511-27-95. Fax 02/514-14-65. 34 rooms, 2 without bath, 14 with shower only, 16 with shower and toilet. 1,280F ($41.30) single without bath; 1,880F ($60.65) double with shower only, 2,280F ($73.55) double with shower and toilet; 3,280F ($105.80) triple with shower and toilet; 3,780F ($121.95) quad. Rates include continental breakfast. Half board 500F ($16.10) extra; full board 900F ($29.55) extra. AE, DC, EURO, MC, V. Métro: Anneessens.

This businessman's hotel is nothing to get excited about, but the rooms are spacious, clean, and well furnished (most with color TV), and it's a 10-minute walk to Grand' Place and 3 minutes from place Rouppe, starting point for buses to Waterloo. The imposing red-brick building on place Anneessens is a school, and there's a monument dedicated to Mr. Anneessens, once one of the merchants who built the beautiful houses on the Grand' Place. Breakfast is served in the hotel, but meals are served in a next-door restaurant. Advance bookings are advisable, as the hotel is often sold out to groups.

Relais la Tasse d'Argent and Hôtel Madou

Rue du Congrès 48 and rue du Congrès 45 (respectively), 1000 Bruxelles. ☎ 02/218-83-75 or 217-32-74. 16 rms, all with bath. 1,500F ($48.40) single; 1,900F ($61.30) double; 2,500F ($80.65) triple. Breakfast 160F ($5.15) extra. No credit cards. Métro: Madou.

Built in two old family houses, these small hotels really make you feel as though you're a guest in a friend's home. The rooms feature half-size bathtubs and large windows overlooking the street. The lovely breakfast room at no. 48 has a grandfather clock and chintz seating, helping to make this an excellent choice. All the rooms in both hotels are newly decorated.

NORTH OF GARE DU MIDI

✪ Hôtel à la Grande Cloche

Place Rouppe 10–12, 1000 Bruxelles. ☎ **02/512-61-40.** Fax 02/512-65-91. 47 rms, 26 with shower only, 4 with bath. TEL. 1,850F ($59.65) single or double without bath, 2,500F ($80.65) single or double with shower only, 3,200F ($103.20) single or double with bath. Rates include continental breakfast. AE, EURO, MC, V. Métro: Anneessens.

This hotel on a small traffic circle 10 minutes on foot from Gare du Midi and another 10 minutes from the Grand' Place, offers clean modern rooms, most with small tiled shower and sink areas; many rooms also have large TVs. The elevator-equipped building even has hairdryers in the hallways and in some rooms.

Hôtel van Belle

Chaussée de Mons 39 (about a 10-minute walk north of Gare du Midi), 1070 Bruxelles. ☎ **02/521-35-16.** Fax 02/527-00-02. 125 rms, 112 with bath. 1,300F ($41.95) single without bath, 2,000F–2,500F ($64.50–$80.65) single with bath; 1,800F ($58.05) double without bath, 2,600F ($83.85) double with bath. AE, DC, EURO, V.

Larger and more formal than most choices in this chapter, the Van Belle offers hotel services such as photocopying and fax machines that smaller budget hotels don't provide. The smaller, cheaper rooms without baths in the old wing have a sink and were recently renovated; the larger rooms in the modern wing have two chairs and a small writing table.

Hôtel Windsor

Place Rouppe 13, 1000 Bruxelles. ☎ **02/511-20-14** or 511-14-94. Fax 02/514-09-42. 24 rms, 9 with shower only. 1,800F ($58.05) single or double without bath, 2,400F ($77.40) single or double with shower only. Rates include breakfast. EURO, MC, V. Métro: Anneessens.

You pass through a quiet little bistro restaurant to get to the guest rooms at this recently renovated hotel. New furnishings, carpets, and wallpaper give the hotel a contemporary feel, and though there are no rooms with full bath (toilets are down the hall), those rooms that don't have a shower do have a bidet. Most rooms also have a phone and a clock radio.

DOUBLES FOR LESS THAN 2,900F ($93.55)
NEAR THE GRAND' PLACE

Hôtel George-V

Rue t'Kint 23, 1000 Bruxelles. ☎ **02/513-50-93.** Fax 02/513-44-93. 17 rms, all with bath. 1,980F ($63.85) single; 1,980F–2,500F ($63.85–$80.65) double. Rates include breakfast. EURO, MC, V. Parking 250F ($8.05) per 24 hours. Métro: Bourse.

On a quiet residential street not far from the Bourse, the George-V is an excellent choice for anyone wishing a private bath. Dark wood, polished brass, and marbled accents give the hotel an air of elegance seldom found in such economical lodgings. In the sparkling little lounge you can have a drink before retiring. The guest rooms were remodeled a few years ago and, if not luxurious, are certainly comfortable.

Residence la Vieille Lanterne
Rue des Grands Carmes 29, 1000 Bruxelles. ☎ **02/512-74-94.** Fax 02/512-13-97. 6 rms, all with bath. 1,700F ($54.85) single; 2,300F ($74.20) double. AE, DC, EURO, MC, V. Métro: Bourse.

A tiny inn with two rooms per floor, this find is diagonally across from the *Manneken Pis*. It can be hard to spot at first—you enter through the side door of a trinket shop selling hundreds of *Mannekin Pis* replicas. You'll feel right at home in the rooms with their old-style windows and recently renovated baths, which have marble counters and tiled walls. New beds and new carpeting were also part of the 1993 renovation. It's a good idea to write ahead to reserve a room; and if you'll be arriving after 2pm, a deposit is required. Note that no breakfast is served.

IN THE AVENUE LOUISE AREA

Hôtel les Bluets
Rue Berckmans 124, 1060 Bruxelles. ☎ **02/534-39-83.** 10 rms, 3 with shower only, 7 with bath; 1 apt. 1,350F ($43.55) single with shower only, 1,750F ($56.45) single with bath; 2,350F ($75.80) double with bath and TV. Rates include breakfast. AE, MC, V. Métro: Hôtel des Monnaies.

If you're searching for classic European charm or you're a fan of American bed-and-breakfasts, you'll certainly enjoy a stay here. You'll feel as though you're staying with friends when you have breakfast in the antique-filled dining room or out in the sun room. A sweeping stairway leads up to the guest rooms, several of which have 14-foot ceilings and ornate original moldings. There are antiques in all rooms and TVs in some. Should you be planning a longer stay or if you'd like the convenience of a kitchenette, there's also an apartment available.

Hôtel Marie-Jose
Rue de Commerce 73, 1040 Bruxelles. ☎ **02/512-08-43.** Fax 02/512-46-04. 23 rms, all with bath. TV. 2,600F ($83.85) single; 2,800F ($90.30) double. Rates include breakfast. AE, DC, EURO, MC, V. Métro: Arts-Loi.

A three-story structure on a quiet side street that's a 10- or 15-minute walk from Gare Centrale (through the Parc de Bruxelles in the center), this hotel (with elevator) welcomes visitors with a cozy flower-graced lobby as well as an upscale restaurant. The room TVs have remote controls.

Sun Hotel
Rue du Berger 38, 1050 Bruxelles. ☎ **02/511-21-19.** Fax 02/512-32-71. 22 rms, 9 with shower only, 13 with bath. TV TEL. 1,750F ($56.45) single with shower only, 2,295F ($74.05) single with bath; 2,800F ($90.30) double with shower only, 3,300F ($106.45) double with bath. Rates include breakfast. AE, DC, EURO, MC, V. Métro: Porte de Namur.

On a dark and narrow street that also houses a couple of upscale restaurants, the Sun was completely renovated a few years ago. The rooms, though small, contain contemporary furnishings, including wall sconces, and the bedspreads are designed to resemble old quilts. Though some rooms are so small and cramped that you can hardly walk around the bed, they're clean and have closets so you can get your bags out of the way. The breakfast room and lobby are contemporary, with lots of marble and a black-and-white color scheme.

PRIVATE ROOMS

Private rooms in Belgium don't represent the substantial savings over hotels that they do in certain other countries, such as Denmark and Sweden, but they provide a colorful alternative to the formal atmosphere of a hotel. **The Windrose,** av. Paul-Dejaer 21a, 1060 Brussels (☎ **02/534-71-91;** fax 02/534-71-92), rents about 70 rooms in Brussels itself and across the country. To reserve a room it's best to write at least two weeks in advance. You must make a minimum two-night reservation and send a 25% deposit and a 500F ($16.10) reservation fee.

Alternatively, you can call when you arrive in town, then call back a few hours later to see if they've found a room for you. Room rates—including breakfast—run 1,000F to 1,350F ($32.25 to $43.55) for a single and 1,600F to 2,200F ($51.60 to $70.95) for a double, without or with a bath. The agency accepts credit/charge cards for bookings of 10,000F ($322) minimum.

SUPER-BUDGET CHOICES
HOSTELS

Brussels offers students and the young-at-heart a powerful lineup of excellent hostels in central locations, most with everything from single rooms to large "sleep-in" rooms.

✪ Auberge de Jeunesse Jacques Brel

Rue da la Sablonnière 30 (a 10- to 15-minute walk from Gare Centrale), 1000 Bruxelles. ☎ **02/218-01-87.** Fax 02/217-20-05. 139 beds. 660F ($21.30) single; 540F ($17.40) per person double; 440F ($14.20) per person quad; 395F ($12.75) dorm bed. Rates include breakfast. Sheets 120F ($3.85) extra. MC, V. Bus 65 or 66 from Gare Centrale to Madou.

Opened in 1987, this youth hostel was formerly a hospital—it still has special facilities for the disabled. Public facilities include a bar, washing machines, a TV room, and two small sun decks. The rooms (with 1 to 14 beds) have large windows, allowing in lots of light, and showers. A 1am curfew is enforced, but the reception is open throughout the day. This hostel is located in the elegant "upper Brussels" area.

Auberge de Jeunesse Jean Nihon

Rue de l'Eléphant 4 (a 20-minute walk from the Grand' Place), 1080 Bruxelles. ☎ **02/410-38-58.** Fax 02/410-39-05. 159 beds, all rms with bath. 660F ($21.30) single; 540F ($17.40) per person double; 440F ($14.20) per person triple or quad; 395F ($12.75) dorm bed. Sheets 120F ($3.85) extra. EURO, MC, V. Métro: Comte de Flandre.

This is Brussels' newest youth hostel, in a neighborhood of apartment buildings. The new building is surrounded by empty lots, which act as a buffer against the neighborhood's urban atmosphere. The rooms have tile baths with separate rooms for the toilet and the shower. Wooden bunk beds are about all you'll find in your room, but public areas include a garden and terrace, self-service facilities, and a TV/video room. A shop and laundry round out the facilities.

CHAB Youth Hotel

Rue Traversière 8 (10 minutes on foot from Gare du Nord and 15 minutes from Grand' Place), 1030 Bruxelles. ☎ **02/217-01-58.** Fax 02/219-79-95. 224 beds, no rms with bath. 650F ($20.95) single; 530 ($17.10) per person double; 440F ($14.20) per person triple or quad; 320F–400F ($10.30–$12.90) dorm bed. Rates include breakfast. Sheets 100F ($3.20) extra. V. Métro: Botanique. Bus 65 or 66 from Gare Centrale.

Located in two buildings across from each other, CHAB offers very pleasant clean rooms with large windows that open like doors onto the street. Both buildings have little gardens in back, and one has a modest kitchen and a snack bar serving meals for 160F to 200F ($5.15 to $6.45) daily from 6:30pm to midnight. The friendly reception gives advice on Brussels's hot spots. A 2am curfew is enforced.

Sleep Well

Rue du Damier 23, 1000 Bruxelles. ☎ **02/218-50-50.** Fax 02/218-13-13. 130 beds, no rms with bath. 640F ($20.65) single; 510F ($16.45) per person double; 430F ($13.85) per person triple or quad; 380F ($12.25) per person in a six-bed room. Rates include breakfast. 10% discount for holders of an FIYTO card or ISIC. Sheets 100F ($3.20) extra. No credit cards. Métro: Rogier.

Just behind the huge City 2 shopping mall and one block from the bustling rue Neuve, Sleep Well enjoys probably the best location of all of Brussels's well-placed hostels. Guests of all ages are welcomed, but a 1am curfew and a 10am to 4pm close-out are maintained. Downstairs, the evening café serves 15 types of beer for 45F to 75F ($1.45 to $2.40). They also sponsor two-hour city tours in summer for only 100F ($3.20) per person.

Youth Hostel Bruegel

Rue due St-Esprit 2 (a 10-minute walk from Gare Centrale), 1000 Bruxelles. ☎ **02/511-04-36.** Fax 02/512-07-11. 135 beds, no rms with bath. 660F ($21.30) single; 540F ($17.40) per person double; 440F ($14.20) per person quad; 395F ($12.75) dorm bed. Rates include breakfast. Those without an IYHF card pay 100F ($3.20) extra. Sheets 120F ($3.85) extra; dinner 270F ($8.70) extra. No credit cards.

This hostel is in an attractive brick building at the side of the Eglise Notre-Dame-de-la-Chapelle, where Jan's father, the great Pieter Brueghel, is buried. The rooms have cinder-block walls, bunk beds, a sink, and large windows. Each floor contains a TV lounge, and a cafeteria is on the premises. A word of caution: Don't change money at the reception, open from 7:30 to 10am and 2pm to midnight—they offer terrible rates.

WORTH THE EXTRA MONEY

Hôtel la Madeleine

Rue de la Montagne 22, 1000 Bruxelles. ☎ **02/513-29-73.** Fax 02/502-13-50. 55 rms, 10 with shower only, 37 with bath. TEL. 1,300F ($41.95) single without bath, 2,000F ($64.50) single with shower only, 2,700F ($87.10) single with bath; 3,000F ($96.75) double with bath. Rates include continental breakfast. ACCESS, AE, EURO, MC, V. Métro: Gare Centrale.

In a superb location, La Madeleine (with elevator) is just one block from the Grand' Place and a few minutes on foot from Gare Centrale. The facilities are generally modest but clean; there's a cheery breakfast room with a white wooden ceiling and red walls.

✪ Hôtel Lambeau

Avenue Lambeau 150, 1200 Brussels. ☎ **02/732-51-70.** Fax 02/732-54-90. 24 rms, all with bath. TV TEL. 2,500F ($80.65) single; 2,900F ($93.55) double or twin. Rates include breakfast. Métro: Montgomery (a 15-minute ride from the train stations) and change there to Georges Henri; the hotel is 20 yards from the Métro exit.

This hotel, built in 1994, meets the highest standards and is an excellent value for the price (at least in Brussels). When I was there shortly after the opening, a European state minister had just checked out. Each room has a color TV with 34 channels, including CNN, as well as a pants press and hairdryer. With very friendly, English-speaking owners, this is a top choice.

Hôtel Mirabeau

Place Fontainas 18–20 (on a small square just off the busy boulevard Le-Monnier), 1000 Bruxelles. ☎ **02/511-19-72.** Fax 02/511-00-36. 30 rms, 6 with shower only, 24 with bath. TV TEL. 1,750F ($56.45) single with shower only, 1,900F ($61.30) single with bath;

2,600F ($83.85) double with bath. Rates include buffet breakfast. AE, DC, EURO, MC, V.
Métro: Anneessens.

The Mirabeau is a good choice if you want a private bath. A TV lounge in the large
combination lobby and breakfast room, and the convenience of an elevator, are
features of this hotel that you might find appealing. The guest rooms have a
contemporary European flavor with modern carpeting and laminate furniture,
including writing desks. Some rooms have a wall of windows that lets in plenty
of light. The bathrooms are modern but tiny.

5 Dining

Although it's not among Europe's least-expensive cities, Brussels has a substantial
number of restaurants where you can dine well at a reasonable cost.

Belgians cook up ingenious specialties, everything from poultry sautéed in beer
to tasty mussels prepared in dozens of sauces. One favorite is mussels steamed in
a vegetable broth, served in a sturdy iron pot. When ordering mussels (a kilo, 2.2
lb., is a typical portion), note that the best time is from September through the
winter; mussels served in the summer are often imported and not as good.

The Belgians also deserve credit for perfecting a mighty culinary quintet of
cheese, waffles, fried potatoes, chocolate, and beer—and no visit to Brussels is complete without a generous sampling of each.

The French may have their name attached to fried potatoes, but it's the Belgians
who mastered the art. Brussels is dotted with dozens of fast-food stands serving
frites wrapped in paper cones. Belgians usually eat their fries with mayonnaise
rather than ketchup; although this method may cause apprehension at first, after
you try it you may be converted forever. Prices run 50F to 65F ($1.60 to $2.10),
depending on the portion and where you buy them; the topping (which you must
specifically ask for) costs 10F to 15F (30¢ to 50¢) extra.

Belgium is also famous for its 400 brands of beer, produced by hundreds of
small breweries throughout the country. Many of these brews are considerably
stronger than those we know in America—the alcohol content can be as high as
12%. Trappist monks produce 30 to 40 brands of the country's strongest beers
(thanks to heavy fermentation). These are also some of the most expensive beers
and can cost up to $5 per bottle.

Brussels is known for its lambic beers, which depend on naturally occurring
yeast for fermentation. These beers are often flavored with fruit and come in bottles
with champagne-type corks. Unlike any other beer in the world, they're more akin
to a sweet sparkling wine. My favorite is Gueze, one of the least sweet. If you prefer
something sweeter, try the raspberry-flavored Framboise or cherry-flavored Kriek.

MEALS FOR LESS THAN 300F ($9.65)
NEAR THE GRAND' PLACE

✪ **Au Suisse**
Bd. Anspach 73–75. ☎ **02/512-95-89.** 65F–120F ($2.10–$3.85). No credit cards. Wed–
Mon 10am–8pm, Tues 10am–7:30pm. Métro: Bourse. SANDWICHES.

The sandwich is a Belgian institution and nowhere is it treated more respectfully
than here. Dozens of fillings are displayed in a glass counter down the right side
of the shop. You can try any of half a dozen types of raw or smoked herring, a
creamy mussel or salmon spread, tuna salads, meat salads, sliced cheeses, flavored

---

Getting the Best Deal on Dining

• Take advantage of the *plat du jour* at lunch and the *menu du jour* at dinner.

• The City 2 shopping mall houses many inexpensive restaurants, where the prices are almost uniformly low.

• Fill up on inexpensive Belgian *patats frites*. A friend of mine traveling through Europe in her youth managed to live on frites for the last few penniless days of her tour.

---

cream cheeses, various hams and salamis, and many more delicious and unusual choices. You then can get your filling in a big hunk of French bread or a hard roll. There are just a few stools at the counter, so it's best to get your sandwich to go.

Den Teepot

Rue des Chartreux 66. ☎ **02/511-94-02.** *Plat du jour* 290F ($9.35); two-course menu 400F ($12.90). No credit cards. Mon–Sat noon–2pm. Métro: Bourse. VEGETARIAN.

If meat and potatoes are not your favorite fare and greasy fries leave you cold, Den Teepot may be just the place for you. Rice and beans and veggies, organically grown and macrobiotically prepared, are the staples here, but, surprisingly, you can also get a beer with your meal. I suggest you try one of the fresh juices—the carrot juice is usually extremely spicy.

Le Bollewinkel

Rue des Bouchers 51. ☎ **02/514-33-54.** Sandwiches 45–125 ($1.45–$4.05); *plat du jour* 240F ($7.75). No credit cards. Mon–Sat 11am–6pm. Métro: Bourse. INTERNATIONAL.

Though most restaurants on rue des Bouchers are overpriced tourist traps, this tiny place uphill from the Galeries St-Hubert serves tasty, filling meals at economical prices. The plat du jour is the only full hot meal available each day, and a list of all the plats du jour for the month is posted in the front window. A recent month's posting included such surprises as paella, Cordon Bleu, roast rabbit, and Hungarian goulash. There are only a handful of tables and the clientele is primarily regulars, but if you persevere you should be able to get a seat.

Ⓢ Salvation Army Restaurant and Hostel

Rue Bodeghem 27 (a five-minute walk from the Grand' Place). ☎ **02/511-17-92.** Continental breakfast 40F ($1.30); dinner 120F ($3.90); supper 60F ($1.95). No credit cards. Mon–Sat 6am–6pm, Sun 7am–10pm. Métro: Annessens. BELGIAN.

This is the cheapest restaurant in town. This self-service eatery has 80 seats at 10 large tables in a high-ceilinged street-level room. Established over 100 years ago, the restaurant offers a continental breakfast, a hot dinner at lunchtime (for example, vegetable soup, spaghetti bolognese, a roll, and coffee), and a supper (bread, meat or cheese, and coffee). It's perfectly respectable, even for women traveling alone.

NEAR THE GARE DU NORD

Restaurant Istanbul

Chaussée de Haecht 16. ☎ **02/218-72-86.** Reservations recommended Fri–Sat night. 220F–430F ($7.10–$13.85); *plat du jour* 295F ($9.50). AE, DC, EURO, MC, V. Daily 11:30am–3pm and 6pm–1am. Métro: Botanique. TURKISH.

A long restaurant with small Turkish carpets and ornaments on the wall, the Istanbul serves tasty grilled fare. Turkish music plays on the radio for most meals, and Friday and Saturday night there's live Turkish music and belly dancing starting at 8pm—at no extra charge. Around the corner from the CHAB Youth Hostel, south of Gare du Nord, Istanbul is one of several low-cost Turkish and Middle Eastern restaurants in the area.

MEALS FOR LESS THAN 400F ($12.80)
NEAR THE GRAND' PLACE

Au Bambou Fleur

Rue Jules-van-Praet 13 (three blocks from the Grand' Place). ☎ **02/502-29-51.** 350F–500F ($11.30–$16.10); lunch special 225F ($8.05). AE, V. Daily noon–midnight. Métro: Bourse. VIETNAMESE.

In recent years there's been quite a proliferation of Vietnamese restaurants in Brussels. They're almost always the cheapest eateries around, and their lunch specials are always a good deal. To help you make a decision, the menu, posted in the front window, has photos of all the dishes.

BETWEEN AVENUE LOUISE & CHAUSSÉE DE WAVRE

☉ Au Trappiste

Av. de la Toison d'Or 7. ☎ **02/511-78-39.** Main courses 180F–390F ($5.80–$12.60); specials up to 600F ($19.35). AE, DC, EURO, MC, V. Daily noon–midnight. Métro: Namur. BELGIAN.

It may seem impossible to find an inexpensive place to eat in the pricey avenue Louise/Chaussée de Wavre area, but this place is an exception. It's easy to spot: next to the Namur Métro stop, diagonally across from the Hilton tower. Au Trappiste has 60 seats in a high beamed-ceilinged dining room with mirrored walls, two large chandeliers, and brass railings. The best deal here is the plat du jour for 480F ($15.50), consisting of vegetable soup plus a main course such as goulash with steamed potatoes, fried fish, breaded veal cutlet, or pasta.

MEALS FOR LESS THAN 500F ($16.10)
NEAR LA BOURSE

✪ In't Spinnekopke

Place du Jardin aux Fleurs 1 (a five-minute walk from the Bourse Métro stop). ☎ **02/511-86-95.** 340F–710F ($10.95–$22.90); plat du jour 295F ($9.50). AE, DC, EURO, MC, V. Mon–Fri noon–3pm and 6–11pm, Sat 6–11pm (Bar, Mon–Fri 11am–11pm, Sat 6–11pm.) Closed Aug and hols. Métro: Bourse. BELGIAN.

My favorite typical local place, this restaurant serves excellent food in a 1762 building. Wood beams and paneling, pink floral wallpaper, pink tablecloths, candles, and roses serve as decorations, capturing a European charm that makes for a special evening out. A large variety of beers is available, and some dishes even come with beer sauces. Prices are a bit high, but worth it.

La Femme du Boulanger

Rue Antoine Dansaert 18. ☎ **02/502-40-26.** Meals 295F–550F ($9.50–$17.75). No credit cards. Mon–Sat noon–3pm and 7–10pm, Sun noon–3pm. Métro: Bourse. BELGIAN.

This 60-seat self-service restaurant has minimal furnishings and is heavily frequented by students. The serving counter has three sections, one for soups and cold buffet foods, one for hot plates, and one for desserts. The buffet (second

Quick Bites

Numerous fast-food Greek places near the Grand' Place make gyros, felafels, and other low-cost items for about 120F ($3.85) each.

The many inexpensive cafeterias and fast-food restaurants in **City 2,** a huge American-style shopping mall on rue Neuve, makes it one of Brussels's great budget centers. The mall, as well as most of its restaurants, is open daily from 10am to 7pm (on Friday to 8pm). Here's a sampling:

City Grill, on the basement level, is a self-service cafeteria. Main courses cost around 220F to 480F ($7.10 to $15.50), the salads are 120F to 340F ($3.85 to $10.95), and the menu of the day, which might be a soup, veal dish, and apple cake, costs 260F to 310F ($8.40 to $10).

Inno Department Store Cafeteria, on rue Neuve, and lined by a pedestrian bridge to City 2, is a self-service cafeteria with many offerings, including pork burgers and anchovies, rumpsteak garni, and other cafeteria specials. Prices are moderate—180F to 375F ($5.80 to $12.10)—so there's often a long line. It's open Monday through Saturday from 9:30am to 7pm (Friday to 8pm).

King Sandwich, also in the basement, specializes in sandwiches for 65F to 140F ($2.10 to $4.50).

You'll also find several restaurants on other floors of City 2, including **Mister Grill and Buffets,** which specializes in pork goulash and fries, and half a chicken with garnishes, in the 250F to 450F ($8.05 to $14.50) range.

At **Pizzeria Donnini,** on the basement level, which specializes in pizza and pasta, you order from a pictorial menu that shows the exact size of the portions, which are huge. Prices run 60F to 310F ($1.70 to $8.85).

---

helpings included) cost 295F ($9.50). On Sunday a complete three-course lunch is offered for 500F ($16.10), with free second helpings, and coffee, tea, or juice.

NEAR THE GRAND' PLACE

Auberge des Chapeliers

Rue des Chapeliers 1–3 (off the Grand' Place). ☎ **02/513-73-38.** Reservations recommended Fri–Sat. 230F–750F ($7.15–$24.20). ACCESS, AE, DC, EURO, MC, V. Sun–Thurs noon–2:30pm and 6–11pm, Fri–Sat to midnight. Métro: Bourse. BELGIAN.

In a 17th-century building where Brussels's best artisans once designed hats, the Auberge des Chapeliers (Inn of the Hat Makers) preserves a charming feel. Behind a beautiful brick facade, the first two floors are graced with wooden beams and paneling and connected by a very narrow wooden staircase. The third floor has windows overlooking the nearby streets. Excellent fries accompany the typical Belgian cuisine. Don't miss this conveniently located and reasonably priced choice.

Cap de Nuit

Place de la Vieille Halle-aux-Blés 28. ☎ **02/512-93-42.** 260F–900F ($8.40–$25.70); *plat du jour* 380F ($12.25). AE, DC, EURO, MC, V. Daily 6pm–6am. Métro: Bourse. ITALIAN/BELGIAN.

Cap de Nuit assures that you'll never go hungry late at night, as it serves up pasta and other dishes all the way to 7am, the latest of any restaurant in town. The modern decor, late hours, and 28 varieties of beer attract a crowd between 20 and 40. The plat du jour, served all night, is the best deal and reliably tasty. Cap de Nuit boasts 200 seats in four connecting rooms.

✪ Restaurant Falstaff

Rue Henri-Maus 23–25. ☎ **02/511-87-89.** Reservations recommended. Main courses 275F–760F ($8.85–$24.50); complete lunch special 340F ($10.95); sandwiches 70F–160F ($2.25–$5.15). AE, DC, EURO, MC, V. Daily noon–5am (lunch special noon–3pm). Métro: Bourse. BELGIAN.

An art nouveau masterpiece with carved wooden ceilings, painted glass, and mirrors, the Falstaff attracts a boisterous crowd. The best value of the day is the lunch plat du jour or the dinner menu du jour. The restaurant has two halves, each with a different menu: an art nouveau part from 1903 and a newer section from 1965. Service can be slow and impersonal, but the place still captures that Belgian joie de vivre.

Shamrock

Rue Jules-van-Praet 27–29. ☎ **02/511-49-89.** 300F–680F ($9.65–$21.95). No credit cards. Daily noon–2:30pm and 7pm–midnight. Métro: Bourse. INDIAN.

Neither the name nor the publike decor even hints that this might be an Indian restaurant, but don't worry—once you see the menu, you'll know you're at the right place. As soon as you sit down at one of the candlelit tables, you'll be brought a papadum (crisp lentil chip) with three sauces to spread on it. It's best if you have several people in your group when you eat here so you can try as many succulent and spicy dishes as possible.

T'Kelderke

Grand' Place 15. ☎ **02/513-73-44.** Main courses 350F–650F ($11.30–$20.95); mussels 325F–745F ($10.50–$24.05). AE, DC, EURO, MC, V. Daily noon–2am. Métro: Bourse. BELGIAN.

T'Kelderke (The Little Cellar) is, as its name implies, a brick-vaulted cellar just a few steps down from the square (on the "upper" side of the square). The food is good and the place features a mix of locals and tourists. The cellar is a striking contrast to the grandiose facade of the Grand' Place but is certainly atmospheric in its own way. The menu focuses on traditional Belgian fare such as pricey mussels and more economical dishes of potatoes mashed with other vegetables and served with a bit of meat.

RUE DES BOUCHERS & PETITE RUE DES BOUCHERS

These two streets boast dozens of inviting restaurants, many with frosted windows and ornate displays of fresh fish outside. Unfortunately, most of these tourist-oriented places are substantially overpriced, often serving food of uneven quality. On the whole, I suggest a stroll through the area to work up your appetite, then a walk to another area of town to find a more reasonably priced restaurant. If you do want to enjoy one minisplurge here, however, try . . .

✪ Chez Leon

Rue des Bouchers 18–22. ☎ **02/511-14-15** or 513-08-48. Mussel dinner 340F–600F ($10.95–$19.35); *plat du jour* (including soup) 340F ($10.95). AE, DC, EURO, MC, V. Daily noon–11pm. Métro: Bourse. BELGIAN

In 1994 Chez Leon served more than 320 tons of mussels, making it Brussels's true king of mussels. Many tourists frequent this bubbling bistro, where the waiters run to and fro at a frantic pace. The three dining rooms feature tables with paper tablecloths and wooden stall seating. The kitchen is to the side as you enter.

FOR DESSERT

Many connoisseurs consider Belgium the world's greatest chocolate confectioner. For Belgians, the real art comes in not merely producing a quality bar of chocolate but in filling that chocolate with goodies, creating the perfect praline.

The **Leonidas** chain of stores sells excellent Belgian pralines for the lowest prices in town, 400F ($12.90) per kilo (2.2 lb.). They have 10 branches, including bd. Anspach 46, off the Bourse (☎ **02/218-03-63**); bd. Adolphe-Max 49–51, parallel to rue Neuve (☎ **02/217-95-55**); and chaussée d'Ixelles 5, off Porte Namur (☎ **02/511-11-51**).

Also, throughout the city look for signs that read VIGAUFRA, where they sell fresh waffles for about 40F to 60F ($1.30 to $1.95).

PICNICKING

You'll find a huge supermarket with a large cold-cut/cheese counter perfect for assembling a picnic lunch in **GB,** in the basement of City 2 on rue Neuve. It's open Monday through Thursday and Saturday from 9am to 8pm and Friday from 9am to 9pm. There's another GB at the corner of rue du Marché-aux-Pullets and rue des Halles, one block from the Bourse. You'll also find ample gourmet food stores in the streets around the Grand' Place.

6 Attractions

SIGHTSEEING SUGGESTIONS

If You Have 1 Day

You'll want to spend your first hours in Brussels at the magnificent Grand' Place, whose elaborate buildings and ornate details are a fairy tale come true. In particular, visit the Gothic Hôtel de Ville de Bruxelles and the Musée de la Ville de Bruxelles (Museum of the City of Brussels).

From the Grand' Place, pay a visit to the defiant *Manneken Pis*, then after lunch head uptown to the impressive Musées Royaux des Beaux-Arts to see its collection of old masters and modern artists. After a few hours in the museum, walk over to the attractive place du Grand-Sablon and its diminutive neighbor, place du Petit-Sablon.

If You Have 2 Days

Spread the above activities at a more relaxed pace over two days and stop in at the Notre-Dame du Sablon church while on place du Grand-Sablon. Also visit the Cathédrale St-Michel et Ste-Gudule near Gare Centrale. Then explore rue Neuve, Brussels's main pedestrian street, and wander about the nearby streets. If you still have extra time, consider a visit to the Musée Instrumental.

If You Have 3 Days

Spend your first two days as outlined above, then on the third day head out to the museum complex at Parc du Cinquantenaire, where you can admire the varied collection of the Musées Royaux d'Art et d'Histoire, the superb Musée Royal de l'Armée et d'Histoire Militaire, and the fun Autoworld. Also consider the Musée du Costume et de la Dentelle (Costume and Lace Museum), near the Grand' Place, and a stroll on the elegant avenue Louise.

Brussels

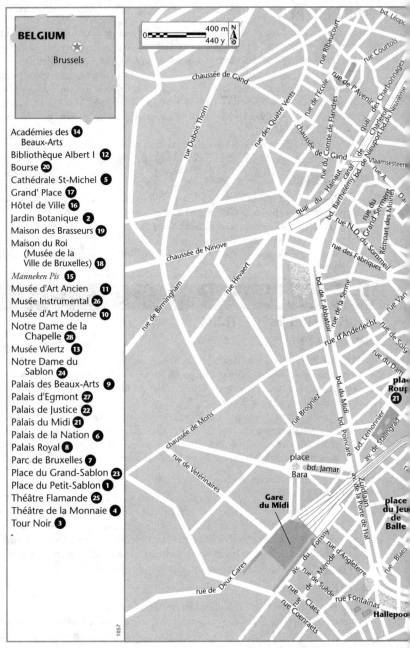

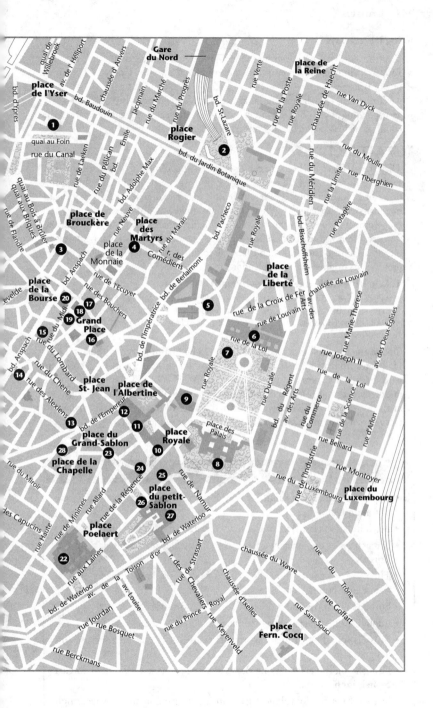

If You Have 5 Days

Visit the massive Atomium from the 1957 Brussels World's Fair and stop in at the Bruparck amusement center directly opposite the Atomium. Consider a picnic in one of Brussels's parks.

Virtually all of Belgium can be visited on a day trip from Brussels, and I suggest spending at least one of your extra days in Brussels seeing another part of the country, such as the medieval wonders of Ghent and Bruges.

TOP ATTRACTIONS

The **Grand' Place** has been the center of the city's commercial life as well as public celebrations since the 12th century. Most of it was destroyed in 1695 by express order of France's Louis XIV; it was rebuilt over the next few years. Prominent merchants and artisans, as well as important guilds, owned these buildings, and each competed to outdo the others with highly ornate facades of gold leaf and statuary, often with emblems of their guilds. Thanks to the town's close monitoring of these reconstructions and later alterations, each building on the square preserves its original baroque splendor.

Hôtel de Ville de Bruxelles (Town Hall)

Grand' Place. ☎ **02/512-75-54.** Admission 80F ($2.55) adults, 50F ($1.60) children. Tues–Fri 9:30am–12:15pm and 1:45–4pm, Sun 10am–noon and 2–4pm. Call or drop by for the exact hours of the English-language tours. Closed Jan 1, May 1, Nov 1 and 11, and Dec 25. Métro: Bourse.

One of the few buildings to survive the 1695 bombardment, the brilliant Town Hall dates from 1402. Its facade shows off gothic intricacy at its best, complete with dozens of statues and arched windows. A 215-foot tower sprouts from the middle, yet it's not placed directly in the center (you'll see 10 windows to the left of the tower and $7^1/_2$ windows to the right). Legend has it that when the architect realized his error, he jumped from the summit of the tower.

❓ Did You Know ?

- About the size of Maryland, Belgium is the second-smallest country in the European Union.
- Belgium has the last Roman Catholic monarchy in northern Europe.
- "French" fries are actually a Belgian specialty and reached their zenith in Brussels.
- The word *spa* comes from the Belgian city of Spa, known for its mineral waters and springs.
- Europe's oldest covered shopping arcade is in Brussels.
- Adolphe Sax, a Belgian, invented the saxophone.
- Brussels was the birthplace of the art nouveau style of architecture and design.
- Flemish- and French-speaking Brussels is one of the few officially bilingual capitals in the world.
- In 1990 King Baudoin abdicated for one day to avoid signing a pro-abortion law that he morally opposed.

You may visit the interior on 30- to 40-minute tours, which start in a room full of paintings of the past foreign rulers of Brussels, who have included the Spanish, Austrians, French (under Napoleon), the Dutch, and finally the Belgians. In the Council Hall you'll see baroque decoration, and in several chambers—such as the Maximilian Room—you'll marvel at 17th-century tapestries so detailed that they even provide perspective. In the room before the mayor's office you'll see a 19th-century painting of Brussels with a river in the town center—a stream later covered up in an attempt to curb malaria. The entire building is still used as the seat of the civic government, and its wedding room remains a popular place to tie the knot.

Musée de la Ville de Bruxelles (Museum of the City of Brussels)

Maison du Roi, Grand' Place. ☎ **02/511-27-42.** Admission 80F ($2.60) adults, 50F ($1.60) children. Apr–Sept, Mon–Thurs 10am–12:30pm and 1:30–5pm, Sat–Sun 10am–1pm; Oct–Mar, Mon–Thurs 10am–12:30pm and 1:30–4pm, Sat–Sun 10am–1pm. Closed Jan 1, May 1, Nov 1, and Dec 25. Métro: Bourse.

This 19th-century structure has served as both a covered bread market and a prison in its previous incarnations. Today it displays a mixed collection associated with the art and history of Brussels. On the ground floor you can admire detailed tapestries from the 16th and 17th centuries, as well as porcelain, silver, and stone statuary. After climbing a beautiful wooden staircase, you can trace the history of Brussels in old maps, prints, photos, and models. And on the third floor the museum shows off dozens of costumes that have been given to the *Manneken Pis* since 1698, including a hotel receptionist uniform, 18th-century ball costumes, and a Japanese kimono complete with headband.

✪ Manneken Pis

Rue de l'Etuve, at the corner of rue de Chêne. Métro: Bourse.

A small bronze statue of a urinating child, the *Manneken Pis* has come to symbolize the city of Brussels. No one knows when this child first came into being, but it's clear he dates from quite a few centuries ago—the 8th century, according to one legend. Thieves have made off with the tyke several times in history. One criminal who stole and shattered the statue in 1817 was sentenced to a life of hard labor. (The pieces were used to recast another version.)

The *Manneken Pis* owns a vast wardrobe, which he wears on special occasions (during Christmas season he dons a Santa suit, complete with white beard). You can see part of his collection in the Musée de la Ville de Bruxelles in the Maison du Roi (above). You'll find the statue at the intersection of rue de l'Etuve and rue du Chêne, four blocks from the Grand' Place. If you want to read about the many legends of the *Manneken Pis,* you'll find an illustrated book for sale in the Musée de la Ville de Bruxelles.

Incidentally, the *Manneken Pis* now has a female counterpart called the **Jeanneke Pis,** located on the dead-end impasse de la Fidélité off rue des Bouchers. It was the 1987 brainstorm of a local restaurateur who wanted to attract business; its lack of grace is an embarrassment to many Bruxellois.

✪ Musées Royaux des Beaux-Arts

Rue de la Régence 3. ☎ **02/508-32-11.** Admission free. Tues–Sun 10am–1pm and 2–5pm. Closed Jan 1, May 1, Nov 1 and 11, and Dec 25. Tram 92, 93, or 94. Bus 20, 34, 38, 71, 95, or 96.

In a vast museum of several buildings, this complex combines the Musée d'Art Ancien (Classical Art) and the Musée d'Art Moderne (Modern Art) under one roof, showing off works from the 14th to 20th century. The collection starts with Hans Memling's portraits from the late 15th century, which are marked by sharp lifelike details, as well as works by Hieronymus Bosch and Lucas Cranach's *Adam and Eve.*

You'll admire the subsequent rooms featuring Pieter Brueghel, including his *Adoration of the Magi.* Don't miss the very unusual *Fall of the Rebel Angels,* with its grotesque faces and beasts. But don't fear—many of Brueghel's paintings are of a less-fiery nature, such as the scenes depicting Flemish village life.

Later artists represented in the collection include Rubens, van Dyck, Frans Hals, Cranach, Guardi, and Rembrandt.

The museum's modern collection is housed in a circular building connected to the main entrance. The overwhelming collection includes works by Matisse, Dalí, Yves Tanguy, Max Ernst, Marc Chagall, Miró, Bacon, and René Magritte. You may want to purchase a museum plan for 10F (30¢) to help you navigate your way through. The Musée d'Art Ancien and Musée d'Art Moderne are connected by an underground passage.

✪ Atomium

Heysel, Laeken. ☎ **02/477-09-91.** Admission 175F ($5.65) adults, 140F ($4.50) children 3–12, free for children 2 and under. Apr–Sept, daily 9am–8pm; Oct–Mar, daily 10am–6pm (Panorama until 9:30pm). Métro: 1A to Heysel, the last stop (a 20-minute trip).

As the Eiffel Tower is the symbol of Paris, the Atomium is the symbol of Brussels, and, as was Paris's landmark, the Atomium was built for a world's fair, specifically the 1958 Brussels World's Fair. Rising 335 feet and looking like a giant plaything of the gods that's fallen to earth, the Atomium represents an iron crystal molecule magnified 165 billion times. Its metal-clad spheres, representing individual atoms, are connected by enclosed escalators and elevators. Within the Atomium is an exhibit on human life and medical research. However, it's the top-most atom of the atomium molecule that attracts most people: a restaurant/observation deck that provides a sweeping panorama of the Brussels metropolitan area.

Mini-Europe

Bruparck, Heysel. ☎ **02/478-05-50.** Admission 370F ($11.95) adults, 290F ($9.35) children 12 and under, free for children 40 inches and shorter. Apr–June and Sept–Oct, daily 9:30am–6pm; July–Aug, daily 9:30am–8pm; Nov–Dec, daily 10am–6pm. Closed Jan–Mar. Métro: Heysel.

Since Brussels is the new capital of Europe, it's fitting that the city is also home to a miniature rendering of all the most notable architectural sights of the Continent. There are even a few natural wonders and technological developments represented. Built on a scale of $^1/_{25}$ of the original, the structures of Mini-Europe exhibit remarkable detail. Though children like Mini-Europe the best, adults also find it interesting.

MORE ATTRACTIONS
MUSEUMS

Musée Instrumental (Instrument Museum)

Place du Petit-Sablon 17. ☎ **02/511-35-95.** Admission free. Tues–Sat 2:30–4:30pm, Sun 10:30am–12:30pm. Tram 92, 93, or 94. Bus 20, 34, 95, or 96.

Only 5% of the museum's immense collection is shown at one time, so the collection rotates periodically. In the permanent exhibit you'll see a piano that fits into a book, a viola with a map of Paris inlaid on the back, one of the first lutes in the world (from the 16th century), and two of the earliest models of a keyboard. In the wind instruments section you'll learn that it was a Belgian, Adolphe Sax, who invented the saxophone. Upon request, small demonstrations are given and the instruments are explained.

Musée Royal de l'Armée et d'Histoire Militaire

Parc du Cinquantenaire 3. ☎ **02/733-44-93**. Admission free. Tues–Sun 9am–noon and 1–4:45pm. Closed Jan 1, May 1, Nov 1, and Dec 25. Métro: Merode; it's opposite Autoworld.

This is one of Brussels's often-forgotten museums, where the huge military collection is one of the finest in Europe. It includes an extensive display of armor, uniforms, and weapons from various Belgian campaigns (such as the Congo), a massive clutter of World War I artillery pieces, an aircraft hangar full of 130 impressive airplanes, and a World War II collection of Nazi flags that brings the Nürnberg rallies to mind. Anyone interested in military history shouldn't miss the superb, though sometimes cluttered, collection.

Musées Royaux d'Art et d'Histoire

Parc du Cinquantenaire 10. ☎ **02/741-72-11**. Admission free. Daily 10am–5pm. Closed Jan 1, May 1, Nov 1 and 11, and Dec 25. Métro: Merode; it's around the corner from the Military Museum and Autoworld.

A vast museum that opens half its collection one day and the other half on the next, this museum shows off antiques, decorative arts (such as tapestries, porcelain, silver, and sculptures), and archeology. Highlights include an Assyrian relief from the 9th century B.C., a Greek vase from the 6th century B.C., the A.D. 1145 reliquary of Pope Alexander, some exceptional tapestries, and colossal statues from Easter Island dating from centuries before Christ. This museum is the largest in Belgium.

Autoworld

Esplanade du Cinquantenaire 11. ☎ **02/736-41-65**. Admission 150F ($4.85) adults, 80F ($2.50) students. Apr–Sept, daily 10am–6pm; Oct–Mar, daily 10am–5pm. Métro: Merode; it's across from the Military Museum.

I'm not a car fanatic, but I found this display of an aircraft hangar full of 500 historic cars fascinating. The collection starts with early motorized tricycles of 1899 and moves on to a 1911 Model T Ford, a 1924 Renault, a 1938 Cadillac that was the official White House car for FDR and Truman, a 1956 Cadillac used by Eisenhower, as well as by Kennedy during his June 1963 visit to Berlin, and more.

Musée Costume et de la Dentelle (Costume and Lace Museum)

Rue de la Violette 6 (near the Grand' Place). ☎ **02/512-77-09**. Admission 80F ($2.60) adults, 50F ($1.60) children. Apr–Sept, Mon–Tues and Thurs–Fri 10am–12:30pm and 1:30–5pm, Sat–Sun 2–4:30pm; Oct–Mar, Mon–Tues and Thurs–Fri 10am–12:30pm and 1:30–4pm, Sat–Sun 2–4:30pm. Closed Jan 1, May 1, Nov 1 and 11, and Dec 25. Métro: Bourse.

Honoring the once-major industry (some 10,000 Bruxellois made lace in the 18th century) that now operates in a reduced but still-prominent fashion, this museum shows off particularly fine lace and costumes from 1599 to the present, with frequent changing exhibitions.

La Maison des Brasseurs (Brewery Museum)

Grand' Place, 10. ☎ **02/511-49-87**. Admisssion 100F ($3.20). Daily 10am–5pm. Métro: Bourse.

This museum dedicated to beer depicts a tiny brewery from the 18th century in a single room. You're given a beer at the end of what will be a brief visit. It's located on the same side of the Grand' Place as the Town Hall.

Special & Free Events

It's only natural that the magnificent Grand' Place should host some of the city's most memorable free events. If you visit April to September, you can watch a free evening **"Sound and Light" show.** Classical music plays as the square's buildings are dramatically highlighted. Or you can stop by at noon when the tower of the Maison du Roi plays golden carillon chimes reminiscent of an earlier European era.

However, the most spectacular event on the Grand' Place is the annual **Ommegang pageant** on the first Thursday in July. During the pageant, noble families dress in historic costumes and parade around the square.

The square still functions as an important **marketplace.** Tuesday through Sunday from 8am to 6pm the Grand' Place hosts a flower market, and on Sunday (as detailed below under "Shopping"), a bird market. During Christmas a large tree is erected at the center and a crèche nativity scene is placed at the lower end of the square.

CHURCHES

Cathédrale des Saints-Michel-et-Gudule
Set back off bd. de l'Impératrice near Gare Centrale. ☎ **02/217-83-45.** Cathedral free; crypt, 40F ($1.30). Summer, daily 7am–7pm; winter, daily 7am–6pm. Métro: Gare Centrale.

Dating from 1226, this cathedral is a gothic masterpiece, highlighted by detailed 16th-century stained-glass windows that are some of the finest in the world. The 15th-century facade of the two matching towers appears strangely unfinished, as they end in square tops rather than long points—yet this is exactly how it was designed. In 1983 extensive cleaning and restorations were started; the process uncovered archeological remains of a Roman church below the cathedral floors. Until the restoration is completed (possibly in 1999) half the interior remains closed.

On Sunday at 10am the Eucharist is celebrated with a choir. In July, August, and September, polyphonic masses are sung by local and international choirs at 10am. Chamber-music and organ concerts are occasionally performed on weekdays at 8pm from August to October. In spring and autumn, mass is sung accompanied by instrumental soloists and readings by actors (in French only).

Notre-Dame du Sablon
Rue de la Régence 3B, off place du Grand-Sablon. ☎ **02/511-57-41.** Admission free. Daily 9am–6pm.

Located between the city park and the Palace of Justice, this late gothic 15th- and 16th-century structure is noted for its fourfold gallery with brightly colored stained-glass windows, illuminated from the inside at night, in striking contrast with the gray-white gothic arches and walls. Also worth seeing are the two baroque chapels decorated with funeral symbols in white marble.

AN AMUSEMENT PARK

The Bruparck is Brussels's amusement park. Built on the site of the 1958 Brussels World's Fair, the Bruparck is home of the Atomium and Mini-Europe (above), the Kinepolis movie complex (see "Films" under "Brussels After Dark," later in this chapter), Bruparck village, a collection of restaurants and cafés (including a restaurant in a 1930s railway car), Oceade (an indoor-outdoor water-sports pavilion with water slides, swimming pools, and saunas), and a planetarium. Admission to Oceade for four hours is 370F ($11.95) for adults and 290F ($9.35) for children. Admission to the planetarium is 130F ($4.20) for adults and 100F ($3.20) for children under 12. Both these latter attractions are open daily in summer, Tuesday through Sunday the rest of the year.

PARKS & GARDENS

The most attractive park in town is the **Parc de Bruxelles,** which extends in front of the Palais Royale. Once the property of the dukes of Brabant, this well-designed park with geometrically divided paths running through it became public in 1776. The many park benches make a fine place to stop for a small picnic. It's also historic: Belgium's first battle for independence (in 1830) was fought here.

A nice park in the center is the **Jardin d'Egmont.** It's often overlooked because it's hidden behind buildings—there are only two small entrance paths. You'll find this sculptured garden between the Palace of Justice and the Royal Palace; enter from rue du Grand-Cerf, or a small footpath off boulevard du Waterloo.

Outside the Musée Instrumental you'll see **place du Petit-Sablon,** with a small sculptured garden at the center surrounded by a wrought-metal gate. Forty-eight statues of ancient guilds surround the quaint garden.

SPECIAL-INTEREST SIGHTSEEING

FOR THE HISTORY BUFF One of Brussels's great sights is the **Waterloo Battlefield** and its nearby museums, detailed under "Easy Excursions" at the end of this chapter.

FOR THE ARCHITECTURE LOVER The **Horta Museum,** rue Américaine 25 (☎ 02/537-16-92), shows off the art nouveau designs, often in iron and glass, of Victor Horta and contains information pertaining to his life and work. Admission is 150F ($4.80), and it's open Tuesday through Sunday from 2 to 5:30pm. To get there, take tram no. 81, 91, or 92; or bus: no. 54 or 60.

Brussels boasts a rich array of other art nouveau and art deco structures. For a list of some of these buildings, refer to the *Brussels Guide and Map,* available from the tourist office.

FOR THE COMIC-BOOK LOVER At the **Belgian Comic Strip Museum,** Waucquez Warehouse, rue des Sables 20 (☎ 02/219-19-80), lovers of Tintin and other Belgian comic-book heroes can see their favorite stars at this unique museum. The building was designed by art nouveau architect Victor Horta. Admission is 150F ($4.80) for adults and 50F ($1.60) for children. It's open Tuesday through Sunday from 10am to 6pm. Take the Métro to Rogier or Botanique.

ORGANIZED TOURS

BUS TOURS Brussels City-Tours, rue de la Colline 8, off the Grand' Place (☎ 02/513-77-44), operates a three-hour tour for 750F ($24.20) and offers several options for day trips across Belgium, Holland, France, and Luxembourg.

For do-it-yourself walking tours of Brussels, refer to the tourist office's *Brussels Guide and Map.*

ALTERNATIVE TOURS Headquartered at rue du Midi 2, **ARAU Tourville** (☎ 02/513-47-61; fax 02/511-68-29) organizes a social tour that attempts to help you "discover not only Brussels's countless treasures, but also problems the city faces." It also runs specialized art tours by coach. "Brussels 1930—Art Deco" runs every Saturday at 9:45am; "Alternative Brussels," every first and third Saturday of the month at 9:45am; and "Brussels 1900—Art Nouveau," every second, fourth, and fifth Saturday at 9:45am. A walking tour, "The Grand' Place and Its Area," takes place every first and third Sunday from May to September and costs 350F ($11.30). Coach tours are priced at 500F ($16.10).

From June 1 to September 15 the **Chatterbus Tour,** rue des Thuyas 12 (☎ 02/673-18-35), operates a three-hour tour daily at 10am (also at 2pm during July only) from the Galeries Saint-Hubert, a shopping mall next to rue Marché-aux-Herbes 90, a few steps off Grand' Place. A walking tour covers the historic center, followed by a bus ride through areas the average tourist will never see. You'll hear about life in Belgium and get a real feel for the city. The price is 520F ($16.60). It's a fascinating experience, but be sure to phone first.

7 Shopping

BEST BUYS Brussels has several **outdoor markets,** where half the fun is finding an alluring item and the other half is bargaining down the price. Of course, you'll also enjoy a stroll along the modern shopping promenades, the busiest of which is the pedestrian **rue Neuve,** which starts at place de la Monnaie, the site of the Opera House, and runs north to place Rogier. Here you'll find numerous boutiques as well as department stores, including **City 2,** a huge shopping mall full of stores and inexpensive restaurants (see "Dining," earlier in this chapter, for details on the latter). One of Brussels's largest modern supermarkets, **Delhaize,** can be found at the corner of rue Marché aux Poulets and boulevard Anspach, diagonally across from La Bourse and next to a Pizza Hut. It's open Monday from 1 to 8pm, Tuesday through Saturday from 9am to 8pm, and Sunday from 9am to 1pm. Watch for the green sign above the door.

U.K. travelers, particularly, may wish to shop at **Marks & Spencer,** rue Neuve 21 (open Monday through Thursday from 9:15am to 6pm, Friday to 8pm, and Saturday to 5pm), or at **W. H. Smith,** av. Adolphe-Max 75 (open Monday through Saturday from 9am to 6:30pm).

Other interesting shopping malls include the **Anspach Center,** off place de la Monnaie, diagonally across from the Opera House; the **Center Monnaie,** across the street; the **Galeries St-Hubert,** the first covered shopping arcade in Europe (from 1845), off rue du Marché-aux-Herbes; and **Galerie Agora,** off the Grand' Place.

For luxury shopping, try the stores on **avenue Louise** and the nearby streets, where you'll find such names as Cartier, Burberry's, Louis Vuitton, Benetton, and Valentino. You may not find any bargains, but there's lots to look at.

You'll find an interesting street for window-shopping near the Grand' Place, **rue des Eperonniers,** which hosts many small shops including antiques, toy, old book, and clothing stores.

Lace is the overwhelming favorite among visitors to Brussels, followed by **crystal, pewter, jewelry,** and **antiques. Chocolate, beer,** and other foods are a more economical favorite of foreign shoppers.

Belgians view **comic books** quite seriously. Hard covers bind comic books—you're meant to treasure and preserve them. Colorful thin volumes often cost about

$10, although you can also find used ones for less. You can also buy comics at several stores between nos. 132 and 206 chausée de Wavre, between rue du Trône and rue Goffart.

OUTDOOR MARKETS   My favorite outdoor market is the **flea market** on place du Jeu-de-Balle, a large cobblestone square a few blocks from Gare du Midi. As at all flea markets, you'll have to sift through lots of junk but can make real finds in the old postcards, comic books, clothes, furniture, African masks, brass fixtures, and other items. The market is set up daily from 7am to 2pm.

For better-quality goods at decidedly higher prices, check out the **antiques market** on place du Grand-Sablon, open Saturday and Sunday. You'll also find quite a few antiques stores, open throughout the week, on streets in the nearby area (try, for example, rue de Rollebeek). Prices are high, but it's a fun place to look around. On Saturday the market is open from 9am to 6pm; on Sunday, from 9am to 2pm.

As you near the Grand' Place on Sunday from 7am to 2pm, the loud chirping and whistling of birds makes it seem as if you're entering a tropical jungle. Yet it's only the **bird market,** where you can admire thousands of birds—from parakeets to ducks. It's an unusual market in the very center of town and is certainly amusing.

Sunday Casbah   Every Sunday hundreds of merchants assemble their wares along the railroad tracks leading to the Gare du Midi, and because many of the merchants are Arabs and southern Europeans, the scene resembles a Middle Eastern casbah. You'll find many excellent food bargains, making it a perfect place to gather provisions for a few days. You can also find household items and many odds and ends at low cost. Hold onto your wallet (busy markets the world over attract pickpockets) and bargain.

The market starts where boulevard du Midi crosses the rail tracks at place de la Constitution, and continues on both sides of the tracks for several blocks. Lemonnier is the nearest Métro stop. It's open Sunday from 6am to 1pm. For a list of other markets, see the *Brussels Guide and Map,* sold at the Brussels Tourist Office.

8 Brussels After Dark

Although Brussels is too conservative and traditional to go really wild at night, it does offer a full array of things to do in the evening. The best list of upcoming events in the weekly English-language *What's On* magazine, available free from the tourist office. It lists dance, opera, live music, film, and TV events for the week, for both Brussels and the rest of Belgium.

The French-language magazine *Kiosque* lists upcoming events with more detailed descriptions and photos than the English-language publications. You can buy it at newsstands for 80F ($2.60).

Keep in mind that the **tourist office** in the Town Hall on the Grand' Place sells concert and theater tickets.

THE PERFORMING ARTS
OPERA, BALLET & CONCERTS

Théâtre Royal de la Monnaie/Opéra National
Place de la Monnaie. ☎ **02/229-12-00,** Tickets 300F–3,000F ($9.65–$96.75), 200F ($6.45) for students under age 25 (available five minutes before a show). Métro: Bourse.

An opera house in the grand style, the Théâtre Royal is home to the Opéra National, which critics have called the best in the French-speaking world. It's also home to the Orchestre Symphonique de la Monnaie, and its resident ballet company has performed all over the world. The box office is open Monday through Saturday from 11am to 6pm.

Théâtre Toone VII

Petite rue des Bouchers 21 (impasse Schuddeveld). ☎ **02/511-71-37.** Tickets 400F ($11.40). Métro: Bourse.

As crazy as the Belgians are about cartoons, it should come as no surprise that the most popular theater in Brussels is a puppet theater. In a tiny room upstairs from a bistro of the same name, such classic tales as *Faust* and *The Three Musketeers* are performed by marionettes. The dialogue is in French, but the plots and characters are so familiar that even if you don't understand a word you'll be able to follow the action onstage. Performances are given Tuesday through Saturday at 8:30pm.

JAZZ

Preservation Hall

Place de Londres 4. ☎ **02/502-15-97.** Métro: Namur.

This basic establishment, notwithstanding the name, has only about 50 seats and is always crowded with jazz fanatics. It's undecorated except for wall mirrors. Founded 30 years ago, it has become one of Brussels's "in" places for New Orleans–type jazz and Dixieland lovers. Open Tuesday, Thursday, Friday, and Saturday from 9pm.

Travers

Rue Traversière 11. ☎ **02/218-40-86.** Cover 300F–250F ($8.05), except Mon, when they perform a free jam session. Métro: Botanique.

Travers is a quintessential small and smoky jazz club with fewer than a dozen tables lit by candles stuck in champagne bottles. Modern art adorns the walls. Between two and five concerts are performed per week; call for the exact schedule. There are also occasional rock and reggae shows. Open Monday through Saturday from 8pm to 2am or later. Concerts start at 8:30pm weeknights, at 10pm Saturday.

FILMS

Most foreign films are subtitled in French and Flemish and cost 220F to 250F ($7.10 to $8.05), except Monday, when prices fall to 150F to 170F ($4.85 to $5.50). Some cinemas offer discount tickets of 150F ($4.85) to students under age 26 and senior citizens.

For a completely different cinema experience, consider a viewing of the sensational IMAX (maximum image) film technology in the **Kinepolis**, bd. du Centenaire 1, in Bruparck (☎ **02/479-76-69**). Films are in either French or Dutch. English versions are occasionally shown; call ahead for details. Admission is 250F ($8.05) for adults, 200F ($6.45) for students and children. To get there, take Métro 1A to Heysel, the last stop.

Bruparck also sports 23 regular cinemas in Kinepolis, making it one of the world's largest movie palaces (see "More Attractions" under "Attractions," earlier in this chapter, for descriptions of the other amusements in Bruparck).

The **City 2 shopping mall,** on rue Neuve, houses eight cinemas.

Musée du Cinema, in the Palais des Beaux-Arts, rue Baron-Horta 9 (☎ 02/ 507-83-70), screens classic films in their original languages every evening, with silent films shown in a different room. Only 50F ($1.60) is charged in advance or 80F ($2.30) on the evening of the show. Children under 16 are not admitted.

CAFES & BARS
IN & NEAR THE GRAND' PLACE

It's always satisfying to grab a chair at a sidewalk café in the Grand' Place and drink in the beauty of the floodlit golden buildings ringing the square. After you've ordered one drink you can remain for as long as you wish.

✪ A la Mort Subite

Rue Montagne-aux-Herbes-Potagères 7. ☎ 02/513-13-18. Métro: Bourse.

A 1911 café with columns, neoclassical ornaments and mirrors, and old small wooden tables in a style that recalls the prewar epoch, A la Mort Subite is a good place to enjoy an afternoon coffee or an evening beer. Coffee costs 60F ($1.95); beer, 65F to 120F ($2.10 to $4.50). Open daily from 10am to 1am.

A l'Imaige Nostre-Dame

8 rue du Marché-aux-Herbes 6. ☎ 02/219-42-49. Métro: Bourse.

In this house dating from 1642, just a block from the Grand' Place, people of all ages enjoy reasonably priced beer amid wooden beams on the ceiling, old wooden tables, painted windows, and an antique ceramic fireplace. Beer costs 75F to 140F ($2.40 to $4.50). Open daily from noon to midnight.

Le Cercueil (The Coffin)

Rue des Harengs 10–12. ☎ 02/513-33-61. Métro: Bourse.

For those with a mischievous sense of the macabre, this bar just off the Grand' Place provides an atmosphere like no other. The tables are glass panes placed over coffins, and when you order certain drinks they'll be served in a ceramic skull. Purple fluorescent lighting keeps the rooms dim, and ecclesiastical music, especially organ music, plays in the background, helping to create an eerie horror-movie atmosphere. Prices are a little high: Half a liter of beer costs 190F ($6.10). Open daily from 11am to 3am.

Cirio

Rue de la Bourse 18. ☎ 02/512-13-95. Métro: Bourse.

On the opposite side of the Bourse from the always-crowded and smokey Falstaff, Cirio is a quiet café popular with older Bruxellois. The prewar atmosphere here is almost tangible, and there's no better café in town for people-watching. Efficient waiters in black vests and bow ties carrying trays of beer, wine, and coffee accompanied by crackers or cookies navigate between little café tables. Art nouveau woodwork, red-and-green-striped banquettes, and lots of polished brass seem to have been perfectly preserved since the late 1800s. Beer costs 66F to 123F ($2.10 to $3.95), and it's open daily from 11am to 1am.

✪ Le Roy d'Espagne

Grand' Place 1. ☎ 02/513-08-07. Métro: Bourse.

The oldest café here, in a 1690 building (once home to Brussels's bakers), Le Roy d'Espagne accommodates guests in several areas. In addition to the outdoor café tables, you can drink in a room that preserves a Flemish interior style of the 17th century—a masterpiece of wooden architecture with a wooden walkway and beams above and a fireplace covered by a black metal hood. From the fourth floor, the view of the Grand' Place is spectacular. Beer costs 70F to 180F ($2.25 to $5.80). Open daily from 10am to 1am.

ELSEWHERE

De Ultieme Hallucinatie

Rue Royale 316. ☎ **02/217-06-14.** Métro: Botanique.

This turn-of-the-century private house is now an art nouveau restaurant as well as an old garden café. Rocky walls and plants decorate one side and a long marble bar occupies the other. There's also a more futuristic bar area downstairs with fluorescent lighting and abstract outer space–style art, a small outdoor café area, and a charming section behind the garden. They have a wide selection of beer, as well as wine, coffee, and a few snacks. Beer begins at 60F ($1.95); a glass of wine is 85F ($2.75); coffee runs 60F ($1.95). The café is open Monday through Friday from 11am to 3am and Saturday and Sunday from 4pm to 3am.

Le Fleur en Papier Doré

Rue des Alexiens 53. ☎ **02/511-16-59.** Métro: Bourse.

A café located in a 17th-century building, this typical beer bar tries to create a "temple of surrealism" with old prints, plates, horns, porcelain, and other objects covering every inch of the walls. The three small rooms house fewer than a dozen tables. On Friday and Saturday from 9 or 10pm an accordion player pumps out some tunes. You'll find this typically charming place off place de la Chapelle. Beer costs 55F to 95F ($1.75 to $3.05); a glass of wine, 75F to 100F ($2.40 to $3.20). Open daily from 11am to 11pm.

A DISCO

Le Garage

Rue Duquesnoy 16. ☎ **02/512-66-22.** Cover 100F ($3.20) Wed–Thurs and Sun, 300F ($9.65) Fri–Sat, which includes three soft drinks or one hard drink. Métro: Gare Centrale.

The first large disco that opened in Brussels (1983), Le Garage accommodates a car to the side of the dance floor, plus a video screen. For the most part, the disco attracts people 18 to 30.

9 Networks & Resources

STUDENTS   Students visiting Brussels enjoy an excellent setup of **youth hostels,** which provide not only a cheap bed but also a great place to meet other students. See "Accommodations," earlier in this chapter.

  Acotra, rue de la Madeleine 51, 1000 Bruxelles (☎ **02/512-70-78**), sells discount student train, plane, boat, and bus tickets and also books places in youth hostels and private rooms. It also sells the ISIC (International Student Identity Card). You'll find this office across a small park from Gare Centrale, toward the Grand' Place. It's open Monday through Friday from 10am to 5:30pm (Thursday to 7pm).

GAY MEN   Rue des Riches-Claires and rue du Marché-au-Charbon (not far from the Bourse) host a few gay establishments. **Macho 2,** rue du Marché-au-Charbon 108, a block from rue des Riches-Claires (☎ **02/513-56-67**), houses a gay men's sauna, swimming pool, steam room, and café. It's open daily from noon to midnight, and on weekends until 6am. Admission is 450F ($14.50), 350F ($11.30) for students.

10 Easy Excursions

WATERLOO   On June 18, 1815, the Grand Alliance of British, Dutch, and Prussian forces, along with a smattering of soldiers from the German principalities, defeated mighty Napoléon Bonaparte and his 74,000 French troops, leaving 40,000 dead. Napoléon himself survived, but his attempt to rebuild his empire was crushed; he was sent to the island of Ste-Hélène, where he died 6 years later at the age of 52.

Bus "W" leaves on the half hour and the hour from a small bus terminal on avenue de Stalingrad in Brussels, one block to the south of place Rouppe. The 11-mile ride takes 50 minutes and costs 90F ($2.90). You can fill in the details of the Battle of Waterloo at the **Wellington Museum,** chaussée de Bruxelles 147, in the village of Waterloo (☎ **02/354-78-06**), or study a 360° panoramic mural and see a short movie of the battle at the **Centre du Visiteur,** route du Lion 252 (☎ **02/354-78-06**), open daily from 9:30am to 6:30pm. The actual battlefield can be surveyed from atop the nearby **Lion's Mound,** a pyramidlike hill behind the center. A souvenir shop in the center sells mementos ranging from tin soldiers ($10) to porcelain figurines of Napoleon on a horse ($120) to a replica of Napoleon's cavalry sword ($1,320).

Admission to the Wellington Museum is 80F ($1.60) for adults, 60F ($1.95) for students and senior citizens, 40F ($1.30) for children 6 to 12. At the Centre du Visiter, to see the giant mural and the short movie costs 275F ($8.85) for adults, 220F ($7.10) for students and seniors, and 170F ($5.70) for children. Entry to the Lion's Mound is 40F ($1.30) for adults and seniors and 20F (65¢) for children. Note that bus "W" stops at both the museum and the visitor center.

OTHER SIDE TRIPS   Most of Belgium is a short distance outside Brussels, making the choices for side trips so many that I can only highlight the possibilities. Consider **Ghent,** often called the "Venice of the North" for its canals and charm; **Bruges,** a medieval monument with a beautiful market square, important sights, and Michelangelo statue; modern **Antwerp,** the hometown of the 17th-century art master Peter Paul Rubens (you can still visit his impressive house), a diamond capital, and a massive port; and **Leuven,** a quaint university town with 22,000 students and architecture dating from hundreds of years ago.

If you want to spend more than a day in Ghent, the **Hotel Cour St. Georges,** Botenmarkt 2 (☎ **091/224-26-40;** fax 091/224-24-24), is a "worth the extra money" choice, in a beautiful 13th-century house with spacious, exquisitely furnished rooms. It's next to the Market Square and charges 2,600F ($83.85) for a single and 3,500F ($112.90) for a double. **Trio's Restaurant,** Donkersteeg 26 (☎ **091/225-15-90**), has only 12 tables but is famous for an excellent menu for 620F ($20). It's closed Tuesday and Wednesday.

In Bruges, the **Hotel Lucca,** Naaldenstraat 30 (☎ **050/342-067;** fax 050/333-464), offers 18 rooms on three floors (no elevator) in a fascinating 13th-century house built 700 years ago by a merchant from Lucca, Italy. Rooms cost 1,500F to 1,800F ($48.40 to $58.05) single, 2,300F ($74.20) double, 3,400F

($109.67) triple, and 3,900F ($125.80) quad; a buffet breakfast is included. **La Sirene d'Or,** Markt 31 (☎ **050/333-776**), an atmospheric restaurant in the heart of Bruges, offers menus for 590F to 1,600F ($19.05 to 51.60).

Belgium's excellent rail network quickly links you up with all of these towns: Leuven is 20 minutes away; Antwerp, 30 minutes; Ghent, 40 minutes; and Bruges, 55 minutes. Note that when arriving by train in Ghent and Bruges, you'll have to take a tram to the city center, about 5 minutes away from the station; the fare is 40F ($1.15).

The national rail company, SNCB, provides several **rail-excursion tickets** to facilitate low-cost trips from Brussels, including "A Weekend at the Sea or Ardennes," which allows half-price travel to those destinations on the weekend; or "Un beau jour à . . . "—day-long excursions to various cities across Belgium. You can also buy a railpass that allows 5 days of travel over a 17-day span. Ask for details at either the tourist office or at any train station.

You can even leave Belgium entirely and be back in Brussels for a late supper that same day—albeit a very ambitious outing. On a rapid train, Paris is only $2^{1}/_{2}$ hours away; Amsterdam and Luxembourg are just under 3 hours; and London, via Eurostar and the Chunnel, $3^{1}/_{2}$ hours.

Budapest

by Beth Reiber

This is a stately, elegant city, with its two sections, Buda and Pest, divided by the huge Danube River (called Duna in Hungarian). Budapest is a capital in the grand style, in the same tradition as Vienna; it's also a logical next stop from Vienna, so close by train that it makes little sense not to visit if you're already in Vienna. Slightly larger than Austria but smaller than the U.S. state of Kentucky, Hungary has about 10 million inhabitants, 2.2 million of whom live in Budapest.

Budapest was a Roman colony early on. The Romans were the first to harness some of the 123 mineral springs to begin the public baths, still a feature of Budapest today. Located on one of the major east-west routes, Budapest through the centuries has been in the path of most European invasions. It was destroyed several times and has been ruled successively by the Mongols, the Turks, and the Habsburgs. All these foreign invaders have left their mark on the city's culture and appearance, from the exotic spices introduced into the cuisine by the Ottoman Turks to the imposing baroque buildings of the Austro-Hungarian empire.

From 1945 to 1990 Hungary was a reluctant member of the Eastern bloc. Hungarians, however, always enjoyed greater freedom than many of their Eastern neighbors and helped lead the way in one of the most amazing stories of our time—the decline of communism and the opening of Eastern Europe to democratic reform. Since its first free elections in more than four decades were held in 1990, the country has been in the midst of even-greater changes. If it has been 10 years since you've been to Hungary—or even just 2—you're in for some big surprises. It's an exciting time to visit Budapest and witness history in the making.

1 Budapest Deals & Discounts

SPECIAL DISCOUNTS   Though some museums offer student reductions, very few discount opportunities are available in Budapest. This shouldn't worry you because, as you'll see, prices are already very low, making Budapest itself a budget best. Even though Hungary is beset with galloping inflation and rising prices for everything from milk to gasoline, the country is still very affordable. In fact, don't be surprised if your money goes further here than in most of

What's Special About Budapest

Museums
- The Hungarian National Gallery, with the world's most complete collection of Hungarian art.
- The Museum of Fine Arts, with works of European masters.

Prices
- A subway ticket for 30¢.
- Accommodations in private homes for less than $12 per person per night.
- Eating like royalty for less than $7.
- Admission fees to museums of less than 80¢.
- Opera tickets for $2.25.

Dining
- Café New York, one of Europe's most splendid dining halls.
- Gundel, with a five-piece orchestra and some of Europe's best cuisine.

Thermal Baths
- There are 200 in Budapest; you can get a 30-minute massage in Budapest for less than $5.50.

other destinations in this book. For example, you can eat very well for a fraction of what the same meal would cost in Vienna. And don't miss the opera—it's
dirt cheap.

Trip Preparations

DOCUMENTS　As of 1990 U.S., Canadian, and U.K. travelers
need a valid passport to enter Hungary. However, at press time, Australian
and New Zealand citizens were still required to obtain a visa. Visas can be obtained
at any Hungarian embassy, consulate, or from IBUSZ, the official Hungarian
travel bureau, which has an office in Vienna. If you're arriving by plane, you can
obtain a visa at Budapest's Ferihegy Airport; likewise, if you're traveling by car
you can apply for a visa prior to your trip.

WHEN TO TRIP　The best time for visiting Budapest and Hungary is
May through October, when weather conditions are generally good. May and
September are lovely, but prolonged rainfall is rare. There are frequent thunder-
storms in summer.

Average Daytime Temperature

	Apr	May	June	July	Aug	Sept	Oct	Nov	Dec
°F	53	62	68	86	82	63	52	42	35
°C	12	17	20	30	28	17	11	6	2

With the exception of the Grand Prix car race and the European
Touring Car race each year, Budapest has only a few special events. The
Spring Festival is Budapest's most famous festival, offering outstand-
ing performances of opera, ballet, folk dancing, art exhibits, and concerts.
The festival features international greats from piano virtuoso Zoltán

Kocsis to Keith Jarrett and Joe Cocker. What's more, prices for tickets are so low that you can attend virtually every event for what it would cost to attend one musical extravaganza in Salzburg.

3 Budapest Specifics

ARRIVING

FROM THE AIRPORT   Ferihegy Airport, 10 miles southeast of the city, consists of two terminals and is linked with the Pest air terminal at Erzsébet tér (formerly Engels tér) by a public minibus that costs 200 Ft ($1.80). Buses depart every half hour or hour for the 35-minute trip. Tickets can be bought from the driver.

Alternatively, there's also a minibus airport Shuttle Bus Service (☎ 1/157-8555) that will deliver passengers anywhere within downtown Budapest for 600 Ft ($5.40) per person. Look for the shuttle service sign in the airport's arrival lobby. In any case, avoid taking a taxi—it'll set you back about 2,000 to 2,200 Ft ($18 to $20). If you do take a taxi, be sure to negotiate the price beforehand.

FROM THE TRAIN STATION   There are three train stations: the **Keleti pu (East Station),** in Pest, for trains to and from Vienna, Paris, Frankfurt, Berlin, or Rome; the **Nuygati pu (West Station),** in Pest, for trains to and from Prague or Berlin; and the **Déli pu (South Station),** in Buda, for connections with Lake Balaton. Each railroad station is also the location of a subway station.

VISITOR INFORMATION

For all kinds of information related to your stay in Budapest—including sightseeing, brochures, maps, museums, cultural programs, weather, and emergencies—visit or phone **Tourinform,** Süto u. 2 (☎ 1/117-9800), near Deák Ferenc tér in Pest, open daily from 8am to 8pm.

For detailed information on hotels, sightseeing tours, and currency rates and exchange, call or go to the **IBUSZ Hotel Service Office,** Petöfi tér 3 (☎ 1/118-4842), near the Duna Inter-Continental Hotel in Pest, open daily 24 hours.

For information on Budapest's events, including concerts, the opera, and special exhibitions, pick up a free copy of the monthly *Programme in Hungary* at Tourinform. **"Budapest Panorama,"** also published monthly and available free at Tourinform, is a four-language cultural, entertainment, and leisure-time brochure that's especially valuable for its good city maps. For even more detailed information, purchase *Budapest Week,* an English weekly sold at selected newsstands for 96 Ft (85¢). It appears on Thursday afternoons and contains all the latest information on everything from films and opera to ballet, folk dancing, pop, rock, and classical music. It also lists all venues, complete with addresses. Giving *Budapest Week* stiff competition is the weekly *Budapest Sun,* which also appears on Thursday and includes an insert with practical information, a day-by-day account of what's happening in Budapest's theaters, concert halls, movie theaters, and other venues, and articles of interest to tourists. It costs 98 Ft (90¢).

CITY LAYOUT

Budapest is bisected by the **Duna (Danube) River** into a right bank and a left bank. Of the city's three main districts, two—**Buda** and **Óbuda**—are found on the left bank, while **Pest** is on the right. In terms of major attractions, most of the main shopping streets, the House of Parliament, the National Museum, the

What Things Cost in Budapest	U.S. $
Taxi from Ferihegy Airport to Budapest city center	18.00
Public transportation within the city	.30
Local telephone call	.10
Double room at the Marriott (deluxe)	230.00
Double room at the Hotel Nemzeti (moderate)	117.00
Double room in the home of Dr. Walter Fleps (budget)	29.00
Lunch for one, without wine, at Bagolyvár (moderate)	7.00
Lunch for one, without wine, at Paprika (budget)	3.00
Dinner for one, without wine, at Gundel (deluxe)	54.00
Dinner for one, without wine, at Kispipa Vendéglö (moderate)	6.50
Dinner for one, without wine, at Bohémtanya (budget)	5.00
Glass of wine	1.80
Half liter of beer	1.35
Coca-Cola in a street café or self-service restaurant	.55
Cup of coffee with milk	1.00
Roll of ASA 100 color film, 36 exposures	6.20
Admission to the National Museum	.70
Movie ticket	2.70
Opera ticket (Hungarian State Opera)	1.80

Museum of Applied Arts, and the Museum of Fine Arts are located in Pest. Buda is the location of Castle Hill, Fisherman's Bastion, Matthias Church, and the National Gallery.

In other words, Pest is the center for major hotels, shopping, dining, banking, and nightlife. Buda, on the other hand, is the historical and cultural part of the city, and Castle Hill has been beautifully renovated with a number of fine buildings. You'll probably want to split your time equally between the two.

Budapest is divided into 23 districts, reflected in postal addresses. District V is the business center of Pest, encompassing the area around Roosevelt tér and Váci út, while District I is Buda's Castle Hill area. To figure out the district from the four-digit postal code, take the middle two numbers: 1052, therefore, is District V; 1135 is District XIII.

The main streets in Pest are **Rákóczi út** (and its extension, Kossuth Lajos utca), stretching a mile from Keleti pu (station) to Erzébet híd; **Teréz körút** (and its extension, Erzsébet körút), running from Blaha Lujza tér to Nyugati pu (station), with the Oktogon subway station halfway along; and the stately 2-mile-long and more than 100-yard-wide **Andrássy út,** impressively lined with theaters, high schools, embassies, and palacelike buildings—it begins near **Deák Ferenc tér** and leads to the monumental **Hösök tere (Heroes' Square),** formerly the site of mass rallies on official holidays. The main shopping street, now also a pedestrian zone, and as elegant as the Merceria in Venice or the Faubourg St-Honoré in Paris, is **Váci út,** running parallel to the Danube from near Erzébet híd to Vörösmarty tér.

Incidentally, after Hungary became a democracy more than 500 street and plaza names were changed back to what they had been 40 years ago. With Lenin and Engels out of favor, Lenin körút became Teréz körút and Erzsébet körút, and Engles tér became Erzsébet tér. Likewise, Népköztársaság became Andrássy út, Tanács körút became Károly körút, and November 7 tér became Oktogon. The old names may still appear on old maps, and some street signs have yet to be changed.

The Hungarian word for street is **utca** (abbreviated "u.") or **út.** A larger boulevard is **körút** (abbreviated "krt."), while a square is **tér.** The word for bridge is **híd.**

Of the seven **bridges** spanning the Danube, only four are of importance for travelers (from south to north): Szabadság híd, linking Fóvám tér in Pest with Szent Gellért tér in Buda; Erzsébet híd, connecting Március 15 tér in Pest with the Gellért Hill area in Buda; Széchenyi lánchíd (the legendary Chain Bridge), reaching from Roosevelt tér in Pest to Clark Adam tér in Buda and Budapest's most beautiful bridge; and Margit híd, which spans the river from Jaszai Mari tér, near the Parliament Building in Pest, via Margit-sziget (Margaret Island), to the Buda side of the river.

GETTING AROUND

BY BUS, TRAM & SUBWAY   Although prices are likely to go up by 1996, public transportation within the city is incredibly cheap. At press time, buses, trams, and subways cost only 35 Ft (30¢). Tickets for all three are sold at newsstands, tobacco shops, and major subway stations (where you'll find automatic ticket machines), but never aboard the conveyance. They must be punched or validated in small machines at the subway turnstiles and aboard the trams and buses.

Tickets are good for only one journey and don't allow a transfer (even if you're transferring from one subway line to another), so you're best off buying several tickets and keeping them on hand. If you'll be traveling a lot, spend 200 Ft ($1.80) for a **day ticket** allowing you to use all buses, trams, and subways throughout the capital. A **seven-day pass** costs 550 Ft ($4.95).

You'll probably end up using the subways the most—there are three lines, number- and color-coded, converging at Deák Ferenc tér and running from 4:30am to 11pm. It's virtually impossible to get lost. The free map issued by Tourinform shows locations of some of the major subway stations. However, if you're going to be in Budapest for any length of time, you may wish to purchase a more detailed map of the city, also available at Tourinform.

BY TAXI   Taxis are also relatively inexpensive. The fare from Keleti pu (train station) to any of the hotels or private homes listed in "Accommodations" should not exceed 700 Ft ($6.30). If you hail a taxi in the street or go to a taxi stand, the fare starts at just 70 Ft (65¢). If you phone for a taxi, the meter starts at 75 Ft (70¢). You can call a taxi by dialing 1/153-3633, 1/122-2222, 1/166-6666, or 1/155-5000.

However, a word of caution about Budapest's taxis is in order. Knowing that foreign visitors are unfamiliar with fares, many taxi drivers intentionally shoot up their fares via a hidden device rigged to their meters. Suddenly, trips that should've cost only 500 Ft ($4.50) may end up being 2,000 Ft ($18). There has been much discussion of regulating taxis—even now, pretty much anyone can operate a taxi privately. It's therefore crucial to negotiate the fare before entering a taxi. The

The Hungarian Forint

For American Readers   At this writing $1 = approximately 110 Ft (or 100 Ft = 90¢), and this was the rate of exchange used to calculate the dollar values given in this chapter (rounded to the nearest nickel).

For British Readers   At this writing £1 = approximately 172 Ft (or 100 Ft = 58p), and this was the rate of exchange used to calculate the pound values in the table below.

Note: The rates given here fluctuate from time to time and may not be the same when you travel to Hungary. Therefore this table should be used only as a guide:

Ft	U.S.$	U.K.£	Ft	U.S.$	U.K.£
10	.09	.06	1,250	11.25	7.25
25	.22	.14	1,500	13.50	8.70
50	.45	.29	1,750	15.75	10.15
75	.67	.43	2,000	18.00	11.60
100	.90	.58	2,250	20.25	13.05
150	1.35	.87	2,500	22.50	14.50
200	1.80	1.16	3,000	27.00	17.40
250	2.25	1.45	3,500	31.50	20.30
300	2.70	1.74	4,000	36.00	23.20
400	3.60	2.32	5,000	45.00	29.00
500	4.50	2.90	6,000	54.00	34.80
750	6.75	4.35	7,000	63.00	40.60
1,000	9.00	5.80	8,000	70.00	46.40

wisest thing to do is to ask the proprietor of your accommodation how much you should expect to pay if you think you're going to be taking a taxi. As stated earlier, most rides within the city shouldn't exceed 700 Ft ($6.30). It's probably best, however, to avoid taking taxis if possible.

BY CAR   **Avis,** located in Pest at Martinelli tér 8 (☎ **1/118-4158** or 118-4240), near the Marriott, rents a compact Opel Corsa for 3,084 Ft ($27.75) daily, plus 30 Ft (25¢) per kilometer. The office is open Monday through Friday from 8am to 8pm, Saturday from 8am to 6pm, and Sunday from 8am to 2pm.

Car-rental agencies with similar prices include **Hertz,** Aranykéz u. 4–8 (☎ **1/117-7533**), and **Europcar,** Üllöi út 60–62 (☎ **1/113-1492**).

FAST FACTS: Budapest

Babysitters   There's no babysitting service in Budapest. However, some of the five-star hotels provide babysitting services for guests.

Banks   The National Bank of Hungary has a main office in Pest at Szabadság tér 8–9 (☎ **1/153-2600** or 112-3223). However, because banks have such short business hours you'll probably find it more convenient to change your money at one of the many travel agencies, such as the IBUSZ Hotel Service, Petőfi tér 3 (☎ **1/118-4842**), open 24 hours. You can even get a cash advance with Visa, MasterCard, and Diners Club at this location. You can also exchange money at any hotel, but at slightly less favorable rates than those offered by banks and travel agencies.

There are even automatic money changers in Budapest now. The most convenient is open 24 hours at the K & H Bank, Károly krt. 20 in the heart of Pest (across from the Viking Söröző Tuborg restaurant). It exchanges U.S. and Canadian dollars, British pounds, and many other currencies, including Japanese yen, into forints at a competitive exchange rate. U.S. $5, $10, and $20 bills are accepted.

There's a 24-hour automatic cash machine for American Express cardholders at **American Express,** conveniently located in the heart of Pest's business district at Deák Ferenc út 10 (☎ **1/267-2022** or 267-2024), just off Vörösmarty Square. Its office is open Monday through Friday from 9am to 5:30pm and Saturday from 9am to 2pm.

Be warned that as you walk around Budapest, you may be approached by people on the street asking whether you wish to exchange dollars for forint at a much more favorable rate than that offered by banks. Don't be tempted! Not only do tourists report being short-changed and cheated in the bargain, but it's against the law.

Business Hours   Most **shops selling food** are open Monday through Friday from 7am to 7pm and Saturday from 7am to 2pm. Other **stores and department stores** are open Monday through Friday from 10am to 6pm and Saturday from 9am to 1pm. Many stay open Thursday until 8pm. **Banks** are open Monday through Friday from 9am to 1 or 2:30pm.

Currency   Hungary's official currency is the **forint (Ft),** also written HuF, and 1 forint equals 100 fillérs (but you'll rarely see a fillér, as they no longer have any practical value). Coins come in 10, 20, and 50 fillérs and 1, 2, 5, 10, 20, 100, and 200 Ft. Banknotes are issued in denominations of 50, 100, 500, 1,000, and 5,000 Ft.

Customs Regulations   There are no special Customs restrictions when entering Hungary. You can import reasonable amounts of tobacco, alcohol, and gifts, and unlimited amounts of non-Hungarian currency. When leaving Hungary, you cannot carry more than 1,000 Ft ($9) with you and can export no more than 4,000 Ft ($36) worth of gifts or goods purchased in Hungary. My guess is that as border restrictions relax, Customs regulations will also become more lenient. If in doubt, ask IBUSZ or Tourinform about the latest developments. To be safe, exchange only what you think you'll need.

Dentist/Doctor   If you need to see a dentist, your best bet is Kiwa Dental, Erzsébet Királyné u. 97/c (☎ **1/252-1421**). For a list of English-speaking dentists or doctors, call your embassy.

Embassies   As a capital city, Budapest is home to the embassies of many foreign countries, including the **United States,** Szabadság tér 12 (☎ **1/112-6450** or 111-9600); **Canada,** Budakeszi u. 32 (☎ **1/275-1200**); the **United Kingdom,** Harmincad u. 6 (☎ **1/118-2888** or 266-2888); and **Australia,** Délibáb u. 30 (☎ **1/153-4233**).

Emergencies   If you need police assistance, phone 07. For the fire department, call 05; for a hospital or an ambulance, 04. The pharmacy at Rákósczi út 86 (☎ **1/322-9613**), near the plush Hungaria Hotel and Keleti pu, is one of the easiest to find. It's open Monday through Friday from 8am to 8pm and Saturday from 8am to 2pm. A list of pharmacies open Sunday is posted on the door.

Holidays   The following holidays are celebrated in Budapest: New Year's Day (Jan 1), Revolution Day (Mar 15), Easter Monday, Labor Day (May 1), Constitution Day (Aug 20), Hungarian Revolution or New Republic Day (Oct 23), and Christmas (Dec 25–26).

Hospitals   Foreigners in need of first aid are handled at any hospital free of charge, though fees are levied for more involved treatment and medical examination. If you need to go to a hospital, the best policy is to call Emergency Medical Service (☎ **1/118-8288** or 118-8012), open 24 hours, with ambulance service, or an ambulance, which will deliver you to the nearest hospital. If it isn't an emergency, try IMS Outpatient Clinic, Váci u. 202 (☎ **1/149-9349**).

Information   For all kinds of information related to your stay in Budapest, see "Budapest Specifics," earlier in this chapter, where you'll find addresses for both IBUSZ and Tourinform.

Laundry/Dry Cleaning   There are many dry cleaners in Budapest though few self-service laundries (*patyolat* in Hungarian). The most centrally located is the Irisz Szalon Patyolat at Rákóczi út 8 (☎ **1/322-1840**), near the Astoria subway station. It has 10 self-service machines, is open Monday through Friday from 7am to 7pm and Saturday from 7am to 1pm, and charges 300 Ft ($2.70) for 5 kilos (11 lbs.) washed, including detergent. Dryers cost 100 Ft (90¢) extra per 15 minutes. It even has a sheet of instructions in English—ask one of the attendants to get it for you.

If you're staying at a private home or guesthouse, your landlord will probably do your laundry for a more reasonable price.

Lost & Found   If you lose something on public transportation (subway, tram, bus), go to BKV, Akácfa u. 15 (☎ **1/321-5230** or 322-1440), near the Oktogon subway stop. If you lose something in a taxi, go to Erzsébet tér 5 (☎ **1/117-2318**). Contact the information window of the train station for items lost on a train. At Keleti pu, phone 322-5615; at Nyugati pu, phone 149-0115; and at Déli pu, go to the office near Track 12 (☎ **1/175-6293**). The windows are open Monday through Friday from 8am to 6pm and Saturday from 8am to 2pm.

For objects lost on the street, in shops, or in museums, contact Tourinform, Sütő u. 2, near Deák Ferenc tér (☎ **1/117-9800**). It's staffed with English-speaking personnel.

Mail   Most post offices (*Posta*) in Hungary are open Monday through Friday from 8am to 6pm and Saturday from 8am to 2pm. The **Central Post Office** is conveniently located in the business district of Pest at Petőfí Sandor u. 13 (☎ **1/117-5500**); it's open Monday through Friday from 8am to 8pm and Saturday from 8am to 1pm. The post offices beside Nyugati pu on Teréz körút and at Keleti pu at Baross tér 11 are open 24 hours. An airmail letter to the United States costs 67 Ft (60¢) for the first 5 grams; a postcard costs 47 Ft (40¢). Mailboxes are red in Hungary.

The **postal code** for Budapest varies according to the district, with 1052 referring to the heart of Pest around the Duna Inter-Continental Hotel, District V.

If you're not sure of the postal code, your best bet is to address a letter to Budapest with H-1000.

Newspapers   *Budapest Week,* an English-language weekly that appears on newsstands and at Tourinform on Thursday afternoon for 96 Ft (85¢), contains information on what's going on in the Hungarian capital, including the performing arts, movies, and concerts. Another local newspaper is the *Budapest Sun,* which also carries information on what's going on. This weekly costs 98 Ft (90¢).

Selected newsstands and hotels carry issues of *Budapest Week,* the *Budapest Sun,* and such well-known English-language newspapers as the *International Herald Tribune.* Libri International Bookshop, in the heart of Pest at Váci u. 32 (☎ 1/118-2718), carries English-language newspapers, as well as guidebooks and fiction in English. It's open Monday through Friday from 10am to 6pm and Saturday from 9am to 1pm.

Photographic Needs   Fotex is a chain of film-processing stores that also deals in Kodak film and processing. A conveniently located Fotex at Váci u. 9 (☎ 1/137-5641), Budapest's main shopping street, is open Monday through Friday from 9am to 9pm and Saturday and Sunday from 10am to 8pm.

Police   The emergency number for the police is 07.

Radio/TV   Radio Bridge, 102.1 FM, airs several programs in English, including hourly Voice of America news reports throughout the day. In addition, Monday through Saturday at 8am and 8pm it airs two 30-minute English-language broadcasts, "Budapest Day" and "Budapest Night," featuring news, business reports, features, and entertainment.

Shoe Repair   Most shoe-repair shops in Budapest are small, servicing the local neighborhood. Ask at your hotel for the nearest repair shop. Otherwise, there's a Mister Minit (an international chain of shoe-repair shops) in the Centrum-Corvin department store at Blaha Lujza tér, open Monday through Friday from 10am to 7pm and Saturday from 10am to 2pm.

Tax   Hotels, private accommodations, and restaurants include a 25% tax in their rates. As for goods, there's a value-added tax (VAT) of 10% to 30% included in the price, with the highest taxes applied to luxury goods. At present, foreigners are not entitled to a refund of the VAT, unlike in most other countries.

Taxis   Refer to "Getting Around" under "Budapest Specifics," earlier in this chapter, for information on calling a taxi and prices.

Telephone   Public telephones and booths are found on streets, in subway stations, and in Budapest's hotels. For a **local call,** insert a 10-Ft (10¢) or 20-Ft (20¢) coin.

The **international country code** for Hungary is 36, while the **city code** for Budapest is 1.

For **international telephone calls,** head for the International Telephone Office, near the main post office on the second floor at Petőfí Sandor u. 17 in Pest. The staff is helpful and will tell you how to make an international call. It's open Monday through Friday from 10am to 6pm and Saturday from 10am to 2pm. Otherwise, if you need an English-speaking operator to assist you, dial 1/267-5555. A three-minute call to North America costs 480 Ft ($4.30).

An alternative to going to the International Telephone Office is to purchase a **telephone card,** available at post offices for 500 Ft ($4.50) or 1,100 Ft ($10) worth of calls. More and more telephones throughout Budapest accept such cards. You can make international direct telephone calls only from the newer red/blue pay phones with a telephone card.

Tipping   Although service is included in restaurant bills, everyone expects to be tipped. As a general rule, add 10% to your taxi fare or restaurant bill. For the violinist who plays at your restaurant table, give 200 Ft ($1.80).

4 Accommodations

One of the changes that I hope will come to Budapest in the near future is more and better accommodations. Although there are the usual first-class hotels beyond your budget, Budapest doesn't have nearly enough medium- and lower-priced hotels to accommodate the growing number of tourists who are flocking to Europe's "undiscovered" capital. Summers are especially overcrowded and overbooked.

Consequently, Budapest relies more heavily on private accommodations to house its tourists than any other major European city. Everyone in town, it seems, rents out rooms to visitors. Officially, these private entrepreneurs must have a special government permit; unofficially, many individuals without permits meet incoming trains to try and rent rooms, and the officials for the most part seem simply to look the other way. On my last several trips to Budapest I was approached by individuals at least six times before I even made it from the train platform to the IBUSZ office at the station. In summer, when accommodations are tight and tourists form long lines at travel agencies trying to book rooms, you're best off trying your luck with an individual who looks trustworthy. Be sure to ask how far away the room is (you don't want to waste time traveling to the town center via a long bus ride) and whether there's a shower. How much you end up paying depends largely on the time of year—but it'll probably be anywhere from $15 to $20 (usually in Western currency) per night for two people.

IBUSZ can book both hotel and pension rooms or private accommodations, but travelers should be aware that in summer months the cheaper accommodations fill up fast. A staff member of IBUSZ suggested trying to arrive early in the morning, since by afternoon all rooms may be filled. (You might have to take a more expensive accommodation the first night and then return to IBUSZ early the next morning.) There's an IBUSZ at Keleti pu, open Monday through Friday from 8am to 7pm and Saturday and Sunday from 8am to 5pm.

A **larger IBUSZ Hotel Service Office** is at Petőfi tér 3 (☎ 1/118-4842), open 24 hours. Different IBUSZ offices handle different private-room accommodations; the one at Petőfi tér has one of the largest lists of private rooms in the city, is usually less crowded, and accepts all major credit and charge cards to pay for accommodations, whether for a private home or a hotel. There's no fee for the booking service, but you must pay for your room at IBUSZ; they'll then issue your accommodations voucher. Private rooms booked through IBUSZ, costing on average 2,000 to 3,500 Ft ($18 to $31.50) for a double, are available for check-in only after 5pm and for a minimum of two nights.

DOUBLES (IN PRIVATE HOMES) FOR LESS THAN $35

Although you may stand a better chance of finding an empty room in a private home if you book through IBUSZ, you might wish to try one of the following

Getting the Best Deal on Accommodations

- Take advantage of winter discounts (even major hotel operators grant significant price reductions off-season).
- Rooms in private homes are the cheapest way to go.
- Ask at your hotel if there are rooms without shower. The staff may assume you want one of the more expensive rooms with a bath.
- If you're willing to stay on the outskirts and spend some time traveling to the city center, you may spend less money for your room.

recommendations if you want to reserve a room in advance or prefer knowing what a place is like before you get there (rooms booked through IBUSZ range from minuscule to spacious). All four private homes listed here prefer payment in U.S. dollars, and rates are about the same as those charged by IBUSZ.

IN PEST

Sándor and Margaritte Toth

Baross u. 98 (south of Keleti Station), 1082 Budapest. ☎ **1/133-3873.** 2 rms, neither with bath. TV. $20–$24 double. Rates include showers. Breakfast $2 extra. No credit cards. Tram 23, 24, or 36 from Keleti pu to the third stop.

The Toths are an older couple who rent very small, basic, and adequately furnished rooms, with satellite color TV and radio. Both hosts are friendly, and their son, Zoltan, speaks English. Take the elevator to the third floor, then look for no. 5 via an open-air corridor facing the inner courtyard.

✪ Townhouser's Lodge

Attila u. 123, 1162 Budapest. ☎ **30-442-331.** Fax 1/342-0795. 5 rms, none with bath. $12 single; $24 double; $36 triple. Rates include showers. Breakfast 300 Ft ($2.70) extra. No credit cards. Take the subway to Örs Vezéer tér; then bus no. 31 to György utca (fifth stop).

Although on Pest's eastern outskirts, this reasonably priced pension is easy to get to and popular with young backpackers. It's actually the home of Béla Tanhauser and his wife, Rose, plus their two daughters and their dogs, Sasha and Dino. This house in a quiet residential area boasts a garden where you can relax in summer and eat breakfast, and guests even have use of a refrigerator and cooking facilities as well as a washing machine for 400 Ft ($3.60) per load. Béla, who speaks English, offers customized van sightseeing tours of Budapest and the surrounding area, including trips to Szentendre and a day's sail on Lake Balaton (city tours cost $10 per person; the trip to Lake Balaton, $25); he even offers horseback riding. The rooms, which come in various sizes and include radios (TVs available), are up on the first and second floors—the only disadvantage is the rather steep stairs.

Incidentally, Béla also rents two apartments in the city center, both with bathroom, bedroom, and kitchen. One sleeps four and goes for 3,600 Ft ($32.40); the other sleeps three and costs 3,000 Ft ($27) per night.

Note: Béla has a cellular phone, which makes dialing him a bit different. If you're calling from outside Hungary, dial the country code (36 from the U.S., 0036 from within Europe) and then the number given above. If you're calling from within Hungary or Budapest, the entire number to call is 06-30-442-331.

IN BUDA

✪ Dr. Walter Fleps

Bogár u. 20b (about 2 miles northwest of the city center), 1022 Budapest. ☎ **1/115-3887.** 2 rms, neither with bath. $29 double. Breakfast $3.50 extra. No credit cards. Take the subway to Batthyány tér; then bus no. 11 to the eighth stop or bus no. 91 from Nyugati pu to the last stop.

My best private-home selection is this ultramodern, spotless, partially glassed-in house with large balconies overlooking the entire city; it's in a rather elegant residential district (where, incidentally, Rubik, of Cube fame, lives). Dr. Fleps, a retired lawyer, speaks excellent English and is extremely helpful with information and tips. His wife, Nelly, offers substantial breakfasts. The bright and sunny rooms are furnished with antiques. There's ample parking on the street.

IN THE OUTSKIRTS

✪ Magaréta Panzió

Fenyö u. 45, 2092 Budakeszi. ☎ **1/176-6922.** Fax 1/176-6922. 6 rms, all with bath. $29 single; $34 double; $42 triple. Rates include breakfast. 10% winter discounts available. No credit cards. Take the subway to Moszkva tér; then bus no. 22 to the last stop, Budakeszi, from which it's an eight-minute walk (look for the signs).

This pension is in the picturesque and peaceful valley of Budakeszi, a well-to-do suburb 9 miles from downtown and 45 minutes away by public transport. Proprietor Elisabeth Kurucz, who speaks perfect English, offers bright and cheerful rooms on the top floor of her home, each carpeted and featuring views of the countryside (her husband, who trains trotter horses, keeps several horses out back). Three rooms have TVs; two have refrigerators. There's also a communal refrigerator for guest use. The only disadvantage to staying here is the long bus ride to and from the center of Budapest (make sure you know the schedule of the last night bus—you wouldn't want to have to come here in a taxi).

DOUBLES FOR LESS THAN $60
IN PEST

Note that most hotels use either U.S. dollars or German marks in calculating room rates, though you can pay, of course, in any currency.

Hotel Medosz

Jókai tér 9, 1061 Budapest. ☎ **1/153-1700** or 153-1434. Fax 1/132-4316. 68 rms, all with bath. Summer, 3,500 Ft ($31.50) single; 6,000 Ft ($54) double. Winter, 2,400 Ft ($21.60) single; 3,900 Ft ($35.10) double. Additional person 500 Ft ($4.50) extra. Breakfast 350 Ft ($3.15) extra. No credit cards. Subway: Oktogon (then a two-minute walk) or Opera (then a four-minute walk).

This budget hotel is a bit worn around the edges, with threadbare carpets in the hallway leading to plain rooms furnished with narrow beds, small wardrobes, worn throw rugs over wooden floors, and old tiled baths. A plus, however, are the double doors leading into each room (which cuts down on corridor noise). In addition, its central location can't be beat.

IN BUDA

⑤ Charles Apartments

Hegyalja u. 23, 1016 Budapest. ☎ **1/175-4379** or 201-1796. Fax 1/175-0255. 20 rms, all with bath. TV TEL. Summer, 64 DM ($42.65) single; 69 DM ($46) double; 83 DM ($55.35) triple. Winter, 60 DM ($40) single; 64 DM ($42.65) double; 77 DM ($51.35) triple. No credit cards. Bus 8, 78, or 112.

This is Buda's best moderately priced accommodation, centrally located just northwest of Gellért Hill. Popular with economically minded business visitors to the capital, it opened a few years ago upon renovation of an older apartment building and offers basic, comfortable rooms complete with satellite TVs, radios, and even kitchenettes. The rooms are cleaned every second day and the sheets changed every fourth day.

✪ Panorama Pension

Fullank u. 7 (2 miles northwest of the city center), 1026 Budapest. ☎ **1/176-4718.** 3 rms, all with bath. Summer, 75 DM ($50) single; 85 DM ($56.65) double. Winter, 55 DM ($36.65) single; 65 DM ($43.35) double. Breakfast 5 DM ($3.35) extra. No credit cards. Bus 11 from Batthyány tér or 91 from Nyugati pu.

At this villalike house with three floors, built in 1986, the rooms are on the mezzanine floor, only a few steps up from street level. This is the most modern of my pension selections (it's a guesthouse with the comfort of a hotel), and all the rooms are adequately furnished, each with a kitchenette, TV lounge, and balcony for sunbathing. The owners speak English. This is a good choice for families of up to six or for longer-staying guests. The only disadvantage is that it's a bit far out, in a residential area of Budapest.

✪ Pension Korona

Sasadi út 127, 1112 Budapest. ☎ **1/186-2460** or 181-2788. Fax 1/181-0781. 14 rms, all with bath. MINIBAR TV. $40 single; $50–$60 double. Rates include breakfast. No credit cards. Bus 7 from Keleti pu to Móricz tér; then 53.

The charming couple running this pleasant, spotless, hotel-like pension with a garden speaks English. There's a free shoeshine machine, and barbecues are held on the lawn. All rooms have a satellite TV and a private terrace or balcony. The restaurant serves excellent Hungarian meals for 600 to 800 Ft ($5.40 to $7.20). The Korona, with ample parking, is located in the southwestern part of town.

✪ Pension Vadvirág

Nagybanyai út 18, 1025 Budapest. ☎ **1/176-4292.** Fax 1/176-4292. 7 rms, all with bath; 1 apt. $40–$50 single; $50–$60 double; $70–$80 apt. Rates include continental breakfast. Use of the basement sauna 1,000 Ft ($9) per hour extra. No credit cards. Take the subway to Moszkva tér; then bus no. 5 to Pasaréti tér, from which it's a 10-minute walk.

This modern two-story house in northwestern Buda, built in 1988, is managed by an English-speaking husband and wife. All the rooms have modern furniture, wall-to-wall carpeting, and plenty of wardrobe space, and three rooms even come with their own private balcony, including an apartment-size room that also has a TV. Surrounding the pension is a pleasant garden where you can sunbathe in summer and where breakfast is served on a terrace overlooking the town. The Vadvirág ("Wildflower") is ideal for families or small groups. The higher prices in each category above reflect peak summer season.

Rózsadomb Panzió

Muraközi u. 18, 1025 Budapest. ☎ **1/135-1291.** Fax 1/135-1291. 6 rms, all with bath; 2 apts. TV TEL. Summer, 85 DM ($56.65) double; 100 DM ($66.65) apt. Winter, 55 DM ($36.65) double; 75 DM ($50) apt. Breakfast 3.60 DM ($2.40) extra. No credit cards. Bus 91 from Nyugati pu to the Vend stop or 11 from Batthyány tér to the Vend stop.

Built on a hill in northwestern Buda, this modern pension contains clean and comfortable double rooms, all with radio and satellite TV; those facing the front (south) even have balconies offering pleasant views of the surrounding residential area. On the third floor are two apartments with the extra conveniences of a refrigerator and a sitting room, perfect for families or small groups. Note, however, that the stairs to the apartments are rather steep (no elevator). All in all, this is a good and inexpensive place to stay in Budapest.

SUPER-BUDGET CHOICES

Backpack Guesthouse
Takacs Menyhért u. 33, 1110 Budapest. ☎ 1/185-5089. 32 beds. 800 Ft ($7.20) per person. No credit cards. Bus 7 or 7A from Keleti pu to Tétényi út (immediately after the rail bridge).

You can't miss this place—the whole facade is covered with graffiti murals (which must cause some disgruntlement among the neighbors on this quiet residential street in Buda). Inside, it's total chaos: five rooms packed full with bunk beds, lockers, people's belongings strewn all over the place, and walls barely visible beneath mountains of postcards and photographs. This guesthouse attracts mainly backpackers, who want nothing more than a cheap place to stay. Be aware that there's no division of the sexes in the sleeping rooms, and the communal kitchen and baths are about as clean as you'd expect with 32 people living under one tiny roof. Still, those who stay here like the camaraderie, especially in the evenings, when everyone gathers around the kitchen table and swaps traveling stories. As the hostel's brochure says, "So much like home, we even have a dog!"

Citadella Szálló
Citadella sétány, 1118 Budapest. ☎ 1/166-5794. Fax 1/186-0505. 15 rms, 8 with shower only, 2 with bath; 60 dorm beds. 50 DM ($33.35) quad without bath, 55 DM ($36.65) quad with shower only, 60 DM ($40) quad with bath; 12 DM ($8) dorm bed. Breakfast 6 DM ($4) extra. No credit cards. Bus 7 from Keleti pu to Móricz tér; then 27 up the-hill to the fortress.

High above the city on Buda's famous Gellért Hill, this youth hostel is actually located in a 150-year-old fortress built by the Habsburgs. Some rooms have great views of the city. Youth-hostel cards are not required and there's no age limit. The dormitory rooms are large and packed with beds, with up to 18 people per room; there are also four-bed rooms. You can't beat the price and it's open all year. Write or call in advance for a reservation.

CAMPING

Camping Hars-Hegyi
Hars-Hegyi u. 5 (2 miles northwest of the city), 1021 Budapest. ☎ 1/115-1482 or 176-1921. Fax 1/176-1921. Sites for 100 RVs and 500 tents, 35 chalets. 300 Ft ($11.70) tent site for two people; 6,000 Ft ($54) chalet. No credit cards. Closed mid-Oct to mid-Apr. Take the subway from Keleti pu to Moszkva tér; then bus no. 22.

In the Buda hills is this huge parklike area with sites for RVs and tents; also available are 35 modern wooden chalets, equipped with showers, toilets, kitchenettes, and refrigerators. Campground facilities include hot public showers, cooking facilities, a snack bar, a restaurant, refrigerators for rent, a playground, and laundry facilities. Note, however, that the campground is open only from mid-April to mid-October.

Mikro Camping
Rozgonyi P. u. 19, 1031 Budapest. ☎ 1/160-9440. 10 tent sites, 4 rms. 800 Ft ($7.20) tent site for two people; 1,200 Ft ($10.80) double. Showers 15 Ft (15¢) extra. No credit cards.

Closed Oct–May. Take the subway to Batthyány tér; then HEV local train 20 minutes to the Romai Furdo stop; then a five-minute walk.

About 20 minutes north of Buda on the HEV local train, this small family-owned establishment is ideal for backpackers and cyclists. Only a few minutes' walk from the Danube, it offers both tent sites and four private rooms, and there are several outdoor swimming complexes nearby. Write or call beforehand for reservations.

Tenniscamp

Csömöri út 158, 1162 Budapest. ☎ **1/163-5584.** Fax 1/271-4013. 55 tent sites. 10 DM ($6.65) tent site for two. Breakfast 4 DM ($2.65) extra. No credit cards. Closed Nov–Apr. Take the subway to Örs Vezéer tér; then bus no. 31 to the fourth stop.

On the eastern edge of Budapest, this campground offers a lot of diversions, including indoor/outdoor tennis courts (racquets and balls are available for rent), billiards, and Bingo. The restaurant serves breakfast and dinner, but there's also a communal kitchen guests can use free, complete with pots and pans and tableware, as well as outdoor grills. There are also shower facilities, and if you don't have your tent, you can rent one for 200 Ft ($1.80) extra. This place is popular with returning guests, so be sure to reserve your site well in advance.

WORTH THE EXTRA MONEY

✪ Hotel Nemzeti

József krt. 4 (off busy Rákóczi út), 1088 Budapest. ☎ **1/269-9310.** Fax 1/114-0019. Telex 22-7710. 76 rms, all with bath. MINIBAR TV TEL. Summer, 140 DM ($93.35) single; 175 DM ($116.65) double. Winter, 85 DM ($56.65) single; 110 DM ($73.35) double. Rates include buffet breakfast. Additional person 35 DM ($23.35) extra. AE, DC, MC, V. Subway: Blaha Lujza tér.

This is my pick for a romantic splurge in the heart of Pest. Built at the turn of the century in ornate art nouveau style, the Nemzeti boasts a lobby full of old-world charm, with marble pillars soaring to arched ceilings etched in gilded stucco and hung with chandeliers. An impressive grand staircase leads upstairs (there are elevators), where you'll find simple but spacious rooms with all the modern conveniences. Most rooms face a quiet inner courtyard. The front desk staff speaks English and can book sightseeing tours, make restaurant reservations, and help obtain theater and opera tickets. Its restaurant alone is worth the visit.

Hotel Stadion

Ifjúság u. 1, 1148 Budapest. ☎ **1/251-2222** or 252-9333. Fax 1/251-2062. Telex 22-5685. 376 rms, all with bath. MINIBAR TV TEL. Summer, 140 DM ($93.35) single; 180 DM ($120) double; 230 DM ($153.35) triple. Winter, 115 DM ($76.65) single; 150 DM ($100) double; 195 DM ($130) triple. Rates include breakfast. AE, CB, DC, MC, V. Subway: Népstadion.

You'll immediately spot this modern seven-story hotel complex because of its size and twin towers. It's very centrally located in Pest, next to the Népstadion subway stop. Facilities include an indoor pool, a solarium, a sauna, a bowling alley, a restaurant, a bar, three elevators, and an English-speaking staff. The hotel doesn't have much character, but it's clean and functional.

5 Dining

Restaurant critics worldwide agree that Hungarian cuisine is among the tastiest in Europe. Equally important is the fact that the price for that cuisine is extremely low: For 800 Ft ($7.20) per meal you can eat well, and for 3,000 Ft ($27) you can dine magnificently.

The basic ingredient in Hungarian food is red pepper, called paprika—you'll find it in soups, main dishes, and even some desserts. Among the most popular specialties, listed on every menu, are *paprika gulyas,* a soup made of beef, onions, paprika, potatoes, and spices; *fogas,* whitefish soup with paprika; *lecso,* a cooked vegetable stew with paprika; *paprika chicken; cabbage leaves* stuffed with bacon, pork, rice, and herbs; *rétes* (apple strudel); and omelets filled with cottage cheese and ground nuts, topped with hot-chocolate sauce.

A restaurant is called an *etterem* in Hungarian; if you're looking for a cup of coffee, look for a sign saying KAVE outside the eatery door. Most restaurants in Budapest are open from about noon to 7 or 10pm. Keep in mind that the closing hours given below are exactly that—the time the restaurant literally locks its doors. Last order is usually an hour or so before closing time.

Excellent wines are the *tokay* (white) and *bikaver* (red, literally meaning "bull's blood"). Hungary's most famous apéritif is an apricot brandy, called *barack.*

MEALS FOR LESS THAN 800 FT ($7.20)
IN PEST

Bagolyvar
Allatkerti út 2. ☎ 1/118-7347. Main courses 400–1,000 Ft ($3.60–$9). AE, DC, MC, V. Daily noon–11pm. Subway: Hösök tere. HUNGARIAN.

Located next to Varosliget (City Park) and under the same ownership as Gundel, Hungary's most famous restaurant, this restaurant serves great home-style Hungarian specialties in an informal yet elegant setting whose atmosphere is reminiscent of a Transylvanian country lodge. In summer there's outdoor dining on the patio, and live accordion music sets the mood nightly beginning at 7pm. The English menu changes daily, with about four choices of soups and salads and half a dozen main courses. Examples include celery-cream soup, lentil soup with sausages, boiled beef with tomato sauce and potato, Hungarian hare stew with dumplings, and pan-fried turkey breast with salad. To make your meal more festive, treat yourself to some Hungarian wine—less than 700 Ft ($6.30) per bottle. Highly recommended.

✪ Bohémtanya
Paulay Ede u. 6 (near Erzsébet tér). ☎ 1/322-1453. Main courses 300–800 Ft ($2.70–$7.20). No credit cards. Daily noon–11pm. Subway: Deák tér. HUNGARIAN.

This student hangout has a deserved reputation as Budapest's best budget restaurant. A very simple establishment with a barlike atmosphere, it has an English menu listing salads, bean soup, carp filet in beer dough, roast pork, roast suckling pig, filet of turkey breast with broccoli sauce, and more. Portions are huge. This place is so popular that you'll probably have to wait for a table if you come during regular mealtimes—but the wait is worth it.

✪ Kispipa Vendéglö
Akácfa u. 38. ☎ 1/342-3969. Reservations recommended at dinner. Main courses 290–500 Ft ($2.60–$4.50); fixed-price meals 740 Ft ($6.65). No credit cards. Mon–Sat noon–1am. Subway: Blaha Lujza tér. HUNGARIAN.

In a modest neighborhood, this simply furnished establishment with a 1920s ambience is a favorite among Hungarians and a great place to celebrate a special occasion. It features live piano music and is decorated with Hungarian advertisements from the first few decades of the century. The English menu lists frogs' legs,

Getting the Best Deal on Dining

- Since Budapest's prices are so low, this is the place to splurge: Meals here cost a third of what they'd be in Austria or Germany.
- Cafeterias are great for simple dining.
- Try local wines and Hungarian beer instead of more expensive imports.

pheasant, venison, grilled trout, duck, veal cutlets, mutton, roast pork, and other exotic dishes. There are also six fixed-price meals, all under $7.

Okay Italia

Szt. István krt. 20 (between Nyugati pu [station] and Margit híd [bridge]). ☎ **1/131-6991.** Salads, soups, antipasta 300–550 Ft ($2.70–$4.95); pasta courses 360–500 Ft ($3.25–$4.50); meat courses 440–1,000 Ft ($3.95–$9). No credit cards. Daily noon–1am. Subway: Nyugati pu. Tram 4 or 6 to Nyugati pu. ITALIAN.

This restaurant has a rather plain interior with tables too close together, but it's staffed by Italians and often packed with Italians living in Budapest (clearly a good sign). The pizzas and pasta are great, with an interesting English menu that includes penne with tomato sauce and olives, sweet chiles, and capers; spaghetti with bacon, egg, and cream; and tagliatelle with meat sauce, mushrooms, ham, and cream. Save room for the ice cream, served only in summer.

Okay Italia has proven so popular that a second branch has opened near Nyugati pu at Nyugati tér 16 (☎ **1/132-6960**), open daily from noon to 1am.

Paprika

Harmincad u. 4 (just off Vörösmarty tér, next to the U.K. embassy). ☎ **1/117-2703.** Soups 140 Ft ($1.25); main dishes 200 Ft ($1.80). No credit cards. Mon–Fri 11am–4pm. Subway: Vörösmarty tér. HUNGARIAN/GERMAN.

For a quick, cheap, and simple meal in the center of Pest, try this self-service cafeteria. It offers half a dozen choices from a Hungarian and German menu, with ordering made easy by an illustrated board and food visibly on display behind the counter. Try the gulash soup, Jokai bean soup, or a main dish such as pork cutlet with potatoes or stuffed pepper; top it off with a glass of inexpensive Hungarian wine. Meals are served on paper plates in the clean and comfortable dining room. You can easily dine here for less than $4.

Self Service

Szende Pal u. 3 (two blocks from Vörösmarty tér, between the Marriot and the Forum). ☎ **1/115-4677.** Salads and soups 100–150 Ft (90¢–$1.35); main courses 200–260 Ft ($1.80–$2.35). No credit cards. Daily 9am–3pm. Subway: Vörösmarty tér. HUNGARIAN.

This very simple cafeteria doesn't have a name and is easy to overlook—there's just a sign in the door listing the daily special and the open hours. It's popular with the local business crowd for its fast service and low prices for Hungarian specialties ranging from bean soup and goulash to stuffed cabbage.

Vegetarium Etterem

Cukor u. 3 (south of Ferenciek tere, off Karolyi Minaly utca). ☎ **1/267-0322.** Appetizers and soups 150–200 Ft ($1.35–1.80); main courses 300–600 Ft ($2.70–$5.40). AE, MC, V. Daily noon–10pm. Subway: Felszabadulas tér; then walk a few minutes south. VEGETARIAN.

This pleasant restaurant is a great alternative to the heavier Hungarian cuisine—and about your only alternative if you're a vegetarian. No smoking is allowed here (a rarity in Europe), and it's decorated with original artwork, huge wooden booths for privacy, and paper lanterns, all of which give it an earthy atmosphere. Evenings feature live classical guitar. The menu, which changes every three months, may include such starters as tomato stuffed with sunflower paste, stuffed mushrooms, and miso soup with tofu, with main dishes ranging from tofu ragoût and stuffed green paprika to tempura and macrobiotic platters, including a seaweed platter.

IN BUDA

⊙ Les Amis Etterem

At the corner of Rómer Flóris and Budai László utca (on Rose Hill). ☎ **1/212-3173.** Reservations recommended. Soups and salads 220–250 Ft ($2–$2.25); main courses 450–1,650 Ft ($4.05–$14.85). No credit cards. Mon–Sat 4pm–1am. Tram 4 or 6 to Margit tér. HUNGARIAN/INTERNATIONAL.

This tiny restaurant is a true gem, offering delicious and hearty portions of Hungarian favorites and continental cuisine. It's usually packed, so try to make a reservation at least a day in advance—there are only five tables. The menu includes Jokai bean soup and consommé with liver dumplings—two Hungarian favorites—and main courses like duck, pork, fish, turkey, steaks, and beef Stroganoff. I recommend the goose-liver risotto; if you've never had the pleasure of eating it, this is a great place to try it.

Tárnok

Tárnok u. 14 (on Castle Hill not far from Matthias Church). ☎ **1/156-1457.** 300–1,000 Ft ($2.70–$9). No credit cards. Daily 10am–10pm. Special "Varbusz MM" minibus from Moszkva tér. SNACKS/SOUPS.

This simple establishment is good for a drink, light lunch, or snack if you're visiting the many area sights. Informal, casual, and popular with young people, it has a limited English menu listing goulash soup, chicken salad, Hungarian mixed cold plate, shrimp cocktail, salad, and a few daily specials. You can come just for a beer or coffee.

MEALS FOR LESS THAN 1,500 FT ($13.50)
IN BUDA

Aranyhordó

Tárnok u. 16 (on Castle Hill not far from Fishermen's Bastion). ☎ **1/156-1367.** Soups 250–330 Ft ($2.25–$3); main courses 900–3,000 ($8.10–$27). AE, MC, V. Restaurant, lunch daily noon–4pm; dinner daily 7pm–midnight (to 10pm in winter). Wine cellar, daily 7pm–midnight (to 10pm in winter). Special "Varbusz MM" minibus from Moszkva tér. HUNGARIAN.

This restaurant is convenient if you're visiting the many nearby attractions. It's actually three establishments in one building, all with the same menu—a ground-floor brasserie, an upstairs formal restaurant, and a wine cellar open only in the evening. I prefer the wine cellar, which resembles the interior of a cave as it winds from room to tiny room. There's Gypsy and accordion music every evening, and the English menu includes grilled chicken, fish, Hungarian paprika veal pork cutlet, goose liver Hungarian style, other grilled dishes, and turkey breast.

IN PEST

Apostolok

Kigyo u. 4 (just off the Váci utca shopping street, near Felszabadulas tér). ☎ **1/267-0290.** Soups and salads 170–300 Ft ($1.50–$2.70); main courses 750–1,600 Ft ($6.75–$14.40). AE, DC, MC, V. Daily 11am–11pm. Subway: Ferenciek tere. HUNGARIAN.

Located in the heart of Pest, this is a beautifully decorated old-world restaurant—stained-glass windows, carved wooden booths and dark-stained wainscoting, an intricately tiled floor, and wrought-iron chandeliers. Its English menu includes all the Hungarian specialties, including Hartobágy pancakes, goose liver, fried carp filet, paprika chicken with gnocchi, roast duck, sholet beans with smoked pork chop, fried chicken, and Hungarian beef stew with potatoes.

❸ Barokk

Mozsár u. 12. ☎ 1/131-8942. Reservations recommended. Soups 270–400 Ft ($2.45–$3.60); main courses 950–2,600 Ft ($8.55–$23.40). AE. Daily noon–midnight. Subway: Oktogon or Opera. HUNGARIAN.

It's hard to believe that this charming restaurant is as inexpensive as it is elegant and small, with a drawing-room atmosphere enhanced by pink brocade tablecloths and matching upholstered chairs, a stucco ceiling, candles on each table, and baroque music playing softly in the background. With only 12 tables, it's intimate, the perfect place for a romantic evening.

Even if you're on a strict budget, you owe it to yourself to dine here. Offering what it describes as "dishes made according to 17th- and 18th-century recipes," the English menu is fun to read, with such colorful descriptions as "Bouillon with Lumplings," "Onyon Sopp," "Trembling Jellied Meat," and, my favorite, "Titbits of tenderloin and ham stitched together with Salvia sauce." All the main courses sound good: filet mignon in extract of mustard and honey; roast knuckle of pork with thyme, braised onions, and potatoes; fried turkey stuffed with ham and nuts; liver and honey; roast duck with curry and apricot jelly, as well as rice with hazelnut and almond; stewed wild boar in red wine with orange and dumplings with plums; and much more. *A word of warning:* Your water glass will be refilled automatically with bottled water, for which, of course, you'll be charged—if you don't want water be sure to say so. Otherwise, this restaurant is highly recommended.

Chicago Brasserie and Restaurant

At the corner of Rákóczi u. and Erszébet u. ☎ 1/269-6753. Appetizers and soups 350–650 Ft ($3.15–$5.85); main courses 650–1,300 Ft ($5.85–$11.70). AE. Mon–Thurs noon–midnight, Fri–Sat to 1am, Sun to 11pm. Subway: Blaha Lujza tér. AMERICAN.

This bar/restaurant could be Anywhere, U.S.A, which is precisely why so many expatriates come here. It features what is arguably the best salad bar in town, as well as a mixed bag of such American favorites as spicy buffalo wings, potato skins, sandwiches, burgers, grilled chicken, enchiladas, fajitas, and barbecued ribs. It also has a children's menu. Don't miss out on the beer—it's brewed right on the premises, with a half liter going for 250 Ft ($2.25).

Múzeum Kávéház Etterem

Múzeum krt. 12 (beside the Hungarian National Museum). ☎ 1/138-4221 or 267-0375. Soups 300–350 Ft ($2.70–$3.15); main courses 700–1,600 Ft ($6.30–$14.40). AE. Mon–Sat noon–1am. Subway: Astoria or Kalvin tér. HUNGARIAN.

This cheerful turn-of-the-century restaurant with an English menu is gaily decorated with colored tiles, etched crossbeams, wainscoting, and a wooden floor. In addition to daily specials, it offers poached salmon with lobster sauce, steak Stroganoff with egg gnocchi, chicken, veal stew, fish, and roast goose. You can dine more cheaply in the café section or simply order a cup of coffee or a beer.

❸ Nemzeti Hotel Restaurant

József krt. 4. ☎ 1/269-9310 ext. 557. Main courses 450–1,500 Ft ($4.05–$13.50). AE, DC, MC, V. Daily noon–11pm. Subway: Blaha Lujza tér. HUNGARIAN/INTERNATIONAL.

Come here if you want a special, romantic evening but find Gundel too expensive (see "Worth the Extra Money," below). Located in the Nemzeti Hotel but with its own sidewalk entrance, this is a refined dining establishment boasting ornately stuccoed tall ceilings, subdued lighting, live music in the evenings, and booths. You might wish to start with Hortobágy pancakes or chicken-liver risotto, followed by Jokai bean soup, and topped with main dishes ranging from fish, paprika chicken, and Hungarian stew to crispy roast duckling, stuffed cabbage, and pork tenderloin. The food is excellently prepared and nicely presented.

Restaurant Matyas Pince

Március 15 tér 7 (near the Erzsébet híd [bridge]). ☎ **1/118-1693.** Reservations recommended. Soups 270 Ft ($2.45); main courses 1,000–2,000 Ft ($9–$18). AE, MC, V. Lunch daily noon–3pm; dinner daily 7pm–midnight. Subway: Ferenciek tere. HUNGARIAN/ INTERNATIONAL.

This tourist-oriented restaurant in Pest has a beautiful interior, 100 seats, English-speaking waiters, and Gypsy music most nights. Phone for a reservation, since this place is often booked by tour groups. The English menu primarily includes Hungarian specialties—from Hungarian paprika chicken or sholet beans with roast duck to smoked pork or stuffed cabbage rolls. Top off your meal with sponge cake with vanilla sauce. There are several dining halls here, including an ornate beer cellar with the same menu as the restaurant.

COFFEEHOUSES

Café Gerbeaud

Vörösmarty tér 7. ☎ **1/118-1708.** Coffee with milk 150 Ft ($1.35); pastry and cakes 35– 125 Ft (30¢–$1.10). No credit cards. Daily 9am–11pm (to 9pm in winter). Subway: Vörösmarty tér. COFFEEHOUSE/SNACKS.

Located on a fashionable square in downtown Pest, the Café Gerbeaud was founded in 1858 by a French entrepreneur, and its white marble tables, mirrored rooms, and stucco ceilings strongly resemble those in other famous mid-19th century coffeehouses in Western Europe. Coffee and pastry here are first class; try a generous helping of the famous Gerbeaud slice (a delicious blend of chocolate and nuts) or the apple strudel (or one of 25 other tempting choices). This is a favorite hangout of reporters, critics, and other literary-minded people.

Café New York

Erzsébet krt. 9. ☎ **1/322-3849.** Large coffee with milk 150–200 Ft ($1.35–$1.80). Daily 9am–10pm. Subway: Blaha Lujza tér. COFFEEHOUSE/SNACKS.

I used to recommend this extraordinary restaurant for a romantic splurge, but capitalism's arrival in Hungary has led to the emergence of restaurants that offer better service and more for your money. Still, this was once one of Europe's most famous restaurants and is not to be missed—all you have to do to soak in its atmosphere is order a cup of coffee. First opened in 1894 as a showcase for the New York Insurance Company, it soon gained a reputation as a haunt for poor writers who, under the benevolence of the maître d' did their work here instead of in their unheated rooms. Today it still has its lovely baroque interior, marble pillars, huge gilt-framed mirrors, and thick carpets. The lavishly decorated lower part, reached via a wide staircase and illuminated by crystal chandeliers, is the dining room. The ground-floor coffee shop sits above the dining room like a balcony, providing a bird's-eye view. In addition to coffee and drinks, the coffee shop has a limited menu of sandwiches, soups, and such dishes as veal gulash with gnocchi or pork with mushrooms, with prices ranging from 200 to 800 Ft ($1.80 to $7.20). Breakfast is served until noon.

Café Ruszwurm

Szentháromság u. 7 (on Castle Hill, near Matthias Church). ☎ **1/175-5284.** Large coffee with milk 150 Ft ($1.35); cakes and pastry 60–150 Ft (55¢–$1.35). No credit cards. Daily 10am–8pm. "Varbusz MM" minibus from Moszkva tér. COFFEEHOUSE/SNACKS.

This Buda café is located in a 17th-century house with Biedermeier furnishings. Founded in 1827, this small place has only two rooms, and its homemade pastries are the best in town. Chocolate torte, fruit cake topped with whipped cream, poppyseed strudel, cinnamon pies, and walnut tarts are among the most popular items. If you don't find a vacant seat, go to the take-out counter and carry some of the tempting pastries to the nearby stone seats of the Fishermen's Bastion, where you can eat them while enjoying the panoramic view over Pest and the Danube.

WORTH THE EXTRA MONEY

Belcanto

Dalszínház u. 8. ☎ **1/269-3101.** Reservations recommended. Soups and salads 270–750 Ft ($2.45–$6.75); main courses 1,300–3,500 Ft ($11.70–$31.50). AE, MC. Daily 6pm–2am. Subway: Opera. CONTINENTAL.

If you can't make it to the opera—or simply like listening to it—this is the place to dine. Just a stone's throw from the opera house, this unusual restaurant employs singing waiters who burst into song at regular intervals. Bona fide opera singers make guest appearances. Unfortunately, the food doesn't quite match the atmosphere and the imported wines are expensive (stick to the Hungarian varieties). Thus make sure you come after the opera, when things are liveliest, though be sure to make a reservation.

Gundel

Allatkerti u. 2. ☎ **1/121-3550.** Reservations recommended. Jacket required for men at dinner. Soups 400–550 Ft ($3.60–$4.95); main courses 1,700–4,000 Ft ($15.30–$36); fixed-price meal 6,500 Ft ($58.50). AE, DC, MC, V. Lunch daily noon–4pm; dinner daily 7pm–midnight. Subway: Hösök tere. HUNGARIAN/CONTINENTAL.

Gundel provides the best of what Hungary has to offer: Not only will you remember the experience for years to come, but also you'll pay only a third of what you'd pay for a similar experience in Vienna. Hungary's most famous restaurant for 100 years is housed in an ornately elegant building on the edge of the city park that recalls the golden age of the Austro-Hungarian Empire. The dining hall looks as if it were straight out of a museum, complete with paintings by Hungarian masters lining the walls, huge vases of flowers, and a five-piece orchestra serenading with waltzes. Little wonder that Elizabeth II chose to dine here in 1993, following in the historic footsteps of such celebrities as the king of Siam, Thomas Mann, Charlie Chaplin, and Richard Strauss. The menu offers a changing selection of fish, duck, beef, and game, along with the world's largest selection of Hungarian wines. Note that men need jackets for dinner—if you don't have one, come for lunch or, even better, dine on the outdoor summer terrace, accompanied by a band playing from the garden pagoda.

6 Attractions

SIGHTSEEING SUGGESTIONS

If You Have 1 Day

If you have only one day to devote to Budapest, spend the morning in Buda on Castle Hill, a picturesque old part of town that has been lovingly restored. Here, along cobblestone streets lined with two-story patrician homes, you'll find Matthias Church, the Fishermen's Bastion next door, as well as the Hugarian National Gallery with its art treasures and the Budapest History Museum tracing the history of the city since Roman times. In the late afternoon, head toward the Pest end of town and stroll down the fashionable Váci pedestrian lane, topping it off with a cup of coffee at Café Gerbeaud. In the evening, attend the opera or splurge for dinner at Barokk or Gundel.

If You Have 2 Days

Spend the first day as described above. On the second, spend the day in Pest, taking in the city's other major attractions—the National Museum, the Museum of Fine Arts, and St. Stephen's Basilica. End the day with a soak in one of Budapest's famous thermal baths.

If You Have 3 Days

Spend Days 1 and 2 as outlined above. On your third day, go to the ancient Roman settlement of Aquincum, in Óbuda, where you can see the ruins of a large amphitheater and visit a museum of Roman archeological finds. In the afternoon, head for Margaret Island, Budapest's most popular recreation area, located right in the middle of the Danube, where you can relax, go swimming, and have a picnic. If it's winter (the Aquincum is open only from May through October), spend the day following your own pursuits or exploring the shops along the Váci.

If You Have 5 Days

Explore the environs of Budapest. Take the Danube Bend Excursion by boat or by bus or skip the tour and head straight for Szentendre, a village with a ceramics museum, an outdoor museum, and lots of shops and boutiques. Another popular destination is Lake Balaton, central Europe's largest freshwater lake and a wine-growing region. See "Easy Excursions," at the end of this chapter, for details.

TOP ATTRACTIONS
ON BUDA'S CASTLE HILL

From Moszkva tér, a special minibus called "Varbusz MM," with a picture of a castle on it, makes runs to and along the ridge of Castle Hill. You can also reach Castle Hill from the Pest side by taking bus no. 16 from Erzsébet tér to Disz tér on Castle Hill.

A more dramatic approach is walking across the Széchenyi lánchid bridge (Budapest's famous Chain Bridge) to Clark Adam tér on the Buda side, and from there taking the funicular to Castle Hill. Running daily from 7:30am to 10pm, it costs 80 Ft (70¢) for adults and 60 Ft (55¢) for children one way. Of course, you can also reach Castle Hill via your own two feet, on a winding path from the Duna River.

Mátyás Templon (Matthias Church)

☎ **1/155-5657.** Admission free. Daily 9am–7pm (to 8pm in summer); mass at 6pm. Special "Varbusz MM" minibus from Moszkva tér, or 16 from Erzsébet tér in Pest and Moszkva tér to Disz tér.

Built in the gothic style in the 13th century with a gold-tiled roof, the colorfully ornate Matthias Church has witnessed many royal marriages (starting with King Matthias Corvin in 1475) and coronations (Maria Theresia in 1740, Franz Josef in 1876, and Karl in 1916, to name but a few). During the Turkish occupation (1542–1686) it was converted into a mosque; in the 1800s it was rebuilt in the neo-gothic style. Today, Catholic mass is held here regularly, and organ concerts of music by Liszt and Kodaly are presented on Friday in summer. The baroque column in front of the church was erected to commemorate the end of a plague in the 18th century.

Halász Bástya (Fishermen's Bastion)

Next to the Matthias Church. Admission free. Daily 24 hours. Special "Varbusz MM" minibus from Moszkva tér, or 16 from Erzsébet tér in Pest and Moszkva tér to Disz tér.

Completed in 1901 in neo-romanesque style on the site of an old fish market, Fishermen's Bastion is the city's landmark. Its arcades, walls, and turrets overlook Pest and the Danube from a unique vantage point, perfect for taking photos of the most attractive areas of Budapest.

✪ Magyar Nemzeti Galeria (Hungarian National Gallery)

✪ In Wings B, C, and D of Buda Castle Palace, Disz tér 17. ☎ **1/175-7533.** Admission 50 Ft (45¢) adults, 20 Ft (20¢) students; free for everyone Sat. Summer, Tues–Sun 10am–6pm (enter by 5:15pm); winter, Tues–Sun 10am–4pm (enter by 3:15pm). Special "Varbusz MM" minibus from Moszkva tér, or 16 from Erzsébet tér in Pest and Moszkva tér to Disz tér.

Devoted solely to Hungarian artists, the National Gallery exhibits Hungary's most treasured artworks. Beginning with early gothic winged altars from the 11th century, the entire history of Hungarian painting and sculpture is represented,

---

❷ Did You Know?

- Buda, Pest, and Óbuda, on both sides of the Danube, did not become one city until 1873.
- Hungarian is not related to most European languages: It resembles languages spoken in western Siberia.
- Budapest's Nyugati pu (station) was built by the Eiffel Company.
- The Parliament Building, erected in 1904, was at the time the largest one in the world.
- As a result of World War I, Hungary lost 68% of its land and 58% of its population.
- Only about one-quarter of Budapest's buildings remained intact after German and Russian fighting during World War II.
- During the 1956 anti-Communist uprising, 190,000 Hungarians fled the country.
- There are 128 listed thermal springs in Budapest.
- Budapest's subway, completed in 1896, was the first in continental Europe—only London's subway (1890) is older.

Budapest

INFORMATION
IBUSZ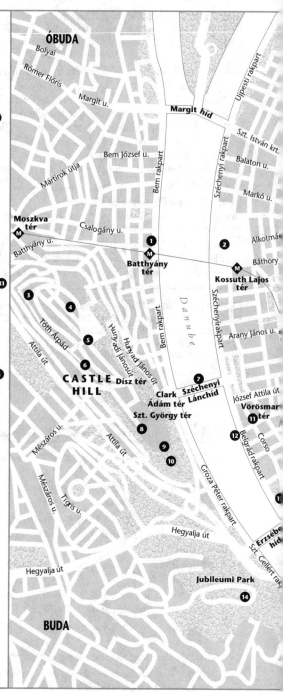
Tourinform 26

TRANSPORTATION HUBS
Erzsébet tér Bus Station 25
Hev Suburban Rail Station 1
International Boat Station 30
Keleti (Eastern) Train Station 28
Nyugati Train Station 20
Vigadó tér Boat Station 12

ATTRACTIONS
Budapest History Museum 10
Chain Bridge
  (Széchenyi Lánchíd) 7
Citadella 14
Ferenc Liszt Memorial
  Museum 21
Golden Eagle Pharmacy 6
Great Synagogue and Museum
  of Hungarian Jewry 27
House of Parliament 2
Hungarian National Museum 31
Inner City Parish Church 29
Matthias Church 5
Military Museum 3
Museum of Applied Arts 32
Museum of Fine Arts 17
Museum of Hungarian Art 9
Museum of Recent History 8
Musical Instruments Museum 4
St. Stephen's Basilica 24
Transport Museum 19

SPA BATHING
Gellért Hotel Baths 15
Széchenyi Baths 16

EVENING
ENTERTAINMENT
Ferenc Liszt Academy
  of Music 23
Hungarian State
  Opera House 22
Pesti Vigadó Concert Hall 11
Petőfi Youth Center 18

Victor Hugo u.

Csanády u.

Visegrádi u.

Balzac u.

Kresz Géza u.

Váci út

Lehel u.

Dózsa György út

Rippl-Rónai u.

Munkácsy u.

Bajza u.

Podmaniczky u.

Hősök tére

16

Kós Károly sétány

17 M

Városliget Park 18

19

20

M **Nyugati Train Station**

Szinyei Merse

Szív u.

Rózsa Ferenc u.

Izabella u.

Kodály körönd

Andrássy út

Városligeti fasor

Bajza u.

Aitósi Dürer

Podmaniczky u.

Csengery u.

Vörösmarty u.

Eötvös u.

Teréz körút

Felső erdősor

Szív u.

Damjanich u.

Dózsa György út

Nagymező u.

Oktogon

M

Andrássy út

21

Király

Rottenbiller u.

Dembinszky u.

Bajcsy Zsilinszky út

Hajós u.

Vörösmarty u.

Dob u.

Rózsa Ferenc u.

István u.

Péterfy Sándor

M **Arany János u.**

22

23

Paulay Ede u.

Csengery u.

Wesselényi u.

Izabella u.

Dohány u.

Thököly út

24

Király

Erzsébet körút

Hársfa u.

28

Keleti Train Station

M

Kerepesi út

25

M

Deák tér

Dob u.

Kertész u.

Akácia u.

Rákóczi út

26

Károly

Wesselényi u.

Blaha Lujza tér

M

Fiumei út

27

Dohány u.

Rákóczi út

Astoria

M

József krt.

Népszínház u.

29

Kossuth L. u.

Múzeum krt.

Bérkocsis u.

Ferenciek tere

M

Déri Miksa u.

31

Krúdy József u.

30

Kálvin tér

M

Baross u.

Baross u.

32

József krt.

Vámház krt.

Szabadság híd

Üllői út

Práter u.

Danube

M

PEST

Ferenc körút

Üllődi út

Ferenc körút

0 | 450 m | N
495 y

Metro M

including medieval stone carvings, frescoes, and room upon room of paintings from the late Renaissance to the 20th century. This place is large, with portraits of famous Hungarians and works by Károly Ferenczy, Mihály Munkácsy, László Paál, Pál Szinyei Merse, and many more. You'll want to spend several hours here.

Legújabbkori Történeti Múzeum and Ludwig Múzeum (Contemporary Historical Museum of Hungary and Ludwig Museum)

In Wing A of Buda Castle Palace. ☎ **1/175-7533.** Admission fees vary according to what's being shown, but average about 80–100 Ft (70¢–90¢). Tues–Sun 11am–6pm (enter by 5:30pm). Special "Varbusz MM" minibus from Moszkva tér, or 16 from Erzsébet tér in Pest and Moszkva tér to Disz tér.

This recently opened museum on Castle Hill is Budapest's only museum devoted exclusively to modern and contemporary art and photography, with changing exhibits. There are also changing exhibits relating to Hungary's history.

Történeti Múzeum (History Museum)

In Wing E of Buda Castle Palace, Szent György tér 2. ☎ **1/175-7533.** Admission 50 Ft (45¢) adults, 20 Ft (20¢) students; free for everyone Wed. Summer, Wed–Mon 10am–6pm; winter, Wed–Mon 10am–4pm. Bus Special "Varbusz MM" minibus from Moszkva tér, or 16 from Erzsébet tér in Pest and Moszkva tér to Disz tér.

Next to the National Gallery, this museum traces 2,000 years of Budapest's history, beginning with excavational finds of the Roman settlement Aquincum, including a Roman helmet, bowls, vases, and a wall mosaic. Be sure to go down into the basement, since the museum is located in the old castle and it's here that you'll find the Albrecht Cellar, constructed in the first half of the 18th century. Its architecture is as interesting as the museum itself, which also contains weapons, sculptures, and ceramics.

IN PEST

Magyar Nemzeti Múzeum (Hungarian National Museum)

Múzeum krt. 14. ☎ **1/138-2122.** Admission 80 Ft (70¢) adults, 40 Ft (35¢) students. Tues–Sun 10am–4:45pm. Subway: Kálvin tér; then a short walk up Múzeum körút.

I wish this museum provided more explanations in English, but at least an inexpensive booklet is available to explain the highlights. Housed in a neoclassical building, this is the country's most important museum, detailing the history of the Hungarian people from prehistoric times to 1849. It contains the nation's most highly venerated objects, the royal regalia of King Stephen: crown, scepter, orb, and coronation robes. These items were returned to Hungary from Fort Knox in 1987, where patriots had safeguarded them from the invading Red Army since 1945. The oldest exhibit is a 50,000-year-old skull found in Hungary. Other objects include a Roman mosaic floor, a Turkish commander's colorful tent, clothing, furniture, a piano used by Beethoven, and Franz Liszt's golden baton. You'll see Hungarians of all ages walking slowly by these priceless symbols.

✪ Szepmuveszeti Múzeum (Museum of Fine Arts)

Dózsa György út 41 (on Hösök tere [Heroes' Square]). ☎ **1/142-9759** or 268-0090. Admission 60 Ft (55¢). Tues–Sun 10am–5pm. Closed Jan–Mar. Subway: Hösök tere.

This museum shows works of the old masters, from the 14th to the 19th century. It's one of Europe's greatest art galleries, with works by Leonardo, Tintoretto, Ghirlandaio, Bellini, Raphael, Dürer, and Cranach exhibited on the ground floor. Spanish masters from the 14th to the 17th century are on the second floor, including the largest collection of El Grecos outside Spain, plus five paintings by Goya.

Drawings and engravings from the 16th to the 19th century are on display on the top floor.

Iparmüvészeti Múzeum (Museum of Applied Art)

Üllöi út 33–37. ☎ **1/217-5222.** Admission 40 Ft (35¢) adults, free for students. Tues–Sun 10am–5:45pm. Subway: Ferenc körút.

This beautiful art nouveau building, constructed before the turn of the century especially for this collection, is bright and airy with a glass-domed atrium. It features changing exhibitions of furniture, glassware, tapestries, jewelry, and other decorative arts, so there's always something new. Both the building and its collections are testimony to the important role Budapest played in European history.

MORE ATTRACTIONS

Aquincum

Kórvin u., in Óbuda. ☎ **1/168-8241.** Admission 50 Ft (45¢) adults, 30 Ft (25¢) students. May–Oct, Tues–Sun 10am–6pm. HEV local train from Batthyány tér to the Aquincum station.

Near the Arpad Bridge are the ruins of this Roman city, which 2,000 years ago had 50,000 inhabitants. Excavation work has been ongoing at this open-air museum since 1870, and discoveries include an amphitheater with a seating capacity of 15,000 and a thermal bath (Budapest has 120 active thermal springs). Most of the Roman finds are in the National Museum in Pest, but some smaller artifacts— weapons, tools, pottery, jewelry, and the like—are exhibited in the nearby Roman Camp Museum, at Szentendrei u. 139 (☎ **1/180-4650**). The day-long Danube Bend Bus tour takes you along the Roman excavation area.

Parliament Building

Kossuth Lajos tér, in Pest. ☎ **1/112-0600.** Tours, 1,500 Ft ($13.50). Tours given May–Oct, Wed and Fri at 10:30am and 2pm. Tours depart from the Erzsébet bus terminal, near the Vörösmarty subway station.

Constructed in neo-gothic style 100 years ago when Budapest was part of the Austro-Hungarian Empire, the stunning 691-room Parliament Building is 820 feet long, 387 feet wide, and 315 feet high, with 27 gates and 88 statues of Hungarian kings and noblemen on the outside walls. Visitors are allowed inside only in groups (and when the Parliament is not is session) on tours offered by IBUSZ that also include a visit to the Hungarian National Gallery.

Szt. István (St. Stephen's Basilica)

Szent István tér, in Pest. ☎ **1/111-0839.** Admission free. Summer, Mon–Sat 9am–5pm, Sun 1–5pm; winter, Mon–Sat 10am–4pm, Sun 1–4pm. Subway: Deák Ferenc tér.

This is the largest church in the city, with two spires, built 150 years ago and named after Hungary's first king, who converted Hungary to Christianity in 1000. It is a combination of many architectural styles, mainly neoclassical and neo-Renaissance. Be sure to visit the small room to the left past the altar; there's a small display there, and if you insert 20 Ft (20¢) into a glass showcase, a hand bone of St. Stephen is illuminated for three minutes.

PARKS & PANORAMAS

On top of 770-foot **Gellért Hill** in Buda (take bus no. 27 from Möricz tér to the last stop), and visible from many parts of Budapest, is a statue erected during Soviet occupation to honor Soviet soldiers who were killed while liberating the city from Nazi occupation in 1944. Since Hungary's real liberation in 1989, however, authorities have changed the name of the monument from Liberation Monument to Freedom Monument, and the names of the Soviet soldiers killed in 1944 that once adorned the monument have been carefully chiseled away. Today a plaque reads, roughly translated, that the monument is dedicated to the memory of everyone who gave his or her life to secure freedom for the Hungarian people. Next to the monument is the **Citadel,** a fortress/former prison built 140 years ago by the Habsburgs and now a restaurant/youth hostel. All tour buses stop here to allow tourists to take photographs. Gellért Hill is the place to go for the best panoramic views of Pest, Castle Hill, and the Danube.

Between Buda and Pest in the middle of the Danube and once a royal hunting ground, the 1-mile-long **Margit-sziget (Margaret Island)** is Budapest's most popular park and largest resort area, with gardens, a pool, outdoor thermal baths, tennis courts, meadows, a game preserve, an open-air cinema, and open-air restaurants. It's ideal for a picnic or relaxing, right in the heart of the city. Walk across Margit híd (bridge) or take bus no. 26 or tram no. 6.

The **Varosliget (City Park)** is Budapest's second-largest park and one of its most popular for family outings. Stretching east from Hösök tere, it contains one of Budapest's most unusual buildings—Vajdahunyad Castle, originally built out of timber and canvas as a temporary structure for an 1896 exposition, with the aim of representing Hungarian architectural styles through the ages. Although some people criticized it as being too kitschy (it does resemble Walt Disney's castle), the majority liked it so much that a fundraiser collected enough money to immortalize it in stone and mortar. Today it contains an agricultural museum, complete with wine cellar, and is particularly striking when lit up at night. Nearby is a boating lake, which is turned into an outdoor ice-skating rink in winter (unfortunately, no skate rentals) and is quite a breathtaking visual sight, especially in the evening. Also in the park is a swimming pool, the famous Szécsenyi thermal baths, a zoo with more than 3,000 animals, a botanical garden, and a big amusement park, open daily from 10am to 6pm (in summer to 9pm), with roller coasters, fun houses, shooting ranges, puppet shows, and dance floors.

ORGANIZED TOURS

Budapest is easy to see on your own. If time is short, however, you might consider joining UBUSZ's **City Tour,** a three-hour trip by bus taking you to the most important sights, including Heroes' Square, Castle Hill, Matthias Church, Fishermen's Bastion, and Gellért Hill. The tour departs daily at 10am (with more departures in summer) and costs 1,700 Ft ($15.30). In addition, if you're in Budapest any time from May through August, you might want to join IBUSZ's **Parliament tour,** since it's the only way you can see the inside of this mammoth building. Tours take place Wednesday and Friday at 10:30am and 2pm and cost 1,700 Ft ($15.30).

SPORTS & RECREATION

THERMAL BATHS   This is my kind of sport! No respectable European would dream of coming to Budapest and not take advantage of the city's famous thermal baths—and you should follow suit. There are approximately 200 medicinal baths in Budapest, where everyone from janitors to politicians can soak away their cares and play chess on floating boards. There are dozens of public baths, but one of the most famous, and certainly most ornate, is the bath at the **Hotel Gellért,** Kelenhegyi út 4–6 (☎ **1/166-6166**), located in Buda at the base of

Gellért Hill beside the Danube. Built in elaborate art nouveau after the turn of the century, the thermal indoor bath, so elegant it looks like a ballroom, has a glass roof that can be removed in fine weather. There's also a large modern outdoor swimming pool with artificial waves, complete with a sunning terrace for nudists. Admission to the thermal baths is 200 Ft ($1.80); if you want a massage, it's 600 Ft ($5.40) for 30 minutes. The swimming pool costs extra. Both bathing suits and towels are available for rent. The baths are open Monday through Friday from 6:30am to 7pm (you must enter by 6pm) and Saturday and Sunday from 6:30am to 1pm (you must enter by noon). Massages are given Monday through Saturday only.

Another famous bath, popular with the local older generation, is the **Király Fürdö,** Fó u. 84 (☎ **1/202-3688**), which features a splendid cupola above an octagonal bath and thermal tubs, salt baths, and massage. It's open on alternating days for men and women. Hours are Monday through Friday from 6:30am to 6pm and Saturday and Sunday from 6:30am to noon.

Finally, another famous bath is **Széchényi Fürdö** in Városliget Park (City Park), Allatkerti krt. 11 (☎ **1/121-0310**), in Pest. Named after a 19th-century aristocrat (his portrait adorns the 5,000-forint banknote), Széchényi is one of Europe's largest public spas and features a gorgeous outdoor thermal bath, open even in the dead of winter (an unforgettable sight if it's snowing, with steam rising primeval-like from the water). Part of the bath stems from the turn of the century, with lavish bronze and mosaic decorations. It's open Monday through Friday from 6am to 6pm and Saturday and Sunday from 6am to 1pm. Entrance to the bath is 150 Ft ($1.35); the closest subway stop is Széchényi Fürdö.

7 Shopping

There are many shopping streets in Budapest, but for a visiting tourist the heart of the **shopping district** is in Pest, in a quadrangle formed by the Danube, József Attila utca, Károly körút, and Kossurth Lajos utca, all near the Deák Ferenc tér subway stop. Váci utca in particular, now a pedestrian zone, is a good hunting ground for souvenir hunters and window-shoppers.

Budapest's best bargains are hand-embroidered handkerchiefs and tablecloths, dolls in Puszta costumes, sheepskin jackets, Tokay wine bottles, packages of paprika, porcelain, pottery, and jewelry.

Try **Népmüveszet Folk Art Centrum,** Váci u. 14 (☎ **1/118-5840**), for a wide selection of Hungarian embroidery, wood carvings, clothing, pottery, and other native products. It's open daily from 9:30am to 6pm. Castle Hill also has souvenir and antique shops.

MARKETS   Budapest's largest and best-known flea market, **Hasznaltcikk Piac,** is held on the southern outskirts of Budapest at Nagykörosi u. 156. Here you'll find stalls selling silver, china, old books, jeans, leather jackets, antiques, and junk, and since the dealers know their wares and their value, you probably won't find any undiscovered treasures. However, it's fun just to browse. It's open Monday through Friday from 8am to 4pm and Saturday from 8am to 2pm. To reach it, take the subway to the Határ út Station, and transfer there to bus no. 54 to the Hasznaltcikk Piac stop, about a seven-minute ride. The market is at the end of Nagykörosi utca, on the left side of the street. Keep your eyes peeled, because it's easy to miss.

8 Budapest After Dark

Because of Hungary's low prices, you should take advantage of Budapest's wonderful concert and stage offerings. There's something going on musically in Budapest virtually every evening of the year, with tickets for many performances starting as low as 250 Ft ($2.25). Particularly outstanding are performances of the Hungarian Symphony Orchestra and the Hungarian State Opera. For information regarding concerts, recitals of guest performers, opera, ballet, and dance, pick up a free copy of the monthly publication *Programme in Hungary* at Tourinform. Other sources of information for what's going on in the capital are *Budapest Week* and the *Budapest Sun,* both published weekly and containing entertainment sections listing concerts, movies, and other events.

Upon your arrival in Budapest, one of your first stops should be the **Philharmonia Booking Office (Nemzeti Filharmonia)** at Vörösmarty tér 1 (☎ 1/118-0441), open Monday through Friday from 10am to 6pm and Saturday from 10am to 2pm, where you can purchase tickets for concerts and the opera (though not at the lowest prices). Tickets for opera and ballet can also be purchased either at the door or at the **Central Theater Booking Office,** Andrássy út 18, open Tuesday through Saturday from 10am to 7pm and Sunday from 10am to 1pm and 4 to 7pm.

THE PERFORMING ARTS

THEATER

The **Madach Theater,** Erzsébet krt. 31, in Pest (☎ 1/322-2015), presents musicals such as *Les Misérables, Cats,* and other Broadway and West End hits. Tickets run 600 to 1,000 Ft ($5.40 to $9). Subway: Blaha Lujza tér.

OPERA HOUSE & CONCERT HALLS

Magyar Állami Operház (Hungarian State Opera)
Andrássy út 22, in Pest. ☎ **1/153-0170** or 131-2550. Tickets 250–1,000 Ft ($2.25–$9). Subway: Opera.

The inside of this opera house is a must see in Budapest—and it won't cost you a lot of money. Indeed, attending an opera or ballet here costs only a fraction of what it costs in other European capitals, and there are few people as enthusiastic about the opera as Hungarians. Built in neo-Renaissance style in the 1880s, the opera house is one of the prettiest on the continent, ornately gilded and decorated with the statues of 16 composers, including Franz Liszt and Ferenc Erkel. Even if you've never been to an opera, you owe it to yourself to attend at least one performance.

Pesti Vigadó (Pester Redoute)
Vigadó tér 2, in Pest. ☎ **1/117-6222.** Tickets 250–1,000 Ft ($2.25–$9). Subway: Vörösmarty tér.

This hall, near Vörösmarty tér, specializes in traditional and contemporary Hungarian music, including performances of the Hungarian Symphony Orchestra. Most concerts begin at 7:30pm.

Zeneakadémia (Academy of Music)
Liszt Ferenc tér 8, in Pest. ☎ **1/342-0179** or 341-4788. Tickets 250–700 Ft ($2.25–$6.30). Subway: Oktogon. Tram 4 or 6 to Király út.

Founded by Ferenc Liszt, the Academy of Music is still an educational institute; Béla Bartók once taught here. Featuring excellent acoustics and rich art nouveau gilding, the academy's concert hall is one of Budapest's main venues for classical concerts, including orchestras, chamber music, and string quartets. The Hungarian Radio Orchestra and Hungarian Symphony Orchestra perform regularly here.

FILMS

Cinemas charge about 300 to 400 Ft ($2.70 to $3.60) for an evening show, half that for a matinee. Movies are shown in their original version, with Hungarian subtitles. Most of the cinemas are found in Pest. Check *Budapest Week* or the *Budapest Sun* for a listing of movies being shown throughout the city in English.

GAMBLING

The **Budapest Casino,** in the Hilton Hotel, Castle Hill in Buda (☎ 1/175-1000), boasts the usual games of roulette, baccarat, blackjack, and one-arm bandits. The minimum stake is 2 DM ($1.35). The doorman at the door will check your passport before letting you in. Admission is 10 DM ($6), half of which goes toward chips for games. It's open daily from 5pm to 4am.

In Pest, there's **Gresham Palast,** Roosevelt tér 5 (☎ 1/117-2502), located near the Atrium Hyatt Hotel. Open daily from 2pm to 4am, it also charges 10 DM ($6) admission, which goes toward chips. No jeans or sports shoes are allowed, and after 8pm men must wear jackets. Be sure to bring your passport.

Last but not least, there's also the **Las Vegas Casino** in the Atrium Hyatt Hotel, also on Roosevelt tér (☎ 1/117-6022 or 266-9052), open daily from 2pm to 5am. It charges $10 admission, which goes toward chips, and again, no jeans or tennis shoes are allowed. Don't forget your passport.

LIVE MUSIC
PIANO BARS

Cafe Pierrot
Fortuna u. 14, Castle Hill, in Buda. ☎ 1/175-6971. Special "Varbusz MM" minibus from Moszkva tér.

Although not as memorable as Miniatür Espresso (below), this piano bar has a convenient location not far from Matthias Church in the Castle Hill district and features live piano music, ranging from jazz to classic and soft rock, every evening beginning at 8pm. It's small and cozy, with an arched ceiling and rattan furniture—a good place to relax after a day of sightseeing. It's open daily from 11am to 1am.

Miniatür Espresso
Buday László u. 10, in Buda. ☎ 1/212-3143. Tram 4 or 6 to the Mechwart liget stop.

With a history stretching back 40 years, this cozy piano bar is an institution and a favorite for travelers who come to Budapest again and again. They come for a bit of nostalgia, confident that little has changed here over the decades—from the lace tablecloths, red wallpaper, and overstuffed red chairs to the soft lighting and soothing piano music played by Makkai Lajos. For the past 40 years it has been run by the motherly Manyi Néni, who has recently passed on the duties to her daughter, Mária, and manager, Agnes. Most likely you'll find both of them there. Admission is free (but don't be tempted by the package of nuts placed on your table—it costs extra). A very civilized place, it's located in Buda, on a hill called Rose Hill west of Margit híd. Open Monday through Saturday from 7pm to 3am.

JAZZ, BLUES & ROCK MUSIC

Black and White

Akácfa u. 13, in Pest. ☎ **1/322-7645.** Cover averages 100 Ft (90¢). Subway: Blaha Lujza tér.

This low-key basement hangout, simple with black tables and chairs, is popular with students for its live music and low prices. Located just 1 1/2 blocks north of Rákóczi út, it offers live music nightly beginning at 8:30pm, mostly Hungarian musicians playing jazz and blues. You won't be broke from spending an evening here—even the pizza is priced under $3. Open Monday through Saturday from 11am to 2am and Sunday from 6pm to 1am.

Picasso Point

Hajós u. 31, in Pest. ☎ **1/132-4750.** Cover 150 Ft ($1.35). Subway: Arany János.

Another casual student hangout, this place offers acoustic jazz, folk rock, or ethnic music three times a week from 8 to 10pm. The ground-floor café has an artsy atmosphere, while in the basement is a disco where the music is so loud you can't hear yourself think. Open daily from noon to 4pm.

Tilos Az A!

Mikszáth Kalman tér 2, in Pest. ☎ **1/118-0684.** Cover 200 Ft ($1.80). Subway: Kalvin tér.

Tilos Az A! is the Hungarian translation of "Trespassers W" from *Winnie the Pooh*, an unlikely name for this alternative hotspot. The top two floors serve as a bar, with music provided by a DJ. The tiny basement, which contains no furniture unless you count its concrete floor, is the venue for live music Monday through Saturday, featuring Hungarian bands which often convey a political or social message in their rock music. Most people here are in their 20s. A good hangout, it's located not far from the National Museum, but you might have problems identifying the place from the outside—look for the "A" above the door and listen for the music. Open Monday through Thursday from 9pm to 3am, Friday and Saturday to 5am, and Sunday to 1am.

BARS

Fregatt

Molnár u. 26 (on the corner of Molnár and Pintér streets), in Pest. ☎ **1/118-9997.** Subway: Ferenciek tere.

This British-style pub is decorated like the interior of a ship, but that's not why anyone comes here. Rather, this is an expatriate bar, crowded with business types, yuppies, and everyone else trying to make a living in Budapest. It may not be your cup of tea, but if you're trying to make contacts in a social setting, this could be the place. Open daily from 5pm to midnight.

Marxim

Kisrókus u. 23, in Buda. ☎ **1/212-4183.** Subway: Moszkvat tér; then a five-minute walk.

The street leading to this unusual bar is fitting—desolate and bleakly industrial, flanked on one side by a Communist-era–looking factory. And there, lo and behold, is a bright-red star signaling Marxim, a pub decorated with socialist-era memorabilia. Where else can you sip a beer and eat a pizza surrounded by chicken wire, Communist posters, red stars, and lighting so bright you feel as if you've been banished to interrogation in the gulag? And as the last insult to Communism, credit cards are accepted. Open Monday through Thursday from noon to 1am, Friday and Saturday from noon to 2am, and Sunday from 6pm to 1am.

A DISCO

Hully-Gully
Lékai J. tér 9. ☎ **1/175-9742.** Cover 400 Ft ($3.60). Subway: Déli pu. Bus 112 to Lékai J. tér.

This is one of Budapest's better discos, with a huge dance floor and—whether you approve or not—two scantily clad dancers who set the pace. It's probably the best place in town to dance the night away. Open daily from 9pm to 5am.

9 Easy Excursions

The easiest way to see the countryside around Budapest is to join one of the several tours offered by IBUSZ. The **Danube Bend Tour by Boat,** for example, is a nine-hour trip along the Danube, with stops at Szentendre with its Kovács Margit Ceramics Museum and shops and at Visegrad with its royal castle ruins. It's offered May through September on Wednesday and Saturday at 8:30am. If you prefer to travel by bus, the **Danube Bend Tour by Coach** takes in Szentendre, Visegrad, and Esztergom with its famous cathedral. This tour departs May through October on Tuesday and Friday at 9am; during the winter months it departs on Saturday only, at 9am. The price for both tours is 5,700 Ft ($51.30).

For further information, contact any IBUSZ office. They will also be able to tell you about full-day tours to Hungary's largest lake, **Balaton,** and to a famous stud farm in **Tok,** complete with an equestrian show. They also have information on hydrofoil trips on the Danube to Vienna and by cruise ship to Passau, Germany, via Czechoslovakia and Austria.

SZENTENDRE Located on the Danube River just north of Budapest, "Saint Andrew" is known for its artists' colony, art shops, and small-town ambience. Its gaily painted houses hold a number of shops, cafés, and galleries. Foremost among its attractions is the **Szabadteri Néprajzi Múzeum (Open-Air Village Museum),** Szabadságforrás út, with its collection of peasant houses and cottages from all over Hungary. It's open from April to October, Tuesday through Sunday from 9am to 5pm.

Be sure, too, to visit the **Kovács Margit Ceramic Museum,** Vastagh György u. 1, with the works of Hungary's most famous ceramicist, including her realistic portraits, biblical figures, grotesque figurines, and jugs and plates with fairy-tale decorations. It's open Tuesday through Sunday from 10am to 6pm.

To reach Szentendre, take the HEV local train from Batthyány tér, a trip of about 45 minutes.

LAKE BALATON After Budapest, Lake Balaton receives more visitors than any other place in Hungary. The largest freshwater lake in central Europe, it is 43 miles long but only 3 miles wide. Its mostly shallow waters warm quickly in the sun, making it popular for swimming, sunbathing, and other summertime pursuits. Its shores are surrounded by hotels and restaurants, while the hills beyond are famous for their vineyards. The main tourist season is from mid-May to about mid-September. Both buses and trains connect the north end of Lake Balaton to Budapest in about 1$\frac{1}{2}$–2 hours. Contact Tourinform for tourist information and IBUSZ if you wish to book accommodations.

10 Copenhagen

by Alice Garrard

For a moment, let's have some fun and create the perfect city. First, we'll lay down a vast network of pedestrian streets, lined with great stores and cafés. Bicycle lanes will span the city, encouraging a quiet, nonpolluting means of transport, and we'll generously spread royal palaces and rich museums throughout. Of course, we'll build our city along a pretty yet functional harbor. Just for fun, let's put an amusement park right in the city center, making carnival rides and concerts accessible to all. Finally, we'll govern our city with a socially minded philosophy that virtually eliminates poverty, crime, and begging.

As you've probably guessed, this is no fantasy—this is Copenhagen. And without a doubt this very real city's richest gift is its quality of life.

Copenhageners are a reflection of a kind and gentle lifestyle. They smile easily, laugh a lot, and will often go out of their way to help a stranger. Copenhageners are known for their terrific sense of humor—they like to poke fun at themselves and others, especially American travelers. The city considers itself the "jazz capital" of Europe, boasting more than its fair share of exceptional talent. And as every stroller along Strøget will discover, the city attracts some of the best street performers in the world.

Even for the value-minded tourist, Copenhagen is a city to love and savor. Getting around is relatively easy—you can walk to almost everything. The hotels and restaurants cater to a variety of budgets and maintain some of the highest standards in Europe. The bars and clubs serve some of Europe's best brews at a fraction of the prices charged in other Scandinavian cities.

This chapter will prove that you can enjoy "wonderful, wonderful" Copenhagen on a budget. And by visiting in 1996 you're in for an extra treat: As Cultural Capital of Europe '96, Copenhagen has many special events, including free entertainment, scheduled throughout the year.

1 Copenhagen Deals & Discounts

BUDGET BESTS Tivoli, the city's biggest tourist draw, provides one of Copenhagen's cheapest thrills. You can get in for 40 Kr ($6.65), half that for kids (see "Attractions," later in this chapter).

What's Special About Copenhagen

Strøget

- World-class shopping and some of Europe's best street performers.

Palaces

- Rosenborg Palace, home of the Danish Crown Jewels and a beautiful park.
- Christiansborg Palace, with its 800 years of history and impressive state rooms.
- Frederiksborg Palace, the "Versailles of northern Europe," 45 minutes from Copenhagen.

Museums

- The Ny Carlsberg Glyptotek, with its ancient and modern art and serene courtyard.
- The spectacular Louisiana Museum of Modern Art, 45 minutes by train from Copenhagen's Central Station.
- The National Museum, Denmark's impressive repository of cultural history.
- The Amalienborg Museum, showcasing official and private royal rooms from 1863 to 1947.

Tivoli

- The geographical and spiritual heart of Danish culture, it has come to life with music, dance, food, and merriment every summer since 1843 and at Christmas since 1994.

The Carlsberg Brewery tour is informative, intoxicating, fun, and free (see "Organized Tours" under "Attractions," later in this chapter). You can see an opera, ballet, or play at the Royal Theater for as little as 40 Kr ($6.65) (see "Copenhagen After Dark," later in this chapter).

SPECIAL DISCOUNTS   The **Copenhagen Card** entitles tourists to free museum entry, free public transportation, and good discounts on a variety of activities throughout the capital. The card is for one, two, or three days and costs 140 Kr ($23.35), 230 Kr ($38.35), or 295 Kr ($49.20), respectively. Cards can be bought at the DSB ticket office in Central Station, the Danish Tourist Board (see "Visitor Information" under "Copenhagen Specifics," later in this chapter), and at many hotels and S-tog stations.

For Students   By flashing an International Student Identification Card (ISIC), young people can get discounts at most of the city's museums, at some concert halls, and on planes, trains, and ferries from Denmark. Check listings throughout this chapter for special student rates.

For Seniors   People over 67 are entitled to half-price tickets at the Royal Theater, reduced admission to some museums, and discounts on ferry trips to Sweden. See the individual listings below for details.

WORTH THE EXTRA MONEY   A trip to the nearby Louisiana Museum in Humlebæk in North Zealand is definitely worthwhile. For details about this stunning repository of modern art and sculpture, see "Attractions," later in this chapter.

2 Pretrip Preparations

REQUIRED DOCUMENTS Citizens of the United States, the United Kingdom, Canada, New Zealand, and Australia need only a passport to enter Denmark.

TIMING YOUR TRIP Copenhagen is at its best from the end of April to the beginning of September. Days are long, Tivoli is open, and sidewalk cafés buzz late into the night. Of course, other seasons have their charms as well, including less precipitation, fewer tourists, and, in general, lower prices. Christmas in Copenhagen is especially endearing; since 1994, Tivoli has opened its doors to the public to make the holidays even brighter, with a special market, play, and ice skating on the lake.

Copenhagen's Average Daytime Temperature & Rainfall

	Jan	Feb	Mar	Apr	May	June	July	Aug	Sept	Oct	Nov	Dec
Temp (°F)	32	31	36	44	53	60	64	63	57	49	42	37
Rainfall "	1.9	1.5	1.2	1.5	1.7	1.8	2.8	2.6	2.4	2.3	1.9	1.9

SPECIAL EVENTS Most of the city's special events are staged during summer, when the tourist season is in full swing. But this year, 1996, when Copenhagen reigns as the official Cultural Capital of Europe, special activities are planned all year long. Festivities usually begin at the end of May with the **Copenhagen Carnival,** a raucous Mardi Gras party replete with costumes and sambas. **Free park concerts** start in June, including a weekly Saturday rock-music festival at Femøren and Sunday concerts in Fælledparken. Free concerts are sometimes held in Nikolaj Church. The 10-day **Copenhagen Jazz Festival,** in the first part of July, and the **Copenhagen Summer Festival,** which emphasizes classical music, from late July to mid-August, highlight the summer's festivities. See the "Special & Free Events" box under "Attractions," later in this chapter, for other happenings, and visit the Danish Tourist Board and Use-It (addresses under "Visitor Information" under "Copenhagen Specifics," later in this chapter) for free event schedules.

BACKGROUND READING Hans Christian Andersen (1805–75) is Denmark's most famous author. His beloved fairy tales include *The Emperor's New Clothes, The Little Mermaid,* and *The Ugly Duckling,* available individually or in Andersen anthologies.

Søren Kierkegaard (1813–55) was a seminal existentialist, deeply influencing later thinkers and future generations. Baroness Karen Blixen (1885–1962), better known by her pseudonym, Isak Dinesen, is perhaps most widely celebrated for *Out of Africa* and *Babette's Feast,* from which award-winning films were made.

Contemporary Danish author Peter Hoeg created a sensation in 1993 with his best-selling *Smilla's Sense of Snow* (set in Copenhagen and Greenland, with a most unforgettable heroine), followed by the less-well-received *Borderliners* in 1994.

3 Copenhagen Specifics

ARRIVING

FROM THE AIRPORT Is it a top-of-the-line department store or an airport? It's both! It's **Copenhagen Airport** (☎ **33-50-93-33**), 6 miles from the city center and the fanciest place to land in Europe.

What Things Cost in Copenhagen	U.S. $
Taxi from Central Station to Kongens Nytorv	5.50
Underground from Central Station to outlying neighborhood	1.60
Local telephone call	.35
Double room at the SAS Royal Hotel (deluxe)	232.50
Double room at the Saga Hotel (moderate)	91.70
Double room at Ms. Tessie Meiling's (budget)	29.15
Lunch for one at Kanal Caféen (moderate)	11.65
Lunch for one at Riz Raz (budget)	6.50
Dinner for one, without wine, at Els (deluxe)	46.00
Dinner for one, without wine, at Café Luna (moderate)	18.60
Dinner for one, without wine, at Københavnercaféen (budget)	10.85
Pint of beer	3.15
Glass of wine	3.35
Cup of coffee in a café	2.30
Coca-Cola in a restaurant	2.00
Roll of ASA 100 color film, 36 exposures	9.15
Admission to Tivoli	6.35
Admission to the Ny Carlsberg Glyptotek Museum	2.50
Movie ticket	10.00
Theater ticket (at the Royal Theater)	6.70

The bank in the arrivals hall is open Monday through Friday from 5:30am to 10pm and Saturday and Sunday from 7:30am to 10pm; but the exchange rate may be high and there's a charge for each traveler's check you cash (see "Banks" under "Fast Facts: Copenhagen," later in this chapter). Public telephones accept a number of foreign coins—including American quarters. There's also a bar/café; a small market; lockers; rental-car counters, including Avis, Budget, Europcar, Hertz, and Pitzner, a Danish company; an information desk; and courtesy baggage carts.

In the adjacent departure hall, the Left Luggage Office (☎ 32-47-47-41), open daily from 6:30am to 10:30pm, charges 20 Kr ($3.35) per bag per day (same price as the lockers, which have a three-day limit), 30 Kr ($5) for bikes and skis. Opposite the lockers, a post office (enter through the red door) is open Monday through Friday from 9am to 5pm.

The **SAS Airport Bus** (☎ 31-54-17-01) departs every 15 minutes and runs between the airport and Copenhagen's Central Station; the trip takes about 25 minutes and costs 30Kr ($5); children under 12 ride free. There are usually several SAS buses parked out front, so be sure you're on the one going downtown; it's marked HOVEDBANEGÅRD/CITY.

City bus no. 250S also makes the run between the airport and Rådhustorget (Town Hall Square) in the city center, a five-minute walk from Central Station, where you can connect with other buses and the S-tog trains. The 45-minute trip costs about 15 Kr ($2.50).

The Danish Krone

For American Readers At this writing $1 = approximately 6 Kr (or 1 Kr = 17¢), and this was the rate of exchange used to calculate the dollar values given in this chapter (rounded to the nearest nickel).

For British Readers At this writing £1 = approximately 9.8 Kr (or 1 Kr = 10p), and this was the rate of exchange used to calculate the pound values in the table below.

Note: The rates given here fluctuate from time to time and may not be the same when you travel to Denmark. Therefore this table should be used only as a guide:

Kr	U.S.$	U.K.£	Kr	U.S.$	U.K.£
1	.17	.10	75	12.50	7.65
2	.33	.20	100	16.67	10.20
3	.50	.31	125	20.83	12.76
4	.67	.41	150	25.00	15.31
5	.83	.51	175	29.17	17.86
6	1.00	.61	200	33.33	20.41
7	1.17	.71	225	37.50	22.96
8	1.33	.82	250	41.67	25.51
9	1.50	.92	300	50.00	30.61
10	1.67	1.02	350	58.33	35.71
15	2.50	1.53	400	66.67	40.82
20	3.33	2.04	450	75.00	45.92
25	4.17	2.55	500	83.33	51.02
50	8.33	5.10	600	100.00	61.22

A **taxi** into town runs about 100 Kr ($16.70). The taxi lane is adjacent to the bus stop.

FROM THE TRAIN STATION Copenhagen's **Central Station** is relatively easy to negotiate. Lockers and shops are located in the center of the station, while more shops, banks, ticket windows, and platform entrances are located around the perimeter. Showers are available for 15 Kr ($2.50), and you can wash clothes for 5 Kr (85¢). A hotel and room reservations service is nearby, in the Danish Tourist Board information office, at Bernstorffsgade 1 (see "Visitor Information," below).

The **luggage-storage office** is open Monday through Saturday from 5:30am to 1am and Sunday from 6am to 1am. The daily rates are 25 Kr ($4.15) per bag or 35 Kr ($5.85) per backpack or bicycle. Alternatively, small lockers cost 20 Kr ($3.35) and big ones are 30 Kr ($5). There are also lockers in a supervised area, and you are given a ticket rather than a key to retrieve your belongings; the cost is 20 or 30 Kr ($3.35 or $5) per day, depending on the size of the locker, with a maximum use of three days.

Den Danske Bank **currency-exchange office,** on the station's platform side, is open daily: from 6:45am to 10pm April 15 to September 30, and from 7am to 9pm October 1 to April 14. Commission rates, competitive with other area banks, are 22 Kr ($3.70) for a cash transaction during normal banking hours (Monday through Wednesday and Friday from 9:30am to 4pm and Thursday from 9:30am to 8pm); at other times, rates rise to 28 Kr ($4.70). Exchanging your traveler's checks for Danish currency can be an expensive transaction; at this writing, the cost per check is 20 Kr ($3.35), with a 40-Kr ($6.70) minimum—so change large denominations at one time. (Better yet, use American Express traveler's checks and exchange them at the American Express office—see "Fast Facts: Copenhagen"— where no fee is charged for the transaction.)

From mid-June to mid-September, travelers can relax and shower for free at the **Interrail Center,** a popular meeting point for backpackers. It's open daily from 6:30am to midnight. There's free luggage storage but no lockers.

Other station facilities include a market, which sells groceries and wine, open daily from 8am to midnight; a post office, open Monday through Friday from 8am to 10pm, Saturday from 9am to 4pm, and Sunday and holidays from 10am to 5pm; and an international telephone bureau called **TeleCom,** open Monday through Friday from 8am to 10pm and Saturday, Sunday, and holidays from 9am to 9pm (☎ **33-14-20-00**).

At the train station, you can also get passport photos taken; rent a bicycle; pick up toiletries; buy flowers, a novel, or souvenirs; enjoy a meal (from a commendable pizza to a delectable Danish buffet); and rent a luggage cart for a refundable 10 Kr ($1.70).

The city's **subway (S-tog)** lines converge at Central Station. Go to Platforms 9 to 12 to catch one of these trains.

VISITOR INFORMATION

Copenhagen Tourist Information is in a modern, convenient location near Tivoli's main entrance, Bernstorffsgade 1 (☎ **33-11-13-25;** fax 33-93-49-69). The most useful publication is the free guide *Copenhagen This Week* (actually published monthly), also available in hotels and tourist spots around town. The staff at the large information desk is patient and helpful and will provide information on everything from hostels and hotels to activities and nightlife to day trips and longer excursions. You can also buy gifts, souvenirs, Tivoli posters, postcards, and stamps or get a light lunch in airy Café Wivex or a brew and burger at Bryg & Burger, next door. The office is open May to September, daily from 9am to midnight; in October and April, Monday through Saturday from 9am to 5pm; and November to March, Monday through Friday from 9am to 5pm and Saturday from 9am to noon.

Nearby, **Use-It,** on the second floor of Huset (The House), Rådhusstræde 13 (☎ **33-15-65-18;** fax 33-15-75-18), is Copenhagen's "alternative" information office. Although the office may appear youth oriented, the information is geared toward budget travelers of all ages. A number of useful free publications are distributed here, including *Playtime,* a booklet with advice on low-cost restaurants, hotels, and sightseeing activities, plus a city map. The energetic young staff can counsel travelers on getting a job, renting an apartment, and almost anything else. Other useful services include a ride board for travelers needing rides or companions to other points in Europe and a terrific room-finding service (see "Accommodations," later in this chapter). There's a big table where you may relax and read the materials; there's also a basket with condoms in it. Another handy service is a free locker for a day, with a 50-Kr ($8.35) refundable deposit; you can leave belongings for a longer period for 10 Kr ($1.70) per day. Use-It is open June 15 to September 15, daily from 9am to 7pm; the rest of the year, Monday through Friday from 10am to 4pm.

CITY LAYOUT

Copenhagen revolves around **Strøget** (pronounced like *strø*-yet), a mile-long pedestrian thoroughfare right in the heart of town. Strøget is actually a string of several streets: Østergade, Amagertorv, Vimmelskaftet, Nygade, and Frederiksberggade. And although this strip seems like a centuries-old essential part of city life, it was declared free of automobiles only in 1962.

Strøget's eastern end runs into **Kongens Nytorv** (King's Square), site of the Royal Theater and the Magasin du Nord department store, and the beginning of **Nyhavn**—once Copenhagen's wild sailors' quarter, now a placid pedestrian area.

Købmagergade, another pedestrian avenue, branches north from the center of Strøget and spawns several smaller pedestrian streets.

The island of **Slotsholmen** lies just a few blocks south of Strøget and is home to Christiansborg Palace, the National Library, and a number of museums.

Strøget's western terminus opens onto **Rådhuspladsen,** Town Hall Square. The wide **Vesterbrogade** continues west past Tivoli Gardens, Central Station (Hovedbanegården), and into lovely residential area of **Frederiksberg,** which also has some cafés, museums, parks, and bed-and-breakfasts.

Some of the suggested reasonably priced hotels are near Central Station.

GETTING AROUND

BY SUBWAY (S-TOG) & BUS   Copenhagen is served by an extensive bus and subway network. Regular service begins daily at 5am (at 6am on Sunday) and continues until 12:30am. At other times there's a limited night-bus service departing from Town Hall Square.

Fares are based on a zone system; rates rise the farther you go. Most destinations in central Copenhagen will cost the minimum 9.50 Kr ($1.60). Buses and subway trains use the same tickets and you can transfer as much as you like for up to one hour.

The subway—called the S-tog—works on the honor system. Either pay your fare in the station you're departing from or stamp your own strip ticket in the yellow box on the platform. In Central Station, the S-tog departs from Platforms 9 to 12.

Similarly, when you board a bus, either pay the driver or stamp your ticket in the machine. It's easy to get away without paying, but beware: Fines for fare dodging are stiff! Bus drivers are exceptionally nice and helpful. Most speak some English, and even if they don't, they have an uncanny ability to know where it is you want to go.

If you plan on traveling by train or bus a lot, buy a 10-ticket strip for 70 Kr ($11.70). Tickets can be bought on buses and at all rail stations. Children 11 and under ride for half price; those 6 and under ride free on buses and those 4 and under ride free on local trains.

Dial 36-45-45-45 for bus information and 33-14-17-01 for S-tog information.

ON FOOT   The compact city center and many pedestrian thoroughfares make walking a breeze. You may be interested in picking up a copy of "Copenhagen on Foot," a well-written booklet of walking tours distributed free by Use-It (see "Visitor Information," above).

BY BICYCLE   Wide bike lanes, long green traffic lights, and beautiful surroundings encourage bike riding for both transportation and recreation. About half of all Danes ride regularly, and even high government officials can sometimes be seen pedaling to work. A guide to biking in and around Copenhagen is distributed free by Use-It (see "Visitor Information," above). You can rent a three-speed at Central Station from **Københavns Cyklebors,** Reventlowsgade 11 (☎ **33-33-86-13**), for about 50 Kr ($8.35) for one day, less if you keep the bike longer; there's a 300- to 400-Kr ($50 to $66.65) deposit. They can also provide a bike map of the city in English, French, and Danish and are open daily from 8am to 6pm.

BY TAXI   The basic taxi fare for up to four people is 15 Kr ($2.50) at the flag drop (make sure your cab has a meter, and note that it's a few kroner more at night and on weekends), then 8 Kr ($1.35) per kilometer (.62 mile) between 6am and 6pm, or 10 Kr ($1.65) between 6pm and 6am and on Saturday and Sunday. Payment by credit/charge card is acceptable. A cab available for hire displays the word FRI. To order a taxi in advance, dial 31-10-10-10 or 31-22-55-55.

BY CAR   Unless you're planning an extended trip outside Copenhagen, you'll find that keeping a car in the city is more trouble than it's worth. Most major U.S. car-rental firms, including Hertz and Avis, have offices in Copenhagen. Compare big-company prices with those charged by local car companies, listed in the "Transport" section of the tourist board publication *Copenhagen This Week.*

In Denmark, drivers must use their lights at all times, even in daytime, and all occupants of the car, including those in the back seat, must buckle their seatbelts.

FAST FACTS: Copenhagen

American Express   The American Express Card & Travel Service office is conveniently located in the middle of Strøget, at Amagertorv 18 (☎ **33-11-50-05**), open Monday through Friday from 9am to 5pm and Saturday from 9am to noon. To report a lost card, call toll free 80-01-00-21; lost checks, toll free 80-01-01-00.

Babysitters   Minerva (☎ **31-22-96-96**) is a multilingual babysitter clearinghouse made up of students of all ages, and it charges only 25 Kr ($4.20) per hour, plus a 25-Kr ($4.20) booking fee. The minimum charge during the day is six hours; in the evening, it's three hours. Reserve Monday through Thursday from 6:30 to 9am and 3 to 6pm, Friday from 3 to 6pm only. On Saturday the office is open from 3 to 5pm only.

Banks   Banks are usually open Monday through Friday from 9:30am to 4pm (Thursday until 6pm). The unfortunate news for travelers is that Danish banks (at this writing) charge 20 Kr ($3.35) per traveler's check, with a minimum 40-Kr ($6.65) fee. This is daunting, especially if your checks are in small denominations. Exchange cash (there's only one fee per transaction) or, better still, use American Express traveler's checks and exchange them, *at no charge*, at the American Express office on Strøoget, or go to Forex at the train station where the fees are lower.

Another way to avoid the heavy-duty bank fee is to purchase items with traveler's checks (rather than Danish cash) in shops where the rate of exchange is good and there's no fee for the transaction; you keep the change and beat the restricted banking hours, too. For such a transaction, a Frommer traveler suggests Sven Carlsen Gift and Art Shop, between Town Hall and Tivoli Gardens, but on the opposite side of the street, at Vesterbrogade 2B (☎ 33-11-73-31).

Business Hours   Shops are usually open Monday through Thursday from 9:30am to 5:30pm (department stores, until 7pm) and Saturday from 9am to 2pm (until 5pm the first Saturday of the month); shops in the train station stay open later. Offices are open Monday through Friday from 9 or 10am until 4 or 5pm.

Currency   The Danish currency is the **krone** (crown), or **kroner (Kr)** in its plural form, made up of 100 **øre.** Banknotes are issued in 20, 50, 100, 500, and 1,000 kroner. Coins come in 25 and 50 øre, and 1, 2, 5, 10, and 20 kroner; the 1-, 2-, and 5-krone coins have a hole in the center.

Dentists   Emergency dental care is provided by Tandlægevagten, Oslo Plads 14 (☎ 31-38-02-51). The office, located near Østerport Station, is open Monday through Friday from 8am to 8pm and Saturday, Sunday, and holidays from 10am to noon. Fees are paid in cash.

Doctors   To reach a doctor outside normal hours, dial 33-12-00-41 Monday through Friday from 9am to 4pm; other times, call 33-96-63-00.

Electricity   The electricity is 220 volts, so you'll need a transformer (often incorrectly called a converter), as well as an adapter plug with two thin round prongs.

Embassies   Denmark's capital is home to the embassies of many nations, including those of the **United States,** Dag Hammerskjölds Allé 24 (☎ 31-42-31-44); **Canada,** Kristen Bernikowsgade 1 (☎ 33-12-22-99); the **United Kingdom,** Kastelsvej 40 (☎ 35-26-46-00); **Ireland,** 21 Ostbanegade (☎ 31-42-32-330); and **Australia,** Kristaniagade 21 (☎ 35-26-22-44). For others, look under "Embassies" in *Copenhagen This Week.*

Emergencies   Dial **112** for police, fire, or ambulance service. No coins are needed when dialing from a public phone. Steno Apotek, Vesterbrogade 6C (☎ 33-14-82-66), is a 24-hour pharmacy across from Central Station.

Eyeglasses   Several optical shops are in and around Strøget. Synoptik, Købmagergade 22 (☎ 33-15-05-38), has a particularly large selection of modern frames. It's open Monday through Thursday from 9:30am to 6pm, Friday from 9:30am to 7pm, and Saturday from 9:30am to 2pm.

Holidays   Copenhagen celebrates New Year's Day (Jan 1), Maundy Thursday, Good Friday, Easter Sunday and Monday, Common Prayer Day (late April), Ascension Day, Whitsunday and Monday (mid-May), Constitution Day (June 5), and Christmas Eve and Christmas Day (Dec 24–25).

Hospitals   Even foreigners staying temporarily in Denmark are entitled to free hospital care in the event of a sudden illness. Rigshospitalet, Blegdamsvej 9 (☎ 35-45-35-45), is the most centrally located hospital. For an ambulance, dial 112.

Information   See "Copenhagen Specifics," earlier in this chapter, for tourist and transportation information. Other important addresses and telephone numbers can be found under the appropriate headings below.

Laundry/Dry Cleaning   Copenhagen has laundries in all areas of town; look for the word *vask* (wash) such as *møntvask* or *vaskeri.* One fairly near the train station, Istedgades Møntvask, at Istedgade 45 and Absalomsgade, is open daily from 7am to 9pm, and charges about 32 Kr ($5.35) for washing, drying, and detergent. Another, Mønt-Vask, Vindsgade 13 at Nørre Farimagsgade, a block from Israels Plads near Ibsens Hotel, is open from 6am to 10pm daily; prices are similar.

For dry cleaning, go to Buen, Vester Farimagsgade 3 (☎ **33-12-45-45**), just one block from Central Station. It's open Monday through Friday from 8am to 6pm and Saturday from 9:30am to 1:30pm, but it's not cheap at about 90 Kr ($15) for a jacket or sweater and a pair of pants.

Lost & Found   If you lost it on a train, try the Lost Property Office at Lyshojgardsvej 80, Valby (☎ **36-44-20-10** for trains). It's open Monday through Friday from 9am to 4pm (Thursday to 6pm). If you lost it on a bus, call the police (see below), and if you lost it somewhere else, try the Copenhagen police at Slots Herrensvej 113, Vanløse (☎ **31-74-88-22**), open Monday through Friday from 9am to 2pm (on Thursday to 5pm).

Mail   Post offices are usually open Monday through Friday from 9 or 10am until 5 or 5:30pm. Some are also open Saturday from 9am to noon. Letters and postcards to North America and Australia cost 5 Kr (85¢), 3.75 Kr (60¢) to other countries in Europe.

You can receive mail marked *Poste Restante* most conveniently (in terms of location and hours) at the post office in Central Station, Monday through Friday from 8am to 10pm, Saturday from 9am to 4pm, and Sunday and holidays from 10am to 5pm. Another convenient post office is two blocks north of Strøget, at 33 Købmagergade (☎ **33-41-02-00**), open Monday through Friday from 9am to 6pm and Saturday from 9am to 1pm. Holders of American Express cards or traveler's checks can pick up personal mail at that company's main office (see "American Express," above), which will hold it for 30 days. American Express does not accept parcels.

Newspapers   There are no English-language newspapers printed in Denmark. However, the *International Herald Tribune, USA Today, The European*, and other papers are widely available. The newsstand opposite Town Hall and those in major hotels have good selections.

You can read newspapers and magazines at Hoved Biblioteket, Kultorvet 2 (☎ **33-93-60-60**), the main public library. It's open Monday through Friday from 10am to 7pm and Saturday from 10am to 2pm.

Photographic Needs   Kontant Foto, Købmagergade 44 (☎ **33-12-00-29**), is the largest camera supply and photo store in Copenhagen. It's open Monday through Thursday from 9am to 5:30pm, Friday from 9am to 7pm, and Saturday from 10am to 2pm. Foto Quick, in Rådhusarkaden, at H. C. Andersens Boulevard and Vesterbrogade, offers one-hour processing but exacts a hefty price: 123 Kr ($18.65) for 24 exposures, 170 Kr ($25.75) for 36 exposures; it's open Monday through Friday from 9am to 5:30pm and Saturday from 10am to 2pm.

Police   In an emergency, dial 112 from any phone—no coins are needed. For other police matters, call Police Headquarters, Polititorvet (☎ **33-14-14-48**).

Radio   English-language newscasts are broadcast on Radio Denmark Monday through Friday at 8:30am on 93.8 FM.

Religious Services   The Cathedral of Copenhagen (Lutheran), Nørregade, is Denmark's most important church; open daily from 8:30am to 5pm. Roman

Catholic services are held in English at the Sacraments Church, Nørrebrogade 27 (☎ **31-35-68-25**), and at St. Ann's Church, Hans Bogbinders Allé 2 (☎ **31-58-21-02**); take bus no. 2 or 11 for the latter. The largest Jewish synagogue is at Krystalgade 12 (☎ **33-12-88-68**). The city's "gay church," Metropolitan Community Church, Knabrostræde 3 (☎ **31-83-32-86**), has services in Danish, but the minister, Mia Andersen, speaks English. Call for times and days of services. For more extensive listings, check the "Churches" section of *Copenhagen This Week.*

Shoe Repair   There's a shoe-repair shop (☎ **31-91-02-20**) in Cityarkaden, near the east end of Strøget, at Østergade 32, as well as a Master Repair (☎ **33-91-00-47**) in the center of Central Station; the latter is open convenient hours, from 8am to 10pm daily.

Tax   Denmark's 25% value-added tax is called MOMS (pronounced "mumps") and is usually included in the prices listed in hotel tariffs and restaurant menus. Many stores offer tourists the opportunity to reclaim sales tax on purchases over 300 Kr ($50); see "Shopping," later in this chapter, for details.

Telephone   The most important thing to note is that in Denmark *you must always dial the area code (31, 32, 33, etc.) before the number*, even when calling from next door.

Making a **local telephone call** costs a minimum of 1 Kr (15¢) for about 2$\frac{1}{2}$ minutes; a tone will sound when you have to add more coins. On older phones, deposit coins before dialing; although unused coins are not returned even if you reach a busy signal, they are credited toward another call. On newer phones—recognizable by their yellow front plate—wait for the answering party to pick up before inserting money. Reach local **directory assistance** at 118. It costs five times as much to make a local call from a hotel room as it does from a pay phone, which you'll usually find in the hotel lobby.

For **international calls** placed through TeleCom, it costs about 20 Kr ($3.05) per minute to call North America and about 9 Kr ($1.35) to call Europe. The easiest way to call North America is via AT&T's "USA Direct" service. If you have an AT&T Calling Card, or call collect, you can reach an American operator from any phone by dialing toll free 800-10010 or 800-10022. Alternatively, you can make long-distance calls from the Central Station's **TeleCom Center** (☎ **33-14-20-00**), located inside the station; it's open Monday through Friday from 8am to 10pm and Saturday, Sunday, and holidays from 9am to 9pm. A second TeleCom Center at the airport is open daily from 6:30am to 10pm. You can also make local calls from TeleCom booths, which is often cheaper than using pay telephones.

Time   There is a six-hour time difference between Denmark and the east coast of the United States (eastern standard time). Daylight saving time is in effect in Denmark from the last Saturday in March until the last Sunday in October.

Tipping   It's usually not necessary. A 15% service charge is automatically added to most restaurant bills. If service has been extraordinary, you might want to round up the bill.

Useful Telephone Numbers   AIDS Information (☎ **33-91-11-19**); Alcoholics Anonymous (☎ **31-81-81-92**).

4 Accommodations

By now, Copenhagen has gotten used to its annual invasion of tourists, and you'll find it nice to know that there are enough budget accommodations to house everyone. As in most European cities, Copenhagen offers several accommodation alternatives, the most economical of which is probably renting a room in a private home.

The **Accommodation Service (Værelseanvisning),** beside Tivoli's main entrance, at Bernstorffsgade 1, specializes in booking private rooms, as well as same-day discounted hotel rooms. The office rents up to 160 private rooms, most 10 to 15 minutes by bus or S-tog from the city center, with rates rarely topping 150 Kr ($25) per person, not including breakfast. The Accommodation Service also works with some of the best hotels in the city, selling same-day space that would otherwise remain empty. There's a 15-Kr ($2.50) per-person booking fee and a deposit required at time of booking. The Accommodation Service desk is open for in-person visits from late May to mid-September, daily from 9am to midnight; the last two weeks of September, daily from 9am to 9pm; throughout October, Monday through Friday from 9am to 5pm, Saturday 9am to 2pm; the rest of the year, Monday through Friday from 9am to 5pm (also Saturday from 9am to noon November to March). Hotels (not private homes) may be booked in advance by contacting **Hotelbooking København,** Bernstorffsgade 1, 1577 København (☎ **33-12-28-80;** fax 33-12-97-23). The advance-bookings desk is open year round, Monday through Friday from 9am to 5pm.

Use-It, a tourist-information desk on the second floor of Huset (an activity center for youth), Rådhusstræde 13 (☎ **33-15-65-16;** fax 33-15-75-18), can provide a full rundown on budget accommodations, including last-minute rooming possibilities posted on its bulletin board. It can also store luggage and hold mail. The office is open daily from 9am to 7pm from June 15 to September 15; the rest of the year, Monday through Friday from 10am to 4pm.

DOUBLES IN PRIVATE HOMES FOR LESS THAN 350 KR ($58.35)
IN THE CENTER

Staying in a room in a private home has several advantages: low cost; a more intimate environment than a hotel, but with privacy; and the opportunity to get to know a Danish host. All the hosts below are English-speaking and well traveled. There's a strong network among hosts, and if one is booked he or she will be able to direct you to another. Each of the following homes has only a handful of rooms available, so always call ahead to avoid disappointment. Out of courtesy to hosts, always let them know when you're to arrive so you don't tie up their time, and be understanding if they can't spend as much time socializing with you as you'd like. More often than not, however, they're amazingly generous with their time. You'll be more than impressed with the lodgings they provide and their sophistication as hosts.

Ms. Turid Aronson

Brolæggerstræde 13, 1211 København K. ☎ **33-14-31-46.** 3 rms, none with bath. 200 Kr ($33.35) single; 280 Kr ($46.65) double; 360 Kr ($60) triple. Breakfast 30 Kr ($5) extra. No credit cards. Bus 2 or 6 from Central Station to the canal.

Getting the Best Deal on Accommodations

- A room in a private home will cost only about half the price of a room in a hotel.
- Try the hotels immediately southwest of Central Station, along Colb- jørnsensgade and Helgolandsgade (off Istedgade). Although many are above our price range, some offer excellent values. The area may have several porno- graphic bookstores and video shops, but it's safe.
- Take advantage of accommodations that include breakfast in the price of the room.
- Ask for a hotel room without a private bath; you usually get a sink. Be sure the bath is nearby and well maintained.

You'll find more upscale lodging in the other private homes listed here, but none more convenient, only a block from Strøget. The rooms are comfortable, spacious, and stocked with brochures of local attractions; guests enjoy sitting around the kitchen table. Two of the rooms are adjacent to the bath, which is tiled with a shower. Brolægerstræde is a short street, only two blocks long, and around the cor- ner from Huset, the popular activity and information center for young people.

✪ Ms. Margrethe Kaae Christensen
Amaliegade 26 (3rd floor), 1256 København K. ☎ and fax **33-13-68-61.** 2 rms, neither with bath. TV. 250 Kr ($41.65) single; 325 Kr ($54.15) double. Additional bed 110 Kr ($18.35) extra; breakfast of bread, bacon, and eggs 45 Kr ($7.50) extra. No credit cards. Bus 1 or 6 from Central Station to Amalienborg Palace.

This is about as close as you'll be able to get to living at the royal Amalienborg Palace 50 yards away. You'll be greeted by the exceedingly friendly and lively Ms. Christensen, whose elegant accommodations were completely refurnished in 1994. The Blue Room has its own sink and a double bed; the Rose Room, its own private entrance and two single beds. Both are supplied with cable TV, coffee- and tea-making facilities, and fruit. They share a bath with tub and shower.

Ms. Solveig Diderichsen
Upsalegade 26, 2100 København O. ☎ **31-38-39-58.** 3 rms, none with bath. TV. 250 Kr ($41.65) single; 300 Kr ($50) double. No credit cards. Take the S-tog or bus 9 to Østerport; then walk to Hjalmar Brantings Plads, turn right, take an immediate left, and you're there.

Solveig Diderichsen's seven-room apartment is 100 years old, with high ceilings, pine floors, and large rooms—two doubles and one single—that are clean, com- fortable, and equipped with good reading lights and coffee-making facilities. Guests share a big bath that has both a tub and a shower, plus a separate toilet. Guests chat with one another around the dining room table or in the airy kitchen. Ethnic restaurants, a bakery, a grocery store, and a post office are nearby, and the Botanical Garden and some of the city's museums are a five-minute walk away through a neighborhood park. The apartment, which Ms. Diderichsen shares with her pet husky, is in a quiet part of the city near the American Embassy. Bus no. 9 comes here from the airport.

Annette and Rudy Hollender

Wildersgade 19, 1408 Copenhagen K. ☎ **31-95-96-22.** 3 rms, none with bath. 210 Kr ($35) single; 270 Kr ($45) double; 400 Kr ($66.65) triple. Breakfast 40 Kr ($6.65) extra. No credit cards. Bus 2 from City Hall, 8 from Central Station, or 9 from the airport.

On Christianshavn, an island a five-minute bus ride from Town Hall, this half-timbered house dating from 1698 is so diminutive it seems like a dollhouse. The three attic guest rooms have exposed beams; all on the third floor, they share a bath on the second. Guests eat breakfast in the comfortable kitchen or, on warm days, at a table in the backyard. Host Annette Hollender checks out local restaurants and attractions, so she can make recommendations to her visitors.

Ⓢ Ms. Tessie Meiling

Sølvgade 34b, 1307 København. ☎ **33-15-35-76** at home, 33-15-28-42 at work. 1 rm, without bath. TV. 150 Kr ($25) single per day, 800 Kr ($133.35) per week; 175 Kr ($29.15) double per day, 1,000 Kr ($166.65) per week. No credit cards. Bus 10 from Central Station to Kronprinsessegade, near the Royal Museum of Art.

Kindergarten teacher Tessie Meiling offers one of the city's best values for a stay of a week or more. The garret apartment, a three-story walk-up in an 1845 house, has a country kitchen with board floors. Wooden cabinets, chests, and tables—and Tessie's artistic hand—are everywhere. Unfortunately, there's only one comfortable room for rent, furnished with two single beds, color TV, cassette player, and good reading lamps. The rates don't include breakfast, but you're welcome to use the kitchen. The shower is in the kitchen, but you have privacy when you use it. The building is near the Royal Museum of Art and Botanical Garden, across from Rosenborg Palace and Garden; the entrance to the apartment is at the back of a narrow walkway.

IN FREDERIKSBERG

Bus no. 1, which stops at most of the homes below, is particularly convenient because it also stops at many of Copenhagen's most popular tourist attractions.

Gurli and Viggo Hannival

Folkets Allé 17, 2000 Frederiksberg. ☎ **31-86-13-10.** 2 rms, 1 with bath. 250 Kr ($41.65) per room. Single travelers may get a discount Nov–Feb. Additional bed 80 Kr ($13.35) extra; continental breakfast for two 20 Kr ($3.35) extra. No credit cards. S-tog: Line C to Peter Bangsvej (toward Ballerup C—*not* Cx). Bus 1 from Town Hall or Central Station to P. G. Ramms Allé; then walk two blocks.

This helpful couple offers a memorable stay in their modern home. The rooms have blond-wood furniture and lots of closet space. Room 12 features a private bath and a small anteroom with a hotplate for boiling water, but Room 11 is equally inviting, with a TV and a full bath downstairs. The bath has a tub and shower, and the pipe-and-cork stairway and framed puzzles in the rooms are particularly unusual. Guests are welcome to borrow from the home's small English-language library. If you call ahead, they may pick you up at the S-tog stop. The Hannibals—she's an artist, he's a retired public school math teacher—are smokers, so smokers will feel particularly at home. They've welcomed visitors here for the past 20 years.

Nils and Annette Haugbølle

Hoffmeyersvej 33, 2000 Frederiksberg. ☎ **31-74-87-87.** 4 rms, none with bath. TV. 240–250 Kr ($40–$41.65) single or double. No credit cards. S-tog: Line C from

Central Station to Peter Bangsvej (fifth stop); then walk three blocks and look for the house (it'll be on the left) with the white fence in front.

The rooms in this modern two-story home are attractive (particularly the new one under the roof)—one has a balcony; each has its own lock. The owners, a doctor and a nutritionist, live downstairs with their three children, away from the second-floor rented rooms. Check out their handy homemade reference file for tourists, complete with maps and brochures. The wood-and-tile bath has a tub and shower. Complimentary tea or coffee is available, and two bakeries and a self-service laundry are nearby.

Ms. Hanne Løye

Ceresvej 1, 1863 Frederiksberg C. ☎ **31-24-30-27.** 3 rms, none with bath. 300 Kr ($50) double. Additional bed 150 Kr ($25) extra. No credit cards. Bus 1 from Central Station to the Frederiksberg City Hall (seventh stop; look for the brick tower with a clock and copper roof); then walk four short blocks.

Old-fashioned furnishings fill the rooms on the second floor of this yellow house with a brown-tile roof, surrounded by a picket fence. The rooms (request the one with the antique mirror at the top of the stairs) are supplied with plates, cups, silverware, and glasses. Ms. Løye does not offer breakfast but does supply hot water for making coffee or tea. You'll find many stores nearby, including restaurants, bakeries, and a supermarket. You can luxuriate in the large bath and read one of the books in English that are scattered about. Two self-service laundries and a dry cleaner are within walking distance. Call ahead.

❍ Ms. Betty Wulff

Jyllandsvej 24, 2000 Frederiksberg. ☎ **31-86-29-84.** 3 rms, none with bath. TV. 240 Kr ($40) double. No credit cards. Bus 1 from Central Station (toward Frederiksberg) to P. G. Ramms Allé.

The wood ceilings and walls make the rooms particularly cozy. The beds are fitted with Swedish health mattresses, and two of the rooms are linked, making them ideal for families. Betty, a scientist with the World Health Organization who has worked at the Scripps Institute in La Jolla, California, serves free coffee and tea throughout the day. You can buy pastries on the corner and munch on them in the front yard; a good Danish restaurant is nearby. You're welcome to store cold food.

If the house is full, ask about a room in her house (built in 1912, now renovated) off Vesterbrogade, near Frederiksberg Park at Jacobys Allé 23 (☎ **31-86-29-84**); the six double rooms have TV (some have a private balcony), and guests may make breakfast in the kitchen and use the garden; prices range from 200 to 300 Kr ($33.35 to $50) double.

HOTEL DOUBLES FOR LESS THAN 320 KR ($53.35)

❍ Hotel KFUM Soldaterhjem

Gothersgade 115, København K. ☎ **33-15-40-44.** Fax 33-15-44-74. 10 rms, none with bath. 195 Kr ($32.50) single; 310 Kr ($51.66) double. No credit cards. S-tog: Nørreport; then walk one block to Gothersgade, turn right, and it's a couple of doors down.

Although originally intended for soldiers, KFUM Soldaterhjem has been taken over by businesspeople and budget travelers searching for the best value in town. The rooms (eight singles and two doubles) are devoid of decoration but are spotless; they provide soap and towels. The second-floor reception doubles as a do-it-yourself piano/TV lounge and snack bar (serving short-order meals for less than $4).

The rooms are all on the fifth floor, a hearty climb. Rosenborg Palace is across from the hotel, and the clean-cut young men of the Royal Guard hang out in the lounge. Reception hours are 8:30am to 11pm Monday through Friday and 3 to 11pm Saturday, Sunday, and holidays; enter the door marked KFUM SOLDATERHJEM. The hotel and café are run by a friendly, competent husband-and-wife team, Preben Nielsen and Grethe Thomasen. This is the only YMCA hotel in Copenhagen; families are welcome.

HOTEL DOUBLES FOR LESS THAN 500 KR ($83.35)
NEAR CENTRAL STATION

The hotels near Central Station are reasonably priced by Copenhagen standards; offer clean, comfortable lodging with breakfast; and are well situated within walking distance of the city's major attractions, including Tivoli, Strøget, and palaces and museums, as well as the Tourist Office. The area attracts some transients, but don't let that put you off. (*Note:* For less than 500 Kr, don't expect a private bath.)

✪ Saga Hotel

Colbjørnsensgade 18–20 (a block from Central Station), 1625 København V. ☎ **31-24-49-44.** Fax 31-24-60-33. 78 rms, 20 with bath. TEL. 250–380 Kr ($41.65–$63.35) single without bath, 400–580 Kr ($66.65–$96.65) single with bath; 350–550 Kr ($58.35–91.65) double without bath, 550–800 Kr ($91.65–$133.35) double with bath; 140–185 Kr ($23.35–$30.83) per person triple or quad. Rates include breakfast. ACCESS, AE, DC, EURO, MC, V.

This perennial standby has long welcomed Frommer's readers with comfortable rooms (7 singles, 53 doubles, 9 triples, 9 quads), a good breakfast, and a 5% discount. Most rooms (with or without bath) have cable TV. The owners/managers, Susanne and Søren Kaas (sister and brother) and Boye Birk, are young and extremely knowledgeable about Copenhagen and ways to save money here, and they're as accommodating as can be. The hotel, decorated in soft colors, has a pleasant breakfast/dining room where it serves a filling potluck supper, complete with Danish meatballs, on Tuesday for 50 Kr ($8.35); it also has a café and bar and sells souvenirs as well as amber and silver jewelry from Poland. The Saga attracts a congenial clientele of all ages and nationalities.

IN VESTERBRO

✪ Hotel Sct. Thomas

Frederiksberg Allé 7 (a 15-minute walk from Central Station), 1621 København V. ☎ **31-21-64-64.** Fax 33-25-64-60. 32 rms, most with shower only. Summer, 350 Kr ($58.35) single; 450 Kr ($75) double. Winter, 199 Kr ($33.15) single; 350 Kr ($85.35) double. Rates include breakfast. DC, EURO, MC, V. Bus 1, 6, 14, 27, or 28 from Central Station (just two or three stops); then a one-block walk.

This pretty four-story building (the oldest on this street) is adorned with faux classical columns and set back slightly from the street. All the rooms were renovated in 1992, but the place retains its old-fashioned charm. Each room is unique; the doubles are spacious (no. 12 especially so), while the singles are small but adequate; many look onto plant-filled courtyards. Most rooms have a private shower, but toilets are in the hallway (five downstairs, three upstairs). This hotel has a home-away-from-home feel. In the cozy sitting room, guests may avail themselves of a TV, maps, brochures, and free coffee and tea. There's a pleasant restaurant next door and a number of reasonably priced ethnic eateries nearby; a laundry and grocery store are three short blocks away. The hotel is one block from Vesterbrogade.

In Frederiksberg

Hotel Cab-Inn

Danasvej 32, Copenhagen, 1910 Frederiksberg C. ☎ **31-21-04-00.** Fax 31-21-74-09. 86 rms, all with bath. A/C TV TEL. 395 Kr ($65.85) single; 480 Kr ($80) double; 565 Kr ($94.15) triple; 650 Kr ($108.35) family room for four. Breakfast 40 Kr ($6.65) extra. ACCESS, AE, DC, EURO, MC, V. Parking 30 Kr ($5). S-tog: Vesterport; then a five-minute walk. Bus 29 to the second stop past the bridge; then walk back half a block.

Small and tidy, the Cab-Inn has tiny high-tech rooms, accessible by magnetic cards, that are reminiscent of cabins on trains or ships, with everything built in. The toilet/shower combo is extremely compact. If claustrophobia isn't a problem, you can save money by staying here, where the motto is "Sleep cheap in luxury." The hotel has a lobby café open 24 hours for guests and a service counter selling toiletries and snacks and renting videos. Complimentary coffee- and tea-making facilities are in the rooms. Rooms for disabled travelers are available, and a solarium is on the premises. If the hotel is full, it has a sister property nearby. Town Hall Square is a 15-minute walk away.

HOTEL DOUBLES FOR LESS THAN 600 KR ($100)
By Nørreport

✪ Ibsens Hotel

Vendersgade 23, 1363 København K. ☎ **33-13-19-13.** Fax 33-13-19-16. 49 rms, some with shower only, 3 with shower and toilet. TV TEL. 420 Kr ($70) single without bath; 550 Kr ($91.65) double without bath, 700 Kr ($116.65) double with shower only, 800 Kr ($133.35) double with shower and toilet. Rates include breakfast. Lower prices available in winter. ACCESS, AE, DC, EURO, MC, V. S-tog: Nørreport.

Managed by Sine Manniche and her two nieces, Ibsens provides old-fashioned ambience (the renovated building dates from 1906), a good location, and a candy jar at the reception desk for guests. Huge antique wooden dressers and decorative cabinets fill the rooms and hallways. Wallpaper is everywhere, even in the toilets. All the guest rooms have TV, hairdryer, and trouser press, and a few have a canopy bed (including cozy single no. 221). Honeymooners like Room 217. Breakfast— an all-you-can-eat affair—is served in an eclectically decorated dining room, a charming place to start the day. The reception area is on the second floor, and there's no elevator (rooms are spread over three floors, and those on the second are most convenient). Pretty Ørsteds Park and the Botanical Garden are nearby, and Strøget is a 10-minute walk away. A laundry is a block and a half away.

Near Central Station

✪ Nebo Missionshotellet

Istedgade 6, 1650 København V. ☎ **31-21-12-17.** Fax 31-23-47-74. 97 rms, half with bath (shower only). TEL. 310–380 Kr ($51.65–$63.35) single without bath, 490–580 Kr ($81.65–$96.65) single with bath; 405–590 Kr ($67.50–$98.35) double without bath, 670–810 Kr ($111.65–$135) double with bath. The higher rates apply in summer. Rates include breakfast. Additional bed 130 Kr ($21.65) extra. ACCESS, AE, DC, EURO, MC, V. Parking 30 Kr ($5) daily.

The Nebo offers comfortable budget rooms (43 singles and 54 doubles) with sinks and phones. This is tops of the three hotels in the area owned by the Church of Denmark, and is capably run by a friendly staff. A few rooms are with-out TVs, but guests are free to use the one in the pretty lobby lounge. If you get a courtyard room, you can enjoy the relaxing sounds of the gurgling fountain outside. Breakfast is a traditional all-you-can-eat buffet served in a pretty room adjacent to a garden, where you can eat outside in summer. The Nebo is half a block from Central Station. Try to stay in late June or July, when rates are lowest.

SUPER-BUDGET CHOICES
HOSTELS

Copenhagen has three International Youth Hostel Federation (IYHF) hostels, open to visitors of all ages. Unfortunately, they're not particularly well located, but good transportation links and good rates counter this disadvantage. Rates differ slightly from one hostel to the next, and preferential prices are given to IYHF cardholders. Sleeping bags are not permitted on the hostels' beds; you must supply your own sheet or rent one from the reception for about 25 Kr ($4.15). IYHF cards can be purchased at any hostel for about 112 Kr ($18.65). In summer, reserve a bed in advance or you may have to go as far as Roskilde (a half-hour train ride away) to find a hostel that can accommodate you. Throughout Denmark, a three-day-maximum stay is usually imposed in summer.

Bellahøj Hostel

Herbergvejen 8, 2700 København. ☎ **31-28-97-15.** 295 beds. 65 Kr ($10.85) per person with the IYHF card, 87 Kr ($14.50) without the IYHF card. Breakfast 35 Kr ($5.85) extra; dinner 65 Kr ($10.85) extra. No credit cards. Closed Jan 2–Feb 2. Bus 2 from Town Hall Square (about 20–30 minutes); then walk to the corner, turn right, and follow Fuglesangs Allé to the hostel.

In a residential area northwest of the city center and across from a park, the Bellahøj has a large, pleasant lobby lounge, laundry facilities, a TV room, a table-tennis room, a vending machine, four showers for men and women on each floor, and lockers (no kitchen). The hostel is open 24 hours but rooms are off-limits from 10am to noon. The 30 rooms (a little on the dingy side) contain 4, 6, or 13 beds each. Families pay 5 Kr (85¢) per person extra to have their own room.

Copenhagen Hostel

Vejlands Allé 200, 2300 København S. ☎ **32-52-29-08.** Fax 32-52-27-08. 529 beds. 65 Kr ($10.85) per person with the IYHF card, 87 Kr ($14.50) without the IYHF card. Breakfast 35 Kr ($5.85) extra; dinner 55 Kr ($9.15) extra. No credit cards. Closed Dec 20–Jan 2. Bus 46 from Central Station (6am–6pm only); other times, 16 or 250S to Mozarts Plads and change to no. 37 or 38.

Copenhagen Hostel has no curfew, but its location, in the middle of a park 2¹/₂ miles south of the city center, can make getting home after midnight tedious. In addition to 60 double and 80 five-bed rooms, there are laundry and cooking facilities, a TV room, kiosk, and table-tennis tables. Check-in is from 1pm to late evening; try to book in advance.

Lyngby Hostel

Radvad 1, 2800 Lyngby. ☎ **42-80-30-74.** 94 beds. 70 Kr ($11.70) per person with the IYHF card, 95 Kr ($15.85) without the IYHF card. Family rooms, 170–420 Kr ($28.35–$70) for a double up to rooms for six. Breakfast 40 Kr ($6.65) extra; dinner 55 Kr ($9.15) extra. No credit cards. Closed Dec 23–Jan 2. S-tog: Lyngby; then change to bus no. 182 or 183 toward Hjortekær.

The smallest of Copenhagen's hostels has fewer than 100 beds. Advance reservations are necessary from September through mid-May. Check-in is between 8am and noon and 4 to 9pm.

OTHER YOUTH CHOICES

Copenhagen has two "unofficial" youth hostels that are good picks for young Eurailers and hearty others (ask about any new possibilities at the Use-It office; see above).

Copenhagen Sleep-In

Per Henrik Lings Allé 6, 2100 København Ø. ☎ **35-26-50-59.** 452 beds. 90 Kr ($15) per person. Rates include breakfast. Closed Sept–June. S-tog: Nørdhavn. No credit cards. Bus 1, 6, or 14 to Idrætsparken.

Established by the government to alleviate tight tourist housing in July and August, the Copenhagen Sleep-in offers one of the cheapest places to sleep in the city. The four-bed rooms are open only in summer and close during the day from noon to 4pm. The location, in Fælled Park, is not as inconvenient as the IYHF hostels, and the price includes breakfast, hot showers, and a guarded luggage-storage room. There are no kitchen facilities, and sleeping bags are required. No curfew.

Vesterbro Ungdomsgaard (City Public Hostel)

Absalonsgade 8, 1658 København V. ☎ **31-31-20-70.** 200 beds. 110 Kr ($18.35) per person with breakfast, 95 Kr ($15.85) without breakfast. Rates include showers and use of lockers. Closed late Aug to early May. From Central Station, walk six blocks along Vesterbrogade to Absalonsgade or take bus no. 6, 16, 27, or 28.

Of Copenhagen's super-budget choices, this private hostel boasts the best location, within walking distance of Central Station. But this also makes it the most expensive of the lot. There are 4 to 10 beds in most rooms, plus a 60-bed dorm. It's open only from early May to late August.

CAMPING

As always, camping is the cheapest accommodations option, though in Copenhagen it's practical only during summer. Sites charge about 40 to 50 Kr ($6.65 to $8.35) per night. You'll also need a camping pass, which is issued by any camp manager, is good for a year, and costs about 25 Kr ($4.20) per person or 50 Kr ($8.35) per family. A full list of legal camping spots is available from the tourist board. **Bellahøj Camping,** Hvidkildevej, 2400 København NV (☎ **31-10-11-50**), about 3 miles from the city center, is the closest and cheapest campground. It's open June through August, 24 hours a day. Take bus no. 2 from Town Hall Square to the "Camping" stop. (And it's nice to know that the Bellahøj Hostel is nearby, in case of serious rain or a sudden cold snap.) Tent camping only is available by the beach at **Strandmølle Camping,** Strandmøllevej 2, 2941 Skodsborg (☎ **42-80-38-83**), where there is tennis, fishing, and a playground.

FARM & COUNTRY HOLIDAYS

You can set up a farm or country holiday in Denmark, in which you either stay with a family and share breakfast only or breakfast and supper with them, or rent a separate cottage on their property and do your own cooking. Rates are quite reasonable, but require a three-night stay; they start at 175 Kr ($29.15) per adult for a room with breakfast included (half price for children 4 to 11 and 25% for younger children); a house for four to six people for a week starts at 2,100 Kr ($350) in summer. For more information, contact the Danish Tourist Board.

LONG-TERM STAYS

If you plan on staying in Copenhagen for some time, visit the Use-It office in Huset (see "Visitor Information" under "Copenhagen Specifics," earlier in this chapter). They can help you with low-cost accommodations in a private apartment or shared student housing.

WORTH THE EXTRA MONEY

Selandia Hotel

Helgolandsgade 12 (two blocks from Central Station), 1653 København V. ☎ and fax **31-31-46-10**. 84 rms, 57 with bath. TV TEL. 390 Kr ($65) single without bath, 600–850 Kr ($100–$141.70) single with bath; 540 Kr ($90) double without bath, 850–1,050 Kr ($141.70–$175) double with bath. Rates include breakfast. Additional bed 200 Kr ($33.35) extra; children 4–12 half price. AE, DC, EURO, MC, V.

This inviting small hotel has a pleasant breakfast room and cheerful yellow hallways with colorful prints. All the rooms are comfortable and have new windows, cable TV, and a pants press. They're decorated in restful, muted colors—sand, salmon, and mint green. All the rooms have sinks, and for those without private bath, the facilities are nearby and quite clean. There are three family rooms on each floor. The larger Absalon Hotel, across the street, is under the same ownership but caters more to business travelers and groups.

BEST WESTERN HOTELS

The following hotels, both outstanding Best Western properties, would far exceed budget prices, except for discounts available with Best Western hotel checks, which must be purchased in the United States.

City Hotel

Peder Skrams Gade 24, 1054 København K. ☎ **33-13-06-66**. Fax 33-13-06-67. 81 rms. TV TEL. 870 Kr ($145) single; 970–1,170 Kr ($161.65–$195) double; about 350 Kr ($58.35) per person with Best Western hotel checks. Rates include breakfast. AE, DC, EURO, MC, V. Bus 28 or 41 from Central Station; or 9 from the airport.

Modern, comfortable, and quiet, this hotel is conveniently a short walk from Strøget, Nyhavn, and the Royal Theatre. The hotel, renovated in 1994, has Danish architecture in the lobby, and many of the rooms feature chairs created by Hans Wegner, who once designed a chair for John F. Kennedy. The rooms have one to five beds, and all have a trouser press and hairdryer. Many of the single rooms are surprisingly spacious. The hotel's sleek stainless-steel bar serves soup, sandwiches, and coffee day and night. A laundry is a block away, and a post office a block and a half away.

✪ Hotel Esplanaden

Bredgade 78 (at Toldbodgade), 1260 København K. ☎ **33-91-32-00**. Fax 33-91-32-29. 116 rms. MINIBAR TV TEL. 655–795 Kr ($109.15–$132.50) single; 865–940 Kr ($144.15–$156.65) double; about 350 Kr ($58.35) per person with Best Western hotel checks. Rates include breakfast. Lower prices on weekends. AE, DC, EURO, MC, V. S-tog: Østerport. Bus 1, 6, 9, or 29 (all stop across the street from the hotel).

Built in 1883 and totally renovated in 1993, the Esplanaden has a pretty entrance and lobby, plus a good location, across from the Citadel (perfect for strolling or jogging). It takes the comfort of its guests seriously, providing umbrellas, hairdryers, and irons as needed; a pay phone at a table in the lobby so guests can avoid the room charge; and free coffee and tea in the dining room at all hours. The rooms are comfortable, the staff is pleasant and helpful, and the breakfast is impressive, with plenty of fresh breads and fruits, cheese, cold cuts, pastries, boiled eggs, and more. The hotel is a short walk from *The Little Mermaid*, the Gefion Fountain, the Fight for Freedom Museum, and Amalienborg Palace. It's a 10-minute walk from Kongens Nytorv, the Royal Theatre, and plenty of nightlife and shopping. A typical Danish restaurant, Cafe Pedersborg, is right next door.

5 Dining

By all means, sample Danish fare whenever possible. The country is famous for its open-face sandwiches, called *smørrebrod*. It literally means "bread and butter," though in reality it's bread complemented with dozens of toppings—from a single slice of cheese to mounds of sweet shrimp. You can let all the stops out and indulge in a typical Danish buffet, which begins with fish, then moves on to meat, cheese, fruit, and dessert; a new plate is provided for each course.

For a hot meal, a good choice for dinner and often offered as a special, consider *frikadeller* (small fried cakes of minced pork, onions, egg, and spices), served with generous portions of potato salad and pickled vegetables. Another popular, filling dish, *biksemad* consists of meat, potatoes, and onions. *Mørbrad*, or braised pork loin, is served with a cream sauce. *Grov birkes* are tasty nonsweet breakfast rolls, and Danish pastries, whichever ones you select, are rich and wonderful ("Napoleon's Hat," for one, is delicious).

No matter what you eat, however, you may wish to follow the Danish custom of drinking a cold Carlsberg or Tuborg beer and an even colder shot of *akvavit*— a 76- to 90-proof potato-based schnapps (the trade name is Aalborg, after the city in Jutland where it's distilled). If coffee's your drink, you'll have to resign yourself to expecting no free coffee refills—that's not the custom here.

Remember that tax and tip are included in the price on the menu, and you're not expected to add anything extra.

A LOCAL BUDGET BEST

Smørrebrod can be found almost everywhere. It takes two or three servings to make a meal, and they're eaten with a knife and fork. Most of the places that sell them are open only during the day, so plan accordingly. Here's a favorite:

Kanal Caféen

Fredriksholms Kanal 18 (a two-minute walk from Christiansborg Palace). ☎ **33-11-57-70.** Reservations recommended at lunch. 30–64 Kr ($5–$10.65). DC, EURO, V. Mon–Fri 11am–4pm and 4pm–7pm (for drinks only). DANISH.

Romantic, old, and authentic, this is the place to come for smørrebrod. It's always crowded with lots of locals, and the atmosphere is friendly, cozy, and Danish. Even if you have to wait for a table, it's worth it. The waiter will hand you a list of more than 30 choices—everything from herring to roast beef to ham with fried egg— and you mark off what you want. What you get is substantial, particularly for smørrebrod. An accompaniment of a large Carlsberg or some cold Aalborg Jubileum schnapps makes a meal here even more memorable. On a canal behind the Parliament Building, the restaurant is in a historic building from the mid-1800s.

Getting the Best Deal on Dining

- Look for small, inconspicuous places off the beaten path.
- *Dagens ret,* the daily special, is a filling meal offered for lunch and/or dinner at a discount price.
- Try the eateries in and around Central Station and the nearby Scala Center, both on Vesterbrogade near Tivoli.
- Also try the restaurants around Grabrodretorv, two blocks north of the middle of Strøget.
- Take advantage of smörgåsbords and other all-you-can-eat restaurants. Although they're not particularly cheap, they offer terrific values.

MEALS FOR LESS THAN 50 KR ($8.35)

Bananrepublikken

Nørrebrogade 13. ☎ **35-36-08-30.** Menu items 24–42 Kr ($6–$7). No credit cards. Sun–Wed 11am–2am, Thurs 11am–4am, Fri–Sat 11am–5am (lunch served 11am–4pm; dinner, 6–10pm). S-tog: Norrebrogade. LIGHT FARE.

Not to be confused with the trendy safari-clothing store, this is a laid-back café with a menu heavy on sandwiches, but you can also get nachos, burgers, and omelets. Live bands perform international music here, usually Thursday through Saturday—the cover runs about 40 Kr ($6.65)—followed by a DJ and disco music late into the night.

Feinsmækker

Larsbjørnsstræde 7. ☎ **33-32-11-32.** 24–34 Kr ($4–$5.70). No credit cards. Mon–Fri 10:30am–5:30pm, Sat 11am–2:30pm. LIGHT FARE/SNACKS.

Cheese, hummus, roast beef, turkey, chicken, ham, salmon, and tuna are the popular smørrebrod fillings at this cozy café with only half a dozen tables. All sandwiches are jumbo-sized and served on French bread. There's also fresh-squeezed orange, apple, and carrot juice; carrot cake (in winter); and all kinds of salads. The eatery is two short blocks north of Frederiksberggade, near the Town Hall side of Strøget and just around the corner from American Express, on Niels Hemmingens Gade.

Govindas

Nørre Farimagsgade 82 (at Gothersgade). ☎ **33-33-74-44.** Buffet 40 Kr ($7.65). No credit cards. Mon–Sat noon–8pm. VEGETARIAN.

This small, slightly out of the way place is popular with vegetarians and others for its food, the all-you-can-eat aspect of it, and the price. It's near the Botanical Garden.

⊛ KFUM Soldaterhjem Cafe

Gothersgade 115 (2nd floor). ☎ **33-15-40-44.** 15–42 Kr ($2.50–$7). No credit cards. Mon–Fri 10am–9:30pm for hot food (snacks until 11pm), Sat–Sun 3–11pm. FAST FOOD/ DANISH.

A real find for low prices and pleasant, if sometimes noisy, surroundings. You can order burgers, chicken, fish, lasagne, pizza, salads, and even Danish hot meals. The dining room is pleasant, casual, and Danish in style. The portions are ample, and the crowd is mostly well-scrubbed young men of the Royal Guard.

Klaptræet

Kultorvet 11. ☎ **33-13-31-48.** 28–44 Kr ($4.70–$7.35). No credit cards. Mon–Thurs 9am–2am, Fri–Sat 9am–5am, Sun 10am–midnight. LIGHT FARE.

One of several inviting eateries at Kultorvet, this bohemian café serves cheap breakfasts, lunches, and light meals to students, travelers, and assorted others. Chili con carne, salads, soups, and sandwiches are among the offerings. Old posters and newspapers double as wallpaper. Order and pay at the bar; they'll bring your food. Kultorvet is a traffic-free pedestrian square, two blocks southeast of Nørreport Station.

Sabines Cafeteria

Teglegaardsstræde 4. ☎ **33-14-09-44.** 30–45 Kr ($5–$7.50). No credit cards. Mon–Sat 8am–2am, Sun 2pm–2am. LIGHT FARE/SNACKS.

This small, undecorated place is not a cafeteria (though it used to be, when Sabine ran it) but a licensed local café with a mixed crowd that has included Mick Jagger. The morning buffet breakfast special features toast, honey, cheese, hard- or soft-boiled egg, yogurt, coffee, and juice or milk, and sells for just 35 Kr ($5.85). Daily specials include smoked salmon, paprika chicken, smoked ham, and more. Copenhageners like to drop in here after a movie; that's a good time for coffee and brandy, which runs 25 Kr ($4.15). Teglegaardsstræde runs perpendicular to Nørre Voldgade, just south of Ørsteds Park.

FAST FOOD

Scala Center

Axeltorv 2. ☎ **33-15-12-15.** 15–52 Kr ($2.50–$8.70). No credit cards. Daily 9am–5am. INTERNATIONAL.

Across from the main entrance to Tivoli, with an entrance on Vesterbrogade, this sparkling center of activity houses a good variety of fast-food stands adjacent to more expensive cafés and international restaurants. Pizza, pasta, smørrebrod, chicken, quiche, hamburgers, and other favorites are all available at moderate prices. Communal tables mean that you can satisfy everyone and still eat together. Scala's ground level features bargain eateries, tops among them Streckess, Th. Sorensen for smørrebrod, and a popular *gelato* counter, Bravissimo. Its third floor is home to more expensive sit-down places. While here you can shop, catch a movie, play pool, or glide up and down in the glass-bubble elevator and take in the scene. The sculpture in front of Scala, by Mogens Møller, symbolizes the sun and the nine planets of the solar system, placed (in small scale) at their equivalent actual distance from the sun.

MEALS FOR LESS THAN 70 KR ($11.65)

⑤ Baron Bolton's Restaurant

St. Kongensgade 17 (near Kongens Nytorv). ☎ **33-11-18-31.** Main courses 39–98 Kr ($6.50–$16.35); children's menu, 25 Kr ($4.15). ACCESS, AE, DC, EURO, MC, V. Summer, daily noon–midnight; rest of the year, Sun–Thurs 5pm–midnight, Sat noon–midnight. INTERNATIONAL.

If you're extra-hungry and enjoy meat dishes, head to Baron Bolton's, tucked in a quiet corner of Baron Bolton's Court. The specialty here is spareribs, served in hefty portions. The menu also features burgers, barbecued chicken, grilled prawns or salmon, and a variety of steaks, all served with a baked potato with herb butter or wedges of french fries, an impressive salad (ask for dressing on the side), and delicious hot rolls. If you've got a big appetite, start with soup of the day or an appetizer such as pickled salmon, chicken wings, or shrimp cocktail, and top it all off with a banana split or fruit pie. It's fairly smoke-free, especially on the lower level, which has high ceilings and good ventilation. The restaurant's patio café is open in summer.

Cafe Wilder

Wildersgade 56 and Sankt Anne Gade (on Christianshavn). ☎ **31-54-71-83.** 19–96 Kr ($3.20–$16). No credit cards. Mon–Fri 9am–2am, Sat–Sun 10am–2am; hot dishes served 6–10pm only. Bus 8. FRENCH/DANISH.

This corner café offers everything from soup and sandwiches to cheese plates to cold salads including chicken pesto. It attracts all ages, many of whom arrive by bike, as well as young parents with a baby carriage in tow. The daily fare is displayed in the counter. It's across from the equally good Cafe Luna (below).

✪ Københavnercaféen (Copenhagen Cafe)

Badstuestræde 10. ☎ **33-32-80-81.** Daily special 65 Kr ($10.85) with five items, 98 Kr ($16.35) with seven items; main courses 52–119 Kr ($8.70–$19.85). AE, DC, EURO, MC, V. Daily 11am–midnight (kitchen open 11:30am–10pm). DANISH.

This café is only half a block from Strøget, yet seemingly miles from the hustle and modernity outside. The menu comes with an English translation, and you won't leave hungry. The daily special features herring, fried filet of fish, roast pork, and bread; the deluxe version adds roast beef, Danish meatballs, chicken, salad, and cheese. Lunch is served until the kitchen closes; dinner, from 5pm. The small place fills up with customers and easy conversation, and it can get smokey. There's free piano music on Sunday in winter; otherwise, guests are free to play whenever the mood strikes.

Restaurant Sporvejen

Grabrødre Torv 17. ☎ **33-13-31-01.** 29–69 Kr ($4.85–$11.50); coffee 12 Kr ($2), and refills 6 Kr ($1). No credit cards. Daily 11am–midnight. AMERICAN.

In an authentic old tram car inside a building, complete with poles and straps, Sporvejen's "tin-can" interior is reminiscent of an American diner. The chef, cooking on a small grill near the front door, dishes your dinner right onto the plate in front of you. Specialties include hamburgers and omelets. It's licensed. Check out the photos of the old streetcars, last seen in Copenhagen in 1972.

✆ Riz Raz

Kompagnistræde 20 (at Knabrostræde). ☎ **33-15-05-75.** Buffet 39 Kr ($6.50) at lunch, 59 Kr ($9.85) at dinner, both half price for children 11 and under; main courses (including buffet) 35–75 Kr ($5.85–$12.50) at lunch, 69–149 Kr ($7.65–$24.85) at dinner. ACCESS, DC, EURO, MC, V. Daily 11:30am–midnight (lunch to 5pm, dinner to midnight; kitchen closes an hour earlier). MEDITERRANEAN.

This narrow, well-lit space has low beamed ceilings, one dining niche opening onto the next, and posters and the work of local artists on the walls. The big draw at lunch and dinner is the reasonably priced buffet. Serve yourself from heavily laden counters, starting with the cold dishes, such as broccoli, black-eyed peas, beets, baby carrots, string beans, cauliflower, cole slaw, red cabbage, rice, couscous, and eggplant in yogurt. Then move on to hot dishes, among them kafta, fava beans, zucchini in tomato sauce, spinach, potatoes, and carrots. Though there's a heavy Mediterranean influence (Greek, Egyptian, and Moroccan dishes are featured prominently), you can always get pasta, and you can request your food spicier, if you prefer it that way. You won't find a more comfortable or welcoming place in all Copenhagen. The service staff is made up of students, most of whom speak several languages. It's fully licensed.

MEALS FOR LESS THAN 100 KR ($16.65)

Axelborg Bodega

Axeltorv 1. ☎ **33-11-06-38.** 35–110 Kr ($5.85–$18.35). AE, DC, EURO, MC, V. Mon–Sat 11am–2am, Sun noon–1am (lunch special served 11am–5pm; the kitchen closes at 9:30pm). DANISH.

Considering that the Circus is across the street, it seems appropriate that this place is loud and boisterous. The tavern's clientele cheer and joke with one another while downing beers the whole time. The Danes use the word *bodega* to refer to a local bar. The menu at this one features open-face sandwiches, tenderloin steak, country ham, cheeses, and omelets for lunch. Beef steak with onions, weinerschnitzel with sautéed potatoes, roast pork rib with red cabbage, and tenderloin with onions, and fried filet of plaice are offered for dinner. You'll spend about $14 if you order with care. Fully licensed.

Bistro

In Central Station. ☎ **33-14-12-32.** Salad and pasta buffet 39 Kr ($6.50) at lunch, 58 Kr ($9.70) at dinner; daily specials (served all day) 49–69 Kr ($8.20–$11.50); main courses (with complimentary salad buffet) 84–132 Kr ($14–$22), half price for kids 11 and under who get the same dish as their parents. ACCESS, AE, DC, EURO, MC, V. Daily 11:30am–10pm (serving until 9:30pm). To get to the Bistro, walk through another restaurant in Central Station, called Spisehjörnet. DANISH.

If you think an outstanding restaurant in a train station is an oxymoron, you're in for a pleasant surprise. At the elegant, airy Bistro, with its columns, arched ceiling, and lights resembling hanging artichokes, choose from several buffets (the restaurant is best known for its cold buffet, priced above our budget but worth the splurge). You can also order à la carte. Menu offerings include farmer steak, pork chops, schnitzel, and fish dishes. On Sunday a special three-course family dinner costs 109 Kr ($18.16) per person.

✪ Cafe Luna

Skt. Annægade 5, Christianhavn. ☎ **31-54-20-00.** Main courses 65–120 Kr ($10.85–$20); lunch 30–65 Kr ($5–$10.85). EURO, MC, V. Daily 9am–10pm. Bus 8. CONTINENTAL/DANISH.

The Cafe Luna excels in tasty food, ample portions, and something travelers rarely get enough of—vegetables. Start with tomato soup or an appetizer of warm goat cheese with olives, and move on to a main course of chopped steak, turkey, fish, or something more exotic like roast veal liver and ox sirloin. The sliced turkey breast in wine sauce that I was served at dinner came with whole-grain bread, broccoli, cauliflower, green beans, cherry tomatoes, red-leaf lettuce, and a side dish of potatoes. Lunch offerings include sandwiches, cold pasta salad, and several salads, including Greek; you can get a three-item smørrebrod for 30 Kr ($5) or three kinds of herring for 42 Kr ($7). There's a daily fish dish. The congenial café, a short bus ride or 20-minute walk from Town Hall Square, has half a dozen tables and a funky frieze that adds spice to the decor.

Cafe Petersborg

Bredgade 76. ☎ **33-12-50-16.** Open-face sandwiches 28–55 Kr ($4.70–$9.20); hot meals at lunch and dinner 55–150 Kr ($9.15–$25). ACCESS, DC, EURO, MC, V. Mon–Fri noon–3pm and 5–8:30pm, Sat–Sun 5–8:30pm. DANISH.

This congenial place (licensed) off the beaten track has good home-cooking, a lively local crowd, and an inviting decor—dark paneling and furniture, exposed beams, three dining areas, and tables trimmed with candles and flowers. Come before or after a visit to the nearby *Little Mermaid.* The English menu lists choices like herring, smoked eel or salmon, ham or mushroom omelet, warm filet of plaice with remoulade, or frikadella (Danish meatballs) with white potatoes and red cabbage.

Pasta Basta

Valkendorfsgade 22 (near Strøget, behind the Holy Ghost Church). ☎ **33-11-21-31.** 60–200 Kr ($10 $33.35); Pasta Basta table 69 Kr ($11.50). ACCESS, DC, EURO, MC, V. Sun–Wed 11:30am–3am, Thurs–Sat 11:30am–5am. INTERNATIONAL.

Except for its name, Pasta Basta has everything going for it: a tastefully decorated modern interior, large windows overlooking a romantic cobblestone street, and an all-you-can-eat buffet with good food. The Pasta Basta table can be ordered as an appetizer. Help yourself to the house wine automatically placed on each table. Measuring stripes down the side of the carafe mean that you pay for only as much as you drink. The new downstairs bar is inspired by whimsy and deserves a peek.

MEALS FOR LESS THAN 140 KR ($23.35)

Barcelona

Fælledvej 21. ☎ **31-35-76-11.** Tapas (appetizers) 45–60 Kr ($7.50–$10); main courses 85–125 Kr ($14.20–$20.85); three-course dinner 155 Kr ($25.85). No credit cards. Café, daily 11am–2am; restaurant, Sun–Thurs 5–10pm, Fri–Sat 5–11pm. Bus 3, 5, or 16. CONTINENTAL.

Affordable for budget travelers at lunch, when its lively tapas bar hops, colorful Barcelona, with its board floors and mixed crowd, is a sophisticated café in the increasingly popular Nørrebro part of town. The dinner menu changes monthly, but beef and fish dishes are always available. A band often performs in the back.

✪ L'Education Nationale

Larsbjørnsstræde 12. ☎ **33-91-53-60.** Reservations recommended for lun (near the Town Hall side of Strøget, a couple of blocks north of Frederiksberggadech, required for dinner. Main courses 90–140 Kr ($15–$23.35). No credit cards. Mon–Sat 9am–3pm and 5:30–10pm, Sun 3pm–midnight. FRENCH.

Eating French in Denmark? Why not? It's a particularly good idea here, where the chef, staff, decor, and food are all French. The charcuterie comes from Lyon, and the pâtés and roulettes are made on the premises. The menu reflects every region of France and changes every few months. Expect generous servings and casual ambience. This is a small place, and it can get smoky. Check out the big French "breakfast" served from 9:30am to 5pm; it includes hearty sandwiches, sausage, and pâté. Reserve a table so you're not disappointed.

Nyhavns Færgekro

Nyhavn 5. ☎ **33-15-15-88.** Buffet (with 11 choices of herring) 68 Kr ($11.35); main dinner courses 135 Kr ($22.50); open-face sandwiches 22–53 Kr ($3.60–$8.85); desserts 37 Kr ($6.20). ACCESS, DC, EURO, MC, V. Daily 11:30am–4pm and 5–11:30pm. DANISH/FRENCH.

This place is unique in Copenhagen because it serves French champagne by the glass. Its desserts—like white-chocolate mousse, profiteroles, petit fours, and tart of the day—are decadent and delectable. Less-indulgent fare for the strong-willed includes 14 open-face sandwiches and traditional Danish meals at lunch (including a daily special), with French fare at dinner. The restaurant has a black-and-white marble floor, a spiral stairway from an old streetcar, and lights that serve as "call buttons" for the friendly servers.

TWO CAFES ON STRØGET

Cafe Europa

Amagertorv 1 (a 10-minute walk from Central Station). ☎ **33-14-28-29**. 13–35 Kr ($2.20–$5.85). No credit cards. Mon–Sat 9am–midnight, Sun 10am–midnight. LIGHT FARE.

Besides an ideal spot along Strøget, the Cafe Europa serves strong coffee and rich desserts, along with breakfast, a variety of sandwiches, beer, and wine to a crowd of all ages. The interior is pleasant—on one wall is a big map of Europe and on another are photographs of well-known European personalities (test your knowledge of them), plus some framed fragments of the Berlin Wall. For those with a penchant for reading while eating, copies of the *International Herald Tribune* and *The European* are readily available.

✪ Cafe Norden

Østergade 61. ☎ **31-11-77-91**. 13–35 Kr ($2.20–$5.85). No credit cards. Mon–Thurs 9am–10pm, Fri–Sat 9am–midnight, Sun 10am–10pm. LIGHT FARE.

On the other side of the Stork Fountain from the Cafe Europa and opposite the Georg Jensen and Royal Copenhagen stores, the Cafe Norden provides the sunniest spot for an afternoon coffee and cake—and the best café au lait. You can also get creamy cappuccino, sandwiches, croissants, pastries, brownies, beer, and wine. There's seating upstairs and the same menu. Order at the bar. The view up Strøget from here is fabulous.

FOR DESSERT

Just look at all the delicious bakeries around Copenhagen and you'll understand why Denmark's pastries are world famous. Don't ask for a danish, though—just point to the dessert that catches your fancy.

✪ Amagertorv Tea Room

On the second floor of the Royal Copenhagen Building, Amagertorv 6. ☎ **33-13-71-81**. 12–24 Kr ($2–$4). No credit cards. Mon–Fri 11am–5pm, Sat 10am–1:30pm (the first Sat of the month 10am–4pm); longer hours at Christmas. DESSERT.

This elegant long room with Venetian chandeliers, large mirrors, and windows punctuated by palms overlooks the rooftops of old Copenhagen. To sit here is to drift back a few centuries. The pastries—pies, cakes, eclairs, and almond confections—are beautifully displayed in the center of the room and served on Royal Copenhagen porcelain, of course. The tea room, which is licensed, provides the perfect setting for sipping wine, sherry, or brandy while listening to strains of "Fly Me to the Moon" or "Bewitched, Bothered, and Bewildered."

Conditori La Glace

Skoubogade 3–5 (at Strøget). ☎ **33-14-46-46**. Cakes 10–20 Kr ($1.70–$3.35); coffee or hot chocolate 25 Kr ($4.20). No credit cards. Mon–Fri 8am–5:30pm (last serving at 5pm), Sat 9am–5pm, Sun 11am–5pm. DESSERT.

Founded in 1870, this dignified café maintains the elegance of a bygone era. Order at the counter and take a seat; when your food is ready, it's brought to your table. Real dessert lovers should try "Sports Cake," the house specialty, whipped cream–topped caramel cream puffs that have been made every day since November 18, 1891. The café has smoking and no-smoking rooms. Skoubogade is a small street off Strøget.

PICNICKING

Pick up an assortment of cheeses, pâtés, and charcuterie at **J. Christian Andersen's,** a tantalizing shop off Strøget, at Købmagergade 32 (☎ **33-12-13-45**). It's open Monday through Thursday from 9am to 6pm, Friday from 9am to 7pm, and Saturday from 9am to 2pm (to 4pm in summer). Look for the Danish cheeses in the center of the store.

WORTH THE EXTRA MONEY

✪ **Els**

Store Strandstræde 3. ☎ **33-14-13-41.** Reservations recommended. Main course at lunch 128 Kr ($21.35); fixed-price lunch 152 Kr ($25.35) for two courses (a main course and your choice of appetizer or dessert), 176 Kr ($29.35) for three courses; fixed-price dinner 276 Kr ($46) for three courses, 346 Kr ($57.70) for four courses. AE, DC, EURO, MC, V. Daily noon–3pm and 5:30–10pm. NEW DANISH.

Visually and culinarily memorable, Els is also outstanding for its location (near Kongens Nytorv), atmosphere, and romance. The original decor dates from 1853, with six murals of women depicting the four seasons and the twin muses of dance and music. The fixed-price menu changes weekly, ensuring the freshest foods available. At dinner, expect to start with lime- and garlic-marinated mussels, duck-liver pàté, or caviar and follow with pheasant, tournedos of veal with morel sauce, or filet of sole. Be sure to try the homemade five-grain bread and the house apéritif, Pousse Rapière.

6 Attractions

SIGHTSEEING SUGGESTIONS

In addition to the shopping streets of Strøget and the wonderful walks of Tivoli, Copenhagen's main sights are the royal palaces, *The Little Mermaid*, a number of marvelous museums, and the well-known Carlsberg Brewery, which can be toured. Experience as many of them as you can.

Note, too, that Copenhagen has been named the Cultural Capital of Europe for 1996, and in honor of that, special events have been planned throughout the year at Tivoli, in museums, and elsewhere in the city.

If You Have 1 Day

Start your morning along Strøget, the world's longest pedestrian street; then explore Kongens Nytorv (King's New Square) and Nyhavn, the old sailors' quarter and one of the most charming parts of the city. After lunch (and Nyhavn is a terrific area for it), take an imperial tour of Christiansborg Palace, visiting the queen's reception rooms and the ancient palace foundations. Reserve the rest of the day and the evening for Tivoli, where you can enjoy everything from old-time carnival fun to concerts featuring the world's top performers in season.

Copenhagen

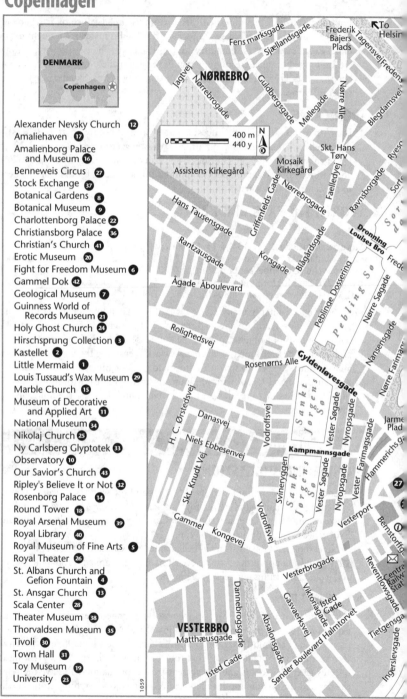

1059

To
Klampenborg
Hovedvej

Lille
Triangel

Carnisons
Kirkegård

Kristianiagade

Østbanegade

1

Ryesgade

Øster Søgade

Sortedam Dossering

Sortedams So

Østerport
Station

Folke Bernadottes Alle

Forbindelsesvej

Dag Hammerskjörds Alle Oslo Plads

Holmens
Kirkegård

Fredensbro

Øster Søgade

Øster Farimagsgade

Øster Farimagsgade

Stockholms Gade

Østre Anlæg

3

2

Grønningen

St. Kongensgade

4

6

Esplanaden

5

Sølvgade

Rigensgade

Suensonsgade

Gernersgade

Skt. Pauls Gade

Bredgade

11

**Botanisk
Have**

7

8

Øster Volgade

Sølvgade

Klerkegade

Fredericiagade

12

13

Gothersgade

9

Øster Farimagsgade

**Rosenborg
Have**

10

Adelgade

Borgergade

15

**Amalienborg
Plads**

Toldbodgade

14

**Kongens
Have**

Kronprinsessegade

St. Kongensgade

Bredgade

16

17

Nørre Voldgade

Frederiksborggade

Gothersgade

Skt. Annæ Plads

steds
ken

Pilestræde

18

Krystalgade

Købmagergade

Skt. Annæ Plads

Inderhavnen

Studiestræde

23

19

20

Østergade

21

Kongens
Nytorv

Nyhavn

22

24

Vestergade

Frederiksberggade

Amagertory

Læderstr.

Komp.

Str.

Højbro
Plads

25

26

Nyhavn

Peder
Skrams
Gade

Havnegade

Wilderskanal

Laksegade

Niels Juelsgade

Holbergsgade

CHRISTIANSHAVN

Rådhus
Pladsen

32

Farvergade

31

ⓘ

Gammel Strand

35

36

Holmens Kanal

37

Børsgade

**Gammel
Dok**

42

Strandgade

Overgaden Neden Vandet

34

38

Tøjhusgade

Inderhavnen

Knippelsbro

Wildersgade

Torvegade

**Our
Savior's
Church**

43

Prinsessegade

H.C. Andersens Boulevard

30

Vester

Vestergade

Ny

Voldgade

39

40

Christians Brygge

41

**Christian's
Church**

Overgaden Oven Vandet

Skt. Annæ Gade

Prinsessegade

33

Brocksgade

Langebro

Langebrogade

Wildersgade

Christmas
Møllers
Plads

Hambrosgade

Mitchellsgade

Langebro

Inderhavnen

Stads graven

Amager Boulevard

Ved Stadsgraven

Sydhavnen

Thors-
havnsgade

To
Airport

Church ✝■   Post Office ⊠   Information ⊘

If You Have 2 Days

Start your second day at the mighty Gefion Fountain and the nearby demure *Little Mermaid* (if you're early enough, you might miss the tour buses). Then make your way to the queen's residence, Amalienborg Palace, and visit the royal rooms now open to the public. The Changing of the Guard takes place outside the palace at noon. Continue your palace perusal with fairy-tale Rosenborg Palace to see the Crown Jewels. Back in the city center, climb the Round Tower for the best view of Copenhagen; if you still have time, visit the Ny Carlsberg Glyptotek to see ancient sculptures and French and Danish art of the 19th and early 20th centuries or the impressive National Museum to learn about the cultural history of Denmark.

If You Have 3 Days

Spend your first two days as suggested above. On the third day, make time to visit Denmark's Fight for Freedom Museum on your way to or from *The Little Mermaid.* Then consider a trip to the Carlsberg Brewery or to the peaceful Botanical Gardens and the nearby Royal Museum of Fine Art and the Hirschsprung Collection.

If You Have 5 Days

Use the first three days as outlined above. On the fourth, visit the Louisiana Museum of Modern Art, the Karen Blixen Museum, and Kronborg Castle in Helsingør (site of Shakespeare's *Hamlet*), all in North Zealand. (Yes, you can do them all in a day, if you start early.) On the fifth day, head west to Roskilde and tour its famous cathedral, final resting place of the Danish monarchy for centuries, and the Viking Ship Museum.

TOP ATTRACTIONS

✪ Tivoli

Vesterbrogade 3. ☎ **33-15-10-01.** Park, 40 Kr ($6.65) adults, 20 Kr ($3.35) children 4–12; rides, 10–20 Kr ($1.65–$3.35) each, and an unlimited-ride ticket is available. Park, mid-Apr to mid-Sept, daily 11am–midnight; Nov 14–Dec 23, limited hours (no rides). Ticket Center, Mon–Sat noon–6pm (also on Sun when events are scheduled). Closed mid-Sept to Nov 13 and Dec 24 to mid-Apr.

When Tivoli opened in 1843, the park was well outside the city center. Today it's Copenhagen's centerpiece, attracting over 4.5 million visitors annually. Tivoli is an integral part of the city and is its main showcase for Danish culture, music, and entertainment. Every day brings with it a full program of open-air concerts, cabaret theater, dancing, pantomime, and other special events. Most are free or fairly priced.

The majority of the performances are staged at night, when the park takes on truly magical proportions. Thousands of lights shimmer through the trees, and every Wednesday, Friday, and Saturday night fireworks light the sky with a cavalcade of color. Don't overlook an afternoon visit, however, especially from May to the first half of June, when 100,000 brightly colored tulips organically paint the park.

Finally, when you're ready for thrills, hop on the old wooden roller coaster, built in 1914. Its incessant creaking gives riders a reason to scream.

Groften and Slukefter are popular spots for a drink. The former, parts of which are open year round, serves Danish food, and the latter, beside the main entrance to Tivoli, features jazz and blues year round.

The **Tivolis Billetcenter** (Tivoli Ticket Center), Vesterbrogade 3 (☎ **33-15-10-12**), sells tickets to concerts and special events in the park. This office also distributes a free daily schedule, and is located next to the park's main entrance.

The Tivoli magic is now part of Copenhagen's Christmas season, when the park hosts a holiday market, a special theatrical production, and ice skating on the lake.

✪ Tivoli Museum

H. C. Andersens Blvd. 22. ☎ **33-15-10-01.** Admission 20 Kr ($3.35) adults, 10 Kr ($1.65) children 6–14. Mid-Apr to mid-Sept, daily 10am–10pm; mid-Sept to mid-Apr, Tues–Fri 10am–4pm, Sat–Sun 10am–5pm.

This evocative museum opened in 1993 and wonderfully complements the park. If you visit Tivoli, this will tell you about its fascinating history, and if you visited Copenhagen when the famous park was closed, this is the next best thing to a visit. You'll learn about the creator of the park, its early days, its legendary performers (including a flea circus that held audiences enthralled for more than 65 years), its pantomime theater (for which the park is well known), its rides, and even its specially made lamps. Start on the ground floor and work your way down, allowing plenty of time because there's lots to see.

✪ National Museum

Ny Vestergade 10. ☎ **33-13-44-11.** Museum, 30 Kr ($5) adults, 15 Kr ($2.50) students and seniors, free for children 15 and under; Victorian House, an additional 30 Kr ($5) adults. Museum, Tues–Sun 10am–5pm; Victorian House, only limited days. Bus 1, 2, 5, 6, 8, or 10.

Cataloguing life in Denmark from the Stone Age to the present, this vast museum across from Christiansborg Palace includes prehistoric finds, ancient burial chambers, traditional farmers' tools, and centuries-old porcelain, furniture, and housewares. Interesting, too, are the displays on the colonization of Greenland, as well as the Victorian House, with its original interior dating from 1890 (tours are available, but you should make a reservation). The museum has a large atrium

❷ Did You Know?

- Denmark is the smallest country in Scandinavia, but Copenhagen (pop. 500,000) is its largest city.
- Denmark has one of the highest standards of living of any EU country.
- Three-quarters of Denmark's land area is devoted to agriculture.
- Denmark has no mountains or rivers, and on average it's only 98 feet above sea level.
- In 1972, Queen Margrethe became the first female monarch in Denmark's history.
- Because of an enormous national effort, only 53 Danish Jews died in World War II.
- The Danes love candles and burn them even at breakfast.
- The average Danish family has 1.2 kids and 5 bicycles.
- About 90% of Danes own their own homes.
- The legal requirement for marriage in Copenhagen is one week's residency.
- Homosexual marriages have been legal in Denmark since 1989.

entry, a pretty café, and a boutique that sells replicas of Viking jewelry and other collectibles. The recently renovated exhibit space is modern and uncrowded, with plenty of room for people to view the displays. Expect to see fewer objects, dramatically presented—nothing staid or predictable here. The interactive computer exhibit is fun and educational, and the exhibits on the Middle Ages and Renaissance, the Ethnographic Collections (10 galleries devoted the earth's peoples), and the Collection of Classical Antiquities should not be missed. Kids have their own Children's Museum and casual eatery on the ground floor.

✪ Rosenborg Palace

Øster Voldgade 4a. ☎ **33-15-32-86.** Summer, 40 Kr ($6.65) adults, 25 Kr ($4.15) students, 5 Kr (85¢) children 5–15; winter, about 30% lower. Jan 3–Apr and Oct 24–Dec 17, Tues, Fri, and Sun 11am–2pm; May and Sept–Oct 23, daily 11am–3pm; June–Aug, daily 10am–4pm. Closed Dec 18–Jan 2. S-tog: Nørreport. Bus 5, 7E, 10, 14, 16, 31, 43, or 184.

The summer residence of King Christian IV (1577–1648) was built during his reign and served as the official royal residence throughout the 17th century. Today visitors may wander through the opulently furnished State Apartments and a dungeon containing the kingdom's most valued possessions, including the Crown Jewels, jewel-encrusted swords, dazzling crowns, opulent necklaces, and other priceless possessions of the royal family. Be sure to see the display featuring the clothing Christian IV wore on the day he lost an eye (an event well known by Danish schoolchildren) and the earrings he had made for his mistress from the bullet fragments. There are no electric lights or heat in the palace, so try to come on a sunny day and allow time to ramble in the sculpted gardens.

Amalienborg Palace

Slotsplads. Bus 1, 6, 9, or 10; or walk from Strøget.

The official residence of Denmark's Queen Margrethe II and her husband, Prince Henrik, is an outstanding example of rococo architecture. Amalienborg is actually a complex of four mansions dating from 1760 that ring a large cobblestone square. An equestrian statue of Frederik V stands at the center of the square, while the Queen's Guards—bearskin hats and all—stand watch around the perimeter. The noontime Changing of the Guard at Amalienborg is as spirited as any, full of pomp and pageantry, but it's performed only when the queen is in residence (mainly during the colder months).

Amaliehavens Kiosk, a block from the palace, at Toldbodgade 34 (☎ **33-11-34-40**), where the tour buses stop, sells cards, souvenirs, stamps, sandwiches, and ice cream, and has a telephone and restroom; friendly owner Poul Jensen is a wealth of information. He accepts U.S. traveler's checks.

Amalienborg Museum

Slotsplads. ☎ **33-12-21-86.** Admission 40 Kr ($6.65) adults, 25 Kr ($4.20) students, 5 Kr (85¢) children. Jan 3–Apr and Oct 23–Dec 18, Tues–Sun 11am–4pm; May–Oct 22 and Dec 26–30, daily 11am–4pm. Closed Jan 1–2 and Dec 19–25. Bus 1, 6, 9, or 10; or walk from Strøget.

In 1994, Amalienborg Palace opened its interior to the public for the first time, revealing regal private and official rooms reconstructed to the period 1863 to 1947. Highlights include the study of King Christian IX, a mix of valuables and victoriana; the more elegant and much less cluttered drawing rooms of his wife, Queen Louise; King Christian X's study, mementos from the Faroe Islands,

Special & Free Events

Throughout 1996, Copenhagen will be nonstop special and free events, when the city is **Cultural Capital of Europe.** Just grab a schedule when you arrive and take advantage of as many of the offerings as possible. Every year, there's always free entertainment associated with the annual 10-day **Copenhagen Jazz Festival,** which starts the first Friday in July.

Grabrødre Torv (Gray Friar Square), a square in the center of Copenhagen, comes alive each summer day with street entertainers, outdoor cafés, and occasional live music concerts. Renovated in traditional Danish style, Grabrødre Torv is a beautiful meeting place for people of all ages.

Nyhavn (the New Harbor), off Kongens Nytorv, a picturesque canal lined by historic buildings, is another summer choice. Once the raucous sailors' quarter, Nyhavn has become a favorite strolling area. During summer the cafés lining Nyhavn's pedestrian street appear to specialize in ice cream and beer. Majestic, tall, fully rigged ships are moored all along the canal, and you can also see where Hans Christian Andersen lived during different periods of his life—at nos. 18, 20, and 67 Nyhavn. Peek into the courtyards at nos. 18 and 20.

Nyhavn's maritime past is still evidenced by a couple of old-time bars and tattoo parlors, such as the one at Nyhavn 17, which has been decorating bodies since 1878 with everything "from wild to mild."

See the tourist board's publication *Copenhagen This Week,* and "Special Events" under "Pretrip Preparations," earlier in this chapter, for more information on unique and interesting city activities.

Greenland, and Iceland, along with an American flag from 1912 and a horseshoe over the door (even kings need luck); and the study of King Frederik VIII, with the original furniture, chandelier, and knickknacks. The museum also houses a costume and jewelry gallery.

Den Lille Havfrue (The Little Mermaid)

Langelinie on the harbor. S-tog: Østerport; then walk through the park. Bus 1, 6, or 9; during the summer a shuttle bus operates between Town Hall Square and the statue.

Like famous monuments the world over, this simple green statue on a rock off the shore will seem smaller than you had imagined it, but it'll make you smile all the same. Locals poke fun at the statue's popularity, and at times they've even vandalized it. Still, this frail bronze figure (actually $1^1/_3$ times human size), created in 1913 by Erik Erikson and inspired by the Hans Christian Andersen fairy tale, remains the most famous monument in Copenhagen. Industrial tanks on the opposite shore create an unsightly background, but adjacent **Kastellet Park,** laid out on the remains of Copenhagen's old ramparts, is a beautiful area for strolling and picnicking (it's open daily form 7am to 5:30pm). Don't miss the nearby Gefion Fountain or the bust of Winston Churchill, adjacent to St. Alban's Church.

✪ Christiansborg Palace

Christiansborg Slotsplads (on Slotsholmen). ☎ **33-92-64-92.** Admission 15 Kr ($2.50) adults, 5 Kr (85¢) children. May–Sept, daily 9:30am–3:30pm; Oct–Apr, Tues–Fri and Sun 9:30am–3:30pm. Bus 1, 2, 6, 8, 9, 10, 28, 29, 31, 37, 41, or 43; or walk from the city center.

Rebuilt early in this century on top of ancient foundations. Christiansborg Palace was home to the royal family until 1794. The ring of water surrounding the tiny island of Slotsholmen resembles a protective moat. Most of the palace's rooms are now used as offices by parliamentary and supreme court officials, though a few of the glamorous royal reception rooms still serve their original purpose. For tourists, admission to the reception rooms is by guided tour only; the tour features 10 regal rooms, including the Throne Room, where the queen regularly receives foreign ambassadors; the Red Room, named for the red velvet on the walls; the Long Hall, still used for state banquets; and the queen's library, which houses 10,000 books. These and other rooms are resplendent with Murano chandeliers, Flemish tapestries, and other impressive details. The palace entrance is beyond the large courtyard, on the left side of the building. Tours start exactly on time and last a too-short 45 minutes.

You can also visit the well-preserved palace ruins (the original foundations of Bishop Absalon's 1167 castle) for an additional charge.

✪ Ny Carlsberg Glyptotek

Dantes Plads 7 (across from the back entrance to Tivoli). ☎ **33-41-81-41.** Admission 15 Kr ($2.50), free for children; free for everyone Wed and Sun. May–Aug, Tues–Sun 10am–4pm; Sept–Apr, Tues–Sat noon–3pm, Sun 10am–4pm. Closed Jan 1, Good Fri, Easter Sun, Whitsunday, June 5, and Dec 24–25. S-tog: Hovedbanegård. Bus 1, 2, 5, 10, 14, 16, 28, 29, 30, 32, 33, 34, or 41; or walk from the city center.

Specializing in ancient art and French and Danish art of the 19th and early 20th centuries, the Glyptotek has impressive Greek statues, Roman portrait busts, and Egyptian and Etruscan art. Founded by brewer/arts patron Carl Jacobsen in 1882, the collection of antiquities has continued to grow and includes Near Eastern, Palmyrene, and Cypriot art, along with extensive works from more recent times. The French sculpture collection features 35 works by Rodin and the complete *ouevre* of Degas. The second-floor modernists are mainly French and include Gauguin (he's represented here by more than 30 works, a collection rivaled only by museums in Amsterdam and St. Petersburg), Corot, Courbet, Manet, Monet, Cézanne, and Renoir; don't miss Gallery 28. The museum is built around a glass-domed conservatory that compels some folks to visit the Glyptotek with little intention of looking at art.

✪ Statens Museum for Kunst (Royal Museum of Fine Arts)

Sølvgade 48-50. ☎ **33-91-21-26.** Admission 30 Kr ($5) adults, free for children 15 and under. Museum, Tues and Thurs–Sun 10am–4:30pm, Wed 10am–9pm; sculpture garden, Thurs–Tues 10am–4:30pm, Wed 10am–9pm. Bus 10, 24, 43, or 184.

The country's largest art museum occupies a monumental building in the Ostre Anlæg park. The Danish art is separated from all the rest, and although there's heavy emphasis on works from the late 18th century, most are overshadowed by outstanding 19th-century landscapes. The foreign-art section is heavy on Dutch and Flemish paintings, though other European modernists (especially French), such as Matisse and Braque, are also well represented. Look for special changing exhibitions.

✪ Louisiana Museum of Modern Art

Gammel Strandvej 13, Humlebæk. ☎ **42-19-07-19.** Admission 48 Kr ($8) adults, 43 Kr ($7.15) students 16 and older and seniors, 15 Kr ($2.50) children 15 and under 16. Mon–Tues and Thurs–Fri 10am–5pm, Wed 10am–10pm, Sat–Sun 10am–6pm. Take the train from Central Station Platform 1 or 2, to Humlebæk, then bus no. 388 from

Humlebæk Station (or a scenic 1-mile walk); a special round-trip train fare is 89 Kr ($14.85).

In North Zealand, about 45 minutes from Copenhagen's Central Station, this stunning museum welcomes 600,000 visitors a year. The wonderful permanent collection includes works by Warhol, Leichtenstein, Calder, Moore, and Giacometti, though the world-class special exhibitions are the main draw. In recent years, Edward Hopper, Robert Mapplethorpe, Alexander Calder, Claude Monet, and Toulouse-Lautrec have been featured. The museum itself, on a spectacular piece of land overlooking the sea, is beautiful. During warmer months, you can picnic on the sprawling grounds.

The man who built the original villa on the property had three wives named Louise, thus the name. It took great courage to open a museum 18 miles from Copenhagen in 1958, but Louisiana was a success from the beginning. Its Children's Museum opened in the fall of 1994.

MORE ATTRACTIONS

Christiania
Christianshavn. Bus 8 from Town Hall Square to the second stop after the bridge.

Organized squatters took over dozens of disused army buildings on the island of Christianshavn in 1971, creating the "Free Town of Christiania." The public, both critical of the city's housing situation and curious about this new solution, generally supported the group, pressuring the government against taking any action. Today, some 900 people live in Christiania. The community, with its piles of garbage, dirt, graffiti, unpaved streets, and sometimes open use of hash and marijuana, looks more like an undeveloped nation than modern Denmark. But these aspects are offset by interesting murals, wonderfully painted houses, and popular nightspots. Tourists are welcome, but they're asked not to take photographs, especially along the main drag, known as "Pusher Street." A restaurant and a jazz club, Spiseloppen and Loppen, respectively, are in the building to your right just inside the main entrance to Christiania; restrooms and a small gallery are in the same building. There is now a vegetarian restaurant called Morgenstedet (no smoking or alcohol).

✪ Den Hirschsprungske Samling (The Hirschsprung Collection)
Stockholmsgade 20. ☎ **31-42-03-36.** Admission 20 Kr ($3.35) adults, 10 Kr ($1.65) students, free for children 15 and under. Wed 10am–10pm, Thurs–Mon 10am–5pm. S-tog: Østerport or Nørreport. Bus 10, 14, 40, 43, or 84.

Tobacco manufacturer Heinrich Hirschsprung bequeathed his vast collection of 19th-century Danish art, notably paintings of people and landscapes, to Denmark in 1911. The striking building constructed specifically to house the collection has 16 exhibition areas, a particularly large one devoted to the works of P. S. Kroyer. Works by Anna and Michael Ancher, Viggo Johansen, and Vilhem Hammershoi are prominently displayed. Furniture designed by the artists—chests, chairs, tables—is exhibited along with the art.

Erotic Museum
Købmagergade 24 (half a block north of Strøget). ☎ **33-12-03-11.** Admission 45 Kr ($7.50).

Interested in lust, passion, erotica? Then visit this uninhibited museum, whose founding director, Ole Ege, was a well-known Danish nude photographer in the

1960s. Exhibits focus on erotica through the ages and include wall paintings from the 1st century, a painted Greek vase from the 6th century, tableaux of Psyche and Amor, and Fanny Hill; and the sex lives (or lack of them) of famous people, including Josephine Baker and Charlie Chaplin. Sex toys and chastity belts are part of the show. The museum is interesting until you reach the last exhibit, a wall of 12 video monitors showing pornographic films from 1930 to the present, in all their predictability. It would've been nice if the display had ended, as it began, on an erotic note. Since it opened in 1992, the museum has stirred great interest, particularly among visitors from places where erotica is usually kept strictly under wraps.

Frihedsmuseet (Denmark's Fight for Freedom Museum 1940–1945)

Churchillparken. ☎ **33-13-77-14.** Admission free. May to mid-Sept, Tues–Sat 10am–4pm, Sun 10am–5pm; mid-Sept to Apr, Tues–Sat 11am–3pm, Sun 11am–4pm. S-tog: Østerport. Bus 1, 6, or 9.

This small but fascinating collection chronicles the nation's underground fight against the Germans who, despite Denmark's pledge of neutrality, occupied the country in 1940. Computerized information, an audiovisual show, and displays on sabotage efforts and prison life, along with a plethora of pictures, are featured. The museum also celebrates the nation's unique and enormously successful efforts to save the country's Jewish citizens.

Grundtvigs Kirke (Grundtvig's Church)

På Bjerget. ☎ **31-81-54-42.** Admission free. Mid-May to mid-Sept, Mon–Sat 9am–4:45pm, Sun noon–4pm; mid-Sept to mid-May, Mon–Sat 9am–4pm, Sun noon–1pm. Closed during official church functions. S-tog: Emdrup. Bus 69 from Town Hall Square, or 10, 16, or 43.

This impressive blond-brick structure, a cross between a simple Danish church (no stained glass, no grand altar) and a gothic cathedral, was completed in 1940 in honor of N. F. S. Grundtvig, the Lutheran parson/poet who wrote 36% of the Danish hymnbook and founded the folk high school movement. The model ship hanging inside was a gift from Queen Alexandrine (Queen Margrethe's grandmother). The church measures 70 feet high on the inside, with a tower soaring 111 feet. Each of its massive columns is made of 10,000 to 12,000 bricks. Concerts are held here.

Københavns Rådhus (Town Hall)

Rådhuspladsen. ☎ **33-66-25-82.** Town Hall, free; clock, 10 Kr ($1.65). Mon–Fri 10am–3pm; guided tours available for a fee.

Copenhagen's imposing red-brick Town Hall (1905) is one of the best-known structures in the city because of its clock tower and location in the heart of town. There's no need to look inside, unless you're a clock fan. The Town Hall is most famous for Jens Olsen's **World Clock,** a gigantic silver-and-gold timepiece located on the ground floor. It began ticking in 1955 and is accurate to within half a second every 300 years! The pillar just east of Town Hall is topped by two men playing lurs, instruments found only in Scandinavia.

Kunstindustrimuseet (Museum of Decorative Art)

Bredgade 68. ☎ **33-14-94-52.** Admission 30 Kr ($5) adults, 20 Kr ($3.35) children. Tues–Sun 1–4pm. Bus 1, 6, or 9.

Housed in a former hospital (1757), this stately rococo museum is laid out around a large tree-filled garden. Its special exhibits never fail to create excitement, while the permanent collection pales by comparison. The museum was renovated in 1994 and 1995. A small café is near the entrance. Note the limited hours.

Legetøjsmuseet (Toy Museum)

Valkendorfsgade 13 (near Grabrødre Torv, or Gray Friar Square). ☎ 33-14-10-09. Admission 25 Kr ($4.20) adults, 12 Kr ($2) children. Sat–Thurs 10am–4pm. S-tog: Nørreport. Bus 2, 5, 14, 16, or 43.

Of more interest to nostalgic adults than to children, the three-story Toy Museum houses almost 5,000 toys from Denmark, Germany, England, and the United States in a converted 200-year-old warehouse. The second floor is a re-created Danish village with 14 houses, each displaying toys with a different theme. Dolls and dollhouses fill the top floor. The oldest toy dates from 1540, and the 1750 Noah's Ark still has all its animals.

Rundetårn (The Round Tower)

Købmagergade. ☎ 33-93-66-60. Admission 15 Kr ($2.50) adults, 5 Kr (83¢) children. Tower, June–Aug, Mon–Sat 10am–8pm, Sun noon–8pm; Sept–May, Mon–Sat 10am–5pm, Sun noon–4pm. Observatory, Oct–Mar, Tues–Wed 7–10pm; June–Aug, Sun 1–4pm; closed Apr–May and Sept.

There are taller buildings in the city, boasting more spectacular views, but none has more charm and history than this ancient observatory. Built by King Christian IV in 1642, the Round Tower has long been loved by locals as an integral part of the cityscape. The observation platform up top can be reached only by climbing the tower's 687-foot internal spiral ramp. En route, you'll pass a large gallery with changing exhibits; it's free and worth a look. At the observation platform, maps point out prominent rooftops around the old city, Rosenborg Palace in the foreground, and Frederiksberg Castle on the horizon.

Thorvaldsen Museum

Porthusgade 2 (Slotsholmen). ☎ 33-32-15-32. Admission free. Tues–Sun 10am–5pm; guided tours in English given Sun at 2pm June–Aug.

The personal museum of Bertel Thorvaldsen (1770–1844), Denmark's most celebrated sculptor, features the artist's graceful creations as well as other works from his private collection. Notable are Thorvaldsen's plaster casts of large monuments from around the world. Among the most striking are his portrayals of Hercules, Venus, Jason, Mars, Vulcan, Mercury, and Christ and the Apostles. Don't miss the monumental equestrian statues or the exhibits in the basement: his personal effects, including two silver spoons (the only cutlery he owned), two flintlock pistols, a silver lorgnette, and a gold snuffbox with his monogram in diamonds (a gift from the city of Turin); his work techniques; and his achievements as a young artist. Audio guides in English are available for a small charge. The museum, which has arched ceilings and striking interiors, is adjacent to Christiansborg Palace. Splendid works in marble by Thorvaldsen may be seen in the Copenhagen Cathedral (Church of Our Lady), for which Bishop Absalon laid the foundations in 1187.

PARKS & GARDENS

In addition to the gardens of Tivoli, Copenhagen boasts several other greens perfect for picnicking. On the grounds of Rosenborg Palace the sculptured gardens of **Kongens Have (King's Garden)** attract ducks, swans, gulls, and people. This is the city's oldest park, and is as popular as ever with hand-holders and strollers alike.

The charming wooded **Botanisk Have (Botanical Garden),** behind the Royal Museum of Fine Arts, is particularly nice on hot summer days. The gates are open daily from 8:30am to 6pm, April to October; until 4pm the rest of the year.

Like most parks in the city, the **Park of the Citadel (Kastellet),** behind *The Little Mermaid,* is laid out on Copenhagen's old ramparts. Adjacent **Churchill Park,** to the south, is noted for St. Alban's English Church and the impressive Gefion Fountain, depicting the legend of the founding of Denmark. And don't overlook the small but winsomely bulldoggish bust of Sir Winston himself in the park.

A ribbon of three artificial lakes cuts through Copenhagen (all rectangular and uninspiring); the most appealing, Lake Peblinge, is the scene of enthusiastic boating, strolling, sitting, and duck-feeding in summer. Nearby, **Ørsteds Park,** with its small lake, pleasant paths, and statues, invites meandering. Cemetery lovers won't be disappointed by the parklike **Assistens Kirkegard,** at Nørrebrogade and Kapelvej, the final resting place of Hans Christian Andersen, Søren Kierkegaard, physicists H. C. Ørsted and Niels Bohr, and tenor sax player Ben Webster (check the directory of famous "residents" at the gate). Nearby, **Fælledparken** is the scene of exuberant outdoor concerts in the summertime.

Frederiksberg Park, adjacent to the zoo, is one of the city's prettiest green places and also the backdrop for summer concerts. Get there quickly and easily from Central Station via bus no. 28 or 41.

North of the city center on Tuborgvej is **Mindelunden i Ryvangen (Memorial Park),** dedicated to Danish civilians who lost their lives during the German occupation of Denmark from April 9, 1940, to May 5, 1945. Among the 158 graves here are those of 31 Danish Jews who died in concentration camps. The location of the park is a former Nazi execution site. To visit, take the S-tog to Hellerup and walk five minutes.

ESPECIALLY FOR KIDS

Copenhagen Zoo

Roskildevej 32. ☎ **36-30-20-01.** Admission 55 Kr ($9.15) adults, 27 Kr ($4.50) children. Summer, daily 9am–6pm; winter, daily 9am–4pm. S-tog: Valby. Bus 27, 28, 39, 145, or 172E.

Founded in 1859 and modernized in recent years, the Copenhagen Zoo is home to 2,000 animals, from Nordic species to Asiatic red pandas to South American giant anteaters. Gorillas and chimpanzees are in the Tropical Zoo, and 16 species of birds in the adjacent Tropical Rain Forest. The children's zoo is terrific, like a farm with cows, llamas, chickens, goats, and other farm animals, as well as a playground, refreshment stand, and Shetland ponies for riding. A train ride within the zoo costs 15 Kr ($2.50), and while there's no commentary and you don't get to see many animals, it does give you a good idea of the lay of the land.

Danmarks Akvarium (Denmark Aquarium)

At Jægersborg Allé and Strandvejen, Charlottenlund. ☎ **31-62-32-83.** Admission 45 Kr ($7.50) adults, 25 Kr ($4.20) children. Mar–Oct, daily 10am–6pm; Nov–Feb, Mon–Fri 10am–4pm, Sat–Sun 10am–5pm. S-tog: Charlottenlund. Bus 6 to Jægersborg Allé.

Opened in 1959, the Denmark Aquarium features fish that inhabit waters around the world, along with some turtles and terrapins. For those with a fascination with bloodthirsty fish, there's a tank of South American piranhas. The train ride to Charlottenlund takes 15 minutes; the beach is within walking distance of here.

Eksperimentarium

In the Tuborg Brewery, Tuborg Havenevej 7, Hellerup. ☎ **39-27-33-33.** Admission 62 Kr ($10.35) adults, 44 Kr ($7.35) children 14 and under, 84 Kr ($12.70) family ticket (good for one adult and one child). Mon, Wed, and Fri 9am–6pm; Tues and Thurs 9am–9pm; Sat–Sun 11am–6pm. S-tog: Hellerup. Bus 6 or 21.

Opened in 1991 and housed in an old bottling hall of the Tuborg Brewery, the Eksperimentarium fuels kids' interest in the natural sciences and modern technology with hands-on exhibits (many explanations in English), microscope-equipped labs, demonstrations (the dissection of a cow's eye, for instance), and computer workshops. There's also a shop and a cafeteria.

Guinness World of Records Museum

Østergade 16 (near Kongens Nytorv). ☎ **33-32-31-31.** Admission 45 Kr ($7.50) adults, 20 Kr ($3.35) children. Daily 10am–8pm.

Newly opened on Strøget in 1995, this museum focuses on world's records of every dimension—a three-dimenional almanac, if you will, of Guinness-like proportions.

❂ Louis Tussaud's Wax Museum

H. C. Andersens Blvd. 22. ☎ **33-11-89-00.** Admission 48 Kr ($8) adults, 20 Kr ($3.35) children. Late Apr to mid-Sept, daily 10am–midnight; mid-Sept to late Apr, daily 10am–10pm. S-tog: Hovedbanegård.

Kids love the beautiful renditions of their favorite fairy tales here: scenes from "Snow White and the Seven Dwarves," "The Princess and the Pea," "The Little Mermaid," "Beauty and the Beast," "Sleeping Beauty," and "The Snow Queen," among others. There are lifelike figures of the Danish kings and queens, from Gorm the Old to reigning Queen Margrethe II; world leaders, inventors, writers, artists, actors, and activists—even a couple of tourists and a homeless person. For the very brave, there's a spooky Chamber of Horrors.

Professor Olsen's Spillerland

Scala Center (3rd floor), Axeltorv 2. ☎ **33-11-50-00.** Admission 30 Kr ($5) adults (which buys six tokens for the pinball machines), free for children 11 and under. Daily 11am–midnight.

At this large family-entertainment arcade with everything from pinball machines to bumper cars, there are even two miniature carousels with three horses. Kids love it—and they get in for free. Many adults are glued to the slot machines in back, less so than the pool tables one floor down.

Ripley's Believe It or Not Museum

Rådhuspladsen 57. ☎ **33-91-89-91.** Admission 45 Kr ($7.50) adults, 20 Kr ($3.35) children. Mon–Thurs and Sun 10am–10pm, Fri–Sat 10am–midnight.

Robert Ripley, a former semiprofessional baseball pitcher, began his travels to farflung places in the 1920s and didn't stop for almost 30 years. Some of the oddities he collected from 198 countries are displayed here, and it'll take at least an hour to see them all.

Tycho Brahe Planetarium

Gammel Kongevej 10. ☎ **33-12-12-24.** Planetarium, 65 Kr ($10.83) adults, 45 Kr ($7.50) children; Omnimax movies extra. Daily 10:30am–9pm. S-tog: Vesterport. Bus 1 or 14.

Another lure for young folks is Western Europe's largest planetarium, with showings of Omnimax movies. Nearly all the shows have an audiocassette translation in English. You'll also learn interesting bits of trivia— for instance, that about

30 tons of dust from space lands on the surface of the earth every day (there's even some cosmic dust on display, along with a moon rock). The hands-on stuff is in English and Danish.

SPECIAL-INTEREST SIGHTSEEING
FOR HISTORY BUFFS

Arbejdermuseet (The Workers' Museum)
Romersgade 22. ☎ **33-93-25-75.** Admission: 30 Kr ($5) adults, 15 Kr ($2.50) children. July–Nov 1, daily 10am–5pm. S-tog: Nørreport.

This museum provides a look at the cultural and social history of Copenhagen's working and middle class in three permanent exhibits: "For Life and Bread," about the effect of industrialization in 1870; "Meager Times," about unemployment in the 1930; and "The 1950s," depicting the prosperous times following World War II. Start at the top floor and work your way down. Cafe & Øl-Halle 1892, the on-premises eatery, looks like the cafés did 100 years ago and serves food and drink from that era as well. Guided tours are available.

✪ Københavns Bymuseum (Copenhagen City Museum)
Vesterbrogade 59. ☎ **31-21-07-72.** Admission free. May–Sept, Tues–Sun 10am–4pm; Oct–Apr, Tues–Sun 1–3pm. Bus 6, 16, 27, or 28.

Many pictures, prints, maps, and models of Copenhagen illustrate the development of the city from antiquity to the present, with some texts in English and Danish. A separate, permanent collection features objects associated with the life of Danish philosopher and author Søren Kierkegaard. Outside the building in warm months, a large-scale model of the city in 1660 draws deserved attention. The museum is now undergoing renovation, which will be completed in 1997. Check out new exhibits in the basement.

Tøjhusmuseet (Royal Arsenal Museum)
Tøjhusgade 3. ☎ **33-11-60-37.** Admission 20 Kr ($3.35) adults, 5 Kr (85¢) children 6–17, free for children 5 and under. Tues–Sun 10am–4pm. Bus 1, 2, 6, 8, 9, 10, 27, 28, 29, 31, or 37.

Those who believe the history of humanity is the history of war will find much of interest here. Housed in the king's arsenal, completed in 1604 with the longest arched hall in Europe, this museum displays a vast collection of weapons spanning several centuries. The first floor, a veritable forest of steel, features tank and artillery displays as well as a long series of cannons. The thousands of personal weapons on the second floor include armor pieces, guns, and swords. Older kids like this museum, too.

FOR ART & ARCHITECTURE BUFFS

Charlottenborg Palace and Exhibition Hall
Nyhavn 2. ☎ **33-13-40-22.** Admission 20 Kr ($3.35) adults, 10 Kr ($1.65) seniors and students, free for children. Thurs–Tues 10am–5pm, Wed 10am–7pm. Bus 1, 6, 7, 9, 10, or 31.

Right on Kongens Nytorv, between Nyhavn and the Royal Theater, this former residence of the royal family, completed in 1683, is now home to the Royal Academy of Fine Arts and students of art and architecture. In the artist-run Exhibition Hall, changing exhibits devoted to art, architecture, decorative arts, and design fill spacious galleries with 10- to 24-foot ceilings. The avant-garde is alive and well here. A pleasant café is on the ground floor.

✪ Davids Samling (The David Collection)

Kronprinsessegade 30. ☎ **33-13-55-64.** Admission free. Tues–Sun 1–4pm. Bus 7, 10, or 43.

This former home of lawyer/businessman/art collector C. L. David, who died in 1960, across the street from the King's Garden, purportedly houses the largest collection of Islamic art in northern Europe. Beautiful calligraphy, pottery, tiles, and tapestries are on the fourth floor. The first three floors are devoted to Danish, French, and English art and decorative arts, respectively.

Gammel Dok (Danish Architecture Center)

Strandgade 27B (Christianshavn). ☎ **31-57-19-30.** Admission: 20 Kr ($3.35) adults, 10 Kr ($1.65) seniors, free for students and children 15 and under. Thurs–Tues 10am–5pm, Wed 10am–8pm. Bus 2, 8, 9, 31, or 37.

The focus here is modern—design, architecture, interiors, textiles, and furniture—as the changing exhibits attest. The term *gammel dok* means "old dock," and the center is in half of a converted warehouse (1882); the other half is studio space for artists. A bookstore/shop and café fill the ground level. The exhibition space and fine views of Copenhagen are on the second floor. The center usually mounts a large, summer-long exhibition.

Nikolaj Church

Nikolaj Plads 12. ☎ **33-93-16-26.** Admission free. Daily noon–5pm. Bus 1, 2, 6, 8, 10, or 43.

Anyone interested in beautiful architecture and modern art should visit the centrally located Nikolaj Church, one of the oldest in Copenhagen and now a museum mounting changing exhibitions primarily of contemporary art. After touring the museum, visit the small café in the church, a pocket of tranquillity for eager sightseers.

Storm P. Museet

Frederiksberg Runddel. ☎ **31-86-05-23.** Admission 20 Kr ($3.35) adults, 1 Kr (15¢) children. May–Sept, Tues–Sun 10am–4pm; Oct–Apr, Wed and Sat 10am–4pm. Bus 18, 27, or 28.

Those with an interest in art as satire and social commentary will want to make the trip to Frederiksberg and the former police station, which now houses the Storm P. Museum. The work of the Danish artist and illustrator Robert Storm Pedersen (1882–1949), known as Storm P., reflects the gap between the haves and the have-nots of the world and reveals his disdain for politicians, critics, and even tourists. His paintings are macabre—a body being pulled from the Seine, for instance, or the indigent. Pedersen's study has been re-created upstairs and includes his extensive pipe collection. A visit here can easily be combined with a look at Morskabs Museet (Danish Museum of Light Theater), with its constantly changing Danish theater–related exhibits; a stroll through Frederiksberg Park, Copenhagen's most beautiful; or a trip to the Copenhagen Zoo.

Teatermuseet (Theater Museum)

Royal Court Theater, Christiansborg Ridebane 18. ☎ **33-11-51-76.** Admission 20 Kr ($3.35) adults, 5 Kr (85¢) children. Wed 2–4pm, Sun noon–4pm.

The Royal Court Theater dates to 1767 and is now used only several times a year because of its age. A board floor slopes down to the orchestra pit, and there are chairs, cushioned benches, and boxes for theatergoers. You can actually walk onto the stage and into the orchestra pit, dressing rooms, and box seats. Busts of famous

Danish actors, dancers, and singers, along with photos and drawings from various productions, line the walls. A lot of attention is paid to Betty Nansen (1873–1943), a well-known Danish actress and one of the country's first female directors. Texts are in Danish, but ask for the brochure in English. Note the limited hours and plan your visit accordingly. (Theater buffs might also be interested in visiting Morskabs Museet, the Danish Museum of Light Theatre, near the entrance to Frederiksberg Park).

ORGANIZED TOURS

WALKING TOURS   Walking tours of Copenhagen often leave from in front of the **Tourist Information Office** (though they are not provided by the tourist office itself); drop by or call to find out current departure times. At this writing, they departed at 10:30am and 2pm, and the price for a two-hour tour was 30 Kr ($5) call 32-97-14-40 for information.

"Copenhagen on Foot," an excellent brochure distributed free by Use-It (see "Visitor Information" under "Copenhagen Specifics," earlier in this chapter, for the address), will guide you through the streets of the city at your own pace.

BUS TOURS   Use-It's free **"Copenhagen by Bus"** brochure takes you through a do-it-yourself tour of all the major sights using city bus no. 6. Those looking for more structure can choose from over a dozen guided bus tours.

Copenhagen Excursions (☎ **31-54-06-06**) offers a 2¹/₂-hour "Grand Tour of Copenhagen" at 150 Kr ($25) for adults, half price for children 11 and under. Tours depart from Town Hall Square (beside the statue of the lur players) April to mid-October, daily at 11am, 1:30pm, and 3pm; the last two weeks of October, daily at 11am and 3pm; the rest of the year, daily at 11am. The company offers a shorter, less-expensive 1¹/₂-hour city tour for 110 Kr ($18.35) for adults and 55 Kr ($9.15) for children, departing Town Hall Square daily at 4pm.

HT Sightseeing Tours (☎ **36-45-45-45**) offers a do-it-yourself bus tour by providing sightseers with their own map when they purchase a ticket. The bus stops at nine selected sites, and tourists are free to get off, explore, and then catch the next tour bus that comes around. Tickets are good for 24 hours and cost 20 Kr ($3.35) for adults (half price with the Copenhagen Card) and 10 Kr ($1.65) for children 10 and under. Tours depart from Town Hall Square June 6 to September 4, daily every half hour from 10am to 4:30pm.

CANAL TOURS   Though no longer as active as it was years ago, the city's waterfront has remained as impressive and interesting as ever. Complemented by a vast network of canals running through the old part of the city, boat tours offer both a relaxing cruise and a good education on the history of the city. Guided tours run from May to the middle of September only, and a quite reasonable one is offered by **Netto-Badene** (☎ **31-54-41-02**), departing daily from 10am to 5pm from Holmens Church, opposite the Stock Exchange. The tour lasts 50 minutes and costs only 15 Kr ($2.50) for adults and 8 Kr ($1.35) for children.

Other guided boat tours, also of 50 minutes' duration, leave from Gammel Strand and Nyhavn, but they cost twice as much (☎ **33-13-31-05**). There's also a half-hour unguided tour to *The Little Mermaid*; another, called "Under 12 Bridges," also unguided, explores the city's canals. Each costs about 36 Kr ($6), 16 Kr ($2.70) for children. Check with the tourist board for current times and itineraries for all tours.

BREWERY TOURS The guided tour of the **Carlsberg Brewery,** Ny Carls-bergsvej 140 (☎ **33-27-13-14**), shows how barley, hops, yeast, and water are combined to produce famous Carlsberg beer. The main brewing hall dates from the turn of the century and is dominated by huge copper kettles and a pungent aroma. The hour-long tour, which involves maneuvering lots of stairs, concludes with a visit to the beer museum, and free samples of the brewery's products. Additional highlights are the unique Elephant Gate, the architecture throughout, and a smaller version of *The Little Mermaid*. The free tours are usually given Monday through Friday at 11am and 2pm, but call to confirm these hours. To get to the brewery, take bus no. 6 from Town Hall Square; look for the Elephant archway.

A visit here may easily be combined with a walk to nearby two public parks (Sondermarken and Frederiksberg) and the zoo, if you start early enough in the day.

7 Shopping

Copenhagen's stores and selections are as wide and varied as any. Everything has its price, however, and here it's usually higher than it is Stateside. Heavy import duties make foreign goods very expensive, which actually is all right, because the most unusual objects here are those of Danish design. Be sure to check out the native silver, porcelain, glassware, and antiques.

STORE HOURS In general, stores are open Monday through Thursday from 9:30am to 5:30pm, Friday from 9:30am to 7pm, and every Saturday from 9am to 5pm in summer and the first and last Saturday of each month the rest of the year. Note that several shops are closed Monday.

GETTING A TAX REFUND Many stores offer non-Scandinavian tourists the opportunity to recover most of the value-added tax (VAT) of 25% on purchases over 300 Kr ($50). Here's how to get the refund (figure on 20% once the handling fee is taken out): After paying, ask the retailer for a Tax Free Check, and leave your purchase sealed until you leave the country. When departing Denmark by train, show both the check and the purchase to an official on board. He or she will validate the check, which must then be returned to the store. If you're flying from Copenhagen, you'll get a cash refund (minus a small commission charge) at the airport's Tax Free Shopping office. Remember not to check luggage containing the purchase until you have received your refund! Questions about tax refunds can be answered by Europe Tax-Free Shopping (☎ **33-52-55-66**).

Shopping Streets

STRØGET All shopping tours should begin on Strøget, the city's mile-long pedestrian thoroughfare and the address of many exclusive stores, such as Royal Copenhagen, Bing & Grondahl, Georg Jensen, Holmegaard, and the upscale department store Illum (peek inside at the marble atrium with its chandeliers and fountain) and the home-furnishings specialty store, Illums Bolighus.

OTHER SHOPPING STREETS A pedestrian street called **Strædet** (it means "the Street," and the word is a combination of Løderstræde and Kompagnistræde) runs parallel to Strøget and has long been known for its antiques stores but is gaining a reputation for its galleries, restaurants, and small upscale shops, as well.

Perpendicular to Strøget, branching north to the Nørreport S-tog, is **Købmagergade,** also free of cars. Several other city shopping streets are reserved

exclusively for walkers and are marked in red on most tourist maps. Besides the upscale shops, Copenhagen has a good number of secondhand stores and small "vintage" boutiques, especially in and around **Larsbjørnsstræde.** Two favorites are the small shop in Kvindehuset (Women's House), Gothersgade 37, open Monday through Friday from noon to 5:30pm, and the well-stocked UFF at Kultorvet 13 (come here for replacement jeans or Nordic sweaters) or Vesterbrogade 37 at Viktoriagade. Other fertile hunting grounds are the shops along **Vesterbrogade.**

INDIVIDUAL SHOPS

BOOKSTORES   Copenhagen has a wealth of bookstores, called *boghandel*, that carry a good selection of travel books and fiction and nonfiction books in English. Tops among them are **Boghallen,** in the Politiken building, Rådhuspladsen 37, a block from Town Hall, near Strøget (☎ **33-11-85-11**), open Monday through Thursday from 9:30am to 5:30pm, Friday from 9:30am to 6:30pm, and Saturday from 9am to 1pm; and **Arnold Busck,** Købmagergade 49 (☎ **33-12-24-53**), open Monday from 10am to 5:30pm, Tuesday through Thursday from 9:15am to 5:30pm, Friday 9:15am to 7pm, and Saturday from 10am to 2pm. Prices for most paperbacks range from 30 to 145 Kr ($5 to $24.15).

DEPARTMENT STORES & SUNDRIES   The fashionable **Magasin du Nord,** at Kongens Nytorv opposite the Royal Theater, is the largest department store in Scandinavia; it also owns **Illum,** on Strøget. The grocery store in **Cityarkaden,** Østergade 32, can supply miscellaneous items such as towels, socks, underwear, wine, candles, and snacks. **Dælls Varehus** department store, Nørregade 12 (☎ **31-12-78-25**), has anything else you might need. The best of the generic souvenir shops is **København Souvenir,** Frederiksberggade 28 (Strøget). **Dælls,** at Fiolstræde and Krystalgade, is a department store that's great if you items like socks, a suitcase, or an umbrella. **Søstrene Grene,** on Strøget, is the city's equivalent to "cash and carry" for household items, with prices starting at 13 ore (a great place to get those wonderful Danish candles).

OTHER SHOPS   By no means overlook the **museum shops** (the one at the National Museum is particularly good for jewelry modeled on Viking amulets). **Artium,** Vesterbrogade 1 (☎ **33-12-34-88**), between Town Hall and Tivoli, has a fine assortment of Scandinavian clothing, glassware, silver, ceramics, and small gift items. For a large assortment of jewelry made from amber, also known as "Nordic gold," visit the **House of Amber,** Kongens Nytorv 2 (☎ **33-11-67-00**), where you'll find a small amber museum upstairs.

The shop of **Tage Andersen,** Ny Adelgade 12, combines floral arrangements, gardening, and high art. The problem is the 40-Kr ($6.65) admission charge to gawk; if you buy something, it goes toward the purchase price. You'll see plants from all over the world, as well as ordinary plants used in extraordinary ways.

Copenhagen Airport has an outstanding selection of **duty-free shops,** about 30 in all.

DENMARK'S LARGEST MALL

In addition to housing myriad cafés and restaurants (see "Dining," earlier in this chapter), the modern **Scala Center,** Axeltorv 2 (☎ **33-15-12-15**), supports a variety of shops, a multiplex cinema, a fitness center, and a dance club. Several stories surround a large atrium where live music is sometimes performed, and plenty of well-placed café tables encourage shoppers to linger. The stores are open on

Monday from 10am to 7pm, Tuesday through Thursday from 10am to 6pm, Friday from 10am to 8pm, and Saturday from 10am to 2pm. Scala Center itself is open Sunday through Thursday from 7am to 2am and Friday and Saturday from 7am to 5am.

AN OUTDOOR MARKET

The lively **Copenhagen Fleamarket,** on Israels Plads, is open every Saturday from May to October. The market specializes in antiques (vintage Georg Jensen, if you're lucky) and bric-a-brac, and is open from 8am to 2pm. Other days it's a fruit and vegetable market. S-tog: Nørreport.

8 Copenhagen After Dark

In Copenhagen, a good night means a late night. On warm weekends hundreds of rowdy revelers crowd Strøget until sunrise, and merrymaking is not just for the younger crowd: Jazz clubs, traditional beer houses, and wine cellars are routinely packed with people of all ages. The city has a more serious cultural side as well, exemplified by excellent theaters, operas, ballets, and a circus that shouldn't be missed. **Half-price tickets** for some concerts and theater productions are available the day of the performance from the ticket kiosk opposite the Nørreport rail station, at Nørrevoldgade and Fiolstræde. It's open Monday through Friday from noon to 7pm and Saturday from noon to 3pm. On summer evenings there are outdoor concerts in Fælled Park near the entrance, near Frederik V's Vej; inquire about dates and times at the Copenhagen Tourist Office.

THE PERFORMING ARTS
THEATER, OPERA & BALLET

Det Kongelige Teater (Royal Theater)
At the south end of Kongens Nytorv. ☎ **33-14-10-02** from 1 to 8pm. Tickets 40–340 Kr ($6.70–$56.70); half price up to one week prior to the performance for those under 26 and over 67. Bus 1, 6, 7, 9, 10, or 31.

Copenhagen's cultural scene is dominated by a single theater, the Royal Theater, home of the famed Royal Danish Ballet, one of the few places in the world regularly staging theater, opera, and ballet under the same roof. Founded in 1748, the theater alternates productions between its two stages. Regular premières and popular revivals keep the stage lit almost every night of the season (it's dark in June and July). The box office is open Monday through Saturday from 1 to 8pm. To get tickets at the box office, pick up a number at the entrance—low numbers are to pick up a reserved seat; high numbers, to buy a ticket. You may also order tickets by fax: 33-12-36-92.

JAZZ, BLUES & ROCK

Copenhagen's love affair with jazz and blues is one of the most passionate in Europe. Danes whole-heartedly embrace jazz as their own, and even though this capital's clubs are not as plentiful as those in New Orleans or Chicago, they challenge the American variety in both quality and enthusiasm.

✪ Ca'feen Funke
Sankt Hans Torv (at Fælledvej). ☎ **31-35-17-41.** Cover 20 Kr ($3.35), but only if there's live music. Bus 5, 10, or 16 from Nørreport to Blegdamsvej.

This small local favorite is rarely visited by tourists. Live bands usually perform blues, soul, or funk on Saturday. Otherwise, you might hear American music from the 1960s and 1970s and amuse yourself, as the locals do, playing backgammon. Bar food is available. Look for the blue facade, and arrive early if you want a seat. Open Monday through Friday from 10am to 2am and Saturday and Sunday from noon to 2am; music usually starts at 9pm.

✪ Copenhagen Jazz House

Niels Hemmingsensgade 10. ☎ **33-15-26-00.** Cover 50–200 Kr ($8.35–$33.35), depending on the band.

This popular addition to the Copenhagen music scene opened in 1991. Expect to hear Danish jazz here 80% of the time, foreign jazz the rest of the time. Once the bands pack up and go home, the disco fires up and goes strong until the wee hours. There's a café at street level. The concert hall in the basement seats 300. Open Wednesday from midnight to 4am, Thursday from 8:30pm to midnight, and Friday and Saturday from 9:30pm to 1am; the disco is open until 5am Thursday through Saturday.

Din's

Lille Kannikestræde 3. ☎ **33-93-87-87.** Cover 30 Kr ($5), which includes a beer.

Din's is a restaurant/bar with a very active stage. Although rock bands sometimes perform here, the intimate back room is best suited to the jazz and blues performances held weeknights (except Tuesday, which is devoted to stand-up comedy, from 9:15 to 11:30pm). On weekends, rock 'n' roll takes center stage. The music starts at 11:30pm. The place opens at 5pm and closes Monday at midnight, Tuesday at 2am, Wednesday at 1am, Thursday at 1:30am, and Friday and Saturday at 4am. The restaurant serves Monday through Thursday from 6pm to midnight and Friday and Saturday from 5pm to 1am.

FREE ENTERTAINMENT

Open since 1989, the multilevel modern **Scala Center,** Axeltorv 2 (☎ **33-15-12-15**), has become a magnet for shopping, grabbing a quick bite to eat, entertainment, and people-watching. Numerous balconies provide a spot to stand or sit and enjoy the wide range of talented musicians who perform everything from jazz to classical guitar to pop several evenings a week on the second-level balcony. Or hop in one of the glass-enclosed elevators and observe the colorful scene as you glide up and down the airy atrium.

FILMS

Copenhagen is a movie city, and most films are in English with Danish subtitles. The going price of a ticket during evening hours is about 60 Kr ($10), but in some places, such as **Palads,** Axeltorv 9 (☎ **33-13-14-00**), the building near the Scala Center that looks like a psychedelic wedding cake and features 19 small cinemas, you pay 45 Kr ($7.50) or less, depending on day and time. Equally good discounts, and more comfortable seating, are available at the five movie theaters at the **Scala Center,** Axeltorv 2 (☎ **33-13-81-00**). Independent cinemas include the **Grand Teatret,** with full bar and café, Mikkel Bryggersgade 8 (☎ **33-15-16-11**), a block from Strøget near Town Hall Square, and the **Delta Bio,** Kompagnistræde 19 (☎ **33-11-76-03**).

THE BAR SCENE
"In" Spots

Cafe Dan Turrell
Store Regnegade 3–5. ☎ **33-14-10-47.**

Opened in 1977 and named after the contemporary Danish author of westerns and murder mysteries, this convivial bar attracts everyone from students to celebrities, who converse over burgers, pasta, quiche, and cappuccino. Light fare runs 42 to 48 Kr ($7 to $8); beer is 21 Kr ($3.50), and wine, 25 Kr ($4.20). Turrell's dust jackets decorate the wall behind the bar, where it's easy to imagine James Dean propped at one end. Open Monday through Wednesday from 9am to 2am, Thursday from 9am to 3am, Friday and Saturday from 9am to 4am, and Sunday from 10am to 2am.

Cafe Victor
Ny Østergade 8. ☎ **33-13-36-13.**

Trendiest of these listings, the Cafe Victor serves crêpes, quiches, and omelets to Copenhagen's beautiful young professionals, schmoozing elbow to elbow. Ceiling-to-floor windows look onto the street, and singles and sightseers often drink or enjoy a small café-style meal at the bar. The surroundings are elegant and most everyone is dressed up; half the clientele comes here to eat (there's also a restaurant on the premises), half to drink. Beer costs 20 Kr ($3.35); wine, 26 Kr ($4.35) and up. Open Sunday through Wednesday from 10am to 2am and Thursday through Saturday from 10am to 4am.

Krasnapolsky
Vestergade 10. ☎ **33-32-88-00.**

This popular restaurant/bar with minimal decor can be laid-back and low-key or loud and boisterous. Drinks from the long well-stocked bar are surprisingly well priced: Beer goes for 20 Kr ($3.35); wine, for 22 Kr ($3.70). Open Monday through Thursday from 10am to 2am, Friday and Saturday from 10am to 6pm, and Sunday from 3pm to midnight.

✪ Peder Oxes Vinkælder
Grabrødretorv 11. ☎ **33-11-11-93.**

Both unabashedly upbeat and terminally crowded, the Vinkælder's basement bar is one of the best in the city, known for its cocktails and beers from around the world, from Rolling Rock to Foster's. The bulk of the crowd can't afford dinner at the popular and pricey restaurant above (go up and sneak a peak at the room with the violins hanging from the wall). Weekend nights require a strong voice to be heard over the music and the crowd, and it can take 15 minutes to get from one end of the bar to the other. Beer costs 15 to 20 Kr ($2.50 to $3.35), wine begins at 25 Kr ($4.20), and mixed drinks run 40 Kr ($6.70). Open daily from noon to 1am.

Old-Time Bars

Hviids Vinstue
Kongens Nytorv 19. ☎ **33-15-10-64.**

This is Copenhagen's most historic wine cellar, faithfully serving citizens since 1723. It's no miracle that Hviids is still open, as it's a great place to drink. The large crowd of locals and visitors always includes a good share of the audience from the Royal Theater, across the street. One cozy seating area leads to another. The Hotel d'Angleterre is just one block away. Beer is 23 Kr ($3.85); wine, 18 Kr ($3). Open Sunday through Thursday from 10am to 1am and Friday and Saturday from 10am to 1:45am; closed Sunday May to August.

Nyhavn 17
Nyhavn 17. ☎ **33-12-54-19.**

Although sailors have been replaced by landlubbers, the spirit of the city's past as an important port still lingers here. You can enjoy a great view of the harbor as well as live music Thursday through Saturday. There's sailing memorablia on the walls, and paintings of exotic women overlook the imbibers. The bar, a real neighborhood type of place, is about 120 years old—the oldest in Nyhavn. Beer and wine go for 20 Kr ($3.35). Open Sunday through Wednesday from 10am to 2am and Thursday through Saturday from 10am to 4am.

GAMBLING

Denmark's first fully licensed casino, the **Casino Copenhagen,** opened in 1990 in the SAS Scandinavia Hotel, Amager Blvd. 70 (☎ **33-11-51-15**; Bus 5, 11, 30, or 33), with great success, offering blackjack, roulette, punto banco, and 140 slot machines. Some 2.5 kilos ($5 \frac{1}{2}$ lb.) of gold, 6,000 light bulbs, and over 10,000 glass-and-wood triangles decorate the place, which is run by Casinos Austria International, the world's largest casino operator. Restaurants, bars, and a weekend disco are on the premises. A jacket and tie are required. Admission is 60 Kr ($10). Bring your passport or another form of identification with you if you plan to play. It's open daily from 2pm to 4am.

DANCE CLUBS

As in other major cities, dance clubs come and go as fast as hiccups, and once gone, they're just as quickly forgotten. If you're really into this scene, ask at your hotel and check the local glossy giveaways (available in most clubs and record stores). Below is a lasting favorite:

Copenhagen Jazz House
Niels Hammingsensgade 10. ☎ **33-15-26-00.** Cover 60–90 Kr ($10–$15), depending on the entertainment.

When it's not a popular jazz hall (and a relatively new one, open since 1991), it's an equally popular disco. After the last strains of jazz have died away for the night, the throb of the disco beat takes over and continues until the wee hours of the morning: Wednesday from midnight to 4am and Thursday through Saturday from 6pm to 5am.

GAY & LESBIAN NIGHTLIFE

Cafe Babooshke
Turensensgade 6. ☎ **33-15-05-36.** Bus 1, 14, or 29.

One of the only clubs in town primarily for lesbians, this is a cozy fully licensed place serving hot and cold food. Changing monthly exhibits feature paintings, graphics, and photographs by women, and from time to time there's live music in the evening. Open Monday through Saturday from 4pm to 1am and Sunday from 4 to 11pm.

✪ **Sebastian Bar & Cafe**
Hyskenstræde 10 (half a block from Strøget, near Helligaands Church). ☎ **22-21-11-79.**

A congenial spot, it's popular with both men and women, and a good place to drop by to learn about Copenhagen's gay scene; ask the bartender or check out the bulletin board. There's occasional entertainment, from opera to disco, and the café food is homemade by the mother and mother-in-law of the owner. You can order burgers and sandwiches at lunchtime; for dinner, choices are pasta, chili, or a hot or cold special. The chocolate mousse comes highly recommended. Happy hour, called Gay Time, is 5 to 9pm daily. Thursday is billiards night for women. Open daily from noon to 1am (the kitchen closes at 10:30pm).

9 Networks & Resources

STUDENTS The **Use-It** office, Rådhusstræde 13 (☎ **33-15-65-18**), is a clearinghouse of information for young people new to Copenhagen (see "Visitor Information" under "Copenhagen Specifics," earlier in this chapter).

Danish-language courses are readily available from several sources in Copenhagen, among them **K.I.S.S. (Danish Language School),** Nørregade 20 (☎ **33-11-44-77**), where courses last 2¹/₂ weeks and cost 210 Kr ($35), including materials. Ask for the "Danish Courses for Foreigners" pamphlet at the Use-It office.

Den Internationale Hojskole (an international folk high school), Montebello Allé 1, 3000 Helsingør (☎ **49-21-33-61**), has a multilingual staff and offers courses in English and other languages.

Rejser, Skoubogade 6 (☎ **33-14-46-33**), specializes in discount train and plane tickets for travelers under 26. **Kilroy Travels Denmark,** Skindergade 28 (☎ **33-11-00-44**), also offers bus, train, plane, and boat discounts to students and people under 26. There's a travel library/bookstore next door called **Kupeen,** where you can research your upcoming journeys, check a ride board for travel companions, and buy English-language travel books (if you have an International Student ID Card, you get a 10% discount).

The main building of **Copenhagen University,** dating from 1479, is in the heart of the city, next to Copenhagen Cathedral. Unfortunately, like many urban schools, the campus lacks the bustle and energy of student life; students prefer to hang out in nearby cafés.

GAY MEN & LESBIANS The city's "gay church" is the **Metropolitan Community Church,** Knabrostræde 3 (☎ **31-83-32-86**). Services, on Sunday at 5pm, are in Danish, but the minister, Mia Andersen, speaks excellent English.

Since May 1989, gay unions (called "registered partnerships," but essentially marriages) and divorces have been legal in Denmark. Gay and lesbian couples have many of the rights of heterosexual married couples, but they cannot adopt or gain custody of children or have a church wedding.

WOMEN **Kvindehuset** (Women's House), Gothersgade 37, at Adelgade (☎ **33-14-28-04**), is a center for women's exchange and informal discussions about everything from politics to art. There's a small but selective secondhand shop on the premises and a table and chairs where you can sit and share coffee and conversation with other women. *The Garlic Press*, the Danish gay magazine, is published here. The Women's House is usually open Monday through Friday from noon to 5:30pm, but call to double-check hours. It's near Kongens Nytorv and Rosenborg Palace.

10 Easy Excursions

For a leisurely trip through the Danish countryside, your best bet may be the **Danish State Railways (DSB) "Special Excursion" ticket.** Not every destination is covered, but trips to the Louisiana Museum of Modern Art (see "Top Attractions" under "Attractions," earlier in this chapter), Roskilde, Odense, Legoland, and other highly touristed destinations certainly are. Call DSB (☎ **33-14-17-01**) for further information.

HELSINGØR (ELSINORE)   Four-hundred years of legal piracy, from the 15th through the 19th century, made Helsingør rich from tolls assessed on passing ships. Today, a walk around this carefully restored old town is proof enough that this was at one time Denmark's most important parcel. A wonderful architectural legacy and other indelible marks have been made on this seaside village by traders from around the world. But Helsingør is most famous for its regal 16th-century **Kronborg Castle** (☎ **49-21-30-78**), supposedly the setting for Shakespeare's *Hamlet.* Whether or not this is true, it is inarguable that the castle is nothing less than majestic. The castle tour features the royal apartments (with paintings and tapestries from the 16th and 17th centuries), the ballroom, the chapel, and other ancient areas.

The castle is open May to September, daily from 10:30am to 5pm; in April and October, Tuesday through Sunday from 11am to 4pm; and November to March, Tuesday through Sunday from 11am to 3pm. Admission is 20 Kr ($3.35) for adults, 10 Kr ($1.65) for children.

Located on the Danish coast 28 miles north of Copenhagen, Helsingør can be reached by train from Central Station in about an hour.

RUNGSTEDLUND   A visit to the Karen Blixen Museum in Rungstedlund can easily be combined with a trip to Kronborg Castle or the Louisiana Museum of Modern Art. The **Karen Blixen Museum,** at Rungsted Strandvej 111 (☎ **42-57-10-57**), is the 400-year-old memorabilia-filled home of the late author (alias Isak Dinesen, 1885–1962) of *Seven Gothic Tales* and the autobiographical *Out of Africa*, opened to the public in 1991. Except for the 17 years she spent in Kenya, Blixen lived here all her life. She was born in the house, originally a wayside inn that her parents bought in 1879, and was educated here by tutors. Karen Blixen's books were published to great acclaim in the United States, which she visited only once, for two months in 1959. You can visit the house (rent a recorded tour, if you like), where you'll see the small, shiny Corona on which she typed her works, as well as walk to her simple grave under a beech tree on Ewald's Hill. The museum and grounds are open May to September, daily from 10am to 5pm; October to April, Wednesday through Friday from 1 to 4pm and Saturday and Sunday from 11am to 4pm. Admission is 30 Kr ($5) for adults, free for children 11 and under; the Copenhagen Card is accepted.

Take the train to Rungsted Kyst, or change at Klampenborg for bus no. 388; the bus stop is about a block from the museum, which is well marked (walk in the direction the bus is traveling).

HILLERØD   A not-so-scenic 45-minute ride from Copenhagen, **Frederiksborg Palace** (☎ **42-26-04-39**) has been called the "Versailles of northern Europe." It was built in Dutch Renaissance style as a royal residence from 1600 to 1620 for Christian IV, who was king of Denmark and Norway for 60 years. Of particular interest are the immense Neptune Fountain, the elaborate, restored three-dimensional ceiling in the Knights Hall, and the chapel, looking just as it did when Christian IV used it.

The palace is open in April and October, daily from 10am to 4pm; May to September, daily from 10am to 5pm; and November to March, daily from 11am to 3pm. Admission is 30 Kr ($5) for adults, 10 Kr ($1.65) for students, and 5 Kr (85¢) for children 6 to 14. Tour cassettes are available in English and other languages.

ROSKILDE   For centuries Danish kings and queens have been laid to rest in the red-brick **cathedral** in Roskilde, most recently King Frederik IX in 1985. Today people visit Roskilde, which lies due west of Copenhagen and a mere half-hour train ride away, primarily to see the cathedral and the impressive royal tombs and the **Viking Ship Museum,** on Strandengen. The museum, open daily, houses five ships raised from the Roskilde Harbor in 1962. Purposefully sunk as barricades around A.D. 1000, they include two warships, two merchant ships, and a small vessel that was either a ferry or fishing boat. Films in English, German, French, Italian, and Spanish about the excavation of the ships are shown.

The **main square** of Roskilde becomes a fruit, flower, vegetable, and flea market on Wednesday and Saturday mornings. Its **palace,** built in 1733, now houses a collection of paintings and furniture from local merchant families.

In summer, excursion boats ply the Roskilde Fjord, and concerts are held throughout the venerable old city, as well as in Roskilde Park on Tuesday night. The enormously popular, four-day **Roskilde Festival** (☎ **42-36-05-48**) is held at the end of June every year. While the emphasis is on rock music, there is also folk, blues, and jazz, along with film presentations and theatrical performances. The festival is one of the oldest and largest in northern Europe, attracting top performers. Tickets are sold in Danish post offices beginning May 1.

The **tourist office** (☎ **42-35-27-00**) is near the cathedral. Trains run frequently between Copenhagen and Roskilde; if you want to explore this area further, take the bus from Roskilde 7km (4¼ miles) west to the charming village of **Gammel Lejre.**

DRAGØR   For a quick change of scene, hop on bus no. 30 or 33 at Town Hall Square (no charge with the Copenhagen Card), and in 40 minutes you'll be strolling the cobblestone walkways of the quaint seaside town of Dragør (rhymes with "sour"), with its small houses with red-tile or thatched roofs.

It's possible to see everything in an hour or two, or linger for lunch or supper in the flower-filled courtyard of the **Hotel Dragør Kro** (1721) or at the **Strand Hotel,** overlooking the harbor. Either of these inns can also provide lodging for the night.

The small **Dragør Museum** (☎ **32-53-41-06**), at the harbor, is open May to September, Tuesday through Friday from 2 to 5pm and Saturday and Sunday from noon to 6pm. There's a small, good camera store, Dragør Foto, on the main drag, Kongevejen 17 (☎ **32-53-78-00**).

The pleasant bus ride to Dragør takes you through tidy Danish communities and farmland.

MALMÖ, SWEDEN   Sweden's third-largest city—undeniably modern but with a 13th-century core—lies directly across the channel from Copenhagen, reachable in less than an hour or two by hydrofoil or boat. Both services depart from Havnegade, at the corner of Nyhavn. Visitors particularly enjoy the architecture in the old part of town, as well as the **Malmö Museum** at Malmöhus, a 15th-century castle. The city has several parks and a $4^1/_4$-mile stretch of sandy beach.

The **ferryboat** from Copenhagen to Malmö takes 90 minutes and costs 10 Kr ($1.65) one way. The **high-speed craft** *(flyvebadene)* at Havnegade/Nyhavn (☎ **33-12-80-88**) takes only 45 minutes and costs 85 Kr ($14.15) each way for adults, 65 Kr ($10.85) for seniors, and 35 Kr ($5.85) for children 2 to 12. A day pass costs 119 Kr ($19.85) round trip, with the following restrictions: Weekdays you must depart between 10am and 2pm; you can travel any time on weekends, but you must return the same day. With the steep competition between the various lines, you may be able to find tickets for much less. At this writing, a high-speed craft called *Pilen*, farther down on Havnegade, offered rates of 30 Kr ($5) per person Monday through Wednesday, Thursday and Friday, 50 Kr ($8.35) Saturday, and 40 Kr ($6.65) Sunday. Whichever boat you take, reserve in advance, remember to bring your passport, and be prepared to change money once you're in Sweden.

For a more in-depth look at the neighboring countries of Denmark and Sweden, ask DSB about **"Around the Sound,"** an inexpensive two-day excursion ticket to Sweden and back via boat and train.

Dublin 11

by Patricia Tunison Preston & John J. Preston

Dublin boasts no spectacular monuments, no grandiose museums, no hilltop castles, and no temples. Yet this city possesses a subtle charm that'll grow on you as you walk its streets and meet its citizens. Although it's a fast-paced capital with more than a million people (nearly one-quarter of Ireland's population) and is the country's largest city, Dublin remains compact and accessible. Unlike most cities of this size, Dublin has not sprouted forests of skyscrapers—it's characterized primarily by low-rise 18th-century buildings and has a distinctly old European feel. In large part Dublin's ambience is due to its inhabitants, 40% of whom are under age 25. They preserve their national heritage in their theater, their literature, and their music—even in the beer they drink.

Founded more than 1,000 years ago, Dublin has long been an important city. The name Dublin comes from the Irish *Dubh Linn* (Dark Pool), named for the black waters of the River Liffey where the first inhabitants built a trading port. Although the Vikings were the first to settle here, Dublin was also home to the Anglo-Normans, who built Christ Church and St. Patrick's Cathedral in the 12th century.

The Irish are a proud people who for centuries struggled against British rule before finally winning their independence in 1949. Much of the conflict, especially during the early years of this century, took place in Dublin. The Irish Nationalist movement, Sinn Féin, was born here, and in 1916 Dublin was the location of the famous Easter uprising, which stimulated Irish nationalism greatly.

The British left a legacy in Dublin's architecture. The simple but elegant Georgian town houses surrounding St. Stephen's Green and Merrion Square, Leinster House (the seat of Irish government), and Dublin Castle's State Apartments are just a few of the important buildings constructed by the British.

1 Dublin Deals & Discounts

BUDGET BESTS The best values in Dublin by far are the city's many bed-and-breakfasts. These are generally small establishments with six or fewer rooms, but what they lack in size they more than make up for in hominess. To stay in a Dublin B&B is to meet the Irish in their own homes, and there's no better way to get to know

What's Special About Dublin

The *Book of Kells*
- A 1,000-year-old copy of the New Testament, one of Ireland's most important treasures.

Irish Music
- Traditional Irish music any night of the week in pubs all over Dublin, most of the time absolutely free.

Wool Sweaters
- A large selection at the Dublin Woolen Mills shop by the Ha'Penny Bridge.

Live Theater
- Productions from a wealth of Irish playwrights past and present are performed.

Literary Landmarks
- Walk in the footsteps of Dublin's three Nobel Prize winners—Joyce, Shaw, and Beckett—by taking a literary pub crawl or soaking up the inspiring exhibits at the Dublin Writer's Museum, James Joyce Cultural Centre, James Joyce Tower, Shaw Birthplace, and other sites.

Ireland than sitting around the breakfast table chatting with your hosts over a huge meal of porridge, soda bread, thick bacon, sausages, eggs, juice, and coffee.

SPECIAL DISCOUNT   Dublin's best special discounts are for traveling on the city's extensive network of buses and commuter trains. Several passes are available, but the best deal is a one-day bus/rail ticket valid for unlimited travel on all city services, priced at IR£4 ($5.80). For IR£8.50 ($12.35) students can get a weekly bus ticket allowing unlimited travel on all buses except the airport coach. You must have a U.S.I.T. card with a C.I.E. Travel Save stamp in order to get one of these passes. The one-day family pass for IR£5.50 ($8) allows two adults and up to four children unlimited use of the bus and suburban rail system during off-peak hours.

WORTH THE EXTRA MONEY   Escorted bus tours, especially those visiting the Wicklow Mountains or the North Coast, are well worth the cost since they'll give you an indication of why Ireland is called the Emerald Isle. If you're traveling with a group and you don't want to take the bus tour, renting a car for a day can be quite affordable. It takes very little time to get out of the city and into the green countryside. Tours cost between IR£10 and IR£23 ($15.50 and $35.65).

2 Pretrip Preparations

REQUIRED DOCUMENTS   Citizens of the United States, Great Britain, Canada, Australia, and New Zealand need only a valid passport to visit Ireland.

TIMING YOUR TRIP   It can be cool and rainy any time of year, so be sure to bring clothes for "damp" days, as Dubliners call their cool wet days.

Dublin's Average Daytime Temperature & Days of Rain

	Jan	Feb	Mar	Apr	May	June	July	Aug	Sept	Oct	Nov	Dec
Temp. (°F)	45	45	49	53	58	63	65	65	62	57	50	47
Days of Rain	12	10	10	10	11	10	10	12	11	10	11	13

Special Events The most important event in Dublin—and all of Ireland—is **St. Patrick's Day,** March 17. Dubliners celebrate their literary heritage each June with the **Dublin Literary Festival.** The focal point of the festival is Bloomsday, June 16, which memorializes James Joyce's character Leopold Bloom. In late September and early October is the **Dublin Theatre Festival.**

BACKGROUND READING Over the years Dublin has been home to an impressive number of playwrights, poets, and novelists. The most notable is James Joyce, who wrote about his turn-of-the-century Dublin in the weighty novel *Ulysses* and his more accessible *The Dubliners,* a collection of short stories. Other famous literary figures include William Butler Yeats, Samuel Beckett, Oscar Wilde, J. M. Synge, George Bernard Shaw, Bram Stoker, and Sean O'Casey. Yeats, Beckett, and Shaw all received Nobel Prizes in literature. Jonathan Swift, author of *Gulliver's Travels,* was dean of St. Patrick's Cathedral from 1713 to 1745.

3 Dublin Specifics

ARRIVING IN DUBLIN

From **Dublin Airport,** 7 miles north of the city, buses run a regular schedule to the **Busáras Central Bus Station.** You can take either the express bus for IR£2.50 ($3.90), which will get you into town in under 30 minutes, or bus no. 41A, which can take as long as an hour but costs only IR£1.10 ($1.70). A taxi into town will cost IR£12 to IR£14 ($18.60 to $21.70).

What Things Cost in Dublin	U.S. $
Taxi from the airport to the city center	15.95
Local telephone call	.29
Double room at the Shelbourne Hotel (deluxe)	284.00
Double room at Georgian House (moderate)	75.40
Double room at Rathoe House (budget)	43.50
Continental breakfast at Kylemore Café	1.45
Lunch for one at the Old Stand (moderate)	8.70
Lunch for one at Bewley's Café (budget)	4.35
Dinner for one, without wine, at the Coq Hardi (deluxe)	50.75
Dinner for one, without wine, at Flanagan's (moderate)	15.25
Dinner for one, without wine, at the Kylemore Café (budget)	7.75
Pint of beer	2.90
Coca-Cola (in a restaurant)	1.10
Cup of coffee	.85
Roll of 100 ASA color film, 36 exposures	7.20
Admission to Dublin Castle	2.20
Movie ticket	4.35–.25
Theater ticket	11.60–3.20

VISITOR INFORMATION

Dublin Tourism, a division of the **Irish Tourist Board (Bord Fáilte),** has its main information center at 14 Upper O'Connell St. (☎ **01/284-4768**), where you can find all sorts of free information about Dublin and the rest of Ireland. Other facilities include a currency-exchange counter, a car-rental counter, and a hotel-reservations desk. Books and maps for sale here can help you learn more about the city. Dublin Tourism also maintains offices at Dublin Airport (☎ **01/844-5387**), at the ferry dock in Dun Laoghaire (☎ **01/280-6984**), and at 18 Eustace St., Temple Bar (☎ **01/671-5717**). The hours for each of the tourist information centers vary depending on the month, but they're generally open Monday through Friday from 9am to 6pm and Saturday from 9am to 1pm, although the information desk at the airport is open daily from 8am to 6pm.

At any of the tourist centers you can also pick up a copy of *Tourism News,* a free tourist information newspaper; the *Dublin Event Guide,* a free biweekly entertainment guide; or *In Dublin,* a biweekly arts-and-entertainment magazine selling for IR£1.50 ($2.35), at any of the tourist centers.

CITY LAYOUT

The **River Liffey** flows from west to east through Dublin. On the **north bank** is the new city, which has as its focal point busy **O'Connell Street,** lined with shops and restaurants. The Busáras Central Bus Station is also on the north side. Connecting the north and south banks of the river are 11 bridges, the largest of which is the O'Connell Street Bridge and the smallest of which is the nearby pedestrians-only Ha'Penny Bridge. On the **south bank** in the old city are most of Dublin's important sites, such as Trinity College, Dublin Castle, Christ Church Cathedral, St. Patrick's Cathedral, the National Gallery, and the National Museum.

GETTING AROUND

Dublin is crowded, and getting around by bus or car can be very time-consuming. If you're going a short distance, it's almost always better to walk, especially since most of the tourist attractions are clustered within the old city. For longer distances, there are a number of transportation options.

BY DART   The Dublin Area Rapid Transit, or DART, commuter train is the best way to get in and out of Dublin if you're staying in Dun Laoghaire or want to take a trip out to Howth Head or Bray Head for a bit of walking around outside the city. Unfortunately, it's not very useful for travel within the city itself. There are only three stops convenient to tourist sites—Pearse Station, beside Trinity College; Tara Station, on the south bank of the Liffey one block from O'Connell Bridge; and Connolly Station. DART fares range from 80p to IR£2.25 ($1.25 to $3.50). The fare to Dun Laoghaire is IR£1.10 ($1.70).

BY BUS   Because of the traffic congestion in the center of Dublin, public buses can be agonizingly slow, but they're still the best way to travel around the city. Almost all the tourist sites can easily be reached by bus. The fare varies according to your destination, with an average fare of 80p ($1.25); the trip to Dun Laoghaire will cost IR£1.10 ($1.70). Exact change is suggested but not necessary.

There are several different **discount bus passes** allowing unlimited travel for one, four, or seven days. These passes range in price from IR£3.30 ($5.10) for a one-day bus pass to IR£14 ($21.70) for a one-week bus and DART pass. You can pick up passes at the main bus office at 59 Upper O'Connell St., across from the

The Irish Punt

For American Readers   At this writing $1 = approximately 64p (or IR£1 = $1.55), and this was the rate of exchange used to calculate the dollar values given in this chapter (rounded to the nearest nickel).

For British Readers   At this writing £1 = approximately 82p (or IR£1 = £1.58), and this was the rate of exchange used to calculate the pound values in the table below.

Note: The rates given here fluctuate from time to time and may not be the same when you travel to the Republic of Ireland. Therefore this table should be used only as a guide:

IR£	U.S.$	U.K.£	IR£	U.S.$	U.K.£
.25	.39	.40	11	17.05	17.38
.50	.78	.79	12	18.60	18.96
.75	1.16	1.19	13	20.15	20.54
1.00	1.55	1.58	14	21.70	22.12
2.00	3.10	3.16	15	23.25	23.70
3.00	4.65	4.74	20	31.00	31.60
4.00	6.20	6.32	25	38.75	39.50
5.00	7.75	7.90	30	46.50	47.40
6.00	9.30	9.48	35	54.25	55.30
7.00	10.85	11.06	40	62.00	63.20
8.00	12.40	12.64	45	69.75	71.10
9.00	13.95	14.22	50	77.50	79.00
10.00	15.50	15.80	75	116.25	118.50

Dublin Tourism information center. Daily combination bus and DART passes are available at all DART stations. To use your bus pass, simply insert it into the small box just inside the door of the bus. The box will stamp your ticket and return it to you.

BY TAXI   Taxis are IR£1.80 ($2.80) to start and 80p ($1.25) per mile after that. Bags are 40p (60¢) extra, and there's a 40p (60¢) extra charge for trips at night and on Sunday. There are taxi stands along O'Connell Street and in front of major hotels. Cab companies you can call include **Co-op Taxis** (☎ **01/676-6666**) and **VIP Taxi Co.** (☎ **01/478-3333**).

ON FOOT   Dublin, though a compact city that can be easily explored on foot, is not an easy city to find your way around. A street in Dublin may change names three times within three blocks, and the street signs, when they're there at all, are posted on the second-floor wall of a corner building. Adding to the confusion is the lack of numbers on buildings in many places and the fact that many streets in Dublin are numbered up one side of the street and down the other, rather than alternating sides. There are exceptions, but they're primarily in the suburbs.

BY BICYCLE   Riding a bicycle in Dublin is not recommended. Traffic is very heavy, streets are narrow, and pedestrians crowd every corner in the city center.

If you're determined to take to the streets on wheels, however, you can rent a bicycle for IR£7 ($10.85) per day or IR£30 ($46.50) per week at the **Bike Store,** 58 Lower Gardiner St. (☎ **01/872-5931**), just around the corner from Isaac's Dublin Tourist Hostel. The Bike Store is open Monday through Saturday from 9:30am to 6pm.

BY RENTAL CAR Renting a car in Dublin is not advisable because of traffic congestion and parking problems, but when exploring the countryside you may wish to go by car. If you do rent a car in Dublin, be sure you can park it off the street—car theft and break-ins are all too frequent. **Budget Rent a Car,** 151 Lower Drumcondra Rd. (☎ **01/837-9611**) and at the airport (☎ **01/844-5919**), is very reliable though it's not the cheapest in town. Expect to pay between IR£30 and IR£65 ($46.50 and $100.75) per day, plus tax and insurance, for their smallest car.

If you're staying in Dun Laoghaire, try **South County Rentals,** Rochestown Avenue (☎ **01/280-6005**). Its least-expensive car rents for IR£25 ($38.75) per day.

FAST FACTS: Dublin

Banks Two convenient banks are the National Irish Bank, 66 Upper O'Connell St. (☎ **01/873-1877**), open Monday through Friday from 10am to 12:30pm and 1:30 to 4pm (on Thursday until 5pm), and the Allied Irish Bank, 100 Grafton St. (☎ **01/671-3011**), open Monday through Friday from 10am to 4pm (on Thursday until 5pm).

Business Hours Regular **office hours** in Dublin are Monday through Friday from 9am to 5pm. **Shops** generally stay open Monday through Saturday from 9am to 6pm, and many offer late shopping until 8 or 9pm on Thursday and Friday nights. Some shops are open Sunday from noon to 5pm.

Currency The basic unit of currency in Ireland is the **punt,** or **Irish pound (IR£),** which is divided into 100 **pence (p).** There are 1p, 2p, 5p, 10p, 20p, 50p, and IR£1 coins and notes of 5, 10, 20, 50, and 100 pounds. We use the symbol IR£ to distinguish the Irish pound from the English pound. Currency can be exchanged at banks, the main post office, and at the Dublin Tourism office at 14 Upper O'Connell St. (see "Visitor Information" under "Dublin Specifics," earlier in this chapter).

Embassies As Ireland's capital, Dublin is home to the embassies of a number of countries, including **Australia,** at Fitzwilton House, Wilton Terrace (☎ **01/676-1517**); **Canada,** at 65 St. Stephen's Green (☎ **01/478-1988**); the **United Kingdom,** at 31 Merrion Rd. (☎ **01/269-5211**); and the **United States,** at 42 Elgin Rd. (☎ **01/668-8777**).

Emergencies Dial **999** for fire, police, and ambulance. For the name and phone number of a physician on duty, ask at your hotel. Leonard's Corner Pharmacy, 106 S. Circular Rd. (☎ **01/453-4282**), is open daily from 9:30am to 10pm.

Eyeglasses See the Talbot Eye Center, at 19a Talbot St. (☎ **01/878-6056**), if you need your glasses repaired or replaced. It's open Monday through Saturday from 9am to 6pm.

Holidays Public holidays in Dublin are New Year's Day (Jan 1); St. Patrick's Day (Mar 17); Easter and Easter Monday; the first Monday in May, June, and August; the last Monday in October; and Christmas (Dec 25–26).

Hospitals   The Mater Misericordiae Hospital, 7 Eccles St. (☎ **01/830-1122**), is a general hospital with an outpatient clinic.

Information   The main information center for **Dublin Tourism,** a division of the Irish Tourist Board (Bord Fáilte), is at 14 Upper O'Connell St. (☎ **01/ 284-4768**). Dublin Tourism also maintains offices at the airport (☎ **01/ 844-5387**), at the ferry dock in Dun Laoghaire (☎ **01/280-6984**), and in Temple Bar (☎ **01/671-5717**). For details, see "Visitor Information" under "Dublin Specifics," earlier in this chapter.

Laundry/Dry Cleaning   Center-city launderettes include the Laundry Room, 8 Lower Kevin St. (☎ **01/478-1774**), and Suds, 60 Upper Grand Canal St. (☎ **01/668-1786**). Take your dry cleaning to Craft Cleaners, 12 Upper Baggot St. (☎ **01/668-8198**).

Lost & Found   The Dublin Bus Lost Property Office is on Earl Place behind Clery's department store, open Monday through Friday from 9am to 12:30pm and 2 to 5pm. You can also inquire about lost property at the Police (Garda) Station, Harcourt Square (☎ **01/673-2222**).

Mail   The General Post Office is located on O'Connell Street, at the corner of Henry Street (☎ **01/872-8888**); it's open Monday through Saturday from 8am to 8pm and Sunday from 10am to 6:30pm. An airmail letter to the United States will cost 52p (80¢) and a postcard to the States will cost 38p (60¢). There's also a foreign-currency exchange here that keeps the same hours as the post office.

Newspapers   The *Irish Independent* and the *Irish Times* are the most informative newspapers.

Photographic Needs   The Camera Shop, 70 Lower Gardiner St. (☎ **01/ 874-7248**), is open Monday through Saturday from 9am to 6pm.

Police   Dial 999.

Radio/TV   Two national, four local, and BBC radio stations are broadcast. TV choices include the BBC, Irish programming, Ulster TV, and satellite programming.

Religious Services   St. Patrick's Cathedral, St. Patrick's Street (☎ **01/ 475-4817**), has Anglican services daily at 8:30am and on Sunday also at 11:15am. St. Mary's Pro-Cathedral, Marlborough Street (☎ **01/874-5441**), has Catholic services on Sunday at 8, 10, and 11am, and 12:30 and 6pm. There's an Orthodox synagogue, Dublin Hebrew Congregation, at 37 Adelaide Rd. (☎ **01/676-1734**).

Shoe Repair   Rapid Shoe Repair, 5 Sackville Place, will repair shoes Monday through Saturday from 9am to 6pm.

Tax   Ireland's VAT (value-added tax) is 17.36% on the price of all goods (except books and children's clothing and footwear). Many stores will refund this amount to foreign visitors. For details, see "Shopping," later in this chapter.

Taxis   See "By Taxi" in "Getting Around," under "Dublin Specifics," earlier in this chapter.

Telephone   Dublin has recently added a seventh digit to its six-digit phone numbers. If your call does not go through, contact an operator.

There's a **local and international phone center** at the General Post Office on O'Connell Street. A local phone call costs 20p (30¢). Pay phones accept either a variety of coins or a phone card (available at post offices). A call to the United States will cost about IR£3.60 to IR£4.80 ($5.60 to $7.45) if dialed directly, or IR£3.86 to IR£5 ($6 to $7.75) if you go through an operator, for three minutes.

Tipping   In restaurants that don't add a service charge, 10% to 15% is the acceptable amount to tip if the service has been good. Taxi drivers don't expect a tip, but if you wish to give one, again, 10% is appropriate.

4 Accommodations

All over Ireland you'll discover delightful bed-and-breakfasts, and Dublin is no exception. The Irish, born with the gift of the gab, are an outgoing lot, and perhaps the best way to get to know a few is to stay in a B&B. For the most part, these are family homes whose owners strive to make you feel like one of the family.

The crime rate in Dublin's city center has been on the rise in recent years, so we recommend that older travelers and those not accustomed to living in an urban environment head out from downtown to find a room. A 15- to 20-minute bus or DART commute will bring you to quiet residential streets where you need not be as concerned for your safety at night. However, young travelers who intend to take advantage of Dublin's many pubs and rock-music clubs will likely want to stay where they'll be within an easy walk of all the action.

Remember: Dublin has recently changed all its phone numbers. If your call doesn't go through, a recording should advise you of the new number. You can dial toll free 1/800-330-330 if you have any difficulty.

DOUBLES FOR LESS THAN IR£35 ($54.25)
IN THE CITY CENTER

✪ Harvey's Guesthouse

11 Upper Gardiner St., Dublin 1. ☎ **01/874-8384.** 10 rms, 6 with bath. May–Oct, IR£18 ($27.90) per person single, double, triple, quad, or quint without bath; IR£20 ($31) per person single, double, triple, quad, or quint with bath. Nov–Apr, IR£2 ($3.10) less per person. Rates include full Irish breakfast. No credit cards. Parking free.

A 10-minute walk from the bus terminal, Harvey's has been in operation for more than 20 years, and its small size ensures personal attention from owner Mrs. Eilish Flood and her son, Robert. This guesthouse is good for families or groups since two of the large rooms can each sleep up to five. Floral sheets and warm duvets are nice touches. There's a private parking area.

Waverly House

4 Hardwicke St., Dublin 1. ☎ **01/874-6132.** 6 rms, 4 with shower. IR£18–IR£20 ($27.90–$31) single without shower; IR£13–IR£15 ($20.15–$23.25) per person double without shower; IR£15–IR£17 ($23.25–$26.35) per person double or triple with attached shower. Rates include full Irish breakfast. No credit cards.

Hardwicke Street is a few blocks from Gardiner Street and in a more attractive area. At the end of this quiet street is a large old church with a picturesque steeple. The Waverly occupies a modernized Georgian town house with a long history of accepting paying guests. In 1903 James Joyce stayed here when the building was used as a boardinghouse, and he based one of his stories in *The Dubliners* on Waverly House. Liz Carty is the proprietor.

Getting the Best Deal on Accommodations

- Bed-and-breakfasts are an Irish institution. Look for them on Gardiner Street near the bus station, along Clontarf Road northeast of downtown, and not far outside the city in the town of Dun Laoghaire.
- Perhaps try accommodations outside downtown Dublin, if you prefer not to climb steep flights of stairs.

DOUBLES FOR LESS THAN IR£40 ($62)
IN THE CITY CENTER

Sinclair House

3 Hardwicke St., Dublin 1. ☎ **01/855-0792.** 6 rms, none with bath. IR£20 ($31) single; IR£30–IR£40 ($46.50–$62) double. Rates include full Irish breakfast. No credit cards.

Less than a 15-minute walk up O'Connell Street from the bridge is this pleasant guesthouse run by Mrs. Maria McMahon. At this 18th-century Georgian town house a full Irish breakfast is served in a large dining room; in the comfortable TV lounge guests can relax, watch TV, or visit with other guests and the hosts. The rooms have clock radios and attractive bedspreads.

✪ Stella Maris

13 Upper Gardiner St., Dublin 1. ☎ **01/874-0835.** 8 rms, 4 with bath. IR£18–IR£20 ($27.90–$31) single; IR£16–IR£18 ($24.80–$27.90) per person double or triple without bath, IR£18–IR£20 ($27.90–$31) per person double or triple with bath. Rates include full Irish breakfast. No credit cards. Parking free.

In one of the restored Georgian town houses along Upper Gardiner Street is the friendly Stella Maris, efficiently run by Mrs. Breeda Smith, who was in the hotel business long before she opened her own B&B. She brings her years of experience into use here. Most of the rooms are large and comfortable, with high ceilings and large windows.

ALONG CLONTARF ROAD

Clontarf Road runs along the north side of Dublin Bay and is about 20 minutes by bus from O'Connell Street. A park with beautiful green lawns located between the bay and the roadway is delightful for evening strolls in summer. Unfortunately, the view across the bay for much of the road's length is of the industrial port of Dublin. Take bus no. 30 from Abbey Street to reach any guesthouse on Clontarf Road.

Bayview

265 Clontarf Rd., Dublin 3. ☎ **01/833-9870.** 3 rms, 2 with bath. IR£20 ($31) single without bath, IR£22 ($34.10) single with bath; IR£28 ($43.40) double without bath, IR£30 ($46.50) double with bath. Rates include full Irish breakfast. No credit cards. Bus 30.

In this small guesthouse you'll be greeted by the genial Mrs. Carmel Drain. Rooms 2 and 3 have large bay windows looking out across the bay. Tea/coffee makers are in each bedroom, and the Irish breakfast is available at 6am for early risers.

Sea Breeze

312 Clontarf Rd., Dublin 3. ☎ **01/833-2787.** 3 rms, all with bath. IR£16 ($24.80) single; IR£32 ($49.60) double. Rates include full Irish breakfast. No credit cards. Closed Dec–Jan. Bus 30.

Sea Breeze is operated by Mrs. Myra O'Flaherty, who goes out of her way to take care of her guests. This 100-year-old house offers the best view on Clontarf Road; try to get Room 4 with the bay window. The sitting room and dining room are both quite spacious. For IR£8 ($12.40), Mrs. O'Flaherty will prepare a four-course meal, though there are also several nearby restaurants.

SOUTH OF CITY CENTER

St. Dunstan's

25A Oakley Rd., Ranelagh, Dublin 6. ☎ **01/497-2286.** 3 rms, none with bath. IR£20 ($31) single; IR£16.50–£19 ($25.60–$29.45) per person double, triple, or quad. Rates include full Irish breakfast. No credit cards. Bus 13 from O'Connell Street.

About 15 minutes south of the city center is Dublin's southern district of Ranelagh, with narrow stone-walled lanes that give this neighborhood the feel of a country village. Your stay in this small red-brick Edwardian town house will be made more enjoyable by the lace-trimmed breakfast room, the tile-and-iron fireplaces, the attractively decorated rooms, and the attentive care of owner Mai Bird.

IN DUN LAOGHAIRE

This Victorian seaside resort (pronounced "Dun Leary"), only 15 minutes by DART train from Dublin's city center, is also the port for ferries to Liverpool and Holyhead in Great Britain. The greatest concentration of guesthouses is on Rosmeen Gardens, a three-minute walk from the Sandycove DART station. You can also reach Dun Laoghaire on bus no. 7, 7A, or 8.

✪ Mrs. Helen Callanan

1 Rosmeen Gardens, Dun Laoghaire, Co. Dublin. ☎ **01/280-6083.** 4 rms, 1 with bath. TV. IR£20 ($31) single without bath; IR£16–IR£17.50 ($24.80–$27.15) per person in shared room without bath, IR£19.50 ($30.25) per person in shared room with bath. Rates include full Irish breakfast. No credit cards. DART: Sandycove. Bus 7, 7A, or 8.

Built in 1900 with a red-brick Victorian facade, this lovely two-story house overlooks Dublin Bay and a nearby public park. The guest rooms, each with a color TV, are spacious and colorfully decorated. Mrs. Helen Callanan is a charming hostess and serves a full Irish breakfast from 7am until midmorning.

Mrs. Anne D'Alton

Annesgrove, 28 Rosmeen Gardens, Dun Laoghaire, Co. Dublin. ☎ **01/280-9801.** 4 rms, 2 with bath. IR£18 ($27.90) single without bath; IR£16 ($24.80) per person in shared room without bath, IR£18.50 ($28.70) per person in shared room with bath. Rates include full Irish breakfast. No credit cards. DART: Sandycove. Bus 7, 7A, or 8.

You'll feel as if you're one of the family at Mrs. D'Alton's cheerful home. All the rooms are very comfortable, with warm duvets on all the beds. There's a cozy TV lounge, and out back, a pleasant garden. The filling Irish breakfast will keep you going through hours of sightseeing.

Mrs. Marie Dunne

30 Rosmeen Gardens, Dun Laoghaire, Co. Dublin. ☎ **01/280-3360.** 4 rms, none with bath. IR£18 ($27.90) single; IR£16 ($24.80) per person in shared rooms. Rates include full Irish breakfast. No credit cards. Closed Nov–Mar. DART: Sandycove. Bus 7, 7A, or 8.

Mrs. Marie Dunne provides a warm welcome to her two-story corner home situated in a quiet cul-de-sac with lovely flower gardens outside. Guests enjoy use of a TV lounge and a cozy dining room. The full Irish breakfast, replete with homemade preserves and breads, is served from 7am each day.

Mrs. Greta McGloughlin

27 Rosmeen Gardens, Dun Laoghaire, Co. Dublin. ☎ **01/280-4333.** Fax 01/280-9331. 3 rms, 1 with bath. TV. IR£28 ($43.40) single without bath; IR£17.50 ($27.15) per person in shared room without bath, IR£21 ($32.55) per person in shared room with bath. Rates include full Irish breakfast. No credit cards. Closed Oct–Apr. DART: Sandycove. Bus 7, 7A, or 8.

Operated by a former Aer Lingus flight attendant, this B&B features a bright and cheery breakfast room overlooking the garden. The guest rooms are comfortably and attractively furnished.

✪ Rathoe House

12 Rosmeen Gardens, Dun Laoghaire, Co. Dublin. ☎ **01/280-8070.** 4 rms, none with bath. IR£20 ($31) single; IR£16–IR£18 ($24.80–$27.90) per person in shared room. Rates include full Irish breakfast. No credit cards. DART: Sandycove. Bus 7, 7A, or 8.

You'll be made to feel like a long-lost relative the moment you walk through the door of Mrs. Valerie Fitzgibbon's Rathoe House. All beds come with electric blankets and down comforters. Mrs. Fitzgibbon is happy to take the time to help you get your bearings in Dublin and serves large Irish breakfasts.

Rosmeen House

13 Rosmeen Gardens, Dun Laoghaire, Co. Dublin. ☎ **01/280-7613.** 5 rms, 1 with bath. IR£20 ($31) single without bath; IR£16 ($24.80) per person in shared room without bath, IR£20 ($31) per person in shared room with bath. Rates include full Irish breakfast. No credit cards. Closed Dec 15–Feb 1. DART: Sandycove. Bus 7, 7A, or 8.

Rosmeen House is an attractive 1920s Spanish-style villa on its own grounds. Guests have use of a drawing room and sun room as well as the dining room. Mrs. Joan Murphy keeps her home immaculately clean. The orthopedic beds all have electric blankets.

SUPER-BUDGET CHOICES
HOSTELS

Avalon House

55 Aungier St., Dublin 2. ☎ **01/475-0001.** Fax 01/475-0303. 45 rms, 8 with bath; 70 dorm beds. IR£14–IR£18 ($21.70–$27.90) single without bath; IR£11–IR£13.50 ($17.05–$20.95) per person double without bath, IR£ 13–IR£14.50 ($20.15–$22.48) double with bath; IR£9–IR£11.50 ($13.95–$17.85) per person quad without bath; IR£7.50–IR£10.50 ($11.65–$16.30) dorm bed. Rates include continental breakfast. AE, MC, V. Bus 16, 16A, 19, or 22.

One of Dublin's newest hostels is housed in an ornate Victorian building constructed in 1879 as a medical school. The carved red sandstone facade is elegant, though the interior of the restored building is much less formal. In addition to the dorms, there are quite a few single and double rooms, and some of the doubles even have private baths. The rooms are small and spartanly furnished but modern and spotless; some have carpeting and others have hardwood floors. Inexpensive meals are served in the spacious lobby dining room, where you'll also find lots of information for visitors to Dublin. The hostel is well located close to Dublin's upscale shopping neighborhoods.

Dublin International Youth Hostel

61 Mountjoy St., Dublin 7. ☎ **01/830-4555.** Fax 01/830-5808. 500 beds. IR£7.50–IR£9.50 ($11.65–$14.75) per night for IYHF members, IR£8–IR£10 ($12.40–$15.50) per night for nonmembers for the first six nights. Rates include full Irish breakfast. EURO, MC, V. Bus 10 from O'Connell Street. Parking in an enclosed private lot.

This newer hostel is housed in what once was a convent. Though most of the accommodations are in large dormitories, there are also a few doubles, triples, and quads. The dining room is a beautiful converted chapel, and the card pay phone is in an old confessional booth. If you stay here, you can also purchase discount train tickets to other parts of Ireland. These tickets are not available anywhere else and are a real savings.

Isaac's Dublin Tourist Hostel

2–5 Frenchman's Lane, Dublin 1. ☎ **01/874-9321** or 836-3877. Fax 01/874-1574. 50 rms, none with bath; 200 dorm beds. IR£17.25 ($26.75) single; IR£14 ($21.70) per person double; IR£5.75–IR£7.50 ($8.90–$11.65) dorm bed (sheets for an additional charge). Continental breakfast IR£1.25 ($1.95) extra; full Irish breakfast IR£1.95 ($3) extra. No credit cards.

Housed in a restored wine-storage warehouse built in the 1700s, this hostel is only 50 yards from the main bus terminal, requires no youth-hostel card, and accepts people of all ages. The ground-floor restaurant/lounge is reminiscent of a German ratskeller with stone walls and huge exposed beams. The self-service restaurant is open to the public. A spacious self-catering kitchen and TV lounge are available to guests.

✪ Kinlay House

2–12 Lord Edward St., Dublin 2. ☎ **01/679-6644.** Fax 01/679-7437. 35 rms, 16 with bath; 80 dorm beds. IR£17.50–IR£18 ($27.15–$27.90) single without bath; IR£12.50–IR£13.50 ($19.40–$20.95) per person double without bath, IR£13–IR£14 ($20.15–$21.70) per person double with bath; IR£11–IR£12 ($17.05–$18.60) per person quad without bath, IR£12–IR£13 ($18.60–$20.15) per person quad with bath; IR£8.50–IR£9.50 ($13.50–$14.75) dorm bed. Rates include continental breakfast. No credit cards. Bus 50, 54, 65, or 77.

Located across from Christ Church Cathedral is this 100-year-old building that was originally a charitable boys' home. It accepts guests of both sexes and all ages, and no hostel card is necessary. All rooms are carpeted, clean, and attractively furnished. Most of the accommodations are in four- and six-bed rooms. Besides a coffee shop and a self-catering kitchen, there's a launderette, TV lounge, study lounge, and recreation room. Note that Kinlay House is situated on a busy street and the noise may bother light sleepers. The hostel is on the edge of the Temple Bar area, Dublin's "left bank," where you'll find plenty of interesting restaurants, pubs, and shops.

✪ Morehampton House

78 Morehampton Rd., Donnybrook, Dublin 4. ☎ **01/668-8866.** Fax 01/668-8794. 16 rms, 2 with bath; 32 dorm beds. IR£12.50–IR£13.50 ($19.40–$20.95) per person single or double; IR£9.95–IR£10.95 ($15.40–$16.95) per person in four- to eight-bed dorm room; IR£7.95–IR£8.95 ($12.35–$13.85) per person in 16-bed dorm room. EURO, MC, V. Bus 10, 46A, or 46B.

Situated in a residential area south of the city center and within a 15-minute walk of St. Stephen's Green, this lovely four-story Victorian house has been recently converted and refurbished as a hostel. It offers a choice of twin rooms and dorm-style accommodations. Facilities include a 24-hour reception desk, a TV room, a common room, a self-catering kitchen, car and bike parking, and lovely gardens.

The Old School House

Eblana Ave., Dun Laoghaire, Co. Dublin. ☎ **01/280-6508** or 280-8777. Fax 01/284-2266.
156 beds. IR£11 ($17.05) per person twin; IR£8–IR£9 ($12.40–$13.95) per person in four-
to six-bed rooms. Some rooms with bath available for IR£1 ($1.55) per person extra.
AE, MC, V. DART: Dun Laoghaire station. Bus 7, 7A, 8, or 46A.

A five-minute walk from the ferry wharf and harbor, this three-story hostel is in
the heart of Dun Laoghaire village, off Lower George's Street. As its name implies,
it was once a school but was converted into lodgings in 1993. About half the rooms
are twins or doubles; the rest are four- to six-bed dorms. Nine ground-floor rooms
have facilities for the disabled. An on-premises cafeteria serves breakfast and
dinner.

WORTH THE EXTRA MONEY

✪ Jurys Christchurch Inn

Christchurch Place, Dublin 8. ☎ **01/475-0111,** or 800/843-6664 in the U.S. Fax 01/475-
0488. 172 rms, all with bath. A/C TV TEL. IR£42–IR£52 ($65.10–$80.60) single, double, or
triple. AE, CB, DC, MC, V. Bus 21A, 50, 50A, 78, 78A, or 78B.

Across from Christ Church Cathedral, this is a new four-story hotel, designed in
keeping with the area's Georgian/Victorian architecture and heritage. This is
the first place of its kind in the city's historic district, offering quality hotel lodgings at guesthouse prices. The rooms, all with contemporary furnishings, can
accommodate up to three adults or two adults and two children—all for the same
price. Facilities include a moderately priced restaurant, a pub lounge, and parking nearby.

✪ Mrs. Elsie O'Donoghue

41 Northumberland Rd., Ballsbridge, Dublin 4. ☎ **01/668-1105.** 8 rms, none with bath.
IR£26 ($40.30) single; IR£48 ($74.40) double; IR£60 ($93) triple. Rates include full Irish break-
fast. No credit cards. Bus 5, 6, 7, or 8.

In the posh Ballsbridge district of Dublin not far from the deluxe Jurys Hotel and
the American Embassy, 15 minutes south of center city, is one of the best splurge
B&Bs in the city. Elsie O'Donoghue's large Victorian home, built in 1877,
features the finest plasterwork ceilings of any guesthouse listed in this chapter.
Breakfast is served in a huge room with a massive mirror over the fireplace.
Mrs. O'Donoghue is extremely helpful to her guests and will make sure you
enjoy your Dublin stay.

The Talbot

95/98 Talbot St., Dublin 1. ☎ **01/874-9202.** Fax 01/874-9672. 42 rms, all with bath;
8 suites. TV TEL. IR£26–IR£36 ($40–$55.80) single; IR£19–IR£30 ($40.30–$55.80) per
person double or twin; IR£72 ($111.60) suite for up to four. Rates include full Irish break-
fast. AE, MC, V. Bus 27A, 31A, 31B, 32A, 32B, or 44A.

Located within two blocks of the Abbey Theatre, the Central Bus Station, and
O'Connell Street, this attractive mansard-roofed guesthouse was originally a trio
of adjoining commercial buildings. Completely renovated and opened to guests in
1994, it blends an old-world ambience with pastel-toned modern furnishings and
fittings. The facilities include a breakfast room with an outdoor deck, an enclosed
parking area, and an elevator—often a rare amenity in older buildings. For groups
of four, the suite rate per person (IR£18/$27.90) is hard to equal for such
stylish digs.

5 Dining

From pub grub to haute cuisine, Dublin has it all—however, the name of the game for cheap eating here is self-service (cafeteria dining). Many very good and inexpensive restaurants, ranging from the massive Bewley's Cafe on Grafton Street to the tiny Cunningham's Coffee Shop across from the National Museum, offer self-service meals. Also keep in mind that breakfast is included in the cost of your room.

LOCAL BUDGET BESTS

✪ Beshoff's

14 Westmoreland St. and 7 Upper O'Connell St. ☎ **01/677-8026.** Fish and chips IR£1.95–IR£5.50 ($3–$8.55). No credit cards. Daily 11:30am–1am. FISH AND CHIPS.

Beshoff's is one of Dublin's oldest and most popular fish-and-chips restaurants, and it now offers two locations, on either side of the O'Connell Street Bridge. The first Beshoff's was founded in 1913 by Russian immigrant Ivan Beshoff. Today the two restaurants offer as many as 20 varieties of fish and chips in an Edwardian oyster-bar atmosphere of black-and-white tiles and marble-top tables. On any given day the catch might include plaice, mackerel, smoked mackerel, shrimp, and monkfish.

MEALS FOR LESS THAN IR£5 ($7.75)
ON THE NORTH BANK

✪ Kylemore Cafe

1–2 Upper O'Connell St. ☎ **01/872-2138.** IR£2.50–IR£5 ($3.90–$7.75); lunch special IR£3.25 ($5.05). No credit cards. Mon–Sat 7:30am–8pm, Sun noon–8pm. IRISH.

This large restaurant on busy O'Connell Street is a cafeteria with style; floor-to-ceiling windows flood the large and always-crowded dining room with light. There are plenty of marble-top tables to seat the throngs of diners who fill the restaurant all day long, so don't be discouraged if it looks full.

ON THE SOUTH BANK

✪ Bewley's Cafe

78 Grafton St. ☎ **01/677-6761.** IR£2–IR£4.50 ($3.10–$7). AE, DC, MC, V. Mon–Wed 7:30am–1am, Thurs–Sat 7:30 or 8am–2am, Sun 9:30am–10pm. IRISH.

Bewley's, a Dublin institution, is always jammed with people despite its 350 seats and three dining areas. It specializes in coffees, teas, and pastries, but you can also get breakfast all day, sandwiches, salads, and hot lunches at their self-service restaurants. There are tables and large booths, and no one will mind if you linger for several hours over coffee and a newspaper or a book.

There are seven other Bewley's branches in the Dublin area, including 11–12 Westmoreland St. and 13 S. Great Georges St.

The Buttery Cafe

Dame Street, Trinity College Campus. ☎ **01/677-3787.** IR£2–IR£3 ($3.10–$4.65). No credit cards. Mon–Fri 8:30am–4pm. Closed late Sept to late June. IRISH.

Another exceptional bargain is this student cafeteria on the Trinity College campus, open to the public in summer only. It's to the left of the campanile and down the stairs. The prices are incredibly reasonable, and you can experience the summer-school atmosphere of this historic campus.

Getting the Best Deal on Dining

- In Dublin you'll find ample opportunities for self-service dining.
- Note that tourist menus provide limited choices but substantial savings.
- Pub grub can often be surprisingly sophisticated and costs less than restaurant fare.

Cunningham's Coffee Shop

35A Kildare St. ☎ **01/676-2952.** IR£1.75–IR£4.50 ($2.75–$7). No credit cards. Mon–Fri 8:45am–5:30pm. IRISH.

This tiny restaurant is hardly bigger than a closet, but it's convenient to the National Museum, which is directly across the street. Duck in for a salad or sandwich if you're in a hurry or linger over quiche, pasta, or pâté.

Dublin Castle Vaults Patisserie & Bistro

Palace St., off Dame St. ☎ **01/679-3713.** Most items IR£1.30–IR£4.95 ($2–$7.65). No credit cards. Mon–Sat 11am–4pm. Bus 50, 54, 50A, 56A, or 77. INTERNATIONAL.

With stone walls, paned windows, and colorful medieval banners, the old vaults of Dublin Castle serve as the setting for this bustling indoor/outdoor café. The menu focuses on pastries, snacks, or such light lunch items as homemade soups, pâtés, quiches, lasagnes, sausage rolls, stuffed baked potatoes, salads, and sandwiches.

✪ St. Teresa's Courtyard Cafe

Clarendon St. ☎ **01/674-8466** or 671-8127. All items 80p–IR£2 ($1.25–$3.10). No credit cards. Mon–Sat 10:30am–4pm. DART: Tara Street station. Bus 16, 16A, 19, 19A, 22A, 55, or 83. IRISH.

Situated in the cobblestone courtyard of early 19th-century St. Teresa's Church, this serene old-world dining room is one of a handful of new eateries inconspicuously springing up in historic or ecclesiastical surroundings. The menu changes daily but usually includes homemade soups, sandwiches, salads, quiches, lasagnes, sausage rolls, hot scones, and other baked goods.

The Well Fed Café

6 Crow St. ☎ **01/677-2234.** IR£2–IR£5 ($3.10–$7.75). No credit cards. Mon–Sat noon–8:30pm. VEGETARIAN.

More than just a restaurant, the Well Fed Café is a gathering place for those who espouse a natural way of life. It specializes in home-cooked vegetarian meals and offers three-course meals. Specialties include vegetable burgers and quiches, tacos, and salads. If you're looking for long-term accommodations or are interested in a yoga class or a lecture on Marxism in Ireland, check the extensive bulletin boards here.

MEALS FOR LESS THAN IR£10 ($15.50)
ON THE SOUTH BANK

✪ Bad Ass Cafe

9–11 Crown Alley. ☎ **01/671-2596.** IR£4.55–IR£9.50 ($7.05–$14.75). AE, EURO, MC, V. Daily 9am–midnight. IRISH.

This restaurant, popular with students and families alike, once employed rock 'n' roller Sinéad O'Connor as a waitress. The spacious split-level dining room is painted red, white, and blue. Along one wall is a large notice board covered with flyers for interesting events in and around Dublin. Reading the menu is half the fun of eating here, where there are often "dinner for two" specials.

Gallagher's Boxty House

20–21 Temple Bar. ☎ **01/677-2762.** IR£5.50–IR£10 ($8.55–$15.50). EURO, MC, V. Daily 11:30am–12:30am. IRISH.

Boxty is a traditional Irish dish made from—you guessed it—potatoes. In this case the potatoes are made into a pancake and rolled around a filling to form an Irish stuffed crêpe. Fillings include beef and horseradish, bacon and cabbage, Indian chickpeas, and many others. The stone walls and stained glass give the restaurant the feel of an old inn or tavern.

Galligan's Cafe & Bistro

6 Merrion Row. ☎ **01/676-5955.** Café snacks IR60p–IR£2.50 (95¢–$3.90); lunch items IR£1.95–IR£4.95 ($3–$7.65); dinner main courses IR£4.95–IR£8.95 ($7.65–$13.85). AE, DC, MC, V. Café, Mon–Fri 7am–7pm, Sat–Sun 8am–7pm. Bistro, daily 5–11pm. IRISH/INTERNATIONAL.

For a light breakfast, snack, or lunch, it's hard to beat the home-cooked fare offered at this self-service eatery just off the north side of St. Stephen's Green. The chalkboard-style menu changes daily but usually includes quiches, pastas, curries, salads, and soups. In the evening, head downstairs to the Bistro, a candlelit enclave with a fireplace, alcoves, rustic furnishings, and table service. The choices usually include warm salads, oven-baked chicken, fresh seafood, and steaks, as well as stir-fried dishes, omelets, and pastas.

National Gallery Fitzers

Merrion Sq. W. ☎ **01/668-6481.** IR£4.95–IR£8.95 ($7.65–$13.85). ACCESS, AE, DC, EURO, MC, V. Coffee daily 10am–noon; lunch daily noon–4pm; tea Tues–Wed and Fri–Sat 2–5pm, Thurs 3–8pm, Sun 2–4:30pm. INTERNATIONAL.

Strategically located next to Gallery VI at the National Gallery on Merrion Square, Fitzers rapidly became one of Dublin's "in" lunch spots after it opened. After gazing at Goyas and before viewing some El Grecos you can try coq au vin or hake Mallorca. Beef cannelloni or vegetarian lasagne might be the perfect accompaniment to a Gainsborough. There's live piano music on Thursday evening and Saturday afternoon, and lots of plants and latticework give Fitzers a garden-party feeling.

✪ The Old Stand

37 Exchequer St. ☎ **01/677-0821.** IR£3.95–IR£9.95 ($6.10–$15.40). ACCESS, EURO, MC. Lunch Mon–Fri 12:30–3pm; dinner Mon–Fri 5–9:30pm, Sat 12:30–8:30pm. PUB GRUB.

To many, the very words *pub grub* are unappealing, and frequently these heavy meals are nothing more than the cheapest eats to be had. However, at the Old Stand pub meals are raised to new heights. For years, Dubliners have been packing this pub at lunch and dinner for such appetizing dishes as smoked salmon salad, chicken Kiev, and chicken Maryland, as well as steaks and sandwiches. You'll find the pub just a couple of blocks off busy Grafton Street.

PICNICKING

In the basement of the **Dunnes Market** on North Earl Street, two doors from O'Connell Street, you'll find almost everything you need for a picnic. Wait to buy your bread across the street at the Kylemore Bakery, which has delicious baked goods and pastries. When you have everything you need, take bus no. 10 to Phoenix Park.

WORTH THE EXTRA MONEY

✪ DeSelby's

17/18 Patrick St., Dun Laoghaire. ☎ **01/284-1761** or 284-1762. IR£4.95–IR£10.95 ($7.65–$16.95). AE, DC, MC, V. Mon–Fri 5:30–11pm, Sat noon–11pm, Sun noon–10pm. DART: Dun Laoghaire station. Bus 7, 7A, 8, or 46A. INTERNATIONAL.

If you're staying at one of the Dun Laoghaire area B&Bs, this busy restaurant is hard to beat for an excellent reasonably priced dinner in a fun atmosphere. Choices include traditional Irish stew, beef Stroganoff, boiled bacon and cabbage, chicken Kiev, pastas, steaks, and half a dozen types of fresh fish, plus American-style burgers and Irish-style mixed grills.

6   Attractions

In A.D. 988 Dublin was founded by traders who settled on the banks of the River Liffey. Since then the city has had a turbulent history as the people constantly struggled for home rule against first the Vikings, then the Normans, and most recently the British. This history is captured in many of the city's important landmarks.

SIGHTSEEING SUGGESTIONS

If You Have 1 Day

Start your day at Trinity College Library where the Book of Kells is on display, then walk over to the National Museum to see exhibits of Irish antiquities. If you have time, briefly visit the nearby National Gallery, with its fine collection of old masters and important Irish artists. After lunch, stroll around Merrion Square and St. Stephen's Green, two public parks-surrounded by dignified Georgian town houses. Walk down Grafton Street and then head over to Dublin Castle. After touring the castle, visit Christ Church Cathedral and St. Patrick's Cathedral. Finish your day at the Brazen Head, Dublin's oldest pub.

If You Have 2 Days

Follow the itinerary above for your first day, then on your second day walk up O'Connell Street to Parnell Square and the Garden of Remembrance, dedicated to people who have died in the cause of Irish freedom. Across from this memorial are the Dublin Writers Museum and the Hugh Lane Municipal Gallery. After touring these two museums, walk back down toward the ILAC Shopping Centre and the colorful produce market on Moore Street. After lunch, you can walk to St. Michan's Church, home to Dublin's own mummies. From here, head for the Irish Museum of Modern Art at the Royal Hospital Kilmainham. Finish the day at the Guinness Hop Store Gallery.

If You Have 3 Days

Spend Days 1 and 2 as described above. On your third day, take a day trip to the Boyne Valley and the north coast to visit burial mounds at Newgrange, the site of the Battle of the Boyne, King William's Glen, and other sites. This trip is also worthwhile for the glimpse of the Irish countryside it affords.

If You Have 5 Days

Schedule another day trip to see the fabulous Irish countryside. Glendalough, a former monastic city, and the Wicklow Mountains make an excellent excursion.

On the morning of your fifth day, take a trip out to Sandycove to see the James Joyce Museum and the Victorian harbor town of Dun Laoghaire. In the afternoon, return to Dublin and take one of the walking tours (see "Organized Tours," below).

TOP ATTRACTIONS

✪ National Museum

Kildare St. ☎ **01/661-8811.** Admission free. Tues–Sat 10am–5pm, Sun 2–5pm. Bus 7, 7A, 8, 10, 11, or 13.

This is Ireland's treasure trove, whose highlights are the displays of golden jewelry found in ancient bog hoards. No one is sure why ancient peoples buried rich caches of gold in inaccessible bogs, but today these unearthed treasures make up this museum's most captivating exhibit. The most famous piece is the Tara Brooch, a large and intricately worked gold pin once used to hold a woman's cloak together. Also in the museum are artifacts from Ireland's Viking past.

National Gallery

Merrion Sq. W. ☎ **01/661-5133.** Admission free. Mon–Wed and Fri–Sat 10am–5:30pm, Thurs 10am–8:30pm, Sun 2–5pm. Bus 5, 7, 7A, 8, 10, 44, 47, 48A, or 62.

This gallery houses a collection of old masters, Irish artists, and the National Portrait Gallery. Among the many works displayed are pieces by Rembrandt, Brueghel, Rubens, El Greco, Gainsborough, and Monet. Near the museum entrance is a statue of George Bernard Shaw, who left one-third of his estate to the museum when he died, saying that he owed his education to the gallery. In the gallery is a moderately priced self-service restaurant (see "Dining," earlier in this chapter).

✪ Trinity College Library

Trinity College Campus. ☎ **01/677-2941.** Library, IR£2.50 ($3.90) adults, IR£2 ($3.10) students and senior citizens, free for children; *The Dublin Experience,* IR£2.75 ($4.25) adults, IR£2.25 ($3.45) children under 18 and senior citizens. Library, Mon–Sat 9:30am–5:30pm, Sun noon–5pm; *The Dublin Experience,* late May to early Oct, daily 10am–5pm. Bus 10.

Trinity College Library, built between 1712 and 1732, is to the right and behind the campanile just inside Trinity College's front gate. Housed in the library's Colonnades exhibition area is the *Book of Kells,* an illustrated and illuminated copy of the gospels created by early 9th-century Irish monks at the monastery of Kells. This exquisitely ornamented volume is the rarest and most important book in Ireland. On the main floor is a bookstore selling works by Irish authors, books about Ireland, and other gifts.

Trinity College is also home to *The Dublin Experience,* a multimedia program that's an excellent introduction to the city's history and people.

Dublin Castle

Dame St. ☎ **01/679-3713.** Admission IR£1.75 ($3.90) adults, IR£1 ($1.55) children. Mon–Fri 10am–12:15pm and 2–5pm, Sat–Sun 2–5pm. Bus 50, 50A, 54, 56A, or 77.

Dublin Castle is about midway between O'Connell Bridge and St. Patrick's Cathedral. The round tower beside the castle's chapel was built by the Normans in the early 13th century and is the oldest part of the castle. Most of the present building, however, was erected in the 18th century by the British as the residence of the viceroys; it now houses the State Apartments and is used for inaugurations of

Irish presidents. The apartments are open to the public, with guided tours held throughout the day. Some fine Georgian plasterwork ceilings can be seen here. Around the outside wall of the attached chapel are more than 90 carved stone busts of British monarchs and other important historical figures.

Christ Church Cathedral

Christ Church Place. ☎ **01/677-8099.** Admission IR£1 ($1.55) adults, 25p (40¢) students. Daily 10am–5pm; tours available by request. Bus 21A, 50, 50A, 78, 78A, or 78B.

One block west of Dublin Castle (above), on a ridge above the site of the original Norse town of Dublin, stands Christ Church Cathedral. Founded in 1038, the present building dates from 1172 and was substantially renovated between 1871 and 1878. Inside you'll find a monument to Strongbow, the ruler who had the cathedral built, and in the crypt you can see the stocks that once stood nearby. You may notice that the north interior wall has a very pronounced outward lean. Don't worry—it's been like this for hundreds of years and the building is in no danger of falling.

St. Patrick's Cathedral

St. Patrick St. ☎ **01/475-4817.** Admission IR£1.20 ($1.85) adults, 60p (95¢) students. Mon–Fri 9am–6pm, Sat 9am–5pm (to 4pm in winter), Sun 10am–4:30pm. Bus 50, 50A, 54, 54A, or 56A.

This cathedral was built less than 25 years after Christ Church Cathedral (above) in an attempt to outdo that building. Jonathan Swift, author of *Gulliver's Travels*, was dean here from 1713 to 1745, and his tomb is to be found within the walls of this impressive Norman cathedral.

✪ Irish Film Centre

6 Eustace St. ☎ **01/679-5744.** Centre, free; *Flashback*, IR£2.30 ($3.55) adults, IR£1.80 ($2.80) seniors and students. Centre, daily 10am–11:30pm; *Flashback*, June–Sept, Wed–Sun at 11am, noon, and 1pm. Bus 21A, 78A, or 78B.

As the Irish film industry marks its 100th anniversary in 1996, this new center is becoming a focal point for local and visiting movie fans alike. It houses several film components under one roof: two movie theaters (cinemas), the Irish Film Archive, a library, a film-themed bookshop and restaurant/bar, and eight film-related organizations. It also offers displays of photos, posters, and memorabilia of the Irish film industry, which has been adding many credits in recent years. In summer, there are showings of the film *Flashback*, a history of Irish film in the past century.

❓ Did You Know?

- No point in Ireland is more than 70 miles from the ocean.
- Dublin's Whitefriar's Church contains the remains of St. Valentine.
- U2 and Sinéad O'Connor both got their start in Dublin.
- There are no snakes in Ireland; according to tradition, St. Patrick banished them from the island.
- Swift, Yeats, and Joyce were all born in Dublin.
- All official documents are published in both Irish and English.
- Dublin's Phoenix Park is the largest enclosed park in Europe.
- Dublin was founded by Vikings.

Dublin

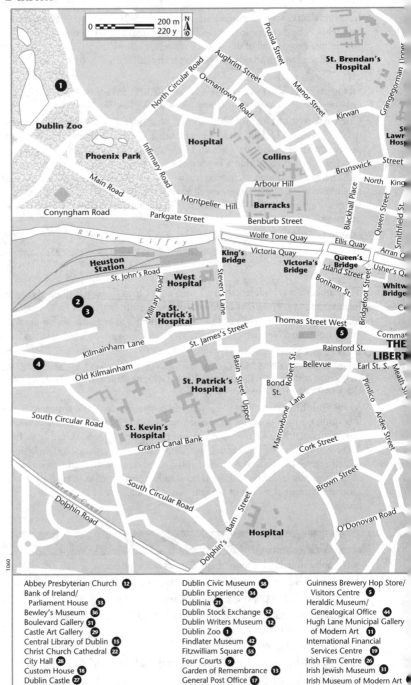

0 ——— 200 m
0 ——— 220 y
N

Dublin Zoo ❶

Phoenix Park

Prussia Street

St. Brendan's Hospital

North Circular Road

Aughrim Street

Oxmantown Road

Manor Street

Kirwan

Grangegorman Upper

S Lawr Hos

Hospital

Collins

Brunswick Street

North King

Arbour Hill

Barracks

Blackhall Place

Queen Street

Smithfield St.

Infirmary Road

Main Road

Montpelier Hill

Benburb Street

Conyngham Road

Parkgate Street

Wolfe Tone Quay

Ellis Quay

Arran Q

River Liffey

Victoria Quay

King's Bridge

Queen's Bridge

Usher's Q

Heuston Station

St. John's Road

Victoria's Bridge

Island Street

Whitw Bridge

West Hospital

Steven's Lane

Bonham St.

Bridgefoot Street

Thomas Street West

Military Road

St. Patrick's Hospital

St. James's Street

Rainsford St.

Cornma

THE LIBER

Kilmainham Lane

Basin Street Upper

Robert St.

Bellevue

Earl St. S.

Meath St

❹

Old Kilmainham

St. Patrick's Hospital

Bond St.

Marrowbone Lane

Pimlico

Ardee Street

South Circular Road

St. Kevin's Hospital

Grand Canal Bank

Cork Street

Brown Street

Grand Canal

Dolphin Road

South Circular Road

Dolphin's Barn Street

Hospital

O'Donovan Road

❷ ❸ ❹ ❺

1060

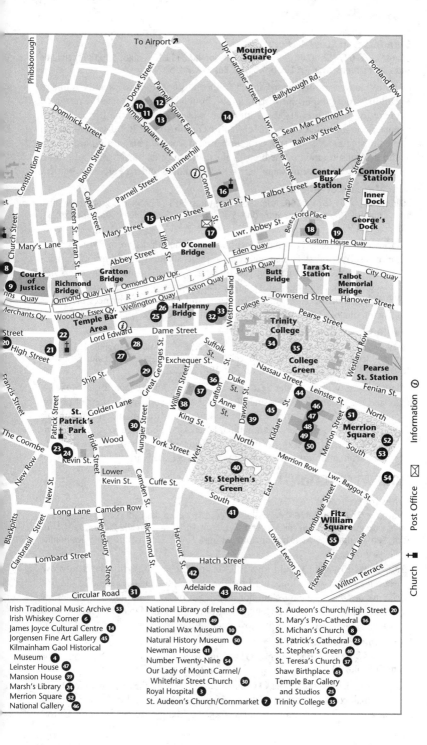

Irish Traditional Music Archive **53**	National Library of Ireland **48**
Irish Whiskey Corner **6**	National Museum **49**
James Joyce Cultural Centre **14**	National Wax Museum **10**
Jorgensen Fine Art Gallery **45**	Natural History Museum **50**
Kilmainham Gaol Historical	Newman House **41**
Museum **4**	Number Twenty-Nine **54**
Leinster House **47**	Our Lady of Mount Carmel/
Mansion House **39**	Whitefriar Street Church **30**
Marsh's Library **24**	Royal Hospital **3**
Merrion Square **52**	St. Audeon's Church/Cornmarket **7**
National Gallery **46**	

St. Audeon's Church/High Street **20**
St. Mary's Pro-Cathedral **16**
St. Michan's Church **8**
St. Patrick's Cathedral **23**
St. Stephen's Green **40**
St. Teresa's Church **37**
Shaw Birthplace **43**
Temple Bar Gallery
and Studios **25**
Trinity College **35**

Church ✝   Post Office ✉   Information ℹ

Guinness Hop Store Gallery

Crane St. ☎ **01/453-6700** ext. 5155. Admission IR£2 ($3.10) adults, 50p (80¢) children and senior citizens. Mon–Fri 10am–4:30pm. Bus 21A, 78, or 78A.

Three blocks west of Christ Church Cathedral, the Guinness Brewery is one of Dublin's most important institutions. Though the brewery itself is not open for tours, at the brewery museum you can learn all about the famous "black porter" or stout that has been brewed in Dublin since 1769. Exhibits explain the brewing process, the coopering of barrels in the days before aluminum kegs, and the transportation of the brew by horse-drawn carts, canal barges, and steam engines. There's a tasting room here as well. Children under 12 are not admitted.

Irish Museum of Modern Art

Military Rd. ☎ **01/671-8666.** Admission free; tours, IR£1 ($1.55) adults, 50p (80¢) children. Tues–Sat 10am–5:30pm, Sun noon–5:30pm. Tours, Sun 12:30–4:30pm. Bus 24, 51, 63, 69, 70, or 90.

Housed in the Royal Hospital Kilmainham, this museum is worth a visit as much for its displays of Irish contemporary art as for its architecture and beautiful manicured grounds. Constructed in the 1680s as a home for army pensioners, it's Ireland's largest building of this vintage that's not a monastery, church, or castle. Special exhibits, lectures, music concerts, and dance performances make this museum one of Dublin's most important cultural centers.

Dublin Writers Museum

18/19 Parnell Sq. N. ☎ **01/872-2077.** Admission IR£2.60 ($4.05) adults, IR£2 ($3.10) students and senior citizens, IR£1.10 ($1.70) children. Daily 10am–5pm. Closed Mon Sept–May. Bus 10, 11, 11A, 11B, 12, 13, 14, 16, 16A, 19, 19A, 22, 22A, or 36.

James Joyce, William Butler Yeats, Oscar Wilde, Brendan Behan, Bram Stoker— Ireland has produced a surprising number of highly acclaimed writers of poetry, prose, and plays. No aspiring writer or student of literature should miss seeing this collection of rare editions, memorabilia, letters, and photos covering Irish literature from the 9th century to the present. The adjacent Irish Writer's Centre provides contemporary writers with a place to meet and work.

MORE ATTRACTIONS

James Joyce Tower

Sandycove. ☎ **01/280-9265.** Admission IR£2 ($3.10) adults, IR£1.60 ($2.50) students and senior citizens, IR£1 ($1.55) children. Apr–Oct, Mon–Fri 10am–1pm and 2–5pm, Sat 10am–5pm, Sun 2–6pm; Nov–Mar, by appointment only. DART: Sandycove; then a five-minute walk. Bus 8.

No James Joyce fan should miss this small museum housed in the Sandycove Martello Tower where Joyce lived for a while in 1904—it's described in the first chapter of *Ulysses.* The museum houses exhibits on Joyce and Dublin at the time *Ulysses* was written. If you pick up a copy of the "*Ulysses* Map of Dublin" you can make this the starting point of a Joyce tour of the city.

Hugh Lane Municipal Gallery

Parnell Sq. ☎ **01/874-1903.** Admission free. Tues–Fri 9:30am–6pm, Sat 9:30am–5pm, Sun 11am–5pm. Bus 10, 11, 11A, 11B, 12, 13, 14, 16, 16A, 19, 19A, 22, 22A, or 36.

At the northern end of Upper O'Connell Street is this old Georgian mansion housing a small collection of primarily French impressionists and early 20th-century Irish artists. The collection includes works by Manet, Monet, Morisot, Corot,

Special & Free Events

Of all Dublin's holidays, **St. Patrick's Day** is the one celebrated with the most enthusiasm. The parade itself is held on March 17, but there are festivities for several days before and after.

Another favorite of Dubliners is the **Liberties Festival,** celebrating life in the Liberties, Dublin's oldest neighborhood. Held each year in mid-June, the festivities include outdoor concerts, exhibitions, guided walks, pageants, and other events.

For fans of James Joyce, June 16 is the day to be in Dublin. On this date the city celebrates **Bloomsday,** in memory of Leopold Bloom, the protagonist of Joyce's *Ulysses* who travels around Dublin on June 16, 1904. Bloomsday is part of the larger **Dublin Literary Festival,** held in mid-June.

In late September and early October, the **Dublin Theatre Festival** is the focus of all Ireland. Featured are new Irish plays, classic revivals, and performances by overseas touring companies.

For free events, nothing in Dublin can beat the free **traditional Irish music** that can be heard every night in pubs all over the city. For details, see "Dublin After Dark," later in this chapter.

Renoir, and Degas, among others. The works on display here were bequeathed to the city of Dublin by Sir Hugh Lane, who drowned in the sinking of the *Lusitania* at the beginning of World War I.

St. Michan's Church

Lower Church St. ☎ **01/872-4154.** Admission IR£1.20 ($1.85) adults, IR£1 ($1.55) students and senior citizens. Tours, Mon–Fri at 10am and 2pm. Bus 34 or 34A.

On the north side of the River Liffey is an unusual Dublin attraction housed in the crypt of a church. The corpses interred in the vaults at St. Michan's have been preserved because of the drying action of the porous limestone walls. Ghoulish visitors are thrilled by these Irish equivalents of Egyptian mummies. Also in this church is an organ on which Handel performed his Dettingen *Te Deum.*

PARKS & GARDENS

Phoenix Park, in western Dublin, is one of the largest urban parks in the world. In such a densely developed city, this vast expanse of green, which can be reached by bus no. 10 from O'Connell Street or no. 25 or 26 from Middle Abbey Street, is a welcome change. Here you'll find the Dublin Zoo, as well as the residences of the president of Ireland and the U.S. ambassador. Rolling hills, ponds where ducks and swans beg for handouts, and a herd of free-roaming deer all make this an excellent place for a picnic.

The **National Botanic Gardens** (☎ **01/837-4388**) are in the northern suburb of Glasnevin and can be reached by bus no. 13 or 19 from O'Connell Street or no. 34 or 34A from Middle Abbey Street. Founded in 1795, the gardens contain more than 20,000 species of plants and a beautiful greenhouse more than 400 feet long. The Botanic Gardens are open daily except December 25. There's no admission charge.

SPECIAL-INTEREST SIGHTSEEING

LITERARY LANDMARKS   Two of Dublin's Nobel Prize–winning writers, James Joyce and George Bernard Shaw, are the focus of downtown sightseeing opportunities with a literary theme. The **James Joyce Cultural Centre,** 35 N. Great George's St. (☎ **01/873-1984**), is devoted to imparting an increased understanding of the life and works of James Joyce, through a series of Joycean exhibits, audiovisual presentations, an archive, and a reference library. It's housed in a restored 1784 Georgian town house, once the home of Denis J. Maginni, a professorial character often featured in Joyce's writings. To add to the authenticity, Ken Monaghan, Joyce's nephew, conducts tours of the house and walking tours through the neighborhood streets of "Joyce Country" in Dublin's northern inner city. Admission is IR£2 ($3.10) per person; with a guided tour of the house it's IR£5 ($7.75) per person, or with a walking tour of "Joyce Country" it's also IR£5 ($7.75) per person. The center is open Tuesday through Saturday from 10am to 4:30pm and Sunday from 12:30 to 4:30pm. To get there, take the DART to Connolly Station or bus no. 1, 40A, 40B, or 40C.

Across the river on the south side of town, literary fans pay homage at the **Shaw Birthplace,** 33 Synge St. (☎ **01/475-0854**). Situated off South Circular Road, this simple two-story terraced house, built in 1838, is the home where George Bernard Shaw was born in 1856. Recently restored, it has been furnished in Victorian style to re-create the atmosphere of Shaw's early days. Rooms on view are the kitchen, maid's room, nursery, drawing room, and a couple of bedrooms, including young Bernard's. Admission is IR£2 ($3.10) for adults, IR£1.60 ($2.50) for students and seniors, IR£1.10 ($1.70) for children 3 to 11. It's open May to October, Monday through Saturday from 10am to 5pm and Sunday from 11:30am to 6pm. Take bus no. 16, 19, or 22.

ORGANIZED TOURS

WALKING TOURS   Small and compact, Dublin lends itself to walking tours. You can set out on your own with a map, but the best way to avoid any hassles or missed sights is to follow one of the four signposted and themed **"tourist trails"**: "Old City Trail," for historic sights; "Georgian Trail," for the landmark buildings, streets, squares, terraces, and parks; "Cultural Trail," for a circuit of the top literary sites, museums, art galleries, theaters, and churches; and the "Rock 'n' Stroll Trail," for a tour of the city's contemporary music enclaves, pubs, breweries, nightspots, and more. Each trail is mapped out in a handy booklet, available for about IR£2 ($3.10) from the Dublin Tourism office, 14 Upper O'Connell St. (☎ **01/284-4768**).

If you prefer an escorted walking tour, there are several firms offering tours led by knowledgeable local guides. Tour times and charges vary, but most last about two hours and cost between IR£4 and IR£6 ($6.20 and $9.60) per person. **Discover Dublin Tours** (☎ **01/478-0191**), with literary, historical, and traditional music themes, departs from various starting points. **Dublin Footsteps** (☎ **01/496-0641** or 845-0772) are tours focused on medieval, literary, 18th-century, or city-center sites, and depart from Bewley's Cafe on Grafton Street or from the Dublin Tourism office. The **Dublin Literary Pub Crawl** (☎ **01/454-0228**) departs evenings from Duke Street. Historical Walking Tours (☎ **01/845-0241**) departs from the front gate of Trinity College; and **Trinity College Walking Tours** (☎ **01/679-4291**) departs from Front Square of Trinity College.

BUS TOURS   For the standard fast-paced, see-it-all-in-under-three-hours bus tour of Dublin, climb aboard the **Dublin Bus** open-deck sightseeing coach. Tours leave from the Dublin Bus office at 59 Upper O'Connell St. (☎ **01/873-4222**) from March to November daily at 10:15am and 2:15pm and December to March on Tuesday, Friday, and Saturday at 10:15am. You can purchase your ticket at the office or on the bus for IR£8 ($12.40) for adults, IR£4 ($6.20) for children. This tour takes in most of the important sights in Dublin but doesn't stop at any of them.

There's another similar bus tour operated April through September in conjunction with the walking-tour Heritage Trail booklets. Tickets for the **Heritage Tour** cost IR£5 ($7.75) for adults and IR£2.50 ($3.90) for children, are good for one day, and allow you to get on and off the bus at various conveniently located stops.

7 Shopping

Grafton Street, a pedestrians-only zone near Trinity College, is Dublin's chic shopping district where trendy boutiques, department stores, and specialty shops proliferate. **Powerscourt Townhouse Centre** and **St. Stephen's Green Centre** are this area's newest focal points and prime examples of Dublin's ongoing renovation and gentrification. In the **Temple Bar area** are unusual shops selling Asian and Latin American imports, secondhand clothes, and hard-to-find records.

RECOVERING VAT & SHIPPING IT HOME   Obtaining a VAT (value-added tax) refund is quite easy in Ireland. Whenever you make a purchase in a shop, ask for a **Cashback voucher.** Be aware that there's a handling charge for this service: IR£3.35 ($5.20) if you spend IR£150 ($232.50) or less, IR£4.35 ($6.75) for IR£150 to IR£300 ($232.50 to $465), and IR£5.35 ($8.30) for more than IR£300 ($465). Refunds may be claimed at the airport Cashback windows before you leave the country or by mail after you return home. If you're leaving by ferry, you must mail the Cashback voucher for a refund. Remember that you may have to show your purchases to Customs before leaving the country in order to get the refund. Look for the cashback tax free shopping sign in shop windows and read the instructions carefully.

If you don't want to carry your purchases while you're traveling, take advantage of the mailing service offered by most shops for an additional charge.

MARKETS   The most interesting city-center market is **Mother Redcaps Market,** Back Lane (☎ **01/854-4655**), housed in an old shoe factory in the heart of the Liberties, one of Dublin's oldest sections. More than 100 dealers exhibit here, with a good selection of arts and crafts, antiques, used books, and locally produced farm cheeses. It's open on Friday and   Saturday from 10am to 5:30pm.

Of the city's open-air food markets, the **Moore Street Market** is legendary. Situated just off Henry Street beside the ILAC Shopping Centre, it's supposed to be the market from which Molly Malone wheeled her wheelbarrow through streets broad and narrow. Today vendors shout for attention (in typical Dublin accents) to sell fruits, vegetables, flowers, and fish Monday through Saturday from 9am to 6pm—or until supplies run out.

In the city's southern suburbs, the most popular choice is the **Blackrock Market,** 19a Main St., Blackrock (☎ **01/283-3522**). More than 60 vendors sell a wide variety of old and new goods at great prices in this indoor/outdoor setting on Saturday from 11am to 5:30pm and Sunday from noon to 5:30pm. Take the DART train to the Blackrock station.

8 Dublin After Dark

From singing pubs to opera to buskers to Broadway-style theater, Dublin offers a wealth of after-dark activities to satisfy tastes of all ages. To find out what's going on, pick up a copy of the biweekly *Dublin Event Guide* newspaper, available free at the Dublin Tourism information office, or the biweekly *In Dublin* for IR£1.50 ($2.35). Here you'll find listings for music performances, stage productions, movie theaters, museum and gallery exhibits, and even TV listings.

THE PERFORMING ARTS
THEATER, OPERA & CLASSICAL MUSIC

Abbey Theatre

Lower Abbey St. ☎ **01/878-7222.** Tickets IR£8–IR£15 ($12.40–$23.25), IR£6 ($9.30) for previews.

Dublin has been known as a theater center since the Abbey Theatre opened in 1904 with William Butler Yeats as its first director. The current theater was built in 1966, 15 years after the original burned down. There are two stages here where you can see the best and latest in contemporary Irish theater. The box office is open Monday through Saturday from 10:30am to 7pm.

Gaiety Theatre

S. King St. ☎ **01/677-1717.** Tickets IR£7–IR£16 ($10.85–$24.80).

Located not far from St. Stephen's Green, this is Dublin's other main venue for contemporary Irish theater. The box office is open Monday through Saturday from 11am to 7pm.

Gate Theatre

Cavendish Row. ☎ **01/874-4045.** Tickets IR£10–IR£12 ($15.50–$18.60), IR£7.50 ($11.65) for previews.

Dublin's opera house is housed in a 200-year-old building that was built as part of the adjacent Assembly Rooms, which themselves were built to help fund the Rotunda Hospital, the first maternity hospital in Europe. The box office is open Monday through Saturday from 10am to 7pm.

National Concert Hall

Earlsfort Terrace. ☎ **01/671-1533.** Tickets IR£6–IR£20 ($9.30–$31).

Dublin's main venue for classical music was originally part of University College, Dublin. The hall stays busy with performances several nights a week for much of the year, and is home to the National Symphony Orchestra. The box office is open Monday through Saturday from 11am to 7pm.

Olympia Theatre

Dame St. ☎ **01/677-7744.** Tickets IR£7.50–IR£15 ($11.65–$23.25).

With its Victorian jewelbox facade and garish red lobby, the Olympia Theatre looks as if it should be home to high-stepping can-can girls. However, it's actually one of Dublin's busier old theaters, hosting everything from contemporary Irish plays to rock concerts. The box office is open Monday through Saturday from 10am to 6:30pm.

The Point

E. Link Bridge, N. Wall Quay. ☎ **01/836-3633.** Tickets IR£10–IR£50 ($15.50–$77.50).

With a seating capacity of 3,000, this is Ireland's newest large theater/concert venue, attracting top Broadway-caliber shows and international stars. The box office is open Monday through Saturday from 10am to 6pm.

FOLK, ROCK & JAZZ

There are dozens of clubs and pubs all over town featuring rock, folk, jazz, and traditional Irish music. Any night of the week you can hear almost any type of music. Check in the *Dublin Event Guide* or *In Dublin* magazine for club schedules.

Two of the city's most popular rock clubs are the **Baggot Inn,** on Baggot Street (☎ **01/676-1430**), and **Whelan's,** at 25 Wexford St. (☎ **01/478-0766**), both of which are open nightly and have live music most nights. Admission charges generally range from IR£2 to IR£6 ($3.10 to $9.30).

FILMS

Movies in Dublin cost IR£3 to IR£5 ($4.65 to $7.75) for adults after 5pm and IR£2 to IR£2.50 ($3.10 to $3.90) before 5pm. There are two multiplex theaters on O'Connell Street and another two blocks away on Mid Abbey Street.

PUBS

You can hardly walk a block in Dublin without encountering a pub. Not only are they watering holes for sipping the dark Guinness stout, but also they offer snacks and meals. Best of all, many of them host live music at night. In any of these pubs music starts around 9pm and continues until 11pm. There's sometimes a small cover charge of IR£1 to IR£3 ($1.55 to $4.65). A pint of Guinness will cost around IR£2 ($3.10).

Brazen Head, 20 Lower Bridge St. (☎ **01/679-5186**), is a couple of long blocks past Christ Church Cathedral and down by the Liffey. At Dublin's oldest pub there are several rooms, each with a slightly different atmosphere. You can have a quiet pint or a meal in one room and join in the music in another.

Davy Byrne's, 21 Duke St. (☎ **01/677-5217**), figured prominently in James Joyce's *Ulysses* and has been famous ever since. However, don't drop by expecting a turn-of-the-century atmosphere. In this upscale neighborhood, Davy Byrne's has had to go with the flow and remodel in pastels and potted plants.

For fans of traditional Irish music, **O'Donoghue's,** 15 Merrion Row (☎ **01/661-4303**), is a must. The Dubliners, one of Ireland's favorite traditional bands, got their start here, and impromptu music sessions are held almost every night. Sometimes bands play in both the front room and the back.

Although Capel Street is looking a bit down at the heels these days, **Slattery's,** 129 Capel St. (☎ **01/872-7971**), continues to be popular for live music of all types, which may be heard in either the upstairs or the downstairs lounge. Traditional Irish music is still the most popular sound here.

DISCOS

For many years, the focal point of Dublin's late-night life was along a one-block strip known as Leeson Street, where a string of ever-changing basement discos thrived. As in many cities, the Dublin audience was always seeking something new, so the names and decors of these places changed almost yearly, making it hard to keep track. There are still a few active clubs along the Leeson Street strip, but in the 1990s the center of nightlife has gradually been shifting toward the Temple Bar district, now recognized as the city's cultural corner or "Left Bank."

Some of the current "in" spots of Temple Bar include **The Kitchen,** a club partly owned by the rock group U2, in the Clarence Hotel, 6/8 Wellington Quay (☎ **01/677-6178**); **Club M,** in Blooms Hotel, Cope Street (☎ **01/671-5622**); and **Bad Bob's Backstage Bar,** 34 E. Essex St. (☎ **01/679-2992**). Two other nearby clubs are also popular: **Lillie's Bordello,** 45 Nassau St. (☎ **01/679-7539**), and **Ri-Ra,** Dame Court (☎ **01/677-4835**). Admission charges at all these places average IR£4 to IR£8 ($6.20 to $12.40). Hours are usually 10 or 11pm until 2am nightly, although some may be closed Sunday or Monday.

9 Networks & Resources

STUDENTS **Trinity College** is the focus of student life in Dublin. On the south side of the River Liffey, at the top of Dame Street, the large campus with its many 18th-century buildings is in the heart of Dublin's old city. At the information office just inside the main gate you can find out more about what's going on at the college.

For general information about the city, young people should check at the office of the **Union of Students in Ireland / Irish Student Travel Service (USIT),** 19 Aston Quay, Dublin 2 (☎ **01/677-8117**). It's a clearinghouse of information and networking resources for those under 25.

GAY MEN & LESBIANS For information on the gay and lesbian scene in Dublin, contact the **National Lesbian and Gay Federation,** 10 Fownes St. (☎ **01/671-0939**), open daily from noon to 5:30pm in the heart of the Temple Bar district. This organization also publishes *Gay Community News,* a monthly newspaper distributed free throughout the city, particularly in the information centers and shops of the Temple Bar district.

10 Easy Excursions

To understand why Ireland is called the Emerald Isle, you must venture beyond the gray walls of urban Dublin into the verdant countryside. You can make several easy day-long excursions from Dublin.

The budget-conscious can hop on the DART train and ride it to the end of the line in either direction. To the north is the peninsula of **Howth,** the northern arm of Dublin Bay. From the Howth station, catch the DART feeder bus to the summit of Howth Head; from there you can walk along quiet paths through green fields back to the village of Howth. At the southern end of the DART line is the village of **Bray.** From here, it's a 3-mile walk around Bray Head to the village of Greystones.

Bus Eireann, Busáras Central Bus Station (☎ **01/836-6111**), offers about 20 half- and full-day excursions from Dublin. Some of the more worthwhile tours are those to the beautiful Powerscourt Gardens in the Wicklow Mountains, the Glendalough and Wicklow Gap tour, and the most interesting one, the Boyne Valley and North Coast tour, which passes through gorgeous green countryside and visits the massive gravesites of Newgrange dating from 2500 B.C. The tours are offered on different days of the week and cost IR£10 to IR£24 ($15.50 to $37.20).

Edinburgh

by Dan Levine

Edinburgh is a city with a long and stormy past. You'll be reminded of that history every time you gaze up at Edinburgh Castle, one of Europe's most arresting sights. You'll recall that past when you follow in the footsteps of Mary, Queen of Scots through the Palace of Holyroodhouse. In the Old Town, the narrow, winding alleys—called closes—will lead you from the 20th-century traffic back to medieval days. In striking contrast to the Old Town's jumble of twisted streets are the wide boulevards and stately town houses of the Georgian New Town. Together, the Old and New Towns, joined by the sloping lawns and ancient trees of Princes Street Gardens, make Edinburgh one of Europe's most historically fascinating cities.

Even though the citizens of Edinburgh take care to preserve their city's history, they don't ignore the finer things in life. The Edinburgh International Festival, held every summer, is one of the world's most popular cultural festivals. And during the rest of the year Edinburgh's many theaters, concert halls, live-music clubs, galleries, and museums are ablaze, catering to the cultural appetite of the Scots. Every block seems to have its own pub, where you can sometimes hear a bit of traditional Scottish music while sipping your pint of ale. Elegant and expensive shops line Princes Street in the New Town, while antiques shops, boutiques, and unusual import stores prevail in the Old Town.

Historic and lively, Edinburgh has much to offer, and if the sun should be shining when you visit, consider yourself very lucky: You will have seen one of Europe's most stunning sights.

1 Edinburgh Deals & Discounts

BUDGET BESTS　The best values in Edinburgh are the many free museums and galleries. These include the two Royal Museums, the Scottish National Gallery, and the Museum of Childhood. Other budget bests include free live music in pubs and clubs and lunch in almost any pub.

SPECIAL DISCOUNTS　If you plan to use the public buses in Edinburgh, be sure to buy a silver **Freedom Ticket,** which costs only £2.20 ($3.30) for adults and £1.50 ($2.25) for children and is good for a day. If you plan to be around for a week, you can get a **City Ridecard** at £9 ($13.50) for adults and £6 ($9) for juniors.

What's Special About Edinburgh

Spectacular Buildings & Streets
- Edinburgh Castle, one of Europe's most stunning sights, set atop a rocky crag in the middle of the city.
- Palace of Holyroodhouse, home of Mary, Queen of Scots and still used by Elizabeth II when she visits Edinburgh.
- The Royal Mile, a fascinating collection of medieval buildings, museums, shops, and pubs along the mile-long street that connects the Palace of Holyroodhouse and Edinburgh Castle.

Woolens
- Numerous factory outlets offer the city's best shopping deals—discount woolens direct from the mills.

Annual Festivals
- Edinburgh International Festival, an annual cultural extravaganza attracting the international theater world's best and brightest.
- Edinburgh Military Tattoo, a musical military parade held each August at Edinburgh Castle.
- Edinburgh International Jazz Festival, featuring international stars and unknowns at various locales around the city.

WORTH THE EXTRA MONEY   In Edinburgh, budget hotels are quite good, attractions admission fees are low, and you won't improve the quality of the food by paying more. The only things you'll have to splurge on is a good bottle of single-malt whiskey or an occasional taxi ride.

2 Pretrip Preparations

REQUIRED DOCUMENTS   Citizens of the United States, Canada, Australia, and New Zealand need only a valid passport for travel to Edinburgh.

TIMING YOUR TRIP   Although it rains all year here and can be gray and overcast for long stretches, summer can also be gloriously sunny and warm. There are even times in winter when the sun shines for several days in a row.

If you're a culture vulture, you won't want to miss the Edinburgh International Festival in late August and early September. If you're interested in attending the festival, be sure to make hotel and airline reservations months in advance. The city is absolutely packed to overflowing during the three weeks of the festival.

Edinburgh's Average Daytime Temperature & Days of Rain

	Jan	Feb	Mar	Apr	May	June	July	Aug	Sept	Oct	Nov	Dec
Temp (°F)	38	38	41	45	50	56	58	58	55	50	42	40
Days of Rain	12	11	11	12	12	10	10	13	11	12	13	13

Special Events   The main focal point of the city's cultural calendar is the annual **Edinburgh International Festival,** which goes on for three weeks in late August and early September. See the "Special & Free Events" box under "Attractions," later in this chapter, for more information.

BACKGROUND READING Sir Walter Scott is Edinburgh's most beloved literary figure and his Waverley novels are its most popular works. Almost as popular is Robert Louis Stevenson, whose collection of poems *A Child's Garden of Verses* (Macmillan, 1981) evokes his childhood in the city. Stevenson's novel *The Strange Case of Dr. Jekyll and Mr. Hyde* (Oxford University Press, 1979) is based on the exploits of a famous local criminal, Deacon Brodie. Robert Burns, idolized by the Scots, brings 18th-century Edinburgh and Scotland to life in such poems as his famous "Scots Wha Ha'e." Sir Arthur Conan Doyle based his character Sherlock Holmes on an Edinburgh surgeon, Dr. Joseph Bell.

3 Edinburgh Specifics

ARRIVING

FROM THE AIRPORT Edinburgh Airport is 10 miles northwest of the city. You may wish to stop by the Edinburgh Tourist Information Desk here before heading into the city. White double-decker Airlink buses regularly make the 25-minute trip into the city. The one-way fare is £3.50 ($5.25). Waverley Bridge is the last stop and is centrally located between the Old Town and the New Town.

Airport taxis will take you into the city center for about £14 ($21). If you can get one of the standard black taxis to give you a ride you'll save a couple of dollars, but these taxis are not supposed to pick up fares at the airport.

FROM THE TRAIN STATION There are two main train stations in Edinburgh: **Waverley Station** and **Haymarket Station.** Waverley Station is the more conveniently located. If you follow the exit signs up the automobile ramp,

What Things Cost in Edinburgh	U.S. $
Taxi from the airport to the city center	21.00
Local telephone call	.15
Double room at the Edinburgh Sheraton (deluxe)	150.00
Double room at the Terrace (moderate)	75.00
Double room at Castle Guest House (budget)	48.00
Continental breakfast in a hotel	4.75
Lunch for one at Tiles Bistro (moderate)	10.50
Lunch for one at the Baked Potato Shop (budget)	4.25
Dinner for one, without wine, at Pompadour (deluxe)	70.75
Dinner for one, without wine, at Pierre Victoire (moderate)	31.50
Dinner for one, without wine, at Queen St. Oyster Bar (budget)	10.50
Pint of beer	2.55
Coca-Cola	1.35
Cup of coffee	1.05
Roll of ASA 100 color film, 36 exposures	6.00
Admission to Edinburgh Castle	7.50
Movie ticket	6.00
Cheapest ticket at King's Theatre	6.00

you'll find yourself on Waverley Bridge. Princes Street and the New Town will be to your right and the Old Town to your left.

VISITOR INFORMATION

The main **Edinburgh Tourist Information Centre** (☎ **0131/557-1700**) is at the corner of Princes Street and Waverley Bridge on the top of the modern underground Waverley Market shopping center. The tourist center is open in May, June, and September, Monday through Saturday from 9am to 7pm and Sunday from 11am to 7pm; in July and August, Monday through Saturday from 9am to 8pm and Sunday from 11am to 8pm; in April and October, Monday through Saturday from 9am to 6pm and Sunday from 11am to 6pm; and November to March, Monday through Saturday from 9am to 6pm. The city operates a 24-hour recorded information hotline (☎ **0891-7757**), with specifics on accommodations, tours, attractions, and restaurants. Calls are charged at 36 to 48 pence (54¢ to 72¢) per minute, depending on when you call. Evenings are cheapest.

For information on events while you're in town, pick up a free copy of the monthly **"Day-by-Day"** at the Tourist Information Centre. It lists events, exhibitions, theater, and music in the city. For more detailed listings, buy the biweekly magazine **The List,** available at newsstands around town for £1.30 ($1.95).

Students who want to find out more about the university scene should head over to the **Edinburgh University Student Centre,** on Bristo Square. There's a large notice board listing events of interest to students. If you're looking for an apartment for a few months or longer, you'll find ads for roommates here.

CITY LAYOUT

Edinburgh is very easy to find your way around. It's divided into an **Old Town** and a **New Town,** separated from each other by Princes Street Gardens. Dominating the Edinburgh skyline is **Edinburgh Castle,** standing high on a hill at the western end of the Old Town. At the opposite end of the Old Town and connected to the castle by the **Royal Mile,** a single street bearing four names along its length, is the **Palace of Holyroodhouse,** the Scottish residence of Elizabeth II and many past kings and queens.

Princes Street, the main thoroughfare of the **New Town,** is bordered on the north side by department stores and some of Edinburgh's most elegant clothing stores. Running the length of Princes Street on the south side is **Princes Street Gardens,** a beautiful park filling the valley between the two sections of the city.

GETTING AROUND

BY BUS Burgundy-and-white Lothian Region Transport double-deckers run frequently to all parts of the city and outlying suburbs. Fares vary according to the number of stops you travel, ranging from 50p to £2 (75¢ to $3). You are expected to have the correct fare when boarding. Deposit your coins in the slot beside the driver and take your ticket. Be sure to hang on to this ticket in case an inspector asks to see it.

You probably won't know how many stops you'll be traveling and thus won't know how much to pay. With plenty of change in hand, ask the driver how much the fare is to your destination or purchase a **Freedom Card** at the Tourist Information Centre for £2.20 ($3.30) and don't worry about the fare. The Freedom Ticket is good for one day and allows you to use the LRT buses as frequently as

The British Pound

At this writing $1 = approximately 67p (or £1 = $1.50), and this was the rate of exchange used to calculate the dollar values given in this chapter (rounded to the nearest nickel). This rate fluctuates from time to time and may not be the same when you travel to Britain. Therefore this table should be used only as a guide:

£	U.S. $	£	U.S. $
.01	.02	6	9.00
.05	.08	7	10.50
.10	.15	8	12.00
.25	.38	9	13.50
.50	.75	10	15.00
.75	1.13	15	22.50
1	1.50	20	30.00
2	3.00	25	37.50
3	4.50	30	45.00
4	6.00	40	60.00
5	7.50	50	75.00

you wish. Freedom Cards are also available at the Ticket Centre on Waverley Bridge.

Monday through Thursday and Sunday, the buses stop running a little after 11pm, but on Friday and Saturday some buses run all night. The night fare is £1.50 ($2.25).

BY TAXI There are taxi stands along Princes Street and at Waverley Station. Fares start at 90p ($1.35) and increase by 10p (15¢) every 300 yards. You can also phone 229-2468 for a cab.

ON FOOT Edinburgh, especially the narrow lanes and closes of Old Town, is best explored on foot. Almost everything you'll want to see is either along or just a few blocks from the Royal Mile, along Princes Street, or on the nearby streets of the New Town.

BY BICYCLE Because Edinburgh is built on a series of hills and ridges, bicycling around the city is not recommended. However, exploring the surrounding countryside by bike is very pleasant. **Central Cycle Hire,** 13 Lochrin Place (☎ **0131/228-6363**), rents bicycles for £6 to £15 ($9 to $22.50), depending on the type of bicycle. Its staff will also help you pick out a route for a day's cycling. It's open Monday and Wednesday through Saturday from 10am to 5:30pm. You can reach the shop by bus no. 9, 10, 11, 16, 18, 23, 27, 30, or 45 from Princes Street; get off by the Cameo Cinema.

BY RENTAL CAR For excursions farther afield, you might want to rent a car. In addition to the major international car-rental agencies, all of which have representatives in Edinburgh, you can try **Total Self Drive,** 45 Lochrin Place (☎ **0131/229-4548**), which offers its smallest cars for about £25 ($37.50) per day with 150 miles free.

FAST FACTS: Edinburgh

Babysitters   If you need a babysitter, contact Guardians Babysitting, 13 Eton Terrace (☎ **0131/343-3870**).

Banks   There are several banks along Princes Street that will change money. They offer the best exchange rate in town and charge a small commission. The Royal Bank of Scotland, 142–144 Princes St. (☎ **0131/226-2555**), is open Monday through Friday from 9:15am to 4:45pm (Thursday to 5:30pm); the Bank of Scotland, 141 Princes St. (☎ **0131/225-6204**), is open the same hours.

Business Hours   Most **shops** are open Monday through Saturday from 10am to 5:30 or 6pm (Thursday to 7:30pm). **Offices** are open Monday through Friday from 9am to 5pm. Some smaller shops may close for lunch.

Consulates   The Consulate of the **United States** is at 3 Regent Terrace (☎ **0131/556-8315**), which is an extension of Princes Street beyond Nelson's Monument. The Consulate of **Australia** is in Hobart House, 80 Hanover St. (☎ **0131/226-6271**). Visitors from Canada and New Zealand should contact their High Commissions in London (see "Fast Facts: London," in Chapter 16).

Currency Exchange   There are currency-exchange counters at the Tourist Information Centre in Waverley Market, at Waverley Station, and at many banks on Princes Street and Royal Mile. The banks charge a smaller fee.

Dentists/Doctors   See "Emergencies," below.

Emergencies   If you need a doctor or dentist, check the Yellow Pages or ask at your hotel. For police assistance or an ambulance, dial 999.

There are no 24-hour pharmacies in Edinburgh. Boots, 48 Shandwick Place (☎ **0131/225-6757**), is a pharmacy that's open Monday through Saturday until 9pm.

Eyeglasses   Boots Opticians, 101–103 Princes St. (☎ **0131/225-6397**), open Monday through Saturday from 9am to 5:30pm (Thursday to 7:30pm), can repair or replace your eyeglasses.

Holidays   Edinburgh celebrates New Year's Day, January 2, the first Monday in May, May 8 (Victoria Day), Christmas Day and December 26 (Boxing Day), and the spring and autumn bank holidays, in mid-April and mid-September, respectively.

Hospital   The Royal Infirmary, 1 Lauriston Place (☎ **0131/229-2477**), is one of the most convenient hospitals.

Information   The **Edinburgh Tourist Information Centre** is on the top (Princes Street level) of the modern Waverley Market shopping mall. See "Visitor Information" under "Edinburgh Specifics," earlier in this chapter, for details.

Laundry/Dry Cleaning   In the Dalkeith Road area is a laundry, simply named Launderette, 210 Dalkeith Rd., open Monday through Friday from 8:30am to 5pm, Saturday from 9am to 2:30pm, and Sunday from 10am to 2:30pm. In the Princes Street area is the Laundromat, 54 Leith Walk, which is an extension of Leith Street one block past Royal Terrace. It's open Monday through Saturday from 8am to 7pm (Wednesday to 6pm) and Sunday from 9:30am to 5pm.

For dry cleaning, try Pullars & Sons, 23 Frederick St. (☎ **0131/225-8095**), open Monday through Friday from 8:30am to 5:30pm and Saturday from 8:30am to 5pm.

Lost & Found   The first place to check if you've lost something in Edinburgh is the Lothian and Borders Police Headquarters, on Fettes Avenue (☎ **0131/ 311-3141**). Another place to try is the Edinburgh Tourist Information Center at Waverley Market. The LRT bus lost property office is at 14 Queen St. (☎ **0131/554-4494**), open Monday through Friday from 10am to 1:30pm. If you lost something on a train, phone 556-2477.

Mail   The Central Post Office is at 2–4 Waterloo Place, at the north end of North Bridge. It's open Monday through Friday from 9am to 5:30pm and Saturday from 9am to 12:30pm.

Newspapers/Magazines   Edinburgh's most informative newspapers are *The Scotsman* and *The Independent. The List* is the city's best listings magazine and is indispensable for goings-on around town.

Photographic Needs   Edinburgh Cameras, 55 Lothian Rd. (☎ **0131/ 229-4416**), open Monday through Saturday from 9am to 5:30pm, will meet all your photo needs.

Police   To reach the police, in an emergency dial 999; otherwise dial 311-3141.

Radio/TV   Edinburgh has several radio and TV stations offering a wide range of programming.

Religious Services   For information on churches and synagogues in Edinburgh, contact the Tourist Information Centre at Waverley Market (☎ **0131/ 557-1700**). An extensive listing of times and locations of services is maintained there.

Shoe Repair   Only a few blocks from the east end of Princes Street, Mister Minit, 22 Frederick St. (☎ **0131/226-6741**), is a convenient place to get your shoes repaired. It's open Monday through Friday from 8:30am to 5:30pm and Saturday from 8:30am to 5pm.

Tax   For details on VAT refunds, see "Shopping," later in this chapter.

Telephone   Public telephones cost 10p (15¢) for the first three minutes and accept coins of various denominations. You can also purchase a phone card, for use in special phones at post offices and newsstands. A three-minute phone call to the United States will cost between £3.90 and £4.50 ($5.85 and $6.75). Alternatively, you can reach an AT&T operator, and receive U.S. rates for collect or credit-card calls, by dialing toll free 0800-89-0011.

Tipping   In most restaurants, tax and service charge are included in the price of the meal, so it's unnecessary to leave any further tip. If a service charge has not been included in the bill, the standard tip here is 10%. Taxi drivers also expect a 10% tip.

4 Accommodations

Despite the city's relatively small size and great popularity with tourists, there are surprisingly few budget hotels in the center. Indeed, Edinburgh's best accommodation deals are 15 to 20 minutes by foot from Waverley Station.

Getting the Best Deal on Accommodations

- Home stays, usually available only in summer, are generally cheaper than hotel rooms—check the tourist office for availability.

- Accommodations about a 10- to 15-minute bus ride out of the city center tend to be cheaper than those in town.

- Try the guesthouses along Dalkeith Road, near the university residence halls.

The cheapest accommodations in Edinburgh, aside from hostels, are home stays. People with an extra bedroom or two in their home will take in paying guests for about £15 ($22.50) per person per night. Home stays are generally available only in the summer, but occasionally in other months as well. The **Edinburgh Tourist Information Centre** in Waverley Market (☎ **0131/557-1700**) has a list of hundreds of home stays, and its staff will also make reservations for you for £3 ($4.50); stop by or phone.

DOUBLES FOR LESS THAN £35 ($52.50)
IN THE CITY CENTER

Castle Guest House

38 Castle St., Edinburgh EH2 3BN. ☎ **0131/225-1975.** 4 rms, none with bath. TV. £19 ($29) single; £34 ($51) double. Rates include full breakfast. No credit cards.

Mr. and Mrs. J. C. Ovens have been accepting guests into their 200-year-old home for more than 30 years. The rooms are all quite cozy and have tea-making facilities and central heating. You can choose from among five breakfasts here. Castle Guest House is less than two blocks from Princes Street and about 10 minutes on foot from Waverley Station. The street affords an excellent view of the castle.

SOUTH OF THE CITY CENTER

Crion Guest House

33 Minto St., Edinburgh EH9 2BT. ☎ **0131/667-2708.** 9 rms, 3 with bath. TV. £17–£23 ($25.50–$34.50) single without bath, £19–£27 ($28.50–$40.50) single with bath; £28–£39 ($42–$58.50) double without bath, £36–£46 ($54–$69) double with bath. Rates include full breakfast. No credit cards. Bus 3, 7, 8, 18, 31, or 37.

Minto Street is one of Edinburgh's budget guesthouse districts, and the Crion is one of the best on the street. The proprietress, Mrs. Cheape, is friendly and has done much to make her small house as homey as possible. Floral-print draperies with matching valances and bedspreads give the guest rooms a country flavor, while in the breakfast room you'll find classic Edinburgh plasterwork wainscoting and an elegant fireplace. The availability of a first-floor room makes this a good choice for those who have problems with stairs.

✪ Gifford Guest House

103 Dalkeith Rd., Edinburgh EH16 5AJ. ☎ **0131/667-4688.** 6 rms, 2 with shower only, 3 with bath. TV. £17–£24 ($25.50–$36) single without bath; £29–£36 ($43.50–$54) double without bath, £34–£40 ($51–$60) double with shower only, £50–£57 ($75–$85.50) double with bath; £53–£65 ($79.50–$97.50) quad without bath, £57–£69 ($85.50–$103.50) quad with shower only. Rates include full breakfast. No credit cards. Free parking. Bus 14, 21, or 33 to Royal Commonwealth Pool.

This spacious old home boasts a beautiful stairwell topped by a huge skylight. Mrs. Margaret Dow, the friendly manager, has three rooms with baths and two with showers. All the rooms are large, with high ceilings, central heating, and tea-making facilities; most have been redecorated recently and contain attractive matching duvets on the beds. The rooms in back (with bath) offer a view of Arthur's Seat and Salisbury Crags.

✪ Kariba Guest House

10 Granville Terrace, Edinburgh EH10 4PQ. ☎ **0131/229-3773.** 9 rms, 5 with shower only, 3 with bath. TV. £17 ($25.50) single without bath; £29–£36 ($43.50–$54) double with shower only, £38–£40 ($57–$60) double with bath; £44–£54 ($66–$81) triple with shower only, £57–£60 ($85.50-$90) triple with bath. Rates include full breakfast. No credit cards. Bus 9, 10, or 27.

This small guesthouse has a very warm, homey atmosphere thanks to owner Agnes Holligan, who's friendly and full of helpful information. A lot of time and energy were put into restoring this Victorian home to its former glory, and the plaster-work cornices and ceilings are particularly attractive. Breakfast is served in the large dining room.

NORTH OF THE CITY CENTER

Blairhaven Guest House

5 Eyre Place, Edinburgh EH3 5ES. ☎ **0131/556-3025.** 9 rms, none with bath. TV. £20 ($30) single; £36 ($54) double. Rates include continental breakfast. No credit cards.

Although the orange-and-white interior of this basic B&B is austere, this house is relatively well located on a quiet street, and the back rooms overlook an attractive garden. Blairhaven, about a 15-minute walk from the city center, is especially recommendable during the busy summer festival season.

Dene Guest House

7 Eyre Place, Edinburgh EH3 5ES. ☎ **0131/556-2700.** 7 rms, 2 with bath. TV. £20 ($30) single without bath; £36 ($54) double without bath, £44 ($66) double with bath. Rates include continental breakfast. No credit cards. Bus 23 or 27 from Hanover Street.

Five minutes north of Waverley Station by bus is the Dene, operated since 1960 by the friendly Donaghue family. The rooms are simply decorated and cozy, and the two four-bed family rooms now have baths. The guesthouse has been completely redecorated. Eyre Place is only three stoplights down the hill and just beyond the modern buildings on the right.

Kisimul Guest House

16 Claremont Park, Edinburgh EH6 7PJ. ☎ **0131/554-4203.** 6 rms, none with bath. TV. £14–£16 ($21–$24) single; £27–£32 ($40.50–$48) double; £41–£47 ($61.50–$70.50) triple. MC, V. Bus 89.

On a street with stately old homes facing a grassy park, you'll find this small but comfortable guesthouse run by the well-traveled Anne and Robert McNeil. The big first-floor rooms are high-ceilinged, characteristic of Georgian Edinburgh, but the top-floor rooms are smaller. All rooms have tea-making facilities and comfortable chairs or a couch.

DOUBLES FOR LESS THAN £45 ($64.50)
IN THE CITY CENTER

Elder York Guest House

38 Elder St., Edinburgh EH1 3DX. ☎ **0131/556-1926.** 14 rms, 3 with shower only, 3 with bath. TV. £23 ($34.50) single without bath; £42 ($63) double without bath, £46 ($69)

double with shower only, £53 ($79.50) double with bath. Rates include full breakfast. No credit cards.

It's a steep climb up to this guesthouse occupying the top floors of an old five-story town house. The rooms are small but adequately furnished with comfortable chairs, new wallpaper, and coffee/tea facilities. The breakfast room is pleasant but the staff is somewhat weary. The hotel is only a couple of blocks from Waverley Station and right beside the intercity bus terminal.

⑤ Terrace Hotel

37 Royal Terrace, Edinburgh EH7 5AH. ☎ 0131/556-3423 or 556-1026. Fax **0131/556-2520.** 14 rms, 11 with bath. TV. Jan–Apr, £22 ($33) single without bath, £31 ($46.50) single with bath; £38 ($57) double without bath, £48 ($72) double with bath. May–Sept, £24 ($36) single without bath, £32 ($48) single with bath; £41 ($61.50) double without bath, £64 ($96) double with bath. Oct–Dec, £22 ($33) single without bath, £31 ($46.50) single with bath; £38 ($57) double without bath, £50 ($75) double with bath. Rates include full breakfast. ACCESS, EURO, MC, V.

This small Georgian-style hotel, on an elegant and usually pricey street, is a great deal. Owner Annie Mann is constantly improving her exceedingly clean hotel. A spacious lounge and separate breakfast room both feature beautiful fireplaces, and the sweeping staircase is illuminated by a huge oval skylight. The guest rooms range from roomy to spacious, and most have 14-foot ceilings that make the rooms seem positively immense. The smallest rooms are on the top floor.

NORTH OF THE CITY CENTER

Ardenlee Guest House

9 Eyre Place, Edinburgh EH3 5ES. ☎ **0131/556-2838.** 8 rms, 6 with bath. TV. £22 ($33) single without bath, £27 ($40.50) single with bath; £38 ($57) double without bath, £55 ($82.50) double with bath. Rates include full breakfast. No credit cards. Bus 23 or 27 from Hanover Street.

Next door to the Dene Guest House (above) is this equally comfortable three-floor guesthouse run by David and Judy Dinse. Here you'll find attractively decorated large rooms with tea-making facilities. Potted plants are a nice touch. You have your choice of how you'd like your eggs fixed each morning.

Ravensdown Bed and Breakfast

248 Ferry Rd., Edinburgh EH5 3AN. ☎ **0131/552-5438.** 7 rms, none with bath. £22 ($33) single; £38 ($57) double; £50 ($75) triple; £63 ($94.50) quad. Rates include full breakfast. No credit cards. Bus 23 from Hanover Street.

The friendly and helpful proprietors, Mr. and Mrs. Leonardo Welch, operate a very pleasant guesthouse offering large, clean rooms. All come with tea-making facilities and comfortable chairs for relaxing. Try to get one of the south-facing rooms—the view of the Edinburgh skyline is magnificent.

WEST OF THE CITY CENTER

Ashdene House

23 Fountainhall Rd., Edinburgh EH9 2LN. ☎ **0131/667-6026.** 5 rms, all with bath. £25 ($37.50) per person; children 10 and under half price in parent's room. Rates include breakfast. No credit cards.

A comfortable two-story brick Edwardian villa, Ashdene is a totally no-smoking B&B located on a quiet leafy street about 10 minutes from the city center. The house is exceptionally well kept and regularly renovated—a new dining room and lounge area are the latest improvements.

Beresford Hotel
32 Coates Gardens, Edinburgh EH12 5LE. ☎ **0131/337-0850.** 10 rms, 5 with bath. TV. £21 ($31.50) per person room without bath, £26 ($39) per person room with bath. No credit cards.

Proprietors Donald and Agnes Mackintosh run the best of the half dozen or so B&Bs on this short block, a stone's throw from Edinburgh's Haymarket BritRail station. Every room in this simple but thoroughly adequate home has a firm bed, a color TV, and coffee/tea-making facilities.

SUPER-BUDGET CHOICES
HOSTELS
Edinburgh's two Y.H.A. hostels are 15 minutes from the city center in elegant and quiet surroundings.

Belford Youth Hostel
6–8 Douglas Gardens, Edinburgh EH4 3DA. 5 rms; 90 dorm beds. ☎ **0131/225-6209.** £25 ($37.50) double; £8.50 ($12.75) dorm bed. Breakfast £2 ($3) extra. MC, V. Free shuttle bus to/from downtown.

Located in a large renovated stone church complete with stained-glass windows and cathedral ceilings, this is one of the most unusual hostels around. It's also one of the least private, since none of the walls reaches to the top of the lofty building, creating dozens of sleeping "cubicles." Doubles are available and represent a particularly good value. Otherwise, there are 4 to 10 beds per room. There's a recreation room with a pool table, a kitchen and laundry for guests' use, and a free bus that regularly makes the 15-minute journey to downtown.

Bruntsfield Youth Hostel
7 Bruntsfield Crescent, Edinburgh EH10 4EZ. ☎ **0131/447-2994.** 172 beds. £7.95 ($12) per night for Y.H.A. members 18 and older, £6 ($9) for Y.H.A. members 17 and under; £10.60 ($16) for nonmembers for the first six nights, after which they receive a membership card. AE, MC. Closed Jan. Bus 11 or 16 from Princes Street to Forbes Road, or 15 to Bruntsfield Hospital.

Completely remodeled in 1992, this hostel offers accommodations in dorms holding 8 to 26 beds each, plus a self-catering kitchen, large lounge, and TV room, all very clean. The spacious lawns of the large park across the street make this hostel an especially good choice in summer.

Eglinton Youth Hostel
18 Eglinton Crescent, Edinburgh EH12 5DD. ☎ **0131/337-1120.** 180 beds. £11 ($16.50) per night for Y.H.A. members 18 and older, £8.80 ($13.50) for Y.H.A. members 17 and under; £12 ($18) for nonmembers for the first six nights, after which they receive a membership card. Rates include continental breakfast. No credit cards. Closed Dec. Bus 3, 4, 12, 13, 22, 26, 28, 31, 33, or 44 to Palmerston Place.

This is the larger of the two official hostels in town, about 400 yards from the Haymarket train station and the same distance from the Gallery of Modern Art. There are 180 beds on three floors, with accommodations in dorms of 6 to 12 beds each, plus a self-catering kitchen, a TV lounge, a self-service laundry, a small grocery, and central heating. Eglinton Crescent is the second left off Palmerston Place.

High Street Hostel
8 Blackfriars St., Edinburgh EH1 1NE. ☎ **0131/557-3984.** 150 beds. £8.50 ($12.75) per person per night (seventh night free). Breakfast £1.30 ($2) extra. No credit cards. From Waverley Station, cross North Bridge and turn left on High Street (second intersection); Blackfriars Street is the second street on the right.

Although this independently operated hostel is not as clean or spacious as the two official ones above, it's conveniently located just off the Royal Mile. No hostel card is necessary to stay here. Beds are in dorms that sleep 6 to 38. The nightly rate doesn't include breakfast but does include showers, luggage-storage facilities, and a self-catering kitchen. Two lounges provide plenty of room for meeting others, and chalkboards and bulletin boards have postings of what's going on in Edinburgh that week.

Pollock Halls

St. Leonard's Hall, 18 Holyrood Park Rd., Edinburgh EH16 5AY. ☎ **0131/667-1971.** 1,000 rms. £25–£27 ($37.50–$40.50) per person. Rates include full breakfast and showers. Closed Oct–May. Bus 14, 21, or 33 to Royal Commonwealth Pool.

For most of the year these are the dormitories for Edinburgh University, but from June to the end of September the 1,000 single and twin rooms are available to the public. There are plenty of facilities, including a self-service laundry, TV rooms, lounges, and bars. Many rooms have excellent views of the nearby Salisbury Crags and Arthur's Seat. The entrance gate is just beyond the Royal Commonwealth Pool complex. Once through the gates, follow the signs to St. Leonard's Hall.

The university also has some rooms available in Patrick Geddes Halls on Mound Place in the Old Town area. These latter rooms are actually more convenient, but the historic seven-story building has no elevator. Only the strong of heart should stay here.

Princes St. Hostel

5 W. Register St., Edinburgh EH2 2AA. ☎ **0131/556-6894.** Fax 0131/557-1519. 70 beds, no rms with bath. £10 ($15) per person in private room; £8 ($12) per person in dorm room. AE, MC, V. To reach the hostel from Waverley Station, turn left onto Princes Street, right onto Andrew Street, then right onto West Register Street.

Opened in 1994 by a young German-American, this hostel occupies the top floor of a small building hidden a block behind Edinburgh's main shopping street. There are four to six bunk beds in each room, and kitchen and laundry facilities are available for guests' use.

WORTH THE EXTRA MONEY

Auld Reekie Guesthouse

16 Mayfield Gardens, Edinburgh EH9 2BZ. ☎ **0131/667-6177.** Fax **0131/662-0033.** 7 rms, all with bath. TV. £28 ($42) single; £54 ($81) double; £66 ($99) triple. No credit cards. Bus 14, 21, or 33.

When Rhona McEwan opened her attractive guesthouse in late 1994, her builder husband fixed every room and added a coffee maker, TV, and clock to each. The windows are large but baths are small, and the whole place feels clean and cheerful. I predict Auld Reekie will be an unqualified success.

Greenside Hotel

9 Royal Terrace, Edinburgh EH7 5AB. ☎ **0131/557-0022.** 12 rms, 8 with bath. TV. £24–£28 ($36–$42) single without bath, £27–£35 ($40.50–$52.50) single with bath; £43–£51 ($64.50–$76.50) double without bath, £47–£58 ($70.50–$87) double with bath. Rates include full breakfast. No credit cards. Closed Jan–Feb.

Royal Terrace is as elegant as its name implies, and at the Greenside you can experience a bit of this elegance at reasonable rates. The guest rooms vary quite a bit from floor to floor, but all have their advantages. In the basement is a suitelike room that extends under the front walk and has an arched ceiling. One back room is absolutely huge and has equally large windows and bath. Taffeta wallpaper enlivens the basement breakfast room, where you can choose either a full Scottish breakfast, complete with oat cakes, or a continental breakfast that includes ham and cheese. The neatly landscaped back garden is made for relaxing on sunny summer afternoons.

5 Dining

Edinburgh is basically a meat-and-potatoes town. Most restaurants and pubs serve the same foods you'd find in London. The local specialty is haggis, a concoction of the heart, liver, and lungs of a sheep, minced and cooked in the sheep's stomach with oatmeal, onions, and seasonings. Scots love it.

LOCAL BUDGET BESTS & FAVORITE MEALS
PUB GRUB

Pubs along the Royal Mile and Rose Street, running parallel to Princes Street, offer plenty of local atmosphere and good prices.

The Café Royal Bistro

17 W. Register St. ☎ **0131/557-4792**. £2.75–£5 ($4.15–$7.50). ACCESS, EURO, MC, V. Mon–Sat noon–5:30pm. PUB GRUB.

Behind the Burger King across from Waverley Market, this café is above the elegant and much more expensive Café Royal Oyster Bar. Very popular with young working people and students, its rooms have an old lived-in feel, and the high ceilings help the pub feel open and airy. Excellent prices on such dishes as shrimp scampi, gammon steak, and poached salmon make this one of my favorite Edinburgh restaurants.

The Royal Mile

127 High St. ☎ **0131/556-8274**. £7.75–£9.50 ($11.65–$14.25); daily special £4 ($6). No credit cards. Mon–Sat 11am–3pm and 6–9:30pm, Sun 12:30–4pm and 6–9:30pm. SCOTTISH.

In this Old Town pub you'll find very good traditional Scottish fare, and the location, midway between the castle and the palace, makes it an ideal lunch spot. The daily special includes soup, a main course, vegetables, and a dessert. You can also try neeps (turnips) and tatties (potatoes) or mince and stovies. This surprisingly elegant pub is popular with government employees from nearby offices.

AFTERNOON TEA

Clarinda's Tea Room

69 Canongate. ☎ **0131/557-1888**. Small pot of tea 75p–£1 ($1.15–$1.50); rolls, sandwiches, and pastries 85p–£1.50 ($1.30–$2.25). No credit cards. Mon–Sat 8:30am–4:45pm, Sun 10am–4:45pm. TEA.

A day spent exploring the Royal Mile can add up to several miles of walking, so if you find your stamina flagging, duck in to Clarinda's for the oh-so-British experience of afternoon tea (you can have it in the morning, too). This tiny cubbyhole of a tea room is only steps from the Palace of Holyroodhouse and dressed in all the finery one would expect from such a place—lace tablecloths, bone china, and antique Wedgwood plates on the walls. There are plenty of teas from which to choose, plus a long list of tempting sweets.

Getting the Best Deal on Dining

- Have an early evening meal—many of the restaurants listed here close at 5:30 or 6pm.
- Try the department stores along pricey Princes Street—surprisingly inexpensive places to eat.
- Eat pub grub or fast food on Sunday—finding a place to eat on Sunday can be a real problem in Edinburgh.

MEALS FOR LESS THAN £5.25 ($7.90)

The Baked Potato Shop

56 Cockburn St. ☎ 0131/225-7572. £2–£3.25 ($3–$4.90). No credit cards. Mon–Sat 9am–9pm, Sun 10am–9pm. STUFFED POTATOES.

If you're in need of some cheap eats while wandering the Royal Mile, you can hardly do better than this hole in the wall. Little bigger than a closet, with seating for only four, the Baked Potato Shop is primarily a take-out place. The potatoes are huge and stuffed with vegetarian fillings (such as curry or cauliflower and cheese) or with chili. However, try the vegetarian haggis—it tastes just like the real thing.

Café Byzantium

9 Victoria St. ☎ 0131/220-2241. Sandwiches £1.75–£2.50 ($2.65–$3.75); buffet lunch £3.75 ($5.65); lunch main courses £3–£3.25 ($4.50–$4.90). No credit cards. Mon–Sat 10am–5:30pm. INDIAN/ENGLISH.

On the top floor of an antique/kitsch market in the middle of trendy Victoria Street, this popular Indian-owned buffet-style restaurant is a terrific choice. Under a Victorian-era vaulted ceiling are about two dozen tables usually filled with both young trendies and older Edinburghers. Meals run the gamut from croissants and toasted sandwiches to heartier fare like Indian curries, macaroni and cheese, and fish and chips. Portions are large, and few meals top £5 ($7.50).

Cornerstone Café

In St. John's Church, West End. ☎ 0131/229-0212. Main courses £2–£4.25 ($3–$6.40). No credit cards. Mon–Fri 11am–9pm, Sat noon–9pm. BRITISH.

A church crypt is the unlikely location of this quality vegetarian café serving well-priced homemade soups, salads, sandwiches, and baked goods. A quiet oasis in the busiest part of town, the Cornerstone is an excellent alternative to department-store fare, and there's outdoor seating during warm weather.

Courthouse Café

Brodie's Close, 304 Lawnmarket, High St. £3.25–£5.75 ($4.90–$8.65). No credit cards. Sept–June, Mon–Sat 10am–4pm; July–Aug, daily 10am–7pm. INTERNATIONAL.

If you know your Edinburgh history, you'll recognize the name attached to this narrow close—Deacon Brodie was the stealthy criminal who inspired Robert Louis Stevenson's *The Strange Case of Dr. Jekyll and Mr. Hyde*. However, the name Courthouse Café derives more from its proximity to the courts than from any literary justice. The kitchen of this spartan café is more than 700 years old, while the dining room itself dates back only 400 years. Imaginative sandwiches and simple lunches are the mainstays. Try the smoked salmon pâté or herring sandwich with sour cream or stop by for a cappuccino and a pastry.

CAFETERIAS

All the major department stores along Princes Street have cafeterias serving economical meals. In addition, many of the smaller stores have small cafés with equally good prices.

Burton's

30 Princes St. ☎ **0131/557-4578.** £3–£5.50 ($4.50–$8.25). ACCESS, V. Mon–Wed and Fri–Sat 9am–5:30pm, Thurs 9am–7:30pm. ENGLISH.

On the fifth floor of this store, reached by an elevator, is the best of the department-store cafeterias, offering a fabulous view of Princes Street Gardens, the castle, and the Old Town. On top of that, the food is good and the servings are generous. As at most cafeterias, desserts are plentiful and cheap.

Jenner's

47 Princes St. ☎ **0131/225-2442.** £2–£5 ($3–$7.50). ACCESS, AE, DC, V. Mon, Wed, and Fri–Sat 9am–5:30pm, Tues 9:30am–5:30pm, Thurs 9am–7pm. ENGLISH.

This department store doesn't have just one cafeteria—it has five restaurants, cafeterias, and coffee shops scattered throughout its large complex. There are menus posted at the Princes Street doors so you can decide which of the restaurants best fits your immediate craving or budget. The first-floor Rose Street Restaurant is best, offering a large selection of hot dishes daily.

MEALS FOR LESS THAN £7.25 ($10.90)

Chez Jules

1 Craig's Close, 9 Cockburn St. ☎ **0131/225-7007.** Main courses £3–£4.50 ($4.50–$6.75). MC, V. Mon–Sat 11am–11pm. FRENCH.

This restaurant is an offshoot of the ubiquitous Pierre Victoire chain, moderately priced French restaurants with imaginative menus. Cheaper and even more packed, what Chez Jules lacks in elbow-room it more than makes up for in food. You can get a big plate of mussels for under £2 ($3), plus a three-course supper, including wine, for around £10 ($15). It's all very French, with candles, red-and-white-checked tablecloths, and Gallic accents, but not too stodgy for a raucous night out.

✪ Henderson's Salad Table and Wine Bar

94 Hanover St. ☎ **0131/225-2131.** £3–£5.50 ($4.50–$8.25). No credit cards. Mon–Sat 8am–10:45pm. VEGETARIAN.

This is another excellent change from the meat-and-potatoes diet. A delicious assortment of salads (served by the scoop) and hot meals is available all day in this large basement restaurant. Batik and stained-glass room partitions, live jazz, and colorful wall hangings create a relaxing atmosphere. Tempting cakes and pies and a large variety of herbal teas are ideal for afternoon tea or dessert.

Ike's Pizza Emporium

158 Rose St. ☎ **0131/225-1010.** Pizzas £7.25–£12.50 ($10.90–$18.75). MC, V. Mon–Thurs noon–10pm, Fri–Sat noon–10:30pm. PIZZA.

There aren't a lot of choices when it comes to pizza, but Ike's serves the best in town. The pies, somewhere between thin crust and deep dish, are made with your choice of all the customary toppings or unusual ones like tuna and banana, prawn and ham, or chicken and sweetcorn. Burgers and steaks are also served.

⑤ Queen St. Oyster Bar

69 Queen St. ☎ **0131/226-2530.** Main courses £3.75–£4.25 ($5.65–$6.40). No credit cards. Mon–Sat noon–1am, Sun 6:30pm–1am. CONTINENTAL.

Without a recommendation from a knowledgeable local, you could easily overlook this tiny seven-table basement bar. Inside, dark woods and delicious aromas combine to create one of the most appealing budget finds in town. Winning appetizers include smoked mussels with horseradish, raw local oysters, and venison pâté. Fish, meat, and vegetarian specials change daily. Spicy chili (made with fresh oysters), ratatouille niçoise (mixed vegetables in tomato sauce), and smoked trout salad (the whole trout) are always available, as are Guinness Stout and a variety of ales.

Tiles Bistro

1 St. Andrew Sq. ☎ **0131/558-1507.** Main courses £3–£4.50 ($4.50–$6.75) for one, £5.50 ($8.25) for any two, £6.75 ($10.15) for any three. MC, V. Mon–Thurs 11am–11pm, Fri–Sat 11am–12:30am, Sun 10am–4pm. CONTINENTAL.

This stunning bar/brasserie, one block north of Princes Street, features beautiful tiled columns and arches, stained glass, an ornate ceiling, and a polished wooden bar featuring half a dozen "real ales." Both bright and lively, Tiles is particularly busy during lunch, when businesspeople and others dine on appetizers like mussels in herbed cream, smoked salmon, and deep-fried Brie. Main courses include chicken-and-ham pie, roast lamb in rosemary sauce, zucchini-and-mushroom bake, and lasagne.

PICNICKING

Marks & Spencer

53 Princes St. ☎ **0131/225-2301.** £1–£2 ($1.50–$3). No credit cards. Mon–Tues 9:30am–5:30pm, Wed 9am–5:30pm, Thurs 9am–8pm, Fri 8:45am–8pm, Sat 8:30am–6pm. SANDWICHES/SALADS.

In the basement of this department store is a supermarket with cooler after cooler of freshly made sandwiches, salads, pasta salads, cakes, cookies, fruits, vegetables, and anything else you might want for a picnic. Best of all, the prices are extremely low and Princes Street Gardens is right across the street. If you feel like taking a walk before eating, head up to the top of Salisbury Crags or Arthur's Seat.

6 Attractions

SIGHTSEEING SUGGESTIONS

If You Have 1 Day

Don't worry. Even if you have only one day in town, you can still see the two most important sights and maybe even a few less important ones. Start the day at Edinburgh Castle, approaching through the Princes Street Gardens, which have a gate opening onto the castle parking lot. This will give you the best feel for the loftiness of Castle Hill. After spending a couple of hours at the castle, head down the Royal Mile, stopping at the Royal Mile pub for lunch. After lunch, tour the Palace of Holyroodhouse, once the throne of Mary, Queen of Scots.

If You Have 2 Days

With two days you can split the Royal Mile into two royal half miles, covering one on the first day and one on the second. This gives you more time to explore the medieval closes and stop at the many small museums along the way. I recommend Lady Stair's House, Huntly House, the John Knox House, St. Giles's Cathedral, and if you have time, a visit to the Brass Rubbing Centre to make your own rubbing. On one of your two days you should also try to visit the National Gallery of Scotland and climb the Scott Monument, both in the New Town along Princes Street Gardens.

If You Have 3 Days

Spend two days in the Old Town visiting the sights already mentioned. On your third day, take a trip outside the city to see the Scottish highlands and a loch or two, preferably Loch Ness, for a chance to glimpse Nessie, the elusive creature rumored to live in the depths of those waters.

If You Have 5 Days

Follow the suggestions above, but add to these a day in the New Town visiting the Georgian House, the Royal Museum of Scotland and National Portrait Gallery, and the Royal Botanic Gardens. If one of your five days happens to be sunny, change your plans and take a picnic lunch up on Salisbury Crags. You can't beat the view from up there! The rest of the day, you might visit the Scottish Gallery of Modern Art or a few more sights along the Royal Mile.

TOP ATTRACTIONS

Many museums that are usually closed Sunday are open on Sundays during the Edinburgh Festival, and some museums that are open only in summer also are open on public holidays.

✪ Edinburgh Castle

Castle Hill. ☎ **0131/244-3101.** Admission £5 ($7.50) adults, £3 ($4.50) senior citizens, £1 ($1.50) children. Apr–Sept, daily 9:30am–6pm; Oct–Mar, daily 9:30am–5pm. Closed Jan 1–3 and Dec 25–26. Lawnmarket buses.

Perched on a hill overlooking Edinburgh, the castle constantly draws the eye. Whether it's catching the first rays of the sun, enshrouded in fog, or brightly

---

❓ Did You Know?

- Greyfriars Bobby, a Skye terrier, kept a 14-year vigil at his master's grave.
- Princes Street Gardens was once a lake.
- More than 17,000 suspected witches were executed in Scotland between 1479 and 1722.
- *The Strange Case of Dr. Jekyll and Mr. Hyde* is based on an actual Edinburgh resident.
- Edinburgh's zoo boasts the world's largest colony of penguins in captivity.
- Founded in 1754, the Royal and Ancient Golf Club in St. Andrews, north of Edinburgh, is one of the world's oldest golfing societies.

Edinburgh

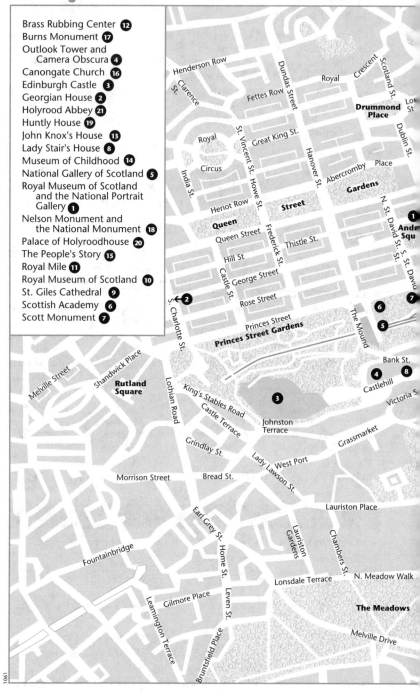

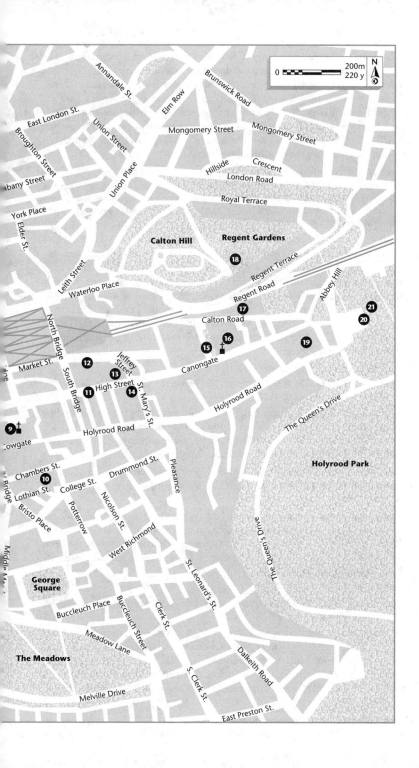

illuminated at night, Edinburgh Castle is the city's most striking sight. The earliest documented use of this natural redoubt as a fortification dates from the late 11th century, though the oldest remaining building is St. Margaret's Chapel, built in the early 12th century. For more than 500 years Edinburgh Castle was under frequent siege, but the constantly expanding fortifications were never successfully stormed. Among the batteries of cannons that protected the castle you'll see Mons Meg, a 15th-century cannon weighing more than 5 tons. Also within these walls are the Scottish crown jewels.

Palace of Holyroodhouse

Canongate. ☎ **0131/556-1096.** Admission £3.50 ($5.25) adults, £3 ($4.50) senior citizens, £1.80 ($2.70) children. Mar–Oct, Mon–Sat 9:30am–5:15pm, Sun 10:30am–4:30pm; Nov–Feb, Mon–Sat 9:30am–4:15pm. Closed Jan 1–3, two weeks in May, the last two weeks of June and the first week of July, and Dec 25–27. Bus 1 or 6.

Built more than 300 years ago for the kings and queens of Scotland, this palace is still the official residence of the queen when she visits Edinburgh each summer. Holyroodhouse was the home of Mary, Queen of Scots, Bonnie Prince Charlie, and Queen Victoria. Uniformed guides will delight in describing to you the grisly death of Queen Mary's personal secretary, David Rizzio, who was murdered by associates of her jealous husband in 1566. Elsewhere in the palace are massive tapestries, ornate plasterwork ceilings, a portrait gallery of the Stuart rulers, the Throne Room, and the State Apartments, still used for entertaining guests during the queen's summer residency.

National Gallery of Scotland

2 The Mound. ☎ **0131/556-8921.** Admission free. Mon–Sat 10am–5pm, Sun 2–5pm. Any Princes Street bus.

At the corner of Princes Street and The Mound, this gallery has an outstanding collection for such a small museum. On display are works by Rembrandt, Raphael, Titian, El Greco, Rubens, van Dyck, Goya, Gainsborough, Monet, Degas, Gauguin, van Gogh, and the Scottish artists Ramsay, Raeburn, and Wilkie.

Royal Museum of Scotland and National Portrait Gallery

1 Queen St. ☎ **0131/225-7534.** Admission free. Mon–Sat 10am–5pm, Sun 2–5pm. Bus 2/12, 4, 4A, 9, or 9A.

The exhibits here all pertain to Scottish history, beginning with the Neolithic period nearly 6,000 years ago and continuing up to the present. Viking, Celtic, and Roman artifacts tell a fascinating story that's an excellent adjunct to the medieval history of Edinburgh. The portrait gallery contains traditional and some not-so-traditional paintings of famous Scots.

Royal Museum of Scotland

Chambers St. ☎ **0131/225-7534.** Admission free. Mon–Sat 10am–5pm, Sun noon–5pm. Lawnmarket or Tron bus.

A Venetian Renaissance facade hides an unusually bright and airy Victorian interior at this museum of natural history, industry, and decorative arts two blocks south of the Royal Mile. Stuffed animals, minerals, steam engines, Egyptian artifacts, and working models of the engines that made the Industrial Revolution possible are on display. The soaring beauty of the main hall is itself reason enough to visit.

✪ Scottish National Gallery of Modern Art

Belford Rd. ☎ **0131/556-8921.** Admission free. Mon–Sat 10am–5pm, Sun 2–5pm. Bus 13.

Housed in an 1820s neoclassical building, the collection here is as fine as that in the National Gallery. Works by Picasso, Matisse, Miró, David Hockney, Henry Moore, Roy Lichtenstein, and many other 20th-century artists are on display both inside the museum and around the spacious grounds.

Scott Monument

E. Princes Street Gardens. ☎ **0131/529-4068.** Admission £1 ($1.50). Apr–Sept, Mon–Sat 9am–6pm; Oct–Mar, Mon–Sat 9am–3pm. Bus 2/12, 3, 4, 4A, 10, 11, 15, 15A, 16, 43, 44, 80, or 80A.

Looking more like a church spire than a monument to a writer, this gothic structure dominates East Princes Street Gardens. In the center of the spire is a large seated statue of Sir Walter Scott and his dog, Maida. The monument rises to a height of more than 200 feet. Visitors are treated to a spectacular view of the city from an observation area at the top of 287 steps.

Nelson Monument and the National Monument

Calton Hill. ☎ **0131/556-2716.** Nelson Monument, £1 ($1.50); National Monument, free. Apr–Sept, Mon 1–6pm, Tues–Sat 10am–6pm; Oct–Mar, Mon–Sat 10am–3pm. Bus 26, 85, or 86.

Erected in memory of Admiral Horatio Lord Nelson, victor at the Battle of Trafalgar, this 106-foot tower atop Calton Hill was built to resemble a telescope, and it offers superb views over the city. The "Greek" ruins beside the monument are all that was built of a monument to commemorate Scottish soldiers and sail-

---

Special & Free Events

For three weeks in late August and early September, Edinburgh goes on a cultural binge. The most famous events, known collectively as the **Edinburgh International Festival,** 21 Market St., Edinburgh EH1 1BW (☎ **0131/ 225-5756;** fax 0131/226-7669), encompass music, performance-art, and theater performances. Tickets are priced at £5 to £35 ($7.50 to $52.50) per show, though money-saving series tickets are available. For tickets, contact the box office by mail, phone, or fax beginning in mid-April.

Other major events are also held during August:

The **Edinburgh Festival Fringe,** 180 High St., Edinburgh EH1 1QS (☎ **0131/228-4051**), features smaller, more offbeat and experimental theatrical performances. Tickets cost £1 to £10 ($1.50 to $15).

The **Edinburgh Military Tattoo,** 22 Market St., Edinburgh EH1 1QB (☎ **0131/225-1188;** fax 0131/225-8627), is a military musical extravaganza held on the esplanade in front of the castle just before dusk. Tickets cost £9 to £18 ($13.50 to $27).

The **Edinburgh International Jazz Festival,** 116 Canongate, Edinburgh EH8 8DD (☎ **0131/557-1642**), features international stars and unknowns at various locales around the city. Tickets cost £3 to £20 ($4.50 to $30).

The **Edinburgh International Film Festival,** 88 Lothian Rd., Edinburgh EH3 9BZ (☎ **0131/228-4051**), screens world premières of films in need of world distribution. Tickets cost £2 to £4 ($3 to $6).

The **Edinburgh Book Festival,** 137 Dundee St., Edinburgh EH11 1BG (☎ **0131/228-5444**), is held in the Scottish Book Center.

ors who died in the Napoleonic Wars. Lack of funds prevented its completion, and now it's one of the most eye-catching structures in all Edinburgh, going by the name of Edinburgh's Disgrace.

Georgian House

7 Charlotte Sq. ☎ **0131/225-2160.** Admission £3 ($4.50) adults, £1.50 ($2.25) students and children. Easter–Oct, Mon–Sat 10am–5pm, Sun 2–5pm. Closed Nov–Apr. Bus 13, 18, 40, or 41A; or walk two blocks over from the west end of Princes Street.

Edinburgh's New Town is a model of 18th-century urban planning. In contrast to the chaos of the Old City, symmetry reigns in the grand boulevards, parks, squares, and elegant rowhouses on this side of Princes Street Gardens. Furnished in original Georgian style, Georgian House shows what life was like in the New Town 200 years ago when this area was indeed new. The furnishings include Chippendale, Hepplewhite, and Sheraton styles, as well as porcelain by Derby and Wedgwood.

MORE ATTRACTIONS

Between Edinburgh Castle and the Palace of Holyroodhouse, along the Royal Mile, are dozens of interesting shops, old pubs, fascinating little museums, and Edinburgh's oldest cathedral. You'll find many of the sights listed here down the narrow closes (alleyways) that lead off the Royal Mile. Regardless of whether they have a specific attraction to offer, all the closes are worth exploring simply for their medieval atmosphere.

St. Giles's Cathedral

High St. ☎ **0131/225-9442.** Cathedral, free; the small Thistle Chapel inside, 50p (75¢). May–Sept, daily 9am–7pm; Oct–Apr, daily 9am–5pm. Bus 1, 6, 34, or 35.

This is the spiritual heart of the Church of Scotland. A church has existed on this site since the 9th century, and parts of this building date from 1120. Since then, many alterations have changed the building immensely. Scottish religious reformer John Knox, who established the Protestant religion in Scotland, became the minister here in 1560. The unusual main spire is in the form of a thistle, one of the symbols of Scotland.

John Knox House

43 High St. ☎ **0131/556-9579.** Admission £2.25 ($3.40) adults, £1.50 ($2.25) senior citizens, £1 ($1.50) children. Mon–Sat 10am–4:30pm. Bus 1 or 6.

Tradition has it that John Knox, leader of the Protestant Reformation in Scotland, lived here between 1561 and 1572. Built in 1490 and a museum since 1853, this may be the oldest house in Edinburgh. The wooden gallery surrounding the upper floors is the last of its kind in the city. Inside are paintings and lithographs of Knox, along with his letters, sermons, and early tracts.

Huntly House Museum

142 Canongate. ☎ **0131/529-4143.** Admission free. June–Sept, Mon–Sat 10am–6pm; Oct–May, Mon–Sat 10am–5pm. Bus 1 or 6.

To learn more about the history of Scotland, and Edinburgh in particular, head for this small museum on Canongate (the lower section of the Royal Mile). In this restored 16th-century town house are exhibits and rooms set up to show how citizens of Edinburgh lived in different centuries of the house's history.

Lady Stair's House

Lawnmarket. ☎ **0131/225-2424** ext. 4901. Admission free. June–Sept, Mon–Sat 10am–6pm; Oct–May, Mon–Sat 10am–5pm. Lawnmarket buses.

In Lady Stair's Close off the Lawnmarket, less than 100 yards from the George IV Bridge, this museum is a must for fans of Scottish literature. Robert Burns, Sir Walter Scott, and Robert Louis Stevenson are commemorated with collections of their works, personal effects, and portraits.

Museum of Childhood

42 High St. ☎ **0131/529-4142.** Admission free. June–Sept, Mon–Sat 10am–6pm; Oct–May, Mon–Sat 10am–5pm. Bus 1 or 6.

With its displays of antique teddy bears, amazingly detailed dollhouses, old board games, and porcelain dolls, this museum is more for adults than for children. However, there are also plenty of exhibits to entertain the kids.

The People's Story

163 Canongate. ☎ **0131/225-2424** ext. 4057. Admission free. June–Sept, Mon–Sat 10am–6pm; Oct–May, Mon–Sat 10am–5pm. Bus 1 or 6.

Most museums focus on the lives of historical figures and artifacts of the wealthy. This, however, is a people's museum that tells the story of the common folk of Edinburgh from the Middle Ages to the present. Sights, sounds, and even smells are reproduced to surround the visitor with the people's story.

Outlook Tower and Camera Obscura

Castle Hill. ☎ **0131/226-3709.** Admission £4 ($6) adults, £3.50 ($5.25) students, £3 ($4.50) senior citizens, £2.50 ($3.75) children. Apr–Oct, daily 9:30am–6pm; Nov–Mar daily 10am–5pm. Bus 1 or 6.

The camera obscura, a device that produces an upside-down image on the wall of a black room, was installed in 1850 and has been a popular attraction ever since. It's like walking inside a huge camera. Also here are exhibits on pinhole photography and holography.

Brass Rubbing Centre

Chalmer's Close, High St. ☎ **0131/556-4364.** Admission free. June–Sept, Mon–Sat 10am–6pm; Oct–May, Mon–Sat 10am–5pm. Bus 1 or 6.

The center provides instruction and replicas of medieval church brasses and Neolithic Scottish stone carvings in all sizes for you to make your own rubbings. There are also ready-made rubbings for sale; rubbings vary in price. The center is housed in an old church and has a number of rubbings and old brasses on display.

Edinburgh Zoo

134 Corstorphine Rd. ☎ **0131/334-9171.** Admission £5 ($7.50) adults, £3 ($4.50) senior citizens and children. Apr–Sept, Mon–Sat 9am–6pm, Sun 9:30am–6pm; Oct–Mar, Mon–Sat 9am–4:30pm, Sun 9:30am–4:30pm. Bus 12, 26, 31, 85, or 86.

The Edinburgh Zoo covers 80 acres of parkland and houses nearly 1,500 animals. The main attraction is the penguin parade, which takes place daily at 2pm from April to September. With more than 100 penguins, this is the world's largest self-supporting captive penguin colony, and they're an unforgettable sight when they go for their afternoon stroll.

PARKS & GARDENS

Edinburgh is filled with parks and gardens. The largest is **Holyrood Park,** which begins behind the Palace of Holyroodhouse. With rocky crags, a loch, sweeping meadows, and the ruins of an old chapel, it's a wee bit of the Scottish countryside in Edinburgh. **Arthur's Seat,** at 823 feet, and the **Salisbury Crags** offer unbeatable views over Edinburgh to the Firth of Forth. This is a great place for a picnic.

The tranquil **Princes Street Gardens** separate the Old Town from the New Town. Old trees and brilliant green lawns fill the valley between the two sections of the city. Along the paved footpaths of the gardens are dozens of wooden benches given by the people of Edinburgh in memory of loved ones. These benches are excellent places to enjoy a picnic lunch or to relax while savoring the views of the city. The gardens are open daily from dawn to dusk. Take one of the Princes Street buses.

Edinburgh's 70-acre **Royal Botanic Gardens,** Inverleith Row (☎ **0131/ 552-7171**), are known for their extensive collection of rhododendrons that flower profusely every spring. With a large arboretum, research facilities, and wild areas providing a sharp contrast to the neatly manicured gardens, this is one of Europe's finest botanical gardens. It's also the second-oldest botanical garden in Britain, established as a physic garden in 1670 by two physicians who used the plants for treating illnesses. The botanic gardens are open November to February, daily from 10am to 4pm; in March, April, September, and October, daily from 10am to 6pm; and May to August, daily from 10am to 8pm. Take bus no. 8, 19, 23, or 27.

SPECIAL-INTEREST SIGHTSEEING

Literary fans should not miss **Lady Stair's House,** a small museum devoted to Scottish writers Robert Burns, Sir Walter Scott, and Robert Louis Stevenson. In addition, if you have the stamina, make a pilgrimage to the top of the **Scott Memorial** in Princes Street Gardens. And on the corner of Lawnmarket and Bank Street is **Deacon Brodie's Tavern,** named for the criminal who inspired Robert Louis Stevenson to write *The Strange Case of Dr. Jekyll and Mr. Hyde.*

ORGANIZED TOURS

WALKING TOURS   Robin's Tours, 66 Willowbrae Rd. (☎ **0131/661-0125**), offers four different walking tours focusing on different aspects of Edinburgh history. The "Grand City Tour" and "The Royal Mile: Old Town" present a standard historical overview, while the "Ghosts and Witches" and "Dr. Jekyll's Ghosts" tours present a darker side of Edinburgh's history. Tickets are £4 ($6) for adults, £3 ($4.50) for students, and £2 ($3) for children. These tours start in front of the Waverley Market Tourist Information Centre.

Grisly, ghostly tours are an Edinburgh specialty, and no one does them better than **The Cadies** (☎ **0131/225-6745**). Their tours of haunted Edinburgh last 1¼ hours, cost £5 ($7.50), and leave from in front of the Witchery Restaurant just outside the gate to Edinburgh Castle. Reservations are required. You can expect strange things to happen on this tour of darkest Edinburgh.

BUS TOURS   Scotline Tours, 87 High St. (☎ **0131/557-0162**), offers a four-hour tour that covers all the city's most important sights and includes stops at both the castle and Holyroodhouse. Tickets are £12 ($18) for adults and £7 ($10.50) for children.

A less expensive option is to choose the **Edinburgh Classic Tour,** which is a day pass for an open-topped double-decker bus that makes a regular circuit past all the major tourist attractions in both Old Town and New Town. You can get on and off the bus to visit an attraction and then catch a later bus. Tickets cost £4.50 ($6.75) for adults and £1.75 ($2.60) for children and are available on the bus.

7 Shopping

Princes Street in the New Town is Edinburgh's main shopping area, with several large department stores and dozens of shops selling designer clothes and other equally expensive items. Also try the Mill Shop store here for bargains in woolens and knitwear.

Victoria Street and **Grassmarket** in the Old Town both have some unusual shops.

Cadenheads Whisky Shop, 172 Canongate, Royal Mile (☎ **0131/556-5864**), sells hundreds of whiskeys, including a good selection of rare single-malts. It's open Monday through Saturday from 10:30am to 5pm.

VAT REFUNDS   In shops all over Edinburgh you'll see signs saying TAX-FREE SHOPPING. These signs refer to the process by which you as a visitor can recover the value-added tax (VAT) that amounts to about 11% of everything you buy. Usually shops will require a minimum purchase of £30 to £50 ($45 to $75). Once the forms are filled out, present them to Customs before leaving the country, along with the purchases themselves. After the forms have been stamped by Customs, mail them back to the store with the envelope provided by the store. Within a few weeks your refund will be mailed to your home address in the form you have requested (such as a check in U.S. dollars).

8 Edinburgh After Dark

For a city of its size, Edinburgh (pop. 450,000) offers an overwhelming array of evening entertainment. Whether your interest is theater, dance, or folk, classical, or rock music, Edinburgh will entertain you for next to nothing. On any given night you might see a play for £5 ($7.50), stop by a pub for a bit of free traditional music, and then head to a disco (get there before 11pm to get in for £3/$4.50) for some late-night dancing—a jam-packed night out for only £8 ($12), not including drinks.

Pick up a free copy of **"Day-by-Day"** at the Tourist Information Centre at Waverley Market. This four-page pamphlet comes out every month and lists exhibitions, theater, music, films, and other information helpful to tourists. The best source of listings information is the biweekly magazine *The List,* available at newsstands around town for £1.30 ($1.95).

THE PERFORMING ARTS

You'll find most of the city's performance venues clustered on or near Lothian Road at the west end of Princes Street. Yes, Edinburgh, too, has a West End theater district.

THEATER & CLASSICAL MUSIC

THEATER   Edinburgh is a theater-goer's dream come true—fine performances and low prices. This is not surprising considering the citizens' love of theater of all kinds, the culmination of which is the annual summer **Edinburgh International Festival.** Tickets start as low as £5 ($7.50) at many theaters, and even the most expensive theaters have tickets for under £8 ($12) for most performances. And it's sometimes possible to catch a free preview. Check *The List* (see above) to find the best deals while you're in town.

The Victorian **King's Theatre,** 2 Leven St. (☎ **0131/229-1201**), has about 1,600 seats and features a wide variety of performances by different repertory companies. Ballet, opera, light opera, pantomime, and drama all show up here. Tickets range from £4 to £19.50 ($6 to $29.25). The box office is open Monday through Saturday from 10am to 8pm.

Located next to the John Knox House, the **Netherbow Arts Centre,** 43 High St. (☎ **0131/556-9579**), is a stage for experimental productions and the best of new Scottish theater. There are sometimes lunchtime performances here. Tickets cost £4 to £7 ($6 to $10.50). The box office is open Monday through Saturday from 10am to 6pm.

Edinburgh's main playhouse, the **Royal Lyceum Theatre,** Grindley Street at Lothian Road (☎ **0131/229-9697**), seats 1,200 and features plays and operas by the resident company. Tickets run £4 to £12 ($6 to $18). The box office is open Monday through Saturday from 10am to 8pm (to 6pm on performance nights).

You can catch new experimental theater productions by English and Scottish playwrights at the large, attractive, and contemporary **Traverse Theatre,** Cambridge Street, off Lothian Road (☎ **0131/228-1404**). Tickets cost £5 to £7 ($7.50 to $10.50). The box office is open Monday from 10am to 6pm, Tuesday through Saturday from 10am to 8pm, and Sunday from 4 to 8pm.

CLASSICAL MUSIC   There are two major halls for performances of classical music: **Usher Hall,** on Lothian Road (☎ **0131/228-1155**), where the Royal Scottish Orchestra performs; and the **Queen's Hall,** Clerk Street (☎ **0131/668-2019**), which is the home of the Edinburgh Symphony Orchestra and showcases other groups as well. Check "Day-By-Day" or *The List* for schedules and programs. Tickets at either hall start at about £5 ($7.50).

FOLK, ROCK & JAZZ

Fans of folk, rock, and jazz can have a field day in Edinburgh, where most clubs offer free live music every night. At most you might have to pay £1.50 to £2.50 ($2.25 to $3.75) on a Friday or Saturday night for the top local bands. Music usually starts around 11pm.

For the greatest concentration of live-music clubs and pubs that feature live music at least one night a week, head for Victoria Street and Grassmarket in Old Town.

For fine traditional music, try **Fiddlers Arms,** 11–13 Grassmarket (☎ **0131/229-2665**), a block west of the end of Victoria Street. On Monday nights local musicians get together to play old favorites in a corner of the pub's front room. Admission is free. Open Monday through Wednesday from 11am to 11pm, Thursday through Saturday from 11am to midnight, and Sunday from 12:30 to 11pm.

In an old church (you can't miss it) that's been converted into a commercial building is one of Edinburgh's most popular spots for live rock music, jazz, and blues, **Preservation Hall,** 9a Victoria St. (☎ **0131/226-3816**). Admission is free Sunday through Thursday but £1.50 ($2.25) on Friday and Saturday. Open daily from 9pm to 2am.

FILMS

The most easily accessible movie theaters are the **Cannon** on Lothian Road, near the western end of Princes Street; the **Cameo** on Home Street (an extension of Lothian Road); and the **Odeon** on Clerk Street, close to Dalkeith Road. The **Edinburgh Filmhouse** on Lothian Road shows foreign films. Tickets run £2 to £4.25 ($3 to $6.35). Early shows are usually less expensive.

EDINBURGH'S PUBS

There's a pub on nearly every block in Edinburgh, and many have live music at least one night a week. In all of them, either a pint of ale or a shot of scotch whiskey will cost £1.20 to £1.60 ($1.80 to $2.40). Most pubs also serve lunch from noon to 2:30pm. Rose Street (parallel to Princes Street) is famous for its pubs.

On the same tiny block as the Guildford Arms (below), the ever-popular **Café Royal,** 17 W. Register St. (☎ **0131/556-1884**), known for its circle bar, appeals to a casual clientele. Stained-glass windows and unusual painted tiles of famous inventors make this café a particularly interesting spot to down a pint. There's also live folk music in the second-floor bistro on Wednesday at 8pm, when there's an admission charge of £3 ($4.50). Open Monday through Saturday from 10am to 11pm and Sunday from 11am to 11pm.

The atmospheric **Green Tree,** 184 Cowgate (☎ **0131/255-1294**), with low ceilings and dark brick walls, is directly under South Bridge, literally in the foundation of the bridge. There's live traditional music on Wednesday at 9pm. It's popular with students from the nearby university. Open Monday through Saturday from 11am to 11pm.

The ornate Victorian **Guilford Arms,** 1 W. Register St. (☎ **0131/556-4312**), behind the Wimpy restaurant by North Bridge, is popular with an older and more upscale clientele. You can't miss the beautiful etched-glass windows. Once inside, you'll be surrounded by the sumptuous decor. Open Monday through Thursday from 11am to 11pm, Friday and Saturday from 11am to midnight, and Sunday from 12:30 to 2:30pm and 6:30 to 11pm.

The small, dark **Malt Shovel,** 13 Cockburn St. (☎ **0131/225-6843**), is an Edinburgh legend that's spawned at least two companion pubs in the area. Besides the free live jazz and traditional music, it has one of the best selections of single-malt whiskeys in town. Open Monday through Saturday from noon to 12:30am.

DISCOS

Discos in Edinburgh generally open their doors around 10pm and stay open until 3 or 4am. Drinks average £1.50 ($2.25) for beer or hard liquor, and many offer special drink prices on certain nights or early in the evening.

Buster Brown's, 25–27 Market St. (☎ **0131/226-4224**), is popular with the under-25 group and features mainstream top-40 dance music. Admission is £3 ($4.50) on Friday and Sunday, £2 ($3) before midnight; £4 ($6) on Saturday, £2 ($3) before 11:30pm. Open Friday through Sunday from 10:30pm to 3:30am.

Century 2000, 31 Lothian Rd. (☎ **0131/229-7670**, is the largest disco in Edinburgh and one of the most popular. Admission is £5 ($7.50), £3 ($4.50) before midnight. Open Friday and Saturday from 10pm to 4am.

9 Easy Excursions

Lothian Region Transport, 14 Queen St. (☎ **0131/554-4494**), offers more than 20 excursions from Edinburgh. Among the best of these is the tour to **Loch Ness and the Grampian Mountains,** available only from early April through early November. The trip costs £22 ($33) for adults and £17.50 ($26.25) for children. Along the way toward the home of the fabled Loch Ness monster, the coach travels through beautiful mountains, forests, fields, and farmland.

For a less expensive all-day excursion, try the trip to beautiful **Loch Lomond.** In summer the tour is combined with a visit to either the Argyllshire or the Trossachs mountains. In winter the tour travels through the Argyllshire mountains. The cost is £13 ($19.50) for adults and £9 ($13.50) for children.

You can also book your tour at the Ticket Centre on Waverley Bridge (☎ **0131/220-4111**).

Florence 13

by Dan Levine

Five hundred years ago, Florence was the center of European culture. It was here in the 14th, 15th, and 16th centuries that many of the most important developments in modern art and architecture took place. Indeed, today we refer to that period as the Renaissance, or "rebirth."

Florence is no longer the axis around which the artistic world revolves, but the taste, elegance, and aesthetic sensibilities that marked the Renaissance are still alive and well. Today the city boasts Europe's richest concentration of artistic wealth. Elegant young Florentines saunter along the narrow cobblestone streets, through the spacious piazzas, and past the great palazzi with the same confidence and pride as their forebears.

Europe's cultural revolution was financed in large part by the Medicis, Florence's ruling family throughout much of the Renaissance. They came to power as bankers and used their wealth to foster the arts. The city is filled with this heritage: Fully half a dozen museums, as well as churches and palaces, house major paintings and sculpture of the period.

However, not only the sights and the history make Florence a special place for visitors. The nuts and bolts of where you stay and what you eat will make this city special around the clock. Many of the budget hotels I've listed are housed in the same 15th- and 16th-century palazzi where the Medicis and the Michelangelos lived. You may find yourself sleeping beneath a ceiling decorated with colorful frescoes or in a bed old enough to have been slept in by Botticelli. The cuisine in this city, situated in the heart of the nation's most fertile agricultural land, is arguably the finest in Italy.

Just as Florence inaugurated a rebirth of creative thought in Europe five centuries ago, it will raise your spirits and lift your thoughts in 1996.

1 Florence Deals & Discounts

BUDGET BESTS   You're likely to find bargains on almost everything in this shopper's paradise. Florence's famous San Lorenzo open-air market stretches for half a dozen blocks, with hundreds of stalls hawking everything from $8 souvenir T-shirts to $400 designer leather coats, often at about half what you'd pay for items of comparable quality back home. Hand-knit all-wool sweaters (at about

What's Special About Florence

The City Itself

- The most significant and most captivating architecture in Italy.
- The surrounding Tuscan countryside, home to some of Italy's most delightful scenery.
- Watching the sun set over the red-tile roofs of the city.
- Taking a passeggiata (stroll) along via Calzaiuoli on a warm night.

Sights

- Michelangelo's David at the Accademia Gallery, which, despite the crowds, is worth the wait.
- The Botticelli Galleries at the Uffizi, some of Europe's brightest and most refreshing museum rooms.
- The rich color and architecture of the Duomo and the adjacent Baptistery and Campanile.

Shopping

- The incomparable prices and variety at the enormous, sprawling San Lorenzo Market.
- The extraordinary quality of the leather goods available throughout the city.
- The trendy boutiques lining via Calzaiuoli and the surrounding streets.

Cuisine

- Enjoying a languorous multicourse meal at any one of the city's terrific restaurants.
- Rich, delicate cream-based pasta sauces.
- Incomparable gelato.

$30) and fashionable leather jackets (beginning at around $200) are the best buys, but budget shoppers will be able to find just about anything here, at reasonable prices.

You can always save money on food and drink by consuming them standing up at one of the city's ubiquitous bars. Prices double—at least—if you sit down.

WORTH THE EXTRA MONEY   To gourmets and gourmands alike, Florence is the culinary capital of Italy. Under "Dining," later in this chapter, you'll find half a dozen restaurants that are particularly worth a splurge.

Florence also has an outstanding selection of charming one-of-a-kind hotels. If you can afford to spend a little bit more on accommodations, you'll inevitably be treated to an extraordinary and memorable stay.

Finally, don't miss the *gelato* (ice cream). At about 3,000 lire ($1.85) per serving, this light, delicious local delicacy is worth every lira.

2 Pretrip Preparations

REQUIRED DOCUMENTS   For information on necessary documents, see Chapter 23 on Rome.

TIMING YOUR TRIP   Florence remains popular and comfortable from April to October, and, thankfully, July and August are not nearly as sweltering as in

Rome. As the inhabitants of many other Italian cities do, Florentines desert their city in August, when many restaurants may be closed for three or more weeks.

Florence's Average Daytime Temperature & Rainfall

	Jan	Feb	Mar	Apr	May	June	July	Aug	Sept	Oct	Nov	Dec
Temp. (°F)	45	47	50	60	67	75	77	70	64	63	55	46
Rainfall "	3	3.3	3.7	2.7	2.2	1.4	1.4	2.7	3.2	4.9	3.8	2.9

Special Events   The highlight of June 24, the feast day of Florence's patron saint, John the Baptist, is the **Calcio Storico,** a rough-and-tumble medieval cross between rugby and soccer played with a wooden ball and few (if any) rules. Teams representing the four original parishes of Florence, clad in 16th-century costume, square off against one another in piazza Santa Croce, competing vigorously for that year's bragging rights. Later on, fireworks light up the night sky.

Nearby Siena has its own medieval grudge match, the **Palio,** on July 2 and August 16. Horses representing 10 of the city's historic districts (*contrade*) race once around the sloping oval main square. The race itself is very brief, but the preparations, parades, and post-Palio celebrations seem to go on forever. Indeed, travelers who have journeyed to Siena in the weeks before a Palio have been known to happen upon impromptu street demonstrations by a hopeful contrada's neighborhood marching band.

What Things Cost in Florence	U.S. $
Taxi (from the train station to piazza della Signoria)	7.00
Public bus (from any point within the city to any other point)	.75
Local telephone call	.13
Double room at the Excelsior (deluxe)	712.50
Double room at the Hotel Morandi alla Crocetta (moderate)	111.90
Double room at the Albergo Mia Cara (budget)	37.50
Continental breakfast (cappuccino and croissant) (at a café)	1.90
(at most hotels)	4.05
Lunch for one at Trattoria del Pennello (moderate)	16.65
Lunch for one at a café (budget)	4.75
Dinner for one, without wine, at Sabatini (deluxe)	110.00
Dinner for one, without wine, at Ristorante Acqua al Due (moderate)	34.20
Dinner for one, without wine, at Procacci (budget)	10.00
Pint of beer (at Fiddler's Elbow)	4.05
Glass of wine (at Chiodo Fisso)	3.50
Coca-Cola to take out (at any café in town)	1.30
Cup of coffee (cappuccino) (at any café in town)	.95
Roll of ASA 100 color film, 36 exposures	5.65
Admission to the Uffizi Galleries	7.50
Movie ticket (at the Astro Cinema)	5.00
Cheapest theater ticket (at the Teatro Communale)	6.25

BACKGROUND READING & VIEWING   Put yourself in the mood to savor this wonderful city by viewing the romantic Merchant/Ivory film *A Room with a View,* based on E. M. Forster's novel of the same name (Bantam). The film evokes the extraordinary charm of one of Europe's most seductive cities.

Mary McCarthy's *The Stones of Florence* (Harcourt Brace Jovanovich) is a readable and excellent source of background on the history and culture of the city.

Irving Stone's biography of Michelangelo, *The Agony and the Ecstasy* (New American Library), adds a fourth dimension to his masterpieces, which you'll be viewing at seemingly every turn in this rich city. *The House of Medici: Its Rise and Fall* (Morrow) by Christopher Hibbert is the best book on Florence's ruling class.

Luigi Barzini's classic *The Italians* (Macmillan) offers a frank, refreshing, and opinionated discussion of the history and culture of his homeland, past and present.

3 Florence Specifics

ARRIVING

BY PLANE   Alitalia, Lufthansa, and about half a dozen other European airlines service Florence's **Amerigo Vespucci Airport** (☎ **055/37-34-98**). Regularly scheduled city buses connect the airport with downtown Florence, make the journey in about 30 minutes, and cost 1,200 lire (75¢) each way. Taxis line up outside the airport's single small terminal and charge about 25,000 lire ($15.65) to the city center.

BY TRAIN   Most Florence-bound trains roll into the **Stazione Santa Maria Novella** (☎ **055/28-87-65**), which you'll often see abbreviated "S.M.N." The station is on the western edge of the city's compact historical center, a leisurely 10-minute walk from the Duomo and 15 minutes from piazza della Signoria and the Uffizi Galleries.

With your back to the tracks, you'll find an Ufficio Turismo information and accommodations service office (☎ **055/28-28-93**) toward the station's left exit. It's open April to October, Monday through Saturday from 9am to 8pm and Sunday from 10:30am to 6:25pm; November to March, the office closes at 9pm. The train information office is near the right exit. Walk straight through the large glass doors into the outer hall for tickets and a bank that changes money Monday through Saturday from 8:20am to 7:20pm. Adjacent to Track 16 is an Albergo Diurno, or day hotel, where you can wash up or take a shower after a long train ride. There's also a 24-hour luggage depot at the head of Track 16 (☎ **055/ 21-23-19**), where you can drop your bags while you search for a hotel. It charges 2,000 lire ($1.25) per piece.

Some trains stop at **Stazione Campo di Marte,** on the east side of the city. There's 24-hour bus service between the two stations.

BY CAR   Driving to Florence is easy; the problems begin once you arrive. Most automobiles are banned from the city center—only those with special permits are allowed in. You can drive into the center to drop off baggage, then you must drive out again to a parking lot. Ask at your hotel which one is closest.

VISITOR INFORMATION

The main train station's **Ufficio Turismo (I.T.A.)** information and accommodations service office (see above) distributes fairly good free city maps, answers simple

The Italian Lira

For American Readers   At this writing $1 = approximately 1,600 lire (or 100 lire = 6.25¢), and this was the rate of exchange used to calculate the dollar values given in this chapter (rounded to the nearest nickel).

For British Readers   At this writing £1 = approximately 2,400 lire (or 100 lire = 4.2p), and this was the rate of exchange used to calculate the pound values in the table below.

Note: The rates given here fluctuate from time to time and may not be the same when you travel to Italy. Therefore this table should be used only as a guide:

Lire	U.S.$	U.K.£	Lire	U.S.$	U.K.£
100	.06	.04	20,000	12.50	8.33
250	.16	.10	25,000	15.63	10.42
500	.31	.21	30,000	18.75	12.50
750	.47	.31	35,000	21.88	14.58
1,000	.63	.42	40,000	25.00	16.67
1,500	.94	.63	45,000	28.13	18.75
2,000	1.25	.83	50,000	31.25	20.83
2,500	1.56	1.04	60,000	37.50	25.00
3,000	1.88	1.25	70,000	43.75	29.17
4,000	2.50	1.67	80,000	50.00	33.33
5,000	3.13	2.08	90,000	56.25	37.50
7,500	4.69	3.13	100,000	62.50	41.67
10,000	6.25	4.17	125,000	78.13	52.08
15,000	9.38	6.25	150,000	93.75	62.50

questions, and makes hotel reservations for a 3,000- to 4,000-lira ($1.85 to $2.50) fee (depending on the quality of the hotel). Especially during the crowded summer months, however, travelers arriving by train may wish to bypass this office and walk a few steps farther to a second municipal office just outside the station. With your back to the tracks, take the left exit, cross onto the concrete median, and turn right; the office will be about 100 feet ahead. This **alternative information center** distributes a wider variety of government tourist publications, including **Firenze Oggi** (*Florence Today*), a helpful 2,000-lira ($1.25) bimonthly. It's usually open daily from 8am to 7:30pm.

The city's largest tourist office is the **Main Municipal Office,** via Cavour 1r (☎ **055/29-08-32** or 29-08-33), about three blocks north of the Duomo. This office is less harried than the busy station offices, offers lots of literature, and boasts an unusually helpful staff. The office is usually open Monday through Saturday from 8am to 7:30pm. A more conveniently located tourist office is near piazza Signoria at chiasso Baroncelli 17r (☎ **055/230-21-24**).

The bilingual **Concierge Information** magazine, available free from the concierge desks of top hotels, contains a monthly calendar of events, as well as information on museums, sights, and attractions. **Firenze Spettacolo,** a 2,500-lira

($1.60) Italian-language monthly sold at most city newsstands, lists the latest in nightlife, arts, and entertainment.

CITY LAYOUT

Florence is a compact city that's best negotiated on foot. No two sights are more than a 20- or 25-minute walk apart, and all the hotels and restaurants listed in this chapter are located in the downtown area.

The city's relatively small, beautiful, and touristy **Centro Storico (Historic Center)** is loosely bounded by the S.M.N. Train Station to the northwest, piazza della S.S. Annunziata to the northeast, and the **Arno River** to the south. The area leading up to the Pitti Palace, just across the river, a few blocks past the ponte Vecchio, is also popular tourist territory.

Piazza del Duomo, dominated by Florence's largest and most famous church and ancillary Baptistery, is at the center of the tourist's city. During your stay, you'll inevitably walk along many of the streets radiating from this imposing square.

Borgo San Lorenzo, running north from the Baptistery, is best known for its excellent outdoor market, which sells everything from marbleized paper-wrapped pencils to leather jackets.

Via Calzaiuoli, Florence's most popular pedestrian thoroughfare and shopping street, runs south from the Duomo, connecting the church with the romantic, statue-filled **piazza della Signoria.** At its midsection, via Calzaiuoli is bisected by the short via Speziali, which opens into **piazza della Repubblica,** a busy shop- and café-ringed square surrounded by expensive shopping streets.

Back on piazza della Signoria, follow the crowds onto via Vacchereccia, turn left, and walk south two blocks to the **ponte Vecchio (Old Bridge),** the Arno's most famous span. Topped with a cluster of tiny jewelry shops, the bridge crosses over to the **Oltrarno** area, a section of artisans and shopkeepers that's best known for the Pitti Palace, just a few blocks past the bridge.

Confused? Climb up through the **Boboli Gardens,** behind the Pitti Palace, and you'll be rewarded with a beautiful bird's-eye view of Florence that'll help you navigate your way around.

STREET NUMBERING There are two systems of street numbering: blue or black (*blu* or *nero*) and red (*rosso*). Blue or black numbers are used for residential and office buildings, including hotels, while red numbers are used to identify all commercial enterprises, including restaurants. In this chapter, red-numbered addresses are indicated by a lowercase "r" following the number.

GETTING AROUND

BY BUS You'll rarely need to take advantage of Florence's efficient A.T.A.F. bus system, since the city is so wonderfully compact. Bus tickets cost 1,200 lire (75¢) and must be purchased before you board. An eight-pack of tickets will run 9,000 lire ($5.65), while a 24-hour pass costs 6,000 lire ($3.75). Tickets are sold at the A.T.A.F. booth at the head of Track 14 in the train station (☎ **055/58-05-28**) and at tobacco shops (*tabacchi*) and most newsstands. Once on board, validate your ticket in the box near the rear door.

Buses no. 13, 14, and 19 run from the train station (most stop outside the exit by Track 16) to piazza del Duomo and from there down via del Proconsolo and past the Bargello to the back side of piazza della Signoria. Buses no. 15, 35, and 36 continue across the Arno and on to the Pitti Palace, in the Oltrarno.

BY TAXI   Cabs can be hailed in the street or called to your restaurant or hotel by dialing 4798 or 4390. Taxis charge 1,250 lire (80¢) per kilometer, but there's a minimum fare of 6,000 lire ($3.75) and most hops around the city average about 10,000 lire ($6.25), including a 10% tip.

ON FOOT   With its 15th-century palazzi lining cobblestone streets that are even older, Florence is one of the most delightful cities in Europe to explore on foot. Florence is very compact. A leisurely walk will take you from one end of the tourist area to the other—from the train station to piazza Santa Croce—in about 25 minutes. The free map given out by the tourist office lacks a street index but may be all you need. The best full map of the city is the yellow-jacketed map by Studio F.M.B. Bologna, available at most newsstands for 7,000 lire ($4.40).

BY RENTAL CAR   Auto-rental agencies in Florence are centered around the Europa Garage on borgo Ognissanti. **Avis** is at no. 128r (☎ **055/68-42-02**) and **Budget** is nearby at no. 134r (☎ **055/28-71-61**); **Eurodollar** has offices across the street at no. 133r (☎ **055/21-86-65** or 28-45-43). Rates start at a steep 112,500 lire ($70) per day with unlimited mileage, plus 13,500 lire ($8.50) per day for insurance. Avis and Budget are open Monday through Saturday from 8am to 8pm and Sunday from 8am to 1pm and 5 to 8pm. Eurodollar is open Monday through Saturday from 8am to 1pm and 2 to 8pm and Sunday from 8am to 1pm only.

Rates are sometimes lower if you make reservations from home at least 48 hours in advance. Plan ahead or consider phoning a friend or relative back home to have the reservations made for you.

Florence's Historic Center, where most hotels are located, is strictly off-limits to all vehicular traffic, except that of local residents. **Parking** near the center will cost about 25,000 lire ($15.60) per day. The garage most convenient to the Historic Center is the Europa, at borgo Ognissanti 96, next to Avis; it's open daily from 6am to 2am. The International Garage, at via Palazzuolo 29, just west of via Porcellana, is only a few blocks away.

FAST FACTS: Florence

Banks   Standard bank hours are Monday through Friday from 8:20am to 1:20pm and 2:45 to 3:45pm; only a few banks are open on Saturday. The Banca Nazionale delle Communicazioni, in the outer hall of the train station, is open Monday through Saturday from 8:20am to 7:20pm. The state railway will change money at any hour at Window 19. **American Express,** at via Guicciardini 49r (☎ **055/27-87-51**), exchanges its traveler's checks without a fee and is open Monday through Friday from 9am to 5:30pm and Saturday from 9am to 12:30pm.

Business Hours   In summer, most **businesses and shops** are open Monday through Friday from 9am to 1pm and 4 to 8pm; on Saturday, most shops are open in the morning only. From mid-September to mid-June, most shops are open Tuesday through Saturday from 9am to 1pm and 3:30 to 7:30pm; on Monday during winter, shops don't open until the afternoon. The exception to this winter rule are *alimentari* (small grocery stores), which are open on Monday morning in low season but closed Wednesday afternoon. In Florence, as throughout Italy, just about everything is closed on Sunday. **Restaurants** are required to close at least one day per week, though the particular day varies from one trattoria to another.

Consulates The Consulate of the **United States** is at lungarno Amerigo Vespucci 38 (☎ **055/239-82-76**), near its intersection with via Palestro; it's open Monday through Friday from 9am to noon and 2 to 4pm. The Consulate of the **United Kingdom** is at lungarno Corsini 2 (☎ **055/28-41-33**), near piazza Santa Trinità; it's open Monday through Friday from 9:30am to 12:30pm and 2:30 to 4:30pm.

Citizens of Australia, New Zealand, and Canada should consult their missions in Rome (see "Fast Facts: Rome" in Chapter 23).

Currency The Italian unit of currency is the **lira,** almost always used in the plural form, **lire.** The lowest unit of currency these days is the silver 50-lira coin. There's also a silver 100-lira piece, a gold 200-lira coin, and a combination silver-and-gold 500-lira coin. Notes come in the following denominations: 1,000, 2,000, 5,000, 10,000, 50,000, 100,000, and 200,000 lire. Occasionally you'll come across a grooved coin with a pictogram of a telephone on it. A remnant of Italy's old pay-phone system, which is gradually being phased out, the telephone *gettone* is worth 200 lire (13¢), the price of a phone call.

Dentists/Doctors For a list of English-speaking dentists or doctors, ask at the American or British Consulate or at the American Express office. Visitors in need of emergency medical care can call Volunteer Hospital Interpreters (☎ **055/ 40-31-26** or 234-45-67) day or night. The interpreters are always on call and offer their services free of charge.

Emergencies In Florence, as throughout Italy, dial **113** for the police. Some Italians recommend the military-trained *Carabinieri* (call **112**), whom they consider a better police force. To report a fire, dial 115. For an ambulance, dial 21-22-22.

For a pharmacy, the Farmacia Communale, at the head of Track 16 in the train station, is open 24 hours daily.

Holidays See "Fast Facts: Rome" in Chapter 23 for details. Florence's patron saint, John the Baptist, is honored on June 24.

Information For the location of the tourist information offices, see "Visitor Information" under "Florence Specifics," earlier in this chapter.

Laundry/Dry Cleaning The Lavanderia Superlava Splendis, via del Sole 29r (☎ **055/21-88-36**), off piazza Santa Maria Novella, is the self-service laundry most convenient to hotels in the train station area. It's open Monday through Friday from 8am to 7:30pm, offers one-day service, and charges about 15,000 lire ($9.40) to wash and dry up to 4 kilos (about 9 lbs.). East of the Duomo is the American-owned Wash & Dry, via dei Servi 105r (☎ **055/436-16-50**). They charge about 10,000 lire for a wash and dry and are open daily from 8am to 9pm. You'll find yet another laundry, the Lavanderia Elen-Sec, at via dei Neri 46r (☎ **055/28-37-47**), on the other side of piazza della Signoria, near Santa Croce. It charges 4,000 lire ($2.50) per kilo (2¹/₄ lbs.), with a 3-kilo minimum. It's open Monday through Friday from 8:30am to 1pm and 4 to 7:30pm (in winter, from 3:30 to 7:30pm); the laundry is closed for three weeks in August.

Lost & Found Oggetti Smarriti is at via Circondaria 19 (☎ **055/36-79-43**), in the area behind the train station.

Mail   Florence's **main post office** is on via Pellicceria, off the southwest corner of piazza della Repubblica. Purchase stamps (*francobolli*) at Windows 21–22. Letters sent "Fermo Posta" (Italian for General Delivery or *Poste Restante*) can be picked up at Windows 23–24. The post office is open Monday through Friday from 8:15am to 7pm and Saturday from 8:15am to noon.

All packages heavier than 1 kilo (2¼ lb.) must be properly wrapped and brought around to the **parcel office** at the back of the building (enter at via dei Sassetti 4, also known as piazza Davanzati). If you're uncertain about Italy's complex parcel-post standards, take your shipment to **Filippo's Pacco Parcel,** via dei Canacci 4r (☎ **055/21-19-12**), off via della Scala near the station, where they'll wrap your shipment for 5,000 to 10,000 lire ($3.15 to $6.25). May to September, Filippo is open Monday through Saturday from 9am to 6:30pm; October to April, Monday through Friday from 9:30am to 1pm and 3 to 6pm.

Remember that you can buy stamps at any *tabacchi* with no additional service charge; ask at your hotel about the current postal rates.

Police   Throughout Italy, dial **113** for the police. Some Italians recommend the *Carabinieri* (call **112**), whom they consider a better-trained police force.

Shoe Repair   For resoling or sewing, try Riparazioni Scarpe Il Ciabattino, at via del Moro 88r, near piazza Santa Maria Novella, not far from the train station. It's open Monday through Friday from 8:30am to noon and 2:30 to 7:30pm and Saturday from 8:30am to noon.

Student Networks & Resources   Florence's university is between the Mercato Centrale and piazza San Marco, the latter being the center of student activity in Florence. The *mensa,* or cafeteria, where students congregate at mealtimes is at via San Gallo 25a. There's a sizable community of American students in Florence for study-abroad programs.

The **Centro Turistico Studentesco (C.T.S.)**, at via dei Ginori 11r (☎ **055/ 28-95-70**), across from the Medici-Riccardi Palace near the San Lorenzo Market, is the best budget travel agent in Florence, selling reduced-price train, air, and ferry tickets. This agency specializes in youth and student fares but is helpful to thrifty travelers of all ages. Note that the staff doesn't make train reservations and doesn't accept credit or charge cards. It's open Monday through Friday from 9:30am to 1pm and 4 to 7pm and Saturday from 9:30am to noon.

Tax   See "Fast Facts: Rome" in Chapter 23 for more information.

Telephone   The telephone area code for Florence is 055.

There are two types of public **pay phones** in regular service. The first accepts coins or special slugs, called *gettone,* which you will sometimes receive in change. The second operates with a phonecard, available at *tabacchi* and bars in 5,000-lira ($3.15) and 10,000-lira ($6.25) denominations. Break off the perforated corner of the card before using it. **Local phone calls** cost 200 lire (13¢). To make a call, lift the receiver, insert a coin or card, and dial.

You can place **long-distance and international phone calls** at the ASST office inside the main post office (see "Mail," above). Several countries also have direct operator service, allowing callers to use telephone calling cards or call collect (reverse charges) from almost any phone. Consult "Fast Facts: Rome" in Chapter 23 for complete information.

Tipping   See "Fast Facts: Rome" in Chapter 23 for more information.

4 Accommodations

Many budget hotels are concentrated in the area immediately to the left as you exit the train station. You'll find most of the hotels in this convenient, if charmless, area on the noisy via Nazionale and the first two side streets off via Nazionale, via Fiume and via Faenza. The area between the Duomo and piazza della Signoria, particularly along and near via Calzaiuoli, is also a good place to look and is a quiet, pleasant place to spend your evenings.

During the peak summer months it's important to arrive early, as many hotels fill up for the next night even before all their guests from the previous evening have checked out. If you have trouble with or are intimidated by the language barrier, try the **room-finding office** in the train station, near Track 16 (see "Arriving" under "Florence Specifics," earlier in this chapter).

A continental breakfast in an Italian hotel is one of the great disappointments of Florence. The usual cost of a roll, butter, jam, and coffee is 6,500 lire ($4.05); you can get the same breakfast for about half that price at any café. Unfortunately, many of the hotels I've listed, especially in the medium- and higher-priced categories, do not make breakfast optional. In the descriptions, if prices are listed "including continental breakfast," you can assume that breakfast is more or less obligatory; if it's optional, almost without exception it's not worth the price.

DOUBLES FOR LESS THAN 78,700 LIRE ($49.20)
NEAR THE DUOMO

Albergo Costantini

Via Calzaiuoli 13 (2nd floor), 50122 Firenze. ☎ **055/21-51-28.** 14 rms, 2 with shower only, 7 with bath. TEL. 54,500 lire ($34.05) single without bath, 68,800 lire ($43) single with shower only or bath; 74,300 lire ($46.45) double without bath, 102,300 lire ($63.95) double with shower only or bath; 139,700 lire ($87.30) triple with bath; 126,500 lire ($79.05) quad without bath. 5% discount Nov–Feb. No credit cards.

The sturdy cot-style beds don't earn raves here, but the perfect location, steps from the Duomo and piazza della Signoria, can't be beat. Recent fixings include new tiling, and excellent English is spoken by Nadia, the friendly manager. This is a good place for older travelers, which the management prefers. Renaissance fans should note that three of the hotel's rooms have frescoed ceilings. The Constantini is open all night.

☉ Locanda Orchidea

Borgo degli Albizi 11 (1st floor), 50122 Firenze. ☎ **055/248-03-46.** 10 rms, 1 with shower only. 43,500 lire ($27.20) single without shower, 44,600 lire ($27.90) single with shower only; 61,200 lire ($38.25) double without shower, 66,300 lire ($41.45) double with shower only; 84,200 lire ($52.65) triple without shower, 90,200 lire ($56.40) triple with shower only. No credit cards. BUS 14 or 23 from the train station; get off at the first stop on via del Proconsolo.

Maria Rosa Cook, the friendly, professional proprietor of this cozy and exceptionally clean pensione, will happily tell you the history of this 12th-century palazzo where Dante's wife was born. Four of her rooms overlook a lovely garden, which all guests are welcome to use. These are the best beds in the house, with especially large windows that let in buckets of sunlight. Ms. Cook, who speaks English and French, is fond of Yankee guests (Red Sox fans are another matter). No curfew.

Getting the Best Deal on Accommodations

- Try one of the budget hotels in the area immediately to the left as you exit the train station.
- Take advantage of the room-finding office in the train station, near Track 16.
- Enjoy an inexpensive breakfast at one of Florence's cafés rather than at your hotel (unless it's included in the room rate).

Soggiorno Brunori

Via del Proconsolo 5 (2nd floor), 50122 Firenze. ☎ **055/28-96-48.** 9 rms, 1 with bath. 69,800 lire ($43.65) double without bath, 77,500 lire ($48.45) double with bath; 94,000 lire ($58.75) triple without bath, 107,800 lire ($67.40) triple with bath; 118,800 lire ($74.25) quad without bath, 144,100 lire ($90.05) quad with bath. Slight reduction for guests who don't take showers. Breakfast 8,000 lire ($5) extra. No credit cards. Closed Jan–Feb. Bus 13, 14, or 19.

The rooms here are a bit tired and show the wear and tear of countless backpackers, but the prices are among the lowest around. The two young English-speaking owners, Leonardo and Giovanni, are exceptionally friendly and full of helpful hints. They'll sell you stamps, help you decipher the train schedules they keep on hand, and offer you a free city map at check-in. Their unusually spacious rooms make this a fine selection for backpacking groups. You may want to ask for one of the three rooms away from the noisy street. There's a 12:30am curfew.

On via Faenza

There are more hotels on via Faenza than on any other block in Florence, as some buildings house as many as six pensiones. Three at no. 56 via Faenza fit into the lowest budget category, while the Albergo Anna and the Albergo Marini, in the same building, are fine choices for those with a bit more money to spend. In the area immediately to the left as you exit the train station, via Faenza is the second left off via Nazionale.

Albergo Azzi

Via Faenza 56 (1st floor), 50123 Firenze. ☎ **055/21-38-06.** Fax 055/21-38-06. 11 rms, none with bath. 78,100 lire ($48.80) double; 107,800 lire ($67.40) triple; 40,200 lire ($25.15) dorm bed. Rates include breakfast. No credit cards.

Reno Mazzapicchio and his partner, Monica Rocchini, operate this cozy, if not always impeccable, dormitory-style pensione. While double and triple rooms are available, most guests pay a flat 40,200 lire ($25.15) per person for a bed in rooms shared with three to five other budget travelers. That's the cheapest bed outside a youth hostel.

Albergo Marcella

Via Faenza 58 (3rd floor), 50123 Firenze. ☎ **055/21-32-32.** 7 rms, 1 with bath. 42,400 lire ($26.50) single without bath; 61,100 lire ($38.20) double without bath, 67,700 lire ($42.30) double with bath; 82,000 lire ($51.25) triple without bath, 89,100 lire ($55.70) triple with bath. No credit cards.

Signor Noto Calogero and his family are always warm and welcoming, offering adequate rooms at low prices. This is a classic ultra-budget-traveler's pensione, in better condition than most others in its class. The management speaks perfect English.

Albergo Merlini

Via Faenza 56 (3rd floor), 50123 Firenze. ☎ **055/21-28-48** or 28-39-39. 12 rms, 2 with bath. 48,400 lire ($30.25) single without bath; 74,300 lire ($46.45) double without bath, 90,200 lire ($56.40) double with bath; 94,100 lire ($58.80) triple without bath, 105,600 lire ($66) triple with bath. Breakfast 10,000 lire ($6.25) extra. No credit cards.

Signora Mary's furnishings would be the envy of any antique collector. Breakfast (optional) is served on a terrace decorated with frescoes by American art students. All in all, though this isn't the best value on the street, it's probably the best value in the building. Perhaps that's why I get so many letters from readers praising this place.

Albergo Mia Cara

Via Faenza 58 (2nd floor), 50123 Firenze. ☎ **055/21-60-53**. Fax 055/230-26-01. 50 rms, 20 with bath. 43,500 lire ($27.20) single without bath, 52,800 lire ($33) single with bath; 60,000 lire ($37.50) double without bath, 74,300 lire ($46.45) double with bath; 22,000 lire ($13.75) hostel dorm bed. Breakfast 7,000 lire ($4.40) extra. No credit cards.

In Florence you can easily pay quite a bit more and get a lot less than you do at Pietro Noto's unusually large modern hotel. He has laid new stonework tiles in every room, installed the latest in plumbing, and even stripped and stained all the window frames. This might not be special if his prices weren't among the lowest in town. A large hostel with dormitory rooms is behind the main hotel.

Albergo Monica

Via Faenza 66B (1st floor), 50123 Firenze. TEL. 54,500 lire ($34.05) single without bath, 57,800 lire ($36.15) single with shower only, 61,100 lire ($38.20) single with bath; 74,300 lire ($46.45) double without bath, 89,100 lire ($55.70) double with shower only, 96,300 lire ($60.20) double with bath; 116,600 lire ($72.90) triple with shower only, 138,600 lire ($86.65) triple with bath. 5% discount for bearers of this book Apr–Oct, 10% discount Nov–Mar. Air conditioning 5,000 lire ($3.15) extra; breakfast 10,000 lire ($6.25) extra. AE, MC, V.

Gracious owner Giovanna Rocchini and her charming English-speaking niece, Monica, run a truly exceptional hotel, complete with spacious rooms kept quite clean and competitively priced. The public areas include a café and a nice outdoor terrace. The quietest rooms are in the back, but this albergo is a good value no matter which room you occupy.

NEAR THE TRAIN STATION

✪ Pensione Burchianti

Via del Giglio 6 (between the train station and the Duomo), 50123 Firenze. ☎ **055/21-27-96**. Fax 055/47-53-87. 14 rms, 7 with bath. 34,100 lire ($21.30) single without bath, 45,700 lire ($28.55) single with bath; 68,800 lire ($43) double without bath, 85,800 lire ($53.65) double with bath; 102,900 lire ($64.30) triple without bath, 117,700 lire ($73.55) triple with bath. Breakfast 5,000 lire ($3.15) extra. No credit cards. From the front of the train station, walk along via Panzani and turn left onto via del Giglio; the hotel is on your right.

It's hard to say enough nice things about this extra-special budget find. Established in the 19th century by the Burchianti sisters, this inspiring pensione in the Renaissance palace of Marquis Salimbeni is jam-packed with atmosphere. It's claimed that Benito Mussolini stayed here, as well as various members of the royal family throughout the ages. Guests today are treated to stained-glass windows, frescoed walls and ceilings, Oriental rugs, and an attention to detail not usually found in low-priced lodgings. There are also a pretty salon and a breakfast room with wood-beamed ceilings.

Pensione Mary

Piazza Independenzia 5 (2nd floor), 50129 Firenze. ☎ **055/49-63-10.** Fax 055/31-76-44. 12 rms, 8 with bath. 50,000 lire ($31.25) single without bath, 65,000 lire ($40.65) single with bath; 80,000 lire ($50) double without bath, 95,000 lire ($59.40) double with bath; 110,000 lire ($68.75) triple without bath, 115,000 lire ($71.90) triple with bath. 10% discount for bearers of this book. Rates include breakfast. Breakfast 5,000 lire ($3.15) extra. No credit cards. From the train station's front exit, turn left onto via Nazionale; the hotel is five blocks ahead, on the east side of piazza Independenzia.

On the top floor of a three-story building (without elevator) on one of Florence's largest squares, this well-lit pensione is popular with students and young-minded others. The wood-paneled halls open into good-size clean rooms.

DOUBLES FOR LESS THAN 119,000 LIRE ($74.40)
NEAR THE TRAIN STATION

Albergo Centrale

Via dei Conti 3 (2nd floor), 50123 Firenze. ☎ **055/21-52-16** or 21-57-61. 18 rms, 9 with bath. TEL. 72,100 lire ($45.05) single without bath, 86,400 lire ($54) single with bath; 113,300 lire ($70.80) double without bath, 132,000 lire ($82.50) double with bath; 163,900 lire ($102.45) triple without bath, 192,500 lire ($120.30) triple with bath. 5% discount for bearers of this book. AE, MC, V. From piazza della Stazione, in front of the train station, walk along via dei Panzani, which quickly becomes via de' Cerretani; via dei Conti is the second left.

Normandy-born manager Mariethérèse Blot is wonderfully obliging and speaks excellent English. She's added a charming French touch to her exceptionally large rooms (such as attractive floral wallpaper) in this former patrician residence known as the Palazzo Malaspina; some rooms feature views of the nearby San Lorenzo Church. The Centrale is particularly well suited for traveling families, and curfew is 1:30am.

Hotel Ausonia

Via Nazionale 24 (3rd floor), 50123 Firenze. ☎ **055/49-65-47.** Fax 055/49-63-24. 20 rms, 12 with bath. 52,000 lire ($32.50) single without bath, 65,000 lire ($40.65) single with bath; 74,000 lire ($46.25) double without bath, 93,000 lire ($58.15) double with bath; 110,000 lire ($68.75) triple without bath, 135,000 lire ($84.40) triple with bath. 5% discount for bearers of this book; 5% discount Nov 15 to mid-Mar. Rates include continental breakfast. AE, MC, V. From piazza della Stazione, in front of the train station, turn left on via Nazionale; the pensione is four blocks ahead on your right.

Run by the friendly English-speaking Delli family, this newly renovated hotel occupies two floors on one of the city's busiest streets. Even though front rooms are equipped with double-paned glass, you might want to request accommodations in back, where it's extra-quiet.

ON VIA FIUME

There are fewer hotels on this street than on the adjacent via Faenza, but two budget-priced places stand out. Via Fiume is the first left off via Nazionale as you walk away from the train station.

Albergo Adua

Via Fiume 20 (2nd floor), 50123 Firenze. ☎ **055/28-75-06.** 7 rms, 4 with bath. 69,900 lire ($43.70) single without bath; 92,400 lire ($57.75) double without bath, 118,800 lire ($74.25) double with bath; 126,500 lire ($79.05) triple without bath, 156,200 lire ($97.65) triple with bath. No credit cards.

This place is plain and a little overpriced for a one-star lodging, but its high carved ceilings, enormous rooms, baths, and windows, plus its remarkably quiet location near the train station, make it noteworthy. The rooms are unusually gracious, and the view of the surrounding rooftops from their windows is pleasant.

Albergo Fiorita

Via Fiume 20 (3rd floor), 50123 Firenze. ☎ **055/28-36-93.** 11 rms, 1 with bath. 57,800 lire ($36.15) single without bath; 97,400 lire ($60.90) double without bath, 118,800 lire ($74.25) double with bath; 126,000 lire ($78.75) triple without bath; 180,400 lire ($112.75) quad without bath. Rates include continental breakfast. No credit cards.

The friendly Masselli family speaks excellent English and offers visitors large rooms with particularly pretty ceilings and favorable rates. The hotel locks up at midnight.

ON VIA FAENZA

In the area immediately to the left as you exit the train station, via Faenza is the second left off via Nazionale.

✪ Hotel Nuova Italia

Via Faenza 26 (around the corner from the San Lorenzo Market), 50123 Firenze. ☎ **055/26-84-30** or 28-75-08. Fax 055/21-09-41. 21 rms, all with bath. TEL. 78,000–95,000 lire ($48.75–$59.40) single; 110,000–140,000 lire ($68.75–$87.50) double. Rates include breakfast. AE, DC, MC, V. From the train station, walk up via Nazionale and turn right onto via Faenza; the hotel is immediately on your left.

It's priced near the top end of our budget, but this standout deserves special mention. The hotel is carefully watched over by English-speaking Luciano and Eileen Viti and their daughter, Daniela. Eileen met Luciano more than 30 years ago, when she stayed at his hotel on the recommendation of *Europe on $5 a Day.* Today the couple is particularly welcoming to our readers, who can expect to be treated like visiting royalty. This is also an ideal selection for families. All rooms have private baths, direct-dial phones, screened soundproof windows, pleasant furnishings, and original art.

Pensione Armonia

Via Faenza 56 (1st floor), 50123 Firenze. ☎ **055/21-11-46.** 7 rms, none with bath. 98,500 lire ($61.55) double; 126,000 lire ($78.75) triple; 164,000 lire ($102.50) quad. Rates include continental breakfast. No credit cards.

Owned by a young English-speaking brother and sister, this small, spotless pensione is more expensive than some others in the building, but it's a step above. Their whitewashed rooms and sparkling tile floors will brighten your day no matter how high the temperature or how thick the crowds.

NEAR THE DUOMO

Hotel Firenze

Via del Corso/piazza Donati 4, 50122 Firenze. ☎ **055/26-83-01** or 21-42-03. Fax 055/21-23-70. 70 rms, 20 with bath. TEL. 49,500 lire ($30.95) single without bath, 62,700 lire ($39.20) single with bath; 79,200 lire ($49.50) double without bath, 92,400 lire ($57.75) double with bath; 114,400 lire ($71.50) triple without bath, 126,500 lire ($79.05) triple with bath. Rates include continental breakfast. No credit cards. TV 10,000 lire ($6.25) extra.

Perfectly located two blocks south of the Duomo, this sparkling, simple lodge has blatantly inexpensive furnishings contrasting with the building's stylish centuries-old facade. Rooms with private bath come with hairdryers and are, in general, much nicer than the bathless rooms.

✪ Pensione Maria Luisa de' Medici

Via del Corso 1, 50122 Firenze. ☎ **055/28-00-48.** 10 rms, 2 with bath. TEL. 93,500 lire ($58.45) double without bath, 106,700 lire ($66.70) double with bath; 132,000 lire ($82.50) triple without bath, 149,000 lire ($93.15) triple with bath; 168,300 lire ($105.20) quad without bath, 74,800 lire ($46.75) quad with bath. Rates include breakfast. No credit cards. Walk a block from piazza della Repubblica to via del Corso.

This charming pensione, named after the very last Medici princess, is perhaps the most imaginative, eclectic, and unusual place to sleep in all of Italy. Each of its rooms is named after a different member of the Medici clan and includes a portrait of that prince or princess. The owner, Dr. Angelo Sordi—physician, amateur historian, and design buff—has furnished each room with 1960s avant-garde Italian furniture that contrasts with the multitude of oversize original Renaissance-style oil paintings and floor-to-ceiling velvet drapes (handmade by his Welsh partner, Evelyn Morris). With 10 enormous rooms, including three triples, two quads, and two rooms that can sleep five, the Maria Luisa is an ideal choice for families on a budget. By the way, Angelo and Evelyn will send you off each morning with a full breakfast that includes cereal and juice.

IN THE OLTRARNO

✪ Pensione La Scalette

Via Guicciardini 13 (2nd floor), 50125 Firenze. ☎ **055/28-30-28** or 21-42-55. Fax 055/28-95-62. 12 rms, 11 with bath. TEL. 72,600 lire ($45.40) single without bath, 96,800 lire ($60.50) single with bath; 115,500 lire ($72.20) double without bath, 159,500 lire ($99.70) double with bath; 214,500 lire ($134.05) triple with bath; 291,500 lire ($182.20) quad with bath. Rates include continental breakfast. MC, V. Bus 31, 32, or 37 from the train station.

Next door to the American Express office and a short block from the Pitti Palace, owner Barbara Barbieri and her family keep their high-ceilinged rooms spotless, as they do each of the half a dozen little sitting rooms you'll find scattered throughout this large top-floor pensione. Every room is spacious and unique. Those in front can be a bit noisy, but the ones in back overlook the Medici's gardens. Breakfasts and dinners (moderately priced) are cooked by the owners themselves and served in a comfortable high-ceilinged dining room. The rooftop terrace offers a stunning view of the Pitti Palace and the Boboli Gardens fanning up the hillside.

✪ Pensione Sorelle Bandini

Piazza S. Spirito 9, 50125 Firenze. ☎ **055/21-53-08.** Fax 055/28-27-61. 12 rms, 3 with bath. 74,000 lire ($46.25) single without bath; 110,000 lire ($68.75) double without bath, 140,000 lire ($87.50) double with bath; 153,000 lire ($95.65) triple without bath, 194,000 lire ($121.25) triple with bath; 195,000 lire ($121.90) quad without bath, 247,000 lire ($154.40) quad with bath. Rates include continental breakfast. No credit cards. Bus 3 or 15 from the train station.

Unassuming from the outside, this cavernous castle, with sweeping views over the red rooftops, is one of Florence's most unusual finds. Everything is oversize in this old palazzo, from the rooms and the furnishings to the gigantic balcony wrapping half the building. It's across the ponte Vecchio, two blocks northwest of the Pitti Palace; enter through the giant iron gates and take the elevator to the second floor.

ELSEWHERE

✪ Hotel Ariston

Via Fiesolana 40, 50122 Firenze. ☎ **055/247-69-80** or 247-66-93. Fax 055/247-69-80. 29 rms, all with bath. TEL. 71,500 lire ($44.70) single; 88,000 lire ($55) double with bath outside room, 104,500 lire ($65.30) double with bath inside room. Rates include breakfast. AE.

Slightly off the beaten tourist track, about a 10-minute walk east of the Duomo, the Ariston offers good value for the money. With the exception of a particularly nice lobby, the hotel is rather simple, though it features several unusual touches, including Oriental carpets on the linoleum floors. Most double rooms come with two single beds pushed together, and in typical European style the curtainless showers splash water throughout the entire bathroom.

Hotel Boston

Via Guelfa 68, 50129 Firenze. ☎ **055/49-67-47.** Fax 055/47-09-34. 20 rms, 13 with bath. TEL. Rates include breakfast. 60,000–70,000 lire ($37.50–$43.75) single without bath, 80,000–95,000 lire ($50–$59.40) single with bath; 100,000–150,000 lire ($62.50–$93.75) double with bath. No credit cards. From the train station, walk three blocks up via Nazionale and turn left onto via Guelfa; the hotel will be on your right.

One of the most beautiful budget hotels in the city, the Boston is peaceful, filled with original art. The first two floors were built in the 17th century and have wooden ceilings and plenty of charm. The rooms on the third floor, accessible by elevator, are equally recommended, fitted with large beds, small baths, and curtains that can block the morning light. In summer, breakfast is served in a bucolic back garden. The above rates are very special for Frommer readers and represent a substantial discount.

SUPER-BUDGET CHOICES

In addition to the inexpensive multibedded accommodations at the Albergo Mia Cara and Albergo Azzi (both above), look to the following hostels for cheap dorm-style rooms.

Ostello Santa Monaca

Via Santa Monaca 6, 50125 Firenze. ☎ **055/26-83-38** or 239-67-04. 111 beds. 20,400 lire ($12.75) per person, plus a one-time sheet-rental fee of 2,000 lire ($1.25)—unless you bring your own. No credit cards. From the train station, walk around to piazza Santa Maria Novella; go along via dei Fossi, which begins at the far left corner of the piazza, until that street ends on the banks of the Arno; cross the ponte alla Carraia (bridge) to the Oltrarno and walk along via de' Serragli; via Santa Monaca will be the third right (about a 10-minute walk).

Much more convenient if not as clean as the remote IYHF youth hostel (below), this privately run hostel is a lively gathering spot for travelers from all over the world, as well as a great place to trade budget tips and meet travel companions. Beware, however, that some readers have reported thefts here. The rooms are closed from 9:30am to 1pm, and the building itself is locked up from 1 to 4pm. If you arrive before 1pm, leave your passport or some other form of ID in the red safety-deposit box next to the reception desk and add your name to the sign-up list for that day; come back to register between 4 and 5:30pm. There's an airtight midnight curfew, and the doors aren't reopened until 6:30am. Breakfast is not available.

Ostello Villa Camerata

Viale Augusto Righi 2–4, 50111 Firenze. ☎ **055/60-14-51.** 400 beds. 23,100 lire ($14.45) per person. No credit cards. Rates include continental breakfast and sheets. Dinner 12,000 lire ($7.50) extra. Bus 17B to the end *(capolinea)* of the route; then a half-mile walk.

Florence's stunningly beautiful IYHF youth hostel is housed in a mammoth 15th-century villa surrounded by a large park and garden. The morning views from this hilltop location are fantastic. The hostel is almost a community unto itself, with movies in English every evening, a bar, and an ultra-budget restaurant serving two meals per day. The hostel accepts IYHF members only, but you can buy a card (valid for a year) on the premises for 33,000 lire ($20.65) or become a member for the night for 6,000 lire ($3.75). In summer, arrive by 2pm, when the reception opens, in order to secure a bed; this popular, peaceful, and dirt-cheap hostel fills quickly. Curfew is 11:30pm year round, and dinner is served from 6:30 to 8pm. Among the most comfortable, least institutional hostels in Europe, this is the only one with baths in some rooms (four to eight beds per room).

WORTH THE EXTRA MONEY

If you blow your budget in one Italian city, make it Florence, and do it at one of these two hotels:

Hotel Mario's

Via Faenza 89 (1st floor), 50123 Firenze. ☎ **055/21-68-01.** Fax 055/21-20-39. 16 rms, all with bath. TEL. 132,000 lire ($82.50) single; 181,500 lire ($113.45) double; 242,000 lire ($151.25) triple; 275,000 lire ($171.90) quad. Rates include full breakfast. AE, DC, MC, V. From the train station, walk up via Nazionale and turn right onto via Faenza.

Traditional Florentine furnishings, right down to the wrought-iron headboards, are everywhere at Mario's. Most rooms look out onto a peaceful garden, a welcome respite from the busy street. The beamed ceilings date from the 17th century, but the building became a hotel only (!) in 1872. Owner Mario Noce and his family run a first-rate ship that's cheap by three-star standards, complete with in-room hairdryers and air conditioning. I've received more letters of praise for Mario's than for any other hotel in Florence. Perhaps it's the fresh fruit they always keep stocked in the rooms.

✪ Hotel Morandi alla Crocetta

Via Laura 50 (1st floor), 50121 Firenze. ☎ **055/234-47-47.** Fax 055/248-09-54. 10 rms, all with bath. TV TEL. 100,000 lire ($62.50) single; 179,000 lire ($111.90) double; 265,000 lire ($165.65) triple. Breakfast 18,000 lire ($11.25) extra. AE, DC, MC, V. Bus 1, 7, 10, 17, or 25 from the train station to piazza San Marco; then walk across to piazza delle SS. Annunziata and go left onto via Gino Capponi; via Laura will be the first right, and you'll find the hotel 200 yards along on your left.

British expatriate Kathleen Doyle has been living here and serving guests since 1929. She boasts that "no one who has come here yet has been disappointed," and it's certainly easy to see why. Each room has its own meticulously planned character—a stained-glass door here, a priceless antique table there. Indeed, the only common thread is the fresh flowers placed daily in every room, carefully chosen to match each room's colors. Mrs. Doyle's son, an officer in the Italian navy, knows exactly what's needed to furnish a particular room and literally has searched the world until he has found the perfect item.

5 Dining

For important information on dining in Italy, see the introduction to "Dining" in Chapter 23 on Rome.

Top among Florence's culinary specialties is *bistecca alla fiorentina*, an inch-thick charcoal-broiled steak. The hills surrounding the city produce the best beef in the country, which is sold by weight and is usually the most expensive item on any menu. Many Florentines sing the praises of *trippa alla fiorentina*, but calves' intestines, cut into strips and served with onions and tomatoes, are not for everyone. *Paglia e fieno*, a mixture of green (spinach-based) and white (egg-based) pasta served in a cream sauce of ham, peas, and (sometimes) mushrooms, is the region's best-known pasta dish. Hearty Tuscan peasant dishes, including *ribollita*, a rich soup of twice-boiled cabbage and bread, and *fagioli all' uccelletto*, a tasty dish of pinto beans smothered in a sauce of tomatoes, rosemary (or sage), and olive oil, also deserve a try. *Crostini di fegatini*, chicken-liver pâté served on small pieces of toast, is a favorite Florentine antipasto. Tuscany's wines—the most famous of which bear the black rooster seal of a true chianti—are as distinctive as the region's meals. Finally, whatever you do, don't miss Florence's gelato—unforgettable ice cream.

There's no one dish or neighborhood that equals good budget dining in Florence. Your best bet is to choose an eatery that will allow you to order just one course—though whether a modest pasta dish will satisfy your appetite may be another matter. While not always the cheapest way to dine, the ubiquitous *menu turistico* (a three-course fixed-price meal) is a good way to contain costs.

Keep in mind that in the listings below, prices are for pasta and meat courses only. Don't forget to add in charges for bread and cover, service, and vegetable side dishes when calculating what you'd expect to pay.

MEALS FOR LESS THAN 15,800 LIRE ($9.90)
NEAR THE TRAIN STATION

Italy and Italy
Piazza della Stazione 25–37r. 3,000–7,500 lire ($1.90–$4.70). No cover charge. No credit cards. Wed–Mon 10am–1am. Exit the train station by Track 16 and cross the street. ITALIAN.

"Italian fast food" may sound sacrilegious, but that's what this cafeteria specializes in. Right down to the modular green plastic furniture and the matching staff uniforms, this place will seem like any roadside hamburger stand in North America. Actually, the food isn't half bad. In addition to burgers, you can choose pizzotto (their own invention, similar to a calzone, stuffed with tomato sauce, cheese, and some meat), spaghetti with one of three toppings, and even french fries. A hamburger alone will set you back 3,000 lire ($1.90).

✪ Nerbone
In the central market, via Santa Casciano, stand no. 292. Sandwiches 4,000 lire ($2.50); pasta and soup 5,000 lire ($3.15); meat dishes 7,000 lire ($4.40). No credit cards. Sun–Fri 7am–2pm, Sat and hols 4–8pm. ITALIAN.

One of the best basic eateries in all Italy, this simple red-and-green food stand, inside Florence's turn-of-the-century meat-and-produce marketplace, is best described as a hole-in-the-wall without any wall. Packed with local working-class types who stand around the marble bar eating, drinking, and talking, Nerbone offers only four small tables next to an adjacent meat counter.

The food here is more flavorful, varied, and plentiful than at most restaurants. Daily specials include an assortment of pastas (penne, rotelli, and the like), fantastic meat and minestrone soups, huge plates of cooked potatoes and other vegetables, and the freshest meat sandwiches imaginable. Service is swift, and wine and beer are sold by the glass.

Pizzeria lo Spuntino
Via Canto de' Nelli 14r. ☎ **055/21-09-20.** Pizza 4,000 lire ($2.50) for a large slice. No credit cards. Tues–Sun 10am–10pm. PIZZA.

This pizzeria would overlook piazza San Lorenzo if it weren't for the San Lorenzo market stalls in front, which effectively block all views. There's always about six

---

Getting the Best Deal on Dining

- Take advantage of an eatery where you can order just one course.
- The ubiquitous *menu turistico* is a great bargain.

---

pizzas to choose from, each sold by weight; tell the barman "*quatro mille*" and you'll get a good-size slice for 4,000 lire ($2.50). There are stools in the front room and tables in back, where you can sit for no extra charge.

Pork's Paninoteca

In the central market, via Santa Casciano, stand no. 14. ☎ **055/21-61-84.** Sandwiches 3,000 lire ($1.90). No credit cards. Sun–Fri 7am–2pm, Sat and hols 4–8pm. ITALIAN SAND-WICHES.

Pork sandwiches are the specialty here, sliced directly from a whole suckling pig resting on the counter. It's not for the squeamish, but those who really enjoy exceptional culinary experiences will love this authentic stand, in the far right corner of Florence's central meat market. A large variety of Tuscan wines are sold by the glass, and other meat sandwiches are also available.

ON VIA PALAZZUOLO, BETWEEN THE TRAIN STATION & THE ARNO

Trattoria

Via Palazzuolo 69r. *Menu turistico* 15,000 lire ($9.40). No credit cards. Sun–Fri 11am–3pm and 7pm–midnight. Closed Aug. Walk two short blocks from the train station, between via dell' Albero and via de' Canacci. ITALIAN.

This nameless one-room trattoria features one of Florence's cheapest *menus turisticos* (its only offering), which includes three courses and wine. Expect to wait outside this colorful hole-in-the-wall with a cadre of hungry locals unless you come early.

NEAR PIAZZA DEL DUOMO

L'Antico Noe

Arco S. Piero 6r. No phone. 3,500–4,500 lire ($2.20–$2.80). No credit cards. Mon–Sat 11am–11pm. SANDWICHES.

A tiny place, under an archway a few blocks from piazza Santa Croce, Noe serves the best sandwiches in Florence to an assorted crowd of workers and students. There are no tables here—you order at the counter and eat your meal standing there or outside, under the span. A large variety of wine is available by the glass, as are an assortment of crostini, small open-face sandwiches topped with a variety of meats, fish, and vegetables.

Procacci

Via Tornabuoni 64r. ☎ **055/21-16-56.** Crostini 3,000–5,000 lire ($1.90–$3.15). No credit cards. Thurs–Tues 11am–8pm. ITALIAN.

Nothing is more Florentine than crostini, little open-face sandwiches topped with a variety of meats and vegetables. This legendary shop, opened in 1885 on one of the city's exclusive commercial streets, lets even budget tourists partake of the historical ritual of pausing around midday or toward evening for a snack and a glass of wine. Ham, salmon, anchovy, liver, tomato, and countless other sandwiches are served in a setting both elegant and charming. You can have a seat, but the traditional way is to remain standing.

✪ Yellow Bar

Via del Proconsolo 39r (at the intersection of via del Proconsolo and borgo degli Albizi, near the Bargello). ☎ **055/21-17-66.** Pizza 8,500–13,500 lire ($5.30–$8.45); pasta courses 9,500 lire ($5.95); meat courses 9,500–19,500 lire ($5.95–$12.20). No credit cards. Wed–Mon 7:30pm–2am. Closed Aug. ITALIAN.

This curious, popular saloon is a cross between an Italian café, a German beer hall, and an American jazz club. In fact, its card lists "piano bar, American bar, pizza, restaurant, and beer-house" as the entertainment credentials. But it's not a bar— it serves meals (not snacks)—and isn't even very yellow. It is an outstanding place to eat, with pasta fresca (fresh pasta) made continuously on the premises, plus reasonably tasty pizza. The piano music that begins at 10:30pm most nights is a sideline to the cuisine. While there's no pressure here to order a full meal, they frown on patrons who come just to drink and are likely to turn you away before about 11pm.

IN THE OLTRARNO

Cabiria Cafe

Piazza S. Spirito 4r. ☎ **055/21-57-32.** 4,500–5,500 lire ($2.80–$3.45). No credit cards. Wed–Mon 8:30am–2am. ITALIAN.

Piazza San Spirito, hiding behind a tangle of back streets, just blocks from the Pitti Palace, is the local's most loved piazza. Once a haven for drug abusers, the square has cleaned up its act, but still claims enough edginess to be an authentic hang-out for the "alternative" crowd. Cabiria Cafe is *the* place to see and be seen, either inside the small fashionable dining room or out at one of the tables overlooking dramatic San Spirito Church. The café is run by sisters Tina and Roberta Giacomo and their mother, Angela, who's a great cook from Naples. A wide variety of straightforward Neapolitan dishes, along with Greek salads and Florentine foods, has equal billing with the full bar that bustles with young trendies.

MEALS FOR LESS THAN 21,000 LIRE ($13.15)
NEAR THE DUOMO

Cibreo

Via Andrea del Verrocchio 4r. ☎ **055/234-11-00.** Pasta courses 8,000–9,000 lire ($5–$5.65); meat courses 15,000–22,000 lire ($9.40–$13.75); fixed-price dinner 30,000 lire ($18.75). AE, MC, V. Tues–Sat 7–11pm. TUSCAN.

Chef/owner Fabio Picchi's 50-seat restaurant has become world-famous for excellent food served in a plain setting with rigorously serious service. Tuscan dishes with English and French touches include spaghetti with turnip leaves, risotto with pumpkin and herbs, pork in chianti, veal with wild berries, and the like. The desserts are made by Fabio's wife, Benedetta.

✪ Ristorante-Pizzeria I Ghibellini

Piazza San Pier Maggiore 8–10r (at the end of borgo degli Albizi, stretching east from via del Proconsolo). ☎ **055/21-44-24.** Pizza 5,000–10,500 lire ($3.15–$6.55); pasta courses 4,000–8,500 lire ($2.50–$5.30); meat courses 8,500–13,500 lire ($5.30–$8.45). AE, DC, MC, V. Thurs–Tues noon–4pm and 7pm–midnight. ITALIAN.

I Ghibellini serves some of the most delicate pasta sauces in Florence in the medium-priced range. Its excellent food combines with its outdoor tables on a quiet piazza, four bright air-conditioned rooms, and long hours to make this one of the most recommendable restaurants in Florence.

Trattoria Le Mossacce

Via del Proconsolo 55r (one block from the Duomo). ☎ **055/29-43-61.** Pasta courses 6,500–7,500 lire ($4.05–$4.70); meat courses 9,500–10,500 lire ($5.95–$6.55); *menu turistico* (available only on request) 20,000 lire ($12.50). No credit cards. Mon–Sat noon–2:30pm and 7–9:30pm. Closed Aug. ITALIAN.

Ask Florentines about this place and they'll tell you "Everyone goes there." In fact, most Florentines have been coming here for so long and are so loyal that they still know and refer to it by its former name, Gastone. Don't be fooled by its narrow doorway or bright ordinary dining room. The food is anything but ordinary here.

BETWEEN PIAZZA DELLA SIGNORIA & PIAZZA SANTA CROCE

This is the one area in Florence where you'll find scads of moderately priced restaurants. The greatest concentration of trattorie is along via dei Neri, which connects piazza della Signoria with piazza Santa Croce and its main cross street, via dei Leoni.

Ristorante Montecatini

Via dei Leoni 6r (steps from the intersection of via dei Leoni and via dei Neri). ☎ **055/28-48-63.** Pasta courses 4,000–6,500 lire ($2.50–$4.05); meat courses 8,500–12,500 lire ($5.30–$7.80); *menu turistico* 21,000 lire ($13.15). AE, DC, V. Thurs–Tues noon–3pm and 7–11pm. Closed Feb. ITALIAN.

If you plan to go with a *menu turistico* in this neighborhood, this is the place to try. It offers an unusually extensive menu, including spaghetti al pesto (a spicy basil sauce from the Genoa region), lasagne, and chicken cacciatore. The pastas are excellent, but the second courses only mediocre. Wine bottles line the walls, the linen tablecloths are changed after each party, and the service is good.

✪ Trattoria da Benvenuto

Via dei Neri 47r (at the corner of via della Mosca), and also at via della Mosca 16r. ☎ **055/21-48-33.** Pasta courses 5,000–6,500 lire ($3.15–$4.05); meat courses 7,500–8,500 lire ($4.70–$5.30). No credit cards. Mon–Tues and Thurs–Sat 12:15–3pm and 7:15–10pm. ITALIAN.

Of the half-dozen restaurants in this area, Benvenuto's offers the least-expensive à la carte dining (though they do insist that you take a full meal) and is the most popular place among Italians. The atmosphere is simple and unassuming, but the food is anything but that.

Trattoria Roberto

Via Castellani 4r (an extension of via dei Leoni toward the river). ☎ **055/21-88-22.** Pasta courses 7,500–9,500 lire ($4.70–$5.95); meat courses 9,500–17,000 lire ($5.95–$10.65); fish courses 12,500–24,000 lire ($7.80–$15); *menu turistico* (including fish course, wine, and dessert) 19,000 lire ($11.90). MC, V. Thurs–Tues noon–3pm and 7–11pm. Possibly closed Aug. SEAFOOD.

Fittingly enough, this restaurant half a block from the river specializes in fish. Its card says so, this news is written in bold letters across the front window, and the display case, placed strategically just inside the door, speaks for itself. Florence is not exactly the seafood capital of Italy, but this is one of the best places in town to indulge your oceanic palate. The attentive service and pleasant atmosphere make this one of the best bets in the area.

NEAR THE TRAIN STATION

Trattoria Enzo e Piero

Via Faenza 105r. ☎ **055/21-49-01.** Pasta courses 6,500–8,000 lire ($4.05–$5); meat courses 7,500–12,500 lire ($4.70–$7.80); menu turistico 19,000 lire ($11.90). AE, DC, MC, V. Mon–Sat noon–3pm and 7–10pm. Walk up via Nazionale from the station; via Faenza is the second street on your left. ITALIAN.

The atmosphere here is pleasant and the service unusually friendly. The menu is in Italian and English, and most of the waiters speak English and will be happy to help you make your selections. The desserts (*dolce*) are especially good here (my favorite is tiramisù). This is a good bet if you'd like to dine in a genuine and reasonably priced trattoria without straying far from the train station.

✪ Trattoria Za-Za

Piazza Mercato Centrale 26r. ☎ **055/21-54-11.** Pasta courses 6,500–10,500 lire ($4.05–$6.55); meat courses 10,500–15,000 lire ($6.55–$9.40). AE, DC, MC, V. Mon–Sat noon–2:30pm and 7–10pm. Closed Aug. ITALIAN.

The walls of this popular locale are lined with chianti bottles and photographs of not-so-famous patrons. At the restaurant's long wooden tables sits an eclectic mix of tourists and local workers. Convenient to the open-air San Lorenzo market, this typical Florentine eatery serves such hearty meals as ribollita and crostini caldi misti at reasonable prices in a rustic setting. While you're waiting to be served, watch the show put on daily in the open kitchen by English-speaking chef Stefano Bondi.

FOR GELATO (ICE CREAM)

Festival del Gelato

Via del Corso 75r (just off via Calzaiuoli). ☎ **055/239-43-86.** 3,000 lire ($1.90) for a small dish. No credit cards. Summer, Tues–Sun 8am–1am; winter, Tues–Sun 11am–1am. ITALIAN GELATO.

Of all the gelaterias in Florence, Festival del Gelato won a recent taste test for serving the best-tasting ice cream in the city—no easy feat. Offering about 50 flavors along with pounding pop music and blinding neon, the gelateria is as much a scene as a substance.

Perche No

Via dei Tavolini 19r (off via Calzaiuoli). ☎ **055/239-89-69.** 3,000 lire ($1.90) for a small dish. No credit cards. Wed–Mon 8am–12:30am. ITALIAN GELATO.

This fine gelateria is called "Why Not?"—a good question indeed.

✪ Vivoli

Via Isole dei Stinche 74 (one block up via dell' Anguillara from piazza Santa Croce). ☎ **055/239-23-34.** 3,000 lire ($1.90) for a small dish. No credit cards. Tues–Sun 9am–1am. Closed Aug and Jan to early Feb. ITALIAN GELATO.

Vivoli is world-famous, but recent taste tests have made me suspect it's now relying a bit too heavily on its reputation. Exactly how renowned is this brightly lit small shop? Taped to the wall is a postcard bearing only "Vivoli, Europa" for the address, yet it was successfully and promptly delivered to this world capital of ice cream.

PICNICKING

Doing your own shopping for food in Italy is an interesting cultural experience since there are few supermarkets. Cold cuts are sold at a *salumeria*. To pick up cheese or yogurt, you'll have to find a *latteria*. Vegetables can usually be found at an *alimentari,* the closest thing Italy has to a grocery store. For bread to put all that between, visit a *panetteria.* Wander into a *pasticceria* to find dessert. And for a bottle of wine to wash it down, search out a *vinatteria.* Via dei Neri, which begins at via de' Benci near piazza Santa Croce and stretches over to the Palazzo Vecchio, is lined with small specialty food shops and is one of the best areas for purchasing food for an outing.

If you prefer to find all you need under one roof, visit the colorful **Mercato Centrale,** Florence's block-long central marketplace. Open Monday through Friday from 7am to 2pm and Saturday from 7am to 2pm and 4 to 8pm, it's located at via dell' Ariento 12, in the midst of the open-air San Lorenzo market, on the block between via San Antonino and via Panicale.

The **Boboli Gardens,** on the opposite side of the green River Arno (see "Parks and Gardens" under "Attractions," later in this chapter), is without a doubt the best picnic spot in town.

WORTH THE EXTRA MONEY

✪ Antica Trattoria Oreste

Piazza S. Spirito 16r. ☎ **055/238-23-83.** Reservations recommended. Pasta courses 8,500–10,000 lire ($5.30–$6.25); meat courses 15,000–22,000 lire ($9.40–$13.75). AE, MC, V. Wed–Mon 7–11pm. ITALIAN.

Tucked away in a pretty corner of a piazza near the Pitti Palace, Trattoria Oreste is truly a local's kind of restaurant, serving top-quality regional dishes in an intimate semiformal atmosphere. Pastas, soups, meats, and other hearty Tuscan dishes change daily but are consistently well prepared and graciously served. The staff speaks virtually no English, but they welcome foreigners with smiles not usually seen in more tourist-weary spots. Oreste may not be particularly cheap, but it's one of my favorite Florentine finds, recommendable for a special night out.

Fiascehetteria da il Latini

Via Palchetti 6r. ☎ **055/21-09-16.** Pasta courses 6,500–8,500 lire ($4.05–$5.30); meat courses 12,500–14,500 lire ($7.80–$9.05); seven-course fixed-price meal 44,000 lire ($27.50). No credit cards. Tues 7:30–10:30pm, Wed–Sun noon–3pm and 7:30–10:30pm. Closed July 20–Aug 10. With your back to the ponte Vecchio, turn left along the river and right into piazza C. Goldoni (opposite Carraia Bridge); then walk one block along via Vigna Nuova and take the first left onto via Palchetti. ITALIAN.

Narcisio Latini and his sons, Giovanni and Torello, operate what must certainly be the busiest, most popular restaurant in town. Even in the dead of winter you'll see a long line of tourists waiting for a cramped seat at one of the long wooden tables. Once you get a table—the wait can be an hour or more—settle in for a raucous, delicious adventure you won't soon forget. Papa Latini watches over the operation with an eagle eye, shouting commands, talking to four people at once, placing phone orders to the Latini family farm 20 miles away (where the wine and most of the food are produced), and never losing control over the wonderful chaos.

There's no written menu—one of the brothers will explain the selection, in rough English. It's all hearty, meaty fare, and you'll spend about 44,000 lire ($27.50) for an unforgettable seven-course feast: an antipasto of prosciutto crudo (ham) and sausage, followed by a pasta course, a main course, a vegetable, ice cream, an *aperitivo* (after-dinner wine), biscotti (almond cookies), coffee, and all the wine and mineral water you can drink. Expect to leave with a full but satisfied stomach.

Il Latini is hard to find but worth every effort.

✪ Ristorante Acqua al Due

Via della Vecchia 40r (at via dell' Acqua, behind the Bargello). ☎ **055/28-41-70.** Reservations required. Pasta courses 8,500–12,500 lire ($5.30–$7.80); meat courses 10,500– 19,000 lire ($6.55–$11.90); *assaggios* 11,500 lire ($7.20) for pasta, 8,500 lire ($5.30) for dessert. No credit cards. Tues–Sun 12:30–3pm and 7:30pm–1am. Closed Aug. ITALIAN.

Italy, of course, is most famous for its pasta, and this is the place to discover what you like best. The specialty of the house is the *assaggio*, a sampling of five types of pasta in various sauces. They also offer a three-part salad assaggio, as well as an assaggio di dolce (desserts) of four super-sweet offerings. There's no English menu, but most of the waiters speak English. No matter how cold it is outside, no matter how hard it's raining, if you don't have a reservation you'll be turned away at this place, one of Florence's best-known eateries. The busy yet comfort-able restaurant is especially popular with the under-30 crowd, but guests of any age can expect to leave here satisfied.

Ristorante Gauguin

Via degli Alfani 24r (about three blocks behind the Duomo). ☎ **055/234-06-16.** Main courses 7,500–14,500 lire ($4.70–$9.05). AE, MC, V. Mon 7–11pm, Tues–Sat 1–3:30pm and 7–11pm. CONTINENTAL/VEGETARIAN.

Jean-Michel Carasso, the affable French owner of this unusual vegetarian restau-rant, is on hand nightly to greet patrons and serve continental meals with distinctly Mediterranean influences. Contemporary original art fills two small rooms and operatic music often fills the air. Menus change frequently but may include vegetable strudel with puréed shallots, smoked trout in herb-and-cheese dressing, stuffed eggplant, or moussaka. Although the restaurant serves no red meat, fish is usually available.

✪ Trattoria del Pennello

Via Dante Alighieri 4r. ☎ **055/239-48-48.** Pasta courses 5,500–8,000 lire ($3.45–$5); meat courses 15,000–17,000 lire ($9.40–$10.65). No credit cards. Tues–Sat 11am–3pm and 7pm– midnight, Sun 11am–3pm. Closed Aug. From via dei Calzaiuoli, turn onto via dei Tavolini, which becomes via Dante Alighieri (if you get lost, just ask anyone for directions to the Casa di Dante, across the street). ITALIAN.

Though his house was just across the street, Dante never dined here. That was his loss. An enormous amount of energy and effort goes into the food at del Pennello, an attractive restaurant with plain white walls, a bright interior, and unassuming plain white curtains. The specialty here is an extraordinary array of two dozen delicious antipasti (appetizers), displayed in the dining room each evening. Prices vary with quantity and dish, but expect to spend 10,000 lire ($6.25) for a healthy sampling. The assortment changes daily, as does the entire menu. Try to get an English-speaking waiter.

6 Attractions

SIGHTSEEING SUGGESTIONS

Seeing all of Florence in a short time requires organization. It's not just that there's so much to see in this great city; it's also that the museums keep short, capricious hours. With the notable exception of the Uffizi Galleries, most museums in Florence close at 2pm, with the last entrance at least 30 minutes (sometimes 45 to 60 minutes) before closing. In addition, each museum is closed a particular day of the week, many on Monday. Churches and the markets are the best places to spend your afternoon touring time, since they usually remain open until 7pm.

If You Have 1 Day

This is a dilemma. There's so much to see in Florence, each attraction as histori-cally significant and aesthetically captivating as the next, that the best approach to one day may be to flip a coin or write the names of sights on slips of paper and pull them out of a hat.

You might begin your day at the Uffizi Galleries, the most important art mu-seum in Europe after the Louvre in Paris. You'd have to race at breakneck speed through the museum's 45 rooms to see everything, so I suggest that you choose a particular period or painter to study and reflect on. Then head over to the Accademia, where there are eight pieces by Michelangelo, one of which is his David, considered one of the greatest Renaissance sculptures. The last visitors are admitted at 1:30pm, and lines can be up to an hour long in summer, so plan to leave the Uffizi by shortly after noon or visit here first.

Have lunch on piazza della Signoria, in the shadow of the Palazzo Vecchio and the Uffizi, for a memorable break from sightseeing. Find time after lunch to visit the Duomo and Baptistery, which remain open until 5pm.

In the late afternoon, head over to the sprawling open-air Mercato San Lorenzo, open until 7pm, to take advantage of the bargains—on leather goods and wool sweaters in particular.

Otherwise, create your own walking tour. Cross the ponte Vecchio into the Oltrarno, Florence's quieter, more workaday quarter, or stroll among the boutiques and palazzi in the area between the Duomo and the river. Finally, try not to miss an opportunity to take in a hearty Tuscan meal at any one of the restaurants I've recommended (see "Dining," earlier in this chapter).

If You Have 2 Days

You may want to spend part of your second day at the Uffizi Galleries again. There's so much to see and to savor here that many people find it most enjoyable and instructive to return to the Uffizi several times, focusing on a different period or style at each visit.

While you're back in the area of the Uffizi, stop at the Palazzo Vecchio. Or visit the many museums of the Pitti Palace, which could easily keep you occupied until 2pm, when they close. Try to make time before 2pm to visit the Bargello, Florence's main sculpture museum, and the Casa Buonarroti, home to an excel-lent collection of early and lesser works by Michelangelo. After a picnic lunch in the Boboli Gardens behind the Pitti Palace, take in the expansive collection of the Duomo Museum, open into the evening.

Also consider that the one-day schedule outlined in the previous section is quite busy. You may want to stretch it over two days.

If You Have 3 Days

The treasures of Florence's half-dozen important churches can easily consume your third day. Fra Angelico's frescoes at San Marco, the tombs of Machiavelli and Dante at Santa Croce, the Spanish Chapel at Santa Maria Novella, the legacy left by the Medici dynasty at their own San Lorenzo and the nearby Medici-Riccardi Palace, and the gothic Orsanmichele will easily combine for a splendid third day of sightseeing in Florence.

> ## A Special Note on Hours
>
> With the exception of churches, all the sights listed here stop admitting visitors at least 30 minutes, and in some cases as much as 60 minutes, before the stated closing time. Tourists can remain inside until the posted closing time, but entrance is forbidden in the last half hour or more.

If You Have 5 Days

Some visitors have fallen so deeply in love with Florence that on their fifth day they've been known to begin selling their possessions and have been seen sitting at a café on piazza della Signoria searching the classified ads for a job and an apartment.

If you have a full five days, I suggest that you stretch the hectic three-day itinerary sketched above over four days. On the fifth, despite Florence's unique pleasures and charms, get out of town. Pisa, Siena, San Gimignano, and nearby Fiesole are all lovely towns that can easily be reached on a day trip (see "Easy Excursions," at the end of this chapter).

TOP ATTRACTIONS

✪ Uffizi Galleries

Piazzale degli Uffizi 6. ☎ **055/2-38-85.** Admission 12,000 lire ($7.50). Tues–Sat 9am–7pm, Sun 9am–2pm; the ticket office closes 45 minutes before the museum.

The Uffizi is one of the most important art museums in the world and should be the first stop in Florence for anyone interested in the rich artistic heritage of the Renaissance. Four centuries of artistic development are housed in this impressive building, originally commissioned by Duke Cosimo de' Medici to house the Duchy of Tuscany's administrative offices (in fact, *uffizi* means "offices").

The gallery consists of 45 rooms where paintings are arranged in chronological order, from the 13th to the 18th century. The superb collection begins in Room 2 in the east wing, with Giotto's early 14th-century *Madonna*, considered by most scholars as the first painting to make the transition from the Byzantine to the Renaissance style. Look for the differences between Giotto's work and his teacher Cimabue's *Madonna in Maestà* on the opposite wall. The museum's best-known rooms are dedicated to Florentine painting on the eve of the Renaissance. In Room 7 are works by Paolo Uccello, Masaccio, Fra Angelico, and Piero della Francesca. As you proceed, look for the elegant Madonnas of Filippo Lippi and Pollaiolo's delightful little panels.

For many, the Botticelli rooms (Rooms 10 to 14) are the axis around which this extraordinary museum revolves. The most stunning and significant of the breathtaking works that fill these rooms are the restored *Primavera* (The Allegory of Springtime) and *The Birth of Venus*.

Other notable works include Leonardo da Vinci's unfinished *Adorazione dei Magi* in Room 15, Rosso Fiorentino's *Putto che Suona in Tribuna* (Cherub Playing a Lute) in Room 18, Lukas Cranach's *Adame e Eva* in Room 20, Michelangelo's *Sacra Famiglia* (Holy Family) in Room 25, Raphael's *Autoritratto* (Self-portrait) in Room 26, Titian's *Flora* and *La Venere di Urbino* (Venus of Urbino) in Room 28, Tintoretto's *Leda* in Room 35, Caravaggio's *Medusa* and *Bacco* in Room 43, Rembrandt's *Autoritratto* (Self-portrait) in Room 44, and Canaletto's *Veduta del Palazzo Ducale di Venezia* (View of the Ducal Palace in Venice) in Room 45.

Since the May 1993 bombing that damaged 37 works of art, the museum has staged an amazing recovery. Only four of those damaged were considered superior examples from the Italian Renaissance; two were destroyed.

✪ Galleria dell' Accademia

Via Ricasoli 60 (between piazza del Duomo and piazza San Marco). ☎ **055/238-86-09** or 2-38-85. Admission 12,000 lire ($6.25). Tues–Sat 9am–7pm, Sun 9am–2pm; last entrance 30 minutes before closing.

A cynic would observe that nowhere else in Europe do so many wait in line for so long to see so little. The Accademia is home to Michelangelo's *David*, generally considered this superior sculptor's greatest work. *David* looms in stark perfection beneath the rotunda of the main room. The statue is now protected by a high glass screen, after a 1991 attack that damaged its left foot. The museum houses seven other Michelangelos, including *The Prisoners*, in the arcade, and the second of his four versions of the *Pietà*. The wait to get in to see *David* can be up to an hour. Try getting there before the museum opens in the morning or around midday.

Duomo

Piazza del Duomo. ☎ **055/21-32-29.** Cathedral, free; cupola ascent, 8,000 lire ($3.15); excavations, 3,000 lire ($1.90). Mon–Fri 9am–6pm, Sat 8:30am–5pm, Sun 1–5pm (cupola and excavations closed Sun); last entrance to ascend the cupola 40 minutes before closing.

The red-tiled dome of Florence's Duomo dominates the skyline in the late 20th century just as it did when it was constructed five centuries ago. At that time it was the largest unsupported dome in the world, a major architectural feat and the high point of architect Filippo Brunelleschi's illustrious career. The cathedral's colorful white-, red-, and green-patterned marble exterior was added in the 19th century and is an interesting contrast to the dark-stone palazzi throughout the rest of the city.

Though much of the interior church decoration has been moved to the Museo dell'Opera del Duomo (below), the cathedral's frescoes and stained glass, by Ghiberti, Donatello, and Uccello, among others, are intact and well worth seeing. In late 1995, restoration work was finally completed on the colorful 16th-century frescos depicting the Last Judgment. When the restorers began their work, they discovered an ugly surprise: A good portion of the work was executed not in "true fresco," but in tempera, which is much more delicate.

---

❷ Did You Know?

- From 1865 to 1870, Florence was the capital of Italy.
- Florentine writers like Dante, Petrarch, and Boccaccio helped turn the Tuscan dialect into Italy's literary language.
- Giotto, Leonardo, Michelangelo, Machiavelli, Donatello, and Galileo were all residents of Florence.
- Although the construction of the cathedral of Santa Maria del Fiore was begun in 1294, the facade was not finished until 1875.
- Florence's Biblioteca Nazionale Centrale serves as the nation's official library; a copy of every book published in Italy is sent here.
- Despite its historic and artistic importance, Florence is only the eighth-largest city in Italy.
- Poet Elizabeth Barrett Browning is buried in Florence's English cemetery.

Florence

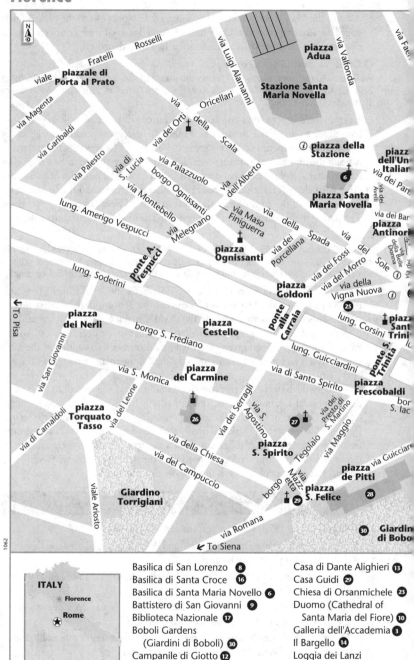

ITALY

Florence

Rome

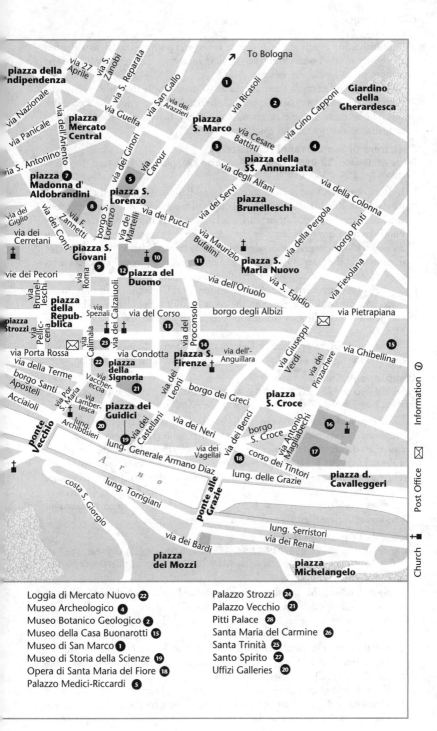

piazza della ndipendenza

via 27 Aprile

via S. Zanobi

via S. Reparata

via Nazionale

via Panicale

via dell'Ariento

via Guelfa

via S. Gallo

via dei Arazzieri

via San Gallo

To Bologna

① ② piazza S. Marco ③ via Cesare Battisti ④

Giardino della Gherardesca

via Ricasoli

via Gino Capponi

ia S. Antonino

piazza Mercato Central

via dei Ginori

via Cavour

piazza della SS. Annunziata

via della Colonna

piazza ⑦ Madonna d' Aldobrandini

⑧

borgo S. Lorenzo

via F. Zannetti

piazza S. Lorenzo

via dei Martelli

via dei Pucci

via degli Alfani

via dei Servi

piazza Brunelleschi

via della Pergola

borgo Pinti

via del Giglio

via dei Conti

via dei Cerretani

piazza S. Giovani ⑨

via Roma

⑫ ✝ ⑩ piazza del Duomo

⑪

via Maurizio Bufalini

✝ piazza S. Maria Nuovo

via S. Egidio

via Fiesolana

vie dei Pecori

via Brunel-leschi

piazza della Repub-blica

via Speziali

via del Corso

via del Proconsolo

borgo degli Albizi

✉

via Pietrapiana

piazza Strozzi

via Pelic-ceria

via Calimala

✝ ⑬ via dei Calzaiuoli

via Porta Rossa

via della Terme

borgo Santi Apostoli

Acciaioli

via Por S. Maria

via Lamber-tesca

⑳

lung. Archibusieri

via Condotta

⑭ piazza S. Firenze ✝

via dell'-Anguillara

via Giuseppi Verdi

via dei Pinzachere

via Ghibellina

⑮

⑫ piazza della Signoria ㉑

via Vacchar-eccia

piazza dei Guidici

⑲

via dei Castellani

via dei Leoni

borgo dei Greci

via dei Benci

borgo S. Croce

piazza S. Croce

via Antonio Magliabechi

⑯ ✝

⑰

Ponte Vecchio

✝

lung. Generale Armano Diaz

via dei Vagellai

⑱

corso dei Tintori

piazza d. Cavalleggeri

costa S. Giorgio

lung. Torrigiani

via dei Neri

Arno

Ponte alle Grazie

lung. delle Grazie

lung. Serristori

via dei Renai

via dei Bardi

piazza dei Mozzi

piazza Michelangelo

Church ✝■   **Post Office** ✉   **Information** ⊙

Loggia di Mercato Nuovo ㉒
Museo Archeologico ④
Museo Botanico Geologico ②
Museo della Casa Buonarotti ⑮
Museo di San Marco ①
Museo di Storia della Scienze ⑲
Opera di Santa Maria del Fiore ⑱
Palazzo Medici-Riccardi ⑤

Palazzo Strozzi ㉔
Palazzo Vecchio ㉑
Pitti Palace ㉘
Santa Maria del Carmine ㉖
Santa Trinità ㉕
Santo Spirito ㉗
Uffizi Galleries ⑳

Brunelleschi's cupola was built double-walled and is strong enough to withstand the hearty tourists who climb the spiraling, dizzying 463 steps leading to the summit for its spectacular view.

Beneath the Duomo's floor are the Scavi della Cripta di San Reparata, the ruins of the 10th-century San Reparata Cathedral that had previously occupied this site. The entrance to the excavations is through a stairway near the front of the cathedral, to the right as you enter.

Battistero di San Giovanni (Baptistery)

Piazza del Duomo. ☎ **055/21-32-29.** Admission free. Mon–Sat 1:30–6pm, Sun 9am–12:30pm and 2:30–5:15pm.

In front of the Duomo is Florence's octagonal Baptistery, dedicated to the city's patron saint, John the Baptist. The highlight of the romanesque Baptistery, constructed in the 11th and 12th centuries, is Lorenzo Ghiberti's bronze exterior doors known as the *Gates of Paradise*, on the side facing the Duomo. The doors were so dubbed by Michelangelo, who, when he first saw them, declared, "These doors are fit to stand at the gates of Paradise." Ten bronze panels depict various scenes from the Old Testament in stunning three-dimensional relief.

The doors at the north side of the Baptistery were Ghiberti's "warm-up" to the Gates and the work that won him the commission for the final set. The doors on the south side, through which you enter, are by Pisano and depict the life of St. John.

The entire Baptistery interior is decorated with gilded mosaics. *The Inferno*, found to the right of and below the Crucifixion scene, is the most dazzling.

Campanile di Giotto

Piazza del Duomo. ☎ **055/230-28-85.** Admission 8,000 lire ($5). Mar–Oct, daily 9am–6:50pm; Nov–Feb, daily 9am–4:20pm; last entrance 40 minutes before closing.

Giotto spent the last three years of his life working on the Duomo's celebrated campanile, or bell tower, and so it's often referred to simply as Giotto's Tower. The bas-reliefs decorating its exterior are copies of works by Andrea Pisano, Francesco Talenti, Luca della Robbia, and Arnoldi (the originals are in the Duomo Museum). The view from the top of Giotto's Tower is about equal to that from the Duomo; there, however, a mere 414 steps here (as opposed to the Duomo's 463). There are fewer crowds on this rooftop, but you won't get the chance to get up close and personal with Brunelleschi's architectural masterpiece here.

Museo dell'Opera del Duomo

Piazza del Duomo 29. ☎ **055/239-87-96.** Admission 8,000 lire ($5) Mon–Sat, free Sun. Mar–Oct, Mon–Sat 9am–7:50pm; Nov–Feb, Mon–Sat 9am–5:20pm; last entrance 60 minutes before closing.

Easily overlooked, this quiet, airy museum behind the cathedral contains all the art and furnishings that once filled the spacious Duomo. Even in the ticket office there's a bust of Brunelleschi, and over the door hang two glazed della Robbia terra-cottas. In the second inner room to your left you'll find sculptures from the cathedral's old gothic facade (destroyed in 1587), including work by the original architect, Arnolfo di Cambio (1245–1302). Also here are a weather-worn but noble *St. John* by Donatello and Nanni di Banco's intriguing *San Luca*.

The highlight of the center room upstairs is the enchanting twin marble choirs by Donatello and Luca della Robbia. In the next room are the original bas-reliefs that decorated the first two stories of the campanile's exterior. Another priceless

Special & Free Events

The **Maggio Musicale,** or "Musical May," is Italy's oldest music festival. Events take place at various outdoor locations throughout Florence, including piazza della Signoria and the courtyard of the Pitti Palace. Zubin Mehta often conducts Florence's own Maggio Musicale Orchestra, and guest conductors and orchestras appear throughout the festival, which, despite its moniker, runs from late April into July. For schedules and ticket information, inquire at one of the tourist offices.

From June to August, the Roman theater in nearby Fiesole comes alive with dance, music, and theater for the **Estate Fiesolana,** or "Summer in Fiesole." A.T.A.F. bus no. 7 travels to Fiesole from the train station and piazza del Duomo. Again, check with the tourist office for details.

and fascinating masterpiece, in the last room on the second floor, is the silver altarpiece with scenes from the life of St. John by Michelozzo and friends.

Among many other points of interest are Donatello's tormented wooden statue of Mary Magdalen and Michelangelo's final *Pietà,* sculpted for his own tomb when he was more than 75 years old. The haunting figure of Joseph is thought to be a self-portrait of the artist—old, tired, and nearly blind. In fact, it's rumored that Michelangelo later tried to destroy the work.

○ Piazza della Signoria, Palazzo Vecchio, and Orcagna's Loggia

Piazza della Signoria. ☎ **055/276-84-65.** Piazza della Signoria, free; Palazzo Vecchio, 8,000 lire ($5) Mon–Fri, free Sun. Piazza della Signoria, daily 24 hours; Palazzo Vecchio, Mon–Fri 9am–7pm, Sun 8am–1pm.

In Italy, all roads lead to Rome, but in Florence all roads lead to the spacious, elegant **piazza della Signoria**—the cultural and physical heart of the city since the 15th century.

The square is dominated by the imposing rough-hewn fortress architecture of the **Palazzo Vecchio**, Florence's city hall for many years and home to Duke Cosimo de' Medici for 10 years. You'll enter through the stunning main courtyard of the palazzo, with its intricately carved columns and extraordinarily colorful ceilings. The highlight of the interior is the massive richly frescoed Salone dei Cinquecento (Hall of the Five Hundred), formerly the city's council chambers and still used for government and civic functions. The richly decorated back rooms of the palazzo offer an intriguing glimpse into how the ruling class of Renaissance Florence lived. The Palazzo Vecchio also houses a modest museum of ancient musical instruments.

A small disk in the ground in front of Ammanati's enormous Neptune fountain marks the spot where the tyrant Savonarola was burned at the stake in 1498. Opposite the Palazzo Vecchio is **Orcagna's Loggia** (also known as the Loggia dei Lanzi), Florence's captivating outdoor sculpture gallery.

Pitti Palace

Piazza de' Pitti. ☎ **055/21-34-40.** Palatina, 12,000 lire ($7.50); Modern Art Gallery, 4,000 lire ($2.50); Argenti, 8,000 lire ($5). Tues–Sun 9am–2pm; last entrance 45 minutes before closing. Walk across the ponte Vecchio, the only bridge in Florence that survived World War II, and continue up via Guicciardini for a quarter of a mile.

Begun in 1458 for the wealthy banker Luca Pitti and later occupied by the Medici family and the Royal House of Savoy, this enormous palace today houses a complex of museums.

The **Galleria Palatina (Palatine Gallery),** on the first floor (☎ **055/21-03-23**), is the star attraction, home to one of the finest collections in Italy after the Uffizi's. In addition to the outstanding Raphaels displayed here, including *Madonna of the Chair, Angelo and Maddalena Doni,* and *Tommaso Inghirami,* the museum's treasures include a large collection of works by Andrea del Sarto; Fra Bartolomeo's beautiful *Deposition from the Cross* and *San Marco;* some superb works by Rubens, including *The Four Philosophers* and his famous *Isabella Clara Eugenia;* canvases by Tintoretto and Veronese; and some absolutely stunning portraits by Titian, including *Pope Julius II, The Man with the Gray Eyes,* and *The Music Concert.*

The **Appartamenti Monumentali (Royal Apartments)** (☎ **055/21-03-23**) are ornate, gilded, and chandeliered, with portraits of the Medicis and furnishings from the days of the House of Savoy. Upstairs, the **Galleria d'Arte Moderna** (☎ **055/28-70-96**) houses an interesting array of Italian impressionist and 20th-century art. Visit the **Museo degli Argenti (Silver Museum),** on the ground floor (☎ **055/21-25-57**), for a look at the treasure of the Medici family.

MORE ATTRACTIONS

Il Bargello

Via del Proconsolo 4 (at via Ghibellina, near the Uffizi). ☎ **055/238-86-06.** Admission 8,000 lire ($3.75). Tues–Sun 9am–2pm.

If a visit to the Accademia has whetted your appetite for more fine Renaissance sculpture, then you'll be interested in the this national museum's outstanding collection. This stark medieval-style building served as the city's jail in medieval times; in the middle of the courtyard is a tank where prisoners used to be tortured and executed. Today Il Bargello, named for the Captain of Justice who ruled from here, houses a number of treasures by Michelangelo, including his first attempt at *David* and his unfinished *Martyrdom of St. Andrew,* as well as *Bacco, Brutus and Madonna Teaching Jesus and San Giovanni to Read.* Among the other important sculptures here are Ammanati's *Leda and the Swan,* Giambologna's *Mercury,* and Donatello's *San Giorgio.* In another room are the two original bronze plaques by Brunelleschi and Ghiberti that were made for the competition to decide who should sculpt the second set of doors for the Bapistry.

Basilica di San Lorenzo and the Cappella dei Principi (Medici Chapels)

Piazza Madonna (at the end of borgo San Lorenzo, near the Medici-Riccardi Palace). ☎ **055/238-86-02.** Admission: San Lorenzo and the Biblioteca Laurenziana, free; Medici Chapels, 8,000 lire ($5). Basilica, daily 7am–noon and 3:30–5:30pm; Medici Chapels, Tues–Sat 9am–2pm, Sun 9am–1pm.

The San Lorenzo Basilica was the Medici family's cathedral as well as the final resting place for most of the clan. The key feature of the main part of the church is the **Biblioteca Laurenziana** (the Laurentian Library), a stunning bit of architecture by Michelangelo containing one of the largest and most valuable collection of manuscripts and codices in the world.

San Lorenzo is best known, however, for the **Medici Chapels.** First visit the New Sacristy, which contains the Michelangelo-designed tombs for Lorenzo de' Medici (with statues of *Dawn* and *Dusk*), and Giuliano de' Medici (with statues of *Night* and *Day*). The Old Sacristy, designed by Brunelleschi and decorated by Donatello, contains also several important works including a sarcophagus by Verrocchio. The other chapels, decorated to their baroque teeth, are less interesting, as are the two rooms behind the altar containing various treasures and religious relics.

Basilica di Santa Croce and the Pazzi Chapel

Piazza Santa Croce. ☎ **055/24-46-19.** Basilica, free; Pazzi Chapel, 3,000 lire ($1.90). Basilica, daily 8am–12:30pm and 3–6:30pm. Pazzi Chapel, Mar–Sept, Thurs–Tues 10am–12:30pm and 2:30–6:30pm; Oct–Feb, Thurs–Tues 10am–12:30pm and 3–5pm.

Begun in 1294, Santa Croce is the largest Franciscan church in the world. The most interesting features inside are the two chapels by Giotto to the right of the altar. Santa Croce is also the final resting place for many of the most renowned figures of the Renaissance. Michelangelo's tomb is the first on the right as you enter. Dante's empty tomb is right next to him, while Machiavelli rests in the fourth. Galileo and Rossini, among others, were also laid to rest here.

The entrance to the tranquil Pazzi Chapel (marked OPERA DI SANTA CROCE) is to the left as you leave the church. Commissioned in 1443 by Andrea de' Pazzi, a key rival of the Medici family, and designed by Filippo Brunelleschi, the chapel is a significant example of early Renaissance architecture. Serving as the church's museum, it houses many works from the 13th through the 17th century and a few of Cimabue's fine works, including his *Crucifixion*, which suffered serious damage in a 1966 flood.

Basilica di Santa Maria Novella

Piazza Santa Maria Novella (around the corner from the train station). ☎ **055/28-21-87.** Basilica, free; Spanish Chapel, 4,000 lire ($2.50). Basilica, Mon–Fri 7–11:30am and 3:30–6:30pm, Sat 7–11:30am and 3:30–5pm, Sun 8:30am–noon and 3:30–5pm; Spanish Chapel, Mon–Thurs and Sat 9am–2pm, Sun 8am–1pm.

The richly decorated gothic interior of this church is covered with frescoes by Lippi, Ghiberti, Ghirlandaio, Brunelleschi, Massaccio, and Giotto, among others. The highlight of this 14th-century green- and white-marble church is the Cappellone degli Spagnoli (Spanish Chapel), covered with an important and captivating series of early Renaissance frescoes by Andrea de Bonaiuto illustrating the history of the Dominican church. The entrance to the Spanish Chapel is immediately to the right as you exit the basilica.

✪ Chiesa di Orsanmichele

Via de' Calzaiuoli (between via dei Lamberti and via Orsanmichele). Admission free. Daily 8am–noon and 3–6:30pm. Walk just a few short blocks up from piazza della Signoria.

The 14th-century Orsanmichele Church is the last remnant of gothic architecture in Florence and was originally built to do double duty as a granary. Inside—among the vaulted gothic arches, stained-glass windows, and 500-year-old frescoes—is the colorful, sumptuous tabernacle by Andrea Orcagna. The niches surrounding the exterior of the church are a virtual history of Florentine sculpture from the 14th through the 16th century. Note Ghiberti's *St. John* (left) and Verrocchio's *St. Thomas* (right) on the front facade.

Museo della Casa Buonarroti

Via Ghibellina 70 (five blocks from the Bargello). ☎ **055/24-17-52.** Admission 8,000 lire ($5) adults, 6,000 lire ($3.75) students. Wed–Mon 9:30am–1:30pm. From piazza Santa Croce, you'll find Casa Buonarroti at the top of via delle Pinzochere, two blocks from the piazza.

This graceful house, which Michelangelo bought and designed for his nephew, was turned into a museum by his heirs. Today it houses two of the master's most important early works: *Madonna alla Scala* (Madonna on the Steps) and *Battaglia dei Centauri* (Battle of the Centaurs), both sculpted in his teenage years when he was still working in relief. The museum also houses a sizable collection of his drawings and scale models, all displayed in magnificent 17th-century halls.

✪ Museo di San Marco

Piazza San Marco 1. ☎ **055/238-86-08.** Admission 8,000 lire ($3.75). Tues–Sun 9am–2pm; the ticket office closes 30 minutes before the museum. From piazza del Duomo, walk down via Ricasoli to its end.

Next door to the San Marco Basilica in what was once a monastery, this small museum is a monument to the work of Fra Angelico. Directly to your right upon entering is a room containing the largest collection of his movable paintings in Florence. The chapter room nearby is home to Angelico's large and impressive *Crucifixion* fresco. At the top of the stairs leading to the monks' cells on the second floor is his stunning and beautiful masterpiece, *The Annunciation.* Each of the cells is decorated with a fresco painted either by Fra Angelico or by one of his assistants under the master's direction.

At the end of the corridor is Savonarola's cell, which includes a stark portrait of the monastery's former prior by his convert, Fra Bartolomeo, as well as his sleeping chamber, notebook, and rosary, and remnants of the clothes worn at his execution.

Palazzo Medici-Riccardi

Via Cavour 1. ☎ **055/2-76-01.** Admission free. Mon–Tues and Thurs–Sat 9am–1pm and 3–5pm, Sun 9am–noon. Walk one block up via de' Martelli from the Duomo.

Built for Cosimo the Elder by Brunelleschi's student Michelozzo, this mid-15th-century palazzo became the prototype for subsequent noble homes. The chapel is covered with magnificent frescoes by Benozzo Gozzoli, who worked several members of the Medici family into his depictions of the Wise Men. Across the courtyard is a second-floor baroque gallery covered with Luca Giordano's frescoes illustrating the Apotheosis of the Medici Dynasty.

PARKS & GARDENS

The lush **Giardini Boboli** (☎ **055/21-33-70**) begin behind the Pitti Palace and fan upward to the star-shaped Belvedere Fortress (☎ **055/234-24-25**), which crowns the hill. Enter the gardens via the rear exit to the Pitti Palace. The gardens, particularly beautiful in the spring, are the best spot in Florence for a picnic lunch. The view from the fortress is stunning, but there's not much to see inside unless there's a special exhibition; ask at the tourist office or look for posters around town.

The Boboli Gardens are open daily from sunrise to sunset; fortress hours vary with exhibitions. Admission to the gardens is 6,000 lire ($3.75); fortress admission is free, but exhibition admission varies.

SPECIAL-INTEREST SIGHTSEEING

Florence's 19th-century ✪ **Jewish synagogue,** an excellent and delightful, if incongruous, example of Moorish architecture, is at via Farini 4 (☎ **055/24-52-52**). The synagogue's caretaker will modestly tell you that "this is the most beautiful synagogue in all of Europe," and she may be right. Call to verify the synagogue's erratic hours, which, when I last visited, were Sunday through Thursday from 11am to 1pm and 2 to 5pm and Friday from 11am to 3pm.

A visit to the synagogue, at the intersection of via Farini and via Pilastri, is best combined with a visit to **piazza Santa Croce** (walk straight up via de' Pepi and turn right when it ends at via dei Pilastri) or the **piazza San Marco / piazza Sant'Annunziata** area (walk out via della Colonna and take the third right at via Farini). Admission is free.

Literary enthusiasts especially will enjoy a pilgrimage to the **Casa Guidi,** the home of Elizabeth Barrett and Robert Browning. The famous couple came to the Casa Guidi in 1847 and remained until 1861, when Barrett passed away. Their home was the center of the Anglo-Florentine community, where they hosted Nathaniel Hawthorne, Margaret Fuller, and other great figures in English and American literature. For the record, Guidi was the family that owned the palazzo in the days of the Medicis. This notable place, which is always staffed by American or British expatriates, is open Monday through Friday from 3 to 6pm, and at the other times by appointment; verify the winter hours. Admission is free. The house is on piazza San Felice (☎ **055/28-43-93**), in the Oltrarno. Piazza San Felice is at the intersection of via Romana, via Mazzetta, and via Maggio, opposite the Pitti Palace.

Dante's House, via S. Margherita 1 (☎ **055/28-39-62**), opened in late 1994, is a three-story building constructed on the site of poet Dante Alighieri's central Florence home. The first floor depicts Florence in the late 13th century, and contains a scale model of the Battle of Campaldino along with reproductions of medieval armor. The second floor has exhibits relating to Dante's wanderings around Verona, Bologna, and Ravenna, and the third floor contains reproductions of famous works of art relating to the poet's compositions. It's worth a look. Admission is 5,000 lire ($3.15) for adults, 3,000 lire ($1.90) for students. It's open in summer, Wednesday through Monday from 10am to 6pm; in winter, Monday and Wednesday through Saturday from 10am to 4pm and Sunday from 10am to 2pm.

While Florence is best known and most often visited for its legacy of art and architecture, the collection of its **Museo di Storia della Scienza (History of Science Museum),** piazza dei Giudici 1 (☎ **055/29-34-93**), on the river behind the Uffizi, is interesting and worth a visit for those with a special interest in the roots of technology. Its halls are filled with 16th- and 17th-century clocks, microscopes, telescopes, surveying instruments and models of the solar system—all lovely as works of art, in addition to having historical and scientific value. The original instruments of Galileo are here, as is a collection of Giovanni Alessandro Brambilla's surgical instruments. The museum is open Monday through Saturday from 9:30am to 1pm; on Monday, Wednesday, and Friday it's also open from 2 to 5pm. Admission is 10,000 lire ($6.25).

ORGANIZED TOURS

Florence is such a small city, and walking through its streets is such a pleasure, that a bus tour is not the most enjoyable way to see this wonderful city.

C.I.T., at the corner of piazza della Stazione and piazza dell'Unità Italiana (☎ **055/21-09-64**), offers two separate half-day bus tours of the city, including visits to the Uffizi Galleries, the Medici Chapels, and the breathtaking piazza le Michelangelo overlooking the city. Each tour costs 40,000 lire ($25). C.I.T. is also the place to inquire about organized tours to other areas of Tuscany.

It's open Monday through Friday from 8:30am to 12:30pm and 3 to 6:30pm, and Saturday from 8:30am to noon.

7 Shopping

In terms of good-value shopping, Florence is easy to categorize: It's paradise. This capitalist capital, where modern banking and commerce began, has something for every taste and price range. Whether you can afford little more than a bargain-priced wool sweater in the open-air market or are looking to carry home your own little piece of the Renaissance's artistic wealth, Florence is for you.

BEST BUYS   Haute couture in Florence is alive and well and living on **via Tornabuoni,** where some of the most recognized names in Italian and international design and fashion share space with the occasional bank, which you may have to rob to afford anything on this chic boulevard.

Via Calzaiuoli is lined with fashionable jewelry and clothing stores and is the city's main shopping street. Stores here are not quite as high fashion or as high priced as those on the gilded via Tornabuoni.

Via del Corso and its extension on the opposite side of via del Proconsolo, **borgo degli Albizi,** is another major shopping street, boasting many of the more avant-garde boutiques in this fashion capital.

If you've arrived in Florence with a Medici-size fortune and hope to leave with a collection to rival the Uffizi, shop on **borgo Ognissanti** near the Arno and **lungarno Corsini** and **lungarno Acciaiuoli** along the river, where you'll find merchants offering fine paintings and sculpture, objets d'art, and antiques. Leather is perhaps what Florence is most famous for. As you get closer and closer to the city, the din of the rumor mill rises to a dull roar, reaching a crescendo when you finally arrive, by which time many travelers have been happily convinced that they must buy a leather coat during their stay. All this is for good reason—for quality, price, and selection, no European city can hold a candle to Florence. Expect to spend $200 to $300 for a leather jacket.

The area around **piazza Santa Croce** is the best place to shop for leather and not much more expensive than the pushcarts at the San Lorenzo Market.

Jewelry shops line both sides of the pedestrian **ponte Vecchio,** the only bridge in Florence that escaped destruction in World War II.

MARKETS   There's nothing in Italy, and indeed perhaps nothing in Europe, to compare with Florence's bustling, sprawling, open-air **Mercato San Lorenzo.** Hundreds of pushcarts crowd together along the streets around the San Lorenzo Church and the Mercato Centrale, offering countless varieties of hand-knit wool and mohair sweaters, leather jackets, handbags, wallets, gloves, and briefcases—not to mention the standard array of souvenir T-shirts and sweatshirts, wool and silk scarves, and other souvenirs.

The market stretches for six blocks between piazza San Lorenzo behind the Medici Chapel to via Nazionale, along via Canto de' Nelli and via dell' Ariento, with stalls also set up along various side streets in between.

The days of bargaining have passed here at the open-air market. Getting a push-cart salesperson to knock 10% or 15% off the posted price should be considered a major accomplishment—and one that happens in only the off-season.

The market operates daily from 9am to 7pm from mid-March to October (closed Sunday and Monday the rest of the year). Almost all vendors accept credit and charge cards.

Much smaller, but still worth a look, is the outdoor **Mercato del Porcellino,** also known as the Straw Market, where about 100 pushcarts crowd together beneath an arcade near piazza della Repubblica. Vendors here offer mostly handbags, scarves, lace products, and souvenirs. The market is named for the bronze boar (*porcellino*) on the river side of the arcade, whose snout has been worn smooth by the countless Florentines who have touched it for good luck.

The Mercato del Porcellino is listed on most maps as "piazza del Mercato Nuovo." From piazza della Repubblica, walk two blocks toward the river and the ponte Vecchio on via Calimala, which begins at the corner of the piazza with the Cinzano and Campari signs. Hours here are generally 9am to 6pm, daily from mid-March to November 3 and Tuesday through Saturday the rest of the year.

ENGLISH-LANGUAGE BOOKSTORES   The **BM Libreria Book Shop,** borgo Ognissanti 4r (☎ **055/29-45-75**), at piazza Goldoni, is the best place in town for top-quality American and British books from both large and small publishing houses. It's open in summer, daily from 8am to 1pm and 3:30 to 7:30pm; in winter, Tuesday through Saturday from 8am to 1pm and 3:30 to 7:30pm.

The biggest and most beautiful English bookstore in town, **Libreria Internazionale Seeber,** via Tornabuoni 68r (☎ **055/21-56-97**), sells a fantastic collection of guidebooks, novels, and art and antiques books. Open Monday from 2 to 7:30pm and Tuesday through Saturday from 9:30am to 7:30pm.

8 Florence After Dark

The best source for entertainment happenings is the Italian-language monthly *Firenze Spettacolo* (2,500 lire/$1.55), offering comprehensive listings on dance, theater, and music events in the city. The magazine is available at most newsstands.

THE PERFORMING ARTS

The two principal performing arts festivals in Florence are the **Maggio Musicale** and the **Estate Fiesolana.** For more information on both, see the "Special and Free Events" box under "Attractions," earlier in this chapter.

One of Italy's busiest stages, Florence's main theater—**Teatro Comunale,** corso Italia 16 (☎ **055/21-08-04** or 21-11-58)—offers everything from symphonies to ballet to plays, opera, and music concerts. The large main theater has 30 or-chestra rows and is topped by horseshoe-shaped first and second galleries. The smaller Piccolo Teatro is rectangular, offering good sightlines from most any seat. Tickets cost 15,000 to 45,000 lire ($9.40 to $28.15), depending on the production.

The excellent, centrally located **Teatro Verdi,** via Ghibellina 101 (☎ **055/ 21-23-20**), schedules regular dance and classical music events, often top-name foreign troupes and orchestras. Tickets cost 10,000 to 35,000 lire ($6.25 to $21.90).

FILMS

The **Astro Cinema,** across from the world-famous Gelateria Vivoli on tiny via Isole dei Stinche, screens films in English every night but Monday (closed in August), for 8,000 lire ($5). A new film is shown every three to six days, so stop by to pick up the latest program (no telephone). To find the Astro, walk along via Ghibellina, which begins behind the Bargello Museum; via Isole dei Stinche will be the first street on the right.

The **Goldoni,** via dei Serragli (☎ **055/22-24-37**), also screens foreign films in their original language, also on Monday (usually at 3:30 and 10:45pm), and also charges 8,000 lire ($5).

BARS, NIGHTCLUBS & DISCOS

Nightlife is not Florence's strongest suit, but it has improved considerably over the last few years.

Chiodo Fisso

Via Dante Alighieri 16r (between via dei Calzaiuoli and via del Proconsolo, one block toward the river from via del Corso). ☎ **055/238-12-90.**

A self-proclaimed "guitar club," this cozy and intimate wine cavern is about the only place to listen to live folk music in Florence. There's no admission charge but relatively steep drink prices. Chianti is the only wine served: A bottle will set you back 25,000 lire ($15.65); a mini-carafe (basically, two glasses), 6,000 lire ($3.75). Beer and mixed drinks run 10,000 lire ($6.25). Open daily from 9pm to 3am; closed two weeks in August.

Fiddler's Elbow

Piazza Santa Maria Novella 7r (about three blocks from the train station). ☎ **055/21-50-56.**

This Irish-style pub is perpetually packed with international travelers and assorted locals. It's one of the few places in town where you can find an authentic pint of Guinness, and for only 6,500 lire ($4.05). Open Thursday through Tuesday from 4:30pm to 12:15am.

Full-Up

Via della Vigna Vecchia 21r. ☎ **055/29-30-06.** Cover 10,000–25,000 lire ($6.25–$15.65).

Located in the city center, near Santa Croce church, this is one of the top dance spaces in Florence with some of the best known DJs. There are plenty of theme evenings, so call to find out what's on. Open Wednesday through Monday from 9pm to 3am.

Space Electronic Disco

Via Palazzuolo 37. ☎ **055/29-30-82.** Cover 20,000 lire ($12.50), which includes the first drink; there's a 5,000-lira ($3.15) discount for bearers of this book.

Revelers will find a more balanced combination of tourists and Italians at this wildly decorated pleasure palace. Its motley collection of artifacts and electronics includes two enormous carnival faces plucked right from an American boardwalk, an open parachute that hangs from the ceiling, an imitation space capsule that sails back and forth across the dance floor, and of course the requisite video screens and lasers. Draft beer costs 6,000 lire ($3.75); mixed drinks, 8,000 lire ($5). Open March to August, daily from 9:30pm to 1:30am; September to February, Tuesday through Sunday from 9:30pm to 1:30am.

Tabasco Disco

Via Pandolfini 26r. ☎ **055/24-33-56.** Cover free–15,000 lire ($9.40).

Florence's top gay dance club is open to both men and women. The dance floor is downstairs, while a small video room and piano bar is up top. There are cabaret shows each Monday, and karaoke most Thursdays. Open Thursday through Tuesdy from 9pm to 3am.

Yab Yam

Via Sassetti 5r. ☎ **055/28-20-18.** Cover 15,000 lire–30,000 lire ($9.40–$18.75).

Known to locals simply as "Yab," this is one of the largest dance clubs in the city center. A full-on light and sound assault in the basement of giant old palazzo near piazza della Repubblica, the club is not related to the famous Yab Jum chain of European nightclubs. Open Sunday, Monday, and Wednesday through Friday from 9pm to 3am.

Zut

Parco delle Cascine. ☎ **0330/26-83-22.** Cover varies from free to 15,000 lire ($9.40).

One of the best new dance clubs, Zut offers something different each night of the week. Sometimes it's hip-hop, sometimes it's techno, and mostly it's acid jazz. The club can hold about 500 people, and often does. Since it's located a 15-minute cab ride from the city center, tourism is minimized. Open Tuesday through Saturday from 10pm to 3 or 4am.

9 Easy Excursions

Tuscany is considered by many to be the most beautiful region of Italy. If you have a car, head toward Siena on the SS 222 through the **Florentine Chianti,** a land of rolling hills that's now usually identified with the production of Chianti Classical Wine (the Gallo Nero, with the black rooster on the label). The road climbs toward the hills of Val d'Ema, passing many centuries-old villas along the way. The road winds down toward Greve in Chianti, a small town with an irregular street plan and ancient marketplace that's worth poking around by foot. The adjacent village of Montefioralle has a medieval castle and the ornately decorated Church of San Stefano.

Three towns, all of which can be reached from Florence on a day trip, are particularly noteworthy.

FIESOLE   Situated on a hill rising above Florence, Fiesole is an important **archeological site,** containing vast 2,000-year-old Etruscan and Roman ruins, including a large amphitheater (☎ **055/5-94-77**). The town center surrounds a large square dedicated to the sculptor Mino da Fiesole (ca. 1430–84). Fronting the square is a romanesque **cathedral,** the 17th-century **Bishop's Palace** (☎ **055/ 5-92-42**), and the **St. Maria Primerana Church** (☎ **055/5-94-00**). Fiesole also offers a splendid panorama of Florence and the countryside below it. Most sites are open in winter, Wednesday through Monday from 9am to 6pm; and in summer, Wednesday through Monday from 9am to 7pm. The town can be reached in 30 minutes by taking municipal bus no. 7 to the end of the line.

SIENA   The "musts" to see in lovely Siena include its stunning **Duomo** and adjacent museum (admission 5,000 lire/$3.15), as well as the **Palazzo Pubblico,** which dominates the unique oval central square, known as the Campo. And if you've dodged one too many errant taxis, you'll especially enjoy the fact that the historic quarter of Siena is car-free.

There is train service from Florence to Siena, but buses are more convenient, since they'll drop you off much closer to the center than the remote train station. S.I.T.A. buses leave Florence for Siena about every 30 minutes from the station at via Santa Caterina da Siena 15r (☎ **055/21-14-87**), located near the train station; exit the station by Track 5, turn left and then right at the next corner, and the bus depot will be right there. The bus journey takes about 75 minutes and costs about 8,000 lire ($5) each way.

PISA   Everybody knows what to see in Pisa, an hour away by train for 12,000 lire ($7.50), round-trip. It's too bad that Pisa is so renowned for its mistakes, though. Were it not for the tilt of the infamous **Leaning Tower,** Pisa's piazza del Duomo would be one of the loveliest squares in the country. To reach it, take the bus marked DUOMO from the train station in Pisa.

Geneva 14

by Nikolaus Lorey

Cool, peaceful Geneva is the quintessential international city. Ever since it hosted its first conference in the 8th century, Geneva has been a privileged site for summit meetings and a favored headquarters of international organizations. Both the Red Cross and the League of Nations were founded here, and the city is home to the multilingual, multinational World Health Organization (WHO), Centre Européen de Recherches Nucléaires (CERN), and countless other representations from the world of acronyms. When Reagan and Gorbachev met for the first time, they chose peaceloving Geneva as their stage.

Despite these ties with the entire world, few places are as conscious as Geneva of its essential quality—that of being first and foremost its own city. Surrounded almost totally by France, Geneva did not join the Swiss Confederacy until 1815, and it still displays its official name with pride: Republic and Canton of Geneva. Separatism is not unheard of. On the Ile Rousseau, the statue of Jean-Jacques Rousseau bears an inscription describing the philosopher simply as a citizen of Geneva—*citoyen de Genève*. Other citizens have included Voltaire, Byron, Lenin, Richard Burton, Alain Delon, Audrey Hepburn, and Romania's exiled King Michael.

Argentine writer Jorge Luís Borges lived here as a child during World War I and returned in his 80s, just a few months before his death; he loyally proclaimed Geneva the one place in the world "most propitious for happiness." When you see the deep-blue lake, with the snow-capped Alps in the distance and the jet d'eau arcing gracefully above the very proper skyline, you may feel the same way.

1 Geneva Deals & Discounts

Is it possible to enjoy Geneva with a budget starting at $50 a day? A friend who works at the United Nations didn't believe it could be done until I showed her how. Indeed, it's possible if you know where to look for the bargains.

In this chapter you'll find a number of inexpensive hotels with double rooms for 90 Swiss francs ($69.75), and this rate includes a continental breakfast. With your remaining francs, you should be able to get lunch and dinner and stay within your budget.

What's Special About Geneva

Lake Geneva
  • One of Europe's most beautiful lakes.
  • Great boat excursions.

The Old City
  • Narrow cobblestone streets and pretty fountains.
  • A great place for a stroll.

The Parks
  • Some 37 acres alongside the lake, with views of the Alps.
  • Great for picnicking and strolling.

The Alps
  • Both the French and the Swiss versions very close to the city.
  • Great for day trips and skiing.

The International Institutions
  • The U.N. and the Red Cross Museum, representative of Geneva's multi-national spirit.

BUDGET BESTS   The best bargains in Geneva are undoubtedly the museums—most are free. An exception is the must-see Red Cross Museum, which charges SFr 8 ($6.20).

If you plan to visit far-flung sections of the city by bus or tram, you'll save money by purchasing a one-, two-, or three-day **transit pass** valid on buses and trams and good for unlimited rides within the city and the outskirts. For only SFr 2 ($1.35) you can have an inexpensive **boat ride** across the blue-green waters of Lake Geneva from one bank to the other.

In summer, head to the parks and quays along the banks of the lake for another Geneva bargain—**free music.** Classical, jazz, and pop music make a wonderful accompaniment to a picnic dinner. In addition, there are free concerts from June to September on Saturday at 6pm at the Cathédrale de St-Pierre and on Sunday and Monday evening at the Eglise de St-Germain, only a block from the cathedral.

And don't pass up the opportunity to have Geneva's delicious **cheese fondue** at least once. This meal is not only filling and entertaining but also one of Geneva's best food bargains.

WORTH THE EXTRA MONEY   The four-star Excelsior hotel will offer reasonable rates to readers who show them this book.

2 Pretrip Preparations

REQUIRED DOCUMENTS   Citizens of the United States, the United Kingdom, Canada, Australia, and New Zealand need only a valid passport. Remember to carry your passport if you visit Chamonix or the Salève in France or if you take a boat excursion that stops at any of the French villages on the south shore of Lake Geneva.

TIMING YOUR TRIP   Despite its proximity to the Alps, Geneva is at a relatively low elevation, less than 3,000 feet. The climate is relatively mild, and rainfall is fairly evenly distributed throughout the year. In winter the rain often mixes with snow.

Geneva's Average Daytime Temperature & Rainfall

	Jan	Feb	Mar	Apr	May	June	July	Aug	Sept	Oct	Nov	Dec
Temp. (°F)	35	29	41	44	60	63	68	65	60	53	41	36
Rainfall "	2.6	2.4	2.8	2.6	2.8	3.3	3.	3.9	3.8	3.4	3.6	3.2

Special Events   The annual **Fêtes de Genève** in the second week of August and **l'Escalade** in mid-december are Geneva's biggest and most popular festivals. The Fêtes de Genève feature live music all over the city, while the focus of the Escalade is a torchlit parade through the streets of the Old City, with hundreds of Genevans dressed in 17th-century costumes. Both celebrations are well worth a special visit.

BACKGROUND READING   *Switzerland for Beginners* (André Deutsch, 1987) by George Mike is an amusing collection of essays on diverse aspects of swiss life. H. M. Waidson's *Anthology of Modern Swiss Literature* (St. Martin's Press, 1985) provides a comprehensive introduction in English to Switzerland's multilingual literature. Writers from all over the world have written about Geneva—Rousseau, Stendhal, Hugo, Hans Christian Andersen, and Rilke. If you read French, you might consider getting a copy of *Genève: Un guide intime* (Autrement, 1986), part of the collection "L'Europe des Villes Rêvées"; this highly personal vision of the city by French author Michel Butor includes an anthology of short pieces on Geneva by the writers mentioned above.

What Things Cost in Geneva	U.S. $
Taxi from the airport to city center	31.00
Public transportation for an average trip within the city	1.70
Local telephone call	.45
Double room at Le Richemond (deluxe)	480.00
Double room at the Hôtel Excelsior (moderate)	140.00
Double room at the Hôtel de la Cloche (budget)	58.15
Lunch for one, without wine, at Café des Antiquaires (moderate)	13.20
Lunch for one, without wine, at Restaurant Manora (budget)	8.50
Dinner for one, without wine, at La Perle du Lac (deluxe)	52.00
Dinner for one, without wine, at Les Armures (moderate)	24.80
Dinner for one, without wine, at La Cave Valaisanne (budget)	16.65
Glass of wine	2.80
Coca-Cola	2.40
Cup of coffee	2.80
Roll of ASA 100 color film, 36 exposures	5.10
Admission to the Red Cross Museum	6.20
Movie ticket	11.60
Theater ticket	18.00

3 Geneva Specifics

ARRIVING

With only 175,000 residents, Geneva is a small city. **Geneva-Cointrin Airport,** though busy with all the comings and goings of employees and visitors to the city's numerous international organizations, is compact and easily negotiated.

Getting into the city from the airport is a breeze. In the air terminal's basement is a station with trains leaving about every 10 to 15 minutes for the six-minute trip to the city's **Gare de Cornavin (Cornavin Station)** (☎ 022/157-33-33). If you happen to be heading for another Swiss city, you may be able to depart directly from the airport station without having to change trains at Cornavin. The train from the airport into the city costs SFr 5.10 ($3.95) one way and runs from 5:30am to 12:20am. Whether you arrive by air or by train, you'll find yourself at Cornavin Station, on the right bank of Geneva.

Taking a taxi into town is highly inadvisable. They take much longer than the train and, costing SFr 40 ($31), are much more expensive.

VISITOR INFORMATION

The **main tourist office,** in the train station (☎ 022/738-52-00), is open July to September, daily from 8am to 8pm; October to June, Monday through Saturday from 9am to 6pm. The helpful staff will make hotel reservations in the city for SFr 5 ($3.85) and elsewhere in Switzerland for SFr 10 ($7.75). Here you can also pick up a free copy of *What's on in Geneva*, a useful publication with information on sightseeing, the performing arts, and special events. A branch of the tourist office is located at 14 place du Molard (☎ 022/311-98-27) with shorter opening hours.

From June 15 to September 15, **CAR (Centre d'Accueil et de Renseignements)** (☎ 022/731-46-47) provides information from a van parked on rue du Mont-Blanc in front of the train station. Hours are daily from 8:30am to 11pm.

Infor Jeunes, 13 rue Verlaine (☎ 022/311-44-22), near place Bourg-de-Four in the Old City, is an information center for young travelers. The staff can answer all sorts of questions about Geneva.

CITY LAYOUT

Geneva is at the western end of **Lake Geneva,** known in French as Lac Léman, site of the impressive jet d'eau. The blue-green waters of the lake meet the **Rhône River,** which divides the city into a left and right bank. On the **rive gauche (left bank)** are the Old City, some major shopping streets, the famous flower clock, the university, and several important museums. On the **rive droite (right bank)** are the train station, the major international organizations, and many attractive parks.

GETTING AROUND

BY BUS & TRAM   Geneva is not very big, so you'll be able to walk almost everywhere. For longer distances, the **Transports publics genevois (TPG)** (☎ 022/308-34-34) offers a fine network of buses and trolleys, as well as one tram—the smoothly gliding no. 12. If you're going three stops or less, the fare is SFr 1.50 ($1.15); for more than three stops the ticket costs SFr 2.20 ($1.70) and is good for one hour with no limits on transfers. Tickets are dispensed from coin-operated machines at every stop.

The Swiss Franc

For American Readers At this writing $1 = approximately SFr 1.29 (or SFr 1 = 78¢), and this was the rate of exchange used to calculate the dollar values given in this chapter (rounded to the nearest nickel).

For British Readers At this writing £1 = approximately SFr 2.18 (or SFr 1 = 46p), and this was the rate of exchange used to calculate the pound values in the table below.

Note: The rates given here fluctuate from time to time and may not be the same when you travel to Switzerland. Therefore this table should be used only as a guide:

SFr	U.S.$	U.K.£	SFr	U.S.$	U.K.£
.25	.19	.11	15	1.63	6.88
.50	.39	.23	20	15.50	9.17
.75	.58	.34	25	19.38	11.47
1	.78	.46	30	23.26	13.76
2	1.55	.92	35	27.13	16.05
3	2.33	1.38	40	31.00	18.34
4	3.10	1.83	45	34.88	20.64
5	3.88	2.29	50	38.76	22.94
6	4.65	2.75	60	46.51	27.52
7	5.43	3.21	70	54.26	32.11
8	6.20	3.67	80	62.01	36.70
9	6.98	4.13	90	69.77	41.28
10	7.75	4.59	100	77.52	45.87

There's also a series of *cartes journalières* (**day passes**). A one-day pass is available for SFr 8.50 ($6.60), a two-day pass for SFr 15 ($11.60), and a three-day pass for SFr 19 ($14.70). Another option are the *cartes multiparcours,* 12 three-stop tickets for SFr 15 ($11.60) or six one-hour tickets for SFr 12 ($9.30). Those staying for longer periods should consider the **monthly passes.** The *carte orange* costs SFr 60 ($46.50), while the *carte vermeil* (for senior and disabled citizens) costs SFr 40 ($31), and the *carte azure* (for those 25 and under), SFr 35 ($27.15).

ON FOOT Unless you want to see both the Old City on the left bank and the international organizations on the right bank in one day, Geneva can easily be explored on foot.

BY BICYCLE A bicycle is an excellent way to visit the countryside around Geneva, but for sightseeing in the city, where the streets of the Old City are steep and made of cobblestones, it's not practical. For cycling in the countryside, pick up a map of the canton of Geneva from the tourist office and head out through farmland and vineyards to the many picturesque small villages.

Multispeed bicycles can be rented at **Cornavin Station** for SFr 15 ($13.15) for half a day or SFr 19 ($14.70) for a full day. Mountain bikes are also available, for SFr 31 ($24.05).

Horizon Motos, at 22 rue de Paquis (☎ **022/738-36-96;** fax 022/738-02-82), also rents mountain bikes, as well as mopeds and motorcycles. The mountain bikes and mopeds are SFr 44 ($34.10) per day and SFr 259 ($200.75) per week. Unless you pay for the rental with a credit or charge card, you'll have to leave a SFr-500 ($378.60) refundable deposit. Motorcycles start at SFr 77 ($59.70) per day. This rate includes insurance and you'll need a valid motorcycle license. Open Monday through Friday from 8am to noon and 1:30 to 7pm, and Saturday to 5pm.

BY BOAT   Shuttling back and forth between the right and left banks of the city in summer are small boats known as **Mouettes Genevoises.** These water buses are the cheapest way to take a cruise on the lake. For as little as SFr 2.20 ($1.70) you can cross from one side of the lake to the other, or for SFr 12 ($9.30) you can get a round-trip ticket that allows you to get off at any of the five stops and get back on a later boat.

BY CAR   Most of the major international car-rental agencies have offices in Geneva. For budget car rentals, try **Léman,** at 6 rue Amat (☎ **022/732-01-43**), where you can rent a Peugeot 106 for SFr 98 ($75.95) per day, with unlimited mileage. Open Monday through Saturday from 8am to 7pm and Sunday from 9am to 5pm.

FAST FACTS: Geneva

Babysitters   The tourist office lists several agencies, including Service de Placement de l'Université, 4 rue de Candolle (☎ **022/329-39-70** or 705-77-02), which you must call between 8am and 1pm and 2 and 4:30pm for service that evening. Le Chaperon Rouge, 4 rue Rodo (☎ **022/781-06-66**), accepts calls daily from 8:30am to 1pm—it's organized by the local Red Cross.

Business Hours   Hours for most **shops** are Monday through Saturday from 8:30am to 6:30pm. **Offices** are open Monday through Friday from 8am to noon and 2 to 6pm.

Consulates   Because of Geneva's important position in global politics, many consulates, as well as missions to the United Nations, are here. These include the consulates of **Australia,** 56–58 rue Moillebeau (☎ **022/734-62-00**); the **United Kingdom,** 37–39 rue Vermont (☎ **022/734-38-00**); **Canada,** 11 chemin du Pré-de-la-Bichette (☎ **022/733-90-00**); **New Zealand,** 28 chemin du Petit-Saconnex (☎ **022/734-95-30**); and the **United States,** 1–3 av. de la Paix (☎ **022/738-76-13**).

Currency   The basic unit of currency in Switzerland is the **Swiss franc (SFr),** which is divided into 100 **centimes.** There are banknotes of SFr 10, 20, 50, 100, 500, and 1,000, and coins of SFr 1/2, 1, 2, and 5, and 5, 10, and 20 centimes. Banks all over Geneva have currency-exchange windows and offer good rates.

Emergencies   Dial 117 for the police, 118 for the fire department. In medical emergencies, dial 372-81-00, or go to the Hôpital Cantonal, 24 rue Micheli-du-Crest (☎ **022/382-33-11**). If you need a dentist, go to one of the cliniques dentaires at 5 chemin Malombré (☎ **022/346-64-44**) and 60 av. Wendt (☎ **022/733-98-00**); both are open daily from 7:30am to 8pm.

Geneva Agenda, published weekly and costing SFr 2 ($1.55) contains addresses and phone numbers of pharmacies open until 9 or 11pm each week; in emergencies dial 111 for urgent pharmaceutical needs, and 144 for an ambulance.

Holidays   Public holidays in Geneva include New Year's Day (Jan 1), Good Friday, Easter Monday, and Christmas Day (Dec 25).

Hotlines   La Main Tendue is a hotline for those in need— call 143.

Information   See "Geneva Specifics," earlier in this chapter.

Laundry   Known in Geneva as a *salon lavoir*, a laundry is usually self-service. The Salon Lavoir, 4 rue de Montbrillant, on the first street behind Cornavin Station, will do your laundry for you for SFr 17 ($13.20). It's open Monday through Friday from 7:30am to 12:30pm and 1:30 to 6:30pm (Thursday to noon) and Saturday from 8am to 12:30pm.

Two laundries in the Plainpalais area are open daily from early morning to late at night and charge only about SFr 15 ($11.60) for you to wash and dry your own clothes. They're at the end of rue des Voisins at 10 rue Jean-Violette, and 200 yards from place du Cirque at 61 bd. St-Georges.

In the Eaux-Vives district, one at 8 rue du 31 Décembre is open daily from 6:30am to 11pm and charges SFr 16 ($12.40) to wash and dry.

Lost & Found   Geneva's efficient Service cantonal des objets trouvés, 7 rue des Glacis-de-Rive (☎ **022/787-60-00**), is open Monday through Thursday from 8am to 4:30pm and Friday from 8am to 4pm. Check here for items lost in shops, restaurants, taxis, buses, and on the street. There are other Lost Property Offices in the airport and the central station.

Mail   The main post office is at 18 rue du Mont-Blanc, two blocks from Gare de Cornavin. It's open Monday through Friday from 7:30am to 6pm and Saturday from 8 to 11am.

Police   In an emergency, dial 117 for the police.

Religious Services   For details, contact the American Church, 3 rue de Monthoux (☎ **022/732-80-78**); the Roman Catholic John XXIII Centre, 35 chemin Adolphe-Pasteur (☎ **022/733-04-83**); or the Jewish Liberal Community, 12 quai du Seujet (☎ **022/732-32-45**).

Tax   The VAT (value-added tax) of 6.5%, levied on items above SFr 500 ($387), is refundable; simply ask the store for a VAT form and present it to the Customs official when leaving the country.

Taxis   Taxicabs are easy to find but not cheap. If you need one, call 331-41-33.

Telephone   A large long-distance phone center is located at Gare de Cornavin, open daily from 7am to 10:30pm. You can also make long-distance calls at the main post office on rue du Mont-Blanc, two blocks from the station. Local calls start at 60 centimes (45¢); telephones accept coins in various denominations. The telephone area code for Geneva is 022.

Tipping   A service charge is usually added to restaurant bills and taxicab fares in Geneva, so it's unnecessary to leave a tip beyond the few centimes you might receive back when you break a franc. However, if a special service is performed by a waiter or cabdriver, a larger tip would be appropriate.

Useful Telephone Numbers   General information, 111; exchange rates, 160; time, 161; weather, 162; road conditions, 163.

4 Accommodations

Despite its reputation as one of the more expensive cities in the world, Geneva has a few inexpensive hotels. The choices are even better in summer, when many student dormitories open up to tourists. These are often the best deals, with attached baths for less than you'd spend for a room without bath in a regular hotel.

It's a good idea to reserve in advance. If you have trouble finding a room when you arrive, remember that the tourist office will make hotel reservations for SFr 5 ($3.90)—see "Geneva Specifics," earlier in this chapter.

DOUBLES FOR LESS THAN SFR 100 ($77.50)
ON THE RIGHT BANK

✪ Hôtel de la Cloche

6 rue de la Cloche, 1201 Genève. ☎ **022/732-94-81.** 8 rms, none with bath. SFr 50 ($38.75) single; SFr 75 ($58.10) double; SFr 90 ($69.75) triple; SFr 130 ($100.75) quad. Rates include continental breakfast. Showers SFr 2 ($1.55) extra for one-night stay, free for longer stays. No credit cards. Bus 1 from Gare de Cornavin. From Gare de Cornavin, walk down rue du Mont-Blanc, turn left onto quai du Mont-Blanc and left again at the fifth street, rue de la Cloche; the hotel is across from the Noga Hilton.

Built in the 1880s, this small hotel was once the apartment of the director of the Grand Casino. Many luxurious features remain, like the beautiful blue-and-white porcelain sink in the bathroom near the entrance (some guests have offered to buy it, according to managers M. and Mme Chabbey).

✪ Hôtel des Tourelles

2 bd. James-Fazy, 1201 Genève. ☎ **022/732-44-23.** Fax 022/732-76-20. 23 rms, 11 with shower and toilet. TV. SFr 70 ($54.25) single without shower, SFr 90 ($69.75) single with shower and toilet; SFr 90 ($69.75) double without shower, SFr 120 ($93) double with shower and toilet. Rates include buffet breakfast. Additional bed SFr 20 ($15.50) extra. AE, EURO, MC, V. Turn right when you come out of Gare de Cornavin, staying to the right of the large church on boulevard James-Fazy; the Tourelles is on the left side of the street just before the bridge over the river.

Named after the turrets on the corner of the building, this is one of Geneva's best budget hotels. The turret rooms are huge, with seating alcoves and views of the river and the Old City. Some rooms have bay windows and antiques; all have color TVs with 30 channels. The hotel is clean and the management friendly.

✪ Hôtel Rio

1 place Isaac-Mercier, 1201 Genève. ☎ **022/731-94-82.** 32 rms, 6 with bath, 10 with shower only. SFr 68 ($52.70) single without bath, SFr 78 ($60.45) single with shower only; SFr 98 ($75.95) double without bath, SFr 98 ($75.95) double with shower only; SFr 98 ($75.95) triple without bath, SFr 120 ($93.02) triple with shower only; SFr 114 ($88.35) quad without bath, SFr 125($96.90) quad with shower only; SFr 98–190 ($75.95–$147.30) room with bath and kitchenette for one to six. Rates include continental breakfast. EURO, MC, V. From Cornavin Station, turn right onto boulevard James-Fazy, which leads right to the hotel.

The Rio, completely modernized in 1994, is ideal for families and small groups. Spread over four floors (with an elevator) of a corner house less than a five-minute walk from the train station, with the reception area on the second floor, it offers good value for the price. The staff is English-speaking and exceptionally friendly and helpful.

Getting the Best Deal on Accommodations

- Student dormitories, available for tourists during summer, are a super bargain.
- For a small fee, the tourist office will make reservations for you if you arrive without them.

Hôtel St-Gervais

20 rue des Corps-Saints, 1201 Genève. ☎ **022/732-45-72.** 26 rms, 2 with shower and toilet. SFr 62 ($48.05) single without shower; SFr 78 ($60.45) double without bath, SFr 98 ($75.95) double with shower and toilet. SFr 105 ($8l.40) double with bath. Rates include continental breakfast. AE, EURO, MC, V. Turn right as you exit Cornavin Station and walk down rue Cornavin to rue des Corps-Saints, which veers off from it where rue Cornavin turns toward the river.

On seven floors of a building with an elevator, the St-Gervais features recently remodeled rooms, most small and geometrically creative; a few are square. The carpets are pretty, the furniture is modern, and everything is spotless. The English-speaking management is friendly. Gare de Cornavin is only a three-minute walk away. Highly recommended.

ON THE LEFT BANK

Hôtel Beau Site

3–4 place du Cirque, 1204 Genève. ☎ **022/328-10-08.** Fax 022/329-23-64. 25 rms with 54 beds, 1 rm with shower and toilet, 10 rms with shower only. SFr 58 ($44.95) single without shower, SFr 68 ($52.70) single with shower only; SFr 78 ($60.45) double without shower, SFr 88 ($68.20) double with shower only, SFr 103 ($79.85) double with shower and toilet; SFr 93 ($72.10) triple without shower, SFr 103 ($79.85) triple with shower only; SFr 103 ($79.85) quad without shower, SFr 113 ($87.60) quad with shower only. Rates include continental breakfast. AE, EURO, MC, V. Bus 1 or 4.

This is a funky old place popular with young travelers. Large high-ceilinged rooms with parquet floors, doors painted red and gray, an antique sewing machine, and a TV lounge with a large overstuffed couch all contribute to the antique atmosphere. If manager Denise Ray is not around, someone at the desk who speaks enough English will check you in.

Hôtel du Lac

15 rue des Eaux-Vives, 1207 Genève. ☎ **022/735-45-80.** 26 rms, none with bath. SFr 58 ($44.95) single; SFr 80 ($62) double; SFr 110 ($85.25) triple. Rates include continental breakfast. No credit cards. Bus 9 from Gare de Cornavin to place des Eaux-Vives.

This immaculate and well-maintained hotel occupies the sixth and seventh floors of a modern apartment building (with elevator). Owners M. and Mme Cagnoli-Spiess are responsible for making this such a delightful place. They take great pride in keeping their hotel in top shape, doing much of the work themselves. All the sixth-floor rooms have balconies, and many rooms have connecting doors so families or two couples can share two rooms.

✪ Hôtel de Prince

16 rue des Voisins, 1205 Genève. ☎ **022/329-85-44.** Fax 022/781-51-19. 24 rms, all with bath. TV TEL. SFr 80 ($72) single; SFr 99 ($76.75) double; SFr 115 ($89.15) triple. Rates include continental breakfast. AE, MC, V. Bus 1 from Gare de Cornavin to Pont d'Arve; then walk across rue de Carouge and turn left at the next intersection.

Near the university in the Plainpalais district, this hotel is an excellent deal. The management is wonderfully friendly, and many rooms have lots of light and minibars—some will be remodeled soon.

DOUBLES FOR LESS THAN SFR 110 ($73.35)
ON THE RIGHT BANK

Hôtel Tor

3 rue Lévrier, 1201 Genève. ☎ **022/732-39-95.** Fax 022/738-41-56. 23 rms, all with bath. TV TEL. SFr 75–100 ($58.15–$77.50) single; SFr 90–130 ($69.75–$100.75) double; SFr 150 ($116.25) triple; SFr 170 ($131.75) quad. Rates include continental breakfast. AE, EURO, MC, V. From Gare de Cornavin, walk down rue du Mont-Blanc and turn left onto rue Lévrier.

On the third floor of an elevator building, the Tor is spacious and well furnished. All rooms have their own tubs or showers and private toilet. The management is pleasant and speaks excellent English. The Tor is close to the bus terminal.

ON THE LEFT BANK

Hôtel Central

2 rue de la Rôtisserie, 1204 Genève. ☎ **022/311-45-94.** Fax 022/818-81-01. 29 rms, all with bath. TV. SFr 60–110 ($46.50–$85.25) single; SFr 70–130 ($54.25–$100.75) double; SFr 110–150 ($85.25–$116.25) triple; SFr 130–190 ($100.75–$147.30) quad. Rates include continental breakfast. No credit cards. Bus 5 or 44 from Gare de Cornavin to Bel-Air.

On the edge of the Old City, a block from rue du Marché—one of Geneva's two main shopping streets—the businesslike Central is convenient for touring and shopping. The rooms may be small but are spotless and have new carpets and modern furnishings. The hotel is on the upper floors of an elevator-equipped building with a shopping arcade on the ground floor.

Hôtel de l'Etoile

17 rue des Vieux-Grenadiers, 1205 Genève. ☎ **022/328-72-08.** Fax 022/321-16-24. 30 rms, all with shower and toilet. TV TEL. SFr 70–80 ($54.25–$62) single; SFr 110–128 ($85.25–$99.20) double; SFr 140 ($108.50) triple. Continental breakfast SFr 6 ($4.65) extra. EURO, V. Bus 1, 4, or 44 from Gare de Cornavin to Ecole-de-Médecine.

In the Plainpalais area, this hotel is much nicer than the street it's on. Refurbished not long ago, the guest rooms are pleasant. Owners M. and Mme Dousse speak English.

Hôtel le Grenil

7 av. de Ste-Clothilde, 1205 Genève. ☎ **022/328-30-55.** Fax 022/321-60-10. 48 rms, 31 with shower and toilet. SFr 100 ($77.50) single without bath, SFr 130 ($100.75) single with bath; SFr 130 ($100.75) double without bath, SFr 150 ($116.25) double with bath; SFr 126 ($97.65) triple without bath, SFr 180 ($139.55) triple with bath; SFr 140 ($108.50) quad without bath, SFr 200 ($155) quad with bath; SFr 25 ($19.35) per person in an eight-bed room. Rates include continental breakfast. AE, DC, EURO, MC, V. Bus 1 or 4 from Gare de Cornavin to place du Cirque; then walk down boulevard St-Georges to avenue de Sainte-Clothilde.

The rooms here are amazingly similar to those you might find in any modern hotel in North America; even more surprising is that Le Grenil is sponsored by the YMCA and the YWCA of Geneva. Besides standard rooms—most with TV, radio, and telephone—the hotel has rooms for the disabled and two dormitories. Other amenities include a TV lounge, a dining room serving lunch and dinner (half board available), an art gallery off the large lobby, and a theater in the basement.

Hôtel Pax

68 rue du 31-Décembre, 1207 Genève. ☎ **022/735-44-40.** Fax 022/786-45-68. 31 rms with 70 beds, 12 rms with shower and toilet. MINIBAR TV TEL. SFr 70 ($46.65) single without bath, SFr 106 ($82.15) single with bath; SFr 98 ($75.95) double without bath, SFr 123 ($95.35) double with bath; SFr 105 ($80.85) triple without bath, SFr 153 ($118.60) triple with bath. Breakfast SFr 9 ($6.95) extra. AE, DC, EURO, MC, V. Bus 9 from Gare de Cornavin to rue du 31-Décembre.

Not as close to the corner as some of the hotels listed here, the Pax is certainly acceptable and moderately priced. Many of the rooms are quite spacious and have large windows. Color TVs are in every room.

SUPER-BUDGET CHOICES
OPEN ALL YEAR

Auberge de Jeunesse

28 rue Rothschild, 1202 Genève. ☎ **022/732-62-60.** 340 beds. SFr 70 ($54.25) double with bath for IYHF members, SFr 84 ($65.10) for nonmembers; SFr 79 ($61.25) quad with bath for IYHF members, SFr 120 ($93) for nonmembers; SFr 23 ($17.80) dorm bed for IYHF members, SFr 30 ($23.25) dorm bed for nonmembers. Youth hostel membership SFr 30 ($23.25) extra. No credit cards. Bus 1 to the Wilson stop; or turn left from Gare de Cornavin an d walk six blocks up rue de Lausanne.

Geneva's official youth hostel has an excellent location less than a 15-minute walk from Gare de Cornavin and two blocks from the lake. Opened in 1987, it's housed in a former hospital and a modern building designed specifically as a youth hostel. The dorm rooms have 6, 8, or 10 beds. Outstanding features include a large glass-walled and glass-ceilinged lobby, a TV lounge, a no-smoking library and quiet room, a self-catering kitchen, rooms for the disabled, and a self-service restaurant featuring *plats du jour* for only SFr 10.50 ($7). There's a midnight curfew here, and the hostel is also closed from 10am to 4pm.

Hôtel les 4 Nations

43 rue de Zurich, 1201 Genève. ☎ **022/732-02-24.** Fax 022/732-20-40. 20 rms, none with bath. SFr 45 ($34.90) single; SFr 70 ($54.25) double. Additional bed (up to four) SFr 30 ($23.25) extra. Breakfast SFr 6 ($4.65) extra. EURO, V. From Gare de Cornavin, turn left onto rue de Lausanne and then right onto rue de Zurich (the second street on the right); it's a seven-minute walk.

This basic hotel with spartan furniture occupies a nondescript four-story house (no elevator) in the rear of a small green-carpeted courtyard. There are showers and a toilet on each floor, and the optional breakfast is served in a hacienda-looking room at street level. The friendly owner, Kurt Kyburz, speaks English. Don't expect comfort here, but the rooms are priced accordingly. This is not necessarily a recommendable hotel for women traveling alone.

Pension St-Boniface

14 av. du Mail, 1205 Genève. ☎ **022/321-88-44.** 140 beds. SFr 45 ($34.90) single; SFr 75 ($58.15) double; SFr 24 ($18.60) dorm bed, SFr 15 ($11.60) if you provide your own sheets. Breakfast SFr 6 ($4.65) extra. No credit cards. Bus 1 from Gare de Cornavin to place du Cirque; then walk three blocks down avenue du Mail.

Open all year, this pension is almost always full, but it's worth a try. There are 140 beds—in dormitories, singles, and doubles. Kitchen facilities are available to guests who want to do their own cooking, and a laundry service is provided for only SFr 2.50 ($1.95) per load.

IN SUMMER ONLY

Cité Universitaire de Genève

46 av. Miremont, 1206 Genève. ☎ **022/346-23-55.** 550 rms, none with bath. SFr 39 ($30.25) single; SFr 53 ($41.10) double; SFr 61 ($47.30) studio. Rates apply to students with official ID card; nonstudents pay 20% more. Breakfast SFr 5 ($3.85) extra; lunch or dinner SFr 14 ($10.85) extra. Refundable key deposit of SFr 30 ($23.25). No credit cards. Three-night minimum stay, shorter periods if space is available. Closed Oct–June. Bus 3 from place des 22 Cantons, near the Notre-Dame Church (off Cornavin Station), to Crêtes de Champel (last stop).

This is the largest and best establishment in this category, open to tourists from July to the end of September. Each room has its own sink, single bed, and desk with chair, and most have fantastic views of the Salève. Studios come with small kitchens. Doubles can be arranged by adding another bed to the room. Breakfast, lunch, and dinner are available in the ground-floor cafeteria.

WORTH THE EXTRA MONEY

Hôtel de l'Union

7 rue Jean-Robert-Chouet, 1202 Genève. ☎ **022/733-99-50.** Fax 022/734-97-92. 48 rms, some with bath. SFr 70 ($54.25) single without bath, SFr 97 ($75.19) single with bath; SFr 135 ($104.65) double with bath. Rates include continental breakfast. Additional bed SFr 25 ($19.35) extra. AE, EURO, MC, V. Bus 3, 10, or 15 from Gare de Cornavin to the Porterie stop; it's next to a tiny post office.

On a quiet side street 50 yards from the bus stop, this modern six-story hotel has charm and atmosphere, and guests are treated with respect. It's ideal for solo travelers: There are 33 single rooms in the house. The rooms are furnished with taste and quite spacious; when I was there, Room 26, for example, was occupied by three jolly Australians. Madame Devid is the cultured manager.

A taxi from the train station will cost about SFr 15 ($11.60); if you're coming directly from the airport, either take bus no. 10 or pay about SFr 25 ($19.35) for a taxi.

⑤ Hôtel Excelsior

34 rue Rousseau, 1211 Genève. ☎ **022/732-09-45.** Fax 022/738-43-69. 60 rms, all with bath. TV. SFr 110 ($85.25) single with toilet and shower, SFr 140 ($108.50) single with toilet and tub; SFr 170 ($131.80) double with toilet and shower, SFr 180 ($139.55) double with toilet and tub. Rates include continental breakfast. Additional bed (up to three) SFr 25 ($19.35) extra. AE, DC, V.

This four-star hotel (with elevator), a three-minute walk from Cornavin Station, has rooms equipped with color TV (20 channels). A street-level restaurant serves meals with beverage for SFr 32 ($24.80) and plats du jour for SFr 14 ($10.85). It's the best deal in Geneva in this hotel category. Ask for Mr. Bühlmann—he'll treat you like a VIP.

5 Dining

Situated in the middle of Europe and containing a bit of the culture of France and Italy—and many other nations—Geneva offers a large variety in the way of food. However, many typical Swiss meals can be exceptional bargains.

Most popular is *fondue* in its three varieties: cheese, into which bread is dipped; beef, in which beef is cooked in a pot of hot oil; and Chinese, in which meat and

> ## Getting the Best Deal on Dining
>
> - Try typical Swiss meals that are exceptional bargains: fondue, raclette, and rösti.
> - Take advantage of the *plat du jour* or, if you're very hungry, the *menu complet.*

vegetables are cooked in a broth. One thing you won't find is chocolate fondue. Though they have wonderful chocolate and love fondue, the Swiss leave the combining of the two to chocoholic Americans. Other Swiss specialties include *raclette*, another cheese dish that features melted cheese over potatoes, and *rösti*, a sort of hash-browned potatoes with onions.

To save money, it's a good idea to stick to the *plat du jour*, or, if you're very hungry, the *menu complet*, which consists of the plat du jour with a soup or appetizer and a dessert. Plats du jour are often available only at lunch, so to save money you might want to eat a large meal at noon and something light in the evening.

MEALS FOR LESS THAN SFR 12 ($9.30)
ON THE LEFT BANK

Grand Passage
50 rue du Rhône. ☎ **022/310-66-11.** SFr 7–21 ($5.40–$16.25). AE, DC, EURO, V. Mon–Fri 8:30am–6:30pm, Sat 8am–5pm. Bus 10 to Molard stop. SWISS.

This department-store cafeteria is the place for an inexpensive lunch in the heart of Geneva's shopping district. Don't confuse this self-service restaurant with the slightly more expensive Restaurant Frañais on the second level in the same building. Here you can get tasty plats du jour for about SFr 14 ($10.85). At the store's place du Molard entrance are several booths selling Middle Eastern fast food for about SFr 7.50 ($5.85).

La Zofage
6 rue des Voisins. ☎ **022/329-51-13.** SFr 8–15 ($6.20–$11.65). No credit cards. Daily 6:45am–midnight. Bus 15 to Plainpalais. SWISS.

This is one of the city's least expensive restaurants. Down a few steps from street level, simply furnished La Zofage is frequented mostly by students. The plat du jour costs about SFr 11 ($8.50) and might be chicken Cordon Bleu with vegetables or potatoes or cannelloni au gratin with a salad.

ON THE RIGHT BANK

Although the concentration of budget restaurants is on the left bank, two right-bank establishments offer excellent deals.

Migros
41 rue des Pâquis. ☎ **022/731-79-50.** SFr 8.90–15 ($6.90–$11.60). No credit cards. Mon 8:45am–6:45pm, Tues–Wed and Fri 7:30am–6:45pm, Thurs 7:30am–8pm, Sat 7:30am–5:45pm. SWISS.

Twelve Migros restaurants are scattered all over Geneva. The largest (100 seats) and most centrally located is diagonally across from the Cornavin Station, to your left at the corner of the rue Lausanne and rue des Alpes. It's two escalators down from street level in the Le Cygne shopping center. Plats du jour start at SFr 8.90

($6.90), and each weekday the restaurant serves at least six inexpensive specials, such as paella, boeuf bourgignon with rice pilaf, or spaghetti bolognese.

⑤ Restaurant Manora

4 rue Cornavin. ☎ **022/731-31-46.** SFr 6.50–18 ($5–$13.95). No credit cards. Mon–Sat 7am–9:30pm, Sun 9am–9pm. SWISS.

One of Geneva's best bargains, Manora is a large self-service restaurant that's packed with people day and night. Plats du jour start at an incredibly low SFr 8.50 ($6.60) for risotto and a vegetable. A filling medium-size plate from the outstanding salad bar costs only SFr 7.80 ($6), and even a large plate of entrecôte steak with fries and a vegetable costs only SFr 18 ($13.95). The large selection of cakes and desserts will tempt you.

MEALS FOR LESS THAN SFR 19 ($14.70)
ON THE LEFT BANK

Au Carnivore

30 place du Bourg-de-Four. ☎ **022/311-87-58.** SFr 15–40 ($11.60–$37). AE, EURO, MC, V. Daily 11am–11:30pm. Bus 26 to Molard stop. SWISS.

The bilevel place du Bourg-de-Four is one of the most beautiful squares in the Old City as well as a great dining spot popular with students, businesspeople, and tourists. As its name implies, Au Carnivore specializes in meats. Although many menu items are beyond our budget, a few lower-priced items make excellent deals.

◎ Café Bourg-de-Four

13 place du Bourg-de-Four. ☎ **022/310-01-98.** SFr 14–24 ($10.85–$18.60). Daily 6:30am–10pm. Bus 10 or 26 to Molard stop. SWISS.

This little restaurant is an excellent place to try rösti, a Swiss version of potato pancakes. You can get this typical dish topped with two eggs for SFr 16 ($12.40) or with ham and two eggs for SFr 18 ($13.95). They also have large salads, a plat du jour for both lunch and dinner, and Yugoslav dishes in the evenings.

Café des Antiquaires

35 Grand' Rue. ☎ **022/311-24-16.** SFr 13–20 ($10.05–$15.50). No credit cards. Mon–Fri 8:30am–2:30pm, Sat 8:30am–10pm. Bus 4 or 5 to Plave Neuve stop. SWISS.

Close to the Hôtel-de-Ville (City Hall) is this small, dark café popular with locals, who get their own large reserved table just inside the front door (don't sit down at the table with the black wrought-iron ashtray). The house specialty is cheese fondue for a reasonable SFr 18 ($14.70), and there are also plats du jour for about SFr 17 ($13.15) Be sure to have a glass of kirsch after your meal to help digest all that cheese—the Swiss would hardly dream of having fondue without this sweet apéritif. In fact, they often have their kirsch in the middle of the meal, calling it *coup du milieu.*

Café du Molard

4 place du Molard. ☎ **022/310-35-53.** SFr 12–40 ($9.30–$31). AE, DC, EURO, V. Daily 7am–midnight. Bus 26 to Molard stop. ITALIAN.

If you're craving good old-fashioned Italian cooking, try this restaurant, which features homemade pasta dishes as well as 15 types of pizza. This place is very popular with young Genevans, who often start a night out on the town here. In summer you can eat at a table out on the square. There are 80 seats inside on two levels and 200 outside in summer.

Dent de Lion

14 rue des Eaux-Vives. ☎ **022/700-27-14.** SFr 14–23 ($10.85–$17.80). Mon–Sat noon–10pm. Tram 22 to Eaux-Vives stop. VEGETARIAN.

This small vegetarian restaurant (26 seats) is always packed at lunch with local businesspeople who wedge themselves into the tiny tables. The plat du jour is SFr 12 ($9.30) and the menu complet, which features the same main dish with a soup and a dessert included, is SFr 20 ($15.50). The plat du jour might be tofu Stroganoff served on a large mound of brown rice with a salad on the side. Take-out is available.

La Cave Valaisanne

Chalet Suisse, place du Cirque. ☎ **022/328-12-36.** SFr 13–25 ($10.05–$19.35). AE, CB, DC, EURO, MC, V. Daily 11am–1am. Tram 15 to Cirque stop. SWISS.

At this popular Swiss restaurant the specialty is fondue. They offer numerous varieties of this cook-it-yourself meal, though the basic cheese fondue is the house favorite. Raclette is also available. Their "lunch-affaire"—oeuf mayonnaise or soup, an entree, and ice cream—for SFr 21.50 ($16.65) is a great deal.

Restaurant les Tropiques

11 rue Sautter. ☎ **022/477-096.** SFr 15–35 ($11.60–$17.10). AE, DC, MC, V. Mon–Fri 7:30am–11pm, Sat 8am–11pm, Sun 9am–6pm. Bus 5 to the last stop. INTERNATIONAL.

Off the beaten track near the City Hospital, this bilevel restaurant offers a large choice of food, from pizza *á emporter* (to take away) to entrecôte flambée au whisky served with Créole rice. Plats du jour are served Monday through Friday for SFr 17 ($13.15). Menus for children are priced at SFr 11 ($8.80). You'll find no tourists here, but will always find a seat.

✪ Taverne de la Madeleine

20 rue Toutes-Ames. ☎ **022/310-60-70.** SFr 11–20 ($8.50–$15.50). No credit cards. Mon–Fri 7am–8pm, Sat 9am–3am. Bus 10 to Molard stop. SWISS.

The simple, cozy restaurant is the oldest in Geneva. It's tucked into a small terrace below the Cathédrale de St-Pierre and across from the much smaller Madeleine Church. Though it doesn't serve alcohol, it's popular, especially at lunch. The restaurant offers several daily specials, including two vegetarian meals. Try the succulent little filets of the Lake Geneva perch, with salad and a huge pile of fries, for SFr 20 ($15.50). Large salads with ham, bacon, eggs, and cheese are SFr 17 ($13.15), while the vegetarian plats du jour average SFr 14 to 16 ($10.85 to $12.80).

PICNICKING

Picnics are your best budget-dining bet in Geneva—with plenty of beautiful parks around the city, try to enjoy at least one picnic while you're here. Moreover, shopping for picnic supplies can be one of the highlights of your trip if you pick them up at the **Halle de Rive** on place du Rive on the left bank. This huge marketplace extending through the whole block is filled with all kinds of delicacies. Stroll through the aisles before making your choices. On market days, every Wednesday and Saturday, place du Rive fills with stalls as farmers from all over the region display and sell the most beautiful produce. In the huge Halle de Rive you'll find dozens of stalls selling fresh breads, cheese, hams, and sausages by the 100 grams or even by the slice. Pick up some beautiful, delicious fresh fruit and a bottle of wine, and you're all set.

WORTH THE EXTRA MONEY

✪ Les Armures

1 rue du Puits-St-Pierre. ☎ **022/310-34-42.** SFr 17–32 ($13.15–$24.80). AE, CB, DC, EURO, MC, V. Daily 11:45am–3pm and 6–11:45pm. MiniBus 17 to rue de l'Hôtel de Ville stop. SWISS.

In the heart of the Old City, beside the arsenal, is a favorite of Genevans. This trilevel restaurant is decorated with suits of armor, swords, shields, and lances, like a real armory. Although there's a wide assortment of pizza, costing only SFr 12 to 15 ($9.30 to $11.60), Swiss dishes are the specialty here: fondue, raclette, and viande séchée (air-dried beef) for SFr 18 to 24 ($13.95 to $18.60). Another popular Swiss specialty is choucroute garni, a dish of sauerkraut accompanied by several types of ham and sausage, for SFr 24 ($18.60). Bill Clinton ate here in early 1994 after meeting with Syria's President Assad: He ordered a choucroute dish (sitting in La Salle des Chevaliers, a small dining room one flight up, at the table next to the only window).

6 Attractions

SIGHTSEEING SUGGESTIONS

If You Have 1 Day

For an overview of Geneva, head first to the Old City. Strolling the narrow cobblestone lanes and climbing the stairways of this once-fortified city on a hill provides a glimpse into the city's medieval history. In the afternoon, head over to the right bank for a visit to the Palais des Nations or the Red Cross Museum, two institutions representative of Geneva's international spirit. Save time to stroll through the lakeside parks and view the jet d'eau and the flower clock, both of which are the symbols of Geneva.

If You Have 2 Days

In the morning, visit another of Geneva's fine museums, such as the Watch and Clock Museum or the Museum of Art and History, and view the Reformation Monument below the walls of the Old City. In the afternoon, try to take a lake cruise to see the beautiful surroundings of Geneva.

If You Have 3 Days

Take a trip to the Alps for some stunning vistas or maybe even some skiing. Mont Blanc, the Continent's rooftop, is possible in a long day, or try the Salève, which can be reached much more conveniently. Both are in France, so be sure to take your passport.

If You Have 5 Days

Geneva's lesser-known museums—the Collections Baur and the Voltaire Museum—may entice you. And then there are the parks, such as the Jardin Botanique. Also try to visit the suburb of Carouge, an unusual old enclave within the modern city. Another possibility is an all-day excursion to the Jura Mountains and the Genevan countryside or to Lausanne or Montreux, two beautiful cities on Lake Geneva.

TOP ATTRACTIONS
THE OLD CITY

With its narrow cobblestone streets and tiny stairways, the Old City of Geneva is a great place for a stroll. Pretty fountains dot the streets, and colorful Swiss and Genevan flags wave between the old buildings. You'll find art galleries and inviting bistros, and bibliophiles will appreciate the shops selling rare books. Geneva was for many centuries a walled city, and you can see part of the walls by walking along rue de la Croix Rouge.

Wandering is the best strategy for knowing the Old City, but there are also several sites you may want to visit: Calvin's church, the 12th-century **Cathédrale de St-Pierre;** the 16th-century **Hôtel-de-Ville** (City Hall), where the Red Cross was founded; the **place du Bourg-de-Four,** which was probably the ancient Roman forum and today is filled with sidewalk cafés; the **Maison Tavel,** Geneva's oldest house and now a museum; and the old **City Arsenal,** with its covered patio, wall mosaics, and cannons.

Maison Tavel

6 rue du Puits-St-Pierre. ☎ **022/28-29-00.** Admission free. Tues–Sun 10am–5pm.

This museum occupies Geneva's oldest house. One of its most interesting exhibits is a large model of the city in about 1850. Made of copper and nickel, the model was built by one man as a hobby. There's also an unusual display of ornately carved doors from several old houses.

OUTSIDE THE OLD CITY

For years Geneva and watches have been synonymous, so it's fitting that one of the sights most associated with this city is the ✪ **flower clock** in the Jardin Anglais (English Garden). All year this clock ticks away with as many as 6,300 flowers filling the area within its 50-foot circumference. The Jardin Anglais is on the left bank at the foot of the pont du Mont-Blanc. From this spot you can walk through one park after another for more than a mile along the left bank of Lake Geneva.

No other sight is more representative of Geneva than the ✪ **jet d'eau,** a huge fountain of water that rises 390 feet into the air on the quai des Eaux-Vives. Visible from all over the city, the jet d'eau rises from the Eaux-Vives Jetty on the left bank but is best seen from the right bank with the Alps and the Old City as a backdrop. The fountain pumps 132 gallons of water per second into the air, and at any given moment 7 tons of water is suspended above the surface of Lake Geneva. The

---

❓ Did You Know?

- Geneva is the most expensive city in Europe (and third in the world).
- The area of Geneva is only one-tenth that of Manhattan.
- Some 25,000 people commute from their homes in France to their jobs in Geneva.
- Geneva was the seat of the League of Nations between the wars.
- The first summit meeting between Mikhail Gorbachev and Ronald Reagan took place in Geneva.

Geneva

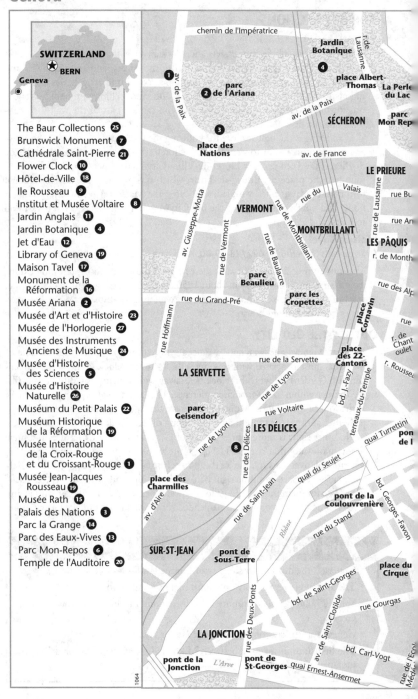

1064

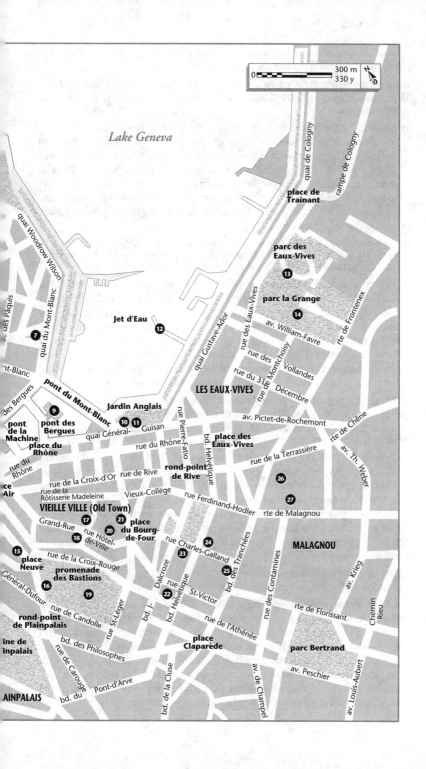

Lake Geneva

0 | 300 m
      330 y

place de
Traînant

quai de Cologny

rampe de Cologny

parc des
Eaux-Vives

13

parc la Grange

14

av. William-Favre

rte de Frontenex

quai Woodrow Wilson

quai du Mont-Blanc

es Pâquis

7

Jet d'Eau **12**

rue des Eaux-Vives

quai Gustave-Ador

rue des Montchoisy

rue de Montchoisy

Vollandes

rue du 31 Décembre

LES EAUX-VIVES

t-Blanc

es Bergues

pont du Mont-Blanc

Jardin Anglais

9

pont
de la
Machine

pont des
Bergues

place du
Rhône

10 11 Guisan

quai Général-

av. Pictet-de-Rochemont

rte de Chêne

av. Th. Weber

rue du Rhône

rue du Rhône

place des
Eaux-Vives

rue Pierre-Fatio

bd. Helvétique

rue de la Terrassière

ce
Air

rue de la Croix-d'Or

rue de Rive

rue de la
Rôtisserie Madeleine

Vieux-Collège

rond-point
de Rive

26

27

rue Ferdinand-Hodler

rte de Malagnou

VIEILLE VILLE (Old Town)

Grand-Rue

17

18

21

rue Hôtel-
de-Ville

20

place
du Bourg-
de-Four

rue Charles-Galland

24

23

MALAGNOU

15

place
Neuve

rue de la Croix-Rouge

Dalcroze

25

bd. des Tranchées

rue des Contamines

av. Krieg

Général-Dufour

16

promenade
des Bastions

19

rue de Candolle

rue St-Léger

rue
St-Victor

22

bd. Helvétique

bd. J-

rue de l'Athénée

rte de Florissant

Chemin
Rieu

rond-point
de Plainpalais

ine de
inpalais

bd. des Philosophes

rue de Carouge

Pont-d'Arve

bd. de la Cluse

place
Claparède

av. de Champel

parc Bertrand

av. Peschier

av. Louis-Aubert

AINPALAIS

bd. du

water jet operates from the beginning of March until the first Sunday of October but may be turned off when the weather is bad.

Musée de l'Horlogerie et de l'Emaillerie (Watch and Clock Museum)

15 route de Malagnou. ☎ **022/736-74-12.** Admission free. Wed–Mon 10am–5pm. Bus 8 to Malagou stop.

A visit to Geneva would not be complete without seeing this museum's extensive collection of clocks, watches, enamel watch cases, and musical snuff boxes. Exquisite clocks and watches that are works of art rather than mere timepieces are displayed on two floors of an old château surrounded by a quiet park. The ticking of timepieces immediately greets you upon entering, and as you wander through the rooms you'll find yourself rushing from one clock to the next as they each mark the hours, half hours, and quarter hours with sonorous chimes and dancing figures.

✪ Palais des Nations

Av. de la Paix. ☎ **022/917-12-34** ext. 4539. Admission SFr 8 ($6.20) adults, SFr 6 ($4.65) students, SFr 3.50 ($2.70) children, free for children 5 and under. Mon–Fri 10am–noon and 2–4pm. Closed Dec 15–31. Bus 8 or F from Gare de Cornavin to the Appia stop.

This massive art deco building was constructed between 1929 and 1936 as the headquarters of the League of Nations, the predecessor of the United Nations, and today it's the U.N.'s European headquarters. Inside are huge conference halls and assembly rooms. An organized tour of the palace is available in several languages, which will give you an idea of the large role Geneva plays in international peacekeeping. Although this is the center of the U.N. in Geneva, there are many more affiliated organizations all over the city. Be sure to call ahead to find out when there'll be a tour in the language you prefer. Identification is required.

✪ Musée International de la Croix-Rouge et du Croissant-Rouge (International Red Cross and Red Crescent Museum)

17 av. de la Paix. ☎ **022/734-52-48.** Admission SFr 8 ($6.20) adults, SFr 4 ($3.10) students. Wed–Mon 10am–5pm. Bus 8 or F from Gare de Cornavin to the Appia stop.

Opened in 1988, the very modern International Red Cross and Red Crescent Museum is directly across the street from the visitors' entrance to the Palais des Nations. The museum chronicles the history of the Red Cross from its founding in Geneva in 1863 by Henri Dunant. The exhibits are minimal while numerous audiovisual presentations, including film footage of wars and natural disasters, give visitors a dramatic look at the work that the Red Cross does. This is one of the most expensive museums in Geneva, but definitely worth the price. Few museums anywhere are as moving.

✪ Monument de la Réformation

Promenade des Bastions. Admission free. Tram 12 to place Neuve.

Located below the highest remaining walls of the Old City, this massive wall more than 330 feet long commemorates one of Geneva's most important historical events—the Protestant Reformation, as preached by John Calvin. Construction of the wall was begun in 1909 on the 400th anniversary of the birth of Calvin, who, though not born in Geneva, lived here for nearly 30 years in the mid-16th century. In the center are four massive statues of Calvin and fellow Reformation leaders Farel, Beza, and Scottish reformer John Knox. On each side of these central figures are smaller statues of important Protestant figures from other nations.

Special & Free Events

Despite its reputation as one of Europe's most expensive cities, Geneva offers a wealth of **free concerts** and other events throughout the year, especially in summer. Along the quays lining both sides of the lake and in the parks extending back from the quays are regular concerts in bandshells and on the lawns. On Saturday nights **concerts and organ recitals** are held at the Cathédrale de St-Pierre in the center of the Old City, and at the much smaller Eglise de St-Germain, only a block away on the Grand' Rue, there are concerts on Sunday and Monday at 6pm in summer. For a listing of events around town, check *Geneva Agenda*, a weekly publication sold at tourist offices and newsstands for SFr 2 ($1.55), or *What's On in Geneva*, published twice a month and handed out free by the Tourist Office and hotels, which lists free events for English-speaking people.

Geneva also has numerous festivals, the most popular of which are the **Fêtes de Genève** during the first week of August and **l'Escalade** in mid-December. The former celebration is marked by revelry and numerous free concerts all over the city. L'Escalade celebrates Geneva's defeat of invading forces in 1602. The festival features hundreds of people in period costumes marching through the streets by torchlight, children in Halloween-like costumes, special meals, and candles. Both events are rather a departure for staid Geneva, and they offer a glimpse of Genevans when they let their hair down.

MORE ATTRACTIONS

Collections Baur

8 rue Munier-Romilly. ☎ **022/346-17-29.** Admission SFr 5 ($3.85) adults, SFr 2.50 ($1.95) students. Tues–Sun 2–6pm. Bus 8 to Florissant.

In a former private home near the Museum of Art and History you'll find this excellent collection of Asian art and ceramics. The collection displays more than 1,000 years of Chinese ceramics as well as exhibiting beautiful antique jade pieces. Watch for the large jade vase with its high-relief images. Japanese swords, lacquer boxes, netsuke, and objects for tea ceremonies are also on display.

Eglise Russe (Russian Church)

3 rue Rodolphe-Toepffer. Admission SFr 1 (75¢). Tues–Sun 9am–noon. Bus 3 to Athénée stop.

Directly across from the Museum of Ancient Musical Instruments is this little jewel-box church. With its gold domes and spires, the church seems oddly out of place in Geneva. It's especially beautiful at night, when lights illuminate the gold domes.

Institut et Musée Voltaire

25 rue des Délices. ☎ **022/344-71-33.** Admission free. Mon–Fri 2–5pm. Bus 7 to Délices or 6 to Prairie.

From 1755 to 1765, French philosopher Voltaire lived in Geneva and his home is now a museum. Seven rooms display original documents relating to Voltaire's life, first editions of his writings, paintings, prints, sculptures, and objects from the 18th century. One of the highlights is a life-size statue of the great philosopher, dressed in a suit he once owned and sitting at his former desk.

Musée d'Art et d'Histoire
2 rue Charles-Galland (three blocks from place du Bourg-de-Four in the Old City). ☎ **022/ 311-43-40.** Admission free. Tues–Sun 10am–5pm. Bus 3 to Athénée stop.

Geneva's largest museum houses a wide variety of art and antiquities. Exhibits range from Egyptian mummies to entire rooms from Swiss châteaux, complete with paneling, antique heating systems, furniture, and the art that was in the rooms when the museum acquired them. Wandering from one lavish room to the next provides an excellent glimpse of the château lifestyle. Another large hall contains all manner of arms and armor from past centuries, including one of the folding ladders used by the Savoyards to scale the walls of the city when they attacked Geneva in 1602. Upstairs in the galleries, several rooms are devoted to turn-of-the-century Swiss artist Ferdinand Hodler. His Alpine landscapes in shades of lavender and blue are especially beautiful.

Musée Historique de la Réformation et Musée Jean-Jacques Rousseau
In the University Library, promenade des Bastions. ☎ **022/320-82-66.** Admission free. Mon–Fri 9am–noon and 2–5pm, Sat 9am–noon. Tram 12 to place Neuve; the museum is inside the park on the right and directly across from the Reformation Museum.

If you're interested in the philosopher Rousseau and can read French, you'll find this two-room museum quite interesting. Documents pertaining to the Reformation, portraits of important figures, and a case filled with Rousseau busts are among the items on display. In an adjoining room you'll also see a folio from a 2nd-century manuscript of Homer's *Iliad.* The museum is on the ground floor of the library, straight ahead as you enter. If the doors are locked during normal hours, ask at the desk to be let in.

Site Archéologique de St-Pierre
At the Cathédrale de St-Pierre. ☎ **022/738-56-50.** Admission SFr 5 ($3.85) adults, SFr 3 ($2.30) children. Tues–Sun 10am–1pm and 2–6pm. MiniBus 17 to rue de l'Hôtel de Ville stop.

Right in the center of Geneva's Old City you'll find one of Europe's largest archeological sites. The cathedral itself dates only from 1160, but during a renovation project evidence was unearthed of a church on this site as long ago as the 5th century. Visitors can now walk through the ages beneath the cathedral and an adjacent chapel and street. Layer upon layer of history has been exposed and left as if the archeologists were still digging. Old wells and a large mosaic floor are evidence of Roman occupation of the site. Located beneath the cathedral, the archeological site has its own entrance, to the right side of the cathedral's main steps.

CAROUGE
Once a separate village on the far side of the narrow Arve River, Carouge was incorporated into the city of Geneva in the early 19th century. However, despite the presence of modern buildings on all sides, Carouge still manages to maintain the feel of a small village much removed from the city. Of particular interest is the **Italian architecture** here, reminiscent of northern Italy, which ruled Carouge in the 18th century. Most of the village's old buildings have been restored and now contain shops, boutiques, restaurants, and discos.

Wednesday and Saturday, Carouge's **market days,** are an especially fun time to visit. Farmers sell their produce under the curiously trimmed plane trees on place du Marché, in the center of which is a small fountain.

You may also want to visit the **Museum of Carouge,** 2 place de Sardaigne (☎ **022/342-33-83**), which contains artifacts pertaining to the history of the village as well as temporary exhibits by local artists. It's open Tuesday through Sunday from 2 to 6pm, and admission is free.

You can reach the Carouge district by taking tram no. 12 from Bel Air (the trip takes only 12 minutes). Be sure to leave at the Marché stop, a few stops after crossing the river l'Arve bridge.

PARKS & GARDENS

The founders of the city of Geneva are to be congratulated for their forethought in preserving the banks of Lake Geneva. Stretching along both banks are several miles of promenades connected to several parks. Many of these parks have been created from the grounds of ancient châteaux, while others surround the modern buildings of the international organizations headquartered here.

ON THE RIGHT BANK   Formerly the grounds of a château, the ✪ **Parc de l'Ariana** surrounds the Palais des Nations on the right bank. When the last owner of the château died without an heir, he donated the grounds to the city to be used as a park, on the condition that it be open to the public forever. Today you can stroll beneath centuries-old cypress and cedar trees and enjoy the peace and quiet surrounding the United Nations' European headquarters.

Directly adjacent to this park is the **Jardin Botanique,** where thousands of trees, shrubs, and flowers from all over the world are on display.

ON THE LEFT BANK   On the left bank, you can walk along quai Gustave-Ador past the jet d'eau and on to the **Parc la Grange** and the adjacent **Parc des Eaux-Vives.** Here you'll find a large rose garden and a beautiful 18th-century château, which is now a popular and expensive restaurant. If it's a warm day and your stroll through the parks has you longing for a dip in the cool waters of the lake, continue another 100 yards or so beyond the Parc des Eaux-Vives to **Genève-Plage,** Geneva's favorite beach.

SPECIAL-INTEREST SIGHTSEEING

John Calvin, who settled in Geneva in 1536, changed the city forever when he split from the Roman Catholic church and devoted himself to the Reformation. For centuries afterward, Geneva was forced to defend itself against the frequent attacks of its Roman Catholic neighbors, who were bent on returning Geneva to the fold. Anyone interested in Calvin's Geneva can arrange for a special guided tour with the Geneva Tourist Office. The tour visits the Calvin Auditorium where he preached, the Reformation Wall, and other sites associated with this religious reformer.

People interested in philosophy and literature will want to visit two museums dedicated to Geneva's other famous residents, **Jean-Jacques Rousseau and Voltaire.** See "More Attractions," above, for more about these small museums.

The Argentine writer **Jorge Luís Borges** lived in Geneva as a child and returned here in his mid-80s. He died in 1986 and is buried in the left bank's Cimetière de Plainpalais.

WALKING TOURS

Geneva is divided into two distinct sections—the old and the new. The Old City preserves Geneva's medieval history with its narrow streets and houses dating from the 13th century. Because buses are not allowed in the Old City, it's necessary to get out and walk.

The **Geneva Tourist Office** in Cornavin Station offers a recorded cassette tour that allows you to hear the history of the Old City as you explore at your own pace. In about 2^1/$_2$ hours the tour covers 2,000 years of Genevan history and provides information on 26 points of interest. For SFr 10 ($7.75) you'll be provided with the tape and a map of the Old City. If you don't have your own tape player, you can use one of the tourist office's, but you'll have to present your passport and leave a SFr-50 ($38.75) refundable deposit.

An alternative to this self-guided tour is the two-hour guided tour offered by the tourist office on Monday, Wednesday, and Friday at 5pm from June to September. The cost of this tour is SFr 10 ($7.75) for adults, SFr 7 ($5.40) for students, and SFr 4 ($3.10) for children 11 and under. In addition to visiting the major sites in the Old City, this tour includes a visit to a private collection of 18th-century furniture and Chinese cloisonné and ends with a sampling of Genevan wines. The tour starts in front of the Town Hall at 2 rue de l'Hôtel-de-Ville.

In addition to these two tours, there are specialized walking tours of the Old City focusing on different periods of history. Contact the Geneva Tourist Office Information Desk in Cornavin Station for details.

BUS TOURS

Keytours, 7 rue des Alpes (☎ **022/731-41-40**), on the right bank, offers a two-hour bus tour pointing out the highlights of both the left and the right banks of Geneva daily at 10am and 2pm from May to October. From November to April the tour runs only once a day, at 2pm, and in spring and fall, twice a day. The tour quickly shows you the highlights of Geneva and includes a brief walk through the Old City. You'll see the shores of the lake with their numerous parks, the flower clock, the jet d'eau (if you visit between March and October), the modern buildings of Geneva's international organizations, monuments, and commercial centers. The cost of the tour is SFr 27 ($20.93) for adults and SFr 14 ($10.85) for children.

7 Shopping

Watches, knives, cheese, and chocolate are among your best buys in Geneva. These are the products for which Switzerland is famous, and you'll find them here in abundance. Check prices carefully, though: Unfortunately, many Swiss watches are currently cheaper in the United States than in Switzerland. Swiss army knives are still a good deal, and as for chocolate—well, Swiss chocolate is incomparable and just isn't the same when you buy it in another country, so indulge yourself while you're here.

The **Chocolatier du Rhône,** 3 rue de la Confédération, with its own tiny café, sells what many consider the best chocolate in the world. A pound of this delectable product costs around SFr 50 ($38.75), but you don't have to buy such a large quantity. Pick and choose a few of your favorites. Make sure you try the prize-winning mocca glacé. A small assortment will cost less than SFr 18 ($13.95).

Geneva's left-bank shopping area is along the exclusive **rue du Rhône** and adjacent streets. Here you'll find shop after shop of designer fashions and expensive watches. Along the winding streets of the **Old City,** you'll find antiques stores and galleries.

For Swiss army knives and watches (if the dollar strengthens), stroll along the pedestrians-only **rue du Mont-Blanc** on the right bank. Shop window after shop window is filled with an endless assortment of watches, knives, and other souvenirs, all at comparable prices.

Note: Before you head out for a day of shopping, remember that shops in Geneva don't open until 1pm on Monday and many of the smaller shops close for lunch between noon and 2pm.

MARKETS   A rare experience is a visit to a Swiss **street market** offering the most perfect produce you'll ever see. You'll find these bustling and beautiful markets near the Cours de Rive on Wednesday and Saturday and in Carouge on place du Marché on Saturday.

Wednesday and Saturday are the days for Geneva's large and busy **flea market,** located on place de Plainpalais. In summer a **book market** is held on place de la Madeleine, at the edge of the Old City below the Cathédrale de St-Pierre. In winter you're likely to find crafts from all over the world on this square. If you're looking for **local crafts,** you'll find them for sale on rue du Rhône near place du Molard on Thursday.

8 Geneva After Dark

Geneva is not known for its nightlife. Few plays are performed in English, and there's little in the way of live popular music. There are, however, regular ballet, opera, and classical-music performances, as you'd expect from such a sophisticated city. The tourist office's monthly "List of Events" has thorough listings.

THE PERFORMING ARTS
CLASSICAL MUSIC, OPERA & BALLET

From September to July, opera and ballet performances are given at the **Grand-Théâtre de Genève,** place Neuve (☎ **022/311-23-11**). The building, which opened in 1879, was modeled on Paris's Opéra Garnier. Destroyed by fire in 1951, it was rebuilt in the same style with a moderized interior. Tickets for opera are SFr 20 to 124 ($15.50 to $96.10), and those for ballet are SFr 20 to 99 ($15.50 to $76.75).

Victoria Hall, 14 rue du Général-Dufour (☎ **022/328-81-21**), is Geneva's main venue for classical-music performances. Tickets cost SFr 20 to 75 ($15.50 to $58.15).

FOLK, ROCK & JAZZ

For free live jazz, try **Halles de l'Ile,** place de l'Ile (☎ **022/311-52-21**), a sophisticated restaurant on an island in the middle of the Rhône River. The building, formerly a marketplace, features a splendid location with large windows opening onto the rushing blue-green waters of the river. Open Monday through Saturday from 8pm to midnight.

Au Chat Noir, 13 rue Vautier, Carouges (☎ **022/343-49-93**), offering hot jazz, rock, soul, and blues nightly, is definitely the *in* place to be. It's open daily from 9pm to 4am. It can be reached by tram no. 12 from Bel Air in 12 minutes (leave at the first stop after crossing the river l'Arve). The bar is about 100 yards off place du Marché. Reservations are recommended on weekends.

If you come on a weekend and it's booked up, you can go across the street to **Bistrobar,** 14 rue Vautier, open daily from 7am to 1am.

FILMS

Read the listings carefully before you go to the movies, which are shown both dubbed into French and in the original language with French subtitles. If the original language of the film you are attending happens to be German and you speak neither German nor French, you'll be out of luck. American and English films are usually shown with subtitles at 6:45 and 10pm. Check the listings in *Geneva This Week*. Subtitled films carry the notation "V.o.s.-tit" ("Version originale, sous-titres"). Tickets cost SFr 15 ($11.60).

BARS & DISCOS

Your best option for bars and discos is the area known as **Carouge** (take tram no. 12). On rue Vautier just off place du Marché you'll find half a dozen or more bars and discos that feature live or recorded rock music. Admission is generally free or only a few francs. Drink prices vary, generally SFr 4.80 to 16 ($3.70 to $12.40), depending on the night's entertainment.

9   Easy Excursions

Geneva is surrounded by water and mountains, and if you're visiting for more than a day, try to make an excursion to the Alps or cruise around Lake Geneva on one of the many excursion boats that ply its blue-green waters every summer. If you're in town for three days or more, try to do both a mountain trip and a lake trip.

THE SALEVE   Standing on Geneva's right bank gazing across at the Old City on the left bank, you can't help but be awed by the massive wall of rock towering at the city's back. This is the Salève, which rises nearly 4,500 feet and commands a spectacular view of Geneva, the lake, the Rhône River, and miles of French and Swiss countryside. To the south the panorama of the Alps with Mont-Blanc rising above the surrounding peaks, and to the north are the Jura Mountains. The peak of the Salève is reached by cable car from the base of the mountain in only three minutes. At the top is a modern observatory, restaurant, and walking and cross-country ski trails. Because the Salève is across the French border, you'll need to bring your passport. However, it's not necessary to change any money for this excursion; they'll accept your Swiss francs at the cable-car ticket window. The round-trip fare is SFr 19 ($12.95) for adults and SFr 12 ($9.30) for children and senior citizens.

To reach the Salève, take bus no. 8 from Geneva to the last stop at the town of Veyrier, which is still on the Swiss side of the border. When you get off the bus, you'll see the border station. Walk through and then follow the signs marked TELEPHERIQUE. It's less than a 10-minute walk.

CHAMONIX & MONT-BLANC   If the Salève whets your appetite for more mountains, a trip into the heart of the French Alps may be just the thing you need. The ski resort of Chamonix, at 3,370 feet, sits at the foot of the Mont-Blanc massif, which rises to 15,625 feet. Surrounding Chamonix are dozens of lesser peaks and glaciers. Although most popular in winter, when skiers flock to the many slopes, this area is beautiful year round. In summer flowers fill the green meadows and tiny Alpine lakes sparkle in the sunlight. But whether you go in summer or winter, pick a sunny day for your visit, for it is under clear skies that you can most fully appreciate the views of the surrounding peaks.

Trains from Geneva to Chamonix, 62 miles south, leave not from Cornavin Station but from the Eaux-Vives Station on the left bank. Tram no. 12 stops in front of this station, but to take this tram you must be on the left bank, since it doesn't cross the river. There's no direct train to Chamonix from Geneva; it's necessary to change trains twice. Your best trains to take for a day in the mountains leave Geneva at 6:40am, 8:26am, 2:43pm, and 5:35pm. The entire journey takes about $2^1/2$ hours; the round-trip fare is SFr 45 ($34.90) in second class, SFr 67 ($51.95) in first class.

From Chamonix, there are three possible ascents out of the valley, all of which present unsurpassed views of peaks and glaciers. The longest and most expensive of these is the ascent by cable car to **L'Aiguille du Midi** at 12,500 feet. The trip is in two stages and costs 180 French francs ($34.60) round-trip, or you can choose to stop at the halfway point, **Plan de l'Aiguille** (7,500 feet), for a round-trip fare of only 70 French francs ($13.45). The last ascent out of the valley is to the resort of **Montenvers** overlooking the Mer de Glâce glacier, which is nearly $4^1/2$ miles long and averages 3,900 feet in width. This is done by electric rack railway. By far the best view and value is from **Le Brevent,** with its stunning panorama of Mont-Blanc, Chamonix nestled in the valley below, and the finger-like glaciers that reach down from the peaks.

Expensive all-day tours to Chamonix are offered from Geneva by **Keytours,** 7 rue des Alpes (☎ **022/731-41-40**), with the cost depending on which ascent you make out of the valley. The excursion for SFr 130 ($100.75), lunch included, offers a trip either to Le Brevent or to La Mer de Glâce. For SFr 153 ($118.60), lunch included, you will climb to L'Aiguille du Midi, and for SFr 182 ($141.10) you can continue past L'Aiguille du Midi, again by cable car, to Helbronner Point on the French-Italian border. This is an additional $3^1/4$-mile trip across snowfields and glaciers. Whether you go by train or escorted motorcoach, don't forget to take your passport—Chamonix is in France.

If you want to stay in Chamonix, try the **Hôtel Chamonix,** 58 place de l'Eglise (☎ **50-53-11-07** in France). A single or double room costs 300F to 360F ($57.70 to $69.25); breakfast is 30F ($5.75) extra. This Alpine town at the foot of Mont Blanc has numerous restaurants and self-service eateries, so no recommendations are necessary. The average price for a meal, with wine, is 120F ($23.10).

LAKE CRUISES   Lake Geneva is a 45-mile-long crescent-shaped body of water, the entire north shore and either end of which are in Switzerland, while the south shore is in France. All along both shores are small villages, châteaux, fields, farms, and vineyards, and framing it all are the ever-present mountains, both the Alps and the Juras. There are numerous tours of the lake, ranging from a short 40-minute trip in a little mouette (water bus) to all-day cruises of the entire lake on sleek yachts. The 40-minute trip leaves from the dock near the flower clock on the left bank and costs SFr 9 ($6.95). The castle of Baron M. de Rothschild; the villa of Empress Joséphine; and Diodati Villa, where Lord Byron stayed in 1816, are some of the sights pointed out on this brief cruise. A two-hour cruise costing SFr 23.50 ($18.20) passes more beautiful villas and châteaux and travels as far as the start of the French portion of the lake's south shore. These cruises leave from quai du Mont-Blanc on the right bank at 10:15am and 3pm from March to November. The all-day cruise costs SFr 55 ($42.60) and leaves from the quai du Mont-Blanc at 9:15am and returns at 10:50pm. This cruise is available daily between late May and late September.

You might want to stay on the lake in Lausanne or Montreux, in good hotels located not more than a five-minute walk from the train station.

In Lausanne, try the **Hôtel du Port,** 4 place du Fort (☎ **021/616-49-30**), a small hotel with only 17 beds. Single rooms cost SFr 54 to 107 ($41.60 to $82.40) and doubles are SFr 99 to 130 ($76.75 to $100.75), breakfast included. An á la carte meal is served for SFr 20 ($15.50). The **Restaurant Mirabeau,** 31 av. de la Gare (☎ **021/320-62-31**), offers filling meals for SFr 20.50 to 27.50 ($15.90 to $21.30). It has 50 seats and is open daily from 11:30am to 2pm and 6:30pm to midnight.

In Montreux, on the lake shore 52 miles east of Geneva, the **Hôtel Elite,** 25 av. du Casino (☎ **021/963-67-33;** fax 021/963-46-94), has 40 beds. Singles are SFr 55 ($42.65) and doubles run SFr 110 to 125 ($85.25 to $96.90). The **Buffet de la Gare,** 22 rue de la Gare (☎ **021/963-12-31**), is a large restaurant in the train station building, serving excellent meals for SFr 15 to 25 ($11.60 to $19.35). It's open daily from 6am to midnight.

Lisbon 15

by Herbert Bailey Livesey

Lisbon invites comparisons with other places, if only because few visitors have a clear image of the city before they first see it. There are points of reference with San Francisco, for it's at the edge of an ocean on the western coast of its continent, built on seven hills traversed by antique trams, with a red-orange suspension bridge spanning its harbor. It's even subject to devastating earthquakes. However, that only skims reality, for despite its location on the Atlantic, Lisbon (pop. 1.5 million) has a pronounced Mediterranean mien. Pastel houses with orange roofs and facades layered with abstract and pictographic tiles tumble down its steep slopes, and the mosaic sidewalks are comprised of irregular chunks of black and white stone.

And there's more: It's not an entirely Latin Mediterranean that Lisbon evokes. The Arabs were here for centuries, and the constricted, twisting streets of the Alfama district hint of Moroccan souks. They and the Crusaders left a fortress that broods from the crest of the highest hill. In addition, the dissolution of the last of Portugal's African colonies in the 1970s and the ensuing return of tens of thousands of overseas citizens ensured that this swiftly became one of the most richly variegated multiethnic, multiracial capitals in Europe.

Legend has it that Ulysses founded Lisbon, but recorded history points to a Roman origin in the 3rd century B.C. In the centuries since, the former Roman city of Olisipo passed through the hands of the Vandals, Visigoths, and Moors en route to becoming the nation's capital in 1260. Echoed in the city's monuments and museums is the 16th-century imperial majesty of a nation whose empire once stretched across many seas and was more than 100 times its own size.

After the devastating 1755 earthquake, which leveled much of the city, Lisbon arose anew under the supervision of the Marquês de Pombal, whose enlightened urban planning continues to serve the city well. The Baixa is an orderly grid of shopping streets sloping gently up from the harbor to the broad, tree-lined avenida da Liberdade. Flanking sidewalk cafés invite lingering, and throughout the city abundant parks and gardens and lively plazas ward off monotony. After a recent fire devastated parts of Baixa and

What's Special About Lisbon

Architectural Highlights
- Mosteiro dos Jerónimos (Jerónimos Monastery), a fine example of the 16th-century Manueline architectural style inspired by Portugal's maritime prowess and vast colonial empire.

Monuments
- Padraño dos Descobrimentos (Monument of the Discoveries), an impressive tribute to Portugal's imperial past coupled with a sidewalk depiction summarizing the past.

Museums
- Museu da Fundaçaño Calouste Gulbenkian (Gulbenkian Foundation Museum), a gem of a museum custom-designed to display its eclectic collection.

Vistas
- From St. George's Castle.
- From the top of the Santa Justa Elevator.
- From Saño Pedro de Alcantara park.

Engineering Highlights
- Ponte 25 de Abril, one of the world's longest single-span suspension bridges.

Neighborhoods
- Strolling through the Alfama's maze of narrow streets for an intimate glimpse of daily Lisbon life.

After Dark
- *Fado,* Portugal's traditional song form, steeped in the full range of human emotion.

Great Towns & Villages
- Sintra, a mountain retreat stocked with romantic palaces and beautiful gardens.

Transportation
- The colorful trams, especially no. 28, which traverses Lisbon's oldest neighborhoods.

---

adjoining Chiado, the remaining ruins revealed that parts of the present city were built atop older structures. Fortunately, most of the damage has been repaired and Pombal's vision retained.

The pace has picked up in Lisbon since Portugal's entry into the European Union (formerly the Common Market). Shops are becoming increasingly chic, restaurants more sophisticated, nightlife hours longer, and, inevitably, prices higher. The dreaded cellular phone and belt beeper are appearing in greater numbers, even though Portugal remains one of the EU's poorer countries. Lisbon's turn at European Cultural Capital is over, and now the city is sprucing up for EXPO '98. Construction is extensive, buildings are getting facelifts, and a new subway line is being urgently dug from Dom Felipe IV plaza down to the harbor. Excavations persistently uncover relics from the Roman, Moorish, and medieval periods, which slows progess.

Still, the contours of the city are changing. Lisbon is percolating, on the move. Yet culture and vestiges of 19th-century technology slow it down, with two-hour lunches, creaking trolleys and funiculars, and traffic-snarling narrow streets. And its spirit—open, companionable, yet exotic and faintly alien—remains the same.

1 Lisbon Deals & Discounts

BUDGET BESTS   Inexpensive eating places abound, many self-described as *cervejarias* (beer halls) or *adegas* (taverns). In some budget restaurants, younger children can eat from their parents' plates and half portions are available. Where portions are large—and they nearly always are—sharing is sometimes permitted. In establishments where diners can choose to sit or stand, standing is always cheaper.

Because Lisbon's touristic nucleus is so compact, most things can be seen and done on foot or for the modest price of a subway or bus ticket.

SPECIAL DISCOUNTS   Most museums are free on Sunday morning, and some are free on Wednesday morning.

For Students   Lisbon's youth and student travel agency, **Tagus Turismo Juvenil,** praça de Londres 9b, between the Alameda and Areeiro metro stops (☎ **01/849-15-31**), offers special rates on flights, car rentals, and sightseeing tours in Portugal and abroad. It's open Monday through Friday from 10am to 1pm and 2:30 to 5:30pm.

Some museums offer free admission to students and senior citizens, so bring along the appropriate ID.

WORTH THE EXTRA MONEY   An evening at a *fado* club (with dinner and entertainment) may run 6,500 Esc ($41.95) per person, but every visitor should experience this Portuguese song form at least once. A dinner reservation guarantees you a seat, but drop in around 11pm just for drinks and pay a minimum, typically 1,500 to 2,500 Esc ($9.70 to $16.15). The music usually goes on until at least 3am.

2 Pretrip Preparations

REQUIRED DOCUMENTS   Citizens of the United States, Canada, the United Kingdom, Australia, and New Zealand require only a valid passport.

TIMING YOUR TRIP   July and August are the peak tourist months, as well as the hottest (though nights are usually cool). Spring and fall are ideal, as the city is often at its greenest.

Lisbon's Average Daytime Temperature & Rainfall

	Jan	Feb	Mar	Apr	May	June	July	Aug	Sept	Oct	Nov	Dec
Temp. (°F)	57	59	63	67	71	77	81	82	79	72	63	58
Rainfall "	4.3	3.0	4.2	2.1	1.7	0.6	0.1	0.2	1.3	2.4	3.7	4.1

Special Events   On June 12 and 13 Lisbon celebrates the **Feast Day of St. Anthony** with *marchas* (strolling groups of singers and musicians). On the evening of June 12 revelers parade in costume along avenida da Liberdade. Festivities include dances, bonfires, and general merriment in the taverns until dawn, especially in the Alfama district. Festivities on **June 24 and 29** in the Alfama honor Lisbon's other popular saints—John, Peter, and Paul.

In July, Sintra holds its annual **music festival.** In August, Estoril does likewise. In the fall, Cascais holds an annual **jazz festival.** Check local newspapers for details.

3 Lisbon Specifics

ARRIVING

FROM THE AIRPORT   From **Portela Airport** to the heart of town is only about 6 miles. Expect to pay about 2,400 Esc ($15.50) for a taxi. The *Linha Verde* (Green Line, no. 90) bus costs 250 Esc ($1.60) and runs from the airport to Santa Apolónia Station every 15 minutes from 7:30am to 10:30pm.

FROM THE TRAIN STATION   From Madrid or Paris, arrivals are at **Santa Apolónia Station,** Lisbon's major terminal, located by the river near the Alfama.

In addition to Santa Apolónia, which serves Lisbon's northern environs, there are three other stations: **Rossio** (with trains to Sintra), **Cais do Sodre** (with trains to the Estoril Coast), and **Sul e Sueste** (with trains to the Algarve).

VISITOR INFORMATION

The main **Portuguese Tourist Office,** at Palácio Foz, praça dos Restauradores (☎ **01/346-33-14** or 342-52-31), is the best source of information. It's open Monday through Saturday from 9am to 8pm and Sunday from 10am to 6pm.

For a listing of useful information, addresses, phone numbers, and events, pick up *What's On in Lisbon* or *Your Companion in Portugal* at the tourist office or any major hotel. The best sources for up-to-the-minute information on entertainment around town are the weekly magazine *Sete* and the newpapers *Diário de Noticias, Correio da Manhañ,* and *Público.* A sometimes useful source is the English-language weekly, *Anglo-Portuguese News.*

CITY LAYOUT

The heart of the city extends some 2 miles from **praça do Comércio** to **praça do Marquês de Pombal** (named after the prime minister who rebuilt the town after the 1755 earthquake). Between praça do Comércio and **Rossio Square** is the **Baixa,** a grid of small shopping streets. Connecting Rossio Square to praça do Marquês de Pombal is **avenida da Liberdade,** Lisbon's somewhat-tattered rendition of the Champs-Elysées.

If you look at Lisbon from the waterfront, to your right is the **Alfama,** crowned by the Castelo Saño Jorge (St. George's Castle). To the left is the **Bairro Alto,** the old inner-city business district that still houses most of the newspaper publishers and fado clubs and has recently become home to chic restaurants, bars, and clubs.

NEIGHBORHOODS   The **Baixa** (literally "Lower Town"), stretching from the river to Rossio Square (site of the Inquisition's auto-da-fés), is a bustling enclave of shops. Such streets as rua do Ouro (Street of Gold) and rua da Prata (Street of Silver) have now diversified their consumer offerings. Rua Augusta and rua de Santa Justa are pedestrian streets lined with boutiques and shops selling leather goods, real and faux jewelry, assorted handcrafts, and more.

The shopping continues along rua do Carmo, rua Garrett, and largo do Chiado, which link the Baixa with the **Bairro Alto** (literally "Upper Town"). Many years ago its steep, claustrophobic streets harbored unsavory characters, but today the Bairro Alto has been pacified to a degree by continuing gentrification.

What Things Cost in Lisbon	U.S. $
Taxi from the airport to Rossio Square	15.50
Metro from Rotunda to Rossio	.42
Local telephone call	.12
Double room at the Hotel da Lapa (deluxe)	290.00
Double room at the Hotel Metropole (moderate)	119.35
Double room at the Pensaño Beira Minho (budget)	29.70
Continental breakfast	2.65
Lunch for one, without wine, at Cervejaria Trindade (moderate)	12.00
Lunch for one, without wine, at Pastelaria Suiça (budget)	6.25
Dinner for one, without wine, at Tágide (deluxe)	28.00
Dinner for one, without wine, at Casanostra (moderate)	13.55
Dinner for one, without wine, at Cubata (budget)	9.55
Large glass of beer	.90–1.60
Coca-Cola in a restaurant	.95–1.20
Cup of coffee	1.25
Roll of ASA 100 color film, 24 exposures	3.90
Admission to Mosteiro dos Jerónimos	2.95
Movie ticket	2.60–3.15
Theater ticket	17.00–21.15

To the north of both the Baixa and the Bairro Alto extends the broad **avenida da Liberdade,** where banks, airline offices, and tour operators rub elbows with cheesy souvenir shops, first-run cinemas, and occasional sidewalk cafés, some of which have space on the central pedestrian promenade.

Rising steep and narrow to the walls of St. George's Castle is the **Alfama,** the ancient Arab quarter. Having miraculously escaped the devastation of the 1755 earthquake, its medieval aspect remains intact, making it one of Lisbon's most colorful neighborhoods. Except for a handful of churches and museums and a smattering of shops and restaurants catering to tourists, this is largely a working-class neighborhood draped with drooping lines of laundry.

Four miles from praça do Comércio is **Belém** (Bethlehem), a Lisbon district that's taking on a separate urban identity of its own. The focal point of Portugal's 16th-century maritime activities, Belém offers several museums and monuments, repositories of folk arts and royal coaches, as well as commemorations of the achievements of Portugal's colonial glories. Here, too, is the eastern end of Europe's longest single-span suspension bridge, the Ponte 25 de Abril.

GETTING AROUND

Taxis are inexpensive enough that even budgeteers may choose to forgo the efficient public transport system at least part of the time.

BY SUBWAY The subway system, shaped like a bent paper clip, is Europe's cheapest—45 Esc (29¢) per ticket when purchased 10 at a time for 450 Esc or

The Portuguese Escudo

For American Readers   At this writing $1 = approximately 155 Esc (or 1 Esc = 0.65¢), and this was the rate of exchange used to calculate the dollar values given in this chapter (rounded to the nearest nickel).

For British Readers   At this writing £1 = approximately 240 Esc (or 1 Esc = 0.41p), and this was the rate of exchange used to calculate the pound values in the table below.

Note: The rates given here fluctuate from time to time and may not be the same when you travel to Portugal. Therefore this table should be used only as a guide:

Esc	U.S.$	U.K.£	Esc	U.S.$	U.K.£
5	.03	.02	1,500	9.68	6.25
10	.06	.04	2,000	12.90	8.33
15	.10	.06	2,500	16.13	10.42
20	.13	.08	3,000	19.35	12.50
25	.16	.10	4,000	25.81	16.67
50	.32	.21	5,000	32.26	20.83
75	.48	.31	6,000	38.71	25.00
100	.65	.42	7,000	45.16	29.17
150	.97	.63	8,000	51.61	33.33
200	1.29	.83	9,000	58.06	37.50
250	1.61	1.04	10,000	64.52	41.67
500	3.23	2.08	12,500	80.65	52.08
1,000	6.45	4.17	15,000	96.77	62.50

55 Esc (35¢) from the vending machine, or 65 Esc (42¢) from the ticket office. It operates daily from 6:30am to 1am.

BY BUS & TRAM   Far more extensive are the bus and tram networks. A module of 10 tickets costs 685 Esc ($4.40) at booths located in most of the major squares (such as Rossio and Figueira) and by the Santa Justa Elevator. Route maps are usually available there as well. Tickets purchased on the bus or tram cost 140 Esc (90¢). Buses and trams run daily from 6am to midnight.

SANTA JUSTA ELEVATOR & FUNICULAR CARS   Near Rossio Square, the **Santa Justa Elevador** links rua do Ouro with praça do Carmo. The fare is 150 Esc (95¢), and hours of operation are Monday through Saturday from 7am to 11pm and Sunday from 9am to 11pm.

Lisbon's three **funicular cars** are the Gloria, from praça dos Restauradores to rua Saño Pedro de Alcantara; the Lavra, from the east side of avenida da Liberdade to campo Martires da Pátria; and the Bica, from calçada do Combro to rua da Boavista. The fare is also 150 Esc (95¢). An unlimited one-day ticket costs 370 Esc ($2.40), and a three-day ticket costs 860 Esc ($5.55). Operating hours are similar to those for the Santa Justa elevator.

SPECIAL TOURIST TICKETS   **Seven-day tickets** valid for all city buses, trams, subways, the Santa Justa Elevator, and the funicular cars cost 1,700 Esc ($10.95). They're sold at the Santa Justa Elevator daily from 8am to 8pm.

Travelers staying in Lisbon a month or more can purchase one of the **Social Passes (*Passes Sociais*),** valid for one month on all forms of public transportation. Adult passes cost 150 Esc (95¢), plus 3,725 to 6,950 Esc ($24.05 to $44.85) per month, and offer various complex options. Social Passes can be purchased at the foot of the Santa Justa Elevator and at ferry, tram, bus, and railroad terminals.

BY TAXI   Cabs, in beige or green and black, can be hailed in the street or found in ranks in major plazas. If the green roof light is on, the taxi is occupied. The initial cost is 250 Esc ($1.60) and each additional 600 feet, or 47 seconds of waiting time, costs 11 Esc (7¢). Luggage weighing more than 30 kilos (66 lb.) is surcharged at 300 Esc ($1.95). Fares increase between 10pm and 6am.

ON FOOT   Most of Lisbon's tourist areas are compact enough to be comfortably covered on foot—but remember that steep hills can make parts of a sightseeing or shopping trip fairly strenuous. Only the sights in the area of Parque Eduardo VII and the Belém district require public transportation or a car.

BY RENTAL CAR   Most international car-rental companies have offices at the airport. Two in-town addresses are **Rupauto,** in the Hotel Tivoli, avenida da Liberdade 185 (☎ **01/352-79-66**); and **Turiscar,** avenida Gomes Pereira 61B (☎ **01/716-29-04**).

Expect to pay a minimum base rate of about 4,000 Esc ($25.80) per day, plus extras and tax. Shop around for special rates.

FAST FACTS: Lisbon

Addresses   Lisbon addresses consist of a street name, a building number, and the story, denoted by a numeral and the symbol °. "Rua Rosa Araújo 2-6°" means the sixth floor at no. 2 on that street. Remember that in Europe the ground floor is not counted as the first floor—6° actually means seven stories up.

Banks   Banks are open Monday through Friday from 8:30am to 3pm; some offer a foreign-exchange service Monday through Saturday from 6 to 11pm. The bank at the airport is always open. Money can be changed on Saturday and Sunday from 8:30am to 8:30pm at the bank at the Santa Apolónia train station. The **American Express** Travel Representative office is at avenida Duque de Loulé 108 (☎ **01/315-50-85** or 315-58-75), open Monday through Friday from 9am to 12:30pm and 2 to 6pm.

Automated-teller machines (ATMs) are widely available, so cash advances can readily be obtained against the major credit or charge cards. Unlike those in neighboring Spain, however, Portuguese ATMs don't recognize CIRRUS or Plus network cards. This will change soon, no doubt, but at this writing the only ATM providing access to CIRRUS and Plus accounts is at the airport.

Business Hours   Typically, **shops** are open Monday through Friday from 9am to 1pm and 3 to 7pm (though some now stay open through lunch) and Saturday from 9am to 1pm; some are also open Saturday afternoon. **Restaurants** are usually open from noon to 3pm and 7 to 11pm or midnight. **Offices** are generally open Monday through Friday from 9am to 1pm and 3 to 5:30pm or 6pm.

Currency   The Portuguese currency unit is the **escudo (Esc),** written 1$00. Fractions of an escudo (centavos) follow the "$"; for example, 100 escudos is written "100$00." Coins are minted in 50 centavos, and 1, 5, 10, 20, 50, 100, and 200 escudos. Notes are printed in 500, 1,000, 2,000, 5,000, and 10,000 escudos.

Doctors English-speaking doctors can be found at the British Hospital, rua Saraiva de Carvalho 49 (☎ **01/60-20-20**). Embassies and hotel concierges can also recommend doctors.

Embassies As a capital city, Lisbon is home to the embassies of many countries, including the **United States,** on avenida das Forças Armadas (☎ **01/726-66-00**), open Monday through Friday from 8am to noon and 1:30 to 4pm; the **United Kingdom,** at rua Saño Domingos a Lapa 37 (☎ **01/396-11-91**), open Monday through Friday from 9am to 1pm and 2:30 to 5:30pm, with the British Consulate at rua de Estrela 4 (☎ **01/395-40-82**), open Monday through Friday from 10am to noon and 3 to 4:30pm; **Canada,** at avenida da Liberdade 144–56, 4° (☎ **01/347-48-92**), open Monday through Friday from 8:30am to 5pm; and **Australia,** at avenida da Liberdade 244-4° (☎ **01/52-33-50**), open Monday through Thursday from 9am to 12:30pm and 1:30 to 5pm and Friday from 9am to 12:20pm.

Emergencies Call **115** for an ambulance, the fire department, and the police. Look in any newspaper or dial 16 for 24-hour pharmacies. Closed pharmacies post notices indicating the nearest open one.

Holidays Holidays in Lisbon are New Year's Day (Jan 1), Freedom Day (Apr 25), Worker's Day (May 1), Camoñes and Portugal Day (June 10), Assumption Day (Aug 15), Day of the Republic (Oct 5), All Saints' Day (Nov 1), Feast of the Immaculate Conception (Dec 8), and Christmas (Dec 25). Other public holidays with shifting dates are Good Friday, Shrove Tuesday, and Corpus Christi.

Hospitals See "Doctors," above.

Information See "Lisbon Specifics," earlier in this chapter.

Laundry/Dry Cleaning Pestox, rua Bernardim Ribeiro 93B (☎ **01/55-66-03**), about 500 yards east of the Rotunda, is open Monday through Friday from 9am to 7pm and charges 1,050 Esc ($6.75) for 4 to 5 kilos (8 to 11 lb.) of laundry on a self-service basis, and 315 Esc ($2.05) per kilo (2.2 lb.), for a minimum of 3 kilos (6.6. lb.) of laundry washed and dried for you. *Tinturaria* is the Portuguese term for dry cleaning.

Language Portuguese is, by turns, as velvety as French, as guttural as German, and as rapid-fire as Spanish. The "s" often sounds like spent waves hissing over hard-packed sand. Older Lisboetas are likely to have French as a second language, while younger people more often learn English in school. Spanish, while by no means the same as Portuguese, has many similarities and might help when other efforts at communication fail.

Lost & Found Check for lost property at Seçaño de Achados da P.S.P. Olivais Sul, praça Cidade Salazar Lote 180 R/C (☎ **01/853-54-03**), open Monday through Friday from 9am to 12:30pm and 1:30 to 5pm.

Mail The Central Post Office (*Correio*), praça dos Restauradores 58, is open daily from 8am to 10pm. The post office at the airport is open 24 hours daily. Letters and postcards to North America cost 135 Esc (85¢). Mailboxes are round, red, and tubular.

Newspapers *Diário de Noticias* is Lisbon's leading daily. The *Anglo-Portuguese News* is a local English-language paper. Foreign-language newspapers are found at many downtown newsstands.

Photographic Needs Fotosport, Centro Comercial Amoreiras, Shop 1080 (☎ 01/342-78-70), is open daily from 10am to 11pm.

Police Call 115 for the police.

Radio/TV Every morning at 8am Radio Comercial broadcasts up-to-the-minute information on Lisbon events in several languages, including English.

Religious Services Since Portugal is predominantly Roman Catholic, finding a mass (in Portuguese) is easy. Other possibilities for worship include the Baptist Evangelical Church, rua Filipe Folque 36, with services on Wednesday at 7:30pm and on Sunday at 11am and 7:30pm; St. George's Church (Church of England), rua de Saño Jorge 6, with services on Sunday at 11am; the Mosque of Lisbon, avenida José Malhoa, with services every day and a special service on Friday; and Shaare Tickva Synagogue, rua Alexandre Herculano 59, with services on Friday from 7:30 to 8pm and on Saturday at 10:30am.

Shoe Repair Silva e Neves Lopes, Lda., rua Rodrigo da Fonseca 182B (near the Hotel Ritz), is open Monday through Friday from 7am to 8:30pm and Saturday from 7am to 1pm.

Tax The value-added tax (IVA in Portugal) is about 16%. See "Shopping," later in this chapter, for refund information.

Taxis See "Lisbon Specifics," earlier in this chapter.

Telephone There's a central telephone office at Rossio Square 68, diagonally across from the National Theater, open daily from 8am to 11pm. Local calls cost 11¢; for long distance within the country, dial "0" (zero) before the two-digit area code and then the number.

To call internationally, dial "00" and then the country and area codes and the number. Some phones are equipped for credit- or charge-card (American Express, Visa, and others—but not phone-company cards) calls. If calling direct from a hotel, however, there may be steep surcharges.

To call collect, or at more economical U.S. calling-card rates, place calls through AT&T's USA Direct by dialing 05017-1-288 or through MCI's Call USA by dialing 05017-1-234. Collect calls, or those at U.S. calling-card rates, can be made through an international operator by dialing 098.

The dial tone for long-distance calls may be unusual, but make sure there's a tone before beginning to dial and that the tone then stops. Dial steadily, without long pauses; the connection can take up to a minute, during which some unfamiliar tones may be heard. Any persistent tone means that the call has failed.

In post offices and at scattered "Credifone" locations, special phones take prepaid cards in 50- and 120-unit denominations (800 and 1,800 Esc/$5.15 and $11.60) sold at post offices; 120 units buys about 3 minutes to the United States at standard rates and over $3^{1}/_{2}$ minutes during the discount periods. International calls can also be made at the Central Post Office, praça dos Restauradores, daily from 8am to 10pm.

Tipping Although restaurant prices usually include a service charge, it's considered appropriate to tip an additional 5% to 10%. Taxi drivers get about 10%

for long rides and 15% to 20% on short rides. Give 100 to 200 Esc (65¢ to $1.30) to porters and bellhops for each bag, depending on their weight and the distance carried. It's customary to leave a similar amount for the chambermaid for each night of a hotel stay.

Useful Telephone Numbers   TAP Air Portugal (☎ **01/386-10-20**), airport information (☎ **01/80-20-60**), train information (☎ **01/87-60-25**), camping and caravanning information (☎ **01/315-27-15**).

4 Accommodations

Budget accommodations abound throughout the city, but the most convenient areas to stay are around the Parque Eduardo VII, along avenida da Liberdade, around Rossio Square, and in the Bairro Alto. Hotels shouldn't be judged solely by the state of their exteriors; go in and ask to see several rooms before deciding. Ask which rooms are quietest and if any have been renovated recently. Some budget lodgings will serve breakfast in your room upon request.

Most of the rates quoted below include VAT, but ask to be sure.

Long-Term Stays   Residências are geared for stays of a week or longer and offer discounts of 10% or more.

DOUBLES FOR LESS THAN 7,000 ESC ($45.15)
NEAR ROSSIO SQUARE

Arco Bandeira

Rua does Sapateiros 226, 1100 Lisboa. ☎ **01/342-34-78.** 10 rms, none with bath. 4,000 Esc ($25.80) single; 7,700 Esc ($49.70) double. No credit cards. Metro: Rossio.

At the top of the Baixa shopping district, a few steps away from the Rossio, Arco Bandeira is five floors up with no elevator. The rooms are scrupulously clean and amply furnished, with firm mattresses and sinks. Traffic is light on the street and the neighborhood seems safe despite the presence of an unobtrusive peep show across the way. Not bad, given the price and location.

Pensaño Beira Minho

Praça da Figueira 6, 2 Esq., 1100 Lisboa. ☎ **01/346-18-46.** 10 rms, 4 with shower. 3,000 Esc ($19.35) single without bath; 5,000 ($32.25) single or double with shower. No credit cards. Metro: Rossio.

Threadbare this place certainly is, with cracked linoleum on the floors and a grungy staircase leading up from the street, but it's clean enough. Right outside is one of Lisbon's most appealing squares, of which most rooms have full views; they even have views of the Castelo Saño Jorge up to the left. The rooms without baths have sinks. Some English is spoken.

Residência do Sul

Praça Dom Pedro IV 59-2° Esq., 1100 Lisboa. ☎ **01/342-25-11.** 21 rms, all with bath. 3,350 Esc ($21.60) single; 3,800 Esc ($24.50) double; 5,000 Esc ($32.25) triple. No credit cards. Metro: Rossio.

In the heart of Lisbon, this very basic lodging shares its entrance with a gift shop. *Dreary* doesn't begin to describe the vestibule or staircase, but the rooms are adequate, even if the furnishings are battered. The price is right, however, and you may find a room here in peak season (July and August), when vacancies are at a premium.

Getting the Best Deal on Accommodations

- Note that *residências* often offer discounts of at least 10% to guests staying more than a week.
- Try your hand at bargaining—hoteliers won't be offended—especially off-season.

IN THE BAIRRO ALTO

✪ Pensaño Londres

Rua Dom Pedro V, 53, 1200 Lisboa. ☎ **01/346-22-03.** Fax 01/346-56-82. 40 rms, 12 with shower only, 13 with bath. 3,000 Esc ($19.35) single without bath, 3,000 Esc ($19.35) single with shower only, 4,000 Esc ($25.80) single with bath; 4,000 Esc ($25.80) double without bath, 5,500 Esc ($35.50) double with shower only. Rates include breakfast. No credit cards. Tram 20 or 24. Bus 15 or 19.

Near the belvedere Saño Pedro de Alcantara, this is a choice hostelry with sculptured ceilings and pleasing furnishings in most rooms, some of which have telephones and all of which have sinks. The refinished staircase and repainted facade and halls are reassuring. For a good view, ask for a fourth-floor room. The reception is on the second floor. Some English is spoken.

Pensaño Sevilha

Praça da Alegria 11-2°, 1200 Lisboa. ☎ **01/346-95-79.** 30 rms, 15 with bath. TEL. 1,575 Esc ($10.15) single without bath; 2,625–4,725 Esc ($16.95–$30.50) single or double with bath. No credit cards. Metro: Avenida.

Just off avenida da Liberdade, this no-frills pension on the parklike praça da Alegria (literally, "Happy Square") is ideal for seasoned budgeteers and backpackers seeking lodging in a central area. The adjacent police station makes the dingy staircase up to the pensaño less intimidating. Most of the good-sized rooms overlook the square. The modern baths are a notch above the dorm-style accommodations. Prices are by no means firm, especially off-season, so bargaining is in order.

AROUND PARQUE EDUARDO VII

Pensaño Pátria

Avenida Duque de Avila 42-6°, 1000 Lisboa. ☎ **01/315-06-20.** Fax 01/57-83-10. 30 rms, 27 with bidet and sink only, 4 with bath. TEL. 4,200 Esc ($27.10) single with bidet and sink, 4,725 Esc ($30.50) single with bath; 5,250 Esc ($33.85) double with bidet and sink, 6,300 Esc ($40.65) double with bath. Rates include breakfast. No credit cards. Metro: Saldanha. Bus 16, 18, 26, or 42.

The Pátria's rooms are basic and cramped but clean, and the management is friendly, although little English is spoken. A sporting-goods store shares the ground-floor entrance; reception is on the sixth floor. The on-premises restaurant serves all meals.

Residênsia Nazareth

Avenida António Augusto de Aguiar 25-4°/5°, 1000 Lisboa. ☎ **01/54-20-16.** Fax 01/356-08-36. 32 rms, all with bath. A/C TV TEL. 5,750 Esc ($37.10) single; 6,750 Esc ($43.55) double. Rates include breakfast. DC, MC, V. Metro: Parque. Bus 31, 41, or 46.

A vaguely Arabic motif of stucco walls and arches in the reception and breakfast/bar areas fades to just a hint in the compact yet well-equipped rooms and baths.

The carpets need replacing. The owners, Senhor Nazir and Senhor Basir of Mozambique, and most of the reception staff speak English. Laundry service is available.

DOUBLES FOR LESS THAN 8,500 ESC ($54.85)

Hotel Internacional

Rua da Betesga 3, 1100 Lisboa. ☎ **01/346-64-01.** Fax 01/347-86-35. 53 rooms, all with bath. A/C TV. 7,500 Esc ($48.40) single; 8,500 Esc ($54.85) double. Rates include breakfast. AE, DC, MC, V. Metro: Rossio.

At this central hotel, room dimensions vary substantially, including ceiling height. Most rooms have an easy chair or two and a desk. Ask to see a couple before registering. The baths may have a shower but no tub. Room safes are a welcome bonus. Guests can get together in the TV salon next to the bar. The creaky floors testify to the building's age.

✪ Pensaño Casal Ribeiro

Rua Braamcamp 10-R/C. Dto., 1200 Lisboa. ☎ **01/386-15-44.** Fax 01/386-00-67. 30 rms, all with bath. TV TEL. 6,000 Esc ($38.70) single; 7,000 Esc ($45.15) double. No credit cards. Metro: Rotunda.

This pension's cream exterior with green trim is promising, carried out in pleasant, if compact, rooms. They're equipped beyond expectations in this category, with TV, radio, and private bath. Guests can meet in the agreeable lounge by the reception desk. English is spoken.

✪ Residence Lisbonense

Rua Pinheiro Chagas 1, 1000 Lisboa. ☎ **01/54-46-28**. 30 rms, all with bath. TEL. 4,500 Esc ($29.05) single; 7,000 Esc ($45.15) double. Rates include breakfast. No credit cards. Metro: Saldanha.

Ensconced in a once-stylish old Lisbon building, the well-maintained Lisbonense (with elevator) occupies four floors. The reception is on the third floor, and there's usually someone on hand who speaks English. The smallish rooms are clean and neat, with warm wood furnishings. Number 311 is a suitelike room with a large bath. All the baths are being updated and room air conditioning is being added. The petite TV lounge doubles as the breakfast room.

Residência America

Rua Tomáz Ribeiro 47, 1000 Lisboa. ☎ **01/352-11-77.** Fax 01/353-14-76. 22 rooms, all with bath. TV TEL. 6,500 Esc ($41.95) single; 8,000 Esc ($51.60) double. Rates include breakfast. AE, DC, MC, V. Metro: Picoas.

This neighborhood is good enough for the Sheraton, right across the street, and an entirely adequate room here goes for a fifth the price of one in the big guy. Security is enhanced by the streetside lobby, which discourages surreptitious entry. On the seventh floor is a bar.

Residência Astória

Rua Braamcamp 10, 1200 Lisboa. ☎ **01/386-13-17.** Fax 01/386-04-91. 82 rms, all with bath. A/C TEL. 5,500–8,000 Esc ($35.50–$51.60) single; 6,500–9,000 Esc ($41.95–$58.05) double. Rates include breakfast. Metro: Rotunda.

Just off the Rotunda, the Astória has squeaky-clean small rooms furnished in light wood. Sculptured ceilings interject a note of old-world charm in this otherwise contemporary lodging. Some rooms have TVs. The owner, Senhor Caldeira, speaks English, as do some of his assistants. Guests have the use of a lounge with a bar.

Residencial Duas Nacoñes

Rua da Victoria 41, 1100 Lisboa. ☎ **01/346-07-10.** Fax 01/347-0206. 55 rms, about half with bath. TEL. 3,740 Esc ($24.15) single without bath, 5,420 Esc ($34.95) single with bath; 6,310 Esc ($40.70) double without bath, 9,460 Esc ($61) double with bath. Rates include breakfast. No credit cards. Metro: Rossio.

In the heart of the Baixa, a few strides off the pedestrian rua Augusta, this economical place is a happy surprise. The high-ceilinged, commodious doubles contain personal safes, and those with baths have tubs long enough to float an NBA point guard. Breakfast is served in a large dining room with blue-and-white scenic tile murals. Renovation work is ongoing, so see your room before accepting. The higher-priced doubles slip over the upper limit of this category, but not by much.

NEAR AVENIDA DA LIBERDADE

○ Residencial Florescente

Rua Portas Saño Antaño 99 (next to the Grand Teatro Politeama), 1100 Lisboa. ☎ **01/342-66-09.** Fax 01/342-77-33. 115 rms, 55 with sink and bidet only, 40 with shower only, 20 with bath. 4,000 Esc ($25.80) single or double with sink and bidet only, 5,000 Esc ($32.25) single or double with shower only, 6,000 Esc ($38.70) single or double with bath. MC, V. Metro: Restauradores.

Discount the Florescente's facade, which badly needed painting on my last inspection. One block off praça dos Restauradores, the Florescente offers small, clean rooms on four floors (no elevator). The street-level reception is welcoming, though the man attending the desk may not be. Some rooms are larger than others or come with TV or piped-in music, so see a few before deciding. Breakfast isn't served, but there are many coffee shops and budget restaurants nearby.

IN THE BAIRRO ALTO

Residencial Camoñes

Travessa do Poço da Cidade 38-1° (near the corner with rua da Barroca), 1200 Lisboa. ☎ **01/346-75-10.** Fax 01/346-40-48 for reservations. 18 rms, 6 with shower only, 8 with bath; 2 suites. TEL. 6,300 Esc ($40.65) double without bath, 8,400 Esc ($54.20) double with bath; 9,450 Esc ($60.95) triple with bath; 10,450 Esc ($67.40) quad; 11,575 Esc ($74.70) room for six. Breakfast 275 Esc ($1.75) extra. Discounts offered for longer stays. No credit cards. Metro: Rossio. Tram 24. Bus 100.

Though the rooms here—divided among three floors, no elevator—are somewhat cramped, they're clean and comfortable, complemented by a cheery breakfast room.

DOUBLES FOR LESS THAN 11,000 ESC ($70.95)
AROUND PARQUE EDUARDO VII

Residência Caravela

Rua Ferreira Lapa 38 (off avenida Duque de Loulé), 1100 Lisboa. ☎ **01/353-90-11.** Fax 01/315-03-19 for reservations. 45 rms, all with bath (14 with shower). TV TEL. 6,930 Esc ($44.70) single; 8,660 Esc ($55.85) double; 10,395 Esc ($67.05) triple. Rates include breakfast. AE, DC, MC, V. Metro: Rotunda. Bus 20 or 22.

Around the corner from the Centro Cultural Americano (where U.S. newspapers and magazines are available for perusal), the Caravela's concrete exterior is unprepossessing. However, its carpeted rooms are comfortable enough, albeit a bit dark and worn here and there. The triples have good-size baths; 14 rooms have showers instead of tubs. Evening socializing is done in a pleasant bar.

Residência Imperador

Avenida 5 de Outubro 55 (near the intesection with avenida Duque de Avila), 1000 Lisboa. ☎ **01/352-48-84.** Fax 01/352-65-37. 43 rms, all with bath. A/C TV TEL. 7,000 Esc ($45.15) single; 8,000 Esc ($51.60) double. Rates include breakfast. AE, DC, EURO, MC, V. Metro: Saldanha. Bus 21 or 44, or 36 Linha Verde.

A few blocks from the Pensaño Pátria (above), the Imperador offers standardized rooms with luggage racks, desks, and sundry furnishings affixed to the wall in the manner of a business hotel. The baths are cheerful, and the staff has some knowledge of English.

IN THE BAIRRO ALTO

Hotel Borges

Rua Garrett 108, 1200 Lisboa. ☎ **01/346-19-51.** Fax 01/342-66-17. 100 rms, all with bath. TEL. 9,000 Esc ($58.05) single; 10,000 Esc ($64.50) double. Rates include breakfast. AE, DC, MC, V. Metro: Restauradores.

Superbly situated off praça de Camões, this busy hotel is bracketed by two of my recommended restaurants, A Brasileira and Bernardí. Even the prestigious haute cuisine emporium Aviz shares the block, should you get the urge to splurge. The hotel's dining room (where all meals are served) has a faded elegance with teardrop chandeliers and a sculptured ceiling. Five floors, served by an elevator, and 100 rooms make this a strong possibility when other places are full. Renovations have begun but will take a while to complete; ask for one of the redone rooms. English is spoken.

Residência Roma

Travessa da Glória 22A-1°, 1200 Lisboa. ☎ **01/346-05-57.** Fax 01/346-05-57. 24 rms, all with bath. TV TEL. 6,000–7,000 Esc ($38.70–$45.15) single; 8,000–9,000 Esc ($51.60–$58.05) double. MC, V. Metro: Restauradores.

A neon sign makes the Roma unmissable. About 60 feet off avenida da Liberdade and freshly painted throughout, this is a very clean, comfortable place to bed down. Rooms 201, 202, and 208 are the most spacious doubles. English is spoken fluently at the front desk (in a glass case nearby is a display of ceramics), and the cozy bar offers 24-hour service.

SUPER-BUDGET CHOICES
A YOUTH HOSTEL

Pousada da Juventuds de Catalazete

Estrada Marginal, 2780 Oeiras. ☎ **01/443-06-38.** 102 beds. June 19–Sept, 1,470 Esc ($9.50) single without bath; 3,255 Esc ($21) double with bath. Feb 19–June 18, 1,260 Esc ($8.25) single; 2,835 Esc ($18.30) double with bath. Oct–Feb 18, 1,155 Esc ($7.45) single; 2,600 Esc ($16.65) double with bath. No credit cards.

This hostel in Oeiras, about half an hour from Lisbon and 15 minutes from Estoril, is open only to members of the International Youth Hostel Federation. It closes at midnight; lights out between midnight and 7am. Smoking, eating, and drinking alcoholic beverages are prohibited. There are single and double rooms; all other rooms have four or six beds—inquire as to per person charge for these. Guests must use a sleeping bag or two sheets when utilizing the hostel's blankets. All three meals are served.

CAMPING

Parque de Campismo de Monsanto

Off the Estoril autostrada. ☎ **01/70-20-61** or 70-20-62. Oct–Apr, 125 Esc (80¢) per person; 125 Esc (80¢) per tent; 110 Esc (70¢) per car. May–Sept, 375 Esc ($2.40) per person; 375 Esc ($2.40) per caravan; 240 Esc ($1.55) for services. No credit cards.

This campground includes all facilities.

WORTH THE EXTRA MONEY

Albergaria da Senhora do Monte

Calçada do Monte 39, 1100 Lisboa. ☎ **01/886-60-02.** Fax 01/887-77-83. 28 rms, all with bath; 4 suites. A/C TV TEL. 12,000–13,000 Esc ($77.40–$83.85) single; 15,000–16,000 Esc ($96.75–$103.25) double, 20,000–22,500 Esc ($129.05–$145.15) double with terrace; 20,000–25,000 Esc ($129.05–$161.30) triple with sitting room. Rates include breakfast. AE, DC, MC, V. Tram 28. Bus 12, 17, 26, or 35.

Only five rooms lack a view in this panoramically perched establishment overlooking all Lisbon. The top-floor café-bar, in particular, offers spectacular sunset views over the Tajo, Alfama, and Bairro Alto. Every room has a beautifully tiled bath, 11 have balconies, and 4 have terraces; most have air conditioning. Since this place is ttucked away on a small street in the Graça area, it's wise to take a cab here the first time; after that, it's a two-block walk to the tram that goes into the heart of town.

5 Dining

By far the best areas for scouting restaurants are the blocks west of rua da Misericórdia and rua do Saño Pedro Alcantara in the Bairro Alto; rua das Portas de Santo Antaño, east of praça dos Restauradores; and rua dos Bacalhoeiros, off the northeast corner of praça do Comércio.

Many restaurants offer an *ementa turística* (tourist menu) that typically includes an appetizer or soup, a main course, dessert, bread, and a beverage for a price often lower than an á la carte main course alone. In places where the *ementa turística* is unappealing or unavailable, consider ordering only a main course. Portions are large, so skipping appetizers, desserts, or both is a cost-paring possibility.

Lisbon's meals are still relatively cheap and built around a number of hearty, earthy dishes. One is *caldo verde,* a soup with mashed potatoes, finely shredded kale, and pieces of peppery sausage cooked in beef broth. Then there's the ubiquitous *bacalhau* (codfish), available in over 300 different recipes. *Carne de porco a alentejana* is pork stewed with clams in a sauce spiced with herbs—a classic. *Barrigas de freira* (literally "nuns' tummies") is a popular egg dish, while *cozido a portuguesa* is a tasty Portuguese version of the New England boiled dinner. Another common and savory dish is grilled sardines—large ones, not like the ones usually found in cans—with a fresh salad. *Açorda,* served almost everywhere, is one of those dishes every native had as a child and loves as an adult. Newcomers may find it less adorable, at least at first. Essentially, it's a porridge of bread, eggs, and parsley or cilantro, tossed with shrimp or fish, and whipped enthusiastically into a fragrant mush. For dessert, try *pudim Molotov,* a cross between a sponge cake and a pudding served with caramel sauce. Any of a dozen types of cheese are also eaten for

---

Getting the Best Deal on Dining

- Try *restaurante-cervejarias*—literally, these are "beer-restaurants."
- A quick, light meal at a snack bar or *pastelaria* will definitely help you keep to your budget.
- Another option is the *tasca*—a down-home, family-style restaurant with good food at budget prices.
- Note that eating and drinking at the bar costs less than doing so at a table; some restaurants even provide barflies with placemats.
- Enjoy a picnic since scenic, relaxing spots are plentiful in Lisbon.
- A true bargain is the *ementa turística* (tourist menu) at lunch.

---

dessert. A special one is *serra da estrêla,* a creamy, smoked, sheep cheese. Breakfast usually consists of coffee and a croissant.

As for wine, it's hard to go wrong ordering the unlabeled house version—*vinho da casa.* Coffee comes in varying forms, among the most popular being *bica* (espresso without milk), *carioca* (espresso with a dash of milk), *garoto* (espresso with more milk), and *galao* (a large glass of coffee with milk).

The practice of charging a *couvert* (cover), already common in other European countries, is surfacing around town. Allegedly a charge for bread, butter and incidentals, it's actually just a transparent way to pad the bill.

MEALS FOR LESS THAN 2,500 ESC ($16.10)
NEAR ROSSIO SQUARE

A Brasileira
Rua Garrett 120–122. ☎ **01/346-95-41.** 250–390 Esc ($1.60–$2.50). No credit cards. Daily 8am–2am. Metro: Rossio. SANDWICHES/SNACKS.

The city's oldest coffee shop, a block from praça de Camões, serves a strong aromatic Brazilian espresso for 155 Esc ($1). The outside tables, next to a sculpture of a suited patron in a fedora, are enjoyable for coffee or quick lunches (note that coffee is served in double portions only, for 210 Esc/$1.35). Inside is a fin-de-siècle coffeehouse where conversations swirl, cards and chess are played, and service is offhand at best. Modern paintings occupy the spaces above the large mirrors.

Bernardí
Rua Garrett 104. ☎ **01/347-31-33.** Appetizers 200–1,500 Esc ($1.30–$9.70); main courses 1,500–2,500 Esc ($9.70–$16.15). AE, DC, EURO, MC, V. Mon–Sat 8am–midnight. Metro: Rossio. PORTUGUESE.

This antiquarian café near A Brasileira (above) is great for a breakfast of coffee and pastries or fresh croissants. A standard version costs 210 Esc ($1.35) at the bar, 600 Esc ($3.85) at a table. Lunch or dinner possibilities include grilled salmon for 2,200 Esc ($14.20) and rice with duck for 1,500 Esc ($9.70). This place is always available for an afternoon or late-night hot chocolate or snack. To imbibe at the bar, prepay at the cashier down on the right and obtain a voucher.

Pastelaria Suiça

Praça Dom Pedro IV 105. ☎ **01/342-80-92.** Main courses 680–1,575 Esc ($4.40–$10.15). No credit cards. Daily 7am–10pm. Metro: Rossio. PORTUGUESE.

A quintessential café experience in the heart of Rossio Square, this always-busy hangout serves Brazilian coffee in a glass for 190 Esc ($1.25), omelets and salads for 680 to 1,200 Esc ($4.40 to $7.75), and sandwiches for 365 to 765 Esc ($2.35 to $4.95). A breakfast of juice, a croissant, bacon, eggs, and coffee can be had for 900 Esc ($5.50). Lunch patrons may be asked to move inside from the highly desirable sidewalk tables unless they've ordered a meal, not just a beverage.

NEAR AVENIDA DA LIBERDADE

Bonjardim

Travessa de Santo Antaño 18. ☎ **01/342-74-24.** Main courses 900–2,300 Esc ($5.80–$14.85); *ementa turística* 1,890 Esc ($12.20). MC, V. Daily noon–11:30pm. Metro: Restauradores. PORTUGUESE.

A slight cut above its nearby sibling of the same name, which is subtitled "Rei dos Frangos" (below), the Bonjardim specializes in grilled meats and fish, with spit-roasted chicken a secondary specialty. Dining downstairs here is preferable to trying upstairs, where service can be elusive.

Bonjardim (Rei dos Frangos)

Travessa de Santo Antaño 11. ☎ **01/342-43-89.** Main courses 880–1,730 Esc ($5.70–$11.15); *ementa turística* 1,650 Esc ($10.65). DC, MC, V. Daily noon–11:30pm. Metro: Restauradores. PORTUGUESE.

This frill-free place calling itself the "King of the Chickens" specializes in spit-roasted golden versions of the eponymous fowl for two for 985 Esc ($6.35). They overshadow the various other grilled meat and fish dishes. The upstairs dining room is a bit more civilized than the one downstairs, where accidentally dipping an elbow in a neighbor's soup is a possibility.

NEAR PRAÇA DO COMÉRCIO

Adega Triunfo

Rua dos Bacalhoeiros 129. ☎ **01/86-98-40.** Main courses 850–1,500 Esc ($5.50–$9.70); *ementa turística* 1,400 Esc ($9.05). AE, DC, MC, V. Mon–Sat noon–3:30pm and 6:30–11pm. Tram 24. PORTUGUESE.

Walk through almost any door on this street and you can have a decent meal at an economical price (see Cubata, below). This place separates itself from most of the others by offering half portions. A basket of chewy bread arrives right off, with little containers of cheese and pâté. Twelve grilled sardines with a side order of açorda is under $10. The blue-and-white tablecloths clash with the avocado imitation-leather chairs, but the staff is friendly, and a few speak English.

✪ Cubata

Rua dos Bacalhoeiros 133. ☎ **01/87-08-77.** Appetizers and salads 650–1,000 Esc ($4.20–$6.45); main courses 820–1,550 Esc ($5.30–$10); *ementa turística* 1,400 Esc ($9.05). No credit cards. Sun–Fri noon–10:30pm. Tram 24. PORTUGUESE.

Unpretentious in appearance both inside and out, Cubata serves tasty economical fare. In addition to the usual repertoire, including caldo verde, haddock filet with steamed tomatoes, and grilled shrimp, there are about 10 daily specials.

In the Bairro Alto

Adega do Teixeira

Rua do Teixeira 39. ☎ **01/342-83-20.** Platos 200–2,250 Esc ($1.30–$14.50); *ementa turística* 2,250 Esc ($14.50). AE, MC, V. Mon–Sat noon–3pm and 7:30–11pm. Metro: Rossio. Tram 24. PORTUGUESE.

Hidden behind the Instituto do Vinho do Porto (see "Lisbon After Dark," later in this chapter) and up a short flight of stairs, this little-known restaurant has outdoor tables under an awning in front of the entrance. The owner, ever anxious to please, comes forward quickly out of the dim interior when a potential patron appears. Given the slightest encouragement, he'll take a guest straight into the kitchen to examine the freshest of fish and peer into the bubbling pots. Seafood is the wise choice here, and the patio the place to eat it (if weather permits).

✪ Baralto

Rua Diário de Noticias 31. ☎ **01/342-67-39.** Soups 120–150 Esc (80¢–95¢); main courses 990–1,150 Esc ($6.40–$7.40); *ementa turística* 1,700 Esc ($10.95). No credit cards. Mon–Fri noon–4pm, Sat–Sun 6:30pm–midnight. Closed late Dec to late Jan. Metro: Rossio. Tram 24. PORTUGUESE.

This small, homey restaurant is frequented at lunch by many professionals working in the area. Avelino Pereira is the owner/waiter, and his wife, Rosa, is the cook, whose rendition of the corvina fish, rojoes (lean, marinated pork), and orange cake are highly recommended. A typical *plato do dia* is grilled salmon, for 1,200 Esc ($7.75).

✪ Cervejaria Trindade

Rua Nova da Trindade 20. ☎ **01/360-21-20.** Main courses 990–1,600 Esc ($6.40–$10.30); *ementa turística* 2,100 Esc ($13.55). AE, MC, V. Daily 9am–2am. Metro: Rossio. Tram 24. PORTUGUESE.

In business since 1836, this lively, cavernous *cervejaria* occupies the site of the former 13th-century Convento dos Frades Tinos, which was leveled by the 1755 earthquake. Several rooms with high arched ceilings and fine blue-and-white tile murals will remind you of the convent. Patrons of this Lisbon institution include journalists and executives, but just about everyone shows up sooner or later. The offerings include several meat dishes, though the kitchen does a better job with seafood, especially shellfish. Beware the pricier items, which include, but are not confined to, spiny lobsters and tiger shrimp. Snacks are available at the standup bar in the second room.

✪ Sinal Verde

Calçada do Combro 42. ☎ **01/342-16-01.** Main courses 890–1,470 Esc ($5.75–$9.50); *ementa turística* 1,995 Esc ($12.85). No credit cards. Mon–Sat noon–3:30pm and 7–10:30pm. Tram 28. PORTUGUESE.

This tidy, welcoming restaurant deservedly does a brisk business. Its decor and furnishings are comparable to those of many of Lisbon's less expensive restaurants, yet are somehow more stylish. The ingredients are fresh, the food mostly cooked to order.

In the Alfama

Sol Nascente

Rua de Saño Tomé 86 (not far down the Alfama hill from Castelo Saño Jorge). ☎ 01/887-72-13. Main courses 950–8,000 Esc ($6.15–$51.60); ementa turística 1,900 Esc ($12.25). AE, DC, MC, V. Tues–Sun 8am–2am. Tram 28. PORTUGUESE.

Don't let the stratospheric upper limit on main courses deter you: That's for lobster, always an exception to Lisbon's usually reasonable prices. The portions for conventional meals are substantial, enough so you can easily skip an appetizer. A plate of five fat grilled sardines, for example, which comes with boiled potatoes, steamed kale, and shaved carrots, costs only 1,200 Esc ($7.75). Choices for dining space include the immaculate large dining room and the tables out on the plaza shared with the Fundaçaño Ricardo Espírito Santo, a museum of the decorative arts.

MEALS FOR LESS THAN 4,500 ESC ($29)
NEAR AVENIDA DA LIBERDADE

Sol Dourado

Rua Jardim do Regedor 19–25. ☎ **01/347-25-70.** Main courses 1,200–3,100 Esc ($7.75–$20); *ementa turística* 2,500 Esc ($16.15). Daily noon–midnight. Metro: Restauradores. PORTUGUESE.

There's no dearth of economical eateries in this vicinity, but this is as good as any and better than most. Sol Dourado specializes in pork with baby clams, one of the humble glories of the Portuguese kitchen. Arroz de marisco, a kind of simple paella, is another option. Attentive service, outdoor tables. The same owners operate Lagosta Real at rua Portes de Saño Antaño 37, and Marisqueria da Baixa on the same street at no. 41.

IN THE BAIRRO ALTO

Bota Alta

Travessa da Queimada 37. ₉ 01/392-79-59. Main courses 1,100–2,100 Esc ($7.10–$13.55). AE, DC, MC, V. Mon–Fri noon–2:30pm and 7–10:30pm, Sat 7–10:30pm. Metro: Rossio. Tram 24. PORTUGUESE.

At night, songs bounce off the walls of the labyrinthine streets of the Bairro Alto, for this section is at the heart of Lisbon's fado district. "High Boot," as this place's name translates, is one of the most popuar bistros in town, attested by framed photos and testimonials from such celebrities as actor John Hurt. It's two rooms are crowded with as many tables as will fit, with old tile dados and mismatched drawings and paintings somehow working as decor. Nutty-tasting brown rice comes with many of the main courses. Fish is the best bet.

✪ Casanostra

Rua da Rosa 84–90. ☎ **01/342-59-31.** Main courses 1,600–2,600 Esc ($10.30–$16.75); *ementa turística* 3,950 Esc ($25.50). MC, V. Tues–Sun noon–midnight, Sat 7pm–midnight. Metro: Rossio. ITALIAN.

Casanostra is the domain of Maria Paola, who imports many of her ingredients from Italy and London to produce authentic Italian cuisine. The work of a prominent Portuguese architect, the decorative style is contemporary trattoria—with downsize industrial lighting, creamy walls, and lime-green chairs. The place seats only 30 and is popular with the young nightclub set, so reserve or go early. The pastas, sorbets, and ice creams are homemade.

Mama Rosa

Rua do Grémio Lusitano 14. ☎ **01/346-53-50.** Pizzas 900–1,300 Esc ($5.80–$8.40); pastas and main courses 1,200–2,600 Esc ($7.75–$16.75); *ementa turística* 2,400 Esc ($15.50). MC, V. Mon–Sat 7pm–2am, Sun 7pm–midnight. Metro: Rossio. Tram 24. PIZZA/ITALIAN.

This comfortable trattoria features traditional red-checked tablecloths and some of the best pizza in town. Good desserts, too.

Papí Açorda

Rua da Atalaia 57–59. ☎ **01/346-48-11.** Main courses 1,150–2,000 Esc ($7.40–$12.90). AE, DC, MC, V. Mon 8–11pm, Tues–Sat 12:30–2:30pm and 8–11pm. Closed two weeks each in July and Nov. Metro: Rossio. Tram 24. PORTUGUESE.

Here's an unexpected touch of class in a blue-collar neighborhood, with three big blown-glass chandeliers in an otherwise minimalist setting of pinkish walls and pink-and-black chairs. Fashionable young strivers make up much of the clientele, and Portugal's president, Mário Soares, is said to be a frequent visitor. Mussels marinhera are a commendable starter—plump nuggets in a cilantro-flecked cream sauce. Main courses are primarily the namesake açordas, for those who've developed a taste for the distinctly Portuguese specialty. Alternatives are available.

✪ Tasca do Manel

Rua da Barroca 24. ☎ **01/346-38-13.** Main courses 850–1,400 Esc ($5.50–$9.05); *ementa turística* 2,000 Esc ($12.90). MC, V. Mon–Fri noon–4pm, Sat–Sun 7pm–midnight. Metro: Rossio. Tram 24. PORTUGUESE.

Almost every item on the menu merits consideration at this eat-in tavern frequented by journalists and assorted other Bairro Alto professionals. The fish is only hours from the depths and the grilled meats are prime choices. Arroz de mariscos (rice with shellfish) is a house specialty. The traditional boiled dinner known as cozido is available, with a half portion for only 980 Esc ($6.30). In fall and winter look for game, especially partridge and hare.

NEAR AVENIDA DA LIBERDADE

Andorra

Rua das Portas de Santo Antaño 82 (off praça dos Restauradores, behind the Central Post Office). ☎ **01/342-60-47.** Main courses 980–7,000 Esc ($6.30–$45.15); *ementa turística* 1,360 Esc ($8.75). MC, V. Mon–Sat 12:30–3pm and 6–11pm. Metro: Restauradores. PORTUGUESE.

This restaurant has a beer-hall look downstairs and a more formal ambience upstairs. One tempting choice is the arroz de cherne (rice with mixed fish). There are outdoor tables most of the year.

THE CHAINS

Yanks looking for tastes of home might seek out the local representative of the Iberian hamburger chain **Foster's Hollywood,** on rua Carlos Alberto Mota Pinto, across from the Amoreiras shopping mall. Burgers are 750 to 1,200 Esc ($4.85 to $7.75). Those hungry for familiar fast food at still lower prices will find a **Burger King** near Foster's Hollywood on rua Carlos Alberto da Moto Pinto and a **McDonald's** at avenida da República 10F. Prices for the usual items run from about 250 to 485 Esc ($1.60 to $3.15). The Portuguese pizza-and-burgers joints, **Abracadabra,** are found at Centro Comercial Imaviz, next to the Sheraton Hotel, and on plaça Dom Pedro IV.

PICNICKING

Celeiro, rua 1 de Dezembro 81 (☎ **01/342-74-95;** Metro: Rossio), is a well-stocked supermarket near Rossio Square that offers such ready-cooked fare as roast chicken at 1,025 Esc ($6.60) per kilo (2.2 lb.). It's open Monday through Friday from 8:30am to 7pm and Saturday from 8:30am to 1pm. MasterCard and Visa are accepted.

A picnic can be enjoyed in many of the city's numerous parks. Favorites are the grounds of the Castelo Saño Jorge atop the Alfama, Saño Pedro de Alcantara in the Bairro Alto, and Parque Eduardo VII, which has picnic tables.

WORTH THE EXTRA MONEY

Cais da Ribeira
Armazém A, Cais do Sodre. ☎ **01/342-36-11.** Reservations required. Main courses 1,400–6,450 Esc ($9.05–$41.60). DC, MC, V. Mon–Fri noon–3pm and 7:30–11pm, Sat 7:30–11pm. Metro: Cais do Sodré. PORTUGUESE.

This former warehouse for the Lisbon fishing fleet has been converted into an immensely popular seafood restaurant. The wide windows provide views of river traffic while patrons tuck into the delectable stew known as caldeirada or any of a dozen specimens from the day's catch, preferably charcoal-grilled. Main courses come with vegetables, so by skipping extras and avoiding the costlier crustaceans you can stay within your budget and have what may be the most memorable meal of your Lisbon stay. The immediate neighborhood gets a little dicey at night, so it might be better to save this for lunch.

6 Attractions

SIGHTSEEING SUGGESTIONS
Since the majority of Lisbon's sights are concentrated within the historic heart of the city, most of the highlights can be seen even with limited time. With only one, or as many as five days, the suggested itineraries below will cover the main attractions.

If You Have 1 Day
After breakfast at Bernardí (see "Dining," earlier in this chapter), take a map and head for the maze of streets that lace the Alfama district. From Rossio Square, head past the shops and boutiques of rua Augusta and turn left onto rua da Conceiçaño. Follow the signs to the Sé (cathedral), a 12th-century structure that has undergone various facelifts. Continue left beyond the Sé and, a bit farther along on the right, stop for the view from the belvedere of Santa Luzia. Follow largo do Contador Mor (directly opposite) to the end and turn left onto chaño da Feira to enter the grounds of the Castelo Saño Jorge (Saint George's Castle). All of Lisbon and the broad River Tajo can be seen from its ramparts.

Wind your way down through the Alfama to praça do Comércio and catch a tram or bus (or taxi) to the Belém area to visit the Mosteiro dos Jerónimos (Jerónimos Monastery). Down by the river is the Torre de Belém (Tower of Belém) and the Monument of the Discoveries.

After lunch in a restaurant in the Bairro Alto, head for the Museu da Fundaçaño Calouste Gulbenkian (Gulbenkian Foundation Museum), whose select collection of exquisite art is superbly displayed in a custom-made setting.

If You Have 2 Days
Spend the morning as outlined above, but have lunch in Belém and then visit the Mosteiro dos Jerónimos, the Museu da Marinha (Marine Museum) at its western end, and the nearby Museu dos Coches (Coach Museum).

On the second day, spend the morning at the Museu da Fundaçaño Calouste Gulbenkian. After lunch in the Bairro Alto, head for the Jardim Botânico and stroll back toward the river along rua Dom Pedro V and rua de Saño Pedro de Alcantara, where there's a small park with a lovely view of downtown Lisbon. Next, visit the 16th-century Igreja de Saño Roque (San Roque Church), whose most dazzling chapel, dedicated to St. John the Baptist, was constructed in Rome in 1742 of lapis lazuli, alabaster, and amethyst. Continue along rua da Misericórdia to praça de Camoñes and turn left through largo do Chiado to rua Garrett, where massive reconstruction is still under way in the wake of the 1988 fire. At the end of rua Garrett, turn left onto rua do Carmo. Both these streets are lined with chic shops and boutiques. At rua de Santa Justa, off to the right is the Elevador de Santa Justa, built by Raul Mesnier de Ponsard, a Portuguese engineer, not by Gustave Eiffel as is often claimed. Follow rua do Carmo into Rossio Square with its pseudo-Moorish train station and stop for a leisurely coffee at one of its cafés.

If You Have 3 Days

Spend the first day strolling leisurely through the Alfama district and seeing the Castelo Saño Jorge; the belvedere of Santa Luzia; the nearby Fundaçaño Ricardo Espírito Santo (Museum of Decorative Arts), with its collection of 17th- and 18th-century Portuguese and colonial furnishings and art objects; the Sé (cathedral) and the nearby Igreja Santo António and Igreja Saño Vicente, the last an impressive building whose cloisters feature exquisite 18th-century tiles. At lunchtime, in good weather, many Alfama families are seen grilling sardines on their stoops. In the vicinity of the castle there are several restaurants for lunch. Because this area is uncommonly picturesque, I suggest that you stroll at leisure for part of the day. No need to worry about getting lost—the Alfama isn't that big and the natives are usually helpful (keep a map handy).

The Museu da Fundaçaño Calouste Gulbenkian can easily fill the morning of the second day. Head to Belém for lunch and in the afternoon visit the Mosteiro de Jerónimos, the Museu da Marinha, the Torre de Belém, the Monument of the Discoveries, the Museu dos Coches, and the Museu Nacional de Arte Antiga (National Museum of Ancient Art).

Spend the third morning in the Bairro Alto as outlined above in "If You Have 2 Days" and the afternoon exploring the shops of the Baixa area between Rossio Square and praça do Comércio. Catch tram no. 28 (Graça) on rua da Madalena to the Igreja da Graça and have a sunset drink at the bar of the Albergaria da Senhora do Monte, calçada do Monte 39.

If You Have 5 Days

Spend three of the days as outlined above, reserving Tuesday or Saturday for a morning visit to the Feira da Ladra flea market. On the afternoon of the fourth day visit the Igreja da Madre de Deus (Church of the Mother of God), beautifully restored inside with tile murals and carved wood, and the nearby Museu do Azulejo (Tile Museum). On the fifth day, go to Sintra, the lush mountain retreat whose fairytale Pena Palace and Paço Real attest to bygone royalty's fondness for this magical place.

TOP ATTRACTIONS

Castelo Saño Jorge (St. George's Castle)
Alfama District. Admission free. Daily 8am–sunset. Bus 37.

Lisbon

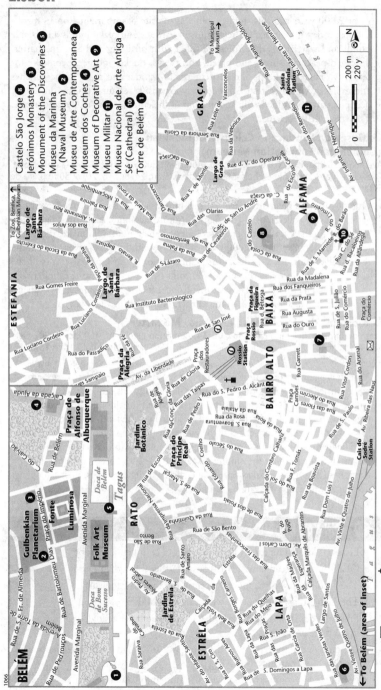

Castelo São Jorge **8**
Jerónimos Monastery **3**
Monument of the Discoveries **5**
Museu da Marinha
(Naval Museum) **2**
Museu de Arte Contemporanea **7**
Museum dos Coches **4**
Museum of Decorative Art **9**
Museu Militar **11**
Museu Nacional de Arte Antiga **6**
Sé (Cathedral) **10**
Torre de Belém **1**

Post Office ⊠ Church ✝

Over 2,000 years ago this strategic hill was the site of important Roman fortifications; today it's a place for relaxation in gardens and playgrounds and beside ponds and waterways. The trees are filled with birdsong and avarian chatter. Uncaged peacocks shriek and preen, and swans, ducks, and geese compete for territory. There are keeps and battlements to wander and many stone benches and tables at which to rest. A moderately expensive restaurant, Casa do Leaño, occupies part of a ruined wall, and in front of the entrance is a small outdoor café. The views are spectacular.

✪ Museu da Fundaçaño Calouste Gulbenkian (Gulbenkian Foundation Museum)

Avenida de Berna 45. ☎ **01/795-02-36.** Admission 200 Esc ($1.30) Tues–Sat, free Sun. Tues–Sun 10am–5pm. Closed hols. Metro: Palhava. Tram 24. Bus 16, 26, or 30 to praça de Espanha.

One of Europe's great art treasures, this museum houses one of the largest privately amassed collections of paintings, furniture, ceramics, sculptures, tapestries, and coins on the Continent. The gift of an Armenian multimillionaire, the made-to-order building contains 5,000 years of history, with Egyptian artifacts from the third millennium B.C., 14th-century Chinese porcelain, Japanese prints of the 17th-century Ukio-e school, Greek gold coins from 500 B.C., stone cylinder seals of Mesopotamia (3000 B.C.), silk carpets from Armenia, and paintings by Rubens, Rembrandt, Gainsborough, Renoir, Turner, Ghirlandaio, and Watteau.

✪ Mosteiro dos Jerónimos (Jerónimos Monastery)

Praça do Império, Belém. ☎ **01/362-00-34.** Admission June–Sept, 450 Esc ($2.90); Oct–May, 275 Esc ($1.75). Tues–Sun 10am–1pm and 2–5:30pm. Closed hols. Tram 15 or 17. Bus 27, 28, 29, 43, or 49.

An extravagant expression of gratitude for the discoveries of Vasco da Gama—who's buried here—and other Portuguese navigators, this monastery contains the gothic-Renaissance Church of Santa Maria, famed for the lacy stonework of its two-tiered octagonal cloisters. Formerly situated on the bank of the river, which has since shifted direction, the church evolved from a chapel built by Prince Henry the Navigator to its current soaring majesty, replete with decorative allusions to the sea and the fruits of the empire it spawned. Besides Vasco do Gama, Luís da Camoñes (Portugal's "Shakespeare"), and three Portuguese kings, their sarcophagi decorated with elephants, are buried here.

❓ Did You Know?

- Lisbon is located on the westernmost part of continental Europe.
- Of all European capitals, only Athens is farther south than Lisbon.
- The Tejo (Tagus) is the longest river on the Iberian Peninsula.
- The Tejo estuary is one of the widest in the world.
- Ponte 25 de Abril, which spans the Tejo, is the longest single-span suspension bridge in Europe.
- Lisbon is one of three places in the world whose Roman Catholic leader bears the title of patriarch.
- Portugal's last colony, Macao, will be returned to China in 1999.
- Portugal's empire was once 100 times the size of the home country.

The Alfama

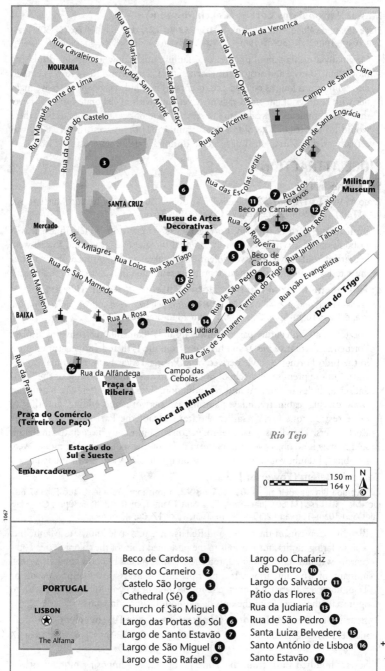

PORTUGAL

LISBON

The Alfama

✝■ Church

Museu Nacional dos Coches (Coach Museum)

Praça Afonso de Albuquerque, Belém. ☎ **01/363-80-22**. Admission 400 Esc ($2.60). Tues–Sun 10am–1pm and 2:30–5:15pm. Closed hols. Tram 15. Bus 14, 27, 43, or 49.

Originally a riding school for the royal family, this is now a museum displaying more than 70 royal and aristocratic coaches, the Cadillacs and Rolls-Royces of their day. Some are as long as railroad cars, decorated in mind-bogglingly excessive manner with lashings of gilt and swags of velvet and swirls of elaborate carving. If ever there were emblems of wealth sure to set the blood of revolutionaries to boil, these would do the trick. The oldest dates from 1581; the newest, from 1824, was actually used by Elizabeth II of England during her 1958 state visit to Lisbon.

MORE ATTRACTIONS

Sé (Cathedral)

Largo da Sé. ☎ **01/86-67-52**. Cathedral, free; cloister, 50 Esc (30¢); Treasury Museum, 300 Esc ($1.95). Daily 9am–5pm. Tram 28 to Graça. Bus 37.

Built in the 12th century by Portugal's first king, Afonso Henriques, this is Lisbon's oldest surviving church. Its original romanesque facade and towers were left largely undamaged by two violent earthquakes, although much of the rest of the exterior and interior has been repeatedly renovated (not always to good effect).

✪ Fundaçaño Ricardo Espírito Santo (Museum of Decorative Arts)

Largo das Portas do Sol 2. ☎ **01/886-21-83**. Admission free. Wed and Fri–Sun 10am–5pm, Tues and Thurs 10am–8pm. Closed hols. Tram 28 to Graça. Bus 37.

Located in a 17th-century palace halfway up the Alfama hill, this museum displays Portuguese decorative pieces and furniture from the 17th and 18th centuries, most in the Indo-Portuguese style derived from Portugal's Far Eastern colonial experience. On the premises is a school of decorative arts, since the work of the foundation includes restoration and reproduction. The artisans here are masters of wood carving, cabinetry, inlay, painting, lacquerwork, and gilding, and they've done restorations for Versailles, Fontainebleau, the Paris Library, and the Rockefellers. They'll also make reproductions of almost any piece in the museum, so if money is no object you can place an order on the spot (though if money were no object, I doubt you'd be reading this budget book). Visits are by guided tour.

Torre de Belém (Tower of Belém)

Off avenida Brasília, Belém. ☎ **01/301-68-92**. Admission: June–Sept, 400 Esc ($2.60); Oct–May, 250 Esc ($1.60). June–Sept, Tues–Sun 10am–1pm and 2:30–6:30pm; Oct–May, Tues–Sun 10am–1pm and 2:30–5:30pm. Tram 15 or 17. Bus 43 or 49.

Blending elements of the gothic and Renaissance in a style known as Manueline, with seafaring motifs and allusions to the purloined fruits of the colonies, this 16th-century watchtower was built as protection against pirates but now contains a small museum of arms and armor. Its upper platform delivers a panoramic view of the Tejo; however, there isn't much else to the interior, so you might simply wish to appreciate the tower from the outside, without paying admission.

Padraño dos Descobrimentos (Monument of the Discoveries)

Avenida Brasília, Belém. Admission 275 Esc ($1.75). Tues–Sun 9:30am–7pm. Tram 15 or 17. Bus 43 or 49.

Several hundred yards from the Torre de Belém, this imposing monument was built in 1960 to commemorate the 500th anniversary of the death of Prince Henry the Navigator, who founded Portugal's first observatory and the Sagres Nautical

The Bairro Alto

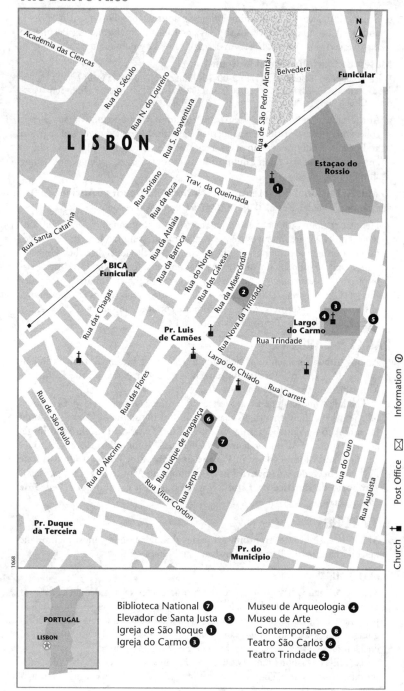

N

Academia das Ciencas

Rua do Século

Rua N. do Loureiro

Rua S. Boaventura

Belvedere

Funicular

Rua de São Pedro Alcântâra

LISBON

Estaçao do Rossio

Rua Soriano

Rua da Rosa

Trav. da Queimada

Rua da Atalaia

Rua da Barroca

Rua do Norte

Rua das Gáveas

Rua da Misercórdia

Rua Nova da Trindade

Rua Santa Catarina

BICA Funicular

Rua das Chagas

Pr. Luis de Camões

Largo do Carmo

Rua Trindade

Rua das Flores

Largo do Chiado

Rua Garrett

Rua de São Paulo

Rua do Alecrim

Rua Duque de Bragança

Rua Serpa

Rua Vítor Cordon

Rua do Ouro

Rua Augusta

Pr. Duque da Terceira

Pr. do Municipio

Information ⓘ

Post Office ✉

Church ✝

1068

PORTUGAL

LISBON ✪

Biblioteca National ❼
Elevador de Santa Justa ❺
Igreja de São Roque ❶
Igreja do Carmo ❸

Museu de Arqueologia ❹
Museu de Arte
  Contemporâneo ❽
Teatro São Carlos ❻
Teatro Trindade ❷

School. It depicts the prince himself leading a throng of sailors, captains, priests, and poets to imperial glory. In the pavement is a map chronicling Portuguese discoveries from 1427 to 1541. An elevator can take you to the top.

Museu da Marinha (Naval Museum)

Praça do Império, Belém. ☎ **01/362-00-10.** Admission 250 Esc ($1.60) adults, 150 Esc (95¢) students 10–18, free for children 9 and under and adults over 65. Tues–Sun 10am–5pm. Closed hols. Tram 15 or 17. Bus 27, 28, 29, 43, 49, or 51.

At the western end of the Mosteiro dos Jerónimos, this museum contains a large collection of maps, maritime paraphernalia, and finely detailed models of ships old and new, including Egyptian and Greek warships dating from 3000 B.C. In an annex across the way is an exhibit of life-size royal barges, galleons, and sailing ships.

✪ Museu Nacional de Arte Antiga (National Museum of Ancient Art)

Rua das Janelas Verdes, Belém. ☎ **01/396-41-51.** Tram Alcantara. Bus 49.

Here are samplings of eight centuries of art (the 12th through the 19th), including ceramics, silver, and tapestries, as well as the most important national collection of Portuguese paintings. Works by Cranach, Velázquez, Brueghel, Holbein, Dürer, and Murillo are on view, as is the unforgettable Hieronymus Bosch masterpiece *The Temptations of St. Anthony.* Don't miss the enormous 17th-century silver platter weighing 2,000 pounds! At this writing, renovations are continuing. Visits to rotating sections of the museum are curtailed, and hours are frequently altered. Call ahead before making the trip to Belém.

PARKS & GARDENS

Among Lisbon's numerous gardens, the finest are the **Jardim Botânico** (Botanical Garden) and the **Jardim da Estrêla.** Its largest parks are the Parque de Monsanto and the Parque Eduardo VII.

The following small parks and terraces offer fine views of the city: *Cristo Rei,* on the other side of the Tagus, has a replica of the statue of Christ in Rio de Janeiro; **Alto de Santa Catarina,** on rua da Santa Catarina; **Castelo Saño Jorge,** at the top of the Alfama; Luenta dos Quarteis, Moinho dos Mochos, Alto da Serafina, and Montes Claros in **Parque de Monsanto; Ponte,** viaduto Duarte Pacheco; **belvedere of Santa Luzia;** Senhora do Monte (great for sunsets); **Zimborio da Basilica da Estrêla,** on largo da Estrêla; and **Saño Pedro de Alcantara.**

CITY TOURS

Along its entire route, **tram no. 28** passes through Lisbon's most picturesque neighborhoods—the Bairro Alto, Alfama, and Graça.

TRAM TOURS

Since 1901 trams have negotiated the intimate alleyways and tight corners of Lisbon's old quarters. Rather than being put out to pasture (as so many of their peers have been throughout the world), Lisbon's aged but doughty trams are still going strong. Carris, the city's tram company, is pleased to offer visitors a pair of enchanting two-hour tram tours through the Portuguese capital.

Its **"Hills of Lisbon"** tour reveals a city of contrasts along a route that penetrates into the heart of the old city and its bustling life and also surveys the bold, bright cityscapes of today's trendier quarters.

"The Tagus Line" tour plies the trail of Portugal's seafaring 15th and 16th centuries. Among the sights visited is one of the great symbols and remarkable achievements born of Portugal's centuries of exploration—the exquisite Jerónimos Monastery, a masterpiece of Manueline architecture.

Both tours depart from praça do Comércio. "The Tagus Line" tour operates daily from July 1 to August 31, departs at 10:30am and 2:15pm, and costs 1,325 Esc ($8.55) for adults, half price for children 4–10; free for those under 4. "The Hills of Lisbon" tour operates daily from May 22 to October 15 several times per day and costs 2,200 Esc ($14.20) for adults, half price for children. Tickets are sold on board.

For exact departure times and additional information, call **01/363-93-43.**

WALKING TOURS

TOUR 1   Start at Rossio Square in the heart of town. Follow rua do Ouro to praça do Comércio with its statue of King José I, then pick up rua da Alfândego de Santarém east out of praça do Comércio and turn left along rua da Madalena to the sign indicating that the Sé (cathedral) is up to the right. On the left is the Igreja Saño António and, a little farther up, the Sé. Follow rua Augusta Rosa (which becomes first Saño Martinho and then rua Limoeiro) to the belvedere of Santa Luzia with its wonderful view of Lisbon and the Tagus.

A little farther up on the left, in largo Portas do Sol, is the Fundaçaño Ricardo Espírito Santo (Museum of Decorative Arts). Returning to the Santa Luzia belvedere and turning right through largo Contador Mor and then going up rua do Funil, you'll come upon chaño da Feira leading up to Castelo Saño Jorge (St. George's Castle). Go back along chaño da Feira and follow rua de Saño Tomé, which becomes calçada da Graça, to the Igreja da Graça by Graça Square. Upon leaving Graça Square, visit the Chapel of Ermida da Senhora do Monte. Turning back a little, go down rua da Voz do Operário until you reach Saño Vicente Square with the church of the same name. Flanking the church is an open space where the Feira da Ladra (Flea Market) is held.

TOUR 2   Start at praça dos Restauradores. Its obelisk was built in memory of national independence won from the Spanish in 1640. Go one block past Rossio Square along rua do Ouro to the Santa Justa Elevator, off to the right. From the top is a marvelous view of downtown Lisbon, the castle, and the Graça area. The adjacent Convent do Carmo houses the Archeological Museum. From the base of the elevator, follow rua do Carmo to the left and go right on rua Garrett to praça de Luís Camoñes. Take a right onto rua da Misericórdia, leading off the praça. This soon comes to the Saño Roque Church. Next to it is the Museum of Sacred Art. Continue up the street a short distance to the park of Saño Pedro de Alcantara with its lovely view. Continue in the direction of praça do Príncipe Real along rua Escola Politécnica. On the right is an entrance to the Jardim Botânico.

ORGANIZED BUS TOURS

Grey Line Tours, avenida Fontes Pereira de Melo 14-12° (☎ **01/57-75-23**), offers various city tours. "Lisboa Turística" is a half-day tour including Rossio, Castelo de Saño Jorge, Alfama, praça do Comércio, Torre de Belém, Padraño dos Descobrimentos, Mosteiro dos Jerónimos, and Museu dos Coches. It departs from Parque Eduardo VII daily at 9:30am and 2:30pm. The price is 4,725 Esc ($30.50); children 3 and under go free and children 4 to 10 are charged half price. "Lisboa a Noite e Casino" includes a panoramic view of Lisbon by night, dinner at a restaurant with performances of Portuguese folk dances and fado, and an optional cabaret show at the Casino Estoril (two drinks included; jacket and tie required). This tour departs from Parque Eduardo VII at 8pm on Tuesday, Thursday, and Saturday from November to March, and daily from April to October. The tour of only Lisbon costs 11,655 Esc ($75.20); with the casino visit it costs 14,280 Esc ($92.15).

Similar tours are also available through **Portugal Tours,** rua D. Estefania, 124-2° (☎ **01/352-29-02**).

7 Shopping

The value-added tax (IVA in Portugal) varies according to the item or service sold—in most cases, from 8% to 16%. Visitors from countries outside the European Union are entitled to a refund of the tax if purchases in a duty-free store total at least 12,080 Esc ($77.95), exclusive of VAT. To obtain the refund, have the shop fill in the front of the Tax-Free Check, then fill in the back. When leaving Portugal, carry your purchases, Tax-Free Checks, and passport in your hand luggage for presentation to Customs. Redeem the stamped checks at the Tax Refund counter for cash or credit on your credit or charge cards. There are Tax Refund counters at the Lisbon airport and the Lisbon harbor. For information, call **01/418-87-03.** Participating stores display the TAX-FREE FOR TOURISTS sign.

Except for several minimalls (such as Imaviz, next to the Sheraton Hotel) and one megamall (Amoreiras, with over 350 shops), small establishments are the norm. The best buys are ceramics, porcelain, pottery, and embroidered and leather goods, but bargains are no longer as common as they once were. The smartest shops are on rua Garrett and the surrounding streets, in an area known as the Chiado, part of which was razed or damaged by the 1988 blaze. Much remains standing though, and reconstruction is well under way.

Rua da Escola Politécnica is the upper end of a long street with five names (rua do Alecrim, rua da Misericórdia, rua de Saño Pedro de Alcantara, rua Dom Pedro V, and rua da Escola Politécnica). Scattered all along here are antiques shops.

MARKETS On Tuesday and Saturday the **Fiera da Ladra ("Thieves" or Flea Market)** goes on until 5pm in campo de Santa Clara behind the Igreja Saño Vicente. Take bus no. 12 from Santa Apolónia Station.

8 Lisbon After Dark

Lisbon's nightlife is gaining momentum. For information on performances and productions, contact the tourist office or the **Agência de Bilhetes para Espectáculos Públicos,** praça dos Restauradores (☎ **01/347-58-23**), open daily from 9am to 10pm. The latter sells tickets to all cinemas and theaters except the National Theater of Saño Carlos, as well as for the frequent concerts by name rock bands stopping in Lisbon on their world tours.

The *Diário de Noticias* also has the latest listings (in Portuguese), as does the weekly magazine *Sete.*

THE PERFORMING ARTS

The season for opera, theater, ballet, and concerts runs from October to May, with additional performances throughout the year. The main venues are the **Teatro**

Nacional de Dona Maria II, in Rossio Square (☎ **01/342-22-10**); the **Teatro Nacional de Saño Carlos,** at rua Serpo Pinto 9 (☎ **01/346-5914**); the **Fundaçaño Calouste Gulbenkian,** avenida de Berna 45 (☎ **01/793-51-31**); the **Teatro Municipal Saño Luís,** rua António Maria Cardoso 40 (☎ **01/347-1279**); and the **Teatro Trindade,** largo da Trinidade 7-A (☎ **01/342-32-00**).

Opera tickets run 500 to 3,000 Esc ($3.25 to $19.35); theater tickets, 1,000 to 2,500 Esc ($6.45 to $16.15). Ballet and concert tickets vary greatly depending on the performance.

Music Clubs

Fado is to Lisbon what jazz is to New Orleans and flamenco is to Seville— a native art that relies on emotion and spontaneity. Don't leave Lisbon without experiencing it. Fado clubs (known as *adegas típicas* or *restaurantes típicos*) serve dinner before and during the entertainment, which usually starts about 10pm. Or you can dine elsewhere and arrive around 11pm to enjoy the show for a minimum charge. Ask how much this is before entering the club—it's typically about 2,500 to 3,000 Esc ($16.15 to $19.35), which will cover two or three drinks.

As riveting as fado can be, an evening of it goes a long way. Alternative entertainments are available. Jazz, rock, and Afro-Brazilian pop are popular, and a number of clubs present live groups several nights a week.

Hot Clube de Portugal

Praça da Alegria 39. ☎ **01/346-73-69.** Cover 500–1,100 Esc ($3.25–$7.10) when there's live music, which begins about 11:30pm. Metro: Avenida.

Come here for the sounds of mainstream and fusion jazz in a traditional subterranean environment, usually blue with cigarette smoke. Open Tuesday through Saturday from 10pm to 2am, with live music Thursday through Saturday.

Lisboa à Noite

Rua das Gáveas 69. ☎ **01/346-85-57.** No cover, but a 2,700-Esc ($17.40) minimum. Metro: Restauradores.

Contrary to what other sources insist, this well-known fado club isn't unusually expensive, although the minimum (which will cover a couple of highballs, a small carafe of wine, and an appetizer/snack) may kick to a higher level when the famous owner/diva, Fernanda Maria, is in residence and performing. The interior is more restrained and attractive than that in most of the breed, as are the routine pitches to buy cassettes and souvenirs. Open daily from 8:30pm to 3am.

Machado

Rua do Norte 91. ☎ **01/346-00-95.** No cover, but a 2,500-Esc ($16.15) minimum. Metro: Restauradores.

Not far from Lisboa à Noite (above), for those who are fado-hopping, Machado has a colorful folkloric setting of bad paintings and signed photos of semicelebrated guests. Every 20 minutes or so, three guitarists take their places at the back of the small stage. The singer stands in front, her shawl pulled tight around her, head thrown back, eyes closed, crying out the ritual of despair and lost love. It's often electrifying, especially when the headliner comes on. Plates of food cost 2,200 to 4,200 Esc ($14.20 to $27.10). Open Tuesday through Sunday from 8pm to 3am.

✪ Parreirinha da Alfama

Beco do Espírito Santo 1. ☎ **01/886-82-09.** No cover, but a 2,100-Esc ($13.55) minimum after 10:30pm. Bus 37.

One of the less expensive quality fado clubs, this place is cozy, and patrons often join spontaneously in the singing. Sets are every 20 minutes from 10pm to 3am. Main courses run 850 to 3,100 Esc ($5.50 to $20). Go later just for music and drinks. Open Monday through Saturday from 8pm to 3am.

✪ Xafarix

Avenida Dom Carlos I 69. ☎ **01/396-94-87.** Tram 15, 16, 17, 18, 29, or 30. Bus 14, 28, 32, 40, 43, or 54.

This friendly small club with nightly live music is owned by Luís Represas, one of Portugal's heartthrob vocalists. The musical idiom varies, but the caliber of the performers is usually high. Open daily from 10pm to 4am.

FILMS

Foreign films are usually subtitled, so recent Hollywood releases can be seen in English, not dubbed into Portuguese, as might be expected. Monday matinees are cheapest, but prices are low anytime. First-run theaters are easily found along avenida da Liberdade and around praça dos Restauradores.

THE BAR SCENE

A burgeoning crop of nightbirds is keeping Lisbon bars and clubs open later and later, sometimes until dawn and beyond. Many of the most popular spots don't even bother to open until 10 o'clock or later.

✪ Bairro Alto

Travessa dos Inglesinhos 50. ☎ **01/342-02-38.** No cover, but a minimum of 680–1,260 Esc ($4.40–$8.15).

In the vanguard of contemporary design, the Bairro Alto is an outpost in the trendy postmodern mold. Though billed as a "bar/pub," it also has a dance floor and, on the upper level, a billiard table. A mixed crowd converses leisurely at the curvaceous bar. This one is tucked away in the labyrinthine upper reaches of the Bairro Alto, so take a cab. Open Wednesday through Saturday from 10pm to 4am.

Harry's Bar

Rua de Saño Pedro de Alcantara 57. ☎ **01/346-07-60.**

Across from one of the most appealing parks and belvederes in the city, this long-lived cocktail lounge (with a picture of Marilyn Monroe on one wall) draws a mixed crowd of couples, gays and lesbians, tourists, artistes, and journalists. Songs by Portuguese pop singers alternate with the likes of Johnny Cash. Cocktails run 450 to 800 Esc ($2.90 to $5.15). Open Monday through Saturday from 10pm to 6am.

Instituto do Vinho do Porto

Rua de Saño Pedro de Alcantara 45. ☎ **01/347-57-07.**

Save this place for after dinner. Behind two massive wood doors in an old building near Harry's Bar is a multiroom lounge featuring Portugal's trademark postprandial tipple. Decorated in dated Eisenhower style, the nonetheless-comfortable retreat is a virtual library of every variety and price level of port wine, some white and dry, most red and semidry or sweet. It may take two or three selections from the big menu to get to a bottle they have open and in stock, but it's a marvelous way to sample one of the nation's proudest products. Glasses of wine cost as little as 120 Esc (75¢) to as much as 9,000 Esc ($58.05) for a rare vintage. Open Monday through Friday from 10am to 11:45pm and Saturday from 11am to 10:45pm.

Pavilhaño Chines Bar
Rua Dom Pedro V 89. ☎ **01/342-47-29.** Tram 24.

This unusual bar goes on for several rooms chockablock with an eclectic and often kitschy collection of toys, collectibles, and oddities, especially from the Far East. The bar in back has a lovely marquetry top, a touch of style amid the rows of souvenir plates, bronze Cupids, cartoons of the Great War antagonists, gobs and gaggles of Victoriana, cases of Toby jugs, ceramics of Buddha, Hussars . . . and Popeye. Beer costs 470 Esc ($2.70) and cocktails run 550 to 750 Esc ($3.55 to $4.85). Open Monday through Friday from 2pm to 2am, Saturday from 6pm to 2am, and Sunday from midnight to 2am.

DANCE CLUBS

Lisbon's classier nightspots are permitted to charge an outrageous cover to keep out the riffraff, but well-dressed, respectable-looking types are usually admitted free. A moderate cover may be charged if the place is full, however.

Fragil
Rua da Atalaia 126. ☎ **01/346-95-78.** Cover varies (some people are charged admission; some aren't). Tram 24.

Opened in 1982, this remains one of the hottest discos in town, popular, it is said, with the film, fashion, and design crowd. The decor changes whenever the owner gets bored, roughly every two or three months. The results are difficult to discern, since the many rooms are kept as dark as the inside of a refrigerator. Drinks run 1,000 to 1,500 Esc ($6.45 to $9.70). Open Monday through Saturday from 11pm or midnight to 6am or later.

✪ Kremlin
Escadinhas da Praia 5. ☎ **01/60-87-68**. Tram 15, 16, 17, 18, 29, or 30. Bus 14, 28, 32, 40, or 43.

The last stop on the beautiful people's nocturnal circuit, this most popular of loud, pounding discos doesn't hit full stride until about 4am and holds a party every month or two when it completely changes its decor. The crowd is mixed, but those in their 20s and early 30s predominate. Drinks run 1,050 to 1,260 Esc ($6.75 to $8.15). Open Monday through Thursday from 2 to 6am and Friday and Saturday from 2 to 10am or later.

Plateau
Escadinhas da Praia 7. ☎ **01/396-51-16.** Tram 15, 16, 17, 18, 29, or 30. Bus 14, 28, 32, 40, or 43.

Next door to Kremlin (above), this is the next-to-last stop on the beautiful people's nocturnal circuit. It's smaller and less distinctive of decor, but the crowd, the mood, and the music are much the same. Drinks run 1,050 to 1,525 Esc ($6.75 to $9.85). Open Tuesday through Saturday from midnight to 4:30am.

✪ Primorosa
Avenida E.U.A. 128-D. ☎ **01/797-19-13.** Cover 2,100 Esc ($13.55), including two drinks. Metro: Entrecampos.

One of Lisbon's enduring discos, Primorosa also has a sedate piano bar (called Cyrrose, meaning "cirrhosis") with live entertainment Monday through Saturday beginning at 11pm. Those who prefer intimacy to the trendy warehouse expanse of many of today's discos will appreciate the cozy nooks and crannies of this club's attractive cavelike decor. Open Saturday through Monday from 11pm to 4am.

9 Easy Excursions

THE ESTORIL COAST   This stretch of Atlantic shore was once favored by native and forcibly expatriated aristocracy and continues to draw some representatives of Europe's dwindling nobility. Unfortunately, development and pollution have taken their toll. **Estoril** itself is some 15 miles from Lisbon and has a casino with a nightclub (☎ **01/468-80-39**), open daily, except Christmas Eve, from 3pm to 3am. Bring your passport for entrance. The cabaret show without dinner costs 5,000 Esc ($32.25), including two drinks. The casino is a rather grave affair, the only whoops and groans coming from the craps table, surrounded by Americans accustomed to a more boisterous form of losing.

Cascais, a few miles farther along, was once a drowsy village that has followed the familiar progression from fishing port to artists' colony to here-comes-everybody. Working boats still find berths among the pleasure craft, and tamarisk and hibiscus struggle for space between boîtes and boutiques. There's a pretty beach, umbrella-covered sidewalk cafés, and a lively nightlife that attracts a mostly younger crowd. For a day in the surf and sun, hop on the train that leaves every half hour or so from the Cais do Sodre Station in Lisbon and get off at Estoril (a half-hour ride), Cascais (a 40-minute ride), or any other stop along the way that strikes your fancy. The round-trip fare to Cascais is 325 Esc ($2.10).

After Cascais, the coast starts to bend north. The temper of the sea changes, raked directly now by the intimidating Atlantic. Wave action has bored gaping cavities into the sheer cliffs at **Boca do Inferno,** a popular photo op. Farther along, the land flattens, the vegetation thins, and fine white sand steams in gusts across the road. Eventually, the land lifts again toward the headlands, pocketing the beaches. Breakers belly into milk-green curls before collapsing in an unending thunderous boil. This is prime windsurfing territory, but both surfers and swimmers must be ultra-careful about the powerful undertow.

SINTRA   An hour in this place of myth and magic has everyone agreeing with Lord Byron, who lived here a while. A "glorious Eden," the poet called this small hilltown of 15,000. At every turn of the road, there's anther battlement, spire, or watchtower. About 18 miles from Lisbon, the town swells regularly with day-trippers from the capital. Botanists thrill to some 90 species of unusual plants thriving in the Sintra hills. Romantics revel in Sintra's two marvelous palaces.

The main square, bordered by pastel shops and houses, is dominated by the huge conical twin chimneys of the **Paço Real** (☎ **01/923-41-18**), also known as the Palácio Nacional de Sintra. The palace is open Thursday through Tuesday from 10am to 1pm and 2 to 5pm. Dating back 1,000 years to the Moors, this was the scene of many memorable moments in Portuguese history. What is seen today dates mainly from the 14th to the 16th century and is largely baroque in character, with gothic, Manueline, and Islamic flourishes. Most impressive are the decorative tilework, tapestries, gilded ceilings, and kitchen, served by those two giant chimneys, all among the best to be seen in Portugal. Yet compared with what's still to be seen, its spaces and decor seem heavy-handed.

An uphill lane leading to **Seteais** becomes a narrow channel between walls with mottled skins of moss and lichen. Bars of sunlight pierce the canopy of oak and eucalyptus from time to time, and high iron gates permit glimpses of the villas they protect. Byron walked the halls of the Palácio dos Seteais, now a hotel. From there, he could see the ocean and, looking still farther up, the golden cupolas of the **Palácio da Pena** (☎ 01/923-02-27), perched 1,300 feet high on a panoramic mountaintop. It's an extraordinary piece of romantic architecture, dating from 1839, when the ruins of a 16th-century monastery began to be adapted for use as a residence. Purists are offended by the palace's agglomeration of styles, but it has nothing to do with aesthetics and everything to do with fantasy. Inspired by the lavish palaces and castles of Bavaria at the time of Mad King Ludwig, Pena is a fanciful pastiche of Moorish, gothic, and Manueline conceits. The Manueline cloister and the chapel remain from the monastery. It's open Tuesday through Friday from 10am to 5pm and Saturday and Sunday from 10am to 1pm and 2 to 5pm.

Admission to both Sintra palaces is 260 Esc ($1.70) October to May, 475 Esc ($3.05) June to September.

Frequent trains run to Sintra from Lisbon's Rossio Station. The trip takes about 45 minutes and costs 325 Esc ($2.10). The local tourist office in praça da República (☎ 01/923-11-57) is open daily from 9am to 7pm.

QUELUZ Just 9 miles from Lisbon, the frosted-pink **Queluz Palace** (☎ 01/435-00-39) is Portugal's rococo rendition of Versailles. The Sun King would have loved it. Built in 1747, it had been a hunting lodge for 200 years before being transformed into a royal residence. Most notable are the Throne Room, Queen's Dressing Room, Don Quixote Chamber, and Music Salon. They are fitted out with Portuguese antiques and tapestries, splendid examples of Arraiolo carpets from the Alentejo region, Italian glassware and marble, Dutch tiles, Austrian porcelain, and Chinese screens. One wing serves as a guesthouse for state visitors, who have included Elizabeth II and former President Reagan. The well-manicured Versailles-like gardens are a fragrant as well as visual delight. A stunning restaurant has been installed in the royal kitchen, with its mammoth fireplace and beamed ceiling. Called, logically enough, the **Cozinha Velha** (☎ 01/435-02-32), its cuisine and service are equal to the setting. A meal there isn't close to inexpensive, averaging about 9,500 Esc ($61.30) for two. Those who decide to take the plunge, perhaps as an appropriate capstone for a visit to the Sintra Mountains, should call ahead to reserve. The restaurant is open daily for lunch and dinner. Queluz Palace is open Wednesday through Monday from 10am to 1pm and 2 to 5pm. Admission October through May is 260 Esc ($1.70); June through September, 470 Esc ($3.05); free Sunday morning and for children under 12; closed holidays.

Without a private car, Queluz is best visited as part of an organized tour. Trains do run from Rossio Square to Queluz, but once there you'll have to take a cab to the palace.

16

London

by Dan Levine

London attracts more visitors than any other European city, and even the briefest glance at this capital's vast and unique offerings will make it clear why. Tourists are drawn by the world-class museums, great shopping, unparalleled theater, and pulsating nightlife. The city's extreme mix of cultures—a relic of empire—gives London the depth and the character that have long kept it at the forefront of the world's art, music, and fashion scenes.

Many travelers who come here hoping to see some vestiges of London's history are disappointed when they see this modern city, where all too often the only things marking the past are the little blue plaques commemorating former residences. Don't despair: The past is alive and well in London—you just have to know how to look for it. With a few notable exceptions, history in the capital is more pronounced socially than architecturally. Though less pronounced than it once was, the British class system stubbornly endures. The scandal-ridden royal family is not just a tourist attraction—it heads a very real aristocracy that continues to wield much of the nation's wealth and power. And despite its declining relevance in today's world, Royal London's pomp and pageantry survive with daily ceremonies like the Changing of the Guard at Buckingham Palace and the Ceremony of the Keys at the Tower of London.

When in London you're in one of the world's most exciting cities. Take advantage of its terrific offerings and unique opportunities. Explore the narrow alleyways of The City, enjoy lunch in a local pub, attend a free concert in a church, and strike up a conversation with the locals. Even though the British Empire is no more, its former capital still flourishes with more than its fair share of cultural activities, entertainment houses, special events, and, of course, history. Have a jolly good time!

1 London Deals & Discounts

BUDGET BESTS Not only does London offer many of the world's "bests," but most of these attractions are either free or priced well below comparable sights Stateside. Most of London's museums are free, as are the main sections of such major attractions as Westminster Abbey and the Houses of Parliament. The Changing of the Guard at Buckingham Palace is also free, along with the

What's Special About London

Attractions

- The Tower of London, combining fascinating history with awesome architecture, colorful pageantry, and good humor.
- The British Museum, as big as it is famous, and the standard by which other great museums are often judged.
- Westminster Abbey, where British monarchs have been crowned for 900 years.

Food & Drink

- Pubs—architecturally or culturally, nothing in England is more special or ubiquitous.

Spectacles

- Covent Garden, once a marketplace and now an upbeat meeting space in the heart of the West End, which reveals London's lightest side.
- Speakers' Corner, where comedians, anarchists, religious fanatics, and would-be politicians compete for your ear every Sunday.

Special Events

- The Chelsea Flower Show, the Notting Hill Carnival, and the Wimbledon Lawn Tennis Championships—so special they're worth planning your trip around.

Flea Markets

- Portobello Road and Camden High Street particularly, which seem to go on forever and offer a full day of fun.

Evening Entertainment

- Great theater—no other city in the world offers such a variety of high-quality productions, and government support for many of the repertory theaters makes tickets affordable.

often-acerbic Speakers' Corner every Sunday in Hyde Park (see "Parks and Gardens" under "Attractions," later in this chapter). Tickets to the London stage are still cheaper than those to comparable New York productions, and cheap seats are regularly available to the opera, ballet, and symphony.

SPECIAL DISCOUNTS   If you're a student or a senior citizen, there are often discounts specially for you.

For Students   Students in England enjoy discounts on travel, on theater and museum tickets, and at some nightspots. The **International Student ID Card (ISIC)** is the most readily accepted proof of student status. This card should be purchased before you leave home, but if you've arrived without one and are a good enough talker (or just happen to be carrying a registrar-stamped and -signed copy of your current school transcript), you can obtain one for about £5.50 ($8.25) at **S.T.A. Travel,** 86 Old Brompton Rd., SW7 (☎ **0171/937-9962** or 937-9921), near the South Kensington tube station. The office is open Monday through Friday from 9am to 6pm and Saturday from 10am to 4pm. Special student discounts and prices are listed throughout this chapter under their appropriate headings.

If you're looking for cheap intra-European flights, try **Campus Travel,** 52 Grosvenor Gardens (☎ **0171/730-8832;** fax 0171/730-5739), which often offers charter flights.

For Seniors   In Britain, senior citizen usually means a woman at least 60 or a man at least 65. Seniors often receive the same discounts as students. Unfortunately for tourists, some discounts are available only to seniors who are also British subjects. More often, however, your passport or other proof of age will also be your passport to cutting costs.

2 Pretrip Preparations

REQUIRED DOCUMENTS   Citizens of the United States, Canada, Australia, and New Zealand need only a valid passport to enter the United Kingdom. However, Customs officials tend to ask younger travelers and suspicious-looking others to prove they have enough cash and/or an onward ticket before admitting them into the country. Some street-wise student travelers avoid this hassle at Passport Control by writing the name of an expensive hotel on their landing cards.

TIMING YOUR TRIP   Seasonal spirit is strong in London. Spring is celebrated with festive fairs and a fresh, friendly attitude as locals shed their coats and restaurateurs return their tables to the sidewalks. Summer means open-air theaters, park picnics, and late-night laughter around bustling Leicester Square. In the autumn, London's churches are decorated with flowers and fruits of the harvest. Fall and winter are best for culture: The opera and ballet seasons are in full swing, and theaters, museums, restaurants, and all the major sights are mercifully free of crowds.

London's Average Daytime Temperature & Rainfall

	Jan	Feb	Mar	Apr	May	June	July	Aug	Sept	Oct	Nov	Dec
Temp. (°F)	40	40	44	49	55	61	64	64	59	52	46	42
Rainfall "	2.1	1.6	1.5	1.5	1.8	1.8	2.2	2.3	1.9	2.2	2.5	1.9

Special & Free Events   The **Charles I Commemoration,** on the last Sunday in January, is solemnly marked by hundreds of cavaliers marching through central London in 17th-century dress. Prayers are said at Banqueting House in Whitehall, where, on January 30, 1649, King Charles I was executed "in the name of freedom and democracy." Free.

The **Chinese New Year** falls in late January or early February (based on the lunar calendar) and is celebrated on the nearest Sunday. Festive crowds line the decorated streets of Soho to watch the famous Lion Dancers. Free.

The **Easter Parade** is London's largest. Brightly colored floats and marching bands circle Battersea Park, kicking off a full day of activities. Free.

The **Chelsea Flower Show** is held annually in May. This international spectacular features the best of British gardening, with displays of plants and flowers of all seasons. The location, on the breathtakingly beautiful grounds of the Chelsea Royal Hospital, helps make this exposition the rose of garden shows. For tickets, contact the Royal Horticultural Society, Vincent Square, SW1 (☎ **0171/ 828-1744**), or check with the British Tourist Authority in your home country (see the Appendix for the address) for the name of the overseas booking agent handling ticket sales this year.

Trooping the Colour celebrates the queen's official birthday on a Saturday in early June. Visitors can catch all the queen's horses and all the queen's men as they parade down the Mall from Buckingham Palace. Free.

The end of June signals the start of the **Wimbledon Lawn Tennis Championships,** the most prestigious event in tennis. Tickets are usually available at the gate for early rounds of play and cost about £9 ($13.50), £4.50 ($6.75) after 5pm. Center-court seats for later rounds are sold by lottery half a year in advance by the All England Lawn Tennis and Croquet Club (☎ **0181/946-2244**). A (very) few center-court seats are sold on the day of the match. To get these seats, camping out in line the night before might be in order.

The **Notting Hill Carnival,** held in late August, is one of the largest annual street festivals in Europe. This African-Caribbean street fair in the community of Notting Hill attracts over half a million people during its two days. Live reggae and soul music combine with great Caribbean food to ensure that a great time is had by all. Free.

Visitors have another chance to see the royals during the **State Opening of Parliament** in late October or early November. Although the ceremony itself is not open to the public, crowds pack the parade route to see the procession. Free.

Early November is also the season for **Guy Fawkes Day,** commemorating the anniversary of the Gunpowder Plot, an attempt to blow up King James I and his parliament. Huge organized bonfires are lit throughout the city, and Guy Fawkes, the plot's most famous conspirator, is burned in effigy. Free.

What Things Cost in London	U.S. $
Taxi from Victoria Station to a Bayswater hotel	12.00
Underground from Heathrow Airport to central London	4.65
Local telephone call	.15
Double room at the Dorchester Hotel (deluxe)	525.00
Double room at the Strand Palace Hotel (moderate)	187.50
Double room at the Oakley Hotel (budget)	55.50
Lunch for one at Daquise (moderate)	13.00
Lunch for one at most pubs (budget)	6.00
Dinner for one, without wine, at the English House (deluxe)	108.50
Dinner for one, without wine, at Bahn Thai (moderate)	19.50
Dinner for one, without wine, at Khan's (budget)	10.25
Pint of beer	2.70
Coca-Cola in a restaurant	1.50
Cup of coffee	1.20
Roll of ASA 100 film, 36 exposures	7.50
Admission to the British Museum	Free
Movie ticket	7.50
Cheapest West End theater ticket	12.00

In the middle of November, the **Lord Mayor's Show** takes to the streets with an elaborate parade celebrating the inauguration of the new chief of The City of London. Colorful floats, military bands, and the lord mayor's 1756 gold State Coach are all part of this famous event. Free.

BACKGROUND READING　　There are too many brilliant British bards to list them all here, but I do feel obliged at least to mention Shakespeare and Dickens. Listed below are some very accessible academic works on British social history. *London Life in the Eighteenth Century* by M. Dorothy George (Academy Chicago Publishers, 1985) is an enlightened and readable study of life in the Georgian period. *The Making of Modern London* by Gavin Weightman and Steve Humphries (Sidgewick and Jackson) is my pick from the mountain of books on the Victorian development of London, and *The Long Weekend* by Robert Graves and Alan Hodge (Norton, 1963) offers a fascinating account of Britain between the wars. *Frommer's Walking Tours: London* offers 12 interesting walks for seeing London's various areas.

3　London Specifics

ARRIVING

FROM THE AIRPORT　　London is served by three major airports: Heathrow, Gatwick, and Stansted. All have good public transport links to central London.

The cheapest route from **Heathrow Airport** is by Underground railway or subway (often called "the tube"). The 15-mile journey takes approximately 45 minutes and costs £3.10 ($4.65) to any downtown station (see "Getting Around," below, for information on transportation discounts). Service is convenient, as the Underground platforms are directly below the airport terminals. But Heathrow is big, and even those with light luggage are advised to use one of the free baggage carts for the long walk to the train. Trains depart every 4 to 10 minutes from 6am to midnight.

Convenient nonstop trains make the 25-mile trek from **Gatwick Airport** to Victoria Station in about 30 minutes. Unfortunately, it costs a hefty £8.60 ($12.90) each way. The station is just below the airport, and trains depart every 15 minutes from 6am to 10pm (hourly, on the hour, at other times).

Stansted Airport is about 30 miles northeast of London. The Stansted Express train makes the 40-minute journey from the airport to Liverpool Street Station for £15 ($22.50) in first class, £10 ($15) in standard class. Trains depart Monday through Friday every half hour from 5:30am to 11pm, Saturday from 6:30am to 11pm, and Sunday from 7am to 11pm.

FROM THE TRAIN STATION　　Trains from Paris arrive at **Victoria Station,** visitors from Amsterdam are deposited at **Liverpool Street Station,** and arrivals from Edinburgh pull into **King's Cross Station.** All three are well connected to the city's extensive bus and Underground network. The stations all contain London Transport Information Centres, luggage lockers, telephones, restaurants, and, of course, pubs.

VISITOR INFORMATION

The **London Tourist Board (LTB)** maintains several Information Centres throughout the capital. Its staff distributes city maps, answers questions, and, in a pinch, can help you find accommodations. When entering England via

The British Pound

At this writing $1 = approximately 67p (or £1 = $1.50), and this was the rate of exchange used to calculate the dollar values given in this chapter (rounded to the nearest nickel). This rate fluctuates from time to time and may not be the same when you travel to Britain. Therefore this table should be used only as a guide:

£	U.S. $	£	U.S. $
.01	.02	6	9.00
.05	.08	7	10.50
.10	.15	8	12.00
.25	.38	9	13.50
.50	.75	10	15.00
.75	1.13	15	22.50
1	1.50	20	30.00
2	3.00	25	37.50
3	4.50	30	45.00
4	6.00	40	60.00
5	7.50	50	75.00

Heathrow, visit the LTB in the arrivals terminal before making your journey into the city; it's open daily from 9am to 6pm. Those arriving via Gatwick or by train from Paris can visit the well-staffed office in Victoria Station's forecourt. The office is open Easter to October, daily from 9am to 8pm; the rest of the year, Monday through Saturday from 9am to 7pm and Sunday from 9am to 5pm. Other LTB Information Centres are in Harrods and Selfridges department stores, both open year round during store hours, and at the Tower of London, open Easter to October only, daily from 10am to 6pm. **Visitorcall** (☎ **0839/123456**) is a recorded service from LTB with 30 lines providing daily information on various topics, including "What's On This Week," "Changing of the Guard," and "Museums." Calls cost 48p (70¢) per minute (36p/50¢ per minute between 6pm and 8am).

The **British Travel Centre,** 12 Regent St., W1, just steps from Piccadilly Circus, provides information on all of Britain. It's open Monday through Friday from 9am to 6:30pm, Saturday from 9am to 5pm, and Sunday from 10am to 4pm. Hours are usually slightly reduced in winter.

For information on Scotland, dial 0171/930-8661; for Wales, dial 0171/409-0969; for all of Ireland, dial 0171/839-8417.

For information about travel by bus, tube, or British Rail, visit a **London Transport Information Centre** in any of the major train stations, or call the London Regional Transport Travel Information Service (☎ **0171/222-1234**), open 24 hours daily.

GETTING AROUND

BY UNDERGROUND (SUBWAY) & BUS   Commuters constantly complain about it, but tourists find London's public transportation network both vast and efficient. Underground stations are abundant, and above ground you can catch one of the famous red double-decker buses. Both the Underground and buses are operated by London Regional Transport (☎ **0171/222-1234**), which maintains fares based on a zone system—you pay for each zone you cross. For most tube trips you'll be traveling within the same zone and the fare will be £1 ($1.50). A **one-day Travelcard** is good for unlimited transportation within two zones on the bus and tube after 9:30am Monday through Friday and anytime during weekends and public holidays. The card costs £2.80 ($4.20) for adults and £1.50 ($2.25) for youths 5 to 15; children 4 and under always ride free. **Weekly Travelcards** valid within the Central London Zone cost £11 ($16.50) for adults and £4.20 ($6.30) for youths 5 to 15. You'll need to present a photo to buy and use the weekly ticket; photo booths are located in tube stations—four passport-size photographs cost £2 ($3).

The tube runs every few minutes from about 5:30am to midnight (7:30am to 11pm on Sunday). Tickets can be purchased from the station ticket window or an adjacent coin-operated machine. Hold on to your ticket throughout your ride; you'll need it to exit. Pick up a handy tube map, distributed free at station ticket windows.

It looks as though the red open-back-platform **buses** will one day be a thing of the past, in favor of the more economical driver-only type. For now you can still make a flying leap onto the departing vehicle. Take a seat, either upstairs or down, and wait for the conductor to collect your fare. On the newer type of buses, pay the driver as you enter and exit through the rear doors. The bus fare within the Central London Zone 1 is £1 ($1.50).

Many tourists shy away from riding buses because their routes can be confusing. Get a free bus map from the tourist office or just ask any conductor about the route and then take advantage of a "top deck" sightseeing adventure. Like the tube, regular bus service also stops after midnight, sometimes making it difficult to get back to your hotel. At night, buses cost £1.70 ($2.55) and have different routes and different numbers from their daytime counterparts. Service is not very frequent either; if you've just missed your night bus, expect a long wait for the next one or hunt down a minicab (see below). The central London night-bus terminus is Trafalgar Square.

BY TAXI   For three or four people traveling a short distance, **black cabs** can almost be economically viable. The fare begins at £1 ($1.50), then climbs at a fast clip. There's an additional charge of 20p (30¢) per person, 10p (15¢) per large piece of luggage, and 60p (90¢) on weekends and after midnight. But the thrill of viewing London's famous monuments from the roomy back seat of a black taxi is almost enough to get your eye off the meter. If you know in advance you'll be needing a cab, you can order one by calling 0171/272-0272.

Minicabs are meterless cars driven by entrepreneurs with licenses. Technically, these taxis are not allowed to cruise for fares but must operate from sidewalk offices—many of which are centered around Leicester Square. Minicabs are handy after the tube shuts down for the night and black cabs suddenly become scarce. Always negotiate the fare beforehand, and if you're approached by a lone driver, hard bargaining is in order.

ON FOOT   London can be a difficult city to negotiate. It seems as though no two streets run parallel, and even locals regularly consult maps, but in the winding streets of The City and in the tourist area of the West End there's no better

London Underground

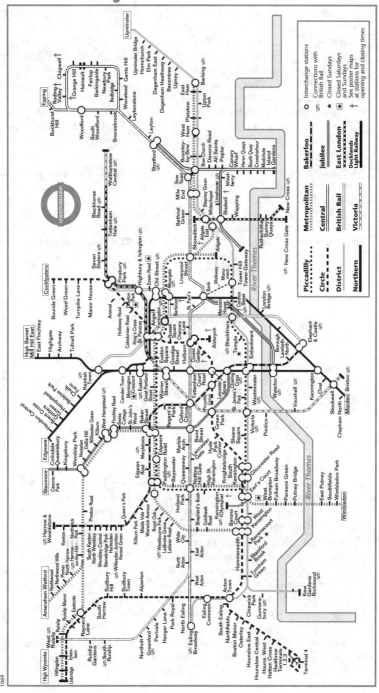

way to go. Be warned that cars have the right-of-way over pedestrians; take care even when the light seems to be in your favor.

BY BICYCLE   Bike lanes are unheard of and cars are unyielding—still, some people do ride. If you want to rent a bike, try **On Your Bike,** 52–54 Tooley St., SE1 (☎ **0171/378-6669**). A 10-speed bike rents for £10 ($15) per day during the week, £15 ($22.50) per day Saturday and Sunday. Substantial discounts are available for weekly rentals. The shop is open Monday through Friday from 9am to 6pm and Saturday from 9:30am to 5:30pm. MasterCard and Visa are accepted. **Yellow Jersey Cycles,** 44 Chalk Farm Rd., NW1 (☎ **0171/485-8090**), rents mountain bikes Monday through Saturday from 9am to 6pm and Sunday from 11am to 5pm.

BY CAR   It's not smart to keep a car in the city, and security measures have closed many streets in The City. However, if you're planning any excursions, a rental is well worth looking into. Rates vary, but expect to pay £25 to £45 ($37.50 to $67.50) per day, depending on the season. The least expensive rentals I've found are from **Practical Used Car Rental,** 111 Bartholomew Rd., NW5 (☎ **0171/284-0199**). **Avis** (☎ **0181/848-8733**) and **Budget** (☎ **toll free 0800/626-063**), both have several branches throughout the city. Gasoline (petrol) costs about £3 ($4.50) per Imperial gallon (about $3.75 per U.S. gallon).

Neighborhood Notes

The City   London is often referred to as a "city of villages" that sprang up around the square mile of the original walled Roman city. Most of the walls have long since disappeared, but the political autonomy of The City of London still separates it from the surrounding areas. The City has always been London's financial center, and it's crammed with tiny streets and a sense of history befitting its ancient beginnings.

The West End   This is the general name of a large, imprecise area west of The City, to Hyde Park. The West End encompasses the Houses of Parliament, Buckingham Palace, and the nation's densest cluster of shops, restaurants, and theaters. You'll get to know this area well.

South Kensington & Chelsea   Beyond the West End, south of Hyde Park, are the fashionable residential areas of South Kensington and Chelsea. Take a close look at these neighborhoods—you've probably never seen so many beautiful city buildings you'd like to own.

The East End   Hugging The City's eastern side is one of London's poorest areas. Traditionally, the East End was undesirable because both the prevailing winds and the flow of the River Thames move from west to east. In the plague-ridden days before sewers, life on the "wrong" side of The City was dangerous indeed. Today the East End is still home to poorer immigrants (mostly from the Indian subcontinent), as well as the capital's famous Cockneys.

Southwark   The borough of Southwark lies across the river from The City, on the south bank of the Thames. Now under heavy reconstruction, Southwark became famous as London's entertainment quarter during Elizabethan times, when theaters and brothels were banned from The City.

FAST FACTS: London

Babysitters   If your request for a recommendation from a member of your hotel staff is answered with a blank stare, phone Childminders, 9 Paddington St., W1 (☎ **0171/935-3000** or 935-2049). Alternatively, try Universal Aunts Ltd. (☎ **0171/738-8937**), a well-known local agency founded in 1921.

Banks   Most banks are open Monday through Friday from 9:30am to 3:30pm, but many stay open until 5pm, and some are open Saturday from 9:30am until noon. Banks generally offer the best exchange rates, but American Express and Thomas Cook are competitive and don't charge a commission for cashing traveler's checks, no matter the brand. **American Express** maintains several offices throughout the city, including 6 Haymarket, SW1 (☎ **0171/930-8422**), near Trafalgar Square. A conveniently located **Thomas Cook** office is at 1 Marble Arch, W1 (☎ **0171/723-1668**). Both offices are open Monday through Friday from 9am to 5pm and Saturday from 9am to noon. Places with the longest hours (sometimes open all night) also offer the worst rates. Beware of Chequepoint and other high-commission bureaux de change.

Business Hours   Stores are usually open Monday through Saturday from 10am to 6pm, but most stay open at least one extra hour one night during the week. Shops in Knightsbridge usually remain open until 7pm Wednesday, while stores in the West End are open late Thursday. Some shops around touristy Covent Garden stay open until 7 or 8pm nightly. Most stores are closed Sunday.

Currency   The basic unit of currency is the **pound sterling (£),** which is divided into 100 **pence (p).** There are 1p, 2p, 10p, 20p, 50p, and £1 coins; banknotes are issued in £1, £5, £10, £20, and £50.

Drugstores   Bliss Chemist, 5 Marble Arch, W1 (☎ **0171/723-6116**), is open daily from 9am to midnight. Boots, 75 Queensway, W2 (☎ **0171/229-1183**), near the Bayswater tube station, is open Monday through Saturday from 9am to 10pm and Sunday from 10am to 8pm.

Embassies/High Commissions   The Embassy of the **United States,** 24 Grosvenor Sq., W1 (☎ **0171/499-9000**), is open to walk-in visitors Monday through Friday from 8:30 to 11am. The High Commission of **Canada,** Macdonald House, 1 Grosvenor Sq., W1 (☎ **0171/258-6600**), is open Monday through Friday from 9am to 5pm. The High Commission of **Australia** is in Australia House, on the Strand, WC2 (☎ **0171/379-4334**), open Monday through Friday from 9am to 1pm. The High Commission of **New Zealand** is in New Zealand House, 80 Haymarket, SW1 (☎ **0171/930-8422**), open Monday through Friday from 9am to 5pm.

Emergencies   Police, fire, and ambulance services can be reached by dialing **999** from any phone. No money is required.

Holidays   Most businesses are closed New Year's Day, Good Friday, Easter Monday, the first Monday in May, and December 25–26. In addition, many stores close on bank holidays, which are scattered throughout the year. There's no uniform policy for museums, restaurants, and attractions with regard to holidays. To avoid disappointment, always phone before setting out.

Information   The **London Tourist Board (LTB)** staffs several information centers, including Victoria Station's forecourt (open daily: Easter to October, from 8am to 7pm; the rest of the year, from 9am to 6pm); and the basement of Selfridges department store, Oxford Street, W1 (open Monday through Wednesday from 9:30am to 7pm, Thursday and Friday from 9:30am to 8pm, and Saturday from 9:30am to 6:30pm).

Mail   Post offices are plentiful and normally open Monday through Friday from 9am to 5pm and Saturday from 9am to noon. The Main Post Office, 24 William IV St., Trafalgar Square, WC2 (☎ **0171/930-9580**), is open Monday through Saturday from 8am to 8pm. Mail boxes are round and red, and well distributed throughout the city.

Newspapers/Magazines   There are a lot of local newspapers in London. In general you'll find that the tabloids sensationalize news more than the respected, larger-format papers. The listings magazine *Time Out* is indispensable for comprehensive information on what's happening in the city. Newsstands are outside almost every tube station, and an unusually good selection of international newspapers and magazines is available at almost every little tobacco shop and food market.

Photographic Needs   Photo processing in London is more expensive than similar services Stateside. Boots The Chemist, 44 Piccadilly Circus, W1 (☎ **0171/734-6126**), offers one-hour photo processing at competitive rates. It's open Monday through Friday from 8:30am to 8pm, Saturday from 9am to 8pm, and Sunday from noon to 6pm.

Police   In an emergency, dial **999** from any phone; no money is needed. At other times, dial the operator (dial 100) and ask to be connected with the police.

Shoe Repair   Most of the major tube stations have "heel bars" that can make quick repairs. More extensive work can be performed in any of the major department stores or at the Complete Cobbler, 28 Tottenham St., W1 (☎ **0171/636-9040**), open Monday through Friday from 8am to 6:30pm and Saturday from 9am to 1pm.

Tax   Unlike the United States, where tax is tacked on at the register, in England a 17.5% value-added tax (VAT) is already figured into the ticket price of most items. Foreign tourists can reclaim the VAT for major purchases. See "Shopping," later in this chapter, or ask at stores for details.

Telephone   England's country code is 44. There are two **London area codes:** 0171 and 0181. If you're calling from inside the United Kingdom but outside the code area, dial the complete area code; if you're calling from outside the United Kingdom, drop the 0 (zero). As in the States, if you're calling from inside the code area, dial just the seven-digit number.

There are two kinds of **pay phones** in normal use. The first accepts coins, while the other operates exclusively with a Phonecard, available from newsstands in £1, £2, £4, £10, and £20 denominations. The minimum cost of a **local call** is 10p (15¢) for the first two minutes (peak hours). You can deposit up to four coins at a time, but telephones don't make change, so unless you're calling long distance, use 10p coins exclusively. **Phonecard** telephones automatically deduct the price of your call from the card. Cards are especially handy if you want to call abroad. Some large hotels and touristy street corners also have telephones that accept major credit and charge cards. Lift the handle and follow the instructions on the screen.

To reach the local operator, dial 100. London information (called "directory enquiries") can be reached by dialing 142, and there's a charge from some phones.

To make an **international call,** dial 155 to reach the international operator. To dial direct, dial 00, then your country code (Australia, 61; New Zealand, 64; South Africa 27; United States, 1), then the local number. You can phone home by dialing a local toll-free number in London and paying with your calling card. To phone Australia dial 0800/89-0061; for New Zealand dial 0800/89-0064; for South Africa dial 0800/89-0027; and for the United States dial 0800/89-0011 (AT&T), 0800/89-0222 (MCI), or 0800/89-0877 (Sprint).

Tipping   Most (but not all) restaurants automatically add a discretionary service charge. The restaurant's policy will be written on the menu. Where a service charge is not included, a 10% to 15% tip is customary. Taxi drivers also expect 10% to 15% of the fare. Note that tipping is rare in pubs.

4 Accommodations

The bed-and-breakfast is one of England's greatest traditions. Morning-meal menus differ but usually include cereal, eggs, bacon or sausage, toast, and all the coffee or tea you can drink. The bad news is that, in general, London's budget hotels are not as nice or as cheap as those on the Continent. The rooms are uniformly small and wear is often evident.

Summer is a seller's market, for the hordes of visitors jousting for coveted hotel rooms keep rates high. But if you sense that rooms are going unoccupied, asking for a reduced rate is definitely in order. In the off-season, prices tumble—sometimes by as much as 30%—and there's often room for further negotiation. Never accept a room until you're sure you've secured the lowest price. Make it clear that you're a budget traveler and be willing to lower your standards. If you're shopping around, make this fact clear. Always ask if they have anything cheaper and note that many hotels will offer a discount for a stay of a week or more. Everyone, especially solo travelers, should ask to see a room before renting it. Most hotels will accommodate a single person in a larger room if it's available, and asking to view it beforehand will encourage this.

Here are a few things to keep in mind when renting a room in London. Although beds are made up daily, sheets are usually not changed during a stay of less than a week. If you need new bedding, request it. Remember that even local telephone calls made from your room can be deathly expensive—inquire about the rate before dialing.

Note: The rates quoted below are accurate for the summer of 1996. Expect reductions before and after the summer season.

DOUBLES WITHOUT BATH FOR LESS THAN £40.50 ($60.75)
BAYSWATER & PADDINGTON

The district of Bayswater runs along the northern edge of Hyde Park and encompasses Paddington Station, one of the city's major gateways to the north. It's a densely packed residential community, populated by a large number of Indians and Pakistanis. It's also jammed with budget hotels. The area's proximity to the park, good restaurants (especially along Queensway and Westbourne Grove), and transportation links to the West End make Bayswater a desirable place to locate. The Central and District Underground lines run to Bayswater and Paddington stations, while buses no. 12, 88, and 289 travel the length of Bayswater Road.

Getting the Best Deal on Accommodations

- Take advantage of off-season rates. Prices tumble—sometimes by as much as 30%—and often there's room for further negotiations.
- Note that many hotels offer discounts to guests staying a week or more.
- Remember to ask if the hotel has anything cheaper.
- Request to see a room before renting it. (Hoteliers are more likely to offer their nicest rooms to travelers who look before they buy.)

---

⑤ Dean Court Hotel

57 Inverness Terrace (one block from Queensway), London W2. ☎ **0171/229-2961** or 229-9982. Fax 0171/727-1190. 16 rms and 25 multishare beds, none with bath. £32 ($48) double; £41 ($61.50) triple; £12 ($18) per person in a multishare per night, £68 ($102) per week. Rates include continental breakfast. No credit cards. Tube: Bayswater.

Brightly decorated rooms (some with antique clothes closets), big breakfasts, a capable management, and an exceptionally kind budget philosophy are all hallmarks of this top budget hotel. Most rooms have tall ceilings and single-size beds. The hotel is on a quiet Bayswater street.

✪ Hyde Park House

48 St. Petersburgh Place, London W2. ☎ **0171/229-1687.** 18 rms, none with bath. TV. £22 ($33) single; £34 ($51) double. Rates include continental breakfast. No credit cards. Tube: Bayswater; then turn left onto Moscow Road and left again at the church.

Announced by a small awning in the middle of a block of rowhouses, this family-run B&B offers a quilt on every bed and a refrigerator in every room. The small rooms are in good condition. The rates include free use of the kitchen and unlimited attention from the family's friendly small dogs.

SUSSEX GARDENS

Despite its quiet-sounding name, Sussex Gardens is one of Bayswater's busiest thoroughfares. Beginning as a traffic circle south of Paddington Station, the long street runs straight up to Edgeware Road. Along both sides of Sussex Gardens there's hardly a house that doesn't announce itself as a hotel. The accommodations are uniformly nondescript, but the rates are good and fierce competition in the off-season means that everything's negotiable.

Albro House Hotel

155 Sussex Gardens, London W2. ☎ **0171/262-2262.** 22 rms, 20 with bath. TV TEL. £25 ($40.50) single without bath, £33 ($54) single with bath; £36 ($58.50) double without bath, £40 ($72) double with bath. Rates include English breakfast. MC, V. Tube: Paddington.

Like most budget hotels in London, this place is not much more than a simple place to lay your head.

✪ Balmoral House

156 Sussex Gardens, London W2. ☎ **0171/402-0118.** 15 rms, 5 with bath. TEL. Rates include English breakfast. MC, V. Tube: Paddington.

One of the best hotels on this busy tree-lined street, Balmoral House features comfortable and very clean singles and doubles with coffee/tea-making facilities and few other frills. Your room comes with a good breakfast.

VICTORIA

The rebuilding of Buckingham House into Buckingham Palace in the 1820s helped transform Victoria into a fashionable neighborhood. Bustling Victoria Station bisects the area, separating pricey Belgravia on its northwest from more accessible Pimlico to the southeast. Much of the area was destroyed during World War II, when houses took the near misses directed at Victoria Station. Happily, most of the rebuilding has been faithful to the original Greco-Roman style. If you're shopping around, note that although there are hundreds of hotels here, the majority are not up to standard. Victoria is known not for its sights, shopping, or entertainment, but for its proximity to Victoria Station, London's transportation hub.

The Ivy House Hotel

18 Hugh St., London SW1. ☎ **0171/834-9663.** Fax 0171/828-9823. 9 rms, none with bath. TV. £25 ($37.50) single; £34 ($51) double; £47 ($70.50) triple; £53 ($79.50) quad. Rates include continental breakfast. AE, MC, V. Tube: Victoria.

Kishan and Joanne Shah, the young husband and wife who run the small Ivy House, began their careers as hoteliers in 1994 and live on the premises with their children. The hotel's three floors of modest rooms are freshly wallpapered and feature new curtains and bedspreads. Besides tea kettles and intercoms, the guest rooms feature few amenities. The Ivy House is a homey place—and its owners are sure to improve it with age.

Melita House Hotel

33–35 Charlwood St., London SW1. ☎ **0171/828-0471.** Fax 0171/932-0988. 19 rms, 12 with baths, 4 with shower only. TV. £32 ($48) single without bath, £35 ($52.50) single with shower only, £40 ($60) single with bath; £38 ($57) double without bath, £45 ($67.50) double with shower only, £50 ($75) double with bath. MC, V. Add 5% when paying by credit card. Rates include continental breakfast. Tube: Victoria. To reach Charlwood Street, turn right off Belgrave Road, south of Warwick Way.

Paul and Tina Gabriele's Melita House is an excellent example of the way quality rises and prices fall just off Belgrave Road. In this spotless charming hotel on a quiet side street, breakfast is served in a ground-floor dining room, a refreshing change from the basements of most hotels.

✪ The Oak House

29 Hugh St., London SW1. ☎ **0171/834-7151.** 6 rms, none with bath. TV. £27 ($40.50) double. No credit cards. Tube: Victoria.

One of my favorite hotels in this area is also one of the closest to Victoria Station, between Eccleston and Elizabeth bridges. Like the hotel itself, the sign hanging outside stands out from those of the other B&Bs on the block. It doesn't take a genius to figure out that resident proprietors Mr. and Mrs. Symington are Scottish. The use of tartan carpeting throughout the hotel is only slightly heavier than the couple's charming accents. There are only six rooms here, all doubles, and each is very small. The conscientious owners have fitted all with orthopedic mattresses, hairdryers, electric shaver outlets, tea/coffee-making facilities, a cutting board, knife, and even a bottle opener. No advance reservations are accepted, so when you get to the station just cross your fingers and call.

CHELSEA & SOUTH KENSINGTON

The expensive residential areas of Chelsea and South Kensington offer little in the way of accommodations for budget travelers. With few notable exceptions, the cost of lodging here reflects location rather than quality. Chelsea gained fame as London's bohemia, a place for writers and artists. Thomas Carlyle, George Eliot, Oscar Wilde, Henry James . . . the list of famous former residents is endless. A room in adjacent South Kensington is only steps away from more than half a dozen top museums and the ritzy boutiques of Knightsbridge.

In addition to the recommendations below, a couple more Chelsea and South Kensington hotels appear in the next price category.

More House

53 Cromwell Rd., London SW7. ☎ **0171/584-2040.** 55 rms, none with bath. £24 ($36) single; £38 ($57) double; £51 ($76.50) triple. Rates include English breakfast. Prices increase by £5 ($7.50) if you stay only one night; 10% discount for stays of one week or more. No credit cards. Closed Sept–May. Tube: Gloucester Road; then turn right and walk five short blocks along Cromwell Road.

This Catholic-run dormitory with an institutional feel is home to foreign students during the school year, but singles and doubles are rented to visitors of all faiths from June to August. The house is well located across from the Science Museum and is extremely functional. There's a refrigerator on every floor, plus microwave ovens for guests' use, laundry facilities, and a licensed bar.

✪ Oakley Hotel

73 Oakley St., London SW3. ☎ **0171/352-5599.** 11 rms, none with bath. £20 ($30) single; £37 ($55.50) double; £46 ($69) triple; £12 ($18) per person in a multishare room. Rates include English breakfast. No credit cards. Tube: Sloane Square; then take a long walk or the no. 11 or 22 bus down King's Road to Oakley Street.

Well-decorated rooms and a fun, friendly atmosphere make this economical hotel a welcome oasis in tab-happy Chelsea. The local council of this chic neighborhood forbids a "hotel" sign, but a knock on the green door will be answered by a friendly Australian. Aside from singles and doubles, the hotel has several multishare rooms at great rates. Guests have free use of the kitchen.

EARL'S COURT

Although it's just west of exclusive Chelsea and Knightsbridge, Earl's Court has been slow to achieve the classy status of its neighbors. There are dozens of hotels here; many are hostel-type multishare accommodations where the quality is often suspect. But the multitude of ultra-budget accommodations means that cheap restaurants, pubs, and services are nearby. The Earl's Court tube station is in the middle of Earl's Court Road, which, along with Old Brompton Road to the south, is the area's chief shopping strip. Affectionately dubbed "Kangaroo Court," Earl's Court is the unofficial headquarters of England's large Australian community.

✪ Aaron House

17 Courtfield Gardens, London SW5. ☎ **0171/370-3991.** Fax 0171/373-2303. 19 rms, 12 with bath. TV. £28 ($42) single without bath, £35 ($52.50) single with bath; £40 ($60) double without bath, £47 ($70.50) double with bath; £50 ($75) triple without bath, £58 ($87) triple with bath; £63 ($94.50) quad with bath. Rates include continental breakfast. MC, V. Tube: Earl's Court Road; then walk about three blocks east, on the west side of Courtfield Gardens.

Aaron House is perhaps the nicest budget hotel in Earl's Court, but the low quality of its competition hardly makes this a rave. The front rooms, all with bath, are particularly large and overlook a peaceful Victorian Square. Every room is fitted with a color TV and coffee/tea-making facilities.

Hotel Boka

33–35 Eardley Crescent, London SW5. ☎ **0171/370-1388**. 52 rms, 23 with shower only. £19 ($24) single without bath, £25 ($37.50) single with shower only; £28 ($42) double without bath, £34 ($51) double with shower only; £11 ($16.50) per person in a multishare room. Rates include continental breakfast. AE, MC, V. Discount for stays longer than one night. Tube: Earl's Court Road; take the Warwick Road exit, cross the street, and turn left onto Eardley Crescent (look for the bright-blue tiled columns).

The best thing about the Boka is its great location, in the middle of an architecturally awesome Victorian crescent. The accommodations here are standard whitewalled rooms, where TVs can be rented for £1 ($1.50) per night.

The Manor Hotel

23 Nevern Place, London SW5. ☎ **0171/370-6018**. 27 rms, 12 with bath. TEL. £23 ($34.50) single without bath, £32 ($48) single with bath; £36 ($54) double without bath, £47 ($70.50) double with bath; £46 ($69) triple without bath, £53 ($79.50) triple with bath. Rates include continental breakfast. Discount for stays of one week or more. No credit cards. Tube: Earl's Court Road.

The owners of the Manor Hotel have replaced the threadbare carpets so they now coordinate with the new wallpaper. The manor is still no palace, but it's thoroughly recommendable and is only two minutes away from the Earl's Court Underground station.

ELSEWHERE AROUND TOWN

Abbeville Guesthouse

89 Abbeville Rd., London SW4. ☎ **0171/622-5360**. 7 rms, none with bath. TV. £16 ($24) single; £26 ($39) double. Rates include continental breakfast. Discounts offered for stays of three nights or more. No credit cards. Tube: Clapham Common; leave at the south exit, walk along Southside Street (with the park on your right) for about 100 yards, and turn left onto Crescent Lane (not Grove), which after 300 more yards crosses Abbeville Road.

In up-and-coming Clapham Common, south of the River Thames, this quiet home offers good accommodations at reasonable rates. Mr. and Mrs. Coleman have been welcoming guests into their home for about three decades, and they know how to please picky people.

✪ Wyndham Hotel

30 Wyndham St., London W1. ☎ **0171/723-7204**. 11 rms, all with shower only. TV. £28 ($42) single; £38 ($57) double; £44 ($66) triple. These rates are for Frommer guide bearers only. Rates include continental breakfast. No credit cards. Tube: Baker Street; then cross Marylebone Road and turn right; Wyndham Street is the fifth on your left.

Tucked away on a quiet Marylebone street, this hotel stands apart from others because of its location and value. All rooms have coffee/tea-making facilities.

DOUBLES WITHOUT BATH FOR LESS THAN £47 ($70.50)

BAYSWATER

Dolphin Hotel

34 Norfolk Sq., London W2. ☎ **0171/402-4943**. 18 rms, 7 with bath. TV. £27 ($40.50) single without bath; £38 ($57) double without bath, £48 ($72) double with bath; £47 ($70.50) triple with bath. Rates include continental breakfast. English breakfast £3 ($4.50) extra. No credit cards. Tube: Paddington.

Norfolk Square is a budget hotel–packed horseshoe around a park just steps south of Paddington Station. There are too many hotels with too few distinguishing marks to mention them all here, but the Dolphin is one. In-room refrigerators, coffee makers, and (sometimes) telephones help this hotel stand out. Otherwise, its recently redecorated rooms are typical of the square and a good bet. Breakfast—whether continental or English—is served in your room.

Lords Hotel

20–22 Leinster Sq., London W2. ☎ **0171/229-8877.** Fax 0171/229-8377. 56 rms, 44 with bath, 12 with shower only. £26 ($39) single without bath, £33 ($49.50) single with shower only, £44 ($66) single with bath; £38 ($57) double without bath, £46 ($69) double with shower only, £57 ($85.50) double with bath; £50 ($75) triple without bath, £57 ($85.50) triple with shower only, £68 ($102) triple with bath. Rates include continental breakfast. No credit cards. Tube: Bayswater; then turn left onto Moscow Road, and right at the Russian Orthodox church (Ilchester Gardens); Lords is two blocks up on your left.

This well-run budget establishment offers basic rooms that are both clean and neat. Some rooms are equipped with TVs and radios, and a few have balconies—all at no extra charge. The hotel caters to people of all ages.

Strutton Park Hotel

45 Palace Court, London W2. ☎ **0171/727-5074.** 28 rms, 25 with shower only. TV TEL. £33 ($49.50) single without bath, £38 ($57) single with shower only; £42 ($63) double with shower only. Rates include English breakfast. AE, DC, MC, V. Tube: Bayswater; then turn left onto Moscow Road and walk about six blocks to Palace Court.

This small pretty hotel offers double rooms only, most with shower only (no private toilets). There's an elevator to take guests up to their rooms and down to a full breakfast.

VICTORIA

Easton Hotel

36–40 Belgrave Rd., London SW1. ☎ **0171/834-5938.** 55 rms, 11 with bath. £32 ($48) single without bath, £42 ($69) single with bath; £42 ($69) double without bath, £53 ($79.50) double with bath; £53 ($79.50) triple without bath, £62 ($93) triple with bath; £72 ($108) quad with bath; £83 ($124.50) five-person family room with bath. Rates include English breakfast. AE, MC, V. Tube: Victoria.

The rooms here are small but adequate, and some on the ground floor let you avoid stairs. An attractive licensed bar almost makes up for the distracting wood paneling on the floor of the breakfast room. The hotel is on a major thoroughfare just behind Victoria Station.

Luna and Simone Hotels

47–49 Belgrave Rd., London SW1. ☎ **0171/834-5897.** Fax 0171/838-2474. 18 rms, 10 with bath. TV TEL. £23 ($34.50) single without bath; £28 ($42) double without bath; £42–£46 ($63–$69) double with bath. Rates include English breakfast. No credit cards. Tube: Victoria.

This excellent family-run hotel is now better than ever. Clean, kindly decorated rooms and a hearty breakfast in a smoke-free dining room have vaulted this place to the budget-hotel pinnacle.

✪ Melbourne House

79 Belgrave Rd., London SW1. ☎ **0171/828-3516.** Fax 0171/828-7120. 15 rms, 13 with bath, 1 suite. TV. £37 ($55.50) single without bath; £50 ($75) double with bath; £74 ($111) triple with bath; £84 ($126) two-room suite with bath. These rates are for Frommer guide bearers only. Rates include English breakfast. No credit cards. Tube: Victoria.

Melbourne House, another of the rare breed of recommendable budget hotels on Belgrave Road, is run by friendly proprietors John and Manuela. The couple totally renovated the hotel in 1992 and offer spacious rooms with tea/coffee-making facilities.

Oxford House Hotel

92–94 Cambridge St. (south of Belgrave Road near Gloucester St.), London SW1. ☎ **0171/ 834-6467.** 17 rms, none with bath. £27 ($40.5) single; £38 ($57) double; £47 ($70.50) triple; £63 ($94.50) quad. Rates include English breakfast. Prices increase by £1 ($1.50) per person if you stay only one night. No credit cards. Tube: Victoria.

This hotel is owned by interior designer Yanus Kader and his wife, Terri. The rooms are comfortable and pretty, featuring floral motifs and coordinated curtains. The beautiful dining area with an open kitchen will remind you of home.

BLOOMSBURY

Bloomsbury's proximity to the West End in general, and to Soho in particular, has long made it a desirable area for visitors. The area gets its energy from its two most important residents: the University of London and the British Museum. Although heavy demand is often reflected in high prices, some bargains are still to be found.

Gower Street

Gower Street's budget hotels are some of the city's most popular. Most of the B&Bs lining this street are so similar to one another that only their addresses distinguish them. Stairs are steep, rooms basic (almost none with bath), and prices fairly uniform. Special touches and extra-friendly management set a few apart from the rest. The best way to reach the Gower Street hotels is from the Goodge Street Underground. Cross onto Chenies Street and turn left onto Gower.

✪ Arran House Hotel

77 Gower St., London WC1. ☎ **0171/636-2186.** Fax 0171/436-5328. 26 rms, 4 with bath. £29 ($43.50) single without bath; £46 ($69) double without bath, £59 ($88.50) double with bath. Rates include English breakfast. MC, V. Tube: Goodge Street.

The Arran House stands out on the block because of its exceptionally kind resident proprietor, Maj. W. J. Richards. The major has ensured that even guests in the front rooms get a quiet night's sleep by soundproofing all the windows. In addition to laundry and coffee/tea-making facilities, the hotel offers light meals, prepared by the owner's son, a professional caterer.

Garth Hotel

69 Gower St., London WC1. ☎ **0171/636-5761.** Fax 0171/637-4854. 17 rms, 5 with shower only, 1 with bath. TV. £29 ($43.50) single without bath, £40 ($60) single with bath; £42 ($63) double without bath, £53 ($79.50) double with shower only; £55 ($82.50) triple without bath, £63 ($94.50) triple with shower only; £67 ($100.50) quad without bath, £74 ($111) quad with shower only. Rates include English or Japanese breakfast. MC, V. Tube: Goodge Street.

The Japanese-run Garth is the unlikely newest addition to Gower Street, a strip whose hotels have come to epitomize the classic English-style bed-and-breakfast. Cleaner than many other local hotels, the Garth suffers from the same limitations that afflict other B&Bs on the block—namely small rooms, street noise, and steep stairs. You can choose from an English-style breakfast or a traditional Japanese morning meal, including rice, seaweed, and a raw egg.

Hotel Cavendish

75 Gower St., London WC1. ☎ **0171/636-9079.** 20 rms, none with bath. £26 ($39) single; £37–£40 ($55.50–$60) double. Rates include English breakfast. No credit cards. Tube: Goodge Street.

This is a nicely furnished, clean, and cozy home run by Mrs. Phillips. The cheaper double rooms are slightly smaller than the more expensive ones.

Jesmond Hotel

63 Gower St., London WC1. ☎ **0171/636-3199.** 15 rms, none with bath. £23 ($34.50) single; £32 ($48) double. Rates include English breakfast. No credit cards. Tube: Goodge Street.

The hotel's proprietors, Mr. and Mrs. Beynon, have been to the United States many times and are acutely aware of American habits and desires. All rooms have coffee- and tea-making facilities.

✪ Ridgemont Hotel

65–67 Gower St., London WC1. ☎ **0171/636-1141.** 35 rms, 4 with bath. TV. £27 ($40.50) single without bath, £37 ($55.50) single with bath; £40 ($60) double without bath, £49 ($73.50) double with bath; £50 ($75) triple without bath, £63 ($94.50) triple with bath; £74 ($111) quad without bath, £84 ($126) quad with bath. Rates include English breakfast. No credit cards. Tube: Goodge Street.

Although it's priced just above our budget, the Ridgemont boasts a friendly atmosphere and warm-hearted Welsh proprietors, Royden and Gwen Rees, making it another good choice along the strip. The Reeses offer complimentary coffee and tea in their lounge.

Bedford Place

Just south of Russell Square, right in the heart of Bloomsbury, is Bedford Place, another hotel-lined block that once figured prominently in these pages. Now almost every hotel here has priced itself above our budget, but if you can afford it, this street is well worth checking out.

CHELSEA & SOUTH KENSINGTON

✪ Magnolia Hotel

104–105 Oakley St. (just off King's Road), London SW3. ☎ **0171/352-0187.** 25 rms, 11 with shower only, 2 with bath. TV. £30 ($45) single without bath, £41 ($61.50) single with bath; £41–£42 ($61.50–$63) double without bath, £46 ($69) double with shower only, £50 ($75) double with bath; £63 ($94.50) triple without bath. Rates include continental breakfast with boiled eggs. AE, MC, V. Tube: Sloane Square; then take a long walk, or bus no. 11 or 22, down King's Road.

This is an extraordinarily well kept bed-and-breakfast with contemporary decor. The smart, clean rooms have recently been recarpeted and painted by the Yugoslavian owners.

EARL'S COURT

Mobray Court Hotel

28–32 Penywern Rd., London SW5. ☎ **0171/373-8285.** 82 rms, 50 with bath. TV TEL. £32 ($48) single without bath, £40 ($60) single with bath; £42 ($63) double without bath, £50 ($75) double with bath; £53 ($79.50) triple without bath, £61 ($91.50) triple with bath; £65 ($97.50) quad without bath, £74 ($111) quad with bath; £76 ($114) quint without bath, £88 ($132) quint with bath; £90 ($135) six-person room without bath, £99 ($148.50) six-person room with bath. Rates include continental breakfast. Rooms with kitchen £11 ($16.50) extra. AE, DC, MC, V. Tube: Earl's Court Road.

A few minutes' walk from the Earl's Court Underground station on a reasonably quiet side street, the hotel offers comfortable rooms outfitted with safes and even trouser presses.

Philbeach Hotel

30 Philbeach Gardens, London SW5. ☎ **0171/373-1244.** 40 rms, 15 with bath. TV. £26 ($39) single without bath, £42 ($63) single with bath; £47 ($70.50) double without bath, £58 ($87) double with bath. Rates include continental breakfast. AE, DC, MC, V. Tube: Earl's Court Road.

One of Europe's largest gay hotels, the Philbeach contains standard budget-hotel rooms, a proper garden, and a decent restaurant and bar. Located in a pretty Victorian town house, the hotel is open to both men and women.

SUPER-BUDGET CHOICES
A PRIVATE HOSTEL

Many hotels offer dormitory accommodations (multishares) where solo visitors share a room with other travelers. If you're traveling with a backpack and arrive at one of London's major railroad stations, you may be handed advertisements for these "unofficial" hotels. These are legitimate, but investigate the location before you commit.

New Kent Hotel

55 Inverness Terrace, London, W2. ☎ **0171/229-9982** or 229-2961. Fax 0171/727-1190. 16 rms, none with bath; 25 multishare beds. £35 ($52.50) double; £42 ($63) triple; £12 ($18) per person in a multishare per night, £68 ($102) per week. Rates include English breakfast. No credit cards. Tube: Bayswater; then cross Queensway onto Inverness Place; Inverness Terrace is just one block away.

This hotel overlooks a quiet Bayswater street not far from bustling Queensway. It's clean, fun, and friendly. There are rarely, if ever, more than four people sharing a room, but if you require more privacy, ask for one of the well-furnished doubles.

IYHF HOSTELS

The **International Youth Hostel Federation (IYHF)** runs four establishments in central London, all very crowded during summer. You have to have a membership card to stay at one of the organization's hostels, available for about £8 ($12) at any of the hostels below. When staying at a hostel, you can save about £1 ($1.50) per night by supplying your own sheets.

✪ Carter Lane Youth Hostel

36 Carter Lane, London EC4. ☎ **0171/236-4965.** 199 beds. £18 ($27) per person per night for travelers over 21. MC, V. Tube: St. Paul's; then turn right, make your way toward the front steps of the cathedral, and follow Dean's Court, a small street, to the corner of Carter Lane.

This top pick, in a wonderfully restored old building that was once a school for choir boys, boasts a good number of singles, and most of the multishare rooms have no more than four beds each. The hostel is in the heart of The City of London on a small backstreet near St. Paul's Cathedral—a location good for sightseeing but poor for dining and nightlife, as everything in The City closes when the bankers go home.

Earl's Court Youth Hostel

38 Bolton Gardens, London SW5. ☎ **0171/373-7083.** 100 beds. £15 ($22.50) per person per night for travelers over 21. MC, V. Tube: Earl's Court Road; then turn right and Bolton Gardens is the fifth street on your left.

In well-positioned but slightly seedy Earl's Court, this hostel is lively, and stores in the area tend to stay open late. Most accommodations are 10-bed dorms.

Holland House

Holland Park, London W8. ☎ **0171/937-0748.** Fax 0171/376-0667. 190 beds. £17 ($25.50) per person per night for travelers over 21. Rates include continental breakfast. MC, V. Tube: Holland Park.

This hostel enjoys the most beautiful setting of all London's IYHF hostels. It's right in the middle of Kensington's Holland Park.

Oxford Street Youth Hostel

14–18 Noel St., W1. ☎ **0171/734-1618.** 87 beds. £18 ($27) per person per night. Rates include sheets. MC, V. Tube: Oxford Circus.

Small and centrally located, this hostel is also the most basic in town. There's a large kitchen for guests' use. Not surprisingly, it costs more to locate here, but if you can get a reservation, it's well worth it.

Ys

Several YMCAs and YWCAs offer reliable accommodations at great prices, and most include dinner daily. Some encourage long-term stays with low weekly rates. In a pinch, phone the **National Council of YMCAs** (☎ **0181/520-5599**) for a list of members with available rooms.

Barbican YMCA

2 Fann St., London EC2. ☎ **0171/628-0697.** Fax 0171/638-2420. 196 rms, none with bath. £21 ($31.50) per person per day without dinner, £116 ($174) per person per week including dinner. Rates include English breakfast. Reserve at least two months ahead. MC, V. Tube: Barbican.

The good news is that this well-located hotel can accommodate almost 250 people. The bad news is that it often does. Make reservations as early as possible.

Indian YMCA

41 Fitzroy Sq., London W1. ☎ **0171/387-0411.** 100 rms, 4 with bath. £28 ($42) single without or with bath. Rates include English breakfast and dinner. Discount for stays of one week or more. No credit cards. Tube: Warren Street.

Although preference is given to Indian citizens and long-term stays, the hotel does maintain a few beds for tourists of other nationalities. Single rooms only.

London City YMCA

8 Errol St., London EC1. ☎ **0171/628-8832.** 111 rms, none with bath. TV. £27 ($40.50) per person per night, £137 ($205.50) per week. Rates include English breakfast and dinner. No credit cards. Tube: Barbican or Moorgate.

Near the Barbican Y (above), this hotel offers a similar standard of accommodation, all in single rooms. Although this place is generally filled with students during the school term, you can probably find space here during summer.

UNIVERSITY ACCOMMODATIONS

From early July to late September (and sometimes during Christmas and Easter), dozens of dormitories open their doors to tourists. The bedrooms are almost all uniformly sparse, and some residence halls offer only singles, but they're inexpensive and centrally located. Try to reserve a space months in advance as the rooms are often packed solid. **King's Campus Vacation Bureau** (☎ **0171/351-6011**) handles tourist bookings for several University of London residence halls.

Carr Saunders Hall

18–24 Fitzroy St., London W1. ☎ **0171/580-6338.** 223 rms, 3 with bath; 78 self-contained apts. £20 ($30) single without bath; £22 ($30) per person per night in apt (minimum four-night stay). Rates include English breakfast. No credit cards. Closed late Sept to early July. Tube: Warren Street.

The best thing about this hall is its location—not the best part of town, but near inexpensive restaurants and the West End. There are only single rooms, and all are small and basic. But there are a communal kitchen and laundry facilities. Couples may be interested in renting one of the hall's apartments with their own private bath and kitchen.

Imperial College

15 Princes Gardens, London SW7. ☎ **0171/589-5111.** 400 rms, none with bath. £20–£26 ($30–$39) per person per night. Rates include continental breakfast. No credit cards. Closed late Sept to early July. Tube: South Kensington.

This South Kensington dormitory offers luxurious accommodations beside Hyde Park and the Royal Albert Hall. The minimum stay in a multishare is one week, but if you're going to be in town that long, you won't mind locating here. Singles are more expensive, though still reasonable by London's standards. When phoning, note that the reception is open from 10am to 1pm and again from 2 to 5pm.

CAMPING

The queen's constables are touchy about people sleeping in London's Royal Parks, and for safety's sake it's probably not a good idea anyway.

Hackney Camping

Millfields Rd., Hackney, London E5. ☎ **0181/985-7565.** Fax 0181/749-9074. £4.50 ($6.75) per adult, £2 ($3) per youth 5–12, free for children 4 and under. No credit cards. Closed Sept to mid-June. Bus 38 from Victoria Station to Clapton Pond; then walk down Millfields Road.

This full-service campground offers hot showers, cooking and laundry facilities, a snack bar, a children's playground, and free baggage storage. Organized social activities include barbecues and live entertainment all summer.

Tent City

Old Oak Common Lane, East Acton, London W3. ☎ **0181/749-9074** or 743-5708. (Winter address: Tent City Ltd., Room 126, Finsbury Business Centre, 40 Bowling Green Lane, London EC1.; ☎ **0171/415-7143**.) 450 beds. £5.50 ($8.25) per person per night. No credit cards. Closed Sept–May. Tube: East Acton.

Tent City offers both campsites and cots for backpackers and budget travelers. Prices are the same for both types of accommodation. There are free hot showers, shaver and hairdryer outlets, free cooking facilities, toilets, laundry facilities, free baggage storage, a snack bar, and free bedding. The camp also has a volleyball court, a football field, nightly entertainment (from small circus acts to live bands), and weekly barbecues.

LONG-TERM STAYS

When you're staying for a month or more, it makes financial sense to rent an apartment (a flat) or a bed-sitting room (a bed-sit, usually a room in a house, often with cooking facilities). Landlords usually require a security deposit equal to one month's rent, returnable when you vacate the space in good condition. The magazines *Loot,* the *London Weekly Advertiser,* and *Daltons Weekly* are all issued on Thursday and contain good listings. The free, alternative weekly *Capital Gay* also has listings. Every Tuesday at 11am **Capital Radio** distributes a free list of available flat shares in the lobby of their Euston Tower building at Euston Road, NW1 (Tube: Warren Street).

Another good place to look for apartments and flat shares is on **newsstand bulletin boards** in the area where you're interested in living. The largest and most famous of these is at 214 Earl's Court Rd., next to the Earl's Court Underground station.

Finally, there are a number of accommodation agencies that'll do the footwork for you. **Jenny Jones Agency,** 40 S. Molton St., London W1 (☎ **0171/493-4801**), specializes in low-cost rentals of three months or more and charges no fees to renters. The office is open Monday through Thursday from 9:30am to 2pm and Friday from 9:30am to 5:30pm. Contact the London Tourist Board for a list of all of London's rental agencies.

WORTH THE EXTRA MONEY

Hundreds of hotels fall just slightly beyond our budget, but the following have been selected for their particularly good value.

Aster House Hotel

3 Sumner Place, London SW7. ☎ **0171/581-5888.** 12 rms, all with bath. TV TEL. £63 ($94.50) single; £71–£89 ($106.50–$133.50) double. Rates include breakfast. AE, MC, V. Tube: South Kensington; then walk three blocks down Old Brompton Road to Sumner Place on your left.

The Aster House is the most beautiful of a number of small B&Bs on this quiet South Kensington street. The pride with which owners Rachel and Peter Carapiet run this hotel will be evident the moment you step into the plushly carpeted interior. All rooms have private facilities featuring amenities usually found in more expensive hotels. Take special note of the award-winning rear garden. The enormous breakfast buffet includes the usual eggs and sausages, as well as health-oriented fresh fruits, cold meats, cheeses, yogurt, and Muesli. The meal is served in L'Orangerie, the beautiful glass-covered pièce de la résistance of this special hotel.

Camelot Hotel

45 Norfolk Sq., London W2. ☎ **0171/262-1980.** Fax 0171/402-3412. 44 rms, 16 with bath, 24 with shower only. TV. £38 ($57) single without bath, £46 ($69) single with shower only, £52.50 ($79) single with bath; £74 ($111) double with bath; £86.50 ($129.75) triple with bath; £115 ($172.50) quad with bath; £144 ($216) five-person room with bath. Rates include English breakfast. MC, V. Tube: Paddington.

Any way you look at it, this artfully decorated hotel is one of the best-value splurges in London. The ultramodern interior, painted in tasteful pastels, combines the looks and services of a top hotel with the charm and prices of something more modest. All rooms have color TVs (with free in-house films), radios, and tea/coffee-making facilities. A cooked breakfast with unlimited helpings is also included. Norfolk Square is in Bayswater, one block south of Paddington station off London Street.

Harlingford Hotel

61–63 Cartwright Gardens, London WC1. ☎ **0171/387-1551.** 44 rms, 40 with bath. TV TEL. £37 ($55.50) single without bath, £49 ($73.50) single with bath; £50 ($75) double without bath; £62 ($93) double with bath; £72.50 ($108.75) triple with bath; £84 ($126) quad with bath. Rates include English breakfast. MC, V. Tube: Russell Square; then walk three blocks north.

The Harlingford is the nicest hotel on Bloomsbury's best-located Georgian crescent. You'll be particularly pleased by the bright ground-floor dining room, where a hearty breakfast is served every morning. The rooms are equipped with coffee/

tea-making facilities and TVs, but let the well-furnished, cozy communal lounge entice you away from the box. A coffee machine on the landing sits next to a free ice dispenser for chilling your bubbly.

Merryfield House

42 York St., London W1. ☎ **0171/935-8326.** 7 rms, all with bath. TV. £36 ($54) single; £48 ($72) double; £69 ($103.50) triple. Rates include English breakfast. Add £2 ($3) per night for stays under four nights. No credit cards. Tube: Baker Street.

This exceedingly friendly hotel is in the Marylebone section of London, just south of Regent's Park, three blocks from the Baker Street Underground station. Each of the compact doubles has a color TV, a hairdryer, and a clock radio. Owner Anthony Tyler-Smith and his cat, Mimi, live on the premises, and if you're lucky enough to get a room in this hotel, you'll enjoy their warm hospitality and a full cooked breakfast served each morning in your room.

5 Dining

Traditional English food is hearty and filling and (sometimes) even delicious. Meals often begin with an appetizer (called a starter) and conclude with coffee and dessert (called sweets or pudding). Vegetables (often called veg) are usually boiled lifeless and served with the main course.

London's ethnic restaurants represent the city's best budget values and add spice to an otherwise bland foodscape. Top Indian chefs and good-quality ingredients keep quality high even in the cheapest of curry houses.

LOCAL BUDGET BESTS
Fish & Chips

Fast-food restaurants have taken their toll in London, but "chippies," as the British call them, are still easy to find. Nowadays, fish and chips are usually offered by Middle Eastern places too, but the most authentic joints won't have a kebab in sight. Several kinds of fish are offered, but when thickly battered and deep-fried, all taste similar; cod is the cheapest. Sitting down will up the price of the meal considerably, so do as most locals do and get it to take away—wrapped in a paper cone, doused with vinegar, and sprinkled with salt. The bill should never top £3.50 ($5.25).

Two of the most popular chippies are **Rock & Sole Plaice,** 47 Endell St. (at Shorts Gardens, near Covent Garden Market) (☎ **0171/836-3785**), open Monday through Saturday from 11:30am to 11pm; and the **North Sea Fish Bar,** 8 Leigh St., WC1 (☎ **0171/387-5892**), just southeast of Cartwright Gardens at Sandwich Street in Bloomsbury, open Monday through Saturday from noon to 2:30pm and 5:30 to 10:30pm.

Pub Grub

Pub food can vary from snacks at the bar to a complete restaurant meal, but it's usually cheap, good, and filling. Most pubs offer food, and there are so many pubs that if you don't like what you see in one, you can move on to the next. The best pubs display their casseroles so you can choose by sight. When they don't, ask the barkeep for a menu and expect an inferior meal. Popular items include bangers and mash (sausages and mashed potatoes), meat or vegetable pies (including cottage pie, made with ground beef and a potato topping), pasties (meat-filled pastries), and ploughman's lunch (a plate topped with bread, cheese, salad, and chutney). Wash it all down with a beer.

Getting the Best Deal on Dining

- Seek out the budget restaurants on the side streets around Covent Garden and Soho—the festive atmosphere of these areas makes finding them fun.
- Look for establishments with a number of taxis parked outside—you can be sure that the food is good and the prices are low.
- Note any restaurants that don't have signs welcoming tourists; they usually care about making you a repeat customer.

Behind the bar, food and drink are kept apart as vigilantly as a rabbi keeps milk from meat. Order and pay for each separately. A good pub lunch will seldom top £4 ($6) and careful ordering can cut that amount almost in half.

Many popular pubs are listed under "London After Dark," later in this chapter. Other pubs known especially for their food include the **Black Friar,** 174 Queen Victoria St., EC4 (☎ **0171/236-5650**), near the Blackfriars Underground station in The City; **De Hems,** 11 Macclesfield St., W1 (☎ **0171/437-2494**), in Soho's Chinatown; **The Sun,** 63 Lamb's Conduit St., WC1 (☎ **0171/405-8278**), between the Russell Square and Holborn Underground stations; **The Lamb and Flag,** 33 Rose St., WC2 (☎ **0171/497-9504**), by Covent Garden Market; and **The Australian,** 29 Milner St., Chelsea SW3 (☎ **0171/589-6027**), which has won numerous awards for its excellent food.

AFTERNOON TEA

As much as the tea itself, it's tradition that makes afternoon tea a pleasant and civilized leisure-class activity. At afternoon tea, the pot is usually served with a spread of sandwiches and sweets that more than make a meal. Accordingly, an authentic tea is expensive and usually served in top hotels, where a jacket and tie are required.

Brown's Hotel, Albemarle and Dover streets, W1 (☎ **0171/493-6020;** tube to Green Park), serves the best fixed-price tea in London. For £16 ($24), you can sit in one of three wood-paneled, stained-glass lounges and feel like a millionaire. Tailcoated waiters will make sure you don't leave hungry, as they fill your table with tomato, cucumber, and meat sandwiches, as well as scones and pastries. Choose from a variety of teas. Tea is served daily from 3 to 6pm.

The **Ritz Hotel,** Piccadilly, W1 (☎ **0171/493-8181;** tube to Green Park), is probably the most famous spot for afternoon tea in the world, and even at £15 ($23) per person you have to book at least a week in advance. There are two sittings, at 3 and 4:30pm daily. Most major credit/charge cards are accepted.

MEALS FOR LESS THAN £7 ($10.50)
IN & AROUND SOHO

✪ Pollo

20 Old Compton St. (near Frith St., a few doors down from the Prince Edward Theater), W1.
☎ **0171/734-5917.** £5–£7 ($7.50–$10.50). No credit cards. Mon–Sat 11:30am–11pm.
Tube: Leicester Square. ITALIAN.

An extremely popular Italian-English restaurant in the heart of the hustle, Pollo offers good food and embarrassingly low prices that keep the masses clucking.

There must be 150 menu items, with few topping £5 ($7.50); even chicken cacciatore or principessa style (with asparagus) is under £4.50 ($6.75). Pastas in a myriad of shapes and sizes are served with a choice of over a dozen red and white sauces. The list of Italian desserts is impressive, too. The atmosphere is lively, but if you don't like crowds, Pollo is not for you.

Prêt à Manger

77 St. Martin's Lane, WC2. ☎ **0171/379-5335**. Sandwiches £2.50–£4 ($3.75–$6). No credit cards. Mon–Fri 8am–10pm, Sat 8am–11pm, Sun 10am–8pm. Tube: Leicester Square. SANDWICHES.

The majority of upscale ready-to-eat foods found at Prêt à Manger are gourmet sandwiches made with trendy ingredients like poached salmon, goat's cheese, tarragon chicken, and hearty herb-laced breads. There's a small selection of salads and sushi, hot croissants, and a huge assortment of cakes. Customers line up cafeteria style, then take their meals to stylish matte-black tables.

Other Prêt à Manger shops are at 12 Kingsgate, Victoria Street, SW1 (☎ **0171/828-1559**); 17 Eldon St., EC2 (☎ **0171/628-9011**); 28 Fleet St., EC4 (☎ **0171/353-2332**); and 298 Regent St., W1 (☎ **0171/637-3836**).

Wong Kei

41–43 Wardour St., W1. ☎ **0171/437-8408**. £5–£8.50 ($7.50–$12.75). No credit cards. Daily noon–11:30pm. Tube: Leicester Square or Piccadilly Circus. CHINESE.

There are many good, cheap Chinese restaurants in Soho, most serving Cantonese fare. Sitting at the end of Chinatown's Gerrard Street and Lisle Street, Wong Kei is one of the cheapest places in the area, featuring an extensive menu. At least a dozen popular dishes, including chicken with garlic sauce and beef with vegetables, cost under £4 ($6). As is the rule at most Chinese restaurants in London, if you want rice you have to order it separately, for 90p ($1.35). Tea is free, and hearty eaters can take advantage of the fixed-price meal including three dishes plus rice for only £5.50 ($8.25) per person (two people minimum).

The Wren at St. James's

35 Jermyn St., SW1. ☎ **0171/437-9419**. Soups, sandwiches, and pies £2–£3 ($3–$4.50). No credit cards. Mon–Sat 8am–7pm, Sun 10am–5pm. Tube: Piccadilly Circus. VEGETARIAN.

Situated inside a popular parish church near Piccadilly Circus, the Wren serves up simple continental breakfasts and imaginative vegetarian lunches that may include a variety of sandwiches and vegetable pies, plus a host of tossed green salads. Interesting and tasty soups, like cream of parsnip or apple, carrot, and cashew, are also always available. Smoking is not allowed in the dining room, and during warm weather outdoor dining is available.

IN THE CITY

Almost everyone in the square mile of The City of London goes home by 6pm, and restaurant workers are no exception. Below are some good lunch selections.

Al's Cafe

11 Exmouth Market, EC1. ☎ **0171/837-4821**. £4–£6 ($6–$9). No credit cards. Tues and Sat–Sun 7am–8pm, Wed–Fri 7am–11pm. Tube: Angel or Farringdon. ENGLISH.

One of London's funkiest cafés is best known for lunch, when it's packed with office types chowing on half-pound bacon cheeseburgers, sausages with grilled onions, and delicious homemade soups like carrot and bean. Most everything comes with thick-cut chips, and a long list of salads and sandwiches are also available. Al's gets high marks for top ingredients that include Italian breads, most always served with a smile.

Ferrari's

8 West Smithfield, EC1. ☎ **0171/236-7545.** £2.50–£5 ($3.75–$7.50). No credit cards. Mon–Fri 5:15am–4pm. Tube: St. Paul's. ENGLISH.

For a little-nicer meal in the same area as Piccolo (below), turn left at the Museum of London and then right onto Little Britain Street until you reach the Smithfield Market, London's wholesale meat center (about six blocks from the St. Paul's Underground station). The restaurant is just across the square. Small and plain, Ferrari's is famous for its sandwich menu, which includes Norwegian prawn and farmhouse pâté. The shop's cakes are irresistible.

Japanese Canteen

394 St. John St., EC1. ☎ **0171/833-3222.** £4–£6 ($6–$4.50). No credit cards. Daily noon–2:30pm and 6–10:30pm. Tube: Farringdon. JAPANESE/PUB.

Lenin and Trotsky used to drink in this funky pub–cum–Japanese noodle shop. Typically dark brown on the outside, the dining rooms are painted white, fitted with blond-wood tables and benches, and enveloped with light rock music. In addition to sushi, the menu includes ramen soup (made with fresh noodles), vegetarian tempura, and small bento box combinations with teriyaki, tempura, and breaded pork cutlets.

Piccolo

7 Gresham St. (just off Martin's Le Grand St.), EC2. ☎ **0171/606-1492.** £2–£3 ($3–$4.50). No credit cards. Mon–Sat 6am–6pm, Sun 6am–2pm. Tube: St. Paul's. ENGLISH.

This sandwich bar, with fewer than a dozen stools all facing the street, is perfect for a quick bite when visiting St. Paul's Cathedral and offers the widest range of sandwiches you're ever likely to come across. Bacon and turkey, roast chicken, and all the standards are priced below £2.50 ($3.75). The shop is between St. Paul's Underground station and the Museum of London.

COVENT GARDEN

Food for Thought

31 Neal St. (across from the Covent Garden Underground station), WC2. ☎ **0171/836-0239.** £3.50–£5.75 ($5.25–$8.75). No credit cards. Mon–Sat 9:30am–8pm, Sun 10:30am–4pm. Tube: Covent Garden. VEGETARIAN.

This most unusual restaurant makes vegetarian food accessible to all palates and wallets. Delicious dishes, such as leek quiche and lasagne, are usually priced around £2.75 ($4.10) and are served downstairs in a small pine-wrapped environment (no smoking). Really tasty soups and salads are also available, as well as a good selection of healthful desserts.

BAYSWATER & PADDINGTON

The Cafe

106 Westbourne Grove (close to Chepstow Rd.), W2. ☎ **0171/229-0777.** £2.50–£5.25 ($3.75–$8). No credit cards. Mon–Sat 7:30am–9pm. Tube: Bayswater. ENGLISH.

The Cafe looks like an American diner. Sit in a booth and open the menu to find sandwiches for about £1 ($1.50), meat pies for about the same, and ice cream for 60p (90¢). The only things missing are the jukebox selectors mounted above each table.

✪ Khan's

13–15 Westbourne Grove, W2. ☎ **0171/727-5420.** £4–£7.25 ($6–$11). AE, DC, MC, V. Daily noon–3pm and 6pm–midnight. Tube: Bayswater; then turn left onto Westbourne Grove from Queensway. INDIAN.

Khan's is famous in these parts for the best Indian food in Bayswater. An airy, cloudlike mural covers the huge walls, as if to create the feeling of a magic-carpet ride. The menu, which includes all the staples, assures that only halal meat is used, conforming to the Muslim dietary code. Curry dishes cost about £3 ($4.50), while a whole tandoori chicken, probably enough for two, is under £4 ($6).

Nahar Cafeteria

190 Sussex Gardens (at the corner of Spring St.), W2. ☎ **0171/402-8129.** £3–£4 ($4.50–$6). No credit cards. Daily noon–10pm. Tube: Lancaster Gate or Paddington. MALAYSIAN.

Though it's short on atmosphere, this basement café offers one of the best meal deals in London—a heaping plate of rice topped with your choice of beef, chicken, or pork in a variety of sweet-and-sour curry-based sauces. For about £4 ($6) you can sample three dishes, served cafeteria style, then brought to matte-black tables. Banana fritters with ice cream and maple syrup is especially recommended for dessert.

BLOOMSBURY

Anwar's

64 Grafton Way, W1. ☎ **0171/387-6664.** £3–£5.25 ($4.50–$8). No credit cards. Daily 10am–10pm. Tube: Warren Street. INDIAN.

Anwar's not only maintains a very high standard of quality but also is one of the cheapest Indian restaurants in London. Few dishes top £4 ($6), and most cost just £3 ($4.50). There's a wide choice of homemade meat and vegetable curries and other Indian specialties, including tandoori chicken for about £3 ($4.50). Anwar's is cafeteria style; help yourself and bring your meal to a Formica-covered table. Despite this "canteen" approach, the food is top-notch.

CHELSEA

Planet Poppadom

366 King's Rd., SW3. ☎ **0171/823-3369.** £4–£6 ($6–$9). No credit cards. Mon–Wed 4pm–midnight, Thurs–Sun noon–midnight. Tube: Sloane Square. INDIAN.

Traditional Indian cooking served in an ultra-contemporary fast-food atmosphere is the "hook" of this new bargain Chelsea restaurant at the bottom of trendy King's Road. There are bar stools for single diners and tables for larger parties, but desserts and coffee aren't served and lingering isn't encouraged.

EAST END

The East End, an amorphous area hugging The City's eastern edge, has always been one of London's poorest areas. The majority of the area's residents have traditionally been newly arrived immigrants from Ireland, the Continent, and the rest of the world. At the turn of the century, the East End was one of Europe's largest Jewish ghettos. Today it's primarily Indian and Bangladeshi, and ethnic restaurants from the subcontinent are in abundance.

Brick Lane Beigel Bakery

159 Brick Lane, E1. ☎ **0171/729-0616.** Bagels and cakes 20p–£1 (30¢–$1.50). No credit cards. Daily 24 hours. Tube: Aldgate East. SANDWICHES.

There's always a line for these tiny bagels (here pronounced "bi-guls"), which are premade into sandwiches filled with cream cheese, salami, chopped herring, or smoked salmon. It's especially busy after midnight, when most everything else in London is shut and a line of taxi drivers runs out the door. There are two adjacent bagel shops on Brick Lane—this one is best. Ironically, both are near the corner of Bacon Street.

Clifton Restaurant

126 Brick Lane, E1. ☎ **0171/377-9402.** Dishes £3.50–£8.25 ($5.25–$12.50); fixed-price dinner £5.75 ($8.50). AE, MC. Daily noon–1am. Tube: Aldgate. INDIAN.

This spacious eatery is one of the most popular on Brick Lane, one of the area's primary thoroughfares. A recommendable introduction to Indian food might include an onion bhaji appetizer, followed by chicken bhuna or tikka masala, with a side of pilau rice and naan bread. The entire filling à la carte meal should cost less than £9.50 ($14.25); fixed-price meals are even cheaper.

Kundan Karahi

108 Brick Lane, E1. ☎ **0171/247-8685.** £3–£6 ($4.50–$9). No credit cards. Daily 11am–11pm. Tube: Aldgate East. INDIAN.

Now a Pakistani stronghold, London's East End is the historical home to the city's newest immigrants. Brick Lane, the East End's primary thoroughfare, is now London's epicenter of currydom. And although some restaurants are actually cheaper, none is better than this eatery, known for its terrific breads, tikkas, paneers, and masalas.

BRIXTON

Jacaranda

11–13 Brixton Station Rd., SW9. ☎ **0171/274-8383.** £5–£7 ($7.50–$10.50). No credit cards. Mon–Sat noon–7pm. Tube: Brixton. CARIBBEAN.

English-style soul food is served in this popular café, where meals are ordered at the counter, then served at your table in unhurried Caribbean time. Huge plates include spicy gumbo, oxtail stew, and plenty of rice and peas. Sandwiches and quiches are also available. Particularly recommended are the house-made cakes, easily big enough for two.

A CHAIN

✪ The Stockpot

Soups 90p ($1.35); main courses £2.75–£3.50 ($4.15–$5.25). No credit cards. Daily 9am–11pm (sometimes varies by location). ENGLISH.

Members of the Stockpot chain are unified by contemporary styling, great central locations, and a generous budget-minded philosophy. Menus change daily and regularly include two homemade soups; a dozen main courses like lasagne, roast lamb, and fish and chips; and an excellent selection of cakes for under £1.50 ($2.25). The food is good, and the prices make all the 'Pots popular.

Central London locations include 273 King's Rd., SW3 (☎ **0171/823-3175**), in Chelsea, a few blocks past the fire station; 6 Basil St., SW3 (☎ **0171/589-8627**), in ultra-fashionable Knightsbridge, between Harrods and Sloane Street; and 40 Panton St., SW1 (☎ **0171/839-5142**), just off Haymarket, one block south of Piccadilly Circus.

MEALS FOR LESS THAN £9 ($12)
SOHO & PICCADILLY

Chuen Cheng Ku

17 Wardour St., W1. ☎ **0171/734-3281**. £4.75–£8 ($7–$12). AE, DC, MC, V. Daily 11am–midnight (dumplings served until 5:45pm). Tube: Leicester Square. CHINESE.

At lunchtime this huge restaurant serves 21 kinds of steamed, fried, or boiled dumplings wheeled to tables on trolleys. Favorites include steamed pork buns and shrimp dumplings, each about £1.75 ($2.65). Adventurers can choose duck's tongue in a sauce of black beans and chili and other exotics. It takes a few servings to get a good feed, and you can have a fulfilling experience for about £8 ($12). Dinner in this red-carpeted, chandelier-hung dining room costs double.

Gaby's Continental Bar

30 Charing Cross Rd. (just off Leicester Sq.), WC2. ☎ **0171/836-4233**. £3–£6.50 ($4.50–$9.75). No credit cards. Mon–Sat 8am–midnight, Sun noon–10pm. Tube: Leicester Square. CONTINENTAL.

This sandwich bar/café has a Middle Eastern slant. A wonderful assortment of such home-cooked specialties as stuffed eggplant and rolled cabbage are displayed in the window. Hungarian goulash and lamb curry are also usually served, and like most main courses they cost less than £5.50 ($8.25), including salad or rice. Everything is made fresh daily according to the chef's mood, and there's always a wide selection of delicious well-priced meals. The restaurant is also known for its sandwiches, especially salt beef (England's approximation of corned beef), cheapest when you buy it to take out for about £3 ($4.50). Gaby's is fully licensed.

New Piccadilly Restaurant

8 Denman St. (just off the bottom of Shaftesbury Ave., a few feet from Piccadilly Circus), W1. ☎ **0171/437-8530**. £3.50–£6.75 ($5.25–$10). No credit cards. Daily 11am–9:30pm. Tube: Piccadilly Circus. ENGLISH/CONTINENTAL.

Postwar decor and a straightforward English café menu combine to make this centrally located eatery a popular budget mainstay. The long dining room is lined with Formica-topped tables on either side, and diners can choose from a large number of unadventurous but well-prepared English-style specialties, like chicken with mushroom sauce and steak risotto for about £4.50 ($6.75). For a pound less, try one of their many pizzas or a pasta dish. Add £1.25 ($1.90) for soup, plus £1.50 ($2.25) for apple pie or ice cream, and you'll have eaten a satisfying three-course meal for about £7.25 ($10.90). The restaurant has no liquor license; patrons are encouraged to bring their own alcohol.

New World

1 Gerrard Place, W1. ☎ **0171/734-0396**. £7–£10 ($10.50–$15). MC, V. Mon–Thurs 11am–11:45pm, Fri–Sat 11am–midnight, Sun 10:45am–10:45pm. Tube: Leicester Square or Piccadilly Circus. CHINESE.

Reminiscent of Hong Kong's massive catering halls, this giant Cantonese palace is one of Chinatown's largest restaurants. The immense menu matches the dining rooms in size and reads like a veritable summary of southern Chinese cookery. All the usual poultry, beef, pork, and vegetable stir-fry dishes are represented. And during lunch, dim sum is served in the traditional manner, via trolley.

Pierre Victoire

6 Panton St., SW1. ☎ **0171/930-6463.** Set lunch £5 ($7.50); dinner £7–£10 ($10.50–$15). No credit cards. Daily noon–4pm and 5:30–11pm. Tube: Piccadilly Circus. FRENCH.

With a comfortable candlelit dining room, decent food, and unbeatable prices, this franchised French restaurant has all the hallmarks of permanence. The bistro food includes roast pork with spinach and garlic, as well as chicken in white wine and cream sauce. Vegetables are served on separate side plates, and fresh bread is included with every meal.

A second version in central London is at 9 William St., SW1 (☎ **0171/ 823-1414**), near the Knightsbridge Underground station.

COVENT GARDEN

Wagamama

4 Streatham St., WC1. ☎ **0171/323-9223.** £6–£8 ($9–$12). Mon–Fri noon–2:30pm and 6–11pm, Sat 12:30–3pm and 6–11pm, Sun 12:30–3pm and 6–10pm. Tube: Covent Garden. No credit cards. JAPANESE.

This Japanese noodle bar is one of the most popular eateries in London. There's always a line to get into the minimalist dining room furnished with basic tables and chairs and a health-oriented Zen-like philosophy. The kitchen's offerings are limited to a variety of vegetarian stir-fries and several kinds of steaming noodle soups. The meals are consistently well prepared and perfectly spiced. Enjoy an ice-cold lager or fresh-squeezed juice while you wait for a table.

SOUTH KENSINGTON

Daquise

20 Thurloe St., SW7. ☎ **0171/589-6117.** £5.75–£8.50 ($8.75–$12.75). No credit cards. Daily 10am–11:30pm. Tube: South Kensington. POLISH.

Near the major museums and steps from the South Kensington tube station, this real find features cabbage in many guises; for example, stuffed with meat or served with veal escalope. The chlodiak soup (ham stock, beetroot, cream, and pickled cucumber) may sound unusual but tastes great. A variety of Polish vodkas and beers is also served, and the friendly, if harried, staff encourage diners to nurse their drinks.

THE CHAINS

✪ Cranks

£5.75–£9 ($8.50–$13.50). No credit cards. Mon–Sat 9:30am–8pm, Sun 10am–7pm. VEGETARIAN.

When Cranks opened its first health-oriented vegetarian restaurant in the early 1960s, the British public laughed. Today more than half a dozen eateries continue to "crank out" innovative, high-quality cuisine at prices that've silenced all snickerers. Lasagne, lentil-and-spinach quiche, satay vegetables, and other tasty dishes are well presented and served in modern, airy, and somewhat fancy settings. A wide selection of herb teas, at about £1 ($1.50) per pot, is available, as well as a good choice of well-priced and organic wines.

Cranks branches include these downtown locations: 8 Adelaide St., WC2 (☎ **0171/836-0660**), where the Strand meets Trafalgar Square; The Market, Covent Garden, WC2 (☎ **0171/379-6508**); Tottenham Street, W1 (☎ **0171/**

631-3912), off Tottenham Court Road two blocks from the Goodge Street Underground station; Barret Street, W1 (☎ 0171/495-1340), across Oxford Street from the Bond Street Underground station; and Marshall Street, W1 (☎ 0171/437-9431), three blocks east of Regent Street in the heart of Soho.

Ed's Easy Diner

£4.25–£7.25 ($6.50–$11). No credit cards. Mon–Fri 11:30am–midnight, Sat 9am–1am, Sun 9am–11pm. AMERICAN.

Ed's Easys are reconstructions of 1950s-style American diners, complete with bobbysoxed waitresses and jukebox selectors. This place flips one of the most authentic burgers in town, which, along with fries and a cola or a milkshake, costs about £7 ($10.50).

Central London locations include 12 Moor St., W1 (☎ 0171/439-1955), just off Cambridge Circus; and 362 King's Rd., SW3 (☎ 0171/352-1956), past the fire station in Chelsea.

Rasa Sayang Restaurant

£5.75–£9.25 ($8.75–$14). AE, DC, MC. Daily noon–10:45pm (varies by location). MALAYSIAN/SINGAPOREAN.

These spick-and-span Southeast Asian eateries were some of the first in London. An unusual menu features dozens of meat and vegetarian dishes topped with traditional sauces. Coconut and fruit sauces are common, as are soups and satays. The restaurants are slightly lacking in atmosphere, but they're well lit, contemporary in style, and often packed.

Central London locations include 38 Queensway, W2 (☎ 0171/229-8417), diagonally across from the Bayswater Underground station; 10 Frith St., W1 (☎ 0171/734-8720), in the middle of Soho; and 3 Leicester Place, WC2 (☎ 0171/437-4556), southwest of Leicester Square.

PICNICKING

There are plenty of supermarkets around offering run-of-the-mill staples. Cold cuts and cheeses from the deli counter are usually cheaper than the prewrapped stuff that hangs in the cooler.

For unusual picnic goodies, try the big and fascinating **Loon Fung Supermarket** at 42–44 Gerrard St., W1 (☎ 0171/437-7332), in the heart of Soho's Chinatown. The most adventurous will try the black-jelly fungus or the steamed, congealed chicken's blood. The rest of us will enjoy dried cuttlefish, a traditional snack that goes great with beer. Loon Fung is open daily from 10am to 7pm.

See "Parks and Gardens" under "Attractions," later in this chapter, for the top picnic spots.

WORTH THE EXTRA MONEY

Bahn Thai

21a Frith St. (just south of Soho Sq.), W1. ☎ 0171/437-8504. £7–£17 ($10.50–$25.50); fixed-price pretheater menu £13 ($19.50). AE, DC, MC, V. Mon–Sat noon–2:45pm and 6–11:15pm, Sun 12:30–2:30pm and 6:30–10:30pm. Tube: Tottenham Court Road. THAI.

In the middle of Soho is one of London's best Southeast Asian restaurants. Two floors of wooden tables, plants, and decorative wall hangings give this exceptional place an authentic feel. But it's the food you've come for, and you won't be disappointed. Excellent, unusual soups, seafood, and rice dishes punctuate a huge and creative menu. The three-course pretheater menu is a particularly good value and even includes coffee.

✪ The English House

3 Milner St., SW3. ☎ **0171/584-3002.** £15.75–£32 ($23.50–$48); fixed-price meals £15.50 ($23.25) at lunch (Mon–Sat), £21 ($31.50) at dinner (Sun). AE, DC, MC, V. Mon–Sat 12:30–2:30pm and 7:30–11:30pm, Sun to 10pm. Tube: South Kensington or Sloane Square. ENGLISH.

Set on a beautiful Chelsea backstreet, the English House looks like the ideal country home. As a fire roars in the cozy dining room, patrons are treated to beautifully prepared traditional English dishes, served by an expertly trained staff. Though the tables are too close together, dining here is romantic, the service is impeccable, and the meal will convince you English food can be wonderful.

Porters Restaurant

17 Henrietta St. (one block south of Covent Garden Market), WC2. ☎ **0171/836-6466.** £11–£15 ($17–$22.50). MC, V. Daily noon–3pm and 5:30–11:30pm. Tube: Covent Garden. ENGLISH.

Porters serves traditional English food with a flair. This large wood-and-fern restaurant offers over half a dozen meat pies, including steak and mushroom, selling for £7.75 ($11.75). Weekends are best, when roast beef and Yorkshire pudding with gravy and roast potatoes is £8.25 ($12.25). Cream teas with scones are served daily from 2 to 5pm for £3.95 ($5.90). Weekends are busy, so expect to wait at the well-stocked bar.

6 Attractions

SIGHTSEEING SUGGESTIONS

Americans are famous for whizzing around Europe's major sights trying to squeeze in as many of the "hits" as their brief vacations will allow. Europeans (who are both geographically closer to one another and enjoy longer holidays) often poke fun at the hectic pace of the American vacation. But when you've come a long way and have only a few days, moving at a fast clip is in order. If soaking up local culture in a Chelsea café is more your cup of tea, you'll have to make modifications to my suggestions.

If You Have 1 Day

Most hotels start serving breakfast at 7:30am, so try to rise early. After breakfast, take the tube to Charing Cross or Embankment (within one block of each other) and cross into Trafalgar Square, London's most famous square and the city's unofficial hub. Here the commercial West End meets Whitehall, the main street of government, and the Mall, the regal road that leads to Buckingham Palace. In the center of the square is Nelson's Column, erected in 1843 to commemorate Nelson's defeat of Napoleon at the 1805 Battle of Trafalgar. The National Gallery is on the top end of the square, while the northeast side is dominated by the Church of St. Martin-in-the-Fields.

Turn down Whitehall and go inside Banqueting House, in the middle of the block, to view the magnificent ceiling painted by Rubens. Across from Banqueting House, visit the home of the Queen's Life Guards, to see the Changing of the Guard Monday through Saturday at 11am and Sunday at 10am and 4pm (not to be confused with the larger affair at Buckingham Palace). Farther down Whitehall, in the middle of the street, you'll see the Cenotaph, dedicated to those British subjects who died during wartime, and just opposite it, behind tall iron gates, is 10 Downing St., home to the prime minister. At the foot of Whitehall lies Parliament Square, site of Big Ben and the spectacular Houses of Parliament. The famous Westminster Abbey is just across Parliament Square. After lunch, take the tube into The City and visit St. Paul's Cathedral.

If You Have 2 Days

Follow the itinerary described above and have time to catch your breath. Take a break from your Whitehall stroll, cross beautiful St. James's Park and arrive at Buckingham Palace at 11:30am for the Changing of the Guard. Or reverse your Whitehall walk, starting in Parliament Square and ending at the National Gallery in Trafalgar Square. After visiting the gallery, continue north along Charing Cross Road, turn right on Long Acre, and visit trendy Covent Garden. In the afternoon of your second day, visit one of the museums listed under "Top Attractions," below.

If You Have 3 Days

Spend Days 1 and 2 as described above. On your third day, visit The City of London and its host of interesting financial, legal, religious, and historic sights. Attractions include the Stock Exchange, the Royal Exchange, the Old Bailey, St. Paul's Cathedral, and St. Bride's Church on Fleet Street. Try to time your sightseeing so you're at St. Bride's for a free lunchtime recital (see "Classical Music" in "The Performing Arts," under "London After Dark," later in this chapter).

In the afternoon of your third day, visit the Museum of the Moving Image on the South Bank, then stroll over to the adjacent South Bank Arts Centre for a late-afternoon drink.

If You Have 5 Days

Spend Days 1 to 3 as described above. On Days 4 and 5, explore London's historic neighborhoods (most notably Chelsea and South Kensington) or partake in the city's active cultural scene. If you like museums, make a pilgrimage to South Kensington: In addition to the Victoria & Albert, there are no fewer than six other museums in this area, including the Natural History Museum, the Science Museum, the Geological Museum, and the Museum of Instruments. Also worth a stop is Kensington Palace, in Kensington Gardens. Home to several members of the royal family, including Princess Margaret, the palace contains many ornate State Apartments and a famous dress collection highlighted by Lady Diana's 1981 wedding gown.

TOP ATTRACTIONS

The British Museum
Great Russell St., WC1. ☎ **0171/636-1555.** Admission free, but £1 ($1.50) donation requested; museum tours, £5 ($9) adults, £3 ($4.50) children 15 and under. Mon–Sat 10am–5pm, Sun 2:30–6pm; 90-minute tours given Mon–Sat at 10:30am and 1:30pm, Sun 3 and 3:30pm. Tube: Holborn or Russell Square.

Britain's largest and oldest national museum houses an unmatched collection of antiquities—many of which are the spoils of empire. Important finds from Egypt, Greece, Rome, and Cyprus share this warehouse of history with spectacular collections from Asia and the Middle East. The Rosetta Stone, at the entrance to the Egyptian Sculpture Gallery (Room 25), is interesting as an artifact yet even more fascinating for the way it changed our understanding of hieroglyphics, which were unread for 1,400 years. The sculptures from the Parthenon, known as the Elgin Marbles (Room 8), are the most famous of the museum's extensive collection of Greek antiquities. Named for Lord Elgin, who took these treasures from Athens, the marbles and other treasures are hotly contested by foreign governments that want their cultural relics back.

To the right of the entrance on the ground floor are the British Library Galleries. Rotating thematic displays come from the library's collection of over eight million books. Included in the permanent exhibit are two copies of the Magna Carta (1215), Shakespeare's First Folio (1623), and the Gutenberg Bible (ca. 1453), the first book printed using movable (hence, reusable) type. The adjacent British Library Reading Room was regularly used by Gandhi, Lenin, George Bernard Shaw, and others. Karl Marx wrote *Das Kapital* here. For tourists, admission to the reading room is with a guide only, Monday through Friday at 2, 3, and 4pm.

Buckingham Palace

The Mall, SW1. ☎ **0171/799-2331** or 930-4832. State Apartments, £8 ($12) adults, £5.50 ($8.25) seniors over 60, £4 ($6) children 16 and under; Queen's Gallery, £3 ($4.50) adults, £2 ($3) seniors, £1.50 ($2.25) children; Royal Mews, £3 ($4.50) adults, £2 ($3) seniors over 60, £1.50 ($2.25) children 16 and under; Gallery and Mews combination ticket, £5 ($7.50) adults, £3.50 ($5.25) seniors, £2.20 ($3.30) children. State Apartments, Aug–Sept only, daily 9:30am–5:30pm. Queen's Gallery, Tues–Sat 10am–5pm, Sun 2–5pm (closed Jan–Feb). Royal Mews, Apr–Sept, Tues–Thurs noon–4pm; Oct–Mar, Wed noon–4pm. Opening times subject to change on short notice. Tube: Victoria, St. James's Park, or Green Park.

As the home of one of the world's last remaining monarchs, Buckingham Palace has strong symbolic interest and is one of the city's top attractions. Built in 1703 for the duke of Buckingham, the palace became the sovereign's official residence in 1837, when Queen Victoria decided to live here (when the queen is at home, the Royal Standard is flown from the flagstaff on the building's roof).

In the summer of 1993, for the first time since it became the official royal residence, Buckingham Palace opened its doors to common tourists (August through September, when the royal family is away on vacation). There are 18 rooms on view, including the Throne Room, the State Dining Room, three drawing rooms, and the Music Room. Tickets to see these State Apartments are on sale from 9am at the ticket office on Constitution Hill, on the south side of Green Park. Hours-long waits should be anticipated. Visitors willing to pay more than twice the admission price can avoid the lines by buying a palace tour through the American tour operator Edwards & Edwards, 50 Main St., 3rd floor, White Plains, NY 10606 (☎ **800/223-6108**). Physically disabled visitors can get a jump on the line by reserving tickets directly from the palace (☎ **0171/839-1377** ext. 4204).

The **Changing of the Guard,** outside Buckingham Palace's front gates, takes place daily just before 11:30am from mid-April through July and on alternate days the rest of the year. (It's canceled during bad weather and for major state events.) The Queen's Foot Guards, with their scarlet coats and bearskin hats, march with lots of shouting and foot stomping in a half-hour ceremony that replaces the sentries who stand guard in front of the palace.

The **Queen's Gallery,** the palace's small art museum, has been displaying rotating exhibits of the royal family's holdings since 1962. The **Royal Mews** is

The British Museum

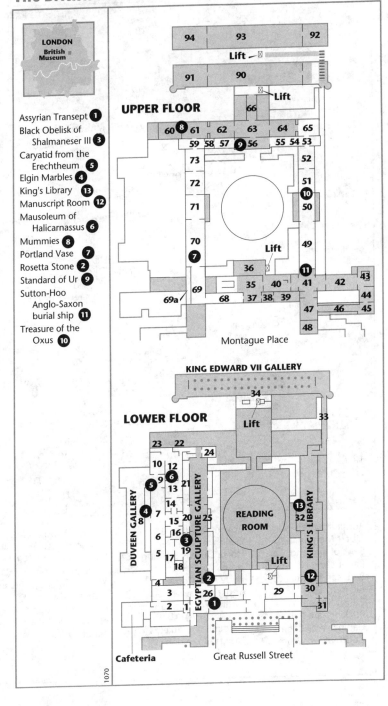

LONDON
British Museum

Assyrian Transept ❶
Black Obelisk of
  Shalmaneser III ❸
Caryatid from the
  Erechtheum ❺
Elgin Marbles ❹
King's Library ⓭
Manuscript Room ⓬
Mausoleum of
  Halicarnassus ❻
Mummies ❽
Portland Vase ❼
Rosetta Stone ❷
Standard of Ur ❾
Sutton-Hoo
  Anglo-Saxon
  burial ship ⓫
Treasure of the
  Oxus ❿

UPPER FLOOR

94   93   92

Lift

91   90

Lift

66

60 ❽ 61   62   63   64   65
59 58 57 ❾ 56   55 54 53
73   52
72   51 ❿
71   50
70   49
❼   Lift
36   11
35 40   41 42 43
69a 69   68 37 38 39   44
47 46 45
48

Montague Place

KING EDWARD VII GALLERY

LOWER FLOOR

34

Lift   33

23   22
      24
10 12 ❻
❺ 9 13   21
❹ 14
8 7   15   20 25   13 32
6   16 ❸   19   READING ROOM
5   17   ❷
4   18   26 ❶   29   12
3   30
2   1   31

Cafeteria   Great Russell Street

DUVEEN GALLERY

EGYPTIAN SCULPTURE GALLERY

KING'S LIBRARY

1070

Inner London

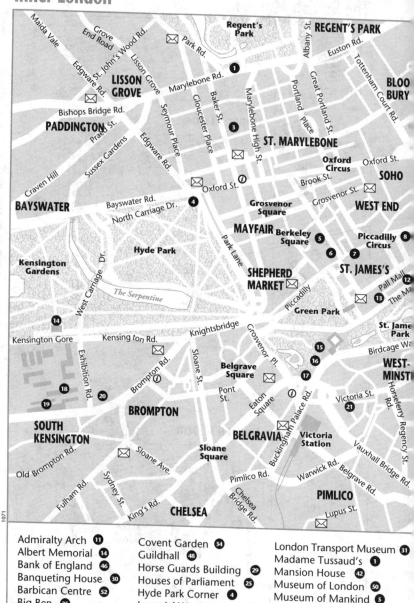

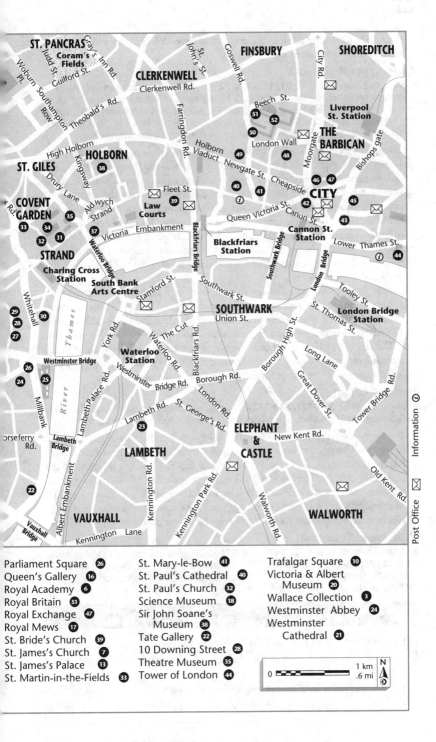

ST. PANCRAS
Coram's
Fields
Gray's Inn Rd.
St. John's St.
Goswell Rd.
FINSBURY
SHOREDITCH
City Rd.
Ludd St.
Guilford St.
Woburn Pl.
Southampton Row
CLERKENWELL
Clerkenwell Rd.
Theobald's Rd.
Beech St.
Liverpool
St. Station
☒
⑤①
⑤②
THE
BARBICAN
High Holborn
HOLBORN
Holborn Viaduct
⑤⓪
London Wall
Moorgate
Bishops gate
⑧
ST. GILES
Kingsway
Drury Lane
④⑨
Newgate St.
Cheapside
☒
④⑧
CITY
④⑥ ④⑦
COVENT
GARDEN
Aldwych
Strand
Fleet St.
③⑨
Law
Courts
☒
④⓪
④①
Queen Victoria St.
Canon St.
④② ☒ ④⑤ ☒
③③ ③④
③⑤
⓪
④③
④④ ⓘ
③② ③①
③⑦
Victoria Embankment
Blackfriars Bridge
Blackfriars
Station
Cannon St.
Station
Lower Thames St.
STRAND
Charing Cross
Station
South Bank
Arts Centre
Stamford St.
Southwark Bridge
London Bridge
Whitehall
②⑨
②⑧
②⑦
Thames
☒ ☒
Southwark St.
SOUTHWARK
Union St.
London Bridge
Station
Tooley St.
St. Thomas St.
③⓪
The Cut
Waterloo Rd.
Blackfriars Rd.
Borough High St.
Long Lane
Westminster Bridge
②⑥
②④ ②⑤
River
Waterloo
Station
York Rd.
Westminster Bridge Rd.
Borough Rd.
London Rd.
Great Dover St.
Tower Bridge Rd.
Millbank
Lambeth
Bridge
Lambeth Palace Rd.
Lambeth Rd.
St. George's Rd.
②③
ELEPHANT
&
CASTLE
New Kent Rd.
orseferry Rd.
②②
LAMBETH
Kennington Rd.
Kennington Park Rd.
Walworth Rd.
☒
Old Kent Rd.
WALWORTH
Vauxhall Bridge
VAUXHALL
Kennington Lane

Information ⓘ
Post Office ☒

Parliament Square ②⑥
Queen's Gallery ①⑥
Royal Academy ⑥
Royal Britain ⑤①
Royal Exchange ④⑦
Royal Mews ①⑦
St. Bride's Church ③⑨
St. James's Church ⑦
St. James's Palace ①③
St. Martin-in-the-Fields ③③

St. Mary-le-Bow ④①
St. Paul's Cathedral ④⓪
St. Paul's Church ③②
Science Museum ①⑧
Sir John Soane's
  Museum ③⑧
Tate Gallery ②②
10 Downing Street ②⑧
Theatre Museum ③⑤
Tower of London ④④

Trafalgar Square ①⓪
Victoria & Albert
  Museum ②⓪
Wallace Collection ③
Westminster Abbey ②④
Westminster
  Cathedral ②①

0 ▮▮▮▮▮▮ 1 km
       .6 mi

N

the Queen's working stables, displaying ornately gilded carriages and live horses in stalls with their names above.

✪ Houses of Parliament

Parliament Square, SW1. ☎ **0171/219-4272** for information. Admission free. House of Commons, public admitted Mon–Thurs 2:30–10:30pm and Fri 9:30am–3pm; House of Lords, public admitted Mon–Wed from about 2:30pm and Thurs from about 3pm, and on some Fris 11am–4pm (line up at St. Stephen's Entrance, just past the statue of Oliver Cromwell; debates usually run into the night, and lines shrink after 6pm). Tube: Westminster.

To most people, the Houses of Parliament, along with their trademark clocktower, are the ultimate symbol of London. Officially known as the Palace of Westminster, the spectacular 19th-century gothic revival building contains over 1,000 rooms and 2 miles of corridors. The clocktower, at the eastern end, houses the world's most famous timepiece. **"Big Ben"** refers not to the clocktower, as many people assume, but to the largest bell in the chime, a $13^{1}/_{2}$-tonner named for the first commissioner of works. Listen to the familiar chime, which has inspired ostentatious doorbells around the world. At night a light shines in the tower whenever Parliament is sitting. Visitors may watch parliamentary debates from the Stranger's Galleries of Parliament's two houses.

Rebuilt in 1950 because of the damage done by a German air-raid attack in 1941, the **House of Commons** remains small. Only 437 of its 651 members can sit at any one time, while the rest crowd around the door and the Speaker's Chair. The ruling party and the opposition sit facing each other, two sword lengths apart.

Debates in the **House of Lords** are not as interesting or lively as those in the more important Commons, but the line to get in is usually shorter, and a visit here will give you an appreciation for the pageantry of Parliament.

National Gallery

Trafalgar Sq., WC2. ☎ **0171/839-3321.** Main galleries, free; Sainsbury Wing, £2–£5 ($3–$7.50). Mon–Sat 10am–6pm, Sun 2–6pm. Tube: Charing Cross or Embankment.

With very few exceptions, the National Gallery's collections encompass the entire history of Western art, with major examples from such masters as Rembrandt, Raphael, Botticelli, Goya, and others. Over 2,000 paintings represent every major school of art. The Sainsbury Wing, which opened in 1991, houses many of the museum's most precious early Renaissance works. A new state-of-the-art Micro Gallery lets you examine any painting in the museum's vast holdings at the touch of a button. There's a great gift shop. Phone for details on current shows.

✪ St. Paul's Cathedral

St. Paul's Churchyard, EC4. ☎ **0171/248-2705.** Cathedral and crypt, £3 ($4.50) adults, £2.50 ($3.75) students and seniors, £2 ($3) children 15 and under; galleries, £2.50 ($3.75) adults, £2 ($3) students and seniors, £1.50 ($2.25) children 15 and under. Mon–Sat 8:45am–4:15pm, Sun for services only. Tube: St. Paul's.

> ## ❓ Did You Know?
>
> - London is the most populous city in Western Europe.
> - In 1960s London two long-lasting fashions were launched: long hair for men and miniskirts for women.
> - London's Heathrow Airport is the busiest in Europe.
> - Harrods is the largest department store in Western Europe.

Dedicated to the patron saint of The City of London, St. Paul's is architect Sir Christopher Wren's masterpiece. Capped by one of the largest domes in Christendom, the great Renaissance edifice is one of the world's few cathedrals ever to be designed by a single architect and completed during his lifetime. Wren is buried in the cathedral's crypt; his epitaph, on the floor below the dome, states "Lector, si monumentum requiris, circumspice" (Reader, if you seek his monument, look around you). You can climb the 259 steps to the Whispering Gallery, just below the dome. Acoustics here are such that even soft sounds can be heard on the other side of the dome. Another steep climb to the Golden Gallery presents you with an unrivaled view of London. The cathedral has been the setting for many important ceremonies, including the funerals of Admiral Lord Nelson (1806) and Sir Winston Churchill (1965) and the wedding of Prince Charles and Lady Diana Spencer (1981).

✪ Tate Gallery

Millbank, SW1. ☎ **0171/887-8000.** Permanent collection, free; temporary exhibits, £5 ($7.50) adults, £3.50 ($5.25) students, seniors, and children. Mon–Sat 10am–5:50pm, Sun 2–5pm. Tube: Pimlico.

This is both London's museum of modern art and the primary gallery for British painting. Large and airy, the gallery holds an especially good cubist collection, many major contemporary pieces by Salvador Dalí, David Hockney, Joan Miró, and plenty of weird postcontemporary others. Among the avant-garde works are regular exhibitions by up-and-coming stars. The architecturally postmodern Clore Gallery houses an extensive collection of Turner's oils and drawings and is one of the most influential mounters of "new edge" exhibitions. If you like your art to push the limits, attend the Tate's free daily one-hour lunchtime lecture at 1pm.

Tower Bridge

E1. ☎ **0171/407-0922.** Admission £5 ($7.50) adults, £3.50 ($5.25) seniors and children 5–15 (last tickets sold 45 min. before closing), free for children 4 and under. Apr–Oct, daily 10am–6:30pm; Nov–Mar, daily 10am–5:15pm. Tube: Tower Hill.

Here's a lyrical London landmark you should try not to miss. Inside is an exhibition examining the 100-year history of the bridge, which includes some clever animatronic characters. You can walk across the footbridges above and examine the hydraulic machinery below, but unless you're particularly fond of heights or Victorian engineering, keep your pounds in your pocket as the best views are from the outside.

✪ Tower of London

Tower Hill, EC3. ☎ **0171/709-0765.** Admission £7.95 ($11.95) adults, £5.95 ($8.95) students and seniors, £5.25 ($7.90) children 5–15, free for children 4 and under. Mar–Oct, Mon–Sat 9am–6pm, Sun 10am–6pm; Nov–Feb, Mon–Sat 9am–5pm, Sun 10am–5pm. Last tickets sold one hour before closing. Beefeater tours given every half hour from 10:45am. Tube: Tower Hill.

Begun by William I (the Conqueror) soon after the Norman Conquest in 1066, this complex has served as a fortress, a royal palace, a treasury, an armory, and a menagerie, but it's best remembered as a prison. The two young sons of Edward IV are thought to have been murdered here in 1485, and Henry VIII's second wife, Anne Boleyn, was executed nearby. Today the closest the Tower comes to torture is the suffocating feeling you get on weekends, when it seems as though everyone in London is here.

The Tower is home the Crown Jewels, displayed in a fortified Jewel House built with moving walkways to help the crowds along. The Imperial State Crown, worn by the monarch at major state occasions, is encrusted with more than 2,800 diamonds and is the world's priciest hat. Other valuables include the exquisite Koh-i-noor diamond, in the crown of the Queen Mother; and the Star of Africa, the largest cut diamond in the world, set in the cross of the Queen Mother's Orb and Scepter.

You can get dizzy exploring the extensive arms and armory displays, but make it a point to see the fascinating Oriental collection, as well as Henry VIII's anatomically exaggerated armor (you'll know it when you see it), in the White Tower. Macabre history continues in the Bowyer Tower, which displays a large collection of historical instruments of torture, including one for henpecking wives.

A visit to the Tower is not cheap—but it's worth every pound. Upon entering, wait by the first gate for the excellent Beefeater-guided free tour.

✪ Victoria & Albert Museum

Cromwell Rd., SW7. ☎ **0171/938-8500,** or 938-8441 for a recording. Admission free (donation requested). Mon noon–5:50pm, Tues–Sun 10am–5:50pm. Tube: South Kensington.

In a city of fantastic museums, the Victoria & Albert is tops. The V&A is the world's greatest repository of decorative arts: If it's pretty and useful—and has been created within the last 15 centuries—you'll likely find it here. Comprehensive collections from around the world stretch for 7 miles and include room upon room of porcelain figurines, costume jewelry, hunting tapestries, enamel washing bowls, carved end tables, silver forks and spoons, musical instruments, gilded mirrors, ceramic bowls and plates, ivory letter openers, wax molds, stained-glass lamps, lace doilies—you name it. The famous Dress Collection covers fashions from the 16th century to the present. A magnificent new Glass Gallery opened in 1995 on Level C. The Twentieth-Century Primary Galleries feature temporary exhibitions of furniture, sculpture, and modern design.

✪ Westminster Abbey

Broad Sanctuary, SW1. ☎ **0171/222-5152** or 222-7110. Abbey, free; Royal Chapels, £4 ($6) adults, £2 ($3) students and seniors, £1 ($1.50) children 15 and under (free to Henry VII Chapel Wed 6–8pm, the only time that photography is permitted). Abbey, daily 10:30am–4pm; Royal Chapels, Mon–Fri 9am–4pm, Sat 9am–2pm and 3:45–5pm. Tube: Westminster.

The Benedictine abbey, which housed a community of monks as early as A.D. 750, was called Westminster (West Monastery) after its location west of The City. In 1050 Edward the Confessor enhanced the site and moved his palace next door, beginning a tradition of church and state that continues to the present. All England's monarchs have been crowned in the abbey since William the Conqueror's coronation on Christmas Day in 1066. Many are buried here too, among a clutter of tombs of statesmen, poets, and benefactors. When not in use, the Coronation Chair (built in 1300) sits behind the High Altar. Incorporated into the chair is the Stone of Scone, which has been associated with Scottish royalty since the 9th century. Captured by Edward I in 1297, the Stone has been stolen back by Scottish nationalists several times (most recently in the 1950s) but always recovered. The abbey's Henry VII Chapel is one of the most beautiful places you may ever see. Added in 1503, the Chapel's exuberant architectural extravagances and exquisite intricate carvings will take your breath away. Comprehensive "Super Tours" condense the abbey's 900-year history into 1½ hours for £6.50 ($9.75) per person.

Westminster

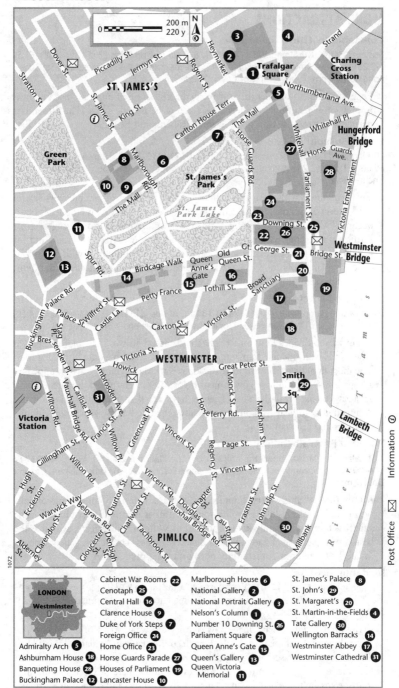

LONDON
Westminster

	Cabinet War Rooms **22**	Marlborough House **6**	St. James's Palace **8**
	Cenotaph **25**	National Gallery **2**	St. John's **29**
	Central Hall **16**	National Portrait Gallery **3**	St. Margaret's **20**
	Clarence House **9**	Nelson's Column **1**	St. Martin-in-the-Fields **4**
	Duke of York Steps **7**	Number 10 Downing St. **26**	Tate Gallery **30**
Admiralty Arch **5**	Foreign Office **24**	Parliament Square **21**	Wellington Barracks **14**
Ashburnham House **18**	Home Office **23**	Queen Anne's Gate **15**	Westminster Abbey **17**
Banqueting House **28**	Horse Guards Parade **27**	Queen's Gallery **13**	Westminster Cathedral **31**
Buckingham Palace **12**	Houses of Parliament **19**	Queen Victoria Memorial **11**	
	Lancaster House **10**		

Post Office ⌧ Information ⓘ

MORE ATTRACTIONS

Courtauld Institute Galleries

Somerset House, The Strand, WC2. ☎ **0171/873-2526**. Admission £3 ($4.50) adults; £1.50 ($2.25) students, seniors, and children 5–15; free for children 4 and under. Mon–Sat 10am–6pm, Sun 2–6pm. Tube: Temple or Covent Garden.

Focusing on quality rather than quantity, this collection of impressionist and post-impressionist paintings is widely considered to be Europe's best. The museum is particularly strong in works by Cézanne, Rubens, and Bellini.

Freud Museum

20 Maresfield Gardens, Hampstead, NW3. ☎ **0171/435-2002**. Admission £2.50 ($3.75) adults, £1.50 ($2.25) students, free for children under 12. Wed–Sun noon–5pm. Tube: Finchley Road.

This museum was the home of Sigmund Freud, founder of psychoanalysis, who lived, worked, and died in this rather plain house after he and his family left Nazi-occupied Vienna as refugees in 1938. On view are rooms containing original furniture, paintings, photographs, letters, and personal effects of Freud and his daughter, Anna. Of particular interest is Freud's study and library with his famous couch and large collection of Egyptian, Roman, and Asian antiquities. Exhibitions and archive film programs are also on view.

Highgate Cemetery

Swain's Lane, Hampstead. ☎ **0181/340-1834**. East side, £1 ($1.50); west side, £3 ($4.50) donation for tour. Times vary; phone for information. Tube: Archway.

Swain's Lane divides London's Highgate Cemetery in two. The old, overgrown "Egyptian" west side filled up years ago and is now accessible only by guided tour. The most famous resident of the east side is Karl Marx, whose grave is topped by a huge bust—the Chinese government helps pay for its upkeep. Highgate is still an active burial ground and its keepers have asked that you to make advance arrangements to visit it. Tours are usually scheduled daily, year round; phone for times and reservations.

National Portrait Gallery

2 St. Martin's Place (around the corner from the National Gallery), WC2. ☎ **0171/306-0055**. Admission free. Mon–Sat 10am–6pm, Sun noon–6pm. Tube: Charing Cross or Embankment.

A walk through this gallery, founded in 1856 as a repository for pictures of politicians and royalty, is like a stroll through centuries of British social history. The gallery is home to the only known portrait of William Shakespeare, as well as the best-known painting of Lady Diana, Princess of Wales. The newest gallery, opened in late 1993, exhibits 20th-century portraiture and photography.

Madame Tussaud's

Marylebone Rd., NW1. ☎ **0171/935-6861**. Admission £7.95 ($11.95) adults, £5.95 ($8.95) seniors, £4.95 ($7.45) children 5–15, free for children 4 and under. Daily 9am–5:50pm. Tube: Baker Street.

Eerily lifelike figures have made this century-old waxworks world famous. The original moldings of members of the French court, to whom Madame Tussaud had direct access, are fascinating. But the modern superstars and the Chamber of Horrors, to which this "museum" donates the lion's share of space, are the stuff tourist traps are made of. Madame Tussaud's is expensive and somewhat overrated.

Bloomsbury & Holborn

British Museum **5**
Courtauld Institute
    Galleries **3**
Dickens's House **6**
Gray's Inn **7**
Inner Temple **13**
Inns of Court
    & Chancery **11**
Jewish Museum **2**
King's College **14**
Lincoln's Inn **9**
Middle Temple **12**
Museum of the Moving
    Image (MOMI) **19**
National Theater **18**
Royal Courts of
    Justice **10**
Royal Festival
    Hall and Queen
    Elizabeth Hall **17**
Royal Opera House **16**
Sir John Soane's
    Museum **8**
Somerset House **15**
University College **1**
University of
    London **4**

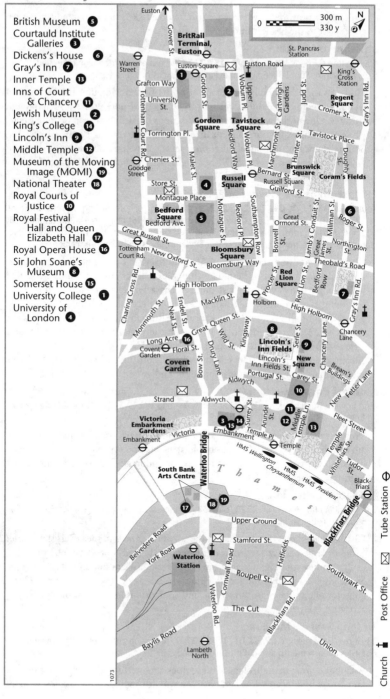

Church   Post Office   Tube Station

Go early to beat the crowds; better still, reserve tickets one day in advance, then go straight to the head of the line.

Museum of Mankind

6 Burlington Gardens, W1. ☎ **0171/437-2224.** Admission free (donation requested). Mon–Sat 10am–5pm, Sun 2:30–6pm. Tube: Piccadilly Circus or Green Park.

Home to the ethnographic department of the British Museum, the Museum of Mankind maintains exhibits relating to a variety of non-Western societies and cultures. One of the world's greatest collections of African art can be found here, while changing exhibitions present themes from Australia, the Pacific Islands, and South America. Only a small selection from the museum's hoard can be shown at any one time. Don't miss the 9-foot-high Easter Island statue brought back by Captain Cook.

✪ Museum of the Moving Image (MOMI)

South Bank, SE1. ☎ **0171/928-3232,** or 401-2636 for a recording. Admission £5.50 ($8.25) adults, £4.70 ($7.05) students and seniors, £4 ($6) children 14 and under. Daily 10am–6pm (last admission at 5pm). Tube: Waterloo is closer, but the short walk over Hungerford Bridge from the Embankment Underground station is more scenic.

This lively hands-on celebration of film and television is one of the city's newest museums—and one of its best. The chronologically arranged exhibits are staffed by costumed actors who never step out of character. The museum itself is as entertaining as a top movie. Displays strike the perfect balance between technology and the culture it produced. You can watch Russian movies on a agitprop train, create your own animated strips for a zoetrope, read the news from a TelePrompTer, then watch yourself on a monitor, and "fly" over London using chromakey technology. The emphasis here is on things British, but MOMI's extraordinarily popular slant is right out of Hollywood.

National Postal Museum

King Edward Building, King Edward St., EC1. ☎ **0171/239-5420.** Admission free. Mon–Fri 9:30am–4:30pm. Tube: St. Paul's.

This three-story museum has an excellent collection of postage stamps from Britain and the world. Over 150 years of philatelic history is covered, from the "penny black" to current issues. Pull out the case on "addresses" to see some interesting 17th-century seals.

✪ Saatchi Collection

98A Boundary Rd., NW8. ☎ **0171/624-8299.** Admission free Fri, £2 ($3) Sat–Sun. Fri–Sun noon–6pm. Tube: St. John's Wood.

Charles Saatchi is as controversial in the art world as he is in the advertising world. Britain's largest private collector of modern art built this personal museum especially to house rotating displays from his vast and brilliant holdings. Each year the Saatchi holds an exhibition focusing on the freshest talent, a show that makes this collector one of the most influential, and contentious, movers on the contemporary art scene.

Sir John Soane's Museum

13 Lincoln's Inn Fields, WC2. ☎ **0171/405-2107.** Admission free. Tues–Sat 10am–5pm (the first Tues of each month also 6–9pm). Tube: Holborn.

A fantastic array of archeological antiquities, architectural drawings, and important works by Hogarth, Turner, and Watteau are housed in the former home of the architect of the first Bank of England. The house is jam-packed with objects, seemingly displayed in a haphazard manner. But enter the small room where Hogarth's *The Rake's Progress* is displayed and ask the guard to show you the room's secret. You'll be convinced that there's a method to the madness.

Wallace Collection

Hertford House, Manchester Sq. (just steps from Oxford St.), W1. ☎ **0171/935-0687.** Admission free (donation requested). Mon–Sat 10am–5pm, Sun 2–5pm. Tube: Bond Street.

It's hard to know which is more impressive, the art and antiques or the house in which they're held. This bountiful haven has a fantastic micro collection of masterpieces by Rembrandt, Rubens, Murillo, and van Dyck, along with superb examples of 18th-century furniture, Sèvres porcelain, clocks, objets d'art, and quite unexpectedly, a most impressive array of European and Asian arms and armor.

PARKS & GARDENS

Hyde Park, the large rectangular expanse often associated with London, is one of the city's most popular greens. As in other Royal Parks, wood-and-cloth chaise longues are scattered about so you, too, can be sitting in an English garden waiting for the sun. Fee collectors will appear from nowhere and demand 60p (90¢) from seated tourists, each of whom is usually ignorant of this cost of relaxation; the benches and grass are free. The park is especially lively on Sunday, when artists hang their wares along the Bayswater Road fence and the northeast corner, near Marble Arch, becomes Speakers' Corner, where anyone can stand on a soapbox and pontificate on any subject. Although this tradition is often touted as an example of Britain's tolerance of free speech, few people realize that this ritual began several hundred years ago when condemned prisoners were allowed some final words before they were hanged on Tyburn gallows, which stood on the same spot. Take the tube to Hyde Park Corner.

A huge misshapen circle north of central London, **Regent's Park** is the city's playground, famous for its zoo, concerts, and open-air theater in summer. A band plays free beside the lake twice daily from May to August. Get there by tube to Regent's Park or Baker Street, or Camden Town for the zoo.

St. James's Park, opposite Buckingham Palace, is perhaps the most beautiful of London's greens. Swans, geese, and other waterfowl, including a family of pelicans, make their home here (feedings daily at 3pm). A central location, a beautiful lake, and plentiful benches make this park perfect for picnicking. Take the tube to St. James's Park.

Adjacent **Green Park** is named for the absence of flowers (except for a short time in spring). But the ample shade from tall trees also makes this park a picnicker's paradise.

The **Chelsea Physic Garden,** 66 Royal Hospital Rd., SW3 (☎ **0171/ 352-5646**), founded in 1673, is the second-oldest botanical garden in England. Behind high brick walls is a rare collection of old and exotic plants, shrubs, and trees, including Asian herbs and a 19th-century fruiting olive tree. Founded by the Society of Apothecaries to teach their apprentices how to identify medicinal plants, the garden has since expanded to include rare species from the New World. Admission is £2.50 ($3.75) for adults, £1.30 ($1.95) for students and children. The garden is open April to October, Wednesday from 2 to 5pm and Sunday from 2 to 6pm. Take the tube to Sloane Square.

The **Royal Botanic Gardens,** better known as ○ **Kew Gardens** (☎ **0181/ 940-1171** or 332-5622), is an important research facility with London's most beautiful indoor/outdoor gardens year round. The architectural brilliance of the iron-and-glass greenhouses and famous Chinese-style pagoda combine with chrysanthemums, rhododendrons, peonies, and one of the world's largest collections of orchids to make a visit to Kew truly unforgettable. The gardens are open daily: November to January from 9:30am to 4pm; in February from 9:30am to 5pm; in March from 9:30am to 6pm; April to August, Monday through Saturday from 9:30am to 6:30pm and Sunday and holidays from 9:30am to 8pm; in September and October from 9:30am to 6pm. Admission is £4 ($6) for adults, £2 ($3) for students and seniors. Kew can be reached by tube in about 30 minutes. From April to October, you can reach the gardens by boat from Westminster Pier, near the Westminster Underground station. The trip upstream takes about 90 minutes and costs £5 ($7.50) for adults, £3 ($4.50) for children 4 to 14, free for children 3 and under.

SPECIAL-INTEREST SIGHTSEEING
FOR THE LITERARY ENTHUSIAST

London boasts an extremely long and rich literary tradition. Geoffrey Chaucer lived above Aldgate, in the easternmost part of The City until 1386, and playwright Joe Orton lived on Noel Road in Islington until his death in 1967. Oscar Wilde, Dylan Thomas, George Orwell, D. H. Lawrence, George Bernard Shaw, Rudyard Kipling, William Blake—the list of authors who made London their home goes on and on. Unfortunately, a little blue plaque is usually all that's left to mark the past, but there are some exceptions.

Dr. Johnson's House

17 Gough Sq., Fleet St., EC4. ☎ **0171/353-3745.** Admission £3 ($4.50) adults, £2 ($3) students and seniors, £1 ($1.50) children 15 and under. May–Sept, Mon–Sat 11am–5:30pm; Oct–Apr, Mon–Sat 11am–5pm. Tube: Blackfriars.

The wonderful Georgian town house where famous lexicographer Samuel Johnson lived and worked, compiling the world's first English dictionary, is now a shrine to him. His original dictionary, which is on display, includes the definition "Dull: to make dictionaries is dull work." There's not much here in the way of furnishings, but the long upstairs room in which Johnson worked is awash in ambience.

Keats's House

Wentworth Place, Keats Grove, NW3. ☎ **0171/435-2062.** Admission free. Apr–Oct, Mon–Fri 10am–1pm and 2–6pm, Sat 10am–1pm and 2–5pm, Sun 2–5pm; Nov–Mar, Mon–Fri 1–5pm, Sat 10am–1pm and 2–5pm, Sun 2–5pm. Tube: Hampstead.

Romantic poet John Keats penned his "Ode to a Nightingale" under a tree in the front garden. Keats died in 1821 at age 26; his house is now a museum displaying letters, books, and memorabilia, along with some of the original furnishings.

○ Thomas Carlyle's House

24 Cheyne Row, SW3. ☎ **0171/352-7087.** Admission £2.80 ($4.20) adults, £1.40 ($2.10) children 16 and under. Wed–Sun 11am–4:30pm. Closed Nov–Mar. Tube: Sloane Square.

This 18th-century Queen Anne town house is on a beautiful backstreet in Chelsea. The Scottish historian/philosopher lived here 47 years, until his death in 1881. His house remains virtually unaltered, to the extent that some of the rooms are without electric light. When the friendly live-in curator is not looking, you can sit in one of the writer's original Victorian chairs or touch a piano that Chopin played.

Dickens's House

48 Doughty St., WC1. ☎ **0171/405-2127**. Admission £3 ($4.50) adults, £2 ($3) students and seniors, £1 ($1.50) children; £5 ($7.50) families (two adults and three children). Mon–Sat 10am–5pm. Tube: Russell Square.

This house was home to one of London's most famous novelists for a short but prolific period. It was here that the writer worked on *The Pickwick Papers*, *Nicholas Nickleby*, and *Oliver Twist*. The author's letters, desk and chair, and first editions are all on display.

FOR THE HISTORY BUFF

It's hard to find much "history" on the streets of London because most of the old buildings have either been demolished or stashed away in a museum. But history can be experienced firsthand by observing age-old ceremonies that are carried out as faithfully today as they were hundreds of years ago. In addition to the aforementioned Changing of the Guard and debates in the Houses of Parliament, plan to attend the **Ceremony of the Keys** at the Tower of London. Every night for the past 700 years the gates of this ancient complex have been ceremoniously locked. You can watch the half-hour-long ritual if you request permission in writing at least one month in advance. Tickets are free. Write to the Resident Governor, Constable's Office, HM Tower of London, London EC 3N 4AB. Include an International Reply Coupon.

Cabinet War Rooms

Clive Steps, King Charles St., SW1. ☎ **0171/930-6961**. Admission £3.90 ($5.85) adults, £3 ($4.50) students, £1.90 ($2.85) children 5–16, free for children 4 and under. Daily 9:30am–6pm (last admission at 5:15pm). Tube: St. James's Park or Westminster.

The British government's World War II underground headquarters—the Cabinet Room, Map Room, Churchill's emergency bedroom, and the Telephone Room (where calls to President Roosevelt were made)—have been restored to their 1940s appearance. It's rather austere but historically fascinating. All visitors receive a free sound guide.

Museum of London

150 London Wall, EC2. ☎ **0171/600-3699**. Admission £3 ($4.50) adults, £1.50 ($2.25) seniors and children 5–15, free for children 4 and under. Tues–Sat 10am–6pm. Tube: St. Paul's, Barbican, or Moorgate.

Behind a monstrous 1970s exterior, built on the site of a 2,000-year-old Roman fort, is an engaging museum of London and Londoners chronologically detailing city life from prehistoric times to the present. Exhibits include a marble head of Mithras (discovered in a nearby Roman temple), a model of old London Bridge (the real one is now in Arizona, U.S.A.), a grizzly cell from Newgate Prison, and the Lord Mayor's ornate 1756 coach (still used each November for the Lord Mayor's Show; see "Pretrip Preparations," earlier in this chapter).

FOR THE ARCHITECTURE LOVER

Inigo Jones and Christopher Wren were two of London's most celebrated architects. Both men designed in the English Renaissance style using Italian and French models, themselves inspired by the architecture of classical Greece and Rome. Jones's Banqueting House (see "Sightseeing Suggestions," above), and St. Paul's Church, overlooking Covent Garden Market, are excellent examples of the era. Wren's most famous work is St. Paul's Cathedral, but his Royal Hospital in Chelsea and Kensington Palace in Kensington are equal testaments to his ingenuity.

Whole areas built in the 18th century celebrate the Georgian period's distinct style. Notice the huge windows fronting houses on Cartwright Gardens, Bedford Square, and other squares around Bloomsbury. The Horse Guards buildings on Whitehall date from this period as well.

Although a variety of styles from this era prevent one from making architectural generalizations, London's most striking buildings are pure Victoriana. My favorites are such unabashedly flamboyant ones as St. Pancras Station (tube to Euston), the Houses of Parliament, and the Royal Courts of Justice on the Strand (the last is open Monday through Friday from 10am to 4:30pm; take the tube to Aldwych or Temple).

✪ Lloyds of London Building
Lime St., EC3. ☎ **0171/327-6210.** Admission free. Tube: Monument or Bank.

There are so many ugly 20th-century buildings in London that Prince Charles is actively fighting against the city's further architectural decline. Located in the center of The City of London, the Lloyds of London Building is a stunning exception. Designed by Richard Rogers (co-architect of Paris's Centre Pompidou), these headquarters to the world's most famous insurance market opened in 1986 to much critical attention. All the "guts" of the building (elevators, water pipes, electrical conduits) are on the exterior, and cranes are permanently affixed to the roof, ready to help with further expansion should it become necessary. At night, special lighting lends an extraterrestrial quality to the site. The building is usually not open to the public, but small groups can make reservations to visit the Underwriting Room of this famous insurance market.

Prince Henry's Room
17 Fleet St., EC4. ☎ **0171/294-1158.** Admission free. Mon–Sat 11am–2pm. Tube: Aldwych or Temple.

Named for King James I's eldest son, this second-floor museum is housed in one of the few buildings to survive the Great Fire of 1666. Built in 1611, the plaster-and-wood building has oak paneling and original ceilings inside. It houses a collection of memorabilia relating to Samuel Pepys, a 17th-century naval leader whose extensive diaries include an abundance of information about the fire and its aftermath.

✪ Westminster Cathedral
42 Francis St., at Ashley Place, SW1. ☎ **0171/834-7452** Cathedral, free; tower, £2 ($3), £1 ($1.50) students and children. Cathedral, daily 7am–8pm; tower, Apr–Oct, daily 9:30am–5:30pm. Tube: Victoria.

Westminster Cathedral, headquarters of the Catholic church in Britain, was completed in 1903. Just a stone's throw from Victoria Station, this spectacular Byzantine-style building stands in stark contrast to the contemporary office buildings around it. The interior marble columns and detailed mosaics are equally majestic. Take a look at the excellent rendering of the cathedral's interior on the wall just inside the front door. From April to October you can take an elevator to the top of the cathedral's landmark white stone–and–red brick tower for an unobstructed view over Westminster.

FOR THE VISITING AMERICAN
Grosvenor Square, W1, has strong U.S. connections and is known to some as Little America. John Adams lived on the square when he was the American

ambassador to the United Kingdom, a statue of Franklin Roosevelt stands in the center of the square, General Eisenhower headquartered here during World War II, and the entire west side is occupied by the U.S. Embassy.

The former **home of Benjamin Franklin,** 36 Craven St., WC2, steps from Trafalgar Square, is just one of many houses formerly occupied by famous Americans. For a complete list, pick up *Americans in London* (paperback; Queen Anne Press, 1988) by Brian Morton, an excellent anecdotal street guide to the London homes and haunts of famous Americans.

ORGANIZED TOURS

WALKING TOURS   London's most interesting streets are best explored on foot, and several high-quality tour companies will help you find your way inexpensively. Excellent walks are offered by **City Walks,** 147C Offord Rd., N1 (☎ **0171/700-6931**), and **The Original London Walks,** P.O. Box 1708, London NW6 (☎ **0171/624-3978**). Both companies operate regularly scheduled theme-based city tours on a daily basis; write or phone for a free brochure or consult the "Around Town" section of *Time Out* magazine. Tours generally cost £4 to £5 ($6 to $7.50) and represent one of the best bargains in London.

One of the most popular tours is offered by **Discovery Walks** (☎ **0171/256-8973**). Their "On the Trail of Jack the Ripper" leaves the Aldgate East Underground station nightly at 8pm; reservations are not required.

BUS TOURS   Bus tours guarantee that you'll catch all the sights, even though you may not have the foggiest idea of where they are in relation to one another. At £9 ($13.50) per person, the panoramic tours offered by **London Transport** (☎ **0171/222-1234**) are cheapest. Buses depart frequently from the Piccadilly Circus Underground station (Haymarket exit), Victoria Station (opposite the Palace Theatre), Marble Arch (Speakers' Corner), and the Baker Street Underground station. From June 10 to September 22, tours run daily from 9am to as late as 7pm; the rest of the year tours are given daily from 10am to 5pm.

Do-it-yourselfers should purchase a **Travelcard** (see "Getting Around" under "London Specifics," earlier in this chapter) and take the front seat on the upper deck of a public double-decker bus. Two of the more scenic bus routes include **no. 11,** which passes King's Road, Victoria Station, Westminster Abbey, Whitehall, Horse Guards, Trafalgar Square, the National Gallery, The Strand, Law Courts, Fleet Street, and St. Paul's Cathedral; and **no. 53,** which passes the Regent's Park Zoo, Oxford Circus, Regent Street, Piccadilly Circus, the National Gallery, Trafalgar Square, Horse Guards, Whitehall, and Westminster Square.

7 Shopping

Even the most jaded capitalists are awed by the sheer quantity of shops in London. The range and variety of goods are so staggering that a quick jump into a store can easily turn into an all-day shopping spree.

The British government encourages tourists to part with their pounds by offering to refund the 17.5% value-added tax (VAT). Not all retailers participate in the refund program, and those that do require a minimum purchase, usually £50 ($75). The reclamation procedure is cumbersome: **To reclaim the VAT,** show the sales clerk your passport and fill out a special form at each shop you visit. Then present the forms and the goods to a Customs officer upon departing Great

Britain. After the official validates your VAT forms, mail them back to the stores where you made your purchases. Several months later you'll receive your refund—in pounds sterling and minus a small commission charge. You can avoid the bank charges usually encountered when cashing foreign-currency checks by using your credit or charge cards for the purchases and requesting that your VAT refund be credited to your account.

DEPARTMENT STORES

Department stores are the city's most famous shopping institutions, and a handful stand out as top attractions as well. All of the following accept American Express, Diners Club, MasterCard, and Visa.

Harrods

87–135 Brompton Rd., SW1. ☎ **0171/730-1234.** Tube: Knightsbridge.

By many estimates, Harrods is the largest department store in the world, selling everything from pins to pianos. The store claims that anything in the world can be bought here—and it may be true. Even if you're not in a shopping mood, the incredible ground-floor food halls are worth a visit. Admire the stained-glass ceiling and the unbelievable fresh-fish fountain in the seafood hall. Open Monday and Tuesday from 10am to 6pm, Wednesday through Friday from 10am to 7pm, and Saturday from 10am to 6pm.

✪ Liberty

210–214 Regent St., W1. ☎ **0171/734-1234.** Tube: Oxford Circus.

Liberty has a worldwide reputation for selling fine textiles in unique surroundings. The pretty old-world store has an incomparable Asian department. Open Monday, Tuesday, Friday, and Saturday from 9:30am to 6pm, Wednesday from 10am to 6pm, and Thursday from 9:30am to 7:30pm.

Marks & Spencer

48 Oxford St., W1. ☎ **0171/935-7954.**

If you're British, this is where you buy your quality underwear. M&S is known for well-priced, quality family clothes—but don't expect the latest fashion trends. Open Monday through Wednesday and Saturday from 9am to 7pm and Thursday and Friday from 9am to 8pm.

Selfridges

400 Oxford St., W1. ☎ **0171/629-1234.** Tube: Marble Arch or Bond Street.

Selfridges seems almost as big and more crowded than its chief rival, Harrods. Opened in 1909 by Harry Selfridge, a salesman from Chicago, this department store revolutionized retailing with its variety of goods and dynamic displays. Open Monday through Wednesday, Friday, and Saturday from 9:30am to 7pm, and Thursday from 9:30am to 8pm.

SHOPPING AREAS

THE WEST END   This is the heart of London shopping, and mile-long **Oxford Street** is its main artery. Its sidewalks are terminally congested—and with good reason. A solid row of shops stretches as far as the eye can see, so if you have only one day to shop, spend it here. At its mid-section, Oxford Street is bisected by **Regent Street,** a more elegant thoroughfare, lined with boutiques, fine china shops, and jewelers. At **Piccadilly Circus,** Regent Street meets Piccadilly, which, along with St. James's Street, Jermyn Street, and the Burlington Arcade, make up one of the swankiest shopping regions in the entire world.

Street fashions can be found in abundance around Covent Garden Market and on Longacre, Shorts Gardens, and Neal Street.

CHELSEA The best shops in Chelsea are along **King's Road,** a mile-long thoroughfare straddling the fashion fence between trend and tradition. In the late 1970s and early 1980s this was the center of punk fashion. Things have quieted down somewhat since then, but the chain-store boutiques are still mixed with a healthy dose of the avant garde.

KENSINGTON This is another trendy area for urban designs. The best young fashion flourishes on **Kensington High Street** in general, and in **Hyper, Hyper,** 26–40 Kensington High St. (☎ **0171/938-4343**), and the **Kensington Market,** 49–53 Kensington High St. (☎ **0171/938-4343**), in particular.

TRADITIONAL SALES

January sales are as British as Christmas pudding (which is usually reduced by 30% and just as edible the next year as the last). All the big department stores start their annual sales just after Christmas, and the smaller shops usually follow suit. For Londoners, the January sales are a rite, and tourists are no less immune to the fever and passion they induce. Several department stores (chiefly Harrods and Selfridges) compete for all-night lines by offering one or two particularly remarkable specials. Be aware that some goods, shipped in especially for the sales, are not as high quality as those offered the rest of the year.

MARKETS

Outdoor markets are where knowledgeable Londoners and bargain hunters shop for food, clothing, furniture, books, antiques, crafts, and, of course, junk. Dozens of markets cater to different communities, and for shopping or just browsing they offer a unique and exciting day out. Few stalls officially open before sunrise. Still, flashlight-wielding professionals appear early, snapping up gems before they reach the display table. During wet weather stalls may close early.

Brixton is the heart of African-Caribbean London and the **Brixton Market,** Electric Avenue, SW9 (tube to Brixton), is its soul. Electric Avenue (immortalized by Jamaican singer Eddie Grant) is lined mostly with exotic fruit and vegetable stalls. But continue to the end, turn right, and you'll see a good selection of the cheapest secondhand clothes in London. Take a detour off the avenue through the enclosed Granville Arcade for African fabrics, traditional West African teeth-cleaning sticks, reggae records, and newspapers oriented to the African-British community. Open Monday, Tuesday, Thursday, and Saturday from 8am to 6pm, Wednesday from 8am to 1pm, and Friday from 8am to 7pm.

The ✪ **Camden Markets,** along Camden High Street, NW1 (tube to Camden Town), is a trendy collection of stalls, in parking lots and empty spaces all the way to Chalk Farm Road, specializing in original fashions by young designers and junk from people of all ages. Cafés and pubs (some offering live music) line the route, making for an enjoyable day out. When you've had enough of shopping here, turn north and walk along the peaceful and pretty Regent's Canal. Open Saturday and Sunday from 8am to 6pm. The **Camden Passage Market,** off Upper Street, NI (tube to Angel), is smaller than Portobello (below) and usually cheaper, too.

Wednesday and Saturday are the best days to pick up bargain jewelry, trinkets, and antiques. Open Wednesday from 9am to 3pm and Saturday from 9am to 5pm.

The ✪ **Portobello Market,** along Portobello Road, W11 (tube to Notting Hill Gate; ask anyone for directions from there), is the granddaddy of them all, famous for its overflow of antiques and bric-a-brac along a road that never seems to end. As at all antiques markets, bargaining is in order here. Saturday between 8am and 4pm is best, as the market consists mainly of fruit and vegetable stalls during the week.

8 London After Dark

London is a cultural cornucopia. As the sun sets and a hush descends on the rest of the land, the capital's theaters, clubs, and pubs swing into action. **Ticketmaster** (☎ **0171/344-4444**) makes credit/charge-card bookings for theaters, opera, ballet, and pop-music concerts. Its hotline is open 24 hours daily. Ticketmaster locations include the London Tourist Board Information Centre, Victoria Station forecourt (open Monday through Saturday from 9am to 7pm and Sunday from 9am to 5pm), and Harrods department store, Knightsbridge (open Monday, Tuesday, and Thursday through Saturday from 9am to 6pm and Wednesday from 9am to 8pm).

Attending a play in London is almost a requirement for any tourist worthy of the name. More theatrical entertainment is offered here than in any other city, at prices far below New York's. Again, the magazine *Time Out* offers a comprehensive roundup of the week's events.

THE PERFORMING ARTS
THEATER

The term West End, when applied to theater, refers to the commercial theaters around Shaftesbury Avenue and Covent Garden. Currently, there are more than 40 such houses where comedies, musicals, and dramas are regularly staged. Tickets cost £10 to £30 ($15 to $45) and are usually most expensive for musicals, as demand for them is highest. But discounts are available. The Society of West End Theatre operates a **discount ticket booth** in Leicester Square, where tickets for many shows are available at half price, plus a £1.50 ($2.25) service charge. Tickets are sold only on the day of performance, and there's a limit of four per person. No credit or charge cards are accepted. The booth is open Monday through Saturday from noon on matinee days (which vary with individual theaters) and from 2:30 to 6:30pm for evening performances. All West End theaters are closed Sunday.

Blockbuster shows can be sold out months in advance, but if you just have to see the most popular show, one of the many high-commission **ticket agencies** can help you out. Always check with the box office first for any last-minute returns. Free West End theater guides listing all the current productions are distributed by tourist offices, hotels, and ticket agencies.

If you have an International Student ID Card (ISIC), you can purchase tickets to top shows at drastically reduced prices. Not all theaters participate in this program, so telephone first for availability. Those that do participate offer their **student-priced seats** on a standby basis half an hour before the performance.

Shakespeare's plays and other classical theater may be seen at the **Royal National Theatre,** South Bank, SE1 (☎ **0171/928-2252**), and at the new

Shakespeare's Globe Theatre, Bankside, SE1 (☎ **0171/928-6406**), an outdoor playhouse built from thatch according to plans for the original 1799 theater.

Some of the best theater in London is performed on the "fringe." Dozens of **fringe theaters** devoted to "alternative" plays, revivals, contemporary dramas, and even musicals are often more exciting than established West End productions, and are consistently lower in price. Expect to pay around £7 to £21 ($10.50 to $31.50). Check *Time Out* for show times.

London's best-kept secret? **Cabaret**—usually a combination of song, dance, comedy, and sex. Basically, anything goes, and uniformly low prices make this one of London's best bets. *Note:* Many cabarets are closed during the Edinburgh International Festival in late summer. Look under "Comedy" in *Time Out* for current offerings.

OPERA & DANCE

Not until the 1946 première of Benjamin Britten's *Peter Grimes* did British opera gain a serious reception. But since then a host of great composers have lifted British opera onto the world stage. The best thing about dance in London (and true to a lesser extent for opera) is that the major houses all offer inexpensive standby seats sold on the day of performance only. Prices at fringe theaters rarely top £7 ($10.50). Check *Time Out* for major programs and current fringe offerings.

London Coliseum

St. Martin's Lane, WC2. ☎ **0171/836-3161** for the box office, 0171/836-7666 for recorded information. Tickets £8–£124 ($12–$186). Tube: Leicester Square or Charing Cross.

The 2,350-seat London Coliseum is home to the English National Opera (ENO), an innovative company that continues to thrill enthusiasts and traditionalists. Operas are always sung in English, and many productions have been transported to Germany, France, and the United States. The ENO season lasts from August to May; visiting companies, often dance, perform during the summer months. The box office is open Monday through Saturday from 10am to 8pm.

Royal Opera House

Bow St., Covent Garden, WC2. ☎ **0171/240-1066.** Tickets £13–£60 ($19.50–$90) for ballet, £23–£130 ($34.50–$195) for opera. Tube: Covent Garden.

Home to both the Royal Opera and the Royal Ballet, this posh theater is rich in history, having first hosted an opera in 1817. Cheap seats are usually available on the day of the performance, though they can be pretty far from the stage. The box office is open Monday through Saturday from 10am to 8pm.

Sadler's Wells Theatre

Rosebery Ave., EC1. ☎ **0171/278-8916.** Tickets £5–£35 ($7.50–$52.50). Tube: Angel.

This is one of the busiest stages in London—and also one of the best. Host to visiting opera and dance companies from around the world, the theater offers great sightlines and terrific prices. Seats are available from 10:30am at the advance box office across the road; the regular box office is open Monday through Saturday from 10:30am to 6:30pm (until 7:30pm on performance nights).

CLASSICAL MUSIC

Barbican Centre

Silk St., EC2. ☎ **0171/638-4141,** or 628-2295 for a recording. Tickets £8–£30 ($12–$45). Tube: Barbican or Moorgate.

Known as "The City's Gift to the Nation," the sprawling, mazelike Barbican Centre has an excellent concert hall that the London Symphony Orchestra calls home. Even if you're not attending a performance, pop down before a show for a free student concert in the foyer. The box office is open daily from 9am to 8pm.

British Music Information Centre

10 Stratford Place, W1. ☎ **0171/499-8567.** Tube: Bond Street.

Britain's clearinghouse and resource center for "serious" music, the center provides free telephone and walk-in information on current and upcoming events. Free recitals are usually offered weekly, often Tuesday and Thursday at 7:30pm; call for exact times.

Royal Albert Hall

Kensington Gore, SW7. ☎ **0171/589-3203.** Tickets £7–£45 ($10.50–$67.50). Tube: Knightsbridge or Kensington High Street.

The Royal Albert attracts top symphonies (when there's no rock concert or boxing match), despite its infamous echo. The box office is open daily from 9am to 9pm.

South Bank Arts Centre

South Bank, SE1. ☎ **0171/928-8800** for the box office, 0171/633-0932 for recorded information. Tickets £5–£50 ($7.50–$75). Tube: Waterloo or Embankment.

The South Bank Arts Centre contains three well-designed modern concert halls. Here, concerts are staged nightly and encompass an eclectic range of styles. The **Royal Festival Hall** is the usual site for major orchestral performances. The smaller **Queen Elizabeth Hall** is known for its chamber-music concerts, and the intimate **Purcell Room** usually hosts advanced students and young performers making their professional debut. In addition, there are free concerts daily in the lobby of the Royal Festival Hall. The box office is open daily from 10am to 9pm.

Wigmore Hall

36 Wigmore St., W1. ☎ **0171/935-2141.** Tickets £4–£20 ($6–$30). Tube: Bond Street or Oxford Circus.

Perhaps the best auditorium in London for both intimacy and acoustics, Wigmore Hall presents instrumental and song recitals, chamber music, and early-music and baroque concerts. Buy the cheapest seats, as it really doesn't matter where you sit. The box office is open Monday through Saturday from 10am to 8:30pm.

Lunchtime Concerts in Churches

In addition to evening performances in the major music halls, lunchtime concerts are regularly scheduled in various churches throughout the city. Church concerts, usually given by young performers, are all free, though it's customary to leave a small donation. A full list of churches offering lunchtime concerts is available from the London Tourist Board.

✪ St. Bride's Church

Fleet St., EC4. ☎ **0171/353-1301.** Admission free. Tube: Blackfriars.

Completed by Christopher Wren in 1703, the tall tiered spire is said to have become the model for wedding cakes when it was copied by a local baker. Concerts here begin at 1:15pm and feature professional musicians or top students on Tuesday and Friday, while Wednesday is devoted to organ recitals. You'll want to arrive early to explore the ancient crypt of this handsome church.

St. James's Church

197 Piccadilly, W1. ☎ **0171/734-4511.** Admission free. Tube: Piccadilly Circus.

When Christopher Wren designed St. James's, he said that this church best embodied his idea of what a parish church should be. In addition to regular lunchtime recitals (Thurday and Friday at 1:10pm), keep an eye out for the occasional inexpensive evening concerts, usually scheduled during summer.

St. Martin-in-the-Fields

Trafalgar Sq., WC2. ☎ **0171/930-0089.** Admission free. Tube: Embankment or Charing Cross.

In the 13th century the church that stood at this central London corner was really "in the fields." Its wide tower-topped portico was the model for many colonial churches in America. Works by Debussy and Schubert are favorites at the weekly hour-long chamber-music recitals here. This church is also known for its above-average choir, and a visit to a full choral Sunday service should not be overlooked. Recitals are given Monday through Friday at 1:05pm.

ROCK

Since the 1960s British rock explosion, London hasn't let up on the number of clubs featuring home-grown talent. The West End in general, and Soho in particular, has a number of intimate places featuring every kind of music known to bandkind. Archaic drinking laws require most late-opening clubs to charge admission, which unfortunately often gets pricey. As usual, check *Time Out* for up-to-the-minute details.

Marquee

105–107 Charing Cross Rd., WC2. ☎ **0171/437-6601.** Cover £5–£7 ($7.50–$10.50). Tube: Tottenham Court Road.

Pink Floyd, David Bowie, Led Zeppelin, The Who, and practically every other rocker you've ever heard of started out playing at Marquee. After more than 30 years and a change of address, this is still the place to hear the bands of the future. Bar prices are refreshingly closer to pub than club. Open daily from 7 to 11:30pm.

Rock Garden

6–7 Covent Garden Plaza, WC2. ☎ **0171/836-4052.** Cover £4.50–£9 ($6.75–$13.50); you can save £1 ($1.50) by arriving before 11pm on weekends. Tube: Covent Garden.

Less hip, but with lots of zip, is the fashion-unconscious Rock Garden. Because this small basement club overlooks touristy Covent Garden Market, most of the 250 or so revelers are usually foreigners. The quality of music varies, as the club's policy is to give new talent a stage. But Dire Straits, The Police, and many others played here before fame visited them, and triple and quadruple bills ensure a good variety. Open Monday through Saturday from 7:30pm to 3am and Sunday from 7:30pm to midnight.

Wag

35 Wardour St., W1. ☎ **0171/437-5534.** Cover £3–£9 ($4.50–$13.50). Tube: Leicester Square or Piccadilly Circus.

Popular with local rockers, the split-level Wag club is a good local hang-out, despite its attitude-heavy management. The downstairs stage usually attracts newly signed cutting-edge rock bands, while dance disks spin up top. The door policy can be selective, but if it's your kind of music, you probably already dress for the part. Open Monday through Thursday from 10pm to 3am, and Friday and Saturday from 10pm to 6am.

In Camden Town & Kentish Town

Many of London's best noise polluters are in Camden Town and adjacent Kentish Town, just east of Regent's Park.

The Bull & Gate

389 Kentish Town Rd., NW5. ☎ **0171/485-5358.** Cover £3–£5 ($4.50–$7.50). Tube: Kentish Town.

Smaller, cheaper, and often better than its competitors, the Bull & Gate is the unofficial headquarters of London's pub rock scene. Independent and unknown rock bands are often served back-to-back by the half dozen. Music is on Monday through Saturday from 9 to 11pm.

Camden Palace

1A Camden Rd., NW1. ☎ **0171/387-0428.** Cover £5–£10 ($7.50–$15). Tube: Mornington Crescent or Camden Town.

The Palace features a variety of music from punk to funk. When the bands stop, records spin, and feet keep moving to the beat. Open Monday through Thursday and Saturday from 9pm to 3am, and Friday from 9pm to 3:30am.

✪ Town & Country Club

9–17 Highgate Rd., NW5. ☎ **0171/265-3334.** Cover £6–£11 ($9–$16.50). Tube: Kentish Town.

This huge ex-theater with a large dance floor, good seating, and a great, varied line-up of bands is one of London's best clubs. All-day festivals are not unheard-of here, and on weekends after 1am there's free bus service to Trafalgar Square. Open Monday through Thursday from 7 to 11:30pm and Friday and Saturday from 7pm to 2am.

JAZZ

You can get information on jazz concerts and events from the **Jazz Centre Society** (☎ **0171/240-2430**) and *Time Out.* Free jazz is offered every Sunday from 12:30pm to 2:30pm on Level 5 of the **Barbican Centre,** Silk Street, EC2 (☎ **0171/638-4141**); tube to Barbican or Moorgate.

✪ Bass Clef

35 Coronet St., N1. ☎ **0171/729-2476.** Cover £3–£7 ($4.50–$10.50). Tube: Old Street.

Many jazz-loving Londoners swear by this intimate, accessible place. The small club features jazz, Latin, and African music, as well as alternative dance nights. Open daily from 8pm to 2am.

Brahms & Liszt

19 Russell St., WC2. ☎ **0171/240-3661.** Cover £5 ($7.50) after 9:30pm. Tube: Covent Garden.

Cockney rhyming slang for "pissed" (as in drunk), Brahms & Liszt is a divey cellar wine bar with nightly live local jazz that's popular with a good cross section of locals, students, and tourists. Descend the "apple and pears" (stairs) with your "china plate" (date) and have a few "pig's ears" (beers). Open Monday through Saturday until 1am, and Sunday until 10:30pm.

The 100 Club

100 Oxford St., W1. ☎ **0171/636-0933.** Cover £5–£8 ($7.50–$12); student discount available. Tube: Tottenham Court Road.

This austere underground club usually hosts jazz nights on Monday, Wednesday, Friday, and Saturday. The stage is in the center of a smoky basement, looking just the way a jazz club is supposed to look. Open Monday and Wednesday from 7:30pm to midnight, Tuesday and Saturday from 7:30pm to 1am, Thursday from 8pm to 1am, and Friday from 8:30pm to 3am.

Ronnie Scott's

47 Frith St., W1. ☎ **0171/439-0747.** Cover £12 ($18). Tube: Leicester Square.

Ronnie Scott's is the capital's best-known jazz room. Top names from around the world regularly grace this Soho stage, but fans be forewarned: This place is pricy. Call for events and show times. Open Monday through Saturday from 8:30pm to 3am.

BARS

Bar Solona

13 Old Compton St., London, W1. ☎ **0171/437-1503.** Cover £4 Fri–Sat after 10pm. Tube: Leicester Square or Tottenham Court Road.

Bar Solona's cute name is matched by an equally charming interior with lots of hidden vaulted nooks, hanging hams, and Flamenco guitarists on week-ends. There's an authentic Spanish atmosphere. Fresh tapas are displayed behind a glass counter, from which you can also order £7.50 ($11.25) jugs of sangría. Unfortunately, the compact subterranean bar, beneath Café Boheme, can become quite smoky. Open daily from 11am to 3am.

Beach Blanket Babylon

45 Ledbury Rd., W11. ☎ **0171/229-2907.** Tube: Bayswater or Westbourne Park.

Named after a kitschy club in San Francisco, BBB, as it's known to locals, looks like a phantasmagorical film set with plaster-sculpted fireplaces, tall towers, purple velvet benches, and a kaleidoscopic window. A gangplank connects the spirited bar to a trendy Mediterranean restaurant that's always full with a see-and-be-seen crowd. Open daily from 11am to 11pm.

FILMS

FIRST RUN If you want to see a first-run film, go to one of the mega-screens, like the **Odeon** (☎ 0171/930-3232) or **Empire** (☎ 0171/437-1234), that ring Leicester Square. These grand old theaters show American blockbusters almost exclusively. Avoid the postage-stamp-size screens of the local multiplex. Most Leicester Square cinemas sell reserved seats at prices that range from £5 to £8 ($7.50 to $12), depending on seat location.

FOREIGN & INDEPENDENT In addition to the Hollywood houses, London is blessed with several top foreign and independent cinemas.

The **Premiere,** in the Swiss Center, Leicester Square, WC2 (☎ 0171/439-4470), is a comfortable alternative movie house. It's heavy on French films, but movies from other Western and Eastern European countries are also routinely shown. Tickets are £5.80 ($8.70). Tube: Leicester Square.

The **Gate Cinema,** at 87 Notting Hill Gate, W11 (☎ **0171/727-4043**), alternates between offbeat and first-release English- and foreign-language films with double features on Sunday afternoon. Tickets are £6 ($9), £4 ($6) for the first performance Sunday through Friday. Tube: Notting Hill Gate.

REPERTORY CINEMAS   Repertory cinemas of note include the **Scala,** 275–277 Pentonville Rd., N1 (☎ **0171/278-0051**), tube to King's Cross; and the **Everyman,** Hollybush Vale, NW3 (☎ **0171/435-1525**), tube to Hampstead. Both are known for their triple bills and prices that rarely top £5 ($7.50).

PUBS & WINE BARS
PUBS

There's nothing more British than a pub. The public house is exactly that: the British public's place to meet, exchange stories, tell jokes, and drink. Many people have tried to build something that looks like a pub outside Britain, but all fail to capture the unique feel of the real McCoy. Americans tend to think of pubs as evening entertainment, but to the British these institutions are all-day affairs. There's no taboo about spending an afternoon in a pub, and on Sunday afternoon the whole family might go to the pub. (Note, however, that children under 14 are not allowed in pubs at all, and no one under 18 may legally drink alcohol.)

Beer is the main drink sold here; don't even try to order a martini in most places. Sold in Imperial half pints and pints (20% larger than U.S. measures), the choice is usually between lager and bitter. Expect to pay between £1.30 and £2.20 ($1.95 and $3.30) for a pint. Many pubs serve particularly good "real" ales, distinguishable at the bar by hand-pumps that must be "pulled" by the barkeep. Real ales are natural "live" beers, allowed to ferment in the cask. Unlike lagers, English ales are served at room temperature and may take some getting used to. For an unusual and tasty alternative to barley pop, try cider, a flavorful fermented apple juice that's so good you'll hardly notice the alcohol—until later.

As a rule, there's no table service in pubs, and drinks (and food) are ordered at the bar. Tipping is unusual and should be reserved for exemplary service.

Most pubs are open Monday through Saturday from 11am to 11pm and Sunday from noon to 3pm and 7 to 10:30pm. A few close daily between 3 and 7pm.

Carpeted floors, etched glass, and carved-wood bars are the hallmarks of most pubs. But each one looks unique, and each has its particular flavor and clientele. Greater London's 5,000-plus pubs ensure that you never have to walk more than a couple of blocks to find one, and part of the enjoyment of pubbing is discovering a special one on your own. But a few tried-and-true pubs are listed below to help you on your way.

The Alma Tavern
41 Spelman St., E1. ☎ **0171/976-1961.** Tube: Aldgate.

A traditional East End "boozer," the Alma was opened in 1854 by Edward Tilney, a soldier who had just returned to London from the Crimean War. Built on the site of an old brewery, the pub has a back garden that sports the original well head from which the water for brewing was drawn. Steve Kane, the tavern's ultra-friendly owner, is a former actor who loves to talk about his establishment's (and his) eventful past. Tell him Frommer's sent you and he'll invite you to take a photo of yourself pulling an English pint behind his bar.

The Ferret and Firkin

114 Lots Rd., SW10. ☎ **0171/352-6645.** Tube: Sloane Square; then bus no. 11 or 22 down King's Road.

The Ferret and Firkin, in Chelsea, offers the best pub night out in London. The beer served is brewed in the basement and really packs a punch. But the best thing about this pub is the nightly piano player whose amplified instrument turns the place into a raucous sing-along. You don't have to be under 30 to crowd in here, but only the younger revelers will know all the words. Nine other Firkin pubs are just as fun and flavorful. Unfortunately, most are difficult to reach.

The Frog & Firkin

41 Tavistock Crescent, W11. ☎ **0171/727-9250.** Tube: Westbourne Park.

Just outside Bayswater's northwestern corner, the Frog & Firkin is a carbon copy of the Ferret in Chelsea (above).

The Lamb & Flag

33 Rose St., WC2. ☎ **0171/497-9504.** Tube: Leicester Square.

The Lamb & Flag is an old timber-framed pub in a short cul-de-sac off Garrick Street in Covent Garden. The pub was dubbed the Bucket of Blood by the poet Dryden after he was almost beaten to death here (no doubt for being too witty at someone else's expense). The pub can be hard to find, but its great atmosphere and above-average food make the search well worth the effort.

Maison Berlemont

49 Dean St., W1. ☎ **0171/437-2799.** Tube: Tottenham Court Road.

Better known as the French House, this pub is an exceptional reminder of Soho's ethnic past. Still run by a member of the Berlemont family, the pub was the un-official headquarters of the French Resistance in exile during World War II, and it continues to attract a fiercely loyal French-speaking clientele.

The Punch Tavern

99 Fleet St. (within walking distance of St. Paul's Cathedral), EC4. ☎ **0171/353-6658.** Tube: Blackfriars.

Although many drinkers come here because this is one of the few taverns in the area with a dart board, the Punch is better known for its extraordinarily impressive Victorian-era gin-palace interior. England's satirical magazine, *Punch*, was founded here by a group that included Charles Dickens. The magazine became unfunny, however, and publication ceased a couple of years ago. Today the Punch Tavern is popular with local office workers. It serves simple pub grub, Burton Ale, Tetley's Bitter, and a wide range of lagers.

The Sherlock Holmes

10 Northumberland St., off Trafalgar Sq., WC2. ☎ **0171/930-2644.** Tube: Charing Cross.

In the upstairs dining room of this popular pub you'll find a re-creation of Holmes's living room at 221B Baker St., while the head of the hound of the Baskervilles and other relevant "relics" decorate the downstairs bar.

The Sun

63 Lamb's Conduit St., WC1. ☎ **0171/405-8278.** Tube: Holborn or Russell Square.

Popular not for its architecture or history but for its remarkable selection of "real" ales and out-of-town brews, the Sun has more than 20 brands on tap, including rotating "guest" beers. Landlord Roger Berman will proudly show you his vaulted cellars during slow periods.

Ye Olde Cheshire Cheese

Wine Office Court, 145 Fleet St., EC4. ☎ **0171/353-6170.** Tube: St. Paul's.

This 1667 historic wooden pub is where Dr. Johnson took his tipple, and it's an attraction in its own right. Ducking through the low doors will transport you back in time, as the cracked black varnish, wooden benches, and narrow courtyard entrance give it authentic period charm. Meals here are delicious and filling but expensive.

Ye Olde Mitre

1 Ely Court, Ely Place off Hatton Garden, EC1. ☎ **0171/405-4751.** Tube: Farringdon.

It's understandable why this tavern is often referred to as London's best-kept secret. This pub is so well tucked down a dingy little alley that first-time visitors often turn back halfway along the passageway fearing that they've gone the wrong way. The pub's delightful Elizabethan interior has long been a favorite haunt of journalists, most of whom work for the *Daily Mirror*, which is located across the road. I suggest you order one of the Mitre's justifiably famous toasted ham-and-cheese sandwiches; they cost only about £1 ($1.50) and go great with beer.

DANCE CLUBS

The hippest Londoners go to "One-Nighters," weekly dance events held at established clubs. The very nature of this scene demands frequent fresh faces, outdating recommendations before ink can dry on a page. The listings magazine *Time Out* is the clubber's bible. Discount passes to dance clubs are sometimes available just inside the front door of Tower Records on Piccadilly Circus. Otherwise, expect to part with a mint to get in. Once inside, beware: £5 ($7.50) cocktails are not uncommon.

The Hippodrome

Charing Cross Rd. (near Leicester Sq.), WC2. ☎ **0171/437-4311.** Cover £8–£13 ($12–$19.50). Tube: Leicester Square.

The popular Hippodrome is London's big daddy of discos, with a great sound system and lights to match. Very touristy, very fun, and packed on weekends. Open Monday through Saturday from 9pm to 3am.

Limelight

136 Shaftesbury Ave., WC2. ☎ **0171/434-0572.** Cover £7–£13 ($10.50–$19.50). Tube: Leicester Square or Piccadilly Circus.

This is the London outpost of a small worldwide chain of churches–cum–dance clubs. The cavernous club features several dance floors and attracts a good-looking crowd. The music is usually mainstream, but phone for special events before heading out. Open Monday through Thursday from 10:30pm to 3am and Friday and Saturday from 10:30pm to 4am.

Ministry of Sound

103 Gaunt St., SE1. ☎ **0171/378-6528.** Cover £12–£15 ($18–$22.50). Tube: Elephant & Castle.

The best regular weekend raver in England has worked hard to keep its underground atmosphere and warehouse style. The vast main floor is frenetic and debauched. No alcohol is served here, but for the all-night dancing multitudes, booze is not the drug of choice. Open Friday and Saturday from midnight to 9am.

United Kingdom

Buckhold Rd., SW18. ☎ 0181/877-0110. Cover £10 ($15).

Three huge club rooms, trippy kitsch and purple decor, and plenty of techno, house, garage, and soul are likely to keep this jumbo club raving through the 1990s. Great DJs give Ministry of Sound (above) a run for its money. Open Friday and Saturday from 10pm to 6am.

FOR GAY MEN & LESBIANS

Brief Encounter

43 St. Martin's Lane, WC2. ☎ 0171/240-2221. Tube: Leicester Square.

A cruisy and popular pub on two levels, Brief Encounter attracts a good mix of young and old beer and cocktail drinkers. The bar is especially popular with the after-work crowd, and because it's around the corner from Covent Garden Market, there are always plenty of tourists here who seem blissfully unaware of the club's gay orientation. Open Monday through Saturday from 11am to 11pm and Sunday from noon to 3pm and 6 to 11pm.

Comptons of Soho

53 Old Compton St., W1. ☎ 0171/437-4445. Tube: Leicester Square or Tottenham Court Road.

A well-established bar with pub hours, Comptons is a great preclub pub as patrons always know what's going on later, and club fliers are available from the barman. Open Monday through Saturday from 11am to 11pm and Sunday from 5:30 to 10:30pm.

First Out Coffee Shop

52 St. Giles High St., WC2. ☎ 0171/636-4748. Tube: Tottenham Court Road.

Breakfast, lunch, and light snacks served all day compliment the café au lait in this good-looking off-the-beaten-track Parisian-style café. Good music, a comfortable atmosphere, and a bulletin board advertising local happenings have made First Out a natural meeting house. Each Friday is a hugely popular women-only night. Open Monday through Saturday from 10am to 11:30pm and Sunday from 1 to 8pm.

Hanger Bar

In Club Soundshaft, Craven St. (behind Heaven, off Hungerford Lane). ☎ 0171/839-5210. Cover £1 ($1.50), refundable with your first drink. Tube: Charing Cross or Embankment.

About 300 people can (and do) pack into this club/bar, open only Monday through Wednesday from 10pm to 3am. It's a great place on two levels, with caged dancers and house sounds—the best-value in mid-week entertainment.

Heaven

Villiers St., WC2. ☎ 0171/839-3852. Cover £5–£10 ($7.50–$15). Tube: Embankment or Charing Cross.

Gay or straight, no trip through clubland would be complete without a visit to this colossal danceteria with two dance floors, three bars, and a stage where live bands sometimes perform. The crowd varies, but the sound system is always great. The club entrance is on a small street between the Charing Cross and Embankment Underground stations. Open Tuesday, Wednesday, Friday, and Saturday from 10pm to 3am.

9 Networks & Resources

STUDENTS The **University of London,** just north and east of Bloomsbury's Russell Square, is the largest school in the city. Like many urban schools, this university has a majority of commuter students and doesn't really have a campus. Bloomsbury unfortunately lacks the verve and bustle of a college community, but the pubs and inexpensive restaurants of the neighborhood serve as frequent student hangouts.

The **University of London Student Union (ULU),** Malet Street, WC1 (☎ **0171/580-9551**), caters to over 55,000 students and may be the largest of its kind in the world. In addition to a gym and fitness center, the Malet Street building houses several shops, two restaurants, a health club, two banks, a ticket-booking agency, and an STA travel office. Concerts and dances are also regularly scheduled here. Stop by or phone for information on university activities. The student union building is open Monday through Saturday from 9:30am to 11pm and Sunday from 9:30am to noon and 12:30 to 10pm. Take the tube to Goodge Street.

GAY MEN & LESBIANS Despite abundant antigay legislation, homophobic hostility is rare in London. There's a large gay community here, supported by a plethora of publications, shops, pubs, nightclubs, cafés, and specialized services. *Capital Gay* is the city's premier "alternative" paper. Written by and for both men and women, this free weekly features previews, reviews, news, and events listings for the gay and lesbian community. *The Pink Paper* is nationally distributed and also free. Both publications are available at gay bars, bookstores, and cafés. At least two monthlies are regularly available at newsstands around town. *Gay Times* is oriented toward men and is known for both news and features; *HIM* supplements its high-quality reporting with glossy photos. The city's popular listings magazine *Time Out* also provides excellent coverage.

Several locally produced guidebooks, written for local and visiting gays and lesbians, are available from several dealers, including the **London Tourist Board Bookshop,** in the Tourist Information Centre, Victoria Station Forecourt, SW1 (☎ **0171/730-3488**), open Easter to October, daily from 9am to 8pm; November to Easter, Monday through Saturday from 9am to 6:30pm and Sunday from 9am to 5pm.

The **Lesbian and Gay Switchboard** (☎ **0171/837-7324**) offers information, advice, and counseling, as well as a free accommodations agency. The line is open 24 hours and always busy.

In addition to stocking the largest selection of gay and lesbian biographies, novels, and "how-to" books around, **Gay's the Word Bookshop,** 66 Marchmont St., WC1 (☎ **0171/278-7654;** tube to Russell Square), holds regular readings and sells calendars, kitsch clothing, jewelry, and associated paraphernalia. Open Monday through Friday from 11am to 7pm, Saturday from 10am to 6pm, and Sunday from 2 to 6pm.

The **London Lesbian & Gay Centre,** 67–69 Cowcross St., EC1 (☎ **0171/608-1471;** tube to Farrington), London's most popular center for gays and lesbians encompasses five floors and includes a theater, disco, two bars, a café, a bookshop, and a women-only floor. This is a great place to get information on the local scene. Open Monday through Thursday from noon to 11pm, Friday and Saturday from noon to 3am (admission until midnight), and Sunday from noon to midnight. Cover charge is £1 ($1.50).

The **Zipper Store,** 283 Camden High St., NW1 (☎ **0171/267-7665;** tube to Camden Town), is London's only licensed gay sex store. Leisure wear, leather wear, and a large assortment of "novelties" can be purchased here. Open Monday through Thursday and Saturday from 10:30am to 6:30pm, Friday from 10:30am to 7pm, and Sunday from 10:30am to 5:30pm.

WOMEN   London is safer than many other cities, but women are advised to take special precautions. Avoid walking alone at night, especially on small, deserted streets. Always carry some emergency money, and don't hesitate to spend it on a taxi if you feel uneasy. The **London Rape Crisis Centre** (☎ **0171/837-1600**) offers immediate help, advice, and counseling to victims.

Spare Rib, a widely distributed monthly magazine, features news and commentary on feminist issues. It's available at larger newsstands around the city. The **Silver Moon Women's Bookshop,** 68 Charing Cross Rd., WC2 (☎ **0171/836-7906;** tube to Leicester Square), is Soho's only dedicated feminist bookseller. In the heart of London's book district, the Silver Moon boasts a huge selection of fiction and nonfiction titles by and for women, as well as nonsexist children's books. It's open Monday through Saturday from 10am to 6:30pm.

Women-only dance events occur almost every night in London, at nightspots all around the city. These clubs are designed for both straights and lesbians who are not looking to attract the attentions of men. Check *Time Out* for the most up-to-date happenings.

10 Easy Excursions

Just a few miles from Trafalgar Square you'll be confronted with an England that's strikingly different from the inner city. The air is cleaner, the people are friendlier, and everything is cheaper.

The **British Travel Centre,** 12 Lower Regent St., W1 (no phone), just south of Piccadilly Circus, offers free leaflets and advice, and can also book trains, buses, and tours. For train journeys under 50 miles, the cheapest ticket is a Cheap Day Return. Try to avoid day trips on Friday, when fares increase to catch the mass exodus of city-dwellers.

HAMPTON COURT PALACE   Hampton Court Palace (☎ **0181/781-9500**) was built in 1514 by Cardinal Thomas Wolsey, who then reluctantly gave it to King Henry VIII under heavy duress. Five of the king's six wives lived here. The State Apartments, added by William and Mary in the 1690s, were designed by Christopher Wren. Some were badly damaged by fire in 1986 but have been painstakingly restored. When the weather cooperates, a visit to this mammoth Tudor structure on 50 landscaped acres is one of the most satisfying day trips from London. Highlights include the huge 16th-century kitchens, the Astronomer's Clock, the Tudor tennis court, and a run through the famous garden maze.

Entrance to the palace, courtyard, and cloister costs £7 ($10.50) for adults and £4.70 ($7.05) for children 15 and under. Guided tours are offered March to September, daily at 11:15am and 2:15pm, and are free with admission. The palace is open April to October, Monday from 10:15am to 6pm and Tuesday through Sunday from 9:30am to 6pm; November to March, Monday from 10:15am to 4:30pm and Tuesday through Sunday from 9:30am to 4:30pm.

Hampton Court is about 15 miles from central London and can be reached by train in 30 minutes from Waterloo Station. From April to October, you can reach Hampton Court by boat from Westminster Pier, near the Westminster Underground station. The trip upstream takes about four hours and costs £7 ($10.50) for adults, £4 ($6) for children 4 to 14, free for children 3 and under.

GREENWICH   Greenwich is only a few miles from Piccadilly Circus, but it feels as though it's eons away. This famous Thames-side town is the traditional docking site of ocean ships that for centuries have traveled up the river to dock here. It's also the place where Greenwich mean time is fixed—you can take a picture of yourself straddling the meridian by the Old Royal Observatory.

The **Royal Naval College** (☎ **0181/858-2154**), commissioned by King Charles II and constructed by Christopher Wren, is one of the most magnificent classical structures in Britain. Admission is free, and it's open to the public Friday through Wednesday from 2:30 to 5pm.

The *Cutty Sark,* King William Walk, SE10 (☎ **0181/858-3445**), now permanently in dry-dock, is open as a museum. This most famous of 19th-century clipper ships made regular tea runs to China covering almost 400 miles of ocean per day. Visitors can roam the beautifully restored decks and examine the masts and rigging. It's open April to September, Monday through Saturday from 10am to 6pm and Sunday from noon to 6pm; October to March, the museum closes an hour earlier. Admission is £3.25 ($4.85) for adults and £2.25 ($3.35) for children 14 and under.

Greenwich can be reached by Docklands Light Railway in 15 minutes from the Tower Hill Underground station or by boat from Westminster Pier, near the Westminster Underground station. Boats depart every half hour from 10:30am to 5pm. The trip downstream takes about 45 minutes and costs £4.60 ($6.90) for adults, £3.60 ($5.40) for children 15 and under. For more information, contact the **Greenwich Tourist Information Centre,** 46 Greenwich Church St., SE10 (☎ **0181/858-6376**).

KEW   Kew is the site of the massive Royal Botanic Gardens. See "Parks & Gardens" under "Attractions," earlier in this chapter, for details.

BATH   An excursion to Bath is one of the most popular day trips from London. Bath was founded by the Romans in A.D. 43, and the glorious ancient ruins are still fed by the only hot-water spring in Britain. The surrounding town, built in the 18th century, is also worth a visit. The **Roman Baths,** as well as the **Pump Room and Museum,** are open in summer Monday through Saturday from 9:30am to 6pm and Sunday from 10am to 4pm; in winter, the sites close an hour earlier (opens at 11am on Sunday).

Bath is about 115 miles from London, reached in 80 minutes by high-speed train from Paddington Station or in three hours by bus from Victoria.

WINDSOR CASTLE   Windsor Castle is the largest inhabited castle in the world, on a site that's been a home to monarchs for more than 900 years. Situated on a bend in the Thames about 20 miles west of London, the castle sits on 4,800 acres of lawn, woodlands, and lakes. You may see Prince Charles playing polo here. And when the royal family is away, you can explore some of the castle's more opulent rooms. The State Apartments are formal ceremonial rooms used for official occasions. They're furnished with fabulous antiques and paintings, including masterpieces by Holbein, Rembrandt, and van Dyck. The Gallery displays a rotating collection of the royal family's art, including paintings by Dalí, Constable, and Chagal. Queen Mary's Dolls' House is a masterpiece in miniature. The house, really a mansion, was built in 1923 on a 1 to 12 scale. Trains to Windsor depart from London's Waterloo Station (☎ **0171/928-5100**) Monday through Saturday every 30 minutes and on Sunday every hour.

Admission is £8 ($12) for adults, £5.50 ($8.25) for children 16 and under; prices are £2 ($3) less on Sunday. The castle is open daily from 10am, closing at 3pm in January and February, 4pm in March, and 5pm April through October. For more information, call 0753/83-1118.

The exclusive Eton College is across a cast-iron footbridge and usually combined with a visit to the palace. The school's students are famous for attending classes in high collars and tails.

Trains from Paddington Station make the journey to Windsor in 50 minutes.

17

Madrid

by Herbert Bailey Livesey

Spain's landlocked capital spreads over a high windswept plateau like wine spilled on aged linen. To the north and west are mountains tall enough to carry snow on their peaks until spring, and rivers rise among them to curl around the city to the west and south. But the plateau, called the Meseta, is a parched tan emptiness right up to the edges of this sprawling city. This may seem to you an odd place for a national capital, until you recognize that this has always been a fractious country, with the centrifugal forces of linguistic and ideological regionalism forever pulling at the fabric of national unity. The 16th- and 17th-century monarchs chose this location for their capital, where only a crude little settlement had previously stood, because it was at the geographic center of the Iberian peninsula and might therefore counteract those separatist compulsions. Climate, access to seaways, mineral deposits, or defendable elvations had nothing to do with the selection. Madrid is a symbol, with scant organic reason for its existence.

That is its strength. Most of its citizens have been "imported" from every other region of Spain, making it a melting pot of the nation's highly diverse strengths, sensibilities, customs, and cultures. It is of, and for, Spain—not Catalunya or Galicia or the País Vasco or Andalucia, the old kingdoms and ministates on the periphery that like to think of themselves as autonomous nations.

Since Franco's death in 1975, Madrid has broken free of the dictator's authoritarian shroud to make a breathless sprint from economic isolation and social stagnation to the dynamic promise of the 21st century. A result is that Europe's highest capital (in altitude) is now also one of its most progressive. Stretched along the expansive Paseo de la Castellana are the corporate headquarters of the nation's vigorous national and international enterprises. Nowadays, the word *mañana* signals progress, not procrastination.

Many first-time visitors are surprised by Madrid's energy and sophistication. Yet scratch the high-tech surface and the core of tradition runs deep and strong. *Tapas, zarzuela, flamenco,* and *churros* continue to be enduring passions among a populace that manages to enjoy the best of both the new order and an old world still recalled.

What's Special About Madrid

Attractions
- Museo del Prado, among the world's great art collections.
- Royal Palace, exemplifying the grandeur of 18th-century Madrid.
- The Teleférico cable car into Casa del Campo, affording a panoramic view of the city in one direction, the Guadarrama Mountains in the other.
- A bus ride up Paseo de la Castellana to admire its surviving mansions and numerous fountains.
- Plaza Mayor, to soak in the history of Madrid just by sitting and watching.
- The lobby lounge of the Palace Hotel with its magnificent stained-glass domed skylight.
- Thyssen-Bornemisza Museum, one of the world's most valuable and important private collections of 13th- to 19th-century artworks, recently purchased by the Spanish government.

Parks
- Retiro Park on Sunday at noon to join Madrileños in the weekend *paseo*.

Restaurants
- *Tapas* bars—try Bocaito or La Trucha for two of the best in town, with genial and helpful bartenders.

Shopping
- The Rastro Flea market on Sunday, overrated but amusing—just don't expect serious bargains and keep a close watch on valuables.

Nightlife
- La Zarzuela, a uniquely Spanish combination of music and dance.
- One of the many *terrazas*—outdoor cafés—on Paseo de la Castellana during a summer evening.

Excursions
- Toledo, encompassing all of Spanish history, encircled by the River Tajo (Tagus), with a magnificent gothic cathedral.

1 Madrid Deals & Discounts

BUDGET BESTS Eating in Madrid need not be expensive. Most restaurants and cafeterias post a changing *menu del día* (available at lunch and sometimes at dinner) that offers soup or salad, a main course, and dessert, plus bread and a glass of wine, for between 900 and 2,000 pesetas ($6.90 and $15.40). Make this the main meal and then in the evening embark on a round of *tasca* (bar) hopping to sample the tasty and filling assorted hors d'oeuvre–size snacks called *tapas*. Or stick to sandwiches or pizzas, which are at least as Spanish as they are American.

For shoppers, the best time to visit Madrid is during the *rebajas* (sales) that take place in January and February and July; all the stores participate, offering discounts that increase as the month goes on.

SPECIAL DISCOUNTS Ask about Iberia Airline's (☎ **800/772-4642**) "Madrid Amigo" promotion.

For Students　Students traveling to Madrid should be sure to have an **International Student Identity Card (ISIC)** with them to benefit from discounts on travel, lodging, and admission prices. Students who arrive without an ISIC can obtain one at **TIVE** (student tourist offices) at Calle José Ortega y Gasset 71 (☎ **1/347-77-00**), or Fernando El Católico 88 (☎ **1/543-02-08**), open Monday through Friday from 9am to 2pm. TIVE also provides information on student discount opportunities.

For Seniors　Senior citizens can obtain **half-price train tickets** on all rail travel from the city. Pick up a copy of *Guía del Ocio* (available at most newsstands) for information about discounts on such events as concerts staged in Madrid's parks.

For Everyone　When planning to do a lot of traveling on Madrid's public transit system, purchase a *bono* for bus or metro (see "Getting Around" under "Madrid Specifics," later in this chapter).

Many of Madrid's more luxurious hotels offer special weekend packages at significantly reduced rates. One of the better offerings is at the Hotel Villa Real; the first-class Carlton, near Atocha Station, has even more attractive weekend deals. For more information and reservations, contact Marketing Ahead, 433 Fifth Ave., New York, NY 10016 (☎ **212/686-9213,** or 800/223-1356).

For EU Citizens　Some museums offer discounted admission charges or are free one day a week for citizens of EU countries.

WORTH THE EXTRA MONEY　To really get a feel for the spirit of Spain, spend the money you've saved from a diet of *tapas* on a flamenco show or zarzuela. Alternatively, splurge on dinner at atmospheric Sobrino de Botín in old Madrid.

2 Pretrip Preparations

REQUIRED DOCUMENTS　American, Canadian, and New Zealand citizens require only a valid passport for stays up to three months. Citizens of the United Kingdom require only an identity card. Australians must have a visa.

TIMING YOUR TRIP　A hoary saying goes that Madrileños suffer nine months of winter and three months of hell. The reality is less extreme. Humidity is usually low, and the hot weeks are from mid-June through August. The most agreeable conditions are during May and early June and from September into October. From November to April the weather is changeable but can be quite acceptable, with high temperatures in the 50s, blue skies, and warm sun. Snow and frost are rare in the city.

Madrid's Average Temperature & Rainfall

	Jan	Feb	Mar	Apr	May	June	July	Aug	Sept	Oct	Nov	Dec
Temp. (°F)	43	45	49	54	61	68	75	74	68	58	48	43
Rainfall "	2	2	1.6	2	1.5	1.2	0.4	0.3	1.3	2	2.4	2

Special Events　Madrid's **Festival of San Isidro** is celebrated during the middle weeks of May with concerts, neighborhood fairs, craft shows, and daily bullfights. Summer and fall have their seasonal festivals, **Los Veranos de la Villa** and **Festival de Otoño**, with myriad concerts and shows to suit all tastes. The **International Jazz Festival** in November attracts some of the world's best players.

Religious festivals are celebrated with parades and pageantry, particularly the Procession of the Three Kings on January 5, Carnaval before Lent, and the solemn processions of the penitents during Holy Week.

BACKGROUND READING   The tourist office (address below) publishes many brochures and leaflets in English on Madrid and environs. For insights into the Spanish culture and character, look into John Hooper's *The Spaniards* (Penguin), Jan Morris's *Spain* (Prentice Hall), and James A. Michener's *Iberia* (Fawcett). These are somewhat dated though still useful. For a comprehensive examination of Madrid's role in the tragedy of the Spanish Civil War, read the definitive account by British historian Hugh Thomas, *The Spanish Civil War.*

3 Madrid Specifics

ARRIVING

FROM THE AIRPORT   Madrid's **Barajas Airport** at (☎ 1/305-83-43 for information) is about 9 miles east of the city center. The airport bus runs from 4:45am to 1:50am (with departures every 15 minutes beginning at 6am) between the airport and Plaza de Colón in the center of the city. The fare is 325 ptas. ($2.50). A taxi costs about 2,000 ptas. ($15.40), depending on traffic, and the journey takes roughly 30 minutes, although during rush hour it could take up to an hour.

FROM THE TRAIN STATION   Trains from France and points in the northeast arrive at Chamartín station. The south of Spain is served by the Chamartín and Atocha stations and the west by the Príncipe Pío (also called Norte) station.

What Things Cost in Madrid	U.S. $
Taxi from the airport to the Hotel Villa Real	18.30
Public transportation within the city	.92
Local telephone call	.12
Double room at the Hotel Villa Real (deluxe)	236.00
Double room at the Hotel Arosa (moderate)	169.60
Double room at the Hostal Riesco (budget)	35.40
Lunch for one, without wine, at D'a Queimada (moderate)	12.90
Lunch for one, without wine, at Mesón Pontejos (budget)	8.60
Dinner for one, without wine, at Jockey (deluxe)	123.85
Dinner for one, without wine, at Bali (moderate)	26.90
Dinner for one, without wine, at Casa Rodríguez (budget)	16.15
Glass of wine or beer	.85–1.40
Coca-Cola	1.25
Cup of coffee	.90
Roll of ASA 100 color film, 36 exposures	6.20
Admission to the Prado Museum	3.25
Movie ticket	4.65
Cheapest theater ticket	5.40

All these stations are on the metro (see "Getting Around," below) for easy access to anywhere in the city. For information from RENFE (Spanish Railways), call 563-02-02 daily from 7am to 11pm. Non-Spanish speakers, however, will probably prefer to have a travel agency make reservations and obtain tickets.

VISITOR INFORMATION

Barajas Airport has a **Tourist Information Center** (☎ 1/305-86-56) that's open Monday through Friday from 8am to 8pm and Saturday from 8am to 1pm. City offices are at Duque de Medinaceli 2 (☎ 1/429-49-51), and in the Torre de Madrid, Princesa 1, Plaza de España (☎ 1/541-23-25); both are open Monday through Friday from 9am to 7pm and Saturday from 9am to 1pm.

The **Municipal Information Bureau** is located at Plaza Mayor 3 (☎ 1/366-48-74). Open Monday through Friday from 10am to 8pm and Sunday from 10am to 2pm, the bureau is only marginally useful, since it's primarily a distribution center for brochures and maps and the attendants aren't much help with additional information.

From July to September in the vicinity of Plaza de España, Puerta del Sol, Plaza Mayor, and Prado Museum, you'll find young people dressed in a distinctive blue-and-yellow uniform whose job is helping tourists and other visitors. They each speak at least two languages other than Spanish and can offer advice on museums, hotels, restaurants, and special interests.

Even without much Spanish it should be possible for you to decipher the weekly *Guía del Ocio*, available at newsstands for 100 ptas. (75¢). It includes information on entertainment, concerts, art exhibitions, sporting events, fairs, processions, and related events. Undubbed movies are designated *V.O.*, and most foreign-language films are from the United States or Great Britain. Thursday's edition of the daily newspaper *El País* has a "Guía" to the week's events, as does Friday's edition of the daily *Diario 16*.

CITY LAYOUT

Madrid is divided into two distinct parts: old and new. In the old part of the city, whose historic and geographical center is the **Puerta del Sol,** the streets curve and twist; in the newer area to the north and east, the streets are laid out in a grid.

Most of the recommended lodgings in this chapter are around the Puerta del Sol. These streets will quickly become familiar: to the north, Calle de Alcalá, Gran Vía (with many theaters, cinemas, and stores), and Plaza de España; to the south, Calle Mayor (off which is Plaza Mayor), Calle de Atocha, and Carrera de San Jerónimo.

Paseo de la Castellana is the main north-south thoroughfare bisecting the city. South of Plaza de Colón it turns into Paseo de Recoletos, and after crossing Alcalá it becomes Paseo del Prado, named for the Prado Museum, which stands on the southeast corner of Plaza de Canovas del Castillo, identified by its Neptune fountain.

Moncloa, the university area, lies northwest of the city, and **Calle de Serrano,** with its smart shops, is east of Castellana between Plaza de la Independencia and Plaza República Argentina.

GETTING AROUND

The tourist office provides a map of Madrid that includes a schematic of the public transit system. The bus and subway networks are efficient and extensive. Buses

The Spanish Peseta

For American Readers   At this writing $1 = approximately 130 ptas. (or 1 pta. = .8¢), and this was the rate of exchange used to calculate dollar values given in this chapter (rounded to the nearest nickel).

For British Readers   At this writing £1 = approximately 204 ptas. (or 1 pta. = .49p), and this was the rate of exchange used to calculate the pound values in the table below.

Note: The rates given here fluctuate from time to time and may not be the same when you travel to Spain. Therefore this table should be used only as a guide:

Ptas.	U.S.$	£	Ptas.	U.S.$	£
5	.04	.02	1,000	7.69	4.90
10	.08	.05	1,500	11.54	7.35
15	.12	.07	2,000	15.38	9.80
20	.15	.10	2,500	19.23	12.25
25	.19	.12	3,000	23.08	14.70
30	.23	.15	4,000	30.77	19.60
40	.31	.20	5,000	38.46	24.51
50	.38	.25	6,000	46.15	29.41
75	.58	.37	7,000	53.85	34.31
100	.77	.49	8,000	61.54	39.21
150	1.15	.74	9,000	69.23	44.12
200	1.54	.98	10,000	76.92	49.02
250	1.92	1.23	11,000	84.62	53.92
500	3.85	2.45	12,000	92.31	58.82

travel in their own lanes on often-congested streets. For general information on public transport, call the **Consorcio de Transportes** (☎ 1/580-19-80). Taxis are plentiful and relatively inexpensive compared to those in other capital cities.

BY SUBWAY   Consulting a map of the metro system, identify the number of the line on which you wish to travel and the name of the station at the end of the line. All the metro stations have a large map at the entrance. A single ticket costs 125 ptas. (95¢), and a *bono* of 10 tickets is a more economical 600 ptas. ($4.60). The subway runs from 6am to 1:30am.

BY BUS   Buses often are more direct than the metro. There are both red and yellow buses, the former more numerous and the latter, called the microbus, more comfortable, with air conditioning. Route information is available from the E.M.T. kiosks in Plaza de Callao, Puerta del Sol, Plaza de Cibeles, and Atocha. The booths also sell a *bonobus* of 10 tickets for 600 ptas. ($4.60); a single ticket is 125 ptas. (95¢). Buses run from 6am to midnight.

ON FOOT   With traffic usually bad, plan to cover distances of under 10 blocks by walking.

BY TAXI   Metered taxis are either white with a diagonal colored band or black with a horizontal red stripe. If they're available, they display a green light on the

Madrid Metro

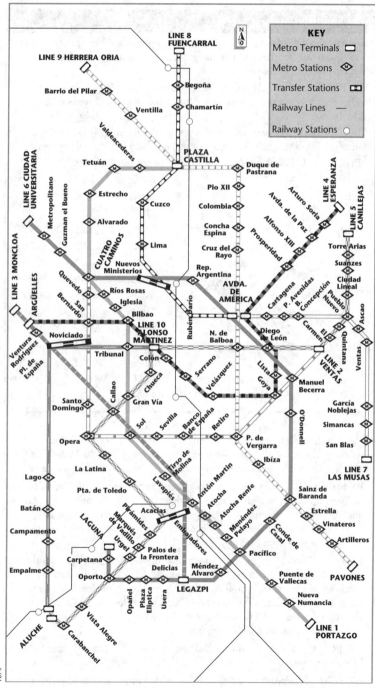

roof and/or a green sign on the windshield saying LIBRE. The meter starts at 150 ptas. ($1.15) and increases 75 ptas. (60¢) per kilometer. There's long list of supplemental fares, including one to or from the airport, 300 ptas. ($2.30); to or from the railway stations, 125 ptas. (95¢); and after 11pm and all day Sunday and holidays, 150 ptas. ($1.15) extra.

BY CAR I strongly recommend that you use a car only for out-of-town excursions, not for getting around Madrid. City traffic is heavy at nearly all hours and the kamikaze habits of native drivers can be hair-raising. Parking spaces on the streets are all but nonexistent. If that isn't discouraging enough, renting a car is expensive, although not quite as bad as in other European countries. It's far cheaper to book a fly/drive package before departing from home. The major car-rental firms are Hertz, Avis, Europcar, and Atesa. Their offerings change, so shopping for the best deal is in order. Many smaller local firms substantially undercut the rates of the big four, but their services are less comprehensive and cars typically have to be returned to the same stations from which they were rented.

FAST FACTS: Madrid

Babysitters Babysitters are known as *canguros* in Spanish. As many hostels are family-run, the daughter or son of the house may oblige. Failing that, check under "Servicio Doméstico" in the telephone directory for agencies that offer babysitting services. Always ask for references.

Banks Money can be changed at any bank advertising CAMBIO; a commission is always charged, which makes cashing traveler's checks in small denominations expensive. A number of U.S. banks have representation in Madrid, Citibank being one of the most visible.

Normal banking hours are Monday through Friday from 9am to 2pm. Some Puerta del Sol bank offices are open in the afternoon and on weekends in summer. In an emergency, the Chequepoint offices found in such heavily touristed locations as the Puerta del Sol are open off-hours and weekends. They don't charge a commission, but their exchange rate is much lower than those prevailing at banks.

The airport branch of Banco Exterior de España is open 24 hours. The **American Express** office, at Plaza de las Cortes 2 (☎ 1/429-57-75), is open Monday through Friday from 9am to 5:30pm and Saturday from 9am to noon.

Automated-teller machines (ATMs) are found throughout the city, especially in tourist and commercial areas. They permit users to obtain cash advances with their credit or charge cards—more important, they provide access to checking and savings accounts through the CIRRUS and Plus networks as long as you have a four-digit Personal Identification Number (PIN). Some Stateside banks charge excessive fees for this service, so that issue should be addressed before leaving for Spain.

Business Hours The Spanish **siesta** survives despite pressures from across the Atlantic and northern Europe. Most businesses operate Monday through Friday from 9am to 6pm, taking a long lunch hour between 2 and 4pm; in summer, offices often close for the day at 3pm. **Banks and government offices** are open Monday through Friday from 9am to 2pm and Saturday from 9am to 1pm. **Shops and many attractions** open at 10am, close for lunch from 1:30 to

5pm, and then reopen until 8pm. One consequence of these working hours is four rush hours per day instead of the usual two.

Consulates The Consulate of the **United States** is in the embassy at Calle Serrano 75 (☎ **1/577-40-00**), open Monday through Friday from 9am to noon and 3 to 5pm. The Consulate of the **United Kingdom** is at Marqués de la Ensenada 16, second floor (☎ **1/308-52-01**), open Monday through Friday from 8am to 2:30pm; the Consulate of **Canada** is in the embassy at Nuñez de Balboa 35 (☎ **1/431-43-00**), open Monday through Friday from 9am to 12:30pm; and the Consulate of **Australia** is at Paseo de la Castellana 143 (☎ **1/579-04-28**), open Monday through Thursday from 8:30am to 1:30pm and 2:30 to 4:45pm and Friday from 8:30am to 2:15pm only.

Currency The unit of currency is the Spanish **peseta (pta.)** with coins of 1, 5, 10, 25, 50, 100, 200, and 500 pesetas. Be aware that the 500-peseta coin is easily confused with the 100-peseta coin. Notes are issued in 500 (only a few left in circulation), 1,000, 2,000, 5,000, and 10,000-peseta denominations.

Dentists/Doctors For bilingual dental and medical attention, call 061 or check with the appropriate consulate for its list of approved dentists and doctors.

Emergencies For the police, dial 091; the fire brigade, 080; an ambulance, 522-22-22. For a 24-hour pharmacy, phone 098. If the nearest pharmacy is closed, it will post a notice giving the address of the closest open one.

Eyeglasses General Optica is one of the larger chains in the country. Most eyeglasses can be made within one hour. Their central locations are at Preciados 22 and Carmen 23 (☎ **1/522-21-21**).

Holidays The majority of Catholic Spain's holidays are religious in origin. Each town celebrates its own saint's day, and in Madrid this is the fiesta of San Isidro, in May, when many businesses close at 2pm all week to enjoy the concerts, plays, art shows, neighborhood fairs, and most important bullfights of the year.

Madrid's holidays are New Year's Day (Jan 1), Epiphany (Jan 6), San José (Mar 19), Maundy Thursday, Good Friday, Easter Sunday, Labor Day (May 1), San Isidro (May 15), Corpus Christi (May or June), Santiago Apóstol (July 25), Feast of the Assumption (Aug 15), Fiesta Hispanidad (Oct 21), All Saints Day (Nov 1), Our Lady of Almudena (Nov 9), Spanish Constitution Day (Dec 6), Immaculate Conception (Dec 8), and Christmas Day (Dec 25).

August is the traditional time when Spaniards flee to the beach or mountains. Consequently, many of the smaller shops and businesses close down for the month.

Hospitals Options are the Hospital La Paz, Castellana 261 (☎ **1/734-26-00**), on the north side of town, or the Hospital 12 de Octubre, Carretera de Andalucia, km 5.4 (☎ **1/390-80-00**), on the south side.

Information See "Visitor Information" under "Madrid Specifics," earlier in this chapter.

Laundry Autoservicio de Lavandería Alba (☎ **1/522-44-63**) is a centrally located laundry (*lavandería*). It charges 1,200 ptas. ($8.55) for washing and drying up to 5 kilos (11 lb.); ironing is extra. It's open Monday through Friday from 9am to 1:30pm and 4:30 to 8pm and Saturday from 9am to 1:30pm. Ask your concierge for the one nearest your hotel. Keep in mind that hotel laundry service is *very* expensive.

Lost & Found   The main office is at Plaza de Legazpi 7 (☎ 1/588-43-46).

Mail   The main post office, Correos, is the grand Palacio de Comunicaciones at Plaza de las Cibeles (☎ 1/536-01-11). It's open for stamps Monday through Friday from 8am to 9pm and Sunday and holidays from 10am to 1pm at Window H. Stamps are also sold at tobacconists (*estancos*). An airmail letter or postcard to the United States is 95 ptas. (75¢).

Newspapers   Foreign-language newspapers and magazines can be found at larger kiosks in the main tourist areas, such as the Puerta del Sol, Gran Vía, and Plaza de las Cibeles.

Photographic Needs   Film and film developing are expensive in Spain, so bring all you need. Otherwise, go to El Corte Inglés, with several branches around town, or to Galeote, Gran Vía 26 (☎ 1/532-24-59).

Police   See "Emergencies," above. Also, during recent summer months, parked outside the Comunidad de Madrid building on the south side of the Puerta del Sol has been a large van marked DENUNCIAS, where crimes can be reported. Failing that, there's an office in the Sol metro station (south side), open daily from 8am to 11pm.

Radio/TV   Tune in to 100.2 FM to pick up Radio Torrejon from the U.S. Air Force base. Hotels with satellite-fed television usually carry two or three English-language channels, often including CNN or Britain's Sky News.

Religious Services   Catholic services in English are held at Alfonso XIII (☎ 1/233-30-32). Other denominations to be found in Madrid are Baptist, at the Community Church of Madrid, Padre Damián 34 (☎ 1/858-55-47); Episcopal (Church of England), at the British Embassy Church of St. George, Núñez de Balboa 43 (☎ 1/576-51-09); Jewish, at the synagogue at Balmes 3 (☎ 1/445-98-35); and Protestant, at the Community Church, Padre Damián 34 (☎ 1/858-55-57).

Shoe Repair   For convenience, go to the heel bar in El Corte Inglés on Calle Preciados (use the basement entrance off Calle Tetuan).

Tax   The government sales tax, known as IVA (value-added tax), is currently 7%. IVA is generally included in the price and can be recovered on goods taken out of the country (for details, see "Shopping," later in this chapter).

Taxis   To call a taxi by telephone, try Radiotaxi (☎ 1/405-12-13), Radioteléfono taxi (☎ 1/547-82-00), or Teletaxi (☎ 1/455-90-08). For further details, see "Madrid Specifics," earlier in this chapter.

Telephone   The minimum charge for **local telephone calls** is 15 ptas. (12¢). Many hotels and hostels tack on a hefty surcharge for long-distance calls. Most public phones have clear instructions in English. Place at least 25 pesetas' worth of coins in the rack at the top and let them roll in as required. Some new high-tech public phones provide on-screen instructions in four languages and accept the **Tarjeta Telefónica,** available in 1,000-pta. ($7.70) and 2,000-pta. ($15.40) denominations at *estancos* (tobacconists), post offices, and the *locutorios telefónicas* (central telephone offices) in Plaza Colón and at Gran Vía 30 (both of which have one USA Direct phone). The *locutorios* are open Monday through Friday from 9am to midnight and Saturday, Sunday, and holidays from noon to midnight. Another central telephone office is at the main post office, Puerta H, on

Plaza Cibeles, open Monday through Friday from 8am to midnight and Saturday, Sunday, and holidays 8am to 10pm.

To call collect or at more economical calling-card rates, dial 900/99-00-11 to access AT&T's USA Direct (to do so from a public phone might require coins or a phone card) or 900/99-00-14 to access MCI's Call USA. When calling from a hotel, check first to make sure there's no service charge or surcharge.

To call **long distance** to the United States and Canada, dial 07, wait for another tone, then dial 1, followed by the area code and number. The average cost of a three-minute call to the United States is approximately 1,800 ptas. ($13.85). Tele-gram and telex facilities are available at the main post office (☎ **1/522-20-00**).

The **telephone area code** for Madrid is 91 when calling from other parts of Spain, only 1 when calling from abroad. In the larger cities, telephone numbers have seven digits, but in many parts of the country six digit numbers are still in use.

Tipping   The custom is widespread, although the amounts expected are often less than those in other countries. The following is a rough guide: In bars, round up the change and always leave at least 10 ptas. (7¢), even after a cup of coffee. In hotels, a service charge is included in the bill, but give the porter 100 ptas. (70¢) per bag; the maid, about 100 ptas for each night stayed; the doorman, 50 ptas. (35¢), or 100 ptas. (70¢) if he goes to some trouble to get a taxi. In restaurants, if the service charge is not included, leave a 10% to 15% tip. Give taxi drivers between 5% and 10%, tour guides 10%, and ushers (theater or bullfight) 50 ptas. (40¢).

4 Accommodations

There are hundreds of hostels in Madrid, all strictly graded and controlled by the tourism authorities. Although they may not have all the conveniences of a hotel, they're usually family-run and more personal.

All the places listed below are in the old part of the city around the Puerta del Sol and Gran Vía. Note that sometimes several hostels are located in the same building; look at the signs at the building's entrance. If one I recommend here is all booked up, it's easy to check out one on another floor. Ask to see the room and the bath before accepting it. Some of the hostels are in houses dating from the 18th and 19th centuries, with high ceilings, elaborate moldings, and some ornate or antique furnishings. Don't be put off by entrances, which can be scruffy-looking. They're often in sharp contrast to the scrupulously clean rooms.

Spanish hotels and hostels typically use twin beds in their rooms; the queen- and king-size beds routinely found in ordinary roadside motels in North America are still relatively rare. Taller clients therefore will want to know that a double bed is called a *matrimonio*. In addition, rooms intended for single occupancy are invariably tiny. People who are willing to spend a little extra for more space can ask for a double for individual use—*doble para uso individual*. The price will be more than a single but less than the full double.

Air conditioning is far from universal. But since Madrid summers can be torrid, readers may want to take particular notice of the accommodations below that have this facility. Rooms advertising "shower only" may have only a small half-bath with a shower and washbasin, sometimes only curtained off from the rest of the room.

Getting the Best Deal on Accommodations

- You can get reductions at some hotels if you pay in cash instead of with a credit or charge card.
- The four-star hotels offer steep weekend discounts more frequently than cheaper hostelries.
- The TIVE office at Calle José Ortega y Gasset 71 provides information on which hostals offer discounts to people carrying an International Student ID Card.

Note: The rates given below do *not* include VAT unless so indicated. Also, remember that the telephone area code for Madrid is 91 when calling from other parts of Spain, only 1 when calling from abroad.

DOUBLES FOR LESS THAN 5,000 PTAS. ($38.45)

Hostal Benamar

San Mateo 20 (2nd floor), 28004 Madrid. ☎ **1/308-00-92.** 22 rms, none with bath. 1,800 ptas. ($13.85) single; 3,200 ptas. ($24.60) double; 4,900 ptas. ($37.70) triple. Rates include VAT. No credit cards. Metro: Tribunal or Alonso Martínez.

The Benamar offers good value for the money. While the rooms don't have baths, each has a basin and is clean and nicely furnished—certainly as comfortable as rooms at some of the more expensive hostels. The manager speaks four languages, including English. There's no elevator.

Hostal Coruña

Paseo del Prado 12 (3rd floor), 28014 Madrid. ☎ **1/429-25-43.** 8 rms, none with bath. 1,800 ptas. ($13.85) single; 3,800 ptas. ($23.10) double; 4,800 ptas. ($36.90) triple. No credit cards. Metro: Antón Martín or Atocha.

They don't come any cleaner or sprightlier than this hostel (with elevator), where the only drawback is the lack of private baths. All rooms are freshly painted, with bare polished floors and crisp coverlets on the double or twin beds, and all have basins. Even the rooms in front, facing the ever-busy Paseo de Prado, are quiet. The Prado is just across the way.

Hostal la Barrera

Atocha 96 (2nd floor), 28012 Madrid. ☎ **1/527-53-81.** 15 rms, 6 with shower only, 3 with bath. 1,900 ptas. ($14.60) single without bath, 2,100 ptas. ($16.15) single with bath; 3,200 ptas. ($24.60) double with shower only, 3,600 ptas. ($27.70) double with bath. No credit cards. Metro: Atocha.

The refurbished Atocha railroad station and the Centro de Arte Reina Sofía are only a short walk down the hill from this newish hostel (with elevator). Señor Mollo offers a gracious welcome and small but spotless rooms with central heating and basins. His children speak English.

Hostal María Cristina

Fuencarral 20 (2nd floor), 28004 Madrid. ☎ **1/531-63-00** or 531-63-09. 18 rms, all with bath. TV TEL. 3,500 ptas. ($26.90) single; 4,600 ptas. ($35.40) double; 6,800 ptas. ($52.30) triple. MC, V. Metro: Gran Vía.

There's no elevator, but a freshly painted staircase leads up to the tidy reception area with its aquarium. Beyond that is a TV lounge/sitting room with wood-paneling and an Oriental rug. The rooms upstairs are furnished with pine beds and tables, the baths small but well appointed. Light refreshments are available.

Hostal Residencia la Perla Asturiana

Plaza de Santa Cruz 3, 28012 Madrid. ☎ **1/366-46-00.** Fax 1/366-46-08. 33 rms, 20 with half bath, 8 with full bath. TV TEL. 2,800 ptas. ($21.55) single without bath, 3,500 ptas. ($26.90) single with bath; 4,700 ptas. ($36.15) double with bath; 6,800 ptas. ($52.30) triple with bath. Rates include VAT. AE, MC, V. Metro: Sol.

This hostel is next to the southeast portal to Plaza Mayor, on Plaza Santa Cruz, which is used mostly as a parking lot and bus stop. The front rooms are large, but ask for one on the south side, since the buses stop at the east side. Besides a comfortable TV lounge, there's a small dining room for breakfast and refreshments.

Hostal Riesco

Correo 2, 28012 Madrid. ☎ **1/522-26-92** or 532-90-88. 26 rms, 13 with shower only, 13 with bath. 3,200 ptas. ($24.60) single with shower only, 4,515 ptas. ($32.25) single with bath; 4,200 ptas. ($32.30) double with shower only, 5,000 ptas. ($38.45) double with bath; 5,800 ptas. ($44.60) triple with bath. Rates include VAT. No credit cards. Metro: Sol.

The Riesco enjoys a superb location, next to the Communidad de Madrid building and a five-minute walk from Plaza Mayor. Pass through the marble lobby and go up to the third floor to discover a hostel featuring a sitting room with deep leather sofas around an inviting fireplace and a large TV. The rooms are well appointed, with desks and chairs (doubles have phones); some have views of the Puerta del Sol.

Hostal Rifer

Calle Mayor 5 (4th floor), 28013 Madrid. ☎ **1/532-31-97.** 12 rms, all with shower or bath. 3,500 ptas. ($26.90) single with shower or bath; 4,000 ptas. ($30.75) double with shower only, 5,000 ptas. ($38.45) double with bath. Rates include VAT. No credit cards. Metro: Sol.

Minutes from the Puerta del Sol and Plaza Mayor, the inviting entrance contains an elevator that takes you up to this small hostel. The pleasant greeting you'll receive will switch from Spanish to English if the lady of the house is on duty. The guest rooms are simply furnished, with marble floors and pressed bedclothes; rooms equipped with showers have basins but no toilets, and the fixtures are enclosed by curtains.

Hostal Riosol

Calle Mayor 5 (2nd floor), 28013 Madrid. ☎ **1/532-31-42.** 12 rms, 6 with shower only, 6 with bath. 2,900 ptas. ($22.30) single with shower only, 3,300 ptas. ($25.40) single with bath; 4,200 ptas. ($32.30) double with shower only, 4,700 ptas. ($36.15) double with bath. Rates include VAT. No credit cards. Metro: Sol.

Two floors down from the Rifer (above) is the conveniently located but small Riosol. Although it isn't as attractively presented as the Rifer, this hostel offers 12 clean, tidy, and renovated rooms (note that the tubs are small). This is an entirely adequate choice if the Rifer is full. The building is kept in good order.

✪ Hostal Sud Americana

Paseo del Prado 12 (6th floor), 28014 Madrid. ☎ **1/429-25-64.** 8 rms, none with bath. 2,200 ptas. ($16.90) single; 4,200 ptas. ($32.30) double. Showers extra. No credit cards. Metro: Antón Martín or Atocha.

Ask for one of the larger front rooms for the light and the view of the Prado. Traffic noise is relatively muted. Señor Pedro Alonso Garrido has been welcoming Frommer readers for more than 30 years to his well-run, nicely decorated hostal with basins in every room. It's in the same excellently maintained building as the Coruña (above).

DOUBLES FOR LESS THAN 7,000 PTAS. ($53.85)

Hostal Continental

Gran Vía 44 (3rd floor), 28013 Madrid. ☎ **1/521-46-40.** 29 rms, all with bath. TEL. 3,600 ptas. ($27.70) single; 5,000 ptas. ($38.45) double. Additional person 35% extra. Continental breakfast extra. MC, V. Metro: Gran Vía.

Along with the slightly more expensive Valencia (below), the Continental is one of several hostels in this centrally located building. This one stands out because the management continues to make improvements, which compensate for the often glum reception. A small TV lounge, where light refreshments are available, adjoins the breakfast room.

Hostal Greco

Infantas 3 (3rd floor), 28004 Madrid. ☎ **1/522-46-32** or 522-46-31. 15 rms, all with bath. TEL. 3,200 ptas. ($24.60) single; 5,300 ptas. ($40.75) double; 7,000 ptas. ($53.85) triple. MC, V. Metro: Banco de España or Gran Vía.

At the Greco, a grandfather clock thunks away in the vestibule off the snug TV salon with its large black-and-white ceramic guard dog. The bedrooms have quirky blond moderne furniture, filling relatively large spaces. The quarters in front have balconies above the fairly quiet street, which is only one block north of the Gran Vía. The staff will do laundry at a reasonable price. Beer and soft drinks are available in the lounge.

Hostal Lisboa

Ventura de la Vega 17, 28014 Madrid. ☎ **1/429-46-76.** Fax 1/420-98-94. 22 rms, all with bath. TEL. 3,800 ptas. ($29.25) single; 5,500 ptas. ($42.30) double. Rates include VAT. AE, DC, MC, V. Metro: Antón Martín or Sol.

Set amid one of Madrid's heaviest concentrations of tapas bars, the Lisboa (with elevator) offers rooms spread over four floors. Some have double beds made of bronze. The small lounge has a TV and VCR. While there's no restaurant or bar on the premises, scores of eating places are within a few minutes' walk to the south and west.

✪ Hostal Matute

Plaza de Matute 11, 28012 Madrid. ☎ **and fax 1/429-55-85.** 25 rms, all with shower or bath. TEL. 3,000–4,000 ptas. ($23.10–$30.75) single with shower or bath; 4,500–6,000 ptas. ($34.60–$46.15) double with shower or bath. Rates include VAT. Continental breakfast 250 ptas. ($1.90) extra. MC, V. Metro: Antón Martín.

Even though Plaza de Matute is in the middle of Calle de las Huertas, one of the prime bar-hopping streets, you'll find peace here. Heavy wood doors are set in an attractive facade painted rose and cream, with shuttered windows behind iron balustrades. A staircase decorated with inlaid marble winds up to the hostel. The fastidious owner speaks good English and is concerned with every detail of his property. The beds have box springs, in a price category where sagging mattresses are the norm. There's also a TV lounge and a tiny breakfast room.

Hostal Sonsoles

Fuencarral 18 (2nd floor), 28004 Madrid. ☎ **1/532-75-23** or 532-75-22. 27 rms, all with bath. TV TEL. 3,400 ptas. ($26.15) single; 5,300 ptas. ($40.75) double. MC, V. Metro: Gran Vía.

The dimly lit entrance here gives way to an attractively furnished lobby and TV lounge with stairs leading to the second floor. A third sitting room, featuring a fishtank, has been created. Double-glazed windows in the rooms facing Fuencarral muffle street noises. The hostel is family-run, promoting the friendly atmosphere, and the husband and children speak some English.

Hostal Triana

Salud 13, 28013 Madrid. ☎ **1/532-68-12** or 532-30-99. 29 rms, 4 with shower only, 25 with bath. TV TEL. 2,400 ptas. ($18.45) single with shower only, 2,800 ptas. ($21.55) single with bath; 5,400 ptas. ($41.55) double with bath. Rates include VAT. MC, V. Metro: Gran Vía, Callao, or Sol.

Just down from the Gran Vía, overlooking the relatively quiet Plaza del Carmen, this is a convenient and ingratiating hostel. Double glass doors open onto a bright lobby with easy chairs, and there's a TV lounge. Some of the decoration, including floral fabrics and lots of white paint and wood, is unusual for Madrid. Go for the larger rooms overlooking the plaza, for they get more light and are more fetchingly decorated, with small balconies. Some English is spoken.

Hostal Valencia

Gran Vía 44 (5th floor), 28013 Madrid. ☎ **1/522-11-15**. 30 rms, 10 with shower and toilet, 20 with bath. TEL. 3,700 ptas. ($28.45) single with shower and toilet; 5,800 ptas. ($44.60) double with bath; 7,900 ptas. ($60.75) triple with bath. Rates include VAT. MC, V. Metro: Calloa or Gran Vía.

Walk through the front door and you'll find this place exuding the companionable atmosphere of a Spanish family home, reinforced by the cordial TV lounge. A justifiable favorite of North American travelers, the hostal (with elevator) is run by the cordial Antonio Ramírez and his American wife, Laurie. The premises have been freshly painted.

Hostal Victoria I

Calle Carretas 7 (2nd floor), 28013 Madrid. ☎ **1/522-99-82**. 18 rms, 16 with bath. TV TEL. 3,500 ptas. ($26.90) single; 5,500 ptas. ($42.30) double with bath; 7,500 ptas. ($57.70) triple with bath. Rates include VAT. AE, MC, V. Metro: Sol.

This small hostel just off the Puerta del Sol has recently been renovated, right down to the matching curtains and bed linen. Señora María Teresa is outgoing, attentive, and justifiably proud of her scrupulously clean establishment. Most rooms are compact, with some downright clautrophobic, so check first. This is the original of three hostels owned by the same family, with top honors going to the Victoria III (below). However, this one is slightly less expensive—and popular year round, so book ahead.

✪ Hostal Victoria III

Carrera San Jerónimo 30 (4th floor), 28014 Madrid. ☎ **1/420-23-57**. 12 rms, all with bath. A/C MINIBAR TV TEL. 3,500 ptas. ($26.90) single; 5,500 ptas. ($42.30) double; 7,000 ptas. ($53.85) triple. Rates include VAT. AE, DC, MC, V. Metro: Sevilla.

Opened in 1993, this is the best of a trio of budget choices in the Puerta del Sol owned and operated by the same conscientious management (see the previous entry). The furnishings are new, the mattresses firm, and all reasonable comforts available, including a common bar/lounge; however, the dimensions are snug. The TV carries CNN and even comes with a remote control. Also rare in this category are the minibars, stocked with beer and soft drinks. The reception is pleasant, although English isn't spoken. At my last visit, the only sign out front was next to the buzzer at the door.

Hotel Residencia Santander

Echegaray 1 (at the corner of Carrera de San Jerónimo), 28014 Madrid. ☎ **1/429-95-51** or 429-66-44. 40 rms, all with bath. TEL. 4,600 ptas. ($35.40) single; 6,000 ptas. ($46.15) double. Rates include VAT. No credit cards. Metro: Sol.

The shiny glass-and-brass doorway on Echegaray leads into a foyer with marble walls and a carved-wood reception desk. The rooms (some with TV) are generally of good size, with parquet floors, dressing table, and wardrobe; some have giant tubs. There's a TV lounge, a cafeteria, and a bar.

DOUBLES FOR LESS THAN 10,000 PTAS. ($76.90)

Hostal la Macarena

Cava de San Miguel 8, 28005 Madrid. ☎ **1/265-92-21.** Fax 1/364-27-5. 25 rms, all with bath. TEL. 3,900 ptas. ($30) single; 6,300 ptas. ($48.45) double; 7,900 ptas. ($60.75) triple; 8,400 ptas. ($64.60) quad. Rates include VAT. AE, MC, V. Metro: Sol.

A friendly welcome awaits beyond the grimy facade of this hostal behind Plaza Mayor, opposite the foot of the Arcos de Cuchilleros stairs leading down to a street full of taverns and restaurants (including the celebrated Sobrin de Botín). The rooms are small but agreeable enough, and there are newer ones upstairs. The TV lounge and breakfast area are pleasant.

Hotel California

Gran Vía 38, 28013 Madrid. ☎ **and fax 1/522-47-02** or 531-61-01. 26 rms, all with bath. A/C TV TEL. 5,900 ptas. ($45.40) single; 7,900 ptas. ($60.75) double; 10,600 ptas. ($81.55) triple. AE, DC, MC, V. Metro: Callao or Gran Vía.

Easily found on the busiest stretch of the Gran Via, amid cinemas and popularly priced restaurants, this three-star establishment shares the second floor with the more expensive Atlántico (below). Although humbler in style and furnishings than its neighbor, the California has a pleasant bar/breakfast room.

Hotel Francisco I

Arenal 15, 28013 Madrid. ☎ **1/548-02-04.** Fax 1/542-28-99. 58 rms, all with bath. A/C TV TEL. 6,300 ptas. ($48.45) single; 8,700 ptas. ($66.92) double; 10,400 ptas. ($80) triple. Rates include breakfast and VAT. Half- and full-board rates available. AE, DC, MC, V. Metro: Opera or Sol.

Under the same ownership as the París (below), this hotel only seconds from the Puerta del Sol is run by the amicable Francisco Martín. The lobby with wood paneling and marble sets the tone for the rest of the hotel. Near the TV lounge's cushy leather chairs is a well-stocked bar. The hotel restaurant is more than adequate to its price range. The guest rooms are a sensible size, well appointed and newly renovated. The rates quoted above are for high season, and bargaining should be productive at other times.

✪ Hotel Mora

Paseo del Prado 32, 28014 Madrid. ☎ **1/420-15-69.** Fax 1/420-05-64. 62 rms, all with bath. A/C TV TEL. 4,950 ptas. ($38.10) single; 6,500–7,500 ptas. ($50–$57.70) double. Metro: Antón Martín or Atocha (but a fairly long walk from either, at least with luggage).

This has to be the top budget hotel choice in the capital, for its superior isn't immediately evident. An impressively furnished spacious lobby with glinting chandeliers sets the tone. The adjacent restaurant attracts a polished crowd for fixed-price meals of 1,000 or 1,500 ptas. ($7.70 or $11.55). Upstairs, the narrow but bright halls lead to rooms of varying configuration yet generally sufficient space. They're crisply furnished in muted tones, with carpeting. The TVs pull in satellite channels in several languages. English is spoken at the front desk. In addition to all that, the Prado Museum is across the street and the Centro de Arte Reina Sofía is only a short walk away.

Hotel París

Alcalá 2, 28014 Madrid. ☎ **1/521-64-96.** Fax 1/531-01-88. 120 rms, all with bath. TV TEL. 7,600 ptas. ($58.45) single; 9,500 ptas. ($73.10) double. Rates include continental breakfast and VAT. AE, MC, V. Metro: Sol.

The París occupies the east corner of the Puerta del Sol, topped by a beloved sign for Tío Pepe sherry. In the public rooms are lots of glass, brass, and red plush. The guest rooms are well appointed, with marble-and-tile baths; some have air conditioning. Ask for a room overlooking Sol. In addition to the bar, restaurant, and TV lounge, there's a patio terrace that's a great place to sit in warm weather.

SUPER-BUDGET CHOICES
YOUTH HOSTELS

For information about reservations at Madrid's youth hostels, call the **International Youth Hostel Federation** (☎ 1/580-42-16).

International Youth Hostel

Calle de Santa Cruz de Marcenado 28, 28015 Madrid. ☎ **1/547-45-32.** 72 beds. 720 ptas. ($5.55) per person per night for members under 26, 865 ptas. ($6.65) for members over 26. Rates include breakfast. No credit cards. Metro: Argüelles.

This youth hostel is heavily used by groups, so always phone first.

Richard Schirrmann Youth Hostel

Recinto de la Casa de Campo, 28011 Madrid. ☎ **1/463-56-99.** 134 beds. 720 ptas. ($5.55) per person per night for members under 26, 865 ptas ($6.65) for members over 26. Rates include breakfast. No credit cards. Metro: Lago.

Another hostel popular with groups. Phone ahead.

CAMPING

Camping Madrid

Carretera Nacional-I, Madrid-Burgos, km 11. ☎ **1/302-28-35.** 764-tent capacity. 500 ptas. ($3.85) per night per adult, 390 ptas. ($3) per child; 385 ptas. ($2.95) per indivi-dual tent, 450 ptas. ($3.45) per family tent; 500 ptas. ($3.85) per car or caravan (RV). No credit cards.

This campsite offers all facilities for camping.

WORTH THE EXTRA MONEY

Hotel Atlántico

Gran Vía 38, 28013 Madrid. ☎ **1/522-64-80.** Fax 1/531-02-10. 79 rms, all with bath. A/C MINIBAR TV TEL. 8,445 ptas. ($64.95) single; 11,378 ptas. ($87.50) double. AE, DC, MC, V. Metro: Callao or Gran Vía.

This three-star hotel is only one of several lodging places housed in this historic beaux arts building, but it's the most impressive. The front desk is up one story (there's an elevator), with an adjacent breakfast room, lounge, and TV salon. Both the public and the private areas have been freshly decorated, often with floral treatments. Extras include hairdryers in the baths. Interior rooms are very quiet. Take a moment to look at the facade, encrusted with carved stone pilasters, balustrades, and garlands.

Hotel Carlos V

Maestro Vitoria 5, 28013 Madrid ☎ **1/531-41-00.** 67 rms, all with bath. A/C TV TEL. 9,345 ptas. ($71) single; 11,760 ptas. ($90.45) double. AE, DC, MC, V. Metro: Sol.

Superbly situated in the pedestrian shopping district north of the Puerta del Sol, within walking distance of almost every major attraction, the Carlos V gives good value at rates only slightly above the highest budget category. In addition to the expected comforts and gadgets, each room has a safe, radio, satellite TV with English channels, and wall-to-wall carpeting. A breakfast nook is located near the tasteful lounge.

Hotel Inglés

Echegaray 8, 28014 Madrid. ☎ **1/429-65-51.** Fax 1/420-24-23. 51 rms, all with bath. TV TEL. 6,800 ptas. ($52.30) single; 10,000 ptas. ($76.90) double. Continental breakfast 500 ptas. ($3.85) extra. AE, DC, MC, V. Metro: Sol.

A large ship model in the front window welcomes guests into the brightly lit lobby and comfortable TV lounge, with deep sofas and armchairs. Just beyond is the bar/cafeteria where breakfast is served. The rooms are well appointed with cupboards and dresser drawers; all have radios and many have sitting areas. Safe-deposit boxes are available. Renovations to the facade should be completed by the time you read this.

5 Dining

There's no shortage of restaurants in Madrid, and it's possible to eat fairly well for relatively low cost. In the old part of the city around the Puerta del Sol and Plaza Mayor, the selection of *cafeterías* offering decent food is enormous. A little to the east, in the area bounded by Calle de las Huertas, Carrera de San Jerónimo, Calle de León, Calle de Echegaray, and Ventura de la Vega, are dozens lively bars and cafeterias. Head north to Calles de Hartzenbusch and Cardenal Cisneros and the surrounding few blocks for scads of inexpensive restaurants and bars serving everything from tortillas and tapas to Italian and German cuisine. In Spain, by the way, a *cafetería* is an informal, inexpensive sit-down restaurant with table service. What Americans call a cafeteria is known as an *autoservicio* here.

FAVORITE MEALS A Spanish *tortilla* is an omelet made with potatoes, onions, and garlic, generally served at room temperature when eaten as a *tapa* (see below). *Gazpacho,* imported from Andalusia and available primarily during summer, is a cold vinegar-based soup made with garlic, tomatoes, bread, and olive oil, served with garnishes of chopped onions, green peppers, and chopped egg, to name but a few. *Paella,* a speciality of the Valencia region, is rice cooked in saffron with bits of chicken and seafood. *Cocido madrileño* is a three-course boiled dinner: first a soup, then vegetables, followed by a stew of beans, sausage, and meat. A popular first course is *judías* (beans), made into a tasty stew. *Perdiz* (partridge) and *codorniz* (quail) appear on menus regularly, along with *cochinillo* (suckling pig) and *cordero asado* (roast leg of baby lamb).

And then there are *tapas,* small portions of food served in almost every bar. They vary in size, quality, and diversity, and it's common to make a complete meal of tapas alone. Popular tapas include *boquerones* (anchovy-size fish marinated in oil or fried), *croquetas* (a kind of fritter with various ingredients), *empanadillas* (pastries filled with tuna or chicken), *setas* (large mushrooms usually fried with garlic), *morcilla* (blood sausage mixed with rice and onions), *pimientos fritos* (fried sweet

---

Getting the Best Deal on Dining

- The *menu del día* offered at lunch (and sometimes at dinner) is a great deal, for it usually comprises a first course of soup or salad, a main course of meat or fish, sometimes dessert and coffee, and always bread and wine.
- Be sure to notice which restaurants fill up with locals. Madrileños know the best dining values.
- Try sampling tapas bars in the evenings, instead of ordering full meals.
- If you stand rather than sit you can save some cash: Many establishments have two prices: *mesa* (table) and *barra* (bar).

---

peppers), *pimientos del padrón* (the saying goes "*unos pican, otros no*"—"some are hot, others not"—tiny, fiery-hot jalapeño-size peppers grilled with oil and salt), *patatas bravas* (roast potatoes with a piquant sauce), *mejillones* (clams), *chipirones in su tinta* (baby squid in their ink), *calamares* (squid), *chorizo* and *salchichón* (sausages), and *queso manchego* (cheese from La Mancha). Warning: *Jamón de Serrano* (air-cured ham) is widely available and delectable . . . though very expensive—a 4-ounce portion can cost $20 or more.

During recent years, an increasing number of foreign restaurants have opened in Madrid. Moroccan, French, German, Chinese, Greek, Japanese, and American foods are seen with ever-greater regularity. Spaniards are slow to accept other cuisines, however, partly because their own are so varied and extensive. And, apart from a few of their tapas, they don't like spicy-hot dishes. That puts a serious crimp in the efforts of chefs trying for authenticity in Szechuan, Hunan, Tex-Mex, Indian, and Mexican dishes, who find they must tone down their recipes more than they'd like. Of the various foreign cuisines, the one best reproduced is Italian. Pastas and pizzas are nearly as common in Madrid as in Chicago and New York, and Spanish cooks have started to learn the meaning of *al dente*. This is why the relatively few foreign restaurants suggested below are primarily Italian.

MEALS FOR LESS THAN 1,500 PTAS. ($11.55)

A Huevo

Jacometrezo 6. ☎ **1/248-51-02.** Breakfast 210–315 ptas. ($1.60–$2.40); combination plates 260–1,800 ptas. ($2–$13.85); *menu del día* 950 ptas. ($7.30). MC, V. Daily 8am–1:30am. Metro: Santo Domingo. SPANISH FAST FOOD.

This plain self-service cafeteria just off the Gran Vía is useful primarily because of its long hours. The basic menu includes breakfasts, sandwiches, and 10 combination plates, most of which have salads on the side. Prices are soothing, including the half roasted chicken, fruit, and drink for only 770 ptas. ($5.90). They run from a low of 270 ptas. ($2.10) for fried eggs and fried potatoes to a high of 1,800 ptas. ($13.85) for steak, roast peppers, mashed potatoes, and salad. Everything can be packaged *para llevar* (to take out).

Artemisa

Ventura de la Vega 4. ☎ **1/429-50-92.** Main courses 900–1,100 ptas. ($6.90–$8.45); *menu del día* 1,155 ptas. ($8.90). AE, V. Mon–Sat 1:30–4pm and 8:30pm–midnight, Sun 1:30–4pm. Metro: Sol or Sevilla. VEGETARIAN.

This inviting restaurant uses very fresh ingredients in compiling its mostly vegetarian dishes. Two of the better choices are vegetable lasagne at 975 ptas. ($7.50) and paella at 800 ptas. ($6.15). Meat-eaters can choose the main course of sausage and kidney beans for 850 ptas. ($6.55). Another branch is at Tres Cruces 4 (☎ **1/521-87-21**), near Plaza del Carmen.

Ballesteros

Ventura da la Vega 6. ☎ **1/429-67-64**. Main courses 600–1,550 ptas. ($4.60–$11.90); *menu del día* 1,365 ptas. ($10.50). V. Mon–Sat 1–4pm and 9pm–midnight. Closed Aug. Metro: Sol. SPANISH.

In a long, narrow room with tables on either side, owner Manolo Ballesteros offers such typical Spanish dishes as stuffed eggplant, veal chops, and steak with a house sauce. His paintings decorate the walls.

La Biotika

Amor de Dios 3. ☎ **1/429-07-80**. Main courses 630–950 ptas. ($4.85–$7.30); *menu del día* 1,155 ptas. ($8.90) Mon–Fri, increased by 10% Sat–Sun and hols. No credit cards. Daily 1:30–4:30pm and 8:30–11:30pm. Metro: Antón Martín. VEGETARIAN/MACROBIOTIC.

Walk through the health-food shop in front to this small, no-frills macrobiotic-vegetarian café that offers salads and rice- and grain-based dishes at minimal prices.

✪ Carmencita

Libertad 16. ☎ **1/531-66-12**. Main courses 900–3,000 ptas. ($6.90–$23.10); *menu del día* 1,000 ptas. ($7.70). AE, DC, V. Mon–Fri 1–4pm and 9pm–midnight. Metro: Chueca. SPANISH.

North of the Gran Vía, this is as marvelously atmospheric as can be imagined, with its extensive tile dadoes, lace curtains inside shuttered windows, and a bust of Juan Carlos I in recognition of a past *plato de oro* award. A typical menu del día (served Monday through Friday at lunch only) consists of lentils followed by deep-fried fish and dessert, with wine. Ink this in at the top of any preferred dining list.

Casa Gades

Conde de Xiquena 4. ☎ **1/522-75-10**. Pizzas and pastas 725–950 ptas. ($5.60–$7.30); main courses 890–2,150 ptas. ($6.85–$16.55); *menu del día* 1,475 ptas. ($11.35). AE, DC, MC, V. Daily 1:30–4pm and 9pm–12:15am. Metro: Chueca. ITALIAN.

Red-and-white checked tablecloths, old photos on the walls, and two galleried seating areas attract a mixed crowd of yuppies and office workers to sample the pizzas and pastas. The menu del día consists of soup or salad, pasta or fish, dessert, beer or wine, and bread.

Madrid I

Carrera San Jerónimo 16. ☎ **1/521-90-31**. Combination plates 550–800 ptas. ($4.25–$6.15); *menu del día* 900 ptas. ($6.90). MC, V. Daily 8:30am–12:30am. Metro: Sol. SPANISH.

Most of the dining bases are covered at this unpretentious emporium east of the Puerta del Sol. In front is a tapas bar; in back, a dining room for *platos combinados;* and upstairs, yet another room with an open buffet Monday through Friday. Pictures of turn-of-the-century Madrid comprise most of the decor. Apart from full breakfasts, lunches, and dinners, they offer pizzas for 675 to 775 ptas. ($5.20 to $5.95) and sandwiches and burgers for 250 to 625 ptas. ($1.90 to $4.80). Assuming you don't expect culinary wonderment, this is a dependable place at any time of day or night.

Mi Pueblo

Costanilla de Santiago 2. ☎ **1/248-20-73.** Main courses 900–1,400 ptas. ($5.90–$10.75); *menu del día* 950 or 1,250 ptas. ($7.30 or $9.60). MC, V. Tues–Sat 1:30–4pm and 8:30–11:30pm, Sun 1:30–4pm. Closed the first three weeks in Aug. Metro: Sol. SPANISH.

Earthenware shades on the hanging lamps, ladderback chairs around the closely spaced tables, and ceramics and craftworks displayed on the walls set the folkloric tone. *Pueblo* means "people" or "town," and this *casera* (home-style) cooking borrows recipes from every region of the country. These include brocheta catalana, a shish kebab of steak and vegetable chunks, and rellenos madrileños, five whole vegetables stuffed with ground meat and delivered to table in a bubbling casserole. Music on the stereo is retro-pop and jazz. Pipe and cigar smoking are forbidden. Now if only the taciturn staff could lighten up and the coffee could be improved.

Museo de Jamón

Victoria 1/Carrera San Jerónimo 6. Combination plates 500–1,450 ptas. ($3.85–$11.15). MC, V. Daily 9am–midnight. Metro: Sol. SPANISH.

A "museum of ham," indeed. This big shiny tapas bar/restaurant a block east of the Puerta del Sol specializes in the most popular edible flesh in Spain. Hams here are mostly air-cured, by a variety of methods. The street-level room has a three-sided bar in the middle and a delicatessen take-out counter to one side. Hams hang like rows of bowling pins high on the walls and above the bar. Portions range from reasonable to stunning—$20 and more for 3 ounces at the high end—so the best way to sample this delicacy is in a sandwich, at 160 to 260 ptas. ($1.25 to $2). Combination plates are less intimidating. Grilled loin of pork with eggs costs 500 ptas. ($3.85) and hake with tomato sauce is 680 ptas. ($5.25). Paella for two is only 1,550 ptas. ($11.90) in the upstairs dining room, where on most nights there's a guitarist.

La Oficina

Carmen 11. ☎ **1/532-71-63.** Combination plates 950–1,700 ptas. ($7.30–$13.10); *menus del día* 950–1,750 ptas. ($7.30–$13.45). MC, V. Daily noon–11pm. Metro: Sol. SPANISH.

Okay, the joke of the name is as lame as can be—"Honey, I have to stay late at La Oficina"—but don't hold that against it. North of the Puerta del Sol, in the pedestrian shopping area around El Corte Inglés, this no-nonsense, bilevel restaurant is largely overlooked by tourists but not by Madrileños. The several *menus del día* and *platos cominados* are filling, tasty, and surprisingly inexpensive. One meal starts with a substantial vegetable-and-chorizo soup and ends with grilled salmon steak with tartar sauce and fried potatoes on the side—1,450 ptas. ($11.15). A *plato* of roast chicken, sausages, a fried egg, and potatoes is only 950 ptas. ($7.30) at the bar. The plentiful tapas at the two long bars feature shellfish and crustaceans (be wary, for some of these are devastatingly expensive). Another entrance is at Preciados 10.

Pontejos

San Cristóbal 11. ☎ **1/531-01-54.** Main courses 900–1,900 ptas. ($6.90–$14.60); *menu del día* 975 ptas. ($7.50). MC, V. Thurs–Tues 9am–midnight. Metro: Sol. SPANISH.

Unpretentious surroundings keep prices down at this popular spot two blocks east of Plaza Mayor. A tiled tapas bar is in front, a tight cluster of tables with blue-and-white cloths is in back. The menu del día is always a bargain, but watch for those days when a hefty helping of paella with crusty homemade bread can be had for 1,050 ptas. ($8.10). The priciest *plato* is roast lamb, but it's worth the 1,900 ptas. ($14.60).

Pozo Real

Pozo 6. ☎ **1/521-79-51.** *Menus del día* 750–2,000 ptas. ($5.75–$15.40). No credit cards. Daily noon–4pm and 8pm–midnight. Metro: Sol. SPANISH.

Even though it's just steps off the heavily traveled Calle Victoria, this is a folksy neighborhood place that sees few tourists, so expect heads to turn when you walk in (the regulars will quickly return to their conversations). Meals, served in the two tiny rooms in back, are simple and straightforward, as might be found in any Spanish home. A sample first course is pastel de verduras, mixed vegetables drizzled with oil and vinegar. Most main courses—broiled fish or chicken, usually—come with fried potatoes or, less often, salad or a vegetable. Flan or fruit can follow. Keep this place in mind for Sunday, when most other restaurants are closed.

Rapid Quick

Puerta del Sol 14. ☎ **1/521-66-16.** Sandwiches 395–630 ptas. ($3.05 $4.85); main courses 550–1,100 ptas. ($4.25–$8.45); *menu del día* 1,000–1,400 ptas. ($7.70–10.75). No credit cards. Mon–Fri 9am–11:30pm, Sat 12:30–11:30pm, Sun and hols 1–11:30pm. Metro: Sol. SPANISH.

It's nothing special, but this self-service restaurant is convenient (at the east corner of the Puerta del Sol) and usually uncrowded, facilitating a quick snack or meal. For breakfast here try hot chocolate and churros, and for a fancier meal at dinner order the grilled salmon and asparagus with two sauces for 1,400 ptas. ($10.75).

⑤ Rodríguez

San Cristóbal 15. ☎ **1/531-11-36.** Main courses 450–1,500 ptas. ($3.45–$11.55); *menu del día* 950 ptas. ($7.30). No credit cards. Fri–Wed 1–4pm and 8–11:30pm. Metro: Sol. SPANISH.

This highly popular family-run restaurant is known for its hearty potajes and cocidos, classic Castilian stews. A plate of paella is only 500 ptas. ($3.85), and a particular treat is fabes con almejas, a soup of white beans, onions, wine, and clams. Only a block off Plaza Mayor, and much cheaper than the restaurants on that square, this is a stellar value.

MEALS FOR LESS THAN 2,500 PTAS. ($19.25)

Bali

San Bernardino 5. ☎ **1/541-91-22.** Main courses 1,000–1,900 ptas. ($7.70–$14.60); *menu del día* 1,700 ptas. ($13.10). AE, V. Tues–Sat 12:30–4pm and 8–11pm, Sun 12:30–4pm. Metro: Plaza de España. INDONESIAN.

Just north of Plaza de España, in an area known for its cheap restaurants, is the slightly more expensive Bali. The decor is tasteful and contemporary, with lots of plants. Rijsttafel, the celebrated Indonesian gastronomic invention, spreads a wealth of small portions of different foods on the table. Translated here as *típico mesa de platos*, the tempting array includes veal, chicken, pork, and vegetables in sauces of coconut, peanut, curry, and pepper. This is a meal for two, with rice, and costs 3,800 ptas. ($29.25). If dining alone, consider the gado-gado, vegetables in peanut sauce.

El Cuchi

Cuchilleros 3. ☎ **1/266-31-08.** Main courses 995–3,225 ptas. ($7.65–$24.80); *menu del día* 1,550 ptas. ($11.90). AE, DC, MC, V. Daily 1–4pm and 8pm–midnight. Metro: Sol. INTERNATIONAL.

This colorful restaurant is at the foot of the stairs leading down through the Arco de Cuchilleros from the southwest corner of Plaza Mayor. The sign above the door reads: "We don't speak English, but we won't laugh at your Spanish." That's a fair indication of the light-hearted attitude of this overseas branch of an Anglo-Mexican chain. Neither the staff nor the management takes themselves seriously. The place is crammed with pictures, tiles, and collections—hats, matchboxes, and a profusion of dried foods hanging on the walls. Many items are a bit expensive, but careful choices (barbecued chicken and mixed salad, for example) can come to less than 2,000 ptas. ($15.40).

D'A Queimada

Echegaray 17. ☎ **1/429-32-63.** Main courses 1,260–2,900 ptas. ($9.70–$22.30); *menu del día* 1,800 ptas. ($13.85); paella 1,260 ptas. ($9.70). MC, V. Daily 11:30am–5pm and 8pm–midnight. Metro: Sol. SPANISH.

You'll have no trouble finding this place: The facade is plastered with garish signs that scream its offerings. The interior is just as gaudy, but the huge pan of paella near the front door reaches out and grabs at appetites. The staff is amiable and the kitchen also turns out dishes from Galicia, in the northwestern corner of the country. Seafood prevails.

La Pampa

Bola 8. ☎ **1/542-44-12.** Main courses 1,450–2,400 ptas. ($11.15–$18.45). Daily 1–4pm and 9pm–midnight. Metro: Opera or Santo Domingo. ARGENTINE.

When the Spanish enthusiasm for exotic finny fare starts to pall, this is the place to go. Grilled meat is the centerpiece—fist-thick slabs of it, charcoal-crusted outside, fragrant juices spilling at the touch of a knife. The only way to get a vegetable here is to order the house salad at the outset (they don't want to clutter up the wooden carving boards with the likes of squash and broccoli). The assortment of steaks and chops meant for two will serve at least three, maybe four. Live music is offered on Thursday. The original branch is at Aparo 61 (☎ **1/528-04-49**); it's closed Monday and has tango musicians some of the other nights.

✪ Spaghetti & Bollicine

Prim 15. ☎ **1/521-45-14.** Main courses 950–1,700 ptas. ($7.30–$13.10). AE, V. Mon–Thurs 2–4pm and 9pm–midnight, Fri 2–4pm and 9pm–1am, Sat 9pm–1am. Metro: Colón or Banco de España. ITALIAN.

Afternoons, tourists and businesspeople fill this trattoria just off Paseo de Recoletos. At night, everyone in the attractive crowd looks to have been born after 1965. Prices are moderate yet fleshed out with little lagniappes. A pretty waitress brings a complimentary glass of sparkling wine and preappetizer of bread topped with chopped tomatoes. At night, she lights a candle. *Primi Piatti* (first courses) are mostly risottos and pastas. A meal-in-itself salad of snapping-fresh greens and vegetables is dressed with fruity olive oil and balsamic vinegar. Some of the properly al dente pastas—puttanesca, for example—are spicier than the Spanish norm.

Toscana

Manuel Fernández González 17. ☎ **1/429-69-50.** Main courses 945–2,600 ptas. ($7.25–$20). No credit cards. Lunch daily 1-4pm; dinner Mon and Wed–Sat 8pm–midnight. Closed Aug. Metro: Sevilla. SPANISH.

Toscana was completely overhauled recently, to compete with the several good tapas bars on this and adjacent blocks. Now it has rough white plaster walls and dark heavy beams that show their adz marks. Hanging here and there are gourds, garlic braids, ceramic pitchers, and (curiously) a baseball bat and glove. The place is jammed most nights, but the squat little tables and stools clear quickly. A man stands behind the bar ladling out portions of the nightly special. That might be morcillo, a veal stew spooned over fries for 700 ptas. ($5.40) or grilled cod with tomatoes for 1,100 ptas. ($8.45).

La Trucha

Nuñez de Arce 6. ☎ **1/532-08-82.** Main courses 945–2,100 ptas. ($7.25–$16.15); *menu de la casa* 2,600 ptas. ($20). No credit cards. Mon–Sat 12:30–4pm and 7:30pm–midnight. Closed July. Metro: Sol. SPANISH.

Trout (*trucha*) is the signature dish of this popular tavern near Plaza de Santa Ana. One version is trucha a La Trucha, in the style of the northern province of Navarre. The whole fish is split open, filled with chopped ham and garlic, and then sautéed. Another is the smoked filets of trout included in the platter of fish and roe called a verbena. This is a popular stop on the tapas circuit, partly because most of the dishes are cooked to order, not merely zapped in the microwave, and the men behind the counter make every new patron feel like an old friend.

Zara

Infantas 5 (one block off the Gran Vía). ☎ **1/532-20-74.** Main courses 260–1,600 ptas. ($2–$12.30); *menu del día* 2,100 ptas. ($16.15). AE, DC, MC, V. Mon–Fri 1–5pm and 8–11:30pm. Closed hols and Aug. Metro: Gran Vía. SPANISH/CUBAN.

The señora at the helm hails from Cuba and has brought her national cuisine to Madrid. That isn't much of a reach, since the Cuban culinary repertoire was heavily influenced by the Spaniards who controlled the island until 1898. What varies primarily is the use of Caribbean tropical fruits and vegetables. The specialties change daily, with perhaps roast pork one day, meatballs and fried eggs another, or chicken escabeche on yet another, all served with rice. Expect to find items like plantains and exotic citrus in unusual combinations.

CAFES

Madrid's traditional cafés, and their younger replications, hold a special place in the lives of its citizens, serving a function somewhere between tapas bars and full-service restaurants. Food, though always available, is decidedly secondary, pushed aside by every Spaniard's favorite occupation: talk. Many of the older cafés, dating back to pre–World War I days and even further, nuture reputations as hotbeds of intellectualism or ideology. Others are favored primarily as meeting places, where a cup of coffee or a beer is the sole price of admission to a table you can hold for hours while you write poetry, read a book, or plan your future.

Café Comercial

Glorieta de Bilbao 7. ☎ **1/531-34-72.** Tapas and sandwiches from 200 ptas. ($1.55). Daily 9am–midnight. Metro: Bilbao. SPANISH.

This authentic outpost began in the last century. Artists and intellectuals have been challenging one another at regular *tertulias* (get-togethers) ever since, reflected in big mirrors hung beneath a towering ceiling. Although this place's reputation is decidedly left-wing radical, no ideological litmus test is set, and most of the patrons seem involved in less cosmic interests. Go only for coffee or drinks and the surroundings, not to eat.

Café Gijón

Paseo de Recoletos 21. ☎ **1/521-54-25.** Tapas 340–1,000 ptas. ($2.60–$7.70); main courses 750–3,150 ptas. ($5.75–$24.25); *menu del día* 1,485 ptas. ($11.40). No credit cards. Daily 9:30am–midnight. Metro: Banco de España. SPANISH.

Hemingway made the Café Gijón famous among Americans, and it's still home to the Spanish tradition of the *tertulia*. That's a more-or-less formal occasion when friends and colleagues get together for discussions of philosophy, the arts, politics, issues of the day . . . or soccer. Outside in the summer or inside in cooler weather, this is a relaxing place to come and sip a coffee or beer or read a newspaper. Be prepared for thick clouds of cigarette smoke.

Café de Oriente

Plaza de Oriente 2. ☎ **1/541-39-74.** Tapas and snacks from 300 ptas. ($2.30). AE, DC, MC, V. Mon–Sat 8:30am–1:30am. Metro: Opera. SPANISH.

A near-legendary priest opened this and other restaurants to steer troubled young men and ex-convicts on a better path. It sits at the edge of its namesake plaza, facing the Royal Palace, which appears especially imposing at night, when illuminated. Outdoors, there are tables; indoors, the look is belle époque, with much use of gilt, brass, and velvet. *Todo* Madrid shows up, some in the tattered mufti of art and music students, many in bespoke suits, and more than a few gorgeous women decked in couture. The dining room in the brick cellar is attractive though far too expensive for these pages.

Círculo de Bellas Artes

Alcalá 42. ☎ **1/531-77-00** or 531-77-06. Tapas from 260 ptas. ($2); *menu del día* 1,050 ptas. ($8.10). No credit cards. Daily 9am–midnight. Metro: Banco de España. SPANISH.

Not only a café but also a cultural center with changing exhibitions upstairs, this place is usually packed. Winter or summer, it's a great place to relax, with lots of deep chairs inside and tables at which to take the sun outside. There's a 105-pta. (80¢) entrance charge to the center.

El Espejo

Paseo de Recoletos 31. ☎ **1/308-23-47.** Tapas 300 ptas. ($2.30); main courses 950–2,450 ptas. ($7.30–$18.85). Daily 9am–midnight. Metro: Banco de España. SPANISH.

Home base is an art nouveau place with a bar in front and a dining room in back. Efficient air conditioning draws out the miasma of smoke that afflicts most of the grand cafés. Better still is the Victorian glass pavilion set out on the median strip bordering the paseo. At one end is a cluster of outdoor tables, at which a piano player often plays for entertainment during warmer months. Both the bar and the pavilion look as if they've been around for a hundred years; it's actually less than two decades.

THE CHAINS

Spanish fast-food chains proliferate. One local favorite, **Vips**, offers sit-down eating from abbreviated menus along with sales of books, magazines, records, tapes, videos, beer, wine, cookies, and meats. Popular from breakfast to late-night munch attacks, it's open daily from 9am to 3am. Menu items run 200 to 235 ptas. ($1.55 to $9.50). A breakfast of a roll or toast and marmalade with coffee or tea is 290 ptas. ($2.25). Vips branches can be found at Gran Vía 43, Princesa 5, Velázquez 84 and 136, Paseo de la Castellana 85, Orense 16 and 79, Paseo de la Habana 17, Julian Romea 4, and Alberto Aguitera 56.

Similar to Vips in every way (except the un-Spanish apostrophe in its logo), **Bob's** offers standard fast-food items for 200 to 1,260 ptas. ($1.55 to $9.70). Burgers come with all the trimmings. Locations include Glorieta de Quevedo 9, Padro Damian 38, Miguel Angel 11, Zurbano 26, and Serrano 41. They're open daily from 9am to 3am.

Foster's Hollywood, on the scene for decades, deals in burgers and fries, barbecued spareribs, and the like at fair prices. Locations in and around Madrid include Tamayo y Baus 1, Velázquez 80, Guzmán el Bueno 100, Magallanes 1, António Morales 3, and Avenida de Brasil 14–16. Most of them are open from 1pm to 1am.

Finally, **Nebraska** is another home-grown cafeteria chain offering a menu del día for 1,315 ptas. ($10.10) in the bar area, and coffee and pastry for 285 ptas. ($2.20). Menus are available in English. Locations in Madrid include Alcalá 18, Gran Vía 32 and 55, Calle Mayor 1, Goya 39, and Bravo Murillo 109 and 291. They're open daily from 9am to midnight.

The usual imports have set up shop. **McDonald's, Burger King, Wendy's, Kentucky Fried Chicken,** and **Pizza Hut** are abundantly apparent at many locations throughout the busiest parts of the city, especially along the Gran Vía, on Puerta del Sol, and in Orense to the north.

PICNICKING

For one-stop shopping, go to the supermarket at **El Corte Inglés** (see "Shopping," later in this chapter) or visit **Casa Mingo** at Paseo de la Florida 2 (☎ **1/547-79-18**) for their take-out roast chicken, cider, and salad (take-out service closed Sunday and holidays). Many bakeshops and gourmet shops sell salads and sandwiches that are perfect for picnics. One such possibility is **Rodilla,** on Plaza Callao, near the Galerías Preciados department store.

Take the mouth-watering booty to **El Retiro park,** the **Parque del Oeste** (northwest of the Royal Palace), or the **Casa de Campo**.

WORTH THE EXTRA MONEY

Sobrin de Botín

Cuchilleros 17. ☎ **1/366-42-17.** Reservations recommended. Main courses 1,075–3,700 ptas. ($8.25–$28.45); *menu del día* 3,645 ptas. ($28.05). AE, DC, MC, V. Daily 1–4pm and 8pm–midnight. Metro: Sol. SPANISH.

A Madrid institution favored by locals and visitors alike, Botín has been in business since the early 18th century, and the ovens still in use aren't much younger. Ernest Hemingway was an enthusiastic patron and even used the restaurant as the place where Lady Brett kissed off Jake Barnes in *The Sun Also Rises*. The vaulted cellars and three above-ground floors are layered with tiles and an entrancing munificence of paintings, posters, ceramics, and other artifacts. The specialties are the slow-cooked roasts central to the Castilian kitchen, especially lamb and suckling pig. While admittedly short of the higher gastronomic achievements available elsewhere in the city (for a good deal more money), the food is quite satisfying. Each evening a *tuna,* a group of minstrels in medieval costume, entertains—yet another reason this obligatory tourist site is virtually on a par with the Prado and the Royal Palace.

6 Attractions

SIGHTSEEING SUGGESTIONS

Recognition of Madrid's magic starts with curiosity and progresses through growing regard to deep affection. It's difficult not to like a place populated with people who spend so much of their time honing their skills at the art of living. As capital for over four centuries, Madrid is naturally the principal repository of the nation's patrimony, its history and culture enshrined in over 50 museums. The glimpses they provide into prehistory, the Roman and Arab epochs, and the golden age of Spain intrigue and delight. Since Madrid reveals itself slowly, the more days you have available for exploring, the better. However, if time is limited, the following suggestions will help you spend it wisely.

Always check museum hours before setting out, particularly at the smaller ones, for they are prone to sudden changes.

If You Have 1 Day

The first stop must be the Museo del Prado. World-famous and justifiably so, this early 19th-century neoclassical building houses a superlative collection of paintings from the gothic period through the High Renaissance, notably by such Spanish masters as Murillo, El Greco, Goya, and Velázquez.

From the Prado, walk or take a bus up to Plaza de las Cibeles with its fountain dedicated to Cybele, the Goddess of Fertility, depicted riding a chariot pulled by lions. On the east side of the plaza is the grandiose Palacio de Comunicaciónes, the main post office. Turn west along Alcalá to the Puerta del Sol.

A plaza shaped like a half moon, the Puerta del Sol is the spiritual heart of Madrid, ground zero for the national roads radiating from Madrid. Calle de Preciados, a pedestrian shopping area, leads off to the north. It's marked by a statue of a bear nibbling at the berries of a *madroño* tree, a vignette serving as the emblem of Madrid. Opposite, the Communidad de Madrid building is topped by a steeple with a large clock. On New Year's Eve, crowds fill the plaza and swallow 12 grapes, one for each toll of the bells.

Continue west down Calle Mayor a few blocks and you'll see a ramp on the left leading off the street through an archway into Plaza Mayor. Café tables spread out into the pedestrians-only plaza in all but the coldest months. They are all but irresistible for an hour or two over coffee or drinks and taking in the shifting scene of buskers, caricaturists, lovers, and poets. (Nurse the drinks and eat elsewhere, for prices are exorbitantly high in the plaza.) Felípe III, who sits astride his horse in the center of the plaza, ordered its construction, one of his relatively rare useful acts. Since the 17th century it has been the site of various dramas, from highly inventive executions during the Spanish Inquisition to fiestas and bullfights. No longer a venue for bloodletting, it sees many other kinds of celebrations, including opera, rock concerts, and fireworks displays. On Sunday mornings, the surrounding arcades buzz with dealers and collectors of stamps and coins.

Next on the "must-see" list is the Palacio Real (Royal Palace). Walk west from Puerta del Sol on Calle del Arenal, past the south side of the Teatro Real, to Plaza de Oriente. The palace faces the plaza from the other side of Calle de Bailén. Cross to the other side, walk down to the south end of the palace, and turn right, toward another statue of Felípe III. From the porch where he sits is a good view of the Campo del Moro park, the larger Casa de Campo park beyond, and, on clear days, the Guadarrama Mountains. Walking back toward Bailén, you'll see the visitors' entrance to the palace on the left. The palace has over 2,000 rooms, only 50 or so open to the public. They're more than enough to give a sense of the opulence with which the Bourbon kings surrounded themselves. The requisite guided tour, conducted in several languages, includes the State Apartments, Library, Royal Pharmacy, Armory, and Carriage Museum.

If You Have 2 Days

Spend the first day as above, but on the second day leave Madrid early for a visit to Toledo, an hour away. See "Easy Excursions," at the end of this chapter, for details of the sights there.

If You Have 3 Days

Three days in Madrid will allow you time to return to the Prado, which can't be absorbed in a single visit. The Prado ticket includes entrance to the Casón del Buen Retiro, an annex three blocks east up Calle de Felípe IV that contains lesser works of the vast Prado collection. Nearby, to the north, is the Museo de Ejército, the military museum. Step across Calle de Alfonso XII, which passes in front of the Casón del Buen Retiro, and into the Parque del Retiro, delightful at any time but particularly from midday on Sunday when Madrileños, dressed in their best, are outside for the *paseo;* the main pathways grow crowded with mimes, musicians, and jugglers. There's something for everyone in the park—formal landscaped

---

Special & Free Events

Every year Madrid launches itself into fiesta after fiesta, with parades, dancing in the streets, fireworks, craft fairs, daily bullfights, and concerts. Check the weekly *Guía del Ocio* ("Leisure Guide") for full details, but the following are the highlights:

Around Christmas and New Year's the city is alive with excitement that culminates in a great gathering beneath the Puerta del Sol's big clock on **New Year's Eve.** Take 12 grapes and pop one in your mouth for each strike of the clock at midnight. Those who are up to the task will have good luck all year.

On January 5 the **Three Kings (Los Reyes)** arrive (by helicopter nowadays) for an exuberant parade on horseback through the streets, during which the children are showered with candy.

In March, the **Madrid Theater Festival** attracts a galaxy of international companies. On the Saturday before Lent begins, hundreds of gaily decorated floats parade down Paseo de la Castellana in a **Carnaval** procession. **Holy Week (Semana Santa)** is celebrated with due solemnity, and processions of the penitents take place all over Madrid, including around the Puerto del Sol. Around **Easter** there's a gathering of horses and their riders from Seville, who step through the streets attired in colorful traditional style, beginning and ending in El Retiro Park.

The most important festival celebrates the patron saint of Madrid, **San Isidro,** in mid-May, with a protracted program of activities and the best bullfights of the year. **"Veranos de la Villa"** provides summer entertainment for the long, warm evenings, including open-air movies at the Cine del Retiro and flamenco shows in another corner of the park. Fall brings Madrid's acclaimed **jazz festival** and the **Feriarte,** Spain's major antiques fair.

The **Fundación Juan March,** Castelló 77 (☎ **1/435-42-40**), offers free concerts from fall to spring, on Monday and Saturday at noon and Wednesday at 7:30pm, changing the theme monthly.

Madrid

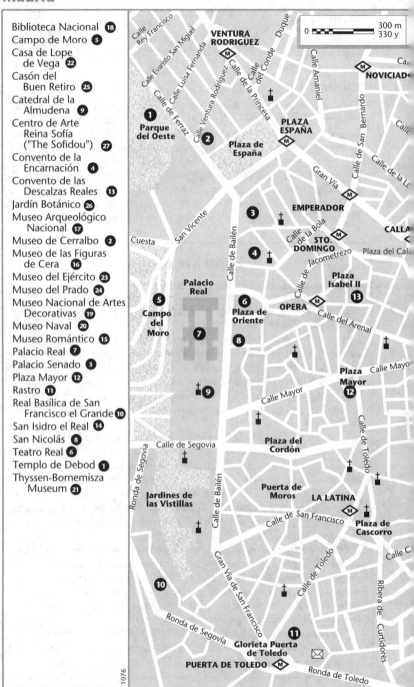

Metro Ⓜ   Church ✝   Post Office ✉   Information ⓘ

gardens and densely wooded areas, boating on the lake, and outdoor bars for people-watching.

On Day 2 visit Toledo as above, and on Day 3 go to the Royal Palace in the morning as described above, spend more time exploring the vicinity of Plaza Mayor, visit the nearby covered market of San Miguel, and then wander down Calle Mayor to see Plaza de la Villa, a cluster of some of Madrid's oldest buildings, including City Hall. The Convento de las Descalzas Reales, founded by Juana of Austria, is sumptuously decorated and deserves a visit. The wealth of art at this still-functioning convent is the bequest of its aristocratic former residents.

If You Have 5 Days

Spend the first three days as described above. On Day 4 choose among a number of fascinating museums, depending on your interest. Those who enjoy weaving and the fabric arts may want to visit the Real Fábrica de Tapices, where tapestries and rugs have been made the same way since the 15th century. The Museo de Artes Decorativas highlights Spanish trends in the decorative arts through the centuries, with a pronounced emphasis on ceramics. At the Museo Lázaro Galdiano are displayed the eponymous collector's idiosyncratic choices in painting, sculpture, silverware, enamels, and ivories, all of which he left to the state, along with the mansion to house them. The Museo Sorolla, in the artist's house, has numerous examples of the Valencian impressionist's work from the turn of the century. Finally, for archeology enthusiasts, the recently revamped collections of the Museo Arqueológico Nacional are excellent, especially the Iberian and classical antiquities.

On your final day, take another trip out of Madrid to Felípe II's Monasterio de San Lorenzo del Escorial (see "Easy Excursions," at the end of this chapter, for details). In the foothills of the Guadarrama Mountains, this somber granite testament to Felípe and pantheon for Spanish kings broods over the plains below. Along with Felipe's austere apartments, the basilica, and museum, visit the great library with its beautifully illuminated manuscripts.

TOP ATTRACTIONS

✪ Museo del Prado

Paseo del Prado. ☎ **1/420-28-36.** Admission 425 ptas. ($3.25). Tues–Sat 9am–7pm, Sun 9am–2pm. Closed Jan 1, Good Fri, May 1, and Dec 26. Metro: Atocha or Banco de España. Bus 10, 14, 27, 34, 37, 45, or M6.

Madrid's most famous museum contains Spanish painting from the 12th to the 18th century as well as Italian masters and painters from the Venetian and Flemish schools. Only a small portion of the holdings is on display at any given time, a fact that has prompted a frustrating search for additional space.

With only a limited amount of time to enjoy this awe-inspiring museum, give priority to the works of Goya, Velázquez, and El Greco, whose *Adoration of the Shepherds* enthralls with its detail and emotion. In the Velázquez rooms, see his portrait of Don Baltasar Carlos, the expressions on the faces of *Los Borrachos* (The Drunkards), and from the last years of his life, *Las Meninas*. Both Velázquez and Goya were court painters, hence the multitude of their paintings here. Goya's cartoons are especially popular, though his brutally candid portraits of the royal family and his somber series of "Black Paintings" also have their admirers. Other important canvases to seek out are those of the Spaniards Ribera, Zurbarán, and Murillo, as well as masterpieces by Hieronymus Bosch (especially the nightmarish *Garden*

The Prado

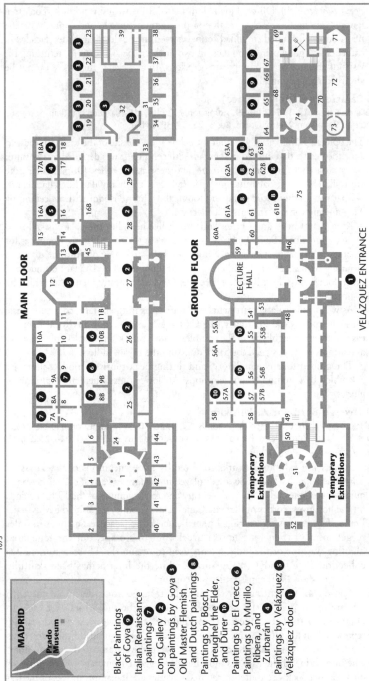

MAIN FLOOR

GROUND FLOOR

VELÁZQUEZ ENTRANCE

LECTURE HALL

Temporary Exhibitions

Temporary Exhibitions

MADRID
Prado Museum

Black Paintings of Goya **9**

Italian Renaissance paintings **7**

Long Gallery **2**

Oil paintings by Goya **3**

Old Master Flemish and Dutch paintings **8**

Paintings by Bosch, Breughel the Elder, and Dürer **6**

Paintings by El Greco **6**

Paintings by Murillo, Ribera, and Zurbarán **4**

Paintings by Velázquez **5**

Velázquez door **1**

1075

of Earthly Delights), Dürer, Titian, Tintoretto, Rubens, and van Dyck. Too often ignored among these riches are the startling gothic diptychs and triptychs on the main floor, all framed in gilded frames carved in the detail accorded facades of cathedrals. A good plan is to focus on two or three specific sections, returning for visits of an hour or so on separate occasions. In any event, the whole cannot be absorbed at one lunge.

✪ Palacio Real (Royal Palace)

Calle de Bailén. ☎ **1/542-00-59.** Admission 790 ptas. ($6.10). Mon–Sat 9am–5pm, Sun and hols 9am–3pm. Metro: Opera. Bus 3, 25, 33, 39, or M4.

The opulent Royal Palace was built for Felípe V on the site of the medieval Alcázar, a fortified castle that burned in the mid-18th century. It was designed by Giovanni Battista Sacchetti in a mix of baroque and neoclassical styles. Of particular note are Italian architect Sabatini's majestic staircase, the many dazzling chandeliers, Gasparini's giddily rococo drawing room, the Throne Room with its ceiling by Tiepolo, and the superb tapestry collection.

King Juan Carlos and Queen Sofía don't live here, but the palace is still used for state functions. Some lucky visitors get to see the State Dining Room set for a banquet: the table, which can seat almost 150, stretching off into the distance, gleaming with silver, gold, and cut glass and illuminated by 15 giant chandeliers. Next door is the Clock Room, where over 60 clocks, mostly French, all strike the hour together.

As well as the palace apartments, the tour takes in the library, coin and music museums, the Royal Pharmacy, the Carriage Museum, and the Royal Armory, easily one of the highlights of the complex, with its imposing displays of weaponry and armor, some designed for battle dogs and the royal toddlers.

The guided tour is mandatory, and during peak tourist periods visitors are assembled by common language groups. At slower times, there are multilingual guides.

✪ Thyssen-Bornemisza Museum

Palacio de Villahermosa, Paseo del Prado 8. ☎ **1/369-01-51.** Admission 650 ptas. ($5). Tues–Sun 10am–7pm. Metro: Banco de España or Atocha. Bus 1, 2, 5, 9, 10, 14, 15, 20, 27, 34, 37, 45, 51, 52, 53, 74, 146, or 150.

This museum exhibits artworks collected by two generations of the Thyssen-Bornemisza family. The works are displayed in the former Palacio de Villahermosa, built between the end of the 18th century and the beginning of the 19th. It stands on the northwest corner of Plaza de Canovas del Castillo, opposite the Museo del Prado. The Prado's directors had hoped to have the palace as an annex in order to get some of their long-unseen works out of storage, but the renovated building was one of the inducements used to obtain the Thyseen-Bornemisza collection. The facade remains intact, while the interior has been skillfully adapted to show off the masterpieces it contains.

Those works, paintings for the most part, range from the end of the 13th century to the present. To a considerable degree, the authorities were eager to obtain the part of the collection covering the last 100 years, a period scantily represented in the capital's museums. To see the artworks in historical order, cross the central court and take the central staircase or the elevator to the second floor. The numbering of the galleries indicates the suggested itinerary, which proceeds on a counterclockwise route. In the first galleries are Italian primitives of the last centuries before the dawn of the Renaissance and their successors, including Tintoretto and Bernini. Also represented are Dutch, Spanish, Flemish, German, and French artists. Of particular note, because they're rarely seen in Spain, are the rooms containing works by such 19th-century American artists as landscapist Albert Bierstadt and portraitist John Singer Sargent and French impressionists and post-impressionists Manet, Monet, Renoir, and Degas. They're followed by examples of the modernist schools and branches that traveled through cubism, constructivism, surrealism, and abstract expressionism, exemplified by artists as diverse as Picasso and Edward Hopper, Dalí and de Kooning, Mondrian and Joseph Cornell.

Monasterio de las Descalzas Reales

Plaza de las Descalzas 3. ☎ **1/542-00-59.** Admission 525 ptas. ($4). Tues–Thurs and Sat 10:30am–12:30pm and 4–5:30pm, Fri 10:30am–12:30pm, Sun and hols 11am–1:30pm. Metro: Sol, Callao, or Opera. Bus 1, 2, 5, 20, 46, 52, 53, 74, M1, M2, M3, M5, or M10.

In the heart of old Madrid, near the Puerta del Sol, this richly endowed royal convent was founded in the mid-16th century in the palace where Juana of Austria, Felípe II's sister, was born. She used it as a retreat and brought the Poor Clare nuns here. For many years the convent sheltered only royal women, typically the daughters of aristocrats who sequestered them until they were old enough for arranged marriages. They did not live a spartan existence, judging from the wealth of religious artwork that surrounded them, including tapestries, sculptures, and paintings by Rubens, Brueghel the Elder, Gérard David, and Titian. The main staircase features trompe l'oeil wall paintings and frescoes, and 16 of the 32 lavishly decorated chapels can be viewed. Compulsory tours are conducted in Spanish by bored guides who impatiently hasten their charges from canvas to tapestry to chapel. Try to slow their pace, for there's much to savor.

✪ Museo Arqueológico Nacional

Serrano 13 (facing Calle Serrano). ☎ **1/577-79-12.** Admission 210 ptas. ($1.60). Tues–Sat 9:30am–8:30pm, Sun and hols 9:30am–2:30pm. Metro: Serrano or Retiro. Bus 1, 9, 19, 51, 74, or M2.

In the same vast building as the National Library, which has a separate entrance on Paseo de Recoletos, the National Archeological Museum houses a profoundly important agglomeration of antiquities from prehistory through the Middle Ages. Arranged chronologically on three floors, the displays are clearly labeled. Most of the artifacts are related specifically to the development of the Iberian Peninsula, though there are some Egyptian and Greek objects. Most illuminating, perhaps, are the rooms devoted to the Iberian period, before sequential conquerors arrived, and those containing relics of the Visigoths, who left relatively little behind. A particular treasure is the *Dama de Elche,* a resplendent example of 4th-century Iberian sculpture, easily equal to the better-known works being produced in Greece

---

❷ Did You Know?

- At 2,120 feet, Madrid is the highest capital in Europe.
- Every month about 20 people who want to be ennobled apply to a special department of the Ministry of Justice.
- Madrid's future cathedral, Nuestra Señora de la Almudena, was begun in 1881 and is still under construction.
- Madrid boasts more bars and nightclubs than any other European city.
- Divorce was legalized in Spain fewer than 20 years ago.

at the time. The Visigothic era, roughly from the 5th to the early 8th century, is represented by bronzes and funerary offerings from Mérida and some intricate votive crowns and jewelry. Galleries farther on contain Roman mosaics, Etruscan pottery, Greek vases, gothic sculpture and architectural fragments, and Mudéjar woodwork. Inside the front gate, to the right after you enter, the Caves of Altamira have been faithfully reproduced. Since access to the real thing, in northwestern Spain, is sharply restricted, these simulations of the 15,000-year-old paintings at least approximate the experience.

MORE ATTRACTIONS

Casa Museo de Lope de Vega

Cervantes 11. ☎ **1/429-92-16.** Admission 200 ptas. ($1.55). Mon–Fri 9:30am–3pm, Sat 10am–2pm. Metro: Antón Martín. Bus 6, 26, 32, 57, or M9.

An extraordinarily prolific 17th-century playwright, Lope de Vega is credited with over 1,800 works. He lived in this house on a street now named for a contemporary he bitterly resented, Miguel de Cervantes, author of *Don Quijote de La Mancha*. The house, relatively modest considering his popular success, has been carefully reconstructed and is a national monument. Inside are his study, bedroom, and kitchen; out back is his garden.

Centro de Arte Reine Sofía

Santa Isabel 52 (at the corner of Atocha). ☎ **1/467-50-62.** Admission 450 ptas. ($3.45). Mon and Wed–Sat 10am–9pm, Sun 10am–2:30pm. Metro: Atocha. Bus 6, 14, 26, 27, 32, 45, 57, or C.

This museum was intended to serve as a repository of 20th-century art, yet its collection is still somewhat sparse and unbalanced, even with the recent acquisition of the holdings of the now-closed Museo de Arte Contemporáneo. Its direction has been controversial from the outset, with some government members contending that it should concentrate on Spanish artists and its directors insisting that its mission should focus on currents in international thought. To date, its successes have usually been with temporary exhibitions rather than with highlights from its permanent collection. A recent triumph was the wresting of Picasso's fabled mural, *Guernica*, away from the Prado, which had held it since its return from the Museum of Modern Art in New York (after Franco's death). It's now the centerpiece of the Reina Sofía, lodged in a separate high-security installation. Largely second-rank work by such mostly Spanish artists as Dalí, Miró, Gris, and Solana supplements the Picasso masterwork. For the moment, the center's most interesting element may be the former 18th-century hospital itself, renovated inside and with new see-through elevator shafts on the exterior.

Museo de America

Avenida Reyes Católicas 6. ☎ **1/549-26-41.** Admission 450 ptas. ($3.50) Tues–Sat, free Sun. Tues–Sat 10am–4pm, Sun 10am–2:30pm. Metro: Montcloa. Bus 46, 62, 82, 83, A, D, or G.

This museum in the University City/Moncloa section has received a $15-million renovation and reopened after being closed for over 13 years. Its expanded galleries are devoted to ethnological and archeological collections from Spain's former colonies in the Americas. Of particular note are those rooms dealing with the social organization and daily lives of the various Native American tribes and nations and the wealth of artifacts related to the observance of their religions. Pre-Columbian jewelry, statuary, and other artifacts are illustrative.

Museo de las Figuras de Cera (Wax Museum)

Paseo de Recoletos 41. ☎ 1/319-46-81. Admission 750 ptas. ($5.75) adults, 500 ptas. ($3.85) children under 12. Daily 10am–2pm and 4–8:30pm (ticket window closes at 2:30pm and 8pm). Metro: Colón. Bus 5, 14, 27, 45, 53, M6, or M7.

More than 400 wax figures should satisfy those who enjoy this sort of commercial enterprise, but Madame Tussaud's this isn't. Prominently featured are scenes from *Don Quijote*, famous bullfighters, and a host of famous and not-so-famous historical and contemporary personages. The museum's principal virtue may be that it's open when other museums are closed. Parents bringing their children and squeamish adults are forewarned that the requisite chamber of horrors graphically depicts a number of grisly tortures employed during the Inquisition.

Museo de Artes Decorativas (Museum of Decorative Arts)

Montalban 12 (off Plaza de las Cibeles). ☎ 1/521-34-40. Admission 210 ptas. ($1.60). Mon–Fri 9am–3pm, Sat–Sun 10am–2pm. Metro: Banco de España. Bus 14, 27, 34, 37, 45, or M6.

This museum is crammed with furniture, leatherwork, wall hangings, ceramics, rugs, porcelain, glass, jewelry, toys, dollhouses, clothes, and lace. After the first floor the museum progresses in chronological order, tracing the development of Spanish interior decoration from the 15th to the 19th century. By the fifth floor, the amplitude may have become numbing to any but scholars and practitioners, but the immense variety of objects still has the capacity to intrigue.

Museo Lázaro Galdiano

Serrano 122. ☎ 1/561-60-84. Admission 315 ptas. ($2.40). Tues–Sun 10am–2pm. Closed hols and Aug. Metro: Avenida America. Bus 9, 16, 19, 51, or 89.

Madrid was the beneficiary of financier/author José Lázaro Galdiano's largess. When he died, he left the city his 30-room turn-of-the-century mansion and his substantial private collection. Every floor attests to his devotion to art: There are paintings from Spain's golden age, including works by Spaniards El Greco, Ribera, Zurbarán, Murillo, and Goya. Among Renaissance Italians represented are Guardi, Tiepolo, and Leonardo, and canvases by Englishmen Gainsborough and Constable are on view. However, the museum is most admired for its comprehensive array of enamels, ivories, and works in gold and silver, most of it created during the Middle Ages. Admittedly, the collection is not always given the careful arrangement it deserves, and the sometimes sullen staff doesn't enhance the experience.

Museo Sorolla

General Martínez Campos 37. ☎ 1/310-15-84. Admission 210 ptas. ($1.50). Tues–Sat 10am–3pm, Sun 10am–2pm. Metro: Rubén Dario or Iglesia. Bus 5, 7, 16, 61, 40, or M3.

The museum of painter Joaquín Sorolla has a homey, down-to-earth quality after the grandeur of some of Madrid's other museums. Sorolla (1863–1923) was born and reared on the coast of Valencia, and his later works were influenced by the French impressionists. Many are seascapes, and he had a knack of painting water so it appears wet on the canvas. The museum is in the house and studio where he lived and worked the last 11 years of his life, and it has been kept (on the ground floor at least) as it was when he died. He was an avid collector, as is evidenced by the large quantity of Spanish ceramics he owned.

Real Fábrica de Tapices (Royal Tapestry Factory)

Fuenterrabia 2. ☎ 1/551-34-00. Admission 50 ptas. (40¢). Mon–Fri 9am–12:30pm. Closed hols and Aug. Metro: Menéndez Pelayo. Bus 10, 14, 26, 32, 37, C, or M9.

Tapestries are still being made in this active 1889 factory as they were when its predecessor opened in the 18th century. Many of the tapestries in the Palacio Real and at El Escorial were made here, with some of the earliest designs by artists as prominent as Goya. The guided tour first enters a room where enormous custom-made carpets are created, then moves on to the room where antique tapestries are painstakingly restored. The final stop is the room where new tapestries are made on vast wooden looms. The tour is in Spanish, but just to observe is illuminating.

Museo del Ejército (Army Museum)

Méndez Núñez 1. ☎ **1/522-89-77.** Admission 50 ptas. (40¢). Tues–Sun 10am–2pm. Metro: Banco de España. Bus 15, 19, 27, 34, 37, or 45.

One of the two remaining buildings of the palace that used to stand in what is now El Retiro park houses this museum. It was founded by Manuel Godoy, who made his spectacular climb from obscurity into the arms of Carlos IV's wife, María Luisa of Parma. Weaponry of every kind—from the surprisingly dainty sword of the semimythical El Cid to firearms from the 1936–39 Civil War—is displayed alongside armor, uniforms, flags, dioramas, miniatures, and thousands of other bits of memorabilia.

Museo Municipal

Fuencarral 78. ☎ **1/588-86-72.** Admission free. Tues–Fri 9:30am–8pm, Sat–Sun 10am–2pm. Metro: Tribunal.

Here the history of Madrid is explained through paintings and prints, documents, scale models, carriages, and costumes. In the basement are two large Roman mosaic floors and other archeological artifacts. Easily as interesting is the eye-popping rococo entrance, crowded with cherubim and warriors, designed by Pedro de Ribera to grace what was formerly an 18th-century hospice for the city's poor.

Museo Naval

Montalbán 2. ☎ **1/379-50-55.** Admission free. Tues–Sun 10:30am–1:30pm. Metro: Banco de España. Bus 10, 14, 27, 34, 37, 45, or M6.

For most North Americans, the highlight of this museum is Juan de la Cosa's map, drawn in 1500, on which America appears for the first time. There are also some intricately detailed ship models, panoramic paintings of sea battles, antique maritime charts, and scores of nautical instruments. A treasure trove for the nautical buff, it's nearly as compelling for devout landlubbers.

Museo Romántico

San Mateo 13. ☎ **1/448-10-45.** Admission 200 ptas. ($1.55). Tues–Sat 9am–6pm, Sun and hols 10am–2pm. Closed Aug. Metro: Alonso Martínez. Bus 37, 40, or M10.

This collection of furniture, paintings, and objets d'art from the Romantic period of the early 19th century was assembled by the philanthropic Marquis of La Vega–Inclán. Housed in an 18th-century baroque mansion, it juxtaposes dollhouses and Goyas with antic flair.

Museo Taurino

Alcalá 237. ☎ **1/725-18-57.** Admission free. Tues–Fri 9:30am–2:30pm, Sun 10am–1pm. Metro: Ventas. Bus 12, 21, 38, 53, M1, or M8.

The Bullfighting Museum is behind the Las Ventas Plaza de Toros. Just about anything to do with the hallowed art-spectacle is on display—from busts of famous fighters to the mounted heads of famous bulls, from swords and capes to sketches, paintings, and scale models. The problem is, it's too far from the city center to justify a special trip for any but the most dedicated aficionado or avidly curious visitor and it's closed when *corridas* are scheduled in the adjoining bullring.

Parque de Atracciones

Casa de Campo. ☎ **1/463-29-00.** Park, 350 ptas. ($2.70); park plus two rides, 650 ptas. ($5); park and all rides, 1,500 ptas. ($11.55) adults, 800 ptas. ($6.15) children 7 and under. Feb–May, Tues–Fri 3–9 or 11pm; Sat–Sun 10am–8pm; June–Nov, Mon–Fri 10am–8pm; Sat–Sun 10am–midnight. Call to verify times, which are subject to frequent change. Metro: Batán. Bus 33 (from Plaza de Isabel II) or 65, and on Sun also from Ventas, Puente de Vallecas, and Estrecho.

Not merely an amusement park, the Parque de Atracciones, set in the spacious Casa de Campo west of the Royal Palace, also has an auditorium that stages spectacular shows in summer (free with admission). Restaurants, electronic games, and a cinema round out the entertainment.

Panteón de Goya

Glorieta de San António de la Florida. ☎ **1/542-07-22.** Admission 200 ptas. ($1.55). Mon–Tues and Thurs–Sat 10am–1pm and 4–7pm. Metro: Norte. Bus 41, 46, 75, or C.

Carlos IV commissioned Francisco de Goya to decorate the ceiling in the dome of the chapel in this 1797 hermitage. His frescoes, depicting the story of St. Anthony of Padua, are populated with plump cherubs and voluptuous angels who were modeled after members of the Spanish court and Madrid society of the day. Some of the women portrayed were rumored to follow dubious professions. Goya is buried here, but somehow his head got lost in transit from Bordeaux, where he was first interred.

Real Academia de Bellas Artes de San Fernando (Royal Academy of Fine Arts of San Fernando)

Alcalá 13. ☎ **1/522-14-91.** Admission 225 ptas. ($1.75). Tues–Fri 10am–7pm, Sat–Mon 10am–2pm. Metro: Sol or Sevilla. Bus 3, 5, 15, 20, 51, 52, or M12.

This center, in a recently restored building east of the Puerta del Sol, offers a wide variety of works by such artists as El Greco, Zurbarán, Sorolla, Ribera, Murillo, Rubens, and Fragonard, plus one room filled with Goyas, these latter of his mature years. After a showy display of these heavyweights in the front galleries, the rooms in back contain a diversity of Chinese terra-cottas, Egyptian bronzes, and small sculptures.

Zoo

Casa de Campo. ☎ **1/711-99-50.** Admission 875 ptas. ($6.75) adults, 450 ptas. ($3.45) children 7 and under. Mar–Oct, daily 10am–9pm; Nov–Feb, daily 10:30am–7pm (ticket office closes half an hour earlier). Metro: Batán. Bus 33 from Plaza de Isabel II, and on Sun and holidays also from Ventas, Puente de Vallecas, and Estrecho.

Madrid's zoo is, not surprisingly, Spain's best, although it doesn't really compare to the superior facilities of San Diego, New York, or Berlin. Most of the animals are housed in open pens rather than cages, separated from the public by ditches. Over 2,000 mammals, birds, and reptiles are grouped according to their continent of origin. Highlights are the two pandas, Chang-Chang and his offspring, Chu-Lin, who was the first panda in Europe to be born in captivity. The Dolphin Show (at 1 and 5pm) also deserves attention.

PARKS & GARDENS

Along with the Casón del Buen Retiro and the building that houses the Army Museum, the 321-acre **Parque del Retiro** is what's left of a 17th-century palace and grounds ordered built by Felípe IV. Now the tree-lined walkways, formal rose garden, Crystal Palace, boating lake, monuments, and grottoes offer a tranquil retreat from the city clangor. Madrileños like to see and be seen, and on the weekend entire three- and four-generation families dress up for the *paseo* through this park.

To the south of the Museo del Prado is the **Jardín Botánico,** in its current location since the 18th century, where visitors can enjoy a wide range of exotic flora. This garden is at its most appealing in spring and summer, of course, but serious gardeners will find plantings of interest even in winter. North and west of the Royal Palace, respectively, are the **Jardines de Sabatini** and the **Campo del Moro.** Just to the north of these is the **Parque de la Montaña,** which contains the Templo de Debod, a 4th-century B.C. Egyptian temple given to Spain in appreciation of its assistance with the building of the Aswan High Dam. The temple and the elevation on which it stands are at the lower end of the larger **Parque del Oeste** (West Park), adjoining **La Rosaleda** (Rose Garden). Bordering these on Paseo Pintor Rosales are several open-air bars, and the eastern terminus of a *teleférico* (cable car) that swings out over the Manzanares River and deep into **Casa del Campo.**

That semiwild preserve, west of the Royal Palace and the city, is an enormous playground for all Madrileños. Here are the zoo, the Parque de Atracciones, the IFEMA (an exhibition center), a boating lake, a sports center, restaurants, and plenty of space to get away from it all.

STROLLING AROUND TOWN

SPECIAL-INTEREST WALKS   Visitors with special interests—in history or architecture, for example—can obtain useful information at the **Patronato Municipal de Turismo (Municipal Tourist Board)** at Calle Mayor 69 (☎ 1/580-00-00). They can suggest more than 40 special-interest routes to follow.

CITY HIGHLIGHTS WALK   Armed with a good map from the tourist office, take the metro or walk to Plaza de la Independencia. Walk south six blocks on Calle Alfonso XII, which borders Retiro Park, to the Puerta de Felípe IV.

With your back to the park, face the **Casón del Buen Retiro,** once an outbuilding of the huge 1631 Palace of the Buen Retiro, most of which was destroyed by the French during the War of Independence (1808—14). The *casón*, part of the Prado, now houses a small collection of 19th-century Spanish paintings. With the casón on the left, walk west down Calle de Felipe IV past the **Military Museum,** glimpsed over to the right. On the left is the **Royal Spanish Academy,** built later but in the same style as the casón. (The first woman member was elected in 1979.) Next on the left is the **Church of San Jerónimo El Real.** This church has always had strong royal connections and was moved from its original site near the river to the healthier heights of the Prado by Isabel and Ferdinand. Built in 1505 in the gothic style, it had a room known as the *cuarto viejo*, where Spanish monarchs could retire in times of mourning and at Lent. Here princes of Asturias were sworn in, Alfonso XIII was married, and his grandson, the current King Juan Carlos, celebrated his accession to the throne in 1975.

The north end of the **Museo del Prado** is another long block down the hill on the left, built in the neoclassical style of the late 18th and early 19th century. Construction began in 1796, but it, too, suffered during the War of Independence and wasn't finished until María Isabel de Braganza, wife of Ferdinand VII, wielded her influence in 1814. In 1819 it opened as an art gallery with 311 pictures. Continuing west, cross over Paseo del Prado on the northern side of Plaza Cánovas del Castillo, with the fountain featuring a statue of Neptune out in the middle. On the other side is the **Palace of Villahermosa,** now housing the collection of the Baron Hans Heinrich von Thyssen-Bornemisza and his fifth wife, Tita.

On the left is the refurbished **Palace Hotel,** built in 1912 on the site of the former Lerma Palace. Just past the Palacio Villahermosa, on the right, is the **Palacio del Congresso de Diputados** overlooking **Plaza de las Cortes.** The neoclassical Spanish parliament building was constructed between 1843 and 1850, and the two fierce lions guarding the entrance were made from bronze cannons captured during the 1860 colonial war in Morocco. Cross over Carrera San Jerónimo in front of the Hotel Villa Real. A tourist office is on the corner of Calle Duque Medinaceli. Turn right and proceed up Calle del Prado, then after one block turn left onto Calle de San Agustín and make the first right onto Calle de Cervantes. This climbs past **Lope de Vega's House** at no. 11. Make a right onto Calle del León at the end and you'll return to Calle del Prado. Just across the street is the **Ateneo,** marked by two lanterns, a gathering place for writers and politicians since 1837. Continue west along Calle del Prado to **Plaza de Santa Ana,** famous for its cafés and tapas bars. As you enter the square, on your right is the **Teatro Español,** an active theater built in the last century on a site where plays have been performed since 1582. Classic Spanish works comprise the current program. Walk west along the left side of the plaza through Plaza del Angel, along the end of Calle de las Huertas, turn left, and then right onto Calle de Atocha, traversing Plaza Jacinto Benavente.

At Plaza de Provincia, walk past the **Church of Santa Cruz,** on your left, to the **Ministry of Foreign Affairs,** also on your left. This neoclassical building has an Italian portal and was once a place to be feared as the court prison. Continue west along Calle de Atocha into **Plaza Mayor,** a logical place to rest while preparing for the rest of the walk.

Take the exit at the far northwest corner and cross Calle Mayor onto Calle Bordadores. Walk north on Bordadores and, with the **Church of San Ginés** on the right, cross over Calle de Arenal and go north on Calle San Martín into Plaza San Martín on your left and Plaza de las Descalzas on your right. Straight ahead is the **Monastery of Descalzas Reale.** On the west side of Plaza San Martín, pick up Calle de la Flora and walk west, and the street will soon become Calle de la Priora. On the left, while you're passing Calle Donados, is the little **Chapel of El Niño de Remedio,** its walls lined with votive offerings from those on whom miracles were bestowed after praying to the image of the Child Jesus. Continue west along Calle del la Priora to **Plaza de Isabel II.** Her statue stands at the near end. On the far side of the plaza is the back of the **Teatro Real**. Walk up Calle de Arrieta to Plaza de la Encarnación and the Monastery. From the plaza turn left (south) onto Calle de la Pavia and come out into **Plaza de Oriente.** The front entrance of the Teatro Real is on the left. Built in the mid-19th century on a site that was once the location of the local washhouse outside the city walls, this was until recently the home of the National Orchestra of Spain. It's been undergoing massive renovations for years but eventually will reopen as an opera house.

The long east face of the **Royal Palace** is seen on the far side of Plaza de Oriente, in the middle of which sits a statue of Felípe V on a rearing horse. This position proved technically difficult for sculptor Pedro Tacco. Guided by the theories of Galileo, he made the rear legs solid metal and left the front ones hollow. At the south end of the palace side is the future cathedral of Madrid, called **Neustra Señora de la Almudena,** begun in 1881 though interrupted in 1931. Only in 1985 were enough funds amassed to begin building again.

Survey the whole scene from the outdoor tables of the Café de Oriente, to the right of the Teatro Real.

ORGANIZED TOURS

Three bus companies offer a variety of tours, ranging from a half-day panoramic tour of Madrid to day-long excursions to such places as Toledo, El Escorial, and Segovia. Morning tours of Madrid cost 3,700 to 4,300 ptas. ($28.45 to $33.10), and a full-day tour to Toledo is 6,910 ptas. ($53.15). For further information, consult one of these three centrally located offices: **Juliá Tours,** Capitán Haya 38 (☎ 1/571-53-00); **Pullmantur,** Sor Angela de la Cruz 6 (☎ 1/556-21-88); and **Trapsatur,** San Bernardo 23 (☎ 1/542-66-66).

The **Madrid Vision Bus** tours museums, avenues, and main streets from April 1 to October 31, making 15 stops along the set route. Passengers may stay on board for the full itinerary, select intermediary stops, or use the service during an entire day, depending on the type of ticket purchased. Departures are Tuesday through Saturday from 9am to 5:20pm and Sunday and Monday from 9am to 2:45pm. Prices range from 525 to 1,100 ptas. ($4 to $8.45). Convenient places to pick up the bus are any of the major museums or at El Corte Inglés department store.

7 Shopping

Madrid's shopping selection is enormous and the service, particularly in the smaller stores, is friendly. Available products include everything to be expected of a modern European capital—from modish clothing boutiques to pipe shops along the two pedestrian walkways, **Calle Preciados** and **Calle del Carmen,** north of the Puerta del Sol. Should the desire for a splurge or a bit of upscale window-shopping arise, head for the **Salamanca** district, between Calles Serrano and Velázquez, Goya, and Juan Bravo, where all the tony designer stores compete for attention. The **AZCA area,** between Paseo de la Castellana and Orense, Raimundo Fernández Villaverde and Avenida General Perón, is also worth a visit (Metro: Nuevos Ministerios) for its range of stores, El Corte Inglés department store, and the new high-fashion mall, **La Moda.** A North American–style mall known as **Madrid-2** is at La Vaguada (Metro: Barrio del Pilar), with over 350 stores offering just about anything, including an excellent food market.

Across from the Prado in the lower floors of the Palace Hotel is **La Galería del Prado,** where gleaming marble, brass, glass, and plants set the stage for some of Madrid's most elegant stores. The **Mercado Puerta de Toledo,** on the site of the old Fish Market, south of the Royal Palace (Metro: Puerta de Toledo), purveys all the latest trends in fashion and design, the best of Spanish crafts and contemporary jewelry, and quantities of antiques in over 150 expensive shops. It's open Tuesday through Saturday from 11am to 9pm and Sunday and holidays from 11am to 2pm.

The major department stores are **El Corte Inglés** and **Galerias Preciados,** both of which have bargain basements (*Oportunidades*) in some of their stores. Branches of El Corte Inglés include Preciados 3, Goya 76, Princesa 42, and Raimundo Fernández Villaverde 79 (at the corner of Paseo de la Castellana). Galerias

Preciados is at Plaza del Callao 1, Goya 87, Ortega y Gasset 2 (at the corner of Serrano), and Madrid-2/La Vaguada. Stores in both chains have some English-speaking salespeople and offer information on VAT refunds, obtainable only on single purchases of more than 86,520 ptas. ($665.50). If you're leaving the country from Madrid airport, a refund can be obtained from the Banco Exterior de España (in the concourse on the other side of Passport Control) upon presentation of the store's signed form subsequently stamped by Spanish Customs.

El Corte Inglés, Galerias Preciados, and the larger shopping centers are open from 10am to 9pm; however, almost everything else closes for lunch at 1:30 or 2pm and doesn't reopen until 5pm. In July and August many stores close on Saturday afternoon, and smaller ones may even close completely for their month's vacation.

January to February and July are the times for the big **sales** (*rebajas*), when every store in Madrid offers tremendous discounts that increase as the month proceeds.

Bargains are no longer to be found in profusion at the famed **El Rastro flea market,** and you can forget about plucking an unsigned Goya drawing or a Roman coin out of the heaps of goods on display. It can be fun to browse, however, always keeping sharp control over purses and personal belongings. The market takes place in the streets of the triangle formed by San Isidro Cathedral, Puerto de Toledo, and Glorieta de Embajadores. Ribera de Curtidores is its main street. On Sunday mornings thousands of Madrileños throng these streets to purchase everything from songbirds to audiotapes to picture frames. Saturday morning is quieter and a better time for browsing through the antiques shops and secondhand stalls. Bargaining is expected.

8   Madrid After Dark

THE PERFORMING ARTS

Madrid's performing arts are undergoing a renaissance. At any time of the year, there's a diverse cultural calendar ranging from theater to contemporary dance to opera. And, there's the ever-popular *zarzuela,* a uniquely Spanish operetta. Theater tickets range from 700 to 2,500 ptas. ($5.40 to $19.25), and on certain days of the week (usually Wednesday, or Sunday's first performance) discounts of up to 50% are available. For details, check the weekly *Guía del Ocio* or the daily entertainment section of the newspaper *El País,* which also publishes a booklet of listings and reviews in its Friday editions. The listings are in Spanish, but they aren't too difficult to decipher. Performances are usually around 7:30pm and 10:30pm.

English-language theatrical productions do alight in Madrid from time to time, but they don't stay long. Visitors who don't understand Spanish are hardly deprived, however, not with the abundant performances of classical and modern dance, symphonies and chamber-music recitals, concerts by touring pop and rock stars, and opera and zarzuela, in which knowledge of the language isn't critical.

It's best to buy tickets at the theater since agencies charge a considerable markup. If the preferred performance is sold out, it may be possible to get tickets at the **Localidades Galicia,** at Plaza del Carmen 1 (☎ **1/531-27-32**), to the left of the Madrid Multicine. It's open Tuesday through Sunday from 10am to 1pm and 4:30 to 7:30pm (closed holidays). It also sells bullfight and soccer tickets.

THEATER, OPERA & ZARZUELA

La Latina, Plaza de la Cebada 2. (☎ 1/365-28-35), presents popular revues and musicals. Metro: Latina.

The privately run **Neuvo Apolo,** Plaza de Tirso de Molina 1 (☎ 1/429-52-38), shows mainly musicals and ballet, plus some *zarzuela*. Metro: Tirso de Molina. The popular **Teatro Calderon,** Atocha 18 (☎ 1/369-14-34), produces good revues, plus flamenco, folkloric, and singing festivals. Metro: Tirso de Molina.

The **Teatro de la Comedia,** Príncipe 14 (☎ 1/521-49-31), shows classic Spanish plays by such authors as García Lorca and Valle Inclán. Metro: Sevilla. Run by City Hall, the smallish **Teatro de la Villa de Madrid,** underneath Plaza de Colón, Jardines del Descubrimiento (☎ 1/575-60-80), puts on plays and concerts of all kinds and is the scene of much activity during the Fall Festival (Festival del Otoño). Metro: Colón.

Grand opera is showcased at the **Teatro Lirico Nacional la Zarzuela,** Jovellanos 4 (☎ 1/429-82-25), until its new home at the Teatro Real is finished, at a still-uncertain date. Until that time, the stage is shared with zarzuela and ballet. Metro: Banco de España or Sevilla.

Along with the Teatro María Guerrero (below), the **Teatro Español,** Príncipe 25 (☎ 1/429-62-97), is an official state theater and is subsidized as such. Classic plays and visiting theater companies are featured, as well as the winning play of the important annual Lope de Vega prize. Metro: Sevilla.

Named after the actress, the state-sponsored **Teatro María Guerrero,** Tamayo y Baus 4 (☎ 1/319-47-69), is also home to the classics. Metro: Banco de España.

CLASSICAL MUSIC

Three years ago the National Orchestra of Spain moved into new quarters at **Auditorio Nacional De Musica (National Auditorium of Music),** Príncipe de Vergara 146 (☎ 1/337-01-00), where 2,000 music lovers can enjoy the best of Spanish and international classical music in a functional modern setting of wood and marble with fantastic acoustics. There's also a smaller concert hall, seating 600. Take the metro to Cruz del Rayo. Recitals and chamber-music groups are often heard at **Fundación Juan March,** Castelló 77 (☎ 1/435-42-40), and **Circulo de Bellas Artes,** Marqués de Casa Riera 2.

FLAMENCO SHOWS

The clubs in which full-bore flamenco is performed are called *tablaos*. Although not the birthplace of the unique Andalucian meld of music and dance, Madrid's tablaos are fairly authentic, if expensive. For the best values, try the **Torres Bermejas,** Mesonero Romanos 11 (☎ 1/532-33-22); **Corral de la Morería,** Morería 17 (☎ 1/265-84-46); or **Café de Chinitas,** Torija 7 (☎ 1/248-51-35). Doors usually open at 9 or 9:30pm and the show starts at about 10:45pm and ends at 12:30am or even later. To save money, go after dinner, when the still-hefty admission charge at least includes one drink. The later performances are usually better anyway, after the tour groups leave and the performers are warmed up. These stages feature large troupes with several dancers, two or three guitarists, and one or two singers, all in costume.

For a more intimate, grittier experience, try **La Soleá,** Cava Baja 27 (☎ 1/265-33-08). The small smoke-filled bar usually has one or two guitarists and two or three singers who try to outdo one another at the hoarse, plaintive *cante hondo* far into the night. No costumes, no dancing, no admission charge.

FILMS

Recently released movies arrive quickly in Madrid. Check in the *Guía del Ocio* for what's on. Undubbed movies are labeled "V.O." (*versión original)* in the listings and on theater posters. Most of the foreign films are in English, with Spanish subtitles. They can usually be found at these theaters: **Alphaville** (four cinemas), Martín de los Héroes 14 (☎ **1/248-72-33**); **Bellas Artes,** Marqués de Casa Riera 2 (☎ **1/522-50-92**); **Bogart,** Cedaceros 7 (☎ **1/429-80-42**); **California,** Andrés Mellado 47 (☎ **1/244-00-58**); and **Renoir** (five cinemas), Martín de los Héroes 12 (☎ **1/559-57-60**).

For classic movies, film commentaries, and foreign films, **Filmoteca,** in the Cine Doré, Santa Isabel 3 (☎ **1/227-38-66**), is the place to go. Movies are generally shown in their original language. Tickets cost 200 ptas. ($1.55); a *bono* for 10 sessions is 1,525 ptas. ($11.75). There's a bar, restaurant, and library here, too.

BARS

ON & NEAR PLAZA DE SANTA ANA

The destination for a grand *tapeo,* Plaza de Santa Ana and the streets that join it are hip-to-hip with beer pubs and ancient taverns. While sherry (*fino*) is the classic tipple with *tapas,* red and white wines and beer are more evident. Ask for a *copa de tinto* or *blanco* for a small tumbler of the wine, or for a *caña* to get a short glass of about 6 ounces of draft beer.

Cervecería Alemana
Plaza de Santa Ana 6. ☎ **1/429-70-33.** Metro: Sol or Antón Martín.

As its name suggests, this was once a popular haunt of German residents; Hemingway liked it, too. It has been in business since 1904, and the bullfighting prints on wood-paneled walls, marble-top tables, and beamed ceiling provide a vintage atmosphere. Open Sunday, Monday, Wednesday, and Thursday from 9am to 12:30am and Friday and Saturday from 9am to 1:30am.

Cervecería Santa Ana
Plaza de Santa Ana 10. ☎ **1/429-43-56.** Metro: Sol or Antón Martín.

Two doors up from the Alemaña, a congenial crowd hangs out in this no-seat bar, which also serves good tapas. Many of the customers are students, not least because the beer is relatively cheap. Open Thursday through Tuesday from 10am to 1am.

La Fontana de Oro
Victoria s/n. ☎ **1/531-04-20.** Metro: Sol.

There's a persistent, if scattered, enthusiasm hereabouts for Irish brews and music, evidenced by this new and fairly persuasive replica of a Dublin pub. Small groups do Irish songs from the elevated stage, at times in Spanish, at others in English. Guinness Stout and hard cider are on tap, but not cheap. It's about midway between the Puerta del Sol and Plaza de Santa Ana, with plenty of better places to eat all around. Open daily from 9am to 5am.

Los Gabrieles
Echegaray 17. ☎ **1/429-62-61.** Metro: Sol or Sevilla.

Pop in here for a quick drink just to admire the extraordinary variety of heavily patterned ceramic tiles covering the walls of the century-old tavern. Open daily from noon to 2am.

Viva Madrid

Manuel Fernández González 7. ☎ **1/310-55-35.** Metro: Sol or Antón Martín.

Students and twentysomething singles have made this 1890 tavern a newly trendy meeting place. Both its facade and its interior are resplendent with intricately patterned tiles, and mythical creatures hold up carved ceiling. Light meals and tapas are served in the room behind the bar. Open daily from 5:30pm to 2:30am.

ALONG CALLE DE LAS HUERTAS

For maxed-out bar-hopping, Calle de las Huertas and its adjoining streets can't be exhausted in a month of Saturday nights. It starts a little bit east of Plaza Mayor but doesn't shift into high gear until Plaza del Angel, south of Plaza de Santa Ana, when it begins running downhill toward Paseo del Prado. Here are some favorites, starting from the top:

Casa Alberto

Huertas 18. ☎ **1/429-93-56.** Metro: Antón Martín.

Cervantes lived upstairs over 380 years ago, and this narrow bar has been in business for almost half that time. It has a stone bar and an elaborately carved wood ceiling. Alberto is popular with a mixed crowd that drops in for its *ambiente* and variety of tempting tapas. Open Tuesday through Saturday from 12:30 to 4pm and 8pm to 1am and Sunday from 1 to 4pm.

Cher's

Huertas 50. ☎ **1/429-83-32.** Metro: Antón Martín.

Both cocktail lounge and disco/bar, this place is named for whom you think. The crowd gets younger as the night wears on toward dawn, but the air of edgy sophistication remains . . . until they crank up the karaoke machine, as much a cliché in Madrid these days as anywhere on the Continent. Open daily from 7pm to 5:30am.

La Fidula

Huertas 57. ☎ **1/429-29-47.** Metro: Antón Martín.

With rock and Latino music roaring out of every other door on Huertas, this retreat makes its statement with recitals by classical performers Friday and Saturday nights from about midnight. The room is cozy even without music. Open daily from 6pm to 3am (until 4am on Friday and Saturday).

Huertas 41

Huertas 41. No phone. Metro: Antón Martín.

Loud. Young. Dancing. Quaffing. Steamy. Energetic. Fun. And with an easy-to-remember name. Open daily from 8pm to 4am.

Muñiz

Huertas 29. No phone. Metro: Antón Martín.

Just a saunter away, this tapas joint hasn't an ounce of Casa Alberto's charm, but its huge selection of well-prepared snacks and *raciones* more than compensates. Open Monday through Saturday from 10am to 1am.

Taberna de Dolores

Plaza de Jesús 4. ☎ **1/429-22-43.** Metro: Sevilla.

This tavern behind the Palace Hotel, a block north of Huertas, has decent if unremarkable tapas; it packs in the customers at least as much for its draft beers as for its food. The cheese or seafood canapés make a savory snack, and three or four of them are a satisfying meal. Open Sunday through Thursday from 11am to 1am and Friday and Saturday from 11am to 2am.

ALONG THE GRAN VÍA

Museo Chicote

Gran Vía 12. ☎ **1/532-67-37.** Metro: Sevilla.

They call this place a "museum" because it's been around since 1931 and is reputed to have been the first cocktail lounge in the city. Hemingway was a regular, which won't come as a surprise, and he met many of his glamourous chums here. The art deco is original, and some of the bartenders look as if they've been on duty almost as long. They can mix up anything you might imagine. The middle-aged clientele and their kids can also get sandwiches and tapas. Open daily from 1pm to 2am.

PLAZA DE SANTA BÁRBARA & SOUTH

✪ Bocaito

Libertad 6. ☎ **1/532-12-19.** Metro: Banco or Chueca.

Consensus points to this as the best tapas bar in town, and although there certainly are other contenders, that opinion has considerable merit. Two doors open onto two sides of the bar, which contains a center counter where two men busily assemble salads and *verbenas* (platters of smoked fish) to order. The black ceiling beams are hung with ceramic plates and copper pots. There are no chairs in the bar area, but a sit-down meal can be had in the back room. Open Monday through Saturday for lunch from 1:30 to 5pm and for dinner from 8:30pm to midnight.

Cervecería Internacional

Regueros 8. ☎ **1/419-48-68.** Metro: Chueca.

The strongest beer in the country is served here, it's alleged, and there's unquestionably a selection from all over the world. There's a beer shop too, plus a restaurant. Open daily from noon to 12:30am.

Cervecería Santa Bárbara

Plaza de Santa Bárbara 8. ☎ **1/319-04-49.** Metro: Alonso Martinez.

The exceptionally long bar here props up the elbows of a demographically diverse crowd of chattering Madrileños. A marble floor, crimson walls with wrought-iron screens, and friendly waiters add to the agreeable atmosphere. This place is also known for its seafood, invariably expensive. Stick to the beer. Open daily from 11am to 11pm.

Santa Bárbara Pub

Fernando VI 3. ☎ **1/319-08-44.** Metro: Alonso Martinez or Chueca.

Around the corner from its cousin, the Cervecería Santa Bárbara, and across from the art nouveau headquarters of the Spanish Society of Authors is what is billed as Madrid's first English pub. You won't find warm beer, but there are authentic touches of Blighty in the central bar and low, round tables. Open Sunday through Thursday from noon to 2am and Friday and Saturday from noon to 3am.

JAZZ BARS

Café Central

Plaza del Angel 10. ☎ **1/369-41-43.** Cover usually about 900 ptas. ($6.90) Mon–Thurs, 1,100 ptas. ($8.45) Fri–Sun. Metro: Sol or Antón Martín.

This is the place for live jazz in Madrid, and as a result it's usually packed with a mix of students, tourists, and Madrid's night beauties. Black bench seating, marble-top tables, and glistening brass set the scene. Performances are from 11pm to 12:30am. While jazz is the main course, the café frequently hosts folkies, blues belters, and performers of related music. Calle de las Huertas runs through this plaza, so the café can be the start or end of an extended pub-crawl. Open daily from 1pm to 2 or 3am.

Café Jazz Populart

Huertas 22. ☎ **1/429-84-07.** Cover sometimes charged. Metro: Antón Martín.

Not far from the Café Central (above), this is a showcase for American blues, Latin salsa, and Caribbean reggae as well as the many shadings of jazz. The large room allows a little individual elbow room and the tone is laid back, at the marble-top bar or the tables ringing the stage. One sour note is the caricature of a blackface minstrel the club uses as a logo. Sometimes there's a cover, sometimes not. In any event, an hour or two here is nearly always cheaper than at the better-known Café Central. Open daily from 6pm to 2 or 3am.

Clamores

Albuquerque 14. ☎ **1/445-79-38.** Cover 525 ptas. ($4.05). Metro: Bilbao or Quevelo.

This is one of the more popular jazz spots, particularly on Monday, when there's dancing. As at many of the clubs featuring jazz, it sometimes strays into other areas. It's also a *xampanyería,* with a great variety of imported champagnes and Spanish *cavas* (sparkling wines). Open daily from 3pm to 3am; live jazz shows are nightly at 11:45pm and 1:15am.

MESONES

On Cava de San Miguel, just west of Plaza Mayor, are several little bars of the type known as *mesones*, each specializing in something different. **La Guitarra** features guitar playing, and its ceiling is covered with sangría jugs, which are for sale. **La Tortilla** has tortillas and beer for two for about 1,000 ptas. ($7.70). The accordionist here asks where patrons are from and plays a song to suit. (He won't refuse a small tip.) There's the **Queso Mesón** for cheese and the **Mesón de Champiñón,** where a plate of plump mushrooms grilled in oil and garlic costs about 575 ptas. ($4.40). The best time to go is Thursday through Saturday between 10pm and 1am.

SUMMER *TERRAZAS*

As the nights become warm in Madrid, outdoor bars spring up. Known as ✪ *Las Terrazas*, the most popular (and expensive) are those along **Paseo de la Castellana** between Cibeles and Emilio Castelar, sometimes referred to as "Madrid's Beach." Among these are El Espejo and Café Gijón (above). The busiest time is late at night, and on Friday and Saturday it can be difficult to move down the sidewalk even at 2am. Sound systems are cranked up to drown out the traffic, a cumulative noise level that doesn't keep the throngs of pretty people from shouting as seductively as possible at each other. For quieter bars frequented by those over 30, head to **Paseo Pintor Rosales** overlooking the Parque del Oeste.

DISCOS

Madrid's most popular discos tend to operate with a selective entrance policy, so dress stylishly and try to look as young, gorgeous, celebrated, and/or rich as possible. Admission charges, usually including one drink, can sail past 2,000 ptas. ($15.40), and even a soft drink inside can cost over 1,000 ptas. ($7.70). They're usually open daily until 4 or 5am, and nothing much happens before 2am. Conversely—or perversely—it's easier to get past the unsmiling gents at the door when arriving before then.

Some discos have a "matinee" period, usually from 7 to 9 or 10pm, attended primarily by teenagers. After closing for an hour or two, they reopen to older patrons.

Archy

Marqués del Riscal 11. ☎ **1/308-21-62.** Cover 2,000 ptas. ($12.50). Metro: Ruben Dario.

In the basement of an old apartment building, the art deco Archy has a restaurant and pub. Hyper-hip when it opened a few years ago, it's settled into a less frantic yet still upper-crusty mode. Several rooms are set aside for drinking; don't show up before midnight in the dining room, and the dance floor is downstairs. Open Monday through Wednesday from 10pm to 4am and Friday and Saturday from 10pm to 5am.

Joy Eslava

Arenal 11. ☎ **1/366-37-33.** Cover 1,500 ptas. ($11.55). Metro: Sol or Opera.

One of those palatial 1930s movie houses was transformed into this popular venue years ago. (Madrid's discos have far longer survival periods than those in the United States.) They tore out the orchestra seats to make room for three bars and a dance floor, but kept the box seats and stage. Laser shows, videos, and a variety of energetic performers keep things moving. The best nights are Friday and Saturday, and because this place is in its postchic phase, it isn't difficult to get past the velvet rope. Matinees are held on Friday and Saturday. Open Monday through Friday from 11:30pm to 5am and Friday through Sunday from 7pm to 6am.

Pacha

Barceló 11. ☎ **1/446-01-37.** Cover 1,500 ptas. ($11.55). Metro: Tribunal.

Another recycled movie palace, this was once the hottest disco in Madrid. It still draws faithful regulars, tourists, and nightbirds who make it one of their several nightly stops. A rectangular bar occupies a space in the old orchestra pit next to the dance floor. A light show complements the music mixed by the DJ in his corner booth. There are "afternoon" sessions on Friday and Saturday. Open Tuesday through Thursday from midnight to 5am, Friday and Saturday from 7pm to 3am, and Sunday from 9pm to 3am.

Palacio de Gaviria

Arenal 9. ☎ **1/526-60-69.** Cover 1,000 ptas. ($7.70). Metro: Sol.

This vintage mansion near the Puerta del Sol has been converted into a *multispacio* with several salons, each serving up expensive drinks and live or recorded music for dancing, from salsa to disco. Sip slowly, since a single cocktail can cost 1,600 ptas. ($12.30) or more. Open daily from 8pm to 3am (until midnight on Sunday).

Teatriz

Hermosilla 15. ☎ **1/577-53-79.** Cover 2,000 ptas. ($12.50). Metro: Serrano or Velázquez.

Those who keep abreast of international design trends should be suitably impressed that this restaurant/cocktail lounge/disco was put together by France's Philippe Starck. It is designed within a inch of its life—even the books on the shelves are bolted into seemingly casual position. Save this for a splurge into the rarefied reaches of Madrid's pulsating nightlife, since a drink or two here would pay for a three-course meal at most of the recommended budget restaurants.

9 Networks & Resources

STUDENTS
THE UNIVERSITIES

There are three universities in and around Madrid—**Complutense, Autonoma,** and one of the oldest universities in the country, **Alcalá de Henares,** 12 miles east of the city. **Complutense,** the largest, is in the northwest corner of Madrid, its many faculties sprawled over several miles of University City. Courses for foreigners are held year round at the Faculty of Philology (Facultad de Filología) in Building A of the Faculty of Philosophy and Letters. The bar in the basement is a great meeting place and one of the most popular on campus. Cheap breakfasts are also available, and the menu del día is 700 ptas. ($5.40). Check the notice board for offers of low-cost lodgings. During May and June the Colegios Mayores (dorms) sometimes have information concerning vacancies in the Cursos para Extranjeros (Courses for Foreigners).

For general information, go to the **Centro de Información Juvenil de la Comunidad de Madrid,** at Caballero de Grácia 32 (☎ **1/580-42-42**), open Monday through Friday from 9am to 2pm and 5 to 8pm. Although the center is directed to the youth of Madrid and the staff's English is limited, they're extremely helpful and will provide computer printouts on just about any topic, from the cheapest hotels and restaurants to friendly bars and discos.

STUDENT HANGOUTS

The branches of the **Bob's** and **Vips** chains are both extremely popular with students (see "Dining," earlier in this chapter, for locations and details). These are also in favor:

Café de Ruíz

Ruíz 11. ☎ **1/446-12-32.** Metro: Bilbao or Tribunal.

For chocolate lovers, tea connoisseurs, or pastry freaks, this is a good place to meet people or catch up on the international press. The crowd changes frequently during the course of the day. Open daily from 2:30pm to 3:30am.

La Chocolateria de San Ginés

Pasadizo de San Ginés 5. No phone. Metro: Sol.

Another must for the chocoholic, this place has been in business since 1894. Drop in for hot chocolate and churros for an early breakfast after a night of partying (it's squeezed between the Joy Eslava disco and the Iglesia de San Ginés). It opens at 4am, when day laborers and night people mingle in the line that forms at the front door. Open Wednesday and Friday through Sunday from 7 to 10pm and 1 to 8am and Tuesday and Thursday from 1 to 8am.

GAY MEN & LESBIANS

In the area known as Chueca (between Calle Hortaleza and Calle Barquillo), several establishments attracting gay men and a smaller number appealing to lesbians have sprung up in recent years. **Librería El Galeón,** Calle Sagasta 4

(☎ 1/445-57-38), is a gay bookstore open Monday through Friday from 9:30am to 1:30pm. **Figueroa,** Augusto Figueroa 17 (☎ **1/521-16-73**), is popular. A couple of blocks away at Libertad 34 is **Blanco y Negro** (☎ **1/231-11-41**). Calle Pelayo is a primary center of gay nightlife, while parallel Calle Hortaleza is a secondary possibility.

WOMEN

Women travelers with a problem or who need information can try the **Instituto de la Mujer** (Woman's Institute) and **Asociación de Mujeres Jóvenes** (Association of Young Women), both located at Almagro 36 (☎ **1/319-68-46**). **Librería de Mujeres,** Calle San Cristóbal (☎ **1/521-70-43**), is a women's center/feminist bookshop near Plaza Mayor.

10 Easy Excursions

SEGOVIA   At any time of year, a trip northwest to Segovia along Routes N1 and C604 leads you through an increasingly dramatic countryside of pine-covered foothills of the Sierra de Guadarrama. Near Rascafría is the 14th-century Monasterio del Paular, part of which is now a hotel. The other part is still a functional Dominican monastery, where tours are permitted.

Turning north, continue over the mountain pass called Puerto de Navacerrada—whose name reveals that it's sometimes closed by snow—and down unto a dusty plain ranked with vineyards and olive groves. Shortly the road reaches **San Ildefonso,** also known as La Granja, the palace built for Felípe V. Its baroque interior and extensive gardens with 26 fountains may be visited.

Segovia is only another 7 miles farther. The town perches on a rocky outcrop, its tawny buildings burnished by the sun. Its landmark structures, pictured often in tourism literature, are the 10-mile-long two-tiered **aqueduct,** built on orders of the Roman emperor Augustus, and the 14th-century fortress called the **Alcázar,** which bears a marked Germanic aspect. The aqueduct, reaching a maximum height of over 27 feet and built without mortar in the late 1st or early 2nd century A.D., is still intact and operational. Most of the fortress (except the towers), on the other hand, is a late 19th-century reconstruction undertaken after a destructive fire. In town are a number of important yet ill-preserved romanesque churches set along the winding streets, plus houses with Mudéjar and hexagonal designs.

If you're on a day trip from the capital, the most begiling spot for a long lunch is the **Mesón de Cándido,** standing in the shadow of the aqueduct on Plaza Azoguejo (☎ **11/428-103**). Parts of it date to 1760, and the walls of its several rooms are encrusted with mementos of those many years of existence. Specialties are Castilian roast pork, lamb, and game.

While a car is desirable for stopping at other sites along the way to Segovia, it isn't essential. The town lies 54 miles north of Madrid and can be reached by train from the Atocha, Chamartín, Recoletos, and Nuevos Ministerios stations. Trains for the two-hour trip cost 1,100 ptas. ($8.45) round-trip. Buses, nearly always faster on middle distances in Spain, depart daily from Empresa La Sepulvedana, Paseo de la Florida 11 (☎ **1/547-52-61** for information). The trip takes 1¹/₂ hours and costs 1,150 ptas. ($8.85).

✪ ARANJUEZ   On the banks of the Río Tajo (Tagus), Aranjuez is a little closer to Madrid, only 29 miles south. The principal reason to make the excursion is the baroque **Royal Palace.** Expanded from a much smaller 14th-century edifice, it was a summer retreat of the Bourbons in the late 18th century, and the leisurely lifestyle shows in the surrounding formal gardens, parklands with stands of majestic elms, and the palace itself. Damaged frequently over the centuries by war and natural disaster, the rambling residence was repeatedly restored, and the existing structure dates primarily from a reconstruction completed in 1752. While it isn't up to the standards of its glory years, by all accounts, there's still much of interest. Of special note is the Porcelain Room or *Cabinet,* its walls and ceilings covered in meticulously painted porcelain made in the factory of Buen Retiro.

Out on the grounds, past numerous ornamental fountains, is the royal hideaway called the **Casa del Labrador** (Laborer's House), erected in 1805 at the behest of Carlos IV. No humble cottage, it's intended to echo the Petit Trianon at Versailles, as lavishly furnished in silks, marble, fine woods, statuary, and porcelains as the main palace.

The town of Aranjuez itself doesn't reward lingering. Even though the surrounding farms are noted for their harvests of prized strawberries and asparagus, no local restaurant really does them justice. If you're traveling by car, eating might best be held off for **Chinchón,** a short detour off the main NIV road to and from Madrid. Two gothic castles and one of Spain's most distinctive main plazas are reason enough to stop off. The houses enclosing the roughly circular plaza have two and three floors of balconies from which citizens have watched bullfights and other celebrations for centuries. Dining possibilities include tapas at any of the several taverns stationed around the plaza or the restaurant of the nearby *parador,* one of a commendable state-owned chain of inns. A particular favorite, though, with enough atmosphere to satisfy the deepest romantic, is the **Mesón Cuevas del Vino,** at Benito Hortelano 13 (☎ 1/894-02-06). Housed in a former olive oil mill and wine cellar, it turns out traditional regional meals of roast pork and lamb. For a *digestif,* try the anis liqueur made in the town and named after it.

Those who wish to avoid the expense and bother of a rental car will find that there are trains about every 30 minutes from Atocha Station that take 45 minutes to Aranjuez and cost 315 ptas. ($2.40) one way. Buses from the Sur Bus Station, Canarias 17 (☎ 1/468-42-00), cost 775 ptas. ($5.95). Something different is the "strawberry train" to Aranjuez that leaves Atocha Station every Saturday and Sunday morning in summer and returns in the evening. Tickets cost 2,200 ptas. ($16.90) for adults or 1,350 ptas. ($10.40) for children 11 and under, and include a visit to the Prince's House, strawberries, and a drink. Call 1/563-02-02 daily from 7am to 11:30pm for full details.

✪ **TOLEDO**   The capital of Visigothic Spain bristles with steeples and towers over the pate of an unlikely hill moated by the Río Tajo. Those familiar with the painting of the city by El Greco, who lived most of his creative life here, will be struck by how closely his 16th-century painting, *View of Toledo,* conforms to the present, in overall impression if not in detail. Toledo is an easy day trip from Madrid, which means it's clogged with tour buses and their human cargoes every day of the year. If possible, stay overnight to get a less-trammeled picture of the city when it's briefly returned to its permanent residents. Otherwise, try to leave Madrid early to avoid the worst of the crush, and wear comfortable shoes to tackle the steep cobblestone streets and alleys. The massive craggy foundation of the city dips and rises over several hills.

Once you're there, the logical first stop is the **cathedral.** Considered one of the most glorious examples of Spanish gothic architecture, most of it was built between the 13th and 15th centuries. Like many Spanish cathedrals, it's nearly enclosed by the town, the surrounding houses snuggling up to and around the bases of its flying buttresses. Surmounted by a 300-foot tower, it has five naves and dozens of side chapels. Highlights are the choir and the richly carved altarpiece. In the Sacristy are paintings by El Greco, Rubens, and Titian, a collection extraordinary not only for its artistry but also for the fact that it hasn't been spirited away to a museum. The cathedral is open Monday through Saturday from 10:30am to 1pm and 3:30 to 6pm, and Sunday from 10:30am to 1:30pm and 4 to 7pm (until 6pm in winter); the last tour is at 12:30pm. Tickets for the cathedral treasury cost 350 ptas. ($2.70).

Next, stop at the **Church of St. Thomas (Santo Tomé)** to see El Greco's famous painting *The Burial of the Count Orgaz*; tickets cost 130 ptas. ($1). Afterward, go on to **Casa y Museo del Greco,** an intriguing example of a 16th-century Toledan house containing a small collection of the artist's paintings, including a view of the city. Queen Isabel had a hand in the building that houses the **Santa Cruz Museum,** which has an impressive Plateresque facade. The paintings within are mostly of the 16th and 17th century, with yet another score by El Greco. It's open Monday from 10am to 2pm and 4:30 to 6:20pm, Tuesday through Saturday from 10am to 6:30pm, and Sunday from 10am to 2pm. Tickets cost 250 ptas. ($1.90).

The **Alcázar** (same hours as above) occupies the highest elevation of the city. Damaged frequently over its centuries as a fortress and royal residence, it was leveled during a Civil War siege. The existing structure is essentially a replica but is built over the old cellars and foundations. Tickets for the Alcázar cost 150 ptas. ($1.15) and it's open Tuesday through Saturday from 9:30am to 1:30pm and 4 to 6:30pm (until 5:30 in winter).

Closer to its original 14th-century state is the **Synagoga del Trásito,** one of Toledo's two surviving synagogues. Past the unassuming exterior are some fine examples of Mudéjar craftsmanship (note the *artesando* ceiling) and a small but compelling museum of Jewish relics and artifacts.

With time and transportation, a most worthwhile outing carries across the Río Tajo to the parador standing on a promontory opposite the city. From its terrace, an unobstructed view of Toledo recalls El Greco's memorable rendition. While meals in the first-class dining room of the parador are well above the budget level, they justify a splurge. Alternatively, a sandwich and a beer can be had in the bar.

Toledo can be reached by train from Atocha Station or by bus from Calle Canarias Sur bus station. The one-way trip is well under two hours by any method of transportation. For further information, call the Toledo Tourist Office (☎ **25/22-08-43**), open Monday through Friday from 9am to 2pm and 4 to 6pm, Saturday from 9am to 7pm, and Sunday from 9am to 3pm. The round-trip train fare is 1,890 ptas. ($14.55).

EL ESCORIAL Felípe II commissioned Juan Bautista de Toledo and his assistant, Juan de Herrera, to build his gloomy Xanadu on this hillside in the Sierra de Guadarrama 34 miles northwest of Madrid. Its purported intent was to commemorate an important victory over the French in Flanders, but the likely real reason was that the ascetic Felípe was increasingly unnerved by the stress of overseeing an empire that bridged four continents. This retreat insulated him from the pressures and intrigues of the Madrid Court. He ruled the troubled empire from his largely unadorned cells here the last 14 years of his life.

The squared-off monastery/palace is typically praised for its massive, brooding simplicity. That impression is allayed inside, where its considerable size and wealth of accoutrements can be appreciated. The extraordinary library reflects the scholarly king's all-embracing intellectual interests, with tens of thousands of volumes and rare manuscripts in many languages and representative of the three primary religions that had existed in Spain. Also within the building is a sizable church with a large frescoed dome, beneath which is a royal pantheon with sarcophagi containing the remains of most of Spain's monarchs since Carlos V. Museums and royal apartments contain canvases by El Greco, Titian, Ribera, Tintoretto, Rubens, and Velázquez, among many.

An all-inclusive ticket is 800 ptas. ($6.15). The monastery is open Tuesday through Sunday and holidays from 10am to 6pm (5pm in winter). The tourist office at El Escorial can be reached at 91/890-59-05.

A pleasant town has grown up around the monastery/palace. Its full name is San Lorenzo de El Escorial and not nearly as touristy as might be expected, given its proximity to Madrid. Avoiding weekends is a good idea, however. There are a number of appealing bars and cafés, some with outside tables, at which to have a snack or sandwich. For a complete meal, a popular moderately priced inn is the 18th-century **La Cueva,** at Calle San Antón 4 (☎ **91/890-15-16**). With care in selection, the cost can be kept at near-budget level.

Trains for El Escorial leave frequently from Atocha, Chamartín, Recoletos, and Nuevos Ministerios stations. They take one hour and cost 735 ptas. ($5.65) round-trip. Buses leave from Empresa Herranz, Isaac Peral 10, Moncloa (☎ **1/543-36-45**), and cost 700 ptas. ($5.40) round-trip.

Munich 18

by Beth Reiber

Named after the *Munichen*, monks who settled more than 1,200 years ago on the banks of the Isar River, Munich is the capital of the state (or Land) of Bavaria and a sprawling city of almost 1.3 million. Home of such industrial giants as BMW and Siemens, Munich is also an important cultural capital of Germany, with four symphony orchestras, two opera houses, dozens of world-class museums, more than 20 theaters, and one of Germany's largest universities. Its diverse student population ensures an active avant-garde cultural scene and a liberal attitude in an otherwise largely conservative region.

Munich is a striking city, largely the product of the exuberant imagination and aspirations of past Bavarian kings and rulers. Royal residences, majestic museums, steepled churches, and ornate monuments celebrate architectural styles from baroque and gothic to neoclassical and postmodern. Add to that wide boulevards, spacious parks, a thriving nightlife, and at least six breweries and you have what amounts to one of Germany's most interesting, exciting, and festive cities.

1 Munich Deals & Discounts

BUDGET BESTS   You can save money by standing up in Munich, whether it's eating or visiting the theater. Eat lunch at an *Imbiss,* a food stall or tiny store selling everything from German sausages and grilled chicken to pizza. Concentrated primarily in Old Town, most even sell beer to wash it all down. If you'd rather sit for a meal, you can often save money by ordering from the *Tageskarte* (changing daily menu) for platters that include both the main course and side dishes. Even better, pack a meal and take it to one of Munich's many beer gardens, where all you'll have to buy is beer. Some beer gardens even offer free concerts.

Standing up is also the cheapest way to see performances of the National Theater and Staatstheater, with tickets costing less than $5.50. And as for Munich's wonderful museums, some are free all day Sunday and public holidays, including the Alte Pinakothek, Neue Pinakothek, Glyptothek, Antikensammlungen, and Bavarian National Museum.

SPECIAL DISCOUNTS   If you're an avid museum fan, consider spending 20 DM ($13.35) for a **museum pass,** good for all 23

What's Special About Munich

Architectural Highlights
- Schloss Nymphenburg, Germany's largest baroque palace.
- The Cuvilliés Theater, the finest rococo tier-boxed theater in Germany.
- The Alte Pinakothek and the Glyptothek, both built in the 19th century by Leo von Klenze, one of Munich's important architects.
- The Residenz, the royal residence of the Wittelsbach family.

Museums
- About 50 museums, galleries, and collections, making Munich one of Germany's most important cultural centers.
- The Alte Pinakothek, one of Europe's most important collections of the old masters.
- The Deutsches Museum, the largest technological museum in the world, where visitors could spend a lifetime.

The Beer Capital of the World
- Six major breweries, in a town of only 1.3 million people.
- Oktoberfest, the world's largest beer festival.
- Beer halls, including the 400-year-old Hofbräuhaus, for a brew and hearty Bavarian meals.
- More than 35 beer gardens.

state-owned museums and valid for eight days. And if you plan on doing a lot of traveling back and forth on Munich's excellent subways, buses, and trams, you can save money by purchasing a **one-day transportation pass** for 10 DM ($6.65), outlined in more detail below.

For Students   If you're a student, your ticket to lower prices is the **International Student ID Card (ISIC)**. With it you can realize substantial savings on museum admission fees, with a deduction of 50% or more off the regular price. In addition, both the opera and the theater offer student discounts for unsold seats on the night of performance—show up about an hour before the performance to see what's available. Make sure to bring your card on your trip, as it's next to impossible to secure one in Germany.

If you need assistance with travel plans, such as securing reduced-price train or plane tickets or a youth-hostel card, a travel agency that deals with student and youth travel is **Studiosus Urlaubscenter,** Amalienstrasse 73 (☎ **089/605 40**); it's in the university district, Schwabing, and is open Monday through Friday from 9:30am to 6pm.

For Seniors   If you're a senior citizen (at least 65 years old), you're entitled to a **50% discount at most museums** in Munich.

2 Pretrip Preparations

REQUIRED DOCUMENTS   The only document needed for citizens of the United States, Canada, Australia, and New Zealand is a valid passport, which allows stays up to three months. Visitors from the United Kingdom need only an identity card.

Students should be sure to bring an International Student ID Card (ISIC) as well.

TIMING YOUR TRIP   Summers can be glorious in Bavaria, and the main tourist season stretches from about April to mid-October. Winters tend to be mild, though snow can fall on the stalls of Munich's outdoor Christmas market.

Munich's Average Daytime Temperature & Rainfall

	Jan	Feb	Mar	Apr	May	June	July	Aug	Sept	Oct	Nov	Dec
Temp.(°F)	33	35	40	50	60	65	70	73	65	50	39	33
Days of Rain	19	16	19	19	21	24	18	17	18	15	17	18

Special Events   Munich's most famous festival is its **Oktoberfest**—actually held in September, from the middle of the month to the first Sunday in October. Although it's certainly worth experiencing at least once, it's also the busiest time of year for Munich. Hotels are full, with rooms often going for about 10% to 20% more than the usual rate, so be sure to reserve far in advance.

Other annual events in Munich include its **Christkindlmarkt,** an outdoor Christmas market held on Marienplatz from the end of November to Christmas Eve; and **Fasching,** Germany's version of Carnival, with elaborate costume balls. Celebrated from January 7 to Shrove Tuesday, Fasching reaches its frenzied peak on Fasching Sunday and Shrove Tuesday, with special events staged at the Viktualienmarkt and Munich's pedestrian-zoned inner city. These two winter

What Things Cost in Munich	U.S. $
Taxi from the airport to Munich's main train station	60.00
U-Bahn from the main train station to Schwabing	2.15
Local telephone call	.20
Double room at the Vier Jahreszeiten Kempinski (deluxe)	310.00
Double room at the Hotel Uhland (moderate)	96.65
Double room at the Pension am Kaiserplatz (budget)	50.00
Lunch for one at Nürnberg Bratwurst Glöckl (moderate)	10.00
Lunch for one at Donisl (budget)	8.00
Dinner for one, without wine, at Aubergine (deluxe)	95.00
Dinner for one, without wine, at Hundskugel (moderate)	26.00
Dinner for one, without wine, at Bella Italia (budget)	9.00
Liter of beer	6.65
Glass of wine	2.35
Coca-Cola in a restaurant	1.75
Cup of coffee	1.60
Roll of ASA 100 color film, 36 exposures	4.00
Admission to the Museum Neue Pinakothek	4.00
Movie ticket	7.35
Ticket to the Nationaltheater (standing room)	5.35

events don't draw nearly the crowds the Oktoberfest does, which means that you should have no trouble finding a hotel room.

BACKGROUND READING   For a pictorial essay on Munich and general background information, pick up a copy of *Munich,* in "The Great Cities" series by George Bailey (Time-Life, 1980). If you're interested in learning more about Bavaria's most famous king, read Wilfrid Blunt's *The Dream King: Ludwig II of Bavaria* (Penguin, 1978).

3 Munich Specifics

ARRIVING

FROM THE AIRPORT   Germany's own Lufthansa provides the largest number of flights to Munich's recently opened **Franz Josef Strauss Airport,** about 17 miles northeast of Munich in Erding. After stopping by the tourist information counter to pick up a map and brochures, proceed to the Flughafen München S-Bahn station, where you can board the S-8, bound for Marienplatz (the center of the city), or the Hauptbahnhof (main train station). Trains leave every 20 minutes, and the trip to the Hauptbahnhof takes about 40 minutes.

Cost of an ordinary ticket is 12.80 DM ($8.55), though if you have a Eurailpass you can the S-Bahn for free. If you don't have a Eurailpass, you can save money by buying a *Streifenkarte* (literally, "strip ticket"), which allows 12 short journeys or 6 longer ones for a cost of 15 DM ($10). Note that the trip from the airport is such a long one that it takes up eight strips on the ticket (fold the ticket to the number 8 slot and then insert it into the ticket machine at the entrance to the station). In any case, the trip into town using the Streifenkarte costs 10 DM ($6.65) compared to the 12.80 DM ($8.55) charged for the ordinary one-way ticket described above. A taxi is prohibitive, costing as much as 90 to 95 DM ($60 to $63.35) one way.

FROM THE TRAIN STATION   If you come by train, you'll arrive at the **Hauptbahnhof,** Munich's main train station, near the center of town; it serves as a nucleus for the city's many tram, U-Bahn (underground subway), and S-Bahn (metropolitan railway) lines. In the train station itself you'll find a tourist information office, a post office, and an information office for obtaining train schedules and making train reservations for travel onward in Europe.

VISITOR INFORMATION

Munich's **main city tourist office, Fremdenverkehrsamt** (☎ **089/23 911**), is in the Hauptbahnhof at its south exit onto Bayerstrasse. Open Monday through Saturday from 8am to 10pm and Sunday from 11am to 7pm, it distributes free maps of the city. For a fee of 5 DM ($3.35) the tourist office here and at the airport will also find a hotel room for you, a valuable service if the accommodations listed in this book happen to be full (otherwise, save yourself the 5 DM by booking directly with the hotel). Another tourist office is at Munich's airport, open Monday through Saturday from 8:30am to 10pm and Sunday from 1 to 9pm. For **recorded information in English,** call 23 91 62 for open hours of museums and 23 91 72 for information on other attractions.

If you want to know what's going on in Munich, pick up a copy of the **Monatsprogramm,** available at the tourist office. Costing 2.50 DM ($1.65), it tells you what's being performed when in Munich's theaters and opera houses and how

The German Mark

For American Readers   At this writing $1 = approximately 1.50 DM (or 1 DM = 67¢), and this was the rate of exchange used to calculate the dollar values given in this chapter (rounded to the nearest nickel).

For British Readers   At this writing £1 = approximately 2.30 DM (or 1 DM = 43p), and this was the rate of exchange used to calculate the pound values in the table below.

Note: The rates given here fluctuate from time to time and may not be the same when you travel to Germany. Therefore this table should be used only as a guide:

DM	U.S.$	U.K.£	DM	U.S.$	U.K.£
.25	.17	.11	20	13.33	8.70
.50	.33	.22	25	16.67	10.8
.75	.50	.33	30	20.00	13.0
1	.67	.43	35	23.33	15.22
2	1.33	.87	40	26.67	17.3
3	2.00	1.30	45	30.00	19.5
4	2.67	1.74	50	33.33	21.74
5	3.33	2.17	60	40.00	26.09
6	4.00	2.61	70	46.67	30.43
7	4.67	3.04	80	53.33	34.78
8	5.33	3.48	90	60.00	39.13
9	6.00	3.91	100	66.67	43.48
10	6.67	4.35	125	83.33	53.35
15	10.00	6.52	150	100.00	65.22

to obtain tickets. In addition, it also lists concerts, both modern and classical, museum hours, and special exhibitions. Although much of the information contained in this pocket-size booklet is in German only, those who don't understand German will also find it useful.

Another good source of information is *Munich Found,* an English-language city magazine published 10 times a year and available at newsstands for 4 DM ($2.65). In addition to articles of local interest, including special exhibitions and events, it contains a calendar for classical music, opera, ballet, theater, rock concerts, and other nightlife activities throughout the period of each issue. The only problem is finding a copy of this valuable magazine—it sells out fast.

CITY LAYOUT

The heart of Old Munich lies directly east of the Hauptbahnhof. Its very center is **Marienplatz,** a cobblestone plaza only a 15-minute walk from the train station and connected to the rest of the city by an extensive subway network. Throughout the centuries it served as a market square, a stage for knightly tournaments, and the site of public executions. Today it's no less important, bordered on one side by the impressive New Town Hall.

Much of the city center is a **pedestrian zone,** and it's here that you'll find Munich's smartest boutiques, most traditional restaurants, oldest churches, and outdoor market, the Viktualienmarkt. Most of Munich's museums are located within an easy walk or short subway ride from the city center.

Schwabing, north of the city center and easily reached by U-Bahn, is home to both Munich's university and its nightlife. Its bohemian heyday was back at the turn of the century, when it served as a mecca for Germany's most talented young artists and writers, including Wassily Kandinsky, Paul Klee, Thomas Mann, and Rainer Maria Rilke. Today Schwabing is known for its sidewalk cafés, fashionable bars, and discos, most found on Leopoldstrasse and Occamstrasse. Although tourist brochures like to call Schwabing "the Greenwich Village of Munich," most of the people milling about here are visitors and tourists, including lots of young people from outlying villages in for a night on the town.

As for other areas worth exploring, the **Englischer Garten** with its wide green expanses and beer gardens stretches northeast from the city center. Munich's Oktoberfest is held at **Theresienwiese,** just south of the Hauptbahnhof, while the **Olympiapark,** home of the 1972 Olympics, is on the northern edge of town. **Schloss Nymphenburg,** the royal family's summer residence, lies to the northwest of town, accessible by subway and then streetcar.

GETTING AROUND

Munich's public transportation system is efficient and convenient, one of the best in the world. But even though it's a large city, many of its major attractions are within walking distance of Marienplatz.

BY SUBWAY   Munich's wonderful underground network, which was created in conjunction with the 1972 Olympics, is the ultimate in German efficiency. I've seldom waited more than a few minutes for a train. What's more, Munich's subway stations have something I wish every city in the world would adopt—maps of the surrounding streets. You never have to emerge from a subway station wondering where you are.

Munich's subway system is divided into the **U-Bahn** (underground subway) and **S-Bahn** (metropolitan railway). Because the S-Bahn is part of the German Federal Railroad, you can use your Eurailpass on these lines. Otherwise purchase a ticket and validate it yourself by inserting it into one of the little machines at the entrance to the track. It's all on the honor system—that is, there's no ticket collector to make sure you have a ticket. However, there are frequent spot checks by undercover controllers—if you're caught without a ticket you'll pay a stiff fine. Munich's public transportation system operates from about 5am to 1am.

One of the best things about Munich's system is that you can make as many free transfers between subways, buses, and trams (streetcars) as you need to reach your destination. A **single journey** to most destinations in Munich costs 3.20 DM ($2.15). Shorter journeys—trips of at most only two stops on the subways or four stops on the tram or bus—cost only 1.60 DM ($1.05). A short journey, for example, is the stretch from the Hauptbahnhof to Marienplatz; a regular journey requiring the 3.20-DM ticket would be from the Hauptbahnhof to Universität.

Much more economical than the single-journey tickets is the *Streifenkarte* (also called a *Mehrfahrtkarte*), a strip-ticket allowing for multiple journeys. These are available for 15 DM ($10) and consist of 12 strips worth 1.25 DM (85¢) each. For short journeys you use only one strip. Most trips in the city, however, require two strips (a total of 2.50 DM/$1.65 for the ride, which is considerably less than the 3.20 DM for the single ticket described above). Simply fold up two segments of the Streifenkarte and insert them into the validating machine.

A simpler solution is to purchase a *Tageskarte* **(day ticket),** allowing unlimited travel on all modes of transportation for one calendar day. A 10-DM ($6.65) Tageskarte is valid for most of Munich proper and includes the entire U-Bahn network. If you want to travel to the far outskirts, purchase the 20-DM ($13.35) card for the entire metropolitan area (about a 50-mile radius). The Tageskarte is especially economical on Saturday, Sunday, or public holidays, when two adults over 18 and up to three children can all travel together using only one Tageskarte for the entire day.

You can purchase Streifenkarte, Tageskarte, and single tickets at the blue vending machines located at U- and S-Bahn stations, as well as from vending machines located at some tram stops and in the second wagon of trams that bear a white-and-green **K** sign. In addition, bus drivers sell single tickets and the Streifenkarte tickets, while tram drivers sell only single tickets. Strip tickets and day tickets are also sold at tobacco and magazine kiosks that display the green-and-white **K** in their window. In addition, day tickets are sold at Munich's tourist offices.

For more information on the various tickets, how to use them, and where to buy them, pick up a free copy of "Rendezvous with Munich" at the city tourist office at the Hauptbahnhof. **Information about Munich's public transportation system (MVV)** is also available by calling 23 80 30 or dropping by the MVV booth at the Hauptbahnhof.

BY BUS & TRAM (STREETCAR)　Buses and trams go everywhere the subway doesn't. As mentioned above, one ticket allows for as many transfers as necessary to reach your destination. The free map provided by the tourist office indicates bus and tram routes for the inner city. For night owls, there are seven bus and three tram lines that run nightly from 1 to 4am, designated by an **N** in front of their number. Contact MVV for more information, including a brochure listing the night lines along with their stops and time schedules.

BY TAXI　Munich's public transportation system is so efficient that you should never have to fork over money for a taxi. If you do take a taxi, you'll pay 3.90 DM ($2.60) as soon as you step inside, plus 2.20 DM ($1.45) per kilometer. If you need to call a taxi, phone 21610, 21611, or 19410. Taxis ordered by phone bring a 1-DM (65¢) surcharge to the bill; luggage is an extra 1 DM (65¢) per bag.

ON FOOT　Another by-product of the 1972 Olympics is Munich's extensive **pedestrian zone,** making it a perfect city to explore on foot. In fact, many of its museums can be reached on foot from the city center. All you need is the map issued by the tourist office to set you off in the right direction.

BY BICYCLE　If you're serious about cycling your way through Munich, be sure to purchase a brochure called "Radl-Touren für unsere Gäste" for 1 DM (65¢) at the tourist office. Although in German, it comes complete with suggested routes and maps for touring Munich by bike.

One of the most convenient places to rent bicycles is **Radius Touristik,** inside the Hauptbahnhof across from Track 30 (☎ **089/59 61 13** or 98 60 15). Open May to October, daily from 10am to 6:30pm, this company charges 20 DM ($13.35) for one day's rental of a single-gear bike, 80 DM ($53.35) for a week; 10% discounts are available for students and readers of this book. More elaborate bikes are available too, as well as a five-hour guided bicycle tour conducted in English every Saturday beginning at 10:30am and costing 45 DM ($30) per person, including bike rental (Frommer readers get a 10% discount).

Another well-known shop renting bicycles is **Aktiv-Rad,** Hans-Sachs-Strasse 7 (☎ 089/26 65 06), near the Frauenhoferstrasse U-Bahn station. Open Monday through Friday from 9am to 1pm and 2 to 6:30pm and Saturday from 9am to 1am, it charges 18 DM ($12) for the whole day and 90 DM ($60) for a week. **FKM,** Grassestrasse 14 (☎ 089/543-8042), near the Hackebrücke S-Bahn Station, is open Monday through Friday from 8am to 5pm. Its rates for a mountain bike begin at 25 DM ($16.65) for the day and 130 DM ($86.65) for a week.

In addition, bicycles are for rent at **several train and S-Bahn stations** in outlying villages of Bavaria, including Freising, Herrsching, Tutzing, and Starnberg. These bicycles rent for only 7 DM ($4.65) a day if you arrive by S-Bahn or train and your ticket costs at least 16 DM ($10.65) (hang on to your ticket for proof) or have a Eurailpass; otherwise you'll pay 13 DM ($8.65) for the day.

BY RENTAL CAR   You'll find counters for all the major car-rental companies at the Franz Josef Strauss Airport. In addition, you'll also find counters for **Hertz** (☎ 089/550 22 56) and **Avis** (☎ 089/550 22 51) at the Hauptbahnhof (Munich's main train station). Other car-rental agencies can be found in the telephone book under the heading "Autovermeitung."

Prices vary, but expect to pay about 169 DM ($112.65) for a one-day rental of an Opel Corsa with unlimited mileage and tax. It pays to shop around, however, since car-rental prices can vary widely depending on the time of the year, the day of the week, and the type of car. Weekend rates, for example, are always lower. And Hertz recently offered a Fiat Punto at a special rate of 55 DM ($36.65) a day, including unlimited mileage and tax.

FAST FACTS: Munich

Banks   Banks are open Monday through Friday from 8:30am to 12:30pm and 1:30 to 3:30pm (until 5:30pm on Thursday). If you need to exchange money outside bank hours, your best bet is the Deutsche Verkehrs-Bank **currency-exchange office** at the Hauptbahnhof, open daily from 6am to 11pm. In addition, the main post office (see "Mail," below) is open for money exchange 24 hours. There's also an automatic money exchange across from the Hauptbahnhof at the Bayerische Vereinsbank on the corner of Bayerstrasse and Schillerstrasse. Open 24 hours, it'll exchange dollar bills in the denominations of $5, $10, $20, and $50 into German marks (DM). **American Express,** Promenadeplatz 6 (☎ 089/29 09 00), is open Monday through Friday from 9am to 5:30pm and Saturday from 9am to 12:30pm. No fee is charged to cash American Express traveler's checks here.

Business Hours   Downtown businesses and shops are open Monday through Friday from 9am to 6pm and Saturday from 9am to 2pm. On the first Saturday of the month (*langer Samstag*), shops remain open until 5pm. Most shops, particularly those in the city center, also stay open until 8 or 9pm on Thursday evening. Note, however, that smaller neighborhood shops may not open for langer Samstag and will generally close from about 12:30 to 2 or 3pm for lunch.

Consulates   The Consulate of the **United States,** at Königinstrasse 5 (☎ 089/ 28 880), is open Monday through Friday from 8am to 11:30am. The

Consulate of the **United Kingdom,** at Bürkleinstrasse 10 (☎ **089/21 10 90**), is open Monday through Friday from 8:45 to 11:30am and 1 to 3:15pm. The Consulate of **Canada,** Tal Strasse 29 (☎ **089/290 65-0**), is open Monday through Thursday from 9am to noon and 2 to 5pm and Friday from 9am to 1:30pm.

Currency   The German **Deutsch Mark (DM)** is divided into 100 **Pfennig.** Coins come in 1, 2, 5, 10, and 50 Pfennig, and 1, 2, and 5 DM. Notes are issued in 5, 10, 20, 50, 100, 200, 500, and 1,000 DM.

Dentists   If you need a dentist in Munich, your best bet is to consult the telephone book for a "Zahnarzt" or contact the American or British consulate. If it's a weekend emergency, telephone 723 30 93; this number can also refer you to a local practice any time of the week. For evening emergencies, go to the Zahnärztliche Klinik, Lindwurm Strasse 2a (☎ **089/51 60-0** or 51 60-29), open from 7pm.

Doctors   If you need an English-speaking doctor, ask the American and British consulates for their list of English-speaking doctors in Munich, or contact an international *Apotheke* (pharmacy).

Emergencies   Important numbers include 110 for the police, 112 for the fire department and paramedics, and 19 222 for an ambulance. The number for medical emergency service is 55 86 61.

   If you're looking for a convenient pharmacy, the Internationale Ludwigs-Apotheke, Neuhauser Strasse 11 (☎ **089/260 30 21** or 260 80 12), on Munich's famous pedestrian lane, is open Monday through Wednesday and Friday from 9am to 6:30pm, Thursday from 9am to 8:30pm, and Saturday from 9am to 2pm (the first Saturday of the month, to 6pm in winter, to 4pm in summer). It's one of the best places to fill international prescriptions; it will also recommend English-speaking doctors. For information regarding the nearest open pharmacy, call 59 44 75.

Eyeglasses   If you need new eyeglasses or repairs to your old ones, Söhnges Optik, Kaufingerstrasse 6 (☎ **089/290 05 50**), can provide service within a few hours. Open Monday through Friday from 9:30am to 6pm and Saturday from 9:30am to 1pm, it's conveniently located near Marienplatz in the center of the city.

Holidays   Because of its large Catholic population, Munich has more holidays than much of the rest of the country. While many museums and restaurants remain open, shops and businesses close. Holidays in Bavaria are: New Year's Day (Jan 1); Epiphany (Jan 6); Good Friday, Easter Sunday and Monday; Labor Day (May 1); Ascension Day, Whit Sunday and Monday, Corpus Christi (all in Apr or May); Assumption Day (Aug 15); German Reunification Day (Oct 3); All Saints Day (Nov 1); and Christmas (Dec 25–26).

   Although it's not an official holiday, note that many museums and shops are also closed for the parade on Faschings Dienstag, the Tuesday before Ash Wednesday.

Hospitals   If you need to go to a hospital, contact your consulate for advice on which one is best for your ailment. Otherwise, call for an ambulance or the medical emergency service (see "Emergencies," above).

Information   The main tourist office (Fremdenverkehrsamt) is in the main train station (Hauptbahnhof). See "Visitor Information" under "Munich Specifics," earlier in this chapter, for information regarding Munich's tourist offices and useful publications on events in Munich.

Laundry/Dry Cleaning A *Reinigung* is a dry cleaner; a *Wäscherei* or *Waschsalon* is a laundry. Coin-operated laundries are found at: Pestalozzistrasse 16 (near Sendlinger-Tor-Platz), Baaderstrasse 19 (near Isartorplatz), Amalienstrasse 61 (near the university), and Kurfürstenstrasse 10 and 14 (in Schwabing). Most laundries close at 6pm. A 24-hour laundry is at Landshuter Allee 77 (near Rotkreuzplatz). Ask the staff at your hotel or pension for the location of the closest Waschsalon. A wash load costs 7 DM ($4.65) while a dryer costs 1 DM (65¢). Detergent is 1 DM (65¢).

Lost & Found If you lose something on the street or on public transportation, contact the city lost-and-found office (Fundbüro) at Arnulfstrasse 31 (☎ **089/12 408-0**), open Monday through Friday from 8:30am to noon and Tuesday from 2 to 5:30pm as well. Items lost on the S-Bahn or on German trains are turned in to the Hauptbahnhof lost-and-found office across from Track 24 (☎ **089/128 66 64**). It's open daily from 6:30am to 11:30pm.

Mail Munich's main post office, Postamt 32, is across from the Hauptbahnhof at Bahnhofplatz 1, 80335 München (☎ **089/5454-2732**). Open Monday through Friday from 7am to 10pm and Saturday, Sunday, and holidays from 8am to 10pm, it's also the place where you can have your mail sent *Poste Restante*. Other post offices are located in the Hauptbahnhof and at Residenzstrasse 2 near Marienplatz. Mailboxes are yellow.

Airmail letters to North America cost 3 DM ($2) for the first 20 grams, while postcards cost 2 DM ($1.35). If you want to mail a package back home (it can't weigh more than 20kg/44 lbs. if sent to the United States), you can buy a box that comes with tape and string at the post office. Boxes come in five sizes and range in price from 2.90 to 5.50 DM ($1.95 to $3.65).

Newspapers Looking for the news in English? Check the Internationale Presse newsstand in the Hauptbahnhof (☎ **089/55 11 7170**), where you can pick up *USA Today*, the *International Herald Tribune*, and the *Wall Street Journal*. It's open daily from 7am to 10:45pm.

Radio & TV Tune into 88.4 FM for Bayern 2's news in English, French, and Italian Monday through Friday at 8:50am; and 1197 AM for Voice of America Europe/Worldwide English Program, with daily news broadcasts on the hour, music, and commentaries.

Photographic Needs There are photography shops throughout the center of Munich, but for film try one of the department stores, where prices are likely to be lower. Kaufhof has two convenient locations, on Marienplatz and on Karlsplatz, while Hertie is right across from the train station at Bahnhofplatz 7.

Police The emergency telephone number for the police is 110.

Religious Services The *Monatsprogramm*, available from the Munich tourist office for 2.50 DM ($1.65), lists churches in various denominations throughout Munich and hours of weekly services. *Munich Found*, an English-language city magazine, also lists churches with English religious services.

Shoe Repair If you've worn your shoes out with walking, give them a tuneup at Mister Minit, a chain of shoe-repair shops. They can be found in most department stores, including Hertie, across from the train station, and Kaufhof, on Karlsplatz and on Marienplatz. There's also a Schuh Reperatur shop in the Hauptbahnhof.

Tax   Germany's 15% federal tax is already included in most hotel and restaurant bills, including all the locales listed in this book. Tax is likewise included in the price of goods, which you can partially recover on items taken out of the country. For information on how you can recover the value-added tax (VAT), refer to "Shopping," later in this chapter.

Telephone   A **local telephone call** costs 30 Pfennig (20¢) for the first three minutes, so put more coins in to be sure you're not cut off (unused coins will be returned). Telephones in some restaurants require 50 Pfennig (35¢). Otherwise, you might wish to purchase a **telephone card,** available in values of 12 DM ($8) and 50 DM ($33.35). The 12-DM card gives you approximately 40 minutes of local telephone calls; the 50-DM card is useful for long-distance calls. Telephone cards are becoming so popular in Germany that many public telephones accept only cards. You can purchase them at any post office.

Incidentally, if you come across a telephone number with a dash, the numbers after the dash are the extension number. Simply dial the entire number as you would any telephone number. For **information** on local telephone numbers, call 01188.

If you're calling Munich from outside the city, use the **area code** 089 from within Germany, 89 from the United States or outside Germany.

For **long-distance calls,** go to the post office instead of calling from your hotel, since hotels usually add a stiff surcharge—even a local call made from your hotel room is likely to cost upward of 50 Pfennig (35¢). The main post office, located across from the Hauptbahnhof, is open until 10pm. It costs 7.80 DM ($5.20) to make a three-minute long-distance phone call to the United States.

Tipping   Tipping is already included in hotel and restaurant bills. However, it's customary to round restaurant bills up to the nearest Mark; if a meal costs more than 20 DM, most Germans will give a 10% tip. Don't leave a tip on the table—include it in the amount you give your waiter. For taxi drivers, it's sufficient to round up to the nearest Mark. Porters should receive 2 DM ($1.35) per bag.

4 Accommodations

Most of Munich's accommodations are clustered around the main train station, the Hauptbahnhof, particularly along Schillerstrasse. While this area may not be the city's most charming, what it lacks in atmosphere it certainly makes up for in convenience. The farther you walk from the station, the quainter and quieter the neighborhoods become.

Although a *pension,* the German equivalent of a bed-and-breakfast, is generally less expensive than a hotel, there's often only a fine line between the two. In any case, the cheaper the room, the greater the likelihood you'll be sharing a bath down the hall. Pensions in Munich often charge a small fee for use of the shower— unless you have a shower in your room. All rooms in pensions and hotels, however, have their own sink. Single rooms, unfortunately, are expensive in Munich; you can save a lot of money by sharing a room.

Getting the Best Deal on Accommodations

- A room without a private shower is usually cheaper than one with a private shower—however, you may be charged extra for each shower you take down the hall. If the charge for a shower is high and there are more than two of you, you might save by taking a room with private shower.

- Accommodations that offer cooking facilities help you save on dining bills.

- Ask if breakfast is included in the room rate—if it's buffet style, you can eat as much as you wish.

- Before placing a call, inquire about the surcharge on local and long-distance telephone calls.

- Note how far the accommodation is from the town center. You might find an inexpensive room on the outskirts but what you'll end up spending for transportation into the city may negate the savings.

Private rooms—those rented out in a private home to tourists—offer some of the cheapest accommodations in the city. They also offer a personal touch to your stay, since in some instances you're living right in someone's home.

Note that floors begin with the "ground floor" (the same as the American first floor) and go up to the first floor (American second), and so on. And remember that if the accommodations below are full, try the tourist office, whose staff will find a room for you for 5 DM ($3.35). All prices here include tax and service charge. The higher prices are those charged April to October, including Oktoberfest, and during major conventions.

ROOMS IN PRIVATE HOMES FOR LESS THAN 90 DM ($60) DOUBLE

Private homes offering rooms are spread throughout the city and listed here in alphabetical order. With the exception of the first one, no rooms have a private bath and breakfast is not offered. Also except for the first one, these homeowners all prefer guests who stay at least three nights.

✪ Frau Audrey Bauchinger

Zeppelinstrasse 37 (across the Isar River from the Deutsches Museum), 81669 München. ☎ **089/48 84 44.** Fax 089/48 91 787. 6 rms, 3 with shower only, 3 with tub/shower and toilet; 2 suites. 40 DM ($26.65) single with shower only; 70 DM ($46.65) double without shower or toilet; 80–105 DM ($53.35–$70) double with shower only; 125–145 DM ($83.35–$96.65) double with tub/shower and toilet; 35 DM ($23.35) per person triple without shower or toilet; 160 DM ($106.65) suite for two, plus 40 DM ($26.65) per extra person. Rates include showers. AE, DC, MC, V. Tram 18 from the Hauptbahnhof to Deutsches Museum. Bus 52 from Marienplatz to Schweigerstrasse (the first stop after the river).

This private home is by far the most modern and best equipped of those listed here. Run by a former teacher from Virginia who married a local antiques dealer, it offers rooms that are clean and pleasant, each unique. There's only one single, which has a shower; others are doubles, some without private bath, others with shower only or with private bath across the hall. The simple triple room is ideal for students, and those looking for greater luxury should ask about the pair of two-room suites complete with private bath and kitchen. Bicycles are for rent, and

Frau Bauchinger gives new arrivals an information sheet on what to see in Munich. Her establishment is easily reached from the airport via S-Bahn. Frau Bauchinger prefers cash; if you pay by credit card, a 5% surcharge will be added to your bill.

Frau Theresa Boiger

Hans-Sachs-Strasse 9, 80469 München. ☎ **089/260 38 35.** 3 rms, none with bath. 50 DM ($33.35) per person for stays of one or two nights, 45 DM ($30) per person for stays of three or more nights. Rates include showers. Heating in winter 3 DM ($2) extra. No credit cards. Tram 20, 25, or 27 from the Hauptbahnhof to Fraunhofer-Müllerstrasse (three stops); then a three-minute walk.

Frau Boiger's apartment is cluttered with mementos of a lifetime spent in a house more than 100 years old. Frau Boiger, who is nearing 80, is a bit of a character. With her smattering of English, she tells guests to ring the doorbell at the front door and then wait for the "modern door-opener"—a key thrown from her upstairs apartment to the street below. (This building predates automatic door buzzers.) Once upstairs, you'll be greeted by her friendly poodle, Bobby. She maintains a refrigerator for guests, who can even cook their own meals if they wish, and everyone is welcome to join her for an evening in front of the TV. Two of her rooms are singles or doubles; the third can accommodate two to four. This area is an interesting part of town, a mixture of antiques shops and gay bars.

Fremdenheim Weigl

Pettenkoferstrasse 32 (just off Georg-Hirth-Platz, about a 10-minute walk south of the train station), 80336 München. ☎ **089/53 24 53.** 3 rms, none with bath. 35 DM ($23.35) single; 70 DM ($46.65) double. Rates include showers. No credit cards. U-Bahn: Theresienwiese. Bus 58 to Georg-Hirth-Platz. If you want to walk, from the Hauptbahnhof's south exit, head down Goethestrasse to Pettenkoferstrasse, then turn right.

The three rooms on the second floor here are owned/managed by Daniela Busetti, who speaks excellent English and is the granddaughter of the original owner. Although she lives in the same building, her apartment is separate from the guest rooms, affording more privacy than the rooms offered by Frau Boiger (above). There's one single room without a sink and two doubles with washbasins.

PRIVATE APARTMENTS FOR LESS THAN 106 DM ($70.65)DOUBLE

Anita Gross

Thalkirchner Strasse 72 (about a 20-minute walk from Marienplatz), 80337 München. ☎ **089/52 16 81.** 2 apts, both with bath. TV TEL. 105 DM ($70) smaller apt for two; 120 DM ($80) larger apt for two, 140 DM ($93.35) for three, 160 DM ($106.65) for four. No credit cards. Bus 58 from the Hauptbahnhof to the Kapuziner Strasse stop.

These two apartments are perfect for those who like being on their own and having all the comforts of home when they travel. They're owned by personable Frau Anita Gross, who lives elsewhere but will pick you up at the train station for 10 DM ($6.65) if given notice of your arrival; this perfect hostess speaks perfect English and provides maps and sightseeing information. Both apartments are modern and cheerful and fully equipped with radio, ironing board/iron, and a kitchenette complete with a refrigerator, a toaster, hotplates, a coffeemaker, pots and pans, and tableware. Even coffee, tea, and sugar are provided free. Bikes are available for rent for 15 DM ($10) per day. The larger apartment, sleeping up to four, has a balcony, replete with table and chairs in fine weather. Be sure to call or write in advance for a reservation.

DOUBLES FOR LESS THAN 91 DM ($60.65)
SOUTH OF THE HAUPTBAHNHOF

Unless otherwise noted, these pensions have the same rates year round.

Hotel-Pension Erika

Landwehrstrasse 8 (a five-minute walk from the train station), 80336 München. ☎ **089/55 43 27**. 30 rms, 10 with shower only, 6 with shower and toilet. 60 DM ($40) single without shower or toilet, 70 DM ($46.65) single with shower only, 90 DM ($60) single with shower and toilet; 90 DM ($60) double without shower or toilet, 100 DM ($66.65) double with shower only, 120 DM ($80) double with shower and toilet. Rates include continental breakfast and showers. AE, DC, MC, V.

This small, personable hotel is owned by Frau Heu. The only building left standing on the street at the end of World War II, it has large clean rooms with high ceilings, some with telephone and TV; those facing the back of the building are virtually free of traffic noise. The hotel's elevator is tiny. In summer, breakfast is served on an outdoor patio.

⑤ Pension Augsburg

Schillerstrasse 18, 80336 München. ☎ **089/59 76 73**. Fax 089/550 38 23. 26 rms, 9 with shower only. 45 DM ($30) single without shower, 55 DM ($36.65) single with shower only; 70 DM ($46.65) double without shower, 85 DM ($56.65) double with shower only; 105 DM ($70) triple without shower, 125 DM ($83.35) triple with shower only. Rates 4 DM ($2.65) per person higher during Oktoberfest. Breakfast 6 DM ($4) extra; showers 3.50 DM ($2.35) extra. No credit cards. Closed Dec 23–Jan 10.

One of many hotels and pensions on Schillerstrasse, Pension Augsburg is probably the most economical and the best for its price. Its reception is on the third floor—there's no elevator—and though rooms are rather bare, no one is complaining at these prices. The rooms are carpeted and clean, and there's hot water all the time. It's owned and managed by Anna and Heinz Paintner. This pension is a two-minute walk from the south side of the train station.

Pension Herzog Heinrich

Herzog-Heinrich-Strasse 3 (a 10-minute walk from the train station), 80336 München. ☎ **089/53 25 75** or 538 07 50. Fax 089/543 83 59. 8 rms, none with bath. 60 DM ($40) single; 85–90 DM ($56.65–$60) double; 110–120 DM ($73.35–$80) triple. Rates include breakfast and showers. No credit cards. U-Bahn: Theresien-wiese. Bus 58 from the Hauptbahnhof to the Georg-Hirth-Platz stop. To walk, turn right out of the south exit of the Hauptbahnhof onto Bayerstrasse, then make a left onto Paul-Heyse-Strasse.

This pleasant pension is owned by a Turkish family, the Ergüls, and offers simple but spotless rooms decorated with wood furniture; a couple of the largest rooms for three or more even have balconies. It's located on the second floor (no elevator). Mr. and Mrs. Ergül, who are friendly and accommodating, speak only a little English, but their children have learned English in school.

⊙ Pension Süzer

Mittererstrasse 1 (150 yards from the train station), 80336 München. ☎ **089/53 35 21** or 53 66 42. Fax 089/53 60 80. 11 rms, 4 with shower and toilet. TEL. 85 DM ($56.65) double without shower or toilet, 105 DM ($70) double with shower and toilet; 120 DM ($80) triple without shower or toilet; 150 DM ($100) quad without shower or toilet. Rates include continental breakfast and showers. AE. From the train station, take a right at the tourist office onto Bayerstrasse and then a left at Mittererstrasse.

This tiny pension is on the third floor (take the elevator to the left or you'll end up at a doctor's office). It's owned by Herr Erol Süzer, an outgoing Turk who speaks excellent English and is eager to answer questions about Munich (though, unfortunately, some of the people working for him do not speak English or German). You can even sign up here for tours of the city. All rooms (no singles) are decorated with Scandinavian-style wood furniture and wainscoting; four have their own refrigerators (with ice cubes!), TVs, and radio alarm clocks. There's also a cable TV with CNN broadcasts in the tiny dining/reception area, where you can buy a beer or coffee for 2 DM ($1.35). Unlimited tea or coffee is served with breakfast. One load of laundry washed and dried costs 10 DM ($6.65). The rates quoted above are special for bearers of this book (not photocopies), which you should show upon arrival—but only if you book directly with the pension.

NEAR THERESIENWIESE

These two pensions with the same rates year round are on the edge of Theresienwiese, site of the Oktoberfest, about a 15-minute walk from the Hauptbahnhof.

✪ Pension Schubert

Schubertstrasse 1, 80336 München. ☎ **089/53 50 87.** 7 rms, 2 with shower only. 50 DM ($33.35) single without shower; 85 DM ($56.65) double without shower, 95 DM ($63.35) double with shower only. Rates include continental breakfast. Showers 3 DM ($2) extra. No credit cards. U-Bahn U-3 or U-6 from Marienplatz to Goetheplatz (two stops).

Located in an older, unadorned building on a tree-lined street, this small pension is a true find. It's owned by outgoing Frau Käthe Fürholzer, who speaks some English, and its walls are decorated with Bavarian mementos and pictures, including a collection of beer-stein tin tops (designed to keep the flies out and the beer fresh in former days). The rooms are clean and orderly in good German fashion.

✪ Pension Westfalia

Mozartstrasse 23 (on the corner of Kobellstrasse), 80336 München. ☎ **089/53 03 77** or 53 03 78. Fax 089/543 91 20. 19 rms, 11 with tub or shower and toilet. TEL. 60–65 DM ($40–$43.35) single without shower or toilet, 80–90 DM ($53.35–$60) single with tub or shower and toilet; 85–95 DM ($56.65–$63.35) double without shower or toilet, 105–125 DM ($70–$83.35) double with tub or shower and toilet; 115–125 DM ($76.65–$83.35) triple without shower or toilet, 135–150 DM ($90–$100) triple with tub or shower and toilet. Rates include buffet breakfast. Showers 3 DM ($2) extra. No credit cards. U-Bahn U-3 or U-6 from Marienplatz to Goetheplatz. Bus 58 from the Hauptbahnhof to Goetheplatz.

A century old, this imposing and elaborate building is just across from the Oktoberfest meadow. The lobby is on the top floor, reached by elevator, where you'll be met by owner Peter Deiritz and his family. Since acquiring the pension in 1990, the Deiritzes have been renovating slowly, making it brighter and more cheerful and adding TVs to rooms. The pension itself is cozy, clean, and comfortable, and the breakfast room and corridor feature 19th-century paintings, all by Munich artists. This is just the kind of place many visitors to Bavaria are looking for.

NORTH OF THE HAUPTBAHNHOF

The accommodations here are all within walking distance of both the train station and Munich's main cluster of museums.

Pension Armin

Augustenstrasse 5, 80333 München. ☎ **089/59 31 97.** Fax 089/59 52 52. 20 rms, none with bath. 60 DM ($40) single; 85–90 DM ($56.65–$60) double; 105–120 DM ($70–$80) triple. Rates include continental breakfast. Showers 2.50 DM ($1.65) extra. Rates about 10% higher during Oktoberfest and major trade fairs. No credit cards. Parking 10 DM ($6.65). Closed from the Fri before Christmas to Jan 7. Walk one block north from the Hauptbahnhof on Dachauerstrasse and turn right onto Augustenstrasse (about a six-minute walk).

Popular with student groups, backpackers, and families, this reasonably priced pension offers plain, uncluttered rooms decorated with dark wooden furniture. Iranian-born owner Armin Georgi speaks English and is happy to dispense information on his adopted hometown as well as book city sightseeing tours. A washer/dryer are available to guests for 11 DM ($7.35) per load, and there's a communal room with TV and a pleasant lobby with drinks available.

Pension Flora

Karlstrasse 49, 80333 München. ☎ **089/59 70 67** or 59 41 35. Fax 089/59 41 35. 45 rms, 5 with shower only, 15 with shower and toilet. 60–70 DM ($40–$46.65) single without shower or toilet, 80–100 DM ($53.35–$66.65) single with shower and toilet; 80–95 DM ($53.35–$63.35) double without shower or toilet, 130 DM ($86.65) double with shower and toilet; 120 DM ($80) triple without shower or toilet, 145 DM ($96.65) triple with shower and toilet; 145 DM ($96.65) quad without shower or toilet, 170 DM ($113.35) quad with shower and toilet. Rates include buffet breakfast. Showers 2 DM ($1.35) extra. No credit cards. Walk six minutes from the north exit of the Hauptbahnhof; it's near the corner of Dachauerstrasse and Karlstrasse.

A family-owned operation since 1956, the first-floor Pension Flora is now run by the original owner's son, Adolf, and granddaughters, Judith and Angy. Great for the price, it features small but clean rooms with wall-to-wall carpeting. A couple of rooms facing away from the street have small balconies. Breakfast is served in a cheerful dining room with a stucco ceiling.

Pension Geiger

Steinheilstrasse 1, 80333 München. ☎ **089/52 15 56.** 17 rms, 10 with shower only. 45–55 DM ($30–$36.65) single without shower, 65 DM ($43.35) single with shower only; 84 DM ($56) double without shower, 95 DM ($63.35) double with shower only; 130 DM ($86.65) triple with shower only. Rates include continental breakfast. Showers 2 DM ($1.35) extra. No credit cards. Parking 3 DM ($2). U-Bahn U-2 to Theresienstrasse (or less than a 10-minute walk from the train station).

Owned and managed for more than 20 years by the personable Frau Huber (who speaks a little English), this clean and well-run pension is near the Technical University and Alte Pinakothek. It's up on the second floor; there's no elevator.

✪ Pension Hungaria

Brienner Strasse 42, 80333 München. ☎ **089/52 15 58.** 12 rms, none with bath. 48–55 DM ($32–$36.65) single; 75–85 DM ($50–$56.65) double; 99 DM ($66) triple; 120 DM ($80) quad. Rates include continental breakfast. Showers 3 DM ($2) extra. No credit cards. U-Bahn U-2 to Königsplatz (one stop, or less than a 10-minute walk from the Hauptbahnhof).

Charming English-speaking Dr. Erika Wolff has owned and managed this delightful small pension since 1957. The reception area is up on the second floor, to which there's unfortunately no elevator. The rooms are bright and cheerful.

IN SCHWABING

If you want to be close to the nightlife in Schwabing yet stay in a quiet neighborhood, this establishment is your best bet.

✪ Pension Am Kaiserplatz

Kaiserplatz 12, 80803 München. ☎ **089/34 91 90** or 39 52 31. 10 rms, 6 with shower only. 45–59 DM ($30–$39.35) single without shower; 75–79 DM ($50–$52.65) double without shower, 79–85 DM ($52.65–$56.65) double with shower only; 105 DM ($70) triple without or with shower only; 120 DM ($80) quad without or with shower only; 150 DM ($100) quint room without or with shower only; 160 DM ($106.65) six-bed room without or with shower only. Rates include continental breakfast and showers. No credit cards. Take any S-Bahn in the direction of Marienplatz, changing there to U-Bahn U-3 or U-6 for Münchner Freiheit.

If you like touches of the Old World, you can't do better than this place for its price category. On the ground floor of a Jugendstil building almost a century old (several architects have offices here—always a good sign), this pension features many rooms decorated with antiques, each in a different style: for example, the English Room, the Farmer's Room, and the Baroque Room, all with high ceilings and a feeling of spaciousness. Extravagantly furnished with chandeliers, sitting areas, lace curtains, or washbasins shaped like seashells, the rooms here are highly recommended. Frau Jacobi, who has run the place for more than 20 years, is very friendly, and what's more, she's a native of Munich. Breakfast is served in your room.

IN THE CITY CENTER

Hotel Erbprinz

Sonnenstrasse 2 (just off Karlsplatz), 80331 München. ☎ **089/59 45 21.** 24 rms, 12 with tub/shower and toilet. TEL. 69 DM ($46) single without tub/shower or toilet, 89–94 DM ($59.35–$62.65) single with tub or shower and toilet; 86–104 DM ($57.35–$69.35) double without tub/shower or toilet, 120–138 DM ($80.70–$92) double with tub or shower and toilet; 133 DM ($88.65) triple without tub/shower or toilet, 172 DM ($114.65) triple with tub or shower and toilet. Rates include continental breakfast. Showers 3 DM ($2) extra. AE, MC, V. Walk five minutes east of the Hauptbahnhof on Schützenstrasse or Bayerstrasse, and take a right on Sonnenstrasse.

This older, second-floor pension (with elevator) offers simple but adequate rooms, and its breakfast room provides a sunny outlook over the Karlsplatz action. Most rooms, however, face the back, where it's much quieter. Note that its cheapest doubles are actually single rooms with a bed only 4¹/₂ feet wide—unless you're more interested in price over comfort, you'll probably want to book the normal, higher-priced double. The higher price in each category is the rate charged during Oktoberfest and major trade fairs.

Pension Diana

Altheimer Eck 15 (between Karlsplatz and Marienplatz), 80331 München. ☎ **089/260 31 07.** Fax 089/26 39 34. 17 rms, none with bath. 55–75 DM ($36.65–$50) single; 79–98 DM ($52.65–$65.35) double. Additional person 40 DM ($26.65) extra. Rates include breakfast and showers. AE, MC, V. S-Bahn and U-Bahn: Karlsplatz; then a three-minute walk.

This simple pension has a great location in the city center. On the third floor (no elevator), it offers small but perfectly adequate rooms; those toward the back are quieter. The corridors, however, are also rather narrow—not for the claustrophobic. The higher prices in each category are those charged in peak season.

BETWEEN THE CITY CENTER & THE ISAR RIVER

Hotel-Pension Beck

Thierschstrasse 36, 80538 München. ☎ **089/22 07 08** or 22 57 68. Fax 089/22 09 25. 44 rms, 8 with shower and toilet. TEL. 45–52 DM ($30–$34.65) single without shower or toilet, 68 DM ($45.35) single with shower and toilet; 72–82 DM ($48–$54.65) double without shower or toilet, 88–108 DM ($58.65–$72) double with shower and toilet; 40 DM ($26.65) per person in a three- to five-bed room without shower or toilet, 45–50 DM ($30–$33.35) per person in a three- to five-bed room with shower and toilet. Rates include continental breakfast and showers. Crib available. No credit cards. Parking 5 DM ($3.35). U-Bahn U-4 or U-5 from the Hauptbahnhof to Lehel; then a five-minute walk. Tram 19 from the Hauptbahnhof to Maxmonument or 20 from the Hauptbahnhof to Mariannenplatz. S-Bahn S-8 from the airport to Isartorplatz; then a three-minute walk.

It's hard to believe that Frau Beck is over 70, so energetically does she run this astonishingly cheap pension (no elevator). Owner since 1950, she speaks very good

English, is talkative, and makes sure that guests know what to see in her beloved Munich. The building itself is more than 100 years old, with rooms spread over four floors in two wings; the cheaper rooms are on the upper floors. One of the best things about this place is that there are small kitchens and refrigerators you can use for free, saving money on meals (ask the reception for plates, pots and pans, and utensils). Frau Beck welcomes families, with one room large enough for five. The rooms, though old, are large, clean, and perfectly adequate, with modern wooden furniture and carpeting, most with TVs and a few with balconies. This pension, a 10-minute walk from the city center, Marienplatz, and the Deutsches Museum, is directly connected to the airport via S-Bahn.

DOUBLES FOR LESS THAN 112 DM ($74.65)
NEAR THE HAUPTBAHNHOF

Hotel Daheim

Schillerstrasse 20 (a three-minute walk from the south exit of the Hauptbahnhof), 80336 München 2. ☎ **089/59 42 49.** Fax 089/59 71 02. 26 rms, 10 with shower only, 8 with tub/shower and toilet. TEL. 79–85 DM ($52.65–$56.65) single without shower or toilet, 105 DM ($70) single with shower only, 110 DM ($73.35) single with shower and toilet; 118 DM ($78.65) double without shower or toilet, 128 DM ($85.35) double with shower only, 148 DM ($98.65) double with tub/shower and toilet; 150 DM ($100) triple without shower or toilet, 175 DM ($116.65) triple with shower only, 185 DM ($123.35) triple with shower and toilet. Rates include continental breakfast and showers. Rates 30%–50% higher during Oktoberfest, major conventions, and trade fairs. AE, MC, V.

On busy Schillerstrasse with its many hotels and pensions, the Daheim is a family-run establishment. The building is a bit old, but the pension itself is perfectly acceptable for the price. Breakfast is served in a lace-curtained room with a good view of Schillerstrasse. Single travelers should note that there are only three single rooms here—the rest are doubles, many of which can be converted into triples; about half the rooms have TVs.

Hotel Haberstock

Schillerstrasse 4 (less than a two-minute walk from the Hauptbahnhof), 80336 München. ☎ **089/55 78 55** or 55 78 56. Fax 089/550 36 34. 67 rms, 24 with shower only, 15 with tub/shower and toilet. TEL. 64–78 DM ($42.65–$52) single without shower or toilet, 82 DM ($54.65) single with shower only, 105 DM ($70) single with shower and toilet; 110 DM ($73.35) double without shower or toilet, 135 DM ($90) double with shower only, 175 DM ($116.65) double with shower and toilet. Rates include breakfast and one shower daily. Rates 10% higher during Oktoberfest. AE, DC, MC, V.

The Haberstock welcomes guests of all ages, businesspeople and tourists alike. Outfitted in the old-fashioned way with two separate doors to eliminate corridor noise, the rooms are simple but tastefully decorated. The hotel itself, typically Bavarian, has nice touches throughout, including ornate gilded mirrors in the lobby and chandeliers.

Hotel Helvetia

Schillerstrasse 6 (a few minutes' walk from the Hauptbahnhof's south exit), 80336 München. ☎ **089/55 47 45.** Fax 089/550 23 81. 46 rms, none with bath. TEL. 65–70 DM ($43.35–$46.65) single; 95–100 DM ($63.35–$66.65) double; 40 DM ($26.65) per person triple, quad, and five-bed rooms. Rates include continental breakfast and showers. Rates 5 DM ($3.35) per person more during Oktoberfest and major conventions. No credit cards.

A good choice on Schillerstrasse is the Helvetia, pleasantly decorated in old-fashioned Bavarian style. The breakfast room has fresh flowers on every table and a TV. The rooms are fairly large, with pine furniture, and many doubles even have two sinks. Most rooms face away from the street, assuring a quiet night's rest.

Hotel Jedermann

Bayerstrasse 95, 80335 München. ☎ **089/53 32 67** or 53 36 17. Fax 089/53 65 06. 55 rms, 34 with shower and toilet. 65–85 DM ($43.35–$56.65) single without shower or toilet, 95–140 DM ($63.35–$93.35) single with shower and toilet; 95–140 DM ($63.35–$93.35) double without shower or toilet, 130–200 DM ($86.65–$133.35) double with shower and toilet; 120–170 DM ($80–$113.35) triple without shower or toilet, 165–220 DM ($110–$146.65) triple with shower and toilet. Rates include buffet breakfast. Crib available. Showers 3 DM ($2) extra. V. Parking 8 DM ($5.35). From the south exit of the train station, near the tourist office, turn right onto Bayerstrasse (less than a 10-minute walk from the Hauptbahnhof).

This delightfully comfortable establishment has been owned by English-speaking Werner Jenke and his family since 1962. Its lobby and rooms were recently renovated, and the breakfast room is a cheerful way to start the day—with an all-you-can-eat breakfast buffet. There are nice touches of antiques and traditional Bavarian furniture throughout, and rooms with baths have the extras of radio, alarm clock, TV, and hairdryer. There are safes in most of the rooms. The higher rates in each category are those charged during major conventions and trade fairs.

IN SCHWABING

Haus International

Elisabethstrasse 87, 80797 München. ☎ **089/12 00 60.** Fax 089/1200-6251. 168 rms, 133 with shower and toilet. 60 DM ($40) single without shower or toilet, 90 DM ($60) single with shower and toilet; 110 DM ($73.35) double without shower or toilet, 150 DM ($100) double with shower and toilet; 150 DM ($100) triple with shower and toilet; 175 DM ($116.65) quad with shower and toilet; 220 DM ($146.65) quint. Rates include continental breakfast and showers. No credit cards. U-Bahn U-2 from the Hauptbahnhof to Hohenzollernplatz; then bus no. 33 to Barbarastrasse.

Built for the 1972 Olympic Games, this tall, modern youth hotel is popular with international school and youth groups, but there's no age limit and no curfew. The rooms are basic but the facilities—restaurant, bar, disco, and pool—are very good. Reserve in advance in writing if you want to stay here, then call a few days before your arrival.

IN THE CITY CENTER

Just a few minutes' walk from Marienplatz, these two older hotels are good if you want to be in the middle of the action; they offer the same rates all year.

✪ Hotel Am Karlstor

Neuhauser Strasse 47 (just off Karlsplatz, popularly known as Stachus), 80331 München. ☎ **089/59 35 96** or 59 66 21. Fax 089/550 36 71. 28 rms, 3 with shower only. TEL. 68–75 DM ($45.35–$50) single without shower, 85–90 DM ($56.65–$60) single with shower only; 100 DM ($66.65) double without shower, 120–125 DM ($80–$83.35) double with shower only; 130–135 DM ($86.65–$90) triple without shower, 150 DM ($100) triple with shower only; 150–155 DM ($100–$103.35) quad without shower. Rates include continental breakfast. Showers 5 DM ($3.35) extra. MC, V. Closed the first two weeks in Jan. S-Bahn: Karlsplatz (one stop, or a five-minute walk east from the Hauptbahnhof on the other side of Karlsplatz).

More than 30 years old, this homey hotel is on the main pedestrian street leading from the train station to Marienplatz. The elevator, situated next to a movie theater, takes you up to the reception area on the fourth floor, which is surprisingly quiet and peaceful considering the traffic outside. The rooms have modern wooden furniture, and there are a lot of repeat guests. With 16 single rooms, it's a good bet for those traveling alone. Owner Herr Henrich Rosenfeld speaks good English; his wife, Robyn, is a native English-speaker.

✪ Hotel Am Markt

Heiliggeistrasse 6, 80331 München. ☎ **089/22 50 14.** 31 rms, 12 with shower and toilet. TEL. 65–70 DM ($43.35–$46.65) single without shower or toilet, 110 DM ($73.35) single with shower and toilet; 112 DM ($74.65) double without shower or toilet, 160 DM ($106.65) double with shower and toilet; 170 DM ($113.35) triple without shower or toilet, 195 DM ($130) triple with shower and toilet. Rates include continental breakfast and showers. No credit cards. Parking 10 DM ($6.65). S-Bahn: From the Hauptbahnhof, take any S-Bahn toward Marienplatz (two stops).

Next to Munich's colorful outdoor market, the Viktualienmarkt, this hotel, renovated in 1988, has flair. The rooms are a bit small, but the breakfast room and entryway are pleasant, tastefully decorated and displaying photographs of some celebrities who have stayed here—and some who haven't. At any rate, the hotel looks more expensive than it is, and you can't beat its location near Marienplatz.

SUPER-BUDGET CHOICES
YOUTH HOSTELS

To sleep in a youth hostel (*Jugendherberge*) in Bavaria, you cannot be older than 26 and must have a youth-hostel card. If you don't have a youth-hostel card, you can purchase one at the youth hostel itself for 36 DM ($24), which is good around the world for one year.

DJH Jugendherberge München

Wendl-Dietrich-Strasse 20, 80634 München. ☎ **089/13 11 56.** 535 beds. 23 DM ($15.35) per person per night. Rates include breakfast, sheets, and showers. No credit cards. U-Bahn U-1 from the Hauptbahnhof to Rotkreuzplatz; then follow the triangular DJH signs.

Munich's largest and oldest youth hostel opens for check-in at 10am and closes its doors at 1am. Like most youth hostels, it offers multiple bunk beds per room. Note that the entrance to the youth hostel is not on Wendl-Dietrich-Strasse but around the corner on Renatastrasse.

DJH Jugendgästehaus München

Miesingstrasse 4, 81379 München. ☎ **089/723 65 50.** 330 beds, no rms with bath. 32.50 DM ($21.65) single; 28.50 DM ($19) per person double; 26.50 DM ($17.65) per person triple or quad; 24.50 DM ($16.35) dorm bed. Rates include breakfast, sheets, and showers. No credit cards. Closed Jan. Take the S-Bahn from the Hauptbahnhof to Marienplatz and then U-Bahn U-3 from Marienplatz to Thalkirchen, from which it's a three-minute walk.

Newer, nicer, and classier than the Jugendherberge (above), this hostel is also a bit farther from the center. The curfew here is also 1am, but you have the choice of singles, doubles, triples, and quads in addition to dormitories.

YOUTH HOTELS
Christlicher Verein Junger Männer (CVJM)

Landwehrstrasse 13 (less than a five-minute walk from the Hauptbahnhof's south exit), 80336 München. ☎ **089/552 14 10.** Fax 089/55 04 282. 34 rms, none with bath. 48–53 DM ($32–$35.35) single; 42 DM ($28) per person double; 39 DM ($26) per person triple. Rates include breakfast and showers. No credit cards.

Accommodating both males and females, this YMCA is popular with groups, particularly from May through October, so be sure to reserve early. Visitors over 27 must pay a 15% supplement to the rates above, and note that unmarried couples must sleep in separate rooms. The rooms, mostly twins, are spartan but adequate and come with sinks. Curfew is at 12:30am, and there's an adjoining restaurant (open Tuesday through Friday evenings only) serving good meals at reasonable prices.

Marienherberge

Goethestrasse 9 (a couple of minutes' walk south of the train station), 80336 München. ☎ **089/555 805.** 50 beds. 35 DM ($23.35) single; 30 DM ($20) per person double or triple; 25 DM ($16.65) dorm bed. Rates include breakfast and showers. No credit cards.

This Catholic-affiliated hostel is for women 18 to 25 only. Ironically, it's located on the same street as several sex shops, and the front door is always locked. Curfew is at midnight. The rooms are simple, most sleeping two or three. There's also one single room and one dormitory-style room with seven beds. Laundry facilities cost only 4 DM ($2.65) per load. Since it's often filled with school groups during the school year, your best bet staying here is during the school vacation in August.

CAMPING

Campingplatz Thalkirchen

Zentralländstrasse 49 (only 2¹/₂ miles from the city center), 81379 München. ☎ **089/723 17 07.** Approximately 2,000 people can be accommodated. 5.50 DM ($3.65) per person; 4–5.50 DM ($2.65–$3.65) per tent, depending on size; 7 DM ($4.65) per auto; 7.50–14.50 DM ($5–$9.65) per camping trailer or RV, depending on size. Showers 1 DM (65¢) extra. No credit cards. Closed Nov to mid-Mar. U-Bahn U-3 to Thalkirchen; then a 10-minute walk.

This municipal campground, open from mid-March to October, is Munich's largest. It's in a parklike setting along the Isar River, with facilities that include washrooms and showers, a bank for money exchange, a snack bar, a supermarket, and even small kitchens. Nearby are the Hellabrunn Zoo and an outdoor heated pool.

Youth Camp Am Kapuzinerhölzl

Franz-Schrank-Strasse, 80638 München. ☎ **089/141 43 00.** 400 sleeping spaces. 7 DM ($4.65) per person. No credit cards. Closed Sept to the end of June. Take U-Bahn U-1 from the Hauptbahnhof to Rotkreuzplatz, then tram no. 12 (marked AMALIENBURGSTRASSE) from Rotkreuzplatz to Botanischer Garten.

Run by the city of Munich from the end of June to August, this huge circuslike tent accommodates young people from around the world who want nothing more than a place to sleep. Located in the Nymphenburg–Botanical Garden area, it's stocked with mattresses and blankets, and tea is served free in the morning. There's also a canteen, showers, and an information bureau. No curfew is observed, and the maximum stay is three nights. It's wise to call beforehand to see whether there's space and also to make sure that the city is still operating it. Every year they talk about doing away with the tent, but the demand is definitely there.

LONG-TERM STAYS

In addition to the recommendations here, the **Hotel-Pension Beck** (above) has cooking facilities on each floor and **Frau Anita Gross** offers two apartments with kitchenettes (above).

Jost Hübner

Bethmannstrasse 15, 85737 München-Ismaning. ☎ **089/96 88 37.** 2 apts, both with bath. 350 DM ($233.35) per week apt for two people. No credit cards. S-Bahn S-8 from the Hauptbahnhof (a 30-minute trip) or from the airport (three stops) to Ismaning; then an 18-minute walk.

English-speaking Herr Hübner rents two apartments, each with a private bath and kitchenette equipped with an electric stove, a refrigerator, a toaster, pots and pans, and utensils. He also has bicycles for his guests to use, and the castle Schleissheim and a lake are nearby. Ismaning, by the way, is older than Munich and near the airport, 7^1/$_2$ miles from the city center. An architect by trade and an enthusiast of old buildings, Herr Hübner has many books on old churches, castles, and buildings in Munich. This place is popular, so book early.

Pension Welti
45 Uhdestrasse, 81477 München. ☎ **089/791 15 42.** 16 apts, all with bath. TV TEL. 70 DM ($46.65) apt for one person; 90 DM ($60.90) apt for two people. No credit cards. Parking 3 DM ($2). Take U-Bahn U-2 to Aidenbachstrasse; then bus no. 64 from Aidenbachstrasse to Plattlinger Strasse.

Each apartment in this pension located in the quiet residential neighborhood of Solln has a fully equipped kitchen. There's even daily maid service and a shopping center nearby where you can buy all your provisions. Although rooms are rented on a daily basis, it's great for longer stays. The owner, Rudolph Keis, was born in Germany but lived in the United States for 12 years.

WORTH THE EXTRA MONEY

Although slightly beyond our budget, these hotels are worth the extra money if it's time for a splurge and you want some extra pampering. All are south of the train station, within walking distance.

Europäischer Hof
Bayerstrasse 31 (across from the Hauptbahnhof's south side), 80335 München. ☎ **089/ 55 15 10.** Fax 089/55151-222. 151 rms, 134 with tub or shower and toilet. TEL. 80–100 DM ($53.35–$66.65) single without shower or toilet, 122–190 DM ($81.35–$126.65) single with shower and toilet; 110–150 DM ($73.35–$100) double without shower or toilet, 140–250 DM ($93.35–$166.65) double with shower and toilet; 175–280 DM ($116.65–$186.65) triple with shower and toilet. Rates include buffet breakfast and showers. Discounts available to holders of this book in July–Aug. AE, DC, MC, V. Parking 12 DM ($8).

You can't get any closer to the train station than this modern hotel with a sleek marble lobby with a courteous staff. Most rooms have been recently renovated with new wallpaper, and all those with baths have cable TVs. No-smoking rooms are available. The higher prices are for the main tourist season (September to October), including Oktoberfest and major conventions. There's a restaurant, and in its elegant breakfast room you can eat as much as you want. From its appearance, you'd expect this place to be more expensive than it is.

Hotel Metropole
Bayerstrasse 43, 80335 München. ☎ **089/53 07 64.** Fax 089/532 81 34. 260 rms, 10 with shower only, 230 with tub/shower and toilet. TV TEL. 90–100 DM ($60–$66.65) single without tub/shower or toilet, 130–150 DM ($86.65–$100) single with shower only, 145–165 DM ($96.65–$110) single with tub/shower and toilet; 130–150 DM ($86.65–$100) double without tub/shower or toilet, 170–300 DM ($113.35–$200) double with tub/shower and toilet. Rates include breakfast and showers. Additional bed 45 DM ($30) extra. AE, DC, MC, V. Parking 21 DM ($14). Walk across the street from the Hauptbahnhof.

This modern hotel has an airy lobby with a two-story atrium topped by a skylight, a friendly staff, and clean, comfortable rooms featuring soundproof windows and TV with remote control. The rooms with showers instead of tubs are cheaper. The higher prices in each category above reflect rates during peak season, including

Oktoberfest and major conventions. Since there are only a few rooms without bath, be sure to reserve in advance if that's important to you. The hotel restaurant serves international food.

✪ Hotel Uhland

Uhlandstrasse 1 (near the Oktoberfest meadow, about a 10-minute walk from the train station), 80336 München. ☎ **089/53 92 77.** Fax 089/53 11 14. 30 rms, all with tub/shower and toilet. MINIBAR TV TEL. 110–170 DM ($73.35–$113.35) single; 145–270 DM ($96.65–$180) double; 180–280 DM ($120–$186.65) triple; 190–310 DM ($126.65–$206.65) quad. Rates include buffet breakfast. Crib available. AE, MC, V. Free parking. U-Bahn U-4 or U-5 to Theresienwiese; then a three-minute walk. Bus 58 from the Hauptbahnhof to Georg-Hirth-Platz (third stop).

The facade of this 100-year-old building is striking—ornate baroque with flower boxes of geraniums at all the windows. In former days each floor of the building was its own grand apartment. It was converted into a hotel more than 40 years ago by the Effinger family, and each room is different. Some have been renovated, and a few even have balconies. Parents take note—there's even a "children's room," complete with bunk beds and a stereo. Note that the higher prices in each category are those charged during Oktoberfest and major conventions.

5 Dining

Typical Bavarian restaurants are boisterous, frequently with wooden tables and chairs, beamed ceilings, and half-paneled walls bearing simple hooks on which you can hang your jacket or hat. You sit wherever there's an empty chair (no one will seat you), making it easy to strike up a conversation with others at your table, especially after a few rounds of beer. In fact, I suspect that restaurants in Munich evolved solely so that its citizenry could eat something as they imbibed their favorite brew. And since this is Bavaria, with its tendency toward excess, the meals are hearty and huge. You don't have to spend a fortune here for atmosphere or the food.

Most of Munich's restaurants are in the city center, clustered around the train station, Marienplatz, and in nightlife districts like Schwabing. Since menus are almost always posted outside the front door, you'll never be left in the dark about prices. Many restaurants offer a *Tageskarte* (daily menu) with special complete meals of the day. In fact, most entrees in Munich's restaurants are complete meals, including a main course and a couple of side dishes (often potatoes and sauerkraut). Prices listed below are for complete meals.

If you want to save money, eat at an *Imbiss,* a stall or tiny hole-in-the-wall where food is served over the counter and you eat standing up. And for your breakfast coffee, go to Tschibo or Eduscho, two chain coffee stores that sell both the beans and the brew. You can bring your own pastry and drink a cup of coffee standing up for 1.95 DM ($1.30).

In addition to the restaurants below, the beer halls mentioned under "Munich After Dark," later in this chapter, also serve food.

FAVORITE MEALS   With its six breweries and the largest beer festival in the world, Munich is probably best known for beer, which is almost a complete meal in itself. Bavarians even drink it for breakfast. The freshest is draft beer, called *vom Fass. Weissbier* is made from wheat instead of barley and is full of nutritious (that's one way to look at it) sediment. In summer, a refreshing drink is a *Radler,* half beer and half lemon soda.

Getting the Best Deal on Dining

- Try Munich's many inexpensive stand-up food stalls (called *Imbiss*), serving Wurst, french fries, beer, and pop.
- Take advantage of the special menu of the day (*Tageskarte*), usually a complete meal in itself.
- Butcher shops and food departments of department stores offer such take-out foods as Leberkäs, grilled chicken, and salads.
- Coffee-shop chains, such as Tcshibo or Eduscho, sell cups of coffee for as little as 1.95 DM ($1.30).
- Ask if there's an extra charge for bread (restaurants in Bavaria charge for each piece of bread consumed) and if the entree comes with vegetables or side dishes.
- Remember to inquire if there's a daily special that's not listed on the menu.

To accompany your beer you might want to order food. For breakfast try *Weisswurst* (literally "white sausage"), a delicate blend of veal, salt, pepper, lemon, and parsley. Don't eat the skin unless you want to astound those around you—it would be like eating the wrapper around a hamburger. Another popular dish is *Leberkäs* (also spelled *Leberkäse*), which translates as liver-cheese but is actually neither one. It's a kind of German meatloaf made of beef and bacon that looks like a thick slab of bologna, often served with a fried egg on top, and it's great with a roll, mustard, and sauerkraut.

Other Bavarian specialties include *Leberknödl* (liver dumplings, often served in a soup or with sauerkraut), *Kalbshaxe* (grilled veal knuckle), *Schweinshaxe* (grilled pork knuckle), *Schweinsbraten* (pot-roasted pork), *Sauerbraten* (marinated beef in a thick sauce), and *Spanferkel* (suckling pig).

MEALS FOR LESS THAN 12 DM ($8)
IN THE CITY CENTER

Bella Italia

Herzog-Wilhelm-Strasse 8 (between Marienplatz and Karlsplatz, in the middle of a grassy median). ☎ **089/59 32 59.** Meals 6–17 DM ($4–$11.35). No credit cards. Daily 11:30am–midnight. U-Bahn: Marienplatz or Karlsplatz. ITALIAN.

This popular chain of Italian-staffed restaurants is the best place in town for inexpensive pizza or pasta, including lasagne, tortelloni, cannelloni, and spaghetti, all between 6 and 15 DM ($4 and $10). This restaurant offers indoor seating as well as outdoor tables under a spread of trees. The pizza Bella Italia—topped with ham, mushrooms, olives, peppers, artichoke, and salami—is especially good.

Buxs

Frauenstrasse 9 (just off the Viktualienmarkt). ☎ **089/29 36 84.** Meals about 10–12 DM ($6.65–$8). No credit cards. Mon–Wed and Fri 11am–8pm, Thurs 11am–9pm, Sat 10am–3pm (to 4:30pm on langer Samstag). U-Bahn and S-Bahn: Marienplatz; then a five-minute walk over the Viktualienmarkt. VEGETARIAN.

This pleasant self-service restaurant is modern, bright, and spotless and offers more than 40 kinds of salad, warm dishes, and desserts, which change daily according to what's fresh. About 90% of the ingredients used are organically grown, without the use of chemicals. You can select as much or as little of each salad or dish as you wish—prices are determined by weighing each plate, with each 100 grams of salad costing 2.60 DM ($1.75) and 100 grams of warm dishes 2.90 DM ($1.95). Expect to spend about 12 DM ($8) for a satisfying meal.

Donisl

Weinstrasse 1 (off Marienplatz). ☎ **089/22 01 84.** Meals 7.20–12 DM ($4.80–$8). AE, DC, MC, V. Daily 9am–11pm. U-Bahn and S-Bahn: Marienplatz. GERMAN.

The Donisl is popular with tourists because of its convenient location and its prices. Its cheapest dish is Weisswurst for 7.20 DM ($4.80), so if you're on a budget come here for breakfast or lunch. Even its main dishes, however, are affordable—the Donisl prides itself on the fact that no meal costs more than 12 DM ($8). Try the Leberkäse, Schweinsbraten, Schweinshaxe, Wiener Schnitzel, or Mastente (duck), each served with a side dish. If all you want is a quick snack, at the entrance to the restaurant is a small *Imbiss* with even lower prices. The restaurant has a bright interior, with an inner atrium complete with skylight, and on its walls are portraits of famous actors.

Hofgarten

On the sixth floor of the Kaufhof department store, Karlsplatz. ☎ **089/512 51 20.** Meals 10–15 DM ($6.65–$10). No credit cards. Mon–Wed and Fri 9am–6pm, Thurs 9am–8pm, Sat 8:30am–1:30pm (on langer Samstag, to 5:30pm in winter, to 3:30pm in summer). S-Bahn: Karlsplatz/Stachus. GERMAN/VARIED.

This self-service cafeteria is your best bet for a meal with a panoramic view of the city. Every day there are changing fixed-price meals for 12 to 14 DM ($8 to $9.35); the soups and salad bar are cheaper. If you want to splurge, try one of the delicious desserts.

Restaurant Marché Mövenpick

Altheimer Eck 14a (entance on Neuhauser Strasse, between Karlsplatz and Marienplatz, across from the Sankt Michaelskirche church). ☎ **089/260 60 61.** Meals 8–15 DM ($5.35–$10). No credit cards. Daily 8am–11pm. U-Bahn and S-Bahn: Marienplatz. GERMAN/INTERNATIONAL.

Despite its official street address, the entrance to this great restaurant is right on the pedestrians-only shopping street called Neuhauser Strasse. A chain of cafeterias belonging to the Swiss-owned Mövenpick group, the Marché is based on a marketplace theme, with counters selling various kinds of food and decorated like a local market. Upon entering, you'll be given a card that's stamped for each item you order. There are two floors, with most of the budget-priced dishes on the lower level. Simply pick up a tray and wander through, stopping at the counters that tempt you the most. In addition to a salad bar, there are other counters selling pasta, main dishes that may range from grilled chicken to pork chops, soups, desserts, fruit juices, and other drinks. It's a good, fast place to fill up on veggies. For a complete meal, expect to spend between 10 and 20 DM ($6.65 and $13.35).

NEAR THE HAUPTBAHNHOF

Nordsee

Schützenstrasse 10. ☎ **089/59 80 52.** Meals 6.50–11 DM ($4.35–$7.35). No credit cards. Mon–Wed and Fri 9am–7pm, Thurs 9am–8:30pm, Sat 9am–3pm (on langer Samstag to 6:30pm in winter, to 3:30pm in summer), Sun 11am–6pm. Walk a few minutes east of the Hauptbahnhof. SEAFOOD.

A chain of fast-food fish restaurants originating on Germany's northern coast, Nordsee makes ordering easy by putting the entire menu (about a dozen choices) on a lighted board with photographs. Simply go through the cafeteria line and choose from the selections of fish sticks, fish sandwiches, fish paella, herring, fish soup, and sole. There's also take-out service.

There's another branch at the Viktualienmarkt (Munich's open-air market) near Marienplatz.

Wienerwald

Bayerstrasse 35. ☎ **089/59 55 71.** Meals 11–20 DM ($7.35–$13.35). AE, DC, MC, V. Daily 9am–midnight. Walk across from the train station's south side (where the tourist office is). GERMAN.

The Wienerwald chain is one of the great success stories of postwar Germany, with more than 20 locations in Munich and hundreds more throughout Germany and Austria. Legend has it that the founder came to Oktoberfest, saw the mass consumption of grilled chicken, and decided to open his own restaurant serving only one item—roast chicken—at a price people could afford. A quarter of a grilled chicken served with a choice of side dish costs less than $6. Other menu items include various chicken dishes, soups, salads, and fish.

Other convenient branches are at Arnulfstrasse 12 (☎ **089/59 70 69**), north of the Hauptbahnhof; Odeonsplatz 6–7 (☎ **089/22 58 30**); Amalienstrasse 23 (☎ **089/28 23 92**); and Wendl-Dietrich-Strasse 5 (☎ **089/16 04 43**).

IN SCHWABING

In addition to the following restaurant, chain restaurants described above with locations in Schwabing include Nordsee and Wienerwald.

Mensa Universität

Leopoldstrasse 13. ☎ **089/38 19 60.** Meals 3–5.50 DM ($2–$3.65). No credit cards. Mon–Thurs 11am–2pm, Fri 11am–1:45pm. Closed Jan 1, Easter, and Dec 25. U-Bahn U-3 or U-6 to Giselastrasse. GERMAN.

Technically for students (including those with international student cards), this cafeteria is so big and busy that if you look anything like a student you won't have trouble getting a meal here. The Mensa is located back from Leopoldstrasse, behind the multistory pink building, in a plain concrete-and-glass two-story structure. Your only problem may be figuring out the system. The daily menus are posted on TV screens, as well as on bulletin boards. There are usually four different meals available at four prices—each with its own colored chip that you buy at one of the ground-floor booths. You then head upstairs to the cafeteria that's dishing out the meal you've selected and hand in the chip when you've picked up your tray. A meal for 3 DM ($2), for example, may consist of beef stew, potatoes, salad, and a roll. If in doubt about what's being offered and which cafeteria to go to, ask one of the students.

A second Mensa, the **Mensa Technische Universität,** Arcisstrasse 17 (☎ **089/ 286 639 10**), is convenient for lunch if you're visiting the Alte and Neue Pinakothek, open the same hours.

MEALS FOR LESS THAN 20 DM ($13.35)
IN THE CITY CENTER

Beim Sedlmayr (Bratwurst-Herzl)

Westenriederstrasse 6. ☎ **089/22 62 19.** Meals 7.50–18.50 DM ($5–$12.35). No credit cards. Mon–Sat 8am–4pm. Closed hols. U-Bahn and S-Bahn: Marienplatz. GERMAN.

This unpretentious restaurant reputedly serves the best Weisswurst in all of Munich, made fresh on the premises each day and costing 6 DM ($4) a pair. Most customers are regulars, locals who stop in before going to work or a day of shopping. It's located near the Viktualienmarkt, Munich's large open-air market. The menu is simple and the prices are reasonable. Other good choices include Leberkäs, one-pot stews, Spanferkel, Schnitzel, or the Schweinsbraten.

Nürnberger Bratwurst Glöckl am Dom

Frauenplatz 9. ☎ **089/22 03 85** or 29 52 64. Meals 10–27 DM ($6.65–$18). No credit cards. Mon–Sat 9:30am–midnight. U-Bahn and S-Bahn: Marienplatz. GERMAN.

Although you could easily spend 30 DM ($20) eating such Bavarian specialties as pork filet or Schweinshaxe, to experience this great establishment all you have to order is its famous Schweinwürstl (six small sausages with sauerkraut) for less than 14 DM ($9.35). Half a liter of beer will cost 4.90 DM ($3.25). Located in the shadows of the Frauenkirche (Church of Our Lady), this is Bavaria at its finest: a rough wooden floor, wooden tables, hooks for clothing, and beer steins and tin plates lining a wall shelf. The restaurant was founded in 1893, totally destroyed in 1945, and rebuilt exactly as it was. Upstairs is the Albrecht Dürer Room, quiet and intimate, but I prefer the ground floor's liveliness. An evening here could possibly be your most memorable in Munich.

Ratskeller

Under the Town Hall, on Marienplatz. ☎ **089/22 03 13.** Meals 10–25 DM ($6.65–$16.65). AE, MC, V. Daily 11am–11pm. U-Bahn and S-Bahn: Marienplatz. GERMAN.

Many town halls contain a cellar restaurant, and Munich's is no exception. This one is cavernous, with low vaulted ceilings, archways, white tablecloths, and flowers on every table. Popular with businesspeople and middle-aged shoppers, this dignified restaurant has an English menu. There's no dress code, but shorts would not be appropriate. In addition to its Bavarian specialties of Spanferkel and suckling pig, it has a salad bar and vegetarian dishes for those tired of pork, as well as Wurst, spaghetti, Leberkäs, and changing specials. This is a good choice for Weisswurst in the morning (costing 6.80 DM/$4.55 a pair), or you might want to come for an afternoon coffee and dessert. Beer and wines are available.

Weinstadl

Burgstrasse 5. ☎ **089/523 27 01.** Meals 13–35 DM ($8.65–$23.35). AE, DC, MC, V. Mon–Sat 11am–11pm. U-Bahn and S-Bahn: Marienplatz. GERMAN.

In contrast to the other restaurants in this section, this one specializes in German wines instead of beer (apparently, Munich was a wine town long before beer took over). Built in 1551 and later serving as a Customs house for wines brought in from Austria, Italy, Hungary, and France to be traded for those of Germany, this restaurant's full of architectural character—a narrow spiral staircase, windows with bull's-eye glass, an arbored courtyard, and a cellar with vaulted ceilings. One of Munich's oldest buildings, it has three floors of dining. Its changing menu may list roast pork with potato dumplings and salad, trout, grilled sausage, and Schnitzel, as well as daily specials.

Weisses Bräuhaus

Im Tal 10. ☎ **089/29 98 75.** Meals 12.50–30 DM ($8.35–$20). No credit cards. Daily 8am–11pm. U-Bahn and S-Bahn: Marienplatz. GERMAN.

This boisterous place is famous for its beer—*Bräuhaus* means "brewery"—and the kind to order here is wheat beer, either Weizenbier or Weissbier. A simple white interior with a wooden floor and long wooden tables, this typical Bavarian restaurant has an English menu whose cheapest and most famous meal is Weisswurst (costing 7.20 DM/$4.80, available only until noon). If you're hungry, order the Bavarian Farmer's Feast—roast and smoked pork, pork sausage, liver dumplings, mashed potatoes, and sauerkraut. Other choices include Leberkäs ("liver cheese" on the English menu), suckling pig, Schweinsbraten, potato pancakes, and breaded calf's head. Or if you want, order just a beer; half a liter costs 5.20 DM ($3.45).

Zum Franziskaner

Perusastrasse 5 (three minutes north of Marienplatz; there's another entrance around the corner at Residenzstrasse 9). ☎ **089/231 81 20.** Meals 10–25 DM ($6.65–$16.65). AE, DC, MC. Daily 8am–midnight. U-Bahn and S-Bahn: Marienplatz. GERMAN.

A lively Bavarian favorite, this restaurant gets so crowded that you may find it difficult to find a seat at prime lunch or dinner times. There are several separate dining rooms, so simply wander through until you find a seat. If you're starving, try the Bavarian sausage platter, with various kinds of Wurst (smoked, blood, liver, onion, and more) as well as radish and bread. Other sections on the English menu include fresh trout, Leberkäs with a fried egg and potato salad, suckling pig with potato dumpling and cabbage salad, Sauerbraten with dumpling, and Wiener Schnitzel. There are also many changing daily specials—unfortunately, they aren't listed on the English menu. You can dine here for less than 10 DM ($6.65) if you order the Weisswurst, served until 3pm and costing 3.70 DM ($2.45) apiece.

SOUTH OF THE HAUPTBAHNHOF

Mariandl Restaurant

Goethestrasse 51 (less than a 10-minute walk south of the Hauptbahnhof, near Beethovenplatz). ☎ **089/53 51 58.** Meals 12.50–30 DM ($8.35–$20). No credit cards. Mon–Fri 11:30am–2:30pm and 6–10:30pm. Closed hols. Bus 58 to Beethovenplatz. GERMAN/VARIED.

This elegant and refined restaurant with a parlorlike atmosphere offers free entertainment as well as dining. From 8pm Monday through Friday musicians play classical music; on Monday it's open mike. Portraits of famous classical composers line the walls, and there are fresh flowers on each table. A changing menu offers a few select complete meals, such as Schnitzel or Sauerbraten, but lighter meals like spaghetti are always available, as are beer, wine, and champagne. The *Mittagsmenü*, or lunch special, offers a two-course meal for about 12 DM ($8).

IN SCHWABING

Gaststätte Atzinger

Schellingstrasse 9 (at the corner of Amalienstrasse, a 10-minute walk from the Alte and Neue Pinakothek). ☎ **089/28 28 80.** Meals 9–19 DM ($6–$12.65). No credit cards. Mon–Tues 10am–1am, Wed–Thurs 10am–2am, Fri–Sat 10am–3am, Sun 1pm–1am. U-Bahn U-3 or U-6 to Universität. GERMAN.

Popular with students who come here to eat, drink, smoke, and talk, this pub/restaurant has terrific prices and atmosphere. Specialties include Schweinsbraten, Schweinshaxe, Schnitzel, fish, spaghetti, Wurst, and Leberkäs. It's in the southern part of Schwabing in an area of bookshops, cheap restaurants, and bars. The daily specials—giant single-platter meals with a main dish and side dishes—are often big enough for two. Half a liter of beer is 4.60 DM ($3.05).

Gaststätte Leopold

Leopoldstrasse 50. ☎ **089/38 38 680.** Meals 12–30 DM ($8–$20). No credit cards. Daily 11:30am–11pm. U-Bahn U-3 or U-6 to Giselastrasse. GERMAN.

Popular with the middle-aged, this Bavarian restaurant can be a haven away from the Schwabing throngs, though later it can get crowded. In summer tables and chairs are set outside, where you can watch the passing crowds on busy Leopoldstrasse, the center stage of nightlife in Schwabing. A large open dining area with a beer-hall atmosphere, it serves typical Bavarian and German fare, as well as changing daily specials.

Munich's First Diner (MFD)

Feilitschstrasse and Leopoldstrasse (behind the Hertie department store). ☎ **089/33 59 15.** Meals 9–22 DM ($6–$14.65). AE, MC. Daily 7:30am–1am. U-Bahn U-3 or U-6 to Münchener Freiheit. AMERICAN.

If you prefer a burger and fries over sausages and sauerkraut, head to MFD, decorated with the requisite chrome and red-vinyl stools and benches. Catering to the youth that make Schwabing their own, it offers loud music, breakfast until noon (including an American breakfast), and an English menu listing salads (meals in themselves), sandwiches, pizza, and pasta. It's a bit of Americana in the heart of Bavaria.

Wok-Man

Leopoldstrasse 68. ☎ **089/39 03 43.** Meals 9–18 DM ($6–$12). No credit cards. Daily 11am–midnight. U-Bahn U-3 or U-6 to Münchener Freiheit. CHINESE.

This casual fast-food cafeteria, easy to find on Schwabing's main boulevard not far from the nightlife district, offers the usual Chinese fare, including fried noodles, sweet-and-sour chicken, fried beef with green peppers and onions, and vegetarian dishes. Even better is its self-service buffet that includes several main dishes, a salad, and appetizers like spring rolls, costing 12 DM ($8) for a small plate and 18 DM ($12) for a large.

STREET EATS

In addition to the locales mentioned here, both the Viktualienmarkt and the Schmankerlgasse, described under "Picnicking," below, offer unlimited choices in fast food and stand-up food stalls. Restaurants listed above with an adjoining *Imbiss* or take-out service include Wienerwald, Nordsee, and Donisl.

NEAR THE HAUPTBAHNHOF

Mathäser Bierstadt

Bayerstrasse 5 (a short walk from the main train station). ☎ **089/59 28 96.** Meals 3.50–9 DM ($2.35–$6). No credit cards. Daily 10am–9:30pm. GERMAN.

This beer hall has an outdoor *Imbiss* at its main entryway, where it sells Wiener (hot dog), Eintopf mit Rindfleisch (a beef stew), Brathuhn (grilled chicken), Weisswurst, and Leberkäs. You can take your order inside and eat it at one of the stand-up tables just inside the door, where you can also order a beer, of course.

IN THE CITY CENTER

Danmark

In the underground passage at Stachus (Karlsplatz). Meals 3.50–8 DM ($2.35–$5.35). Mon–Wed and Fri 9am–7pm, Thurs 9am–9pm, Sat 9am–3pm (to 7pm on langer Samstag). S-Bahn and U-Bahn: Karlsplatz/Stachus. INTERNATIONAL.

It's hard to miss this busy *Imbiss* in the middle of the passageway beneath the Stachus at Karlsplatz. Different counters offer Wurst and hot dogs, pizza, hamburgers, sandwiches, gyros, Chinese dishes, and beer. There are stand-up counters where you can eat.

Räucheronkel

Orlandostrasse 3 (near the Hofbräuhaus, a seven-minute walk from Marienplatz). ☎ **089/ 22 45 09.** Meals 4–12 DM ($2.65–$8). No credit cards. Mon–Fri 7am–6pm, Sat 7am–1pm. GERMAN.

This cafeteria-style *Imbiss* (popular with the working class) is connected to its own butcher shop and has chest-high tables where you can stand and eat. No one here speaks English, so you'll just have to point. Choices usually include Weisswurst, Leberknödel soup, Schweinsbraten, dumplings, Gulasch, Kalbsbraten, Leberkäs, grilled chicken, salads, and sausages. This is also a good place to buy picnic ingredients.

Vinzenz Murr

Rosenstrasse 7 (a minute from Marienplatz). ☎ **089/260 47 65.** Meals 4–10 DM ($2.65– $6.65). No credit cards. Mon–Wed and Fri 8am–6:30pm, Thurs 8am–8:30pm, Sat 8am–2pm (to 6pm on langer Samstag). GERMAN.

This is the most convenient location of a chain of Munich butcher shops that have a stand-up *Imbiss* in addition to meats and take-out service. Sandwiches, Schweineschnitzel, pizza, salads, cheeses, breads, and Leberkäs are just some of the selections. There's also an extensive salad bar.

IN SCHWABING

Hut's Pizza Station

Feilitzschstrasse 11. ☎ **089/34 24 97.** Meals 3.50–6 DM ($2.35–$4). No credit cards. Daily 1pm–1am. U-Bahn U-3 or U-6 to Münchener Freiheit. PIZZA.

This is one of several take-out establishments in Schwabing, catering primarily to the hordes of young people who come here for a night on the town. Although its main seller is pizza by the slice for 3.50 DM ($2.35), it also sells curry Wurst and gyros with tzaziki.

PICNICKING

Check out "Street Eats," above, since the localities there all offer take-out food.

Department stores (such as Hertie across from the train station or Kaufhof on Marienplatz) have basement food departments. These sell fruits and vegetables, cheese, sausages, breads, drinks, and cakes, as well as ready-made salads, Leberkäs, grilled chicken, and more.

If you want more traditional surroundings, the **Viktualienmarkt** can't be beat. Munich's most famous outdoor market, dating from the early 1800s, is a colorful affair with permanent little shops and booths and stalls set up under umbrellas. Wurst, bread, cakes, honey, cheese, wine, fruits, vegetables, flowers, and meats are sold here, and in the middle of the market there's even a beer garden, where you're welcome to sit at one of the outer tables (only at those without a tablecloth) and eat your purchase. There are also a lot of stand-up fast-food counters. The market is open Monday through Friday from 8am to 6pm and Saturday from 8am to 2pm.

Another good place to search for picnic ingredients is **Schmankerlgasse,** an underground passage leading from the Hertie department store near the Hauptbahnhof to Karlsplatz. Schmankerlgasse is lined with booth after booth of food stalls, each specializing in something different, including pita-bread sandwiches, fish, vegetarian dishes, Chinese food, pasta, sausages, desserts, croissants, fresh fruit juices, salads, cheeses, and vegetables. You can either stand and eat it here, sit at one of the tables, or take it with you. Schmankerlgasse is open Monday through Wednesday and Friday from 9am to 6:30pm, Thursday from 9am to 8:30pm, and Saturday from 8:30am to 2pm (first Saturday of the month, 8:30am to 6pm).

If you want to picnic in style, head for the finest delicatessen in town, **Alois Dallmayr,** Dienerstrasse 14 (☎ **089/21350**). Its meats, cheeses, wines, grilled chicken, breads, fruits, vegetables, caviar, chocolates, teas, coffees, and cakes are expensive—you can even have things gift-wrapped here. It's open Monday through Wednesday and Friday from 9am to 6:30pm, Thursday from 9am to 8:30pm, and Saturday from 9am to 2pm.

And where can you go to eat your goodies? Try **along the Isar River** or somewhere in the huge expanse of the **Englischer Garten.** Better yet, take your food to one of the **beer gardens** in the section below, where all you have to buy is one of those famous mugs of foaming beer.

BEER GARDENS

Munich's beer gardens are as fickle as the weather—if the weather's bad, the beer gardens don't open. By the same token, if suddenly in the middle of February the weather turns gloriously warm, the beer gardens start turning on the taps.

Generally speaking, however, beer gardens are open on sunny days from May to September or October, usually from 10 or 11am to midnight. Ranging in size from tiny neighborhood gardens that accommodate a few hundred people to those that seat several thousand, beer gardens number about 35 in and around Munich, making it the beer-garden capital of the world. Many of the larger ones boast traditional Bavarian bands on weekends. The smallest beer available is usually a liter—after all, you're here to drink beer—which costs about 9 DM ($6) if you fetch it yourself and 10 DM ($6.65) if you order it from a waitress.

Caution: Many of the beer gardens are in the middle of huge parks, making them a bit difficult to find. Take note of how you got there; it's even harder to find your way out of the park after you've had a few liters of beer.

These four beer gardens allow you to bring your own food: **Augustiner Keller,** Arnulfstrasse 52 (☎ **089/59 43 93**), about a 10-minute walk northwest of the Hauptbahnhof; **Viktualienmarkt,** in the city center near Marienplatz (☎ **089/ 29 75 45**), closed Sunday and holidays (described under "Picnicking," above); **Chinesischer Turm,** in the Englischer Garten (☎ **089/39 50 28**), reached by taking the U-Bahn (U-3 or U-6), to Giselastrasse; and **Hirschgarten,** Hirschgartenstrasse 1 (☎ **089/17 25 91**), near Nymphenburg Palace (take the S-Bahn to Laim).

WORTH THE EXTRA MONEY

Haxnbauer

Münzstrasse 8 (near the Hofbräuhaus, a five-minute walk from Marienplatz). ☎ **089/ 22 19 22.** Meals 15–30 DM ($10–$20). AE, DC, MC, V. Mon–Sat 5pm–midnight. Closed Christmas to mid-Jan, and July–Aug. U-Bahn and S-Bahn: Marienplatz. GERMAN.

This restaurant with an English menu claims to sell more pork and veal Haxn than any other place in the world. You can see meats roasting in the front window. Inside, the atmosphere is subdued and dignified, a good place to come for a quiet evening. Note the old copper bar (polished every day) and the collection of old firemen's helmets, some 100 years old.

Another Haxnbauer is around the corner at Sparkassenstrasse 2 (☎ 089/ 22 19 22) with the same English menu, open daily from 11am to midnight year round.

Hundskugel

Hotterstrasse 18 (a five-minute walk from Marienplatz). ☎ **089/26 42 72.** Meals 16–40 DM ($10.65–$26.65). No credit cards. Daily 11am–11pm. U-Bahn and S-Bahn: Marienplatz. GERMAN.

In operation since 1440, this may well be Munich's oldest restaurant. Its facade, brightly lit and decorated with flower boxes, hints at what's waiting inside— intimate rooms with low-beamed ceilings, little changed over the centuries. It serves Bavarian and German traditional food, including Spanferkel with dumplings and Kraut salad, Tellerfleisch (beef cooked in meat stock and cut into slices), and the Hundskugel Spezial (broiled pork tenderloin with potatoes, mushrooms, and vegetables, baked with cheese), an experience you won't forget. A three-course daily special, below 20 DM ($13.35), is available until it runs out.

Prinz Myshkin

Hackenstrasse 2 (off Sendlinger Strasse, a few minutes' walk from Marienplatz). ☎ **089/ 26 55 96.** Appetizers and soups 7–15 DM ($4.65–$10); pizza 14–19 DM ($9.35–$12.65); main courses 17–30 DM ($11.35–$20). AE, MC, V. Daily 11am–11pm. U-Bahn and S-Bahn: Marienplatz. VEGETARIAN.

If you want to splurge on something other than German cuisine, this trendy restaurant serves vegetarian dishes in a refined, relaxed setting. Boasting a high vaulted ceiling, artwork, candles on every table, and background music that's likely to be soft jazz, it serves a variety of changing salads, soups, and appetizers; these may include vegetarian quiche, Japanese miso soup, or a wild rice salad. In addition to pizza, it offers innovative main dishes ranging from various ravioli to a Thai-inspired dish of paprika, mushrooms, onions, pineapple, and bananas in a coconut-curry sauce. Monday through Friday from 11:30am to 2pm it offers a fixed-price business lunch for less than 15 DM ($10).

6 Attractions

SIGHTSEEING SUGGESTIONS

To see the best of what Munich has to offer, you could easily spend a week in the city. After all, with the possible exception of Berlin, Munich has more first-class museums than any other city in Germany and is the cultural capital of the nation. If, however, you have less than a week, the suggestions below will guide you to the most important attractions.

If You Have 1 Day

Begin with a breakfast of Munich's famous Weisswurst at a traditional Bavarian restaurant. To get a feel for the atmosphere of this Bavarian capital, then stroll through Old Town. Start at Stachus (Karlsplatz) and walk down the pedestrian lane of Neuhauser Strasse with its many shops and boutiques, stopping at the venerable Frauenkirche, Munich's largest church and most celebrated landmark. Continue to Marienplatz, the heart of the city, where you'll find the Neues Rathaus (New Town Hall). You can take an elevator up to the Rathaus tower for a view over the city.

From Marienplatz, head for St. Peter's Church, affectionately called Alte Peter (Old Peter) by the townspeople. Then visit the Viktualienmarkt, Munich's colorful open-air market, where you might want to eat lunch at one of its many stand-up food stalls or at the beer garden located in its center.

In the afternoon, head toward the Deutsches Museum, the world's largest technological museum. If you still have the energy, the time, and the inclination, rush to the Neue Pinakothek with its collection of famous old and new masterpieces. Spend the evening at one of Munich's famous beer halls.

If You Have 2 Days

Spend your first morning as outlined above, but in the afternoon devote yourself to the Neue Pinakothek, with its collection of late 18th- and 19th-century works, and the most famous works from the Alte Pinakothek (now under renovation).

On Day 2, spend the morning at the Deutsches Museum. In the early afternoon visit Nymphenburg Palace, summer residence of the Wittelsbach Electors of Bavaria and Germany's largest baroque palace.

If You Have 3 Days

Spend your first day entirely in Old Town as outlined above, but include in your walk visits to the Residenz, the official residence of the Wittelsbach family, and its Treasure House. Nearby is the Cuvilliés Theater, one of the most beautiful rococo theaters in Germany. You should also pay a visit to the Stadtmuseum, the Municipal Museum, with displays relating to the history and development of Munich. End the day with a stroll through the Englischer Garten, stopping off for a liter at its Chinesischer Turm beer garden.

Spend Day 2 at the Deutsches Museum and Nymphenburg Palace. On Day 3 visit the Neue Pinakothek; the Antikensammlungen, with its collection of antiquities; the Glyptothek, with one of Europe's finest collections of Greek and Roman sculpture; and the Lenbachhaus, devoted to Munich's artists.

If You Have 5 Days

Spend the first three days as outlined above. On Day 4, head for the Haus der Kunst, repository for art since the beginning of the 20th century. Nearby is the great Bavarian Museum, relating to the history of Bavaria with an outstanding collection of nativity scenes. Spend the afternoon shopping or visiting the BMW Museum and the Olympic Village. Or go to Dachau, a former concentration camp that's been set up as a memorial to those who died under Hitler's regime. On the fifth day, take an excursion to Neuschwanstein, Germany's most famous castle, in the foothills of the Bavarian Alps.

TOP ATTRACTIONS

If museums are high on your list, you can save money by spending 20 DM ($13.35) on a **combination ticket** that will allow you entrance into all 23 state museums, including the Neue Pinakothek, Bavarian National Museum, Glypothek, Antikensammlungen, and the Haus der Kunst. Valid for eight days, it can be purchased at any of the state museums. Remember, too, that many museums (with the exception of the Deutsches Museum and Nymphenburg) are free on Sunday and holidays.

✪ Alte Pinakothek

Barer Strasse 27. ☎ **089/238 05215.** Currently closed for renovations, with an expected reopening in 1997; until then, major works are on display at the Neue Pinakothek.

If you visit only one museum in Munich, this should be the one. Begun as the private collection of the Wittelsbach family in the early 1500s, it contains virtually all European schools of painting from the Middle Ages to the beginning of the 19th century. It has one of the largest collections of Rubens in the world (61 of his works), not to mention galleries filled with German, Dutch, Flemish, Italian, Spanish, and French masterpieces. Represented are Dürer, Cranach, Altdorfer, Brueghel, Rembrandt, Raphael, Leonardo, Titian, Tiepolo, El Greco, Velázquez, Murillo, Poussin, and Lorrain. The museum contains galleries of religious allegorical paintings, portraits of peasants and patricians, Romantic landscapes, still lifes, and scenes of war and hunting. They're housed in an imposing structure built by Leo von Klenze between 1826 and 1836 and modeled on Venetian Renaissance palaces.

Although it's difficult to pick the stars in the collection, Dürer is well represented with his *Four Apostles, The Baumgartner Altar, Lamentation for the Dead Christ,* and, my favorite, his famous *Self-portrait.* Watch for Titian's *Crowning with Thorns,* Rembrandt's *Birth of Christ* with his remarkable use of light and shadows, Rubens's *Self-Portrait with His Wife in the Arbor* and *Last Judgment,* and Brueghel's *Land of Cockaigne.*

In Albrecht Altdorfer's *Battle of Alexander,* which took him 12 years to complete, notice the painstaking detail of the thousands of lances and all the men on horseback. Yet Alexander the Great on his horse is easy to spot amid the chaos, as he pursues Darius fleeing in his chariot. Another favorite is Adriaen Brouwer of the Netherlands, one of the best painters of the peasant genre. The Alte Pinakothek has 17 of his paintings, the largest collection in the world. *Cabinet 10,* where Brouwer has captured the life of his subjects as they drink at an inn, pay cards, or engage in a brawl, is delightful.

Neue Pinakothek

Barer Strasse 29. ☎ **089/238 05195.** Admission 6 DM ($4) adults, 3.50 DM ($2.35) senior citizens, 1 DM (65¢) students and children; free for everyone Sun and hols. Tues and Thurs 10am–8pm; Wed and Fri–Sun 10am–5pm. U-Bahn U-2 to Königsplatz; then a 15-minute walk. Tram 18 to Pinakothek. Bus 53 to Schellingstrasse.

❓ Did You Know?

- Munich (München in German) means "home of the monks."
- In 1919, workers and soldiers in Munich proclaimed a Communist republic—it was short-lived.
- The Nazi party was founded in Munich.
- Nearly 40% of Munich was destroyed during World War II.
- The first waltz in the world was danced here in 1740, even earlier than in Vienna.
- During Oktoberfest, 72 oxen broiled whole on the spit, 30,000 grilled fish, 400,000 pairs of pork sausage, and 700,000 chickens are devoured—and over a million gallons of beer are consumed.

Across from the Alte Pinakothek is the Neue Pinakothek, with its comprehensive view of European painting in the 19th century (and, until the 1997 reopening of the Alte Pinakothek, selected works of European masters from the 15th to the 19th century). Included in the collection are examples of international art from around 1800 (David, Goya, Gainsborough, Turner), as well as German and French impressionism, symbolism, and art nouveau. Corinth, Slevogt, Liebermann, Cézanne, Gaughin, Rodin, van Gogh, Degas, Manet, Monet, and Renoir all have canvases here.

The building itself is a delight, designed by Alexander von Branca and opened in 1981 to replace the old museum destroyed in World War II. Using the natural lighting of skylights and windows, it's the perfect setting for the paintings it displays. Follow the rooms chronologically, starting with Room 1.

✪ Deutsches Museum

Museuminsel 1 (Ludwigsbrücke). ☎ **089/21791.** Admission 8 DM ($5.35) adults, 5 DM ($3.35) senior citizens, 3 DM ($2) students and children. Daily 9am–5pm. Tram 18 to Deutsches Museum. S-Bahn: Isartor.

I've been to the Deutsches Museum more than any other museum in Munich and still haven't seen it all. The largest technological museum of its kind in the world, the Deutsches Museum is divided into 30 departments, including those relating to physics, shipping, rocks and minerals, vehicles, musical instruments, aviation, glass technology, writing and printing, photography, textiles, and weights and measures. There's also a planetarium.

You can see the first German submarine, 50 historic automobiles (including the first Benz of 1886), and the original airplanes of the Wright brothers. You can descend into the bowels of a salt mine or test your memory. Would you like to watch the developing of a black-and-white photograph? What was Columbus's route to the New World? What does the nervous system of a turtle look like? What makes the museum fascinating for adults and children alike is that there are buttons to push, gears to crank, and levers to pull.

Nymphenburg Palace and Marstallmuseum, Amalienburg, and the Royal Pavilions

Schloss Nymphenburg 1. ☎ **089/17 908-668.** Combination ticket to everything, 6 DM ($4) adults in winter, 8 DM ($5.35) in summer; 4 DM ($2.65) senior citizens, students, and children in winter, 5 DM ($3.35) in summer. For Nymphenburg Palace, Amalienburg, and Marstallmuseum only, 4.50 DM ($3) adults in winter, 6 DM ($4) in summer; 3 DM ($2) senior citizens, students, and children in winter, 4 DM ($2.65) in summer. Nymphenburg Palace and Amalienburg, summer, Tues–Sun 9am–12:30pm and 1:30–5pm; winter, Tues–Sun 10am–12:30pm and 1:30–4pm. Marstallmuseum, summer, Tues–Sun 9am–noon and 1–5pm; winter, Tues–Sun 10am–noon and 1–4pm. Badenburg, Pagodenburg, and Magdalenenklause, summer, Tues–Sun 10am–12:30pm and 1:30–5pm; closed Oct–Mar. Take U-Bahn U-1 to Rotkreuzplatz; then tram no. 12 (going toward Amalienburg Strasse) to Schloss Nymphenburg.

The former summer residence of the Wittelsbach family who ruled over Bavaria, Nymphenburg Palace is Germany's largest baroque palace. Construction began in 1664 but took more than a century to complete; then the palace stretched 625 yards long and looked out over a park of some 500 acres. You could spend a whole day in just the sculptured garden, with its statues, lakes, and waterfalls, and in its park pavilions (each a miniature palace in itself). But first visit the main palace and the nearby Marstallmuseum for its outstanding collection of carriages.

Munich

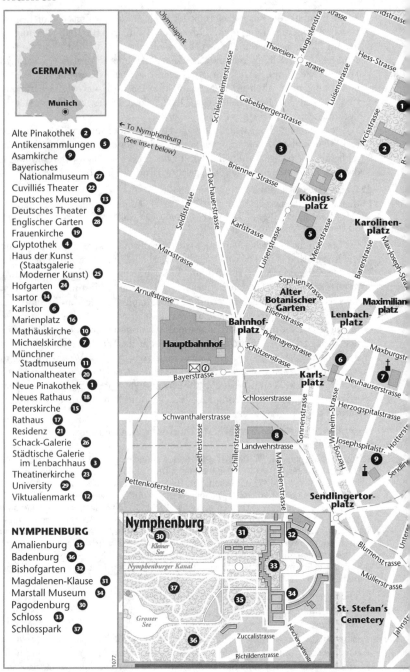

GERMANY

Munich

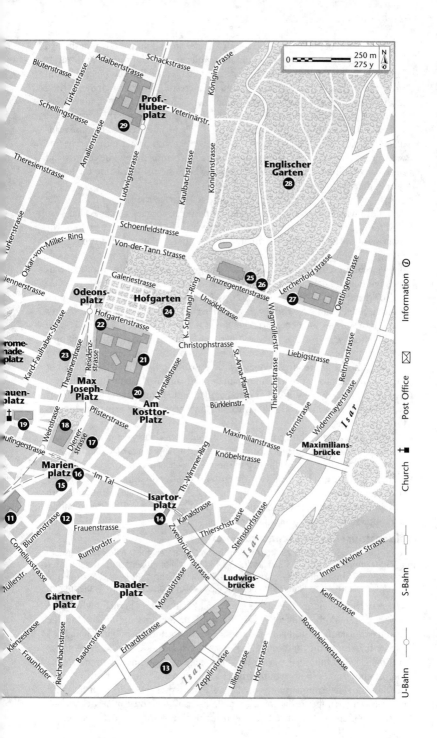

Blütenstrasse

Adalbertstrasse

Schackstrasse

Königinstrasse

Schellingstrasse

Türkenstrasse

Amalienstrasse

Prof.-Huber-platz

㉙

Veterinärstr.

Theresienstrasse

Ludwigstrasse

Kaulbachstrasse

Königinstrasse

Englischer Garten

㉘

Türkenstrasse

Oskar-von-Miller-Ring

Schoenfeldstrasse

Von-der-Tann Strasse

Lerchenfeld strasse

Oettingenstrasse

iennerstrasse

Galeriestrasse

Prinzregentenstrasse

㉕ ㉖

Odeonsplatz

Hofgarten

㉔

K. Scharnagl-Ring

Unsöldstrasse

㉗

Card-Faulhaber-Strasse

romenadeplatz

Hofgartenstrasse

㉒

Wagmüllerstr.

Liebigstrasse

Reitmorstrasse

㉓

Theatinerstrasse

Residenzstrasse

㉑

Christophstrasse

St.-Anna-Pfarrstr.

Thierschstrasse

Sternstrasse

Widenmayerstrasse

Isar

auenplatz

Max Joseph-Platz

㉒⓪

Am Kosttor-Platz

Marstallstrasse

Bürkleinstr.

†

⑲

Weinstrasse

Pfisterstrasse

Maximilianstrasse

Maximiliansbrücke

ufingerstrasse

⑱

Dienerstrasse

⑰

Knöbelstrasse

Th.-Wimmer-Ring

Marienplatz ⑯

Im Tal

⑮

Isartorplatz

⑪

Blumenstrasse

⑫

Frauenstrasse

⑭

Kanalstrasse

Thierschstrasse

Steinsdorfstrasse

Isar

Corneliusstrasse

Rumfordstr.

Zweibrückenstrasse

Innere Weiner Strasse

Müllerstr.

Gärtnerplatz

Baaderplatz

Morassistrasse

Ludwigsbrücke

Kellerstrasse

Klenzestrasse

Reichenbachstrasse

Baaderstrasse

Fraunhofer-

Erhardtstrasse

⑬

Isar

Zepplinstrasse

Lilienstrasse

Hochstrasse

Rosenheimerstrasse

0   250 m / 275 y   N

U-Bahn —○—   S-Bahn —□—   Church † ■   Post Office ⊠   Information ❼

There are no palace tours—you simply wander around on your own in the two wings open to the public. The main attractions are the glorious Grand Marble Hall, richly decorated with stucco work and frescoes, the Brussels tapestries, and the Chinese lacquer cabinet, but the most interesting in gossip circles is King Ludwig I's Gallery of Beauties. The 36 portraits, commissioned by Ludwig, represent the most beautiful women in Munich in his time. Among them are Marie, Queen of Bavaria (mother of Ludwig II), and Lola Montez, a dancer whose scandalous relations with Ludwig I prompted an 1848 revolt by a disgruntled people who forced Ludwig's abdication. (Lola Montez was banished from the country and moved to California in the United States, where she made a name for herself during the Gold Rush days.)

Just outside the main palace (to the left as you face the ticket booth) is the **Marstallmuseum,** with its splendid collection of state coaches, carriages, and sleds used for weddings, coronations, and special events. Housed in what used to be the royal stables, the museum culminates in the fantastic fairytalelike carriages of Ludwig II, which are no less extravagant than his castles. On the first floor above the Marstallmuseum is a collection of Nymphenburger porcelain, with its beautiful and delicate figurines, tea services, plates, and bowls.

Now head for the park. To your left is **Amalienburg,** a delightful small pink hunting lodge unlike anything you've ever seen. Considered one of the world's great masterpieces of rococo art, this lodge was built by architect François de Cuvilliés for Maria Amalia, Charles Albert's wife. She used to station herself on a platform on the roof to shoot game that were driven past her. The first couple of rooms in this lodge are simple enough with drawings in the spirit of the hunt, but then the rooms take off in a flight of fantasy, with an amazing amount of decorative silver covering the walls with vines, grapes, and cherubs. Its Hall of Mirrors is as splendid a room as you're likely to find anywhere, far surpassing anything in the main palace.

In the park are also three pavilions: the **Magdalenenklause,** designed as a meditation retreat for Max Emanuel, complete with artificially made cracks in the walls to make it look like a ruin; the **Pagodenburg,** an elegant two-story tea pavilion, with an interior of Dutch tiles on the ground floor and Chinese black-and-red lacquered chambers upstairs; and **Badenburg,** Max Emanuel's bathhouse with its Chinese wallpaper and two-story pool faced with Dutch tiles (this qualifies as Europe's first indoor swimming pool).

Residenzmuseum and Schatzkammer

Max-Joseph-Platz 3. ☎ **089/29 06 71.** Admission (separately for the Residenzmuseum and Schatzkammer) 5 DM ($3.35) adults, 3 DM ($2) senior citizens and students, free for children 15 and under. Tues–Sun 10am–4:30pm. U-Bahn U-3, U-4, U-5, or U-6 to Odeonsplatz. Tram 19 to Nationaltheater (or easy walking distance from Marienplatz).

Whereas Nymphenburg Palace was the Wittelsbach summer home, the Residenz was the family's official in-town residence for four centuries up until 1918. The **Residenzmuseum,** a small part of the residence, is open to the public. Though it's a mere fraction of the total palace, it's so large that I wonder how its inhabitants ever managed to find their way around. There are court rooms, apartments, bedrooms, and arcades in everything from Renaissance and baroque to rococo and neoclassical. The Antiquarium is the largest Renaissance room north of the Alps; in the Silver Chamber is the complete table silver of the House of Wittelsbach— some 3,500 pieces. The Ancestors Hall contains the portraits of 121 members of

Special & Free Events

Munich's most famous event of the year is the **Oktoberfest**, which is held from the middle of September to the first Sunday in October. The celebration began in 1810 to honor King Ludwig I's marriage, when the main event consisted of a horse race in a field called Theresienwiese. Everyone had so much fun that the celebration was held again the following year, and then again and again. Today the Oktoberfest is among the largest fairs in the world.

Every year the festivities get under way with a parade on the first Oktoberfest Sunday, with almost 7,000 participants marching through the city streets in folk costumes. Most activities, however, are at the Theresienwiese, where huge beer tents sponsored by local Munich breweries dispense both beer and merriment, complete with Bavarian bands and singing. Each tent holds up to 6,000 people, which gives you at least some idea how rowdy things can get. During the 16-day period of the Oktoberfest, an estimated six million visitors guzzle over a million gallons of beer and eat 700,000 broiled chickens. Pure gluttony, and a lot of fun! In addition to the beer tents, there are also carnival attractions and amusement rides. Entry to the fairgrounds is free, though rides—and of course, beer— cost extra.

Munich's other major event is **Fasching (Carnival)**, which culminates in a parade through town on Shrove Tuesday.

the Wittelsbach family—eerie because of the way their eyes seem to follow you as you walk down the hall. Be sure, too, to see the Emperor's Hall, the Rich Chapel, the Green Gallery, and the Rich Rooms.

In the Residenz is the **Schatzkammer (Treasure House)**, housing an amazing collection of jewelry, gold, silver, and religious items belonging to the Bavarian royalty, including swords, crowns, scepters, goblets, bowls, toiletry objects, serving platters, and more, each more fantastic than the last. Nothing is plain and simple—indeed, most items are studded with bulging diamonds, rubies, and emeralds.

Cuvilliés Theater

Residenzstrasse 1 (just north of the Residenzmuseum). ☎ **089/29 68 36** or 29 06 71. Admission 2.50 DM ($1.65) adults, 1.50 DM ($1) senior citizens and students, free for children 14 and under. Mon–Sat 2–5pm, Sun and hols 10am–5pm. Closed approximately 80 days a year due to performances; telephone beforehand to make sure it's open. U-Bahn U-3, U-4, U-5, or U-6 to Odeonsplatz.

Also known as the Altes Residenztheater, this small but sumptuous work of art is considered the finest rococo tier-boxed theater in Germany. Seating 500 spectators, it was built by François de Cuvilliés in the mid-1700s, destroyed in World War II, and painstakingly rebuilt with original materials—the magnificently carved and gilded woodwork had been stored in safety during the war. (Cuvilliés was considered the best architect and interior decorator of the South German rococo style. Of very short stature, he began his career as a court jester.)

Glyptothek

Königsplatz 3. ☎ **089/28 61 00.** Admission 5 DM ($3.35) adults, 3 DM ($2) senior citizens, 1 DM (65¢) students; combination ticket for both Glyptothek and Antikensammlungen,

8 DM ($5.35) adults, 4 DM ($2.65) senior citizens and students; free for everyone on Sun. Tues–Wed and Fri–Sun 10am–4:30pm, Thurs noon–8:30pm. U-Bahn U-2 to Königsplatz.

The Glyptothek and the Antikensammlungen across the square form the largest collection of classical art in what was West Germany. The Glyptothek houses Greek and Roman statues, busts, and grave steles in a beautiful setting of plain white brick and domed ceilings, reminiscent of a Roman bath, and one of the best examples of neoclassicism in Germany. Built by architect Leo von Klenze, the building was commissioned by King Ludwig I, whose dream was to transform Munich into another Athens. Indeed, the Glyptothek does resemble a Greek temple.

In Room II (to your left as you enter the museum) is the famous *Barberini Faun*, a large sleeping satyr dating from about 220 B.C. In Room IV is the grave stele of Mnesarete, which depicts a dead mother seated in front of her daughter. Also in the museum are sculptures from the pediments of the Aphaia Temple in Aegina, with scenes of the Trojan War, as well as a room filled with Roman busts.

Antikensammlungen

Königsplatz 1. ☎ **089/59 83 59.** Admission 5 DM ($3.35) adults, 3 DM ($2) senior citizens, 1 DM (65¢) students; combination ticket for both Glyptothek and Antikensammlungen, 8 DM ($5.35) adults, 4 DM ($2.65) senior citizens and students; free for everyone on Sun. Tues and Thurs–Sun 10am–4:30pm, Wed noon–8:30pm. U-Bahn U-2 to Königsplatz.

The architectural counterpart of the Glyptothek across the square, the Antikensammlungen houses the state's collection of Greek, Roman, and Etruscan art. The focus is on Greek vases (primarily Attic from the 6th and 5th centuries B.C.). Small statues and terra-cotta and bronze objects round out the collection. Particularly striking is the Greek and Etruscan gold jewelry, including necklaces, bracelets, and earrings.

MORE ATTRACTIONS

Bavaria Film Tour

Bavariafilmplatz 7, Geiselgasteig. ☎ **089/649 37 67.** Admission 14 DM ($9.35) adults, 9 DM ($6) children; stunt show, 9 DM ($6). Daily 9am–4pm. Closed Nov–Feb. Tram 25 to Bavariafilmplatz.

Although tours of Germany's largest film studio are in German only, you may wish to join the 1¹/₂-hour tour if you're a film buff or speak German. Among the internationally known films produced by Bavaria Film are *Cabaret, Das Boot* (the submarine used in the movie is on display), and *The Never-Ending Story.* The stunt show, which runs from April to September, costs extra.

Bayerisches Nationalmuseum

Prinzregentenstrasse 3. ☎ **089/211 24-1.** Admission 3 DM ($2) adults, 3 DM ($2) senior citizens, 1 DM (65¢) students, 50 Pfennig (35¢) children; free for everyone on Sun and hols. Tues–Sun 9:30am–5pm. U-Bahn U-4 or U-5 to Lehel. Tram 20.

Down the street from the Haus der Kunst, the Bavarian National Museum emphasizes the historical and cultural development of Bavaria, as well as the rest of Europe, from the Middle Ages through the 19th century. The museum complements the Alte Pinakothek, showing what was happening in other genres of art and crafts at the same time painters were producing their masterpieces.

Glass, miniatures, ivory carvings, watches, jewelry, clothing, textiles and tapestries, toys, porcelain (particularly Nymphenburg and Meissen), medieval armor, and religious artifacts and altars are just some of the 20,000 items on display.

Outstanding are the wood carvings of Tilman Riemenschneider (notice the facial expressions of the 12 Apostles in Room 12), as well as works by Erasmus Grasser, Michael Pacher, Johann Baptist Staub, and Ignaz Günther, to name only a few.

One delightful thing about this museum is that the architecture complements the objects on display. The Late Gothic Church Art Room, for example (Room 15), is modeled after a church in Augsburg, providing a perfect background for the religious art it displays. Similarly, Room 9 is the Augsburg Weavers Room, while Room 10 is the interior of a cozy inn from gothic times in Passau.

My favorite floor is the basement. Part of it is devoted to folk art, including furniture and complete rooms showing how people lived long ago. Notice the wooden floors and low ceiling (to save heat). The other half of the museum houses an incredible collection of nativity scenes (*Krippe*) from around Europe. Some of the displays are made of paper, while others are amazingly lifelike. Both the vastness and the quality of this collection are impressive. Don't miss it.

Note: Due to renovations, parts of the museum will be closed until 2000. If you're interested in a specific collection, call ahead to make sure it's open at the time of your visit.

BMW Museum

Petueilring 130. ☎ **089/3822-33 07.** Admission 5.50 DM ($3.65) adults, 4 DM ($2.65) students, senior citizens, and children; 12 DM ($8) family ticket. Daily 9am–5pm (you must enter by 4pm). U-Bahn U-2 or U-3 to Olympiazentrum; then a five-minute walk.

Anyone interested in cars, motorcycles, and the history of the automobile should see this museum. Housed in a super-modern building, it features video films (including one describing how the future was imagined by people in the past—essentially, technology as threat), slide shows, and actual displays of motors and cars from the days of the "oldies" to the age of the robot. What's more, the museum relates it all to what was taking place in the world at the time, putting it in historical perspective. It also asks questions about the future of technology and mankind.

Deutsches Jagd- und Fischermuseum (German Hunting and Fishing Museum)

Neuhauser Strasse 22 (on the corner of Augustiner Strasse). ☎ **089/22 05 22.** Admission 5 DM ($3.35) adults, 3 DM ($2) students and seniors, 1 DM (65¢) children. Tues–Wed and Fri–Sun 9:30am–5pm, Mon and Thurs 9:30am–9pm. U-Bahn: Marienplatz.

This special-interest museum devoted to the hunt and the rod is conveniently located in the center of the city, not far from Marienplatz. A bronze statue of a wild pig marks its entrance, and inside is an array of mounted wild animals, birds, fish, antlers, rifles, crossbows, and elaborate royal hunting sleds from the 17th and 18th centuries, as well as a huge collection of fishing hooks and lures. This is, perhaps, a place of escape for hunters and fisherfolk while spouses hunt for shopping bargains in the vicinity.

Münchner Stadtmuseum

St. Jakobsplatz 1. ☎ **089/233 223 70.** Admission 5 DM ($3.35) adults, 2.50 DM ($1.65) senior citizens and students, free for children 5 and under; 7.50 DM ($5) family ticket (two adults and one child 14 or under). Tues and Thurs–Sun 10am–5pm, Wed 10am–8:30pm. Walk from Marienplatz toward Sendlinger-Tor-Platz.

Whereas the Bavarian National Museum traces the history of the state, the Munich City Museum relates the history of the city—but that's not all. The Puppet-Theater Collection is outstanding, with puppets and theater stages from around the world, while the musical-instrument collection on the fourth floor displays European instruments from the 16th to the 20th century and primitive instruments from around the world.

There are sections devoted to beer brewing (with explanations in German only), medieval weaponry, and the history of photography. The museum's most valuable pieces are the 10 Morris Dancers carved by Erasmus Grasser, completed in 1480 for display in Munich's old town hall. The morris (or morrice) dance, popular in the 15th century, was a rustic ambulatory dance performed by companies of actors at festivals. The museum also features rooms illustrating life in Munich in the 17th, 18th, and 19th centuries, including parlors, dining rooms, kitchens, and bedrooms.

Münchner Tierpark Hellabrunn (Munich Zoo)

Siebenbrunner Strasse 6. ☎ **089/62 50 80.** Admission 9 DM ($6) adults, 6 DM ($4) senior citizens and students, 4 DM ($2.65) children 4–14, free for children 3 and under. Summer, daily 8am–6pm; winter, daily 9am–5pm. U-Bahn U-3 to Thalkirchen. Bus 52.

Munich's zoo is home to 5,000 animals and includes the Elephant House (built in 1913), an aviary, and an aquarium, plus all the usual zoo inhabitants in environments that mimic native habitats. A good excursion with children, it also has a petting zoo and playgrounds.

Staatsgalerie Moderner Kunst (State Gallery of Modern Art)

In the Haus der Kunst, Prinzregentenstrasse 1. ☎ **089/21 12 70.** Admission 5 DM ($3.35) adults, 3 DM ($2) senior citizens, 1 DM (65¢) students and children; free for everyone on Sun and hols. Tues–Wed and Fri–Sun 10am–5pm, Thurs 10am–8pm. U-Bahn U-3 or U-6 to Odeonsplatz (then a 10-minute walk) or U-4 or U-5 to Lehel (then an 8-minute walk). Tram 20. Bus 53.

The State Gallery of Modern Art is housed in the west end of a massive columned building called the Haus der Kunst. The building is a product of Hitler's regime, built in 1937, and it now displays much of the modern art Hitler tried to suppress. Devoted to art of the 20th century, it has a large collection of German art, particularly Klee, Marc, Max Ernst, Kirchner, and Beckmann. Other highlights are cubism, American abstract expressionism, surrealism, and art of the 1920s and 1930s. On display are works by Braque, Corinth, Salvador Dalí, Kandinsky, Kokoschka, Matisse, Mondrian, Moore, Picasso (14 of his works), and Warhol. The east wing of the Haus der Kunst features changing exhibitions, for which there's a separate entrance fee.

Städtische Galerie im Lenbachhaus

In the Lenbach House, Luisenstrasse 33 (off Königsplatz, not far from the Glyptothek). ☎ **089/233-0320.** Admission 6 DM ($4) adults, 3 DM ($2) senior citizens and students, 9 DM ($4.40) family ticket; special exhibits, 8 DM ($5.35) adults, 4 DM ($2.65) senior citizens and students, 12 DM ($8) family ticket. Tues–Sun 10am–6pm. U-Bahn U-2 to Königsplatz.

The City Gallery is the showcase for Munich's artists, in a setting that couldn't be more perfect. The museum is the former Italianate villa of artist Franz von Lenbach, built at the end of the last century. Some of the rooms have been kept as they were then.

Although landscape paintings from the 15th to the 19th century, as well as examples of German Jugendstil, are part of the collection, the great treasure of the gallery is the collection of the Blaue Reiter (Blue Rider) group of artists. Wassily Kandinsky, one of the great innovators of abstract art, was a key member of this Munich-based group, and the Lenbach House has an outstanding collection of

Kandinsky's work from his early period shortly after the turn of the century to the outbreak of World War I. Other Blue Rider artists represented include Paul Klee, Franz Marc, August Macke, and Gabriele Münter.

ZAM—Zentrum für Aussergewöhnliche Museum (Center for Out-of-the-Ordinary Museums)

Westenriederstrasse 26. ☎ **089/290 41 21.** Admission 8 DM ($5.35) adults, 5 DM ($3.35) students, senior citizens, and children older than 3. Daily 10am–6pm. Walk five minutes from Marienplatz or a couple of minutes from Isartorplatz.

Munich's newest museum complex is actually seven museums in one, each one unique. Where else, for example, can you find a museum devoted to the chamber pot? Other collections are devoted to pedal cars (the largest collection in the world, according to the *Guinness Book of World Records*), the life of Kaiserin Elisabeth of Austria, corkscrews, keys, and the Easter rabbit! Each collection has its own room, and the entire complex can be viewed in about an hour. Explanations are only in German but there's an English pamphlet.

PARKS & GARDENS

The **Englischer Garten** is one of the largest city parks in Europe. Despite its name, it owes its existence to an American rather than an Englishman. Benjamin Thompson, who fled America during the Revolution because of his British sympathies, was instrumental in the park's creation and landscaping. Stretching 3 miles along the Isar River right in the heart of the city, today it offers beer gardens, sunbathing (including nude sunbathing, a surprise to quite a few unsuspecting tourists), and recreation.

Much more formal are the 500 acres of **Nymphenburg Park,** already described under "Top Attractions," above. On the north end of Nymphenburg Park is the **New Botanical Garden,** but the most conveniently located garden is the **Hofgarten,** located right off Odeonsplatz and laid out in the Italian Renaissance style of the 17th century.

ORGANIZED TOURS

With this guidebook and a good map, and with the help of Munich's great transportation system, you shouldn't need to spend money on an organized tour. For those who prefer to be guided, Panorama Tours of the Gray Line offers sightseeing trips of Munich lasting 1 to 2½ hours. The 1-hour trip is adequate, with buses departing from in front of the Hertie department store, across from the Hauptbahnhof, daily at 10am and 2:30pm (also at 11:30am May to October). The fare is 15 DM ($10) for adults and 8 DM ($5.35) for children. Day-long excursions are also offered, including those to castles (Neuschwanstein among them), and to Rothenburg, Herrenchiemsee, Berchtesgaden, and Dachau.

For more information, drop by the **Panorama Tours** office at Arnulfstrasse 8 (☎ **089/59 15 04**), to the north of the Hauptbahnhof. The office is open Monday through Friday from 9am to 6pm (in summer, from 7:30am to 6pm), Saturday from 7:30am to noon, and Sunday from 7:30 to 10am.

7 Shopping

As Germany's fashion center, Munich has upscale boutiques, department stores, and designer names, located primarily in the pedestrian-zoned Old Town. If you're interested in souvenirs—beer mugs, the blue-and-white simple pottery of Bavaria, porcelain—your best bet in terms of price is the department stores, including **Hertie** (across from the Hauptbahnhof), **Karstadt** (on Karlstor, right off Stachus, and at Neuhauser Strasse 44), and **Kaufhof** (Karlsplatz 21–24 and on Marienplatz).

Another good place to hunt for Bavarian and German souvenirs and gifts is along **Orlandostrasse,** about a five-minute walk from Marienplatz near the Hofbräuhaus. This small pedestrian lane has several souvenir shops selling T-shirts, beer steins, dolls in Bavarian costume, pipes, postcards, Christmas-tree ornaments, and nutcrackers.

If you have lots of money and want to purchase a Bavarian dirndl, check out **Wallach,** Residenzstrasse 3, which has been selling traditional clothing since 1900. This shop also sells ceramics, some toys and gift items, shawls, bed sheets, beer steins, and pewter.

Most shops are open Monday through Friday from 9 or 9:30am to 6pm and Saturday from 9am to 2pm. In addition, most shops are also open Thursday evening until 8:30pm and on the first Saturday of the month (*langer Samstag*) until 5pm.

If you purchase more than 60-DM ($40) worth of goods from any one store and you're taking your purchases out of the country, you can **recover part of the value-added tax (VAT),** 15% in Germany. Many shops, including those listed above, will issue a Tax Cheque at the time of purchase. Fill in the reverse side, and upon leaving the last European Union country you visit in Europe, present the articles to Customs. Airports in Berlin, Frankfurt, Munich, and other large cities have counters that will refund your money immediately.

MARKETS Munich's most famous market is the **Viktualienmarkt,** dating from the early 1800s. Here you can buy bread, cheese, honey, cakes, fruit, wine, vegetables, and much, much more. It's a wonderful place to obtain picnic supplies. The market is open year round, Monday through Friday from 8am to 6pm and Saturday from 8am to 2pm.

If you're here in December, enjoy the **Christkindlmarkt** on Marienplatz, a colorful hodgepodge of stalls offering everything from Bavarian foods to Christmas decorations. It's held from the beginning of December to Christmas Eve.

Even better is the **Auer Dult,** a flea market lasting eight days and held three times a year, in April, July, and October. It has been a Munich tradition for more than 600 years, currently held on Mariahilfplatz (take bus no. 52 from Marienplatz). Everything from spices, leather goods, jewelry, and sweaters to antiques, kitchen gadgets, and ceramics is sold, and there are also rides and amusements for children. For more information, contact the tourist office.

8 Munich After Dark

Since commercial ticket agencies sell opera and theater tickets at a higher price to make a profit, it makes sense to buy your tickets directly from the theater or opera. To find out where to purchase tickets in advance, buy a copy of the *Monatsprogramm,* issued monthly for 2.50 DM ($1.65). It lists all the major theaters and what's being played when. Another publication listing operas, plays, classical concerts, rock and jazz concerts, movies, and more is *Munich Found,* an English-language magazine costing 4 DM ($2.65).

Both the Nationaltheater (the Bavarian State Opera House) and the Staatstheater am Gärtnerplatz (opera, operettas, ballet, and musicals) offer **standing-room tickets** for 8 to 20 DM ($5.35 to $13.35). You can purchase these tickets in advance, and they may be your best bet to see popular performances. For performances that are not sold out students can get a **discount** at the Nationaltheater by standing in line about an hour before the show and presenting their International Student ID Card. These are discount tickets for seats, starting at about 6 DM ($4). Otherwise the normal price of a seat runs about 15 to 65 DM ($10 to $43.35).

THE PERFORMING ARTS
THEATER & OPERA

Cuvilliés Theater

Residenzstrasse 1. ☎ **089/2185 19 20.** Tickets 30–250 DM ($20–$166.50) for opera, 7–60 DM ($4.65–$40) for plays. U-Bahn U-1 or U-2 to Fraunhoferstrasse.

Also known as the Altes Residenztheater, this theater seating 500 is considered Germany's finest rococo tier-boxed theater. It features opera and classical plays. The box office, at Max-Joseph-Platz 1 (☎ **089/22 57 54**), is open Monday through Friday from 10am to 6pm and Saturday from 10am to 2pm.

Münchner Kammerspiele–Schauspielhaus

Maximilianstrasse 26. ☎ **089/237 213 28.** Tickets 9–57 DM ($6–$38). Tram 19 to Maximilianstrasse.

Contemporary plays from German playwrights, including Brecht, Böll, and Handke, are presented here. The box office is open Monday through Friday from 10am to 6pm and Saturday from 10am to 1pm.

Nationaltheater (Bayerische Staatsoper)

Max-Joseph-Platz (a three-minute walk from Marienplatz). ☎ **089/2185-1920.** Tickets 15–250 DM ($10–$166.50) for opera, 9–130 DM ($6–$86.65) for ballet. U-Bahn and S-Bahn: Marienplatz.

With opera performed in its original language, the Nationaltheater's Bavarian State Opera House is famous for its progressive versions of the classics. It also stages ballet. The box office, at Maximilianstrasse 11, is open Monday through Friday from 10am to 1pm and 2 to 6pm and Saturday from 10am to 1pm.

Residenztheater

Max-Joseph-Platz 1. ☎ **089/22 57 54.** Tickets 19–65 DM ($12.65–$43.35). S-Bahn: Marienplatz.

The Bayerisches Staatsschauspiel performs classics in German, including Schiller, Goethe, Shakespeare, and Pirandello. The box office is open Monday through Friday from 10am to 6pm and Saturday from 10am to 1pm.

Staatstheater am Gärtnerplatz

Gärtnerplatz 3. ☎ **089/201 67 67.** Seats 16–86 DM ($10.65–$57.35), standing room 8–12 DM ($5.35–$8); student tickets, seats 10 DM ($6.65), standing room 4–6 DM ($2.65–$4). Bus 52 or 56 to Gärtnerplatz.

Light opera, operetta, ballet, and musicals are beautifully performed here, usually in German, from *My Fair Lady* to *The Nutcracker* and *The Barber of Seville*. The box office is open Monday through Friday from 10am to 6pm and Saturday from 10am to 1pm.

CLASSICAL MUSIC CONCERTS

Gasteig

Rosenheimer Strasse 5. ☎ **089/48 09 80.** Munich Philharmonic Orchestra 40–200 DM ($26.65–$133.35). S-Bahn: Rosenheimer Platz. Tram 18 to Gasteig.

Completed in 1985, the Gasteig serves as the stage for Munich's major concerts. Its largest concert hall, the Philharmonie, seats 2,400 and features performances of the Munich Philharmonic Orchestra, the Munich Bach Orchestra and Chorus, the Bavarian Radio Symphony Orchestra, and guest orchestras and ensembles. The Kleiner Konzertsaal (Small Concert Hall) features a wide range of musical talent, from flamenco guitar to concerts of Renaissance and baroque music. The Gasteig also contains several smaller concert halls, as well as the Munich City Library and the Richard Strauss Conservatory. The box office is open Monday through Friday from 10:30am to 2pm and 3 to 6pm and Saturday from 10:30am to 2pm.

Prinzregenten-Theater

Prinzregentenplatz 12. ☎ **089/29 16 14 14.** Tickets 30–65 DM ($20–$43.35) for most orchestra concerts. U-Bahn U-4 to Prinzregentenstrasse.

Performances of the Bayerischen Staatsorchester (Bavarian State Orchestra), piano recitals, guest orchestras and ensembles, and ballets take place in this theater.

LIVE-MUSIC HOUSES

✪ Bunterhund

11 Occamstrasse, Schwabing. ☎ **089/34 72 89.** Cover 5–10 DM ($3.35–$6.65). U-Bahn U-3 or U-6 to Münchner Freiheit.

My favorite nightspot in Schwabing, the Bunterhund is the new name of the original Schwabinger Brettl. With a 30-year history, it's the only establishment that carries on the bohemian spirit of old Schwabing, where musicians from around the world can perform to an appreciative audience. Not just anyone can get up and play. Musicians audition beforehand, so you can be assured they're good. This place is tiny—come early for a seat. Open daily from 8pm to 1am.

Unterfahrt

Kirchenstrasse 96, Haidhausen. ☎ **089/448 27 94.** Cover 16–25 DM ($10.65–$16.65); Sun jam session 5 DM ($3.35). S-Bahn and U-Bahn Ostbahnhof; then a five-minute walk. Bus 54 to Haidenauplatz.

This informal and relaxed jazz locale is more proof that Munich is fast becoming one of Europe's prime spots for jazz, "from old-time to no time," and is popular with a slightly older crowd of jazz enthusiasts. On Sunday there's a jam session from 9pm, and from October to April there's free jazz on Sunday from 10am to 2pm. Open Tuesday through Thursday and Sunday from 8pm to 1am and Friday and Saturday from 8pm to 3am.

BEER HALLS

Augustiner Bierhalle

Neuhauser Strasse 16 (on Munich's main pedestrian lane in Old Town, between Stachus and Marienplatz). ☎ **089/551 99 257.** U-Bahn and S-Bahn: Stachus or Marienplatz.

About 10% cheaper than its sister Augustiner Restaurant, next door, the Bier-halle is much smaller than the other two establishments listed here, with correspondingly lower prices. It still, however, has typical Bavarian decor, with dark wood-paneled walls, wooden tables, and simple hooks for hats and coats. Specialties here include pancake soup with browned onions, Leberkäs, sliced radish, and a menu that changes daily. Half a liter of beer begins at 5.20 DM ($3.45). Open Monday through Saturday from 9am to midnight.

Hofbräuhaus

Platzl 9. ☎ **089/22 16 76.** U-Bahn and S-Bahn: Marienplatz.

Without a doubt, the Hofbräuhaus is the most famous beer hall in the world. In 1989 it celebrated its 400th birthday. Everyone who has ever been to Munich has probably spent at least one evening here, and you'll probably want to do the same. There are several floors in this huge place, but the main hall is the Schwemme on the ground floor. It features your typical Bavarian brass band, waitresses in dirndls, and tables full of friendly Germans who often break into song and link arms as they sway back and forth. If you've never been to the Oktoberfest, this place will give you an idea what it's like. German food is available (there's also a restaurant up on the first floor), including various sausages, Leberkäs, boiled pork knuckle with sauerkraut and potatoes, a plate of sliced radish, and roast chicken. The Hofbräuhaus, owned by the State of Bavaria, is in the city center. A liter of beer costs 9.20 DM ($6.15). Open daily from 10am to midnight.

Mathäser Bierstadt

Bayerstrasse 5 (between Stachus and the Hauptbahnhof). ☎ **089/59 28 96.** U-Bahn and S-Bahn: Stachus.

This place is massive, with various rooms, but follow the oompah music up a half flight of stairs to the beer hall. Claiming that it pours more beer than anywhere else (it advertises 5,000 seats), the Bierstadt caters to locals rather than to tourists and is sometimes packed even in the middle of the day. In summer you can sit in an outdoor courtyard, and in the morning you can come here for Weisswurst. The menu lists the usual fare of roast Schweinshaxe, sausages, suckling pig, Leberkäs, sliced radish, chicken, and more. The beer is Löwenbräu, and a liter will set you back 9.60 DM ($6.40). Open daily from 8am to midnight.

FILMS

To find out what's playing, either buy a newspaper or try to get a copy of *Munich Found,* which lists the various cinemas and their schedules. The average price of a movie ticket is 10 to 12 DM ($6.65 to $8). Those that show movies in their original language include:

Cinema, Nymphenburger Strasse 31 (☎ **089/55 52 55;** U-Bahn U-1 to Stiglmaierplatz), specializes in contemporary films in both German and English. This is one of your best bets for seeing Hollywood's most recent releases.

The Filmuseum, Jakobsplatz 1 (☎ **089/233 223 48;** U-Bahn and S-Bahn: Marienplatz, then a three-minute walk southeast), is part of the Munich City Museum, with film festivals held on different themes (recent festivals have included Charlie Chaplin films, Fritz Lang films, and samurai flicks from Japan). There are usually two showings daily. Admission is 8 DM ($5.35).

Museum-Lichtspiele, Lilienstrasse 2 (☎ **089/489 12 96;** S-Bahn: Rosenheimer Platz), near the Deutsches Museum and Ludwigsbrücke bridge, has three screens showing first-run films in their original language, including many new Hollywood releases. For more than 18 years, it has also featured daily showings of *The Rocky Horror Picture Show*, complete with specially designed staging for audience participation. **Neues Arena Kino,** Hans-Sachs-Strasse 7 (☎ **089/ 260 32 65;** U-Bahn U-1 or U-2 to Frauenhofer; Tram 20, 25, or 27 from the Hauptbahnhof to Frauenhofer-Müllerstrasse, then a three-minute walk), shows international offbeat cult, avant-garde, science fiction, and old and new classics, often in the original language. There are several showings nightly.

THE BAR SCENE
IN SCHWABING

Once the center of everything bohemian in Munich, Schwabing today is more likely to be filled with out-of-towners than with natives. Still, it's definitely worth a stroll through Munich's most famous night district, and the crowds are still huge in summer. The busiest streets are the main boulevard, Leopoldstrasse, and the smaller side streets Feilitzschstrasse and Occamstrasse, near the Münchener Freiheit subway station. Below are a few recommendations to whet your thirst:

Flotte

Occamstrasse 8. ☎ **089/33 48 46.** U-Bahn U-3 or U-6 to Münchener Freiheit.

This bar has been here on Occamstrasse for more than 15 years and features a DJ playing rock 'n' roll or golden oldies of the 1950s and 1960s. It's simply decorated, with the usual wooden floor, large bar area, and wooden tables. Half a liter of beer goes for 5.50 DM ($3.65). Open daily from 7pm to 1am.

Haus der 111 Biere

Franzstrasse 3. ☎ **089/33 12 48.** U-Bahn U-3 or U-6 to Münchener Freiheit.

The 111 kinds of beer from 25 countries around the world are the claim to fame of this establishment. Its two floors are often packed with people from around the world as well, and it's easy to strike up a conversation. Bottles and cans of beer cost around 6 to 18 DM ($4 to $12). Open Monday through Friday from 4pm to 1am and Saturday, Sunday, and holidays from 3pm to 1am.

Nachteule

Occamstrasse 7. ☎ **089/39 96 56.** U-Bahn U-3 or U-6 to Münchener Freiheit.

The "Night Owl" claims to be the oldest bar left in Schwabing, established in the dark ages of 1960. A small, simple locale with a tiny dance floor, Nachteule is a place where anyone can feel at home—and, judging from the rather mixed clientele, it's a place where many of them do. Half a liter of beer runs 4.80 DM ($3.20). Open Tuesday through Thursday from 7pm to 1am and Friday and Saturday from 7pm to 2am.

Turbo

Occamstrasse 5. ☎ **089/34 99 01.** U-Bahn U-3 or U-6 to Münchener Freiheit.

This tiny place, complete with a disc jockey who plays oldies, really packs them in, and in case you're interested, there seem to be many more men than women. The specialty here is the "*ein meter Pils oder Alt*," which is a 1-meter wooden board with 15 small beers on it. For 0.4 liters of beer you'll pay 5.80 DM ($3.85); for "*ein meter Pils oder Alt*," 41 DM ($27.35). Open daily from 7pm to 1am.

IN THE CITY CENTER

Iwan

Josephspitalstrasse 15 (on the corner of Sonnenstrasse). ☎ **089/55 49 33.** S-Bahn: Karlsplatz/Stachus.

This trendy bar decorated in red, black, and gray is a convenient place for a drink, day or night, and draws a mixed crowd from gays to aspiring actors. It's nestled in an inner courtyard. In summer there's outdoor seating, and the liquor menu is extensive. A third of a liter of beer costs 4.50 DM ($3) and up. Open in summer, daily from noon to 2am; in winter, Monday through Thursday from 11am to 2am, Friday and Saturday from noon to 3am, and Sunday from 5pm to 2am.

DISCOS

Discos in Munich are suffering from a tendency toward elitism. Most have doors with one-way mirrors that can be opened only from the inside—so the bouncer can look over potential customers and decide whether they're of the right material to be let in. Far Out, in the center of Old Town, gets so crowded on the weekends that you might not get in. In winter, coats must be checked (for a small fee).

Far Out

Am Kosttor 2 (near the Hofbräuhaus, a seven-minute walk northeast of Marienplatz). ☎ **089/22 66 62** or 22 66 61. Cover 5 DM ($3.35) Wed–Thurs and Sun, 10 DM ($6.65) Fri–Sat.

People come here primarily to dance, evident from the conspicuous lack of seating. It gets so crowded on weekends that the doorman lets in only regular patrons. Go on a weeknight, when the admission is also lower. On Wednesday the music tends to be mellower, drawing in an older crowd. There are more than 70 cocktails on its menu, and sandwiches and ice cream are also available. A third of a liter of beer costs 4.50 DM ($3). Open Wednesday from 9pm to 4am and Thursday through Sunday from 10pm to 4am.

Sunset

Leopoldstrasse 69. ☎ **089/39 03 03.** U-Bahn U-3 or U-6 to Münchener Freiheit.

This small basement establishment is more democratic than most, allowing as many as will fit through its doors. Here, 0.4 liter of beer goes for 6.80 DM ($4.55). Open daily from 8pm to 4am.

9 Easy Excursions

DACHAU   About 12 miles from Munich is Dachau, site of Germany's first concentration camp under the Hitler regime and now a memorial to those who died under the Nazis. Some 200,000 prisoners—Jews, Gypsies, and opponents of the regime—passed through Dachau's gates, of whom 32,000 lost their lives.

At the **KZ-Gedenkstätte Dachau (Concentration Camp Memorial)**, Alte Römerstrasse 75 (☎ **08131/1741**), two of the camp's original 30 barracks have been rebuilt, and also on display is the crematorium. The former workshops and offices have been made into a museum, with photograph after photograph illustrating the horrors of the Holocaust. They show the expressionless faces of children with eyes of the old. There are bodies piled high on top of one another, and there are lines of people quietly waiting to be executed. Documentaries are shown in English at 11:30am and 3:30pm.

Visiting the Dachau concentration camp is not pleasant, but perhaps it's necessary: A plaque near the exit of the museum reminds us that those who forget the past are destined to repeat it. If you need something a bit uplifting after visiting the concentration camp, walk through the older medieval city in the center of Dachau, which has a history stretching back 1,200 years.

Admission to the Dachau memorial is free and it's open Tuesday through Sunday from 9am to 5pm. To get there, take S-Bahn S-2 going toward Petershausen to Dachau (about a 20-minute ride), and then bus no. 722 to Robert-Bosch-Strasse.

NEUSCHWANSTEIN   You've probably seen pictures of Neuschwanstein—a fairytale castle perched up on a cliff above the town of Hohenschwangau (☎ **08362/81035**), created by the extravagant Bavarian King Ludwig II. Even if you've never seen it, you'll probably still recognize it, for this is the castle that served as the model for the castle at Disneyland.

Construction on King Ludwig II's most famous castle began in 1869, but it was still not finished at the time of Ludwig's mysterious death in 1886 (his body, as well as the body of his doctor, was found floating in a lake, but no one has ever proven whether he was murdered or committed suicide). Neuschwanstein, one of several overly ornate castles Ludwig left to the world, is a lesson in extravagance, with almost every inch covered in gilt or stucco.

Admission to the castle is 10 DM ($6.65) for adults, 7 DM ($4.65) for students and senior citizens, free to children 14 and under. It's open April to September, daily from 8:30am to 5:30pm; October to March, daily from 10am to 4pm. To get here, take the train from Munich's Starnberger Bahnhof (next to the Hauptbahnhof) to Füssen, about a two-hour trip; from Füssen, take a bus to Hohenschwangau.

Paris 19

by Darwin Porter & Danforth Prince

What do Jim Morrison, Oscar Wilde, Isadora Duncan, and Frédéric Chopin have in common? Two things: None was a native Parisian yet all died in the French capital and are buried in the city's grand and melancholy Père-Lachaise Cemetery. Of all the world's cities, Paris has entered most deeply into people's imagination as the quintessential city. Men and women have come here from every continent, and when you see the graves of so many legendary foreigners at Père-Lachaise, next to Molière, Proust, Piaf, and other French luminaries, you'll understand that Paris is the capital not only of France but also, in a way, of the Western world.

The urban splendor of the City of Light and of its famous landmarks is legendary: the River Seine and the bridges spanning it; Notre-Dame, Sacré-Coeur, and Sainte-Chapelle; the Eiffel Tower and Arc de Triomphe. While strolling through Paris, you'll find it also offers astoundingly beautiful streets, parks, and neighborhoods: the Latin Quarter with its labyrinthine side streets and the Marais with its 17th-century mansions; the Luxembourg and Tuileries gardens and the Bois de Boulogne; the *grands boulevards* and avenue des Champs-Elysées; the historic place de la Concorde and diminutive place de Furstemberg.

Yet millennia-old Paris is no dusty museum. In many ways it's more modern than most North American cities. Sleek designs brighten the solid gray facades, computers called minitel have replaced phone books in many places, and the swift RER trains, part of the Métro, traverse the city in minutes. And then there are the controversial futuristic public works of the last two decades: the Centre Pompidou, I. M. Pei's Louvre pyramids, the Grande Arche de la Défense, La Villette, the Opéra de la Bastille, and the new Cité de la Musique. Despite its many illustrious dead, Paris is very much alive and vibrant.

1 Paris Deals & Discounts

Many people imagine that Paris is super-expensive—and it is compared to many major U.S. cities. A double room at the Ritz will cost $600 per night and dinner for two at a top restaurant will cost $300 plus, but you can still enjoy the city at a fraction of that cost if you live as the Parisians do and employ some creative money-saving techniques.

What's Special About Paris

Performing Arts
- Performances at Paris's world-renowned stages: the Comédie-Française and the Opéra de la Bastille.

Attractions
- Viewing the city from the top of a famous monument: the Eiffel Tower or the Arc de Triomphe.
- Exploring historic neighborhoods, such as the Latin Quarter and the Marais.
- Walking along the Seine, Paris's moody river.
- Discovering the smaller museums, such as the Musée de l'Orangerie and the Musée Nissim de Camondo.
- Biking around the vast Bois de Boulogne and relaxing in the intimate place des Vosges, two of Paris's many beautiful parks and squares.

Architecture
- Ultramodern structures, such as the Centre Pompidou, the Louvre pyramids, the Grande Arche de la Défense, and the Cité de la Musique.

Restaurants
- Paris's great restaurants, among the best in the world, definitely worth the splurge.
- Sidewalk cafés, where you can watch the world go by.

BUDGET BESTS   It's hard to find an acceptable hotel room under $80 for a double unless you're willing to tolerate some less-than-meticulous housekeeping or prepared to stay at a hostel or in a hotel room without a private bath or toilet. Choose a hotel room with only as much plumbing as you personally need. Walking down the hall to the bath, shower, or toilet will save you a lot of money. If bathless rooms are not for you, there are still some good, clean, and well-equipped hotels with rooms at around $80 for a double. Note, though, that even these properties will offer rooms that most North Americans will find small; most average city apartments are small and space is at a premium in Paris, so don't expect spaciousness for your money. Expect to find even tinier bathrooms; elevators that barely accommodate one person, never mind a person plus suitcase; and narrow spiral staircases. Don't expect air conditioning either.

As for dining, here we'll demur from the general opinion: Not all Parisian food is good; in fact, it seems that in the last few years standards at budget restaurants have declined greatly. The standard prix-fixe menu at a typical bistro isn't what it used to be and you're as likely to be faced with a boiled chicken instead of a true *poulet rôti* and to pay $40 or $50 for an inferior meal for two. In addition, the menus of most budget restaurants are similar and extremely boring and the less-expensive dishes tend to be items like pig's feet, andouillettes, or tripe, which many Americans can't stomach (no pun intended). We suggest you take advantage of the best values Paris has to offer—the delectable items gloriously displayed in the windows of boulangeries, pâtisseries, charcuteries, crèmeries, and épiceries or at the street markets. Bring a good knife, corkscrew, and dining accoutrements (or purchase some paper and plastic versions) and enjoy your own feasts in one of the city's parks or gardens. Obviously, you'll want to take some of your meals in traditional restaurants, so we'll direct you to some of the best choices. Look for the prix-fixe *menu du jour* (also known as *le formule*) or simply order the *plats du jour*, made from the best buys at the daily market. Try to avoid ordering special wines; most restaurants will feature *vin de pays* (a little better quality than *vin ordinaire*) by the glass or quarter- or half-liter pitchers.

Also you can do as the French do and frequent the wine bars, tearooms, crêperies, and even pizzerias where you can find good-quality meals for reasonable prices. Remember that there are cafés and then there are cafés—Deux Magots and Café Flore were at one time frequented by intellectual luminaries; today they're filled with tourists and others paying exorbitant prices for nostalgic ambience; frequent the cafés that locals pop into at lunch or late afternoon and you'll save yourself some money and enjoy a far more authentic experience. By the way, you can save substantially by taking your coffee or other beverage while standing at the bar. It'll cost double if you sit down, although at the end of a day's sightseeing you may think it's worth the extra expense.

Walk and use the Métro (purchase a *carnet*—see "Special Discounts," below) to get around. As for sightseeing bargains, the bridges, monuments, squares, parks, churches, and shop windows of Paris are free and filled with romance and many of the museums offer reduced admission one day a week. Serious museum-goers, though, will want to consider purchasing the Carte Intermusées (see "Special Discounts," below), a card granting a discount and allowing you to enter around 60 Paris museums.

SPECIAL DISCOUNTS   The best discounts are provided by the RATP (public transportation) cards and the Carte Intermusées.

If you plan to use public transportation frequently, consider the **Carte Orange,** an economical weekly or monthly pass—63F ($12.10) for a week's unlimited travel (*coupon hebdomadaire*) or 219F ($42.10) for a month's pass (*coupon mensuel*). The only catch is that you must provide a little photo of yourself, and this will increase the price a bit. The weekly Carte Orange must be bought any time from Monday through Wednesday morning, and it's valid through Sunday; get the monthly card on the first or second day of each month.

Otherwise, buying a *carnet* for 41F ($7.90) is also a good deal; a single ticket is 7F ($1.35).

The **Carte Intermusées,** good for entry into 60 museums and monuments in Paris and the Ile de France region, is sold at the museums and at major Métro stations. It comes in three varieties: 60F ($11.55) for one day, 120F ($23.05) for three days, and 170F ($32.709) for five days. For the price of the card, you can avoid the ticket lines and walk right into the Louvre, the Musée d'Orsay, the Orangerie, the Picasso Museum, the Panthéon, and the Châteaux de Versailles, Malmaison, and Fontainebleau, to mention only a few. But even if you don't buy this card, you can save money by visiting the museums on the day they offer free or reduced admissions. The Louvre, for instance, has reduced admission on certain days (see "Attractions," later in this chapter).

Another money-saver is the VAT refund. As in other European Union countries, you can often get a refund on the hefty value-added tax (TVA in French) levied on retail purchases. If you purchase more than 2,000F ($384.60) worth of goods in a single shop, ask the shopkeeper to make out an export sales invoice (*bordereau*)—make sure it has the name and address of the store on it—which you'll show to the French Customs officer when you leave the country (at the airport, on the train, at the highway border post—remember to show it!). In a number of weeks the shop will send you a check for the amount of the refund. Not all shops participate in the program, so ask before you buy.

For Children & Youth   Anyone under age 18 is admitted free to France's national museums.

If you have a child under age 16 and plan to travel in France by train, explore the possibility of buying a **Carte KIWI** for the child. At 435F ($82.70) it's not cheap, but it may be a good deal in the long run. With this card, the child gets a 50% discount on trips that start in the *période blanche* or *période bleue* (white period or blue period) of the train riders' calendar, some 300 days a year, and everybody accompanying the child (up to four people, who don't need to be relatives) also benefits from a 50% discount. For more information, get the brochure "Votre enfant voyage en train," with an English section, from any train station.

For Students & Under-25s   Students are privileged people in France. All sorts of reductions are offered to holders of a valid **International Student Identity Card (ISIC).** It can be obtained before you leave from the Council on International Educational Exchange (CIEE), 205 E. 42nd St., New York, NY 10017 (☎ **212/ 438-2643,** or 800/GET-AN-ID), for $16. In Paris, the ISIC is sold at the **AJF,** 119 rue St-Martin (see "Visitor Information" under "Paris Specifics," later in this chapter), for 60F ($11.55), provided you show proof of your student registration and bring a passport-size photograph. You can gain admission to national museums at half price and reductions on train, bus, plane, and even cinema and theater tickets. Flash your ISIC whenever you take out your wallet to pay for something—even if no reduction is advertised. You'll be astounded at the number of discounts granted. For more on student savings, see "Visitor Information" under "Paris Specifics," later in this chapter.

If you're not a student but are between 18 and 24, you may be entitled to many of the same reductions on all sorts of sights and transportation tickets. Ask whenever you're going to pay for something—your passport should serve as proof of your age.

For Seniors   Drop in at one of Paris's railroad stations and buy a **Carte Vermeil** for 140F ($26.90), valid for one year. With this card, travelers over 60 will get reductions of up to 50% on certain train trips (starting in the *période bleue*), plane and bus fares, theater tickets, and national museum admissions.

Even without the Carte Vermeil you may be entitled to some discounts, especially on museums and sights. Always ask before paying.

2 Pretrip Preparations

REQUIRED DOCUMENTS   For visits of less than three months, all that U.S., Canadian, and New Zealand citizens need is a valid passport. Australian travelers need a visa in addition to a passport. U.K. travelers need only a National Identity Card.

TIMING YOUR TRIP   Although April in Paris may sometimes be too cold for some travelers, spring and fall are normally the best times to be in the city. Temperatures are usually mild, and the performing arts and other cultural activities are in full swing. In winter, the lack of sunshine and the occasional bitter-cold wind can be disappointing, but then again, there's so much to see and do inside that you won't miss the picnics in the parks.

Like winter, summer can be mild or extreme, depending on the year and your luck. The number of foreign tourists increases, and many Parisians, especially in August, head for the coast or the mountains. The city is transformed, and the banks of the Seine become a makeshift beach: Paris-Plage. Cultural life dwindles and many restaurants, cafés, and shops close for up to a month; the French call it the *fermeture annuelle* (annual closing). The long hours of daylight, though, will give you more time to explore the city and its street life.

Paris's Average Daytime Temperature & Rainfall

	Jan	Feb	Mar	Apr	May	June	July	Aug	Sept	Oct	Nov	Dec
Temp. (°F)	38	39	46	51	58	64	66	66	61	53	45	40
Rainfall "	3.22	2.9	2.4	2.7	3.2	3.5	3.3	3.7	3.3	3.0	3.5	3.1

Special Events   In the first weeks of January, the big Parisian stores have their annual sales and you'll find bargains galore. This is also the month when Paris's boat show is held at La Défense: the **Salon International de la Navigation de Plaisance.**

On July 14, **Bastille Day,** celebrating the day the Revolutionary mob stormed the Bastille, enormous celebrations are held around the city, ending with fireworks

What Things Cost in Paris	U.S. $
Taxi from Charles de Gaulle Airport to the city center	40.40
Taxi from Orly Airport to the city center	32.69
Public transportation for an average trip within the city (from a Métro *carnet* of 10)	.79
Local telephone call	.38
Double room at the Ritz (deluxe) 600.00	
Double room at the Hôtel St-Jacques (moderate)	91.35
Double room at the Hôtel du Globe (budget)	58.65
Lunch for one at Au Vieux Casque (moderate)	17.25
Lunch for one, without wine, at L'Incroyable (budget)	12.50
Dinner for one, without wine, at Maxim's (deluxe)	169.00
Dinner for one, without wine, at Bofinger (moderate)	33.90
Dinner for one, without wine, at La Petite Hostellerie (budget)	11.55
Glass of wine (quarter liter)	2.50
Coca-Cola	3.50
Cup of coffee (regular)	3.00
Roll of ASA 100 color film, 36 exposures	7.70
Admission to the Louvre	7.70
Movie Ticket	9.60
Theater ticket (at the Comédie-Française)	25.00

near the Eiffel Tower. Also in July is the end of the **Tour de France,** when thousands crowd the Champs-Elysées to witness the finish of this passion-inspiring month-long bicycle race.

New Year's Eve is called the **Fête de St-Sylvestre,** and it's a night when people go out for enormous multicourse table d'hôte meals in their favorite restaurants. Places at the banquet table are reserved in advance and can cost as much as $200 per person—but what a feast! Note that it can be difficult to find a simple, normal meal on New Year's Eve.

At virtually any time of year, there seems to be some sort of music, dance, or drama festival taking place in Paris. Contact the French National Tourist Board in the United States for a complete list (see the Appendix for a mailing address and phone number).

BACKGROUND READING   Probably more books have been written about Paris than about any other European capital. Here are some personal favorites: Janet Flanner's *Paris Was Yesterday* (Harcourt Brace Jovanovich) is a collection of articles written for *The New Yorker* on diverse aspects of the city's life in the 1920s and 1930s; many of the themes explored can still be observed today. Dealing with the same period—and the Lost Generation—is Hemingway's *A Moveable Feast* (Scribner's). Some classic novels include Dickens's *A Tale of Two Cities* (Putnam), set during the French Revolution, and Henry James's *The American* (Norton) and *The Ambassadors* (Penguin), both tales contrasting France and America. French writers, of course, have also masterfully captured Paris in literature: Proust's long, rich *Remembrance of Things Past* (Random House); Colette's romantic novels, such as *Chéri* (Ballantine) and *Gigi* (Farrar, Straus & Giroux); and Simone de Beauvoir's *Memoirs of a Dutiful Daughter* (Schoenhof), a critical account of the author's bourgeois upbringing. Finally, Argentinian Julio Cortázar's *Hopscotch* (Pantheon) is an experimental novel about literary and bohemian life set in the city's streets and garrets. For insight into French society and city life today, read *France Today* by British journalist John Ardagh and also Theodore Zeldin's *The French*.

3 Paris Specifics

ARRIVING

FROM THE AIRPORTS   Paris has two airports handling international traffic: Charles de Gaulle and Orly.

The largest, busiest, and most modern is **Aéroport Charles-de-Gaulle** or CDG (☎ 1/48-62-22-80), sometimes called Roissy–Charles-de-Gaulle, 14¹/₂ miles northeast of downtown. Terminal 1 (Aérogare 1) is used by foreign airlines; Terminal 2 (Aérogare 2) is reserved for Air France, its affiliate Air Inter, and some foreign airlines, including Air Canada. A shuttle bus (*navette*) connects the two terminals with one another.

There are several ways of getting to and from the airport. The cheapest option is the Roissy bus leaving every 15 minutes for place de l'Opéra; it takes 45 minutes and costs 35F ($6.75). The RER suburban train line stops at Terminal 2 (look for the Aéroport Charles-de-Gaulle 2 stop). A shuttle bus connects terminal 1 to the RER train station named Aéroport Charles-de-Gaulle 1. From the station, RER Line B3 trains depart about every 15 minutes on the half-hour trip into town, stopping at the Gare du Nord, the mammoth Châtelet–Les Halles Métro interchange, and the RER stations of St-Michel, Luxembourg, Port-Royal, and Denfert-Rochereau, before heading southward out of the city again. A ticket into town on the RER costs 37F ($7.10) in second class or 56F ($10.75) if you want to go first class (not worth it).

Besides the RER, Air France runs shuttle buses from both terminals to the Porte-Maillot Métro station, next to Paris's huge convention center on the western end of the city, and to place Charles-de-Gaulle–Etoile and the Arc de Triomphe, near some of the budget hotels listed below. There are several buses per hour charging 48F ($9.25) for the 40-minute trip.

A taxi into town from Charles de Gaulle takes between 40 and 50 minutes and costs about 210F ($40.40) from 7am to 8pm, about 40% more at other times.

Charter flights and some international airlines, including American Airlines, arrive at **Aéroport d'Orly** or ORY (☎ **1/49-75-77-48** for Orly Sud, 1/49-75-78-48 Orly Ouest), 8$^{1}/_{2}$ miles south of the city center. The airport has two terminals: French domestic flights land at Orly Ouest; inter-European and intercontinental flights arrive at Orly Sud. Shuttle buses connect the two Orly terminals and other shuttles connect them to Charles de Gaulle Airport every 30 minutes or so.

There are six ways to get into town from Orly. Air France operates coaches from Exit E on the arrival level in Orly Ouest and Exit F Platform 5 in Orly Sud into their downtown terminal at Les Invalides. The trip takes about 30 minutes and leaves every 12 to 15 minutes, costing 35F ($6.75). You can request that the bus stop at Montparnasse-Duroc.

An airport shuttle bus leaves every 15 minutes for the RER Pont de Rungis Aéroport d'Orly, where you board a Line C2 train that stops at several downtown stations, including St-Michel, Invalides, and Gare d'Austerlitz (35 minutes). This airport shuttle leaves from Exit F on the arrival level at Orly Ouest and from Exit H Platform 1 at Orly Sud. The cost is 28F ($5.40) for second class and 42F ($8.05) for first class.

You can also take the Orlyval service using RER Line B. This departs from Exit F near the baggage claim area at Orly Sud and Exit W Hall 2 on the departure level at Orly Ouest. You'll connect at the Antony station—total trip time to Châtelet is about 30 minutes for a cost of 50F ($9.61)

The Orly bus operates from Exit J arrival level in Orly Ouest and Exit H Platform 4 in Orly Sud to Denfert-Rochereau for 30F ($5.75).

Finally, the JetBus leaves from Orly Ouest at Exit C arrival level and Exit 1 Platform 2 at Orly Sud. The connecting stop is the Villejuif–Louis-Aragon station, reached in about 15 minutes for 21F ($4.05). From here you can travel on Métro Line 7 into town.

A taxi from Orly into the city costs about 170F ($32.69) and takes 40 to 50 minutes.

Note: Useful telephone numbers: Info RATP for Orly bus, Roissy bus, and Orlyval, 1/43-46-14-14; Info Cars Air France, 1/42-99-25-00 (CDG) or 1/41-75-44-40 (Orly); Info SNCF for RER service information, 1/45-82-50-50.

FROM THE TRAIN STATIONS   Paris has six major train stations. For information, call the **Société Nationale des Chemins de Fer (SNCF)** (☎ **1/45-82-50-50**) and ask for someone who speaks English or go to a travel agent or the station information booths.

Coming from northern Germany and Belgium, you'll probably arrive at the **Gare du Nord** (some trains from London arrive here as well). Other trains from London and Normandy come into the **Gare St-Lazare,** in northwest Paris. Trains from the west (Brittany, Chartres, Versailles) head to the **Gare de Montparnasse;**

The French Franc

For American Readers   At this writing $1 = approximately 5.20 francs (or 1 franc = 19¢), and this was the rate of exchange used to calculate the dollar values given in this chapter (rounded to the nearest nickel).

For British Readers   At this writing £1 = approximately 8.50 francs (or 1 franc = 11p), and this was the rate of exchange used to calculate the pound values in the table below.

Note: The rates given here fluctuate from time to time and may not be the same when you travel to France. Therefore this table should be used only as a guide:

F	U.S.$	U.K.£	F	U.S.$	U.K.£
1	.19	.12	75	14.42	8.82
2	.38	.24	100	19.23	11.76
3	.58	.35	125	24.04	14.71
4	.77	.47	150	28.85	17.65
5	.96	.59	175	33.65	20.59
6	1.15	.71	200	38.46	23.53
7	1.35	.82	225	43.27	26.47
8	1.54	.94	250	48.08	29.41
9	1.73	1.06	275	52.88	32.35
10	1.92	1.18	300	57.69	35.29
15	2.88	1.76	350	67.31	41.18
20	3.85	2.35	400	76.92	47.06
25	4.81	2.94	450	86.54	52.94
50	9.62	5.88	500	96.15	58.82

those from the southwest (the Loire Valley, Bordeaux, the Pyrenees, Spain) to the **Gare d'Austerlitz;** those from the south and southeast (the Riviera, Lyon, Italy, Geneva) to the **Gare de Lyon.** From Alsace and eastern France, Luxembourg, southern Germany, and Zurich, the arrival station is the **Gare de l'Est.** All train stations are next to a Métro station bearing the same name.

FROM THE BUS STATION   International buses pull into Paris's **Gare Routière Internationale** (International Bus Terminal) at 35 av. Porte-de-la-Villette, in the 19th arrondissement, the northeastern part of the city. This is not a wonderful part of town, with crime problems. The Métro station here is Porte-de-la-Villette; to go downtown, take Line 7 heading toward either Mairie d'Ivry or Villejuif–Louis-Aragon.

VISITOR INFORMATION

FOR EVERYONE   At the airports are small information offices, and for a fee their staff will help you to make a hotel reservation. But the prime source of information is the **Office de Tourisme et des Congrès de Paris,** 127 av. des Champs-Elysées, 8e (☎ **1/49-52-53-54;** Métro: Charles-de-Gaulle–Etoile or George-V), open daily from 9am to 8pm. For a fee, the staff will make a hotel reservation for you on the same day you want a room: 8F ($1.55) for hostels and foyers, 20F ($3.85) for one-star hotels, 25F ($4.80) for two-star hotels, 40F ($7.70) for three-star hotels. The office and its reservation service are often very busy in the summer season—you'll probably have to wait in line. The Office de Tourisme has six auxiliary offices: at the Gare du Nord (open May to October, Monday through Saturday from 8am to 9pm and Sunday from 1 to 8pm; November to April, daily from 1 to 8pm); at the Gare de l'Est and Gare de Lyon (open May to October, Monday through Saturday from 8am to 9pm; November to April, until 8pm); at the Gare d'Austerlitz (open Monday through Saturday from 8am to 3pm); at the Eiffel Tower (open May to September, daily from 11am to 6pm); and at the Gare Montparnasse (open May to October, daily from 8am to 9pm; November to April, until 8pm).

FOR STUDENTS   Paris, with its huge student population, both native and foreign, has all sorts of organizations providing information on student-travel discounts:

Accueil des Jeunes en France (AJF), 119 rue St-Martin, 4e (☎ **1/42-77-87-80;** Métro: Rambuteau; RER: Châtelet–Les Halles), is across place Pompidou from the entrance to the Centre Pompidou. AJF helps students find student restaurants and obtain inexpensive lodgings, meal vouchers, student cards, and discount train, bus, and plane tickets. This central booking office is open all year, Monday through Saturday from 9am to 4pm. It also has an office in the Latin Quarter, at 139 bd. St-Michel, 5e (☎ **1/43-54-95-86**), open Monday through Friday from 10am to 6pm; and an office at the Gare du Nord (☎ **1/42-85-86-19;** Métro: Gare du Nord), normally open June to September, Monday through Friday from 7:30am to 10pm.

Union des Centres de Recontres Internationales de France (UCRIF), 72 rue Rambuteau, 1er (☎ **1/40-26-57-64;** Métro: Louvre-Rivoli), operates more than 63 hostels throughout France; though catering to groups, it has an information/reservation service for individuals.

CITY LAYOUT

The River Seine divides Paris into the **Right Bank** (*Rive Droite*) and the **Left Bank** (*Rive Gauche*). The right (north) bank of the river is where you'll find the Louvre, the Opéra Garnier, the Grands Boulevards, and much of monumental Paris. Generally speaking, this is the higher-priced part of town. On the left (south) bank are the areas associated with the Sorbonne and student life; generally speaking, these are the less-expensive areas.

The heart of medieval Paris was the Ile de la Cité and the areas immediately surrounding it; as Paris grew it absorbed many of the once-distant villages, and today these are *arrondissements* (districts) of the city proper—consequently, each of the 20 arrondissements has a character of its own. They're numbered from 1 to 20 starting at the center around the Louvre and progressing in a clockwise spiral. The key to finding any address in Paris is looking for the number of the arrondissement, which will be rendered either as a number followed by "e" or "er" (1er, 2e, and so on) or, more formally, as part of the postal code (the last digit or the last and penultimate digits indicate the arrondissement—75007 indicates that the address is in the 7th arrondissement, 75017 means that the address is in the 17th arrondissement, and so on).

Each arrondissement possesses a unique character and a unique place in the hearts of Parisians. On the Right Bank, the **1er** is home to the Musée du

Paris by Arrondissement

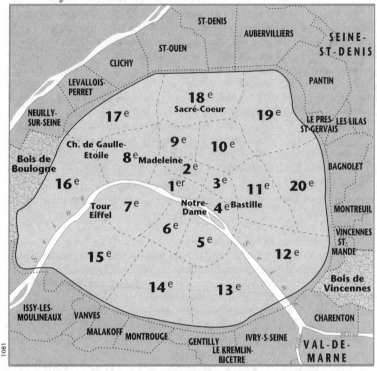

ST-DENIS

AUBERVILLIERS

SEINE-
ST-DENIS

ST-OUEN

CLICHY

PANTIN

LEVALLOIS-
PERRET

18ᵉ
Sacré-Coeur

19ᵉ

NEUILLY-
SUR-SEINE

17ᵉ

LE PRES-
ST-GERVAIS

LES LILAS

Ch. de Gaulle-
Etoile

9ᵉ

10ᵉ

Bois de
Boulogne

8ᵉ Madeleine
2ᵉ

BAGNOLET

16ᵉ

1er

3ᵉ

11ᵉ

20ᵉ

Tour
Eiffel

7ᵉ

Notre-
Dame

4ᵉ Bastille

MONTREUIL

6ᵉ

VINCENNES
ST-
MANDE

5ᵉ

15ᵉ

12ᵉ

Bois de
Vincennes

14ᵉ

13ᵉ

ISSY-LES-
MOULINEAUX

VANVES

CHARENTON

MALAKOFF

MONTROUGE

GENTILLY
LE KREMLIN-
BICETRE

IVRY-S-SEINE

VAL-DE-
MARNE

Louvre, place Vendôme, rues de Rivoli and St-Honoré, Palais Royal, and Comédie-Française—an area filled with grand institutions and grand stores; at the center of the **2e** is the Bourse (stock exchange), making it the city's financial center; most of the **3e** and the **4e** is referred to as the Marais, the old Jewish quarter that in the 17th century was home to the aristocracy—today it's a trendy area of boutiques and restored mansions as well as the center of Paris's gay and lesbian community. On the Left Bank, the **5e** is known as the Latin Quarter, home to the Sorbonne and Panthéon and associated with the intellectual life that thrived in the 1920s and 1930s; the **6e,** known as St-Germain-des-Prés, stretches from the Seine to boulevard du Montparnasse and is also associated with the 1920s and 1930s—as well as being a center for art and antiques, it boasts the Palais and Jardin du Luxembourg within its boundaries. The **7e,** containing both the Tour Eiffel and Hôtel des Invalides, is a residential district for the well-heeled.

On the Right Bank, the **8e** epitomizes monumental Paris—with the triumphal avenue des Champs-Elysées, the Elysées Palace, and the fashion houses along avenue Montaigne and the Faubourg St-Honoré. The **18e** is home to Sacré-Coeur and Montmartre and all that the name conjures of brilliant bohemian life painted most characteristically by Toulouse-Lautrec. The **14e** incorporates a large part of Montparnasse, including its cemetery, while the **20e** is where the the city's famous lie buried in Père-Lachaise and where today the most recent immigrants from North Africa live. Beyond the arrondissements stretch the vast *banlieue* (suburbs) of Greater Paris, where the majority of Parisians live.

GETTING AROUND

BY SUBWAY (METRO) The Métro is fast, clean, safe for the most part, and easy to navigate. The first Métro line was opened in 1900. It's operated by the Régie Autonome des Transports Parisiens (RATP), just like the city buses.

The Métro has 13 lines and more than 360 stations (there's bound to be one near your destination), and it's connected to the RER (Réseau Express Régional), with four lines that stop at only a few stations, crisscrossing the city in minutes and connecting downtown Paris with its airports. The trains run from 5:30am to past midnight, finishing up their final runs before 1am. Both the Métro and the RER operate on a zone system, at a different fare per zone, but it's unlikely that you'll be traveling any farther than the first zone.

A single ticket (*un billet*) costs 7F ($1.35), but if you ask for *un carnet* (a booklet) you'll get 10 (loose) tickets for 41F ($7.90), dropping the price per ticket to only 79¢. If you're going to be in Paris for a few days, it may be a better idea to get a weekly or monthly unlimited-ride Carte Orange; see "Special Discounts" under "Paris Deals & Discounts," earlier in this chapter.

Be sure to keep your ticket until exiting the train platform and passing the *limite de validité des billets.* An inspector may ask to see it at any time before that.

The older Métro stations are marked by curvaceous art nouveau gateways reading MÉTROPOLITAIN; others are marked by M signs. Every Métro stop has maps of the system, and these are also available at ticket booths. Once you decide which Métro line you need, make sure you're going in the right *direction:* On Métro Line 1, "Direction: Esplanade de la Défense" indicates a westbound train, while "Direction: Château de Vincennes" is just the opposite. To change train lines, look for the orange CORRESPONDANCE signs; blue signs reading SORTIE mark the exits.

Near the exits there's always a *plan du quartier,* a pictoral and detailed map of the streets and buildings surrounding each Métro station, with all exits marked. It's often a good idea to consult this before you climb the stairs, especially at large stations; you may want to use a different exit stairway so as to be on the other side of a busy street or closer to where you're going.

For more information on the city's public transportation, stop in at either of the two offices of the Services Touristiques de la RATP, at 53 bis quai des Grands-Augustins, 6e (☎ **1/40-46-42-17;** Métro: St-Michel), or at place de la Madeleine, 8e (☎ **1/40-06-71-45;** Métro: Madeleine); or you can call 1/43-46-14-14 for information.

Pickpocket Warning: Most of the time the Métro is quite safe. However, precautions are in order in the northern parts of the city and in deserted stations or in those long corridors between stations late at night. As a tourist, you're a special mark. You may feel safer riding in the first train car, where the engineer is. Watch out for pickpockets, especially on the Métro. In Paris, these include bands of ragamuffins who'll quickly surround you, distract you by waving something in your face, pick your pockets clean, and disappear, all within seconds. *Don't let them near you.* Be rude if you have to.

BY BUS Although generally slower than the Métro, buses allow you to see the sights as you ride. They take the same tickets as the Métro and also operate on a zone system, shown on charts in each bus.

BY TAXI Parisian taxis are fairly expensive and also scarce because there are only 15,000 on the streets. Look for them at specially marked taxi ranks at key locations.

Paris Métro

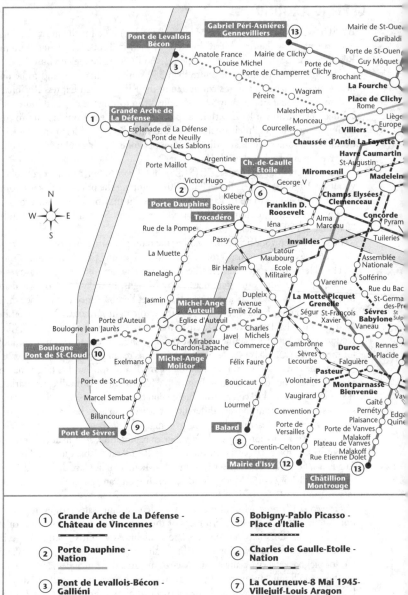

Légende des lignes

1. Grande Arche de La Défense - Château de Vincennes

2. Porte Dauphine - Nation

3. Pont de Levallois-Bécon - Galliéni

3B. Porte des Lilas - Gambetta

4. Porte de Clignancourt - Porte d'Orléans

5. Bobigny-Pablo Picasso - Place d'Italie

6. Charles de Gaulle-Etoile - Nation

7. La Courneuve-8 Mai 1945- Villejuif-Louis Aragon

7B. Pré-St-Gervais - Louis-Blanc

8. Balard - Créteil-Préfecture

108.2

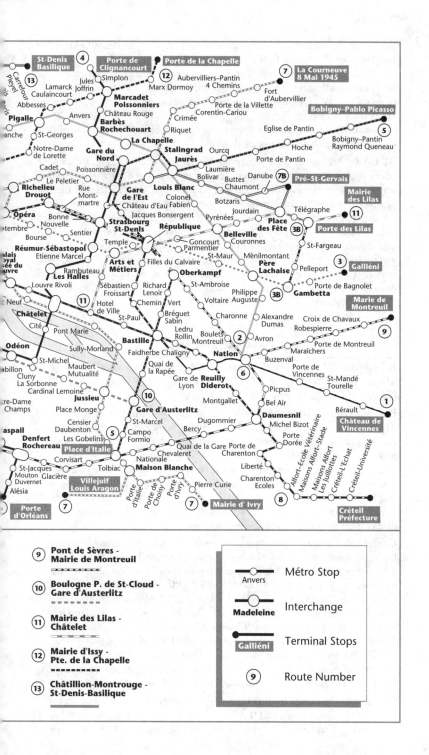

For one to three people, the drop rate in Paris proper is 13F ($2.50) plus 3.23F (60¢) for every kilometer from 7am to 7pm, after which rates rise to 5.10F ($1) per kilometer. You'll pay supplements from taxi ranks at train stations and at the Air France shuttle-bus terminals of 6F ($1.15) for luggage, and, if the driver agrees to do so, 5F (95¢) for transporting a fourth person or 3F (60¢) for a pet. Higher tariffs apply daily from 7pm to 7am.

Taxi drivers are required by law to transport disabled customers and to help them with wheelchairs, luggage, and the like.

BY CAR Because of Paris's narrow streets and difficult parking, we strongly advise you against driving in the city. Even for out-of-town excursions, the best way to go is on the extensive train and bus network. Rental cars and fuel are expensive, and traffic fines are positively staggering. Renting a car from one of the major companies will cost about 1,144F ($220) for a week with unlimited mileage plus about $20 per day for collision insurance and 18.6% tax for a total of $427—and that's provided you book it and prepay it in the United States. If you rent on the spot it'll most likely cost you more. If you must, call Hertz, Avis, or Budget and book *before you leave.* All these companies and others have car-rental desks at the airports, at the train stations, and at Air France's Aérogare des Invalides (Métro: Invalides).

FAST FACTS: Paris

Babysitters   There are several agencies in Paris offering babysitting services: Allo Maman Poule (☎ **1/47-48-01-01**) or Kid Service, 159 rue de Rome, 17e (☎ **1/47-66-00-52;** Métro: Gare-St-Lazare).

Business Hours   Normally, **banks** are normally open Monday through Friday from 9am to noon and 1 or 1:30 to 4:30pm. Some banks have long hours on Saturday morning. Some currency-exchange booths are open very long hours—see "Currency Exchange," below.

The *grands magasins* (**department stores**) are generally open Monday through Saturday from 9:30am to 6:30pm; **smaller shops** close for lunch and reopen around 2pm, but this has become rarer than it used to be. Many stores stay open until 7pm in summer; others are closed Monday, especially in the morning. Large **offices** remain open all day, but some also close for lunch.

Consulates   If you have a passport, immigration, legal, or other problem, contact your consulate. Call before you go there, as they often keep strange hours and observe both French and home-country holidays. The Consulate of **Australia** is at 4 rue Jean-Rey, 15e (☎ **1/40-59-33-00;** Métro: Bir-Hakeim). The Consulate of **Canada** is at 35 av. Montaigne, 8e (☎ **1/44-43-29-00;** Métro: Franklin-D.-Roosevelt or Alma-Marceau). The Consulate of **New Zealand** is at 7 ter rue Léonardo-de-Vinci, 16e (☎ **1/45-00-24-11** ext. 280 from 9am to 1pm; Métro: Victor-Hugo). The Consulate of the **United Kingdom** is at 9 av. Hoche, 8e (☎ **1/42-66-91-42;** Métro: Madeleine). The Consulate of the **United States** is at 2 rue St-Florentin, 1er, off the northeastern corner of place de la Concorde (☎ **1/42-96-12-02;** Métro: Concorde).

Currency   The French **franc (F)** is divided into 100 **centimes.** There are coins of 5, 10, and 20 centimes, and $^1/_2$, 1, 2, 5, and 10 francs. Sometimes there are two types of coins for one denomination, especially after the 1989 bicentennial of the French Revolution, when new commemorative coins were minted. Bills come in denominations of 20, 50, 100, 500, and 1,000 francs.

Currency Exchange   Call a commercial bank or look in the financial pages of your newspaper to find the current rate of exchange. You'll get slightly less than this rate when you exchange money. Always ask if there's a fee or commission charged on the transaction. A big fee or commission can wipe out the advantage of a favorable exchange rate.

Banks and *bureaux de change* (exchange offices) almost always offer better exchange rates than hotels, restaurants, and shops, which should be used only in emergencies. We've always found very good rates, no fees or commissions, and quick service at the **Comptoir de Change Opéra,** 9 rue Scribe, 9e (☎ 1/47-42-20-96; Métro: Opéra; RER: Auber). It's open Monday through Friday from 9am to 5:15pm and Saturday from 9:30am to 4:15pm. The *bureaux de change* at all train stations (except Gare de Montparnasse) are open daily; those at 63 av. des Champs-Elysées, 8e (Métro: Franklin-D.-Roosevelt), and 140 av. des Champs-Elysées, 8e (Métro: George-V), 200 rue de Rivoli (Métro: Tuileries), and 9 rue Berger, 1er (Métro: Les Halles), keep long hours.

With a grand Paris office, **American Express,** 11 rue Scribe, 9e (☎ 1/47-77-70-07; Métro: Opéra, Chaussée-d'Antin, or Havre-Caumartin; RER: Auber), is extremely busy with customers buying and cashing traveler's checks (not the best rates for exchange transactions), picking up mail, and solving travel problems. It's open Monday through Friday from 9am to 6:30pm; the bank is also open Saturday (same hours), but the mail-pickup window is closed.

Dentists   You can call your consulate and ask the duty officer to recommend a dentist. For dental emergencies, call SOS Dentaire (☎ 1/43-37-51-00) daily from 9am to midnight.

Doctors   Call your consulate and ask the duty officer to recommend a doctor. Otherwise, call SOS Médicins (☎ 1/47-07-77-77), a 24-hour service.

Emergencies   For the police, call 17. To report a fire, dial 18. For an ambulance, call 15 or SAMU (☎ 1/45-67-50-50). For SOS Help in English call 1/47-23-80-80.

Paris has a number of all-night pharmacies, including the Pharmacie Dhéry, 84 av. des Champs-Elysées, 8e (☎ 1/45-62-02-41; Métro: George-V), in the Galerie des Champs shopping center.

Holidays   France has lots of national holidays, most tied to the church calendar. On these days, shops, businesses, government offices, and most restaurants close. They include New Year's Day (Jan 1); Easter Monday (late Mar or early Apr); Labor Day (May 1); Ascension Thursday (in May or June, 40 days after Easter); Whit Monday, also called Pentecost Monday (51st day after Easter, in June or July); Bastille Day (July 14); Assumption Day (Aug 15); All Saints Day (Nov 1); Armistice Day (Nov 11); and Christmas Day (Dec 25).

In addition, schedules may be disrupted on Shrove Tuesday (the Tuesday before Ash Wednesday, in Jan or Feb) and Good Friday (late Mar or early Apr).

Hospitals   Two hospitals with English-speaking staff are the American Hospital of Paris, 63 bd. Victor-Hugo, Neuilly-sur-Seine (☎ 1/46-41-25-41; Métro: Les Sablons), west of Paris proper; and the British Hospital of Paris, 3 rue Barbès Levallois-Perret (☎ 1/46-39-22-22; Métro: Anatole-France), north of Neuilly, over the city line northwest of Paris. *Note:* Only patients with adequate medical insurance should use the American Hospital: it's a private hospital where room rates are about $600 per day—without doctors' fees. The emergency department is basically $62 per day, but this doesn't include x-rays and other tests, if required. So you'd better phone before going.

Hotlines   SOS Help is a crisis line where English is spoken; call 47-23-80-80 daily from 3 to 11pm. The Comité National pour la Réadaptation des Handicapés, 38 bd. Raspail, 7e (☎ **1/53-80-66-66;** Métro: Sèvres-Babylone), is an information service for disabled people; it's open Monday through Friday from 9:30am to noon and 2:30 to 8pm.

Information   See "Visitor Information" under "Paris Specifics," earlier in this chapter.

Laundry/Dry Cleaning   To find a laundry near you, ask at your hotel or consult the Yellow Pages under "Laveries Automatiques." Take as many 10F, 2F, and 1F pieces as you can. Dry cleaning is "nettoyage â sec"; look for shop signs with the word PRESSING. Washing and drying 6 kilos (13¼ lb.) of stuff usually costs about 40F ($7.70).

Lost & Found   The central office is Objets Trouvés, Prefecture de Police, 36 rue des Morillons, 15e (☎ **1/45-31-14-80;** Métro: Convention), at the corner of rue de Dantzig; for objects left in a taxi, ask for extension 4208. It's open Monday and Wednesday from 8:30am to 5pm, Tuesday and Thursday from 8:30am to 8pm, and Friday from 8:30am to 5:30pm. For Lost and Found on the Métro, call 40-06-75-27.

If you lose your Visa or MasterCard (Visa is Carte Bleue and MasterCard is Eurocard in France), call 42-77-11-90, 24 hours a day. For lost American Express traveler's checks, call toll free 19/05-90-86-00; for AMEX cards, 47-77-72-00.

Mail   Large post offices (PTT) are normally open Monday through Friday from 8am to 7pm and Saturday from 8am to noon; small post offices may have shorter hours. There are many post offices scattered around the city; ask anybody for the nearest one. Airmail letters within Europe cost 2.80F (55¢); to the United States, 4.30F (85¢); to Australia, 5.80F ($1.10).

The city's main post office is at 52 rue du Louvre, 75001 Paris (☎ **1/40-28-20-00;** Métro: Louvre-Rivoli), open 24 hours a day for urgent mailings, telegrams, and telephone calls. This is where you should go to pick up *Poste Restante* (general delivery) mail; be prepared to show your passport and pay a small fee for each letter you receive.

Police   Dial 17 in emergencies.

Religious Services   All major religions are represented in Paris. Here are some specifics: St. Joseph's Roman Catholic Church, 50 av. Hoche, 8e (☎ **1/42-27-28-56;** Métro: Charles-de-Gaulle–Etoile); American Cathedral in Paris (Episcopal), 23 av. George-V, 8e (☎ **1/47-20-17-92**); American Church (Episcopal), 65 quai d'Orsay, 7e (☎ **1/47-05-07-99;** Métro: Invalides); International Baptist Fellowship, 23 rue Beaunier, 14e (☎ **1/43-95-68-58**); Lutheran Church, 16 rue Chauchat, 9e (☎ **1/47-70-80-30;** Métro: Richelieu-Drouot); Eglise Grecque Orthodoxe (Greek Orthodox), 7 rue Georges-Bizet, 16e (☎ **1/47-20-82-35;** Métro: Alma-Marceau); Cathédrale Orthodoxe Alexandre-Nevsky (Russian Orthodox), 12 rue Daru, 8e (☎ **1/42-27-37-34;**

Métro: Courcelles); Association Israélite de Paris (Jewish), 17 rue St-Georges, 9e (☎ **1/40-82-26-26;** Métro: Le Peletier); Mosquée de Paris (Muslim), place du Puits-de-l'Ermite, 5e (☎ **1/45-35-97-33;** Métro: Monge).

Tax   For information on France's TVA (value-added tax), see "Special Discounts" under "Paris Deals & Discounts," earlier in this chapter.

Taxis   See "Getting Around" under "Paris Specifics," earlier in this chapter.

Telephone   Pay telephones take coins of 1F, 2F, and 5F; the minimum charge for a **local call** is 2F (40¢). Most pay phones, though, take only telephone debit cards called *télécartes,* which can be bought at post offices and at *tabacs* (cafés and kiosks that sell tobacco products). The cost of the call is automatically deducted from the "value" of the card as recorded on its magnetized strip. The télécarte comes in 50- and 120-unit values, costing 40F ($7.70) and 96F ($18.45), respectively. If you don't plan to make many phone calls, a télécarte may not be a very good idea, since you may end up not using its entire value. They come in very handy, though, for making long-distance calls. For **international calls,** dial 19, then the country code (for the United States and Canada it's "1"), then the area or city code, then the local number. To place a collect call to North America, dial 19/33-11 and an English-speaking operator will assist you. Otherwise, use access codes to your telephone credit card companies. For AT&T USA Direct dial 19/00-11. Save money by calling North America after 10pm or between 2am and noon and on Sunday.

To call **long distance in France** dial 16, then the local number.

Avoid making any phone calls from your hotel room; some hotels charge at least 3F (60¢) for local calls.

Tipping   Service is supposedly included at your hotel, but it's still customary to tip the bellhop about 6F ($1.15) per bag, more in expensive splurge hotels. You might use 5% of the daily room rate as a guideline. If you have lots of luggage, tip a bit more. Though your *addition* (restaurant bill) or *fiche* (café check) will bear the words *service compris* ("service charge included"), it's customary to leave a tip. In a fancy restaurant, 10% to 12% will do; in a cheap place, 8% to 10% is fine; in a café, a few coins, perhaps totaling more than 5% but less than 10%, is good.

Remember, service has supposedly already been paid for. Taxi drivers expect 10% of the fare as a tip. At the theater and cinema, tip the usher who shows you to your seat 2F (40¢). In public toilets, there's often a posted fee for using the facilities. If not, the maintenance person will expect a tip of about 2F (40¢). Put it in the basket or on the plate at the entrance. Porters and cloakroom attendants are usually governed by set prices that are displayed. If not, give a porter 5F to 8F (95¢ to $1.55) per suitcase, and a cloakroom attendant 2F to 4F (40¢ to 75¢) per coat.

4   Accommodations

Anyone who has ever seen *An American in Paris* and planned a trip to the capital of France has probably dreamed of staying in some quaint, cozy little hotel on a pretty square or a narrow side street, right in the midst of a neighborhood bursting with charm. Well, there aren't many such hotels left in the 1990s, but with careful planning you can stay in one—and on a budget, too.

Regarding budget accommodations, keep in mind the provisos we mentioned earlier in the chapter. Note, too, that in France you'll pay more for a room with twin beds than for a room with one double bed. When you make a reservation, be precise about what kind and how many beds you want in your room.

A room with a shower or tub doesn't necessarily mean that the room has a toilet as well. There are rooms with a toilet and shower, rooms with a toilet only, and rooms with a shower only. The trend these days is to renovate small hotels and put a shower, toilet, bidet, and sink in each room, so those marvelously cheap bathless rooms are dwindling but haven't entirely disappeared.

Ask to see a room before checking in, and if you don't like it, ask to see another. As for price, the rates given below are for the high summer season and are correct as this book goes to press. No one has promised to maintain the rates quoted here, so the rate you pay may be a bit higher or lower than that quoted. Also, in high season you may be required to take breakfast with your room.

The **Office de Tourisme et des Congrès de Paris,** on the Champs-Elysées, will help you find a room for a fee (see "Visitor Information" under "Paris Specifics," earlier in this chapter). In summer, this service is likely to be in demand, and there may be quite a line of people waiting, so get there early. The French government rates each hotel from one to four stars: One star denotes a simple, basic hotel; four stars signify a high-class one. In many of the following descriptions we've noted this rating.

DOUBLES FOR LESS THAN 400F ($76.90)

NEAR THE SORBONNE

The Sorbonne area, with its bookstores, café life, and famous boulevards, lives deep in the imagination of many visitors to Paris. Besides the university and the busy intersections of boulevards St-Michel and St-Germain, you'll find several other Parisian icons: the Jardin du Luxembourg, the Panthéon, and (only 15 minutes away on foot) Notre-Dame. Hotels in this area cater to students and budgeteers. You can find rock-bottom digs or very comfortable lodgings, as you wish.

Grand Hôtel St-Michel

19 rue Cujas, 75005 Paris. ☎ **1/46-33-33-02** or 46-33-65-03. Fax 1/40-46-96-33. 61 rms, all with shower only. TV TEL. 300F–360F ($57.70–$69.25) single; 410F ($78.85) double; 480F–510F ($92.30–$98.10) triple. Breakfast 35F ($6.75) extra. AE, DC, JCB, MC, V. Métro: Cluny–La Sorbonne. RER: Luxembourg.

This hotel has six floors of basic rooms, most with little balconies, some (especially nos. 64 and 67) with fine views over the Paris roofs. The hotel has for some time been undergoing a renovation and a substantial number of rooms have already been redecorated and freshened up. The breakfast room is light and airy with its tile floor and fresh white photograph-decorated walls.

Hôtel de la Faculté

1 rue Racine, 75006 Paris. ☎ **1/43-26-87-13.** Fax 1/46-34-73-88. 19 rms, all with shower only. TEL. 350F–390F ($67.30–$75) single or double. Continental breakfast 29F ($5.60) extra. MC, V. Métro: Odéon or St-Michel.

In a prime Latin Quarter location steps off the busy boulevard St-Michel, this modest hotel holds some surprises. The tiny lobby leads to a minuscule elevator and a winding staircase. Down the narrow hallways are guest rooms with new rustic furnishings. Everything may seem a bit squeezed in here, but the prices won't squeeze your budget.

Getting the Best Deal on Accommodations

- Try for a room with one double bed instead of two twin beds.
- Making reservations is strongly advised, especially in summer, when budget rooms may be occupied.
- A room without a bath can be marvelously cheap.

Hôtel des Allies

20 rue Bertholet (a five-minute walk from bd. St-Michel), 75005 Paris. ☎ **1/43-31-47-52.** Fax 1/45-35-13-92. 43 rms, 10 with bath (some with shower). 180–220 F ($34.55–$42.25) single or double without bath, 295 F ($56.65) single or double with bath; 230–280 F ($44.15–$53.75) triple without bath, 380 F ($72.95) triple with bath. Breakfast 28F ($5.40) extra; showers 15F ($2.90) extra. MC, V. Métro: Censier-Daubton or Pont-Royal.

This hotel, owned and managed by friendly M. Albessard since 1964, occupies a good location in a quiet area. The house door is locked at 10:30pm, but guests are given keys. Street parking is possible.

Hôtel Gerson

14 rue de la Sorbonne, 75005 Paris. ☎ **1/43-54-28-40.** Fax 1/44-07-13-90. 24 rms, 17 with shower only. 220F ($42.30) single without bath, 300F ($57.70) single with shower only; 300F ($57.70) double without bath, 360F ($69.25) double with shower only; 420F ($80.75) triple with shower only. Continental breakfast 30F ($5.75) extra; showers 25F ($4.80) extra. MC, V. Métro: Cluny–La Sorbonne. RER: Luxembourg.

The Gerson is in the very heart of the Latin Quarter, just a few steps down the hill from place de la Sorbonne. It's the quintessential low-budget hotel, with soft beds and many nicks in the woodwork, but it has clean rooms, some with private baths, that are quite reasonable.

Hôtel Marignan

13 rue du Sommerard, 75005 Paris. ☎ **1/43-54-63-81.** 30 rms, 1 with bath, 6 with toilet only. 190 F ($36.50) single without bath; 310–390 F ($59.50–$63.35) double without bath, 410 F ($78.70) triple with toilet but no bath; 480 F ($92.15) quad without bath, 560 F ($124.80) quad with bath. Rates include continental breakfast and showers. No credit cards. Métro: Maubert-Mutualité (then a two-minute walk) or St-Michel (then a six-minute walk).

The rooms in this six-floor walk-up have recently been renovated by owners Paul and Linda Keniger—he's French and looks like Steven Spielberg and she's from California. Carved stucco ceilings, tile baths, and wood dressers are now features of the rooms, along with brand-new carpeting and beds. The Kenigers provide a warm, friendly atmosphere and work hard to keep their guests satisfied. There are few questions about Paris or France that Paul can't answer. Families with children are especially welcome (rare in Paris). Guests have use of a washer/drier and iron. Off-season, the kitchen can be used, and all year round, after breakfast, you can bring your own food to the small dining room.

NEAR MONTPARNASSE

Hôtel des Bains

44 rue Delambre, 75014 Paris. ☎ **1/43-20-85-27.** Fax 1/42-79-82-70. 41 rms, all with shower or bath. TV TEL. 367F ($70.60) single or double with one bed; 418F ($80.40) double with two beds; 548F ($105.40) triple; 600F ($115.40) quad. Buffet breakfast 43F ($8.25) extra. No credit cards. Parking 65F ($12.50). Métro: Edgar-Quinet.

Named for the public baths that once occupied this building and completely renovated and modernized, this six-floor hotel (no elevator) is a good choice for families
or small groups. All rooms have safes and hairdryers as well as TVs with cable. The
house is in a quiet area, and the reception area is at street level.

NEAR ST-MICHEL & NOTRE-DAME

Even closer to the Seine, still in the midst of the vibrant street life of the Latin
Quarter, are several good lodging choices.

✪ Hôtel du Globe

15 rue des Quatre Vents, 75006 Paris. ☎ **1/46-33-62-69.** 15 rms, 14 with bath (tub or
shower). 405 F ($77.75) single or double with bath (tub), 305 F ($58.55) single or double
with bath (shower), 255 F ($48.95) single or double without bath. Continental breakfast 35F
($6.75) extra. No credit cards. Métro: St-Sulpice.

This hotel doesn't look like much from the outside, but as soon as you enter you'll
know that great care has been taken in decorating this charming old building.
Every room has the basic necessities, but all are decorated uniquely—most with
a floral pattern and lace accents. One of my favorites is salmon-colored Room 7.
There's no elevator, but you probably won't mind climbing the wonderful narrow
staircase. Room prices vary according to size and amenities.

Hôtel Henri IV

25 place Dauphine, 75001 Paris. ☎ **1/43-54-44-53.** 21 rms, none with bath. 140F ($26.90)
single; 2205F ($42.30) double. Rates include continental breakfast. Showers 15F ($2.90)
extra. No credit cards. Métro: Pont-Neuf.

On a small chestnut-lined square on the Ile de la Cité, near Notre-Dame, this five-
floor house (no elevator) is more than 400 years old; the hotel has been here since
1892. The rooms are spacious, with medieval parquet floors, high ceilings, and
enormous windows (ask for no. 1, with a view of the square). There's hot and cold
running water in each room, plus a toilet and shower on every floor. The reception area is one creaky flight of stairs up. To find this unique historical hotel, walk
over pont Neuf and turn left.

Hôtel le Home Latin

15–17 rue du Sommerard, 75005 Paris. ☎ **1/43-26-95-15.** Fax 1/43-29-87-04. 58 rms, all
with bath. TV TEL. 365F ($70.20) single; 430F ($82.70) double; 495F ($95.20) twin; 595F
($114.40) triple. Continental breakfast 35F ($6.75) extra. V. Métro: Maubert-Mutualité or
St-Michel.

After extensive renovations, this hotel has attained two stars. Europeans love modern conveniences, and the Hôtel le Home Latin has them all, even down to the
automatic sliding glass doors at the entrance. Done in coral shades, each of the
fresh and clean rooms has a small bath and a table and chairs. The hotel is fairly
large and quiet, but if you're worried about traffic noise ask for a room at the
back. A room here might be on the high side of your budget, but you won't be
disappointed.

Hôtel St-André-des-Arts

66 rue St-André-des-Arts, 75006 Paris. ☎ **1/43-26-96-16.** Fax 1/43-29-73-34. 34 rms, 25
with shower only or shower and toilet. TEL. 233F ($44.80) single without bath, 298F ($57.30)
single with shower and toilet; 426F ($81.90) double with shower and toilet; 519F ($99.80)
triple with shower and toilet; 542F ($104.25) quad with shower and toilet. Rates include
continental breakfast. MC, V. Métro: Odéon (then cross boulevard St-Germain and walk down
rue de l'Ancien-Comédie to rue St-André-des-Arts, on the right).

The St-André is the stereotype of the romantic Latin Quarter hotel: On a crooked street filled with art galleries and cafés sits this half-timbered 17th-century building with rough stone. The hotel has tiny rooms, high ceilings, and great prices. The front-desk clerk speaks English.

NEAR THE JARDIN DU LUXEMBOURG

There's an exceptional hotel several blocks from the southwest corner of the Jardin du Luxembourg. The neighborhood is quite nice, and the Métro will whisk you over to Odéon or St-Michel in a matter of minutes.

Grand Hôtel Léveque

29 rue Cler, 75007 Paris. ☎ **1/47-05-49-15.** Fax 1/45-50-49-36. 50 rms, 12 with sink only, 3 with shower only, 35 with shower and toilet. 195F–230F ($37.50–$44.25) single or double without bath; 300F ($57.70) single or double with shower only; 325F–365F ($62.50–$70.209) single or double with shower and toilet. Continental breakfast 30F ($5.75) extra. MC, V. Métro: Ecole-Militaire or Latour-Maubourg.

The Grand Hôtel Léveque is a large establishment on a colorful pedestrian street with a busy marketplace during the day. About half the rooms have been renovated recently, with showers and toilets installed in most; the renovated rooms are at the high end of the price scale. The staff is helpful and, if you ask, may be able to give you one of the rooms on the fifth floor with partial but panoramic views of the Eiffel Tower. If you need complete quiet, ask for a back room.

Hôtel de Nevers

3 rue de l'Abbé-de-l'Epée, 75005 Paris. ☎ **1/43-26-81-83.** 26 rms, 9 with bath, 8 with shower only. 173F ($33.25) single without bath, 263F($50.60) single with shower only, 293F ($56.35) single with shower and toilet; 286F ($55) double with shower only, 356F ($68.45) double with shower and toilet; 409F ($78.65) triple with shower and toilet. Rates include continental breakfast. Showers (for those rooms without bath) 15F ($2.90) extra. No credit cards. Métro: Luxembourg.

This 200-year-old house offers basic rooms. Backpackers traveling in groups of four or five will pay less here than in a hostel. It's located in a quiet area, next to a small tree-lined square, and managed by Mme Allanic, a jolly lady who speaks some English.

Hôtel des Academies

15 rue de la Grande-Chaumière, 75006 Paris. ☎ **1/43-26-66-44.** 21 rms, 17 with shower or shower and toilet. TEL. 190F ($36.55) single with sink and toilet only; 255F ($49.05) single or double with shower only, 295F–310F ($56.75–$59.60) single or double with shower and toilet. Rates include showers. Continental breakfast 30F ($5.75) extra. No credit cards. Métro: Vavin.

On a quiet side street southwest of the Jardin du Luxembourg, this hotel is proper and comfortable, with hearteningly low prices. The decor in the lobby and guest rooms is eclectic at worst, kitschy at best. There's no elevator, but rooms on the fourth and fifth floors are cheaper, so the climb pays for itself.

NEAR THE EIFFEL TOWER

The Eiffel Tower neighborhood is in the 7th arrondissement, a very proper district of leafy streets and fine residences, including the art nouveau creations of architect Jules Lavirotte on avenue Rapp (no. 29 is his masterpiece). There are many restaurants and food shops on avenue Bosquet, rue de Grenelle, and rue St-Dominique, but this is primarily a quiet residential area.

Hôtel Eiffel Rive Gauche

6 rue du Gros Caillou, 75007 Paris. ☎ **1/45-51-24-56.** Fax 1/45-51-11-77. 30 rms, all with bath. TV TEL. 250F–450F ($48.10–$86.55) single; 290F–460F ($55.75–$88.45) double; 440F–550F ($84.60–$105.75) triple. Breakfast 35F ($6.75) extra. AE, EURO, MC, V. Métro: Ecole-Militaire.

This modern hotel is a few minutes' walk from the Eiffel Tower. Maximum rates are for larger rooms, but rooms in the lower-priced category are adequately furnished and comfortable. There's a pretty breakfast room. Direct fax service is offered but charges are hefty and be warned that if you make a collect call from the hotel, a steep surcharge will be added to your bill.

NEAR THE ARC DE TRIOMPHE

Place de l'Etoile, renamed place Charles-de-Gaulle–Etoile, holds the tremendous Arc de Triomphe. Baron Haussmann's 12 grand avenues, including the Champs-Elysées, radiate from the vast square. The proper and respectable neighborhoods north of here hold offices, showrooms, restaurants, and hotels.

When you arrive at the enormous Charles-de-Gaulle Métro station, check the *plan du quartier* for your hotel's location and take the exit closest to the street you're seeking. This will stop you from circling the vast square above ground and save you a good 15 minutes.

Hôtel Deux Avenues

38 rue Poncelet, 75017 Paris. ☎ **1/42-27-44-35.** Fax 1/47-63-95-48. 32 rms, 10 with shower only, 11 with bath. 220F ($42.30) single without bath, 280F ($53.85) single with shower only, 340F ($65.40) single with bath; 250F ($48.10) double without bath, 300F ($57.70) double with shower only, 380F ($73.10) double with bath; 480F ($92.30) quad with bath. EURO, Continental breakfast 27F ($4.25) extra. MC, V. Métro: Charles-de-Gaulle–Etoile (then walk down avenue de Wagram from the Arc de Triomphe, cross avenue des Ternes, and turn right onto rue Poncelet) or Ternes (then walk down avenue de Wagram and turn onto the first street to the left).

Since 1900 this hotel has been in this location near a colorful street market and will appeal to younger readers who like busy surroundings.

Hôtel Niel

11 rue Saussier-Leroy, 75017 Paris. ☎ **1/42-27-99-29.** 36 rms, some with shower only or bath. TEL. 205F ($39.40) single without bath, 265F ($50.95) single with shower only; 305F ($58.65) single with bath; 260F ($50) double without bath, 320F ($61.55) double with shower only, 360F ($69.25) double with bath. Rates include continental breakfast. Showers (for those in rooms without bath) 25F ($4.80) extra. MC, V. Métro: Ternes.

This large hotel has a feeling of simplicity, propriety, and tidiness. The helpful receptionist will tell you that each room is unique, but you'll see that all are good and clean and come with reading lamps over the beds (rare in Paris).

NEAR THE GARE DU NORD

Hôtel de Londres et d'Anvers

133 bd. Magenta (about 200 yards from the Gare du Nord), 75010 Paris. ☎ **1/42-85-28-26.** Fax 1/42-80-04-73. 64 rms, all with bath. TV TEL. 310F ($59.60) single; 370F ($71.15) double. Continental breakfast 37F ($71.15) extra. AE, EURO, MC, V. Métro: Gare du Nord (then walk up rue de Dunkerque and bear left until you reach place de Roubaix, from which you can see the hotel's vertical blue sign; it's about an eight-minute walk).

This two-star hotel is popular with traveling salespeople and recommended to small groups. The spotless rooms contain standard furniture, wall-to-wall carpeting, and soundproof windows. There are 10 singles.

Hôtel de Milan

17 rue St-Quentin, 75010 Paris. ☎ **1/40-37-88-50.** Fax 1/46-07-89-48. 53 rms, 19 with shower or bath. 140F ($26.90) single without bath, 160F ($30.75) single with toilet only, 250F ($48.10) single with bath; 170F ($32.70) double without bath, 190F ($36.55) double with toilet only, 300F ($57.70) double with bath; 420F ($80.75) triple with bath. Continental breakfast 20F ($3.85) extra; showers 18F ($3.45) extra. No credit cards. Métro: Gare du Nord (then walk down rue St-Quentin and on the right you'll see the blue-painted hotel with a blue sign).

A basic hotel occupying six stories of a renovated 200-year-old house, the Milan is recommended to younger readers and backpackers. Monsieur Rault is the English-speaking owner. The hotel has an elevator leading to the fourth floor, and rooms with TVs are available at a slightly higher charge. At the end of the street is a covered market hall, a good place to buy food.

✪ New Hôtel

40 rue St-Quentin, 75010 Paris. ☎ **1/48-78-04-83.** Fax 1/40-82-91-22. 41 rms, all with bath (tub or shower). TV TEL. 322 F ($61.80) single with shower, 403 F ($77.40) single with tub; 370 F ($71.05) double with shower, 451 F ($86.60) double with tub; 527 F triple ($101.20) triple with shower, 557 F ($106.95) triple with bath; 570 F ($109.45) quad with shower, 650 F ($124.80) quad with bath. Rates include beakfast. AE, DC, EURO, MC, V. Métro: Gare du Nord.

This hotel is one of the best deals in Paris. The building (with elevator) is in front of the Gare du Nord, to the left when you leave the train or Métro station. The rooms, spread over six floors, are clean and modern. Breakfast is served in a basement room with brick walls and rustic furnishings. The staff is helpful—they even sell Métro tickets and will assist you confirming flights, checking timetables, or answering general questions.

NEAR THE GARE DE L'EST

Hôtel des Voyageurs

9 rue du 8-Mai-45, 75010 Paris. ☎ **1/40-34-54-34.** Fax 1/40-34-00-84. 43 rms, 23 with bath (shower or tub). 203F ($39.05) single without bath, 263F ($50.60) single with shower; 260F ($43.45) double without bath, 296F ($56.90) double with shower, 306F ($58.85) double with tub. Continental breakfast 25F ($4.80) extra; showers 20F ($3.85) extra. DC, JCB, MC, V. Métro: Gare de l'Est.

This hotel is ideally located across from and to the right of the Gare de l'Est's main entrance. While the rooms are rather small, the reasonable rates make it a good choice. The hotel has an occupancy rate of more than 80%, so phone before arriving if you don't have a reservation.

Hôtel Jarry

4 rue Jarry, 75010 Paris. ☎ **1/47-70-70-38.** Fax 1/42-46-34-45. 36 rms, 22 with shower or bath (tub or shower). 140F ($26.90) single without bath, 180F ($34.60) single with shower only, 200F ($38.45) single with bath (shower), 230F ($44.25) single with bath (tub); 170F ($32.70) double without bath, 210F ($40.40) double with shower only, 230F–260F ($44.25–$50) double with bath (tub or shower); 320F ($61.55) triple with bath (tub). Continental breakfast 18F ($3.45) extra. AE, DC, EURO, MC, V. Métro: Gare de l'Est or Gare du Nord.

This basic but clean hotel is in a good location in a quiet area. The front desk is covered 24 hours. It's on a small side street off boulevard de Strasbourg.

Hôtel Paradis

9 rue de Paradis (off rue du Faubourg St-Denis), 75010 Paris. ☎ **1/47-70-18-28.** Fax 1/45-23-38-32. 50 rms, 42 with shower. TV. 215F–240F ($41.35–$46.15) single without shower, 260F–285F ($50–$54.80) single with shower; 300F ($57.70) double without shower,

330F–360F ($63.45–$69.25) double with shower; 475F–505F ($91.35–$97.10) triple. Rates include continental breakfast. V. Métro: Gare de l'Est or Gare du Nord.

On a small side street off a busy shopping street, the four-floor Paradis (with elevator) is recommended for all age groups. The room furnishings are a little old-fashioned, but each room has a color TV and soundproof windows. The English-speaking owners assured me that they would treat holders of this book like VIPs.

✪ Little Hôtel Regina
89 bd. de Strasbourg, 75010 Paris. ☎ **1/40-37-72-30.** Fax 1/40-36-34-14. 33 rms, 23 with shower and toilet. TEL. 190F ($36.55) single with toilet only, 290F single with shower and toilet; 310F ($59.60) double with shower and toilet. Continental breakfast 25F ($4.80) extra. MC, V. Métro: Gare de l'Est.

This six-floor hotel (with elevator) has been under the same family management since 1960. It's practically facing the main exit of the Gare de l'Est. The rooms are large, with ample wardrobe space, new mattresses, and instant hot water; some rooms have TVs. Try to book no. 17, which features a full view of the station. Older readers will find it convenient.

NEAR THE GARE ST-LAZARE

Hôtel de Genève
36 rue de Londres, 75009 Paris. ☎ **1/48-74-33-99.** Fax 1/40-16-96-46. 30 rms, all with bath. MINIBAR TV. 410F ($78.85) single; 430F ($82.70) double; 525F ($100.95) triple. Continental breakfast 25F ($4.80) extra. AE, EURO, MC, V. Métro: St-Lazare.

The six-floor Genève has clean, tastefully furnished rooms, each with a cable color TV, hairdryer, safe, and soundproof windows. The staff is helpful, and the hotel is recommended for all age groups.

Hôtel de Parme
61 rue de Clichy, 75009 Paris. ☎ **1/48-74-40-41.** 36 rms, half with shower only or bath. 180F ($34.60) single or double without bath, 230F ($44.25) single or double with shower only, 250F–280F ($48.05–$53.85) single or double with bath; 240F ($46.15) triple without bath, 300F ($57.70) triple with bath. Continental breakfast 30F (5.75) extra; showers 20F ($3.85) extra. No credit cards. Métro: Gare St-Lazare (then a 10-minute walk up rue d'Amsterdam; turn right across rue de Parme) or Place-Clichy.

This is a pleasant and well-run hotel with rooms on five floors connected by an elevator. The English-speaking manager, M. Cornilleau, has been with the hotel since 1970. Somewhat off the tourist routes, the Parme usually has vacant rooms when all the other hotels around St-Lazare are booked up.

DOUBLES FOR LESS THAN 580F ($111.35)
NEAR THE SORBONNE

Hôtel Claude-Bernard
43 rue des Ecoles, 75005 Paris. ☎ **1/43-26-32-52.** Fax 1/43-26-80-56. 29 rms, all with bath, 5 suites. TV TEL. 395F ($75.95) single with shower only; 545F ($104.80) double with shower only; 600F ($115.40) double with bath; 700F ($134.60) triple; 780 F ($149.75) suite for two, plus 100 F ($19.20) for each extra person. Continental breakfast 35F ($6.75) extra. AE, DC, MC, V. Métro: Maubert-Mutualité.

It'll be evident from the moment you enter its lobby that the three-star Claude-Bernard keeps exceedingly high standards. The congenial rooms have a tasteful crimson wallpaper, sleek baths, and perhaps a semi-antique piece like a writing desk. The suites are particularly attractive (although more expensive), with great couches and seats. A sauna is available for a 70F ($13.45) charge.

Hôtel des Grands-Ecoles

75 rue Cardinal-Lemoine, 75005 Paris. ☎ **1/43-26-79-23.** Fax 1/43-25-28-15. 47 rms, 39 with bath (tub or shower). TEL. 320F ($61.55) single without bath, 470F ($90.40) single with bath; 360F ($69.25) double without bath, 620F ($119.25) double with bath. Continental breakfast 40F ($7.70) extra; additional bed 100F ($19.25) extra. CB, MC, V. Métro: Cardinal-Lemoine or Monge.

Housed in two separate buildings and tucked away from the street in a lovely garden, the Grands-Ecoles will make you feel as if you're in the French countryside. The owners have decorated and renovated the 18th-century bourgeois home with floral wallpapers and pink and green accents. A room in the main house will cost you a little more than a room in the annex; the main building has an elevator. Breakfast is served in the main house at café-style tables with lace cloths.

NEAR ST-MICHEL & NOTRE-DAME

✪ Hôtel Abbatial St-Germain

46 bd. St-Germain, 75005 Paris. ☎ **1/46-34-02-12.** Fax 1/43-25-47-73. 43 rms, all with bath. TEL. 480F–620F ($92.30–$119.25) single; 580F–750F ($111.55–$144.25) double; 850F ($163.45) triple. Continental breakfast 40F ($7.70) extra. AE, EURO, MC, V. Métro: Maubert-Mutualité.

The higher you go in this hotel, the better the rooms get. You enter through a little hallway of mirrors and faux marble and climb a flight of stairs to the pleasant reception area. From there, an elevator will take you to the cheerful, airy rooms, some of which have French windows with pleasant views. All rooms also have in-room safes. In addition, you'll benefit from cordial proprietors and a superb location.

Hôtel St-Jacques

35 rue des Ecoles (at the corner of rue Valette), 75005 Paris. ☎ **1/43-26-82-53.** 40 rms, 35 with bath (shower or tub). TEL. 180F ($34.60) single without bath, 320F ($61.55) single with shower only, 410F ($78.85) single with bath; 475F ($91.35) double with bath; 550F ($105.75) triple with bath. Continental breakfast 35F ($6.75) extra. AE, MC, V. Métro: Maubert-Mutualité.

On busy rue des Ecoles, the two-star St-Jacques has attractive prices and rooms that for the most part are large. The furniture is rather basic, but there are some fine architectural details and the rooms have recently been renovated. When you choose a room, keep in mind the traffic on the main street.

IN THE FAUBOURG ST-GERMAIN

In the 18th century, Parisian aristocrats built elegant *hôtels particuliers* (private mansions) west of boulevard St-Germain in what soon became the *quartier chic par excellence*. Those mansions still stand, occupied for the most part by embassies and ministries. But rather than being a museum, the Faubourg St-Germain is one of Paris's most lively areas, with countless boutiques and antiques shops as well as *épiceries* (food shops), *pâtisseries* (pastry shops), and *boulangeries* (bakeries). This area is a few blocks away from the tourist maelstrom, and the relative calm will allow you to get better acquainted with the subtle moods of the city.

✪ Hôtel de Nevers

83 rue de Bac, 75007 Paris. ☎ **1/45-44-61-30.** Fax 1/42-22-29-47. 11 rms, all with bath. MINIBAR. 375F ($72.10) single; 410F–440F ($78.85–$84.60) double or twin. Continental breakfast 30F ($5.75) extra. No credit cards. Métro: Rue du Bac.

The building that houses this Hôtel Nevers (there's another one near the Jardin du Luxembourg; see above) used to be a convent, and it's presently *classé*, which means that any restorations must respect the original architecture. That precludes an elevator, so you'll have to climb the never-ending beautiful white staircase. The rooms, in their antique primness, are cozy and pleasant, two (nos. 10 and 11) with large terraces.

BETWEEN PLACE DE L'OPERA & PLACE PIGALLE

Hôtel Navarin et d'Angleterre

8 rue Navarin, 75009 Paris. ☎ **1/48-78-31-80.** Fax 1/48-74-14-09. 26 rms, some with toilet only, 24 with bath (shower or tub). TV TEL. 285F ($54.80) single with toilet only; 340F ($65.40) double with bath. Breakfast 30F ($5.75) extra. MC, V. Métro: St-Georges or Notre-Dame-de-Lorette.

This four-story walk-up has been managed by the charming Maylin family for the past 25 years. You'll seldom find more warmth and charm in a hotel than here, where each room is unique. In summer, breakfast (from 7:30 to 9:30am) is served in a small garden with an acacia tree and a fountain. If you book a room facing this garden, you'll be awakened by singing birds—unusual for a big city like Paris. The rooms were modernized in 1990, but the old-fashioned sitting room and antique furniture in the lounge still radiate a fin-de-siècle atmosphere. Readers believing in old values will love this place.

NEAR THE EIFFEL TOWER

Hôtel de la Tour Eiffel

17 rue de l'Exposition, 75007 Paris. ☎ **1/47-05-14-75.** 23 rms, all with bath. TV TEL. 330F ($63.45) single; 380F ($73.010) double. Continental breakfast 30F ($5.75) extra. MC, V. Métro: Ecole-Militaire.

Next to the Romanian embassy and with a view of the statues in its garden, this hotel is neither quaint nor romantic, but rather modern and comfortable. The well-appointed rooms have pleasant furnishings and color TVs, and the baths are up-to-date. The management is efficient and cordial and, if you wish, will serve a fine breakfast in your room.

Hôtel Rapp

8 av. Rapp, 75007 Paris. ☎ **1/45-51-42-28.** Fax 1/43-59-50-70. 16 rms, all with bath. TEL. 255F ($49.05) single; 340F–360F ($65.40–$69.25) double. Continental breakfast 25F ($4.80) extra. MC, V. Métro: Alma-Marceau. RER: Pont de l'Alma.

Virtually in the shadow of the Eiffel Tower and close to the Seine (the nearest Métro station is across the river on the Right Bank), the Rapp is small, quiet, and rather modern. The manager, who speaks English, extols the convenience and security of being near several embassies. The rooms are well appointed, with fine dark furniture and yellow draperies, and everything is clean. Parking is easy on this street; you pay 17F ($3.25) with a hotel card.

NORTH OF THE ARC DE TRIOMPHE

Ⓢ Hôtel des Deux Acacias

28 rue de l'Arc de Triomphe, 75017 Paris. ☎ **1/43-80-01-85.** Fax 1/40-53-94-62. 31 rms, all with bath (tub or shower). TV TEL. 335F–405F ($64.40–$77.90) single; 340F–380F ($65.40–$73.10) double. Rates include continental breakfast. AE, EURO, MC, V. Métro: Charles-de-Gaulle–Etoile (take the avenue Carnot exit).

This excellent budget hotel is on a quiet street just two blocks north of the Arc de Triomphe. Its rooms are plain but neat and not faded, all with color TVs. The woman at the front desk is efficient and amiable.

NEAR PLACE DE LA REPUBLIQUE

Hôtel des Arts-et-Métiers

Rue Borda, 75003 Paris. ☎ **1/48-87-73-89.** Fax 1/48-87-66-58. 16 rms, 9 with bath (shower), 5 with shower only. 150F ($28.85) single without shower, 180F ($34.60) single with shower only; 220F ($42.30) double without shower, 250F ($48.10) double with shower only; 270F ($51.90) single or double with shower and toilet. Continental breakfast (with unlimited coffee) 25F ($4.80) extra. AE, V. Métro: Arts-et-Métiers.

At this six-story hotel, which takes its name from a cluster of art and handcraft schools in the area, the front desk is open 24 hours. The rooms on the top two floors are the cheapest (there's no elevator); the higher-priced rooms have a shower or shower and toilet. The owner, Madame Bey, is eager to please her guests, 50% of whom are from the States, Australia, and Japan, most of them students. The hotel is especially recommended for the younger generation.

NEAR PORTE MAILLOT

Porte Maillot is the site of the Palais des Congrès, Paris's convention center, and is several blocks west of the Arc de Triomphe along avenue de la Grande-Armée. This is where the Air France bus from Charles de Gaulle Airport drops you, and you can connect with the Métro (Porte-Maillot) or RER (Neuilly–Porte-Maillot). The area has many hotels, some of which are bargains. Though you're on the edge of the city, the Métro whisks you to the center easily and cheaply.

Hôtel de Palma

46 rue Brunel, 75017 Paris. ☎ **1/45-74-74-51.** Fax 1/45-74-40-90. 37 rms, all with bath. TV TEL. 430F–450F ($82.70–$86.54) single; 470F–485F ($90.40–$93.25) double; 600F ($115.40) triple. Rates include continental breakfast. MC, V. Métro: Argentine. RER: Neuilly–Porte-Maillot.

If you like comfort but don't want to pay top franc for it, head for the Palma. It may be a bit far from the city center, but the Château-de-Vincennes Métro will take you rapidly and directly to the avenue des Champs-Elysées, place de la Concorde, Louvre, and Bastille—with easy connections to the Latin Quarter. The Palma has a large, pleasant lobby and well-kept rooms with modern tiled baths and color TVs. The management is very professional.

SUPER-BUDGET CHOICES

YOUTH HOSTELS

Paris has plenty of youth hostels (*auberges de jeunesse*) and *foyers* (literally "homes") to accommodate the hordes of young travelers who descend on the city every summer. Quality differs greatly from place to place, but the superior hostels offer excellent value. While some are huge and impersonal and occupy similarly huge and impersonal buildings, other hostels are warm places where you can meet people from all over the world. Some, as you'll see from our listings, occupy historic buildings that are both comfortable and handsome. Many of these hostels welcome travelers regardless of age.

A Paris hostel is an especially good deal for solo travelers. As single rooms in hotels become scarce in summer and other periods, you may have to choose between paying for a double room or paying for a bed at a hostel. The major draw-back of hostels for some people—whether or not they're traveling alone—is the day lock-out and the night curfew. If having a place to take an afternoon nap is essential or late nightlife is what you came to Paris for, then perhaps staying at a hostel, with all the savings this implies, is not the best choice.

Many hostels don't accept reservations from individuals (they do so only for school and other large groups). In those cases the best strategy is to show up at the hostel where you want to stay as early as possible in the morning—8 o'clock or earlier. You can also call ahead to find out what your chances are for getting a bed. Believe us, for some hostels, like those run by the Accueil des Jeunes en France (see below), all this trouble is really worth it. Once you're "accepted," make sure you tell your host how many nights you plan to stay (five is the maximum at some places).

If you arrive in the city late in the day and don't want to start calling up or going to hostels that may already be full, it's a good idea simply to head for one of the offices of the **Accueil des Jeunes en France (AJF)**. This organization exists to find inexpensive beds for young people, and it'll book you a bed for that night. If you want to stay at one of its own hostels (they're all great), tell it so. Its main office is at 119 rue St-Martin, 4e (☎ **1/42-77-87-80;** Métro: Rambuteau; RER: Châtelet–Les-Halles), across from the entrance to the Centre Pompidou. See "Visitor Information" under "Paris Specifics," earlier in this chapter, for the location of the other offices.

The **Office de Tourisme et des Congrès de Paris** will also book you a bed in a hostel for an 8F ($1.55) fee. See "Visitor Information" under "Paris Specifics," earlier in this chapter, for other organizations that provide information on budget accommodations.

Centre International de Paris/Opéra

11 rue Thérèse (off avenue de l'Opéra), 75001 Paris. ☎ **1/42-60-77-23.** 68 beds. 125F ($24.05) per person per night. Rates include continental breakfast. Lunch or dinner 60F ($11.55) extra. No credit cards. Open July–Oct 15. Métro: Pyramides or Palais-Royal–Musée-du-Louvre.

Run by the UCRIF (Union des Centres de Rencontres Internationales de France), this small hostel is clean and welcoming, and at times it feels even cozy. Each room has three to eight beds, with showers and toilets on each floor. Its location is excellent, not far from the Louvre and the Palais-Royal.

The same people run several other hostels in Paris, including those at 20 rue Jean-Jacques-Rousseau (☎ **1/42-36-88-18;** Métro: Louvre-Rivoli, Palais-Royal–Musée-du-Louvre, or Châtelet–Les-Halles); 44 rue des Bernardins (☎ **1/43-29-34-80;** Métro: Maubert-Mutualité), in the Latin Quarter; and 5 rue du Pelican, 1er (☎ **1/40-26-92-45**), near Les Halles.

Young and Happy Hostel

80 rue Mouffetard, 75005 Paris. ☎ **1/45-35-09-53.** Fax 1/47-07-22-24. 85 beds. 100F ($19.25) per person per night, 637F ($122.50) per week. Rates include breakfast. Sheet rental 12F ($2.30) extra. No credit cards. Métro: Place-Monge.

In the heart of the student area, 10 blocks east of the Sorbonne, this hostel is usually booked with groups, so phone to make sure there are beds available before heading over. Most rooms have six beds. The hostel is closed for cleaning from 11am to 5pm, and there's a 1am curfew. The staff organizes guided mountain-bike tours around Paris for 118F ($22.70), and they'll send faxes for a fee.

❂ Youth Hostel le Fauconnier

11 rue du Fauconnier, 75004 Paris. ☎ **1/42-74-23-45.** Fax 1/42-71-61-02. 15 rms, 89 dorm beds. 168F ($32.30) single; 148F ($28.45) twin; 120F ($23.10) dorm bed. Rates include continental breakfast. No credit cards. Métro: St-Paul-le-Marais or Pont-Marie.

Of all Parisian youth hostels, Le Fauconnier is my favorite. Run by Les Maisons Internationales de la Jeunesse et des Etudiants (MIJE), it's in a historic *hôtel particulier* on a quiet street in the Marais, near the Seine. Despite the groups that sometimes overrun it, Le Fauconnier has a touch of elegance, with a pleasant courtyard and a beautiful staircase. All rooms have private showers and there are some singles and doubles, thus affording more privacy than is customary at youth hostels.

Other MIJE hostels are nearby: **Maubuisson** at 12 rue des Barres (☎ **1/42-74-23-45**) with 114 beds; and **Fourcy** at 6 rue de Fourcy (☎ **1/42-74-23-45**) with 206 beds.

UNIVERSITY ACCOMMODATIONS

Foyer International des Etudiants

93 bd. St-Michel, 75006 Paris. ☎ **1/43-54-49-63.** 160 beds. 160F ($30.75) single; 220F ($42.30) double. Rates include continental breakfast and showers. No credit cards. Open July–Sept. Métro: Luxembourg.

Open to traveling students from July through September, this university residence has an excellent location and is quite comfortable.

WORTH THE EXTRA MONEY

❂ Hôtel Jardin des Plantes

5 rue Linne, 75005 Paris. ☎ **1/47-07-06-20.** Fax 1/47-07-62-74. 33 rms, all with bath (shower or tub). MINIBAR TV TEL. 420F ($80.77) single with shower only, 510F ($98.10) single with bath; 450F ($86.55) double with shower only, 560F ($107.70) double with bath; 660F ($126.90) triple; 740F ($142.30) quad. Continental breakfast 40F ($7.70) extra; additional bed 100F ($19.25) extra; use of sauna 70F ($13.45) extra. DC, MC, V. Métro: Jussieu.

This two-star hotel owes its name to its location across from the vast Jardin des Plantes, the botanical gardens created on the order of Louis XIII's doctors in 1626 and first called the Jardin Royal des Plantes Médicinales. There are still some 15,000 medicinal herbs at the gardens, and some regal comforts can be found at the nearby hotel: a roof terrace, sauna, vaulted cellar with a fireplace, and glass-fronted sidewalk café adjoining the lobby. Each room's tiled bath has a hairdryer. The more expensive rooms open onto the sunny terrace.

Hôtel St-Louis Marais

1 rue Charles V, 75004 Paris. ☎ **1/48-87-87-04.** Fax 1/48-87-33-26. 15 rms, all with bath. 510F ($98.10) single; 610F ($117.30) double with one bed, 710F ($136.55) double with two beds. Continental breakfast 40F ($7.70) extra. EURO, MC, V. Métro: Sully, Bastille, or St-Paul.

This charming hotel in a 300-year-old building was originally a convent for the Celestines, a Benedictine order. The rooms have antique furniture and beamed ceilings, and all rooms with two beds have a tub in the bath. There are no TVs and the lack of an elevator provides some inconvenience, but those looking for a small hotel with a cultivated atmosphere will like this place.

❂ Hôtel Sully St-Germain

31 rue des Ecoles, 75005 Paris. ☎ **1/43-26-56-02.** Fax 1/43-29-74-42. 31 rms, all with bath. TV TEL. 600F ($115.40) single; 750F ($144.25) double or twin; 850F ($163.45) triple; 950F ($182.70) quad. Rates include buffet breakfast. MC, V. Métro: Maubert-Mutualité.

Beautifully furnished in the European style of the Middle Ages, this highly recommended three-star hotel features antique carpets, *dernier-cri* plumbing, and an original suit of knight's armor in the lounge. Each room features a safe, a hairdryer, and the soundproof windows. A two-person Jacuzzi is available for 100F ($19.25) extra, while use of the exercise room is free. Laundry is washed in the house. The manager/owner, M. Gibon, speaks English well and is a font of information about Paris. The restaurant offers several prix-fixe menus starting at 95F ($18.25). If the Sully is booked up, try the hotel next door, furnished in art deco style and under the same management.

5 Dining

Brillat-Savarin, author of the 1825 gastronomic classic *Physiology of Taste*, wrote: "To eat is a necessity; to eat well is an art." This dictum still defines the attitude of many a Parisian toward food. Eating is such a passion here that it even shapes the cityscape. Almost every street corner has a bistro or café, and these, not banks or department stores, dominate the major intersections. It's not unusual to find entire streets lined with small restaurants.

Here are just a few dining notes. Despite what you may have learned in high-school French, never say *"Garçon!"* to a waiter. Use *"Monsieur, s'il vous plaît!"* or *"Madame, s'il vous plaît!"*

Most restaurants in Paris are open for lunch from noon to 2:30pm and for dinner from 7 to 10pm. For a quick meal outside these times, go to a café: Most serve light one-course meals. But choose your café carefully: A prime location often carries a higher price tag. Buying a sandwich or a crêpe from a sidewalk booth is the cheapest alernative (see "Street Eats," below).

Unless breakfast is included in the price of your hotel room, go to a sidewalk café for your morning *café au lait* and croissant. If you stand at the counter, the price will be about 40% lower than if you sit and have a waiter serve you.

At a restaurant, for lunch or dinner, the least-expensive choice will be the *plat du jour,* a main course garnished with vegetables that makes a perfectly adequate meal. The best value, though, is usually the *menu du jour,* a fixed-priced meal of three to five courses, usually with two or three choices for each course. House wine, either red or white, is sometimes included, the standard measure being a quarter-liter carafe (*un quart*).

For a simple meal, head for a café and order an omelet, sandwich, soup, or salad. French sandwiches, made on crusty fresh baguettes, are disappointing at first glance, with somewhat meager fillings, but they taste good because the bread is exceptional. Omelets come plain with just a sprinkling of herbs or filled with cheese, ham, or other hearty additions. Or try a salad niçoise, a huge bowl filled with lettuce, boiled potatoes, hard-boiled eggs, capers, tomatoes, olives, and anchovies. These dishes make a filling, pleasant meal for 40F to 60F ($7.70 to $11.55).

If you want a free glass of water (as opposed to its bottled counterpart), ask for *une carafe d'eau* ("ewn *kah*-rahf doh"). *Café* means an espresso; order a *café au lait* if you want it with milk. By the way, Paris has a full complement of American-style fast-food eateries, such as McDonald's and Pizza Hut. Parisians, too, respond to the appeal of uniform quality and (relatively) quick service, but you'll discover that fast-food prices are higher here than in the United States.

Getting the Best Deal on Dining

- At sidewalk booths you can buy inexpensive sandwiches and crêpes.
- Choose a sidewalk café for breakfast, unless the meal is included in the price of your hotel room.
- The *menu du jour* is a great choice for lunch or dinner.
- The *plat du jour* or *plat garni* is usually cheaper than the full-course menu.
- Note that it's less expensive to eat standing at a counter rather than sitting at a table.
- Try some of the budget restaurants along rue de la Huchette and rue Xavier-Privas.

MEALS FOR LESS THAN 75F ($14.40)
IN THE LATIN QUARTER

✪ A la Bonne Crêpe

11 rue Grégoire-de-Tours, 6e. ☎ **1/43-54-60-74.** Three-course lunch with crêpe for the main course 54F ($10.40); crêpes à la carte dishes 12F–70F ($2.30–$13.45); quarter-liter pitcher of cider 22F ($4.25). No credit cards. Mon–Sat noon–2pm and 7–11pm. Métro: Odéon. FRENCH/BRETON.

The region of Brittany is known for its crêpes (French pancakes) and ciders, and in this restaurant seating 30 you can combine these goodies into lunch or dinner. Savory crêpes filled with cheese, meat, seafood, or other hearty ingredients make the main course, and sweet crêpes filled with jam or chocolate are a wonderful dessert. The cider is the alcoholic kind, Brittany's answer to beer. Rue Grégoire-de-Tours is a tiny street beginning between nos. 140 and 142 bd. St-Germain and running north toward the Seine.

La Dinette

59 rue Dauphine, 6e. ☎ **1/43-54-35-15.** Three-course meal 45F ($8.65); drinks 12F–16F ($2.30–$3.10). No credit cards. Daily 10:30am–11pm. Métro: Odéon. CHINESE.

This very attractive Chinese take-out place also has dining tables. The food, on display in steam tables by the door, is a blend of Asian and French tastiness and beauty. The menu du jour offers soup, pâté, or salad, then shrimp dumplings or a main dish made with beef, pork, or chicken, plus Cantonese—all for one low price.

Le Petit Vatel

5 rue Lobineau, 6e. ☎ **1/43-54-28-49.** Two-course prix-fixe lunch 61F ($11.75); *plat garni* at dinner 55F ($10.60); daily specials 45F ($8.65); à la carte dishes 40F–68F ($7.70–$13.05). MC, V. Mon–Fri noon–3pm and 7pm–midnight, Sat noon–midnight, Sun 7pm–midnight. Métro: Mabillon (then walk up rue Mabillon and turn left onto rue Lobineau). FRENCH.

One of Paris's most charming eateries, Le Petit Vatel has 22 seats (a few on the sidewalk in summer) in a pocket-size dining room. The daily specials may be stuffed cabbage, rice sautéed with seafood, moussaka, or roast chicken, all served with a vegetable or salad. The two-course lunch consists of a choice of an appetizer, cheese or a dessert, and a choice of the daily special or a plat garni. A quarter liter of red wine is 13F ($2.20). The restaurant is named after a famous chef who worked for Louis XIV. A candlelit meal at this jewel is something you'll long remember.

NEAR THE GARE ST-LAZARE

Restaurant le Bandol

10 rue de Parme, 9e. ☎ **1/48-74-13-59.** *Menu du jour* 60F ($11.55), à la carte meals 80F ($15.40). MC, V. Mon–Sat 11am–3pm and 7pm–1am. Métro: St-Lazare (then from the Gare St-Lazare, walk up rue de Amsterdam and turn left shortly before reaching place Clichy) or Clichy. FRENCH.

The 50-seat Bandol is off the beaten track and thus frequented by French customers—you may be the only foreigner eating here. The food is filling and tasty. Try the minestrone or the snails as a starter, followed by steak or roast chicken, then cheese and coffee.

Croq Passion

8 rue d'Isly, 8e. ☎ **1/42-93-16-62.** *Plat du jour* 36F ($6.90); light fare 18F–20F ($3.45–$3.85). Mon–Fri 7am–3:30pm. Métro: St. Lazare. FRENCH.

This tiny eatery is mainly for people in a hurry, but the food is first class. Its take-out sandwiches (try the one with Roquefort and walnuts) are best-sellers with people who work in this busy part of Paris. The *plat du jour* might be escalope de saumon à la ciboulette (filet of salmon with chives) or poulet à l'indienne (curried chicken). About a dozen salads are offered, plus some delicious desserts, including lemon meringue pie.

NEAR THE CHAMPS-ELYSEES

Feri's Restaurant à Emporter

8 rue de Ponthieu, 8e. ☎ **1/42-56-10-56.** Main courses 29F–40F ($5.60–$7.90); less for salads and sandwiches. No credit cards. Daily 8am–6am. Métro: Franklin-D.-Roosevelt. FRENCH/DELI.

Feri's is a little storefront deli/take-out with excellent food at good prices. After 11am a line begins for lunch pickup, and the place stays busy until after supper. Main courses might be roast chicken, pot au feu (a hearty stew), or spaghetti. You can drop in anytime for croissants, pain au chocolat (a chocolate-filled croissant), and other snacks, and from dinnertime through 6am you can get fresh pizzas.

NEAR PLACE DE LA REPUBLIQUE

The Calypso

4 bd. Jules-Ferry, 11e. ☎ **1/43-55-69-09.** 14F–42F ($2.70–$8.10). No credit cards. Mon–Sat 9am–4pm. Métro: République. SOUPS/SNACKS.

This always-crowded tiny eatery (10 tables inside and 12 more on the sidewalk in summer) is decorated with books, pictures, and tropical plants. The menu is à la carte only and offers soups, casseroles, and light dishes. The apple crumble is the house specialty, prepared personally by owner Madame Evelyne. Fourteen kinds of tea are available. Servings are generous.

NEAR THE ARC DE TRIOMPHE

Restaurant Monte Carlo

9 av. de Wagram, 17e. ☎ **1/43-80-14-39.** *Plats du jour* 25F–30F ($4.80–$5.75), prix-fixe menu 39F ($7.50); à la carte dishes 28F–50F ($5.40–$8.65). No credit cards. Daily 11am–11pm. Métro: Charles-de-Gaulle–Etoile. FRENCH.

The well-lit modern Monte Carlo contains rattan chairs and contemporary furnishings; half the seats are reserved for nonsmokers. A la carte items include roast chicken, pasta with meat sauce, breaded veal cutlets, and stewed rabbit with rice. On each table is a pitcher of fresh water. Service is quick, and the restaurant is popular and recommendable.

NEAR THE BASTILLE

Spaghetterie Il Carretto

164 av. Ledru-Rollin, 11e. ☎ 1/43-79-91-21. *Plat du jour* (Mon–Fri only), wine included, 69F ($13.25); pizzas 48F–50F ($9.25–$9.60). AE, EURO, MC, V. Daily noon–3pm and 7pm–midnight. Métro: Ledru-Rollin. ITALIAN.

The best-sellers at this place, decorated in typical Italian style, are pizzas and pasta dishes. Try the spaghetti with eggplant sauce or the fusilli flavored with melted cheese—*una poesia!* Orders are taken and served personally by owner Signor Bonomo.

NORTH OF THE LOUVRE

Ma Normandie

11 rue Rameau, 2e. ☎ 1/42-96-87-17. *Menus du jour* 59F–115F ($11.35–$22.10). AE, EURO, MC, V. Mon–Sat 11:30am–2:30pm. Métro: Pyramides, 4-Septembre, or Bourse. FRENCH.

Near the small square in front of the Bibliothèque Nationale, Ma Normandie serves well-prepared food in homey surroundings. A cheerful waiter will greet you when you come in and show you to a table in the ground-floor dining room or upstairs. This is a good place to order such French staples as jambon cru d'Auvergne, pave de rumsteak au poivre garni (steak in pepper sauce), or boeuf bourguignon, as well as more elaborate dishes. The bread's delicious and the wines are great.

⑨ Restaurant l'Incroyable

26 rue de Richelieu or 23 rue de Montpensier, 1er. ☎ 1/42-96-24-64. Three-course *menu du jour* 65F ($12.50) at lunch, 75F ($14.40) at dinner. No credit cards. Mon noon–2:15pm, Tues–Fri noon–2:15pm and 6:30–9pm, Sat noon–2:15pm. Closed Jan. Métro: Palais-Royal–Musée-du-Louvre (then walk up either rue de Richelieu or rue de Montpensier behind the Comédie-Française). FRENCH.

This little place, open for more than 50 years, is justly named "the Incredible," for where else could you have a four-course lunch in appealing old-fashioned surroundings for such a low price? Dark bentwood furniture, old plaques and pictures on the walls, and (in good weather) a few little tables out in the passageway make this restaurant truly French. The food is simple but good, with many choices on the menu du jour.

MEALS FOR LESS THAN 100F ($19.20)
IN THE LATIN QUARTER & ST-GERMAIN-DES-PRES

✪ Au Vieux Casque

19 rue Bonaparte, 6e. ☎ 1/43-54-99-46. *Menu du jour,* wine included, 90F ($17.30); *plats du jour* 48F–58F ($9.25–$11.15); à la carte dishes 35F–70F ($6.75–$13.45). V. Mon–Sat 7–11:15pm. Métro: St-Germain-des-Prés or Mabillon. FRENCH.

Au Vieux Casque has lots of atmosphere, boasting a wood-and-stucco ground-floor dining room, a stone-vaulted cellar, and an upstairs room with rough-hewn beams.

You can see the chef at work on the ground floor, preparing updated classic French meals a cut above those at similar places—such as a delicate tomato salad to start, followed by a turkey cutlet in a cream sauce with rice, and ending with Camembert, fruit, or a dessert. This is definitely a superior establishment.

Aux Charpentiers

10 rue Mabillon, 6e. ☎ **1/43-26-30-05.** *Plats du jour* 75F–95F ($14.40–$18.25); three-course prix-fixe 120F ($23.10) at lunch, 150F ($28.85) at dinner; à la carte dishes 70F–120F ($13.45–$23.10). AE, DC, MC, V. Daily noon–3pm and 3–11:30pm. Métro: Mabillon. FRENCH.

During the Middle Ages and Renaissance, the carpenters' guildhall was next door to this restaurant, and that's how Aux Charpentiers got it name. The walls are decorated with photographs and plans of carpentry, including models of wooden vaults and roof structures. This bilevel restaurant seats 170. The 150F ($28.85) dinner menu offers a choice of four appetizers, such as warm Lyon sausage with potato salad or hare pâté flavored with sweetened onions and oranges. There follows a choice of five main courses that might be chicken breast with tarragon or daube of beef provençal with a zesty orange confit. Desserts may include clafoutis Mirabelles or soufflé glacé au Grand Marnier. Other à la carte dishes range from roasted Bresse chicken to grilled filet mignon.

✪ La Petite Hostellerie

35 rue da la Harpe (just east of boulevard St-Michel), 5e. ☎ **1/43-54-47-12.** *Menu du jour* 60F ($11.55) for three courses, 85F ($16.35) for four courses; wine 16F ($3.10). AE, DC, MC, V. Mon 6:30–10:30pm, Tues–Sat noon–2pm and 6:30–10:30pm. Métro: St-Michel or Cluny–La Sorbonne. FRENCH.

Founded in 1902, this restaurant has two dining rooms: a small and usually crowded ground-floor one and a larger (seating 100) upstairs one featuring attractive 18th-century woodwork. People come for the cozy ambience and decor, decent French country cooking, polite service, and excellent prices. The 85F ($16.30) menu might feature such favorites as coq au vin, canard à l'orange, or entrecôte à la moutarde. Start with onion soup or stuffed mussels and finish with cheese or salad followed by pêches Melba or tarte aux pommes. Rue de la Harpe is a side street running north of boulevard St-Germain.

Le Grenier de Notre-Dame

18 rue de la Bûcherie (near Notre-Dame and boulevard St-Michel), 5e. ☎ **1/43-29-98-29.** *Menu du jour* 85F ($16.35) for three courses; à la carte dishes 45F–125F ($8.65–$24.05). AE, DC, MC, V. Wed–Mon noon–2:30pm and 7:15–10:45pm. Métro: Maubert-Mutualité. FRENCH/VEGETARIAN.

At this well-established vegetarian restaurant, fresh flowers fill the dining room and small lamps grace every green-clothed table—and the food is outstanding. We especially recommend the cassoulet végétarien (with white beans, onions, tomatoes, and soy sausage) and the lentilles maraîchères (with lentils, carrots, and onions). And don't forget the desserts, such as tarte de tofu, for which Le Grenier has a well-deserved reputation.

✪ Restaurant des Beaux Arts

11 rue Bonaparte, 6e. ☎ **1/43-26-92-64.** Three-course *menu du jour,* wine included, 75F ($14.40). No credit cards. Daily noon–2:30pm and 7–10:45pm. Métro: St-Germain-des-Prés. FRENCH.

Across from Paris's famous Ecole Nationale Supérieure des Beaux-Arts (School of Fine Arts) is what many see as a typical Parisian artists' eatery, with bentwood furniture, long tables covered in white paper, and wood-paneled walls. Specialties include navarin d'agneau (lamb stew), coq au vin, and confit de canard (duck leg cooked in its own grease with mushrooms). The portions are large. If the downstairs dining room is full, try upstairs.

IN THE 15TH ARRONDISSEMENT

⑤ Le Café du Commerce

51 rue du Commerce, 15e. ☎ **1/45-75-03-27.** Three-course meal, wine included, 65F–130F ($12.50–$25); à la carte dishes 55F–79F ($10.60–$15.20). AE, DC, JCB, MC, V. Daily noon–11:30pm. Métro: Emile-Zola, Commerce, or La Motte–Picquet. FRENCH.

Not far from the Eiffel Tower, Le Café is one of the best dining bargains in this general area of unpretentious stores and busy commercial streets. The list of dishes is astounding: about 15 appetizers, five fish dishes, 16 main courses, seven vegetable side dishes, four cheeses, and more than a dozen desserts. The 65F ($12.50) menu will provide oeuf dur mayonnaise, poulet sauce estragon (chicken tarragon), fruit compôte and a quarter liter of red or rosé wine. The 130F ($24.95) menu features some choice—warm goat cheese on a bed of lettuce or a plate of crudités followed by either breast of duck with a green-pepper sauce or skate with a caper sauce. Crème caramel or chocolate mousse for dessert plus half a liter liter of wine are included.

EAST OF THE OPERA GARNIER

⑤ Chartier

7 rue du Faubourg Montmartre, 1er. ☎ **1/47-70-86-29.** Three-course *menus du sugges-tion,* wine included, 80F–160F ($15.40–$30.75); à la carte dishes 35F–48F ($6.75–$9.25). V. Daily 11:45am–3pm and 6:30–10pm. Métro: Montmartre. FRENCH.

Established in 1896 near Montmartre and now a historic monument, Chartier has long been a budget favorite offering great value in authentic French surroundings. Globe brass chandeliers and other decorative elements adorn the interior. On the menu are about 100 items. Prices are low enough that a three-course repast is easy on the budget, even if you don't choose the fixed-priced meal.

Le Drouot

103 rue de Richelieu, 2e. ☎ **1/42-96-68-23.** Three-course *menus du suggestion,* wine included, 80F–160F ($15.40–$30.75); à la carte dishes 35F–48F ($6.75–$9.25). V. Daily 11:45am–3pm and 6:30–10pm. Métro: Richelieu-Drouot. FRENCH.

Le Drouot is another faithful old budget eatery, with an upstairs working-class dining room straight out of the 1940s. The food is delicious, the waiters are efficient, and the clientele is loyal. Sample dishes include salmon with béarnaise sauce, leg of lamb with white beans, trout amandine, and beef bourguignon. The fixed-price menus offer a choice of three complete meals.

NEAR THE ARC DE TRIOMPHE

Etoile Verte

13 rue Brey, 17e. ☎ **1/43-80-69-34.** *Menus du jour* 69F–145F ($13.25–$27.90); à la carte dishes 45F–80F ($8.65–$15.40). Daily 11:30am–3pm and 6:30–11pm. EURO, MC, V. Métro: Charles-de-Gaulle–Etoile (then walk down avenue de Wagram and turn left at the second street; rue de Brey is slightly downhill). FRENCH.

A highly popular restaurant with 105 seats, this place is heavily booked on week-days by employees working in this busy district. A la carte offerings include spaghetti bolognese, roast chicken, pepper steak, and entrecôte. The 100F ($19.20) prix-fixe menu offers several appetizers, including shrimp-and-avocado cocktail and smoked salmon with kiwi salad; these can be followed by lamb chop grilled with herbs and cheese or dessert. A quarter liter of red wine is included, too. The 69F ($13.25) menu is an excellent value.

NEAR THE GARE DU NORD

Restaurant Terminus
23 rue de Dunkerque, 10e. ☎ **1/42-85-05-15.** Main courses 77–129 F ($14.80–$24.75); *plat du jour* (lunch only) 85F ($16.35). AE, EURO, MC, V. Daily 7am–1am. Métro: Gare du Nord. FRENCH/INTERNATIONAL.

In front of the Gare du Nord, the Terminus has a decor in art deco and Liberty styles. The specialties are seafood and choucroute, but other dishes are offered as well, including lamb, spaghetti bolognese, and cheese platters. The chocolate mousse is superb. The best-seller here in the evenings is an enormous seafood platter—scampi, mussels, calamari, and much more for 200F ($38.45). The waiters speak English.

IN THE MARAIS

Marais Plus
20 rue des Francs-Bourgeois, 3e. ☎ **1/48-87-01-40.** Breakfast, brunch, light lunch, or dinner 48F–95F ($9.25–$18.25). AE, MC, V. Daily 10am–7:30pm. Métro: St-Paul. FRENCH.

The Marais district contains a number of restaurants but only one tea shop like this. Here you can buy postcards, toys, T-shirts, guidebooks, and globes or head for one of the 50 small café tables in the back and upstairs. Menu choices include salads, sandwiches, and simple light meals, plus croissants and other delicious baked goodies. The crowd is often young, sophisticated, and good-natured.

STREET EATS

In Paris you can find a large variety of very affordable street food sold everywhere from the Latin Quarter to outside the *grand magasins* on the Right Bank. Tasty sandwiches, crêpes, frites, and (in cold weather) delicious roast chestnuts are just a few of the items available. The crêpes are especially good—freshly made and filled with your choice of ingredients: cheese, ham, egg (or a combination of these); chocolate and nuts; apricot jam; or some other treat. Prices run 12F to 30F ($2.30 to $5.75), depending on the filling.

PICNICKING

For a truly French picnic, the magic words are *charcuterie, épicerie, boulangerie,* and *pâtisserie* (butcher shop, grocery store, bakery, and pastry shop). *Charcuterie* used to refer to a butcher who specialized in pork, but today it refers to a gourmet store selling cold meats, pâtés, salads, breads, rolls, cakes, and pastries—all delectably displayed.

The best place to eat your picnic lunch is in the nearest park. My favorites are the Jardin des Tuileries and the Parc Monceau, both on the Right Bank, but equally charming are the place des Vosges in the Marais, with handsome benches; the vast Jardin du Luxembourg on the Left Bank; and the Parc du Champ-du-Mars by the Eiffel Tower. And there are many smaller intimate spots—so many that it's not hard to find a pleasant spot to enjoy a picnic meal.

WORTH THE EXTRA MONEY

✪ A Priori Thé

35–37 Galerie Vivienne (entrances at 6 rue Vivienne and 4 rue des Petit-Champs), 2e. ☎ **1/42-97-48-75.** Lunch 75F–95F ($14.40–$18.25); brunch 135F ($25.95) Sat, 146F ($28.10) Sun. MC, V. Mon–Fri noon–6pm, Sat noon–6:30pm, Sun 1–6pm. Métro: Bourse, Palais-Royal–Musée-du-Louvre, or Pyramides. FRENCH/TEAROOM.

Among the most beautiful of Paris's 19th-century shopping arcades is the Galerie Vivienne, with high ceilings and elegant stores. You can enjoy both the gallery and a good repast at A Priori Thé, a cleverly named tearoom that serves coffee, a large assortment of teas, main dishes, sandwiches, salads, and desserts. The menu changes each month. The American management here has created a harmonious and appealing blend of Parisian and New World styles.

Bistrot de la Mer Fauchon

30 place de la Madeleine, 8e. ☎ **1/42-66-92-63.** *Formule* 120F ($23.10), 140F ($26.90), and 160F ($30.75). AE, DC, JCB, MC, V. Mon–Sat 11:45am–3pm and 7–11pm. Métro: Madeleine. FRENCH.

Fauchon is one of the city's food spectaculars, and its five restaurants only enhance its reputation (also see Brasserie Fauchon and Trattoria Fauchon, below). The seafood at this bistro is the freshest and the atmosphere elegant. The 120F ($23.05) formule offers a main course (*plat*), a dessert, and coffee. Your choices might be moules marinières, half a lobster, and a variety of oysters. The 140F ($26.90) formule consists of an appetizer, a main course, and coffee. Start with a selection from langoustines (small lobsters), herring salad, rilletes of salmon with toast, fusili salad with seafood, salmon tartare, or curried mussels.

Brasserie Bofinger

5–7 rue de la Bastille, 4e. ☎ **1/42-72-87-82.** Two-course prix-fixe, with a glass of wine, 140F ($26.90); three-course Grand Siècle menu, including half a bottle of wine, 166F ($31.90). AE, MC, V. Mon–Fri noon–3pm and 6:30pm–1am, Sat–Sun noon–1am. Métro: Bastille. FRENCH/ALSATIAN.

Bofinger, opened in 1864, is one of the city's best-loved restaurants. Its belle époque decor—dark wood, gleaming brass, bright lights, waiters with long white aprons—will transport you back to the 19th century. The menu features many Alsatian specialties, including choucroute (sauerkraut), and excellent French classics, including oysters and foie gras. The prices are actually moderate for Paris. There are 200 seats on two levels.

Brasserie Fauchon

30 place de la Madeleine, 8e. ☎ **1/42-66-92-63.** *Formules* 109F ($20.95), 115F ($22.10), and 140F ($26.90). AE, DC, JCB, MC, V. Mon–Sat 7pm–1am. Métro: Madeleine. FRENCH.

Founded in 1886, Fauchon is one of the world's great food stores. It also operates five restaurants, only three within our price range (also see Bistrot de la Mer Fauchon, above, and Trattoria Fauchon, below). The brasserie is decked out in salmon pink and black. The dishes are classic, from the appetizers to the main dishes—warm goat cheese, fish soup, roast leg of lamb with white beans, lamb kidneys, and boeuf bourguignon. All the desserts, such as chocolate mousse and the pastries, are delectable.

Chez Maître Paul

12 rue Monsieur-le-Prince, 6e. ☎ **1/43-54-74-59.** Reservations recommended. Main courses 80F–145F ($15.40–$27.90); three-course fixed-price meal, including half a bottle of

wine, 180 F ($34.55). AE, DC, MC, V. Mon–Fri noon–2:30pm and 5pm–closing, Sat 5pm–closing. Métro: Odéon. FRENCH COUNTRY.

Small but comfortable, Chez Maître Paul serves specialties from the Franche-Comté region of eastern France. Try the saucisson chaude avec pommes à l'huile (hot sausage with potatoes in oil) to start and follow it with poulet sauté au vin rouge d'Arbois (chicken sautéed in red wine with mushrooms and tomatoes). If you're not interested in either of those, we'd recommend the champignon à la greque (cold mushroom salad) or the filet de veau (filet of veal). The fixed-price menu includes wine and you can have your choice of a plate of cheeses or dessert. This place is a little pricey but well worth the extra money.

L'Enoteca

25 rue Charles-V, 4e. ☎ **1/42-78-91-44.** Main courses 55F–95F ($10.60–$18.25). EURO, MC, V. Daily 7:30–11:30pm. Métro: Sully-Morland. ITALIAN.

Located in the Marais in a charming old stone building, L'Enoteca is a local budget favorite. The interior is as rustic as the exterior, with small plain wood tables and exposed-beam ceilings. The menu includes such traditional favorites as spaghetti, ricotta-filled ravioli, and lasagne with zucchini. There are several meat dishes as well as a menu of "wines of the week."

Le Procope

13 rue de l'Ancienne-Comédie, 6e. ☎ **1/43-26-99-20.** Main course plus appetizer or dessert (served 11am–8pm) 99F ($19.05); *menu complet* at lunch 130F ($25). AE, MC, V. Daily 8am–2am. Métro: Odéon. FRENCH.

In operation since 1686, Le Procope bills itself as the oldest restaurant in the world and has entertained such luminaries as Voltaire, Benjamin Franklin, Marat, and Verlaine. This historic place makes for a memorable Parisian meal, with little crystal chandeliers, mirrors, dark oil paintings, and snowy linens. Many French classics are represented on the long menu, so you can choose from history's best. To save, order the two-course fixed-price lunch or drop in just for coffee and pastry.

✪ Trattoria Fauchon

30 place de la Madeleine, 8e. ☎ **1/42-66-92-63.** Cold specialties 39F–70F ($7.50–$13.45); pasta 35F–70F ($6.75–$13.45); hot dishes 39F–90F ($7.50–$17.30). AE, DC, JCB, MC, V. Mon–Sat 11:45am–3pm and 7–11pm. Metro: Madeleine. ITALIAN.

This handsome trattoria offers a variety of classic specialties using the exquisite ingredients found at Fauchon. Among the seven or so cold specialties are salade de haricots toscane (with tomatoes, tuna, green beans, and olives in a Balsamic dressing), salade de fenouil (fennel, olives, tomatoes, and hard-boiled eggs), or a shellfish sampler of oysters, shrimp, and other seafood. Ravioli, lasagne, and tagliatelle carbonara with bacon and cream sauce are just three of the marvelous pasta dishes.

6 Attractions

SIGHTSEEING SUGGESTIONS

If You Have 1 Day

To start seeing Paris as early as possible, try to have breakfast in a sidewalk café rather than in your hotel, and then begin at Kilométre 0: marked on the Parvis in front of Notre-Dame. All distances in France are measured from this point on the Ile de la Cité. From here, cross the River Seine to the Musée du Louvre on the

Right Bank. Focus on a few rooms in a particular section, as it takes months to see the collection in its entirety.

From the museum, stroll through the Jardin des Tuileries to place de la Concorde. Walk down avenue des Champs-Elysées to the Arc de Triomphe; near the Champs-Elysées are several budget restaurants where you can have lunch. Note that Métro Line 1 runs in a straight line from the Louvre to the Arc de Triomphe (Métro: Charles-de-Gaulle–Etoile), with several stops along the way, an alternative to walking that'll also save you some time.

From the Arc de Triomphe, walk down avenue Kléber to place du Trocadéro (or take the Métro to Trocadéro) for some splendid views of the Eiffel Tower.

Finally, head for the Latin Quarter (catch the RER at Champ-de-Mars, southwest of the Eiffel Tower on the Seine, to St-Michel) and get lost in its narrow mazelike streets between the river and boulevard St-Germain-des-Prés. This is an excellent area for dinner.

If You Have 2 Days

On the first day, follow the above itinerary from Notre-Dame to the Arc de Triomphe, but see the Louvre in a more relaxed fashion and take a different route from place de la Concorde to avenue des Champs-Elysées: Walk up rue Royal (with a view of the Eglise de la Madeleine, the church with the Greek columns, at the end) and turn left on rue du Faubourg St-Honoré to stroll past the Palais de l'Elysée and the most fashionable shops in Paris. To head back to the Champs-Elysées, turn left on avenue Marigny at place Beauveau. After visiting the Arc de Triomphe, take Métro Line 1 to St-Paul, in the heart of the Marais; walk east on rue St-Antoine and turn left on rue de Brague to see place des Vosges. The Musée Picasso and place de la Bastille are both near here.

Explore the Left Bank on your second day. Start at the Eiffel Tower and stroll past the Invalides, with the Tomb of Napoléon, through the Faubourg St-Germain, a district of elegant 18th-century mansions (the Musée Rodin and Musée d'Orsay are here). Head back to the Latin Quarter.

If You Have 3 Days

Combine the above itineraries with visits to the Centre Pompidou and to Montmartre and Sacré-Coeur. You'll also have time to explore the parks: the Jardin du Luxembourg on the Left Bank or Park Monceau on the Right Bank.

If You Have 5 Days

Five days is a sensible time to stay in Paris, and if you have a week or 10 days, so much the better. You'll probably have time to see the Sainte-Chapelle and the Conciergerie on Ile de la Cité, explore more museums, and visit the château of Versailles, the cathedral at Chartres, or the renamed Disneyland Paris outside the city.

Special & Free Events

The Office de Tourisme et des Congrès de Paris publishes a monthly list of special events, including music festivals, concerts, opera performances, exhibits, plays, and sports events. Ask for the *Manifestations du mois.*

Also see "Timing Your Trip" under "Pretrip Preparations," earlier in this chapter, for a list of annual special events.

TOP ATTRACTIONS

❂ Musée du Louvre

Quai du Louvre, 1er. ☎ **1/40-20-53-17**, 40-20-51-51 for recorded information, 40-20-52-09 for hours of tours in English. Admission 40F ($7.70) adults, 20F ($3.85) after 3pm and all day Sun, free for children 17 and under with ID. Wed 9am–10pm, Thurs–Mon 9am–6pm (Richelieu Wing open until 10pm Mon). Métro: Palais-Royal–Musée-du-Louvre.

Formerly a royal palace, the Louvre is perhaps the greatest museum in the world. It's certainly one of the largest: If you were to spend five minutes looking at each object in its collection from opening time to closing, it would take you almost a decade to see it all. The *Venus de Milo,* the *Winged Victory,* and the *Mona Lisa* are only three of the masterpieces housed in its collections, which are divided into seven departments: Asian antiquities; Egyptian antiquities; Greek, Roman, and Etruscan antiquities; sculpture; prints and drawings; paintings; and objets d'art. A great way to begin exploring this wealth of art is to take the 90-minute guided tour.

The Richelieu Wing, inaugurated in 1993, houses the museum's collection of French paintings from the Middle Ages to the late 18th century, the gallery of medieval French sculpture, the Oriental antiquities section (a rich collection of Islamic art), and Les appartements Napoléon III, which were reproduced in all their bourgeois splendor. Constructed from 1852 to 1857, the Richelieu Wing has virtually been rebuilt, adding some 230,000 square feet of exhibition space. In 165 rooms, plus three covered courtyards, about 12,000 works of art are displayed. The wing also contains the upscale Café Richelieu and the Café Marly, accessible only from the Louvre's main courtyard, the Cour Napoléon.

The enormous glass pyramid designed by I. M. Pei is the museum's exciting entrance. Of all the *grands projets* supported by former President Mitterrand during the last decade, this was probably the most audacious. Oblivious to it all, the photogenic pyramid has become one of Paris's landmarks. The renovations have also greatly expanded exhibition space and turned the Louvre into a most comfortable museum, with six dining facilities and excellent book and gift shops.

Arc de Triomphe

Place Charles-de-Gaulle–Etoile, 8e. ☎ **1/43-80-31-31.** Admission 32F ($6.15) adults, 21F ($4.05) ages 18–25 and over 60, 10F ($1.90) children 12–17, free for children 11 and under. Apr–Sep, daily 9:30am–4:30pm; Oct–Mar, daily 10am–4:30pm. Closed Jan 1, May 1 and 8, July 14, Nov 11, and Dec 25. Métro: Charles-de-Gaulle–Etoile.

The world's largest triumphal arch was commissioned by Napoléon in honor of his Grande Armée and its 128 victories. The arch was far from complete by the time France's imperial army had been swept from the field at the Battle of Waterloo, and was not completed until 1836. Although it has come to symbolize the greatness of France and her spirit (or, as Victor Hugo described it, a "stone built on glory"), it has also witnessed some of the country's defeats, as when German armies marched through the arch and down the Champs-Elysées in 1871 and again in 1940. Beneath the arch, under a gigantic tricolor flag, burns an eternal flame honoring France's Unknown Soldier, buried here in 1920 in memory of those who lost their lives in World War I. Several outstanding 19th-century sculptures cover the arch, including Rude's *La Marseillaise,* seen on the Champs-Elysées side, and his relief the *Departure of the Volunteers.*

On the inner walls under the vault are inscribed the names of the 128 battles of the Republic and the Empire, along with the names of the 600 generals who took part in them. Victor Hugo lay in state under the arch in 1885 before being

The Louvre

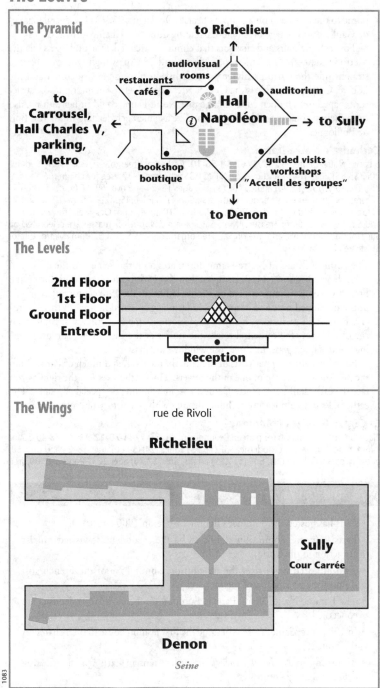

The Pyramid

to Richelieu

audiovisual rooms

restaurants cafés

auditorium

Hall Napoléon

to Carrousel, Hall Charles V, parking, Metro

→ to Sully

bookshop boutique

guided visits workshops "Accueil des groupes"

to Denon

The Levels

2nd Floor
1st Floor
Ground Floor
Entresol

Reception

The Wings

rue de Rivoli

Richelieu

Sully
Cour Carrée

Denon

Seine

1083

borne to the Panthéon on a pauper's hearse. On August 25, 1944, Général Charles de Gaulle paid homage here before parading down the Champs-Elysées.

To reach the stairs and elevators that climb the arch, take the underpass (via the Métro entrances). From the top, 162 feet and 284 steps high, you can see in a straight line the Champs-Elysées, the obelisk in place de la Concorde, and the Louvre. On the other side is the Grande Arche de la Défense, a multipurpose structure shaped like an open cube so large that Notre-Dame could fit beneath it. Also from the top you can see the elegant parklike avenue Foch, leading to the vast Bois de Boulogne.

Cathédrale Notre-Dame

6 Parvis Notre-Dame, 4e. ☎ **1/42-34-56-10.** Cathedral, free; towers, 35F ($6.75) adults, 20F ($3.85) ages 18–24 and over 60, 7F ($1.35) children 7–17, free for children 6 and under; Treasury, 15F ($2.90) adults, 10F ($1.90) ages 18–24 and over 60, 5F (95¢) children 7–17, free for children 6 and under. Cathedral, Sun–Fri 8am–6:45pm, Sat 8am–12:30 and 2–6:45pm; towers and crypt, daily 9:30am–7:30pm (10am–4:30pm Oct–Mar); museum, Wed and Sat–Sun 2:30–6pm; Treasury, Mon–Sat 9:30am–5:45pm. Six masses are celebrated on Sun, four on weekdays, and one on Sat. Free organ concerts Sun at 5:30pm. Métro: Cité or St-Michel. RER: St-Michel.

The gothic loftiness of Notre-Dame dominates both the Seine and the history of Paris. It was begun in 1163, completed in the 14th century, pillaged during the French Revolution, and restored by Viollet-le-Duc in the 19th century. Polyphonic music developed here and Napoléon audaciously crowned himself in this sanctuary. But for all its history, it's the art of Notre-Dame that still awes. Built in an age of illiteracy, the cathedral retells the stories of the Bible in its portals, paintings, and stained glass; its three rose windows are masterful.

For a look at the upper parts of the church, the river, and much of Paris, climb the 387 steps to the top of one of the towers. The south tower (on the right as you face the cathedral) holds Notre-Dame's 13-ton bell, rung on special occasions. The cathedral's museum features exhibits dealing with the history of Notre-Dame.

✪ Centre Georges Pompidou

Place Georges-Pompidou (or plateau Beaubourg), 4e. ☎ **1/44-78-12-33,** 44-78-40-86 for information. Musée d'Art Moderne, 35F ($6.75) adults, 24F($4.60) ages 18–24 and over 60; one-day pass to all exhibits, 60F ($11.55) adults, 40F ($7.70) ages 18–24 and over 60, free

---

❓ Did You Know?

- Paris has hosted the Summer Olympics twice: in 1900 and 1924.
- Paris's Centre Pompidou claims to be the second-most-visited tourist attraction in the world.
- Two hundred years after the Revolution, about 15% of the French still support the restoration of the monarchy.
- The Banque Nationale de Paris is Europe's top bank as far as deposits are concerned.
- In 1989, Yves Saint-Laurent became the first fashion house to offer shares on the Bourse.
- According to *National Geographic,* pedestrians in Paris will step in dog droppings every 286th step.

for children 17 and under. Mon and Wed–Fri noon–10pm, Sat–Sun and hols 10am–10pm. Métro: Rambuteau, Hôtel-de-Ville, or Châtelet–Les-Halles.

The full name of this gigantic futuristic arts center is Centre National d'Art et de Culture Georges Pompidou, and because it's been called "the most avant-garde building in the world" it was despised by many when it was built. The center's bold exoskeletal architecture and the bright colors of the painted pipes and ducts that crisscross its transparent facade were considered jarring in the traditional old Beaubourg neighborhood.

Since then, many detractors have become grudging admirers. You'll recognize the center when you see it: Those enormous colorful pipes run in mazes to bind its exterior, and translucent escalators of incredible length follow along its outer walls, trundling visitors among the various levels. The square in front of the center is always filled with people watching the acrobats and other street performers.

Besides being a venue for changing exhibits, the center houses the Musée National d'Art Moderne–Centre de Création Industrielle, tracing art, architecture, and design from 1905 to the present, plus a public library. The permanent collection includes works by Matisse, Picasso, Braque, Léger, Kandinsky, and Pollock.

Note: The Centre Pompidou will be undergoing renovation throughout 1996 but will remain open, although some galleries may close from day to day.

✪ Musée d'Orsay

62 rue de Lille/1 rue de Bellechasse, 7e. ☎ **1/40-49-48-14,** 40-49-48-48 for the information desk. Admission 35F ($6.75) adults, 24F ($4.60) ages 18–24 and over 60, free for children 17 and under; reduced admission Sun. Tues–Wed and Fri–Sat 10am–6pm, Thurs 10am–9:45pm, Sun 9am–6pm (June 20–Sept 20 the museum opens at 9am). Métro: Solférino. RER: Musée-d'Orsay.

Once a railroad station, this turn-of-the-century building (featured in Orson Welles's film *The Trial*) houses an astounding collection of art dating from 1848 to 1914. Works from the Louvre and the old Musée du Jeu de Paume—repository of an unsurpassed collection of impressionist masterpieces—were transferred here in the mid-1980s, and the Musée d'Orsay is now one of the world's great art museums. Thousands of paintings, watercolors, pastels, sculptures, objets d'art, items of furniture, architectural displays, and even photographs and movies are housed in this brilliant glass-roofed building.

✪ Musée Picasso

In the Hôtel Salé, 5 rue de Thorigny, 3e. ☎ **1/42-71-25-21.** Admission 27F ($5.20) adults (14F $2.70 Sun), 17 F ($3.25) ages 18–24 and over 60, free for children 17 and under. Apr–Sep, Wed–Mon 9:30am–6pm; Oct–Mar, Wed–Mon 9:30am–5:30pm. Métro: Chemin-Vert or St-Paul.

The Hôtel Salé, a renovated mansion in the Marais, houses the world's greatest collection of Pablo Picasso's works. After his death in 1973, the artist's estate arranged to donate this enormous collection in lieu of French inheritance taxes, which were also enormous. Besides Picasso's own paintings, sculptures, ceramics, engravings, and sketches, which number in the thousands, the museum displays works by the artist's favorite painters, including Corot, Cézanne, and Matisse.

✪ Sainte-Chapelle

4 bd. du Palais, Ile de la Cité, 1er. ☎ **1/43-54-30-09.** Admission 27F ($5.20) adults, 18F ($3.45) ages 18–25 and over 60, 10F ($1.90) children 12–17, free for children 11 and under. Apr–Sept, daily 9:30am–6:30pm; Oct–Mar, daily 10am–5pm. Closed Jan 1, May 1, Nov 1 and 11, and Dec 25. Métro: Cité or Châtelet. RER: St-Michel.

Paris

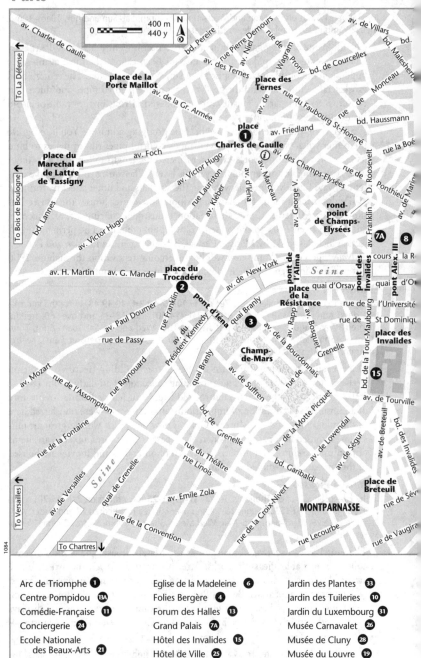

Arc de Triomphe ❶
Centre Pompidou ⓭A
Comédie-Française ⓫
Conciergerie ㉔
Ecole Nationale
   des Beaux-Arts ㉑

Eglise de la Madeleine ❻
Folies Bergère ❹
Forum des Halles ⓭
Grand Palais ❼A
Hôtel des Invalides ⓯
Hôtel de Ville ㉕

Jardin des Plantes ㉝
Jardin des Tuileries ❿
Jardin du Luxembourg ㉛
Musée Carnavalet ㉖
Musée de Cluny ㉘
Musée du Louvre ⓳

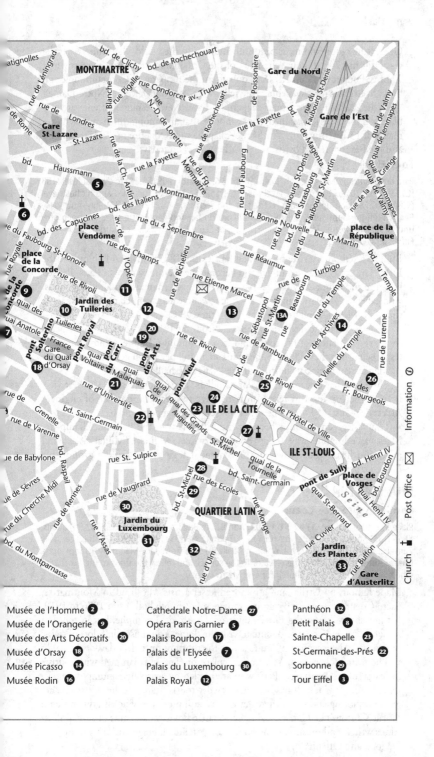

Musée de l'Homme ②
Musée de l'Orangerie ⑨
Musée des Arts Décoratifs ⑳
Musée d'Orsay ⑱
Musée Picasso ⑭
Musée Rodin ⑯

Cathédrale Notre-Dame ㉗
Opéra Paris Garnier ⑤
Palais Bourbon ⑰
Palais de l'Elysée ⑦
Palais du Luxembourg ㉚
Palais Royal ⑫

Panthéon ㉜
Petit Palais ⑧
Sainte-Chapelle ㉓
St-Germain-des-Prés ㉒
Sorbonne ㉙
Tour Eiffel ③

One of the oldest and most beautiful churches in the world, the Sainte-Chapelle was built in 1246 to house the relics of the Crucifixion, including the Crown of Thorns, bought by Louis XII (St. Louis) from the Emperor of Constantinople and brought to Paris for safekeeping (the relics were later transferred to Notre-Dame).

In the *chapelle haute* (upper chapel), Old and New Testament scenes are emblazoned in 15 perfect stained-glass windows that are among the highest achievements of 13th-century art. The Sainte-Chapelle survived a fire in the 17th century and the beauty created by its master artisans lives on today.

Tour Eiffel

Parc du Champ-de-Mars, 7e. ☎ **1/45-50-34-56.** Elevator, 20F ($3.85) to the first level (188 ft.), 38F ($7.30) to the second level (380 ft.), 55F ($10.90) to the third and highest level (1,060 ft.); walking up the stairs to the first and second levels, 12F ($2.30). July–Aug, daily 9am–midnight; Sept–June, daily 9:30am–11pm (in fall and winter the stairs are open only until 6:30pm). Métro: Trocadéro, Bir-Hakeim, or Ecole-Militaire. RER: Champ-de-Mars–Tour Eiffel.

Built as a temporary structure to add flair to the 1889 Universal Exhibition, the Eiffel Tower managed to survive and become the soaring symbol of Paris. Praised by some and damned by others (like writers Guy de Maupassant and Huysmans, who called it "a hollow candlestick"), the tower created as much controversy in its time as I. M. Pei's Louvre pyramid did in the 1980s.

Take the Métro to Trocadéro and walk from the Palais de Chaillot to the Seine to get the full effect of the tower and its surroundings. Besides panoramic views (especially when the Trocadéro fountains are in full play), you get a free show from the dancers and acrobats in front of the Palais de Chaillot.

The tower has elevators in two of its pillars. Expect long waits. The best view is from the top level, where historians have re-created the office of engineer Alexandre-Gustave Eiffel. The tower has several restaurants and bars.

The vast green esplande beneath the Eiffel Tower, the Parc du Champ-de-Mars, extends all the way to the 18th-century Ecole Militaire (Military Academy) at its southeast end. Now a formal lawn, it was once a parade ground for French troops.

MORE ATTRACTIONS

Basilique du Sacré-Coeur

Place St-Pierre, 18e. ☎ **1/42-51-17-02.** Admission: Basilica, free; dome, 15F ($2.90) adults, 8F ($1.55) students 6–25; crypt 10F ($1.90) adults, 5F (95¢) students 6–25. Basilica, daily 7am–10:30pm. Dome and crypt, Apr–Sept, daily 9:15am–7pm; Oct–Mar, daily 9:15am–6pm. Métro: Abbesses (then take the elevator to the surface and follow the signs to the *funiculaire,* which takes you up to the church for one Métro ticket).

Made famous by Utrillo and a hundred lesser artists who lived in Montmartre, Sacré-Coeur is a vaguely Byzantine-romanesque church built from 1876 to 1919. It's not as familiar as the Eiffel Tower or the Arc de Triomphe, but it, too, is a romantic symbol of Paris. Be sure to visit the dome. You must climb lots of stairs, but the view is sweeping: 30 miles across the rooftops on a clear day.

The primary square in Montmartre, place du Tertre, is jammed with tourists in search of a stereotypical Paris who are hassled by artists demanding their permission for a portrait. It has become a tawdry tourist trap, but the side streets are worth exploring and so are the vineyard that still produces wine and the museum on rue Cortot. The Cimetière du Montmartre holds the remains of several illustrious writers and musicians, including Zola, Stendhal, Fragonard, Degas, Berlioz, Delibes, and Offenbach.

1st Arrondissement

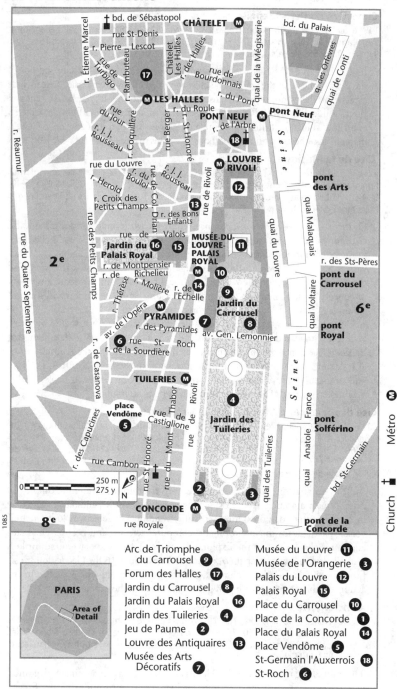

Cimetière du Père-Lachaise

16 rue du Repos, 20e. Admission free. Mar 15–Nov 5, Mon–Fri 8am–6pm, Sat 8:30am–6pm, Sun 9am–6pm; Nov 6–Mar 14, Mon–Fri 8am–5:30pm, Sat 8:30am–5:30pm, Sun 9am–5:30pm. Métro: Père-Lachaise.

In eastern Paris, Père-Lachaise is the most famous cemetery in the city and one of the most beautiful in the world. The illustrious men and women buried here include greats from the worlds of art, literature, and music: Molière, Ingres, Balzac, Chopin, Bizet, Wilde, Bernhardt, Proust, Modigliani, Apollinaire, Isadora Duncan, Colette, Stein and Toklas, Piaf, Jim Morrison, and Simone Signoret, to name only a few. A map of the cemetery with many famous gravesites marked costs 10F ($1.90).

Cité de la Musique

221 av. Jean-Jaurès, 19e. ☎ 1/44-84-45-00, or 44-84-44-84 for ticket sales and information. Public areas, free; museum, undetermined at press time; concerts, 60F–160F ($11.40–$30.40). Public areas, Wed–Sun noon–6pm; museum, Tues–Sun (hours undetermined at press time). Métro: Porte-de-Pantin.

Of the half dozen *grands travaux* conceived by the Mitterrand administration, this testimony to the power of music scheduled to open in October 1995 has been the most widely applauded and in some ways the most etherial, intangible, and innovative. Set at the city's northeastern edge, in what used to be a rundown and depressing neighborhood few Parisians thought about, it incorporates a network of concert halls, a library and research center for the categorization and study of all kinds of music from around the world, and a museum.

Designed as an interconnected complex of bulky post-cubist shapes by noted architect Christian de Portzamparac, the Cité is a kind of "Centre Beaubourg" of music, eclectic and multinational, with archives documenting such musical forms as folk songs from Brittany and Siberia, classical music from North Africa, jazz, and unusual interpretations of French baroque. Concerts will be scheduled Wednesday through Saturday at 8pm and Sunday at 4:30pm.

Cité des Sciences et de l'Industrie, La Villette

30 av. Corentin-Cariou, 19e. ☎ 1/40-05-80-00 (administration). Exhibitions (including the *Argonaut*), 45F ($8.65), 25F ($4.80) after 4pm, free for children 6 and under; Géode, 55F ($10.60); cinéaxe, 32F ($6.15); three-in-one combination ticket, 119F ($22.90); Cité des Enfants, 20F ($3.85). Tues–Sat 10am–6pm, Sun 10am–7pm. Closed May 1 and Dec 25. Métro: Porte-de-la-Villette.

Built as an abattoir, this structure was converted into a museum complex of extraordinary ambition. At the Explora, view exhibits, shows, and models and play interactive games demonstrating scientific techniques. Subjects include the universe, space, Earth, the environment, computer science, and health. The planetarium is also located in the Explora. There's an adventure playground for kids 3 to 12, and the submarine the *Argonaut* to be explored. In the Géode, four to six films are shown on a huge hemispheric screen that enfolds the audience in the action. At the cinéaxe, breathtaking simulations are to be experienced.

✪ Conciergerie

1 quai de l'Horloge, Ile de la Cité, 1er. ☎ 1/43-54-30-06. Admission 26F ($5) adults, 17F ($3.25) ages 18–26 and over 60, 7F ($1.35) children 7–17, free for children 6 and under. Apr–Sept, daily 9:30am–6:30pm; Oct–Mar, daily 10am–5pm. Métro: Cité, Châtelet, or St-Michel. RER: St-Michel.

This building dates from the Middle Ages, when it was an administrative office of the Crown, but it's most famous for its days as a prison during the French

Revolution. Those destined for the guillotine were imprisoned here during the Reign of Terror, including Marie Antoinette and other members of the royal family. You can visit the dank cells where these unfortunates spent their last days and hours and marvel at the vagaries of fate.

Les Egouts de Paris (Paris Sewers)

Pont de l'Alma (at the corner of quai d'Orsay and place de la Résistance), 7e. ☎ **1/47-05-10-29.** Admission 25F ($4.80) adults, 20F ($3.85) ages 6–24 and over 60. Sat–Wed 11am–5pm. Closed three weeks in Jan. Métro: Alma-Marceau. RER: Pont de l'Alma.

Those who have read Victor Hugo's *Les Misérables* or seen old movies of World War II Resistance fighters will want to visit the sewers of Paris—not as beautiful as the city above ground but enormously interesting. Paris's sewer system is actually an engineering marvel, laid out under Napoléon III by Belgrand, at the same time when the *grands boulevards* were being laid out under the direction of Baron Haussmann. If the mechanical guts of a great city interest you, get in line for a visit on one of the few afternoons when a glimpse is offered.

La Grande Arche de la Défense

1 Parvis de la Défense, 92040 Paris la Défense. ☎ **1/49-07-27-57.** Admission 35F ($6.75) adults, 25F ($4.80) children 4–18, free for children 3 and under. Apr–Sept, daily 9am–7pm; Oct–Mar, daily 9am–6pm. RER: La Défense.

This 35-story arch completes the great design conceived by Le Nôtre in the 17th century that envisaged a continuous line of perspective running from the Arc de Triomphe du Carrousel in the courtyard of the Louvre, down the avenue des Champs-Elysées, and through the Arc de Triomphe to La Défense. The Arche was built in 1989 to Johan Otto von Spreckelsen's design as the architectural center-piece of the suburb of La Défense.

Hôtel des Invalides

Place des Invalides, 7e. ☎ **1/44-42-37-72.** Admission 35F ($6.75) adults, 24F ($4.60) children 7–18 and seniors over 60, free for children 6 and under. Apr–Sept, daily 10am–6pm (Tomb of Napoléon, 10am–7pm June–Aug); Oct–Mar, daily 10am–5pm. Closed Jan 1, May 1, Nov 1, and Dec 25. Métro: Latour-Maubourg, Invalides, or Varenne.

Louis XIV built this majestic building as a hospital and home for wounded war veterans. These functions are still performed here, and there's office space for numerous departments of the French armed forces. But most visitors come to see the Tomb of Napoléon, a great porphyry sarcophagus lying beneath the golden dome of the Invalides. The emperor's body was transferred to this monumental resting place in 1840, almost two decades after his death on the remote South Atlantic island of St-Hélène, where he was in exile.

If you like military lore, visit the Musée de l'Armée, featuring thousands of weapons, spear- and arrowheads, suits of armor, cannons, battle flags, booty, and every other sort of military paraphernalia.

Musée Carnavalet

23 rue de Sévigné, 3e. ☎ **1/42-72-21-13.** Admission 35F ($6.75) adults, 25F ($4.80) ages 18–24 and over 60, free for children 17 and under. Tues–Sun 10am–5:40pm. Métro: St-Paul (then walk east on rue St-Antoine and turn left on rue de Sévigné).

In the Marais, the Musée Carnavalet is also known as the Musée de l'Histoire de Paris, and it details the city's history from prehistoric times to the present. Paint-ings, signs, items of furniture, models of the Bastille, and Marie Antoinette's per-sonal items are all on display. The museum is housed in two splendid mansions, the Hôtel Le Peletier de St-Fargeau and the Hôtel Carnavalet, once the home of Madame de Sévigné, the 17th-century writer of masterful letters.

Musée National du Moyen Age / Thermes de Cluny

6 place Paul-Painlevé, 5e. ☎ **1/43-25-62-00.** Admission 27F ($5.20) adults (18F/$3.45 Sun), 18F ($3.45) ages 18–24 and over 60, free for children 17 and under. Wed–Mon 9:15am–5:45pm. Métro: Cluny–La Sorbonne.

This is Paris's museum of medieval art. Wood and stone sculptures, brilliant stained glass and metalwork, and rich tapestries, including the famous 15th-century *The Lady and the Unicorn,* with its representation of the five senses, are among the exhibits. The Hôtel de Cluny, in which the museum is housed, is one of the city's foremost examples of medieval architecture. Some parts date back to Roman times, and you can see the ruins of thermal baths.

○ Musée Marmottan

2 rue Louis-Boilly, 16e. ☎ **1/42-24-07-02.** Admission 35F ($6.75) adults, 15F ($2.90) children 12–18, free for children 11 and under. Tues–Sun 10am–5:30pm. Métro: La Muette.

On the edge of the Bois de Boulogne, this jewel contains a veritable cache of Monets that were donated to the Academy des Beaux-Arts by Monet's son. Among them are the *Impression at Sunrise* that gave its name to the impressionist movement, *The Houses of Parliament,* and *African Lilies,* plus numerous paintings of Giverny.

Musée de l'Orangerie

Place de la Concorde, 1er. ☎ **1/42-97-48-16.** Admission 27F ($5.20) adults (18F/$3.45 Sun), 18F ($3.45) ages 18–25 and over 60, free for children 17 and under. Wed–Mon 9:45am–5pm. Métro: Concorde.

Since 1984 the Orangerie has housed the renowned Jean Walter and Paul Guillaume art collection. It was sold to the French state by Domenica Walter, who had married both men. The collection, though comprising fewer than 150 paintings, all from the periods of impressionism to the 1930s, is truly remarkable. Among the painters represented are Cézanne, Renoir, Rousseau, Matisse, Derain, Picasso, Laurencin, and Soutine. The lower floor contains Monet's aqueous *Nymphéas.* The Orangerie's intimate rooms are refreshing after the vastness of the Louvre.

Musée Rodin

In the Hôtel Biron, 77 rue de Varenne, 7e. ☎ **1/44-18-61-10.** Admission 27F ($5.20) adults (18F/$3.45 Sun), 18F ($3.45) ages 18–24 and over 60, free for children 17 and under. Apr–Sept, Tues–Sun 9:30am–5:45pm; Oct–Mar, Tues–Sun 9:30am–4:45pm. Métro: Varenne.

Sixteen rooms in the 18th-century Hôtel Biron contain many of Auguste Rodin's masterpieces. *The Thinker* is here, in several incarnations, and so are *Balzac, The Burghers of Calais,* and *The Gates of Hell.* Look also for the few works by Camille Claudel, Rodin's mistress and a brilliant sculptor herself. The sculpture garden is delightful.

Panthéon

Place du Panthéon, 5e. ☎ **1/43-54-34-51.** Admission 27F ($5.20) adults, 18F ($3.45) ages 18–25 and over 60, 10F ($1.90) children 12–17, free for children 11 and under. Apr–Sept, daily 10am–6:30pm; Oct–Mar, daily 10am–5:30pm. Métro: Cardinal-Lemoine or Maubert-Mutualité.

This neoclassical building with a huge dome was originally a church: It was commissioned by Louis XV in thanksgiving for his having recovered from a serious illness and called the Eglise Ste-Geneviève (after Paris's patron saint). Following the Revolution it was renamed the Panthéon and rededicated as a necropolis for France's secular heroes. In the crypt beneath the dome are the tombs of Voltaire, Jean-Jacques Rousseau, Victor Hugo, Louis Braille (inventor of the reading system for the blind), Emile Zola, and other outstanding figures.

HISTORIC SQUARES

Serene and rational yet intimate and endearing, **place des Vosges** in the Marais (Métro: St-Paul; then walk east on rue St-Antoine and turn left on rue de Brague) is Paris's oldest and perhaps most beautiful square. Henri IV planned it in the early 17th century on the spot where Henri II had been killed in a tournament. Originally known as place Royale, it retains its royal heritage in the white fleurs-de-lis crowning each row of rose-pink brick houses. After the Revolution, it became place de l'Indivisibilité and later place des Vosges, in honor of the first département that completely paid its taxes. Among the famous figures connected with the square are Madame de Sévigné, who was born at no. 1 bis, and Victor Hugo, who lived at no. 6 for 16 years and whose house presently contains the Musée Victor-Hugo.

The fashionable promenades and romantic duels of the 17th century are long gone, and antiques dealers, booksellers, and cafés compete today for your attention. Children play and older residents chat—all in all, an affable slice of Parisian life.

Place Vendôme (Métro: Tuileries, Concorde, or Madeleine) features some of the most fashionable addresses in Paris. Here you'll find the Hôtel Ritz and such luxurious stores as Van Cleef et Arpels. The July Column in the center was commissioned by Napoléon to honor those who fought and won the Battle of Austerlitz, and Austrian cannons were used in its construction. Among its famous residents was Chopin, who died at no. 12 in 1849.

PARKS & GARDENS

Formerly a forest and a royal hunting preserve, the **Bois de Boulogne** (☎ 1/40-67-97-02; Métro: Les-Sablons, Porte-Maillot, or Porte-Dauphine) in the 16th arrondissement is the largest park in Paris. Napoléon III donated the *bois* to the city of Paris, and Baron Haussmann, his town planner, created the Service Municipal des Parcs et Plantations to help transform it into a park. Today it's a vast reserve of more than 2,200 acres with jogging, horseback riding, bicycle trails (you can rent a bike at the *bois*), two lakes for boating, the famous Longchamp and Auteuil racecourses, the beautiful Jardin Shakespeare in the Pré Catelan, and the Jardin d'Acclimatation, Paris's children's amusement park.

The **Jardin des Tuileries,** between the Louvre and place de la Concorde (☎ 1/42-60-38-01; Métro: Tuileries or Concorde), was laid out in the 1560s by Catherine de Médicis, wife of Henri II. A century later, Le Nôtre, creator of French landscaping, redesigned it in the classical style. Today it's a restful green space adorned with statues, including beautiful Maillols in the midst of Paris. Its odd name comes from the clay earth of the land here, once used to make roof tiles called *tuiles.*

Commissioned by the widow of Henry IV, Marie de' Medici, the **Jardin du Luxembourg** (☎ 1/43-29-12-78; Métro: Odéon; RER: Luxembourg) is one of Paris's best-loved parks. It's located south of the Latin Quarter and is popular with students and a favorite with children, who love the *parc à jeux* (playground) and the *théâtre des marionettes* (puppet theater). Besides pools and fountains and statues of queens and poets—including those of Hérédia, Baudelaire, and Verlaine—there are tennis courts and spaces for playing boules.

It's hard to believe that the quiet **Jardin du Palais Royal** (Métro: Louvre), sheltered between three covered arcades stretching behind Cardinal Richelieu's Palais Royal, were once the site of dramatic events that launched the French Revolution; it was also a veritable pleasure garden during the 18th century, filled with gambling dens and other, more lascivious attractions. Today the garden's most controversial aspect are the prison-striped columns built in 1986 by sculptor Daniel Buren. Note, too, Pol Bury's steel-ball sculptures decorating the fountains.

Of Paris's parks and squares, the English-style **Parc Monceau** (☎ 1/42-27-39-56; Métro: Monceau or Villiers; Bus: 30 or 94) is probably the most romantic. A favorite of Marcel Proust, it contains a number of odd features, including a pyramid, ancient columns, and several tombs of an unknown origin. The park is in the heart of a well-heeled residential district, and some nearby streets (such as rue Rembrandt and avenue Velásquez) feature handsome architecture. Two excellent small museums are also in this area: the Musée Nissim-de-Camondo, 63 rue de Monceau, 8e (☎ 1/45-63-26-32), with an extraordinary collection of 18th-century furniture and decorative arts; and the Musée Cernuschi, 7 av. Velásquez, 8e (☎ 1/45-63-50-75), specializing in Chinese art.

SPECIAL-INTEREST SIGHTSEEING

No matter what special interest you may have, there's probably something in Paris just for you. For a start, there are more than 100 museums specializing in all sorts of subjects, arcane and otherwise. The following list barely scratches the surface: **Fondation Le Corbusier** (20th-century architecture), 8–10 square du Docteur-Blanche, 16e (☎ 1/42-88-41-53; Métro: Jasmin; **Musée d'Art Juif** (Jewish art), 42 rue des Saules, 18e (☎ 1/42-57-84-15; Métro: Lamarck-Caulaincourt); **Musée de l'Homme** (anthropology and ethnography), in the Palais de Chaillot, 17 place du Trocadéro, 16e (☎ 1/44-05-72-72; Métro: Trocadéro); **Musée des Arts de la Mode** (fashion), in the Palais du Louvre, 107–109 rue de Rivoli, 1er (☎ 1/44-55-57-50; Métro: Tuileries or Palais-Royal–Musée-du-Louvre); **Musée du Cinéma,** in the Palais de Chaillot, 1 place du Trocadéro, 16e (☎ 1/45-53-74-39; Métro; Trocadéro); and **Musée National des Arts d'Afrique et d'Océanie** (African and Pacific art), 293 av. Daumesnil, 12e (☎ 1/44-74-84-80; Métro: Porte-Dorée).

ORGANIZED TOURS

BUS TOURS   Paris is the perfect city to explore on your own, but if your time or leg muscles don't permit doing so, consider taking an introductory bus tour. The most prominent company is **Cityrama,** 4 place des Pyramides, 1er (☎ 1/44-55-60-00; Métro: Palais-Royal–Musée-du-Louvre). Its two-hour "orientation tour" of Paris costs 150F ($28.85), and it also features half- and full-day tours for 260F ($50) and 450F ($86.55), respectively. Tours to Versailles and Chartres are a better bargain, but the popular nighttime tours of Paris are expensive.

BOAT TOURS   Among the most favored ways to see Paris is by the *bateaux-mouches,* sightseeing boats that cruise up and down the Seine. They sail from the pont de l'Alma on the Right Bank (☎ 1/42-25-96-10, or 48-59-30-30 for reservations, 40-76-99-99 for schedules; Métro: Alma-Marceau). From March through mid-November departures are usually on the hour and the half hour, while in winter there are 4 to 16 cruises per day, depending on demand. The voyage lasts 1¼ hours and costs 40F ($7.70). Special reserved-seats tours, including meals, are run at lunchtime for 350F ($67.30), at teatime on weekends for 250F ($48.10), and at dinner for 580F ($111.55).

Boats also leave from the quai Montebello on the Left Bank. For information, call 43-26-92-55.

Another option is the **BATOBUS,** a ferry service that cruises for several miles through the heart of Paris from April to September making five stops: at La Bourdonnais–Tour Eiffel, near the Eiffel Tower (Métro: Trocadéro or Bir-Hakeim; RER: Champ-de-Mars); Solférino–Musée-d'Orsay; quai Malaquais, opposite the Louvre; quai Montebello–Notre-Dame; and Hôtel de Ville (Métro: Hôtel-de-Ville). Hop on or off the boat at any stop. The fare is 40F ($7.70), and there are one-, three-, and seven-day passes as well. For information call 44-11-33-44.

7 Shopping

Paris is at the forefront of the world of fashion and design, and you can visit (if not purchase anything in) the boutiques of the great couturiers: **Chanel,** 31 rue Cambon, 1er (☎ **1/42-86-28-00;** Métro: Concorde or Madeleine); **Lanvin,** 22 rue du Faubourg St-Honoré, 8e (☎ **1/42-65-14-40;** Métro: Concorde); **Hermès,** 24 rue du Faubourg-St-Honoré, 8e (☎ **1/40-17-47-17;** Métro: Concorde); and **Dior,** 30 av. Montaigne, 8e (☎ **1/40-73-54-44;** Métro: Franklin-D.-Roosevelt).

More to the point for budget travelers are the *grands magasins,* Paris's great **department stores.** They sell all sorts of French goods, often at great prices, and are very experienced at helping you with VAT refunds (see "Special Discounts" under "Paris Deals & Discounts," earlier in this chapter). Try **Galeries Lafayette,** 64 bd. Haussmann, 9e (☎ **1/42-82-34-56;** Métro: Havre-Coumartin), and **Printemps,** 64 bd. Haussmann, 9e (☎ **1/42-82-50-00;** Métro: Chaussée-d'Antin). These most attractive stores stand directly behind the Opéra Garnier and are open Monday through Saturday from 9:30am to 6:30pm.

The largest department store is **La Samaritaine,** 19 rue de la Monnaie, 1er (☎ **1/40-41-20-20;** Métro: Pont-Neuf or Châtelet–Les Halles), between the Louvre and pont Neuf. It's housed in several buildings with art nouveau touches and has an art deco facade on quai du Louvre. The fifth floor of store no. 2 has a fine restaurant that's not expensive; look for signs to the panorama, a free observation point with a wonderful view of Paris. La Samaritaine is open Monday, Wednesday, and Saturday from 9:30am to 7pm and Tuesday and Friday from 9:30am to 10pm.

Many of the city's **museums** have great museum shops selling arts, crafts, books, and high-quality souvenirs at reasonable prices.

BOOKSTORES Paris has several English-language bookstores carrying American and English books and maps and guides to the city and other destinations. Try **Brentano's,** 37 av. de l'Opéra, 2e (☎ **1/42-61-52-50;** Métro: Opéra), open Monday through Saturday from 10am to 7pm; or **Galignani,** 224 rue de Rivoli, 1er (☎ **1/42-60-76-07;** Métro: Tuileries), open Monday through Saturday from 10am to 7pm.

Most famous of all is **Shakespeare & Company,** 37 rue de la Bûcherie, 5e (Métro or RER: St-Michel), Sylvia Beach's congenial shop frequented by Hemingway, Fitzgerald, Gertrude Stein, and other luminaries in the 1920s, when Beach published the first complete version of Joyce's *Ulysses.* The shop was then located on rue de l'Odéon; its successor is just off place St-Michel.

And last, but not least, **W. H. Smith,** 248 rue de Rivoli (☎ **1/42-60-37-97;** Métro: Concorde), offers Paris's largest selection of paperbacks in English. It's open Monday through Saturday from 9am to 6:30pm.

MARKETS For a real shopping adventure, come to the vast **Marché aux Puces de la Porte de St-Ouen,** 17e (Métro: Porte-de-Clignancourt). The Clignancourt flea market, as it's commonly known, features several thousand stalls, carts, shops, and vendors selling everything from used blue jeans to antique paintings and furniture. *Note:* Watch out for pickpockets. It's open Saturday, Sunday, and Monday from 7:30am to 7pm.

More comprehensible, and certainly prettier, is the **Marché aux Fleurs** (Métro: Cité), the flower market in place Louis-Lepine on the Ile de la Cité. Come Monday through Saturday to enjoy the flowers, whether you buy anything or not; on Sunday it becomes the **Marché aux Oiseaux,** an equally colorful bird market.

8 Paris After Dark

Nightlife in Paris is bewilderingly diverse. Whatever you want to see or do is here. Theater is wonderful. Opera, ballet, and classical music performances are world-class. Movie listings are incredibly varied, and there are numerous bars and dance clubs.

Several local publications provide up-to-the-minute listings of performances and other evening entertainment. Foremost among these is *Pariscope: Une Semaine de Paris,* a weekly guide with thorough listings of movies, plays, ballet, art exhibits, clubs, etc. You can buy it at any newsstand for 3F (60¢).

For **half-price theater tickets,** go to the Kiosque-Théâtre at the northwest corner of the Madeleine church (Métro: Madeleine). You can buy tickets only for that same day's performance. The little panels all around the kiosk indicate whether the performance is sold out (little red man) or whether they still have tickets (little green man). The Kiosque-Théâtre is open Tuesday through Friday from 12:30 to 8pm, Saturday from 12:30 to 2pm for matinees and 2 to 8pm for evening performances, and Sunday from 12:30 to 4:30pm. A second ticket counter, selling tickets at a 50% discount is in the basement section of the Châtelet–Les Halles Métro Station, with the same open hours, and a third is located at Gare Montparnasse.

Students can often get last-minute tickets by applying at the box office an hour before curtain time. Have your ISIC with you.

THE PERFORMING ARTS

THEATER

The classics of Molière, Racine, and other French playwrights are staged in marvelous performances at the 300-year-old refurbished **Comédie-Française,** 2 rue de Richelieu, 1er (☎ **1/40-15-00-15,** 40-15-00-00 for recorded information in French; Métro: Palais-Royal–Musée-du-Louvre). Schedules are varied with the addition of more modern works and plays translated from other languages. Prices average 50F to 200F ($9.60 to $38.45), with last-minute seats even cheaper. The box office is open daily from 11am to 6pm, and you can buy tickets up to two weeks in advance.

Pariscope has full listings of the other theaters in the city.

OPERA

The city's principal operatic stage is the **Opéra de la Bastille,** on place de la Bastille, 12e (☎ **1/40-01-17-89,** 44-73-13-00 for opera and concert tickets,

43-43-96-96 for tape-recorded programming information, 47-42-53-71 for ballet tickets, 44-73-13-99 for information; Métro: Bastille). Opened to commemorate the 1989 bicentennial of the French Revolution, this modernistic performance center was designed by the Uruguayan-Canadian architect Carlos Ott and has brought new life to the Bastille neighborhood. Tickets cost 60F to 650F ($11.55 to $125) for opera, 50F to 370F for ballet, and 45F to 225F for concerts. The box office is open daily from 11am to 6:30pm.

DANCE

For classical ballet and other dance performances, come to the **Opéra Garnier,** place de l'Opéra, 9e (☎ **1/40-01-17-89;** Métro: Opéra; RER: Auber). Formerly Paris's great lyrical stage—and also the Opera House that the Phantom called home—this grand building from the age of Napoléon III is in itself worth the price of a ticket. Originally called the Opéra, it beame known as the Opéra Garnier with the opening of the Opéra de la Bastille (above). The Opéra Garnier closed in 1995 for extensive repairs; it's scheduled to reopen in 1998. Performances have moved to the Opéra de la Bastille.

CLASSICAL MUSIC

More than a dozen Parisian churches regularly schedule free or inexpensive organ recitals and concerts, among them **Notre-Dame** (☎ **1/43-29-50-40;** Métro: Cité) on Sunday at 5:45pm; the **Eglise St-Sulpice** (Métro: St-Sulpice); and the **American Church,** 65 quai d'Orsay (☎ **1/47-05-07-99;** Métro: Invalides).

Other concerts are held in numerous halls throughout the city. The Orchestre de Paris plays in the **Salle Pleyel,** 252 rue du Faubourg St-Honoré, 8e (☎ **1/45-61-53-00;** Métro: Ternes), where tickets range from 50F to 350 F ($9.60 to $67.20); the **Théâtre du Châtelet,** 1 place du Châtelet, 1er (☎ **1/40-28-28-98,** or 42-33-00-00 for recorded information); and the **Cité de la Musique,** 221 av. Jean-Jaurès, 19e (☎ **1/44-84-45-00,** or 44-84-44-84 or ticket sales and information), where concerts cost 60F to 160F ($11.40 to $30.40).

Again, *Pariscope* carries full listings.

VARIETY THEATER

The world-famous **Folies-Bergère,** 32 rue Richer, 9e (☎ **1/44-79-98-98**), was closed for years but reopened in 1993 with great pomp and is again one of the main attractions in Paris's colorful theater scene. There are 1,600 seats, costing 150F to 280F ($28.85 to $53.85); 600F ($115.40) for the dinner and show. You can enter from 8:30pm; shows (Tuesday through Sunday) start punctually at 9:15pm, and when the curtain goes up nobody is allowed to come in. It's no longer presenting revues complete with the cancan; instead today's show is a musical comedy that features songs from the 1960s. The next show has not been determined but will be some kind of musical. The nearest Métro station is rue Montmartre; from there it's a five-minute walk.

JAZZ

Parisians seem to have an insatiable craving for American music, especially jazz, and so Paris has a very vibrant jazz scene. Look through current listings in *Pariscope* for the jazz masters you admire, then take the Métro to the club.

Caveau de la Huchette

5 rue de la Huchette, 5e. ☎ **1/43-26-65-05.** Cover 60F ($11.55) Sun–Thurs, 70F ($13.45) Fri–Sat, 55F ($11.05) weekdays for students under 25. Métro: St-Michel. RER: St-Michel.

This is Paris's jazz club of long standing, popular with both foreigners and locals of all ages who want to listen and dance to good jazz. With a capacity of 400, the club has four rooms and two levels. Drinks begin at 22F ($4.25), but there's no minimum so you buy only what you want. Open daily from 9:30pm to 4am.

New Morning

7–9 rue des Petites-Ecuries, 10e. ☎ **1/45-23-51-41.** Cover 120F ($23.10). Métro: Château-d'Eau.

When the Lounge Lizards played here, the audience was skeptical until they were totally seduced by the music, but once they were convinced, the concert lasted until 4am. New Morning is probably Paris's best jazz club, and the audience must be one of the toughest in the world to win over. The best New York groups perform here. Concerts usually start at 9pm.

FILMS

The diversity of movies being shown at any time in Paris is bewildering. The glitzy theaters along the Champs-Elysées show new big-name films, both French and foreign. Smaller cinemas located on both banks of the Seine show the classics, as well as lesser-known titles from all over the world. Look in *Pariscope* for what's on.

"V.O." next to a listing stands for *version originale*, which means that the soundtrack will be in the original language of the film; "V.F." (*version française*) means that the film has been dubbed in French; *sous-titres* are subtitles. Movie tickets cost about 50F to 60F ($9.60 to $11.55), depending on the cinema and the film that's playing. Students can sometimes get reductions on ticket prices; other discounts are offered during the daytime on weekdays.

NIGHTCLUBS

Paris nightclubs are world-famous. The names Lido, Folies-Bergère, Crazy Horse Saloon, and Moulin Rouge are mimicked in dozens of other big cities, and grand revues with music, colorful costumes, variety acts, comedians, and plentiful nudity are a Paris specialty.

The heyday of the great supper-club revues was before World War II, before Technicolor movies with stereo sound, and certainly before the advent of television. Spectacular shows are still staged, but today they're expensive and somewhat self-conscious.

If you must see a Paris spectacular, be prepared to spend at least $100 per person, perhaps as much as $200—drinks can cost as much as $35 apiece. Then choose from among these places: **Moulin Rouge,** 82 bd. de Clichy, 18e (☎ **1/46-06-00-19;** Métro: Blanche); **Lido de Paris,** 116 bis av. des Champs-Elysées, 8e (☎ **1/40-76-56-10;** Métro: George-V); and the **Crazy Horse Saloon,** 12 av. George-V, 8e (☎ **1/47-23-32-32;** Métro: George-V).

DANCE CLUBS

The clubs of Paris must be among the hippest/chicest in the world. At present, many Parisian circles seem to favor salsa, rap, reggae, and Eurotechdisco, and they fastidiously extol the virtues of going out on weeknights, to avoid the suburban crowds who come into the city on Friday and Saturday nights. The later you go, the better. However, everything can change overnight.

Pigalls

77 rue Pigalle, 9e. ☎ **1/45-26-04-43.** Cover 100F ($19.25). Métro: Pigalle.

A somewhat decadent feeling pervades this place, perhaps because of its neighborhood. The music is disco and new wave. There are sculptures on the walls. The crowd is less than wild, but fashion-conscious nevertheless. If you come around 2am, you may have to wait around half an hour to get in, but at 4am you'll be admitted right away. Drinks 60F ($11.55). Open daily from midnight until very late.

Rex Club

5 bd. Poissonière, 2e. ☎ **1/42-36-83-98.** Cover 70F ($13.45). Métro: Bonne-Nouvelle.

Go down about a thousand steps and you'll find everything is big, gray, mirrored, and high-tech. There's smoke smelling like strawberry. Are things made of rubber? Habitués are young and wear clothes like silver while dancing alone. Tuesday is a big rap party; Wednesday is for bands; Friday is Eurodisco. Open daily from 11:30pm to dawn.

GAY & LESBIAN PARIS

Gay life is centered mostly around Les Halles and Le Marais, with the greatest concentration of gay clubs, restaurants, bars, and shops located between the Hôtel-de-Ville and Rambuteau Métro stops. Gay discos come and go so fast that even a magazine devoted somewhat to their pursuit, *Gai Pied,* has a hard time keeping up. That magazine is sold at many news kiosks, as is *Lesbia,* a monthly national lesbian magazine.

Banana Café

13 rue de la Ferronnerie, 1er. ☎ **1/42-33-35-31.** Métro: Châtelet–Les Halles.

It's considered one of the most popular gay bars in the Marais, a ritualized stopover for European gay men, and some gay women, visiting or doing business in Paris. Set on two floors of a 19th-century building, it has walls the color of an overripe banana, dim lighting, and a well-known happy hour where the price of drinks is reduced every day between 4:30 and 7pm. The street level features just a bar. The cellar level contains music alternating between a live pianist and recorded disco. Although it's a worthy place for a drink and maybe a dialogue throughout the day, it's at its most crowded and animated every night after 11:30pm. Thursday through Saturday nights, go-go dancers of virtually any sexual persuasion perform from spotlit platforms in the cellar. Open daily from 4:30pm to 5am.

Le Bar Central

33 rue Vieille-du-Temple, 4e. ☎ **1/48-87-99-33.** Métro: Hôtel-de-Ville.

Le Bar Central is one of the leading bars for gay men in the Hôtel de Ville area. In fact, it's probably the most famous gay men's bar in Paris today. The club has established a small hotel upstairs with a few facilities and only seven bedrooms. Both the bar and its little hotel are in a 300-year-old building in the heart of the Marais. The hotel caters to gay men, less frequently to lesbians. Beer runs 14F to 17F ($2.65 to $3.25). Open daily from 4pm to 2am.

La Champmeslé

4 rue Chabanais, 2e. ☎ **1/42-96-85-20.** Admission free. Métro: Pyramides.

With dim lighting, background music, and comfortable banquettes, La Champmeslé offers a cozy meeting place for women. It is, in fact, the leading women's bar of Paris. The club is housed in a 300-year-old building decorated with exposed stone and heavy ceiling beams, with "retro"-style furnishings evocative of the 1950s. Every Thursday night one of the premier lesbian events of Paris—a cabaret—begins here at 10pm. Entrance and drinks cost the same on Thursday as any other day; drinks run 35F ($6.65). Josy is the charming entrepreneur who established this place in the mid-1970s. Open daily 6pm to 2am.

Le Palace Gay Tea Dance

8 rue du Faubourg-Montmartre, 9e. ☎ **1/42-46-10-87.** Cover 40F ($7.60) before 6pm, 60F ($11.40) after 6pm. Métro: Rue Montmartre.

If you're gay, this is *the* gathering place in Paris on a Sunday afternoon. Men are welcomed into this chatty, gossipy, fun environment whether or not they've come to dance. It's an international crowd, and if you don't want to drink beer or liquor, you can always sip coffee. For more details about Le Palace, see Le Privilège, below. Open Sunday from 4 to 11pm.

Le Privilège

In the basement of Le Palace, 8 rue du Faubourg-Montmartre, 9e. ☎ **1/47-70-75-02.** Cover 40F ($7.60) before 6pm, 60F ($11.40) after 6pm. Métro: Rue Montmartre.

This bar is one of the most popular watering holes in Paris for lesbians, who arrive wearing everything from leather and sunglasses to silk scarves and lipstick. It's most popular with women between midnight and around 4am, after which it's usually relinquished to a crowd of mostly gay men. You may be rather intensely "screened" at the door before being allowed inside. For hours, prices, and further details, see Le Palace (above).

AFTER HOURS

Where do you go after it's all over? In the old days, late-night revelers would make their unsteady way to Les Halles to watch the market open and have one last wake-up drink. However, Les Halles is now gone—but not completely.

Perhaps the last vestiges of Les Halles are the fishmongers' stands set up along rue Montmartre in the early morning. If a fishmonger is going to get up at 2:30 or 3am to set up shop, he or she is going to need something bracing to open the eyes and fight off the chill. This is where they come to get it, among tiled murals of the old produce markets. Always noisy and reassuring, **Le Cochon à l'Oreille** ("A Pig in Your Ear"), 15 rue Montmartre, 1er (☎ **1/42-36-07-56**), will revive and delight you if anything can. It's open Monday through Saturday from 4am to 4pm. Take the Métro to Les Halles.

9 Networks & Resources

FOR STUDENTS   See "For Students" in "Visitor Information" under "Paris Specifics," earlier in this chapter, for more data.

The **Centre Régional des Oeuvres Universitaires (CROUS)**, 39 av. Georges-Bernanos, 5e (☎ **1/40-51-36-00;** Métro: Port-Royal), is a university group that provides data about low-cost student dormitory housing in Paris, where a minimum stay of two days is imposed, although no student can stay for more than a month. It also provides data on many university restaurants that feature very basic but still-nourishing meals at prices that are among the lowest in Paris. It's open Monday through Friday from 9am to 5pm.

One privately run establishment catering most of the year to students is the **Maison d'Etudiants J. de Ruiz de Lavison,** 18 rue Jean-Jacques Rousseau, 1er (☎ **1/45-08-02-10;** Métro: Louvre or Palais-Royal). It offers inexpensive lodgings for about 50 male students, usually French-born men from the provinces, ages 18 to 23, for about nine months during the academic year. In summer, from mid-June to late August, it opens its doors to nonstudents, male and female, and houses them in simple rooms with one or two beds. (In summer, about 70 beds are available, and the minimum stay is reduced to four days.) With breakfast included, overnight rates are 200F ($38) in a single and 260F ($49.40) in a double. Advance reservations are essential. The building is owner-managed by Mme Michelle Besnier, and has a small but charming garden in the back.

FOR GAY MEN, LESBIANS & BISEXUALS   "Gay Paree," with one of the world's largest homosexual populations, has dozens of clubs restaurants, organizations, and services. Other than publications (see below), one of the best sources of information on gay and lesbian activities is the **Centre Gai & Lesbien,** 3 rue Keller, 11e (☎ 1/43-57-21-47; Métro: Bastille). Well equipped to dispense information and to coordinate the activities and meetings of gay people from virtually everywhere, it's open daily from 2 to 8pm. On Sunday it adopts a format known as *Le Café Positif* and features music, cabaret, and information about AIDS and sexually transmitted diseases.

A gay hotline, theoretically designed as a way to creatively counsel those with gay-related problems, is **SOS Ecoute Gay** (☎ 1/48-06-19-11). Someone will respond to calls Monday through Friday from 6 to 10pm. A separate hotline specifically intended for victims of homophobia or gay-related discrimination, **SOS Homophobie** (☎ 1/48-06-42-41) offers a panel of French-trained lawyers and legal experts who provide advice and counsel Monday through Friday from 8 to 10pm.

Another helpful source is **La Maison des Femmes,** 8 Cité Prost, 11e (☎ 1/43-48-24-91; Métro: Charonne), offering information about Paris for lesbians and bisexual women. Informal dinners and get-togethers are sponsored at irregular intervals. Call any Monday, Wednesday, or Friday from 3 to 8pm for further information.

A publication, *Gai Pied's Guide Gai* (revised annually) is the best source of information on gay and lesbian clubs, hotels, organizations, and services—even restaurants. Women might also like to pick up a copy of *Lesbia,* to check the ads if for no other reason. These publications and others are available at Paris's largest and best-stocked gay bookstore, **Les Mots à la Bouche,** 6 rue Ste-Croix-de-la-Bretonnerie, 4e (☎ 1/42-78-88-30; Métro: Hôtel de Ville). It's open Monday through Saturday from 11am to 11pm and Sunday from 2 to 8pm. Both French- and English-language publications are inventoried.

10 Easy Excursions

VERSAILLES   Louis XIV, who reigned from 1643 to 1715, commissioned the **Château de Versailles** (☎ 1/30-84-74-00) and its vast grounds and gardens. Construction lasted for 50 years, and the result is simply astounding. Fourteen miles southwest of Paris, Versailles is one of France's great tourist attractions.

Guided tours take you through parts of the château. Highlights include the Royal Apartments and the famous **Hall of Mirrors,** where the armistice ending World War I was signed. Save time for the **Grand Trianon,** which functioned as the royal guesthouse, and the **Petit Trianon,** loved by Marie Antoinette. The **gardens** at Versailles, with their fabulous system of waterworks, are also worth special consideration. Water shows called *grand eaux* are played May through September on Sunday afternoons, and there's also one night show per month, with the fountains marvelously illuminated. For schedules, ask at the tour office in Paris, or at the tourist office in the town of Versailles, 7 rue des Réservoirs (☎ 1/39-50-36-22), only a short walk from the palace.

The palace is open Tuesday through Sunday: from 9am to 6:30pm May 2 to September 30, to 5:30pm the rest of the year. The grounds are open daily from dawn to dusk. Admission to the palace is 42F ($8.10) for adults, 28F ($5.40) for ages 18 to 24 and over 60, and 28F ($5.40) for all on Sunday. Admission to the Grand Trianon is 23F ($4.40), and to the Petit Trianon, 13F ($2.50).

To get to the château at Versailles, catch RER Line C5 at the Gare d'Austerlitz, St-Michel, Musée d'Orsay, Invalides, Pont de l'Alma, Champ-de-Mars, or Javel station, and take it to the Versailles Rive Gauche station, from which there's a shuttle bus to the château. The 35F ($6.75) trip takes about half an hour. A regular train also leaves from the Gare St-Lazare to the Versailles Rive Gauche RER station.

CHARTRES   "For a visit to Chartres, choose some pleasant morning when the lights are soft, for one wants to be welcome, and the Cathedral has moods, at times severe." Thus wrote Henry Adams in *Mont St-Michel and Chartres,* and, yes, the cathedral may at times have severe moods—gray and cold like winter weather in the Ile de France region—but it's always astoundingly beautiful, with its harmonious architecture and lofty stained-glass windows.

The ✪ **Chartres Cathedral** is one of the greatest creations of the Middle Ages. It survived both the French Revolution, when it was scheduled for demolition, and the two world wars. Take one of the excellent guided tours of the cathedral and save some time to stroll through the graceful, tranquil town of Chartres.

Admission to the cathedral is free. It's open daily: April to September, from 7:30am to 7:30pm; October to March, from 7:30am to 7pm. Ask at the Chartres tourist office (☎ **1/37-21-50-00**), outside the cathedral, about tours in English.

Tours of the crypt are given at 11am and 2:15, 3:30, and 4:30pm (in summer, also at 5:15pm). The crypt tour costs 10F ($1.90) for adults, 7F ($1.35) for ages 18 to 24 and over 60, free for children 17 and under. The tower is open April to September, Monday through Saturday from 9:30 to 11:30am and 2 to 5:30pm and Sunday from 2 to 5:30pm; October through March, Monday through Saturday from 10 to 11:30am and 2 to 4pm and Sunday from 2 to 4pm. Admission to the tower is 20F ($3.85) for adults, 9F ($1.75) for young people and seniors.

Trains run frequently from Paris's Gare Montparnasse to Chartres. A round-trip ticket costs 126F ($24.25) and the trip takes about an hour each way.

DISNEYLAND PARIS   This spectacular entertainment park, 20 miles east of Paris about halfway between Charles de Gaulle and Orly airports, opened in April 1992 as Euro Disney—now it's called **Disneyland Paris** (☎ **1/49-41-49-10**). It's one-fifth the size of Paris itself and features 39 attractions in five entertainment lands, including Main Street U.S.A., Frontierland, Adventureland, Fantasyland, and Discoveryland. The latest feature is Space Mountain, which opened in 1995 and claims to catapult riders from a cannon from Earth through the Milky Way to the moon. Outside the park are hotels, a 27-hole golf course, swimming pools, tennis courts, restaurants, and a Congress Center, Le New York Coliseum, complete with a grand ballroom and a Radio City Music Hall.

Daily admission in peak season is 195F ($37.50) for adults and 150F ($28.85) for children 3 to 11; off-season, 150F ($28.85) for adults and 120F ($23.10) for children 3 to 11. Children 2 and under are admitted free.

The park is open Monday through Friday from 9am to 6pm and Saturday and Sunday from 10am to 7pm. To get there from Paris, take RER Line A to Marne-la-Vallée, a 40-minute trip costing 37F ($7.10) for a second-class ticket; frequent trains shuttle between Chessy and the resort (call 1/43-36-14-14 for information). If you're traveling by car, take Hwy. A-4; ample parking space is available.

Prague 20

by Dan Levine

If you can visit only one city in Eastern Europe, try to make it Prague. The capital of the Czech Republic is a dreamy wonderland of cobblestone streets and sandstone buildings with hundreds of spires that rise out of the morning mist and reflect the last crimson glimmers of sunset. The city center's narrow, winding lanes are the embodiments of romanticism. Prague Castle tops a hill, and a river runs through the city. Old Town truly seems magically removed from reality; it's hard to get caught up in the tension and strife of everyday life here. Visitors often take circuitous routes to their destinations just to reexperience the enchantment of Charles Bridge or watch shadows lengthen around Old Town Square.

The entire city center is a museum that has seemingly been untouched by the centuries. However, it's far from frozen in time. Prague is a dynamic metropolis in the middle of momentous change. The fall of the Communist regime, which ruled over Czechoslovakia for some 40 years, opened the city to the most dramatic transformation in its long history.

1 Prague Deals & Discounts

BUDGET BESTS Prague's expensive hotels may stretch your budget. Private rooms are always the best buy; a double may cost 750 to 1,400 Kč ($27.80 to $50) as against 2,600 Kč ($92.85) or more in a hotel.

Restaurants are still reasonably priced, almost all within range of the frugal traveler. Be sure to check your bill carefully, however—there are many unscrupulous waiters in Prague's restaurants, so be alert for "errors." Museums and entertainment are inexpensive, so you don't have to go out of your way to save money. Bus and rail fares are still incredibly low.

Students with an International Student Identity Card (ISIC) receive a range of discounts, from lower museum admissions to reduced travel fares.

2 Pretrip Preparations

REQUIRED DOCUMENTS U.S. citizens and British subjects need only a passport to enter the Czech Republic. Canadians, Australians, and New Zealanders must obtain visas before traveling.

What's Special About Prague

Monuments
- Old Town Square, one of Europe's most attractive, combining gothic, Renaissance, baroque, and rococo architecture.
- Charles Bridge, Prague's oldest bridge and the symbol of the city.

Castles
- Prague Castle (Pražskýhrad), dating from the city's golden age in the 14th century, dominating the west side of the Vltava River.
- Karlštejn, 45 minutes from Prague, a well-preserved structure from 1348, built to house the crown jewels of the Holy Roman Empire.

Historic Buildings
- Royal Palace, home of Bohemian kings and princes from the 9th to the 16th century.
- Old Town Hall, from the 11th century, with its 14th-century tower.
- Powder Tower, a 140-foot tower, the only one remaining from Prague's medieval fortifications.

Museums
- European Art Museum, with one of central Europe's finest collections.
- National Museum, a neo-Renaissance building displaying the nation's archeological and historical past.
- Czech National Gallery, with a major collection of Bohemian painting and sculpture.
- St. Agnes Convent, housing within its gothic halls a gallery of 19th-century Czech art.

Places of Worship
- St. Vitus Cathedral, a massive 14th-century gothic structure containing the tombs of St. Vitus and St. Wenceslas (of Christmas carol fame).
- Týn Church, with its twin 260-foot spires, where Jan Hus first heard Reformation sermons.
- Old New Synagogue, Europe's oldest remaining Jewish house of worship.

Parks & Gardens
- Letná Park, with its Renaissance gardens and Royal Summer Palace.
- Waldstein Palace Gardens, surrounding the first baroquepalace in Prague.

Events & Festivals
- Prague Spring Music Festival, from mid-May through June, with music and cultural events performed in the city's major concert halls.
- Prague City of Music Festival, in November, with concerts around town.

TIMING YOUR TRIP   From almost all perspectives, May to September is the best time to visit Prague: The weather is warm, the streets are lively, all the restaurants and sights are open long hours, and cultural events like concerts and theater are in full swing. The off-season promises lower rates and fewer crowds.

Prague's Average Daytime Temperatures

	Jan	Feb	Mar	Apr	May	June	July	Aug	Sept	Oct	Nov	Dec
Temp. (°F)	27	29	37	46	55	61	64	63	57	47	38	31
Temp. (°C)	–3	–2	3	8	13	16	18	17	14	8	3	–1

Special Events   From mid-May to June, the city hosts the ✪ **Prague Spring International Music Festival.** If you plan to attend, get tickets as far in advance as possible through Čedok, or you can write ahead for schedules and tickets to the Prague Spring International Music Festival, Hellichova 18, 11800 Praha 1 (☎ **2/51-04-22** or 53-02-93; fax 2/53-60-40).

BACKGROUND READING   Milan Kundera is the Czech Republic's best-known writer. His most famous work, *The Unbearable Lightness of Being,* is set around the 1968 Warsaw Pact invasion and was turned into a movie starring Daniel Day-Lewis and Juliette Binoche 20 years later. Iva Pekarková, one of the few top female Czech novelists whose works are translated into English, published her first novel, *Truck Stop Rainbows,* at age 23. Arnošt Lustig, a survivor of Czechoslovakia's Nazi-era Terezín concentration camp, shared the 1991 *Publishers Weekly* Award for best literary work with John Updike and Norman Mailer.

Václav Havel is not only the Czech Republic's first leader but also a respected author/playwright. His *Letters to Olga* is a book of selected letters Havel wrote to his wife while in prison in the early 1980s. The author's most recent essay

What Things Cost in Prague	U.S. $
Taxi from Ruzyně Airport to the city center	10.75
Metro, tram, or public bus anywhere in Prague	.20
Local telephone call	.04
Double room at the Hotel Paříž (deluxe)	245.00
Double room at the Hotel Evropa (moderate)	79.00
Double room at the Hotel Juventus (budget)	61.00
Lunch for one at the Knights of Malta (moderate)	10.00
Lunch for one at most pubs (budget)	3.00
Dinner for one, without wine, at Parnas (deluxe)	30.00
Dinner for one, without wine, at Adria (moderate)	11.50
Dinner for one, without wine, at Country Life (budget)	5.50
Half liter of beer	.55
Coca-Cola in a restaurant	.70
Cup of coffee	1.00
Roll of ASA 100 film, 36 exposures	7.50
Admission to the National Museum	1.05
Movie ticket	1.05
Cheapest National Theater ticket	2.85

collection is *Summer Meditations*. Finally, no Czech reading list would be complete without reference to Franz Kafka. *The Collected Novels of Franz Kafka* (Schocken), which includes *The Castle* and *The Trial*, binds most of the writer's claustrophobic, paranoid works into a single volume.

3 Prague Specifics

ARRIVING

FROM THE AIRPORT   Prague's **Ruzyně Airport** (☎ **02/36-77-60** or 36-78-14), 12 miles west of the city center, has a bank for changing money (usually open daily from 7am to 11pm), several car-rental offices (see "By Rental Car" under "Getting Around," below, for complete information), and telephones that work. Taxis are plentiful and line up in front of the airport. The fancy cars parked directly in front of the terminal will cost about twice the price of the rickety Škoda and Lada taxis waiting off to the right.

Warning: The majority of Prague's taxi drivers will take advantage of you; obtaining an honestly metered ride from the airport is close to impossible (see "Getting Around," below). The fare *should* be no more than 250 Kč ($8.95) to Wenceslas Square. If you pay only twice this, consider yourself lucky.

ČSA, the Czech national airline, operates an airport shuttle to and from its main office in downtown Prague, every 30 minutes or so from 7:30am to 7:30pm. The ČSA main office, at Revoluční 25, is centrally located, about five blocks from the náměstí Republiky metro station. The shuttle costs just 30 Kč ($1) per person.

Hardcore budgeteers can get into town on city bus no. 119, which delivers passengers from the airport to the Dejvická metro station (Line A). The bus/subway combination into the city center costs just 12 Kč (45¢).

FROM THE TRAIN STATIONS   Passengers traveling to Prague by train typically pull into one of two centrally located stations: Hlavní Nádraží (Main Station) or Nádraží Holešovice (Holešovice Station). Both are on Line C of the metro system and offer a number of visitor services, including currency exchange, a post office, and a luggage-storage area.

Hlavní Nádraží, Wilsonova třída, Praha 2 (☎ **02/24-21-76-54**), is both the grander and the more popular of the two; however, it's also seedier. The station's basement holds a 24-hour luggage-storage counter that charges 20 Kč (70¢) per bag per day. Although cheaper, the nearby lockers aren't secure and should be avoided. Also located beneath the station's main hall are surprisingly clean public showers that are a good place to refresh yourself for just 30 Kč ($1.05); the showers are open Monday through Friday from 6am to 8pm, Saturday from 7am to 7pm, and Sunday from 8am to 4pm. On the station's second floor you'll find the train information office (marked by a lowercase "i"), open daily from 6am to 10pm; and on the top floor is a tattered restaurant recommendable only to the most famished. From the main train station it's a 5-minute stroll to the "top" end of Wenceslas Square or a 15-minute walk to Old Town Square. Metro Line C connects the station to the rest of the city. Metro trains depart from the lower level, and tickets, which cost 6 Kč (20¢), are available from the newsstand near the metro entrance. Taxis line up just outside the station and are plentiful throughout the day and night.

Nádraží Holešovice (☎ **02/24-61-58-65**), Prague's second station, is usually the terminus for trains from Berlin and other points north. Although it's not as

The Czech Koruna

For American Readers   At this writing $1 = approximately 28 Kč (or 1 Kč = 3.5¢), and this was the rate of exchange used to calculate the dollar values given in this chapter (rounded to the nearest nickel).

For British Readers   At this writing £1 = approximately 42 Kč (or 1 Kč = 2.4p), and this was the rate of exchange used to calculate the pound values in the table below.

Note: The rates given here fluctuate from time to time and may not be the same when you travel to the Czech Republic. Therefore this table should be used only as a guide:

Kč	U.S.$	U.K.£	Kč	U.S.$	U.K.£
1	.04	.02	350	12.50	8.33
5	.18	.12	400	14.28	9.52
10	.36	.24	450	16.07	10.71
15	.54	.36	500	17.86	11.90
20	.71	.48	600	21.43	14.29
25	.89	.60	700	25.00	16.66
50	1.79	1.19	800	28.57	19.05
75	2.68	1.79	900	32.14	21.43
100	3.57	2.38	1,000	35.71	23.81
150	5.36	3.57	1,250	44.64	29.76
200	7.14	4.76	1,500	53.57	35.71
250	8.93	5.95	2,000	71.43	47.62
300	10.71	7.14	2,500	89.29	59.52

centrally located as the main station, its more manageable size and position at the end of metro Line C make it almost as convenient.

FROM THE BUS STATION   The **Central Bus Station Praha–Florenc,** Křižíkova 5, Praha 8 (☎ **02/24-21-10-60**), is a few blocks north of the main railroad station. Most local and long-distance buses arrive at this terminal, situated just beside the Florenc metro station, which is on both metro Lines B and C. Smaller bus depots are at **Želivského** (metro Line A), **Smíchovské nádraží** (metro Line B), and **nádraží Holešovice** (metro Line C).

VISITOR INFORMATION

Despite tourism's terrific importance to the nascent capitalist Czech economy, the country's politicians haven't yet gotten around to properly funding an official visitors' agency. Čedok, Na příkopě 18 and Václavské náměstí 24 (☎ **2/24-19-71-11;** fax 2/232-16-56), once the country's official state-owned visitors bureau, is now just a traditional semiprivate travel agency. As at others in town, its staff prefers selling tickets and tours to dispensing free information.

The **American Hospitality Center,** Melantrichova 8, Praha 1 (☎ **2/24-22-99-61** or 24-23-04-67; fax 2/24-22-93-63) is certainly hospitable and is the best place to get brochures, guides, advice, and information on citywide events. Opened at the behest of the mayor of Prague by two American businessmen of Czech ancestry, the center is staffed almost exclusively by bilingual Czechs who are as happy to dispense advice as they are to sell tickets and tours; they also make hotel reservations. The center is open daily from 8am to 8pm.

The **Prague Information Service (PIS)**, Na příkopě 20 (☎ **2/54-44-44** or 26-40-22), between Wenceslas Square and náměstí Republiky, is one of the city's largest Czech-owned tourist offices, offering brochures on upcoming cultural events as well as tickets to sightseeing tours and concerts. In summer, it's usually open Monday through Friday from 8am to 7pm and Saturday and Sunday from 9am to 3pm; winter hours are slightly shorter. A second PIS office is inside the main railway station (see "Arriving," above).

CITY LAYOUT

The **Vltava River** bisects Prague. **Old Town (Staré Město)** and **New Town (Nové Město)** are on the east (or right) side of the river, while **Hradčany** (castle district) and **Malá Strana** (Lesser Town) are on the river's west (or left) bank.

Bridges and squares are Prague's most prominent landmarks. The **Charles Bridge,** the oldest and most famous of the 15 spanning the Vltava, is in the middle of the city. **Old Town Square,** a few winding blocks east of the Charles Bridge, is, appropriately enough, the center of Old Town. Several important streets radiate from this hub, including fashionable Pářižská to the northwest, historic Celetná to the east, and Melantrichova, connecting to **Václavske náměstí (Wenceslas Square)** to the southeast.

On the west side of Charles Bridge is **Mosteká,** a three-block-long thoroughfare running into **Malostranské náměstí,** Malá Strana's main square. **Hradčany,** the castle district, sits just northwest of the square, while a second hill, Petřín, is just southwest of the square.

FINDING AN ADDRESS When reading maps, searching for addresses, or navigating your way around Prague, you should know that *ulice* (abbreviated "ul.") means "street," *třída* means "avenue," *náměstí* (abbreviated "nám.") is a "square" or "plaza," *most* means "bridge," and *nábřeží* means "quay." In Czech none of these words is capitalized, and in addresses, street numbers follow the street name (for example, Václavské nám. 25).

GETTING AROUND

BY METRO, BUS & TRAM Prague's public transportation network is both vast and efficient—one of the few reliable Communist-era legacies. The city's metros, trams, and buses share the same price structure and ticket system. As of this writing, **tickets** cost 6 Kč (20¢) each for adults and 3 Kč (10¢) for children 10 to 16; rides are free for those 9 and under and over 70. The same tickets are valid on the city's entire public transportation network and can be purchased from orange coin-operated machines in metro stations or from most newsstands. Hold on to your ticket throughout your ride; you'll need it to prove that you've paid if you're confronted by a ticket collector. A money-saving **booklet of 25 tickets** (*ekologicke jízdenky*) costs just 115 Kč ($4.10). If you're planning to stay for a couple of weeks or more, it makes sense to buy a **one-month or three-month pass** (*mesíčni jízdenka*), which cost 300 and 750 Kč ($10.70 and $26.80), respectively. These can be purchased at the "DP" windows of any metro station. After the first week of the month, passes are available only at the Dopravní podnik (transport department) office on Na bojišti, near the I. P. Pavlova metro station.

Metro trains operate daily from 5am to midnight and run every two to six minutes or so. The three lettered lines (A, B, and C) intersect with one another at various points around the city. The most convenient central Prague stations are Můstek, at the foot of Vácslavské náměstí (Wenceslas Square); Staroměstská, for Old Town Square and Charles Bridge; and Malostranská, serving Malá Strana and the Castle District.

The city's two dozen electric **tram (streetcar)** lines run practically everywhere. You can never get too lost—no matter how far from the center you travel there's always another tram with the same number traveling back. You never have to hail trams; like trains, they automatically make every stop. The most popular tram, no. 22 (alternatively dubbed the "tourist tram" or the "pickpocket express"), steals past top sights like the National Theater and Prague Castle.

As with other means of public transportation, **bus** riders must purchase tickets in advance, from either a newsstand or a metro station machine, and validate them on boarding. Regular bus service stops at midnight, after which selected routes run reduced schedules, usually only once per hour. If you just miss a night bus, expect a long wait for the next.

BY FUNICULAR   The funicular, a kind of cable car on a track, dashes up and down Petřín Hill every 10 minutes or so from 9:15am to 8:45pm (see "Attractions," later in this chapter). The incline tram makes only two stops—one at the Nebozízek Restaurant in the middle of the hill—and requires the same 6-Kč (20¢) ticket as other means of public transport. The funicular departs from a small house in the park just above the middle of újezd in Malá Strana.

BY TAXI   Taxis can be hailed in the streets or found in front of train stations, large hotels, and popular tourist attractions.

Warning: The majority of cab drivers routinely rip off unsuspecting tourists. When you get into a taxi, the meter should start no higher than 10 Kč (35¢). When you're riding within the city center, it should then climb at 12 Kč (45¢) per kilometer. You'll see two numbers on the taxi meter: The one on the left that keeps climbing is the fare; the one on the right will read "1," "2," "3," or "4." The higher the number, the faster the meter runs. When you're riding in the city center, if the rate window doesn't read "1," you're getting ripped off. Taxis at Wenceslas and Old Town squares are particularly notorious.

If you phone for a taxi, chances are pretty good that you'll be charged the official rate, as your trip is logged in an office and becomes a matter of public record. However, taxi drivers are allowed to start the meter when they get the call, so by the time the car arrives, it'll already have some crowns on it. Two of the larger taxi companies with English-speaking dispatchers are **AAA Taxi** (☎ **02/34-24-10** or 32-24-44) and **RONY Taxi** (☎ **02/692-19-58**).

BY RENTAL CAR   If you're staying in central Prague, don't drive. However, driving around the Czech Republic is relatively straightforward and car-rental rates are low compared with those of Western European cities. **Europcar,** Pařížská 26 (☎ **02/24-81-12-90**); **Hertz,** Karlovo nám. 28, Praha 2 (☎ **02/29-78-36**); **Budget,** at Ruzyně Airport (☎ **02/316-52-14**); and **Avis,** E. Krásnohorské 9, Praha 1 (☎ **02/231-55-15**), have offices in Prague. Local Czech car-rental companies sometimes offer lower rates. Compare **A Rent Car,** Opletalova 33, Praha 1

(☎ **02/24-22-98-48** or 24-21-15-87); or **ESO Car,** Husitská 58, Praha 3 (☎ **02/27-88-88;** fax 2/27-22-11 or 82-10-76).

FAST FACTS: Prague

American Express   For travel arrangements, traveler's checks, currency exchange, and other member services, visit the city's sole American Express office, Václavské nám. (Wenceslas Square) 56, Praha 1 (☎ **02/24-21-99-92;** fax 2/24-22-77-08). It's open Monday through Friday from 9am to 6pm and Saturday from 9am to noon, although it sometimes closes for lunch from 1:30 to 2pm. To report lost or stolen cards, call 24-21-99-78.

Business Hours   Most **banks** are open Monday through Friday from 9:30am to 3:30pm; some are also open on Saturday from 9:30am until noon. **Offices** are generally open Monday through Friday from 8am to 4pm. **Pubs** are usually open daily from 11am to midnight. Most **restaurants** are open for lunch from noon to 3pm and for dinner from 6 to 11pm. **Stores** are usually open Monday through Saturday from 10am to 6pm, but those in the tourist center keep longer hours and may be open on Sunday as well. Be aware that many of the small food shops that keep long hours charge up to 20% more for all their goods after 8pm or so.

Currency   The Czech crown (koruna), abbreviated Kč, is divided into 100 hellers. There are five banknotes and nine coins. Notes, each of which bears a forgery-resistant metal strip and a prominent watermark, are issued in 100, 200, 500, 1,000, and 5,000 crown denominations. Coins are valued at 10, 20, 50, hellers and 1,2,5, 10, 20, and 50 crowns.

Currency Exchange   When changing money in Prague, you'll get a better rate for cash than for traveler's checks. Banks generally offer the best exchange rates, but American Express and Thomas Cook are competitive and don't charge commission for cashing traveler's checks no matter the brand. Beware of CheckPoint and other private money-changing places that deceptively charge obscenely high commissions—often 10%. Don't be afraid to use your credit and charge cards; I've found that bank-card exchange rates are not only favorable but regularly to my advantage when conversion costs are figured in. There's one **American Express** office in Prague (see above). **Thomas Cook** is across Wenceslas Square at Václavské nám. 47 (☎ **02/24-22-95-37;** fax 2/26-56-95); it's open Monday through Friday from 9am to 5pm and Saturday from 9am to noon.

Automated-teller machines (ATMs) are located throughout the city center, and many accept foreign cards linked to the CIRRUS network. Some of the most convenient Prague 1 locations include Na příkopě 5; Václavské nám. (Wenceslas Square) 42; and by the Kotva department store at nám. Republiky 8. ATMs at the above locations are all open 24 hours.

Doctors/Dentists   The Diplomatic Health Center for Foreigners, Na homoice 724, Praha 5 (☎ **02/52-92-21-46** weekdays, 52-92-11-11 evenings and weekends), provides 24-hour emergency health care as well as referrals to specialists. There's a 1,000-Kč ($35.70) examination deposit, which may be returned depending on the services rendered.

Drugstores   An emergency pharmacy is at Václavské nám. 8 (☎ **02/ 24-22-75-32**).

Embassies   The Embassy of the **United States** is at Tržiště 15, Malá Strana, Praha 1 (☎ **02/24-51-08-47**), open Monday through Friday from 8am to 4pm; **Canada,** Mickiewiczova 6 Hradčany, Praha 6 (☎ **02/24-31-11-08**), open Monday through Friday from 9am to 9pm; and the **United Kingdom,** Thunovská 14, Praha 1 (☎ **02/24-51-04-39**), open Monday through Friday from 9am to noon. The nearest Australian embassy is in Vienna (see "Fast Facts: Vienna" in Chapter 29).

Emergencies   Prague's police and fire services can be reached by dialing **158** from any phone. To call an ambulance, dial 155.

Eyeglasses   A number of spectacle shops are located on Na příkopě and Wenceslas Square. Even if you forgot to bring your prescription with you, Lunettes Optika, Václavské nám. 51, Praha 1 (☎ **02/26-47-74**), can fit prescription glasses in about one hour. It's open Monday through Friday from 9am to 7pm and Saturday from 9am to 5pm. Visus Optik, Na příkopě 13, Praha 1 (☎ **02/24-21-24-54**), has a good selection of fashion frames and sells contact lens solutions. It's open Monday through Friday from 9am to 7pm and Saturday from 9am to 6pm.

Hospitals   In an emergency, dial 155 for an ambulance. University Hospital Motol, Vúvalu 84 (Motol), Praha 5 (☎ **02/52-95-10-70**), is particularly welcoming to foreigners and assures patients of English-speaking doctors. The doctors also make house calls.

Laundry/Dry Cleaning   Laundry Kings, 16 Dejvická, is an American-style coin-operated laundry. Washes cost 110 to 150 Kc ($3.95 to $5.35) per load, depending on how much drying power you need. There's someone there to do it for you for just 35 Kc ($1.25) additional, but this service takes at least 24 hours. Irons are available free for patrons' use. From the Hradcanska metro station, take the "Praha Dejvice" exit and turn left. Laundry Kings is open daily from 8am to 10pm.

Rapid Service, Francouzská 15, offers both dry cleaning and American-style shirt laundering. There are two other Rapid Service locations, at Dejvická 30 and Jecna 29.

Lost Property   If you lose something in Prague, it's probably gone for good, but optimists might try visiting the city's Lost Property Office, Bolzanova 5 (☎ **02/24-22-61-33**).

Luggage Storage/Lockers   The Ruzyně Airport Luggage Storage Office (☎ **02/36-78-14**) never closes and charges 55 Kč ($1.95) per item per day. Left-luggage offices are also available at the train stations, Hlavní Nádraží and Nádraží Holešovice. Both charge 20 Kč (70¢) per bag per day, and both are technically open 24 hours; if your train is departing late at night, double-check to make sure someone will be around. Luggage lockers are available in all of Prague's train stations, but they're not secure and should be avoided.

Finally, you don't need to tell the bellhop of a well-located fancy hotel that you're not one of its guests. At an economical average of 50 Kč ($1.80) per item, your bags can stay at the Páříž—even if you can't.

Newspapers/Magazines Two high-quality English-language newspapers are published here. *Prognosis,* published every Friday, is the more artsy of the two—a kind of *Village Voice,* with in-depth stories about Czech and Slovak social life. The ***Prague Post,*** published each Wednesday, is straighter and newsier. Between them, these papers offer the most comprehensive and up-to-date visitor information available.

The Czech-language ***Pěehled,*** a monthly listings booklet, is an excellent publication with information on theaters, galleries, concerts, clubs, films and other events around town. It costs 10 Kč (35¢) and is simple enough for non-Czechs to understand.

Photographic Needs Photo processing in Prague is more expensive than similar services Stateside. Fotografia Praha, Václavské nám. 50 (☎ 02/26-33-04), with 10 branches in Prague, is one of the best sources for most photographic needs.

Police In an emergency, dial 158. For other matters, contact the Central Police Station, Konviktská 14 (Staré Město), Praha 1 (☎ 02/24-13-11-11).

Post Office The main post office is at Jindřišská 14 (☎ 02/24-22-88-56), off Václavské náměstí, open 24 hours. This branch can send and receive faxes, and even has a special window for stamp collectors. There's also a post office on the lower level of the main train station, open Monday through Friday from 8am to 8pm and Saturday from 8am to 1pm; another one is inside the castle across from St. Vitus Cathedral, open daily from 8am to 7pm. There's also one at the airport.

Restrooms My first pick for restrooms are the lobby-level lavatories in the city's better-known hotels. Most restaurants and pubs also have restrooms you can use if you ask politely first.

Tax A 23% value-added tax (VAT) applies to most restaurant, hotel, and shop items and is included in the menu, rate card, or ticket price, rather than tacked on at the register.

Telephone The country code for the Czech Republic is 42. Prague's telephone area code is 02.

There are two kinds of pay phones in normal use. The first accepts coins while the other operates exclusively with a Phonecard, available from post offices and some hotels for 100 Kč ($3.60). The minimum cost of a **local call** is 1 Kč (4¢). You can deposit several coins at a time, but telephones don't make change, so unless you're calling long distance, use 1-Kč coins exclusively. Phonecard telephones automatically deduct the price of your call from the card. Cards are especially handy if you want to call abroad, as you don't have to continuously chuck in the change.

The fastest, most convenient way **to call the United States** from Europe is through USA Direct. This service bypasses the foreign operator and automatically links you to an AT&T operator in America. The access number in the Czech Republic is 0042-000-101. The same service is also offered through MCI: Dial 0042-000-112.

Tipping Rules for tipping are not as strict in Prague as they are in the United States, but when you're presented with good service, 10% to 15% is appreciated. Taxi drivers should get about 10%—unless they've already ripped you off, in which case they should get a good scolding.

Check restaurant menus to see if service is included before leaving an additional tip. Note that tipping is rare in pubs.

4 Accommodations

You may have heard about how cheap things are in Prague, but for reasons of supply and demand that doesn't pertain to hotels. Some experts believe that the situation is finally changing: As competition stiffens, quality is rising and prices are falling. Let's hope it's true.

There are several ways you can save money on hotels in Prague. Keep prices down by traveling off-season and off the beaten track. Politely negotiate the price of the room, especially if you sense that there are plenty of empty ones to choose from—you might find yourself paying 25% less than you expected. Negotiate a trade-off: a lower price for a smaller room, one without a TV, or one on the top floor. Ask if they'll offer a better rate if you stay several nights. If you're a student or an older traveler, ask for a special discount. Be pleasant, not pushy. Make it clear that you're shopping around; if the proprietor is not easily persuaded, try elsewhere or hope for better luck next time.

One of the least-expensive ways to keep a roof over your head is by taking advantage of hostels. Listed below are several places offering multishare accommodations.

ROOMS IN PRIVATE APARTMENTS Rooms in private apartments are a traveler's best defense against Prague's sky-high hotel rates. While heavy demand has encouraged most hotel owners to overprice their rooms, there's a glut of private apartment dwellers itching to trade accommodations for cash. Although few of these apartments are in the city center, most are within walking distance of a subway, tram, or bus stop. If you arrive in Prague by train, chances are you'll be approached by grandmothers offering their spare bedrooms. Several agencies carry listings and make reservations for tourists wishing to stay in private apartments. These include **Ave Ltd.,** in the train stations Hlavní Nádraží and Nádraží Holešovice (☎ **2/24-22-32-26;** fax 2/24-22-34-63); **Čedok,** Na příkopě 18 (☎ **2/24-19-71-11;** fax 2/232-16-56); and **Prague Suites,** Melantrichova 8, Praha 1 (☎ **2/24-22-99-61** or 24-23-04-67; fax 2/24-22-93-63).

DOUBLES FOR LESS THAN 2,100 KČ ($75)
NEAR OLD TOWN SQUARE

Pension Unitas
Bartolomějská 9, Praha 1. ☎ **2/232-77-00.** Fax 2/232-77-09. 12 rms, none with bath. 900 Kč ($32.15) single; 1,200 Kč ($42.85) double; 2,500 Kč ($89.30) triple. No credit cards.

Owned by the Sisters of Mercy (the nuns, not the rock band), this ascetically decorated hotel is just about as simple as you can get but is fantastically located in the middle of Old Town. Occupied by the Czech Secret Police in the 1950s, the basement room was once a prison where Václav Havel was incarcerated. You, too, can stay in the President's Cell, P6, though conditions don't seem to have improved much since Havel's day. It's cheerier upstairs, where the rooms are bright but basic. Smoking and drinking are banned, and there's a 1am curfew.

NEAR NÁMĚSTÍ REPUBLIKY

⑤ Axa

Na poříčí 40, 11000 Praha 1. ☎ **2/24-81-25-80.** Fax 2/232-21-72. 127 rms, 100 with bath; 5 suites. TEL. 1,500 Kč ($54) single with bath; 1,000 Kč ($37.70) double without bath, 2,500 Kč ($89.30) double with bath; 1,800 Kč ($64.30) triple without bath, 3,100 Kč ($110.70) triple with bath; from 2,000 Kč ($71.45) suite. Rates include continental breakfast. Children under 6 stay free in parents' room. MC, V. Metro: Line B to náměstí Republiky or Florenc.

Built in 1932 and completely overhauled in 1992, the Axa is a typical Prague hotel: drab outside and sterile inside. The lobby and rooms are white, functional, and almost devoid of decoration. The small front desk acts as a check-in, concierge, money exchange, and even newsstand. Frills are few, and so are towels. The beds are "Eastern European Specials"—thin mattresses on sofalike pullout beds. In addition to a simple bath that lacks counter space, most guest rooms contain little more than a narrow closet, a table, and two chairs; most have TVs. On the positive side, the Axa occupies a good location, close to náměstí Republiky; there's a six-lane indoor lap pool; and the rooms without private facilities are one of the best deals in Prague.

Opera

Těšnov 13, Praha 1. ☎ **2/231-56-09** or 231-57-35. Fax 2/231-24-77. 58 rms, 12 with bath. May–Sept, 1,100 Kč ($39.30) single without bath, 1,500 Kč ($53.60) single with bath; 1,500 Kč ($53.60) double without bath, 2,000 Kč ($71.40) double with bath; 1,900 Kč ($67.85) triple without bath, 2,400 Kč ($85.70) triple with bath. Oct–Apr, rates drop 10%. R ates include breakfast. AE, MC, V. Metro: Line B to Florenc.

As with many Prague hotels, you'll approach the stately Opera with great hopes—then will be disappointed that the interior lacks even a shred of the facade's charm. Popular with German tour groups, the Opera provides the most basic accommodations and services. Budget-style pine furnishings are set off by garish orange curtains. Rooms without private baths are outfitted with sinks, and all rooms have small original etchings on the walls.

The Opera is recommendable for being relatively clean and modestly priced when compared with others in the neighborhood. The hotel offers laundry/dry-cleaning services, and there's a restaurant/snack bar on the ground floor.

ON WENCESLAS SQUARE (VÁCLAVSKÉ NÁMĚSTÍ)

Hotel Evropa

Václavské nám. 25, Praha 1. ☎ **2/24-22-81-17** or 24-22-81-18. Fax 2/24-22-45-44. 104 rms, 50 with bath; 3 suites. 1,300 Kč ($46.45) single without bath, 2,100 Kč ($75) single with bath; 2,200 Kč ($78.60) double without bath, 2,800 Kč ($100) double with bath; 2,800 Kč ($100) triple without bath, 3,500 Kč ($125) triple with bath; 3,600 Kč ($128.60) quad without bath, 4,200 Kč ($150) quad with bath; from 3,900 Kč ($139.30) suite. Rates include breakfast. AE, MC, V. Metro: Line A or B to Můstek.

Erected in 1889 and rebuilt in the art nouveau style from 1903 to 1905, the Evropa remains one of the most magnificent turn-of-the-century structures in Prague. The fantastic statue-topped facade is wrapped with hand-sculpted wrought-iron railings. Seats on the outdoor terrace of the ground-floor café are some of the city's most coveted—for style and people-watching, not for food or service.

The rooms are adequate at best, shabby at worst. The best ones are the front doubles, six with balconies overlooking Wenceslas Square; these are relatively large and have high ceilings. The furnishings are limited to beds and a table, with belle art practically unknown. The baths contain aging tubs, hand-held showers, and few towels. The worst rooms are windowless, bathless, charmless boxes tucked way in the back. There's no trick to getting a good room here—luck is the only mitigator. Reservations are accepted by fax. Even if you choose not to check-in, the hotel is definitely worth checking out.

NEAR NÁMĚSTÍ MÍRU

Hotel Juventus
Blanická 10, Praha 2. ☎ **2/25-51-51.** Fax 2/25-51-53. 20 rms, none with bath. 1,000 Kč ($35.70) single; 1,700 Kč ($60.70) double. Rates include breakfast. No credit cards. Metro: Line A to náměstí Míru.

This is just about as basic a place as you can find in central Prague. The rooms are downright sparse—no phones, TVs, or even clocks. However, you'll get a writing desk and high ceilings. A couple of small paintings on the walls constitute the decorations. All rooms have sinks with cold and hot running water (sometimes). The management is considering adding showers to all rooms, an improvement that will likely raise rates. I hope they also renovate the shabby lobby bar, in which patrons must strain to hear one another over the ever-trumpeting TV.

DOUBLES FOR LESS THAN 3,200 KČ ($114)
NEAR NÁMĚSTÍ REPUBLIKY

Atlantic
Na poříčí 9, Praha 1. ☎ **2/24-81-10-84.** Fax 2/24-81-23-78. 60 rms, all with bath; 1 suite. TV TEL. 2,850 Kč ($101.80) single; 3,400 Kč ($121.45) double; 3,950 Kč ($141.10) suite. Rates include breakfast. Additional person 700 Kč ($25) extra. AE, MC, V. Metro: Line B to náměstí Republiky.

Built in 1845 and named the English Court, this hotel catered to society's elite until it fell into disrepair around the turn of the century. Rebuilt in 1935, the five-story Atlantic has never reclaimed its past prestige; instead, it's become one of the best in its moderate class, notable for a fine location and ample (though simply furnished) rooms. It would be a mistake to expect too much from this place, which completed its last makeover just months before the Communist regime fell in 1989. Behind the lobby is a pleasant wood-paneled restaurant/lounge, and the hotel offers laundry, dry cleaning, theater booking, and other concierge services.

NEAR NÁMĚSTÍ MÍRU

Anna Hotel
Budečská 17, Praha 2. ☎ **02/25-75-39** or 24-24-60-32. 23 rms, all with bath. 1,900 Kč ($67.85) single; 3,000 Kč ($107.15) double. No credit cards. Metro: Line A to náměstí Míru.

The area behind the immense National Museum on Wenceslas Square is called Vinohrady and was once planted with the king's vineyards. Today it's a good-looking working-class neighborhood largely unknown to tourists. The Anna Hotel is located here, about 15 minutes' walk from Wenceslas Square. The hotel is spartan and clean, with few decorations and bright white baths. The nearby restaurants and pubs are as authentically Czech as you can get—at prices that most tourists in Old Town only dream of.

Hotel Luník

Londýnská 50, Praha 2. ☎ **2/25-27-01.** Fax 2/25-66-17. 35 rms, all with bath. 1,900 Kč ($67.85) single; 2,200 Kč ($78.60) double. Rates include breakfast. No credit cards. Metro: Line A to náměstí Míru.

Behind the Luník's off-white faux-stucco front, which brandishes beautiful wooden windows, is a hotel so modest you'd think that you're in a hostel. A small elevator takes guests up to 31 identical twin-bedded doubles and four singles that have matching wooden beds and closets but no chairs, desks, or lamps. However, some have TVs. The only redeeming features of the hotel's complete 1992 gutting and rebuilding are showers that are pleasantly tiled from floor to ceiling and full-length mirrors.

IN KAMPA

Hotel Kampa

Všehrdova 16 (Malá Strana), Praha 1. ☎ **2/24-51-04-09.** Fax 2/24-51-03-77. 85 rms, all with bath. TEL. 1,900 Kč ($67.85) single; 3,000 Kč ($107.15) double; 4,200 Kč ($150) triple. AE, MC, V. Metro: Line A to Malostranská.

On one of the cutest and quietest streets in Prague, the Kampa occupies what was an armory built at the beginning of the 17th century. Although the hotel was renovated in 1992, the rehab was under the direction of the most modest decorator. The rooms are incredibly simple and despite their price will not be acceptable to first-class travelers. Singles are literally furnished with one single bed and a stand-alone wardrobe. There's no decoration on most walls, and the baths are compact. The doubles are larger and marginally nicer. Try to get one of the doubles with an extra bed, as these are the largest rooms. The restaurant serves lunch and dinner, but the smartest guests dine elsewhere.

ELSEWHERE

Botel *Albatros*

Nábřeží Ludvíka Svobody (at the end of Revoluční on the River Vltava), Praha 1. ☎ **2/24-81-05-41** or 231-36-00. Fax 2/24-81-12-14. 80 rms, all with bath; 4 suites. TEL. 2,019 Kč ($72.10) single; 2,546 Kč ($90.95) double; 4,037 Kč ($144.20) triple; from 4,509 Kč ($161) suite. Rates include breakfast. AE, MC, V. Tram 5, 14, 26, or 53.

The permanently moored blue-and-white *Albatros* is a converted hotel boat, or "botel." It's no *Queen Mary*, though. The rooms are predictably cramped, just large enough to accommodate two single beds and a tiny table. At the near end of the berth is a diminutive closet and bath devoid of counter space. There's a radio in each room, but no TV. Suites, toward the back of the boat, are exceptions to these otherwise restricted accommodations. Particularly bright and large, each enjoys wraparound windows. Although there's a small restaurant on the boat, guests will have more fun on the lively bar barge docked just behind the *Albatros*.

Hotel Ostaš

Orebitská 8, Praha 3. ☎ **2/627-93-86.** Fax 2/627-94-18. 30 rms, all with bath; 2 suites. TEL. 1,400 Kč ($50) single; 2,600 Kč ($92.85) double; 3,000 Kč ($107.15) triple; from 4,400Kc ($157.15) suite. Rates include breakfast. No credit cards. Tram 133, 168, or 207.

Known primarily to German tour groups, the Ostaš is nothing to write home about—and just barely good enough to be included here. The ascetic rooms contain little more than beds and bureaus. And although the hotel was completely remodeled in 1992, the furnishings and lighting are strictly functional, only suites have TVs, and guests cannot obtain an outside line directly from their bedside phones. Rates here are stiff even by Prague standards. If you do decide to stay here, hard bargaining is in order.

SUPER-BUDGET CHOICES
YOUTH HOSTELS

There are several dormitory-style accommodations in Prague. Unfortunately, most are far from the center, necessitating both a metro and a bus ride to reach them. Still, they're cheap, and you'll meet lots of other travelers there.

Hostel Sokol

Hellichova 1, Praha 1. ☎ **2/53-45-51** ext. 397. 100 beds. 200 Kč ($7.15) per person. No credit cards. Closed Oct–May.

There's a lot lacking at this hostel: The beds are packed 10 to 12 per room, the management enforces a 12:30am curfew, and cleanliness is suspect. But the Sokol earns mention here for its absolutely fantastic location: in the heart of Malá Strana, a short walk from Charles Bridge. Open only from June to September, the hostel is closed daily between 10am and 3pm.

Hostel Týnská

Týnská 17, Praha 1. ☎ **2/231-25-09.** 80 beds. 210 Kč ($7.50) per person. Rates include breakfast. Closed Oct–May.

There's not much to recommend about this hostel open from June to September, except for its superlative location 150 feet from Old Town Square. About 40 bunk beds are crammed into a single subterranean gymnasium, bisected by a long partition separating men and women. The baths are far from spotless, but the showers are hot. A currency-exchange desk and a luggage-deposit box are available, and the hostel is open 24 hours.

The Strahov Hostels

Spartakiádní, Praha 6. 1,500 beds (no rms with bath). 230–280 Kč ($8.20–$10) per person. Closed Oct–May. From the city center, take metro Line A to Dejvická, then bus no. 143, 149, or 217 to Strahov Stadium; it's a 20-minute trip in all.

Across from the giant Strahov Stadium, the Strahov Hostels were built to house athletes for intra–Eastern European Olympic-style games that were held annually before the fall of Communism. Today these dozen concrete high-rises are students' homes throughout the school year and budget tourist hotels during summer, June to September only. Most rooms are doubles, none has a private bath, and all are open 24 hours.

At least four companies have contracted with the city to operate these summer hostels. Accommodations in each are identical, but services and prices vary slightly. **ESTEC Hostel** (☎ **02/52-73-44**) is the best known, probably because it runs the buildings closest to the road, which are the ones tourists first see. The **Petros** (☎ **02/35-44-43**) and **Sakbuild** (☎ **02/35-44-42** or 52-06-55) hostels are immediately adjacent to each other and should be compared for price before committing.

5 Dining

While conversations in the West always return to love, discussions in Prague always revert to food. Foreigners swap restaurant tips like trading cards—my favorite Chinese place for your best local pub—and when it comes to cuisine, no expatriate is opinionless. News about new restaurant openings travels fast, and menu and chef changes are familiar topics of conversation. Seldom will any single eatery gain high marks for an entire menu. "Choose carefully" is tacked onto every restaurant recommendation, along with an implied disclaimer that it was good last time—but next time, who knows? I've been to an untold number of restaurants where the preparations were excellent but the ingredients were (to Western standards) substandard: Meals made with fruit that should have been juiced and chicken that should have been ground into fast-food "nuggets." It's hard not to pity the proud chefs who have to do the best they can with low-quality ingredients. Prague's chefs do their best with game. When it's available, order goose, duck, or venison and you'll rarely be disappointed.

MEALS FOR LESS THAN 170 KČ ($6)
NEAR WENCESLAS SQUARE (VÁCLAVSKÉ NÁMÊSTÍ)

Country Life
Jungmannova 1, Praha 1. Main courses 25–55 Kč (90¢–$2). No credit cards. Mon–Thurs 9am–6:30pm, Fri 9am–3pm. Metro: Line B to Národní třida. VEGETARIAN.

Among dried beans, fresh breads, and shelves of biblical books, this Seventh Day Adventist–run health-food store/restaurant offers a strictly meatless menu served cafeteria style in pleasant, woody surroundings. Appetizers like bread with tofu spread, tomatoes, cucumbers, and shredded cabbage are followed by main courses that include spicy goulash; vegetable salads; zesty wheat-bread pizza topped with red pepper, garlic, and onions; and vegetable burgers served on multigrain buns with garlic-yogurt dressing. Everything is available to go. After procuring your food from the counter, carry your plate up to the small dining loft.

A second Country Life, offering a similar menu with only stand-up dining, is at Melantrichová 15, Praha 1. It's open Monday through Thursday from 8:30am to 7pm, Friday from 8:30am to 2:30pm, and Sunday from noon to 6pm.

Harvey's
Václavské nám. 18, Praha 1. ☎ 02/24-23-90-16. 26–60 Kč (95¢–$2.15). No credit cards. Daily 7am–midnight. Metro: Line A or B to Můstek. BURGERS.

The sole Czech outpost of Canada's most popular hamburger chain, Harvey's not only sells burgers to rival McDonald's (across the street) but also serves healthful grilled chicken-breast sandwiches and uses fresh vegetables that are unheard of at the U.S.–based chain. Harvey's is also one of the few eateries in the city to keep such long hours.

Obchod Čerstvých Uzenin
Václavské nám. 36. 30–55 Kč ($1.05–$2). No credit cards. Mon–Fri 7:30am–7pm, Sat 8am–6pm, Sun 10am–4:30pm. Metro: Line A or B to Můstek. CZECH DELICATESSEN.

On the ground floor of the Melantrich Building, from which Václav Havel addressed the throngs during the 1989 revolution, this delicatessen is something you should try not to miss. Vegetarians hurry past the meaty aromas wafting over the short line of patrons that often forms out the door. The front of the shop is a take-out deli offering dozens of kinds of cooked and smoked meat, sausage, and salami. In back is a small restaurant where cooked meats and beer are served without side dishes or airs, just a dollop of mustard and a slice of dense bread. You have to eat standing up, but the selection is extensive, you can't get it any fresher, and prices are pure Czech. Expect to pay about 55 Kč ($2) for a plate of meat and a beer.

NEAR OLD TOWN SQUARE (STAROMĚSTSKÉ NÁMĚSTÍ)

Bona Vita

Dlouha 4 (one block from Old Town Square, behind and to the left of the Jan Hus statue), Praha 1. ☎ **02/231-13-76.** 35–40 Kč ($1.25–$1.45). No credit cards. Mon–Sat 10am–10pm, Sun 11am–10pm. Metro: Line A to Staroměstská. HEALTH/ INTERNATIONAL.

This unusual cafeteria-style restaurant, opened as a showplace for a local packaged soy product, demonstrates all the wonderful things that can be done with dried soy meat. The chewy results include soy with curry, stir-fried soy, soy with chili, soy burgers, and other somewhat-inventive dishes. Chicken, steak, and sandwiches are also available. The dining room is clean and bright, with mirrored walls and blond wood furnishings.

Hogo Fogo

Salvátorská 4, Praha 1. ☎ **02/231-70-23.** Main courses 35–70 Kč ($1.25–$2.50). AE, MC, V. Mon–Fri noon–midnight, Sat–Sun noon–2am. Metro: Line A to Staroměstská. CZECH.

It's hard to determine exactly what attracts Hogo Fogo's loyal following of Americans and Czechs in their 20s. The bare basement dining room is unremarkable, the service is sluggish, and most of the food is just tolerable. There are some menu stand-outs, however (lentil soup and fried cheese are two); the rock music is good, and everything's incredibly cheap, especially for a restaurant just two blocks from Old Town Square. Half liters of beer are just 30 Kč ($1.05), and diners can sit all day if they wish.

IN MALÁ STRANA

Jo's Bar

Malostranské nám. 7, Praha 1. Main courses 100–170 Kč ($3.60–$6.10). No credit cards. Daily 11am–1pm. Metro: Line A to Malostranská. MEXICAN.

A chief hangout for U.S. visitors in their 20s, Jo's is packed most evenings and weekends with those craving something other than pork and potatoes. Unfortunately for the house, however, that craving isn't for the restaurant's mediocre Mexican cooking—it's for the beer, plus the camaraderie with other English speakers. Jo's is kind of a dive, but in a country where breakfast is practically an unknown meal, this place saves the day with passable breakfast burritos and other egg dishes. For good tacos, guacamole, and salsa, wait until you return home.

NEAR NÁMĚSTÍ MÍRU

Na Zvonařce (At the Bell)

Šafaříkova 1, Praha 2. ☎ **02/69-10-04-48.** Main courses 30–80 Kč ($1.05–$2.85). V. Daily 10am–11pm. Metro: Line C to I. P. Pavlova. CZECH.

First a pub for bellmakers, then a dingy Communist-era restaurant, Na Zvona_ce has blossomed into one of the best all-around Czech restaurants in Prague. You'll find a book-size menu (in English), relatively good service, a terrific shaded outdoor patio, and top-of-the-line food. And this real find is reasonably priced. Meals are strictly Czech favorites: roast duck with dumplings and cabbage, pork tongue with potatoes . . . you get the idea. When it's available, Na Zvona_ce makes one of the best grilled whole trouts in town. Beef in cream sauce with wheat dumplings also gets high marks, along with great Plžen Urquell beer.

Radost F/X

Bělehradská 120, Praha 2. ☎ **02/25-12-10.** Main courses 50–80 Kč ($1.80–$2.85). MC, V. Daily noon–6am. Metro: Line C to I. P. Pavlova. VEGETARIAN.

One of Prague's only real vegetarian restaurants, Radost is recommendable for its good soups, like garlicky spinach and oniony lentil, and its hearty sandwiches, like tofu with stir-fried vegetables. Some disappointments are anchovyless Greek salad and lackluster pizzas, but for the most part Radost is worthy of praise.

The restaurant, looking more like a café than a serious dining establishment, is located above a popular American-style dance club of the same name (see "Prague After Dark," later in this chapter). Radost is also one of the only restaurants that's open all night. Its fine Bloody Marys complement the 5am breakfasts.

MEALS FOR LESS THAN 350 KČ ($12.50)
NEAR WENCESLAS SQUARE (VÁCLAVSKE NÁMĚSTÍ)

Gany's

Národní třída 20, Praha 1. ☎ **02/29-76-65** or 29-72-23. Reservations suggested. Main courses 70–150 Kč ($2.50–$5.35). AE, DC, MC, V. Daily 8am–11pm. Metro: Line A or B to Můstek. CZECH/INTERNATIONAL.

Don't be discouraged by the disheveled entrance leading up two dingy flights to this restaurant. Ignore the Riviera Disco and enter a bona-fide institution that's, literally and figuratively, one of Prague's brightest restaurants. Gany's is a successful amalgam of new and old: Its fabulously understated art nouveau interior, complete with original globe chandeliers, has been perfectly restored and enlivened with trendy period-style oil paintings. Gany's curious combination of cuisines means a choice of starters like smoked salmon, battered and fried asparagus, and ham au gratin with vegetables, plus entrees encompassing trout with horseradish to beans with garlic sauce. In between is an arm's-length list of chicken, beef, veal, and pork dishes, each drowned in a complementary, if not extraordinary, sauce.

Kmotra Pizzeria

Jirchářích 12 (about three blocks from K-Mart), Praha 1. ☎ **02/24-91-58-09.** Pizzas 150–250 Kč ($5.35–$8.95). No credit cards. Daily 11am–1am. Metro: Line B to Národní třída. ITALIAN.

This Neapolitan-style restaurant serves the best thin-crust pizza in Prague. The cavernous dining rooms, on two floors, seem perpetually packed, and the wait can be long at the height of the dinner hour. The crowd can get loud, but it's always lively and fun.

NEAR NÁMĚSTÍ REPUBLIKY

Red, Hot, & Blues

Jakubská 12, Praha 1. ☎ **02/231-46-39.** Reservations suggested. Main courses 95–270 Kč ($3.40–$9.65). AE, MC, V. Daily 11am–11pm. Metro: Line B to náměstí Republiky. AMERICAN/CREOLE/CAJUN.

There are two rooms in this trendy American-owned eatery: a small front bar and a slightly larger dining room where live jazz is played nightly. During summer, a ceilingless atrium opens for eating and drinking and the musicians often move outside, too. Popular with Americans in their 20s who seem happy to be eating anything other than roasted meats, this restaurant attracts few connoisseurs with its food. The most recommendable choices are the avocadoless nachos and excellent toasted vegetable and chicken sandwiches, both served on French bread. Red,

Hot, & Blues shines brightest on Saturday and Sunday, when it serves the only good à la carte brunch in town. There's a full bar.

Zlatá Ulička (Golden Lane)

Masná 9, Praha 1. ☎ **02/232-08-84.** Main courses 90–150 Kč ($3.20–$5.35). No credit cards. Daily 10am–midnight. Metro: Line B to náměstí Republiky. CZECH/ SERBIAN.

Hidden among Old Town's back streets near St. Jakub's Church and named after the Hradčany street of colorful 16th-century cottages, the pint-sized Zlatá Ulička is one of central Prague's unique finds. Designed by a Sarajevo architect, the interior has been transformed into a surreal Renaissance-era courtyard, surrounded by yellow-and-blue faux-cottage facades complete with shingle roofs. Stereo speakers sing from birdcages, a ladder climbs to nowhere, and several gold plaques, inscribed with wistful Serbian-language poems, are embedded in the floor. One translates in part "maybe tomorrow the ships will come."

Many of the dishes served here may seem similar to those found at any number of Czech restaurants, but once you taste your food you'll discover its Serbian qualities: savory spices that are almost completely absent in Bohemia. Whole trout is pan-fried in olive oil with garlic and parsley, giant homemade hamburgers are enlivened with a medley of piquant spices, while the very traditional Serbian shish kebab alternates marinated veal and vegetables. Other items worth mentioning include the grilled mushrooms appetizer, French-style crêpes, and veal medallions fried and topped with cheese, sour cream, and mushroom sauce.

NEAR NÁM STÍ MÍRU

Elite

Korunni 1, náměstí Míru, Praha 2. ☎ **02/25-88-44.** Reservations suggested. Main courses 95–175 Kč ($3.40–$6.25). No credit cards. Daily 11am–10pm. Metro: Line A to náměstí Míru. CZECH/ITALIAN.

There are two Elites in the same restaurant: The first is a large downstairs dining room that's too bright, loud, and impersonal; the second is up on the balcony, where shadows are long and conversations intimate. The menu, the same in both places, curiously combines Czech and Italian dishes. All the local "hits" are here, including chicken, cabbage, duck, and beef. If you don't expect Roman standards, you'll find the Italian offerings surprisingly enjoyable, pizzas notwithstanding. Of the half a dozen pasta entrees, the tagliatelle with salmon-cream sauce rates best. Like other pasta dishes here, it's loaded with big chunks of meat and filling enough to constitute an entire meal.

CAFES & TEAROOMS

Cafe Evropa

Václavské nám. 25, Praha 1. ☎ **02/24-22-81-17.** Café au lait 31 Kč ($1.10); pastries 30–100 Kč ($1.05–$3.60). AE, MC, V. Daily 7am–midnight. Metro: Line A or B to Můstek. CAFE.

Spin through the etched-glass revolving door into the other-worldliness of Prague's finest art nouveau café. Built in 1906, the Evropa is bedecked with period chandeliers and hand-carved woods, all made more elegant by musicians who entertain every afternoon. Drinks are expensive and service is terrible, but compared to Western standards it's cheap and few diners are in a mood to hurry. There's a 20-Kč (70¢) cover charge after 3pm.

Dobrá Čajovna

Václavské nám. 14, Praha 1. Small pot of tea 35 Kč ($1.25). No credit cards. Mon–Sat noon–9:30pm, Sun 3–9:30pm. Metro: Line A or B to Můstek. TEA.

Inside this café's intimate pillow-covered cavern, you'll find it difficult to discern whether you're in Prague or Pakistan. Hidden at the end of a narrow passage, across Wenceslas Square from the Ambassador Hotel, Dobrá Čajovna is truly one of the city's greatest hidden finds. It's not for everyone, mind you: Most patrons sit on the floor, and the teahouse has a decidedly New Age bent. Order at the front counter, which doubles as a health and spiritual-gift shop, then take a seat in the tea den.

A second, even more exotic Dobrá Čajovna is inside the Roxy dance club (see "Prague After Dark," later in this chapter), open from 5pm to midnight.

Dolce Vita

Široká 15 (half a block off Pařížská), Praha 1. ☎ 02/232-91-92. Cappuccino 35 Kč ($1.25); pastries 35–110 Kč ($1.25–$3.95). No credit cards. Daily 8am–11pm. Metro: Line A to Staroměstská. CAFE.

In Prague's old Jewish Quarter is the city's finest Italian café. An excellent espresso machine, operated by people who know how to use it, is the café's primary draw. But comfortable seating, a good-looking see-and-be-seen crowd, and light pastries and ice creams are great pluses.

The Globe

Janovského 14, Praha 7. Sandwiches and desserts 70–110 Kč ($2.50–$3.95). No credit cards. Daily 10am–midnight. Metro: Line C to Vltavská. Tram 1, 3, 5, 8, 12, 14, 17, 25, or 26. CAFE.

Prague's only bookstore/coffeehouse is not only the best place in the city for used paperback literature and nonfiction but also one of the most conducive places for young U.S. expatriates to meet. The smart-looking bar serves espresso-based drinks, sandwiches, salads, and desserts and stocks a full bar.

WORTH THE EXTRA MONEY

Vínárna u Maltézských Rytířů (Wine Tavern of the Knights of Malta)

Prokopská 10, Praha 1. ☎ 02/53-66-50 or 53-63-57. Reservations recommended. Main courses 115–350 Kč ($4.10–$12.50). AE, MC. Daily 11am–11pm. Metro: Line A to Malostranská. CZECH.

For price, service, and a warm welcome, Nadia and Vitězslav Černík's Knights of Malta is one of the best small restaurants in Malá Strana. There are just 4 tables in the dignified ground-floor dining room, with another 10 or so in the cavernlike cellar.

A short menu usually indicates intelligent preparations and fresh food, and the somewhat meager list here is no exception. Chateaubriand, filet mignon, pork filet, and shish kebab are four of the five main courses; the fifth is Prague's all-purpose vegetable au gratin. It's likely Nadia will recommend something special, such as the wonderful chicken with pineapple and walnuts that she created for *Prague Post* editor-in-chief Alan Levy. If you phone in advance and say that Frommer's sent you, Nadia will promise to save you a piece of her homemade apple strudel—a scrumptious yet not-too-sweet nutty fruit pie that's served warm.

6 Attractions

SIGHTSEEING SUGGESTIONS

If You Have 1 Day

The best sights in Prague are outside. Walk around Old Town Square, Charles Bridge, and Wenceslas Square and get lost in the tiny winding cobblestone alleys of Old Town and Malá Strana.

If You Have 2 Days

Spend your first day as suggested above. On your second, visit Prague Castle in the morning and spend the afternoon around Old Town Square, visiting Old Town Hall, the Old New Synagogue, and the Old Jewish Cemetery.

If You Have 3 Days

After visiting the above-mentioned sights on Days 1 and 2, expand your sightseeing to include the Strahov Monastery and the Municipal House (Obecní dům) and explore New Town (Nové Město).

If You Have 5 Days Or More

Visit the National Galleries and the Bertramka/Mozart Museum. Take your time and visit some of the city's cafés and pubs. Take an organized tour or visit one or more of the towns that surround Prague.

TOP ATTRACTIONS

Pražský Hrad (Prague Castle)

Hradčany. ☎ **02/33-37-33-68** or 333-71-11. Admission: Castle, 90 KČ ($3.20); St. Vitus Cathedral and Golden Lane, free. Daily 9am–5pm (to 4pm in winter). Metro: Line A to Malostranská or Hradčanská.

The huge hilltop complex known collectively as Prague Castle encompasses dozens of houses, towers, churches, courtyards, and fountains. A visit to the castle could easily take an entire day (or even more), depending on how thorough your exploration is.

St. Vitus Cathedral is not just the most dominant part of the castle but also, historically, the most important. Constructed in A.D. 926 as the court church of the Přemyslid princes, the cathedral has long been the center of Prague's religious and political life. It was named after St. Vitus, a wealthy 4th-century Sicilian martyr who became Bohemia's major patron saint. Of the massive gothic cathedral's 21 chapels, the **Chapel of St. Wenceslas** stands out as one of the few indoor sights in Prague that every visitor really should try to see. Decorated with paintings from the 14th to the 16th century and encrusted with hundreds of pieces of jasper and amethyst, the chapel sits atop the site of the famous saint's grave.

The **Royal Palace,** in the castle's third courtyard, was the residence of Bohemian kings and princes for over 700 years, beginning in the 9th century. Massive vaulted Vladislav Hall, the interior's centerpiece, was used for coronations and special occasions. The adjacent Diet was where the king met with his advisers and where the supreme court was held. In the 20th century, Czechoslovakia's presidents have been inaugurated here.

Prague

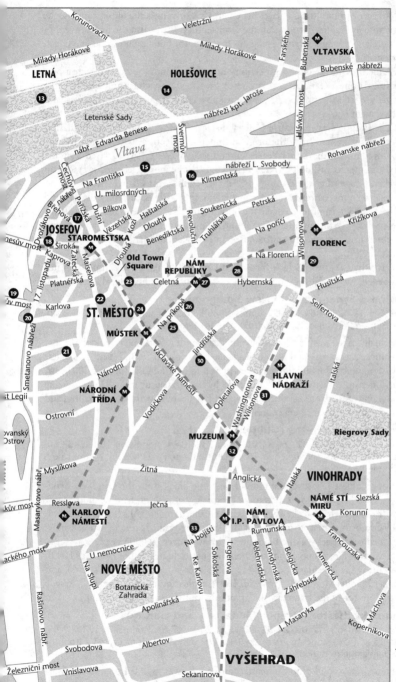

Adjacent to the Royal Palace, **St. George's Convent** is the oldest romanseque structure in Prague, dating from the 10th century. It was also the first convent in Bohemia. No longer serving a religious function, the building now houses a Czech art museum.

A picturesque street of 16th-century houses built into the castle fortifications, **Golden Lane** (Zlatá ulička) is one of Prague's most charming roads. Once home to castle sharpshooters, the houses now contain small shops, galleries, and refreshment bars.

The **Prague Castle Picture Gallery** displays European and Bohemian master-pieces, but few are from the original imperial collection, which was virtually destroyed during the Thirty Years' War. Of the works that have survived from the days of Emperors Rudolph II and Ferdinand III, the most celebrated is Hans von Aachen's *Portrait of a Girl* (1605–10), depicting the artist's daughter.

Like seemingly everything else in Prague, the castle is currently undergoing major changes. In order to make the building more accessible to the public, plans are under way to remodel and rebuild, the enhancements to be paid for by revenues from restaurants, coffeehouses, and even a hotel that are proposed for the castle site.

Visit the **Prague Castle Information Center**, Vikářská 37, behind St. Vitus Cathedral, for a good selection of guidebooks, maps, and other related information.

Staronová Synagóga (Old New Synagogue)

Červená 2. ☎ **02/24-81-00-99**. Admission 80 Kč ($2.85) adults, 40 Kč ($1.45) students. Sun–Fri 9:30am–5:30pm. Metro: Line A to Staroměstská.

Originally called the New Synagogue (to distinguish it from an even older one that no longer exists), the Old New Synagogue, built around 1270, is Europe's oldest Jewish temple. The building has been prayed in continuously for over 700 years, only interrupted between 1941 and 1945 by the Nazi occupation. The synagogue is also one of the largest gothic buildings in Prague, built with vaulted ceilings and fitted with Renaissance-era columns.

Starý Židovský Hřbitov (Old Jewish Cemetery)

U Starého hřbitova. ☎ **02/24-81-00-99** or 232-18-14. Admission 100 Kč ($3.60) adults, 50 Kč ($1.80) children. Sun–Thurs 9am–5:30pm, Fri 9am–3pm. Metro: Line A to Staroměstská.

Europe's oldest Jewish burial ground, just one block from the Old New Synagogue, was begun in 1439. Because the local government of the time didn't allow Jews to bury their dead elsewhere, graves were dug as much as 12 bodies deep, with each tombstone placed in front of the last. The result is one of world's most crowded cemeteries—a one-block area filled with over 20,000 graves.

The most famous people buried here are the celebrated Rabbi Loew (d. 1609), who made the legendary Golem (a clay "monster" to protect Prague's Jews), and banker Markus Mordechai Maisel (d. 1601), at the time the richest man in Prague and protector of the city's Jewish community during Rudolph II's reign.

Strahovský Klášter (Strahov Monastery and Library)

Strahovské nádvoří. ☎ **02/24-51-11-45** or 24-51-03-55. Admission 30 Kč (1.05) adults, 15 Kč (55¢) students. Tues–Sun 9am–12:15pm and 1–5pm. Tram 22 from the Malostranská metro station.

Strahov, the second-oldest monastery in Prague, was founded high above Malá Strana in 1143 by Vladislav II. It's still home to Premonstratensian monks, a schol-arly order closely related to the Jesuits. Unfortunately, the monks' dormitories and refectory are off-limits. What draws visitors here are the monastery's ornate libraries, which hold almost a million volumes. Over the centuries the monks have assembled one of the world's best collections of philosophical and theological texts, including many illuminated manuscripts and first editions. The Philosophical Library's 46-foot-high ceilings are decorated with carved wood and frescos. Ancient wooden printing presses, downstairs in the Museum of Czech Literature, are also worth visiting.

The monastery also houses several two-dimensional altars and the remains of St. Norbert, a 10th-century German-born saint who founded the Premonstratensian order. His bones were brought here in 1627, when he became one of Bohemia's 10 patron saints.

Staroměstské Radnice (Old Town Hall) and Orloj (Astronomical Clock)

Staromestské náměstí (Old Town Square). ☎ **02/24-48-20-88** or 24-48-27-51. Admission: Tower, 15 Kč (55¢) adults, 10 Kč (35¢) students and children. May–Oct, Tues–Sun 9am–6pm; Nov–Apr, Tues–Sun 9am–5pm. Metro: Line A to Staroměstská.

Crowds congregate hourly in front of the Old Town Hall's Astronomical Clock to witness the glockenspiel spectacle that occurs daily from 8am to 8pm. Constructed in 1410, the clock has long been an important symbol of Prague. According to legend, when the timepiece was remodeled at the end of the 15th century, clock artist Master Hanus was blinded by members of the Municipal Council so he could not repeat his fine work elsewhere. In retribution, Hanus threw himself into the clock mechanism and promptly died. The clock was out of kilter for almost a century.

It's not possible to determine the time of day from this timepiece; you have to look at the clock on the very top of the Old Town Hall's tower for that. This astronomical clock, with all its hands and markings, is meant to mark the phases of the moon, the equinoxes, the season and the day, and innumerable Christian holidays.

When the clock strikes the hour, viewers are treated to a kind of medieval morality play. Two cuckoo-clock doors slide open and the statues of the 12 Apostles glide by, while the 15th-century conception of the "evils" of life—the skeleton of Death, a preening Vanity, a corrupt Turk, and an acquisitive Jew—shake and dance below. At the conclusion of World War II, the horns and beard were removed from the moneybag-holding Jew, who's now politely referred to as "Greed."

It's worth climbing the Town Hall tower for an excellent view over the red rooftops of Old Town Square and the surrounding area.

MORE ATTRACTIONS

České Muzeum Vytvarných Umení (Czech Museum of Fine Arts)

Celetná 34, Praha 1. ☎ **02/23-22-46-27.** Admission 20 Kč (70¢) adults, 10 Kč (35¢) students. Tues–Sun 8am–6pm. Metro: Line B to nàmestí Republiky.

Located in the House of the Black Madonna, one of Prague's finest cubist buildings, the new Museum of Fine Arts is dedicated to cubist art, a form that flourished in Prague early in this century. The best works include an Otto Gutfreund bronze statue and an oak chair designed by Pavel Janák. The museum also houses a collection of Czech modern art and is hosting major international exhibitions beginning with one from New York City's Whitney Museum of American Art.

Obecní dům (Municipal House)

Nám. Republiky 5, Praha 1. ☎ **02/232-58-58.** Metro: Line B to náměstí Republiky.

The architectural part of the art nouveau movement that swept across Europe in the second half of the 19th century developed in tandem with the Continent's Industrial Revolution. Innovative building materials—primarily steel and glass—opened endless possibilities for artistic flourishes and embellishments. Architects abandoned traditional pseudohistorical-style stone structures for ones more in keeping with their asthetics. There are several excellent examples of whimsical art nouveau architecture in Prague, though none is more flamboyant that the Municipal House (Obecní dům), built between 1906 and 1911. The building has been an important cultural symbol since the country of Czechoslovakia was signed into existence here in 1918. The building is Prague's outstanding monument to itself and its citizens, lushly encrusted inside and out with paintings and ornaments. The recently renovated facade is one of the city's most eye-catching. The interior is an extravaganza of painted murals, mosaics, sculptures, stained glass, and ironwork. Its most important room, Smetana Hall, has a roof made of stained-glass windows and is the home of the Prague Symphony Orchestra.

Lennon Wall

Velkopřevprské náměstí, Praha 1. Metro: Line A to Malostranská.

One of the city's most photographed attractions is this colorful graffiti-covered wall on a quiet side street in Malá Strana's Kampa neighborhood near the Charles Bridge. Named after the famous Beatle whose huge image is spray-painted in the wall's center, this is a kind of pilgrimage site for young locals and tourists who regularly pay homage with flowers and candles.

Following his 1980 murder, John Lennon became a hero of pacifism and subculture throughout Eastern Europe, and this monument was born. During Communist rule, the wall was regularly whitewashed, only to be repainted by the city's faithful. When the new democratically elected government was installed in 1989, it's said that the French ambassador, whose stately offices are directly across from the wall, phoned Prague's mayor and asked that the city government refrain from interfering with the monument.

Národní Muzeum (National Museum)

Václavské nám. 68, Praha 1. ☎ **02/24-23-04-85.** Admission 30 Kč ($1.05) adults, 15 Kč (55¢) students, free for children 5 and under, and for everyone on the first Mon of each month. Wed–Mon 9am–5pm. Metro: Line A or C to Muzeum.

The National Museum, dominating upper Wenceslas Square, looks so much like an important government building that it even fooled the Communists who fired on it during their 1968 invasion. If you look closely you can still see shell pockmarks. The second-oldest museum in the Czech lands, it was opened in 1893. Built in neo-Renaissance style, the museum now houses two floors of exhibits. On the first floor is an exhaustive collection of Czechoslovakian minerals, rocks, and meteorites. Only 12,000 of the museum's collection of over 200,000 rocks and gems are on display, all neatly arranged in old wooden cases.

The second floor features exhibits on the ancient history of these lands, as well as zoological and paleontological displays. Throughout the "prehistory" exhibit are cases of human bones, preserved in soil just as they were found. Nearby, a huge lifelike model of a woolly mammoth is mounted next to the bones of the real thing, and half a dozen rooms are packed with more stuffed-and-mounted animals than you could shake a shotgun at.

Palác Kinských (Kinský Palace)

Staroměstské náměstí (Old Town Square), Praha 1. ☎ **02/24-81-07-58.** Admission 30 Kč ($1.05) adults, 15 Kč (55¢) students; free for children 5 and under, and for everyone on the first Mon of each month. Tues–Sun 10am–6pm. Metro: Line A to Staroměstská.

Housing graphic works from the National Gallery collection, the rococo Kinský Palace boasts a permanent collection of works by Georges Braque, André Derain, and other modern masters, including Pablo Picasso, whose 1907 *Self-portait* has virtually been adopted as the National Gallery's logo.

Good-quality international exhibitions have included Max Ernst and Rembrandt retrospectives, as well as shows on functional art and crafts.

Bertramka/W. A. Mozart Museum

Mozartova 169, Praha 5. ☎ **02/54-38-93.** Admission 60 Kč ($2.15) adults, 45 Kč ($1.60) students. Daily 9:30am–6pm. Tram 2, 6, 7, 9, 14, or 16 from the Anděl metro station.

Mozart loved Prague and when he visited the composer often stayed here. Now a museum, the villa is filled with the usual displays that include his written work and his harpsichord. There's also a lock of Mozart's hair, encased in a glass cube. Much of the Bertramka villa was destroyed by fire in the 1870s, but Mozart's rooms, where he finished composing the opera *Don Giovanni*, have miraculously remained untouched.

PARKS & GARDENS

My favorite Prague park, **Kampa** is near the foot of the Charles Bridge in Malá Strana and was named by Spanish soldiers who set up camp here after the Roman Catholics won the 1620 Battle of White Mountain. The park as it is today wasn't formed until the period of Nazi occupation, when the private gardens of three noble families were joined. It's the perfect place to picnic.

Prague Castle's **Královská Zahrodna (Royal Garden),** once the site of the sovereign's vineyards, was founded in 1534. Dotted with lemon trees and surrounded by 16th-, 17th-, and 18th-century buildings, it's consciously and conservatively laid out with abundant shrubbery and fountains. The park is open Tuesday through Sunday from 9am to 5pm, and admission is 5 Kč (20¢). Take metro Line A to Malostranská or Hradčanská.

Looming over Malá Strana, adjacent to Prague Castle, lush green **Petřínské Sady (Petřín Hill)** is easily recognizable by the miniature replica of the Eiffel Tower topping it. The huge park is dotted with gardens and orchards that bloom in spring and summer. Throughout are a myriad of monuments, churches, a mirror maze, and an observatory. Hunger Wall, a decaying 21-foot-high stone wall that runs up through Petřín to the grounds of Prague Castle, was commissioned by Charles IV in the 1360s as a medieval social project designed to provide jobs for Prague's starving poor. Take tram no. 12 or 22 to újzed.

Part of the excitement of the **Valdštejnská Zahrada (Waldstein Gardens)** is their location, behind a 30-foot wall on the back streets of Malá Strana. Elegant, leafy gravel paths—dotted by classical bronze statues and gurgling fountains—fan out in every direction. Laid out in the 17th century, the baroque park was the personal garden of Gen. Albrecht Waldstein (1581–1634), commander of the Roman Catholic armies during the Thirty Years' War. These gardens are the backyards of Waldstein's palace—Prague's largest—which replaced 23 houses, three gardens, and the municipal brick kiln. The Waldstein Gardens are open May to September, daily from 9am to 7pm. Take metro Line A to Malostranská.

7 Shopping

BEST BUYS   Not only are **garnets** the Czech national gem, but the reddish stones are also among the country's top exports. There are at least five specific kinds of garnets in the world; Bohemian garnets are of the "Pyrope" type, an amalgam of calcium and magnesium that's almost always deep red. Handmade glass is another Czech specialty. Of the country's estimated 200 glass artists, about half a dozen have international reputations. In addition to hand-blown functional pieces, galleries are full of unusual sculptures.

Other good buys include handmade wooden toys and traditional puppets available from stands and shops in all the major tourist areas. Plenty of original arts and crafts are sold on Charles Bridge and on main squares and streets.

Note: While some European countries encourage tourists to part with the dollars by offering to refund the value-added tax (VAT), the Czech Republic offers no such program.

BOOKSTORES

The Globe, Janovského 14, Praha 7, stocks over 10,000 titles and is the best place in the city for used paperback literature and nonfiction. Take metro Line C to Vltavská or tram no. 1, 3, 5, 8, 12, 14, 17, 25, or 26. **U Knihomola (The Bookworm)**, Mánesova 79, Praha 2 (☎ **02/627-77-70**), is a large shop near Jîrího z Poděbrad metro station (Line A) with a wide selection of English-language books upstairs and a comfortable café downstairs. It's open Monday through Saturday from 9am to midnight and Sunday from 9am to 6pm.

OTHER SHOPS

Granát Turnov
Dlouhá třída 30, Praha 1.

Granát Turnov, the monopoly controling the Czech Republic's garnet industry, is *the* place to visit if you're serious about shopping for garnets. Expect to pay between 600 and 900 Kč ($20 and $30) for a middle-priced ring or bracelet that incorporates one of these jewels. Open Monday through Friday from 9am to 5pm.

K-Mart
Národní třída 26, Praha 1. ☎ **02/26-23-41.**

The Prague K-mart is the first of 13 Czech stores now owned by the company, the best place to go for most any necessity. Since K-Mart took over the Communist-era shop that once stood here, sparkling display cases and Muzak have replaced drab displays and the din of mumbling shoppers. Open Monday through Wednesday from 8am to 7pm, Thursday and Friday from 8am to 8pm, Saturday from 9am to 6pm, and Sunday from 10am to 5pm.

Loutkami
Nerudova 47, Malá Strana.

This busy shop offers what's probably the widest selection of puppets, old and new, for sale anywhere in Prague. There are many kinds of puppets—including hand, glove, rod, and marionettes—but no ventriloquist dummies. Open Monday through Saturday from 9am to 6pm.

Moser

Na příkopě 12. ☎ **02/22-18-51** or 22-18-52.

The Jewish Moser family opened Prague's most prestigious crystal shop in 1857 and continued to produce their own works until the Nazis forced them to flee during World War II. Prague's Communist government nationalized the firm but managed to retain the company's exacting standards. Even if you're not buying, this inimitable old-world shop is definitely worth a browse. Open Monday through Friday from 9am to 7pm and Saturday from 9am to 1pm.

8 Prague After Dark

Turn to the two English-language newspapers, *Prague Post* and *Prognosis,* for listings on cultural events and nightlife around the city. *ProGram,* a Czech-language weekly with more comprehensive listings, is easy enough for non-Czechs to decipher and available at most metro station newsstands. **Ticketpro** (☎ **02/24-23-21-10**), Prague's computerized ticket service, sells seats to most events around town. You can purchase tickets by phone using a credit or charge card (American Express, Diners Club, MasterCard, or Visa) or visit one of its many central Prague locations: PIS, Staroměstské nám. 22; PIS, Na příkopě 20; American Hospitality Center, Melantrichova 8, Praha 1 (☎ **02/24-22-99-61** or 24-23-04-67; fax 2/24-22-93-63); Melantrich, Václavské náměstí; Reduta, Národní 20; or Laterna Magika, Národní 20. You should know that tickets are sometimes—but not always—cheaper when purchased directly from theater box offices.

THE PERFORMING ARTS
CLASSICAL MUSIC

Czech Philharmonic Orchestra
In the Rudolfinum, náměstí Jana Palacha, Praha 1. ☎ **02/24-89-31-11** or 24-89-33-52. Tickets 350–450 Kč ($12.50–$16.10). Metro: Line A to Staroměstská.

Despite the economic problems that have plagued the organization since the fall of Communism, Prague's most prestigious orchestra is still world-class.

Prague Symphony Orchestra
In the Rudolfinum, náměstí Jana Palacha, Praha 1. ☎ **02/24-89-32-27.** Tickets 250–350 Kč ($8.95–$12.50). Metro: Line B to náměstí Republiky.

The city's second orchestra regularly performs in many churches around Prague, as well as outside and in select gardens during summer. Most of the concerts are now performed at the Rudolfinum while the orchestra's home stage at the Municipal House (Obecní dům) is being refurbished.

THEATER COMPANIES

Most of the city's theater offerings are staged in the Czech language, but there are several active English-language troupes, especially during summer. These vary annually with the arrival and departure of touring troupes, so check the listings in the local English-language newspapers for the latest.

Image Black Light Theatre
At Theatre Image, Pařížská 4, Praha 1. ☎ **02/232-91-91** or 231-44-58. Tickets 100–170 Kč ($3.60–$6.10). Metro: Line A to Staroměstská.

Black-light theater is popular in Prague, with performances on up to six separate stages at any one time. The concept is simple: Actors and props coated with luminescent paints cavort under black lights that illuminate only bright objects. The result is a pantomime show packed with light comic entertainment and exceptional Houdini-esque visual tricks.

Národní Divadlo Marionet (National Marionette Theater)

Žatecká 1, Praha 1. ☎ **02/232-34-29** or 232-25-36. Tickets 100–240 Kč ($3.60–$8.60). Metro: Line A to Staroměstská.

Marionette theater is a centuries-old tradition in Bohemia. One of the most popular and accessible Czech cultural treasures, puppet theater is performed in almost every town in the country, and many families have collections of traditional marionettes. Both the marionettes and their costumed operators are part of the action, which usually includes humor and song. Productions run the gamut from whimsical interpretations of Mozart's *Don Giovanni* to serious stagings of ancient Greek literary classics. Performances are usually scheduled nightly. The box office is open Tuesday through Sunday from 10am to 8pm.

OPERA

National Opera

In the National Theater (Národní divadlo), Národní 2, Praha 1. ☎ **02/24-91-34-37.** Tickets 80–500 Kč ($2.85–$17.85). Metro: Line B to Národní třída.

Although this is not a particularly adventurous company, the National Opera is well regarded, and sometimes attracts internationally acclaimed heavyweight soloists to its stage.

Státní Opera (State Opera Company)

In the State Opera House, Wilsonova 4, Praha 2. ☎ **02/24-22-76-93** or 24-22-98-98. Tickets 80–500 Kč ($2.85–$17.85). Metro: Line A or C to Muzeum.

The State Opera is slightly more flamboyant than its rival, staging grand productions of time-honored hits like *Rigoletto, Don Giovanni, Aïda,* and *Madame Butterfly.* To the disappointment of the medium's most serious fans, however, the State Opera offers these big-money crowd-pleasers almost exclusively. The box office is open daily from 10am to 5pm and one hour before performances.

Stavovské Divadlo (Estates Theater)

Ovocný třída 6, Praha 1. ☎ **02/24-21-50-01.** Tickets 200–600 Kč ($7.15–$21.45). Metro: Line A or B to Můstek.

In a city full of spectacularly beautiful theaters, the massive pale-green Estates ranks as one of the most awesome. Built in 1782, this is the only theater in the world that's still in its original condition from Mozart's day. Simultaneous English translation, transmitted via headphone, is available for most plays staged here. The box office is open Monday through Friday from 10am to 6pm and Saturday and Sunday (performance days only) from noon to 1pm and 2:30 to 6pm; and half an hour prior to curtain time.

DANCE

National Ballet

At the National Theater (Národní divadlo), Národní 2, Praha 1. ☎ **02/24-91-34-37.** Tickets 200–500 Kč ($7.15–$17.85). Metro: Line B to Národní třída.

Although most of its top talent has gone West since 1989, the ballet still puts on a good show.

THE CLUB & MUSIC SCENE

The Prague club and music scene is limited but lively. Each summer, several top international names stop here on their tours of Europe, but these events are relatively few and far between. Czech musicians and bands perform around town almost nightly and are definitely worth checking out.

ROCK & DANCE CLUBS

Bunkr

Lodecká 2, Praha 1. ☎ **02/231-07-35.** Cover 20–70 Kč (70¢–$2.50), but usually none after 2am. Metro: Line B to náměstí Republiky.

A long, deep basement that once was a 1950s Civil Guard bunker/bomb shelter, Club Bunkr opened in November 1991, followed a few months later by a like-named street-level café. Despised by its neighbors, the club features loud DJ nights and a plethora of live bands. Owner Richard Nemcok has honest credentials: He was jailed by the socialists and signed Charter 77 before immigrating to the United States in 1981. Packed with lots of young 20-something European tourists, Bunkr is sometimes laughed at by knowledgeable locals. Still, it's hard to argue with its success; Havel has been spotted here, and every time I'm here I have a lot of fun. The music usually starts at 9pm. The café is open daily from 11am to 3am; the club, daily from 6pm to 5am.

Lávka

Novotného lávka 1, Praha 1. ☎ **02/24-21-47-97.** Cover 40–70 Kč ($1.45–$2.50). Metro: Line A to Staroměstská.

Because of its location next to the Old Town foot of the Charles Bridge, Lávka attracts a lot of tourists. This isn't such a bad thing, however, because this club is also one of the nicest in town, offering a large bar, a good dance floor, and fantastic outdoor seating. Straightforward dance hits attract a good-looking young crowd. Open daily from 9pm to 4am.

Malostranská Beseda

Malostranské nám. 21, Praha 1. ☎ **02/53-90-24.** Cover none–70 Kč ($2.50). Metro: Line A to Malostranská. Tram 12 or 22 to Malostranská náměstí.

This *Beseda,* or "meeting place," on Malá Strana's main square is located in a building that was once the area's town hall. Situated on the second floor of the arcaded side of the square, the club consists of little more than two smallish rooms—one holds the bar, the other a stage on which live bands perform most nights. Although this is not the best place to hang out, it's hard to beat when a good band is playing. Open daily from 7pm to 1am; music usually begins at 8pm.

Radost F/X

Bělehradská 120, Praha 2. ☎ **02/25-12-10.** Cover 40–80 Kč ($1.45–$2.85). Metro: Line C to I. P. Pavlova.

Popular with a very mixed gay and model crowd, Radost is built in the American mold: a subterranean labyrinth of nooks and crannies and a pulsating dance floor with good sightlines for wallflowers. It's worth going just to stare at the spectacular painting hanging over the back bar. Open daily from 9pm to 5am.

Roxy

Dlouhá 33 (about two blocks toward Old Town Square from Revoluční třída), Praha 1. Cover 10–30 Kč (35¢–$1.05).

The best club in Prague is a subterranean dance space that was once an art deco theater and still has its deteriorating balcony overlooking the dance floor. There are several private nooks and plenty of seating at tables and on stairs, and good dance disks spin on weekends. Open Sunday through Thursday from 8pm to 2am and Friday and Saturday from 8pm to 4am.

JAZZ

Agharta Jazz Centrum

Krakovská 5, Praha 1. ☎ **02/24-21-29-14.** Cover 50–100 Kč ($1.80–$3.60). Metro: Line A or C to Muzeum.

Relatively high prices guarantee this small jazz room a predominantly foreign clientele. Upscale by Czech standards, the Agharta jazzery regularly features some of the best music in town—running the gamut from standard acoustic trios to Dixieland to funk and fusion. Hot Line, the house band led by Agharta part-owner and drummer extraordinaire Michael Hejuna, regularly takes its keyboard-and-sax Crusaders-like sound to this stage. Bands usually begin at 9pm. Open daily from 8pm to midnight.

Reduta Jazz Club

Národní 20, Praha 1. ☎ **02/24-91-22-46.** Cover 80–120 Kč ($2.85–$4.30). Metro: Line B to Národní třída.

Reduta is a smoky subterranean jazz room that looks exactly like a jazz cellar is supposed to look. An adventurous booking policy means that there are different bands playing almost every night of the week. It's open Monday through Saturday from 9pm to 2am; music usually starts around 9:30pm.

BARS & BEER HALLS

Chapeau Rouge

Jakubská 2.

Hidden on a small Old Town back street, this French-owned drinkery has a good bar with Guinness on tap, and provides service with a sneer. There are two large rooms, both with pink pastel walls, industrial metal wall sconces, plank floors, and a good sound system playing contemporary rock music. Open daily from noon to 3am.

Molly Malones

U obecního dvora 4 (about four blocks from Old Town Square), Praha 1. ☎ **02/231-62-22.** Metro: Line A to Staroměstská; then take Kozi třída (behind and to the right of the Jan Hus statue) past the clock and the trees.

With Guinness on tap and a warm fireplace, Molly Malones is a good approximation of an Irish pub. The cozy two-room interior is popular with foreigners. Open daily from noon to 3am.

U Fleků

Křemencova 11. ☎ **02/29-32-46.** Cover 30 Kč ($1.05) for admission to the garden when the band performs. Metro: Line B to Národní třída.

Originally a brewery dating from 1459, U Fleků is Prague's most famous beer hall—and the only one that still brews its own beer. It's a huge place with a myriad of timber-lined rooms and a large, loud courtyard where an oompah band performs. The ornately decorated medieval-style wood ceilings and courtyard columns are charming but not very old. The recipe for U Fleků's special dark beer is the real thing—and very good as well. It's not available anywhere else; they brew only enough to service their own restaurant. Sausages, goulash, and other traditional foods are served (but not recommended). Open daily from 10am to midnight.

Velryba (The Whale)

Opatovická 24, Praha 1. ☎ **02/24-91-23-91.** Metro: Line B to Národní třída.

Velryba was opened in July 1992 as a Czech literary café and quickly caught on with the city's intellectuals and theater types. Sort of down and dirty, the pub has become one of Prague's trendiest cafés, a "real" place that doesn't particularly appreciate foreign tourists. In addition to café drinks, Velryba serves well-priced pasta and Czech dishes. Open daily from 11am to 2am.

9 Easy Excursions

Just as New York City is not representative of the United States and London does not embody all of England, Prague is very different from the towns that surround it. Even if you don't have much time, try to spend a day outside the city to explore the countryside.

Most of the destinations listed below are accessible from Prague by train. It's important that you know which of Prague's several stations your train is departing from; check with **Čedok,** Na příkopě 18 and Václavské nám. (Wenceslas Square) 24 (☎ **02/24-19-71-11;** fax 2/232-16-56). Long-haul trains in the Czech Republic are very popular, especially in summer and on Friday and Sunday evenings, so although seats can be purchased up until the moment of departure, prebooking is recommended.

KARLŠTEJN (KARLSTEIN) & KUTNÁ HORA Medieval **Karlštejn castle,** 17 miles southwest of Prague, was founded by Charles IV in 1348 and hasn't changed much since. Probably the most popular short trip from Prague, this dramatic-looking castle was once the Royal Treasury. It's more spectacular from the outside than from the inside, which is accessible only by guided tour. Tours are offered Tuesday through Sunday from 9am to 7pm and cost 30 Kč ($1.05). Trains depart from Prague's Smíchov Station hourly throughout the day and take about 40 minutes to reach Karlštejn.

Kutná Hora, a medieval town that grew fantastically rich from the silver deposits beneath it, is probably the second most popular day trip from Prague. Small enough to be seen in a single day at a brisk pace, the town's ancient heart is much decayed, but it's also mercifully free of the ugly Communist-era functionalist-style buildings that plague many of the country's small towns. Kutná Hora's main draw is the macabre **Bone Church (Kostnice),** filled with human bones assembled in bizarre sculptures. It's located a mile up the road in Sedlec; board a local bus on Masarykova Street. Kutná Hora is best reached by bus, which departs from the terminal at Prague's Želivského metro station and takes about 90 minutes.

KARLOVY VARY (CARLSBAD) Famous for its **thermal spas,** Karlovy Vary annually attracts over 80,000 people who come specifically for a spa treatment lasting two weeks or more; tens of thousands of others come just for a day or two. In addition to the treatment spas, the city offers countryside beauty. There are about 60 miles of **walking paths** around the hills and woods surrounding Karlovy Vary, and those taking the cure often enjoy lengthy strolls there. The town's many **pedestrian promenades,** lined with turn-of-the-century art nouveau buildings, are also truly beautiful.

Day-trippers to Karlovy Vary can experience the waters on an "outpatient" basis. The **State Baths III** (☎ 017/256-41) welcomes tourists with mineral baths, massages, saunas, and a cold pool; it's open for men on Tuesday, Thursday, and Saturday, and for women on Monday, Wednesday, and Friday from 7:45am to 3pm. **Vojenský lážensky ustav,** Mlýnské nábřeží 7 (☎ 017/222-06), offers similar services and costs about 1,000 Kč ($35.75) per day.

Frequent express buses make the trip from Prague's Florenc station to Karlovy Vary's Horakova náměstí in about 2^1/$_2$ hours. The trip costs 80 Kč ($2.85) each way. Take a 10-minute walk or local bus no. 4 into Karlovy Vary's town center. Avoid taking the train from Prague, which takes over four hours on a circuitous route.

ČESKÉ BUDĚJOVICE Southern Bohemia's well-preserved Renaissance town of České Budějovice is steeped in history and small enough to be seen comfortably in a day. At its center is one of the largest squares in central Europe, containing the ornate **Fountain of Sampson,** an 18th-century water well that was once the town's principal water supply.

The **Černa Vez (Black Tower),** U Černé věže (☎ 038/386-38), is the most famous symbol of České Budějovice. This 232-foot-tall 16th-century tower was built as a belfry for the adjacent Church of St. Nicholas. Visitors regularly ascend the tower's 255 steps for a glimpse of downtown and the surrounding countryside. Admission is 30 Kč ($1.05) for adults and 15 Kč (55¢) for students. The 13th-century **Church of St. Nicholas** (☎ 038/989-67), one of the most important sights in České Budějovice, was a bastion of Roman Catholicism during the 15th-century Hussite rebellion. The church's flamboyant white-and-cream 17th-century baroque interior shouldn't be missed.

Express trains from Prague make the trip to České Budějovice in about three hours and cost about 150 Kč ($5.35) in first class, 90 Kč ($3.20) in second class.

ČESKÝ KRUMLOV Český Krumlov—a living gallery of elegant Renaissance-era buildings housing charming cafés, pubs, restaurants, shops, and galleries—is one of the prettiest towns in all of Bohemia. Even the United Nations Educational, Scientific, and Cultural Organization (UNESCO) agrees: In 1992, UNESCO named Český Krumlov a World Heritage Site for its historical importance and physical beauty. Bustling since medieval times, the town has undergone centuries of embellishment that have left it exquisitely beautiful.

Reputedly the largest castle in Bohemia, after the Prague Castle, **Český Krumlov Château** (☎ 0337/20-75) was constructed in the 13th century as part of a private estate. Throughout the ages the castle has been passed on to a variety of private owners, including the Rožmberk family, the largest landholders in Bohemia. Perched high atop a rocky hill, the château is open to tourists from April to October only, exclusively by guided tour. Visits begin in the palace's rococo Chapel of St. George, continue through portrait-packed Renaissance Hall, and end with the Royal Family Apartments, outfitted with ornate furnishings that include Flemish wall tapestries and European paintings. Tours last one hour and cost 135 Kč ($4.80) for adults and 70 Kč ($2.50) for students.

The only way to reach Český Krumlov by train from Prague is via České Budějovice, a slow ride that will deposit you at a station relatively far from the town center. The 3^1/$_2$-hour bus ride from Prague usually involves a transfer in České Budějovice. The bus station in Český Krumlov is a 15-minute walk from the town's main square.

TEREZÍN Prague's Jewish population was decimated during World War II, when the occupying Nazi army deported most of Bohemia's Jews to the **Terezín Concentration Camp,** located 30 miles northwest of the city. There were no gas chambers, mass machine-gun executions, or medical testing rooms here. Terezín was a "show" camp, used by the Nazis to demonstrate to the world (via the International Red Cross) that Jews, Gypsies, homosexuals, and political prisoners were not being mistreated. However, thousands died here, most from disease and starvation. For most inmates, Terezín was little more than a stopping-off point on their way to greater suffering and death at Auschwitz or Buchenwald. Of the 139,654 prisoners sent to Terezín, only 17,472 were left to be liberated at the war's end.

Today the Terezín Camp exists as a memorial to the dead and a monument to human depravity. Visitors can tour the camp's dank cells and execution fields and visit an adjacent museum that exhibits historical and personal artifacts illustrating camp life. Several short documentary films are available for viewing on request, including a Nazi-made propaganda piece.

Terezín Camp (☎ **0416/922-25**) is open daily from 8am to 4:30pm. Admission costs 75 Kč ($2.70) for adults and 40 Kč ($1.45) for students and children 11 and under. To reach Terezín from Prague's Florenc bus station (metro Line C), take any bus from stand no. 17 or 19. The ride takes about an hour and costs 40 Kč ($1.40) each way. Prague-based **Wittmann Tours** (☎ **02/231-28-95**) offers irregularly scheduled group tours to Terezín on most Sundays and Thursdays. Tours depart from the Jewish Community Center, Maiselova 18, near the Old New Synagogue, and cost 675 Kč ($24.10) for adults and 500 Kč ($17.85) for students.

21 Rome

by Dan Levine

Rome is many things to many people. It's the ancient Rome of the Forum and Colosseum, where the intrigues of the Roman Empire played themselves out and from where emperors dispatched armies to conquer most of Europe and the Middle East. It's the pope and the Vatican, the headquarters of Catholicism and a pilgrimage destination for millions of believers. It's the Sistine Chapel and the Vatican Museums, custodians of some of humankind's most important works of art. It's the capital of a country with a particularly distinctive and enjoyable cultural personality. And it's the chaos of a place settled 2^1/$_2$ millennia before the advent of the automobile—a city bursting at the seams with both refugees and fashionable shops from around the world. And some come just for the food.

The more the Eternal City changes, it seems, the more it stays the same. The 1994 political scandal that unraveled Italy's government was but the latest imbroglio in a bureaucratic landscape that for centuries has been one of Europe's most volatile. The crowds and the noise and the heat are all part of the living history book that's Rome.

1 Rome Deals & Discounts

BUDGET BESTS   Rome is a very expensive city, with almost nothing that can be called a genuine bargain. Only a few sights don't charge an entrance fee, including most churches and the Pantheon. However, one of the greatest joys of Roman life is the evening *passeggiata,* or stroll, on via del Corso and around piazza di Spagna— that's free.

SPECIAL DISCOUNTS   Many places in Rome reduce rates for students and are listed in this chapter. If you need help leaving Rome, visit the **Centro Turistico Studentesco (CTS),** via Genova 16 (☎ **06/4-67-91**), off via Nazionale. It offers discounted plane, train, bus, and boat journeys for travelers under 26. CTS is open Monday through Friday from 9am to 1pm and 3 to 7pm and Saturday from 9am to 1pm.

WORTH THE EXTRA MONEY   Don't be discouraged by the hefty 13,000-lira ($8.15) admission to the Vatican Museums and Sistine Chapel. While this is one of the most expensive attractions in Italy, it's also one of the most interesting and important—and worth every lira.

What's Special About Rome

Ace Attractions
- Piazza Navona, filled with cafés, artists, and tourists.
- The Spanish Steps, a favorite gathering point of locals and tourists alike during the early-evening *passeggiata* (walk).
- The Fountain of Trevi, where tossing a coin over your shoulder into the fountain assures a return visit to the Eternal City.

Ancient Monuments
- The Colosseum, the 50,000-seat stadium of the Roman Empire.
- The Roman Forum, the political and economic center of the vast Empire.
- The Pantheon, one of the ancient city's best-preserved structures—an inspiration for all of Western architecture.
- Ostia Antica, a well-preserved vast Roman city from the 2nd century A.D.

Food
- So many excellent restaurants—it's hard to get a bad meal.

Museums
- The Vatican Museums, home to the Sistine Chapel and $4^1/2$ miles of art.
- Capitoline Hill, one of the world's finest sculpture museums.

Parks
- Villa Borghese, a large park of rolling hills near the town center.

Spectacles
- Wednesday audiences with the pope and Sunday blessing.
- Opera at the Terme di Caracalla—summertime opera performances inside ancient Roman baths.

Shopping
- Some of Europe's trendiest stores near piazza di Spagna.
- Porta Portese, a vast Sunday flea market.

Religious Shrines
- St. Peter's, the spiritual center for the world's Catholics.
- Six other Catholic pilgrimage churches, plus many lesser churches filled with rich artwork.

Couples, especially, will find that spending a little extra on accommodations is also worth the money. Even a top budget hotel is far from spectacular, but it'll get you a room away from the decidedly unromantic area around the Stazione Termini, where most cheap rooms are located. It's a shame to come all the way to a city so rich in history and stay in such a relatively drab location.

2 Pretrip Preparations

REQUIRED DOCUMENTS   Italy requires all non-E.U. visitors to carry a passport, but it does not require visas from U.S., Canadian, Australian, or New Zealand travelers.

TIMING YOUR TRIP   The main tourist season is April through October, when temperatures and room rates are highest. August is not the best time to visit. The heat is oppressive and the city just about deserted, since thousands of Romans take this time to vacation and many shops close for the month. Indeed, there's a saying that "Only the dogs remain in Rome during Ferragosto."All hotels and sights, as well as most restaurants, remain open, but many small businesses, such as laundries and grocers, are closed.

Rome's Average Daytime Temperature & Rainfall

	Jan	Feb	Mar	Apr	May	June	July	Aug	Sept	Oct	Nov	Dec
Temp.(°F)	49	52	57	62	70	77	82	78	73	65	56	47
Rainfall"	3.6	3.2	2.9	2.2	1.4	0.7	0.2	0.7	3.0	4.0	3.9	2.8

Special Events   There are two very special times to be in Rome: Easter and Christmas. If you plan to visit at these holiest of times, especially during Easter, make reservations *far* in advance. Rome honors its patron saints, Peter and Paul, on June 29.

BACKGROUND READING & VIEWING   Rome's ruins are all the more fascinating if you know something about the context in which they were built and used.

Edward Gibbon's *History of the Decline and Fall of the Roman Empire* (Fawcett, 1987) has been a landmark scholarly work ever since it was written in the 18th century. Robert Graves's *I, Claudius* and *Claudius the God* (Random House, 1977) and H. V. Morton's *A Traveller in Southern Italy* (Dodd, 1987) are lighter reads that triumphantly succeed in taking the reader back into the age of the emperors. If you don't feel like reading *I, Claudius* or its sequel, you can always view the hit PBS TV series on video before you leave home.

While it may at times be a bit dense for the average train ride, there's nothing quite like Latin literature for setting the scene of ancient Rome. Especially recommended are Virgil's *Aeneid,* an epic poem about the founding of Rome; Plutarch's *Lives* (Modern Library, 1967), which contrasts the Roman and Greek civilizations by comparing individual Greeks and Romans; and Petronius's *Satyricon* (Harvard University Press), one of the few surviving examples of an ancient novel and a window into the decadent politics and society of ancient Rome.

Finally, I recommend Luigi Barzini's classic *The Italians* (Macmillan, 1977), an opinionated and refreshingly frank look at the history and culture of his homeland.

3 Rome Specifics

ARRIVING

FROM THE AIRPORT   Most international flights land at **Leonardo da Vinci Airport,** also known as **Fiumicino** (☎ **06/6-59-51**), 18 miles from downtown Rome. Immediately after Passport Control (but before Customs) you'll see two tourist information desks to your left, one for Rome and the other for the rest of Italy. The Rome desk has a good map and some useful brochures; it's open Monday through Saturday from 8:30am to 7pm. When it's closed, maps are available from nearby racks. An adjacent bank changes money at reasonable rates; it's open daily from 7:30am to 11pm.

In the main arrivals hallway you'll find a luggage-storage office, open 24 hours, which charges 5,000 lire ($3.15) per bag per day.

There's a train station in the airport terminal. Express trains to Rome's Stazione Termini take about 30 minutes and cost 13,000 lire ($8.15) each way. Local trains

What Things Cost in Rome	U.S. $
Taxi (from the train station to piazza di Spagna)	6.30
Public bus	.95
Local telephone call	.13
Double room at the Excelsior (deluxe)	325.00
Double room at the Hotel Venezia (moderate)	134.40
Double room at Pensione Papà Germano (budget)	37.50
Continental breakfast	
(at any café/bar)	1.90
(at most hotels)	5.30
Lunch for one at Fiaschetteria Beltramme (moderate)	16.75
Lunch for one at Volpetti (budget)	6.85
Dinner for one, without wine, at Toulà (deluxe)	95.50
Dinner for one, without wine, at Taverna Fieramosca (moderate)	17.35
Dinner for one, without wine, at the Marco Polo Bar (budget)	8.55
Pint of beer (at the Fiddler's Elbow)	3.95
Glass of wine (at the Druid's Den)	2.00
Coca-Cola to take out	1.45
Cup of coffee (cappuccino) (at any café in town)	1.00
Roll of color film, 36 exposures	4.40
Admission to the Vatican Museums and the Sistine Chapel	8.15
Movie ticket	6.30
Cheapest theater ticket (at the Terme di Caracalla)	15.65

are almost as frequent and cost 9,500 lire ($4.40) each way. But these terminate at Tiburtina Station, where you have to change to a subway to Termini, a journey of about an hour.

The average price for a taxi ride to or from the airport is 70,000 lire ($43.75); taxis, yellow or white, line up in front of the airport terminals.

Charter flights sometimes land at the city's smaller **Ciampino Airport** (☎ **06/7934-0297**). Yellow ACOTRAL buses leave this airport every half an hour or so and deposit passengers at Cinecittà station, the last stop on Line A of the Metropolitana. From there, take the subway to Rome's central rail station or beyond. The complete journey takes about 45 minutes and costs 3,000 lire ($1.90).

FROM THE TRAIN STATION   Most Rome-bound trains arrive at the sprawling silver **Stazione Termini**. You'll almost certainly be approached by touts claiming to work for a tourist organization. These people really work for individual hotels and will say almost anything to sell you a room. Unless you know something about Rome's layout and are somewhat travel savvy, it's best to ignore these salespeople.

The official Ente Provinciale per il Turismo (EPT) tourist board staffs a hard-to-find small window at the head of Track 3 (☎ **06/487-12-70**). It's usually open daily from 8:15am to 7:15pm. Pick up a free map, as well as a brochure on

The Italian Lira

For American Readers At this writing $1 = approximately 1,600 lire (or 100 lire = 6.25¢), and this was the rate of exchange used to calculate the dollar values given in this chapter (rounded to the nearest nickel).

For British Readers At this writing £1 = approximately 2,400 lire (or 100 lire = 4.2p), and this was the rate of exchange used to calculate the pound values in the table below.

Note: The rates given here fluctuate from time to time and may not be the same when you travel to Italy. Therefore this table should be used only as a guide:

Lire	U.S.$	U.K.£	Lire	U.S.$	U.K.£
100	.06	.04	20,000	12.50	8.33
250	.16	.10	25,000	15.63	10.42
500	.31	.21	30,000	18.75	12.50
750	.47	.31	35,000	21.88	14.58
1,000	.63	.42	40,000	25.00	16.67
1,500	.94	.63	45,000	28.13	18.75
2,000	1.25	.83	50,000	31.25	20.83
2,500	1.56	1.04	60,000	37.50	25.00
3,000	1.88	1.25	70,000	43.75	29.17
4,000	2.50	1.67	80,000	50.00	33.33
5,000	3.13	2.08	90,000	56.25	37.50
7,500	4.69	3.13	100,000	62.50	41.67
10,000	6.25	4.17	125,000	78.13	52.08
15,000	9.38	6.25	150,000	93.75	62.50

museums and *Un Ospite a Roma,* the city's best free monthly tourist information booklet. This office also makes hotel reservations—use it if you're in a pinch.

There are two huge identical-looking exits on either side of the station's main hall. Head toward Track 22 for hotels designated below as "to the left of the station"and turn toward Track 1 for hotels "to the right of the station."

The entrance to the Metropolitana, Rome's two-line subway system, is downstairs (you'll see an illuminated M surrounded by a red circle pointing the way). Most of the city's buses begin their journeys in piazza dei Cinquecento, in front of the train station.

There's a branch of the Banca Nazionale delle Communicazioni between the entrance to Tracks 8 to 11 and 12 to 15. You can exchange currency here Monday through Saturday from 8:30am to 7:30pm.

In the station's massive outer hall is the Informazioni Ferroviarie, which answers questions about train times, and nearby is a perpetually crowded long bank of ticket windows.

VISITOR INFORMATION

For those arriving by train, the most convenient **tourist information office** is the one at the head of Track 3. (See "From the Train Station," above, for complete information.)

Rome's main **Ente Provinciale per il Turismo (EPT)** office, via Parigi 5 (☎ **06/488-37-48**), also distributes a few meager brochures and offers a free hotel reservation service. It's open Monday through Saturday from 8:15am to 7:15pm. To get reach the main office from the train station, exit through the front doors, cross the enormous bus lot called piazza dei Cinquecento, look for the Grand Hotel, and turn right onto via Parigi.

CITY LAYOUT

Stazione Termini, the main railroad station, on **piazza dei Cinquecento,** marks the eastern edge of the tourist's city. The broad, busy **via Nazionale** begins at piazza della Repubblica, just a short walk away, and stretches down to **piazza Venezia** at the eastern edge of Old Rome. Southeast of piazza Venezia are the Roman Forum and the Palatine Hill (the centermost of the seven hills on which the city was founded), stretching along the once-ostentatious **via dei Fori Imperiali,** which connects piazza Venezia with the Colosseum.

Via del Corso stretches north from piazza Venezia to **piazza del Popolo,** which marks the northern edge of tourist Rome. About two-thirds of the way to piazza del Popolo, via Condotti runs east to **piazza di Spagna,** and the Spanish Steps, the city's chic shopping area. East to piazza del Popolo (and north of piazza di Spagna) is **Villa Borghese,** the city's principal park.

To the west of piazza Venezia and stretching toward the river lies **Old Rome,** an area of narrow winding streets, aging buildings, and generally excellent restaurants and charming cafés. Corso Vittorio Emanuele is the main boulevard traversing this neighborhood. Across the Tiber (Tevere) River is **Vatican City** and south of the Holy See is **Trastevere,** one of the city's most colorful residential neighborhoods.

GETTING AROUND

The free **map** of Rome distributed by the tourist office is remarkably comprehensive for a city this size, though its lack of an index makes street-finding tough. The best map, listing every vicolo and largo, is the yellow city plan produced by the Istituto Geografico de Agostini, available at bookstores for a whopping 12,000 lire ($7.50).

BY SUBWAY   Rome's **Metropolitana** subway system has just two lines, both of which stop at Stazione Termini. They connect most of the city's major hubs, but

---

A Traveler's Advisory

Watch out for pickpockets and thieving children. The former are clever, preying on unwary travelers, especially on buses and the Metropolitana. If you take the obvious precautions, however, you shouldn't have much trouble. The ubiquitous thieving children, on the other hand, are brash and bothersome and a real social problem. Routinely, a band of six or more unaccompanied children rove major tourist areas, wielding pieces of cardboard or a newspaper. They'll approach their target and begin babbling plaintively, waving or shoving the cardboard or newspaper into your face. Meanwhile, their free hand is rummaging through your pockets or purse. I've found that a modest challenge, rather than retreat, is the most effective defense. Yell back at them, stamp your foot, and invoke the name of the *polizia*—preferably before they actually reach you and begin their ploy. Of course, if you spot them before they spot you, do whatever you can to avoid these fearless, obnoxious criminals.

unfortunately neither goes anywhere near Trastevere. **Line A** is the most useful to the average tourist, with stops at piazza della Repubblica, piazza Barberini, piazza di Spagna, piazza del Popolo (Flaminio), and the Vatican (Ottaviano). In the opposite direction from Termini, Line A travels southeast past piazza San Giovanni to the Catacombs and other outlying sights. **Line B,** meanwhile, begins at Termini and heads southwest by way of via Cavour and the Colosseum.

Tickets cost 1,500 lire (95¢) each or 13,000 lire ($8.15) for 10 and can be purchased at tobacco shops (*tabacchi*), at most newsstands, and from machines in the stations. You can also buy a **one-day pass,** good on all buses and the Metropolitana, for 5,000 lire ($3.15), or a **one-week pass** for 20,000 ($12.50). The Metropolitana operates daily from 5:30am to midnight.

BY BUS & STREETCAR   There are three major drawbacks to Rome's public bus and streetcar system—traffic, crowds, and petty thieves. Downtown congestion can be so bad that you're sometimes better off on foot. When navigating this sprawling city by bus, remember **bus no. 64.** This indispensable line, sometimes called "the pickpocket bus," begins right behind the ticket booth at the train station, travels along via Nazionale, passes through piazza Venezia, and continues across the heart of the Old City along via Vittorio Emanuele, ending just off St. Peter's Square.

Bus no. 492 also makes the Termini–Vatican trip, on a longer route, by way of piazza Barberini, piazza Colonna, piazza Venezia, largo di Torre Argentina, and piazza Navona; bus no. 492's western terminus is piazza Risorgimento, up via della Porta Angelica from the entrance to St. Peter's Square, and convenient to the entrance to the Vatican Museums. Other key lines from the station include **bus no. 27,** which travels to the Colosseum, and **bus no. 75 and 170,** which cross the river into Trastevere.

You can buy bus tickets at a small gray-metal office in the corner of piazza dei Cinquecento, in front of the Stazione Termini. It's open daily from 6am to 11:30pm. The adjacent bus information window is open daily from 7:30am to 7:30pm.

Bus fare is 1,500 lire (95¢); tickets must be stamped in the red boxes at either end of the bus.

ON FOOT   Rome is not a pedestrian's paradise. It's spread out and crowded with cars. Sidewalks are extremely narrow, if they exist at all. Still, the heart of Old Rome, around the Spanish Steps and piazza Navona, is a joy to wander through.

BY TAXI   Taxi fares begin at 6,400 lire ($4) and click upward by 300 lire (20¢) every 250 yards. There's a 3,000-lira ($1.90) supplement for all rides between 10pm and 7am, a 1,000-lira (65¢) add-on for travel on Sunday and holidays, and 500 lire (30¢) extra per bag. If you order a taxi by telephone, the meter goes on when they receive the call, not when you begin riding. Finally, there's a whopping 14,000-lira ($8.75) surcharge for rides to the airport, though curiously they tack on just 10,000 lire ($6.25) for travel from the airport downtown.

Beware of unmetered cabs, which are illegal and unlicensed and charge sometimes exorbitant, uncontrolled rates. To call a taxi, dial 3570, 3875, or 4994.

BY RENTAL CAR & SCOOTER   Renting a car to get around Rome is pointless. Parking spots are scarce and only cars with special permits may enter the historic center.

For excursions out of the city, try **Hertz**, via Veneto 156 (☎ **06/54-79-91**); or **Avis**, piazza Esquilino 1c (☎ **06/478-01-50**).

Keep in mind that rates can be considerably less—as much as half the price or better—if you make reservations from your home country at least 48 hours in advance. Plan ahead or consider phoning a friend or relative back home to have reservations made for you.

For scooters and motorcycles, visit the **Scoot-A-Long** agency at via Cavour 302 (☎ **06/678-02-06**), near largo Ricci, two long blocks from the Cavour Metropolitana stop. Mopeds, with a top speed of 30 m.p.h., cost 45,000 lire ($28.15) per day, including insurance and unlimited mileage; there's a 200,000-lira ($125) refundable deposit, which you can pay with a credit or charge card; the actual rental fee must be paid in cash. Vespas that reach 60 m.p.h. at full throttle are 55,000 lire ($34.40) per day, with a 300,000-lira ($187.50) deposit. For weekly rates, multiply the daily rate by six. They're open daily from 9am to 7pm. You can take their bikes out of the country, but not on the autostrada.

BY BICYCLE   Heavy traffic and crazy drivers make bicycling around Rome somewhat unnerving. But mountain biking in the historic center or up in the large Villa Borghese park are singular experiences. **I Bike Rome,** via Veneto 156 (☎ **06/322-52-40**), rents bikes for 6,000 lire ($3.75) per hour, 15,000 lire ($9.40) per day, or 45,000 lire ($28.15) per week. They're open daily, year round, from 8:30am to 8pm.

You can also rent bikes from an **outdoor dealer,** immediately to your right as you exit the piazza di Spagna Metropolitana stop. Prices there are 7,000 lire ($4.40) per hour or 25,000 lire ($15.65) per day. It's open daily, from 9am to midnight March to October, from 9am to 8pm the rest of the year. Both places require a document as deposit.

FAST FACTS: Rome

Banks   Standard bank hours are Monday through Friday from 8:30am to 1:30pm, then again from about 2:45 to 3:45pm; only a few banks are open Saturday, and then usually mornings only. There's a bank in the train station, between the entrance to Tracks 8 to 11 and Tracks 12 to 15, that usually exchanges currency Monday through Saturday from 8:30am to 7:30pm and Sunday from 8am to 2:15pm. The **American Express** office, piazza di Spagna 38 (☎ **06/6-76-41**), exchanges traveler's checks (no fee) and is open Monday through Friday from 9am to 5:30pm and Saturday from 9am to 12:30pm.

Business Hours   In summer, most **businesses and shops** are open Monday through Friday from 9am to 1pm and 4 to 8pm; on Saturday shops are only open in the morning. From mid-September to mid-June, most shops are open Tuesday through Saturday from 9am to 1pm and anywhere from 3:30 or 4:30 to 7:30pm; on Monday in winter, shops don't open until the afternoon. In Rome as throughout the rest of Italy, just about everything except restaurants is closed on Sunday. **Restaurants** are required to close at least one day per week; the particular day varies from one trattoria to another. Most serve from noon to 3pm and 7:30 to 10:30pm.

Currency   The Italian unit of currency is the **lira,** almost always used in the plural form, **lire.** The lowest unit of currency these days is the silver 50-lira coin. There is also a silver 100-lira piece, a gold 200-lira coin, and a combination silver-and-gold 500-lira coin. Notes come in the following denominations: 1,000,

2,000, 5,000, 10,000, 50,000, 100,000, and 200,000 lire. Occasionally you'll come across a grooved coin with a pictogram of a telephone on it. A remnant of Italy's old pay-phone system, which is gradually being phased out, the telephone *gettone* is worth 200 lire (13¢), the price of a phone call.

Doctors/Dentists   For a list of English-speaking doctors and dentists, consult your embassy. At the private (and expensive) Salvator Mundi clinic, viale Mura Gianicolensi 67 (☎ **06/58-60-41**), you're certain to find English-speaking doctors and staff.

Embassies   The Embassy of the **United States**, via Veneto 121 (☎ **06/ 4-67-41**), is open Monday through Friday from 8:30am to 12:30pm and 2 to 5:30pm. The Embassy of the **United Kingdom** is at via XX Settembre 80a (☎ **06/482-54-41**); the Embassy of **Canada** is at via Zara 30 (☎ **06/440- 30-28**); the Embassy of **Australia** is at via Alessandria 215 (☎ **06/85-27-21**); and the Embassy of **New Zealand** is at via Zara 28 (☎ **06/440-29-28**)—they're all open Monday through Friday from 9:30am to 12:30pm and 2 to 4pm.

Emergencies   In Rome and throughout Italy, dial **113** in case of fire or in order to reach the police. The military-trained *Carabinieri* offer similar services (call **112**). For an ambulance, dial 5100.

Holidays   Italy is a religious country and its calendar is packed with holidays. The national holidays are New Year's Day (Jan 1), Epiphany (Jan 6), Easter Sunday and Monday, Liberation Day (Apr 25), Labor Day (May 1), Assumption Day (Aug 15), All Saints Day (Nov 1), Immaculate Conception (Dec 8), and Christmas and Santo Stefano (Dec 25–26). The city of Rome honors its patron saints, Peter and Paul, on June 29.

Information   For information on local tourist offices, see "Visitor Information" under "Rome Specifics," earlier in this chapter.

Laundry   There are few self-service launderettes in Italy. At the *lavandaria* at via Montebello 11 (☎ **06/474-55-03**), near the train station, they'll wash for 3 kilos (6¹/₂ lbs.) for you for 15,000 lire ($9.40) and 5 kilos (11 lbs.) for 25,000 lire ($15.65). It's open Monday through Friday from 9am to 7pm and Saturday from 9am to 1pm.

Lost & Found   Oggetti Rinvenuti is at via Nicolò Bettoni 1 (☎ **06/ 581-60-40**), open Monday through Saturday from 9am to noon.

Mail   Rome's main post office, piazza San Silvestro 19, 00187 Roma, is located near piazza di Spagna. For stamps (*francobolli*), visit Windows 22 to 24, on the right side as you enter. You can also buy stamps at face value at almost all *tabacchi* (tobacconists).

Many Romans prefer to use the more efficient postal service at the Vatican. If you're in the pope's neighborhood, bring your mail, and get some cool stamps too. The Vatican post office is adjacent to the information office in St. Peter's Square in the left wing. It's open Monday through Friday from 8:30am to 7pm and Saturday from 8:30am to 6pm. There's sometimes a mobile postal stand on the right side of the square, too.

Tax   The value-added tax (IVA in Italy) is already included in the price of most products and services. The tax is refundable to non–E.U. citizens who spend more than 525,000 lire ($328.15) in any one store. See "Shopping," later in this chapter, for details.

Telephone   There are two types of public pay phones in regular service. The first accepts coins or special slugs, called *gettone*, which you'll sometimes receive in change. The second operates with a phonecard, available at tabacchi and bars in 5,000-lira ($3.15) and 10,000-lira ($6.25) denominations; break off the perforated corner of the card before using it. Local phone calls cost 200 lire (13¢). To make a call, lift the receiver, insert a coin or card, and dial.

To phone the United States collect, or with your calling card, phone AT&T's USA Direct (☎ **06/172-10-11**), MCI's Call USA (☎ **06/172-10-22**), or US Sprint (☎ **06/172-18-77**). You can also call 06/172-10-01 for Canada, 06/172-10-61 for Australia, and 06/172-00-44 for the United Kingdom.

The area code for Rome is 06.

Tipping   In cafés, its customary to leave a 100-lira (6¢) or 200-lira (13¢) coin on the counter with your empty espresso cup. If you've been sitting down, 200- to 500-lira (15¢ to 35¢) is more like it. If service is exceptional, an additional tip of 5% or more is appropriate, though not expected. For taxis, tip up to 10%— service is not included in their fares.

4 Accommodations

Budget hotels are concentrated on either side of Stazione Termini, a run-down immigrant-heavy neighborhood that's far from anyone's romantic notion of Rome.

The few remaining budget pensiones and hotels in central Rome are better located and more expensive than those located by the station, but they're not necessarily better. The station-area hotels I've included were selected for their for fine standards of comfort and relatively good value. If you arrive in Rome without a reservation, try to arrive early; the best places fill up by around midday. The city's tourist offices can help you find a room, but the lines can stretch on forever.

Rentals in Italy, 1742 Calle Corva, Camarillo, CA 93010 (☎ **805/987-5278,** or 800/726-6702), rents apartments in most Italian cities and throughout the country. A regularly updated catalog, which lists all their Italian offerings, costs $15. But if you're planning to remain in one place for a week or more, you can't beat the quality and price of these private accommodations. **Interhome,** 124 Little Falls Rd., Fairfield, NJ 07004 (☎ **201/882-6864**), offers a similar service, with rentals starting at about $230 per week for a studio apartment.

The prices below are quoted for the summer of 1996—expect discounts before and after the season. By Italian law, triple rooms cost 35% more than double rooms and maximum rates must be posted in the room.

Breakfasts in Italian hotels are usually expensive and disappointing. Go to a nearby café instead.

DOUBLES FOR LESS THAN 65,500 LIRE ($40.95)

Those seeking to spend the minimum amount of money in Rome won't find many comforts. However, if funds are truly tight, the following provide rock-bottom rates, usually with few frills.

TO THE RIGHT OF THE TRAIN STATION

The neighborhood on either side of the Stazione Termini is rather unappealing, but there are budget accommodations in this area. The area to the right of the train station (exit by Track 1) is marginally more attractive and peaceful than the area

---

Getting the Best Deal on Accommodations

- Remember to make reservations, which usually require one night's deposit. During summer, these are a necessity.
- If you arrive without a reservation, head to the tourist office in the train station or go to the main office—the staff will help you reserve a room.

---

to the left—a fact vehemently disputed, naturally, by all those in the hotel business on the opposite side of the station.

Hotel Bolognese

Via Palestro 15 (1st, 2nd, and 3rd floors), 00185 Roma. ☎ **06/49-00-45.** 21 rms, 7 with shower only, 2 with bath. 38,000–43,500 lire ($23.75–$27.20) single without bath, 55,500 lire ($34.70) single with shower only; 62,500; lire ($39.05) double without bath, 76,500 lire ($47.80) double with shower only, 82,000 lire ($51.25) double with bath; 85,000 lire ($53.15) triple without bath, 109,000 lire ($68.15) triple with bath. No credit cards. As you exit Stazione Termini by Track 1, turn left and walk along via Marsala, which becomes via Volturno; after three blocks, turn right on via Montebello and the hotel is four blocks ahead past the corner of via Palestro.

When owner Giorgio Calderara isn't carefully watching his hotel and ensuring his guests's happiness, you'll find him painting in a closet-size studio—in fact, all the canvases you see in the halls and rooms are his. The five newly renovated rooms on the first floor (three with balconies) are a remarkable bargain, but that's not to take anything from the well-kept rooms on the two upper floors. Breakfast is not available.

Hotel Galli

Via Milazzo 20 (2nd floor) (100 yards from the station), 00185 Roma. ☎ **06/445-68-59.** 13 rms, 1 with bath. 39,500 lire ($24.70) single without bath; 58,000 lire ($36.25) double without bath, 65,500 lire ($40.95) double with bath; 82,000 lire ($51.25) triple without bath, 103,000 lire ($64.40) triple with bath. Breakfast 8,500 lire ($5.30) extra. No credit cards. Exit the train station by Platform 1, turn right, and take the first left onto via Milazzo.

They speak only enough English here to check you in, but the Galli is inexpensive in any language. The rooms are ample though basic and nondescript. Don't worry—the musty odor disappears quickly once you open a window.

Locanda Marini

Via Palestro 35 (3rd floor), 00185 Roma. ☎ **06/44-00-58.** 10 rms, none with bath. 48,000 lire ($30) double; 80,000 lire ($50) triple; 22,000 lire ($13.75) per person in shared rooms. No credit cards. To get here, see the directions for Pensione Katty, below.

The Marini's rooms are as spartan as those at the Katty across the hall, but they're a bit brighter—meaning that the place feels less like a dormitory—and owner Antonia Marini is gracious and friendly. Likewise, the prices here are nearly identical to the Katty's, and Antonia never puts more than three guests in a room. The building has no elevator.

Locanda Otello

Via Marghera 13 (4th floor), 00185 Roma. ☎ **06/49-03-83.** 6 rms, none with bath. 31,500 lire ($19.70) single; 59,000 lire ($36.90) double. No credit cards. Walk only a few steps from the side exit of Stazione Termini by Track 1.

The Otello has exceptionally big, bright rooms for a location so close to the station. Its friendly proprietors understand only a bit of English, and likewise ask only a bit of money from their guests.

Pensione Katty

Via Palestro 35 (3rd floor), 00185 Roma. ☎ **06/444-12-16.** 10 rms, 2 with bath. 48,000 lire ($30) double without bath; 82,000 lire ($51.25) double or triple with bath; 24,000 lire ($15) per person in shared rooms. Refundable 2,000-lire ($1.25) key deposit required. No credit cards. Head up via Marghera, which begins opposite the train station exit by Track 1, then walk up four blocks to via Palestro and turn left; the hotel is on the left side of the street via San Martino della Battaglia and Gaeta.

Luigi and Maria Idda offer accommodations at bargain-basement rates—indeed, some of the lowest in Rome. This is a one-of-a-kind place, the last of a dying breed of pensione that rents by the bed rather than by the room. There are never more than three beds per room. Four blocks from the station, this hotel (no elevator) is just far enough away to be out of earshot and sight of the cacophony and seediness that blights the area.

If the Katty is full, they'll send you to the nearby **Pensione Lucy**, via Magenta 13 (☎ **06/495-17-40**), with similar prices.

✪ Pensione Papà Germano

Via Calatafimi 14 (about eight blocks from the Stazione Termini), 00185 Roma. ☎ **06/48-69-19.** 13 rms, 2 with bath. 38,000 lire ($23.75) single without bath; 60,000 lire ($37.50) double without bath, 70,000 lire ($43.75) double with bath; 70,000 lire ($43.75) triple without bath, 78,000 lire ($48.75) triple with bath; 23,000 lire ($14.40) per person in shared rooms. MC, V. Exit the train station by Track 1, turn left, and walk along via Marsala, which becomes via Volturno; turn right onto via Calatafimi and the hotel will be half a block ahead on your left.

Though he tops the list in just about every budget travel guide, owner Gino insists that word of mouth is his best advertising, keeping his pensione filled 365 days a year. In any case, this place truly is a budget standout, mostly because of Gino himself. Terminally happy, he loves his job, tirelessly offering help, advice, books, maps, and so on to even the one-day visitor. He keeps his 13 modern rooms spotless, despite the heavy traffic, and he's also one of the very few hoteliers left in Rome who rents by the bed, an important factor for solo travelers. Perhaps the one drawback is that because the place is so small, noise carries far—don't expect to sleep late. In the end, though, this pensione is worthy of all the accolades it gets. (In case you're wondering, the place is named for Gino's father.)

TO THE LEFT OF THE TRAIN STATION

In the area to the left of the station, the streets are wider, the traffic is heavier, and the noise level is higher than in the area to the right of the station. There are scores of hotels here, but few are good choices for budget-minded, safety-conscious travelers.

NEAR THE ROMAN FORUM

Albergo Perugia

Via del Colosseo 7, 00184 Roma. ☎ **06/679-72-00.** 11 rms, 4 with shower only, 2 with bath. TEL. 42,500 lire ($26.55) single without bath; 62,500 lire ($39.05) double without bath, 75,500 lire ($47.20) double with shower only or bath; 88,000 lire ($55) triple without bath, 103,500 lire ($64.70) triple with shower only or bath. No credit cards. Metropolitana: Colosseo (then turn right down the massive via dei Fori Imperiali, and right again onto the first small street, called via del Tempio della Pace; after a third right turn, at the intersection with via del Colosseo, the hotel is just ahead on your left).

Location is everything for the four-floor Perugia (no elevator). A short walk from the Colosseum in a quiet neighborhood, this budget place has unfortunately ignored the basics: The floors and curtains could use a wash, the walls could use some decorations, and everything could use a fresh coat of paint. But the owners are nice and their prices are relatively low. Breakfast is not available.

DOUBLES FOR LESS THAN 93,000 LIRE ($58.15)
TO THE RIGHT OF THE TRAIN STATION

Pensione Corallo

Via Palestro 44 (6th floor), 00185 Roma. ☎ **06/445-63-40.** 11 rms, 5 with bath. 50,500 lire ($31.55) single without bath, 62,000 lire ($38.75) single with bath; 73,000 lire ($45.65) double without bath, 87,000 lire ($54.40) double with bath; 101,000 lire ($63.15) triple without bath, 121,000 lire ($75.65) triple with bath. No credit cards. Exit the train station by Track 1, walk straight for four blocks along via Marghera, turn left onto via Palestro, and the hotel is three blocks ahead (take the back elevator up to the fire-engine-red reception desk).

This is a classic family-run place, where the ever-professional and courteous Toni Cellestino or his wife is always on hand to make sure guests are properly cared for. The couple doesn't speak much English, but a bargain is a bargain in any tongue. While the slightly musty rooms can be best described as unremarkable, eight come with a modest flower-decked balcony, most overlooking a quiet courtyard.

TO THE LEFT OF THE TRAIN STATION

Hotel Giugiu

Via dei Viminale 8 (2nd floor), 00184 Roma. ☎ **06/482-77-34.** 12 rms, 2 with shower only, 4 with bath. 62,500 lire ($39.05) single without bath; 81,500 lire ($50.95) double without bath, 95,000 lire ($59.40) double with bath. Rates include continental breakfast. No credit cards. Exit the train station by Track 22, turn right, and walk about four blocks, with the bus lot on your right; turn left on largo di Villa Peretti and the hotel will be two blocks ahead on your left, across from the Hotel Columbia, at the head of via dei Viminale.

A neon sign sticks out over the slightly forbidding entrance, though once you're inside, friendly owner Mr. Chindamo will make you feel at home. This small pensione boasts 14-foot ceilings and medium-size rooms that show some wear. Still, the location is good, in a safe neighborhood a block from the Teatro dell' Opera.

⑤ Pensione Cortorillo

Via Principe Amedeo 79a (5th floor), 00185 Roma. ☎ **06/446-69-34.** 7 rms, none with bath. 67,000 lire ($41.90) single; 80,000 lire ($50) double; 107,000 lire ($66.90) triple. Discounts up to 30% during slow periods. Breakfast 8,500 lire ($5.30) extra. No credit cards. To get here, see the directions for the Pensione di Reinzo, below.

Signora Iolanda Cortorillo is delighted to have celebrated her silver anniversary in this book—she's as warm and gracious as she was more than 25 years ago, and she still runs one of the least-expensive listings in this chapter. The rooms are spacious and clean, especially considering the price. All overlook the interior courtyard, which makes them feel peaceful despite the noisy neighborhood. All in all, this is an exceptional value. Another thing that hasn't changed in all these years: Signora Cortorillo still speaks hardly a word of English, though her daughter is almost always there to help. Also note that they prefer not to take reservations in summer.

Pensione di Rienzo

Via Principe Amedeo 79a (2nd floor), 00185 Roma. ☎ **06/446-71-31.** Fax 06/446-91-42. 20 rms, 6 with shower only. 63,500 lire ($39.70) single without shower, 76,000 lire ($47.50) single with shower; 82,000 lire ($51.25) double without shower, 97,500 lire ($60.95) double with shower. Discounts up to 30% during slow periods. No credit cards. Exit the train station by Track 22, turn left, walk half a block, and turn right onto via Gioberti (Bar Tavola Calda

Etna is on the corner); after two blocks, turn left onto via Principe Amedeo and, when you reach no. 79a, take the stairs on the right side of the courtyard.

Owner Balduino di Rienzo hosts budget-minded travelers in what is certainly one of Rome's best rock-bottom-priced hotels. Indeed, when you inquire about his prices he's proud to say, "Little, very little." A shy, pleasant man, he speaks enough English to check you in and out, with his daughter often at hand for the big questions. His rooms are generally spacious and clean, and the baths are modern.

NEAR THE ROMAN FORUM

Albergo Apollo

Via dei Serpenti 109, 00184 Roma. ☎ **06/488-58-89.** 11 rms, none with bath. 73,000 lire ($45.65) double. No credit cards. Bus 64 from the train station about five stops to the Palazzo delle Esposizioni on via Nazionale (then walk two blocks west and turn left onto via dei Serpenti; the hotel is two blocks down on your left).

The rooms are bare and run-down here, with some antique closets and desks, but the area is respectable, across from the Bank of Italy in a characteristic Roman neighborhood. You'll especially enjoy leaving your hotel and seeing the Colosseum in the distance down the street. Four rooms on each floor share two baths.

NEAR PIAZZA NAVONA

Albergo Abruzzi

Piazza della Rotonda 69, 00186 Roma. ☎ **06/679-20-21.** 25 rms, none with bath. 54,500–71,000 lire ($34.05–$44.40) single; 82,000–93,000 lire ($51.25–$58.15) double. No credit cards. Bus 64 to largo di Torre Argentina (then walk four blocks north along Minerva or via Argentina; the hotel is directly ahead, in front of the Pantheon).

Unbelievably, this basic budget hotel directly overlooks the Pantheon and the adjacent piazza. It's somewhat noisy, but you can't get more central than this. The hotel's four floors are filled with medium-size rooms, most with queen-size beds. The more expensive rooms have the piazza view, while the cheaper (and quieter) ones are in the rear.

NEAR CAMPO DE' FIORI

The area surrounding campo de' Fiori, Rome's best open-air flower market, is beautiful, historic, and well located. From here you can walk to the Pantheon, the Trevi Fountain, and even the Spanish Steps. When you're tried of walking, it's nice to know that hotels near this campo are also close to the no. 64 bus route.

Albergo Della Lunetta

Piazza del Paradiso 68, 00186 Roma. ☎ **06/686-10-80.** Fax 06/689-20-28. 37 rms, 15 with bath. TEL. 45,000 lire ($28.15) single without bath, 65,500 lire ($40.95) single with bath; 85,000 lire ($53.15) double without bath, 120,000 lire ($75) double with bath; 114,500 lire ($71.55) triple without bath, 155,000 lire ($96.90) triple with bath. No credit cards. Bus 26 from the train station to largo di Torre Argentina (then walk west—in the direction the bus was going—along corso Vittorio Emanuele; after three blocks, turn left on via Paradiso and the hotel is half a block ahead).

A favorite of American students studying in Rome, the labyrinthine Lunetta is simply decorated, with fading floral wallpaper, and has small baths. Its best virtue is its location, near the large corso Vittorio Emanuele toward campo de' Fiori.

Albergo Sole

Via del Biscione 76, 00186 Roma. ☎ **06/6880-6873** or 687-94-46. Fax 06/689-37-87. 60 rms, 4 with shower only, 25 with bath. 75,000 lire ($46.90) single without bath, 80,000 lire ($50) single with shower only, 100,000 lire ($62.50) single with bath; 105,000 lire

($65.65) double without bath, 130,000–160,000 lire ($81.25–$100) double with bath. No credit cards. Bus 26 from the train station to largo di Torre Argentina (then follow the directions for the Lunetta, above, but continue across piazza Paradiso onto via Biscione).

A longtime favorite of Rome cognoscenti, the Sole offers simple aging rooms in what the owner says is the oldest hotel in Rome, dating from 1462! Of course, the area is even more ancient—the hotel is built above the remains of a Roman theater from 55 B.C. The attractive courtyard garden in back is the highlight of the place.

○ Hotel Piccolo

Via dei Chiavari 32, 00186 Roma. ☎ 06/6880-2560 or 689-23-30. 16 rms, 6 with shower only, 3 with bath. 66,500 lire ($41.55) single without bath, 74,500 lire ($46.55) single with shower only; 86,000 lire ($53.75) double without bath, 97,500 lire ($60.95) double with shower only, 109,000 lire ($68.15) double with bath. No credit cards. Bus 64 to largo di Torre Argentina (then walk west—in the direction the bus was going—for two blocks and turn left onto via dei Chiavari; the hotel is three blocks ahead on your right).

You enter this smartly modern hotel through a contemporary cast-iron gate that contrasts well with the small old-fashioned stone street in front. A modern marble-lined entrance leads up to the first-floor reception and rooms that won't disappoint you. The recently redecorated guest quarters are spacious, with spotless baths. The Piccolo is a shining star in one of Rome's top locations.

BETWEEN PIAZZA DI SPAGNE & PIAZZA DEL POPOLO

The ritzy area around the Spanish Steps is a favorite of visitors to Rome and boasts perhaps the most expensive in everything from stores to hotels. The following listings thus offer unusually good values.

Hotel Pensione Parlamento

Via delle Convertite 5, 00187 Roma. ☎ 06/684-16-97 or 6992-1000. 17 rms, 9 with bath. TEL. 64,000 lire ($40) single without bath, 92,500 lire ($57.80) single with bath; 86,000 lire ($53.75) double without bath, 110,000 lire ($68.75) double with bath. Rates include breakfast. No credit cards. Metropoitana: Spagna (then exit onto piazza di Spagna and walk to via Condotti; turn left onto via del Coreo, then left onto via delle Convertite).

A basic family-run budget hotel, the Parlamento gets good marks for its lovely flowered rooftop terrace. In addition to beds and bureaus, the guest rooms come with radios. The pensione's biggest drawback is the 75-step climb up an elevatorless building. If you're hearty, however, you'll be rewarded with accommodations that are a particularly good value.

○ Pensione Fiorella

Via Babuiono 196, 00187 Roma. ☎ 06/361-05-97. 8 rms, none with bath. 73,500 lire ($45.95) single; 92,500 lire ($57.80) double. Rates include continental breakfast. No credit cards. Metropolitana: Line A to Flaminio (then walk through the arch to piazza del Popolo; via Babuino is the leftmost of the three streets that fan out from the piazza).

The orange-and-green tile floors of this delightfully simple little pensione are kept sparkling by Antonio and Caterina Albano. This is the sort of place that'll make you want to extend your stay just so you can be here. It's one of the nicest places in this price range, in any part of town. Note that reservations are accepted only a day before checking in, and the doors are locked shut nightly at 1am.

NEAR CASTEL SANT' ANGELO

Near the Vatican, across the river from the historic city center, hotels in this region are a good bet for quiet and a local charm often missing from lodgings in more bustling tourist areas.

◐ Pensione Marvi

Via Pietro della Valle 13, 00193 Roma. ☎ **06/686-56-52** or 6880-2621. 7 rms, all with bath. 80,000 lire ($50) single; 103,500 lire ($64.70) double; 155,000 lire ($96.90) triple. Rates include continental breakfast. No credit cards. Bus 492 from the train station to the first stop across the river or 64 to Castel Sant' Angelo (then walk from the bus stop to the "far" side of Castel Sant' Angleo; via Pietro della Valle is between the castle and via Crescenzio—there's no sign, just a gold doorbell high up to the left of the building's big green door).

Adventurers looking for a wonderfully authentic Roman homestay would do well to look no further than this pensione on a quiet residential street. No English is spoken here, but guests are welcomed by a warm smile and simple yet comfortable surroundings. It's one of Rome's best values. The breakfast is served in a pretty dining room.

DOUBLES FOR LESS THAN 127,000 LIRE ($78.75)
TO THE RIGHT OF THE TRAIN STATION

Hotel Pensione Astoria Garden and Montagna

Via Vittorio Bachelet 8, 00185 Roma. ☎ **06/446-99-08.** 32 rms, 20 with bath. TEL. 69,000 lire ($43.15) single without bath, 80,500 lire ($50.30) single with bath; 114,500 lire ($71.55) double without bath, 149,000 lire ($93.15) double with bath; 166,500 lire ($104.05) triple without bath, 218,000 lire ($136.25) triple with bath. Rates include continental breakfast. AE, CB, DC, MC, V. From the train station, walk up via Marghera and go left on via Varese for three blocks (via Vittorio Bachelet is not listed on most maps, but is in fact the continuation of via Varese between via Vicenza and piazza dell'Independenza).

Manager Signor Vannutelli runs this hotel for the Montagna family in good old-fashioned Roman style, with a spacious lobby, lots of old wood, and colorful floral bedspreads that add an air of distinction. Breakfast is served on the glass-enclosed veranda in the lovely back garden/courtyard during the warmer months.

⑤ Hotel Romae

Via Palestro 49, 00185 Roma. ☎ **06/446-35-54.** Fax 06/446-39-14. 20 rms, all with bath. TV TEL. 93,000 lire ($58.15) single; 132,000 lire ($82.50) double; 164,000 lire ($102.50) triple. Rates include continental breakfast. AE, MC, V. Exit the train station by Track 1, walk straight for four blocks along via Marghera, and turn left onto via Palestro; the hotel is three blocks ahead on your left.

Though this hotel is just a bit above our budget, it represents one of Rome's best values. The friendly reception area contains a small espresso bar/lounge, and each sparkling-clean room has a bath, a TV, and even a hairdryer. All rooms are fresh and crisp, but those on the second floor are particularly recommendable. Owners Francesco Boccaforno and Lucy Baumhauer speak excellent English and have guaranteed these rates to Frommer's readers through 1996.

TO THE LEFT OF THE TRAIN STATION

⑤ Hotel Morgana

Via Turati 37, 00185 Roma. ☎ **06/446-72-30.** Fax 06/446-91-42. 70 rms, 66 with bath. TV TEL. 109,000 lire ($68.15) single with bath; 95,500 lire ($59.70) double without bath, 177,000 lire ($110.65) double with bath; 217,000 lire ($135.65) triple with bath; 271,500 lire ($169.70) quad with bath. Rates include continental breakfast. AE, DC, MC, V. Exit the train station by Track 22, go left half a block, turn right up via Gioberti, and via Turati—a continuation of via Amendola—is the first left off via Gioberti; the Morgana is on the left on the first block, just a block after the name change.

It's hard to say enough good things about brothers Mauro, Nicolà, and Roberto di Rienzo and their comfortable budget hotel, where they offer exceptionally discounted rates to bearers of this book. With spotless white walls, recessed lighting, and modern baths, their ultramodern hotel is one of the best values in the city; some rooms even have brass beds. The brothers boast that they "won't rent a room they wouldn't sleep in themselves." Always extraordinarily professional, all three speak excellent English and one is always around to dispense information about the city. The all-you-can-eat breakfast is served in a spacious bright room. If you reserve ahead, their airport van will pick you up and deliver you to the hotel for free.

Near Piazza di Spagna

This handful of hotels is in one of the ritziest neighborhoods in town—and the prices certainly reflect that.

Hotel Marcus

Via del Clementino, 94, 00186 Roma. ☎ **06/6830-0320.** Fax 06/683-25-67. 15 rms, all with bath. TV TEL. 91,000 lire ($56.90) single; 114,000 lire ($71.25) double; 145,000 lire ($90.65) triple. Breakfast 10,500 lire ($6.55) extra. AE, V. Metropolitana: Spagna (then exit into piazza di Spagna; turn left and then right onto via Condotti, the street that runs right into the Spanish Steps; follow this street for seven blocks—its name changes to become via Fontanella Borghese, then via del Clementino).

On a large street a few blocks from the Spanish Steps, the Marcus offers large, serviceable rooms. Salvatore, the owner, has managed this pleasant pensione for over 25 years. And even though the hotel's in the center of the hustle and bustle, the double windows he installed in all the rooms help cut out the noise.

Pensione Erdarelli

Via Due Macelli 28, 00187 Roma. ☎ **06/679-12-65** or 678-40-10. Fax 06/679-07-05. 37 rms, 21 with bath. 79,000 lire ($49.40) single without bath, 98,000 lire ($61.25) single with bath; 126,000 lire ($78.75) double without bath, 137,500 lire ($85.95) double with bath; 158,500 lire ($99.05) triple without bath, 186,000 lire ($116.25) triple with bath. Rates include continental breakfast. Air conditioning 20,000 lire ($12.50) per night extra. AE, MC, V. Metropolitana: Spagna (then exit onto piazza di Spagna and turn left onto via Due Macelli; the hotel's two blocks ahead, on your right).

Operated by the Erdarelli family since 1935, this simple and somewhat dated pensione is perfectly situated, within walking distance of the Spanish Steps. Most rooms, on five floors, offer high ceilings and good views. The top-floor accommodations are smaller but come with private balconies. The view from Room 11 is particularly memorable, as it overlooks the baroque Church of Santa Andrea delle Frate. The above rates are special for Frommer readers.

Pensione Lidia Venier

Via Sistina 42, 00187 Roma. ☎ **06/679-17-44.** Fax 06/884-14-80, Attn: Lidia Venier. 30 rms, 10 with shower only, 10 with bath. 86,000 lire ($53.75) single without bath, 97,500 lire ($60.95) single with shower only, 109,000 lire ($68.15) single with bath; 121,000 lire ($75.65) double without bath, 144,000 lire ($90) double with shower only, 270,000 lire ($168.75) double with bath. Rates include continental breakfast. AE, DC, V. Metropolitana: Piazza Barberini(then walk up via Sistina and you'll come upon the pensione on the left just after the intersection with via Crispi).

You ascend an elegant winding marble staircase to the reception area, and from here you're dispatched to one of the clean, modern rooms, some even complete with frescoed ceilings. The breakfast is served in a room with painted ceilings and picnic tables and hard wooden benches. Despite these fine touches, the prices remain moderate. There's a 2am curfew.

NEAR PIAZZA NAVONA

✪ Pensione Navona

Via dei Sediari 8, 00186 Roma. ☎ **06/686-42-03** or 6880-3802. 22 rms, 10 with bath. 71,000 lire ($44.40) single without or with bath; 109,000 lire ($68.15) double without or with bath. Rates include continental breakfast. No credit cards. Bus 64 to largo di Torre Argentina. Via dei Sediari is a small street between piazza Navona and the Pantheon, best reached from piazza S. Andrea d. Valle; walk a long block north on Rinascimento, turn right onto via dei Sediari, and the hotel is just ahead on your right.

Wrapped around an open courtyard, this pretty first-floor pensione is full of character. Recent renovations have made the rooms comfortable if not stylish. The hotel occupies a grand palace built in 1360 and holds architectural surprises at every turn. The baths are fully tiled, and the high ceilings lend an open, airy feel. The owners, the Australian-born Natale family, speak fluent English.

Pensione Mimosa

Via S. Chiara 61 (2nd floor) ($1\frac{1}{2}$ blocks from the Pantheon), 00186 Roma. ☎ **06/6880-1753.** 12 rms, 3 with bath. 57,000 lire ($35.65) single without bath; 87,000 lire ($54.40) double without bath, 103,500 lire ($64.70) double with bath. Rates include continental breakfast. No credit cards. Bus 64 from the train station to largo di Torre Argentina (then walk two blocks north on via de Torre Argentina, turn left on via S. Chiara, and the hotel is half a block up on the left).

An aging place (the building is from the 1500s) with few frills, the Mimosa features an excellent location in the heart of Rome. The low rates and location make the place a favorite of American students spending a semester in Rome. Guests get copies of the front-door key so they can return at any hour. The owner's two sons speak English.

NEAR CAMPO DE' FIORI

Hotel Campo de' Fiori

Via del Biscione 6, 00186 Roma. ☎ **06/6880-6865** or 687-48-86. Fax 06/687-60-03. 27 rms, 4 with shower only, 9 with bath. TEL. 100,000 lire ($62.50) double without bath, 115,000 lire ($71.90) double with shower only, 170,000 lire ($106.25) double with bath. Rates include continental breakfast. MC, V. Bus 64 from the train station to largo di Torre Argentina (then continue west—in the direction the bus was going—along corso Vittorio Emanuele; after three blocks, turn left onto via Paradiso, a small street that spills into piazza Paradiso, and continues as via del Biscione to the hotel; it's a seven-block walk in all).

They've mastered the art of the unique at this hotel in the heart of the historic district. Each small room with bath is decorated in a different regional style, carried out in meticulous detail with generous use of mirrors and occasionally gaudy details. The "rustic" room, for instance, feels uncannily like a Tuscan farmhouse. The rooms without bath have average furnishings, mini-chandeliers hanging over the beds, and floral wallpaper. Half a dozen rooms enjoy a view of the vibrant campo de' Fiori, the open-air flower market, and all guests have access to the pocket-size roof garden, with its view of St. Peter's. There's no elevator connecting the hotel's six stories, but the management here has made up for it by providing the most elegant four-story climb in Rome: There are few windows on the way up the marble stairs, but they've painted colorful floral scenes to brighten the ascent. The management is gradually adding a bath—and an individual style—to each room currently lacking this.

Hotel Smeraldo

Vicolo dei Chiodaroli 9, 00186 Roma. ☎ **06/687-59-29.** Fax 06/6880-5495. 35 rms, 14 with shower only, 4 with bath. A/C TV TEL. 86,000 lire ($53.75) single without bath or with shower only, 103,500 lire ($64.70) single with bath; 103,500 lire ($64.70) double without bath or with shower only, 126,000 lire ($78.75) double with bath; 126,000 lire ($78.75) triple without bath or with shower only, 166,500 lire ($104.25) triple with bath. Breakfast 6,000 lire ($3.75) extra. AE, MC, V. Bus 26 from the train station to largo di Torre Argentina (then turn south/left onto via de Torre Argentina; take the second right, via di S. Anna, and tiny vicolo dei Chiodaroli is just ahead on your left).

An incredible value in a charming area of the historic center, this highly recommended choice features a modern reception behind granite floors. An elevator takes you to all four floors, where the rooms are simple but clean. Those with baths are some of the shiniest I've seen in accommodations of this category. The place is often full, so it's a good idea to reserve ahead of time.

BETWEEN PIAZZA DI SPAGNA & PIAZZA DEL POPOLO

Residenza Brotzky

Via del Corso 509 (3rd floor), 00186 Roma. ☎ **06/361-23-39.** 13 rms, all with bath. 72,000 lire ($45) single; 108,000 lire ($67.50) double; 149,000 lire ($93.15) triple. No credit cards. Metropolitana: Line A to Flaminio (then walk through the large Roman arch called Porta del Popolo to piazza del Popolo and continue straight across the square and two blocks down via del Corso).

On via del Corso, one of Rome's main shopping streets, where the ancient Romans once held chariot races, the Brotzky is quiet, as many rooms overlook an inner courtyard. Although the rooms are simple, with aging plumbing, the *residenza* features a panoramic terrace upstairs affording fantastic views of town. Breakfast is not served, but there are tables here for a picnic or relaxation. The place is often full, so try to reserve ahead of time.

IN THE VIA NAZIONALE AREA

Via Nazionale is the wide boulevard running between piazza della Repubblica and piazza Venezia. From the front door of Stazione Termini, walk up to piazza della Repubblica (diagonally to the left across piazza dei Cinquecento), walk to the left around this circular piazza, and turn left onto via Nazionale.

✪ Pensione Elide

Via Firenze 50 (1st floor), 00184 Roma. ☎ **06/488-39-77** or 474-13-67. 14 rms, 4 with shower only, 5 with bath. TEL. 76,000 lire ($47.50) single without bath, 89,000 lire ($55.65) single with shower only; 101,000 lire ($63.15) double with shower only, 113,500 lire ($70.95) double with bath. Breakfast 7,500 lire ($4.70) extra. V. From the train station, walk clockwise around piazza della Repubblica to via Nazionale; via Firenze is the second street on the right.

This remarkable place is operated by one of Rome's friendliest families—appropriately named the Romas. The floors and the new modern baths always sparkle, and the prices are surprisingly low. They even change the wallpaper and paint the ceilings every year, which is quite an undertaking for such a small and inexpensive place. Ask for Room 16 or 18, both of which have unique carved and painted wooden ceilings. Everyone gets to enjoy the similarly decorated breakfast room. There's a 1:30am curfew.

NEAR THE VATICAN

Hotel Adriatic

Via Vitelleschi 25, 00193 Roma. ☎ **06/6880-6386.** 27 rms, 22 with shower only. TEL. 74,500 lire ($46.55) single without shower, 97,500 lire ($60.95) single with shower; 101,000 lire ($63.15) double without shower, 128,000 lire ($80) double with shower; 128,000 lire

($80) triple without shower, 172,000 lire ($107.50) triple with shower. No credit cards. Bus 64 from the train station to borgo Sant' Angelo (near St. Peter's pass under the nearby portal; then continue one block along via Porta Castello until you reach via Vitelleschi, where you turn left).

Lanfranco Mencucci, his wife, and his son, Marino, take great pride in their hotel and see to it that their modern rooms and baths are kept clean and attractive. They also have a small terrace with fruit trees and a rose trellis.

Hotel Bramante

Vicolo delle Palline 25, 00193 Roma. ☎ 06/654-04-26. 20 rms, 10 with bath. 80,000 lire ($50) single with bath; 103,500 lire ($64.70) double without bath, 137,500 lire ($85.95) double with bath; 137,500 lire ($85.95) triple without bath; 218,500 lire ($136.55) quad with bath. Breakfast 12,000 lire ($7.50) extra. AE, DC, MC, V. Bus 64 from the train station to the last stop (then walk through the nearby portal and continue along largo del Colonnato for three portals; at the third, go left and the hotel will be directly on your left).

In a charming old building begun in the 14th century, this place is clean, comfortable, and about as close to the Vatican as you can get, even if the linoleum floors and tan wallpaper don't really match the old-Roman flavor of the neighborhood. The top floors have nice beamed ceilings. The ivy-covered breakfast terrace has a view of the Colonnato del Vaticano, the special escape wall connecting the Vatican with the Castel Sant' Angleo. Owner Giuliana Belli was actually born in this building.

SUPER-BUDGET CHOICES

Each summer a handful of Roman university dormitories are turned into **unofficial youth hostels,** charging ultra-low rates usually similar or identical to those at the Ostello Foro Italico. Their locations change just about every year, so you'll need to check with the tourist office when you arrive. Consider, however, that these locations, like the official IYHF hostel, are often distant from the central part of the city.

Centro Universitario Marianum

Via Matteo Boiardo 30 (two blocks from piazza San Giovanni in Laterano), 00185 Roma. ☎ 06/700-54-53. 90 rms, none with bath. TEL. 66,500 lire ($41.65) per person single or double. Rates include three meals daily. No credit cards. Closed Nov–June 15 and Aug 1–21. Metropolitana: Manzoni (then walk two blocks toward the Colosseum on viale Manzoni and turn left onto via Matteo Boiardo).

A dormitory for local students much of the year (it's open only June 15 to July and August 21 to October), this place has that unmistakable institutional air, but it's good for those who want to pay one modest price for a bed and three square meals (served at 8am, 1pm, and 8pm). The Centro caters primarily to groups, but individual travelers are welcome if there's a vacancy. Note that there's a midnight curfew.

Ostello Foro Italico

Viale Olimpiadi 61, 00194 Roma. ☎ 06/323-62-67. 350 beds. 114,500 lire ($71.55) per night. Rates include continental breakfast and sheets. Dinner 12,500 lire ($7.80) extra. No credit cards. Metropolitana: Line A to Ottaviano (then bus no. 32 to the sixth stop).

Unfortunately, the hostel is far from anything else in Rome, located out by the Olympic Stadium, about an hour's commute from the train station and the rest of the city center. And with few windows and no neighborhood charm, it rates as one of the less-appealing youth hostels in Italy. Rooms contain 6, 7, 12, or 20 beds. An International Youth Hostel Federation membership card is required, but it can be purchased on the spot for 40,000 lire ($25). Despite its name, the youth hostel accepts travelers of any age. It's open from 7 to 9am and from 2pm until the 11pm curfew.

WORTH THE EXTRA MONEY

✪ Ara Pacis Hotel

Via Vittoria Colonna 11 (3rd floor), 00193 Roma. ☎ **06/320-44-46** or 320-44-47. Fax 06/562-16-17. 36 rms, 33 with bath. TEL. 114,500 lire ($71.55) single; 172,000 lire ($107.50) double; 206,000 lire ($128.75) triple. Rates include continental breakfast. AE, MC, V. Bus 492 or 910 from the train station to the first stop across the river.

Think wood—rich, dark, stained wood. Wood doors, shutters, and antique furniture filling the rooms and halls. And inlaid wooden ceilings, which you'll find in almost all the enormous rooms. This hotel has been in business since the turn of the century, and the management has clearly worked hard to preserve the character it must have had back then. Even the entranceway is impressive and will make the weariest budget traveler feel like a returning emperor. Yet convenience is not lacking: Modern baths resembling ship-cabin facilities were recently installed in almost all rooms. Ask for one of the seven rooms with their own terrace. A delightfully European, Roman kind of place.

The hotel is on the Vatican side of the Tiber, halfway between the ponte Cavour and piazza Cavour. Look for the large bust of Minerva on the wall to the right as you step off the elevator.

Hotel Venezia

Via Varese 18, 00185 Roma. ☎ **06/445-71-01** or 446-36-87. Fax 06/495-76-87. 59 rms, all with bath. TV TEL. 155,000–190,000 lire ($96.90–$118.75) single; 210,000 lire ($131.25) double; 285,000 lire ($178.15) triple. AE, CB, DC, MC, V. From the Stazione Termini, walk three blocks up via Marghera (which begins opposite the exit by Track 1) to its intersection with via Varese; the hotel is right there on the left.

Swiss expatriate Rosemarie Diletti and her daughter, Patrizia, have beautified this unique 18th-century building with their own personal touches. Antiques, rugs, and various historical pieces fill the ample-size rooms. Several top-floor accommodations have sunny balconies, and all rooms have traditional Murano-glass chandeliers and hairdryers. The staff is both fluent in English and exceedingly helpful around the clock. And when the clock strikes breakfast, look forward to a huge buffet, which usually includes fruit from the owner's garden. The Venezia is close enough to the train station to be convenient and easily reached, but in a quiet neighborhood nonetheless. Discounts will be given to bearers of this book.

5 Dining

In New York, London, and other major cities, it's often not the native dishes that are so special, but rather those that the countless immigrants who settle and open restaurants import from home. The same can be said of Rome.

Here you can sample foods from the farthest provincial reaches of the Republic without ever stepping out of range of the Metropolitana. Most Rome restaurants proudly announce somewhere on their menu or business card (*bigliettino*) the region where their specialties originated, and often go further to identify one or two particular house specialties. *Spaghetti alla carbonara* (with a sauce of bacon and eggs) and *saltimbocca alla romana* (veal wrapped or covered in ham slices) top the list of homespun Roman specialties, but don't be afraid to go

---

Getting the Best Deal on Dining

- Take advantage of the all-inclusive fixed-price meals known as the *menu turistico* and *menu del giorno*.
- Try dining in a self-service pizzeria or a *rosticceria*, an Italian cafeteria.
- Café/bars are great budget refuges for lunch.

---

beyond these. Ask the host for recommendations of the region—carbonara may not be the wisest selection at an Abruzzese trattoria.

A traditional Italian meal consists of a first course (*primo piatto*), usually a pasta dish; a second course (*secondo piatto*) of meat, fish, or chicken; a vegetable side dish to accompany the main course (*contorno*); and dessert (*dolce*). Most places expect their diners to take at least two courses, and will invariably "remind" you of this lest you "forget."

The ubiquitous tourist menu (*menu turistico* or *menu del giorno*) is an all-inclusive fixed-price meal that usually ranges from 12,500 to 21,000 lire ($7.80 to $13.15) and consists of a pasta course, a main course, a vegetable side dish, bread, cover and service charges, and often wine and dessert or fruit. The one disadvantage to this budget option is that you'll usually be offered only a very limited selection of ordinary, uninteresting dishes to choose from.

Pane e coperto ("bread and cover charge"), ranging from 1,000 to 2,500 lire (65¢ to $1.55) per person, is an inexpensive but unavoidable menu item that'll be new to most travelers. For better or worse, it's a charge you'll have to pay at restaurants simply for the privilege of eating there. Also note that a tip (*servizio*) of 10% to 15% will automatically be added to your bill.

Breakfast   Avoid buying hotel breakfasts if at all possible. Always expensive and often unsatisfying, they cannot compare with a visit to an Italian café-bar where you stand at the counter for a delicious cappuccino and a pastry or two for 3,000 to 4,000 lire ($1.90 to $2.50).

Stand Up   Another uniquely Italian custom to watch out for in Italian bars and cafés is the difference between prices *alla banca* (at the bar) and those *alla tavola* (at a table). You'll rarely see Italians sitting down to savor their cappuccino because sit-down prices on all items are at least twice those if you stand at the bar—three times as much in the most heavily touristed places.

A Final Note   Keep in mind that in the listings below, prices are given for pasta and main courses only. Don't forget to add in charges for bread and cover, service, and vegetable side dishes when calculating what you can actually expect to pay.

MEALS FOR LESS THAN 12,000 LIRE ($7.50)
NEAR THE MAIN TOURIST OFFICE

✪ **Marco Polo Bar**
Largo S. Susanna 108 (just off largo S. Susanna toward via Vento). ☎ **06/482-48-69.** Complete meal 12,000 lire ($7.50). No credit cards. Mon–Sat noon–3pm and 6:30–10pm, Sun noon–3pm. Metropolitana: Piazza della Repubblica (then a five-minute walk). ITALIAN.

A popular café/bar, the Marco Polo offers the lowest full-meal price around in a small self-service area beyond the cappuccino makers and pastry counters. The dining area is attractive for self-service, with dark-wood walls and private tables. Since you fetch the food yourself, you don't pay a service or cover charge.

OFF VIA NAZIONALE

✪ Pizzeria Est! Est! Est!

Via Genova 32. ☎ **06/488-11-07.** 9,500–11,500 lire ($5.95–$7.20), cover and service included. No credit cards. Tues–Sun 6–11:30pm. Closed three weeks in Aug. From piazza della Repubblica, take a left off via Nazionale onto via Genova. ITALIAN.

Open since the turn of the century, this is the oldest pizzeria in Rome. Is it the best? Only you can judge. The decor hasn't changed much in more than 90 years—diners still eat a wooden tables astride antique woodwork. Though it's not Rome's cheapest pizzeria, it's certainly the most storied and may be the best.

NEAR PIAZZA NAVONA

Dar Filettaro

Largo dei Librari 88. ☎ **06/696-40-18.** Cod filet 5,000 lire ($3.15) each. No credit cards. Mon–Sat 11am–10pm. SALT COD.

A true local favorite near campo de' Fiori, Dar Filettaro offers only one item: fried salt-cod filets, a true Roman specialty. There's not much in the way of atmosphere here, but the loyal patrons come with only one tasty thing on their minds.

Pizzeria Baffetto

Via del Governo Vecchio 114 (at the corner with via Sora near piazza Navona, in the area behind the Chiesa Nuova). ☎ **06/696-16-17.** 8,000–11,000 lire ($5–$6.90). No credit cards. Mon–Sat 11am–1am. Closed 15 days in Aug. ITALIAN.

Ask any Roman where to go for pizza and invariably he or she will mention this place first. Of the three pizzerias I list, this is the cheapest, smallest, and most crowded, its two bright rooms always packed with young Romans, no matter what the time or the weather (and spilling out to a few streetside tables in summer). If you're in a hurry or especially hungry, arrive to grab a table as soon as it opens.

Volpetti

Via della Scrofa 31–32 (near the intersection with via dei Portoghese, just a few minutes from the north end of piazza Navona). ☎ **06/686-19-40.** Pasta courses 6,000–7,000 lire ($3.75–$4.40); meat courses 6,000–11,000 lire ($3.75–$6.90). No credit cards. Mon–Sat 7am–8:30pm. ITALIAN.

An upscale food store/*rosticceria*, Volpetti is best suited for a quick meal, as it offers only stand-up dining at metal counters. Despite this inconvenience, the place is quite attractive and the food excellent. Via della Scrofa runs roughly parallel to the Tiber River.

NEAR THE COLOSSEUM

Snack Bar Venezia

Via Cavour 207. ☎ **06/48-45-40.** Pasta courses 6,000–8,000 lire ($3.75–$5); meat courses 7,000–11,000 lire ($4.40–$6.90). No credit cards. Mon–Sat noon–2:30pm. Metropolitana: Cavour (then walk down via Cavour toward the Colosseum). ITALIAN.

A clean, modern café/bar, the Venezia serves up some tasty pasta for lunch only from the back bar. You can eat at a counter or at one of the few tables here.

MEALS FOR LESS THAN 19,000 LIRE ($11.90)
NEAR PIAZZA NAVONA & LARGO DI TORRE ARGENTINA

✪ L'Insalata Ricca

Largo dei Chiavari 85. ☎ **06/6880-3656.** Pasta courses 6,000–9,000 lire ($3.75–$5.65); meat courses 8,500–12,000 lire ($5.30–$7.50); salads 4,500–8,000 lire ($2.80–$5). No credit cards. Thurs–Tues 12:30–3pm and 6:45–11pm. Bus 64 from the train station to largo di Torre Argentina (then walk west—in the direction the bus was going—for two blocks and turn left onto via dei Chiavari; it's not far from piazza Navona). ITALIAN.

Translated literally, this excellent budget trattoria's name means "the rich salad." The selection of second courses may be relatively limited, but you can always find at least 10 salads, eight unique and delicious first courses, and a handful of daily specials. You'll find it easy to save money here by ordering just a pasta dish and salad, enough to satisfy the heartiest appetite for little more than 16,000 lire ($10). Indeed, unlike places where they insist you take a full meal, the management boasts that their trattoria was created to provide a place where diners could order just one course or a salad. The menu is multilingual, and there's always a line for the excellent and inexpensive food served at this tiny one-room restaurant. No smoking is allowed.

Pizzeria Le Maschere

Via dei Monte della Farina 29. Pizza 9,000–12,000 lire ($5.65–$7.50), plus a steep 2,000-lira ($1.25) *coperto* per person and 15% service. AE, DC, MC, V. Tues–Sun 7pm–midnight. Bus 64 from the train station to largo di Torre Argentina (one short block in from via Arenula, the main boulevard running between largo di Torre Argentina and ponte Garibaldi). ITALIAN.

Stick to the thin-crust pizza here or you'll end up spending 22,000 lire ($13.75) or more on a full meal of specialties from Calabria, the owner's home province. As pizza goes, the pies are expensive, but the setting is enchanting. *Maschere* means "masks," and the walls of the often-crowded large dining area are covered with them. Tables are set out on a quiet piazza in summer.

Ristorante Il Delfino

Corso Vittorio Emanuele 67 (just past largo di Torre Argentina). ☎ **06/686-40-53.** *Menu turistico* 18,000 lire ($11.25); pizza 8,000–9,000 lire ($5–$5.65); pasta courses 6,000–8,000 lire ($3.75–$5); meat courses 9,000–11,000 lire ($5.65–$6.90). AE, DC, MC, V. Tues–Sun 8am–9pm. Bus 64 from the train station or piazza Venezia to largo di Torre Argentina. ITALIAN.

Rome's biggest self-service restaurant offers an exceptional selection of dishes, including pizza that's available all day (unlike in most pizzerias, where the ovens are fired up only for the dinner hour). It's a bright, cheery palace, with polished green stone floors and piped-in pop music and less of a fast-food atmosphere than many of the newer self-services in town. It even offers an English/American-style breakfast of two eggs, bacon, toast, juice, and coffee for about 9,500 lire ($5.95).

Trattoria Da Sergio

Vicolo delle Grotte 27. ☎ **06/686-42-93.** Pizza 5,500–9,000 lire ($3.45–$5.65); pasta courses 4,500–8,000 lire ($2.80–$5); meat courses 9,000–12,500 lire ($5.65–$7.80). No credit cards. Mon–Sat 12:30–3:30pm and 7:30pm–midnight. Bus 64 from the train station to largo di Torre Argentina (then go down via Arenula toward the river and continue until reaching piazza Cairoli; turn right onto via dei Giubbonari and take the fifth left). ITALIAN.

For good home-cooking at moderate prices you'll enjoy Da Sergio, where every day a new pasta specialty emerges. When I visited, I enjoyed the gnocchi, which the owner had made earlier in the day. The simple interior includes hams hanging from the ceiling as well as a crowd of loyal locals.

Trattoria L'Insalata Ricca 2

Piazza Pasquino 72 (near piazza Navona, at one end of via Santa Maria dell' Anima). ☎ **06/6880-7881.** Pasta courses 6,000–9,000 lire ($3.75–$5.65); meat courses 8,500–12,000 lire ($5.30–$7.50); salads 4,500–8,000 lire ($2.80–$5). No credit cards. Tues–Sun 12:30–3pm and 7:15–11:30pm. ITALIAN.

Once you eat here you'll discover why the owners opened a second place under the same name. The atmosphere is rustic—rare in Rome—with wood-beamed ceilings, copper pots and wine jugs dangling from the roof, and a hand-painted sign out front.

NEAR THE COLOSSEUM

✪ Da Sabatino

Via del Boschetto 28 (between via Nazionale and the Colosseum). Pasta courses 5,000–7,500 lire ($3.15–$4.70); meat and poultry courses 7,000–10,500 lire ($4.40–$6.55). No credit cards. Mon–Sat noon–4pm and 7pm–midnight. Metropolitana: Cavour (then about a five-minute walk). ITALIAN.

A simple, very Roman restaurant—outside you'll see only a sign reading FRASCATI above the small plain door—with imitation woodwork and a mix of prints and paintings on the wall, Da Sabatino offers some of the lowest à la carte food prices in town. Only two people work here: Sabatino, who serves the tables and chats with the loyal clientele, and his wife, who tends to all the cooking. Both have honed their skills—Sabatino is entering his 50th year at the place.

Trattoria Da Pasqualino

Via dei Santi Quattro 66 (a block from the Colosseum toward San Giovanni in Laterano). ☎ **06/700-45-76.** Pasta courses 7,000–10,000 lire ($4.40–$6.25); meat and fish courses 8,000–16,000 lire ($5–$10). AE, V. Tues–Sun noon–3pm and 8pm–midnight. Follow via dei Fori Imperiali past the Colosseum and just before it turns into via Labicana, turn right; then take the second left. ITALIAN.

The 100-year-old Da Pasqualino boasts a remarkable location. Yet despite its proximity to Rome's foremost sight, the prices here are remarkably reasonable and the ambience is very typical, with mostly Italians dining.

NEAR THE TREVI FOUNTAIN

Tourists flock by the busload to throw their loose lire into the gaudily baroque Trevi Fountain; legend has it that those who do so will be sure to return to Rome. Tourists also come for the neighborhood's several moderately priced trattorias.

Here are several good picks, but you might shop around in this compact area, since others offer competitive prices.

Rosticceria/Tavola Calda Al Picchio

Via del Lavatore 39–40. ☎ **06/6710-9926.** Menu turistico (with six options, all including wine) 18,000–24,000 lire ($11.25–$15); pasta courses 4,500–8,000 lire ($2.80–$5); meat courses 7,000–13,000 lire ($4.40–$8.15). No credit cards. Tues–Sun noon–3:30pm and 6–10:30pm. Closed two weeks in Feb. ITALIAN.

This restaurant is a bit more pleasant than its neighbors and can cater to your every whim, with six *menu turisticos*. Its choices are advertised in six languages. The ambience is a bit unusual for Rome: tables under a long barrel vault more reminiscent of a Czechoslovakian beer hall than an Italian eatery. If you prefer, they also offer a self-service *rosticceria* with counter seating to the front of the restaurant.

Trattoria della Stampa

Via dei Maroniti 32 (a small street that begins at largo del Tritone off via del Tritone). ☎ **06/ 6710-9919.** Pasta courses 6,000–8,000 lire ($3.75–$5); meat courses 9,000–12,000 lire ($5.65–$7.50). No credit cards. Mon–Sat 12:30–3pm and 6:30 or 7–10 or 10:30pm. Metropolitana: Barberini (then a short walk). ITALIAN.

This is a typical place in the heart of Rome and a favorite of journalists (the name means "trattoria of the press"). The plain woodwork is decorated with onions, red peppers, and wine—all ingredients favored by owner Antonio Bucci, who presides over the kitchen.

Pizzeria La Fontana di Venere

Vicolo dei Modelli 56. ☎ **06/678-2753.** Pizza and pasta 7,000–10,000 lire ($4.40–$6.25). MC. Mon–Sat 11:30am–2:30pm and 6pm–midnight. Face the Trevi Fountain and turn left; the restaurant is around the corner on your left. PIZZA/PASTA.

A traditional Roman kitchen, this small restaurant near the Trevi Fountain serves decent pizzas, along with very good lasagne, spaghetti, and the occasional risotto.

IN TRASTEVERE

Trastevere is the artists' and writers' quarter of Rome. "Everyone has his own favorite trattoria in Trastevere," so the Romans tell you. My favorite budget value is Mario's, but there are many others in this area just waiting to be discovered.

Da Corrado

Via delle Pelliccia 39. ☎ **06/580-60-04.** Pasta courses 7,500–9,500 lire ($4.70–$5.95); meat courses 9,500–19,000 lire ($5.95–11.90). No credit cards. Tues–Sun noon–3pm and 7pm–midnight. ITALIAN.

In the neighborhood known for its colorful restaurants, Da Corrado is kaleidoscopic. A quintessential working-class eatery, it serves excellent pastas, meats, and salads along with generous amounts of wine and spirits. The repartee is sometimes heated, often humorous, and always part of the fun. There's no menu, and the bill is usually toted up on your paper tablecloth.

✪ Trattoria Mario's

Via del Moro 53. ☎ **06/580-3809.** *Menu turistico* 17,000 lire ($10.65); pasta courses 4,500– 6,000 lire ($2.80–$3.75); meat courses 8,000–10,000 lire ($5–$6.25). No credit cards. Mon–Sat noon–4pm and 7pm–midnight. Closed second half of Aug. Bus 170 from the train station or piazza Venezia to the first ponte Garibaldi stop (then turn right onto via del Moro and walk toward ponte Sisto, looking for the trattoria halfway down on the left). ITALIAN.

This charming place, decorated with the work of neighborhood artists and operated by three generations of Mario's family, offers one of the better food values in Rome. The 17,000-lira ($10.65) *menu turistico* is the cheapest outside the train station's immediate vicinity and full of variety, making it a big favorite of visitors.

NEAR STAZIONE TERMINI

This is certainly the best Roman neighborhood for budget dining, though neither the surroundings nor the food is particularly pleasant. Here are a few exceptions to the rule:

Hostaria-Pizzeria La Reatina

Via San Martino della Battaglia 17. ☎ **06/49-03-14.** Pizza 5,500–9,500 lire ($3.40–$5.95); pasta courses 4,500–7,000 lire ($2.80–$4.70); meat courses 7,000–12,000 lire ($4.40–$7.50). *Coperto* and service 2,000 lire ($1.25) extra. No credit cards. Sun–Fri noon–3pm and 6:30– 11:30pm. Closed 15 days in Aug. Via San Martino della Battaglia runs between piazza

Indipendenza and viale Castro Pretorio; the restaurant is the on the right, just past the intersection with via Villafranca. ITALIAN.

There's no menu turistico here, but with the moderate à la carte prices you'll have no trouble filling up for less than you'd pay for a fixed-price dinner someplace else. A three-course meal here (without wine) shouldn't be more than 18,000 lire ($11.25). Don't expect much in the way of atmosphere—just hearty, inexpensive food and a satisfied local clientele. Pizza is served, but only in the evening. The service is not always the most attentive.

La Diligenza Rossa

Via Merulana 271. ☎ **06/488-57-48.** Pasta courses 6,000–8,000 lire ($3.75–$5); meat courses 10,500–13,500 lire ($6.55–$8.45). No credit cards. Tues–Sun 11am–11pm. With your back to the central train station, turn left onto via Cavour, then left again onto via Merulana; the restaurant is on your right. ITALIAN.

Loosely translated as "The Red Coach Grill," La Diligenza Rossa offers an arm-long list of Italian specialties served in a comfortable downscale dining room. Seating is on bentwood chairs at plastic-covered wooden tables. Recommendable first courses include tortellini consommé and minestrone with rice and pasta. Next, try the chicken breast sautéed cacciatore or marsala style or, better yet, order saltimbocca or osso buco. A variety of pizzas is also served, prepared in the restaurant's signature copper-top pizza oven.

MEALS FOR LESS THAN 26,000 LIRE ($16.25)
NEAR PIAZZA NAVONA

Again, this is a top-notch neighborhood for finding good food at reasonable prices.

Antica Trattoria Pizzeria Polese

Piazza Sforza Cesarini 40 (just off corso Vittorio Emanuele, the main boulevard running through Old Rome, between piazza di Chiesa Nuova and the Tiber). ☎ **06/686-17-09.** Pasta courses 8,000–11,000 lire ($5–$6.90); meat courses 9,500–20,000 lire ($5.95–$12.50). MC, V. Wed–Mon 12:15–3pm and 7–11pm. ITALIAN.

The large menu here changes regularly—the last time I visited they were featuring no fewer than 17 second-course selections. The menu is not translated, but most of the waiters speak English. You can order such specialties as fettuccine alla Sforza (with a sauce of cream and mushrooms), fracostine di vitello alla fornata (veal in a white-wine sauce), or abbacchio al forno (roast lamb). The Polese remains busy year round, with tables out on the piazza in summer and rustic old chandeliers over the tables inside. This is an excellent selection for the medium-price category, where you can expect to spend 22,000 to 33,000 lire ($13.75 to $20.65) for a plentiful, hearty, and delicious meal, including wine.

Trattoria Da Luigi

Piazza Sforza Cesarini 24. ☎ **06/686-59-46** or 6880-5463. Pasta courses 8,500–10,500 lire ($5.30–$6.55); meat courses 11,500–17,000 lire ($7.20–$10.65). AE, DC, V. Tues–Sun noon–3pm and 7pm–midnight. ITALIAN.

On the same square as the Polese (above), this place is similarly priced and just about as popular and well established. Also like its nearby competitor, it has outdoor tables in summer and red lampshades over the tables. It's kept darker and more romantic, though, and is tastefully decorated with the old theater posters and mirrors advertising various English liquors. Perhaps it's the latter that makes tourists and expatriates prefer this place, while more Italians can be found at the Polese. They don't seem to mind if you order only a pasta dish here; I especially recommend the penne alla vodka in a rich tomato-cream sauce.

NEAR THE VATICAN

✪ Taverna-Ristorante Tre Pupazzi

Borgo Pio 183 (at the corner of via Tre Pupazzi). ☎ **06/686-8371.** *Menu turistico* (including dessert) 21,000 lire ($13.15); pizza 8,500–10,000 lire ($5.30–$6.25); pasta courses 8,500–16,000 lire ($5.30–$10); meat and fish courses 11,000–21,000 lire ($6.90–$13.15). AE, MC, V. Mon–Sat noon–3:30pm and 7pm–midnight. Borgo Pio is two short blocks from, and parallel to, via della Conciliazione, at the corner of Vicolo del Campanile. ITALIAN.

This cozy and charming 17th-century-style taverna comes highly recommended from nearby hoteliers and many other Romans as well. Its 21,000-lira ($13.15) *menu turistico* is acceptable considering the restaurant's delightful atmosphere and proximity to St. Peter's. Service can be slow, however.

NEAR STAZIONE TERMINI

If you must eat in this neighborhood and can afford this price range, you'll find either of these places acceptable:

Hostaria Angelo

Via Principe Amedeo 104 (between via Gioberti and via Cattaneo). ☎ **06/731-22-63.** *Menu turistico* 23,000 lire ($14.40); pasta courses 5,000–8,000 lire ($3.15–$5); meat courses 8,500–12,000 lire ($5.30–$7.50). AE, DC, MC, V. Thurs–Tues 11am–3pm and 6–11pm. ITALIAN.

Angelo's atmosphere is pleasant enough, featuring checkered floors and wood paneling. Its clientele includes a good mix of Italians and tourists. Stick to the ample menu turistico, which includes a choice from among 10 second courses—otherwise you're likely to spend 24,000 lire ($15) or more.

Trattoria da Alfredo

Via Principe Amedeo 126a. ☎ **06/446-42-98.** *Menu turistico* 21,000 lire ($13.15) without wine, 24,000 lire ($15) with wine; pasta courses 5,000–7,000 lire ($3.15–$4.40); meat courses 9,500–12,000 lire ($5.95–$7.50). AE, MC, V. Mon–Sat noon–3pm and 6:30–11pm. ITALIAN.

A few steps beyond the Trattoria Angelo, with atmosphere and service a few notches below, Alfredo's is nonetheless a good choice. The menu turistico includes an unusually wide selection of main courses, including veal, chicken, liver, and fish.

PICNICKING

Piazza Vittorio Emanuele, near the train station, is Rome's principal open-air daily food market. There's also a modest-size outdoor covered market (the **Mercato Rionale**) at via Flaminia 60, near piazza del Popolo, plus plenty of little shops in between where you can pick up meat, cheese, and drinks; the market's open Monday through Saturday from 7am to 2pm. The market in **campo de' Fiori** is especially characteristic and photogenic. There's an **open-air food market** near the train station year round, Monday through Saturday from 6am to about 2pm, on via Montebello, on the two blocks between via Volturno and via Goito. There are numerous *panetterie, pasticcerie,* and *salumerie* in storefronts behind the street vendors.

Doing your own food shopping in Italy can be an interesting cultural experience, since supermarkets are very rare. Cold cuts are sold at the *salumeria*. To pick up cheese or yogurt, you'll have to find a *latteria*. Vegetables can usually be found at an *alimentari*, the closest thing Italy has to a grocery store. For bread to put all that between, visit a *panetteria*. Wander into *pasticceria* to find dessert. And for a bottle of wine to wash it down, search out a *vinatteria*.

The **Villa Borghese,** Rome's only downtown park, is the place to take your fixings for an imperial picnic.

WORTH THE EXTRA MONEY
NEAR THE FORUM & THE COLOSSEUM

Ristorante-Pizzeria Su Recreu
Via del Buon Consiglio 17. ☎ **06/679-49-18.** Pizza 11,000–13,000 lire ($6.90–$8.15); pasta courses 10,000–13,000 lire ($6.25–$8.15); meat courses 17,000–20,000 lire ($10.65–$12.50); fresh fish 11,000–21,000 lire ($6.90–$13.15) per 100 grams (roughly a quarter pound). AE, DC, MC, V. Tues–Sun noon–3pm and 7:30pm–1:30am. Metropolitana: Cavour (then walk along via Cavour away from the train station and take the third left onto via del Cardello, one block past via degli Annibaldi; the pocket-size via del Buon Consiglio is immediately on your right). ITALIAN.

The sign over the door—LOCALE TIPICO SARDO—means "typical Sardinian restaurant." That tells it all about this popular restaurant with white stucco walls, closely packed tables, and Sardinian artifacts hanging from walls and ceiling. The food is outstanding, the atmosphere lively. Popular dishes include risotto alla pescatore (a rice-and-seafood combination), pane frattau (very thin bread stuffed with tomato, cheese, and egg), linguine con bottarga (with fish roe), homemade ravioli stuffed with spinach ricotta cheese, and fresh fish.

IN TRASTEVERE

✪ Taverna Fieramosca
Piazza de' Mercanti. ☎ **06/589-02-89.** Pizza 7,500–17,000 lire ($4.70–$10.65); meat courses 9,000–24,000 lire ($5.65–$15); vegetables 6,000–8,000 lire ($3.75–$5). No credit cards. Mon–Sat 7pm–midnight. Closed one week in Aug. Bus 170 from the train station or piazza Venezia to the first stop across the river, viale Trastevere (then walk along via dei Genovesi for five short blocks and turn right onto via Santa Cecilia to piazza de'Mercanti). ITALIAN.

This delightful place bills itself as an authentic medieval taverna—and that's exactly what it is. Cannons hang from the ceiling, suits of armor stand at attention in the corner, and all eating is done at long wooden tables. They carry the theme to the extreme and don't serve any pasta, which came to Italy with Marco Polo toward the end of the Middle Ages. Indeed, the only modern intrusion is the eating utensils. This Middle Ages mess hall enjoys a devout following of Romans and tourists alike. The menu here is a 24- by 36-inch souvenir poster, and during the evening guitar and accordion players add to the revelry. In summer 200 seats are placed on the piazza outside.

NEAR THE HISTORIC CENTER

Fiaschetteria Beltramme
Via della Croce 39. Pasta courses 9,500–13,000 lire ($5.95–8.15); meat courses 13,000–24,000 lire ($8.15–$15). No credit cards. Mon–Sat noon–3pm and 7:45–10:30pm. Closed Aug. Metropolitana: Piazza di Spagna (via della Croce begins at piazza di Spagna, at the corner where the Mondi shop is situated). ITALIAN.

The sketches on the wall were done by artists who frequent this tiny one-room institution that's been serving Roman specialties for more than a century. In fact, it's so well known among the city's artists and intellectuals that there's neither a menu nor a sign (other than FIASCHETTERIA) out front identifying it as a place to eat. Owner Luciano Guerra points out that this is a "locale known to the national art authorities," though he doesn't say whether it's the food or the milieu—or the combination of the two—that attracts them.

Ristorante Valle "La Biblioteca"
Largo Teatro Valle 9. ☎ **06/6880-1357.** Reservations recommended, especially on Sat. Pasta courses 11,000–12,000 lire ($6.90–$7.50); meat courses 17,000–26,000 lire ($10.65–$16.25). AE, DC, MC, V. Mon–Sat 8pm–1 or 2am. Bus 64 or 170 from the train station to largo di Torre Argentina (then walk in the same direction the bus was traveling and turn right at piazza di Sant' Andrea della Valle). ITALIAN.

This is one of Rome's older restaurants, known to everyone simply as La Biblioteca (The Library), for its exceptionally exhaustive wine collection lining almost every inch of its walls. Some might call the place gaudy or even tacky, but it does have a certain charm and the food is excellent. You don't get to be this old without it. They also feature live music and dancing every night. Expect to spend at least 39,000 lire ($24.40) per person without wine.

6 Attractions

SIGHTSEEING SUGGESTIONS

A word to the wise about sightseeing in Rome: Just about all the sights of significance, except the Vatican and other churches, are closed Monday. During the rest of the week museums and attractions close by 2pm, and stop admitting visitors 3o to 60 minutes before that.

If You Have 1 Day

Rome wasn't built in a day, so don't expect to see it all that quickly either. You'll just have to make the choice a historical tour that includes the Colosseum and Forum, a spiritual and artistic tour that includes St. Peter's and the Vatican area, or an architectural and cultural visit through the historical center's tangle of streets, encompassing the Spanish Steps, piazza Navona, and the Trevi Fountain, among other sites.

If You Have 2 Days

Spend your second day at whichever place—the Fourm/Colosseum, St. Peter's/Vatican, or historical center area—you weren't able to get to on your first day.

If You Have 3 Days

What should you not miss once you've covered the Rome's most significant areas? The twin museums on the Capitoline Hill are something of a must-see, followed by the Etruscan Museum and the Galleria Borghese in the Villa Borghese.

If You Have 5 Days

If you've already managed to see all of Rome's top sites—an especially difficult task considering the capricious opening days and hours of most—leave the city to explore Tivoli or Ostia Antica.

TOP ATTRACTIONS

With the exception of churches, all the sights listed below stop admitting visitors at least 30, and in some cases as much as 60, minutes before the listed closing time.

⊙ The Forum, Palatine Hill, and Circus Maximus

Via dei Fori Imperiali. ☎ **06/699-01-10.** Forum and Palatine Hill, 12,000 lire ($7.50); Circus Maximus, free. Sun, Tues, and hols 9am–2pm; Mon and Wed–Sat, June–July 15 9am–7pm, May and July 16–Aug 15 9am–6:30pm, Apr 16–30 and Aug 16–31 9am–6pm, Mar 16–Apr 15 and Sept 9am–5:30pm, Feb 16–Mar 15 and Oct 9am–5pm, Nov–Jan 15 9am–4:30pm. Last admission is one hour before closing. Closed Jan 1 and May 1.

The **Roman Forum (Foro Romano)** is a wonderfully intact slice of ancient Rome, where, with a little imagination, you can envision the life and vibrancy of the city as it was 2,000 years ago. This area was for a long time the seat of commerce and government, where Romans came to conduct all business, imperial and mercantile.

Archeologists began uncovering the site early in the last century and are still digging here today. As you descend into the main part, the life of the Eternal City flowers before you—the triumphal arches at either end, the remains of several imperial temples, the odd, lonely marble column sprouting up from the earth, or the slice of marble edifice lying on the ground carved with a few letters or words of an inscription.

The Arch of Titus marks the east end of the Forum, nearest the Colosseum, while the bigger and more impressive Arch of Tiberius stands at the west end. Rising above the Forum, accessible from stairs near the Arch of Titus, is the **Palatine Hill**. Rome was built on seven hills, beginning with this one. The palace ruins and the remains of the other buildings and gardens here are less impressive than those of the Forum below but significant nonetheless.

Only the outline of the narrow oval known at the **Circo Massimo (Circus Maximus)**, where Roman chariot races took place, remains. To view the Circus, now an open expanse of grass, go to the southern side (far left edge as you enter) of the Palatine Hill. You can also jog there today.

The main entrance to the Forum is on via dei Fori Imperiali, a huge boulevard created by World War II dictator Benito Mussolini as a place to hold military parades. Another entrance to the Palatine Hill and Forum is down via di San Gregorio from the Colosseum, to the left as you exit. If you're in a hurry and would prefer to see only the Forum, you can make a quick getaway (and it's only an exit, not an entrance) behind the Arch of Titus, the closest exit to the Colosseum.

The Colosseum and the Arch of Constantine

Via dei Fori Imperiali. ☎ **06/700-42-61.** Colosseum, street level of interior, free; upper levels, 8,000 lire ($5). Wed and hols 9am–2pm; Mon–Tues and Thurs–Sat, June–July 15 9am–7pm, May and July 16–Aug 15 9am–6:30pm, Apr 16–30 and Aug 16–31 9am–6pm, Mar 16–Apr 15 and Sept 9am–5:30pm, Feb 16–Mar 15 and Oct 9am–5pm, Nov–Jan 15 9am–4:30pm. Last admission to the upper levels is one hour before closing. Closed Jan–Feb 15. Metropolitana: Colosseo.

Every major city has at least one icon that symbolizes it: the Eiffel Tower in Paris, the Houses of Parliament and Big Ben in London, the Grand Canal and the gondolas in Venice, and the **Colosseum (Colosseo)** in Rome. It's most impressive from the outside, a mammoth remnant of the golden age of the Roman Empire. Completed in the 1st century A.D., it was in this 50,000-seat stadium that Christians were thrown to the lions and other public events took place. Its legendary crumbled look is due mostly to the fact that it was used for centuries as a quarry for other Roman construction projects. The original "floor" of the structure is also gone, revealing the labyrinthine underground network where prisoners, lions, and general provisions were kept.

The Roman Forum & Palatine Hill

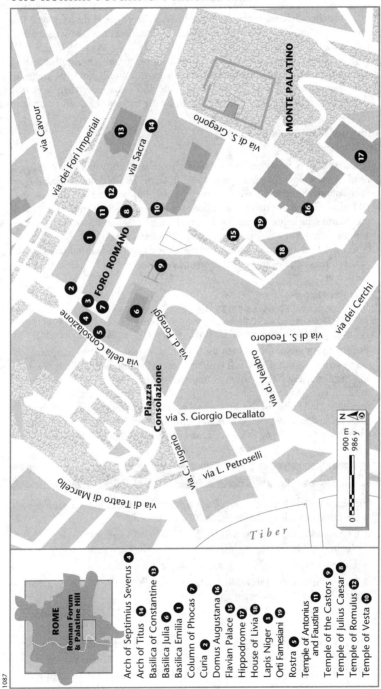

MONTE PALATINO

via di S. Gregorio

via Cavour

via dei Fori Imperiali

via Sacra

FORO ROMANO

via d. Foraggi

via della Consolazione

Piazza Consolazione

via S. Giorgio Decallato

via C. Jugario

via L. Petroselli

via di Teatro di Marcello

via d. Velabro

via di S. Teodoro

via dei Cerchi

Tiber

N

0   900 m
     986 y

1087

To clamber up to the higher levels, go to the stairway just to the left as you face the main entrance. In recent years various of the three upper levels have been closed for reconstruction and reinforcement.

As you step out of the Colosseum, you'll see the grandest triumphal arch of them all, the **Arch of Constantine**, to your left. Ironically, in 1994 archeologists found evidence that the arch is actually 350 years older than originally thought, meaning it would have been built by the emperor Hadrian rather than Constantine.

Augustus's and Trajan's Forums
Via dei Fori Imperiali.

If you walk away from the Colosseum on via Alessandrina, you'll find Augustus's Forum on the right side and Trajan's Forum on the left. Neither of these is open to the public, but you can see everything you need to from the sidewalk above.

Trajan's Forum is certainly the highlight of this imperial walk, with its 25 standing columns, including the intricately carved Trajan's Column (Colonna Traiano), a stunning series of bas-reliefs winding up a monumental pillar.

Via dei Fori Imperiali ends at piazza Venezia, which is dominated by the stark-white winged chariots of the ostentatious 19th-century Vittorio Emanuele Monument.

✪ The Pantheon
Piazza della Rotonda. ☎ **06/36-98-31.** Admission free. July–Sept, daily 9am–6pm (light permitting); Oct–June, Mon–Sat 9am–4pm, Sun 9am–1pm. Bus 64, 170, or 175 to largo di Torre Argentina (then walk up via de' Cestari for three blocks to piazza della Rotonda).

The Pantheon may not have been the first building in Rome, but it's certainly the oldest structure in the city still entirely intact. The original building, built by Marcus Agrippa during the reign of Augustus Caesar (around 27 B.C.) as a temple to all the gods, was a rectangular structure. All but the front columns and portico were later destroyed by fire, and when it was rebuilt by the emperor Hadrian (A.D. 130), it took on its present round form. It served later for a time as a church and even for a while as a fish market, and today is the best-preserved monument

---

❷ Did You Know?

- Rome's population at the end of the 1st century was one million people; by the 6th century it was less than 50,000.
- Construction of Rome's subway had to be stopped frequently so that archeologists could examine newly found vestiges of the city's past.
- There are more than 300 monumental fountains in Rome.
- According to author John Gunther, by the mid-1960s there had been no fewer than 230,000 books written about Rome.
- The 1985 treaty between Italy and the Vatican ended Rome's title of "sacred city."
- The Vatican may be the smallest country in the world, but it contains the largest residence—the Vatican Palace.
- The Spanish Steps were actually designed by the French but received their name from the nearby Spanish Embassy.

to the industry of classical Roman civilization. Note that all light for this marvelous structure comes from the hole in the center of the ceiling.

To the lay person, this dome is much more impressive than the Duomo in Florence, since this one is so immediate, beginning just about 50 feet above the patterned marble floors. The great artist Raphael is buried here, in the illuminated tomb to the left as you enter.

Museo Conservatori and Museo Capitoline

Capitoline Hill, piazza del Campidoglio. ☎ **06/6710-2074.** Piazza, free; museums, 10,000 lire ($6.25) for both, free the last Sun in each month. Piazza, daily 24 hours. Both museums, Apr–Sept, Tues 9am–1:30pm and 5–8pm, Wed–Fri 9am–1:30pm, Sat 9am–1:30pm and 8–11pm, Sun 9am–1pm; Oct–Mar, Tues 9am–1:30pm and 5–8pm, Wed–Fri 9am–1:30pm, Sat 9am–1:30pm and 5–8pm, Sun 9am–1pm; last entrance is 30 minutes before closing.

The smallest of Rome's seven hills, the Capitoline was the political and religious center of the imperial city, and for many centuries since it has been home to Rome's Palazzo Senatorio (city hall). The hill's sweeping front steps, designed by Michelangelo, lead from piazza Venezia up to this majestic plateau, while the back side of the summit enjoys a terrific view of the Forum below—especially beautiful on a moonlit night.

Sharing this tiny square are the Museo dei Conservatori, on the right as you reach the top, and the Museo Capitoline, opposite; together, they make up the oldest and perhaps the finest sculpture museum in the world. Don't miss the mosaics from Hadrian's villa or the collection's most famous works, including *The Dying Gaul, Boy Extracting a Thorn from His Foot, Old and Young Centaurs,* and *The Capitoline Wolf.*

St. Peter's Basilica

St. Peter's Sq. Piazza and basilica, free; to ascend the cupola, 6,000 lire ($3.75) on foot, 7,000 lire ($4.40) with elevator halfway. Piazza, daily 24 hours. Basilica, Mar–Sept, daily 7am–7pm; Oct–Feb, daily 7am–6pm. Elevator/stairs up the cupola, Mar–Sept, daily 8am–6pm; Oct–Feb, daily 8am–4:30pm. Note that, for security reasons, it may be difficult to get into the square and the basilica on Wednesday morning if you don't have a ticket for the pope's weekly public audience (see below).

St. Peter's Square is in fact is not a square but a beautiful oval piazza ringed by a majestic colonnade and dominated by two stately fountains at the center.

The absolutely enormous St. Peter's Basilica is the second-largest church in the world (a pale imitation in the Ivory Coast recently became the largest) and the spiritual center for millions of Catholics. Throughout the center aisle of the church are markers indicating the size of other major cathedrals in the world—dwarfs by comparison.

Although there has been a church on this site since the 4th century—as long as Christianity has been the official Roman religion—the present structure was not begun until the early 16th century and completed more than 100 years later. Immediately to the right as you enter is Michelangelo's best and most moving *Pietà*—he did four of these statues, this one when he was 25 years old. The sculpture is now protected by bulletproof glass after a 1978 attack on the artwork.

St. Peter's tomb is said to be beneath Bernini's captivating canopied altar. Downstairs you'll find the tombs of a number of popes and other saints.

Visitors can climb the cupola for a terrific view of the Vatican complex and the rest of Rome. The entrance is at the far right end of the church as you enter. Be aware, though—there are still 330 steps after the elevator has taken you to the end of its line.

Rome

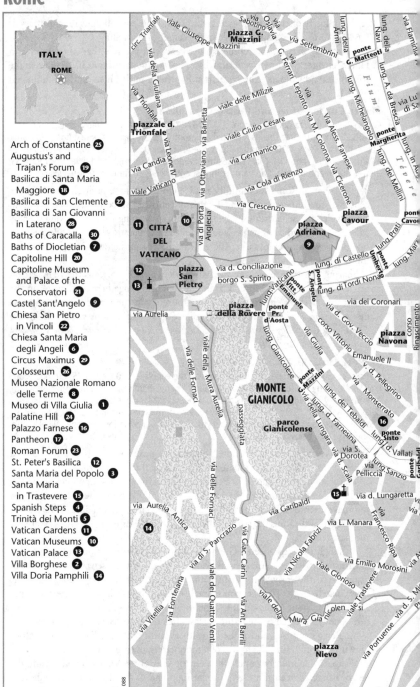

Church †■ Post Office ⊠ Information ⓘ

Mass is celebrated almost every hour on the hour from 7am to noon, and 5pm, seven days a week. The pontificale, or main Sunday mass, happens at 10:30am.

Note: A dress code prohibiting shorts, tank tops, and skirts above the knee is enforced at all times in the church.

The Vatican is in fact a sovereign country of a few hundred citizens and is protected (theoretically) by its own militia, the curiously uniformed Swiss guards.

There's a **Vatican Tourist Office** on the left side of the square as you face the basilica (☎ **06/6988-4466** or 6988-4866), open Monday through Saturday from 8:30am to 6:30pm. They'll sell you a map of the Vatican for 2,000 lire ($1.25), accept reservations for tours of the Vatican Gardens (see below), point you in the right direction for papal-audience tickets, and otherwise try to answer any questions you might have. A shuttle bus leaves from in front of this office for the entrance to the Vatican Museums daily every 30 minutes from 8:45am to 1:45pm in summer, 8:45am to 12:45pm in winter; the fare is 2,000 lire ($1.25).

✪ Vatican Museums and Gardens

Viale Vaticano. ☎ **06/6988-3333.** Gardens, see the text below; museums, 13,000 lire ($8.15), free to all the last Sun of the month. Gardens, see the text below. Museums, July–Sept and the two weeks before and after Easter, Mon–Sat and last sun of the month 8:45am–5pm; Oct–June, Mon–Sat and last Sun of the month 9am–1:45pm. Last visitors are admitted one hour before closing. The entrance to the Vatican Museums is on viale del Vaticano, a fair hike from St. Peter's Square, on the north side of Vatican City; if you're not up to a 10- to 15-minute trek, take the shuttle bus from the Vatican City Tourist Office on St. Peter's Square (see text above). Metropolitana: Ottaviano; then about a six-block walk to the entrance. Bus 492 from the train station and old city area.

The Vatican is home to a mind-boggling collection of artistic, historical, and monetary treasures. The 4¹/₂ miles of corridors forming the Vatican Museums complex will take you through five outstanding museums, the breathtaking Raphael Rooms, and Fra Angelico's only work in Rome, all culminating in the unparalleled Sistine Chapel. And that's just what's indoors.

You'll enter the Vatican Museums through a series of long corridors hung with tapestries from the Raphael School. At the end of these halls, the **Raphael Rooms** commence. Commissioned by Pope Julius II in the 16th century, these salons are covered with frescoes that glorify the papacy.

The intense, grim *Incendio di Borgo* (Fire in the Borgo), in the first room, depicts a 9th-century conflagration in the area between the Vatican and the river that was extinguished by the miraculous intervention of Pope Leo IV. The second room, known as the Stanza della Segnatura, includes Raphael's depiction of *Truth* (on the wall directly in front of you as you enter). Clockwise, the other scenes are *Goodness, Theology,* and *Beauty.* Raphael painted himself into *Truth*—he's the man in the black cap in the lower right-hand corner. And in the lower left corner of *Theology,* look for the old St. Peter's Basilica.

The third room, the Stanza di Eliodoro, shows the pope asking Attila the Hun to cease and desist in A.D. 410. The Sala di Constantino, the final room, was actually painted by a student of Raphael. Notice that this less-skilled painter used black to signify shadowing, whereas the master employed darker shades of the same color.

Following the Raphael Rooms you'll come on the somber, contemplative, and more formal **Cappella di Beato Angelico,** a small chapel decorated with the only work of Fra Angelico in Rome. In fact, the scenes in his work look more like Florence and Tuscany than Rome, a testament to the artist's homesickness.

If you're interested in the Vatican's **Museum of Modern Religious Art,** visit this collection now, before descending to the Sistine Chapel—the Vatican traffic cops operate a one-way museum. The collection—55 rooms' worth— was commissioned by Pope Paul VI, who feared that the religious artistic tradition was fading.

The Vatican Museum complex also includes an **Egyptian Museum,** with relics from the Roman conquest of that kingdom; an **Etruscan Museum,** on a par with the collection at Rome's Villa Giulia (below); and the **Pio-Clementine Museum,** an excellent museum dedicated to classical sculpture.

The Vatican has graciously put together a brochure outlining four suggested itineraries of its enormous complex, ranging in length from 90 minutes to five hours, which you can pick up at the entrance.

From the corridors of tapestries you'll doubtless see the lush **Vatican Gardens.** Guided tours of the Vatican City grounds are the only sort available—public access is otherwise not allowed. From March through October, tours leave Monday, Tuesday, and Thursday through Saturday at 10 or 11am from the tourist information office on St. Peter's Square; November to February, tours run only on Tuesday, Thursday, and Saturday. The tour costs 16,000 ($10). Reservations for garden tours are required year round; in summer, it's recommended that you reserve several days in advance. Reservations can be made in person only (with a passport or ID in hand), and payment is required when you make the reservation.

✪ Capella Sistina (Sistine Chapel)

Vatican Museums, viale Vaticano. Admission included in the 13,000-lira ($8.15) admission to the Vatican Museums. The Sistine Chapel is part of the Vatican Museums complex and follows the same hours (see above).

In Italy, all roads lead to Rome. In Rome, all roads lead to the Vatican. And in the Vatican, all roads lead to the Sistine Chapel. Thousands of slightly distracted tourists wander anxiously through the Raphael Rooms and other parts of the Vatican Museums through which all visitors must pass to get to the chapel, with that inquiring "Are we there yet?" look on their face.

What they're all waiting for is, of course, the stunning ceiling painted by Michelangelo between 1508 and 1512. Everything about the Sistine Chapel is simply awe-inspiring. Besides the absolute splendor of Michelangelo's work and the fact that he painted on such a huge horizontal surface, consider that he did it in 30-minute bursts of effort, since frescoes are painted on wet plaster. Also consider, as your neck gets sore bending backward so you can gaze at the work, what it must've been like to stand like that continually and still produce one of the greatest works of art ever. What's more, anxious to return to his native Florence, he got the job done quite quickly.

The Sistine Chapel was, in fact, not built as a chapel at all, but rather was meant to be a vault—note its rectangular shape. Its homeliness as a place of worship was not lost on Pope Sixtus IV, who commissioned the frescoes that adorn its walls; the left wall shows the story of Moses, while the right side details the life of Jesus. Sixtus IV's successor and nephew, Pope Julius II, still wasn't pleased with the look of the place, so he asked Michelangelo to connect the two walls. Michelangelo, a sculptor by trade, had no interest in doing the ceiling, but the pope forced him to do it. (Indeed, if you study his figures, you'll see that they appear more like sculptures than paintings.)

Papal Audiences

Each Wednesday when the pope is in Rome, he speaks with the general public. The regular time for this public session is 11am—usually 10am during summer. However, this can change from one week to the next, so be sure to check when you arrive. Audiences take place outside in St. Peter's Square during the warmer months and in various interior rooms when it's cold or wet; again, check when you pick up your tickets.

There are several ways to get free tickets to see the pope. Tickets are rarely "sold out," but you must request them at least the day before. The most convenient way to reserve is to call the American Paulist fathers at the **Church of Santa Susanna**, via XX Settembre 14 (☎ **06/482-75-10**); tickets must be picked up on Tuesday afternoon between 4 and 6pm. Via XX Settembre runs parallel to via Nazionale, one block farther away from the train station. Santa Susanna is on the block between via Orlando, which radiates from piazza della Repubblica, and via Torino.

Alternatively, you can contact the helpful **Foyer Unitas**, via S. Maria dell' Anima 30 (☎ **06/686-59-51**), to reserve tickets a few days before the event. (See "Organized Tours," below, for more information.)

You can also reserve tickets at the **Prefettura**, up the stairs under the colonnade on the right side of St. Peter's Square as you face the basilica (where the ellipse meets the rectangular area directly in front of the church). The Prefettura is open Monday through Saturday from 9am to 1pm. The address for written inquiries is Prefettura della Casa Pontifica, Città del Vaticano 00120.

Finally, you can also work through the **Bishop's Office for United States Visitors to the Vatican**, via dell' Umiltà 30, 00187 Roma (☎ **06/678-91-84**; fax 06/686-75-61), but only by writing before you arrive in Rome or calling at least a week beforehand. In any case, it's best to have a letter of introduction from your local priest.

If you can't make a Wednesday audience, you can catch up with the pope on Sunday promptly at noon, when he appears at his library window on St. Peter's Square to recite the Angelus, a traditional prayer, and issue his weekly blessing to the world.

Each of the scenes on the ceiling displays a different day in the Creation, as told in the book of Genesis. The crowning glory of the room is the tremendously powerful *Last Judgment*, commissioned years later by Pope Paul III, who insisted it be painted over the altar (until that time, depictions of the Last Judgment had always been displayed at the church exit). Look for the face of both Michelangelo and St. Bartholomew, who's holding his own skin.

Debate has raged for years over the ground-breaking cleansing of the ceiling, which took place during much of the 1980s. Only two individuals—the best art conservators in the world—were allowed to touch the priceless plaster. Some in the art world insist that Michelangelo's work has been forever altered, while others (myself included) are awe-struck by the stunning palate—and the creative use of shadow—that the restoration has uncovered.

No flash photography is allowed, there are no guided tours (briefings are conducted in the halls and museum rooms preceding the chapel), and—ostensibly—no talking is permitted inside the Sistine Chapel.

Castel Sant' Angelo

Lungotevere Castello. ☎ **06/687-50-36.** Admission 8,000 lire ($5). Mon 2–5:30pm, Tues–Sat 9am–1pm, Sun 9am–noon.

On the banks of the Tiber and connected to the Vatican by a wall that includes a secret escape tunnel is the imposing Castel Sant' Angleo. Built by the emperor Hadrian in A.D. 139 as his mausoleum, it has subsequently served many purposes, at various times having been used as a fort, a prison (Cellini slept here, as did the notorious Cenci family), and, most notably, a papal refuge. Highlights of the fortress include the weapons and uniform exhibits, the Pauline Hall, the Perseus Room, and the Library.

Museo di Villa Giulia (Etruscan Museum)

Piazza Villa Giulia 9. ☎ **06/320-19-51.** Admission 8,000 lire ($5). Tues–Sat 9am–7:30pm, Sun 9am–1pm. Metropolitana: Flaminio; then a good 30-minute walk or take bus no. 48. Bus 910 from the train station, or 48 from the Flaminio Metropolitana stop.

This fine museum happens to be in a lovely villa at one end of the Villa Borghese, Rome's main urban park. As archeological museums go, this one is rather impressive, home to the world's finest collection of Etruscan relics. No one is quite sure where the Etruscans came from or when or where they landed, but they apparently settled in southern Tuscany, where the artifacts that fill this museum were discovered. Scholars agree that they brought with them a highly developed culture, as evidenced by their exceptionally advanced art and sculpture. They're believed to have ruled Rome for a century or more beginning in the 7th century B.C.

The museum, packed with archeological treasures, offers a stunning window into their civilization, mostly in the form of pottery (downstairs), through there's also a fine collection of bronze implements (upstairs), plus several outstanding larger sculpted pieces. The highlights of the first floor include the two figures of Apollo in Room 7, and the *Sarcofago degli Sposi* in Room 9, a remarkably well preserved sarcophagus with a half-reclining married couple on top. Among the most impressive pieces upstairs is a 2-foot-tall bronze figure in Room 15, *Veiovis di Monterazzano* from the 1st century A.D., found near Viterbo in 1955, and an Etruscan chariot in Room 18.

Galleria Borghese

Piazzale del Museo Borghese. ☎ **06/854-85-77.** Admission 4,000 lire ($2.50). Tues–Sat 9am–2pm, Sun 9am–1pm. Last admission is 30 minutes before closing. Bus 910 from the train station, or 56 from piazza Barberini or piazza Venezia, to the park entrance closest to the museum. To get here from the Villa Giulia, walk around behind the museum along viale delle Belle Arti, past the Modern Art Museum on your left, and straight into the heart of the park on viale di Villa Giulia; when you get to the top of the hill, you'll see a path branching off to the left and sign directing you to the Galleria Borghese; this very pleasant 20-minute amble looks longer on a map than it actually is.

At the opposite end of the Villa Borghese park from the Etruscan Museum is the Galleria Borghese, with an excellent collection of both paintings and sculpture. Indeed, it's about the only good old-fashioned art museum in Rome. The first floor is home to Bernini's moving *Rape of Persephone*, as well as his *Apollo and Daphne*, plus Canova's erotic sculpture of the housemistress herself, Princess Pauline

Borghese (Napoléon Bonaparte's sister). Upstairs you'll come on Raphael's *Descent from the Cross*; paintings by Titian, Botticelli, and Rubens; and a wide collection of grim portraits by Caravaggio. Unfortunately, the building has been undergoing major renovation; parts of the museum may be closed this year.

Basilica di San Giovanni in Laterano (Saint John in Lateran)

Piazza San Giovanni in Laterano 4. ☎ **06/6988-6433.** Admission free. Daily 7am–6pm. Metropolitana: San Giovanni (then walk through the portal at the walls of Rome and the church will come into sight).

The oldest church in Rome, San Giovanni in Laterano is the city's hometown cathedral, where the pope comes to celebrate mass on certain holidays. Indeed, the crimson building to the right as you face the church was the papal residence from the 4th through the 14th century.

Statues of the 12 Apostles line the main hall of the church. Those on the left (as you enter) are by Bernini, and those on the right by Borromini, the principal architect for most of the structure you see today.

Chiesa di Santa Maria degli Angeli (Saint Mary of the Angels)

Piazza della Repubblica. ☎ **06/488-08-12.** Admission free. Daily 7:30am–noon and 4–6:30pm.

Michelangelo converted part of the Baths of Diocletian into this church just around the corner from the Museo Nazionale Romano delle Terme. Its airy interior and beautiful marble floors are surrounded by huge paintings that would be the pride of any less-ornamented city.

MORE ATTRACTIONS

Chiesa di San Pietro in Vincoli (Saint Peter in Chains)

Piazza di San Pietro in Vincoli 4a. ☎ **06/488-28-65.** Admission free. Daily 7am–12:30pm and 3:30–6pm. Metropolitana: Piazza Cavour (then walk left across via Giovanni Lanza to via di Monte Polacco, trudge up the three endless flights of stairs that are this street, and turn right at the top; after a few hundred yards you'll come upon a piazza and the church to the left) or Colosseo (then walk up largo Polveriera and go left on via Eudossiana to the church).

The chains that held St. Peter, the patron saint of Rome, can be seen under the high altar of this church. The chief attraction is not the chains, however, but rather Michelangelo's fabulous, if unfinished, *Moses*, complete with a marvelously carved waist-length beard (it's sitting on top of the tomb of Pope Julius II, to the right as you face the altar).

Among the treasures of the church are a piece of the table from the Last Supper (facing the apse door), the heads of Saints Paul and Peter (in the tabernacle), and a great bronze door from the Senate of the Roman Forum (now in the middle part of the main entrance).

Santurario Scala Santa

Piazza San Giovanni in Laterano. ☎ **06/759-46-19.** Admission free. Daily 6:15am–12:30pm and 3–7pm. Metropolitana: San Giovanni (then walk through the portal in the walls of Rome and the church will come into sight).

The building off to the left and across the street as you exit the Basilica of San Giovanni in Laterano houses the Holy Stairs (Scala Santa), the original 28 marble steps from Pontius Pilate's villa—now covered with wood for preservation—that Christ is said to have climbed on the day he was condemned to death. According to a medieval tradition they were brought from Jerusalem to Rome by

The Piazza di Spagna Area

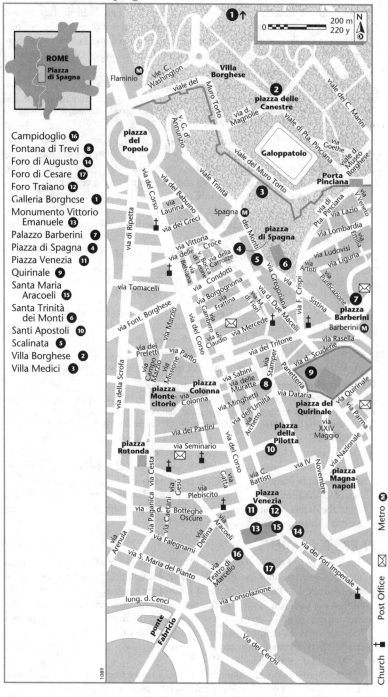

ROME
Piazza
di Spagna

Metro **M**

Post Office ⊠

Church ✝ ▪

Constantine's mother, Helen, in 326, and the stairs have been in their present location since 1589. Today pilgrims from all over the world come here to climb the steps on their knees. This is one of the holiest sites in Christendom; please show respect for those worshipping here and refrain from talking or taking pictures.

Basilica di San Clemente

Piazza di San Clemente, via San Giovanni in Laterano. ☎ **06/731-57-23.** Main church, free; excavations, 3,000 lire ($1.90). Mon–Sat 9am–noon and 3:30–6pm, Sun 10am–noon and 3:30–6pm. Metropolitana: Colisseo (then a long one-block up via Labicana; it's a 10-minute walk from the Basilica di San Giovanni in Laterano).

While so much of Rome is glorious and monumental, a visit to the several layers of San Clemente will give you a feel of what it was like to have been an early Christian in Rome. Beneath this plain 12th-century structure are the remains of two earlier structures, dating from the 4th and 1st centuries A.D., respectively.

The medieval **Triumph of the Cross** mosaic in the apse of the church is particularly noteworthy, as are the two intact and well-preserved 11th-century frescoes: one, scenes from the legend of St. Alexis, and the other, St. Clement celebrating mass.

Basilica di Santa Maria Maggiore (Saint Mary Major)

Piazza Santa Maria Maggiore. ☎ **06/48-31-95.** Admission free. Summer, daily 7am–8pm; winter, daily 7am–7pm. Only a short walk from Stazione Termini, the church can be entered at either end, from piazza Santa Maria Maggiore in the front or from via Cavour in the back.

One of the seven pilgrimage churches in Rome, this basilica houses relics of the Holy Crib below the altar and a 5th-century triumphal arch above. Its other features include two richly decorated chapels—the right one in the Renaissance style, the left one baroque—and a stunning 13th-century mosaic in the apse. The ceiling is decorated with gold brought back from America by Columbus.

Cimitero Monumentale dei Padri Cappucini

Via Veneto 27. Admission 2,000 lire ($1.25). Summer, daily 9am–noon and 3–6:30pm; winter, daily 9am–noon and 3–6pm. Metropolitana: Barberini (then walk up the right side of via Veneto and take the stairs on the right side of the Chiesa Immacolata Concezione at via Veneto 27).

This is perhaps the most unusual and unique sight in the country: Every inch of its walls and ceilings is adorned with the skeletal remains of 4,000 Capuchin friars who died between 1528 and 1870. It's of no special religious significance; their sign of explanation reads simply that these bones "speak eloquently to the visitors about the drama of a life which is passing" and urges prayer and meditation. This is a grisly, haunting, and curiously popular place.

PARKS & GARDENS

Rome is a city of stone, not of green. Nonetheless, those who need a fix of fresh air should venture into the **Villa Borghese,** Rome's urban park, located on the north side of the Old City. You'll find some of the best views over Rome from the edge of the park here, as well as countless hills and trees and a duck pond inside the massive area. The park is best approached from the Spagna or Flaminio Metropolitana stations, on the south and west sides of the park, or by taking bus no. 910 from the station, or bus no. 56 from piazza Barberini or piazza Venezia, to the east side of the greenlands.

For other natural edification, turn to the **Vatican Gardens** (see "Top Attractions," above) or **Tivoli** (see "Easy Excursions," later in this chapter).

ORGANIZED TOURS

INTENSIVE TOURS   Rome's best tours—and, indeed, perhaps Europe's most remarkable guided visits—are free and operated by Josefa Koet and Leideke Galema, two Dutch nuns who run the **Foyer Unitas Ecumenical Centre,** an ecumenical study center on the fourth floor of the Palazzo Pamphilj at via Santa Maria dell' Anima 30 (☎ **06/686-59-51**), just off piazza Navona. Their tours and evening slide presentations were prompted by the fact that there were countless Catholic groups in the city offering guidance and tours for Catholic visitors, but few organizations catering to non-Catholics. Their tours were designed with non-Catholics in mind, though travelers of any faith are welcome to join.

What's the catch? Well, these are not ordinary tours. They're for the budget traveler who has a serious and intense interest in the history and culture of this spectacular city—and in examining particular sights in great depth. They may spend an entire morning, for example, showing a group a single building or one particular area of the Forum. They may spend hours discoursing on the history of one of the city's catacombs, or conducting a group through a few of the Vatican Museums. They don't rush from place to place, but rather relate to you everything they know about a particular place.

The Palazzo Pamphilj is one short block up via di Sant' Agnese in Agone from piazza Navona. If you're coming from corso Vittorio Emanuele, you'll find via Sant' Agnese on the left just past the fountain at the center of piazza Navona. They're open Monday through Friday from 9am to noon and then again from 4:30 until 6:30pm, Saturday from 9am to noon only. If you come at another time, you can take a program from the elevator door and call in a reservation later during office hours. You can simply show up at the date, time, and meeting point listed, but they recommend that you call to confirm, in case one of them is not feeling well or museum hours have changed. Note: They don't operate their tours during July and August.

BUS TOURS   For the standard bus tour, my recommendation is **Carrani Tours**, via Vittorio Emanuele Orlando 95 (☎ **06/488-05-10** or 474-25-01). They've been in business since 1927—about as long as buses have roamed the Roman roads. Most of their 20 tours range in price from 38,000 to 44,000 lire ($23.75 to $27.50). You can pick up their brochure in just about every hotel and pensione in Rome, or at their headquarters a block up from piazza della Repubblica. Note that they'll usually come and pick you up at your hotel.

7 Shopping

The value-added tax (IVA in Italy) is included in the stated price of all consumer goods and most services. The average tax is 19%, but it goes as high as 35% on some luxury items. You are entitled to a refund of the tax paid if you spend more than 525,000 lire ($328) in any one store. Get a receipt from the shopkeeper, show it to a Customs official at the border (who can ask to see the goods), then mail the stamped receipt back to the merchant within 90 days. Your refund will be mailed to you.

BEST BUYS   The streets around **piazza di Spagna** are the most fashionable addresses in Rome. Along the streets to the west of the square, particularly **via Condotti,** you'll find all the best Italian and international names in clothing and footwear. Needless to say, prices in this high-rent neighborhood are as stratospheric.

Rome's most popular—and most popularly priced—shopping area is **via Cola di Rienzo** near the Vatican, running from piazza del Risorgimento to the ponte souvenir shops, as well as pharmacies, supermarkets, and small department stores, all with prices considerably more moderate than those across the river. This is where the average middle-income Roman comes to shop. To get here, take the Metropolitana to Lepanto or Ottaviano.

Via Nazionale and **via del Corso** are also fine areas for window-shoppers (and those with fewer lire to spend, too). Here you'll find many of Rome's department stores.

Finally, **Old Rome,** particularly north of piazza Venezia and between piazza Navona and the Trevi Fountain, is the place to wander for handicrafts and one-of-a-kind shops and boutiques.

MARKETS   You can find everything from 17th-century candelabra and antique doorknockers to 5,000-lira ($3.15) cassette tapes and 20,000-lira ($12.50) shoes at Rome's seemingly endless **flea market at Porta Portese** in Trastevere. Countless vendors and just plain folks set up shop here every Sunday from roughly 7 or 8am to about 1 or 2pm. Most of the wares (mostly clothes) on sale here are pretty chintzy and of little interest to the tourist, but the market is a sight in and of itself. Unlike the open-air market in Florence, you'll see precious few tourists and thousands of Romans. Still, watch out for pickpockets.

Bus no. 27 will take you here from the train station and downtown; get off at the second stop after the river, on via Ettore Rolli, just past the corner of via Panfilo Castaldi; the market, whose size varies with the meteorological and economic climate, stretches at least to via Pietro Ripari and piazza Ippolito Nievo, which is on the no. 170 bus line.

The best of the many markets specializing in flowers and produce is on **piazza Campo de' Fiori.** The small but colorful market, crammed with fresh fruit and vegetables, is open Monday through Saturday from 7 or 8am to about 1 or 2pm. In spring and fall look for untrimmed artichokes on long stalks. Autumn brings Muscat grapes and porcini mushrooms.

A handful of pushcarts offering used books, etchings, lithographs, art reproductions, antique jewelry, and other odds and ends and one-of-a-kind items sets up Monday through Saturday from 9am until about 6pm (4:30pm in winter) at **piazza Borghese,** near ponte Cavour. To find them, walk out via Condotti from piazza di Spagna and continue for $2^1/_2$ blocks past via del Corso on via della Fontanella Borghese.

Piazza Vittorio Emanuele, south of Stazione Termini, is the site of Rome's biggest daily open-air food market, open Monday through Saturday roughly from 8am to 2pm.

8 Rome After Dark

Un Ospite a Roma, a free magazine available from the concierge desks of top hotels, is full of current information on what's happening around town. *Trova Roma*, a weekly listings magazine inserted in the Thursday edition of *La Repubblica* newspaper, is indispensable for its coverage of movies, music, art, opera, dance, and the like. Most newsstands stock extra, free copies of *Trova Roma* in case you weren't able to pick it up on Thursday.

THE PERFORMING ARTS
OPERA & BALLET

Open-air opera and ballet at the **Terme di Caracalla**, via delle Terme di Caracalla, are one of the great summer events of Italy. The stage is set amid the ruins of this one-time Roman bathhouse, which indeed often becomes part of the production. Usually two operas and a ballet are put on here each summer, with shows three or four times a week in July and August. The production of *Aída* is particularly memorable.

Tickets cost 25,000 to 65,000 lire ($15.65 to $40.65) for the opera or 20,000 to 50,000 lire ($12.50 to $31.25) for the ballet.

The main opera house ticket office, on via Firenze, on the block between via Nazionale and via del Viminale (☎ **06/488-36-41** for information), is open Tuesday through Sunday from 9:30am to 6pm; the box office at the Terme is open from 8 to 9:30pm on performance days. Take bus no. 93 from the train station to the Terme.

If there are no performances at the Terme di Caracalla when you visit, you can attend a performance at the **Teatro dell'Opera,** via Firenze 72 (☎ **06/48-16-01**), a plain white building almost remarkable for its ugly facade. Tickets cost 15,000 to 100,000 lire ($9.40 to $62.50). The box office is open Tuesday through Saturday from 10am to 4pm and Sunday from 10am to 1pm.

JAZZ

Rome also sports a fair variety of small jazz clubs with frequent performances of local musicians (you'll find most of them listed in the entertainment sections of Italian newspapers).

One favorite is the **St. Louis Music City,** via del Cardello 13a (☎ **06/474-50-76**). A long cavernous club with a jazz stage at one end, this place also has a restaurant area and a pool table off to the side. Entrance is free, but you must become a club member first, a formality which will set you back 10,000 lire ($6.25). Happily, club owner Mario Ciampa has traditionally offered a 50☎ discount on membership to bearers of this book. It's still not cheap, however. If you sit at one of the tables near the stage, expect to pay 5,000 to 10,000 lire ($3.15 to $6.25) per drink. There's live music almost every night from 10:30pm or so. Via del Cardello is halfway between the Colosseum and via Cavour.

FILMS

English-language movies in Italy are almost always dubbed. The one exception in Rome is at the **Pasquino,** in Trastevere at vicolo del Piede 19a (☎ **06/580-36-22**), which maintains a cult following among American expatriates in Rome. Prices here are lower than at most other theaters, only 7,000 lire ($4.40) as opposed to 10,000 lire ($6.25) elsewhere in town. Films at the Pasquino change every day or two; check the local newspapers for listings.

CAFES & GELATERIAS

When in Rome, do as the Romans do: Enjoy a leisurely dinner at some hidden-away trattoria's outdoor tables or while away the night at a café in a peaceful neighborhood.

The outdoor cafés on the pedestrians-only **piazza della Rotonda,** in the shadow of the Pantheon, are perhaps the best places to be on warm summer nights.

Cappuccino prices are a steep 4,000 lire ($2.50). The long, oval **piazza Navona,** with the overly baroque fountain in the center, is also popular at night.

The **Spanish Steps** on piazza di Spagna are almost a sight in and of themselves. There are no cafés actually on the staircase, but on warm summer nights the place is buzzing with the sounds of (mostly) young people from all over the world just sitting around, hanging out, and generally having a good time.

And from piazza di Spagna it's always pleasant to stroll over to the **Fontana di Trevi** by night.

Of the cafés near the Spanish Steps, the **Antico Caffè Greco,** via Condotti 86, is the standout, being the oldest in Rome. Open Monday through Saturday from 8am to 8:40pm. **Cafe Gelateria Fontana di Trevi,** piazza Fontana di Trevi 90, is the most popular of the several *gelaterie* (ice-cream shops) ringing the piazza. Try their cornetto, a chocolate-covered croissant stuffed with whipped cream, chocolate cream, or custard. Small pizzas and sandwiches are also sold here. In summer it's open daily from 7am to 2am; in winter, Thursday through Tuesday from 7am to midnight.

The famous ✪ **Gelateria Tre Scalini,** piazza Navona 28, is the headline hangout on this square. Its most noteworthy dessert is tartufo, the ice-cream confection by which all other ice-cream confections in this gelato-rich country are judged. This homemade delicacy is the richest mound of chocolate you can imagine, packed with bittersweet chocolate chips and a cherry buried somewhere inside—or as some would say, a mound of bittersweet chocolate chips held together by a smidgen of chocolate ice cream all crowned with whipped cream. Open in summer, Thursday through Tuesday from 8am to 1:30am; in winter, Thursday through Tuesday from 8am to 1am.

Some locals prefer the ice cream at ✪ **Giolitti,** via Uffici del Vicario 40 (☎ **06/679-42-06**), a fancy café sporting a turn-of-the-century look with marble floors and hanging chandeliers, but no outdoor tables. It's on a small street between piazza Navona and piazza Colonna. Open Tuesday through Sunday from 7am to 2am.

BARS

Several of Rome's favorite watering holes are along via del Governo Vecchio, a charming narrow back street near piazza Navona. All the cafés here are equally cozy (read: small). Poke into **Enoteca il Piccolo** at nos. 74–76, the **Crêperie Mizzi** at no. 112, and **Il Merlio Maschio** at no. 12. This is one of the few areas in Rome—or in Italy, for that matter—where you can find a subdued, comfortable place to sit and leisurely enjoy a few drinks. Small snacks are also available. Most bars along this street are open every night until 2am.

In 1993, Andrea and Georgio, English-speaking Italian friends, returned from a trip to the United States and decided to open a bar together in central Rome. The result is **Locale,** vicolo del Fico 3 (☎ **06/87-90-75**), a well-planned three-room drinkery that features happy hours and loud live music most every night. Admission ranges from free to 12,000 lire ($7.50). Open daily from 7pm to 2am.

For a budget drink, you can't do better than **Vineria Reggio,** campo de' Fiori 15 (☎ **06/654-32-68**), a small wine store/bar that specializes in small glasses of prosecco (sparkling wine) for only 1,500 to 2,000 lire (95¢ to $1.25). Quintessentially Roman, Reggio's patrons either stand along the long bar or sit on adjacent wooden benches. Open Monday through Saturday from 9:30am to 1pm and 5pm to 1am.

DISCOS

One thing Romans who aren't millionaires don't do is dance much, since it can be prohibitively expensive: Expect to spend 40,000 to 50,000 lire ($25 to $31.25) just for entrance and a few drinks. Top clubs in 1995 were **Billow,** via Campania 37 (☎ **06/482-18-90**); and **Promozione Incontro,** via dell'Imbrecciato 263 (☎ **06/5528-6800**). The entrance is hidden on via della Magliana.

9 Easy Excursions

✪ **TIVOLI**   Tivoli is lov-e-ly, even if it is a bit worn out from all the tourists who flock here each day. The **Villa d'Este** (☎ **0774/2-20-70**), a delightful tiered water park built by Cardinal d'Este in the 16th century, is the more interesting of the two villas here. Amazingly enough, the villa's 500 fountains, conduits, and waterfalls operate entirely by gravity—quite an engineering feat. Nearby is the much older **Villa Adriana** (☎ **0774/53-02-03**), a motley collection of replicas of all the beautiful places that the emperor Hadrian had seen in the world.

Both are open daily from 9am until an hour before sunset. Entrance is 10,000 lire ($6.25) for the Villa d'Este, 8,000 lire ($5) for the Adriana.

Tivoli is some 45 minutes outside Rome, accessible by a bus marked AUTOBUS PER TIVOLI, which leaves every 15 to 20 minutes from via Gaeta just west of via Volturno, near Stazione Termini; the fare is 5,000 lire ($3.15) each way. It's easier to take the bus to the Villa d'Este, then take bus no. 2 or 4 from there to the Villa Adriana.

✪ **OSTIA ANTICA**   A vast, astonishingly well preserved ancient Roman city in a pastoral setting without any nearby sign of modernity, Ostia Antica captures the essence of Imperial Rome in the middle of the 2nd century A.D. It's especially worth visiting if you won't have a chance to go to Pompeii, for here you'll see such dazzling details of Roman architecture as mosaic floors, marble walls, a few wall paintings—details by and large missing from the Roman Forum.

Ostia Antica is open daily from 9am to 7pm March to September, and daily from 9am to 5pm the rest of the year. Last entrance is one hour before closing. Admission is 12,000 lire ($7.50).

To get to Ostia Antica, take the Metropolitana Line B to the Magliana station and transfer there to a suburban train which connects with Ostia Antica in half an hour. When you arrive, walk across a bridge over a highway and continue straight in that direction for 5 to 10 minutes.

22 Salzburg

by Beth Reiber

Salzburg is famous for its magnificent Alpine scenery, its fortress and perfectly preserved baroque inner city, and its music festivals, as well as for being Mozart's birthplace. Although it has only 150,000 inhabitants, this city is one of the world's leading cultural centers, especially for classical music. A short journey by train or car from Munich, Salzburg is a convenient stopover for anyone traveling from Germany to Vienna or Italy. Like most European cities, it's divided by a river, the Salzach, into left and right banks, connected by 10 bridges. The names of both the town and the river derive from the salt mines in the region, which brought Salzburg fame and fortune.

Mozart's birthplace on Getreidegasse is a magnet, attracting more than a million visitors annually. Every year in January, July, August, and on Easter, Wolfgang Amadeus's genius is celebrated in world-renowned music festivals, with such conductors in the past as Leonard Bernstein, James Levine, and Herbert von Karajan and such singers as Fischer-Dieskau, Pavarotti, and Baltsa. Salzburg's perfectly preserved center on the left bank, with its baroque structures, brooding fortress above the old city, 17th-century streets, gaily flowered horsecarts, and strolling shoppers (many dressed in colorful dirndls) creates an enthralling setting and mood, made even more magical by the scenery on every side. The city, filled with architectural wonders, is known as the Austrian Rome. Little wonder that many travelers count Salzburg as one of Europe's most beautiful and charming towns.

1 Salzburg Deals & Discounts

BUDGET BESTS   In Salzburg, you'll find **open-air food and drink stalls**—called *Imbiss* or *Würstelbude*—at every second street corner. They sell wieners, hamburgers, sandwiches, Leberkäse, soft drinks, and beer (in cans) for much less than a restaurant would charge: a Coca-Cola is 16 S ($1.50); a hot dog, 30 S ($2.85); a beer, 26 S ($2.50). You'll find a convenient Imbiss in the center of the Altstadt (Old City) at Alter Markt, selling Würste (sausages), french fries, and drinks. It's open throughout the year, Tuesday through Saturday from 5pm to midnight and Sunday from 2pm to midnight. On a rainy or cold day, the **self-service counters** in university cafeterias, department stores, and butcher shops can be considered moneysavers.

What's Special About Salzburg

Music

- The Salzburg Festival in August, one of the world's best for opera.
- Concerts almost daily in Mirabell Palace, the Residenz, or the Fortress.
- Other festival extravaganzas throughout the year.
- Free brass-band concerts in summer.

The Sound of Music Film Locations

- Schloss Leopoldskron (closed to the public), the Nonnberg Abbey, Festspiel-haus, and Mirabell Garden.

Architectural Highlights

- Hohensalzburg, a medieval fortress above the city.
- The Residenz, residence of the archbishop of Salzburg, rebuilt in the baroque style.
- The Dom (cathedral), the finest example of an early baroque building north of the Alps.
- Hellbrunn Palace, a summer residence for the archbishops and famous for its trick fountains.
- Churches in Salzburg by famed architect Fischer von Erlach, including the Collegiate Church, Holy Trinity Church, and St. John's Hospital Church.

Romantic Walk

- Along the Salzach River at night, with a view of the floodlit Hohensalzburg.

Finally, it can be relaxing and enjoyable indeed to sit in the small open-air café at **Mirabellgarten,** Salzburg's most scenic and popular public park and garden, sipping a small beer and munching a roll while admiring the surrounding baroque buildings, the Hohensalzburg silhouette, and the Alpine skyline (and the pigeons hunting for your breadcrumbs).

Be sure to visit the City Tourist Office, Mozartplatz 5 (☎ **0662/84 75 68**), for up-to-date information on such **free events** as concerts or folklore evenings that may take place during your stay. During summer, for example, there are free brass-band concerts in the Mirabellgarten on Wednesday at 8:30pm and Sunday at 10:30am. There are also free concerts given throughout the school year by students at the music school Mozarteum.

SPECIAL DISCOUNTS   There are **discounts** on admission fees to museums and reduced cable-car fares granted to students and children under 15, provided you can show proof of age (passport) or an International Student ID Card. These reductions vary from 20% to 50%.

Anyone under 26 can purchase heavily reduced rail and flight tickets by contacting **Ökista,** Wolf-Dietrich-Strasse 31 (☎ **0662/88 32 52**), open Monday through Friday from 9:30am to 5:30pm.

WORTH THE EXTRA MONEY   Salzburg is famous the world over for its music, presented throughout the year in a number of **festivals and concerts.** Tickets to these concerts are not always inexpensive and are not even always available unless you order them months in advance. But it's worth the effort and the money to take advantage of being in one of the music capitals of the world. See the

"Special & Free Events" box under "Attractions" and also "Salzburg After Dark," later in this chapter, for more information.

2 Pretrip Preparations

REQUIRED DOCUMENTS   All that Australian, New Zealand, Canadian, and U.S. citizens need for entry into Austria for stays up to 90 days is a valid passport. British subjects need only an identity card.

TIMING YOUR TRIP   Salzburg's season is year round. In fact, winter is one of the most beautiful times of year, especially when a fresh blanket of snow covers the hills surrounding the city. Summers are pleasant, rarely so hot that they're uncomfortable. The main tourist seasons are Easter, May through September, and the Christmas holidays, when many hotels in the medium and upper range raise their rates.

Salzburg's Average Daytime Temperature & Rainfall

	Jan	Feb	Mar	Apr	May	June	July	Aug	Sept	Oct	Nov	Dec
Temp. (°F)	28	35	37	45	55	64	68	70	60	50	39	33
Rainfall "	2.5	2.6	2.8	3.5	5.3	6.8	7.5	6.4	3.6	2.9	2.7	2.7

Special Events   Throughout the year Salzburg hosts annual music festivals. The year kicks off with **Mozart Week,** held at the end of January, followed by the **Salzburg Easter Festival.** Most famous is the **Salzburg Festival,** which is held throughout August and has a history stretching back 70 years. It features opera, plays, concerts, chamber music, and a number of other events. Autumn brings the **Salzburg Cultural Days,** a two-week musical event held in October with more opera, ballet, and concerts. Since these festivals are popular, you should make hotel reservations at least a month or two in advance if you wish to visit Salzburg during these times, especially in August.

3 Salzburg Specifics

ARRIVING

FROM THE AIRPORT   The **Flughafen** (airport), Innsbrucker Bundesstrasse 95 (☎ **0662/8580-0**), a mile southwest of the city, is larger than Innsbruck's and much smaller than Munich's. Daily flights are operated to and from Frankfurt, London (Heathrow), Amsterdam, Paris, Zurich, and Vienna. Bus no. 77 takes you to Salzburg's main train station for 22 S ($2.10); taxis charge about 140 S ($13.35) for the same trip.

FROM THE TRAIN STATION   Salzburg is about 1¹/₂ to 2 hours from Munich by train and about 3 hours from Vienna. All trains arrive at the **Hauptbahnhof** (main train station), on the right bank of the city center at Südtiroler Platz (☎ **0662/1717**). Buses depart from Südtiroler Platz to various parts of the city, including the Old City (*Altstadt*) across the river. It's about a 20-minute walk from the Hauptbahnhof to the heart of the Altstadt.

BY CAR   If you come by car, ask your hotel proprietor where the nearest garage is located. Street parking (metered) is not only costly but also practically impossible to find, especially on the left bank with its narrow streets and pedestrians-only

What Things Cost in Salzburg	U.S. $
Taxi from the airport to the train station or hotel	13.35
Public transportation (bus or trolleybus)	2.10
Local telephone call (per minute)	.09
Double room, with continental breakfast, at the Hotel-Pension Trumer Stube (deluxe)	119.05
Double room, with continental breakfast, at the Hotel Amadeus (moderate)	57.15
Double room, with continental breakfast, at Pension Sandwirt (budget)	41.90
Lunch for one, without wine, at Sternbräu (moderate)	15.00
Lunch for one, without wine, at Mensa im Mozarteum (budget)	4.75
Dinner for one, without wine, at K & K (deluxe)	27.00
Dinner for one, without wine, at Wienerwald (moderate)	11.00
Dinner for one, without wine, at Wilder Mann (budget)	7.50
Half liter of beer	2.85
Glass of wine (one-eighth liter)	2.40
Coca-Cola (in a restaurant)	2.00
Cup of coffee with milk (in a restaurant)	3.00
Roll of ASA 100 color film, 36 exposures	6.65
Admission to Mozart's Birthplace	5.90
Movie ticket	8.10
Concert ticket (to the Festspielhaus)	22.85

zones. Note that if you're staying at one of the hotels in the inner city's pedestrian zone, you can still drive to your hotel for check-in. In the Altstadt, you're required to stop at a ticket booth to obtain permission to drive to your hotel. In any case, once there, ask the proprietor of your hotel where you should park. You can reach most of Salzburg's sights on foot.

VISITOR INFORMATION

There's a small **tourist information kiosk** on Platform 2a of the Hauptbahnhof, Südtiroler Platz (☎ **0662/87 17 12** or 87 36 38), where you can pick up a map for 10 S (95¢) or obtain hotel reservations by paying a 50-S ($4.75) deposit per person that goes toward your hotel payment. In addition, a 30-S ($2.85) fee for the service is charged for two people; for three or more, the fee is 60 S ($5.70). This office is open during winter, daily from 9am to 7pm; in summer, daily from 9am to 8pm. Be sure to pick up a map of the city.

The main **City Tourist Office (Fremdenverkehrsbetriebe der Stadt Salzburg)** is in the heart of the Old City at Mozartplatz 5 (☎ **0662/84 75 68,** 889 87-330 or 889 87-331). Open in summer (May to September) daily from 9am to 8pm and in winter Monday through Saturday from 9am to 6pm, it also books hotel rooms, hands out city maps and brochures, and sells sightseeing, concert, and theater

The Austrian Schilling

For American Readers At this writing $1 = approximately 10.50 S (or 1 S = 9¢), and this was the rate of exchange used to calculate the dollar values given in this chapter (rounded to the nearest nickel).

For British Readers At this writing £1 = approximately 16.50 S (or 1 S = 6p), and this was the rate of exchange used to calculate the pound values in the table below.

Note: The rates given here fluctuate from time to time and may not be the same when you travel to Austria. Therefore this table should be used only as a guide:

S	U.S.$	U.K.£	S	U.S.$	U.K.£
1	.09	.06	100	9.50	6.05
2	.19	.12	150	14.30	9.10
3	.29	.18	200	19.05	12.10
4	.38	.24	250	23.80	15.15
5	.48	.30	300	28.55	18.20
6	.57	.36	350	33.35	21.20
7	.67	.42	400	38.10	24.25
8	.76	.48	450	42.85	27.25
9	.85	.54	500	47.60	30.30
10	.95	.60	600	57.15	36.35
15	1.43	.90	700	66.65	42.40
20	1.90	1.21	800	76.20	48.50
25	2.38	1.51	900	85.70	54.55
50	4.76	3.03	1,000	95.25	60.60

tickets. Be sure to pick up a free copy of "Veranstaltungen," a monthly brochure that lists the various concerts in Salzburg's many music halls.

CITY LAYOUT

Most attractions are on the left bank of the Salzach River, in the **Altstadt (Old City).** Much of the Altstadt is now a pedestrian zone, including Getreidegasse with its many shops, Domplatz, and Mozartplatz. The Altstadt is where you'll find such attractions as Mozarts Geburtshaus (Mozart's Birthplace), the Festival House complex, the cathedral, the Catacombs of St. Peter, the Haus der Natur (Museum of Natural History), and Salzburg's landmark, the **Hohensalzburg.** In fact, it's this fortress, towering above the Altstadt on a sheer cliff, that makes Salzburg such a beautiful city, even from afar. It's lit up at night, making a walk along the **Salzach River** one of the most romantic in Austria.

The **Hauptbahnhof** is on the opposite (right) side of the Salzach River, about a 20-minute walk from the Altstadt. This part of the city is newer and also contains the Mirabellgarten and a number of hotels and shops.

GETTING AROUND

BY PUBLIC TRANSPORTATION A quick, comfortable public transportation system is provided by 19 **bus lines,** charging 22 S ($2.10) per ticket or 75 S

($7.15) for a set of five, which reduces the single-trip price to $1.40. Tickets are good for a single journey, including transfers to reach your final destination. If you think you'll be traveling a lot by bus, you might also wish to purchase a **24-hour ticket** for 32 S ($3.05) or a **one-day pass** for 36 S ($3.40), which allows you to use all of Salzburg's buses, ride the funicular up to the fortress, take the Mönchsberg lift and the tramway (Salzburg–Bergheim). Note that children 5 and under can travel for free on Salzburg's buses and that children 6 to 15 can travel for half price. Note, too, that prices may go up in 1996.

You can purchase only single tickets from bus drivers. Sets of five reduced-fare tickets and the one-day passes can be purchased from more than 120 tobacco shops throughout the city, marked with a sign that says *tabak trafik*. For more information about Salzburg's public transportation system, call 0662/62 05 51-0.

BY TAXI The average taxi fare from the train station to a hotel or private home within the city limits is 100 S ($9.50), and 140 S ($13.35) to the airport or into the outskirts. Fares start at 30 S ($2.85) as soon as you climb into a taxi; from 10pm to 6am fares start at 40 S ($3.80); luggage is an extra 5 S (50¢) each. To telephone for a taxi, call 8111 or 66 1715.

ON FOOT Walking around Salzburg, especially in the Altstadt on the left bank with its many pedestrian zones, is a pleasure. In fact, because Salzburg is rather small and compact, you can walk to most of its major attractions. One of the best walks in the city is along the top of Mönchsberg from Café Winkler to the fortress, about a 30-minute walk.

BY BICYCLE Cycling is becoming more and more popular, evident from the ever-increasing bike paths through the city. If you feel like a long ride, try the bike path beside the Salzach River that goes all the way to Hallein, 9 miles away.

You can rent bicycles year round at the **Hauptbahnhof** (main train station) at Counter 3 (☎ **0662/8887-5427**). About 50 standard and mountain bikes are available (no racing bikes) for 90 S ($8.55) a day. If you have a Eurailpass or a ticket valid for that day, the cost is only 50 S ($4.75).

BY RENTAL CAR It's much less expensive if you arrange for car rental before coming to Europe. If you need a car in Salzburg, go to **Hertz,** Ferdinand-Porsche-Strasse 7 (☎ **0662/87 66 74**), across from the train station near the Hotel Europa, or to its airport office (☎ **0662/85 20 86**). The downtown office is open Monday through Friday from 8am to 6pm and Saturday from 8am to 2pm, while the airport branch is open daily from 9am to 1:30pm and 3 to 8pm. Daily rental of a Fiat Panda, including 20% tax and unlimited mileage, is 696 S ($66.30).

Nearby is **Avis,** Ferdinand-Porsche-Strasse 7 (☎ **0662/87 72 78**). It's open Monday through Friday from 7:30am to 6pm and Saturday from 8am to noon and charges 858 S ($81.70) for a one-day rental of an Opel Corsa, including unlimited mileage and 20% tax. However, because there are always special weekend prices and other promotions, it pays to shop around.

FAST FACTS: Salzburg

Babysitters Students at Salzburg's university earn extra money by babysitting. Call 0662/8044-6001 or 8044-6002, Monday through Friday from 10am to noon and also Monday and Thursday from 2 to 4pm.

Banks   Banks are open Monday through Friday from 8:30am to 12:30pm and 2 to 4:30pm. If you need to **exchange money** outside these hours, try the Wechselstube (Exchange Office) (☎ **0662/87 13 77**) at the Hauptbahnhof, open daily from 7am to 10pm in summer and 7:30am to 9pm in winter. In the Altstadt, a bank with particularly long hours is the Rieger Bank, Alter Markt 15 (☎ **0662/ 84 13 89**). It's open Monday through Friday from 9am to 6pm and Saturday from 9am to 4pm, with even longer hours during summer, including Sunday service. You can also exchange money at the post office in the train station, open 24 hours, as well as at the main post office, Residenzplatz 9 (☎ **0662/84 41 27**), Monday through Friday from 7am to 7pm and Saturday from 8 to 10am. The **American Express** office is on Mozartplatz (☎ **0662/84 25 01**), next to the tourist office. It's open Monday through Friday from 9am to 5:30pm and Saturday from 9am to noon.

Business Hours   Shops are usually open Monday through Friday from 8 or 9am to 6:30pm (some close for an hour or two at noon) and Saturday from 8 or 9am to noon or 1pm. On the first Saturday of the month (called *langer Samstag*), many shops remain open until 5pm.

Consulates   The Consulate General of the **United States** is at Herbert-von-Karajan-Platz 1 (☎ **0662/84 87 76**), open Monday, Wednesday, and Friday from 9am to noon. The Consulate of the **United Kingdom** is at Alter Markt 4 (☎ **0662/84 81 33**), open Monday through Friday from 9am to noon. Citizens of Australia, Canada, and New Zealand should contact their respective embassies in Vienna (see "Fast Facts: Vienna" in Chapter 27).

Currency   The Austrian currency is the **Schilling,** written ASch, AS, ÖS, or simply S (as I have). A Schilling is made up of 100 Groschen (which are seldom used). Coins are minted as 5, 10, and 50 Groschen, and 1, 5, 10, 20, 25, and 50 Schilling. Banknotes appear as 20, 50, 100, 500, 1,000, and 5,000 Schilling.

Dentists/Doctors   If you need a doctor or dentist, your best bet is to head to one of Salzburg's hospitals; the largest is St. John's Hospital, Müllner Hauptstrasse 48 (☎ **0662/4482-0**). Or ask your hotel concierge for the address of the hospital closest you, or inquire at your consulate. If you need an English-speaking doctor during the weekend, call 141.

Emergencies   For the police, phone 133; to report a fire, 122. For urgent medical assistance on the weekend, or an English-speaking doctor, call 141; for an ambulance, 144.

Two pharmacies useful to travelers are the 200-year-old Alte Hofapotheke, Alter Markt 6 (☎ **0662/84 36 23**), a wonderful old-world drugstore a few blocks from the Mozart house; and Salvator Apotheke, Mirabellplatz 5 (☎ **0662/87 14 11**). Both are open Monday through Friday from 8am to 12:30pm and 2:30 to 6pm and Saturday from 8am to noon. The names and addresses of pharmacies open on Saturday afternoon, Sunday, and holidays are posted in every pharmacy window.

Holidays   Holidays celebrated in Salzburg are New Year's Day (Jan 1), Epiphany (Jan 6), Easter Monday, Labor Day (May 1), Ascension Day, Whit Monday, Corpus Christi, Assumption Day (Aug 15), Austria Day (Oct 26), All Saints' Day (Nov 1), Immaculate Conception (Dec 8), and Christmas (Dec 25–26).

Hospitals   Hospitals in Salzburg include St. John's Hospital, Müllner Hauptstrasse 48 (☎ **0662/4482-0**); Accident Hospital, Dr.-Franz-Rehrl-Platz 5 (☎ **0662/6580-0**); Hospital of the Barmherzigen Brüder, Kajetanerplatz 1 (☎ **0662/84 45 31-0**); and Diakonissen Krankenhaus im Diakonizzentrum, Guggenbichlerstrasse 20 (☎ **0662/6385-0**).

Information   The main tourist office is at Mozartplatz 5 (☎ **0662/84 75 68**). For more information, refer to "Visitor Information" under "Salzburg Specifics," earlier in this chapter.

Laundry   There's a self-service laundry on Südtiroler Platz in front of the train station: Constructa, Kaiserschützenstrasse 10 (☎ **0662/87 62 53**), open Monday through Friday from 7am to 7pm and Saturday from 7am to 1pm. It charges 118 S ($11.25) for 6 kilos (13^1/4 lb.) washed and dried.

Lost & Found   All lost-and-found objects are registered with the Polizei (police) at Alpen Strasse 90. The Fundbüro (☎ **0662/6383-2330** or 6383-2331) is the lost-and-found office, open Monday through Friday from 7:30am to 12:30pm. Phone information is given Monday through Friday from 7:30am to 3:30pm.

Mail   The main post office (Hauptpostamt) is in the center of the Altstadt at Residenz Platz 9 (☎ **0662/84 41 21-0**). It's open Monday through Friday from 7am to 7pm and Saturday from 8 to 10am. Have your mail sent here for Poste Restante. There's a branch post office beside the train station on Südtiroler Platz (☎ **0662/88 9 70-0**), open 24 hours daily. Postcards to North America cost 8.50 S (80¢), while airmail letters cost 10 S (95¢) plus 1.50 S (14¢) for each 5 grams.

Photographic Needs   For film or quick development of prints, there's a Niedermeyer photo shop at Schwarzstrasse 10 (☎ **0662/87 36-41**), on the right bank of the Salzach River between the Staatsbrücke and Makartsteg bridges. It's open Monday through Friday from 8:30am to 6pm and Saturday from 8:30am to noon (from 9am to 5pm on the first Saturday of the month).

Police   The emergency number for the police is **133.**

Shoe Repair   There's a Mister Minit, which provides quick service for shoe repairs, in a shopping mall called Kiesel-Passage at the corner of Rainer and Elisabethstrasse, about a two-minute walk from the Hauptbahnhof. It's open Monday through Friday from 9am to 1pm and 2 to 6:30pm and Saturday from 9am to 1pm. There's also a Mister Minit in the Forum department store across from the train station.

Tax   Government tax and service charge are already included in restaurant and hotel bills. If you have purchased goods for more than 1,000 S ($95.25), you're entitled to a refund of part of the value-added tax (VAT); see "Shopping," later in this chapter.

Telephone   Telephone booths are painted either silver with a yellow top or green and are found on major roads and squares. For **local calls,** use a 1-S (9¢) coin for each minute—insert more coins to avoid being cut off (unused coins will be returned).

Note that telephone numbers are gradually being changed in Salzburg. If you have problems making a connection or need a number, dial 1611 for information. And if you come across a number with a dash, as in 6580-0, the number after the dash is the extension number. Simply dial the entire number.

Because hotels add a surcharge to telephone calls made from guest rooms, make your **international calls** from a post office. The cost of a three-minute call to the United States is 42 S ($4). If you're going to make a lot of local calls or wish to make international calls from a pay phone, purchase a **telephone card** from any post office, available in values of 50 S ($4.75), 100 S ($9.50), or 200 S ($19.05); then just insert the card into slots of special telephones found virtually everywhere.

Salzburg's **city code** is 0662 within Austria, 662 if you're calling Salzburg from another country.

Tipping   A service charge is included in hotel and restaurant bills, and taxi fares. If you're satisfied with the service, tip up to 10% of the bill in taxis, hotels, restaurants, and beauty salons.

4 Accommodations

Most of Salzburg's budget accommodations are on the outskirts of town and in neighboring villages, easily reached in less than 30 minutes by bus. The cheapest rooms are often those rented out in private homes, with a shared bath down the hall. However, they're usually equipped with a sink and are clean.

A bit higher priced are bathless doubles in a small pension (often called a *Gasthof* or *Gästehaus*). Not surprisingly, prices are usually higher in establishments more centrally located. In addition, many of the higher-priced accommodations charge even more during peak season, including Easter, May to September, and Christmas. At the beginning of January, when tourism is at its lowest, some hotels close down completely.

If the recommendations below are full, the **Salzburg City Tourist Office** at the train station and on Mozartplatz will book a room for you for a 30-S ($2.85) fee (for one or two people) or a 60-S ($5.70) fee (for three or more) and a deposit. In addition, **Bob's Special Tours** (☎ 662/84 95 110) will book accommodations, including rooms in private homes, for a 30-S ($2.85) fee.

If, however, you've already booked a room with one of my recommendations, please honor the reservation by showing up. In summer, it's become common practice for some establishments to employ hustlers at the train station to recruit customers fresh off the train. Some of these accommodations are so far out in the countryside that you may as well be in Germany; and some recruiters even go so far as to claim that they represent accommodations travelers may have already booked, only in the end to deliver them someplace else.

Remember that telephone numbers are being changed in Salzburg. If you can't reach any of the accommodations below, dial 1611 for information.

DOUBLES FOR LESS THAN 450 S ($42.85)
IN THE CITY

Pension Junger Fuchs

Linzer Gasse 54, 5020 Salzburg. ☎ **0662/87 54 96.** 20 rms, none with bath. 240–300 S ($22.85–$28.55) single; 380–440 S ($36.20–$41.90) double; 500–550 S ($47.60–$52.40) triple. No credit cards. Bus 1, 2, 5, or 6 from the Hauptbahnhof to Makartplatz.

This is the inner city's cheapest pension and looks as if it's been here forever. The old stone stairway leading to the upper floors (no elevator) is narrow and probably medieval; the rooms themselves date from this century but look no less weary.

Getting the Best Deal on Accommodations

- Inquire about the winter discounts offered by medium- and upper-range hotels.
- Note that lower prices are charged for accommodations in surrounding villages.
- Look for accommodations offering cooking facilities, which will help you save on dining bills.
- Ask if there's an extra charge for taking a shower and if breakfast is included in the room rates.
- Before making a call, find out if there's a surcharge on local and long-distance calls.

Though bare, small, and simple, the rooms are nevertheless adequate, with a sink, hooks to hang up your coat, a bed, and a table. Some may smell of cigarette smoke, so it wouldn't hurt to ask to see your room first. Basically, this is just a cheap place to sleep, in a convenient location.

Pension Sandwirt Auer

Lastenstrasse 6a (behind the train station), 5020 Salzburg. ☎ **0662/87 43 51.** 10 rms, 3 with shower only. 280–330 S ($26.65–$31.40) single without shower; 440–460 S ($41.90–$43.80) double without shower, 500–550 S ($47.60–$52.40) double with shower; 600 S ($57.15) triple without shower, 660 S ($62.85) triple with shower; 760 S ($72.40) quad without shower, 800 S ($76.20) quad with shower. Rates include continental breakfast and showers. No credit cards. Take the overhead bridge from Platforms 12 and 13 in the Hauptbahnhof.

This simple pension (without elevator) is a good choice for backpackers who aren't too fussy and don't require much more than a bed. Although it's a bit run-down, its prices are among the lowest in town, and its spartan rooms are clean and perfectly acceptable. Set back from the road behind another building, it's thus protected a bit from the noise of trains coming and going.

IN THE OUTSKIRTS

Hotel Grödig

Neue-Heimat-Strasse 15, 5082 Grödig. ☎ **06246/73 523.** Fax 06246/73 523-7. 14 rms, all with bath (some with tub, some with shower). MINIBAR TV TEL. 200 S ($19.05) per person. Rates include continental breakfast. No credit cards. Bus 55 from the Hauptbahnhof to the Neue Heimat stop in Grödig.

In the center of Grödig, a small village about 3 miles from Salzburg, this personable small hotel offers comfortable rooms equipped with radios; most have terraces with views of Untersberg.

⑤ Pension Schiessling

Anif 17, 5081 Salzburg. ☎ **06246/72 4 85.** 12 rms, 2 with shower and toilet. 200 S ($19.05) single without shower or toilet, 250 S ($23.80) single with shower and toilet; 350 S ($33.35) double without shower or toilet, 450 S ($42.85) double with shower and toilet. Rates include continental breakfast and showers. 10% surcharge for stays of only one night. No credit cards. Bus 55 from the Hauptbahnhof to Anif Hotel Friesacher (20 minutes).

This pension in the village of Anif, south of Salzburg, has an on-premises dairy, with 30 cows and a bull in the barn. Some rooms are in the farmhouse; most are in a more modern structure across the street. Breakfast is served in a pleasant room with a terrace. Anif is known for its *Heurige* (wine taverns), so there's more to do here in the evening than in most small villages. This pension is one of the best budget accommodations near Salzburg.

DOUBLES (IN PRIVATE HOMES) FOR LESS THAN 505 S ($48)
IN THE CITY

These accommodations are in private homes, which sometimes offer less privacy but are good opportunities for getting to know the Austrians. Note, however, that they all prefer guests to stay longer than one night.

Frau Brigitte Lenglachner

Scheibenweg 8, 5020 Salzburg. ☎ 0662/43 80 44. 6 rms, 4 with shower and toilet. 270 S ($25.70) single without shower or toilet; 450 S ($42.85) double without shower or toilet, 500 S ($47.60) double with shower and toilet; 650 S ($61.90) triple without shower or toilet. Rates include continental breakfast and showers. 40 S ($3.80) extra for one-night stays. No credit cards. Walk from the Hauptbahnhof across the Salzach River via the Pioniersteg bridge (about a 15-minute walk).

This small two-story cottage is owned by a traditionalist who wears dirndl costumes and speaks English. Look at her guestbook—it's full of praise. The rooms, all with sinks, are pleasant and spotless and have the look of traditional Austria. In addition to the rooms listed above, there's a double equipped with a bunk bed for 380 S ($36.20). This place is popular, so try to reserve in advance.

Frau Trude Poppenberger

Wachtelgasse 9, 5020 Salzburg. ☎ 0662/43 00 94. 2 rms, neither with bath. 280 S ($26.65) single; 450 S ($42.85) double. Rates include continental breakfast and showers. No credit cards. Walk from the Hauptbahnhof across the Salzach River via the Pioniersteg bridge (about a 20-minute walk).

Frau Poppenberger offers two rooms with balconies in her private home and breakfasts with homemade cakes. She'll pick you up at the train station, and her husband, who speaks fluent English, will happily provide sightseeing information.

Frau Maria Raderbauer

Schiesstattstrasse 65, 5020 Salzburg. ☎ 0662/43 93 63. 5 rms, 3 with shower and toilet. 270 S ($25.70) single without shower or toilet; 500 S ($47.60) double without or with shower and toilet; 750 S ($71.40) triple with private shower and toilet across the hall. Rates include continental breakfast and showers. No credit cards. Walk from the Hauptbahnhof across the Salzach River via the Pioniersteg bridge (about a 20-minute walk).

This two-story private house in a quiet neighborhood is surrounded by rose bushes and has sparkling-clean rooms. The triple has a balcony, as well as its own bath across the hall. Frau Raderbauer, who speaks English, will pick up guests at the station.

Frau Hilde Radisch

Scheibenweg 5, 5020 Salzburg. ☎ 0662/42 47 12. 3 rms, none with bath. 275 S ($26.20) single; 450 S ($42.85) double. Rates include continental breakfast and showers. No credit cards. Walk from the Hauptbahnhof across the Salzach River via the Pioniersteg Bridge (about a 15-minute walk).

This is another good choice in private accommodations. Frau Radisch, a talkative septuagenarian, has an ivy-covered two-story house with a garden and serves homemade marmalade for breakfast. She has one single room without a sink and two double rooms with sinks and adorned with such antiques as a coffee grinder and kitchen scales.

Rudy and Friedl Simmerle

Wachtelgasse 13, 5020 Salzburg. ☎ **0662/42 75 53.** 2 rms, 1 with toilet. 420 S ($40) double. Rates include continental breakfast. Showers 25 S ($2.40) extra. No credit cards. Walk from the Hauptbahnhof across the Salzach River via the Pioniersteg bridge (about a 20-minute walk).

The Simmerles are a retired couple who speak fluent English. Their two rooms—one with its own toilet and the other with a sink—are large and well furnished. Living here is like being their guest, and if you phone one or two days in advance and let them know when you're arriving, they'll come pick you up after receiving a second phone call confirming that you've arrived. This home is in the northwestern part of the city.

IN THE OUTSKIRTS

✪ Blobergerhof

Hammerauerstrasse 4, 5020 Salzburg. ☎ **0662/83 02 27.** Fax 0662/82 70 61. 6 rms, all with shower and toilet. 350 S ($33.35) single; 500–550 S ($47.60–$52.40) double. Rates include continental breakfast. No credit cards. Bus 1 from the Hauptbahnhof to Hanuschplatz, then 60 from Hanuschplatz to Kaserer (about 20 minutes); then a couple of minutes' walk.

This picturesque Salzburg-style farmhouse with flowerboxes is managed by a wonderful English-speaking mother and daughter who receive repeated kudos from readers. Its rooms are spacious, and it's neat as a pin. They raise chickens, so you can always be assured of fresh eggs, and there's a fine restaurant across the street. They'll pick you up at the station.

Gästehaus Gassner

Moosstrasse 126b, 5020 Salzburg. ☎ **0662/82 49 90.** 10 rms, 7 with shower and toilet. 400 S ($38.10) double without shower or toilet, 600 S ($57.15) double with shower and toilet. Rates include buffet breakfast. No credit cards. Bus 1 from the Hauptbahnhof to Hanuschplatz, then 60 from Hanuschplatz to the Felleitner (10 minutes) stop, in front of the house.

This modern home south of the city has well-furnished, clean, spacious rooms, some with minibar, TV, and telephone. The breakfast room faces a field, and in summer you can eat breakfast on the outdoor terrace. There's also a laundry room. Except in the morning, someone will pick you up at the station, and the owner speaks English.

Frau Elfriede Kernstock

Karolingerstrasse 29, 5020 Salzburg. ☎ **0662/82 74 69.** Fax 0662/82 74 69. 6 rms, 4 with shower and toilet. 440 S ($41.90) double without shower or toilet, 500 S ($47.60) double with shower and toilet; 750 S ($71.40) triple with shower and toilet; 1,000 S ($95.25) quad with shower and toilet. Rates include continental breakfast and showers. No credit cards. Bus 77 from the Hauptbahnhof to Karolingerstrasse.

On the western edge of town, this beautiful private bungalow has hand-painted furniture, spacious rooms and closets, and very clean toilets. One of the rooms with private bath has a small kitchen; another has a balcony. If she's not busy with guests, English-speaking Frau Kernstock will pick you up at the bus stop if you call from the station. While you're having breakfast, you'll hear the soundtrack from *The Sound of Music.*

Frau Mathilde Lindner

Kasern am Berg 64, 5020 Salzburg. ☎ **0662/45 66 81** or 45 67 73. 8 rms, none with bath. 150–180 S ($14.30–$17.15) per person. Rates include continental breakfast and showers. No credit cards. Bus 1, 2, 5, or 6 from the Hauptbahnhof to Mirabellplatz, then 15 from

Mirabellplatz to Kasern (15 minutes); then a 10-minute walk uphill. Train: From the Hauptbahnof to Kasern.

This nice Alpine cottage is on top of a high hill northeast of Salzburg, with a great view of the mountains. Four rooms have access to a balcony, and there's a garden for sunbathing. The rooms, which should be reserved at least one day in advance, are furnished with wooden beds, wardrobes, chairs, tables, and sinks. If she has time, Frau Lindner will pick you up from the station; if you're arriving by car, take the Autobahn Nord exit. If you have a Eurailpass, you can ride for free on a local train (the Regionalzug) from the Salzburg Hauptbahnhof to Kasern, a four-minute ride. Families are welcome.

Frau Moser

Kasern am Berg 59, 5020 Salzburg. ☎ **0662/45 66 76.** 4 rms, none with bath. 180 S ($17.15) single; 340–360 S ($32.40–$34.30) double. Rates include continental breakfast and showers. No credit cards. Bus 1, 2, 5, or 6 from the Hauptbahnhof to Mirabellplatz, then 15 from Mirabellplatz to Kasern (15 minutes); then a 10-minute walk uphill. Train: From the Hauptbahnhof to Mariaplain.

Frau Moser's husband is a hunter, as is evident from the more than 100 sets of antlers decorating the walls of this private home. Not far from Frau Lindner's (above), it also offers a great view of Salzburg, and its upper-priced doubles have their own balcony. The breakfast room has a panoramic view of the Alpine scenery as well, and there's a terrace and garden. If you telephone upon your arrival in Salzburg, she'll give instructions on how best to reach Kasern via a local train (the Regionalzug, only a four-minute ride from Salzburg's Hauptbahnhof) and will meet you at the station in Kasern.

Frau Marianne Schoibl

Saalachstrasse 6, 5020 Salzburg. ☎ **0662/42 21 59.** 3 rms, all with shower only. 500 S ($47.60) double. Rates include continental breakfast. No credit cards. Bus 1 from the Hauptbahnhof to Leiner/Stadium, then 29 to Saalachstrasse.

The ideal place for a long stay, this small and cozy bungalow-type private home is in a quiet area northwest of town. The host is very helpful. The rate includes use of a kitchenette with a refrigerator and other equipment.

Frau Rosemarie Steiner

Moosstrasse 156c. 5020 Salzburg. ☎ **0662/83 00 31.** 6 rms, 3 with shower and toilet. 250 S ($23.80) single without shower or toilet; 460 S ($43.80) double without shower or toilet, 480 S ($45.70) double with shower and toilet. Rates include continental breakfast and showers. No credit cards. Bus 1 from the Hauptbahnhof to Hanuschplatz, then 60 from Hanuschplatz to Kaserer (about 20 minutes); then a couple of minutes' walk.

This modern three-story house south of town offers adequately furnished clean rooms, three with balconies. There's also a TV lounge and a kitchen, and the owner, who speaks English, is happy to give sightseeing advice.

⑤ Eveline Truhlar

Lettensteig 11, 5082 Fürstenbrunn. ☎ **06246/73 3 77.** 1 rm, with shower and toilet. 450 S ($42.85) double; 600 S ($57.15) triple; 800 S ($76.20) quad. Rates include continental breakfast. No credit cards. Bus 1 from the Hauptbahnhof to Hanuschplatz, then 60 from Hanuschplatz to the last stop in Fürstenbrunn.

Last but certainly not least in this list of inexpensive accommodations is Eveline's spacious room with its modern private bath, radio, and huge terrace offering a panoramic view of Untersberg. The owner, who has managed Bob's Special Tours for more than 15 years, speaks excellent English, will pick you up at the station, and knows Salzburg in and out. This is one of the best bargains around, and the tiny village of Fürstenbrunn should appeal to those who enjoy the countryside and walks through the woods.

DOUBLES FOR LESS THAN 605 S ($57.60)
IN THE CITY

Gasthof Römerwirt
Nonntaler Hauptstrasse 47, 5020 Salzburg. ☎ **0662/82 94 23.** 35 rms, 15 with shower and toilet. 380 S ($36.20) single without shower or toilet, 550 S ($52.40) single with shower and toilet; 600 S ($57.15) double without shower or toilet, 700 S ($66.65) double with shower and toilet; 850 S ($80.95) triple without shower or toilet, 1,000 S ($95.25) triple with shower and toilet. Rates include continental breakfast and showers. No credit cards. Free parking. Closed Nov–Feb. Bus 5 from the Hauptbahnhof to Nonntal (10 minutes).

In a quiet area behind Mönchsberg on the left side of the river is this modern three-story pension with spacious but spartan rooms (it reminds me of a dormitory). Proprietor Herr Wallner is helpful about what to do in Salzburg and speaks English. There's ample free parking.

○ Pension Bergland
Rupertgasse 15, 5020 Salzburg. ☎ **0662/87 23 18.** Fax 0662/872 31 88. 17 rms, 5 with shower only, 12 with shower and toilet. TEL. 440 S ($41.90) single with shower only, 500 S ($47.60) single with shower and toilet; 580 S ($55.25) double without shower or toilet, 780–840 S ($74.30–$80) double with shower and toilet; 960 S ($91.40) triple with shower and toilet. Rates include continental breakfast and showers. No credit cards. Free parking. Closed mid-Nov to mid-Dec.

This pension, owned by the Kuhn family for more than 80 years, is on three floors of a modern building on a residential street, about a 10-minute walk across the river from the Old City. It has a cozy bar/lounge equipped with a piano and guitar, plus a small English library. The rooms are spotless and cheerfully decorated with Scandinavian furniture and original artwork by the owner, English-speaking Peter Kuhn. Some rooms have radios; others have TVs. There are bicycles for rent, and it's located about a 15-minute walk south of the Hauptbahnhof.

IN THE OUTSKIRTS

○ Gasthof Fürstenbrunn
Fürstenbrunnerstrasse 50, 5082 Fürstenbrunn. ☎ **06246/73 3 42.** 11 rms, all with shower and toilet. 560–580 S ($53.35–$55.25) double; 760–780 S ($72.40–$74.30) triple; 900 S ($85.70) quad. Rates include continental breakfast. No credit cards. Bus 1 from the Hauptbahnhof to Hanuschplatz, then 60 from Hanuschplatz to Fürstenbrunn (about 20 minutes).

In a quiet location 5 miles south of Salzburg at the foot of Untersberg mountain, this is a very cheerful guesthouse, with plants in the hallway, large immaculate rooms, and wooden furniture gaily painted Austrian style (*Bauernmöbel*). Owners Manfred and Heidelinde Schnöll speak some English and will pick you up at the train station. The guesthouse's popular restaurant, Gasthof Schöll, serves lunch and dinner. It's a great place to stay if you enjoy the wooded countryside.

Pension Helmhof
Kirchengasse 29, 5020 Salzburg. ☎ **0662/43 30 79.** Fax 0662/43 30 79. 16 rms, 12 with tub/shower and toilet. TEL. 350 S ($33.35) single without tub/shower or toilet, 420 S ($40) single with tub/shower and toilet; 550 S ($52.40) double without tub/shower or toilet, 700 S ($66.65) double with tub/shower and toilet; 680 S ($64.76) triple without tub/shower

or toilet, 900 S ($85.70) triple with tub/shower and toilet. Rates include continental breakfast and showers. No credit cards. Bus 2 from the Hauptbahnhof to Rudolf-Biebl-Strasse, then 29 to Schmiedingerstrasse.

In Liefering on the northeastern edge of town, this pension may still have rooms when other pensions in the town center are booked up. This attractive country house has a red roof, green shutters, balconies off most rooms, and flowers on the windowsills. The owner speaks English, and there's a tiny outdoor pool.

DOUBLES FOR LESS THAN 890 S ($84.75)
IN THE CITY

Gasthof Auerhahn

Bahnhofstrasse 15 (a 10-minute walk north of the Hauptbahnhof), 5020 Salzburg. ☎ **0662/ 45 10 52.** Fax 0662/451 05 23. 16 rms, all with shower and toilet. TV TEL. 520–650 S ($49.50–$61.90) single; 880–980 S ($83.80–$93.35) double; 1,000 S ($95.25) triple. Rates include continental breakfast. AE, DC, MC, V.

This well-furnished small hotel is across from a secondary railroad track (used once or twice a day, causing little noise). It's family owned, with a pleasant restaurant serving typical Austrian food, popular with neighborhood people. The rooms are upstairs, along corridors that have a hunting-lodge feel, with heavy beams, painted *Bauernmöbel,* and gaily painted doors. Recently renovated, all rooms have cable TVs with CNN. The only disadvantage to staying here is that it's a bit far from the Altstadt.

Hotel Amadeus

Linzer Gasse 43–45, 5020 Salzburg. ☎ **0662/87 14 01** or 87 61 63. Fax 0662/876 16 37. 27 rms, 23 with tub/shower and toilet. TV TEL. 380–420 S ($36.20–$40) single without tub/ shower or toilet, 620–750 S ($59.05–$71.40) single with tub/shower and toilet; 600–750 S ($57.15–$71.40) double without tub/shower or toilet, 980–1,320 S ($93.35–$125.70) double with tub/shower and toilet; 1,200–1,550 S ($114.30–$147.60) triple with tub/shower and toilet. Rates include buffet breakfast and showers. AE, DC. Bus 1, 2, 5, or 6 from the Hauptbahnhof to Makartplatz.

This small family-owned hotel (with elevator) has a great location in the city center, within walking distance of almost everything. Guests have their choice of rooms facing either the street or a beautiful and peaceful cemetery (where Mozart's wife is buried). Recently renovated, the rooms are cheerful and pleasant and have TVs with cable programs in English, including CNN. The higher prices in each category are for the peak tourist season, including May to September. The buffet breakfasts are substantial, offering eggs, cereals, and cold cuts.

✪ Pension Chiemsee

Chiemseegasse 5, 5020 Salzburg. ☎ **0662/84 42 08.** Fax 0662/84 42 08 70. 6 rms, all with shower only. 400–480 S ($38.10–$45.70) single; 750–880 S ($71.40–$83.80) double. Rates include buffet breakfast. Additional person 200 S ($19.05) extra. MC, V. Bus 5, 6, 51, or 55 from the Hauptbahnhof to Mozartsteg; then a two-minute walk.

Right in the Altstadt, this tiny pension is a true find and is owned by friendly Barbara Schwaiger, who lived in the United States for two years and gained experience working for hotels in Vienna before returning to her hometown to open her own pension. As expected, she speaks perfect English and is more often than not dressed in the traditional dirndl. First mentioned in documents in 1488, the house itself is 1,000 years old—note how worn the stone stairway is. The reception and small but pleasant breakfast room are up on the first floor, while guest rooms are on the third (no elevator). The rooms are simple but clean, with prices based on the room size and the season. Because it has only six rooms, it's best to reserve well in advance.

IN THE OUTSKIRTS

✪ Parkpension Kasern

Wickenburgallee 1, 5020 Salzburg. ☎ **0662/50 0 62.** Fax 0662/51 1 88. 14 rms, all with tub/shower and toilet. TV. 500–650 S ($47.60–$61.90) single; 800–1,100 S ($76.20–$104.75) double. Rates include continental breakfast. Additional person 200 S ($19.05) extra. MC, V. Bus 1, 2, 5, or 6 from the Hauptbahnhof to Mirabellplatz, then 15 from Mirabellplatz to Kasern.

This is a lovely country house set in a park on the northern outskirts of town. Built in 1870 as a private mansion, it's now in its fourth generation of owners and features exquisite artistry throughout. Most rooms are large, with tall ceilings and antique furniture; a recent addition includes six modern rooms as well. All have cable TV with CNN. There's a fine garden where guests can sit outside in summer. Proprietor Felicitas Eichhausen and her husband speak excellent English. This pension is 15 minutes by bus from the city center.

SUPER-BUDGET CHOICES
YOUTH HOSTELS

⑤ International Youth Hotel

Paracelsusstrasse 9. 5020 Salzburg. ☎ **0662/87 96 49.** Fax 0662/87 88 10. 140 beds. 160 S ($15.25) per person double; 140 S ($13.35) per person quad; 120 S ($11.40) dorm bed. Showers 10 S (95¢) extra. No credit cards. Walk 10 minutes south of the train station.

This is the best budget choice in town. It's centrally located (a 15-minute walk to the Altstadt), and there's no curfew or age limit. There are four doubles; the rest are quads and dormitory-style rooms with six to eight beds each. All rooms have sinks, lockers are available, and there's a coin-operated laundry. The bar is open until midnight, and breakfast and dinner are available. *The Sound of Music* is shown free daily at 2:30pm. Sightseeing tours are offered. The only drawback is that you can reserve a bed only one day in advance of your arrival, so call early in the morning. The young staff all speak English.

Jugendgästehaus Salzburg

Josef-Preis-Allee 18, 5020 Salzburg. ☎ **0662/842 67 00.** Fax 0662/84 11 01. 390 beds. 245 S ($23.35) per person double with shower and toilet; 195 S ($18.55) per person quad with shower only; 145 S ($13.80) dorm bed. Rates include continental breakfast and showers. One-night stay 10 S (95¢) extra; box lunch or dinner 65 S ($6.20) extra. No credit cards. Bus 5 from the Hauptbahnhof to Justizgebäude; then a three-minute walk.

This official youth hostel is open all year. If you're not a card-carrying member, you can still stay here for 40 S ($3.80) extra per night. Amenities include a TV room, steel lockers, a coin-operated laundry, a self-service restaurant, rental bikes for 80 S ($7.60) per day, and a games room for table tennis. There's a midnight curfew.

Jugendherberge Aigner Strasse

Aigner Strasse 34, 5026 Salzburg. ☎ **0662/62 32 48.** Fax 0662/62 32 48-13. 105 beds. 135 S ($12.85) per person. Rates include continental breakfast, sheets, and showers. No credit cards. Bus 6 from the Hauptbahnhof to Volksgartenbad, then 49 from Volksgartenbad to the Finanzamt stop.

This is another official youth hostel, open all year and offering rooms that sleep two to eight. There's no age limit, but if you're not a youth-hostel member you must pay 40 S ($3.80) extra per night. Facilities include a TV room and table tennis. It's in the southern part of Salzburg, about a 25-minute walk from the Altstadt and the Hauptbahnhof.

CAMPING

Camping Ask Salzburg West

Karolingerstrasse 4, 5020 Salzburg. ☎ **0662/83 42 23.** 49 S ($4.65) per adult, 25 S ($2.40) per child; 30 S ($2.85) per tent; 45 S ($4.30) per car; 55–70 S ($5.25–$6.65) per RV. Showers 10 S (95¢) extra. No credit cards. Closed mid-Sept to mid-May. Bus 77 from the Hauptbahnhof to Karolingerstrasse.

This camping ground is on the western edge of the city. It's open from mid-May to mid-September.

Camping Ost-Gnigl

Parscherstrasse 4, 5023 Salzburg. ☎ **0662/64 41 43** or 64 41 44. 40 S ($3.80) per adult, 20 S ($1.90) per child; 22 S (2.10) per tent; 30 S ($2.85) per car; 35 S ($3.35) per RV. Rates include showers. No credit cards. Closed Oct to mid-May. Bus 1, 2, 5, or 6 from the Hauptbahnhof to Mirabellplatz, then 29 from Mirabellplatz to Minnesheimstrasse.

This campground has a good location on the eastern edge of town with easy access to the city center by bus. It's open from mid-May to September.

WORTH THE EXTRA MONEY

✪ Hotel-Pension Trumer Stube

Bergstrasse 6, 5020 Salzburg. ☎ **0662/87 47 76** or 87 51 68. Fax 0662/87 43 26. 22 rms, all with shower and toilet. TV TEL. 480–680 S ($45.70–$64.75) single; 780–1,250 S ($74.30–$119.05) double; 1,100–1,600 S ($104.75–$152.40) triple; 1,300–1,800 S ($123.80–$171.40) quad. Rates include continental breakfast. AE. Bus 1, 2. 5, or 6 from the Hauptbahnhof to Mirabellplatz.

This is a great place for a splurge, centrally located just across the river from the Altstadt, a five-minute walk from Mozart's Birthplace. Ideal for couples and families, it's owned by the charming Hirschbichlers, both of whom speak English and are eager to give tips on sightseeing and help make concert and tour bookings. The pension was recently renovated (with an elevator) and the rooms are spotless and cozy, with cable TV with CNN. The above rates reflect both the low- and high-season rates for each category.

✪ Hotel Wolf

Kaigasse 7, 5020 Salzburg. ☎ **0662/843 45 30.** Fax 0662/842 42 34. 15 rms, all with tub/shower and toilet. TV TEL. 580–840 S ($55.25–$80) single; 930–1,490 S ($88.55–$141.90) double. Rates include buffet breakfast. AE. Bus 5, 6, 51, or 55 from the Hauptbahnhof to Mozartsteg; then a two-minute walk.

This small pension has one of the best locations, in a quiet pedestrian zone at the foot of the Hohensalzburg. The structure itself dates from the 14th century and is a national monument, but inside it's super-modern with all the conveniences, including an elevator. Try to book Room 15, 17, or 18—each has antique furniture. Every room is different. The owner wears dirndl costumes and speaks excellent English. The highest prices are for July and August.

5 Dining

Salzburg's inexpensive restaurants are distributed on both banks of the Salzach River, many conveniently clustered in and around the Altstadt. Most feature specialties typical of Austria and southern Germany, such as *Leberknödelsuppe* (soup with liver dumplings), *Knoblauchsuppe* (garlic soup), *Bauernschmaus* (a combination dish of pork, ham, sausage, dumplings, and sauerkraut), *Tafelspitz* (boiled beef with vegetables), *Gulasch* (Hungarian stew), *Leberkäs* (a German meatloaf), or *Wiener Schnitzel* (breaded veal cutlet). The only real Salzburg dish is *Salzburger Nockerl*, a dessert made of eggs, flour, butter, and sugar, and sometimes called a "pregnant omelet." When served at your table it looks round and fluffy like a blimp, but when you start eating it the air escapes and the Nockerl looks like a plain omelet. Try it at least once while in Salzburg.

LOCAL BUDGET BESTS

Mensa im Mozarteum

Mirabellplatz 1. ☎ **0662/87 35 06.** Fixed-price meals (for nonstudents) 40–50 S ($3.80–$4.75). No credit cards. Mon–Fri 11:30am–2pm. Closed July 7–15, Sept 1–16, and Dec 21–Jan 7. Bus 1, 2, 5, or 6 from the Hauptbahnhof to Mirabellplatz. AUSTRIAN.

This student *mensa* (cafeteria), in the Mozarteum music school, serves fixed-price meals to both students and nonstudents, though students pay about l0 S (95¢) less than the prices above. The menu changes daily, usually with three or four choices available. It's conveniently located on the right side of the Salzach, between the train station and the Altstadt, less than a 10-minute walk from each. The only problem is that the mensa, buried in a basement, is a bit difficult to find. Ask a student for directions.

⑤ Mensa der Universität

Churfürstenstrasse (between Alter Markt and Domplatz). ☎ **0662/8044 69 09.** Fixed-price meals 32 S ($3.05) for students, 42 S ($4) for nonstudents. No credit cards. Mon–Thurs 8am–6pm, Fri 8am–3pm. Closed July–Aug and Dec 21–Jan 6. AUSTRIAN.

This student mensa is conveniently in the center of the Altstadt and has longer open hours than most mensas. It offers two complete meals daily, with slightly higher prices charged for nonstudents. In any case, it's a real bargain.

MEALS FOR LESS THAN 100 S ($9.50)
IN THE OLD CITY

✪ Augustiner Bräustübl Mülln

Linderhofstrasse or Augustinergasse 4 (north of Mönchsberg). ☎ **0662/43 12 46.** 30–70 S ($2.85–$6.65). No credit cards. Mon–Fri 3–10:30pm, Sat–Sun and hols 2:30–10:30pm. Bus 1, 2, 5, or 6 from the Hauptbahnhof to Mirabellplatz, then 27 from Mirabellplatz to Augustinergasse; or 1 from the Hauptbahnhof to Hanuschplatz, then 27 from Hanuschplatz to Augustinergasse. AUSTRIAN.

This is a great place for a meal, either in its beer garden or in one of the huge beer halls upstairs. Known among locals as Augustinerbräu Müllnerbräu (because of the area it's in, Müllner), this is a brewery where the star of the show is the brew, costing 24 S ($2.30) for a half liter or 48 S ($4.60) for a liter that you fetch yourself. You can bring your own food, but there are also various counters selling sausages and cold cuts, cheese, pretzels, bread, hamburgers, grilled chicken, Gulaschsuppe, salads, boiled pork with horseradish, beef with creamed spinach and potatoes, and

---

Getting the Best Deal on Dining

- Try the daily specials (*Tagesgericht*), which are usually complete meals offered at discount prices.
- Take advantage of butcher shops and food departments of department stores, which usually offer such take-out food as Leberkäs and grilled chicken.
- Dine at an inexpensive *Imbiss,* or food stall, selling Wurst, snacks, and beer.
- Ask if there's an extra charge for each piece of bread consumed and if your main course comes with vegetables or side dishes.

---

more. Pick and choose and create your own dinner. This is a crowded and noisy place, just as a brewery should be. Unfortunately, the drinking halls can also be quite smoky.

Nordsee

Getreidegasse 27. ☎ **0662/84 23 20.** 60–100 S ($5.70–$9.50). No credit cards. Mon–Sat 9am–11pm, Sun and hols 11am–11pm (to 7pm in winter). Bus 1 from the Hauptbahnhof to Hanuschplatz. SEAFOOD.

Nordsee is a chain of fast-food fish restaurants that originated in northern Germany. This self-service place is conveniently located on the same street as Mozart's Birthplace, offering fishburgers, fish sandwiches, cod filet with potato salad or pickles in white-mustard sauce, and more. Take-out service is also available.

Schwaighdfer

Kranzlmarkt 3. ☎ **0662/84 27 09.** 55–110 S ($5.25–$10.50). No credit cards. Mon–Sat 9am–7pm, Sun and hols 10am–5pm. Bus 1 from the Hauptbahnhof to Hanuschplatz. AUSTRIAN.

This Austrian-style deli offers more than 20 kinds of salad, ranging from 30 to 50 S ($2.85 to $4.75), and such main courses as Gulasch, Schweinebraten with salad, Tafelspitz, stuffed green peppers, and other Austrian specialties. It's a tiny place, with just a few seats in the back where you can eat your meal. Take-out service is also available.

Spaghetti & Co.

Getreidegasse 14. ☎ **0662/84 14 00.** Pizza and pasta 60–110 S ($5.70–$10.50). AE, DC, MC, V. Sun–Thurs 10:30am–11:30pm, Fri–Sat 10:30am–12:30am. Bus 1 from the Hauptbahnhof to Hanuschplatz. PASTA/PIZZA.

Near Mozart's Birthplace in the middle of the Altstadt, this is one branch of a chain of spaghetti parlors offering more than a dozen spaghetti dishes, as well as pizza, soups, and salads. It also has a do-it-yourself salad bar, with a large plate costing 69 S ($6.55).

NEAR THE HAUPTBAHNHOF

Kieselpassage

Rainerstrasse 19–23 (at the corner of Elisabethstrasse). ☎ **0662/88 26 91.** 20–75 S ($1.90–$7.15). No credit cards. Mon–Sat 9am–6pm, Sat 9am–noon (to 4:30pm the first Sat of the month). AUSTRIAN.

The Kieselpassage is a small indoor shopping mall about a three-minute walk from the Hauptbahnhof (look for an orange building). In its basement is a food court, with counters selling breads, pastries, salads, and such dishes as grilled chicken,

Gulaschsuppe, Wiener Schnitzel, and daily specials. The only disadvantage is that there aren't many places to sit down—you may end up eating at one of the several stand-up counters. Also in the basement is a store selling fruit, vegetables, and food.

Oregano

In the Forum department store, Südtirolerplatz 11. ☎ **0662/505 36.** 50–100 S ($4.75–$9.50). No credit cards. Mon–Fri 9am–5:30pm, Sat 9am–11:30am (to 4:30pm the first Sat of the month). AUSTRIAN.

This self-service restaurant is up on the first floor of Forum, Salzburg's largest department store, which faces the train station. It serves two excellent daily Tagesgerichte for 55 and 70 S ($5.25 and $6.65) with soup, a main dish, and salad. In addition to a salad bar, there are many à la carte choices, and with drinks and dessert you can eat like royalty for less than $10. There's a no-smoking section.

MEALS FOR LESS THAN 160 S ($15.25)
IN THE OLD CITY

Bärenwirt

Müllner Hauptstrasse 8. ☎ **0662/43 03 86.** Soups, salads, and appetizers 38–98 S ($3.60–$9.35); main courses 68–188 S ($6.45–$17.90). No credit cards. Thurs–Tues 11:30am–9pm. Bus 49 from Hanuschplatz to Müllnersteg. AUSTRIAN.

On the Müllner hill within a 10-minute walk from the center of the Altstadt, this cozy restaurant with wood-paneled walls is a typical Austrian *Gaststätte* (neighborhood family-owned inn) where most customers are regulars, the owner doubles as the main chef, and the owner's English-speaking wife is the charming hostess, dressed in traditional dirndl. In summer, treat yourself to a Strudel on the little terrace overlooking the Salzach.

○ Gasthaus Wilder Mann

Getreidegasse 20 or Griesgasse 17. ☎ **0662/84 17 87.** 55–140 S ($5.25–$13.35). No credit cards. Daily 11am–9pm (last order). Closed Sun in winter. Bus 1 from the Hauptbahnhof to Hanuschplatz. AUSTRIAN.

This simple popular restaurant has wooden tables, a wood-plank floor, and antlers on the wall. This is where the locals come to drink, eat, and gossip, and you may well be the only non-Salzburger around. The menu lists Bauernschmaus, Gulasch, Bratwurst, Schnitzel with ham and cheese baked over it, turkey with mushroom sauce, and pork chops. Watch for the reasonable daily specials. Wilder Mann translates as "Wild Man," an appropriate name. It's located in a narrow passageway between Getreidegasse and Griesgasse.

Pizzeria Peppone

Gstättengasse 15. ☎ **0662/84 32 84.** Pizza and pasta 70–120 S ($6.65–$11.40); meat dishes 130–225 S ($12.40–$21.40). DC, MC, V. Daily 11:30am–1:30pm and 5:30–11:30pm. Bus 1 from the Hauptbahnhof to Hanuschplatz. ITALIAN.

You can choose from dozens of pizzas and pasta dishes in this 130-seat restaurant near the lift to Café Winkler. Specialties include many varieties of pizza, spaghetti pomodoro, picatta milanese (Italian version of Wiener Schnitzel) with fries, and frittura mista (fried mixed fish). It also has pizza by the slice for 25 S ($2.40).

⊗ Sternbräu

Getreidegasse 34–36 or Griessgasse 23. ☎ **0662/84 21 40.** Main courses 85–195 S ($8.10–$18.55). No credit cards. Daily 11:30am–10:45pm. Bus 1 from the Hauptbahnhof to Hanuschplatz. AUSTRIAN.

This is one of Salzburg's best moderately priced restaurants, a huge place with seating both inside and out in a courtyard garden (a great place for a beer). The menu is extensive, listing such Austrian favorites as Bauernschmaus, Wiener Schnitzel with fries and salad, Tafelspitz, rumpsteak with herb butter and salad, pork cutlet, fresh fish, and grilled steak.

Stiegl-Bräu-Keller

Festungsgasse 10. ☎ **0662/84 26 81.** 80–150 S ($7.60–$14.30). No credit cards. Daily 11am–midnight. Closed Oct–Apr. Bus 5, 6, 51, or 55 from the Hauptbahnhof to Mozartsteg. AUSTRIAN.

Carved out of the rock of a mountain, the Festungsberg, a few hundred yards off Residenz Platz, this is a typical Austrian beer-cellar restaurant popularly called Stieglkeller. It has outdoor beer gardens as well as indoor seating. Try the Leberknödelsuppe, roast chicken, or the Salzburger Nockerl.

Wienerwald Restaurant

Griesgasse 31. ☎ **0662/84 34 70.** 69–160 S ($6.55–$15.25). AE, DC, MC, V. Daily 10am–12:30am. Bus 1 from the Hauptbahnhof to Hanuschplatz. AUSTRIAN.

This place has rooms decorated like those of a Swiss chalet, with comfortable seats. There are more than 300 restaurants of this chain in Austria, Germany, and Switzerland, where the specialty is spit-roasted chicken. An especially good deal is the quarter grilled chicken, with a choice of side dish. Other items on the menu include soups, casseroles, salads, club sandwich, turkey, steak, and grilled salmon. There's also a salad bar. It's popular with families and has a no-smoking section.

Yuen China Restaurant

Getreidegasse 24. ☎ **0662/84 37 70.** 90–185 S ($8.55–$17.60). AE, DC, MC, V. Daily 11:30am–11:30pm. Bus 1 from the Hauptbahnhof to Hanuschplatz. CHINESE.

This restaurant, on the same street as Mozart's Birthplace and entered via a courtyard and up a flight of stairs, looks authentic with its dragon motif on the ceiling, hanging Chinese lanterns, and a tank of exotic goldfish. In addition to the usual beef, chicken, pork, and vegetable dishes, it offers daily specials.

NEAR THE HAUPTBAHNHOF

Rosenkavalier

In the Hauptbahnhof. ☎ **0662/87 23 77-15.** Salads 30–70 S ($2.85–$6.65); main courses 75–130 S ($7.15–$12.40). AE, DC, MC, V. Daily 11am–7pm. AUSTRIAN.

Normally I avoid restaurants in train stations, but this is clearly an exception. It's a very civilized establishment, with tall ceilings and a turn-of-the-century atmosphere embellished with white tablecloths and classical or piano music playing softly in the background. The menu is fairly standard, including salads, soups, and such Austrian specialties as Kavalierspitz (boiled rump of beef), Schnitzel, Gulasch, grilled pike-perch, and Cordon Bleu, as well as lasagne and spaghetti. As is usual in Austria, main dishes come with such side dishes as salad or potatoes, making them complete meals. A good place for a meal while waiting for a train connection.

CAFES & KONDITOREIS

Salzburg is famous for its coffeehouses and pastry shops, where you can linger over pastry and coffee or a glass of wine, read the newspapers available (including the *International Herald Tribune*), and watch the passersby. In summer, many cafés have outdoor seating. Inside you'll be tempted by the delectable confections, heavily garnished with whipped cream. If you prefer, you can also take some pastries away for consumption on a park bench or in your hotel.

As well as the establishments listed below, another recommended coffeehouse is **Café Glockenspiel,** Mozartplatz 2 (☎ **0662/84 14 03**), near the tourist office.

Café Bazar

Schwarzstrasse 3 (on the right side of the Salzach River near the Staatsbrücke). ☎ **0662/ 87 42 78.** *Melange* (large coffee with milk) 35 S ($3.35); desserts 25–60 S ($2.40–$5.70). Mon 10am–6pm, Tues–Sat 7:30am–11pm. No credit cards. COFFEEHOUSE/SNACKS.

This fancy coffeehouse features chandeliers and large windows affording views of the river. It's popular with students from the nearby Mozarteum as well as with older people perusing the daily newspaper. In addition to coffee and desserts, it serves snacks and daily specials.

Café Mozart

Getreidegasse 22. ☎ **0662/84 37 46.** Small *Mocca* 27 S ($2.55); coffee with milk or cream 35 S ($3.35); desserts 25–40 S ($2.40–$3.80). Mon–Sat 9am–8pm, Sun 11am–8pm. No credit cards. COFFEEHOUSE.

The upstairs coffeehouse is appropriately named, as it's on the same street as Mozart's Birthplace. Although the house is 700 years old, the café dates back only 150 years. This refined and quiet Konditorei is where the locals tend to go for their meditative cups of coffee (try the *Mocca,* a strong Viennese coffee), along with some delicious Torte and Strudel, of course. The specialty of the house is its rich chocolate cake.

Café Tomaselli

Alter Markt 9. ☎ **0662/84 44 88.** *Melange* (large coffee with milk) 35 S ($3.35); desserts average 25–60 S ($2.40–$5.70). Mon–Sat 7am–9pm, Sun 8am–9pm. No credit cards. COFFEEHOUSE.

Established in 1705, the Café Tomaselli is still going strong. In fact, it's so popular that you may have to wait to get a seat. In summer, extra chairs are placed out on the cobblestone square. Have a *Melange* (large cup of coffee with milk) and dessert or choose from the pastry tray or the display case. There's also wine, beer, soft drinks, and snacks, plus ice cream in summer.

Konditorei Fürst

Brodgasse 13. ☎ **0662/84 37 59.** Large coffee with cream 33 S ($3.15); desserts 25– 40 S ($2.40–$3.80). Mon–Sat 8am–8pm, Sun and hols 9am–8pm. No credit cards. COFFEEHOUSE.

Across the square from Tomaselli is this younger upstart, founded in 1884. There are 50 varieties of cakes, pastries, and confections here, most heavily garnished with whipped cream. Try the Mohrenkopf, Mozartkugel, or Linzertorte—sinful!

PICNICKING

Kaufhaus Forum, across from the Hauptbahnhof at Südtirolerplatz 11 (☎ **0662/ 50536**), has a food department in the basement. Come here for the basics of cheese, sausage, bread, and fruit, as well as prepared foods like Leberkäs. It's open Monday through Friday from 9am to 6pm and Saturday from 8:30am to noon (to 5pm on the first Saturday of the month).

In the Altstadt, a wonderful place for inexpensive food is **Schwaighofer,** Kranzlmarkt 3 (☎ **0662/84 27 09**), located near the Staatsbrücke. This tiny hole-in-the-wall specializes in deli meats and sausages, cheeses, 20 kinds of salads, and such dishes as Gulaschsuppe, Tafelspitz, and stuffed green pepper. There are even a few tables where you can sit down to eat your goodies. It's open Monday through Saturday from 9am to 7pm and Sunday and holidays from 10am to 5pm.

If it's a nice day, you may want to join the other sun worshipers on the benches in the **Mirabellgarten** or along the **Salzach River.** Another good place to eat your purchases is at the **Augustiner Bräustübl Mülln,** a brewery described in "Meals for Less Than 100 S ($9.50)," above.

WORTH THE EXTRA MONEY

✪ K & K

Waagplatz 2 (near the tourist office and American Express) ☎ **0662/84 21 56.** Appetizers and soups 60–110 S ($5.70–$10.50); main courses 120–230 S ($11.40–$21.90); fixed-price lunch 180 S ($17.15); table charge 20 S ($1.90) per person (upstairs only). AE, DC, MC, V. Daily 11:30am–2pm and 6–9:30pm. Closed Sun in winter. AUSTRIAN.

This cozy and civilized first-floor restaurant features fresh flowers, heavy wooden tables, and soft classical music. Note the stone fish tank upstairs, filled with today's fresh trout. The interesting menu changes daily, listing typical Austrian cuisine as well as Austrian dishes with a twist. Thus, in addition to the usual Tafelspitz, grilled chicken breast, and trout, there may be cauliflower and broccoli layered with ham or perhaps a delicious spinach ravioli with parmesan.

By the way, there's another dining room on the ground floor. It's much more casual (and not quite as special as the restaurant upstairs), but it's open throughout the day from 11:30am to 9:30pm and offers basically the same menu without the table charge which is levied upstairs.

✪ Stiftskeller St. Peter

St. Peter-Bezirk 1 (near St. Peter's Monastery at the foot of the Mönchsberg). ☎ **0662/ 84 12 68-0** or 84 84 81-0. Soups, salads, and appetizers 40–125 S ($3.80–$11.90); main courses 90–225 S ($8.55–$21.40). AE, MC, V. Daily 11:30am–2pm and 5–10pm. AUSTRIAN.

This is probably the most popular first-class restaurant in Salzburg. It serves international food as well as local specialties, including fresh trout, boiled beef with chives, veal ragoût, beef Gulasch, and numerous daily specials. Its traditional desserts are great—try the Salzburger Nockerl. There are various dining rooms, each unique but all with a medieval ambience. In short, this place is a delight. It's under the management of St. Peter's Monastery, which dates from 803.

6 Attractions

SIGHTSEEING SUGGESTIONS

If You Have 1 Day

Start the morning with a tour of the Hohensalzburg Fortress and its museums. You might want to take the funicular up the hill, then walk back down into the city (about a 20-minute walk). Spend the afternoon in the Altstadt, strolling through its pedestrian lanes. Be sure to see Mozart's Birthplace on the famous Getreidegasse, Salzburg's most picturesque street. Notice the many wrought-iron shop signs: In the days when many people were illiterate, they served a useful purpose. Other places to visit include the Dom (cathedral) and the beautiful cemetery at St. Peter's. Top off the day with a beer at Augustiner Bräustübl Mülln. In the evening, take a stroll along the Salzach River, where you'll have a view of the fortress, all lit up.

If You Have 2 Days

To the attractions above, add the Hellbrunn Palace, 3 miles south of the city (open only from April to October). Its park with the trick fountains is unique. Try to include a visit to the Haus der Natur (Museum of Natural History), one of the best of its kind in the world; the Residenz State Rooms; and the National Costume Museum—all in the Altstadt. In late afternoon, take the lift (elevator) to the Café Winkler, a casino/café. It's worth the trip to the top just for the view, the best in all Salzburg. If you feel like a hike, you can walk from the Café Winkler along the ridge to the fortress in about half an hour, with great photo opportunities along the way. In the evening, get dressed up and go to one of Salzburg's many musical events, such as a concert in the fortress, its festival houses, the Mozarteum, or the Residenz.

If You Have 3 Days

Spend the first two days as outlined above. On the third day, head for Untersberg, a mountain 7 miles south of Salzburg where you have a lovely view of the city and the Alps. In the afternoon, take a stroll through the Mirabellgarten, topping it off with a sauna or swim at the adjoining Kurhaus.

If You Have 5 Days

Consider taking Bob's Bavarian Mountain Tour, a four-hour guided (in English) excursion covering the major Sound of Music film locations and a visit to Berchtesgaden. Another interesting option is to take a do-it-yourself excursion to Hallein's salt mines (open from April through October).

TOP ATTRACTIONS

✪ Mozarts Geburtshaus (Mozart's Birthplace)

Getreidegasse 9. ☎ **0662/84 43 13.** Admission 62 S ($5.90) adults, 47 S ($4.45) students and senior citizens, 17 S ($1.60) children. June–Aug, daily 9am–7pm; Sept–May, daily 9am–6pm. Bus 1 from the Hauptbahnhof to Hanuschplatz, or 5 or 6 from the Hauptbahnhof to Rathausplatz.

This is, without doubt, the most heavily visited attraction in Salzburg. Wolfgang Amadeus Mozart was born in this third-floor apartment in 1756 and lived here with his family until 1773. The museum exhibits his piano (he started composing when he was four) and the violin he played as a small boy. A plaque marks the spot where his cradle stood. Of the several paintings of Amadeus and his family, only one is thought to be a true likeness of the musical genius—the unfinished one by the piano, done by Mozart's brother-in-law.

In addition to the rooms where the family lived, there are a few adjoining rooms decorated in the style of a typical burgher's house during Mozart's time.

But most fascinating are the models of various stage settings for Mozart's operas, showing the interpretations through the ages. The dozens of models, all originals, range from an 1810 production of *Don Giovanni* in Munich to a 1930 productionof *Die Zauberflöte* staged in Berlin. A must-see.

Festung Hohensalzburg (Hohensalzburg Fortress)

Mönchsberg 34. ☎ **0662/80 42 21 23.** Grounds only and Sound and Vision Show, 30 S ($2.85) adults, 15 S ($1.40) students and children; grounds, tour, and museums, 60 S ($5.70) adults, 55 S ($5.25) senior citizens, 35 S ($3.35) students, 30 S ($2.85) children. Conducted tours, July–Aug, daily 9am–5:30pm; Apr–June and Sept–Oct, daily 9:30am–5pm; Nov–Mar, daily 10am–4:30pm. Fortress grounds, July–Sept, daily 8am–7pm; Apr–June and Oct, daily

8am–6pm; Nov–Mar, daily 9am–5pm. Rainermuseum closed Oct–Apr. Take the funicular (22 S/$2.10 one way or 32 S/$3.05 round-trip for adults; half price for children) or it's a 30-minute walk from the Altstadt.

This medieval fortress/castle dominates the city. Built between the 11th and the 17th centuries as a residence for the prince-archbishops who ruled Salzburg for more than 500 years, it's a perfectly preserved medieval fortress. Perched high above the city on a cliff, it contains the **State Rooms** of the former archbishops and two museums. The State Rooms, with their coffered ceilings and intricate iron-work, can be visited only if you join one of the tours. Unfortunately, tours are conducted in English only when enough English-speaking visitors are present to warrant it. To avoid disappointment, pay only the 30-S ($2.85) admission fee to the fortress grounds and then head immediately to the tour office. If there's a tour in English, you can always pay the difference there.

The tour takes visitors through dark corridors and unfurnished chambers, including a dismal **torture chamber.** In the fortress is also a huge open-air **barrel organ,** which used to ring out at the end of the day to signal the closing of the city gates. Now it's played three times a day from Easter to October. In the living quarters of the former archbishops is a late gothic porcelain stove dating from 1501, the most valuable item in the fortress.

The tour concludes at the **Burg Museum,** with its displays of weapons used in peasant revolts, furniture, and a macabre collection of medieval torture devices. The other museum, the **Rainermuseum,** displays more weapons.

If you don't take the tour, the base admission fee allows you to wander through the fortress grounds, courtyards, and viewing platforms and includes entrance to the "Sound and Vision Show," a multimedia presentation of Salzburg and the fortress.

The easiest way to reach the fortress is by funicular. However, it's not cheap, and you still have to pay admission once you reach the top of the hill. If you're on a tight budget, you might wish to approach the fortress on foot. A path lead-ing from the Altstadt and winding up the hill, offering changing vistas on the way, makes a pleasant walk. As an alternative, you may wish to go up by funicular and come down on foot.

Residenz

Residenzplatz 1. ☎ **0662/8042-2690.** State Rooms tours, 45 S ($4.30) adults, 35 S ($3.35) senior citizens and students, 15 S ($1.40) children 15 and under; Residenzgalerie, 45 S

❓ Did You Know ?

- For over 1,000 years, Salzburg's powerful bishops ranked as princes of the Holy Roman Empire.
- There's mist or fog in Salzburg about one out of every seven days.
- Renaissance and baroque influences in the architecture have earned Salzburg the title the "Austrian Rome."
- For a time, Mozart was Konzertmeister to the archbishop of Salzburg, but since he was almost never in town he received no salary.
- Salzburg's music festival has been held almost every year since 1920.
- American forces in Austria were headquartered in Salzburg from 1945 to 1956.

Salzburg

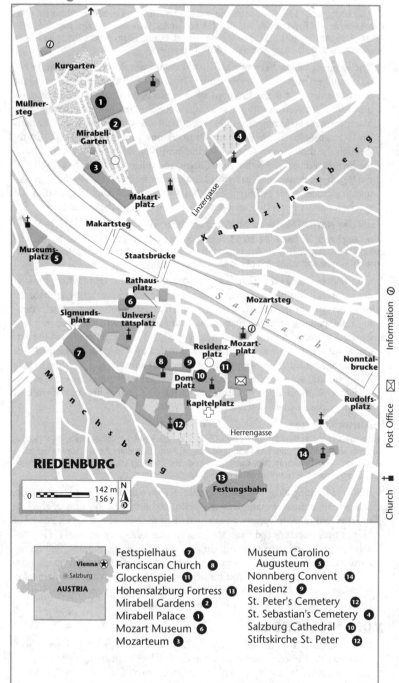

Kurgarten

Müllner-
steg

Mirabell-
Garten

Makart-
platz

Linzergasse

Kapuzinerberg

Makartsteg

Museums-
platz ⑤

Staatsbrücke

Salzach

Rathaus-
platz

Mozartsteg

Sigmunds-
platz

Universi-
tätsplatz

Mozart-
platz

Nonntal-
brucke

Residenz-
platz

⑦

⑧ ⑨ ⑪

Dom-
platz ⑩

Rudolfs-
platz

Kapitelplatz

⑫

Herrengasse

⑭

RIEDENBURG

Mönchsberg

0   142 m
     156 y

N

⑬

Festungsbahn

Information ⓘ

Post Office ✉

Church ✝ ■

Vienna ★

Salzburg

AUSTRIA

Festspielhaus ⑦
Franciscan Church ⑧
Glockenspiel ⑪
Hohensalzburg Fortress ⑬
Mirabell Gardens ②
Mirabell Palace ①
Mozart Museum ⑥
Mozarteum ③

Museum Carolino
  Augusteum ⑤
Nonnberg Convent ⑭
Residenz ⑨
St. Peter's Cemetery ⑫
St. Sebastian's Cemetery ④
Salzburg Cathedral ⑩
Stiftskirche St. Peter ⑫

($4.30) adults, 35 S ($3.35) senior citizens and students, free for children; combination ticket (State Rooms and Residenzgalerie), 70 S ($6.65) adults. State Rooms tours, July–Aug, daily 10am–4:30pm (last tour); Sept–June, Mon–Fri at 10am, 11am, noon, 2pm, and 3pm. Residenzgalerie, daily 10am–5pm (closed Wed in winter).

The Residenz, in the heart of the Altstadt, dates from the mid-12th century but was rebuilt extensively during the 16th, 17th, and 18th centuries. It served as the official residence of the archbishops when it was deemed safe for them to move down from the fortress into the city (after you've toured both places, you won't blame them for preferring the more elegant Residenz). Conducted 40-minute tours (in German only) of the **Residenz Prunkräume (State Rooms)** take visitors through the throne room (considered the most beautiful room of the Residenz), the bedroom of the archbishop, the library, and other chambers. Be sure to visit the **Residenzgalerie** too. A gallery of European art from the 16th to the 19th century, it includes works by Dutch, French, Italian, and Austrian baroque artists. Of special interest are paintings that depict Salzburg through the centuries.

Haus der Natur (Museum of Natural History)

Museumsplatz 5. ☎ **0662/84 26 53.** Admission 45 S ($4.30) adults, 30 S ($2.85) students and children. Daily 9am–5pm. Bus 1 from the Hauptbahnhof to Hanuschplatz; then turn right onto Griesgasse and at the end of it is Museumsplatz.

On five floors in 80 exhibition rooms, practically everything that lives or grows on our planet is brilliantly displayed. Exhibits include stuffed prehistoric animals; the twin roots of a fir tree hundreds of years old; live tarantulas; a rock crystal weighing 1,360 pounds; such abnormalities as a calf with two heads, a chicken with four legs, and a deer with three; a giant model of a DNA molecule; models of the Saturn V rocket; and pieces of moon rock donated by President Nixon in 1973. There's also an aquarium with fresh- and seawater animals, as well as the Reptile Zoo with 200 scaly creatures, including a collection of poisonous snakes and alligators. Without a doubt, this is one of the best natural-history museums in Europe. Unfortunately, descriptions are only in German.

Hellbrunn Palace

Three miles south of the city. ☎ **0662/82 03 72.** Palace, 48 S ($4.55) adults, 24 S ($2.30) students and children; park and Orangerie, free. Apr and Oct, daily 9am–4:30pm (last tour); May–Sept, daily 9am–5pm (last tour); July–Aug, also evening tours 6–10pm. Closed Nov–Mar. Bus 55 from the Hauptbahnhof to Hellbrun (a 20-minute ride).

Built as a hunting lodge and summer residence for Salzburg's prince-bishops, the palace is an impressive example of the wealth and comfort controlled by absolute rulers at that time. It features, like the palace of the tsars in Leningrad, dozens of hidden trick fountains and water sprays in its large baroque gardens. This is probably the only conducted tour in Europe in which laughing, running, and hiding is expected of the tourist. Tours through the palace last approximately 45 minutes.

Be sure, too, to visit the **Volkskundemuseum (Folklore Museum),** located in the Monatsschlösschen on the palace grounds. (By the way, not far away is the Hellbrun Zoo, worth a visit if you have kids.)

MORE ATTRACTIONS

If you plan to visit the Museum Carolino Augusteum, the Spielzeug Museum (Toy Museum), the cathedral excavations, and the Folklore Museum in Hellbrunn, you can save money by buying a combination ticket to all four for 60 S ($5.70) for adults and 20 S ($1.90) for students and children.

Catacombs of St. Peter's Church

St. Peter-Bezirk 1. ☎ **0662/844 57 80.** Church and cemetery, free; catacombs tour, 12 S ($1.15) adults, 8 S (75¢) senior citizens, students, and children. Church, daily 9am–5pm. Catacombs tour, May–Sept, daily on the hour 10am–5pm; Oct–Apr, daily at 11am, noon, and 1:30, 2:30, and 3:30pm. Bus 1 from the Hauptbahnhof to Hanuschplatz; then walk to the end of Sigmund Hafnergasse, turn left to Domplatz, and the church is next to the Dom.

This church in the Altstadt has a lovely rococo interior and is surrounded by one of the most picturesque cemeteries I've ever seen, beautifully arranged and worth a walk through. At the entrance to the catacombs (against the cliff) are two of the cemetery's most important tombs—those of Mozart's sister, Nannerl, and Haydn's brother, Johann Michael Haydn. If you have time, you might wish to join a guided tour of the catacombs (for a minimum of five, conducted usually in German but sometimes also in English). You'll visit two rooms carved in the face of the cliff, the first dating from A.D. 250 and built by Roman Christians for secret religious ceremonies. Be forewarned—there are a lot of stairs on this 20-minute tour. In January and February, tours are given infrequently—check the notice board at the entrance for the next tour.

Dom (Cathedral)

Domplatz. ☎ **0662/84 41 89.** Dom, free (but donations appreciated); Dom museum, 40 S ($3.80) adults, 30 S ($2.85) senior citizens, 10 S (95¢) students, 5 S (50¢) children. Dom, daily 6am–8pm (to 6pm in winter); Dom museum, mid-May to mid-Oct, Mon–Sat 10am–5pm, Sun 11am–5pm. Dom museum closed mid-Oct to mid-May. Bus 1 from the Hauptbahnhof to Hanuschplatz; then walk to the end of Sigmund Hafnergasse, turn left, and you've reached Domplatz.

Salzburg's Dom, in the center of the Altstadt, was built in the 8th century but destroyed by a fire in the 16th century. The present Dom, commissioned by Archbishop Wolf-Dietrich and designed by an Italian architect, is considered the finest example of an early baroque building north of the Alps. This is where Mozart was baptized and engaged as a court organist, and it's famed for its three bronze doors and its 4,000-pipe organ. Treasures of the Dom are on display in the museum, to the right of the front door.

Domgrabungsmuseum (Cathedral Excavations)

Residenzplatz. ☎ **0662/84 52 95.** Admission 20 S ($1.90) adults, 10 S (95¢) students and children. Wed–Sun 9am–5pm. Closed Nov–Easter. Bus 1 from the Hauptbahnhof to Hanuschplatz.

Special & Free Events

Salzburg's most famous annual event is the **Salzburg Festival,** which attracts music lovers from all over the world. It's therefore understandable that tickets are hard to come by and impossible to get once the festival is under way—from the end of July to the end of August. To find out what's being performed, contact the Salzburg Festival, Postfach 140, 5020 Salzburg (☎ **0662/8045**). Among the highlights are Mozart's operas, Hugo von Hofmannsthal's *Everyman,* performances of the Salzburg Marionette Theater, and guest philharmonic orchestras.

For **free concerts,** your best bet is the Mozarteum, where concerts are given regularly by students. In summer, free brass-band concerts are held in Mirabell Garden on Wednesday at 8:30pm and on Sunday at 10:30am.

Around the corner from the Dom entrance (to the left if you're facing the Dom's massive doors) is a museum showing the history of the Dom since the 8th century, with excavation work showing ruins of the foundation.

Mönchsberg and Café Winkler

Mönchsberg. ☎ **0662/84 77 38.** Mönchsberg Lift (elevator), 15 S ($1.40) one way and 25 S ($2.40) round-trip adults, half price for children. Elevator, Mon 9am–7pm, Tues–Sun 9am–11pm. Café, Tues–Sat 11am–11pm, Sun 11am–5pm. Bus 1 from the Hauptbahnhof to Hanuschplatz.

Salzburg's other conspicuous hilltop building is the Café Winkler, which contains a café and sits high above the city. The best reason for coming here, however, is the view—Salzburg's most impressive. In front of you are all the churches, a stretch of the Salzach River, and the Hohensalzburg Fortress. Also of interest is the *Sattler Panorama,* a huge 360° mural of Salzburg, painted in 1825, that was taken throughout Europe as proof that Salzburg was a beautiful city worthy of a visit.

If you feel like a hike, take the path that skirts the top of the ridge to the fortress, about a 30-minute walk. Café Winkler can be reached via the Mönchsberg Lift, an elevator that whisks visitors to the top. The elevator is at Gstättengasse 13, departing at least every 15 minutes.

Museum Carolino Augusteum

Museumsplatz 1. ☎ **0662/84 31 45.** Admission 40 S ($3.80) adults, 15 S ($1.40) students and children. Tues 9am–8pm, Wed–Sun 9am–5pm. Bus 1 from the Hauptbahnhof to Hanuschplatz; then turn right onto Griegasse and at the end of it is Museumsplatz.

Beginning with Salzburg's founding as a Roman settlement in the 1st century A.D., this collection documents Salzburg's cultural history through the ages with a presentation of locally produced art and crafts. Included are Roman mosaics, vases, and bronze figures; paintings; sculptures; religious art; ceramics; musical instruments (my favorite department); jewelry; glassware; coins; and furniture. Of particular interest are models of Salzburg in 1612 and 1860, which show how little the Altstadt has changed in the past few centuries.

St. Sebastian Friedhof (Cemetery)

Linzer Gasse 41. Admission free. Daily 7am–7pm. Bus 1 or 5 from the Hauptbahnhof to Mirabellplatz or Makartplatz.

And now for some ancient gossip: Three of Salzburg's most famous people are buried here. Best known, perhaps, are two members of Wolfgang Amadeus Mozart's family—his father, Leopold, and his wife, Constanze. The talk around Salzburg is that Amadeus was actually in love with Constanze's sister, but when the sister refused him he settled for Constanze, who reputedly resembled her sister. After Amadeus's death, Constanze married Georg Nikolaus Nissen, who ended up writing Mozart's first biography.

Another famous person buried here is Archbishop Wolf-Dietrich von Raitenau, who more than anyone else was responsible for the Salzburg of today, turning it from a medieval town into a Renaissance and baroque city. Educated in Rome and related to the Medicis, Wolf-Dietrich wished to transform Salzburg into a dazzling city that would rival the great cities of Italy. He set about rebuilding the Dom (cathedral), started construction on the Residenz, and built a palace (Mirabell Palace) for himself and his mistress, who bore him 12 children. A bit too flamboyant for an archbishop, Wolf-Dietrich was eventually imprisoned.

Finally, Doctor Paracelsus, an alchemist who worked tirelessly to find cures for leprosy and dropsy, is buried here as well.

Bürgerspital Spielzeug Museum (Toy Museum)

Bürgerspitalgasse 2. ☎ **0662/84 75 60.** Admission (including the Punch-and-Judy show Wed and Fri at 3pm) 30 S ($2.85) adults, 10 S (95¢) students and children. Tues–Sun 9am–5pm. Bus 1 from the Hauptbahnhof to Hanuschplatz.

Housed in the former Salzburg Municipal Hospital, this delightful museum displays every conceivable sort of toy—from a hand-carved Noah's Ark to a merry-go-round, from model trains to dolls, cutouts, and cardboard theaters—all dating from the 16th century to the present. There's also folk art and temporary exhibits. You'll see more adults than children as visitors here.

Trachtenmuseum (National Costume Museum)

Griesgasse 23. ☎ **0662/84 31 19.** Admission 30 S ($2.85) adults, 20 S ($1.90) students and children. Mon–Fri 10am–noon and 2–5pm, Sat 10am–noon. Bus 1 from the Hauptbahnhof to Hanuschplatz; then turn right onto Griesgasse and the museum will be on your left.

Those who plan to buy dirndls should go here first: Traditional Salzburg dress, past and present (and a few lederhosen, sweaters, hats, and jackets), from the 18th to the 20th century, is on exhibit.

PARKS & GARDENS

The most famous garden in town, now a public park, is the **Mirabellgarten** (Mirabell Garden), on the right bank of the river. *Mirabell* is the Italian word for "beautiful view" and, designed in the 17th century in baroque style with statues, marble putti, fountains, and ponds, it offers a good view of the Hohensalzburg Fortress. In the middle of the grounds is a palace built by Archbishop Wolf-Dietrich for his mistress and now used for concerts and administrative offices. The park itself is a popular place for a stroll, and its benches are always full with Salzburg's office workers and older people catching a few rays. The Orangerie is free, and in spring the garden comes alive with 17,000 tulips. A small open-air cafeteria sells beverages and snacks.

Adjoining the garden is the **Kurpark,** a tree-lined area with a small hill called Rosenhügel, a good spot for taking snapshots, with an indoor swimming pool.

Smaller parks are found at the foot of **Kapuzinerberg** and **Mönchsberg,** all with benches that invite picnicking,

ORGANIZED TOURS

In a city as small as Salzburg that can be so pleasurably covered on foot, it really isn't necessary to book a bus tour unless you desire to visit out-of-town sights. For readers planning more than a two-day stay, here's a list of the excursions to consider.

Bob's Special Tours, near Mozartplatz in the heart of the Altstadt at Chiemseegasse 1 (☎ **0662/84 95 110**), offers three four-hour tours, all of which cost 300 S ($28.55). The *"Sound of Music* Tour" includes a short city tour and takes in most of the major filming locations, including Leopoldskron Palace, the lake district, and the church where the wedding took place. The second tour, the "Bavarian Mountain Tour," includes some *Sound of Music* sights, as well as the gardens of Hellbrunn and Berchtesgaden in Germany (passport required). Both tours depart daily at 9am and 2pm, with pickup at any guesthouse or hotel in Salzburg. The third excursion, good for cloudy and rainy days, visits the salt mines in Berchtesgaden (entrance fees extra). Finally, the "Eagle's Nest Tour," offered daily May to October, takes in the view of the Bavarian Alps and costs 520 S ($49.50). Tours are small and personable, in buses that seat 8 to 20.

Another tour company is **Salzburg Panorama Tours** (☎ **0662/87 40 29**). In addition to its city tour, "*Sound of Music* Tour," and "Bavarian Mountain and Saltmines Tour," it offers two tours of the surrounding countryside: "Lakes and Mountains" is a four-hour circular tour through Salzburg's lake district—Fuschl See, Mondsee, and Wolfgang See, stopping at the famous Weisses Rössl Hotel. This tour operates at 2pm daily, for 300 S ($28.55) per person. The "Bavarian Mountain Tour" is a four-hour tour that crosses the German border twice (bring your passport). The tour proceeds via Hellbrunn and Anif to Berchtesgaden and Königssee. You'll see Hitler's former residence (what's left of it, anyway) from your bus window. The tour leaves daily at 2pm, at a cost of 300 S ($28.55) per person.

And, finally, one more tour company is **Salzburg Sightseeing Tours**, Mirabellplatz 2 (☎ **0662/88 16 16**), the first company to offer a "*Sound of Music*" tour (its bus even appeared in the film)—it still offers a four-hour "The Most Unique *Sound of Music* Tour" for 300 S ($28.55). For a quick impression of the city, you might wish to join its one-hour tour offered four times a day for 170 S ($16.20), or, if you have a bit more time, join the two-hour "Mozart City Tour," which takes in the Dom, St. Peter's Church, Hellbrunn Palace, and even a trip to the Winkler Café for a panoramic view of the city, at a cost of 220 S ($20.95). From May to October there's also the "Grand City Tour," a 3 1/2-hour bus and walking tour of the city, including wine tasting at St. Peter's, for 380 S ($36.20). Excursions into the countryside include trips to the Eagle's Nest and the surrounding countryside, as well as a tour of the salt mines in Hallein, which includes a trip by cable car, an open-air Celtic museum, and entrance to the mines, for 420 S ($40). Note that as a special service to holders of this book, readers are entitled to a 10% discount on all tours; students and families receive further reductions.

7 Shopping

Austrian artisanry is of high quality, with correspondingly high prices for sweaters, dirndls, leather goods, jewelry, and other local goods. Most shops are concentrated in the Altstadt along Getreidegasse and Alter Markt, as well as across the river along Linzer Gasse.

If in any one store you make purchases that total more than 1,000 S ($95.25), you're entitled to a refund of the value-added tax (amounting to 10% to 32%, depending on the item). Ask the store clerk for a U-34 form, which you present to Customs upon departing the last European Union country on your way home. If, for example, you're flying back to the United States from Frankfurt, present your U-34 form, receipt from the shop, and goods purchased to the Customs officer at the Frankfurt airport.

MARKETS   Salzburg has two well-known markets. **Grüner Markt (Green Market)** is held in the Altstadt, in front of the Universitäts church on Universitätsplatz (behind Mozart's Birthplace). It features stalls selling vegetables, fruit, flowers, and souvenirs, as well as a stand-up food stall selling sausages. It takes place Monday through Friday from 6am to 6pm and Saturday from 6am to 1pm.

On the other side of the river, in front of St. Andrews Church near Mirabellplatz, is the **Schrannenmarkt.** This is where Salzburg's housewives go to shop and socialize, purchasing vegetables and locally grown products. It's held every Thursday (on Wednesday if Thursday is a public holiday) from 6am to 1pm.

8 Salzburg After Dark

As the birthplace of Mozart and site of the Salzburg Festival (see the "Special & Free Events" box under "Attractions," earlier in this chapter), the city boasts a musical event almost every night of the year. To find out what's going on where, stop by the City Tourist Office, Mozartplatz 5 (☎ **0662/84 75 68**), to pick up a free copy of *Wochenspiegel* as well as a monthly brochure.

The cheapest way to buy theater tickets is by going directly to the theater box office. A ticket agency, such as **Polzer,** Residenzplatz 3 (☎ **0662/84 65 00**), will charge a stiff 20% commission. The **Salzburg Ticket Service.** which also charges a 20% commission, is conveniently located at the City Tourist Office on Mozartplatz (☎ **0662/84 22 96** or 84 03 10). Selling tickets for all concerts, it's open Monday through Friday from 9am to 6pm and Saturday from 9am to noon; in July and August, daily from 9am to 7pm.

Tickets for the Salzburg Festival must be booked months in advance.

THE PERFORMING ARTS
OPERA, DANCE & MUSIC

Festspielhaus

Hofstallgasse 1. ☎ **0662/80 45-0.** Tickets for orchestra concerts 240–540 S ($22.85–$51.40); during the Salzburg Festival, 300–3,900 S ($28.55–$371.40). Bus 1 from the Hauptbahnhof to Hanuschplatz, or 5 or 6 from the Hauptbahnhof to Rathausplatz.

This is where opera, ballet, and concerts are performed and major events of the Salzburg Festival take place. Performances are in the 1,324-seat Kleines Haus (Small House) or the 2,170-seat Grosses Haus (Large House), and it's best to buy your tickets in advance; the box office for the Salzburg Festival is at Hofstallgasse 1 (☎ **0662/84 45 01**); for orchestra concerts, given September through June, it's at Waagplatz 1A (☎ **0662/84 53 46**), near the tourist office. The box office is open Monday through Friday from 8am to 6pm; performances are usually at 7:30pm.

Mozarteum

Schwarzstrasse 26. ☎ **0662/87 31 54.** Most tickets 180–650 S ($17.15–$61.90). Bus 1, 5, or 6 from the Hauptbahnhof to Mirabellplatz.

Orchestra concerts and chamber-music and organ recitals are presented in this hall. As part of a music school, it occasionally features free concerts by students. The Mozarteum is located on the right bank of the river, near Mirabell Garden. The box office is open Monday through Thursday from 9am to 2pm and Friday from 9am to 4pm; performances are at 11am and/or 7:30pm.

Schlosskonzerte

In the Mirabell Palace, Mirabellplatz, and in the Residenz, Residenzplatz 1. ☎ **0662/87 27 88.** Tickets 280–300 S ($26.65–$28.55). Bus 1, 5, or 6 from the Hauptbahnhof to Mirabellplatz (Mirabell Palace) or Rathausplatz (Residenz).

The Salzburger Schlosskonzerte (Salzburg Palace Concerts) take place throughout the year in the Mirabell Palace and the Residenz. The chamber-music series presents Mozart's music as well as music from the baroque to the contemporary. Concerts are held in small ornately baroque rooms, much as they were during Mozart's time. The box office, at Griesgasse 6, is open Monday through Friday from 9am to noon and 2 to 5pm; performances are almost daily at 8pm.

Festungskonzerte

Hohensalzburg Fortress, Mönchsberg 34. ☎ **0662/82 58 58.** Tickets 300–330 S ($28.55–$31.40). Take the funicular from Festungsgasse.

Salzburg's landmark, the Hohensalzburg Fortress, features concerts called the Festungskonzerte in the medieval Prince's Chamber from May to the end of October and during Easter and December. The Salzburger Mozart-Ensemble is featured as well as guest musicians. The box office, at A.-Adlgasser-Weg 22, is open daily from 9am to 9pm; performances are given at Easter, mid-May through October, and in December daily at 8 or 8:30pm.

THEATER

Salzburger Landestheater

Schwarzstrasse 22. ☎ **0662/87 15 12.** Tickets 100–590 S ($9.50–$56.20). Bus 1, 5, or 6 from the Hauptbahnhof to Makartplatz.

Comedies, dramas, and musicals are performed here, as well as ballet, operas, and operettas. During August the theater takes part in the Salzburg Festival. The Landestheater has a central location on the right bank of the Salzach, just south of Mirabell Garden. The box office is open Tuesday through Saturday from 10am to 1pm and 5:30 to 7pm; performances are usually Tuesday through Sunday at 7 or 7:30pm.

Salzburger Marionettentheater

Schwarzstrasse 24. ☎ **0662/87 24 06.** Tickets 250–400 S ($23.80–$38.10). Bus 1, 5, or 6 from the Hauptbahnhof to Makartplatz.

Next to the Landestheater, the Salzburger Marionettentheater was founded in 1913 and is one of Europe's largest and most famous marionette theaters. The company has toured throughout the world, including Argentina, Australia, Japan, and the United States, not to mention almost every country in Europe. It presents operas and operettas from Easter to September, including *The Magic Flute, Die Fledermaus, The Barber of Seville, The Marriage of Figaro,* and *Don Giovanni.* The box office is open Monday through Saturday from 9am to 1pm; performances are usually Monday through Saturday at 7:30pm, with matinees occasionally at 4pm in July and August.

FILMS

The easiest to find are the **Central Lichtspiele,** Linzer Gasse 17 (☎ 0662/87 22 82); **Elmo Kino,** St.-Julien-Strasse 5 (☎ **0662/87 23 73**), on the right bank; and **Mozartkino,** Kaigasse 33 (☎ **0662/84 22 22**).

The first performance usually starts at 2:30pm, the last at 10pm. The average ticket price is 85 to 95 S ($8.10 to $9.05) for evening shows, 50 S ($4.75) for matinees.

For alternative, offbeat, or international films, the best place to go is the **Salzburger Filmkulturzentrum,** Giselakai 11 (☎ **0662/87 31 00**), just off Linzer Gasse and Steingasse, across the river from the Altstadt. It shows films in their original language, with German subtitles, and all seats are 85 S ($8.10).

THE BAR SCENE

For an alternative night scene, try **Steingasse,** a narrow, ancient cobblestone street on the right bank that leads uphill from the Staatsbrücke (bridge), hugging the side of the Kapuzinerberg hill. There are some trendy shops here, as well as some rather exclusive nightclubs (with one-way mirrors and no windows). And, yes, that tiny house at Steingasse 24 with the red light beckoning brightly is what you think it is.

In addition to a stroll on Steingasse, there are also a couple of breweries in Salzburg that are congenial for an evening out.

Augustiner Bräustübl Mülln

Augustinergasse 4. ☎ **0662/43 12 46.** Bus 27 from Mirabellplatz or Hanuschplatz to Augustinergasse.

This brewery, popularly known as Augustinerbräu or Müllnerbräu, is one of the cheapest places in town for a brew, with seating either outdoors in its beer garden or in one of its massive dining halls. There are also counters selling sausages, pretzels, and other foods that go well with beer, which goes for 24 S ($2.30) for a half liter. It's open Monday through Friday from 3 to 10:30pm and Saturday, Sunday, and holidays from 2:30 to 10:30pm.

Fridrich

Steingasse 15. ☎ **0662/87 62 18.** Bus 1, 2, 5, or 6 to Mirabellplatz.

For a drink along Steingasse on the right bank of the river, try this tiny modern bar. It's housed snugly in what used to be a blacksmith's shop, in a 14th-century building boasting its original arched ceiling. There's a sign on the door that says this place is for members only, but that's enforced only if the place gets too full. A tiny glass of wine begins at 36 S ($3.40). Open daily from 5pm to 1am.

Shrimps

Steingasse 5 (just off Linzer Gasse). ☎ **0662/87 44 84.**

This bar/restaurant is a cozy and popular place for both a meal and drinks, with a low vaulted ceiling and candles to set the mood. Soups, salads, seafood, pasta, and rice dishes dominate the menu, while the recorded music ranges from classical to jazz, blues, and swing. A quarter liter of beer or a small glass of wine goes for 22 S ($2.10). Open Monday through Friday from noon to 11pm.

Urbankeller

Schallmooser Hauptstrasse 50. ☎ **0662/87 08 94.** Cover 100–150 S ($9.50–$14.30) Fri, free Mon–Thurs and Sat. Bus 29 to Canavalstrasse.

This cellarlike establishment with a vaulted ceiling served as a wine cellar and ice-storage room back in 1636. Today it's a *Heuriger* (wine tavern) and restaurant, featuring jazz music every Friday evening except holidays and during the months of July and August. It offers a self-service counter of salads, cheeses, and sausages. There's also a restaurant with waitress service. Wine begins at 38 S ($3.60). The music includes local groups such as the Salzach River Stompers, as well as jam sessions and guest bands. It's on the right bank of the Salzach, about a 30-minute walk from the Hauptbahnhof, or a short bus ride. Open Monday through Saturday from 5pm to midnight.

Die Weisse Bräustüberl and Bräugasthof Rupertihof

Rupertgasse 10 and Virgilgasse 9. ☎ **0662/87 22 46** or 87 64 81. Bus 29.

This brewery, which specializes in wheat beer, serves its beer in two establishments located next to each other. The Bräugasthof Rupertihof, on Rupertgasse 10, is a large restaurant with waiter service and changing menus offering such dishes as pepper steak and Gulasch. It's open Monday through Friday from 5pm to midnight and Saturday from 6pm to 1am. The Bräustüberl (open daily from 11am to 11pm), behind the Bräugasthof, is smaller and less formal—you fetch your own beer and can dine on sausages and pretzels. Beer costs 34 S ($3.25) for a half liter. In fine weather, you'll probably want to sit outside in the beer garden. These places are on the right bank of the Salzach, about a 15-minute walk from the Hauptbahnhof.

9 Easy Excursions

UNTERSBERG   Untersberg, the mountain dominating Salzburg, is 6,115 feet above sea level, 7 miles south of the city in St. Leonhard. Visiting Untersberg is certainly worth the extra money, and probably will be one of the highlights of your stay in Salzburg. To get there, take bus no. 55 from the train station to St. Leonhard, the last stop, and change to the cable car to ride to the top of the mountain. You'll have a glorious view of Salzburg and the Alps. A marked path leads to the peak in about 20 minutes (bring good walking shoes if you plan to hike); if you prefer, you can sit in the restaurant there and enjoy the view.

The round-trip fare for the cable car (☎ **0662/87 12 17** or 06246/724 77) is 190 S ($18.10) for adults, 90 S ($8.50) for children. The cable car operates daily: July to September, from 8:30am to 5:30pm; March to June and October, from 9am to 5pm; November to February, from 10am to 4pm. It's closed for maintenance for two weeks in April.

HALLEIN   Hallein, 10 miles south of Salzburg, is famous for its **salt mines** near a mountain, the Dürrnberg. The mines (☎ **06245/85 285-15**) have been operated since Roman times. Take an early train from Salzburg to Hallein. In Hallein, follow the signs to the ground station of the funicular up the Dürrnberg. At the top of the mountain, take the footpath (a five-minute walk) to the Dürrnberg salt-mine entrance. A one-hour salt-mine tour (in German only) is conducted by a uniformed miner. He'll give you a coverall to protect you from cold, humidity, and dirt, then seat you on the bench of a small electric car. You'll see a huge saltwater lake, slide down twice on wooden rails, and listen to lectures on salt production. This excursion will take half a day, and is highly recommended if you travel with kids, even though the tour is in German (if you're lucky your tour guide may speak some English and make a few translations for your sake).

The salt mines are open daily: mid-April to mid-October from 9am to 5pm and in winter from 11am to 3pm. The tour costs 160 S ($15.25) for adults and 80 S ($7.60) for children. Note that children must be at least 4 years old to go on the tour.

Stockholm 23

by Alice Garrard

On a map, Stockholm appears cold and remote, a city disjointedly dotted across numerous islands, sliced into pieces by icy artic waters, and positioned as far north as Siberia. Yet to visit this breathtaking cosmopolitan city is to enter a romantic dream of old-world Europe. With remarkable grace, the Swedes have tamed their environment.

Up close, Stockholm is the most beautiful capital in Scandinavia-indeed, it's one of the most beautiful cities in the world. By day the narrow winding streets of Gamla Stan (Old Town) gracefully give way to the vast openness of Skansen. At night, world-class restaurants and glamorous clubs speak eloquently of Stockholm's sophistication, and lights from some of Europe's grandest buildings beckon passersby across well-kept ocean inlets.

Not surprisingly, the Swedish people mimic their environment. From afar, locals may appear reserved. However, when you delve into their culture and begin to meet the people, you'll find their openness, warmth, and hospitality boundless.

1 Stockholm Deals & Discounts

BUDGET BESTS Opera and philharmonic tickets can be had practically for a song, and the city's many playhouses are also reasonably priced. Outdoor summer concerts and other warm-weather events are usually free, as are a host of year-round special events and activities. During winter, open-air ice skating in the heart of the city is both exhilarating and inexpensive. Anytime, a stroll along the waterfront or a walk through Old Town is fun and free.

SPECIAL DISCOUNTS On heavy sightseeing days, the **Stockholm Card** will prove itself one of the city's most outstanding values. Just 175 Kr ($23) per day or 525 Kr ($69.05) for three days buys you unlimited rides on the public transport network, admission to most of the city's museums, free guided city sightseeing tours, and a guidebook to Stockholm. It also provides boat sightseeing at half price, as well as a one-way ticket to Drottningholm Palace. The card may be purchased at the tourist information counter at Sweden House and at Hotell Centralen at Central Station and is valid for one adult and two children under age 18.

You'll find a reliable **free map** at the back of the free tourist board publication *Stockholm This Week*.

What's Special About Stockholm

Gamla Stan (Old Town)
- Narrow streets and alleyways that make you get lost—in direction and time.
- The city's densest cluster of shops, restaurants, and nightspots.

Special Parks
- Skansen, a memorable open-air museum and picnic spot.
- Djurgården, a forested island in the heart of the city perfect for jogging and strolling.
- Kungsträdgården, the city's main park for ice skating, concerts, and people-watching.

Waterfront
- Boasting some of Europe's most glorious buildings and views (don't forget your camera when you cross the bridge to Djurgården).

Festivals & Events
- Especially during summer, including the Jazz and Blues Festival, the Water Festival, Sailboat Day, and the Stockholm Marathon.
- The Nobel Prize ceremonies in December, one of the world's biggest annual events.

Sweden's enormously high taxes on alcohol are quite sobering. If you want to tipple without taking out a mortgage, buy **duty-free alcohol** before entering the country. Ditto for tobacco. Overseas visitors may import up to one quart of alcohol and 200 cigarettes.

For Students   A valid student ID will get you discounts at some museums and at cultural events, such as the opera and ballet.

For Seniors   Travelers 65 and over receive most of the same discounts as students—and more. Take advantage of the reduced fares on subways and buses. The listings below have even more heartening discount news.

WORTH THE EXTRA MONEY   Stockholm County encompasses about 24,000 small islands that will make you believe you're a million miles from anywhere. Most are uninhabited; a few were inhabited hundreds of years ago (and contain interesting ruins); others are jammed every summer with vacationing city-dwellers. The Stockholm Information Service (see "Visitor Information" under "Stockholm Specifics," later in this chapter) will be happy to help you plan an excursion, as either a day trip or an overnight stay. Ferries are usually frequent and cheap, hotels are more charming and less expensive than in the city, and camping is always free. It's really unusual to have such a pristine expanse adjacent to a major city. I'd advise you to make the most of this incomparable opportunity to take to the islands and seas at a relatively low cost. See "Easy Excursions," at the end of this chapter, for further details.

2 Pretrip Preparations

REQUIRED DOCUMENTS   Citizens of the United States, Canada, Great Britain, Australia, and New Zealand need only a passport to visit Sweden.

TIMING YOUR TRIP   Without question, most of Stockholm's special events and free outdoor concerts happen during summer. But spring and autumn are probably the prettiest times of year, and while citizens of many other countries think of winter as something to wait out, Swedes revel in this season (expect a dry cold in December, so bring warm shoes).

Stockholm's Average Daytime Temperature & Rainfall

	Jan	Feb	Mar	Apr	May	June	July	Aug	Sept	Oct	Nov	Dec
Temp. (°F)	27	26	31	40	50	59	64	62	54	45	37	32
Rainfall "	1.7	1.1	1	1.2	1.3	1.7	2.4	3	2.4	1.9	2	1.9

Special Events   The **Stockholm Marathon** is usually run in early June, attracting thousands of local and world-class runners. The June **Midsummer Celebration** falls on the Friday nearest to the longest day of the year. Special events, most free, include folk music and dancing and fill the city's parks and other outdoor spaces.

The **Stockholm Jazz and Blues Festival** is held for 10 days from the last weekend of June through the first weekend of July. Programs for this annual event will be available through the Stockholm Information Office.

Bellman Week, in mid-July, honors 18th-century court poet Carl Michael Bellman. Revelers, many in period costume, celebrate with poetry and music at Gröna Lund and various other city parks. The annual 10-day **Stockholm Water Festival** in early August, established in 1991, celebrates the element that makes Stockholm such a lovely city, where swimming and fishing in the center of town are long-standing traditions. Festivities include live entertainment, music, dancing, sporting events, fireworks, the world's largest crayfish festival, and the awarding of the Stockholm Water Prize, $150,000 in cash that goes to an individual or organization that has made an outstanding contribution to water conservation.

The **Women's 10K Run,** scheduled each August, has traditionally attracted more than 25,000 entrants. **Sailboat Day,** during the first weekend in September, is an excuse for the city's aquatic pleasurecraft to show off. From Sunfish to schooner, the harbor becomes a showcase for boats of all sizes.

The exciting week-long **Stockholm Open tennis championships** are held the last week of October or the first week of November in the Globe Arena.

The **Nobel Prizes,** named after the Swedish inventor of dynamite, Alfred Nobel, are awarded on December 10 for excellence in physics, chemistry, medicine, literature, and economics. The prizes have been awarded since 1901 (the Peace Prize in Oslo, all others in Stockholm).

Lucia, the festival of lights, is celebrated on December 13, the shortest day (and longest night) of the year. This is one of the most popular and colorful of all Swedish festivals, designed to "brighten up" an otherwise dark period. The festivities continue on the nearest Sunday, when a Lucia Queen is crowned with candles during a ceremony in Skansen. Concerts are held throughout the city from morning till night.

Finally, few locals miss the **Christmas Markets,** beginning four weeks before the holiday and held daily in the squares of Gamla Stan (Old Town) and every Sunday (on a much larger scale) in Skansen. Stalls are filled selling handcrafts, gifts and other seasonal items, and traditional foods such as smoked reindeer meat, cloudberry jam, ginger cookies, and hot glögg.

BACKGROUND READING   Noted Swedish authors include Vilhelm Moberg, most famous for his works on the Swedish-American experience, especially *The Emigrants* (Warner); Per-Anders Fogelstrom, whose novels are set in Stockholm; dramatist August Strindberg, famous for the realism of his plays; Selma Laberlof, who penned such works as *The Wonderful Adventures of Nils*; and Astrid Lindgren, author of dozens of children's books.

Those interested in the Vikings can try Johannes Brondsted's *The Vikings* (Penguin) or Frans Bengtsson's *The Long Ships* (William Collins Sons).

If you want to read about the politics, economics, and culture of Sweden, you can order free fact sheets from the **Swedish Information Service,** which has offices in the United States at 1 Dag Hammarskjöld Plaza, 45th Floor, New York, NY 10017-2201 (☎ **212/751-5900;** fax 212/752-4789), and at 1099 Wilshire Blvd., Suite 1100, Los Angeles, CA 90024-4314 (☎ **310/575-3383;** fax 310/477-8331). In Stockholm, the **Swedish Institute,** with more of the same enlightening pamphlets, is conveniently located on the second floor of Sweden House, at Kungsträumdgården (☎ **8/789-20-00**). Dozens of well-written and well-researched publications seem to leave no stone unturned. The institute also sells a wide variety of English-language books about Sweden and by famous Swedish authors. It's open Monday through Friday from 9am to 6pm during summer (until 5pm in winter).

3   Stockholm Specifics

ARRIVING

FROM THE AIRPORT   Stockholm's **Arlanda Airport** is 28 miles north of town. Four rainbow-striped buses (☎ **8/600-10-00**) leave the airport, and you want the one to Stockholm City. Take it to City Terminal. It costs 50 Kr ($6.60) for everyone except kids 15 and under, who ride free with a parent. The journey takes 40 minutes, and buses run about every 10 minutes from 6:35am to 11pm, afterward according to the arrival times of specific flights. Taxis are available at the airport, but the ride into town will run about 300 Kr ($39.45).

You can change money at several places in the baggage-claim area, before you reach Customs (rates are reasonable, hours long). Adjacent red telephones offer local calls for up to three minutes for 2 Kr (25¢). Beyond Customs, you'll find a post office, a bank, and representatives from most of the major car-rental companies. Downstairs is the Left-Luggage Office (☎ **8/797-62-28**); charges are 25 Kr ($3.30) per bag per day, and the office never closes. Lockers cost 20 to 25 Kr ($2.65 to $3.30).

Pick up a city map from the information office at the airport (☎ **8/797-61-00**), which is open 24 hours, and you'll soon be making your way easily around the city. There are six day rooms with a bed, toilet, and shower at the airport if you need a brief rest.

FROM THE TRAIN/BUS STATION   Stockholm's train station, **Central Station,** Vasagatan 14, and bus station, **City Terminal (Cityterminalen),** Klarabergsviadukten 72, are across from each other and connected underground by escalators. The trilevel Central Station can be confusing; the more modern bilevel City Terminal is easy to maneuver and seems more like an international airport than a bus station. It has an information desk inside to the left of the

What Things Cost in Stockholm	U.S. $
Taxi from Central Station to the National Museum	9.50
T-Bana from Central Station to an outlying neighborhood	1.70
Local telephone call	.25
Double room at the Grand Hotel (deluxe)	351.60
Double room without bath at the Queen's Hotel (moderate)	65.80
Double room without bath at the Tre Små Rum (budget)	52.65
Lunch for one, without wine, at Bistro Jarl (moderate)	9.15
Lunch for one, without wine, at Café Blå Porten (budget)	6.50
Dinner for one, with wine, at Stadhuska[um]llaren (deluxe)	93.40
Dinner for one, without wine, at Michelangelo (moderate)	11.50
Dinner for one, without wine, at Nicki's Café (budget)	6.60
Pint of beer in a bar	5.30
Coca-Cola in a café	2.25
Cup of coffee in a café	1.90
Roll of ASA 100 color film, 36 exposures	7.75
Admission to the Vasa Museum	5.90
Movie ticket	8.55
Budget theater ticket	9.85

entrance, a money-exchange window (look for the yellow-and-black sign), and a kiosk selling international newspapers.

Since neither the bus nor the train station is within walking distance of hostels or most budget hotels, you'll probably have to take the subway to your lodging. But that's easy enough: From the lower level of Central Station you can connect directly to the subway system. Just follow the signs that say T-BANA or TUNNELBANA.

The ground level of the train station is home to the tourist office and the helpful Hotell Centralen, where you can book hotel rooms (see "Accommodations," later in this chapter, for further details). Look for a sign with a white "i" on a green background pointing the way.

Baggage carts, lockers, and showers are also available. The lockers cost 15, 20, or 25 Kr ($2, $2.65, or $3.30), depending on size, for 24 hours, but it's much safer to make use of the Left-Luggage (Resgods) Office (☎ 8/762-25-49), which charges 40 Kr ($5.25) per bag per day. It's open daily from 7am to 9pm.

Train tickets are sold on the ground floor; Tracks 16 are for trains heading north and Tracks 10 to 18 for those heading south. The ground floor is also home to telephones, train information (SJ Information), and a currency exchange called Forex, open daily from 8am to 9pm (look for the big yellow-and-black Forex sign).

There is a large market on the lowest level, along with clean bathrooms—there's a 5-Kr (65¢) charge to use them—and large showers, which cost 20 Kr ($2.65). An attendant is on duty.

The Swedish Krona

For American Readers   At this writing $1 = approximately 7.6 Kr (or 1 Kr = 13¢), and this was the rate of exchange used to calculate the dollar values given in this chapter (rounded to the nearest nickel).

For British Readers   At this writing £1 = approximately 12.13 Kr (or 1 Kr = 8p), and this was the rate of exchange used to calculate the pound values in the table below.

Note: The rates given here fluctuate from time to time and may not be the same when you travel to Sweden. Therefore this table should be used only as a guide.

Kr	U.S.$	U.K.£	Kr	U.S.$	U.K.£
1	.13	.08	75	9.87	6.18
2	.26	.16	100	13.16	8.24
3	.39	.25	125	16.45	10.31
4	.52	.33	150	19.74	12.37
5	.66	.41	175	23.03	14.43
6	.79	.49	200	26.32	16.49
7	.92	.58	225	29.61	18.55
8	1.05	.66	250	32.89	20.61
9	1.18	.74	300	39.47	24.73
10	1.32	.82	350	46.05	28.85
15	1.97	1.24	400	52.63	32.98
20	2.63	1.65	450	59.21	37.10
25	3.29	2.06	500	65.79	41.22
50	6.58	4.12	600	78.95	49.46

For information about rail service within Sweden, call 020/75-75-75; for international rail service, 8/22-79-40. For bus information, call 8/700-51-47 or Swebus (☎ **020/64-06-40**); for airport bus departures, call 8/600-10-00. If you're too loaded down to get to the airport bus from your hotel by local transportation (and vice versa), at this writing Taxi Kurir offers transport for 70 Kr ($9.10) that includes both taxi and bus fare, a great deal (☎ **8/30-00-00**).

VISITOR INFORMATION

After getting settled in your room, your first stop in Stockholm should be **Sweden House (Sverige Huset),** Hamnagatn 27, off Kungsträdgården.

On the ground floor you'll find the **Stockholm Information Service** (☎ **8/789-24-90**), the country's main tourist office. Even if you desire no other information, make sure you get your free copy of *Stockholm This Week* for its lists of special and free events and good map. The Stockholm Card (described in "Budget Bests" under "Stockholm Deals and Discounts," earlier in this chapter) can be purchased here, as can city tour and archipelago excursion tickets. This office sells stamps and will reserve a hotel room for you for a service charge of 40 Kr ($5.25), plus a 10% deposit on the room. They can also reserve a room at one of the city's youth hostels, for a service charge of 15 Kr ($2). The reservations desk can also book summer cottages and overnight packages, as well as sell tickets to concerts and soccer games.

The 160-page *Discover Stockholm* book for 69 Kr ($9.05) is a good investment and souvenir of your trip; a map of Stockholm and surrounding areas costs 10 Kr ($1.30). You can also buy posters, cards, and gift items here. There's a convenient bathroom on the premises, but you have to pay 5 Kr (65¢) to use it, and someone must buzz you into it. The Stockholm Information Service is open June to August, Monday through Friday from 9am to 6pm and Saturday and Sunday from 9am to 5pm; in September, Monday through Friday from 9am to 6pm and Saturday and Sunday 9am to 3pm; and the rest of the year, Monday through Friday from 9am to 6pm and Saturday and Sunday from 10am to 3pm.

The **Swedish Institute Bookshop,** on the second floor of Sweden House (☎ 8/789-20-00 from 9:30am to 12:30pm; fax 8/20-72-48), features an extensive collection of English-language books about Swedish life, coffee-table tomes, novels, records, cassettes, CDs, children's books, art books, and fact sheets on Sweden's social, political, and economic issues. It's open Monday through Friday from 9am to 6pm and Saturday from 10am to 2pm year round.

Hotell Centralen, in the main hall of Central Station (☎ 8/24-08-80; fax 8/791-86-66), makes hotel reservations (see "Accommodations," later in this chapter), answers general questions, and distributes free maps. It's open May to September, daily from 8am to 9pm; the rest of the year, Monday through Friday from 8am to 5pm.

SL Center, on the lower level of Sergels Torg (☎ 8/686-11-97; if it's busy, or if you need only information about times for buses, subways, and local trains, call 8/600-10-00), offers information about local subway and bus transportation and sells a good transport map for 35 Kr ($4.60), as well as tickets for the system. It's open Monday through Thursday from 8:30am to 6:30pm and Friday from 8:30am to 5:30pm.

CITY LAYOUT

It helps to picture the city as the group of islands it really is, even though, for all intents and purposes, bridges and tunnels connect them as one. Fortunately for visitors, only a handful of the thousands of islands in the Stockholm archipelago are important tourist destinations.

NORRMALM The heart of modern Stockholm, Norrmalm is actually on the mainland, in the northernmost part of the city center. It's where you'll arrive at the train station, shop in the major stores, and probably find a hotel. **Drottninggatan,** the major pedestrian shopping street, runs approximately north-south and bisects Norrmalm. Along this thoroughfare are the important squares of **Sergels Torg** (the active center of Norrmalm) and **Hötorget,** home to Åhléns and PUB department stores, respectively. Branching east from Sergels Torg is **Hamngatan,** a short street lined with chain-store outlets, the NK department store (Sweden's largest), Sweden House (home of the Stockholm Information Service), and **Kungsträdgården** (half park, half street, and host to many free outdoor events). **Birger Jarlsgatan,** a few blocks east of Kungsträdgården, leads to the Royal Dramatic Theater and the American Express office and is filled with interesting shops and cafés as far as Sturegallerian, the trendy new shopping gallery at **Stureplan.**

ÖSTERMALM Flanking Norrmalm on the east, this upscale neighborhood is home to the Royal Library, the Museum of History, shops, hotels, and restaurants.

KUNGSHOLMEN Due west of Norrmalm, Kungsholmen is home to Stockholm's striking City Hall, where the Nobel Prize banquet is held annually.

GAMLA STAN   In Swedish, Gamla Stan means **Old Town,** and on the city's tourist maps this district's small island is always in the center. Pretty buildings, cobblestone streets, narrow alleyways, and interesting shops provide a welcome counterpoint to Norrmalm's big-city landscape. In olden days, fast currents on either side of the island forced sea merchants to portage their goods to vessels waiting on the other side. The paths these porters pounded are now the oldest extant streets in Stockholm and are well worth exploring.

SÖDERMALM   South of Gamla Stan lies Södermalm, an area once considered the "bad" side of town. Today, as the city gentrifies, Södermalm's rents have skyrocketed and chic restaurants, bars, and clubs have moved in. You might stay in one of Södermalm's budget hotels or private rooms, and you're well advised to visit the cliffs overlooking Stockholm Harbor.

SKEPPSHOLMEN   East of Gamla Stan, across a narrow channel, lies tiny, pretty Skeppsholmen, home to two popular youth hostels (and the Museum of Modern Art, which is being rebuilt and will reopen here in 1998). The quiet streets on the island, as well as the islet connected to it, are perfect for strolling.

DJURGÅRDEN   Farther east still is Stockholm's tour de force, the magnificent Djurgården (Deer Garden), which encompasses many of the city's top sights. This shady neck of land with lush oak groves would be any lumberjack's delight but, thankfully, has been protected for centuries by the government, which has historically maintained the area as a grazing ground for the king's deer. The *Vasa* Ship Museum and the massive outdoor Skansen folk museum are the area's top draws, though several other good museums are located here, too.

GETTING AROUND

Subways (called Tunnelbana) and buses are operated by SL, the city transportation network, and charge according to a zone system—the price increases the farther you go. Most places you'll visit in central Stockholm will cost 13 Kr ($1.70), payable at the Tunnelbana and bus entrance.

In addition to the **Stockholm Card** (described in "Special Discounts" under "Stockholm Deals & Discounts," earlier in this chapter), several discounts are available. SL sells **day passes** only. A one-day unlimited-use pass for the Stockholm area and the Djurgården ferries costs 60 Kr ($7.90); a three-day pass is 115 Kr ($15.15).

People under 18 and senior citizens can buy half-price tickets for all forms of public transportaton. For more information about routes, times, and prices, call 8/600-10-00.

BY SUBWAY (TUNNELBANA OR T-BANA)   Stockholm is blessed with a fast and far-reaching subway system called the T-Bana. It's easy to use and you'll probably never go more than a few stops or wait more than five minutes for a train. Color-coded maps are on station walls and printed in most tourist publications. Timetables for each train are also posted. Escalators in some subway stations are steep enough to rival London's. More than half the city's 99 subway stations are distinctive for the permanent artwork and other decoration they display. Especially eye-catching are Kungsträdgården, T-Centralen, Rådhuset, Solna, and Slussen.

One ticket costs 13 Kr ($1.70) and is good for one hour (use it as often as you want), or you can get a strip of 20 coupons for 85 Kr ($11.20). A one-day tourist card for unlimited use in the Stockholm area costs 60 Kr ($7.90) for adults, 35 Kr ($4.60) for children and seniors; and a three-day tourist card is 115 Kr ($15.15) for adults, 75 Kr ($9.85) for children and seniors. Unlimited transportation is included in the cost of the Stockholm Card.

If you're paying with cash or using a strip ticket, pass through the gate and tell the person in the ticket booth where you're going. He or she will either ask for your fare or stamp your ticket. If you have a Stockholm Card, just flash it. Sometimes the ticket collector is absent; in these instances, few commuters wait for the collector to return—they just walk through.

Note: Most subway stops have several well-marked exits; save yourself time (and avoid walking several blocks out of your way) by checking your map and choosing the exit closest to your destination. Trains are shorter during less heavily trafficked periods, such as evenings, so stand toward the center of the platform for boarding.

BY BUS Buses run where subways don't, comprehensively covering the city. Enter through the front door and pay the driver, show your Stockholm Card, or have your strip ticket stamped. If you plan on making extensive use of buses, buy a transport map from the Stockholm Information Office or the SL Center (addresses listed under "Visitor Information," above). Many buses depart from Normalmstorg, catercorner to Kungsträdgården and two blocks from Sweden House.

BY FERRY Ferries ply the waters between Gamla Stan (and Slussen) and Djurgården year round, providing the best link between these two highly touristed areas. In summer, boats depart every 15 minutes from 9am to midnight (to 10:40pm on Sunday); in winter, daily from 9am to 6pm. The ride costs about 15 Kr ($2) for adults, half price for seniors and those 7 to 18 years old. Check with the Stockholm Information Service for more details.

BY TAXI Beware! The meter starts at 23 Kr ($3.05), and a short ride can easily come to 60 Kr ($7.90), but the tip is included in the price. You can order a cab by phone, but there may be an additional charge. Avoid gypsy cabs; always take one with a yellow license plate with the letter T at the end of the number. Taxi Stockholm (☎ **8/15-00-00**) and Taxi Kurir (☎ **8/30-00-00**) are two companies with set prices, so they're always a good bet. But always ask if there's an extra charge for a pickup. Taxi Kurir offers transport from your hotel to the airport bus that includes both the taxi and the bus fare for only 70 Kr ($9.20); for this service call 8/686-10-10.

ON FOOT Walking is the most delightful way to get to know the city. You'll have to explore Gamla Stan on foot as cars are banned from most of the streets. Djurgården and Skeppsholmen are other popular haunts for strolling.

BY BICYCLE Bicycling is particularly recommended for exploring Djurgården, and bikes are available for rent just to your right after you cross the bridge onto the island from **Skepp o Hoj** (☎ **8/660-57-57**) from 9am to 9pm daily, May to August. It's most economical to rent for a full day, at 100 Kr ($13.15) for 24 hours; or you can pay by the hour, at 40 Kr ($5.25) for the first hour and 35 Kr ($4.60) per hour thereafter. The company's name means "Ship Ahoy." (They also rent boats and skates.)

BY RENTAL CAR Unless you're planning an extended trip outside Stockholm, you'll find that keeping a car in the city is more trouble than it's worth. Most major American car-rental firms, including Hertz and Avis, have counters at the airport and offices in Stockholm. Local companies are usually cheaper and are listed under "Biluthyrning" in the phone book and in the "Transportation" section of *Stockholm This Week*. Swedish law requires that motorists drive with their lights on day and night.

FAST FACTS: Stockholm

American Express   The Stockholm office gets a gold star from travelers for friendliness and helpfulness. Catercorner from the Royal Dramatic Theater at Birger Jarlsgatan 1 (☎ **8/679-78-80**), it can exchange money and hold or forward mail (see "Mail," below), and there's a cash machine on the premises. The office is open Monday through Friday from 9am to 5pm (to 6pm June to August) and Saturday from 10am to 1pm. For 24-hour refund assistance, call 020/795-155.

Babysitters   To find a babysitter, ask the proprietor of your hotel or guesthouse for a recommendation. Deluxe hotels also usually keep a list of babysitters and might be of assistance.

Banks   Most banks are open Monday through Friday from 9:30am to 3pm. Some in central Stockholm stay open later.

Exchange rates rarely vary from bank to bank, but commissions do. These fees can be very high, around 35 Kr ($4.60) for a traveler's-check transaction; however, you may often exchange up to six checks per transaction, so it's a good idea to change as much money as you think you'll need at one time. There may be no fee to change cash, but the rate is lower. Competitive rates are also offered by many post offices, including the main branch, which keeps long hours (see "Mail," below). The exchange window (Forex) at the train station is open daily from 8am to 9pm. Cash American Express traveler's checks at the American Express office at no extra charge.

Business Hours   Shops are usually open Monday through Friday from 9:30am to 6pm and Saturday from 9:30am to 2pm. Larger stores may maintain longer hours Monday through Saturday and may open Sunday as well. Most offices are open Monday through Friday from 9am to 5pm.

Currency   You'll pay your way in Stockholm in Swedish **kronor (Kr)** or crowns (singular, **krona**), sometimes abbreviated SEK, which are divided into 100 **öre**. Bills come in denominations of 10, 20, 50, 100, and 1,000 kronor. Coins are issued in 50 öre, as well as 1, 5, and 10 kronor. For currency exchange, see "Banks," above, and "Mail," below.

Dentists   Emergency dental care is available at St. Eriks Hospital, Fleminggatan 22 (☎ **8/654-11-17**, or 644-92-00 after 9pm). Regular hospital hours for walk-ins are 8am to 7pm. At other times, phone first.

Doctors   Normally, emergency medical care is provided by the hospital closest to the area you're staying in. For information, as well as advice regarding injuries, contact Doctors on Duty (☎ **8/644-92-00**). City Akuten, a privately run infirmary at Holländargartan 3 (☎ **8/11-71-02**), can also provide help but at a cost of about 300 to 500 Kr ($39.45 to $65.80) a visit. Also check the telephone directory under "Hälso- och sjukvård" in the blue pages at the beginning of the *Företag* phone book for clinics listed by neighborhood and you may be able to visit a local doctor for less money than the amount noted above.

Embassies　The Embassy of the **United States** is at Strandvägen 101 (☎ **8/783-53-00**); the Embassy of **Canada**, at Tegelbacken 4 (☎ **8/613-99-00**); the Embassy of the **Republic of Ireland**, at Östermalmsgatan 97 (☎ **8/661-80-05**); the Embassy of the **United Kingdom**, at Skarpögatan 6–8 (☎ **8/667-01-40**); the Embassy of **Australia**, at Sergels Torg 12 (☎ **8/613-29-00**). New Zealand does not maintain an embassy in Stockholm; inquiries should be made through the New Zealand Embassy in The Hague (☎ **31-70/346-93-24**).

Emergencies　For police, fire department, or ambulance service, call **90-000**.

Eyeglasses　Many streets have an *Optiker* that can repair or replace broken glasses. Tollare, Hamngatan 37 (☎ **8/20-13-33**), in the Gallerian shopping mall, has friendly service and a good selection of frames in contemporary styles. It's open Monday through Friday from 9:30am to 6:30pm, Saturday from 9:30am to 4pm, and Sunday from noon to 4pm. Or try NK Optik, in the NK department store at Hamngatan 18–20 (☎ **8/762-87-78**), open Monday through Friday from 10am to 7pm, Saturday from 10am to 5pm, and Sunday from noon to 5pm (possibly shorter hours in summer). It's on the ground floor in the back of the store.

Holidays　Sweden celebrates New Year's Day (Jan 1), Epiphany, Good Friday, Easter and Easter Monday, May Day (May 1), Ascension Day (Thursday of the sixth week after Easter), Whit Sunday and Monday (also called Pentecost), Midsummer Day (Saturday closest to June 24), All Saints' Day (the Saturday following Oct 30), and Christmas (Dec 24–26).

Hospitals　For the hospital closest to you, phone Doctors on Duty (☎ **8/644-92-00**) or visit City Akuten, Holländargartan 3 (☎ **8/11-71-02**), a privately run infirmary.

Information　The Stockholm Information Service is in Sweden House, Hamngatan 27 (☎ **8/789-24-00**). Other tourist offices and sources of information are mentioned in "Visitor Information" under "Stockholm Specifics," earlier in this chapter.

Laundry/Dry Cleaning　Many of the hotels listed in "Accommodations" offer laundry facilities. There's a self-service laundry, Tvättomatten, at Västmannagatan 61 (☎ **8/34-64-80**), beside the Hotel Gustav Vasa, where for 55 Kr ($7.25) you can wash and dry 5 kilos (11 lb.) of dirty clothes. The cost includes washing powder, and you should plan to arrive at least two hours before closing; it's open Monday through Friday from 9am to 6pm and Saturday from 10am to 2pm. Tvättomatten will also wash or dry clean your clothes for you for the same price.

Lost & Found　If you lost it on a bus or the T-Bana, check at the SL office at the Rådmansgatan stop (☎ **8/736-07-80**). If you lost it on a train, check the lost-and-found office on the lower concourse of Central Station (☎ **8/762-20-00**). If you lost it at the airport, call the airport lost and found (☎ **8/797-60-80**). If you lost it somewhere else, check with the Police Lost and Found Office, Bergsgatan 39 (☎ **8/769-30-00**).

Mail　The main Stockholm Post Office, Vasagatan 28–34 (☎ **8/781-20-40**), is diagonally across from Central Station. It's open Monday through Friday from 8am to 6:30pm and Saturday from 10am to 2pm; the one in Central Station is open later. Most local post offices are open Monday through Friday from

9am to 6pm and Saturday from 9 or 10am to 1pm. A centrally located post office three blocks from Sweden House and the NK department store, at Regeringsgatan 65 (☎ **8/781-21-38**), is open Monday through Friday from 8:30am to 6:30pm and Saturday from 10am to 1pm.

You can receive mail either at the main post office (marked *Poste Restante* with a "hold until" date) or at American Express. The mail service at American Express, Birger Jarlsgatan 1 (☎ **8/679-78-80**), is free; the mail is delivered here daily about 10am. The charge to forward mail is 20 Kr ($2.65). Open Monday through Friday from 9am to 5pm (to 6pm June to August) and Saturday from 10am to 1pm.

Newspapers   The *International Herald Tribune, USA Today,* and *The European* are available at newsstands all around town and in most hotel news shops. The latest American and British magazines are also readily available. A broad selection of periodicals is available at Pressbyran, at Norrmalmstorg (where the buses converge, a block from Sweden House), open Monday through Friday from 8am to 10pm, Saturday from 10am to 10pm, and Sunday from 10am to 9pm; or Press Specialisten, Sveavägen 52 (☎ **8/21-91-13**), open Monday through Friday from 10am to 6pm and Saturday from 11am to 3pm. Be forewarned that your favorite magazine will be a lot more expensive here; for instance, *Us* magazine cost a startled reader 49 Kr ($6.45).

Expressen, a liberal tabloid, and *Dagens Nyheter*, an independent newspaper, are Stockholm's largest-selling dailies. Even if you can't read Swedish, you might be interested in scanning their advertising and nightlife pages.

Finally, foreign periodicals can be read free at Culture House (Kulturhuset), Sergels Torg, third floor (see "Visitor Information" under "Stockholm Specifics," earlier in this chapter), and at the Municipal Library (Stadsbiblioteket), Sveavägen 73 (☎ **8/729-86-00**), open Monday through Thursday from 10am to 8:30pm, Friday from 10am to 6pm, and Saturday and Sunday from noon to 4pm.

Pharmacy   For 24-hour service, go to C. W. Scheele, Klarabergsgatan 64 (☎ **8/24-82-80**).

Photographic Needs   Film can be purchased and processed on almost every street in the city center, especially in the major tourist areas. One-hour film processing is available at Central Station. For camera supplies and one-hour processing, try Kodak Image, Hamngatan 16 (☎ **8/21-40-42**), open Monday through Friday from 9:30am to 6pm and Saturday from 10am to 3pm.

Department stores often have two-for-the-price-of-one sales on film in summer, and the Fotoquick chain offers good prices year round; look for shops in Central Station, and at Drottninggatan 19, Sergels Torg 12, and St. Eriksgatan 34.

Police   For emergencies, dial 90-000. For other matters, contact Police Headquarters (Polishuset) at 8/769-30-00. Or pay a visit in person to police headquarters at Bergsgatan 52, open 24 hours daily.

Radio/TV   There are several FM radio stations in the Stockholm area. Radio Sweden, at 89.6 FM, broadcasts programs in English and other languages; call 8/784-74-00 for times. If you have an AM receiver, you may hear broadcasts all the way from Moscow—and beyond. There are three national television channels and some local cable channels; programming seems to favor nature and news shows. When foreign movies are shown (usually at night), they are subtitled.

Religious Services Some 92% of Swedes belong to the Church of Sweden, a Lutheran church, though they're not big on religion or church-going. The Stockholm Cathedral (Storkyrkan), Old Town (☎ **8/723-30-00**), consecrated in 1279, holds regular services, and is open to the public. Two Protestant Sunday services in English are held at Santa Clara Church, Klara Östra Kyrkogatan 8, near Central Station (☎ **8/723-30-29**), and at Immanuel Church, an international, interdenominational fellowship, at Kungstensgatan 17 (☎ **8/15-12-25**). Other houses of worship include Stockholm Cathedral (Roman Catholic), Folkungagatan 46 (☎ **8/640-00-81**), and the modern, centrally located Santa Eugenia Catholic Church, Kungsträdgårdsgatan 12 (☎ **8/679-57-70**); and the Great Synagogue (Jewish-Conservative), Wahrendorffsgatan 3A (☎ **8/679-29-00**). For more listings, call Stockholm's church-information number (☎ **8/781-01-00**).

Shoe Repair There's a while-you-wait shoe repair at Mister Minit, on the ground floor opposite the elevator in the NK department store at Hamngatan 18–20 (☎ **8/762-85-83**); it's open Monday through Friday from 10am to 7pm and Saturday from 10am to 5pm.

Tax Sweden is legendary for its painfully high income taxes—as much as 72% in the top bracket. Fortunately, visitors to Stockholm need concern themselves only with the VAT (value-added tax) placed on most goods and services. A VAT of 21% is applied to entertainment, restaurants, and food; hotel rooms and other travel-related expenses are taxed 12%; and everything else is taxed 25%. Actually, you won't really have to worry about this either, as the VAT is already added into the tag price of most store items, restaurant menus, and hotel tariffs.

Many stores offer non-Scandinavian tourists the opportunity to recover the VAT on purchases over 100 Kr ($13.16). See "Shopping," later in this chapter.

Telephone/Fax The area code for the Stockholm area is 8, and all numbers listed in this chapter assume that prefix, unless otherwise noted.

Public phones are fairly straightforward. **Local calls** cost 2 Kr (26¢) for the first few minutes, and one more krona for every couple of minutes after that (depending on distance). Phones accept 50-öre, 1-Kr, 5-Kr, and 10-Kr coins. As in many cities, it's hard to find a coin-operated phone when you need one; in Stockholm it's easier and definitely more convenient (though the cost is the same) to buy a telephone card, called a **Telekort,** from most any newsstand and use it in the growing number of phones that accept cards rather than coins.

The easiest way to make **international calls** to North America is via AT&T's USA Direct service. If you have an AT&T Calling Card, or call collect, you can reach an American operator from any phone by calling 020/795-611.

Alternatively, international calls can be made from the TeleCenter Office on the Central Station's ground floor (☎ **8/456-74-94**), open daily from 8am to 9pm. A call to the United States or Canada costs 18.75 Kr ($2.50) per minute daily from 10pm to 8am; from 8am to 10am (and all day Sunday) rates fall to 14.40 Kr ($1.90) per minute. Long-distance rates are posted.

For **directory assistance,** dial 0018. For directory listings or other information for Stockholm or other parts of Sweden only, dial 07975; for other parts of Europe, dial 07977.

The Stockholm telephone directory consists of three books: The one designated *Företag* is for companies and organizations; *Privatpersoner*, for individuals; and *Gula Sidorna* is the yellow pages.

The Telecenter will also hold **faxes** for you (sent to fax number 8/20-33-10); ask the sender to specify "hold for [your name]" on the fax, or if they include your local telephone number, the office will contact you when it arrives. Receiving a fax costs about 12.50 Kr ($1.65) for the first page and 6.50 Kr (85¢) for each additional page. The TeleCenter is open daily from 8am to 9pm, except major holidays. All major credit and charge cards are accepted.

Tipping A 10% service charge is routinely included in hotel and restaurant bills. Further tipping is unnecessary unless service is extraordinary; in that case, round up the amount—say, from 85 Kr to 90 Kr (but this would be at dinner; in Stockholm, it's never customary to tip at lunch).

4 Accommodations

Sure, you've heard about Stockholm's sky-high hotel prices. But less-expensive options exist—so, armed with this guide, you're sure to find an affordable bed.

There's no budget-hotel-packed street in the city. Budget hotels are few and far between and are listed below along with some accommodation alternatives. It's surprisingly common for Stockholm's city-dwellers to supplement their incomes by sharing their homes with tourists. Those who open their homes to foreigners are exceedingly friendly, well traveled, and interested in meeting new people, and they give a lot of themselves to ensure their guests are comfortable. There seems to be an unofficial network of private-room renters, so even if the home you phone is full, chances are good that the owners will refer you to a friend who has room. Here are a few alternatives to emptying your wallet for a room:

A DISCOUNTING SERVICE On the ground level of Central Station, **Hotell Centralen** (☎ **8/24-08-80;** fax 8/791-86-66) can sometimes offer cut-price rooms for same-day occupancy during slow periods. Of course, not all hotels discount rooms, but those that do usually lower their rates as the day wears on. The 40-Kr ($5.25) booking fee is waived if you book in advance by telephone or fax. The office is open June to August, daily from 7am to 9pm; in September and May, daily from 8am to 7pm; and October to April, daily from 8am to 5pm.

A ROOM-FINDING SERVICE **Hotelltjänst,** Vasagatan 15–17, 4th Floor, 11120 Stockholm (☎ **8/8/10-44-37,** 10-44-57, or 10-44-67; fax 8/21-37-16), rents more than 50 rooms in private homes across Stockholm at excellent set rates. In fact, it's hard to beat their charge of 250 Kr ($32.90) single, 370 Kr ($48.70) double, with shared bath. There are no service fees, but a minimum two-night stay is required; ask for a place near a subway or bus stop (first, take a look at the private homes listed in this chapter). In addition, Hotelltjänst sometimes offers select hotel rooms at a deep discount often as much as 50% in summer. This can mean high-quality singles for about 450 Kr ($59.20) and doubles for 600 Kr ($78.95). You can reserve hotel rooms anytime in advance; private rooms, 10 days ahead. The office is two long blocks from Central Station; turn right when you get off the elevator. It's open Monday through Friday from 9am to noon and 1 to 5pm.

ROOMS IN A PRIVATE HOME Some locals have been renting rooms to tourists for years, and their rates and locations prove them to be excellent values. Some sure-to-please choices are listed below.

HOSTELS Don't shy away from hostels, especially if you're traveling alone. Most of the city's hostels have four-bed rooms with reasonable prices. All have

Getting the Best Deal on Accommodations

• Try renting a room in a private home.

• A room-finding service can find you cut-price rooms.

• Hostels are excellently priced, well-maintained, clean lodgings for people of all ages.

exceptionally high standards and are clean, and two occupy the city's best location. See "Super-Budget Choices," below, for details.

DOUBLES FOR LESS THAN 450 KR ($59.20)
IN PRIVATE HOMES

Staying in a private home costs less than a hotel and affords the opportunity to get to know Swedish people in their own environment. Call ahead to book a room and let the hosts know your arrival time so they don't spend hours waiting for you.

✪ Ms. Eva Abelin

Skeppargatan 49B, 11458 Stockholm. ☎ 8/663-49-57. 3 rms, none with bath. 275 Kr ($36.20) per person. Breakfast 25 Kr ($3.30) extra. No credit cards. T-Bana: Red line to Östermalmstorg; take the Sibyllegatan exit and then walk to Skeppargatan (less than five minutes) and turn left to the apartment building, which is next to a flag shop.

This place has it all: a central location, elegant facilities, and an engaging, gracious host. Ms. Abelin, an avid art collector, rents a large double room with a sink and TV, a smaller double right across from the bath, and a single around the corner from the bath. All rooms are comfortable, with plenty of light, pleasing decor, interesting artwork, a writing table, a chest of drawers, and hanging space for clothes. The bath is large, with a big tub and a hand-held shower, plus candles if you're in the mood for an atmospheric soak. Guests enjoy sipping coffee and chatting at the kitchen table. It's convenient to walk to the attractions in Norrmalm and on Djurgården from here.

⑤ Ms. Ingrid Ollén

Störtloppsvägen 34, 12947 Stockholm. ☎ 8/646-68-68. 2 rms, neither with bath. 175 Kr ($23.05) single; 250 Kr ($32.90) double; 300 Kr ($39.45) triple. Breakfast 30 Kr ($3.95) extra. No credit cards. T-Bana: Red line to Västertorp; exit the station following the arrow toward Störtloppsvägen, then turn left on that street and walk two blocks; when you reach the *apotek* (pharmacy), walk behind that building to find the entrance.

A 15-minute ride from the center in a pleasant neighborhood that includes a bank, a post office, two grocery stores, a café, and two pizzerias, this place offers two double rooms (one with TV) with complimentary cooking privileges. One room is beside the full bath, the other beside the kitchen. Ms. Ollen is a retired nurse, not to mention a world traveler and avid swimmer, who has welcomed people from 40 countries to her home. Guests can use the laundry for 25 Kr ($3.30) and there's an open-air pool nearby.

✪ Ms. Pernilla Wilton

Bastugatan 48A, 11825 Stockholm. ☎ 8/84-14-79 or 84-17-25. Fax 8/84-14-79. 1 rm, without bath. TV. 250 Kr ($32.90) single; 390 Kr ($51.30) double. No credit cards. T-Bana: Mariatorget; then take the Torkel Knutssonsgatan exit.

On a quiet street in Södermalm, in one of city's most attractive neighborhoods, Pernilla Wilton offers a spacious room with a full-size bed (more can be added to accommodate a family) and plenty of books and tourist materials to read. Added to that, it's in a 19th-century house with a cozy Swedish ambience and a view of Lake Malaren and the city, most notably the striking City Hall. Guests are assured a warm welcome here and may use the kitchen. English and German are spoken. Gamla Stan is a 15-minute walk (or two underground stops) away. Always call ahead to be sure the room is available and to get directions.

IN HOTEL ROOMS

Hotell Örnsköld

Nybrogatan 6, 11434 Stockholm. ☎ **8/667-02-85.** Fax 8/667-69-91. 4 rms, 1 with toilet only, 2 with bath (with shower). 195 Kr ($25.65) single without bath, 250 Kr ($32.90) single with toilet only, 450 or 475 Kr ($59.20 or $62.50) single with bath. Rates include breakfast. AE, DC, EURO, MC, V. T-Bana: Line 13, 14, or 15 to Östermalmstorg (Östermalmstorg exit), just one stop from Central Station.

These small, basic singles rent on a first-come, first-served basis, for the lowest rates in town. There's barely room for you and your bag, and the toilet and shower are a walk away from the room that has neither (it does have a phone). The rooms with full bath also have phones and TVs; the room with toilet only has neither. Still, the location is central, a block from the American Express office. Other rooms in this upscale hotel are beyond this book's budget. It's near the Royal Dramatic Theatre.

⑤ Tre Små Rum

Högbergsgatan 81, 11854 Stockholm. ☎ **8/641-23-71.** Fax 8/642-88-08. 6 rms, none with bath. TV. 300 Kr ($39.50) single; 400 Kr double ($52.65). Rates include continental breakfast. No credit cards. T-Bana: Mariatorget; when you exit the subway, turn right on Swedenborgsgatan and right again on Högbergsgatan, and the hotel is three blocks away.

Jakob Vunarndt, the enthusiastic young owner, got the idea for this little hotel during his travels in Europe. Its motto is "cheap and clean"; it's modern, too, but not unlike a hostel in the sense that the rooms are small (and a little claustrophobic and dark). The beds are comfortable, though, and Jakob puts fruit in each room. Guests share two toilets and two large showers. Door cards are provided instead of keys. The hotel did not accept credit cards at this writing, but that may change in the future. It books up quickly, so call ahead. Tre Små Rum is in a quiet neighborhood on Södermalm, near reasonably priced cafés and a laundry.

DOUBLES FOR LESS THAN 550 KR ($72.35)

Wasa Park Hotell

St. Eriksplan 1, 11320 Stockholm. ☎ **8/34-02-85.** Fax 8/30-94-22. 14 rms, none with bath. TV TEL. 360–395 Kr ($47.35–$51.95) single; 495–520 Kr ($65.15–$68.40) double. Breakfast 30 Kr ($3.95) extra (although in summer it's sometimes included in the room price); additional person 125 Kr ($16.45) extra. EURO, MC, V. T-Bana: St. Eriksplan, four stops from Central Station.

Some of the older rooms here are old-fashioned, while the new doubles resemble those you might find in a first-class hotel, with sharp gray carpets, dark-wood furniture, and TVs. The quality can vary, so if you're not pleased with what you're offered, ask to see another room or two; no. 16 is a pleasant twin, no. 18 an inviting single. The public baths (one with tub) are clean, and the hallways have wooden floors. The location is great, in Norrmalm's arty quarter opposite Vasa Park. The entrance to the hotel is through the arch to the right of the Thai restaurant on Sankt Eriksplan. The airport bus stops outside, and the T-Bana station is one block away.

WEEKEND & SUMMER DISCOUNTS

✪ Hotell Anno 1647

Mariagränd 3, 11646 Stockholm. ☎ **8/644-04-80.** Fax 8/643-37-00. 42 rms, 29 with bath (with shower). TV TEL. Most days in summer and Fri–Sat year round, 395 Kr ($51.95) single with sink only, 590 Kr ($77.65) single with bath; 495 Kr ($65.15) double with sink only, 790 Kr ($103.95) double with bath; minisuites and suites available at reduced rates. Mon–Thurs the rest of the year, prices almost double. Rates include breakfast. AE, DC, EURO, MC, V. T-Bana: Slussen.

This pretty hotel has undergone many renovations since its erection in 1647. Although updating has made it more modern, the Anno 1647 still jealously guards its "country inn" roots. The rooms with bath are substantially nicer than those without, but pretty hardwood floors and tasteful furnishings in mauve and green or gray make all the accommodations more than adequate. A café serves lunch and snacks, and beer and wine are sold in the lobby. There's no elevator, so if you dislike stairs, ask for a ground-floor room. (The no-smoking rooms, however, are on the fourth floor.) The hotel provides some excellent views of the harbor and Gamla Stan. The entrance is on narrow Mariagränd, off Götgatan, and is just a block from the subway.

Queen's Hotel

Drottninggatan 71A (near the intersection of Olof Palmes Gata), 11136 Stockholm. ☎ **8/24-94-60.** Fax 8/21-76-20. 30 rms, 7 with shower only, 10 with bath (with shower). TV TEL. Sat–Sun, 400 Kr ($52.65) single without bath, 450 Kr ($59.20) single with shower only, 495 Kr ($65.15) single with bath; 500 Kr ($65.80) double without bath, 550 Kr ($72.35) double with shower only, 695 Kr ($91.45) double with bath. Sun–Fri, prices rise considerably. Rates include breakfast. ACCESS, AE, DC, EURO, MC, V. From Central Station, turn left on Vasagatan, right on Olof Palmes Gata, and left again on Drottningatan—a 10-minute walk in all.

On Stockholm's busiest shopping street, this pleasant hotel has 10 newer rooms that have full bath (with shower) and an in-room iron, plus 20 older rooms (16 doubles and 4 small singles), a TV lounge, and an old-fashioned elevator. Breakfast is served in a cheerful country-style dining room. The staff is friendly and helpful; if you have an early flight or train, they'll prepare an early breakfast tray for you. Over the years, this hotel has been popular with English-speaking travelers, especially those from the United States, the United Kingdom, Australia, and New Zealand.

SUPER-BUDGET CHOICES

Brygghuset

Norrtullsgatan 12N (near the corner of Frejgatan), Stockholm. ☎ **8/31-24-24** for information, 8/785-75-10 for reservations. Fax 8/31-02-06. 57 beds. 120–150 Kr ($15.80–$19.75) per adult, 95 Kr ($12.50) per child 4–12; discounts with an International Student Identity Card (ISIC). Sheets 35 Kr ($4.60) extra. No credit cards. Closed Sept–May. T-Bana: Odenplan; then take the Odenplan exit and walk three blocks up Norrtullsgatan.

During most of the year this building serves as a community center for various local events. During summer (June to August) the "community" is expanded to include world travelers who are accommodated in two-, three-, four-, and six-bed rooms. It's good for families, who can wash clothes here; the atmosphere and prices are inviting; and a full breakfast is available next door for 40 Kr ($5.25). A 2am curfew is enforced, except during the Water Festival. No sleeping bags are allowed.

✪ Columbus Hotell & Vandrarhem

Tjärhovsgatan 11, 11621 Stockholm. ☎ **8/644-17-17.** Fax 8/702-07-64. 90 hotel beds; 44 rms, 2 with bath. Hotel, 390 Kr ($51.30) single; 490 Kr ($64.45) double. Hostel, 250 Kr ($32.90) single; 300 Kr ($39.45) double; 120 Kr ($15.80) per person in family or dorm rooms. Breakfast 45 Kr ($5.90) extra. Paper sheets 30 Kr ($3.95) extra; cotton sheets 45 Kr ($5.90) extra; towels 15 Kr ($1.95) extra. AE, DC, EURO, MC, V. T-Bana: Medborgarplatsen; Tjärhovsgatan is five blocks east, about an eight-minute walk.

A hotel/hostel on the island of Södermalm, the Columbus is pretty with a cordial staff. The separate hotel section consists of 16 rooms sharing a shower and toilet; each has a TV and phone. The hostel has rooms with two to eight beds each, lockers, and three showers for men and for women on each of the three floors. The public baths are passable but not sparkling. In a quiet area of the city, the building dates from 1780; it has a small café serving beer and wine, a small kitchen for guests, secure baggage room, a room with a sun bed for those who want an artificial Nordic tan, and an outdoor café in summer. A children's playground and an indoor pool are nearby. There's no curfew. The maximum hostel stay is five nights.

Hotel/Hostel *Gustaf AF Klint*

Stadsgårdskajen 153, 11645 Stockholm. ☎ **8/640-40-77** or 640-40-78. Fax 8/640-64-16. 32 cabins, none with bath. In the hotel part, 380 Kr ($50) single; 480 Kr ($63.15) double. In the hostel part, 120 Kr ($15.80) per person. Breakfast 40 Kr ($5.25) extra; paper sheets 35 Kr ($4.60) extra; cotton sheets 55 Kr ($7.25) extra; towels 10 Kr ($1.30) extra. AE, DC, EURO, MC, V. T-Bana: Slussen; use the Södermalmstorg exit and take the stairs down to the riverbank—you'll see the ship to the right.

This floating hotel/youth hostel rigged with lights is on the riverbank just across from Old Town. When the *Klint* served as a radar sounder mapping out the ocean floor, the officers lived in what is now the hotel part of the ship (4 singles and 3 doubles), while the deckhands occupied what is now the hostel part (6 doubles and 17 quads). The hotel section is slightly more spacious than the hostel's cramped quarters; all the cabins are equipped with bunk beds. During summer the ship's deck-top bar and café are open, with a lovely view of Stockholm's harbor. Year round, cheap dinners are served in a sometimes-smoky pub below deck.

IYHF HOSTELS

There are four "official" International Youth Hostel Federation (IYHF) hostels in Stockholm, offering excellently priced, well-maintained lodgings. Two, on Skeppsholmen, probably offer the best-located lodgings in the city (they fill up by 8am in summer). All are similarly priced and offer lower rates to IYHF card-carriers. If you aren't a member, you have to get a Welcome Card and pay an extra 35 Kr ($4.60) per night for up to six nights, after which you gain member status.

Finally, the Swedish Hostel Federation emphasizes that its hostels are not just for young people. If hosteling suits your travel style, age is unimportant.

✪ AF *Chapman*

Västra Brobänken, Skeppsholmen, 11149 Stockholm. ☎ **8/679-50-15.** Fax 8/611-98-75. 136 beds, no rms with bath. 95 Kr ($12.50) per person with the IYHF card, 130 Kr ($17.10) without. Breakfast 40 Kr ($5.90) extra. Paper sheets 30 Kr ($3.95) extra; towels 10 Kr ($1.30) extra. EURO, MC, V. Closed mid-Dec to Apr 1. T-Bana: Kungsträdgården. Bus 65 (until 5:30pm) from Central Station.

The towering fully rigged masts of this gallant tall ship are a Stockholm landmark. The vessel sailed through the world under British, Norwegian, and then Swedish flags for about half a century before establishing itself as a hostel in 1949. Today the ship is permanently moored on the island of Skeppsholmen. The hostel is extremely popular, so arrive early to reserve a bed. The reception is open from 7am to noon and 3pm to 2am. The hostel imposes a five-night maximum stay and closes in winter. The rooms are closed daily from 10am to 3pm for cleaning, and a 2am curfew is enforced. You can buy disposable sheets, supply your own, or use a sleeping bag. There's no kitchen, laundry, or TV room, but you may watch TV across the street at the STF Vandrarhem. Toilets and showers (only two for women) are in the corridor. Each room has a locker, but you must supply your own lock. The common area (and the café on the deck in summer) is conducive to meeting people; browse through the budget-conscious Stockholm information booklet provided by the staff.

Långholmen Hostel and Hotel

Långholmen (P.O. Box 9116), 10272 Stockholm. ☎ **8/668-05-00.** Fax 8/84-10-96. 254 beds. TV TEL. Hotel (including breakfast), daily in summer and Sat–Sun year round, 425 Kr ($55.90) single cell with shower, 650 Kr ($85.55) double cell with shower; Mon–Fri the rest of the year, 690 Kr ($90.80) single cell with shower, 890 Kr ($117.10) double cell with shower. Hostel, 97 Kr ($12.75) per person with the IYHF card, 130 Kr ($17.10) without. Half price for children under 12. Breakfast 50 Kr ($6.60) extra; cotton sheets 35 Kr ($4.60) extra; towels 13 Kr ($1.70) extra. AE, DC, EURO, MC, V. T-Bana: Hornstull; then follow the directions below.

For over $2^1/2$ centuries Långholmen Prison, on the island of the same name, housed some of the country's worst criminals. Painstaking renovations, true to the building's integrity, have culminated in one of the fanciest, most unusual hostels in the world. The decor is an enjoyable cross between prison institutional and ultramodern Scandinavian. Most rooms have private baths, radios, TVs, and telephones, and high-quality beds that pull down Murphy style from the walls. No-smoking rooms are available.

A member of the Swedish Hostel Federation, the Långholmen rents similar rooms at both hostel and hotel prices. Sheets and towels are not provided in the hostel half, and you're expected to clean the hostel room when you leave. No curfew is imposed, and guests are permitted to use the kitchen and laundry facilities and borrow an iron or hairdryer. You can even swim in the lake in front of the hotel. On winter weekdays, when the hotel tends to fill up, only 28 beds are available at hostel prices.

A wine-and-cheese cellar, a 24-hour cafeteria, a restaurant, a pub, and banquet rooms are on the premises. Guided tours of the prison museum are available in English.

From the Hornstull T-Bana station, follow Långholmsgatan toward Västerbroplan. Turn left on Hogalidsgatan and cross the first small bridge you come to onto the island, a 10-minute walk in all. It's easier to get here by car, but if you're walking the circuitous route, enter the Långholmen compound where you see the glass walkway. During summer there's boat service from Stadshusbron, near Central Station. Call the reception for departure times.

STF Vandrarhem/Hostel Skeppsholmen

Västra Brobänken, Skeppsholmen, 11149 Stockholm. ☎ **8/679-50-17.** Fax 8/611-71-55. 152 beds, no rms with bath. 95 Kr ($12.50) per person with the IYHF card, 130 Kr ($17.10) without; if it's available, a bed in the 15-bed room is a bargain at 60 Kr ($7.90). Breakfast 45 Kr ($5.90) extra. Paper sheets 30 Kr ($3.95) extra; towels 10 Kr ($1.30) extra. EURO, MC, V. Closed mid-Dec to mid-Jan. T-Bana: Kungsträdgården. Bus 65 (until 5:30pm) from Central Station.

Across from the AF *Chapman* (above), this three-story yellow hostel often picks up the ship's overflow in its 13 doubles, 13 triples, 13 quads, and one 15-bed room for men and a 6-bed room for women. The doubles, triples, and quads are well sized and have sinks, and some feature magnificent views of Old Town. The reception is open from 7am to 2pm and 3pm to 2am. There are lockers, a small shop for snacks and sundries, museum prints in the rooms and hallways, and several common areas with benches and tables for relaxing or watching TV. The dining room serves terrific porridge (try it the Swedish way, with milk and apple butter). This hostel provides more privacy than the *Chapman.* Smoking is not allowed; curfew is at 2am.

Zinkensdamm Hostel and Hotel

Zinkens väg 20, 11741 Stockholm. ☎ **8/668-57-86.** Fax 8/616-81-20. 500 beds. 95 Kr ($12.50) per person with the IYHF card, 130 Kr ($17.10) without. Breakfast 45 Kr ($5.90) extra. Cotton sheets 40 Kr ($5.25) extra; towels 12 Kr ($1.60) extra. T-Bana: Zinkensdamm; then follow the directions below.

Zinkensdamm is the largest hostel in Sweden. The rooms are clean, and a kitchen is available free. Use of the washing machines and dryers costs 35 Kr ($4.60). The reception sells a wide variety of candy and sweets, as well as postcards. The atmosphere is relaxed, the staff friendly. The grounds have picnic tables, roses, and trees, and there's a park nearby where bicycles can be rented. The hostel is open 24 hours.

The hostel is a bit of a walk from the Zinkensdamm T-Bana station. Proceed east along Hornsgatan (where there's a good bakery), follow the rock outcropping, turn left down the steps between nos. 103 and 107, and follow the path down the hill. The hostel is the brown building on the left. It's on western Södermalm; as always, call ahead before setting out.

WORTH THE EXTRA MONEY

✪ Wellington Hotel

Storgatan 6, S-11451 Stockholm. ☎ **8/667-09-10.** Fax 8/667-12-54. 51 rms, all with bath (tub or shower). TV TEL. May–Sept, Hotel Cheque about $60 per person. Daily in summer and Sat–Sun year round, 600 Kr ($78.95) single; 750 Kr ($98.70) double. Mon–Fri the rest of the year, 850–1,200 Kr ($111.85–$157.90). Rates include breakfast. AE, EURO, DC, MC, V. T-Bana: Östermalmstorg.

Except for the economical Hotel Cheques offered by Best Western and special summer and weekend rates, this prize of a small hotel would far exceed budget status. Its staff is so friendly that guests often linger in the living room–like lobby chatting with them. From the comfortable rooms, decorated in soft colors and outfitted with a pants press and hairdryer, you can hear the soft sound of church bells on the hour. The sauna, free to guests, is beautifully appointed, with a changing room, terry-cloth robes, soft towels, lotion and shampoo, shower, toilet, and sun bed. Add to that a breakfast room (with filling fare), concierge service, and two no-smoking floors. The top floors afford memorable rooftop views.

5 Dining

For tourists on a budget, meals can sometimes seem more like a chore than a delight. Food in Stockholm is priced higher than in most other European cities, but in addition to good-value lunch specials (below), there are a number of great budget eateries.

Getting the Best Deal on Dining

- Note that lunch specials are large and considerably less expensive than dinner.
- Try department-store cafeterias, pasta and pizza houses, and vegetarian restaurants for dinner.

Although price limitations mean that you're unlikely to enjoy a full-fledged Swedish smörgåsbord, you can try other local specialties, including herring (*strömming*), pea soup (*ärtsoppa*, usually served on Thursday), eel, Swedish meatballs, dill meat fricasse and *pytt i panna* (a simple tasty meat-and-potato hash).

If you're in Stockholm during the Christmas season, when tables are trimmed with traditional colorful holiday cutlery, be sure to sample ginger cookies and *glögg*, a potent traditional drink of fortified hot mulled wine with raisins and almonds. And don't forget to visit the Swedish pastry shops—some of the best in Europe!

Many restaurants compete for noontime midweek business with fantastic lunch specials. Most cost only 50 to 80 Kr ($6.60 to $10.50), and unless otherwise noted, prices for all lunch specials listed here include a main course, salad, bread, and a non-alcoholic drink. Lunch is usually served from 11am to 2pm (check individual listings). Adjust your eating habits to take advantage of specials that make a large lunch considerably less expensive than dinner. If you don't see a daily special (*dagens rätt*) posted, ask for it.

For dinner, look to pasta and pizza houses or one of a number of vegetarian restaurants (some of Stockholm's prettiest eateries). To save even more money, avoid alcohol; state control keeps prices extremely high.

It's not customary to tip in Swedish restaurants (a service fee has been incorporated into the prices), but Swedes occasionally do tip at dinner for exceptional service. Even then, they simply round up the amount; for instance, for a 76-Kr tab, they'd leave 80 Kr.

MEALS FOR LESS THAN 50 KR ($6.60)
IN NORRMALM

Coffee House
Odengatan 45 (near Dobelnsgatan). ☎ **8/673-23-43.** 14–50 Kr ($1.85–$6.60); lunch special 45 Kr ($5.90). No credit cards. Mon–Fri 7am–7pm (breakfast 7–10am), Sat–Sun 9am–6pm (breakfast 9–11am). T-Bana: Rådsmansgatan. LIGHT FARE.

This friendly place with tiled floor and round tables fills with local folks and the low hum of conversations. The lunch special, served from 11am to closing, includes a sandwich, juice, and coffee. Quiche and large salads are also available, and good coffee or tea comes with a free refill (help yourself from the table inside the door). There's a high chair for tots. The Lebanese owners, the three Makdessi-Elias brothers, will make you feel most welcome. Its homey atmosphere appeals to people of all ages.

Kungstornet
Kungsgatan 28 (a block from Sveavägen). ☎ **8/20-66-43.** 18–55 Kr ($2.35–$7.25). No credit cards. Mon–Thurs 7am–11pm, Fri 7am–midnight, Sat 8am–midnight, Sun 9am–10pm. T-Bana: Hötorget. LIGHT FARE.

What you see is what you get: decor from the 1950s, seating upstairs and down, and a counter filled with sandwiches and pastries. You can also get quiche, stuffed avocados, and salads, and the lunch prices include bread and coffee. For an afternoon pick-me-up, there's a dessert-and-coffee combo costing 29 Kr ($3.80).

✪ Nicki's Café

Jungfrugatan 6. ☎ **8/662-14-74.** Breakfast 14–46 Kr ($1.85–$6.05); sandwiches 15–25 Kr ($1.95–$3.30); hefty salad 45 Kr ($5.90); daily special 50 Kr ($6.60). No credit cards. Mon–Fri 7:30am–2:30pm. Closed four weeks in summer, usually July to early Aug. T-Bana: Östermalmstorg. LIGHT FARE.

The hours here aren't great, but the prices are. This tiny café, less than half a block from Hedvig Eleonara Church, has only nine tables, red-and-white-checked tablecloths, and white hanging lamps. Prices are reasonable (for Stockholm), especially if you like breakfast; coffee and tea cost 8 Kr (95¢). The special comes with bread, cheese, and coffee. Help yourself to the bread and cheese from the table by the window, as well as to the veggies on your own table. A typical special is a full plate of roast lamb with tasty potatoes au gratin. Make this your big meal of the day.

✪ Pastafamiljen

Hamngatan 15. ☎ **8/678-27-47.** Menu items 25–40 Kr ($3.30–$5.25). No credit cards. Mon–Fri 10am–6pm, Sat 11am–3pm. T-Bana: Kungsträdgården. ITALIAN.

Wedged into the front corner of a bookstore a block from Sweden House, this little eatery represents one of Stockholm's best dining deals. Order your pasta salad (portions are so hefty they're hard to finish), panini, or pizza at the counter and try to snag one of the half-dozen tables. Otherwise, you'll have to make do at the bar. Help yourself to water and bread at the counter. The café au lait here is particularly popular, and the books all around give the place a special atmosphere (and food for thought). Weekdays, it's less crowded after 2pm, when the office workers in the area head back to their desks and duties.

Pastafamiljen has another large and inviting location on Södermalm, on the corner of Hornsgatan and Blecktornsgatan (open Monday through Friday from 11am to 7pm and Saturday from 11am to 4pm).

✪ Restaurang Riddar Klara

Klarabergsviadukten 63 (a raised street above Vasagatan), top floor. ☎ **8/20-80-20.** 10–45 Kr ($1.30–$5.90); salad bar only, 12 Kr ($1.60). Mon–Fri 8am–6pm (breakfast served 8–10am). T-Bana: T-Centralen. SWEDISH/VEGETARIAN.

Originally a restaurant for the employees of the Swedish post office, it's now open to the public. The location, a couple of minutes' walk from Central Station, is a bit difficult to find but worth the effort (walk up the stairs opposite the Royal Viking Hotel, then double back in the direction of the train station). The daily special costs only 42 Kr ($5.50) for an entree—a fish, meat, pasta, or vegetarian dish—rice or potatoes, and all the salad you can handle. Add bread and coffee and it costs 48 Kr ($6.30). Besides low prices, the cafeteria affords a fine view of City Hall, the water, the Old Town, and Södermalm. Coffee comes with refills. The place gets crowded midday with postal workers, so try to time your visit for before 11:30am or after 12:45pm. At the reception desk, ask for a visitor's card to the restaurant, then take the elevator or escalator to the top floor. In summer, you can sit outside and enjoy the panoramic view. Do as the regulars do and return your tray to the cart or conveyor belt when you've finished.

On Gamla Stan

Hermans Lilla Gröna

Stora Nygatan 11. ☎ 8/411-95-00. Reservations suggested. 53–62 Kr ($6.95–$8.15); lunch special 55 Kr ($7.25). No credit cards. Mon–Fri 11am–8pm (lunch special 11am–3pm), Sat noon–8pm, Sun 1–7pm (to 9pm in summer). T-Bana: Gamla Stan. VEGETARIAN.

This friendly small place serves only a couple of dishes each day, many Asian-inspired. The food is dependably tasty and servings are generous, so diners leave satisfied. The lunch special includes a drink, bread, and coffee or tea. The restaurant's owner, Herman Ottoson, owns half a dozen vegetarian eateries in Stockholm. This was one of his first, and it's still quite popular. You can eat on barstools or at tables.

MEALS FOR LESS THAN 70 KR ($9.20)

In Norrmalm

Leonardo

Sveavägen 55. ☎ 8/30-40-21. Reservations recommended. Pizza and pasta 72–78 Kr ($9.45–$10.25); fish and meat dishes 128–152 Kr ($16.85–$20); lunch special (including bread, salad, espresso, and small glass of beer, juice, or soda) 50 Kr ($6.60). AE, DC, EURO, V. Mon–Fri 10:30am–midnight, Sat–Sun noon–midnight (lunch special served 10:30am–2:30pm). T-Bana: Rådmansgatan. Bus 52. ITALIAN.

A refurbished Stockholm standard, it has gray-and-peach decor, sconces, mirrored walls, and a gleaming cappuccino machine. An authentic Italian staff and chef, a good menu, and great food are the real testaments to this trattoria's success. An attractive special packs folks in at lunch, but to stay under budget at dinner you'll have to limit yourself to pasta and pizza (made with mozzarella and fresh tomatoes and supposedly the only oven pizza in Sweden); also take advantage of the chalkboard specials, priced from 59 to 89 Kr ($7.75 to $11.70). The restaurant is half a block from the Rådmansgatan T-Bana station. Fully licensed.

NK Cafeteria (NK Cafeet)

On the fourth floor of the NK department store, Hamngatan 18-20. ☎ 8/762-80-00. Sandwiches 35–62 Kr ($4.60–$8.15); pastries 13–27 Kr ($1.70–$3.55). Mon–Fri 10am–7pm, Sat 10am–5pm, Sun noon–5pm. T-Bana: Kungsträdgården. LIGHT FARE.

Cheerful, relaxed, and brightly lit, this is a point-and-pay kind of place, adjacent to a full-service (more expensive) restaurant called Plates. NK has other cafés scattered about, and there's a grocery store on the lowest level.

✪ Teater Baren (Theater Bar)

On the second floor of the Culture House, Sergels Torg 3. Daily special 54 Kr ($7.10); salad buffet 45 Kr ($5.90); menu items 65–75 Kr ($8.55–$9.85). ER, MC, V. Mon–Fri 11am–3pm, Sat–Sun 11am–5pm. T-Bana: T-Centralen; take the Sergels Torg exit. SWEDISH/VEGETARIAN.

This is a great place to come for lunch, for the food and the view, overlooking animated Sergels Torg. Arrive before noon or after 1pm to avoid the crunch. The daily special includes a fish, meat, or vegetarian hot dish with bread, salad, soda or light beer, and coffee; and if you want dessert, cookies are only 2 Kr (25¢) each. Hungry for veggies? The salad bar is outstanding, with 10 items to choose from, including sprouts and fresh broccoli and cauliflower. At the end of your meal, return your tray to the cart. There's really only one drawback here: you have to pay 5 Kr (65¢) to use the toilet.

On Djurgården

✪ Café Blå Porten

Djurgårdsvägen 64. ☎ **8/662-71-62.** 40–70 Kr ($5.25–$9.20). No credit cards. Tues–Thurs 11am–9pm, Fri 11am–4:30pm, Sat–Sun 11am–5pm. Bus 44 or 47. Ferry: From Slussen or Gamla Stan. LIGHT FARE.

There are not many restaurants on this museum island, and those that are here cater almost exclusively to hungry, stranded tourists. This bohemian cafeteria-style café is an exception, catering equally to students and art enthusiasts who visit the adjacent Liljevalch Art Gallery, where exhibits change every 12 weeks. The café has an inviting atmosphere and serves soups, salads, quiche, and cold and hot meals, along with wine and beer. Sandwiches, cookies, fruit, and desserts, set out on wooden tables, are also available. Café Blå Porten (it means Blue Door, and there is one) is beside the gallery, and in summer customers spill out into the art gallery's tree- and plant-filled courtyard. It's particularly busy on weekends.

On Södermalm

Strömmen

Södermalms Torg. ☎ **8/643-44-70.** 40–90 Kr ($5.25–$11.85); lunch special 50 Kr ($6.60). AE, MC, ER, V. Mon–Fri 7am–10pm, Sat noon–10pm, Sun noon–9pm. T-Bana: Slussen (take the Södermalmstorg exit). SWEDISH.

This is a coffee shop with a rooftop-restaurant view, and its perch above the harbor, in the free-standing blue building across the square from the Slussen T-Bana station, is one of the best locations in Stockholm. In addition to some of the cheapest dinner dishes in town, Strömmen serves breakfast, so if you're in the mood for an early-morning walk across Gamla Stan and then to Södermalm, make this your goal for coffee and a roll. Lunch comes with bread, salad, and soda, coffee, or light beer, and every seat has a panoramic view.

For the Lunch Special

Stockholm's ubiquitous lunch specials are its saving grace for the budget tourist. Except in the most heavily touristed areas, almost every restaurant offers a good meal at prices substantially lower than those at dinner. When striking out on your own, note that a crowded restaurant usually means good food at low prices. The following eateries, all in Norrmalm, are above our budget at dinnertime but offer excellent lunch specials.

Bistro Jarl

Birger Jarlsgatan 7. ☎ **8/611-76-30.** Lunch specials 59–80 Kr ($7.75–$10.55); main courses 90–160 Kr ($11.85–$21.05). ACCESS, AE, DC, EURO, MC, V. Daily 11:30am–2:30pm and 6pm–1am. SWEDISH/FRENCH.

The centrally located Bistro Jarl's lunch special comes with homemade bread, a salad, and a main dish that's either meat, fish, or vegetarian. And homemade pies are available if you're still hungry at the end of the meal. The elegant and intimate café has lace curtains, high ceilings, teardrop chandeliers, and linen tablecloths—plus good food—and there are newspapers and backgammon for distractions. Check the chalkboard menu for the day's offerings. The bistro is near the Royal Dramatic Theater, the American Express office, and Sweden House.

City Lejon

Holländargatan 8 (just off Kungsgatan, two blocks north of Hötorget square). ☎ **8/23-00-80.** 57–98 Kr ($7.50–$12.90); lunch specials from 45 Kr ($5.90). AE, EURO, MC.

Mon–Thurs 10am–9pm, Fri 10am–10pm, Sat 11:30am–6pm (lunch special Mon–Fri 10:30am–3pm). T-Bana: Hötorget. SWEDISH.

The great draw here is the lunch special, one of the best values in town. This place bustles, mainly with local office workers, and gets quite busy around noon. A continuous series of wooden doors covers the restaurant's walls, complemented by wooden tables and low-wattage stained-glass hanging lamps. The food here is good and filling, and the weinerschnitzel and plank steak are particularly popular.

⊛ Getingboet

Sveavägen 9–11 (a block from Sergels Torg and the Culture Center). ☎ 8/21-29-35. Lunch specials 46–51 ($6.05–$6.70); main courses 99 Kr ($13.05); bar menu 29–46 Kr ($3.80–$6.05). ER, MC, V. Mon–Fri 11am–11pm, Sat noon–11pm (lunch served until 3pm). T-Bana: T-Centralen (Sergels Torg exit). SWEDISH.

Far from the well-trafficked tourist track, Getingboet ("Wasp's Nest") has a loyal local crowd. The restaurant's menu changes monthly but always includes pasta and meat or fish dishes, and at lunch you can also get an open-face sandwich with bread and salad. The casual bar upstairs has a limited chalkboard menu, a big-screen TV, and a stage where rock 'n' roll bands perform Wednesday through Saturday nights; the cover is 40 Kr ($5.25). The restaurant fills up in the evenings with a lively theater crowd. Beer costs 29 Kr ($3.80) and wine is 31 Kr ($4.10).

MEALS FOR LESS THAN 110 KR ($14.50)
ON GAMLA STAN

Maharajah

Stora Nygatan 20. ☎ 8/21-04-04. Main courses 59–99 Kr ($7.75–$13). DC, ER, MC, V. Mon–Fri 11am–11pm, Fri–Sat 11am–midnight, Sun 1–11pm. INDIAN.

A little removed from the heavily touristed areas of Gamla Stan, this is a quiet, pretty place with soft lighting and lots of woodwork. It serves standard Indian favorites—tandoori, curries, kebabs, vindaloo, and vegetarian dishes—along with a variety of wonderful breads, including nan, paratha, and chapati.

Michelangelo

Västerlånggatan 62. ☎ 8/21-50-99. Pizza and pastas 62–84 Kr ($8.15–$11.05); meat and fish dishes 129–179 Kr ($16.95–$23.55); lunch special 55–70 Kr ($7.25–$9.20). AE, DC, EURO, MC, V. Mon–Fri 11am–midnight, Sat and hols noon–midnight, Sun noon–11pm (lunch special served Mon–Fri 11am–2:30pm). T-Bana: Gamla Stan. ITALIAN.

Stucco walls, pictures of the Sistine Chapel, Italian rock 'n' roll, and candlelit tables are the hallmarks of this restaurant. Downstairs you can eat in one of several brick cellar rooms with fish tanks and cherub statuettes. The menu includes a large assortment of pizza, pasta, fish, and steak, along with daily specials. The location is on the main pedestrian drag, in the heart of Old Town, a two-minute walk from the Gamla Stan T-Bana station.

In Norrmalm & Östermalm

Capri

Nybrogatan 15. ☎ 8/662-31-32. Pizza 68 Kr ($8.95); pasta 78 Kr ($10.25); fish and meat dishes 105–165 Kr ($13.80–$21.70). Prices include bread, salad, and service. ACCESS, AE, DC, EURO, MC, V. Mon–Fri 4:30pm–midnight, Sat noon–midnight, Sun 1–11pm. T-Bana: Östermalmstorg. ITALIAN.

Although this place also serves meat and fish dishes, it's the extensive pasta and pizza menu, not to mention the courteous service and well-prepared dishes, that attracts budgeteers. Capri's vaulted ceiling is reminiscent of Italy's Blue Grotto. If you come for dinner, look for the nightly special, usually less expensive than the regular menu. The restaurant is just west of Östermalms food hall, two blocks from the Östermalmstorg T-Bana station.

○ Gröna Linjen

Mäster Samuelsgatan 10 (at Norrlandsgatan). ☎ **8/611-92-96.** All-you-can-eat meal (including main course, soup, and salad bar) 65 Kr ($8.55) at lunch, 75 Kr ($9.85) at dinner. No credit cards. Mon–Fri 10:30am–8pm, Sat 11am–8pm (to 6pm off-season). Closed hols. T-Bana: Hötorget or Östermalmstorg (take the Stureplan exit for the latter). VEGETARIAN.

This was the house of Sweden's prewar Conservative Party leader, and eating here still feels like dining in a private home. The restaurant, which opened as Sweden's first vegetarian restaurant in 1940, features vintage ceramic fixtures, white furniture, pastel walls, four dining areas including a reading room (don't miss the fireplace in the middle room), and an unlimited supply of a great variety of foods. Enter through a modest doorway. The restaurant is on the third floor, but there's an elevator.

Hard Rock Cafe

Sveavägen 75 (at the corner of Odengatan, two blocks north of the Rådmansgatan T-Bana station). ☎ **8/16-03-50.** 55–180 Kr ($7.25–$23.70). AE, DC, EURO, MC, V. Sun–Thurs 11am–midnight, Fri–Sat 11am–3am. T-Bana: Rådmansgatan. AMERICAN.

Is it a tourist attraction or a restaurant? Cynics hate to admit it, but the Hard Rock is perennially packed and, price aside, flips the best burger in town for 89 Kr ($11.70). You can also get a slightly less expensive BLT for 65 Kr ($8.55). (You can spend a lot more, but why not go to a fancier place to do so?) The café does have character, with walls exhibiting rock 'n' roll memorabilia, and whether you like it or not, the chain has successfully promoted itself as the unofficial American emissary to the world. The T-shirt shop closes at 10:30pm.

Örtagården (Herb Garden)

Nybrogatan 31. ☎ **8/662-17-28.** Reservations recommended at night. All-you-can-eat mini-smörgåsbord 65 Kr ($8.55) Mon–Fri until 5pm, 80 Kr ($10.55) Mon–Fri after 5pm and all day Sat–Sun. DC, EURO, MC, V. Mon–Fri 10:30am–9:30pm, Sat 11am–8:30pm, Sun noon–8:30pm. T-Bana: Östermalmstorg. VEGETARIAN.

Floral furniture, pastel-green woodwork, and a ceiling hung with glass chandeliers will have budget-minded travelers convinced they're in the wrong place. However, Örtagården offers one of the best deals in town with its huge smörgåsbord and comfortable surroundings. Help yourself to the hot and cold dishes (including soup, salads, fruits, and fresh vegetables), take a seat in the pleasant dining room, and pay when you leave. Desserts cost extra but are not expensive, and wine is served. Meat dishes are available at lunch only, so vegetarian and nonvegetarian friends can dine contently together. At lunch and dinner, a classical pianist performs and reservations are suggested. Örtagården is on the second floor, in the same building as Östermalms food hall but with a separate entrance.

MEALS FOR LESS THAN 160 KR ($21.05)
ON SÖDERMALM

Hannas Krog

Skanegatan 80. ☎ **8/643-82-25.** Reservations highly recommended. Main courses 70–150 Kr ($9.20–$19.75). DC, EURO, MC, V. Mon–Fri 11am–2pm and 5pm–midnight, Sat–Sun 4pm–midnight. T-Bana: Medborgarplatsen. INTERNATIONAL.

Situated on Södermalm, Stockholm's equivalent to New York's SoHo, Hannas Krog attracts a lively crowd. You can sit at the bar and chat with the locals and staff or opt for a bite to eat in one of the cozy dining areas. During summer, they open up the huge windows looking onto the street and provide outdoor seating. A second bar on the lower level has plenty of music, sometimes live; and across the street you'll find Hannas Deli, an offshoot of the successful restaurant.

ON KUNGSHOLMEN

Salt

Hantverkargatan 34. ☎ **8/652-11-00.** Reservations suggested. Main courses 74–160 Kr ($9.75–$21.05). AE, DC, EURO, MC. V. Daily 5pm–1am. T-Bana: Rådhuset. SWEDISH.

The owners first opened Pepper (which still exists) and now Salt, in a quiet part of Kungsholmen. Salt is constantly crowded and unabashedly patriotic, with authentic Swedish fare, Swedish beer, Swedish music, and tables made of Swedish birch. Herring is always on the menu, along with plenty of other Swedish dishes.

FAST FOOD & PICNIC SUPPLIES

The high-quality fast-food eateries and fresh food markets around Hötorget square are essential knowledge for budget travelers. Here you can buy picnic supplies, stop for a snack, or have a full meal.

On the south side of the square, enter though the glass doors of **Hötorgshallen** and take the escalator down to this great gourmet market. Almost magically, you seem to descend onto a veritable cornucopia of high-quality picnic supplies and prepared foreign foods. Head for the coffee bar or sample a kebab in pita or a falafel for about 28 Kr ($3.70). Hötorgshallen has been around since 1880 but was rebuilt in 1958; it houses 35 stands selling fresh breads, meats, fish, and cheeses, with the eating stalls along the sides. You can get fresh fish lunches and dinners—and sit down—at a popular spot called Kajsas Fisk, where the daily specials cost 55 to 65 Kr ($7.25 to $8.55). By the escalator, Piccolino Café sells sandwiches. Hötorgshallen is open Monday through Friday from 9:30am to 6pm and Saturday from 9:30am to 3pm.

Fruits, vegetables, and a variety of other picnic supplies are also available at the **outdoor market** on Hötorget square itself. It's open Monday through Friday from 9am to 6pm (until 4pm Saturday) year round.

The ✪ **Saluhall,** on Östermalmstorg at the corner of Nybrogatan and Humelgårdsgatan, is the fanciest food market of the lot—and Sweden's oldest. Inside the striking brick building, nearly two dozen stalls, a few doubling as casual restaurants, offer high-quality fish, meats, cheeses, fresh produce, and Swedish specialties such as biff Lindström (beef patties with capers and beets). Figure on spending 60 to 110 Kr ($7.90 to $14.45). It's open Monday from 10am to 6pm, Tuesday through Friday from 9am to 6pm, and Saturday from 9am to 3pm.

For picnic staples and general foods, try the supermarket in the basement of **Åhléns department store** on Drottninggatan (☎ 8/676-60-00). Alternatively, **ICA** and **Konsum** are two of the largest supermarket chains around.

WORTH THE EXTRA MONEY

✪ **Le Bistrot de Wasahof**

Dalagatan 46 (across from Vasa Park, two blocks from the T-Bana stop). ☎ **8/32-34-40.** Reservations recommended. Dinner 73–175 Kr ($9.60–$23.05). AE, DC, EURO, MC, V. Mon–Sat 5pm–1am, Sun 5pm–midnight. T-Bana: Odenplan. SWEDISH/FRENCH/ITALIAN.

This bubbling bistro is not tremendously above our budget and is recommended for a special night out. Just south of Odengatan, the restaurant is in a theater-filled area known as Stockholm's "Off-Broadway." The crowd is arty, the food tasty, and the atmosphere convivial. The paintings, dating from 1943, depict the life of 18th-century Swedish musician Carl Michael Bellman. Seafood platters for one or two are available; try the oysters—they're imported from France and particularly popular. The menu changes monthly.

Rolfs Kök

Tegnergatan 41. ☎ **8/10-16-96.** Reservations recommended. Main courses 90–170 Kr ($11.85–$22.35). AE, DC, EURO, MC, V. Mon–Fri 7:30am–1am, Sat 5pm–1am, Sun 5–1am. T-Bana: Rådmansgatan; then walk three blocks. SWEDISH/INTERNATIONAL.

For a gourmet restaurant, this place is reasonable, and the food is outstanding: Swedish with Thai, French, Italian, and Indian influences, served on hot oversize plates. You can sit at the bar in the center of the restaurant and watch the skillful cooks work their culinary magic. The restaurant's design was partly inspired by the Shaker movement and partly by new Swedish design. Everything is done in light wood, in a minimalistic way. This is a friendly place, so you might find yourself talking to the people dining at the next table. The ambience is casual, and the crowd ranges in age from 20 to 50. Save room for dessert.

A Super-Splurge

Stadshuskällaren (City Hall Cellar)

Stadshuset, Kungsholmen. ☎ **8/650-54-54.** Reservations required for Sat at least two days in advance. Two-course lunch 175 Kr ($23.05); Nobel dinner 710 Kr ($93.40) per person. AE, DC, EURO, MC, V. Mon–Fri 11:30am–11pm, Sat 2–11pm. T-Bana: T-Centralen. Bus 62. SWEDISH.

You don't have to be a Nobel Prize winner or even the significant other of one to sit down to an authentic Nobel dinner. The restaurant that orchestrates the prestigious banquet each year can also arrange Nobel dinners for individuals—your choice of any Nobel menu since the first, in 1901. Imagine dining (as laureates actually did in 1989, to pick a year at random) on appetizers of quail eggs and smoked-eel and sole pâté, followed by a main course of tender moose in a berry sauce, and the perennial Nobel dessert, ice cream enveloped in spun sugar. Fine champagne and wines of outstanding vintage accompany the meal. Granted, you pay mightily for the experience, but it's unforgettable, foodwise and otherwise. The cellar restaurant in City Hall looks much as it did when it opened in 1922.

6 Attractions

SIGHTSEEING SUGGESTIONS

If You Have 1 Day

Start your day in Djurgården with a visit to the *Vasa* Ship Museum and the vast outdoor Skansen folk museum. After a picnic lunch or a bite to eat in Café Blå Porten, in Djurgården, set your sights on Gamla Stan (Old Town) for an afternoon stroll (there are organized walking tours in summer; ask about them at the Tourist Information Office). Take your time wandering around Stockholm's oldest streets and admiring the city's pretty port views.

If You Have 2 Days

Spend the first day as described above. On the second, explore modern Stockholm's Norrmalm district. A visit to Kungsträdgården park is a must and in winter might include an ice-skating session. During summer, keep an eye out for the regularly scheduled special events here. It's also easy to go from here to Kungsholmen and tour Stockholm's renowned City Hall, or to either the National Museum, rich in Swedish and European art, or the Museum of National Antiquities and its impressive Gold Room.

If You Have 3 Days

On the third day, make the short trip to Drott-ningholm Palace to see the Swedish royal couple's house and gardens. Later, back in Stockholm's Old Town, compare Drottningholm with the older Royal Palace, and visit Storkyrkan, Stockholm's cathedral and the oldest building in town.

If You Have 5 Days

Continue your museum-hopping at the Millesgården, the Museum of National Antiquities, the National Art Museum, and any other that might interest you. Take an archipelago cruise or a trip to one of the many islands around the city.

TOP ATTRACTIONS

In trying to decide what to see and do in Stockholm, keep in mind that the city's museums are busiest on weekends; most are closed on Monday but stay open late on Thursday night. Discounted admission prices are often available for students and seniors.

ON DJURGÅRDEN

Many of Stockholm's best sights are clustered on Djurgården, the island that was once the king's hunting ground, east of Gamla Stan (Old Town). Beautiful, thick forests and sweeping harbor vistas gracefully combine with several well-designed sightseeing attractions.

The most enjoyable way to get here in warm weather is by ferry from Gamla Stan. Buses and a trolley will also get you here; buses no. 44 and 47 stop at the two top attractions, described below, and bus no. 69 will take you to the tip of the island and other attractions. It's also fun to take just for the inexpensive "unguided tour" it provides.

✪ Vasamuséet (*Vasa* Museum)

☎ **8/666-48-00.** Admission 45 Kr ($5.90) adults, 30 Kr ($3.95) students, 10 Kr ($1.30) children 7–15. Early June to late Aug, daily 9:30am–7pm; the rest of the year, Thurs–Tues 10am–5pm, Wed 10am–8pm. Closed Jan 1, May 1, Dec 23–25, and Dec 31. Ferry: From Slussen (on Södermalm). Trolley: 7, departing in summer and on weekends year round from across the street from the Royal Dramatic Theater. Bus 44 or 47.

When the warship *Vasa* set sail on its maiden voyage in August 1628, it was destined to become the pride of the Swedish fleet. But even before it reached the mouth of Stockholm harbor, the 64-cannon man-o'-war caught a sudden gust of wind, fell on its side, and sank to the bottom of the sea. Forgotten for centuries, the boat was discovered in 1956 by marine archeologist Anders Franzén. Today this well-preserved highly ornamented wooden vessel is the most frequently visited attraction in Stockholm.

Stockholm

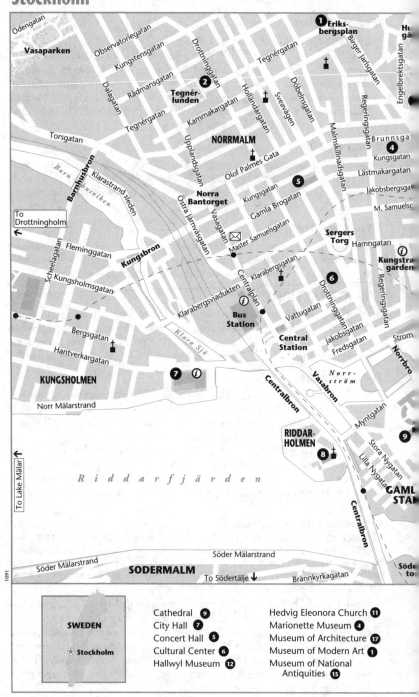

Cathedral **9**
City Hall **7**
Concert Hall **5**
Cultural Center **6**
Hallwyl Museum **12**

Hedvig Eleonora Church **11**
Marionette Museum **4**
Museum of Architecture **17**
Museum of Modern Art **1**
Museum of National
Antiquities **15**

SWEDEN

★ Stockholm

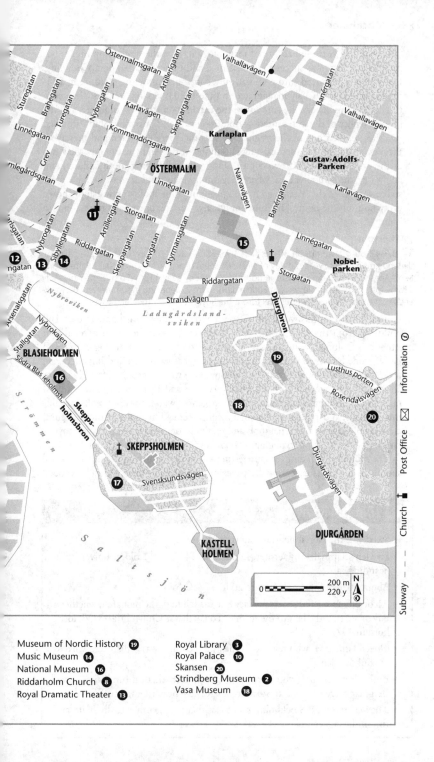

Museum of Nordic History **19**
Music Museum **14**
National Museum **16**
Riddarholm Church **8**
Royal Dramatic Theater **13**

Royal Library **3**
Royal Palace **10**
Skansen **20**
Strindberg Museum **2**
Vasa Museum **18**

Subway - - - Church ✝ Post Office ⊠ Information ⊘

It took five years and advanced technology to raise the fragile ship intact, but in 1961 the *Vasa* was successfully reclaimed and placed in a temporary building. In 1988 it was moved into a climatically controlled museum, a stunning $35-million building officially inaugurated in June 1990, marking the latest chapter in this ship's long history. Be sure to see the carvings on the bow and stern and the life-size replica of the ship's interior. An exhibit called "The Sailing Ship," installed in 1995, displays one of the original six sails that were recovered and preserved; the *Vasa*'s sails are the oldest existing sails in the world. And you can now view two of the original masts and two copies, along with the rigging. Both children and adults love the computer area, where they can try their hand at constructing a more stable version of the *Vasa*. Catch the 25-minute film about the warship, shown every hour on the hour. The museum has a good café, open daily from 11am to 7pm.

✪ Skansen

☎ **8/442-80-00.** Admission 30–50 Kr ($3.95–$6.60) adults, free–10 Kr ($1.30) children, depending on time of year and day of week. Museum grounds, May–Aug, daily 9am–10pm; Sept–Apr, daily 9am–5pm. Historic houses, May–Aug, daily 11am–5pm; Sept–Apr, daily 11am–3pm. Ferry: From Slussen (on Södermalm). Tram 7, departing in summer and on weekends year round from across the street from the Royal Dramatic Theater. Bus 44 or 47.

Founded in 1891, this wonderful 75-acre outdoor museum is home to over 150 buildings from the 16th to the early 20th century—it's a Swedish version of America's Colonial Williamsburg, displaying traditional Nordic log cabins and native stone houses in their original settings. Weather-beaten and imperfect, yet thoroughly charming, many of the buildings here were transported from locations all across Sweden. Some cottages (rural dwellings and 18th-century town houses) maintain their original interiors, including painted wooden walls, fireplaces, spinning wheels, old plates, and assorted folk decor. Throughout the museum, craftspeople, using traditional tools and methods, demonstrate the former ways of farming, metalworking, typography, bookbinding, and 15 other trades.

The museum's buildings are interesting in and of themselves, but Skansen's real success is due to its exceptionally peaceful surroundings on a naturally wooded

---

❓ Did You Know ?

- Sweden is the largest neutral country in Europe.
- Sweden's Uppsala Universitet, founded in 1477, is the oldest university in Scandinavia.
- About 40% of Stockholmers are 20 to 44 years old.
- According to a 1980 succession act, the first child of the monarch, whether a boy or a girl, is the heir to the throne. Today that is Crown Princess Victoria, born in 1977.
- Queen Christina, who reigned in the 17th century, was actually crowned as king of Sweden.
- Both Greta Garbo (who portrayed Queen Christina on film) and Ingrid Bergman were students at Stockholm's Royal Theater Dramatic School.
- The water around Stockholm is so clean that people can actually swim and fish in the city center.

peninsula. In addition, there's a particularly endearing zoo. There may not be many animals here that you haven't seen before, but the open design makes it feel more like a farm than a zoo.

Restaurants (including Tre Byttor, which specializes in foods from olden times) and food stands are scattered throughout the area, but, if the weather is nice, it's fun to pack your own lunch and find a welcoming spot for a picnic.

During summer, try your foot at folk dancing with the locals. Dances are scheduled on Sunday at 2:30 and 4pm, the rest of the week at 7pm.

A map of Skansen, sold at the museum's entrance, will definitely come in handy. There's also a gift shop.

In Gamla Stan (Old Town)

Getting lost in Gamla Stan's timeless maze of car-free streets is one of Stockholm's greatest pleasures. Pretty shades of pastel separate the short, squat buildings along cobblestone streets. Exposed drainpipes run past wooden storm shutters protecting first-floor windows. Black metal streetlamps illuminate storefronts and metal hooks for hoisting cargo hang over garret windows.

Also known as Old Town, Gamla Stan is the city's most heavily touristed area and although you may catch a glimpse of a contemporary office interior or pass some high-fashion window displays, its quiet, historical charm stoically maintains an authentic ancient atmosphere.

Medeltidsmuséet (Museum of Medieval Stockholm)

Strömparterren. ☎ **8/20-61-68.** Admission 30 Kr ($3.95) adults, 20 Kr ($2.65) seniors and students, 5 Kr (65c) children 5–17, free for everyone Wed 3–6pm only. July–Aug, Tues–Thurs 11am–6pm, Fri–Mon 11am–4pm; Sept–June, Tues and Thurs–Sun 11am–4pm, Wed 11am–6pm. T-Bana: Kungsträdgården or Gamla Stan. Bus 62 or 43.

Digging for an garage beneath the Parliament Building led to surprising archeological finds and the eventual creation of this museum (a recipient of the European Museum of the Year award), which shelters part of the city wall from around 1530 and a cemetery wall from around 1300, as well as myriad artifacts from 13th-century Stockholm. Particularly impressive are the vaulted passageway leading from the entrance (and the present) into the medieval city; an imaginative exhibit on spiritual life (you'll swear you're in a medieval cloister, with brick flooring, limestone pillars, and sandstone capitals); the Ridderholm ship (ca. 1520), excavated in 1930; and the eerie Gallows Hill, which reveals the way justice used to hold sway here. Plenty of skulls are displayed, many with a hole left by the arrow from a crossbow. A lot of texts are in English as well as Swedish. The museum is free late Wednesday afternoon. To enter it, go down the stairs in the middle of Norrebron, the bridge leading to Gamla Stan (or Norrmalm, depending on which way you're headed).

✪ Stockholms Slott (Royal Palace)

Off Skeppsbron. ☎ **8/789-85-00.** Admission 30 Kr ($3.95) adults, 15 Kr ($1.95) students, 10 Kr ($1.30) children 7–18. May, Tues–Sat 10am–3pm, Sun noon–3pm; June–Aug, Tues–Sat 10am–3pm, Sun–Mon noon–3pm; Sept–Apr, Tues–Sun noon–3pm. T-Bana: Gamla Stan.

A royal residence has stood on this spot for more than 700 years, and the existing palace, rebuilt between 1697 and 1754, reflects a time when Sweden flourished as one of Europe's major powers. Encompassing 608 rooms, it's used by the Swedish king for ceremonial tasks and official state functions. The complex is huge and, although the massive stone facade is somewhat uninspired, the 18th-century Royal Apartments are grand, with flamboyantly painted ceilings, opulent chandeliers,

---

Special & Free Events

In addition to the special events outlined in "Timing Your Trip" under "Pretrip Preparations," earlier in this chapter, a full schedule of special and free happenings will keep you busy. Always check with the tourist office and their publication, *Stockholm This Week*, for the most up-to-date information.

During summer, Norrmalm's park, **Kungsträdgården,** adjacent to Sweden House, comes alive almost daily with classical-music concerts, rock bands, theater performances, and various other attractions. During the winter, an outdoor ice rink opens its gates here, providing some of the best inner-city skating anywhere.

Summertime also means frequent **free and almost free concerts** in other parts of Stockholm. Folk dancing is performed Monday through Saturday evening and Sunday afternoon at the Skansen outdoor museum. Parkteatern (the Parks Theater) provides free open-air performances in the city's parks throughout summer.

---

ornate tapestries, and other royal riches on permanent display. (Note that the apartments can close without notice for special occasions.)

Be sure to visit the Royal Armory (separate entrance and admission) to see the ceremonial armor for horses and riders, along with royal finery including coronation robes and wedding costumes fit for a king (or queen), as well as the royal coaches (anyone who loves horses will be thrilled by a number of these exhibits). Forgo the Royal Treasury (separate entrance and admission) unless you have a thing for baubles; there are many stairs to maneuver for only two fairly small rooms.

At noon (1pm on Sunday) you can see the Changing of the Guard in the palace courtyard. In summer, the spectacle includes the guards' parade and music.

Storkyrkan (Stockholm Cathedral)

Trångsund (next to the Royal Palace). ☎ 8/723-30-00. Admission 10 Kr ($1.30) in summer; concerts free–180 Kr ($23.70). Daily 9am–4pm (to 6pm in summer). T-Bana: Gamla Stan.

Founded in the 13th century, this church has seen some of Sweden's most important religious ceremonies, including coronations and royal marriages. As the oldest building in Stockholm still used for its original purpose, it bears testimony to the city's changing past. Every Saturday at 1pm, and on Sunday once or twice a month, concerts featuring the church's huge 18th-century organ are performed here.

ON KUNGSHOLMEN

✪ Stadshuset (City Hall)

Hantverkargatan 1. ☎ 8/785-90-00. Stadshuset, 30 Kr ($3.95) adults, free for children 11 and under; tower, 15 Kr ($1.95) adults, free for children. Tours, June–Aug, daily at 10am, 11am, noon, and 2pm; Sept, daily at 10am, noon, and 2pm; the rest of the year, daily at 10am and noon. Tower visits, May–Aug, daily 10am–4:30pm (closed Sept–Apr). T-Bana: Rådhuset.

Stockholm's landmark City Hall is home to the annual Nobel Prize banquet and may be visited only by guided tour. The tour's highlight is undoubtedly the Golden Hall, lavishly decorated with over 19 million 23-karat-gold tiles. Dinners honoring Nobel Prize winners were originally held in this room, but swelling guest lists have forced the party to relocate to the even-larger Blue Hall (which isn't blue). Marble floors, stone columns, and gothic motifs throughout make City Hall look and feel much older than its 70 years. In summer only you may climb to the top of the distinctive tower, topped by three gleaming crowns.

IN NORRMALM & ÖSTERMALM

National Museum

Blasieholmen (at the foot of the bridge to Skeppsholmen). ☎ 8/666-42-50. Admission 50 Kr ($6.60) adults, 25 Kr ($3.30) students and seniors, free for children 15 and under. Tues 11am–8pm, Wed–Sun 11am–5pm.

Although it stocks masterpieces by stars like Rembrandt, Rubens, El Greco, and Renoir, this pleasant and manageable museum, which turned 200 in 1992, is not labyrinthine like Paris's Louvre. There are English-language tours in summer, and the collection is well marked (in Swedish and English) and nicely displayed. Be sure to visit the third-floor gallery with mid-19th- to mid-20th-century Swedish painters, including Anders Zorn, Carl Larsson, and Ernst Josephson. The third floor also houses works by Renoir, Degas, Rodin, and Corot, along with 16th- and 17th-century French, Italian, Flemish, and Dutch painters. The second-floor Department of Applied Arts features over 28,000 pieces of porcelain, glassware, silverwork, and jewelry, including a contemporary Swedish design gallery. The museum has a shop and café.

✪ Historiska Muséet (Museum of National Antiquities)

Narvavägen 13–17. ☎ 8/783-94-00. Admission 55 Kr ($7.25) adults, 45 Kr ($5.90) students and seniors, 30 Kr ($3.95) children 7–15, free for children 6 and under. Tues–Wed and Fri–Sun 11am–5pm, Thurs 11am–8pm. T-Bana: Östermalmstorg. Bus 44, 47, 56, or 69.

If you come for no other reason than to view the opulent Gold Room, a spiral gallery of gold and silver treasures, some dating from the 5th century—including the Dune Hoard, the largest medieval treasure in Scandinavia, consisting of 150 items that were probably buried in A.D. 1361—a visit here would be worthwhile. (Don't miss the 14th-century gold buckle the size of a small pizza.) Viking stone inscriptions, 10th-century coins, and ancient armor are also displayed in the museum. The collection, which complements that of the Nordic Museum, shows daily life from the dawn of time to the Middle Ages. The museum shop has a fine collection of English-language history books and copies of Viking jewelry in gold and silver.

Moderna Muséet och Fotografiska Muséet (Museum of Modern Art and Museum of Photography)

Birger Jarlsgatan 57C. ☎ 8/666-42-50. Admission 40 Kr ($5.25) adults, 20 Kr ($2.65) students and seniors, free for children 15 and under, half price for everyone on Thurs. Tues–Thurs noon–7pm, Fri–Sun noon–5pm. T-Bana: Rådmansgatan; then a five-minute walk on Tegnergatan. Bus 46 to Tegnergatan (it stops in front of the museum).

Conveniently open late twice a week, the Museum of Modern Art and Museum of Photography are excellent choices for evening sightseeing, especially on Thursday, when the admission is half price. Housed in the 19th-century Tram Depots until 1998, when an impressive new building will open on the island of Skeppsholmen, these museums showcase changing exhibitions of Swedish and international contemporary art, along with works from the outstanding museum collections. A well-stocked museum shop and a restaurant/café are on the premises.

MORE ATTRACTIONS
ON DJURGÅRDEN

Nordiska Muséet (Museum of Nordic History)

Djurgården. ☎ **8/666-46-00**. Admission 50 Kr ($6.60) adults, 30 Kr ($3.95) seniors, 20 Kr ($2.65) students, 10 Kr ($1.30) children 7–15. Tues–Wed and Fri–Sun 11am–5pm, Thurs 11am–8pm. Ferry: From Gamla Stan to Djurgården. Trolley 7, departing in summer and on weekends year round from across the street from Norrmalmstorg. Bus 47 or 69.

In an impressive stone building, this ethnographic museum documents changes in Nordic life over the past 500 years. You'll learn how Swedes lived, dressed, and worked, and track the culture's evolution to the current day. Start with the Nordic folk costumes on the lower level and work your way up. The museum's large café offers a daily lunch special. In the children's museum, kids get to dress up and pretend they're Swedish pioneers. A shop selling books, cards, and gift items is on the premises. The striking (often dusty) statue in the entry is of Gustav Wasa, by the well-known Swedish sculptor Carl Milles.

✪ Thielska Galleriet (Thiel Gallery)

Sjotullsbacken 6–8. ☎ **8/662-58-84**. Admission 40 Kr ($5.25) adults, 20 Kr ($2.65) students and seniors. Mon–Sat noon–4pm, Sun 1–4pm. Bus 69.

Built as a gallery to house the burgeoning collection of banker/art patron Ernst Thiel, it was bought by Sweden and opened to the public in 1924, when Thiel went bust. One room is devoted to Carl Larsson, and there are works by Gauguin, Vuillard, Anders Zorn, Carl Wilhelmson, and Ernst Josephson. Climb to the tower room to see the two dozen Munchs and a fine view of the archipelago. On the grounds are works by Rodin and Norwegian scultor Gustav Vigeland.

✪ Aldemarsudde

Prins Eugens väg 6. ☎ **8/662-28-04**. Admission 40 Kr ($5.25) adults, 30 Kr ($3.95) students and seniors, free for children 15 and under. June–Aug, Tues and Thurs 11am–5pm and 7–9pm, Wed and Fri–Sun 11am–5pm; Sept–May, Tues–Sun 11am–4pm. Bus 47.

This former palace of Prince Eugen (1865–1947) not only is known for its glorious architecture and truly palatial view but also has been made famous by the artworks of Prince Eugen himself. The "artist prince," as Eugen is known, was a prolific painter, and he's said to be among the finest landscape painters of his generation (this is arguable). The prince also collected art, particularly that of his contemporaries, and his collection of turn-of-the-century Swedish art is one of the finest in Sweden; this collection and the prince's own work are exhibited in the palace's gallery annex. The principal rooms on the ground floor of the original building remain largely as they were during the prince's lifetime, while the two upper floors, including his studio on the top floor, are used mainly for special exhibitions, which are a big draw. The small house adjacent to the palace has exhibits on the life of Prince Eugen. The gardens are filled with flowers and sculpture by Carl Milles and Auguste Rodin and afford a magnificent view of the sea approach to Stockholm.

IN NORRMALM

✪ Hallwylska Muséet (Hallwyl Museum)

Hamngatan 4. ☎ **8/666-44-99**. Admission 40 Kr ($5.25) adults, 20 Kr ($2.65) students, free for children 6 and under. Tues–Sun noon–3pm; the English-language tour is at 1pm on Sun only. T-Bana: Kungsträdgården.

Stockholm's most eccentric museum is a magnificent turn-of-the-century private residence filled with 70 years' worth of passionate collecting by Countess Wilhelmina von Hallwyl. On display is everything from buttons to Dutch and Swedish paintings, European china and silver, umbrellas, and weapons. The Hallwyls, who lived here from 1898 to 1930, had three daughters, one of whom, Ellen, became a sculptor and studied with Carl Milles; and they had a modern bathroom before the king did! Admission to the house is by one-hour guided tour only. Arrive early—they book quickly. You'll wish you could stay longer.

Kulturhuset (Cultural Center)

Sergels Torg 3. ☎ **8/700-01-00.** Admission 30 Kr ($3.95) adults, 20 Kr ($2.65) students and seniors, free to children 11 and under; theater production, concert, and some exhibition prices vary. Tues–Thurs 10am–7pm, Fri 10am–6pm, Sat–Sun noon–5pm. T-Bana: T-Centralen.

Built in 1974, the Kulturhuset was designed to expose Swedes to other cultures, but it's equally effective at exposing other cultures to one another. Several galleries, stages, and cafés put the space to excellent use, and the large third-floor library supplies thousands of records (which you may listen to with headsets), 200 newspapers, and 500 magazines. People from all over the world come here to catch up on local news. There's an information desk on the lower level and chess boards on the Sergels Torg level, near the entrance. The glass sculpture outside the building, *Vertical Accent,* by Edvin Ohrstrom, is particularly striking at night, when it's lit.

ON SÖDERMALM

Katarina Elevator

Södermalms Torg, Slussen. Admission 5 Kr (65¢), free for children 6 and under. Mon–Sat 7:30am–10pm, Sun and hols 10am–10pm. T-Bana: Slussen.

The Katarina Elevator itself is not the attraction—the seven-story view it provides is. Just over the bridge from Gamla Stan, the elevator lifts visitors to a perch high above the port. If you're feeling strong, take the stairs up the cliff behind the elevator, but don't miss this spectacular view of Stockholm.

ON LIDINGÖ

✪ Millesgården

Carl Milles väg 2. ☎ **8/731-50-60.** Admission 40 Kr ($5.25) adults, 35 Kr ($4.60) students and seniors, 15 Kr ($1.95) children 7–16, free for children 6 and under. May–Sept, daily 10am–5pm; Oct–Apr, Tues–Sun 11am–4pm. T-Bana: Ropsten; then bus to Torsvik (the first stop; pedestrians cannot cross the bridge on foot); from here, walk about 8 minutes, following the signs to the Millesgården (the entire trip will take about 40 minutes).

One of the greatest Swedish artists, sculptor Carl Milles (1875–1955) lived and worked in the United States from 1931 to 1951, when he returned to Stockholm to design and build a garden on a hill beside his home on the island of Lidingö. The Millesgården is a little time-consuming to get to, but those who are eager enough will be rewarded with the opportunity to gaze at the artist's most important works, including the monumental *Hand of God,* overlooking all of Stockholm. In Milles's house, also open to the public, is his unique collection of art objects from ancient Rome and Greece and of medieval and Renaissance art. This breathtaking site, also the final resting place for Milles and his wife, beautifully complements the artist's works.

PARKS & GARDENS

Parks are one of Stockholm's loveliest assets, and many have already been mentioned above. Bring a picnic to **Skansen** or to anywhere on the wooded peninsula of **Djurgården. Waldemarsudde** and **Millesgården** are also excellent strolling grounds, as is the entire island of **Skeppsholmen.** In Norrmalm, take your lunch to the **Kungsträdgården,** a bustling urban park and the city's summer meeting place.

Tanto Lunden, with tiny cottages and carefully tended gardens near the city center, was created in Stockholm in 1919 so that city workers who couldn't afford a country home could nonetheless benefit from country living. The one-room cottages, which are rented from the city for 50 years, look more like dollhouses, with their equally tiny yards filled with birdhouses and compost heaps. To get here, take bus no. 43 or the T-Bana to Zinkensdamm. Zinkens väg, where you'll find the Zinkensdamm Hostel and Hotel, dead-ends into Tanto Lunden; climb the wooden steps and enter a world in miniature. Don't overlook delightful house at no. 69.

SWIMMING

If you're a swimmer and have missed having the opportunity to mark off some laps since traveling in Europe, head for Stockholm's 1904 art nouveau **Centralbadet,** at Drottninggatan 88 (☎ 8/8-24-24-01), half a block from the Queen's Hotel, at the far end of the courtyard. Here you'll find a 75-foot pool, along with a steam room, sauna, Jacuzzi, gym, water workouts, and solarium spread throughout three floors—all yours for only 69 Kr ($9.10). Don't fret if you didn't bring a bathing suit; you can rent one here, along with a towel and robe, and, if you're in the mood to splurge, indulge in a half-hour or hour-long massage (about $26 and $52, respectively). On the ground level is a little café with ceiling fans and wicker furniture. It's usually open Monday through Friday from 6am to 9pm, Saturday from 8am to 8pm, and Sunday from noon to 8pm, but always call ahead to confirm times.

ESPECIALLY FOR KIDS

The award-winning **Marionettmuséet (Marionette Museum),** Brunnsgatan 6 (☎ 8/10-30-61), is an enchanting place, with displays of 1,000 puppets—string, shadow, glove, even battery-driven—from around the world, particularly Sweden and Asia. Visitors may play with some of them. Ask at the desk for exhibit descriptions in English. There is free coffee, and you may even sit and have tea in the Japanese room. Admission is 15 Kr ($1.95) for adults, 10 Kr ($1.30) for children over 14, and 5 Kr (65¢) for children 3 to 14 (free for kids 2 and under). On certain weekend afternoons, puppet theater performances are given in the adjacent marionette theater (Marionetteatern), at an additional charge. The museum is open from August to May, Tuesday through Sunday from 1 to 4pm.

"Please touch" is the modus operandi at the ✪ **Musikmuséet (Music Museum),** Sibyllegatan 2 (☎ 8/666-45-30). Kids get to play many of the instruments displayed here, among them conga drums, xylophone, harp, stringed instruments, and synthesizer. Adults can enjoy the texts in English. Downstairs, "Ljudion" ("The Audio"), a room downstairs, reads your movements and translates them into music, while "Kloink" is a music workshop where visitors actually get to play instruments. "Tutti" is a permanent exhibit of musical instruments from around the world, from the 17th century to the present day. The museum shop sells cassettes, CDs, records, books (mostly in Swedish), and posters. It's open Tuesday through Sunday from 11am to 4pm; admission is 20 Kr ($2.65) for adults and 10 Kr ($1.30) for children.

Another favorite with kids is the **Tekniska Muséet (National Museum of Science and Technology),** Museivägen 7, Djurgården (☎ **8/663-10-85**), where they get to experiment to their hearts' content, as well as view steam engines, aircraft, vintage cars, and more. It's open Monday through Friday from 10am to 4pm and Saturday and Sunday from noon to 4pm; admission is 25 Kr ($3.30) for adults, 10 Kr ($1.30) for students, 50 Kr ($6.60) for a family. Within walking distance is the 507-foot **Kaknäs TV Tower** (☎ **8/667-80-30**), which provides a panoramic view of Stockholm and the archipelago. Inside is a souvenir shop and a tourist information office. The tower is open April 15 to September 15, daily from 9am to 10:30pm; the rest of the year, Tuesday through Thursday from 10am to 5pm. Admission is 20 Kr ($2.65) for adults and 12 Kr ($1.60) for children. To get here or to the National Museum of Science and Technology, take bus no. 69 from opposite Åhléns department store.

OMNIMAX fans will find a new theater, along with a modern planetarium, together called Cosmonova, in the **Naturistoriska Riksmuséet (Swedish Museum of Natural History),** Frescativägen 40 (☎ **8/666-51-30**). The films, a skillful blend of the scientific, the geographic, and the dramatic, rarely fail to envelop and awe their audiences. Tickets are 60 Kr ($7.90) for adults, 50 Kr ($6.60) for students and seniors, and 30 Kr ($3.95) for children 16 and under. The theater, planetarium, and museum all are open daily from 10am to 8pm. Call for ticket availability and showtimes; then hold on to your seat.

SPECIAL-INTEREST SIGHTSEEING

FOR THE LITERARY ENTHUSIAST   Admirers of Swedish dramatist August Strindberg (1849–1912) can visit the **Strindberg Museum,** Drottninggatan 85 (☎ **8/411-53-54**), in a reconstruction of his 24th and last residence in Stockholm (1908–10). The apartment is filled with authentic furniture and details and includes a replica of the author's library, crammed with books and neatly stacked newspapers. Strindberg, an avid book collector, read with pen in hand and often scribbled comments in the margins, including epithets like "Lies!" and "Stupid jackass" when he disagreed with an author. Besides getting an intimate glimpse into Strindberg's life, it's fun to see the old apartment building with its marble stairs and cage elevator. The museum is open Tuesday through Friday from 10am to 4pm (on Tuesday also from 6 to 8pm) and Saturday and Sunday from noon to 4pm. Admission is 20 Kr ($2.65) for adults, 15 Kr ($1.95) for students, and free for children 13 and under. Take the T-Bana to Rådmansgatan.

FOR THE HISTORY BUFF   Stockholm was founded in the 13th century and, despite the fancy boutiques that now line the streets of **Gamla Stan,** you can still get a feeling for what it must have been like here hundreds of years ago. Cars are banned from most streets, and the area's narrow alleyways still exude ancient charm. Wander along Österlånggatan and Västerlånggatan, following the path where the old city walls once stood.

Those interested in the Vikings and early Swedish history will enjoy a triumvirate of museums, starting with the **Historiska Muséet (Museum of National Antiquities),** Narvavägen 13–17 (☎ **8/783-94-00**), with a collection depicting life here from the dawn of time to the Middle Ages. Next in the historical chain of progression is **Skansen,** which shows how Swedes have lived (and in what kinds of structures) over the past 400 years, and the **Museum of Nordic History,** which details how Sweden became a modern society (see the museum entries above under "Top Atractions" and "More Attractions," above).

FOR THE ARCHITECTURE LOVER　Stockholm's most stunning edifices line the water. Most of these gorgeous buildings were erected around the turn of the century and are maintained in excellent condition. The city's picture-postcard beauty can be summed up in one spot: on **Djurgårdsbrom,** the bridge connecting Djurgården (where Skansen is located) to the rest of the city.

The **Arkitekturmuséet (Swedish Museum of Architecture),** on Skeppsholmen (☎ 8/463-05-00), mounts exhibitions on architecture and maintains archives of photographs, drawings, and models of Swedish architecture. It's open mid-November to March, Tuesday through Sunday from 11am to 4pm (Tuesday until 6pm); the rest of the year, Tuesday through Sunday from 11am to 5pm (Tuesday until 8pm). Admission is free from mid-November to March; the rest of the year, 20 Kr ($2.65) for adults, 15 Kr ($1.95) for students and seniors, free for children 14 and under. Take bus no. 65 or the T-bana to Kungsträdgården.

The **Stockholms Stadsmuseum (City of Museum of Stockholm),** in Slussen near the subway exit (☎ 8/700-05-00), depicts Stockholm in centuries past in drawings and models. Texts are in Swedish only, but visitors should still find the first and second floors well done and interesting. The museum has a good café and is open September to May, Tuesday, Wednesday, and Friday through Sunday from 11am to 5pm and Thursday from 11am to 9pm; June to August, Tuesday, Wednesday, and Friday through Sunday from 11am to 5pm and Thursday from 11am to 7pm. Admission is 30 Kr ($3.95) for adults and 20 Kr ($2.65) for students and seniors; free for children.

ORGANIZED TOURS

City Sightseeing (☎ 8/11-70-23) operates three-hour bus tours of Stockholm year round, leaving daily from the Opera House at 2pm, and also at 5pm mid-April to early October. The cost is 230 Kr ($30.25) for adults, half price for children 6 to 11. From early June to early August, one-hour tours also leave from the Opera House at 10am, 11am, noon, 2pm, and 3pm; the cost is 75 Kr ($9.85) for adults, half price for children 6 to 11. Ask about their combination excursions that include walking, touring by bus, and/or taking a boat.

Stockholm Sightseeing (☎ 8/24-04-70) provides boat tours of the city, departing from Strömkajen, in front of the Grand Hotel. (Locals insist that the best way to explore their city is by boat.) Get tickets at the kiosk topped with yellow flags with a red S on them. The company's "Under the Bridges of Stockholm" tour takes two hours and costs 120 Kr ($15.80) for adults, half price for children 6 to 11; it's offered from mid-April to mid-December. The hour-long "Royal Canal Tour" runs from mid-May to early September and costs 75 Kr ($9.85).

Strömma Sightseeing (☎ 8/23-33-75) offers a "Great Archipelago Boat Tour" with a guide from early June to mid-August for 60 Kr ($7.90), half price for children 6 to 11, except for evening cruises. The boat leaves from Nybroplan, in front of the Royal Dramatic Theatre; it goes as far as Vaxholm (see "Easy Excursions," at the end of this chapter).

7 Shopping

A whopping 25% goods tax makes shopping in Sweden expensive, and you can get most items at home for less money. On the positive side, Swedish stores usually stock items of the highest quality. Favorite buys include crystal, clothing, and Scandinavian-design furniture. Take a good look at some of the high-tech designs that've made Scandinavia famous. You might decide to take home a souvenir that will bring you joy for years.

Many stores offer **tax rebates** to tourists spending over 101 Kr ($13.30). Here's how to get your refund: When you make your purchase, ask the retailer for a Tax Free Check (valid for one month) and leave your purchase sealed until you leave the country. At any border crossing on your way out of Sweden (or at repayment centers in Denmark, Finland, or Norway), show both the check (to which you have added your name, address, and passport number) and the purchase to an official at the tax-free desk. You'll get a cash refund of about 16% to 18% in U.S. dollars (or seven other currencies) after the service charge has been taken out (remember not to check the purchase in your luggage until after you receive the refund). At Arlanda Airport there are separate booths for VAT purchases that are to be checked as baggage and those that are to be carried on the plane, so be sure to get in the right line for your refund. Allow enough time before your flight in case there's a crowd. For more information, call 024/74-17-41.

Shopping hours in Stockholm are usually Monday through Friday from 9:30am to 6pm and Saturday from 9:30am to 2pm. Department stores are sometimes open on Sunday as well.

BOOKS   The best prices, along with a large selection of books, are found at **Akademibokhandeln,** at Regeringsgatan and Mäster Samuelsgatan (☎ **8/613-61-00**), open Monday through Friday from 9:30am to 6pm and Saturday from 10am to 2pm (3pm in winter); check out the bargain bin. Fiction is upstairs, in the back on the left. Large and impressive, **Hedengrens Bokhandel,** at Sture-plan 4 in Sturegallerian (☎ **8/611-51-32**), has big travel and fiction sections downstairs; you'll also find a nice architecture section. A paperback, fiction or nonfiction, will run you 75 to 115 ($9.85 to $15.15) wherever you buy it.

BEST BUYS   For the best shopping and window-shopping in Stockholm, stroll along the quiet streets of **Gamla Stan** (particularly Västerlånggatan), filled with boutiques, art galleries, and jewelry stores. Similarly winsome shops and galleries may be found along the Hornsgats-Puckeln (the Hornsgatan-Hunchback, a reference to the shape of the street), on **Södermalm.** Other streets that tempt browsing include Hamngatan, Birger Jarlsgatan, Biblioteksgatan, and Kungsgatan, all in **Norrmalm.**

Drottninggatan is a pedestrian street leading from Hötorget square past the Kulturehuset into Gamla Stan, but most of the stores along it aren't as appealing as those you'll find elsewhere.

NK (Nordiska Kompaniet), Hamngatan 18–20 (☎ **8/762-80-00**), across from Sweden House, is the Harrods of Stockholm. The stunning department store, now actually an assortment of independent shops under one roof, is built around a four-story atrium, and the quality merchandise is beautifully displayed. There are several cafés in the store. The ground-level information desk is quite helpful. It's open Monday through Friday from 10am to 7pm, Saturday from 10am to 5pm, and Sunday from noon to 5pm.

For more reasonable prices, visit **Åhléns City** department store (pronounced like Orleans), a block from Central Station at Klarabergsgatan 50 (☎ **8/676-60-00**). This is a good place to buy Swedish-designed crystal, ceramics, and gift items (all on the ground floor). It's open Monday through Friday from 9:30am to 7pm, Saturday from 9:30am to 6pm, and Sunday from noon to 4pm.

Gallerian, at Hamngatan 37, is a centrally located mall where you can buy luggage and day packs (near the main entrance), toys, cheap postcards (toward the back), and other items. Its upscale cousin, **Sturegallerian,** is at Stureplan 4.

On Södermalm, near the Medborgarplatsen T-Bana station, is a fairly new mall called **Söderhallarna,** which consists of two buildings, the Saluhallen and the Björkhallen. It's the perfect place for those who like to combine shopping with dining out, movie-going, and contemplating modern Swedish architecture.

The **Swedish Institute Bookshop,** on the second floor of Sweden House, Hamngatan 27 (☎ **8/789-20-00**), has a wealth of books about the art and culture of Sweden, CDs, cassettes, records, and children's books, including many by Astrid Lindgren. For toys, shop at **Stor & Liten,** in the Gallerian shopping center, Hamngatan 37 (☎ **8/23-13-90**), and **Leka Samman,** on Södermalm at Hornsgatan 50A (☎ **8/714-96-00**).

For famous Swedish crystal and porcelain, visit **Duka,** at the Consert House, Kungsgatan 41, at Sveavägen (☎ **8/20-60-41**). For handcrafts, including textiles, yarns, baskets, rugs, pottery, and items in wood and metal, browse through **Svensk Hemslöjd,** Sveavägen 44 (☎ **8/23-21-15**), operated by the Swedish Handicraft Society.

For quality secondhand clothing, check out a commission shop called **Cattis,** Linnegatan 33, at Jungfrugatan (☎ **8/663-77-70**), in an upscale neighborhood. The shop has an impressive selection of clothes and reasonable prices and is open Monday through Friday from 10am to 6pm and Saturday from 11am to 4pm.

For camping or outdoor gear, **Frilufts Magasinet,** Sveavägen 73, at the corner of Odengatan (☎ **8/34-20-00**), has a wide assortment.

If Scandinavian-design furniture, lamps, glass, ceramics, and other household objects intrigue you, don't miss **IKEA,** Kungens Kurva (☎ **8/740-80-00**), which claims to be the largest home-furnishings store in the world. The store is 25 minutes from the city center and is served by a special free bus, which leaves from Regeringsgatan 13 (opposite Fritzes bookshop) Monday through Friday from 11am to 5pm (returning hourly on the half hour). Otherwise, take the T-Bana to Skärholmen. The store does not accept credit or charge cards. IKEA is open Monday through Friday from 11am to 8pm, Saturday from 10am to 5pm, and Sunday from 11am to 5pm.

8 Stockholm After Dark

Stockholm's "living arts" are well supported with state funds. As a result, the price of high-quality "serious" entertainment is extremely reasonable. Moreover, good public funding means that performing-arts houses don't have to rely on a conservative public—they can experiment with new and interesting ideas.

The city's concert hall, opera house, and theaters are closed in summer, but, luckily, three deals are offered in their place. **Free open-air park performances** by **Parkteatern** (the Parks Theater) begin in June and continue throughout the summer; **Sommarnättskonserterna (Summer Night Concerts),** on the main staircase of the National Museum, start in July and run through the end of August; and **folk-dancing at Skansen** takes place Monday through Saturday at 7pm.

Also in summer, **jazz cruises** provide an exhilarating way to experience Stockholm from the water while enjoying upbeat entertainment under the stars. This is also a good way to meet Swedish people, and the boats usually stop at a friendly island so revelers can dance and socialize on shore.

Churches—the cathedral, on Gamla Stan; Jacob's Church, near the Opera House; and Hedvig Eleonora, in Östermalm, to name a few—often host free evening (and afternoon) concerts. Check listings under "Music" in *Stockholm This Week* or look for announcements posted in front of individual churches.

On the late-night front, all is well. The nightlife in what once was a fairly staid capital has undergone a major change over the last decade or so. Today, late-nighters can engage in the city's thriving café culture, listen to live rock and jazz, and dance into the wee hours—usually at Kungsträdgården or on Gamla Stan or Södermalm.

Always check the tourist office, *Stockholm This Week,* and local newspapers (especially *Dagens Nyheter* from Thursday through Sunday) for details on upcoming events.

THE PERFORMING ARTS

Almost every capital has its national houses, where the biggest-budgeted performances are staged. But it's the proliferation of "alternative" theater and music that divides cities with great culture from all the rest. Stockholm is one such city, and an opportunity to visit one of its smaller playhouses should not be passed up. Check *Stockholm This Week* for a full list of current performances. Not many theaters are open in summer, but you'll find plenty of concerts.

CLASSICAL CONCERTS, OPERA, THEATER & BALLET

Berwaldhallen (Berwald Concert Hall)
Strandvägen 69. ☎ **8/784-18-00.** Tickets 40–290 Kr ($5.25–$38.15).

This award-winning hexagonal structure built into a granite hillside is home to the **Stockholm Radio Symphony Orchestra.** Call or check the entertainment section of local papers for a schedule and times for upcoming concerts. The box office, at Oxenstiernsgatan 20, is open Monday through Friday from 11am to 6pm.

Engelska Teatern (English Theater Company)
Nybrogatan 35. ☎ **8/662-37-32.** Tickets 150–200 Kr ($19.75–$26.30).

The company stages productions in English on stages throughout the city. The office is open Monday through Friday from 10am to 5pm; call for specific information.

✪ Filharmonikerna i Konserthuset (Stockholm Concert Hall)
Hötorget 8. ☎ **8/786-02-00** for information, 10-21-10 for the box office. Tickets 40–190 Kr ($5.25–$25); students and seniors get a 15% discount.

This hall is home to the **Royal Stockholm Philharmonic Orchestra,** and performances are usually on Wednesday, Thursday, and Saturday from August to May, while touring companies sometimes light up the stage on other days throughout the year. Carl Milles's sculpture *Orpheus* is outside the building. The box office is open Monday through Friday from 11am to 6pm and Saturday from 11am to 3pm.

Kungliga Dramatiska Teatern (Royal Dramatic Theater)

On Nybroplan. ☎ **8/667-06-80.** Tickets 90–180 Kr ($11.85–$23.70) for the large stage, 180 Kr ($23.70) for the small stage; those 19 and under pay half price; those 20 to 26 and seniors always get a 10% discount, but only on Sunday.

This is one of the great playhouses of Europe. The plays performed here are almost exclusively in Swedish (with the exception of touring companies), but that shouldn't deter you. During summer the theater offers a daily guided tour for 15 Kr ($1.95) at 3pm; the rest of the year, at 5:30pm on Saturday only. It's usually closed for two weeks in summer. The box office is open Monday from noon to 6pm, Tuesday through Saturday from 10am to 7pm, and Sunday from noon to 4pm.

Operan (Opera House)

Gustav Adolfs Torg. ☎ **8/24-82-40.** Tickets 120–290 Kr ($15.80–$38.15), with a 20% discount for students; there are some side seats (with an obstructed view) for 80 Kr ($10.55) and "listening seats" (no view, but not standing room) for only 20 Kr ($2.65).

The Operan, built in 1898, houses the **Royal Swedish Opera** and the **Royal Swedish Ballet.** Most of the operas performed in this beautifully restored house are in the original language, with an emphasis on such popular works as *La Traviata, Madame Butterfly*, and *Aïda*. The Royal Ballet presents classics like *The Nutcracker, Don Quixote,* and *Romeo and Juliet* as well as contemporary works. The season runs from the end of August to the beginning of June. Call or visit the box office for a current schedule. The box office is open Monday through Friday from 11am to 7:30pm (to 6pm when no performance is scheduled) and Saturday from 11am to 3pm (later on performance days).

CABARET

Restaurang och Cabare Studio

St. Eriksplan 4. ☎ **8/33-63-05.** T-Bana: St. Eriksplan.

Le Studio is an appealing local place popular with theatergoers (there are numerous stages in the area) and cabaret lovers. Warm and lively, the room seems full even when business is slow—which is rare. During summer, café tables line the street and the crowd flows out the door. Swedish and international cabaret acts appear here year round Wednesday through Sunday. It's is a few doors from the T-Bana station. Open Monday through Friday from 11am to 1am, Saturday from noon to 1am, and Sunday from 4pm to 1am; shows start at 8, 9, or 10pm, depending on the act.

JAZZ, ROCK & BLUES

Engelen

Kornhamnstorg 59B (in Gamla Stan). ☎ **8/20-10-92.** Cover none–60 Kr ($7.90), depending on the group. T-Bana: Gamla Stan.

Engelen (the name means "Angel") provides a stage for local bands nightly. The live music is upstairs from 8:30pm until midnight, while dance discs spin below until 3am in Kolingen. The early to mid-20s crowd arrives early (before 10pm), especially on weekends, when it's packed. The cover usually isn't enforced until 9pm, so it pays in more ways than one to come early. (Strix, a free rock club, is in the same building.) Open daily from 5pm to 3am.

Fasching

Kungsgatan 62. ☎ **8/21-62-7,** or 21-93-65 for upcoming performances. Cover 60–170 Kr ($7.90–$22.35), depending on the entertainment; occasionally free. T-Bana: T-Centralen.

This club serves up plenty of contemporary jazz, Afro and Latino music, and some blues. It hosts a jazz lunch Monday through Friday from 11am to 2pm. Evening entertainment is offered Monday through Friday from 6pm and Saturday from 7pm (hours can be irregular, so be sure to call ahead).

Globen (Globe Arena)

Johanneshov. ☎ 8/725-10-00 for information, 600-34-00 for the box office. Tickets 240–350 Kr ($30.25–$46.05) for concerts, about 100 Kr ($13.15) for ice hockey. T-Bana: Globen.

Stockholm's futuristic Globe Arena measures 279 feet high by 361 feet wide and seats 16,000. It has hosted such well-known stars as Roxette, Bruce Springsteen, Diana Ross, Liza Minnelli, and Luciano Pavarotti. If you're not a megaconcert fan, you might enjoy taking in an ice-hockey game here. The box office is open in summer, Monday through Friday from 10am to 4pm; in winter, Monday through Friday from 10am to 6pm and Saturday from 10am to 3pm.

Kaos

Stora Nygatan 21 (in Gamla Stan). ☎ 8/20-58-86. Cover: None Sun–Thurs, and Fri–Sat before 7:30pm; 20–40 Kr ($2.65–$5.25) Fri–Sat after 7:30pm; none for the Sat–Sun jam session at 2pm.

In a house dating from 1760, Kaos has been around for about 30 years and claims to be the oldest music club in Sweden. Visually and musically, there's definitely a sense of walking into the 1960s when you enter. The informal café/club has live music nightly. Sunday from 9pm on is dedicated to the blues, Wednesday is for boogie-woogie, and a free jam session is held at 2pm on Saturday and Sunday. Several nights a week, especially on weekends, an additional stage is opened downstairs in the vaulted cellar, where a second band plays.

Mosebacke Etablissement

Mosebacke Torg 1–3. ☎ 8/641-90-20. Cover 40–140 Kr ($5.25–$18.40), depending on the band; free outdoors in mid-Aug. T-Bana: Slussen.

Mosebacke attracts an older crowd with its cabarets and packs in people of all ages who come to listen to local rock, blues, and jazz bands. The big plus for budgeteers is the free outdoor entertainment in summer from 7 to 11pm nightly. Call for the schedule. Open in summer, daily from 11am to midnight; the rest of the year, daily from 5pm to midnight.

✪ Stampen

Stora Nygatan 5 (in Gamla Stan). ☎ 8/20-57-93 or 20-57-94. Cover 50–100 Kr ($6.60–$13.15), depending on the band. T-Bana: Gamla Stan.

Stampen, a Stockholm tradition since 1968, is the city's lively center for jazz, soul, funk, blues, and traditional rock 'n' roll, with two bands performing nightly. The upstairs stage is beneath a ceiling sporting a contra bass, a Christmas tree, a wooden sleigh, and other whimsical decor. The second stage is in the more subdued downstairs room where you can enjoy the music while dancing. Like many of the city's other live-music clubs, Stampen is in Gamla Stan. Open Monday through Thursday from 8pm to 1am, Friday and Saturday from 8pm to 2am, and Sunday from 1pm to 5am.

THE BAR SCENE

Because of the astronomical price of alcohol, most customers nurse their drinks for a long time and understanding waiters don't hurry you. For budget tourists, even a short hop to the local watering hole must be considered a splurge. With that in mind, here are some favorites:

Bakfickan (Back Pocket Bar)
Operakällaren, Kungsträdgården. ☎ **8/20-77-45.**

This well-kept secret—from visitors anyway—is as tiny as its name implies. Patrons sit around the bar (where service is quickest) or at bar stools along the tiled walls. The quietest time is 2 to 5pm. Good food is available all day and includes such dishes as salmon or venison served with vegetables and bread. Daily food specials run 60 to 95 Kr ($7.90 to $12.50). A glass of wine is 46 Kr ($6.05); beer, 44 Kr ($5.80). Open Monday through Saturday from 11:30am to midnight.

✪ Black & Brown Inn
Hornsgatan 50B (on Södermalm). ☎ **8/644-82-80.**

This is the place to come when you're in the mood to sample many kinds of beer. Scottish and Irish music and classic hits play constantly in this landmark tavern, decked out with booths, windowseats, plaid wallpaper, and, in the back room, beer-coaster decor (check it out). Fish and chips, burgers, and Guinness sausage with coleslaw and chips complement the beers. Food costs 21 to 98 Kr ($2.75 to $12.90). There are two ciders on draft. A bottle of beer costs 29 Kr ($3.80) and up; draft beer begins at 37 Kr ($4.85). Prices are discounted 30% during happy hour (from opening until 7pm). Open Monday through Wednesday from 4pm to midnight, Thursday from 4pm to 1am, Friday and Saturday from 3pm to 1am, and Sunday from 2pm to 11pm.

Tennstopet
Dalagatan 50 (at Odenplan). ☎ **8/32-25-18.**

You'll have to fight local artists and journalists for a seat at the bar of Stockholm's oldest pub, with a bright-red awning outside and equally red decor inside. There's a dart room in back and a couple of cozy tables in between it and the crowded bar area. A restaurant on the premises serves traditional Swedish fare in a pretty setting, but the prices exceed our book's budget. Bottles of Bass Pale Ale, McEwan's Export, Guinness Stout, and other imports run 37 Kr ($4.85). Open Monday through Thursday from 3pm to 1am, Friday from 3pm to 3am, Saturday from 1pm to 3am, and Sunday from 1pm to 1am.

A GAY & LESBIAN BAR/DISCO

Hus 1
Sveavägen 57. ☎ **8/30-83-38.** T-Bana: Rådmansgatan. Bus 52.

This casual place, housed in Stockholm's Gay Center (see "Networks and Resources," later in this chapter), has soft lights and soft music. If you're hungry, there's plenty to eat: burgers, sandwiches, fish and chips, pytt i panna (Swedish stew), and steak, along with a daily pasta special. Most dishes run 29 to 35 Kr ($3.80 to $4.60); the daily special, including a main course and a large beer, costs 50 Kr ($6.60). Food is served Sunday through Thursday from 6 to 11pm and Friday and Saturday from 6pm to midnight. Hus 1 also operates as the largest gay disco in the Scandinavian countries Wednesday through Saturday. It's half a block from the Rådmansgatan T-Bana station on a pretty tree-lined street. Open Monday through Saturday from 6pm to 3am and Sunday from 6pm to midnight. Admission of 60 Kr ($7.90) is charged only on Friday and Saturday.

DANCE CLUBS

If starting late means it's good, then Stockholm's dance clubs are very good. Most are open for dinner; then there's a lull for a few hours before the die-hards arrive around midnight. The nature of this scene requires constant new places, so ask around and check the listings in newspapers and magazines for the latest.

Café Opera
On Kungsträdgården, behind the Opera House. ☎ **8/11-00-26.** Cover none before 11pm, 65 Kr ($8.55) 11pm–2am.

Café Opera is the most exclusive place in town, and even the men who stand guard at the door are drop-dead gorgeous. While some people choose to eat the expensive dinners here, the real socializing starts with the dancing after midnight. Drinks are appropriately expensive. To escape the frenzy for a while, turn right instead of left when you enter, pass through the Opera Bar, where artists and journalists gather, and make your way to the congenial Bacfickan, or Back Pocket Bar (above). Open Monday through Saturday from 11:30am to 3am and Sunday from 1pm to 3am.

Daily News Café
On Kungsträdgården, behind the Opera House. ☎ **8/21-56-55.** Cover none Wed–Thurs and Sun, 60 Kr ($7.15) Fri–Sat after 10pm.

The Daily News Café is just doors away from its rival, Café Opera (above). With an elaborate light show and good sound system, this place is more dance-oriented than the Opera. The crowd doesn't arrive until late, and when they do you'll think you're in a New York City club. The drinks are ridiculously priced. There's live music upstairs and a disco downstairs; both get going around 10pm. Open Wednesday through Saturday from 7pm to 3am and Sunday from 8pm to 3am.

Göta Källare
In the Medborgarplatsen subway stop, on Södermalm. ☎ **8/642-08-28.** Cover 25 Kr ($3.30) Mon–Tues before 9:30pm, 85 Kr ($11.20) after 9:30pm; 50 Kr ($6.60) Wed–Thurs before 9:30pm, 85 Kr ($11.20) after 9:30pm; 55 Kr ($7.25) Fri–Sat before 9:30pm, 90 Kr ($11.85) after 9:30pm. T-Bana: Medborgarplatsen (turn right as you come up the stairs from the subway if you're coming from Norrmalm or Gamla Stan).

Well-dressed couples (most aged 40 to 60) who like to dance cheek-to-cheek congregate here to enjoy the live bands, large dance floors, Platters-style music, and one another. Live music for 45 minutes alternates with disco for 15 minutes, and food is served. On Sunday there's a tea dance. You've got to be at least 25 to get into this fun place. Open Monday through Saturday from 8pm to 3am.

FILMS

Tickets for most films, including American blockbusters and other international hits, generally cost 65 Kr ($8.55). Most foreign films are screened in their original language with Swedish subtitles. The **Saga** movie house, at Kungsgatan 24, has six cinemas that are small but have staggered rows so heads don't get in the way. You'll have your choice of a number of first-run English-language films here.

9 Networks & Resources

STUDENTS Students who plan to study in Stockholm or elsewhere in Sweden can get a handbook of information about housing, health services, work permits, Swedish-language courses, sports and social activities, and other matters by contacting the **Federation of Student Unions,** Körsbärsvägen 2 (Box 5903), 11489 Stockholm (☎ **8/674-54-00**). To visit them in person, take the T-Bana to Tekniska Högskolan; call ahead for hours.

Killroy Travels, Kungsgatan 4 (☎ 8/23-45-15), is the place for low-cost student and youth rail and air tickets; the maximum age for the latter is 34. It's usually open Monday through Friday from 9:30am to 5pm. The office is one block from Birger Jarlsgatan at Stureplan.

Transalpino, Birger Jarlsgatan 13 (☎ 8/679-98-70), offers discount plane tickets for students to age 35 with valid ID. It's usually open Monday through Friday from 10am to 5:30pm.

GAY MEN & LESBIANS Many local gays and lesbians gather at **RFSL-Huset,** Sveavägen 57 (☎ 8/736-02-12 for information, or 24-74-65 for the switchboard 8–11pm; or 736-02-10 for the help line). This large building is headquarters to most of Stockholm's gay and lesbian organizations and also houses a restaurant, disco, and bookstore. Pick up a free flyer at the bookstore, which is to the left after you enter the building. The center is open daily, usually from noon to 3pm.

Hus 1 (☎ 8/30-83-38) is a casual eatery serving light fare like burgers, pasta, and fish and chips. And if you're in the mood for a beer and a game of pool, that's possible, too (see "The Bar Scene" under "Stockholm After Dark," earlier in this chapter). A disco in the back of the building is open Monday through Saturday from 6pm to 3am and Sunday from 6pm to 12pm. The first Friday of the month is lesbian night, but men are still welcome at the bar. Admission of 60 Kr ($7.90) is charged only on Friday and Saturday.

Hjarter Dam (Queen of Hearts), Polhemsgatan 23 (☎ 8/653-57-39), is a popular meeting place/café for gays and lesbians. It serves Swedish fare in informal, friendly surroundings.

Rosa Rummet (Pink Room Bookstore), Sveavägen 57 (☎ 8/736-02-15), has postcards and a good selection of Swedish- and English-language books on current gay issues. It's open Monday through Thursday from 3 to 8pm, Friday from 3 to 6pm, and Saturaday and Sunday from 1 to 4pm.

Get to the RFSL-Huset complex via the T-Bana to Rådmansgatan or bus no. 52, which stops on Sveavägen. Look for the rainbow PRIDE sign out front.

10 Easy Excursions

DROTTNINGHOLM The palace of the present-day Swedish King Carl XVI Gustaf and Queen Silvia is open to visitors year round. The 17th-century rococo structure is just 7 miles from the city center (perfect for a half-day trip). In addition to the State Apartments, the palace grounds encompass a theater dating from 1766 and a beautiful Chinese Pavilion.

Drottningholm Slott (Drottningholm Palace) (☎ 8/759-03-10) was built for Sweden's Queen Eleonora in 1662. This four-story palace with two-story wings has often been referred to as "little Versailles." The interior dazzles with opulent furniture and art from the 17th through the 19th century, including painted ceilings framed by gold, ornate chandeliers, and Chinese vases. Ample sculptured gardens surround the palace, and from time to time visitors may even spot the down-to-earth royal couple taking a stroll. Admission is 30 Kr ($3.95) for adults and 10 Kr ($1.30) for students. The palace is open May to August, daily from 11am to 4:30pm; in September, Monday through Friday from 1 to 3:30pm and Saturday and Sunday from noon to 3:30pm.

The palace's **Drottningholm Court Theater** (☎ 8/759-04-0600) is one of the world's oldest extant stages still using original backdrops and props; it stands exactly as it was on opening night in 1766. Eighteenth-century ballets and operas are still performed here, authentic down to the original costumes. Inquire at the Stockholm Information Service for a schedule of the period operas and ballets held from May to September. Even if no show is scheduled, visit the wonderful museum next door. Admission is 30 Kr ($3.95) for adults and 10 Kr ($1.30) for children. The theater is open May to August, daily from noon to 4:30pm; in September, daily from 1 to 3:30pm.

The **Kina Slott (Chinese Pavilion)** is near the end of the palace park. Many of Europe's grand old palaces were inspired by the exotic architecture of Asia. This pavilion was constructed in Stockholm in 1753 as a royal birthday gift and quietly floated downriver so it would surprise the queen when it arrived. The pavilion was a particular favorite of King Gustavus III, who loved to pass summer days here with his court. Admission is 25 Kr ($3.30) for adults and 10 Kr ($1.30) for students and seniors. The pavilion is open April to October, daily from 1 to 3:30pm; May to August, daily from 11am to 4:30pm; in September, Monday through Friday from 1 to 3:30pm and Saturday and Sunday from noon to 3:30pm.

There are two ways of reaching Drottningholm. The first, and most exciting, is **by steamboat,** which takes 50 minutes and costs 70 Kr ($9.20) round-trip for adults or 50 Kr ($6.60) for children 6 to 11. Boats leave from Stadshusbron, beside Stockholm's City Hall, daily: on the hour from 10am to 4pm and at 6pm June to mid-August, and 10am to 2pm (to 4pm on weekends) from May to early June and mid-August to early September. Call Strömma Kanalbolaget (☎ **8/23-33-75**) for more information.

Stockholm Sightseeing (☎ **8/24-04-70**) offers round-trips to Drottningholm in turn-of-the-century boats. You can also take the T-Bana to Brommaplan, then connect to any Mälarö bus for Drottningholm.

VAXHOLM   Local ferries and tour boats make the pleasant hour-long trip to Vaxholm, a popular island destination in the archipelago, many times a day. This is a small place, ideal for a half-day excursion, and you'll be able to get your bearings right away.

To familiarize youself with Vaxholm once you've disembarked, follow the path along the water, passing the **information office** (☎ **8/541-314-80** or 541-315-00)—ask for a map if it's open—and the sign for the fortress museum (see below), to the **lookout** at the old Portuguese battery. From this serene spot, you can stroll down the hill and sit on the rocks by the water.

From here, make your way to the **main square** of the town; follow Vallgatan, crossing Fiskaregatan and Kilgatan. Turn right on Lotsgatan, which leads to the main square and the town hall, built in 1885 and rebuilt in 1925. You'll also find some shops on the square. From here, follow Rådhusgatan back to the waterfront and the information office.

If you want to treat yourself to a good (but not inexpensive), elegantly served meal with a view of the harbor and boats scudding to and fro, visit the restaurant in the **Vaxholm Hotel.**

The **Vaxholm Fortress,** constructed between 1548 and 1863 to protect the inlet to Stockholm, is open from mid-May to August; admission is 30 Kr ($3.95) for adults, 15 Kr ($2) for seniors and children 7 to 12. You can get there in five minutes by boat.

The ferry to Vaxholm takes about an hour, calling at several islands along the way, and costs 35 Kr ($4.15) one way, 70 Kr ($8.35) round-trip. It departs from in front of the Grand Hotel; call **Waxholmsbolaget** (☎ **8/679-58-30**) for more information. Bus no. 670 will get you back to Stockholm if you don't want to wait for the return boat.

MARIEFRED   The perfect day trip, a visit to Mariefred on Lake Malaren includes a boat ride, a pretty little town that's easy to explore on foot, an "old-time" train station and steam railway, a bookshop that's been around since 1897, and a castle with compelling nooks and crannies and a portrait collection from the 16th century to the present.

Gripsholm Castle (☎ 0159/101-94), on a spit of land south of the town, is home to the National Portrait Gallery, with 1,200 of its 4,000 portraits on display. There's a multitude of rooms and portraits to see, outstanding among them the ceiling and paneling in Duke Karl's Chamber, the tiled fireplace in Princess Sofia Albertina's Study, the King's Bedchamber with a 17th-century ivory clock, the paneling and wall hangings in the Council Chamber, the White Drawing Room, the domed ceiling of Gustav III's Theater, the Sentry Corridor (a portrait of Jenny Lind hangs here), the Large Gallery (a portrait of King Carl XVI Gustaf and his family hangs here, along with one of Lovisa Ulrika, whose attendants are depicted as hens), and the Tower Room, where you'll find modern portraits, including Dag Hammarskjöld, Greta Garbo, and Ingmar Bergman. Room 52 houses some compelling self-portaits.

A guidebook in English is helpful but costs about $4. Admission is 30 Kr ($3.95) for adults, 15 Kr ($1.95) for students and children. The castle and portrait gallery are open May to August, daily from 10am to 4pm; in April and September, Tuesday through Sunday from 10am to 3pm; and October to March, only Saturday and Sunday from noon to 3pm.

There are shops, an inviting café called **Konditori Fredman,** the town hall around the main square, and some charming streets to explore. **Gripsholms Vardshus,** the town's upscale hotel, has a public bar and a restaurant, called skankrum, that serves substantial meals.

Many visitors never realize there's a **boardwalk** in Mariefred (walk in the opposite direction of the church and the pier) leading past moored boats and houses with red-tile roofs peaking out to sea. There are benches where you can sit and gaze at the bullrushes, and beyond them, the church steeple and castle domes.

In summer, a coal-fired steamboat called the *S/S Mariefred* makes the trip to Mariefred from Stockholm; sit on the right side for the best views and photo opportunities. The pretty trip, which offers splendid views of City Hall as the boat leaves Stockholm, takes a little more than an hour and costs 160 Kr ($21.05) round-trip, half price for children 15 and under. Snacks and drinks are served on board. In May, the boat departs Stockholm at 10am only on Saturday and Sunday; from mid-June to mid-August, it leaves Tuesday through Sunday at 10am (no sailing on Monday). It returns from Mariefred at 4:30pm (5pm on Saturday); double-check the departure time with the crew before you go exploring.

In summer, you may also travel to Mariefed by train—the last leg of the journey, from Läggesta to Mariefred (change trains at the small terminal called Läggesta Södra), is in a turn-of-the-century steam-powered train.

SIGTUNA & UPPSALA   Another getaway that fills a single day to perfection takes you to **Sigtuna,** founded in A.D. 970. Home to 2,500 people, this picturesque town has a beautiful waterfront walkway, historic ruins, a church, a museum, an old-fashioned café (Tant Bruns Kaffestuga, or "Auntie Brown's"), a revered hotel dating from 1907, a summer hostel, shops, and a helpful tourist office that serves its visitors coffee and cake. Plan to arrive at 10am, when the tourist office and cafés open. If you're pressed for time, do a quick transit by walking along Storagatan to the museum and hotel (pick up a map and information on the church at the tourist office along the way), then double back following the waterfront walkway, head up to Town Hall Square, have coffee at Auntie Brown's, and visit St. Mary's Church and the ruins next to it.

You can get to Sigtuna on your Stockholm Card; take the train to Märsta, then change for the local bus, whose departure is coordinated with the train's arrival; the one-way trip takes about an hour. There's also a boat trip from Stockholm to Sigtuna in summer.

The university city of **Uppsala** is only 22 miles from Sigtuna, so you might want to take an extra day, hop on another bus, and visit it, notably the cathedral and the university grounds. If you do visit, be sure to have coffee and pastry at Ofvandahls Café, at St. Olofsgatan and Syssomansgatan, a local tradition. The trip between Sigtuna and Uppsala is not covered on the Stockholm Card.

ARCHIPELAGO EXPLORATION   Greater Stockholm's beloved archipelago is 150 miles long and made up of 24,000 or so nearby islands (Vaxholm, above, is only one of them), starting just beyond Djurgården. If you want to explore the archipelago in depth, buy the **16-day ferry pass,** called a Batluffarkortet, for 265 Kr ($34.85).

If you don't have 16 days to devote to island-hopping, consider an excursion of one or two days to **Finnhamm** (plenty of natural beauty, tranquillity, and a memorable youth hostel—a three-story house with dormer windows facing the sea—with 13 rooms for two or four people, cottages for four, kitchen facilities, or three meals a day), **Sandhamm** (there's a town here that's popular with the yachting set; you can take the ferry one way and come back by bus), and **Utö,** famous for its bread. For a day's outing in summer, consider the **Feather Islands (Fjaderholmarna),** where there's an aquarium, a pub, a restaurant, a shop that sells smoked fish, and a building filled with handcrafts; locals pack a picnic when they go. The Stockholm Information Service can provide the particulars.

FERRIES TO FINLAND   It's easy to get from Stockholm to Helsinki or Turku in Finland on a budget—or to Åland, the pretty Finnish island between Sweden and Finland that's popular with nature lovers. Ferry traffic is heavy and competition fierce, resulting in reduced rates for travelers. The ferries are modern and most have discos, pools, saunas, and shops. Prices for cabins sleeping four people start at 125 Kr ($14.90) one way to Åland, 160 Kr ($19.05) to Turku, and 300 Kr ($35.70) to Helsinki; travel time is about $6^1/_2$, 12, and 17 hours, respectively. For more information, contact **Silja Line** (☎ **8/22-21-40**), **Viking Lines** (☎ **8/714-56-00**), **Birka Cruises** (☎ **8/714-55-20**), or **Anedin-Linjen** (☎ **8/24-79-85**).

24 | Venice

by Dan Levine

Certainly, the tourists are inescapable. And prices can be double what they are anywhere else in Italy. And, yes, it's not the cleanest city in Europe. But this, after all, is Venice. Visitors flock here for a very good reason—beauty. They come to see the rio Frescada canal flowing slowly past the houses painted subdued shades of red, green, and violet. They come to travel the truly grand Canal Grande as it winds past stately Renaissance palazzi. They come to experience the unparalleled tranquillity of campo Santa Margherita, where only the sound of the fish hawker or children playing football pierces the stillness. And they come to ride the gondolas and *motoscafo* that slowly and skillfully ply the waters of the city. Underneath the bizarre beauty and sometimes-stifling tourism, Venice is a living, breathing city that seems almost too exquisite to be genuine.

Venice was at the crossroads of the Byzantine and Roman worlds for centuries, a fact that lends to its unique heritage of art and architecture. And although traders and thinkers no longer pass through "La Serenissima" as they once did, it's nonetheless at a crossroads: an intersection in time between the Renaissance world that built it and the modern world that keeps it afloat—which includes the budget traveler.

1 Venice Deals & Discounts

BUDGET BESTS   You've probably heard it said a hundred times: The best free sight in Venice is the city itself. And there's something else you can't buy anywhere—the quiet. You'll hear conversations going on in dozens of languages, but never an automobile horn or a failing car muffler. Just the occasional murmur of a *motoscafo* making its way through the narrow side canals of the city.

Venice's many festivals and special events (see "Special Events" under "Pretrip Preparations," later in this chapter) are also budget bests. Most of the revelry is free, and even at the Film Festival and the Biennale there are a number of free and inexpensive screenings and exhibits.

You can always save money on food and drink by consuming them standing up at one of the city's ubiquitous bars. A 3,000-lira ($1.90) panino (sandwich) and a cappuccino at 2,000 lire ($1.25) make a quick and satisfying lunch. Prices double—at least—if you sit down.

What's Special About Venice

The City Itself
- The silence—no sirens, no motorcycles, no diesel exhaust, just children playing, dogs barking, fish merchants hawking, and the like.
- The fact that beneath it all Venice is a living, breathing, proud, even thriving city.
- The canals—need I say more?
- The subdued, weather-beaten pastel colors of the city's houses, every one of which is somewhat askew.

Events & Festivals
- The Carnevale, when Venetians and tourists alike take to the streets in vivid porcelain masks for days of bacchanalian revelry.
- The annual Venice International Film Festival, the next best thing to Cannes—including some free screenings.
- The Biennale: In Italy's museums, art history is exhibited; at this biennial celebration, art history happens.

Sights
- The modern art on display at the Peggy Guggenheim Collection, arguably the finest modern-art museum in Europe.
- The open expanse of piazza San Marco, such a contrast to the rest of this tiny city of narrow, labyrinthine alleys and canals.
- Seeing how precious little has changed in Venice since the 15th-century canvases on display at the Accademia.
- Watching local artisans make the famous hand-painted porcelain Carnival masks (*maschere*).

Cuisine
- Seafood, particularly spaghetti alle vongole.

The Romance
- A moonlight gondola ride—though expensive and exclusively for tourists, it really is wonderfully romantic.

SPECIAL DISCOUNTS   Anyone between 16 and 26 with a pocket-size photo can pick up at the tourist office a free **"Venice for the Young" pass** entitling the holder to various discounts across the city.

2 Pretrip Preparations

WORTH THE EXTRA MONEY   Just about everything in Venice, from accommodations to public transportation to dry cleaning, costs significantly more than in any other Italian city. However, I think this one-of-a-kind city is worth every lira.

REQUIRED DOCUMENTS   See "Pretrip Preparations" in Chapter 21 on Rome.

TIMING YOUR TRIP   May and September are the best months to visit. July and August are hot, though the real crowds come at the height of summer rather than just before or after. Visiting Venice in April or October is hit or miss; it can still be cool and damp but delightfully uncrowded.

Venice can be considerably cheaper from the first of November through mid-March, when many hotels observe the low-season (*bassa stagione*) prices that are about 25% to 40% lower than the regular rates. Of course, this is a double-edged sword: If your hotel were in a cold, wet, flooded city, you'd discount the room rates, too.

Venice's Average Temperature & Rainfall

	Jan	Feb	Mar	Apr	May	June	July	Aug	Sept	Oct	Nov	Dec
Temp. (°F)	43	48	53	60	67	72	77	74	68	60	54	44
Rainfall "	2.3	1.5	2.9	3.0	2.8	2.9	1.5	1.9	2.8	2.6	3.0	2.1

Special Events   During the week and a half before Ash Wednesday, Venetians take to the streets for **Carnevale.** Revelers dance along dressed in centuries-old costumes and hiding behind the colorful porcelain masks you see year round in gift shops all over town. Countless other events fill the calendar for the entire month leading up to Ash Wednesday. Contact the tourist office for full details on the 1996 festivities.

The **Voga Longa** (literally "long row"), a 30km (18-mile) rowing "race" from San Marco to the Lido and back, has been revived recently after centuries of

What Things Cost in Venice	U.S. $
Water taxi (for journey up to seven minutes)	16.70
Public boat (from any point within the city to any other point)	1.50
Local telephone call	.13
Double room at the Gritti Palace (deluxe)	350.55
Double room at the Hotel American (moderate)	135.00
Double room at Albergo Al Gambero (budget)	61.90
Continental breakfast (cappuccino and croissant)	
(at a café/bar)	2.20
(at most hotels)	5.30
Lunch for one at Trattoria alla Madonna (moderate)	17.25
Lunch for one at any café in town (budget)	5.00
Dinner for one, without wine, at Harry's Bar (deluxe)	82.50
Dinner for one, without wine, at Antica Locanda Montin (moderate)	27.55
Dinner for one, without wine, at Snack-Pizzeria Beau Brummel (budget)	5.25
Pint (*grande*) of beer at any café in town	3.25
Glass (*bicchiere*) of wine at any café in town	.75
Coca-Cola (to take out)	1.65
Cup of coffee (cappuccino) at any café in town	1.30
Roll of color film, 36 exposures	6.90
Admission to the Palazzo Ducale	6.25
Movie ticket	6.25
Cheapest theater ticket (at Teatro La Fenice)	18.75

disinterest. It takes place in May; for exact dates in 1996, consult the tourist office. The event itself is colorful, if not much of a race; it's mostly a fine excuse for a party.

Stupendous fireworks fill the night sky and hearty revelry the night air during the **Festa del Redentore,** on the third Saturday night and Sunday in July. The celebration, which marks the July 1578 lifting of a plague that had gripped the city, is centered around the Chiesa del Redentore on the Giudecca. Two pontoon bridges link piazza San Marco with the Giudecca for the occasion, and boats full of revelers fill the Giudecca Canal.

The **Venice International Film Festival,** held in late August and early September, is perhaps the finest summer celebration of celluloid in Europe after Cannes. Films from all over the world are shown in various venues across the city—and often outside in the many *campi.* Ticket prices vary but are usually modest; many outdoor screenings are free.

Venice hosts the latest in modern painting and sculpture from dozens of countries during the **Biennale,** an international modern-art show that fills the pavilions of the gardens at the east end of Castello throughout the summer of every even-numbered year. Many great modern artists have been "discovered" at this world-famous show. Note that the gardens are marked "Esposizione Internazionale d'Art Moderna" on most maps; take vaporetto Line 1 or 4 to the Giardini stop.

The **Regatta Storica,** which takes place on the Grand Canal on the first Sunday in September, is first a seagoing parade, second an excuse for a party, and third a genuine regatta. Just about every seaworthy gondola in Venice, richly decorated for the occasion and piloted by *gondolieri* in colorful period costumes, participates in this maritime cavalcade.

Finally, the ultimate anomaly: Venice's irrepressible civic boosters have arranged for an annual **October Maratona (Marathon),** starting at Villa Pisani on the mainland and ending up along the Zattere for a finish at the Basilica di Santa Maria della Salute on the tip of Dorsoduro.

Other notable events include the **Festa della Salute,** on November 21, and the **Festa della Sensa,** on the Sunday following Ascension Day.

BACKGROUND READING   My favorite is Mary McCarthy's *Venice Observed* (Harcourt Brace Jovanovich). John Ruskin's *The Stones of Venice* (DaCapo) is still the classic volume of art history. And read Luigi Barzini's classic *The Italians* (Macmillan) for a frank, refreshing, and opinionated discussion of the history and culture of Italy, past and present.

3 Venice Specifics

ARRIVING

FROM THE AIRPORT   Flights land at the **Aeroporto Marco Polo,** due north of the city on the mainland (☎ **041/260-61-11**). Of course, the most fashionable and most traditional way to arrive in the city is by sea. The Cooperative San Marco (☎ **041/522-23-03**) keeps that tradition alive, operating a *motoscafo* (shuttle-boat) service between the airport and piazza San Marco for 15,000 lire ($9.40) each way. Call for the daily schedule of 10 or so round-trips, which changes with the season, or drop by the headquarters at San Marco 978 (on calle dei Fabbri). A private water taxi into town will almost cost more than your flight did, about 110,000 lire ($68.75).

The Azienda Trasporti Veneto Orientale (ATVO) bus (☎ **041/520-55-30**) connects the airport with piazzale Roma. Buses leave roughly every hour, cost 5,000 lire ($3.15), and make the trip in about 30 minutes. Local ACTV bus no. 5 (☎ **041/78-01-11**) is cheaper still, at 1,500 lire (95¢) per person. Buses leave from the airport and piazzale Roma every hour at 40 minutes after the hour.

FROM THE TRAIN STATION   Trains from all over Europe arrive at the Stazione Venezia–Santa Lucia (☎ **041/71-55-55**). To get there, all trains must pass through a station marked VENEZIA–MESTRE. Don't be confused: Mestre is a charmless industrial city on the mainland.

At the far right end as you come off the tracks at Santa Lucia is the luggage depot near the head of Track 8. If you're planning to strike out on your own to look for accommodations, leave your heavy gear here. The depot charges 1,500 lire (95¢) per piece per day and is open 24 hours daily. There's an Albergo Diurno (day hotel) at the far right side of the station as you face the tracks; it's open daily from 7am to 8pm and charges 5,500 lire ($3.45) for a shower.

The official city tourist board, **Azienda Autonoma de Soggiorno e Turismo** (☎ **041/71-52-88**), staffs a surly office between the station's large front doors. It's open daily from 8am to 8pm.

The **train information** office (☎ **041/71-55-50**), marked with a lowercase "i," is across from the tourist board office in the station's main hall. It's staffed daily from 8am to 9pm.

Two banks for **currency exchange** keep long hours (usually until 9pm) and compete with each other for business. Compare their rates before exchanging money.

Finally, on exiting the station you'll find the docks for vaporetto Lines 2 and 5 to your left; Line 1 is to your right.

BY CAR   Warning! There are three parking garages in Venice with vastly differing rates. **Garage Comunale,** on piazzale Roma (☎ **041/522-23-08**) is the cheapest, charging 15,000 lire ($9.40) per day for an average-size car. The **Tronchetto Garage,** on a small island adjacent to the Venetian Causeway (☎ **041/520-75-55**), charges 30,000 lire ($18.75) per day. If your hotel is a member of the Venetian Hoteliers Association, it may be able to supply you with a 40% discount voucher for this garage. To reach Venice from the Tronchetto Garage, take public waterbus no. 17 or 82, not the private boats that are famous for cheating tourists. Your last choice for parking would be **Garage San Marco,** on piazzale Roma (☎ **041/523-22-13**); this privately owned lot charges about 50,000 lire ($31.25) per day for an average-size car.

VISITOR INFORMATION

In addition to the tourist office inside the train station (see "Arriving," above), there's a second **tourist office** at San Marco 71, just off calle dell' Ascensione (☎ **041/520-99-55**), in the far left arcade at the opposite end of piazza San Marco from the basilica. The office maintains a remarkably spotty schedule: The staff's best guess, when I last visited, was Monday through Saturday from 8:30am to 3:45pm.

CITY LAYOUT

Keep in mind as you wander seemingly hopelessly among the *fondamenti* and *calli* of Venice that the city was not built to make sense to those on foot but rather to those plying its canals. No matter how good your map and sense of direction, time after time you'll get wonderfully lost.

The Italian Lira

For American Readers   At this writing $1 = approximately 1,600 lire (or 100 lire = 6.25¢), and this was the rate of exchange used to calculate the dollar values given in this chapter (rounded to the nearest nickel).

For British Readers   At this writing £1 = approximately 2,400 lire (or 100 lire = 4.2p), and this was the rate of exchange used to calculate the pound values in the table below.

Note: The rates given here fluctuate from time to time and may not be the same when you travel to Italy. Therefore this table should be used only as a guide:

Lire	U.S.$	U.K.£	Lire	U.S.$	U.K.£
100	.06	.04	20,000	12.50	8.33
250	.16	.10	25,000	15.63	10.42
500	.31	.21	30,000	18.75	12.50
750	.47	.31	35,000	21.88	14.58
1,000	.63	.42	40,000	25.00	16.67
1,500	.94	.63	45,000	28.13	18.75
2,000	1.25	.83	50,000	31.25	20.83
2,500	1.56	1.04	60,000	37.50	25.00
3,000	1.88	1.25	70,000	43.75	29.17
4,000	2.50	1.67	80,000	50.00	33.33
5,000	3.13	2.08	90,000	56.25	37.50
7,500	4.69	3.13	100,000	62.50	41.67
10,000	6.25	4.17	125,000	78.13	52.08
15,000	9.38	6.25	150,000	93.75	62.50

Snaking through the city like an inverted S is the **Canal Grande (Grand Canal),** the wide main artery of aquatic Venice. Scores of short and narrow canals cut through the interior of the two halves of the city, flowing gently by the doorsteps of centuries-old palazzi and endlessly frustrating the landlubbing tourists trying to navigate the city on foot.

Only three bridges (*ponti*) cross the Grand Canal: the **ponte degli Scalzi,** just outside the train station; the elegant white marble **ponte Rialto,** connecting the districts of San Marco and San Polo at the center of town; and the wooden **ponte Accademia,** connecting campo Morosini in San Marco with the Accademia museum across the way in Dorsoduro.

The city is divided into six districts, or *sestieri.* **Cannaregio** stretches from the train station east to the Rialto Bridge. To the east beyond Cannaregio (and skirting piazza San Marco) is the **Castello** quarter. The sestiere of **San Marco** shares this side of the Grand Canal with Castello and Cannaregio, occupying (roughly) the area west of piazza San Marco and the Rialto Bridge. **San Polo** is across the Rialto Bridge, stretching west to just beyond campo dei Frari and campo San Rocco. **Santo Croce** is next, moving north and west, stretching all the way to piazzale Roma. Finally, you'll find **Dorsoduro** on the opposite side of the Accademia Bridge from San Marco. Not confused enough yet? For the record, each sestiere is divided further into an indeterminate number of *parrochie,* or neighborhoods. These indications don't appear on maps and are of little or no use to the navigating tourist.

Within each sestiere, there are no street numbers but simply one continuous string of 6,000 or so house numbers, which wind their way among the canals and calli in a fashion known to no living person. The format for addresses is this chapter is the name of the sestiere followed by the house number within that district (which comprises the building's mailing address), followed by the name of the street on which you'll find that address: for example, San Marco 1471 (on salizzada San Moisé), Venezia.

Venice shares its lagoon with several other islands. Opposite piazza San Marco and Dorsoduro is the **Giudecca,** a tranquil working-class place where you'll find the youth hostel and a handful of hotels, restaurants, and bars. The **Lido di Venezia** is the city's beach; it separates the lagoon from the open sea. **Murano, Burano,** and **Torcello** are popular tourist spots northeast of the city.

Finally, the industrial city of **Mestre,** on the mainland, is the gateway to Venice.

GETTING AROUND

To be a successful tourist in Venice, imagine yourself as a child's miniature battery-operated toy car—when driven into a wall or other obstacle, it instantly turns and continues on its way. Time and again, you'll think you know exactly where you're going, only to wind up at the end of a dead-end street or at the side of a canal with no bridge to get to the other side. Just remind yourself that the city's physical complexity—that is, getting lost—is an integral part of its charm. With its countless stepped footbridges and almost no elevators in any of the buildings, Venice is one of the worst cities in the world for the physically disabled.

The free map offered by the tourist office has good intentions, but it doesn't even show, much less name or index, all the pathways of Venice. For that, pick up the yellow-jacketed map (*pianta de città*) produced by **Studio F.M.B. Bologna,** for 10,000 lire ($6.25) at any newsstand. This map also shows all the vaporetto stops and lines.

BY BOAT   The various areas and islands of the city are linked by a comprehensive *vaporetto* system of about a dozen lines operated by the Azienda del Consorzio Trasporti Veneziano (ACTV) (☎ **041/78-01-11**). Transit maps are available at the tourist office (see above) and at most ACTV stations.

The fare on most boats, including Lines 1 and 52 (those most utilized by tourists) is 2,400 lire ($1.50). Express boats, most notably Line 82, cost 3,500 lire ($2.20). Most lines run daily every 10 to 15 minutes from 7am to midnight, then hourly until morning. Note, however, that not all stations sell tickets after dark; settle up with the conductor on board, or gamble on a 30,000-lira ($18.75) fine.

The 14,000-lira ($8.75) **Biglietto 24 Ore** entitles the bearer to 24 hours of unlimited travel on any ACTV vessel. The **Biglietto 3 Giorni,** covering three full days of unlimited travel, may seem steep at 20,000 lire ($12.50), but single-fare trips can add up quickly. The **Biglietto Isole,** a ticket valid for unlimited one-day travel in one direction on Line 12 (which services the islands of Murano, Mazzorbo, Burano, and Torcello) costs 5,000 lire ($3.15).

Line 1, an *accellerato,* is the most important for the average tourist, making all stops along the Grand Canal and continuing on to the Lido. **Line 82,** a *diretto,* also travels the Grand Canal, though it stops only at piazza San Marco, the Accademia Bridge, the Rialto Bridge, and the train station before circling

Dorsoduro and crossing the lagoon to the Lido. **Line 52,** the *circolare,* is another major line, circling the perimeter of the city and crossing the lagoon to Murano on one side and the Lido on the other. **Line 12** also crosses the waves to Murano, continuing on to Burano and Torcello.

There are just three bridges spanning the Grand Canal. To fill in the gaps, *traghetti* gondolas cross the canal at seven or so intermediate points. You'll find a traghetto station at the end of any street named "calle del Traghetto" on your map (see map recommendation above). The fare, regulated by the local government, is 1,000 lire (65¢).

BY WATER TAXI   *Taxi acquei* (water taxis) prices are high and not for the average tourist. For journeys up to seven minutes, the rate is 27,000 lire ($16.70); 500 lire (30¢) click off for each additional 15 seconds. There's an 8,500-lira ($5.30) supplement for night service (10pm to 7am), and a 9,000-lira ($5.65) surcharge on Sunday and holidays; note that these two supplements cannot be applied simultaneously. If they have to come get you, tack on another 8,000 lire ($5).

There are six **water-taxi stations** serving various key points in the city: the train station (☎ **041/71-62-86**), piazzale Roma (☎ **041/71-69-22**), the Rialto Bridge (☎ **041/523-05-75**), piazza San Marco (☎ **041/522-97-50**), the Lido (☎ **041/526-00-59**), and Marco Polo Airport (☎ **041/541-50-84**). **Radio Taxi** (☎ **041/523-23-26** or 522-23-03) will come pick you up any place in the city, for a surcharge of course.

ON FOOT   Get a map. Then look for the ubiquitous yellow signs that direct travelers toward five major landmarks: Ferrovia (the train station), piazzale Roma, the Rialto Bridge, piazza San Marco, and the Accademia Bridge.

FAST FACTS: Venice

Banks   Banks are normally open Monday through Friday from 8:35am to 1:35pm and 2:45 to 3:45pm or 3 to 4pm (usually the latter); only a few banks and the American Express office (see "Currency Exchange," below) are open on Saturday; those banks that are open on Saturday follow an 8:35 to 11:35am schedule. Both exchange offices at the train station are open seven days a week.

Business Hours   Standard hours for **shops** are 9am to 12:30pm and 3 to 7:30pm Monday through Saturday. In winter shops are closed on Monday morning, while in summer it's usually Saturday afternoon that they're closed; most grocers are closed on Wednesday afternoon throughout the year. In Venice and throughout Italy, just about everything is closed on Sunday. **Restaurants** are required to close at least one day per week, though the particular day varies from one trattoria to another.

Consulates   The Consulate of the **United Kingdom** is at Dorsoduro 1051 (☎ **041/522-72-07**), at the foot of the Accademia Bridge; it's open Monday through Friday from 9am to noon and 2 to 4pm. The United States, Canada, and Australia have consulates in Milan, about three hours away by train. (The U.S. Consulate in Milan is at largo Donegani 1051 [☎ 02/29-03-51], open Monday through Friday from 9am to noon and 2 to 4pm.) Along with New Zealand, they all maintain embassies in Rome (see "Fast Facts: Rome" in Chapter 21).

Currency   The Italian unit of currency is the **lira,** almost always used in the plural form, **lire.** The lowest unit of currency these days is the silver 50-lira coin.

There is also a silver 100-lira piece, a gold 200-lira coin, and a combination silver-and-gold 500-lira coin. Notes come in the following denominations: 1,000, 2,000, 5,000, 10,000, 50,000, 100,000, and 200,000 lire. Occasionally you'll come across a grooved coin with a pictogram of a telephone on it. A remnant of Italy's old pay-phone system, which is gradually being phased out, the telephone *gettone* is worth 200 lire (13¢), the price of a phone call.

Currency Exchange   In addition to the banks mentioned in "From the Train Station" under "Venice Specifics," earlier in this chapter, you can change money at the **American Express** office, San Marco 1471, on salizzada San Moisé (☎ **041/520-08-44**). If you're standing with your back to the Basilica di San Marco, exit the piazza by way of the arcade at the far left end and bear slightly to the right; you'll see a mosaic sign in the pavement pointing the way. The office is open for banking in summer, Monday through Friday from 8am to 8pm and Saturday from 9am to 12:30pm; in winter, Monday through Friday from 9am to 5:30pm and Saturday from 9am to 12:30pm. For all other services, it's open throughout the year Monday through Friday from 9am to 6pm and Saturday from 9am to 1pm.

Dentists/Doctors   For a short list, check with the Consulate of the United Kingdom or the American Express office.

Emergencies   In Venice and throughout Italy, dial **113** to reach the police. Some Italians will recommend that you forgo the police and try the military-trained *Carabinieri* (phone **112**), in the opinion of some a better police force. For an ambulance, phone 523-00-00. To report a fire, dial 520-02-22; on the Lido, 526-02-22.

Holidays   See "Fast Facts: Rome" in Chapter 21. Venice's patron saint, St. Mark, is honored on April 25.

Information   See "Visitor Information" under "Venice Specifics," earlier in this chapter.

Laundry   The self-service laundry most convenient to the train station is the Lavaget at Cannaregio 1269, to the left as you cross the ponte alle Guglie from Lista di Spagna. The Lavanderia a Gettone Gabriella, San Marco 985, on calle Terrà delle Colonne (☎ **041/522-17-58**), is the best place in the piazza San Marco neighborhood. To find it, exit the piazza underneath the clock tower, continue straight along Merceria dell' Orologio, turn left onto Merceria San Zulian, cross a small bridge onto calle Fiubera, then take your first right and then your first left. If you get lost, ask someone to point you toward the Hotel Astoria. Both are open Monday through Friday from 8:30am to 12:30pm and 3 to 7pm; the rate at both locations is about 16,000 lire ($10) for up to 4.5 kilos (10 lb.).

At the Lavanderia a Gettone SS. Apostoli, at Cannaregio 4553a, on salizzada del Pistor, just off campo SS. Apostoli (☎ **041/522-66-50**), you pay 12,000 lire ($7.50) for a load of 4.5 kilos (10 lb.), or 20,000 lire ($12.50) for 8 kilos (17 lb.). This place is open Monday through Friday from 8:30am to 12:30pm and 3 to 7pm. It's (relatively) convenient to the Rialto Bridge area.

Lost & Found   The central Ufficio Oggetti Rinvenuti (☎ **041/78-82-25**) is in the annex to the City Hall (known as the "Municipio" in Italian), at San Marco 4134, on calle Piscopia o Loredan, just off riva del Carbon on the Grand Canal, near the Rialto Bridge (on the same side of the canal as the Rialto vaporetto station). Look for scala (stairway) C; the lost-and-found office is in the "Economato" section on the "Mezzanino" level, one flight up. The office is ostensibly open only on Monday, Wednesday, and Friday from 9:30am to 12:30pm, but there's usually someone available weekdays from 9:30am until the building closes at 1:30pm.

There's also an Ufficio Oggetti Smarriti at the airport (☎ **041/260-64-36**), and an Ufficio Oggetti Rinvenuti at the train station (☎ **041/71-61-22**); it's right at the head of Track 14 and is open Monday through Friday from 8am to 4pm.

Mail   Venice's Posta Centrale is at San Marco 5554, on salizzada Fontego dei Tedeschi (☎ **041/522-06-06**), just off campo San Bartolomeo, near the foot of the Rialto Bridge on the San Marco side of the Grand Canal. This office is usually open Monday through Saturday from 8:15am to 7pm. Stamps are sold at Window 12.

If you're at piazza San Marco and need postal services, walk through sottoportego San Geminian, the center portal at the opposite end of the piazza from the basilica. This post office is open Monday through Friday from 8:15am to 1:30pm and Saturday from 8:15am to 12:10pm.

Remember that you can buy stamps (*francobolli*) at any *tabacchi* with no additional service charge; ask at your hotel about the current postal rates.

Pharmacies   Venice's many drugstores take turns staying open all night. To find out which one is on call tonight in your area, ask at your hotel or dial 523-05-73.

Police   In an emergency, dial 112 or 113. For other business, dial 270-82-03.

Shoe Repair   If your hotel manager doesn't know of one closer, try the shoe repair shop at Dorsoduro 871, on calle Nuova Sant'Agnese, on the main route between the Accademia and the Peggy Guggenheim Collection.

Tax/Tipping   See "Fast Facts: Rome" in Chapter 21.

Telephone   The telephone area code for Venice is 041. See "Fast Facts: Rome" in Chapter 21 for information on using pubic pay phones and international calling.

4 Accommodations

Hotels are more expensive in Venice than in any other city in Italy. Whatever you've been spending in other parts of the country, you can plan on spending about $1^1/_2$ times that amount here. But it's worth it!

In June and September and during special events year round, it can seem that there are no budget lodgings in Venice, especially if you arrive after noon. Arrive as early as you can, for time literally is money. The tourist office in the train station will book rooms for you, but the lines are long and (understandably) the staff's patience is sometimes thin.

Finally, keep in mind that hotels observe a high- and a low-season price schedule. Be sure to ask when you arrive at a hotel whether it in fact has an off-season price. High season in Venice runs from March 16 to October 31, with a lull during July and August. Some hotels close altogether from December to February.

Getting the Best Deal on Accommodations

• If possible, try to stay at a hotel where breakfast is not obligatory.

• Arrive in the city before noon, when it's more likely you'll find a budget room.

• If you're on an especially tight budget, think about spending the night in Padova.

DOUBLES FOR LESS THAN 90,000 LIRE ($56.25)
ON OR NEAR LISTA DI SPAGNE

The Lista di Spagna, immediately to the left as you exit the train station, is full of budget hotels. This area is comparatively charmless, but that's like complaining that your caviar is too cold.

Albergo Adua

Cannaregio 233a (on Lista di Spagna, on the right, about two blocks from the train station), Venezia. ☎ **041/71-61-84.** 12 rms, 4 with bath. 45,000 lire ($28.15) single without bath, 68,000 lire ($42.50) single with bath; 65,000 lire ($40.65) double without bath, 95,000 lire ($59.40) double with bath; 84,000 lire ($52.50) triple without bath, 108,000 lire ($67.50) triple with bath; 96,000 lire ($60) quad without bath, 144,000 lire ($90) quad with bath. Breakfast 8,000 lire ($5) extra. MC, V.

This is a delightful family operation, with an unusually elegant entrance, comfortable rooms (up to five of which may share a bath), and one of the friendliest families in Venice. Patriarch Stefani's son, Luciano, and daughter, Lucia, are bubbly, helpful, and efficient, speaking perfectly adequate English. They've been in business more than 30 years—and have been included in this book nearly that long; although the furnishings are straight out the 1970s, the place hasn't gotten old yet. Breakfast is served in their kitchen or in bed.

Albergo Santa Lucia

Cannaregio 358 (on calle della Misercordia, the second left off Lista di Spagna), Venezia. ☎ **041/71-51-80.** 18 rms, 7 with bath. 57,000 lire ($35.65) single without bath; 69,000 lire ($43.15) double without bath, 109,000 lire ($68.15) double with bath; 126,000 lire ($78.75) triple without bath, 154,500 lire ($96.55) triple with bath. Rates include continental breakfast. MC, V. Closed two weeks in Jan or Feb.

You'll recognize this place by its flower-decorated stone terrace with sun chairs, a place filled with roses, oleander, ivy, and birds chirping—though the rooms themselves are rather plain. Breakfast is served in an old-fashioned way, with coffee and tea brought in sterling-silver pots. Friendly owner Emilia Gonzato Parcianello doesn't speak English, but her son, Gianangelo, does.

Archie's House

Cannaregio 1814 (just off rio San Leonardo 30), Venezia. ☎ **041/72-08-84.** 7 rms, 1 with bath. 50,000 lire ($31.25) double; 25,000 lire ($15.65) per person in shared rooms. Showers 1,500 lire (95¢) extra. Call to check low-season rates (Oct–May), which are usually about 30% off the standard price. Singles not available in summer. No credit cards. From the train station, turn left and walk straight along Lista di Spagna, cross the first bridge (ponte alle Guglie), and continue on rio San Leonardo; you'll find Archie's on your right just past Cannaregio 1745 (on the right) and the Hotel Leonardo (on the left).

This place is an ultra-budget institution: Archie Baghin (an English version of Arcadio) and his Taiwanese wife, Chuen-Lih, offer spartan accommodations that are just about the cheapest in Venice. Though he hails from nearby Vicenza, Archie has lived in 12 countries and has picked up a Ph.D., as well as French, German, English, Greek, and Chinese, among other languages, along the way. In 1977 he settled down here and "for fun" got into the rooming-house business. Archie is full of helpful hints about all the countries he's called home at one time or another, not to mention Venice. No reservations are accepted.

Casa David

Cannaregio 180 (2nd floor) (a few steps in from Lista di Spagna), Venezia. ☎ **041/71-54-46.** 4 rms, none with bath. 33,000 lire ($20.65) single; 55,000 lire ($34.40) double; 76,000 lire ($47.50) triple. No credit cards. From the station, walk about two blocks along Lista di Spagna and turn right down a narrow alley, just past the Hotel Continental at Cannaregio 170; the casa is a few doors ahead on your left.

With only four rooms to rent, compact Casa David really feels like the home it is. In addition to great prices, guests are treated to spacious double rooms as well as big smiles from the proprietors, who speak very little English.

Casa Ottolenghi

Cannaregio 180 (3rd floor) (a few steps in from Lista di Spagna), Venezia. ☎ **041/71-52-06.** 5 rms, none with bath. 62,500 lire ($39.05) double. No credit cards. From the station, walk about two blocks down Lista di Spagna and turn right down a narrow alley, just past the Hotel Continental at Cannaregio 170; the casa is a few doors ahead on your left.

This is just a tiny place, but owner Oscar Bordin's prices are just as small. Breakfast is not available.

Hotel Rossi

Cannaregio 262 (on calle delle Procuratie), Venezia. ☎ **041/71-51-64** or 71-77-84. 20 rms, 8 with bath. TEL. 53,000 lire ($33.15) single without bath, 66,000 lire ($41.25) single with bath; 76,500 lire ($47.80) double without bath, 171,500 lire ($107.20) double with bath; 133,000 lire ($83.15) triple with bath. Rates include continental breakfast. AE, MC, V. Closed early Jan to mid–Feb. From the train station, walk along Lista di Spagna; calle delle Procuratie is the fifth left, just before campo San Geremia.

This pleasant little place offers adequate rooms and a quiet courtyard next door—though not my favorite, it's an acceptable standby in this convenient neighborhood. Steep staircases lead to three floors. In low season you may be able to avoid the mandatory breakfast.

✪ Locanda Bernardi-Semenzato

Cannaregio 4366 (on calle de l'Oca), Venezia. ☎ **041/522-72-57** or 522-24-24. 18 rms, 5 with bath. 42,500 lire ($26.55) single without bath, 52,000 lire ($32.50) single with bath; 67,500 lire ($42.20) double without bath, 96,500 lire ($60.30) double with bath; 113,500 lire ($70.95) triple without bath, 126,000 lire ($78.75) triple with bath. Breakfast 5,500 lire ($3.45) extra. MC, V. Closed Jan–Feb. From the Ca d'Oro vaporetto stop (no. 6), walk straight ahead to Strada Nova, turn right, and look for the sign on your left above Cannaregio 4309, just before you reach campo SS. Apostoli; this will be calle Duca; then walk up and take the first right onto calle de l'Oca.

The rooms at this cozy locanda are plain, with little on the walls, but they're kept clean and homey—and remarkably cheap—by the young English-speaking Pepoli family and their two charming children. Access to the rooftop terrace is included in these ultra-budget rates.

NEAR THE TRAIN STATION

Alloggi da Bepi

Santa Croce 158 (on fondamenta Minotto), Venezia. ☎ **041/522-67-35.** Fax 041/523-27-65. 10 rms, 3 with bath. 55,000 lire ($34.40) single without bath; 82,500 lire ($51.55) double without bath, 104,500 lire ($65.30) double with bath. Rates include continental breakfast. MC, V. From the railway station, cross the Grand Canal on ponte degli Scalzi and turn right onto fondamenta San Simeon Piccolo; turn left before the first footbridge, walk several blocks along the curvy pathway, turn left onto fondamenta Minotto, and the hotel is just ahead, on your left.

Although this small three-story hotel offers few amenities, its quiet location and manageable prices make it particularly recommendable. There's nothing fancy about the basic beds and baths here—they're just clean and comfortable. The hotel's affable owners, Primo and Flora, speak little English but are eager to please.

Locanda Stefania

Santa Croce 181a (on fondamenta Tolentini), Venezia. ☎ **041/520-37-57.** 17 rms, 7 with bath. 42,500 lire ($26.55) single without bath, 51,500 lire ($32.20) single with bath; 69,000 lire ($43.15) double without bath, 91,500 lire ($57.20) double with bath; 109,000 lire ($68.15) triple without bath, 126,000 lire ($78.75) triple with bath. No credit cards. Closed Nov 15–Mar. From the train station, cross ponte degli Scalzi right out front, turn right, and walk along the Grand Canal until you reach the first canal, rio Tolentini; here, turn left along fondamenta Tolentini and, when this canal makes a sharp right at campazzo dei Tolentini, follow the canal and the locanda will be on your left.

From the outside the Stefania looks as though it were frozen in the act of falling down, but once indoors you'll find a refreshing and excellent budget choice run by the Girardi family. It features plain, exceptionally spacious rooms with large windows, in a relatively quiet neighborhood. Ask for one of the three rooms with frescoed ceilings.

NEAR PIAZZA SAN MARCO

This is the highest-rent neighborhood in this high-rent city, with the exception of the handful of places listed below.

✪ Alloggi ai do Mori

San Marco 658 (on calle larga San Marco), Venezia. ☎ **041/520-48-17** or 528-92-93. Fax 041/520-53-28. 12 rms, 3 with bath. 45,500 lire ($28.45) single without bath; 88,000 lire ($55) double without bath, 114,500 lire ($71.55) double with bath; 97,500 lire ($60.95) triple without bath; 120,000 lire ($75) quad without bath. Additional person 34,000–40,000 lire ($21.25–$25) extra; breakfast 3,000 lire ($1.90) extra. MC, V. From the San Marco vaporetto stop (no. 15), head to the piazza, where you should exit underneath the clock tower; turn right at the first opportunity and you'll find the hotel on the left, just before Wendy's.

Antonella, the energetic owner of this small budget wonder, isn't just an incredibly hospitable hotelier, she's a friend who goes out of her way to make Frommer readers feel particularly special. On three floors up unusually steep stairs, the hotel offers rooms that are petite but charming; most have interesting views, and some have beamed ceilings. Although they're smaller than the more accessible lower-floor rooms, accommodations on the top floor are coveted for their basilica views—you can almost reach out and touch San Marco. The hotel is just steps from piazza San Marco and is named for the statue of two Moors that ring the bells atop the nearby clock tower. For reservations, telephone between 9am and 6pm.

✪ Hotel Locanda Remedio

San Marco 4412 (on calle del Remedio), Venezia. ☎ **041/520-62-32.** Fax 041/521-04-85. 14 rms, 11 with bath. TEL. 59,500 lire ($37.20) single without bath, 73,000 lire ($45.65) single with bath; 74,000 lire ($46.25) double without bath, 99,500 lire ($62.20) double with bath. Breakfast 7,700 lire ($4.80) extra. No credit cards. Exit piazza San Marco under the clock, turn right onto calle larga San Marco, left on calle dell'Angelo, and right onto calle del Remedio; the hotel will be on your right.

In Venice, where there are so many hotels, it's a pleasure to discover one that's truly special. The Remedio is just such a place, offering huge rooms in an ancient palace just minutes from piazza San Marco. Not all accommodations are created equal here, however. Make sure you get one of the grand rooms on the main floor. Room 27 has a fantastic ceiling fresco, and like others on the same floor it features oversize hand-carved beds and bureaus.

Locanda Casa Petrarca

San Marco 4386 (on calle Schiavone), Venezia. ☎ **041/520-04-30.** 6 rms, 3 with bath. 45,500 lire ($28.45) single without bath; 89,000 lire ($55.65) double without bath, 114,500 lire ($71.55) double with bath; 104,500 lire ($65.30) triple without bath, 132,000 lire ($82.50) triple with bath. Breakfast 9,000 lire ($5.65) extra. No credit cards. See the text below for directions to the locanda.

Nellie must be one of the kindest and most delightful women in Italy. Always smiling and happy, she could bring sunshine to the Bridge of Sighs. She patiently dispenses advice in English more refined than that of most of her guests. What's the catch? She has just six rooms, including one tiny single, and could never accommodate even a fraction of those who want to be her guests. A real one-of-a-kind place, tucked away at canal side on a dead-end calle, Nellie's nest is hard to find—but patience, like her warmth, is a virtue.

From campo San Luca, near the Rialto Bridge (vaporetto: Rialto), walk away from the Grand Canal on calle dei Fuseri (look for the Tarantola Bookstore on the corner), take the second left onto calle Ungheria, then go right onto calle Schiavone; no. 4386 is on the left. Be careful at night, as two budget travelers somehow missed her door and walked right into the canal at the end of the calle. Having trouble finding campo San Luca? As you step off the vaporetto at Rialto, turn right, walk along the Grand Canal, and turn left onto calle del Carbon (just after San Marco 4176), which runs right into campo San Luca.

Locanda Silva

Castello 4423 (on fondamenta del Remedio), Venezia. ☎ **041/522-76-43.** 25 rms, 7 with bath. 51,500 lire ($32.20) single without bath; 86,000 lire ($53.75) double without bath, 109,000 lire ($68.15) double with bath; 126,000 lire ($78.75) triple without bath, 171,500 lire ($107.20) triple with bath. Rates include continental breakfast. No credit cards. Closed Dec–Jan. Exit piazza San Marco on calle dell' Anzolo, take the second right, and cross the canal (you'll be on calle del Remedio at this point); turn left onto fondamenta del Remedio when this street ends.

I've seen better but I've also seen worse. This spacious place, on a peaceful canal not far from piazza San Marco, is kept clean and comfortable—and modestly priced—by Signor Ettore and his daughter, Sandra.

⑤ Pensione Casa Verardo

Castello 4765 (at the foot of ponte Storto), Venezia. ☎ **041/528-61-27.** Fax 041/523-27-65. 12 rms, 8 with shower only, 2 with bath. 49,500 lire ($30.95) single without bath; 71,500 lire ($44.70) double without bath, 82,500 lire ($51.55) double with shower only, 93,500 lire ($58.45) double with bath; 121,000 lire ($75.65) triple with shower only, 132,000 lire ($82.50) triple with bath; 40,000 lire ($25) per person quad or quint with bath. Breakfast 7,500 lire ($4.70) extra. MC, V. Take the Line 1 or 82 vaporetto to San Zaccaria; walk up calle delle Rasse to campo SS. Filippo e Giacomo; exit the campo on calle Rimpeto la Sacristia, which begins at Bar Europa, and the door to the pensione will be right there once you cross ponte Storto, the first bridge.

You know you'll be staying in a friendly family's home the moment you step through the door of this centrally located and exceptionally reasonably priced pensione. Copies of famous Renaissance masterpieces decorate the walls of the oversize rooms, which are charmingly cluttered with huge antiques. Though it's just a short walk from piazza San Marco, the Verardo is on a quiet canal and is one of the few places where you can step outside and not see anyone selling anything. See the cover of this book for the view from the pensione's rooftop.

NEAR THE ACCADEMIA

Antica Locanda Montin

Dorsoduro 1147 (on fondamenta di Borgo), 31000 Venezia. ☎ **041/522-71-51.** Fax 041/ 522-33-07. 7 rms, none with bath. 45,500 lire ($28.45) single; 80,000 lire ($50) double; 91,000 lire ($56.90) triple. Breakfast 5,500 lire ($3.45) extra. AE, DC, MC, V. Closed Jan or Feb. See the text below for directions to this locanda.

Operated by the Carretin family for almost 50 years, the Montin boasts a uniquely offbeat interior that warrants high marks from its trendy, budget-conscious clientele. The rooms, which enjoy views of a quiet canal or an interior courtyard, are furnished with oversize wooden beds and a clutter of art. The hotel closes at 1am.

The Montin is about equidistant from the Zattere vaporetto stop (Line 52 or 82) on the Giudecca Canal, and the Ca' Rezzonico stop (Line 1) on the Grand Canal. From the former, turn left along the Zattere and take the first right onto calle Trevisan, which becomes fondamenta di Borgo after the first bridge. From Ca' Rezzonico, walk straight ahead on calle del Traghetto and take the third left after you pass campo San Barnabà; this is calle delle Turchette, which, after the first bridge, becomes fondamenta di Borgo.

Hotel Galleria

Dorsoduro 878a (at the foot of the Accademia Bridge), Venezia. ☎ **041/520-41-72** or 528-58-14. 10 rms, 6 with bath. 65,000 lire ($40.65) single without bath; 90,000 lire ($56.25) double without bath, 120,000 lire ($75) double with bath; 155,000 lire ($96.90) triple with bath; 185,000 lire ($115.65) quad with bath. Rates include continental breakfast. No credit cards. Cross the Accademia Bridge from San Marco or step off the vaporetto (Line 1 or 82) at the Accademia stop and you'll see the Galleria to the left of the museum.

Spending the night here is like staying at the Ca' d'Oro. Step through the great green doors, with brass gargoyle doorknobs, and saunter up the marble staircase to the reception area, complete with red velvet wallpaper and designer carpets. From there you'll be led to the modern rooms, where you'll rest under enormous down comforters, beneath what must be the only carved ceilings in a hotel in Italy. Six rooms overlook the Grand Canal; this is perhaps the only place remotely in this price range with Grand Canal views.

IN SAN POLO

⑤ Locanda Ca' Foscari

Dorsoduro 3887 (on calle Marconi, at the foot of Crosera), Venezia. ☎ **041/522-58-17.** 12 rms, 2 with shower only, 1 with bath. 45,500 lire ($28.45) single; 69,000 lire ($43.15) double; 109,000 lire ($68.15) triple; 126,000 lire ($78.75) quad. Rates are with or without shower or bath. Breakfast 7,000 lire ($4.40) extra. No credit cards. Closed two months between Nov and Feb. From the train station, take vaporetto Line 1 or 82 to San Tomà from the wharf, walk up to calle Campaniel and turn left; once across the first canal, turn immediately right onto fondamenta Frescada, then left onto calle Marconi.

Though one of the most modestly priced hotels in Venice, this family-run locanda is remarkably bright and spacious, with big windows in most rooms, soothing pink and lavender ceilings, and even textured wallpaper and a roof garden—all the details that make a difference for the traveler on a shoestring budget. A fine choice, especially for groups of three of four.

IN THE EASTERN END OF CASTELLO

✪ Locanda Sant' Anna

Castello 269 (on corte dei Bianco), Venezia. ☎ **041/520-42-03** or 528-64-66. 8 rms, 3 with shower only, 3 with bath. 45,500 lire ($28.45) single without bath; 62,500 lire ($39.05) double without bath, 80,500 lire ($50.30) double with shower only, 97,500 lire ($60.95) double with bath; 126,000 lire ($78.75) triple with shower only, 143,000 lire ($89.40) triple with bath. Breakfast 6,500 lire ($4.05) extra. No credit cards. Closed mid–Jan to mid–Feb. See the text below for directions to this locanda.

Though one of the most remote hostelries I've listed, the Sant' Anna is one of my top choices. In a peaceful location far from the major tourist traffic, this ultramodern, elegant locanda is ideal for families or any others who want to come home in the evening and simply relax. The place has a newer, almost institutional feel, but many of the good-size rooms feature large windows overlooking a wide canal. The sitting room, a veritable jungle of plants kept in perfect health by the ever-attentive Vianello family, is especially nice, with Murano chandeliers.

From the Giardini vaporetto stop (no. 18) on Line 1, 52, or 82, walk through the park ahead of you and slightly to your left (it's called viale Garibaldi on your map). Turn right when this tree-lined boulevard ends, walk along the right side of rio de Sant' Anna canal, at which point you'll be walking along fondamenta de Sant' Anna. Go left over the second bridge, walk straight ahead, and take the second right onto corte di Bianco.

DOUBLES FOR LESS THAN 110,000 LIRE ($68.75)
ON OR NEAR LISTA DI SPAGNA

Exit the train station and turn left for this wide boulevard, which begins just past ponte degli Scalzi.

Hotel Dolomiti

Cannaregio 73 (on calle Priuli), Venezia. ☎ **041/71-51-13** or 71-66-35. Fax 041/71-66-35. 50 rms, 20 with bath. TEL. 57,000 lire ($35.65) single without bath, 103,000 lire ($64.40) single with bath; 86,000 lire ($53.75) twin without bath, 126,000 lire ($78.75) twin with bath; 103,000 lire ($64.40) double without bath, 160,000 lire ($100) double with bath; 126,000 lire ($78.75) triple without bath, 183,000 lire ($114.40) triple with bath. Breakfast 11,000 lire ($6.90) extra. No credit cards. Closed Nov 15–Feb. Take the first left off Lista di Spagna onto calle Priuli.

An unremarkable exterior gives way to large, clean, but ordinary rooms at this lodging house just a few steps from the train station. Unfortunately, there's no elevator in this four-story hotel. Sergio, the manager, speaks good English.

Hotel Guerrini

Cannaregio 265 (on calle delle Procuratie), Venezia. ☎ **041/71-51-14**. 32 rms, 23 with bath. 69,000 lire ($43.15) single without bath, 103,000 lire ($64.40) single with bath; 91,000 lire ($56.90) double without bath, 137,500 lire ($85.95) double with bath; 171,500 lire ($107.20) triple with bath; 195,000 lire ($121.90) quad with bath. Breakfast 13,000 lire ($8.15) extra in season, 6,000 lire ($3.75) during winter. No credit cards. Closed mid-Jan to mid-Mar. Take the fourth left off Lista di Spagna onto calle delle Procuratie.

The Guerrini has been in the Mazzo family for over half a century, a fact reflected in the efficient professionalism and helpfulness of their English-speaking staff. Their place is clean, if a bit sterile, with uninspiring yellow walls and a few objets d'art thrown in. If only they could put as much effort and elegance into their rooms as they have into their marble-tiled, chandelier-bedecked lobby. Ask for a room in the main building, as opposed to the more mundane annex across the street.

Hotel Leonardo

Cannaregio 1385 (on calle della Masena), Venezia. ☎ **041/71-86-66.** 16 rms, 8 with bath. TEL. 69,000 lire ($43.15) single without bath, 91,500 lire ($57.20) single with bath; 103,000 lire ($64.40) double without bath, 148,500 lire ($92.80) double with bath; 148,500 lire ($92.80) triple without bath, 194,500 lire ($121.55) triple with bath. Rates include continental breakfast. Showers (for those in rooms without bath) 3,000 lire ($1.90) extra. MC, V. Closed Jan. From the train station, walk along Lista di Spagna and cross the first bridge, ponte alle Guglie; continue straight on rio Terrà San Leonardo and calle della Nasena will be the sixth left after the bridge (look for the sign on the left above Cannaregio 1382, just before campiello Anconetta).

There's an air of faded elegance (read: time for a renovation) about this homey place, operated by Maria Teresa Gonzato, the sister of the woman who owns the Albergo Santa Lucia (above). Nonetheless, the place is clean and tastefully decorated, and all the furniture and headboards are either upholstered or carved.

NEAR PIAZZA SAN MARCO

Albergo al Gambero

San Marco 4687 (on calle dei Fabbri), Venezia. ☎ **041/522-43-84** or 520-14-20. Fax 041/520-04-31. 30 rms, 1 with shower only, 3 with bath. 60,500 lire ($37.80) single without bath; 99,000 lire ($61.90) double without bath, 110,000 lire ($68.75) double with shower only, 126,500 lire ($79.05) double with bath; 132,000 lire ($82.50) triple without bath, 148,500 lire ($92.80) triple with shower only, 170,500 lire ($106.55) triple with bath; 165,000 lire ($103.15) quad without bath, 187,000 lire ($116.90) quad with shower only, 214,500 lire ($134.05) quad with bath. These prices are for Frommer readers only. Rates include continental breakfast. No credit cards. From the Rialto Bridge vaporetto stop, turn right along the canal, cross the small footbridge, then turn left onto calle dei Fabbri; the hotel is about five blocks ahead, on your right.

One of Venice's newest budget hotels occupies an enviable location midway between piazza San Marco and the Rialto Bridge. The Gambero's smallish, basically furnished rooms are par for the course, though guests in any of the canalside rooms will enjoy the serenades of the passing gondoliers. High ceilings make rooms on the first two floors preferable.

Hotel Atlantico

Castello 4416 (on calle del Remedio), Venezia. ☎ **041/520-92-44.** Fax 041/520-93-71. 36 rms, 26 with bath. TEL. 83,000 lire ($51.90) single without bath, 98,000 lire ($61.25) single with bath; 110,000 lire ($68.75) double without bath, 180,000 lire ($112.50) double with bath; 143,000 lire ($89.40) triple without bath, 230,000 lire ($143.75) triple with bath. Rates include continental breakfast. No credit cards. See the text below for directions to this hotel.

Laura Innocenti's spacious rooms are complemented by pretty common areas, modern baths, and old-world charm. Some top-floor rooms have a view of the nearby Bridge of Sighs.

Though the Atlantico is about five minutes from piazza San Marco, it's very quiet for the area. From piazza San Marco, head out calle larga San Marco, which is the first right as you exit the piazza under the clock tower; go left at calle va al ponte de l'Anzolo (the last calle before calle larga San Marco goes over a small bridge—you'll find the Ristorante all'Angelo on the corner), and the first right will be ramo dell' Anzolo, which becomes calle del Remedio once you cross the first bridge.

⑤ Hotel Riva

San Marco 5310 (on ponte dell'Angelo), Venezia. ☎ **041/522-70-34.** 19 rms, 17 with bath. 90,000 lire ($56.25) single with bath; 95,000 lire ($59.40) double without bath, 120,000 lire

($75) double with bath. Rates include breakfast. No credit cards. See the text below for directions to this hotel.

Completely renovated from head to toe, this fantastic budget bargain, fronting a quiet canal close to piazza San Marco, is one of the best-value finds in the city. All three floors of rooms have been gutted and redone, complete with new windows and reinforced walls that make each accommodation feel both bright and wonderfully private. The top-floor rooms have original wood-beamed ceilings.

To reach the hotel from piazza San Marco, head out calle larga San Marco, which is the first right as you exit the piazza under the clock tower; go left at calle va al ponte de l'Anzolo (the last calle before calle larga San Marco goes over a small bridge—you'll find the Ristorante all'Angelo on the corner), and follow the street straight, over two bridges to the hotel.

NEAR THE ACCADEMIA

Pensione alla Salute (Da Cici)

Dorsoduro 222 (on fondamenta Ca' Balà), Venezia. ☎ **041/523-54-04** or 522-22-71. Fax 041/522-22-71. 58 rms, about 30 with shower only or bath. TEL. 68,500 lire ($42.80) single without bath, 97,000 lire ($60.65) single with shower only; 97,500 lire ($60.95) double without bath, 148,500 lire ($92.80) double with bath; 137,500 lire ($85.95) triple without bath, 183,000 lire ($114.40) triple with bath. Rates include continental breakfast. No credit cards. Take vaporetto Line 1 to the Santa Maria della Salute stop (no. 14); walk straight ahead to the first bridge on your right, cross it, and walk as straight ahead as you can to the next canal, where you'll turn left (before crossing the bridge) onto fondamenta Ca' Balà.

The elegant lobby, lovely terrace garden, and cozy cocktail bar of this exceptionally large hotel give way to 58 excellent rooms, most with high ceilings and huge windows. The Salute is in a quiet residential neighborhood, near the Guggenheim Collection, that sees few tourists. Breakfast is served outdoors in summer. This is the medium-priced place to try when you arrive in the late afternoon and every place else is *completo* (full).

SUPER-BUDGET CHOICES

Foresteria della Chiesa Valdese

Castello 5170 (at the end of calle lunga Santa Maria Formosa), Venezia. ☎ **041/528-67-97.** 43 beds, no rms with bath; 2 apts. 34,000 lire ($21.25) per person double or triple; 23,000 lire ($14.40) dorm bed; 137,500 lire ($85.40) four-bed apt with bath and kitchen (four- to seven-night minimum). The 8,000-lira ($5) breakfast is often mandatory. No credit cards. Walk to the end of calle lunga Santa Maria Formosa; the calle begins at the Bar all' Orologio on campo Santa Maria Formosa, which is just about equidistant from piazza San Marco and the Rialto Bridge.

Those lucky enough to find a place at this elegant 16th-century palazzo will find wonderfully charming accommodations at almost impossibly low prices. Each room in this old-world hideaway opens onto a balcony overlooking a quiet canal. The frescoes that grace the high ceilings in the doubles and two of the dorms are by the same artist who decorated the Correr. The four-room apartments, complete with kitchen facilities, are the best budget choice in town for traveling families. The reception is open from 9am to 1pm and 6 to 8pm only.

HOSTELS & DORMITORIES

Foresteria Domus Cavanis

Dorsoduro 912a (on rio Antonio Foscarini), Venezia. ☎ **041/528-73-74.** 90 beds in 45 rms, none with bath. 51,500 lire ($32.20) single; 82,500 lire ($51.55) double; 126,000 lire

($78.75) triple; 171,500 lire ($107.20) quad. Rates include continental breakfast. Full board also available. No credit cards. Closed Oct–May. From the Accademia stop on vaporetto Line 1 or 82, walk to the left around the museum, then walk straight ahead on rio Antonio Foscarini; the Domus Cavanis will be halfway down on your right.

While the rooms in this converted dormitory—open to tourists June through September only—are rather plain, the beds are narrow, and the place is popular with groups, Padre Ferdinando Fietta runs a tip-top place with extraordinary rates. The institutional-looking building surrounds a concrete playground.

Ostello Venezia

Giudecca 86 (on fondamenta Zitelle), Venezia. ☎ and fax **041/523-82-11.** 300 beds. 21,000 lire ($13.15) per person. Youth hostel card available on premises for 30,000 lire ($18.75) or you can buy a hostel card on an installment basis for 5,000 lire ($3.15) per night for six nights. Rates include continental breakfast, sheets, and showers. No credit cards. Take vaporetto Line 82 from the docks to the right as you exit the train station to the Zitelle stop, at the eastern end of the Giudecca, and turn right as you step off the boat.

Modern and efficiently run by Claudio Camillo, this is Venice's largest dormitory. What's more, the view of the tip of Dorsoduro and piazza San Marco in the distance is positively awesome. The three-night maximum stay is usually enforced only in summer. Arrive by midafternoon to guarantee yourself a bed in summer. From July to September registration opens at noon; the remainder of the year the check-in starts at 5pm. The rooms are closed until 5pm all year, and curfew is 1pm. This youth hostel is open to budget travelers of all ages. Remember to add the 4,800-lira ($3) round-trip cost of the vaporetto to the net cost of staying at this hostel. The ample dinner, at 13,000 lire ($8.15) for three courses and fruit, is one of the best food values in town. Mealtimes are usually 6 to 9pm.

FOR WOMEN ONLY

Casa delle Studente Domus Civica

San Polo 3082 (at the corner of calle Chiovere and calle Campazzo), Venezia. ☎ **041/72-11-03.** 95 beds, no rms with bath. 34,000 lire ($21.25) single; 62,500 lire ($39.05) double. No credit cards. Open June–July and Sept (not Aug). See the text below for directions to this casa.

This is an unremarkable institutional place for women only, open just June, July, and September (not August); the rest of the year it's a dormitory for students at the local university. Don't plan on any carousing, as they enforce an 11pm curfew. All rooms are singles and doubles, and breakfast is not available.

From the train station, cross ponte degli Scalzi right out front, turn right, and walk along the Grand Canal until you reach the first canal, rio Tolentini. Here, turn left along fondamenta Tolentini; when this canal makes a sharp right at campazzo dei Tolentini, turn left onto corte dei Amai, which will lead you right to the corner of calle Chiovere and calle Campazzo, just after you cross the rio delle Meneghette canal.

WORTH THE EXTRA MONEY

Venice will cost you more across the board than you're accustomed to paying elsewhere in Italy. Here are my splurge recommendations in this city of splurge:

Hotel American

Dorsoduro 628 (on rio de San Vio), Venezia. ☎ **041/520-47-33.** Fax 041/520-40-48. 29 rms, all with bath. A/C MINIBAR TV TEL. 100,000–180,000 lire ($62.50–$112.50) single; 150,000–270,000 lire ($93.75–$168.75) double. Rates include continental breakfast. Additional person 30,000–50,000 lire ($18.75–$31.25) extra. AE, MC, V. From the Accademia vaporetto stop, turn left along the Grand Canal, pass the Accademia Bridge, then turn right onto rio Terrà Foscarini; turn left, go down the first passageway, cross the small footbridge, then turn right onto rio di San Vio and the hotel is on your left.

Despite its decidedly unromantic name, the Hotel American is my top splurge recommendation for both style and substance. The perfect combination of charm and utility, this three-story hotel is liberally dressed with lovely Oriental carpets, polished woods, flowery country-style wallcoverings, and plenty of original art. The best choices here are the larger corner rooms and the nine overlooking a quiet canal; some even have small terraces. Every room is outfitted with traditional Venetian-style furnishings that usually include carved headboards and Murano glass chandeliers.

Locanda Sturion

San Polo 679 (on calle del Sturion), Venezia. ☎ **041/523-62-43.** Fax 041/522-83-78. 11 rms, all with bath. A/C TV TEL. Summer, 110,000 lire ($68.75) single; 180,000 lire ($112.50) double. Winter, 80,000 lire ($50) single; 100,000 lire ($62.50) double. These rates reflect discounts for bearers of this book. Rates include continental breakfast. Additional bed 50,000 lire ($31.25) extra. AE, V. From the Rialto vaporetto stop, cross the bridge, turn left at the other side, and walk along the water; calle del Sturion will be the fifth street on the right, just before San Polo 740.

Though there's been a pensione on this site since 1290, a 1992 gutting and rebuilding has made the Sturion into a contemporary moderately priced hotel. Owned and operated by Sandro Rossi, his Scottish wife, Helen, and their daughter, Nicolette, the hotel is perched four flights (and 69 tiring steps) above the Grand Canal—one of the only reasonably priced places in Venice where you can savor a view of the city's bustling central waterway and your morning cappuccino at the same time. Unfortunately, only two rooms offer water views; the rest have a charming lookout over the Rialto rooftops.

5 Dining

Venice does not lack for restaurants, many of which specialize in Adriatic seafood. *Spaghetti alle vongole* (in clam sauce) is a local staple, as is *seppie nere con polenta*—stewed cuttlefish served in its own black ink over polenta, a thick porridge made from corn flour. *Spaghetti bigoli in salsa* (in anchovy-and-onion sauce) is harder to find but equally distinctive. Needless to say, fresh grilled fish (*pesce alla griglia*) is always available. Finally, there's the ubiquitous *frittura mista*, a mixture of fried seafood. Other, more earthly dishes include *risi e bisi* (rice with peas), *pasta fagioli* (bean-and-pasta soup), and every youngster's favorite, *fegato alla veneziana* (liver and onions).

Eating cheaply in Venice is not easy. Pizza is by no means a local specialty, but it nonetheless represents about the only way to save money. Standing up at a café or *rosticceria* is uniformly less expensive than sitting down, if not very comfortable.

Note: Keep in mind that the listings below show prices for pasta and meat courses only. Don't forget to add in charges for bread and cover, service, and vegetable side dishes when calculating what you can actually expect to pay.

MEALS FOR LESS THAN 16,000 LIRE ($10)
ON OR NEAR LISTA DI SPAGNA

This is the most heavily touristed area of town, and you're not likely to get much in the way of authentic Venetian cuisine; however, the restaurants along this stretch are cheap and convenient to the many hotels recommended in the neighborhood.

Getting the Best Deal on Dining

- Standing up at a café or rosticceria is uniformly less expensive than sitting down.
- Pizza may not be a *local* specialty, but it's certainly a way to save to money.

Snack-Pizzeria Beau Brummel

Cannaregio 160a (on Lista di Spagna). ☎ **041/71-57-07.** Pizza-and-beer or spaghetti-and-wine fixed-price meal 9,500 lire ($5.95); *menu turistico* 15,000, or 21,000 lire ($9.40 or $13.15); pizza and pasta courses 7,500–10,000 lire ($4.70–$6.25); meat courses 11,000–17,500 lire ($6.90–$10.95). No cover charge. AE, DC, MC, V. Thurs–Tues 9am–10pm. ITALIAN.

While throughout most of Venice and Italy you'll be frowned on and still charged a dollar or more for *coperto* if you order just one course and a drink, at this tourist spot doing so is encouraged. You can choose from pizza and a beer or spaghetti and a glass of vine, both at 9,500 lire ($5.95), with no added charges. Beau Brummel's atmosphere is slightly less tacky and more Italian than its neighbor and competition next door, Gino's.

Trattoria Spaccanapoli

Cannaregio 1518 (on rio Terrà San Leonardo). ☎ **041/71-61-70.** *Menu turistico* 12,000–31,000 lire ($7.50–$19.40). Minimum 15,000 lire ($9.40) per person. MC, V. Wed–Mon noon–2:30pm and 5–10pm. Closed Jan–Feb. Walk to the end of Lista di Spagna; you'll find it on the right side of the road at the far foot of ponte alle Guglie, the bridge that crosses Canale di Cannaregio. ITALIAN.

With outdoor tables and a dark, romantic interior, this place is a cut above some of its more touristy neighbors along this strip leading from the station. Nonetheless, it caters to every traveler's whim and budget with countless fixed-price meals. Indeed, it's functionally impossible to order à la carte, since every combination you could come up with is covered by one of the all-inclusive specials; there are a dozen fixed-price options from 13,000 to 14,000 lire ($8.15 to $8.75) alone. Exceptionally pleasant and authentic.

NEAR PIAZZA SAN MARCO

✪ Pizzeria al Vecio Canton

Castello 4738a (at the corner of Ruga Giuffa, calle Ruta, and calle della Corona, off campo Santa Maria Formosa). ☎ **041/528-51-76.** Pizza 6,000–10,500 lire ($3.75–$6.55); pasta courses 7,000–9,500 lire ($4.40–$5.95); meat courses 10,500–18,000 lire ($6.55–$11.25). AE, CB, DC. Tues–Wed 7–10:30pm, Thurs–Mon noon–2:30pm and 7–10:30pm. Closed Aug and for one to two weeks at Christmas. From campo SS. Filippo e Giacomo, exit on salizzada San Provolo, cross the bridge and take the first left, then go left again over the next bridge onto corte Rotta. ITALIAN.

Good pizza is hard to find in Venice, and I mean that in the literal sense. Tucked away at the corner of two tiny streets, this may be one of the best-hidden *pizzerie* in Italy, but its charming atmosphere and tasty fixings are worth the time you'll spend looking for the place. Inside is both intimate and friendly, with just 10 tables surrounded by wooden chairs and a service staff that speaks decent English.

Vino, Vino

San Marco 2007 (on ponte delle Veste). ☎ **041/523-70-27.** Main courses 4,000–7,500 lire ($2.50–$4.70). No credit cards. Wed–Mon 10am–1am. With your back to the Basilica di

San Marco, exit the piazza through the arcade on the far left side; pass the American Express office, cross over the canal, turn right onto calle Veste, and Vino Vino is just ahead on your left. ITALIAN.

As its name suggests, Vino Vino is a restaurant masquerading as a wine bar. In addition to dozens of varietals, sold by the bottle or glass, half a dozen Venetian specialties are always available, usually displayed under glass so you can see what you're ordering. After placing your order, settle into one of about a dozen wooden tables squeezed into two simple storefront-style rooms. The high quality of the food is consistent enough to keep the restaurant popular with locals all day.

NEAR CAMPO DEI FRARI

✪ Ristorante al Giardinetto

San Polo 2909 (on calle del Cristo, just off fondamenta della Dona Onesta). ☎ **041/522-41-00** or 522-28-82. *Menu turistico* 21,000 lire ($13.15); pizza and pasta courses 6,000–11,500 lire ($3.75–$7.20); meat courses 10,000–19,000 lire ($6.25–$11.90). AE, MC, V. Tues–Sun noon–2pm and 7–10pm. Closed Dec 20–Jan. See the text below for directions to this ristorante. ITALIAN.

It's hard to resist the budget-priced pizza here, served outside under a charming grape arbor just steps from a quiet canal. But the fish is outstanding as well—owner Livio picks up fresh seafood at the nearby campo della Pescaria each morning. You may never want to leave.

To find it, take vaporetto Line 1 or 82 to San Tomà, walk straight ahead along calle del Traghetto, turn left at the end of this short calle and then take the first right (before you go over the bridge) onto fondamenta del Forner, which becomes fondamenta della Dona Onesta.

NEAR THE RIALTO BRIDGE

Antica Trattoria da Marco

San Polo 900 (on campiello del Sansoni). ☎ **041/522-65-65.** Pizza 7,000–11,500 lire ($4.40–$7.20), most priced at 8,500–10,500 lire ($5.30–$6.55). No credit cards. Tues–Sun noon–2:30pm and 7–10pm. From the foot of the Rialto Bridge on the San Polo side of the Grand Canal, turn left and walk along the Grand Canal for five blocks, turn right onto calle del Paradiso, and walk ahead for about four blocks to campiello del Sansone. ITALIAN.

The old-fashioned feel of this cozy place is complemented by the soothing jazz and rhythm and blues that's played continuously. The pizza is so good that at the end of the restaurant's first year in business the owner dropped everything else from the menu.

✪ Rosticceria San Bartolomeo

San Marco 5423 (on calle della Bissa). ☎ **041/522-35-69.** *Menu turistico* 10,500, 13,500, or 18,500 lire ($6.55, $8.45, or $11.55) in the ground-floor dining room, and 21,000 or 30,000 lire ($13.15 or $18.75) upstairs; pasta courses 6,000–7,000 lire ($3.75–$4.40) in the ground-floor dining room, about 20% more upstairs; meat and fish courses 10,500–13,500 lire ($6.55–$8.45) in the ground-floor dining room, about 20% more upstairs. No cover charge downstairs. MC, V. Summer, Tues–Sun 9am–2:30pm and 4:30–9:30pm; winter, Tues–Sun 9am–2:30pm and 4:30–8:40pm. Closed two weeks in Jan. See the text below for directions to this rosticceria. ITALIAN.

With 17 pasta dishes, 12 meat courses, and about that many seafood dishes, this place can satisfy any combination of culinary desires. What's more, since all the food is displayed under the long glass counter, you don't have to worry about any mistranslating—you'll know exactly what you're ordering. There's no *coperto* if you take your meal standing up (or sitting on stools) in the aroma-filled ground-floor eating hall, and as in any stand-up place, there's no implicit or explicit requirements that you take more than one course. For those who prefer to linger, head to the dining hall upstairs, though you can do much better than this institutional setting. This appears to be the most popular *rosticceria* in Venice—and for good reason.

From campo San Bartolomeo, at the foot of the Rialto Bridge on the San Marco side of the Grand Canal, take the underpass to your left (if the bridge is at your back) marked SOTTOPORTEGO DELLA BISSA; you'll come across the rosticceria at the first corner. Note that while this place still calls itself the "San Bartolomeo" on its menus and business cards, the sign above the entrance reads GISLON.

Cantina do Mori

San Polo 429 (on via do Mori). ☎ **041/522-54-01.** 1,500–2,000 lire (95¢–$1.25). No credit cards. Fri–Wed 11am–2pm and 4:30–8:30pm. Cross the Rialto Bridge, walk to the end of the market stalls, turn left, then immediately right, and look for the small wooden sign hanging on the left side of the street. SANDWICHES.

Pizza is the fuel of Naples and crostini (open-face sandwiches) the soul food of Florence. In Venice it's *tramezzini*—small white-bread sandwiches filled with thinly sliced meats, cheeses, and vegetables. They are traditionally washed down with a small glass of wine, called an *umbra* (shadow) when taken late in the afternoon.

Hidden on a tiny backstreet two blocks from the Rialto Bridge, Cantina do Mori is a rustic stand-up popular with local fishermen and construction workers. It's well known among locals for serving the absolute best sandwiches made with home-prepared mayonnaise.

Rosticceria Teatro Goldoni

San Marco 4747 (on calle dei Fabbri). ☎ **041/522-24-46.** *Menu turistico* 19,500 lire ($12.20); pizza and pasta courses 6,000–9,000 lire ($3.75–$5.65); meat courses 9,000–12,000 ($5.65–$7.50). No credit cards. Thurs–Tues 10am–2:30pm and 5–9pm. Closed one week sometime in Jan or Feb. ITALIAN.

As at all *rosticcerie*, you can see exactly what you're getting and don't have to pay any cover charge. Specialties here include pollo alla veneta (Venetian-style chicken) and fegato alla veneziana (liver and onions). It's just off campo San Luca, near the Rialto Bridge.

MEALS FOR LESS THAN 29,500 LIRE ($18.50)
NEAR PIAZZA SAN MARCO

Le Bistrot

San Marco 4687 (on calle dei Fabbri). ☎ **041/522-43-84.** Appetizers and crêpes 7,500–12,500 lire ($4.70–$7.80); pasta courses 10,500–12,500 lire ($6.55–$7.80); pizza and meat and fish courses 10,500–19,000 lire ($6.55–$11.90). No credit cards. Wed–Mon 11:45am–3pm and 7pm–1am. From the Rialto Bridge vaporetto stop, turn right, walk along the canal, cross the small footbridge, then turn left onto calle dei Fabbri; Le Bistrot is about five blocks ahead, on your right. VENETIAN/CONTINENTAL.

One of the few popularly priced sit-down restaurants serving dinner past midnight, Le Bistrot is equally recommendable during the day. Meals are served either in a bright and airy back dining room or outside (from April to October) on a small side street beside a narrow canal. The front bar features a piano that customers are encouraged to play.

Appetizers include garlic-boiled clams and mussels as well as baked cheese with ham. Various pastas are topped with squid, wild mushrooms, artichokes, or, more simply, tomatoes and basil. Shrimp and cod highlight the seafood entrees, while rack of lamb, duck, and frog's legs dominate the meat entrees.

✪ Trattoria alla Rivetta

Castello 4625 (on salizzada San Provolo). ☎ **041/528-73-02.** Pasta courses 6,000–9,000 lire ($3.75–$5.65); fish courses 9,500–14,500 lire ($5.95–$9.05); other second courses 10,000–13,500 lire ($6.25–$8.45). AE, MC, V. Tues–Sun noon–2:30pm and 7–10pm. Closed mid-July to mid-Aug. Walk behind the Basilica di San Marco to campo SS. Filippo e Giacomo; the trattoria is literally tucked away next to a bridge just off the side of the campo with the FARMACIA sign at the corner. SEAFOOD.

There are scores of places in this price range in Venice, but the alla Rivetta has that extra something that makes all the difference in a meal. Lively, popular, and thoroughly authentic, this is your best bet for genuine Venetian cuisine and company in the San Marco area. All sorts of fish—the specialty—decorate the window of the plain, brightly lit place, where you'll be welcomed heartily by the staff. Be sure to try the antipasto di pesce and whatever is penciled in as the daily special. Expect to wait for a table, even in winter. This is an excellent place to experiment, as everything is prepared very well.

Trattoria Bandierette

San Marco 813 (on calle Fiubera). ☎ **041/522-06-25.** *Menu turistico* 18,000 lire ($11.25); pasta courses 7,000–7,500 lire ($4.40–$4.70); meat courses 12,000–14,500 lire ($7.50–$9.05). No credit cards. Wed–Mon noon–2:30pm and 7–9:30pm. Closed Jan 15–Mar 15. Exit the piazza under the clock tower, which is to the left as you face the basilica; go left, cross ponte dei Ferali, and the Bandierette will be on your left. ITALIAN.

This family-run trattoria advertises *cucina casalinga* ("home-cooking") and has exceptionally low prices for a place so close to piazza San Marco. The staff is very friendly, especially considering the location in the heart of the tourist quarter.

NEAR THE ACCADEMIA

Taverna San Trovaso

Dorsoduro 1016 (on fondamenta Priuli not far from the Accademia). ☎ **041/520-37-03.** *Menu turistico* 20,000 lire ($12.50); pizza and pasta courses 6,000–11,500 lire ($3.75–$7.20); meat courses 9,500–13,500 lire ($5.95–$8.45); fish courses 16,000–23,000 lire ($10–$14.40). AE, DC, MC, V. Tues–Sun noon–2:30pm and 7–9:30pm. Closed a few days around Christmas. Walk to the right around the Accademia, take an immediate right onto calle Gambara, and turn left when this street ends at a canal; the San Trovaso will on your left. ITALIAN.

Dining here is like eating in a wine cellar. Bottles line the wood-paneled walls and the vaulted brown ceilings add an intimate touch. The menu turistico includes wine, dessert, and frittura mista (mixed fried seafood). Both the wine-cellar room downstairs and the more modern air-conditioned quarters upstairs are frequently packed with happy patrons enjoying the excellent food and fine service. Fegato alla veneziana (liver and onions) and grilled fish are the taverna's claim to fame. They also prepare an excellent gnocchi and a competent osso buco.

NEAR CAMPO DEI FRARI

✪ Trattoria della Dona Onesta

Dorsoduro 3922 (on calle della Dona Onesta). ☎ **041/522-95-86.** Pasta courses 5,000–9,000 lire ($3.15–$5.65); meat courses 10,000–13,000 lire ($6.25–$8.15). MC, V. Mon–Sat noon–2:30pm and 7–10pm. Closed Aug and around Christmas. See the text below for directions to this trattoria. ITALIAN.

This unpretentious place might not catch your eye (even if you could find it) unless you peeked through the curtains to see all of its 11 tables filled. There aren't even pictures on the walls—the staff's energy is devoted to the food, excellent and reasonably priced by Venetian standards. I suggest you try the cioccolatina (chocolate liqueur in frozen cream).

The Dona Onesta is difficult to find but worth the effort. Turn off Crosera, which runs perpendicular to the Grand Canal between campo San Pantalon and campo dei Frari, at Dorsoduro 3930, near the Hotel Tivoli. The restaurant is right at rio Frescada canal. Alternatively, take vaporetto Line 1 or 82 to San Tomà, walk straight ahead along calle del Traghetto, turn left at the end of this short calle, and then take the first right (before you go over the bridge) onto fondamenta del Forner, which becomes fondamenta della Dona Onesta. Continue on Dona Onesta and turn left across the first bridge.

PICNICKING

Doing your own shopping for food in Italy can be an interesting experience since there's no such thing as a supermarket. See the Rome chapter for details.

Venice's principal market, commonly referred to as the **Mercato Rialto,** begins on the San Polo side of the Rialto Bridge and continues along the Grand Canal to campo della Pescaria, just about directly across the canal from the Ca' d'Oro vaporetto stop. You'll find the vendors there Monday through Saturday roughly from 7am to 1pm, though the fish merchants usually take Monday off.

An open-air market specializing in fresh fish and vegetables sets up shop on the spacious **campo Santa Margherita,** open roughly Tuesday through Saturday from 8:30am until 1 or 2pm. A more colorful market, however, is the nearby produce market operating from the side of **a boat moored just off campo San Barnabà.** This market is open roughly from 8am to 1pm and 3:30 to 7:30pm, daily except Wednesday afternoon and Sunday. You should have no trouble filling out your picnic spread with the fixings available at the various shops lining the sides of the campo, including an exceptional *panetteria* (Rizzo Pane) at no. 2772, a fine *salumeria* at no. 2844, and a good shop for wine, sweets, and other picnic accessories next door.

Also try **via Giuseppe Garibaldi,** in the eastern end of the Castello sestiere, where vendors are in business Monday through Saturday, roughly from 8:30am to 1:30pm. This is the second-largest market in the city after the Rialto. (On Saturday, you'll find clothes, kitchen utensils, and other miscellaneous items for sale here as well.) You'll find the market along **rio Terrà San Leonardo,** between ponte alle Guglie and campiello Anconetta, to be the most convenient to the train station. Finally, you might try **campo Santa Maria Formosa.**

Unfortunately, Venice doesn't have much in the way of green space for a picnic. The park at the eastern end of Castello (see "Parks & Gardens" under "Attractions," later in this chapter) is hardly worth the trek or the money you'll spend getting there.

WORTH THE EXTRA MONEY

It's remarkably easy to spend 45,000 lire ($28.15) or more on dinner anywhere in this city. But there are three very special places where your money will be well spent.

Antica Locanda Montin

Dorsoduro 1147 (on fondamenta di Borgo). ☎ **041/522-71-51.** Pasta courses 7,000–10,500 lire ($4.40–$6.55); meat courses 12,000–20,000 lire ($7.50–$12.50); fish courses 12,000–29,000 lire ($7.50–$18.15). AE, DC, MC, V. Tues 12:30–2:30pm, Thurs–Mon 12:30–2:30pm and 7:30–10pm. See the text below for directions to the locanda. SEAFOOD.

Signora Carrettin, the iconoclastic owner, has put together the best modern-art collection outside the Guggenheim on the walls of this popular unpretentious restaurant. In fact, hardly an inch of wall shows between the paintings and drawings that are stacked five high. You know a place must be good when it's this crowded, at these prices, in such an out-of-the-way location. There's also a terrific garden out back.

The Montin is about equidistant from the Zattere vaporetto stop (Line 5) on the Giudecca Canal and the Ca' Rezzonico stop (Lines 1 and 2) on the Grand Canal. From the former, turn left along the Zattere and take the first right onto calle Trevisan, which becomes fondamenta di Borgo after the first bridge. From Ca' Rezzonico, walk straight ahead on calle del Traghetto and take the third left after you pass campo San Barnabà; this is calle delle Turchette, which, after the first bridge, becomes fondamenta di Borgo.

Trattoria alla Madonna

San Polo 594 (on calle della Madonna). ☎ **041/522-38-24.** Pasta courses 6,000–7,500 lire ($3.75–$4.70); meat courses 12,000–14,500 lire ($7.50–$9.05); grilled fish 7,500 lire ($4.70) per *etto* (roughly a quarter pound). AE, MC, V. Thurs–Tues noon–3pm and 7–10pm. Closed Dec 24–Jan. From the foot of the Rialto Bridge on the San Polo side of the Grand Canal, turn left; calle della Madonna will be the second street on your right (look for the big yellow sign). ITALIAN.

You'll find art, art, and more art here, always original and usually stacked two or three high on the walls of this trattoria, one of the city's most famous. The place is enormous—the five dining rooms have high beamed ceilings—but there's rarely an empty table. The food and service are terrific and much sought after. Specialties include risotto con frutti di mare (rice with seafood) and any fish "alla griglia" (grilled). Expect to spend about 42,000 lire ($26.25) per person for a full meal, including wine.

✪ Trattoria da Remigio

Castello 3416 (on calle Bosello). ☎ **041/523-00-89.** Pasta courses 4,000–5,000 lire ($2.50–$3.15); meat and fish courses 7,500–10,500 lire ($4.70–$6.55). AE, MC, V. Mon 1–3pm, Wed–Sun 1–3pm and 7pm–midnight. See the text below for directions to this trattoria. ITALIAN.

After hearing reports that his restaurant's quality was suffering, Remigio's owner, who was on an extended vacation, rushed back to Venice to save his reputation. Once again, Remigio has risen to reclaim its title as my favorite Venetian restaurant. Famous for its straightforward renditions of Adriatic classics, Remigio is the kind of place where you can order a simple bowl of spaghetti with tomato sauce and expect it to be one of the best meals you've ever had. Fish dishes, sold by weight, are especially recommendable, as is any antipasto. There are only two smallish dining rooms here, so even late on a winter weekday you can expect a wait.

The best way to reach this hidden restaurant is to ask a local. To attempt finding it on your own, exit piazza San Marco toward the water and turn left onto riva degli Schiavoni. Cross three bridges, then turn left onto calle della Pietà, which jogs left into calle Bosello. The restaurant is about three blocks ahead on your left.

6 Attractions

SIGHTSEEING SUGGESTIONS

If You Have 1 Day

I have a radical suggestion: If you have just one day in Venice, don't bother with any of the sights. Not the Basilica di San Marco, Accademia, or Peggy Guggenheim Collection. Instead, just wander aimlessly among the labyrinth of streets and passageways, because this city of canals is its own most extraordinary attraction. For its look, way of life, and history, Venice has no match in Europe. Some of the plainer neighborhoods, off the beaten tourist track, include eastern Castello, the Ghetto area (once the Jewish quarter) in northern Cannaregio, and the island of Giudecca.

If You Have 2 Days

Once you've thoroughly taken in the city's best sight—itself—move on to the lesser attractions. First among them has to be the Basilica di San Marco and the Palazzo Ducale, both on piazza San Marco. While you're on the square, you might as well take in the Museo Correr and ride the elevator to the top of the Campanile di San Marco for a terrific view of the entire lagoon.

If You Have 3 Days

Turn over your third day in Venice to its art. Visit the Accademia for a look at the city's Renaissance heritage and the nearby Collezione Peggy Guggenheim for one of Europe's best displays of 20th-century artworks. If you have time after this, take in either the Ca' Rezzonico or the Ca' d'Oro for a look at the interior of one of the palazzi that line the Grand Canal.

If You Have 5 Days

The remainder of the city's sights will carry you through a fourth day. For Day 5, I suggest that you explore the rest of the lagoon: Murano, Burano, Torcello, and the Lido.

TOP ATTRACTIONS

✪ Basilica di San Marco

San Marco, piazza San Marco. ☎ **041/522-52-05.** Admission: Basilica, free; galleries, museum, and Loggia dei Cavalli, 3,000 lire ($1.90) adults, 2,000 lire ($1.25) students; Tesoro and Pala d'Oro, 3,000 lire ($1.90) adults, 2,000 lire ($1.25) students. Summer, Mon–Sat 9:30am–5:30pm, Sun 2–5:30pm; winter, Mon–Sat 9:30am–4:30pm, Sun 1:30–4:30pm. Last entrance 30 minutes before closing time.

Venice for centuries was Europe's principal gateway to the East, so it should come as no surprise that the architectural style for the sumptuously Byzantine Basilica di San Marco, complete with several bulbed domes, was borrowed from Constantinople. Legend has it that in 828 four Venetians—a monk, a priest, and two enterprising merchants—conspired to smuggle the remains of St. Mark from Alexandria. Thus St. Mark replaced the Greek St. Theodore as Venice's patron saint. Through the subsequent centuries, Venetians vied with one another in donating gifts to this church, the saint's final resting place.

And so it is that San Marco's interior came to be so exquisitely gilded, every inch covered in colorful mosaics added over some seven centuries. For an up-close look

The Basilica of San Marco

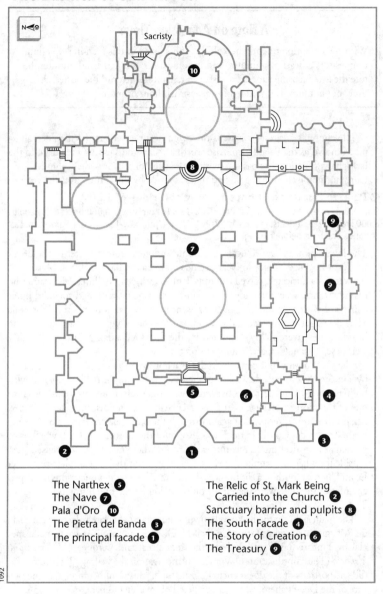

Sacristy

The Narthex **5**
The Nave **7**
Pala d'Oro **10**
The Pietra del Banda **3**
The principal facade **1**

The Relic of St. Mark Being
  Carried into the Church **2**
Sanctuary barrier and pulpits **8**
The South Facade **4**
The Story of Creation **6**
The Treasury **9**

at many of the most remarkable of these, pay the admission to go upstairs to the galleries. Also up here is the Loggia dei Cavalli, the patio above the entrance, from which you can enjoy a closer look at the church's exterior and can mingle with copies of the famous four bronze horses brought to Venice from Constantinople in the 13th century (the originals have been moved inside to the otherwise not terribly interesting museum).

A Note on Admission Times

With the exception of churches, all the sights listed in this section stop admitting visitors at least 30 minutes, and in some cases as much as 60 minutes, before the listed closing times. Tourists can remain inside until the posted closing time, but entrance is forbidden in the last half hour or more.

The church's greatest treasure is the magnificent jewel-encrusted golden altarpiece known as the Pala d'Oro. Also worth a visit is the Tesoro (Treasury), to the far right as you enter the basilica, with a collection of the Crusaders' plunder from Constantinople and other gold and relics amassed by the church over the years.

✪ Palazzo Ducale and ponte dei Sospiri (Bridge of Sighs)

San Marco, piazza San Marco. ☎ **041/522-49-51.** Admission 10,000 lire ($6.25) adults, 6,000 lire ($3.75) students. Easter–Oct, daily 8:30am–7pm; Nov–Easter, daily 9am–4pm. Last entrance one hour before closing.

The lovely pink Palazzo Ducale, the home and government center of the doges (dukes) who ruled Venice for years, stands between the Basilica di San Marco and the water. Its intricately carved columns, famed 15th-century Porta della Carta (the main entrance, where the doges' proclamations were posted), and splendid inner courtyard with a double row of Renaissance arches give way, via the enormous Scala dei Giganti staircase, to the wood-paneled courts and meeting rooms of the interior; these were richly decorated by the finest Venetian painters, including Veronese, Titian, Carpaccio, and Tintoretto.

The first room you'll come to is the spacious Sala Quattro Porte, with works by Tintoretto. The Sala del Collegio, the next main room, is richly decorated with both Tintorettos and 11 pieces by Veronese. A right turn from this room leads into one of the most impressive of the spectacular interior rooms, the richly adorned Senato (Senate). After passing again through the Sala Quattro Porte, you'll come to the Stanza del Consiglio dei Dieci (Room of the Council of Ten), which is of particular historical interest as this is the room where justice was dispensed. Just outside the adjacent chamber, the Sala della Bussola, is the last complete Bocca dei Leoni ("lion's mouth"), a slit in the wall into which secret denunciations of alleged enemies of the state were placed for quick action by the much feared Council of Ten.

The main sight on the next level down—indeed in the entire palace—is the Sala del Maggior Consiglio (Great Council Hall). This enormous space is made special by Tintoretto's *Paradiso* above the doge's seat and Veronese's *Il Trionfo di Venezia* (The Glorification of Venice) in the oval on the ceiling. Tintoretto also did the portraits of the doges encircling the top of this chamber; note that the picture of the Doge Faliero, who was convicted of treason and beheaded in 1355, has been blacked out. Exit the Great Council Hall via the tiny doorway on the opposite side of Tintoretto's *Paradiso* to find the enclosed ponte dei Sospiri (Bridge of Sighs), which connects the palace with the grim Prigioni (Prisons). The bridge is named for the sighs of Casanova. But contrary to popular myth, it was not despair over a romance that gave it its name, but rather his sadness at being led to the adjacent jail.

Readers who understand Italian may be interested in the Itinerari Segreti del Palazzo Ducal (Secret Itineraries of the Palazzo Ducale)— guided tours of otherwise restricted quarters of this enormous, impressive palace. Make reservations for the tours, which cost 10,000 lire ($6.25) and begin at 10am and noon, at the "Direzione" at the Palazzo Ducale, or call 520-42-87.

Campanile di San Marco (Bell Tower)

San Marco, piazza San Marco. ☎ **041/522-40-64.** Admission 5,000 lire ($2.50) adults, 2,500 lire ($1.55) students. June–Aug, daily 9am–9pm; Sept–May, daily 10am–4pm.

What's a beautiful Italian city without a bell tower that tourists can climb to get a spectacular view of the surrounding area? Well, this campanile, located in piazza San Marco, is less elegant than others in Italy, but the view of the entire lagoon is really something.

Galleria dell' Accademia

Dorsoduro, at the foot of the Accademia Bridge. ☎ **041/522-22-47.** Admission 12,000 lire ($7.50). July–Sept, Mon–Sat 9am–7pm, Sun 9am–1pm; Oct–June, Mon–Sat 9am–2pm, Sun 9am–1pm. Take vaporetto Line 1 or 82 to the Accademia stop (no. 12).

The Accademia is the definitive treasure house of Venetian painting, which is exhibited chronologically from the 13th through the 18th century. There's no one hallmark masterpiece in this collection; rather, this is an outstanding and comprehensive array of works by all the greats of Venice, including Carpaccio, Tintoretto, Mantegna, Veronese, Titian, Canaletto, Bellini, and Tiepolo, among others. Most of all, though, the works open a window onto the Venice of 500 or 600 years ago. Indeed, you'll see in the canvases how little Venice, perhaps least of any city in Europe, has changed over the centuries.

✪ Collezione Peggy Guggenheim

Dorsoduro 701 (on calle San Cristoforo). ☎ **041/520-62-88.** Admission 10,000 lire ($6.25) adults, 5,000 lire ($3.15) students, free for everybody Sat 6–9pm. Sun–Mon and Wed–Fri 11am–6pm, Sat noon–9pm. Take vaporetto Line 1 or 82 to the Accademia stop (no. 12); walk around the left side of the Accademia museum, take the first left, and walk straight, following the signs—you'll cross one canal, then walk alongside another, until turning left when necessary.

❓ Did You Know?

- In the 9th century, the body of St. Mark was supposedly transported from Egypt to Venice.
- Richard Wagner died in 1883 at the Palazzo Loredan Vendramin-Calergi, overlooking the Grand Canal.
- The Grand Canal is bordered by about 200 palaces.
- UNESCO's worldwide campaign to save Venice was launched in 1966, after terrible floods in November of that year.
- Venice's *vaporetti* were originally fueled by steam, hence their name ("little steamers").
- In accordance with laws against opulent decoration, gondolas have been painted black since the 16th century.
- The average age of Venetians is the highest in Europe.
- The population of Venice in the 19th century was nearly 200,000; today's it's 85,000.
- The population of Venice doubles during Carnevale.

Venice

 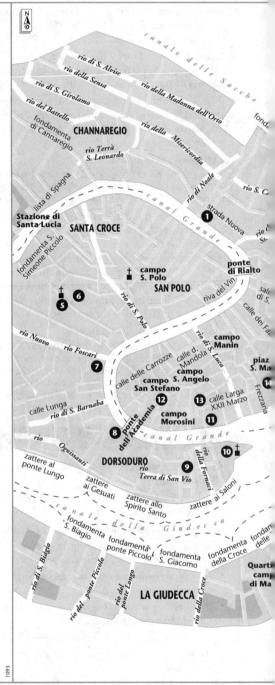

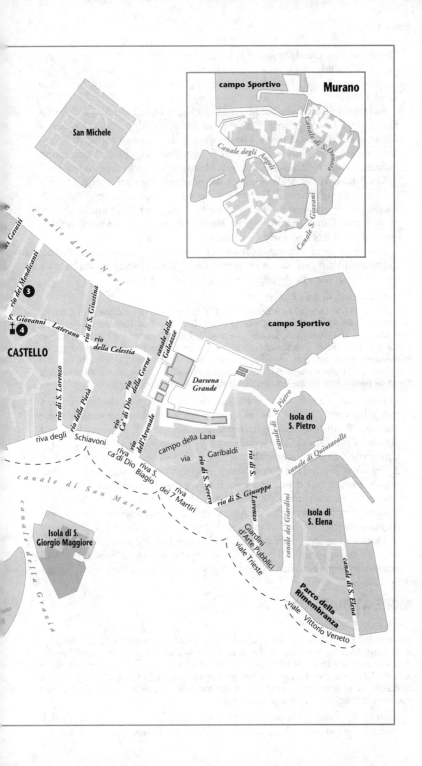

One of the most visited attractions in Venice, this collection of painting and sculpture was assembled by eccentric and eclectic American expatriate Peggy Guggenheim. She did a fine job of it, covering all the major movements in art since about 1910.

Among the major works are Magritte's *Empire of Light*, Picasso's *La Baignade*, Kandinsky's *Landscape with Church (with Red Spot)*, Metzinger's *The Racing Cyclist*, and Pollock's *Alchemy*. The museum is also home to several of Ernst's haunting canvases, Giacometti's unique figures, Brancusi's fluid sculptures, and numerous works by Braque, Dalí, Léger, Mondrian, Chagall, Miró, and others.

The Palazzo Venier dei Leoni, Peggy Guggenheim's home throughout her life in Venice, is a sight in itself. The graves of her canine companions share the lovely interior garden with several of the collection's sculptures, while the patio at the side of the Grand Canal, watched over by Marino Marini's **Angel of the Citadel,** is one of the best spots to simply linger and watch the canal life.

Note the museum's unique hours—it's open when many others are closed. Also, the museum staff is made up entirely of young English-speaking students on internships, so don't be shy about speaking English with them.

Scuola Grande di San Rocco

San Polo 3058 (on campo San Rocco, adjacent to campo dei Frari and the Frari Church). ☎ **041/523-48-64.** Admission 8,000 lire ($5). Apr–Oct, daily 9am–1pm and 3:30–6:30pm; Nov–Mar, Mon–Fri 10am–1pm, Sat–Sun 10am–4pm. Take vaporetto Line 1 or 82 to the San Tomà stop; from there, walk straight ahead on calle del Traghetto and turn right and then immediately left across campo San Tomà; then walk as straight ahead as you can, on ramo Mandoler, calle Larga Prima, and finally salizzada San Rocco, which leads into the campo of the same name—look for the crimson sign behind the Frari Church.

This museum is a vast monument to the work of Tintoretto—the largest collection of his work anywhere. The collection, the richest of the many schools (*scuole*) that once flourished here, begins upstairs in the Sala dell' Albergo. The most notable of the enormous, powerful canvases is the moving *La Crocifissione* (The Crucifixion). In the center of the gilt ceiling of the Great Hall, also upstairs, is *Il Serpente di Bronzo* (The Bronze Snake). Among the eight huge, sweeping paintings downstairs, each depicting a scene from the New Testament, *La Strage degli Innocenti* (The Slaughter of the Innocents) is the most noteworthy, so full of dramatic urgency and energy that the figures seem almost to tumble out of the frame. As you enter the room, it's on the opposite wall and at the far end of the room.

There's a guide to the paintings inside posted on the wall just before the entrance to the museum. There are a few Tiepolos among the paintings, as well as a solitary work by Titian. Note that the works on or near the staircase are not by Tintoretto.

MORE ATTRACTIONS

Basilica dei Frari

San Polo 3072 (on campo dei Frari). ☎ **041/522-26-37.** Admission 1,000 lire (65¢), free on holidays. Mon–Sat 9am–noon and 2:30–6pm, Sun 3–5:30pm; hours can be erratic in winter. Take vaporetto Line 1 or 82 to the San Tomà stop; from there, walk straight ahead on calle del Traghetto, turn right and then immediately left across campo San Tomà; then walk as straight ahead as you can, on ramo Mandoler, then calle larga Prima, and turn right when you reach the beginning of salizzada San Rocco.

Around the corner from the Scuola Grande di San Rocco, this gothic church houses the grandiose tombs of two famous Venetians: Canova and Titian. It's also home to Titian's *Assumption of the Virgin*, behind the high altar, and his *Virgin of the Pesaro Family*, in the left nave. Through a door on the right as you face the altar, in the Sacristy, you'll see Bellini's triptych *Madonna and Child*.

Ca' d'Oro (Galleria Giorgio Franchetti)

Cannaregio between 3931 and 3932 (on the narrow calle Ca' d'Oro). ☎ **041/523-87-90.** Admission 4,000 lire ($2.50). Daily 9am–2pm. Take vaporetto Line 1 to the Ca' d'Oro stop; the entrance is 50 yards away.

The 15th-century Ca' d'Oro is the best-preserved and most impressive of the patrician palazzi lining the Grand Canal. The ornate beamed ceilings provide the setting for sculptures, furniture, tapestries, impressive bronze and iron work from Venetian churches, and an art gallery whose two most important canvases include Mantegna's gripping, haunting *San Sebastiano* immediately as you enter and Titian's *Venus* on the top floor, as well as lesser paintings by Tintoretto, Carpaccio, van Dyck, Giorgione, and others. For a delightful stop, step out onto the palazzo's balcony, overlooking the Grand Canal.

Ca' Rezzonico (Museo del 700 Veneziano)

Dorsoduro (on fondamenta Rezzonico). ☎ **041/522-45-43.** Admission 8,000 lire ($5) adults, 5,000 lire ($3.15) students. Mon–Thurs and Sat 10am–4pm, Sun 9am–12:30pm. Take vaporetto Line 1 to Ca' Rezzonico; from the vaporetto dock, walk straight ahead to campo San Barnabà, turn right at the piazza and go over one bridge, then take an immediate right for the museum entrance.

This 18th-century canalside palace offers an intriguing look into what living in a grand Venetian palazzo was like. Furnished with period paintings, furniture, tapestries, and artifacts, this museum is one of the best windows into the life of Venice of 200 years ago, as seen through the tastes and fashions of the Rezzonico clan.

Museo Correr

San Marco, piazza San Marco. ☎ **041/522-56-25.** Admission 8,000 lire ($5) adults, 5,000 lire ($3.15) students. Daily 10am–4pm. Last entrance is 45 minutes before closing time; call ahead to check the hours, since they often change as special-event and traveling exhibitions pass through the city.

This museum, which you enter through an arcade at the end of piazza San Marco, opposite the basilica, is no match for the Accademia but does include some interesting scenes of Venetian life among its paintings. And while the Ca' Rezzonico shows what life in a palazzo on the banks of the Grand Canal was like, the fine collection of artifacts on exhibit here gives an interesting feel for aspects of the day-to-day life in this city. There are even a few pieces of armor and old-time weaponry.

Carpaccio's *Le Cortigiane* (The Courtesans), in Room 15 on the upper floor, is the collection's notable masterpiece. For a lesson in just how little this city has changed in the last several hundred years, head to Room 22 and its anonymous 17th-century bird's-eye view of Venice. Most of the rooms have a sign with a few paragraphs in English explaining the significance of that sala's wares.

PARKS & GARDENS

Alas, there's not much in the way of parks or gardens in this maritime city of stratospheric real-estate values. In fact, the only acceptable set of gardens is at the far eastern end of the Castello sestiere, where the Biennale takes place every two years; look for "Esposizione Internazionale d'Arte Moderna" on your map. Vaporetto Lines 1 and 4 stop at the Giardini station nearby.

SPECIAL-INTEREST SIGHTSEEING

FOR THE BOAT LOVER   One of the most interesting sights you'll see in
Venice is the **Tramontin Gondola Factory** at Dorsoduro 1542, on fondamenta
Ognissanti. Nearly half the 400 sleek black boats that ply Venice's canals today
have been made by one of the four generations of the Tramontin family, who have
labored at this craft—and in this location—since 1884.

Though the boats have no modern equipment and rarely move at any great
speed, putting one together is a fascinatingly exact science. The right side of the
gondola is lower, for instance, since the gondolier always stands on the left. If the
Tramontini worked continuously, assembling just one of these would take some
40 to 45 working days. Today's father-son team puts just three new boats into
service each year, carefully crafting each from the seven types of wood—mahogany,
cherry, fir, walnut, oak, elm, and lime—necessary to give the boat its various characteristics. They don't do all the work, but they do put all the pieces together; the
painting, the *ferro* (the iron symbol of the city affixed to the bow), and the wood
carving, for instance, are all farmed out to various local artisans.

To find their place from the Zattere, the seaside boulevard on the Guidecca
Canal in Dorsoduro (on vaporetto Lines 52 and 82), walk up calle Cartelotti (also
known as Corteleto), which begins at no. 1470, and turn left onto fondamenta
Ognissanti when this short street ends. (It's near the Ospedale Giustinian, if you're
asking directions.) Don't be shy—just walk right in.

They're on the job Monday through Friday from 9am to noon and then from
2 to 6pm; note that they're away on vacation for most of August.

FOR THE ROMANTIC   A **gondola ride,** one of the great traditions of Europe,
really is as romantic as it looks. However, only royal Romeos and Juliets can
afford it. The going rate is 80,000 lire ($50) for up to 50 minutes, for up to five
passengers per vessel; there's a 20,000-lira ($12.50) surcharge after dark. And what
of the accompanying musicians and serenading *signore* that've made gondoliering
so famous? Well, a musical ensemble is so expensive it must be shared among
several boats traveling together. Travel agents are about the only people in town
who book musical accompaniment.

There are 12 gondola stations spread throughout Venice, including piazzale
Roma (☎ **041/522-05-81**), the train station (☎ **041/71-85-43**), the Rialto
Bridge (☎ **041/522-49-04**), and piazza San Marco (☎ **041/520-06-85**).

But before your dreams fade away, read on: To tourists, gondolas mean
romance, but to Venetians they're a basic form of transportation. There are just
three bridges that cross the Grand Canal, and traghetto gondolas ferry the general
public back and forth at seven other points along the way. You'll find on your map
a traghetto gondola station at the end of any street with the name "calle del
Traghetto." There's one, for instance, right alongside the San Tomà vaporetto
station, and next to Ca' Rezzonico. The ride is short and you must stand, but at
only 1,000 lire (65¢) each way, it's priced for the local citizenry, not the wealthy
tourists.

7 Shopping

Scores of boutiques fill the narrow pathways between the Rialto Bridge and piazza
San Marco. The budget-conscious should know, though, that they'll find better
value to the south in Florence and Rome.

Venice is uniquely famous for several local products, including the intricately carved multicolored **glassware** from the island of Murano and the delicate **lace** of the factories on Burano.

Manu, San Marco 1228 (☎ **041/522-92-94**), in a tiny alley between calle Frezzeria and fondamenta Orseolo, steps from piazza San Marco, is one of the best places to buy antique glass beads and handmade jewelry. Relatively unknown to tourists, this unflashy shop stocks many unusual, hard-to-find items.

Dimodi, in campo SS. Filippo e Giacomo, behind the Basilica di San Marco (☎ **041/523-51-87**), is typical of Venice's small, upscale accessory shops. Here you'll find custom jewelry, scarves, gloves, ties, and umbrellas, all made in Italy.

Everywhere—and I mean *everywhere*—you'll see shops selling hand-painted porcelain **Carnevale masks** (*maschere*). These make excellent souvenirs, and since they're priced by size and intricacy of design, they can meet any budget. There's no window-shopping quite like watching the masks being made. There are several ateliers (studio factories) around town where you can watch these artisans in action. My favorite is the **Ca' Macana,** at Dorsoduro 3172, on calle delle Botteghe, around the corner from the Ca' Rezzonico (☎ **041/520-32-29**). Other noteworthy studio factories offering these handcrafts and other gifts include **Riflesso di Venezia,** at Dorsoduro 2856, on calle lunga San Barnabà; **Metamauco,** at San Marco 1735, on calle Frezzeria (☎ **041/528-58-85**); and **Cristal Star,** at San Marco 1017, on calle dei Fabbri (☎ **041/523-49-68**).

8 Venice After Dark

Whether or not you're in Venice during the summer festival season, be sure to visit one of the tourist information centers for current English-language schedules of events. Up-to-date entertainment listings are posted in the offices.

Other sources of information include the music section of the **Venice Department of Culture** (☎ **041/520-92-88**), for current serious music offerings, and the weekly tourist-oriented magazine *Ospite de Venezia,* available free from most major hotels.

THE PERFORMING ARTS

Several Venetian churches regularly host classical-music concerts by local and international artists. The **Chiesa de Vivaldi,** known officially as the Chiesa de Santa Maria della Pietà, is a popular venue, as is the Frari Church, and a host of others around the city. Information, schedules, and tickets are available from Agenzia Kele & Teo, ponte dei Baretteri, San Marco (☎ **041/520-87-22**), and other ticket agencies around town.

Close to the Rialto Bridge, the **Teatro Goldoni,** San Marco 4650/b, on calle Goldoni near campo San Luca (☎ **041/520-75-83**), is known for its winter theater season, which regularly features well-known international productions. Tickets run 20,000 to 40,000 lire ($12.50 to $25). The box office is open Monday through Saturday from 10am to 1pm and 4:30 to 7pm.

The famous **Teatro la Fenice,** San Marco 2549, on campo San Fantin (☎ **041/521-01-61** or 521-03-36), is the city's principal stage for opera, music, theater, and (sometimes) dance. A concert here is not just a show, it's an experience. Tickets cost 30,000 to 150,000 lire ($18.75 to $93.75). The box office is open daily from 9:30am to 12:30pm and 4 to 6pm, and from 30 minutes before curtain time.

Both contemporary and classic plays are staged in Italian at the **Ridotto Theater,** calle Vallaresso, San Marco (☎ 041/522-29-39), just a stone's throw from St. Marks Square. Recent productions have included works by Shakespeare, Molière, Alan Ayckbourn, and Neil Simon. Tickets range from 17,000 to 35,000 lire ($10.65 to $21.90). The box office is open Monday through Saturday from 10:30am to 12:30pm and 4:30 to 6:30pm.

BARS

Devil's Forest Pub

San Marco 5185 (on calle Stagneri). ☎ **041/520-06-23.** At the foot of the Rialto Bridge on the San Marco side of the Grand Canal is campo San Bartolomeo; calle Stagneri begins at the right end of campo San Bartolomeo if you're coming off the bridge—look for the Banca Commerciale Italiana on the corner.

One of the city's newest watering holes, the Devil's Forest is designed to look like a British pub, complete with a carved-wood bar, interior stained glass, and a good selection of draft beers, including Guinness Stout. A pint of beer costs 7,000 lire ($4.40), while simple pasta dishes and sandwiches run 6,000 to 8,000 lire ($3.75 to $5). Dart and backgammon boards are available to patrons. Open Tuesday through Friday from 8am to midnight and Saturday and Sunday from 8am to 1am.

Paradiso Perduto

Cannaregio 2540 (on fondamenta della Misericordia). ☎ **041/72-05-81.** From the train station, walk along Lista di Spagna, past campo S. Geremia, and across the first bridge onto rio Terrà San Leonardo; turn left onto rio Terrà Farsetti, cross the bridge, turn right onto fondamenta della Misericordia, and the bar will be straight ahead on your left.

Good food at reasonable prices would be enough to regularly pack this restaurant, but its biggest draw is the live jazz performed on a small stage several nights a week. Extremely popular with American and other foreigners living in Venice, this bar is largely devoid of tourists, primarily because it's hard to find and off the beaten path. If you feel like eating, you'll find a good selection of well-prepared pizzas and pastas for under 10,000 lire ($6.25); arrive early for a table. Beer runs 6,000 lire ($3.75). Open Thursday through Tuesday from 7pm to 1 or 2am.

FILMS

There are five cinemas in Venice and two on the Lido that often screen American, British, and Australian films. Call or check entertainment listings to see whether the movies are *versione originale* (in their original language, with Italian subtitles). On movie posters around town it's usually abbreviated "*v.o.*"

The **Accademia,** at Dorsoduro 1019 (☎ **041/528-77-06**), on calle Corfu opposite El Souk disco, and the **Olimpia,** San Marco 1094, on campo San Gallo (☎ **041/520-54-39**), are the two most centrally located theaters, and most likely to show films in English. Tickets cost 10,000 lire ($6.25). The Olimpia is closed Monday.

CAFES

For tourists and locals alike, Venetian nightlife centers around the city's many cafés, themselves tucked away in some of the world's prettiest piazzas. **Piazza San Marco** is the most popular, if also the most expensive and touristed place to linger over a cappuccino. The **Caffè Florian,** at San Marco 56a–59a, on the side of the piazza nearest the water, is the most famous (closed Wednesday); on the opposite side of the square at San Marco 133–34 is the **Café Lavena.** At both spots, a cappuccino at a table will set you back at least 7,000 lire ($4.40).

For just plain relaxing, at a lower price and level of pretension, I'm fond of the three places on **campo Santa Margherita,** a huge open campo about half-way between the train station and Ca' Rezzonico. Other popular squares for café life include **campo Sant'Angelo** and **campo Santo Stefano. Campo San Bartolomeo,** at the foot of the Rialto Bridge, and nearby **campo San Luca** are the most popular gathering spots in town; you'll see Venetians of all ages milling about engaged in animated conversation.

Note that most cafés are open Monday through Saturday from 8pm to midnight.

9 Easy Excursions

MURANO, BURANO & TORCELLO   Venice shares its lagoon with three other principal islands. Murano is famous throughout the world for the products of its glass factories. Lace is the claim to fame of Burano. And nearby Torcello is home to the oldest church in Venice.

Guided tours of the three islands are operated by the **Serenissima Company,** with departures from a dock between piazza San Marco and the Hotel Danieli, right next to the wharf for the *motonave* to the Lido (☎ **041/522-85-83** or 522-42-81). The four-hour, 40,000-lira ($25) tours leave daily at 9:30am and 2:30pm.

You can also visit these islands on your own. Vaporetto Lines 12, 13, and 52 make the journey to Murano, and Line 12 continues on to Burano and Torcello.

THE LIDO   Venice's Lido **beaches** are more scene than substance. For bathing and sunworshiping, there are much nicer beaches in Italy. But the parade of wealthy Italian and foreign tourists (plus a few Venetians) who frequent this *litorale* throughout summer is an interesting sight indeed. There are two beach areas at the Lido: **Bucintoro,** at the opposite end of viale Santa Maria Elisabetta from the vaporetto station; and **San Niccolò,** a mile away, and reached by bus B. You'll have to pay 12,000 lire ($7.50) per person (standard procedure throughout Italy) unless you patronize the public beach at the end of bus Line B.

Vaporetto Lines 1, 6, 52, and 82 cross the lagoon to the Lido from the San Zaccaria–Danieli stop near San Marco. From the Lido–Santa Maria Elisabetta vaporetto stop, walk straight ahead along viale Santa Maria Elisabetta to reach the beach (or take bus A). Bus B goes to San Niccolò.

25 Vienna

by Beth Reiber

Being in Vienna sometimes makes me wish I had a time machine—not that it would be easy to decide which century to zero in on. Perhaps the last half of the 18th century, when Vienna resounded with the music of Haydn and Mozart and Empress Maria Theresa ruled from her glittering Schönbrunn Palace. Or maybe the first decades of the 20th century, when Freud was developing his methods of psychoanalysis, Klimt was covering canvases with his Jugendstil figures, and Vienna was whirling to Strauss waltzes.

But I'll settle gladly for Vienna today. Music is still the soul of this city, the manifestation of its spirit—from chamber music and opera to jazz concerts and alternative rock. The Habsburgs, rulers of Austria for six centuries, left behind a rich architectural legacy of magnificent baroque and rococo buildings and palaces, beautifully landscaped gardens, and fabulous art collections from the far corners of their empire.

Vienna, however, is not resting on past laurels. After the Austro-Hungarian Empire was carved up into several countries following World War I, Vienna was a capital without an empire, and when the Iron Curtain fell after World War II, it was suddenly on the edge of Western Europe, far from other major capitals. Now that Eastern Europe has opened up and the emphasis has shifted farther east, however, Vienna is again in the center. A springboard for travel to and from Budapest, Prague, and beyond, Vienna has reblossomed into the international city it once was. Vienna is "in," with chic boutiques, good restaurants, and a burgeoning nightlife.

1 Vienna Deals & Discounts

BUDGET BESTS The most wonderful thing you can do for yourself is go to a performance at the Staatsoper (State Opera). Standing-room tickets start at only $1.90, for which you're treated to extravaganzas held on one of Europe's most renowned stages. Even sit-down tickets are not prohibitively expensive, starting at $9.50.

The rest of Vienna is affordable, too. Try at least one meal at a *Beisl,* a typical blue-collar pub, where you can get hearty home-cooked meals for as little as $8. But don't forget Vienna's wonderful wine cellars, where you can soak in the lively atmosphere for the price of a glass of wine.

What's Special About Vienna

Music
- The Staatsoper (State Opera), one of Europe's best.
- Beethoven, Haydn, Mozart, Schubert, and Johann Strauss, whose homes are open to the public.
- Music festivals galore, including the Operetta Festival, the Haydn Festival, the Schubert Festival, and the Summer of Music.

Museums
- The Treasury, with the jewels and riches of the Habsburg family.
- The Museum of Fine Arts, with its paintings by the old masters.
- Museums of 19th- and 20th-century art, including the Belvedere gallery and the Museum of Modern Art.
- Special-interest museums, from the Sigmund-Freud-Haus to the Doll and Toy Museum.

Coffeehouses
- A wide range of coffeehouses, from the elegant Demel to the egalitarian-minded Cafe Hawelka.
- At least 20 varieties of coffee, from *Mokka* to *Melange*.
- Tortes, cakes, and desserts!

Architecture
- Schönbrunn, one of Europe's most impressive baroque palaces.
- Imposing buildings of the 19th century, including the Museum of Fine Arts and Museum of Natural History, the State Opera House, and the Parliament.
- Works by such innovative architects of the 20th century as Adolf Loos and Otto Wagner, and, more recently, several whimsical buildings by Hundertwasser.

And if you want to save money, eat at a *Würstelstand,* a sidewalk food stand selling various kinds of Wurst and a roll for $2.20 to $3.35. They're located throughout the city and are as much a part of the Viennese scene as the opera house.

SPECIAL DISCOUNTS   As is the case elsewhere in Europe, there are many special discounts for students visiting Vienna. But this city also offers a number of special deals for everyone.

For Students   If you're a student with bonafide identification, you're entitled to savings of 50% or more off the admission price of museums in Vienna. You can also obtain theater tickets to the Staatsoper, Burgtheater, or Akademietheater for 50 S ($4.75), but only if you can show current student status with a valid university identification card. To be on the safe side, be sure to bring both your university card and an **International Student Identity Card (ISIC).**

If you've arrived in Vienna without an ISIC, you can obtain one at **Ökista,** where you can also purchase cheap airline flights and train tickets (for youths under 26). There are three locations: Türkenstrasse 6 (☎ **01/401 48 0**), Karlsgasse 3 (☎ **01/505 01 28**), and Reichstratsstrasse 13 (☎ **01/402 15 61**). All three are open Monday through Friday from 9:30am to 5:30pm.

For Everyone All **municipal museums** (including the residences of Mozart, Beethoven, Haydn, and Johann Strauss; the Vienna Historical Museum; and the Clock Museum) are free Friday morning.

If you're interested in seeing the famous **Spanish Riding School,** consider going to one of the morning training sessions, when tickets cost 80 S ($7.60). If you're willing to stand, you can see the **Vienna Boys' Choir** free of charge (they perform at Sunday mass). And if you plan on traveling a lot by public transportation, be sure to buy a "strip ticket," or a 24-hour or 72-hour ticket, described in more detail below.

2 Pretrip Preparations

REQUIRED DOCUMENTS Citizens of the United States, Canada, Australia, and New Zealand need only a valid passport for stays up to 90 days. British subjects need only an identity card.

TIMING YOUR TRIP Vienna is at the same latitude as Seattle and the northern tip of Maine, and its climate is moderate and generally agreeable. May, June, and September are usually the nicest months; snow can cover the ground from December through February.

Vienna's Average Daytime Temperature & Days of Rain

	Jan	Feb	Mar	Apr	May	June	July	Aug	Sept	Oct	Nov	Dec
Temp. (°F)	30	32	38	50	58	64	68	70	60	50	41	33
Days of Rain	3	3	3	4	5	5	4	5	5	4	4	3

Special Events If your sole reason for coming to Vienna is the theater, avoid July and August—the Staatsoper, Volksoper, Burgtheater, and Akademietheater are all closed during these months. In addition, in July and August there are no performances of either the Spanish Riding School or the Vienna Boys' Choir. However, there are many other musical events that are part of Vienna's Summer of Music festival.

It's not surprising that many of Vienna's festivals and events revolve around music. The **Operetta Festival** in early February stages productions at the Volksoper. In March there's a **Haydn Festival,** while the **Wiener Festwochen (Vienna Festival)** in May and June features music, theater, dance, and art.

July and August feature Vienna's **Summer of Music** with its many concerts at Schönbrunn Palace, at memorial sites (such as the Haydn House), and at the Rathaus (City Hall). The annual **Schubert Festival** is in November; December is the month of the outdoor **Christmas bazaar,** with stalls selling handcrafted items and decorations in front of the Rathaus, on Spittelberg, and on Freyung.

BACKGROUND READING For a better appreciation of Vienna and its history, read Charles Osborne's *Schubert and His Vienna* (Knopf, 1985) or Hilde Spiel's *Vienna's Golden Autumn, 1866–1938* (Weidenfeld, 1987). A vivid portrayal of Maria Theresa and her times is presented by Edward Crankshaw in *Maria Theresa* (Atheneum, 1969). *The Spell of the Vienna Woods: Inspiration and Influence from Beethoven to Kafka* (Holt & Co., 1994) by Paul Hofmann takes readers on historical tours of the Vienna Woods, the 540 square miles of woods around the capital that have served as a playground for royalty and commoners through the ages. For a personal account of Vienna's darker history, a gripping story of the fate of a Jewish family is given by George Clare in his *Last Waltz in Vienna: The Rise and Destruction of a Family, 1842–1942* (Holt & Co., 1981).

3 Vienna Specifics

ARRIVING

FROM THE AIRPORT   Vienna's airport, **Schwechat** (☎ **01/711 10-0** or 711 10-2231), is 11 miles southeast of the city center. A shuttle bus departs about every 20 or 30 minutes for the City Air Terminal, near the center of town next to the Hilton. The trip takes about 20 to 30 minutes, depending on traffic. From the City Air Terminal you can catch the U-Bahn (subway) at the Landstrasse station.

Less frequent are the shuttle buses to the Südbahnhof (a 20-minute trip) and the Westbahnhof (a 35-minute trip), Vienna's two train stations, with departures every hour. In any case, the cost of the shuttle bus to the City Air Terminal or the train stations is 70 S ($6.65) one way.

Taxis charge about 350 to 400 S ($33.35 to $38.10) for the same trip. If you make arrangements a day in advance, however, C & K Airport Service (☎ **01/ 608 08**) will deliver you to or from the airport for 270 S ($25.70).

FROM THE TRAIN STATION   Vienna has two main train stations. If you're arriving from Germany, Switzerland, France, Salzburg, or other points west or

What Things Cost in Vienna	U.S. $
Taxi from the airport to the city center	38.00
U-Bahn from Stephansdom to Schönbrunn	1.90
Local telephone call (1 min.)	.09
Double room at the Hotel Sacher (deluxe)	371.00
Double room at Pension Pertschy (moderate)	102.85
Double room at Pension Wild (budget)	56.20
Lunch for one, without wine, at Gasthaus Witwe Bolte (moderate)	14.00
Lunch for one, without wine, at Naschmarkt (budget)	6.50
Dinner for one, without wine, at Hauswirth (deluxe)	33.00
Dinner for one, without wine, at Crêperie-Brasserie Spittelberg (moderate)	14.00
Dinner for one, without wine, at Schnitzelwirt (budget)	7.50
Half liter of beer	3.40
Glass of wine (one-eighth liter)	2.00
Coca-Cola (in a restaurant)	2.30
Cup of coffee (in a restaurant)	2.50
Roll of ASA 100 color film, 36 exposures	6.50
Admission to the Kunsthistorisches Museum	4.30
Movie ticket (depends on where you sit)	6.65–9.50
Theater ticket (standing room at the Staatsoper)	1.90

north, in most cases you'll arrive at the **Westbahnhof (West Station).** A subway line (the U-3) connects the Westbahnof with Stephansplatz in the center.

If you're arriving from the south or east—say, from Italy, Hungary, Greece, or countries of the former Yugoslavia—you'll most likely arrive at the **Südbahnhof (South Station).** Take Tram D from in front of the station if you're heading for the Ring and the city center. Tram no. 18 travels between the two train stations.

Since the opening of Eastern Europe, **Franz-Josefs-Bahnhof** has become important for train travel to and from Prague. Take tram D for the city Ring and the city center; tram no. 5 travels to the Westbahnhof. The U-4 Friedensbrücke stop is about a five-minute walk from the station.

For information on train schedules, call 01/1717.

VISITOR INFORMATION

For information on Vienna, including the current showings and times for the opera, theater, Spanish Riding School, and Vienna Boys' Choir, drop by the **Vienna Tourist Board,** Kärntner Strasse 38 (☎ **01/211 14-0** or 513 88 92), on the corner of Philharmoniker Strasse, near the Sacher Hotel; it's open daily from 9am to 7pm. Be sure to pick up a free copy of the *Wien Monatsprogramm,* issued every month and available at the Tourist Board—it tells what's going on in Vienna's concert halls, theaters, and opera houses.

If you're looking for detailed information, be sure to purchase a 50-S ($4.75) English-language booklet published by the city government called **"Vienna from A to Z,"** also available at the Tourist Board. Its alphabetical listings are keyed to the unique, numbered plaques you'll find affixed to the front of every building of historical interest in Vienna. You'll spot these plaques everywhere: They're heralded by little red-and-white flags in summer. By referring to the number on the plaque with the corresponding number in "Vienna from A to Z," you'll have the English translations.

The tourist office will also book hotel rooms for a 40-S ($3.80) fee. Next door to the tourist office is the travel agency **Intropa** (☎ **01/51 514**), which sells theater tickets, books sightseeing tours, and exchanges money. In summer it's open daily from 9am to 5:30pm; in winter, Monday through Friday from 9am to 5:30pm and Saturday from 9am to 1pm.

If you're arriving at Vienna International Airport, there's a tourist office in the Arrivals Hall, open daily from 8:30am to 9pm. A tourist office at the Westbahnhof is open daily from 6:15am to 11pm, while another one at the Südbahnhof is open daily from 6:30am to 10pm May to October and 6:30am to 9pm November to April. Both will book hotel rooms.

CITY LAYOUT

Vienna's old city center is delightfully compact, filled with tiny cobblestone streets leading to majestic squares. In the center is **Stephansplatz** with Vienna's most familiar landmark, St. Stephen's Cathedral (Stephansdom). From here it's a short walk to the Hofburg (the official residence of the Habsburgs), the Kunsthistorisches Museum (Art History Museum), and the Staatsoper. **Kärntner Strasse,** much of it pedestrian, is Vienna's main shopping street and leads from Stephansplatz past the Staatsoper to **Karlsplatz.**

Circling the **Altstadt (Old City)** is "the Ring," as Vienna's **Ringstrasse** is commonly called. This impressive boulevard is 2½ miles long and 187 feet wide, built in the mid-1800s along what used to be the city's fortifications (hence its shape

The Austrian Schilling

For American Readers   At this writing $1 = approximately 10.50 S (or 1 S = 9¢), and this was the rate of exchange used to calculate the dollar values given in this chapter (rounded to the nearest nickel).

For British Readers   At this writing £1 = approximately 16.50 S (or 1 S = 6p), and this was the rate of exchange used to calculate the pound values in the table below.

Note: The rates given here fluctuate from time to time and may not be the same when you travel to Austria. Therefore this table should be used only as a guide:

S	U.S.$	U.K.£	S	U.S.$	U.K.£
1	.09	.06	100	9.50	6.05
2	.19	.12	150	14.30	9.10
3	.29	.18	200	19.05	12.10
4	.38	.24	250	23.80	15.15
5	.48	.30	300	28.55	18.20
6	.57	.36	350	33.35	21.20
7	.67	.42	400	38.10	24.25
8	.76	.48	450	42.85	27.25
9	.85	.54	500	47.60	30.30
10	.95	.60	600	57.15	36.35
15	1.43	.90	700	66.65	42.40
20	1.90	1.21	800	76.20	48.50
25	2.38	1.51	900	85.70	54.55
50	4.76	3.03	1,000	95.25	60.60

as a circle around the Altstadt). Everything inside the Ring is known as the First Bezirk ("precinct," denoted by 1010 in addresses). The rest of Vienna is also divided into various precincts.

Trams run along the tree-shaded Ring, which is divided into various sections, known as Opernring (home of the Staatsoper), Kärntner-Ring, Burgring (where you'll find the Hofburg and the Kunsthistorisches Museum), and Schubert Ring. **Schönbrunn,** Vienna's top sight, is a few miles southwest of the city center, easily reached by U-Bahn from Karlsplatz.

GETTING AROUND

Vienna's transit network consists of five **U-Bahn (subway) lines,** trams, **buses,** and several **rapid transit and commuter trains.** Unfortunately, a good free map depicting tram and bus lines, which is what most tourists need, does not exist. Luckily, most of Vienna's attractions are within walking distance of one another.

If you think you'll be using Vienna's public transportation system extensively, you may wish to purchase a large **map** with the U-Bahn, bus, and tram lines outlined throughout for 15 S ($1.40) from the **Informationsdienst der Wiener Verkehrsbetriebe,** in the underground Opernpassage at Karlsplatz and in the U-Bahn station at Stephansplatz. Both are open Monday through Friday from

6:30am to 6:30pm and Saturday and Sunday from 8:30am to 4pm. The staff can answer questions, such as which bus to take to reach your destination. You can also call for information by dialing 01/587 31 86.

Fares　A single ticket (good for the tram, bus, S-Bahn, or the U-Bahn) costs 17 S ($1.60) if purchased in advance, which permits as many transfers as you need to reach your destination as long as you keep moving in the same direction. Advance tickets can be purchased from machines found in U-Bahn stations and ticket booths or from tobacconist shops. Tickets purchased from bus or tram conductors, on the other hand, cost 20 S ($1.90). I suggest, however, that instead of single tickets you purchase the *Vierfahrtenstreifenkarte,* a strip ticket that allows four rides for 68 S ($6.45). These must be purchased in advance, either from ticket booths at the Karlsplatz or Stephansplatz U-Bahn station or from automatic machines at all U-Bahn and train stations (look for the VOR FAHRKARTEN sign). In addition, there's also a **24-hour ticket** available for 50 S ($4.75), a **72-hour ticket** for 130 S ($12.40), or an **eight-day pass** for 265 S ($25.25), which you can use for any eight days you wish, not necessarily in succession. You must validate all tickets yourself by inserting them into machines at the entryway of S-Bahn and U-Bahn platforms or on buses and trams. Children up to age 6 can travel for free, while those 7 to 15 travel for half the fare.

BY U-BAHN (SUBWAY)　The most important U-Bahn line for visitors is U-4, which stops at Karlsplatz before continuing to Kettenbrückengasse (site of Vienna's outdoor market and weekend flea market) and Schönbrunn. U-2 travels around part of the Ring, while U-1 has a station at Stephansplatz. U-4, U-2, and U-1 all converge at Karlsplatz. U-3 connects the Westbahnhof with Stephansplatz and beyond.

BY TRAM　Although the U-Bahn and buses are gradually taking over most of the tram routes, trams are still heavily used for traveling around the Ring (trams no. 1 and 2) and for transportation between the Südbahnhof and the Ring (tram D) and the Westbahnhof and the Burgring (tram no. 58). Tram no. 18 travels between the Westbahnhof and the Südbahnhof.

BY BUS　Buses crisscross the entire city. Three buses (1A, 2A, and 3A) go through the inner city Monday through Saturday and there are eight buses in operation throughout the night from Schwedenplatz to the suburbs (including Grinzing) on weekend nights and nights before public holidays. Information on both buses and trams can be obtained at the Informationsdienst der Wiener Verkehrsbetriebe (information office of the Vienna transport service), in the underground passageway linking the Oper and Karlsplatz and the U-Bahn station at Stephansplatz.

BY TAXI　If you need a taxi, you can call 31 300, 81 400, 40 100, or 60 160. The base price is 24 S ($2.30), plus an additional 12 S ($1.15) for taxis summoned by phone and 10 S (95¢) in the evenings from 11pm to 6am and all day Sunday and holidays. Each additional kilometer is 12 S ($1.15). Luggage is 12 S ($1.15) extra.

ON FOOT　You can do almost all your sightseeing in Vienna on foot. You can walk from one end of the Altstadt to the other in about 10 minutes. Even the walk from the Ring to either train station is only half an hour or so.

BY BICYCLE　There are more than 200 miles of marked bike paths in Vienna. From May to September, bikes may be taken along for half fare in specially marked cars of the U-Bahn Monday through Friday from 9am to 3pm and from 6:30pm to the end of the day, on Saturday after 9am, and all day Sunday and holidays.

The most popular places for bike rentals and tours are at the amusement center of Prater and along the banks of the Donaukanal (Danube Canal), with several bike-rental agencies at both these spots. The most centrally located is probably the bike shop **Radverleih Salztorbrücke** at Salztorbrücke, north of Stephansplatz on the Donaukanal (☎ **01/535 34 22**). It's open April to mid-October, daily from 10am to 7pm. Other bike shops are located at the Praterstern station and Am Kaisermühlendamm station. Charges are generally 50 S ($4.75) for one hour or 200 S ($19.05) for the whole day.

During summer, rental bikes are also available at the Westbahnhof and Südbahnhof. If you have a Eurailpass or a valid train ticket for that day, the cost of a day's rental is 50 S ($4.75). Otherwise, bikes rent for 90 S ($8.55) for one day.

For more information on biking, contact the Vienna Tourist Board, where you can pick up a pamphlet called "See Vienna by Bike," complete with recommended routes.

BY RENTAL CAR   Car-rental agencies include **Avis,** Opernring 3–5 (☎ **01/587 62 41**), **Budget Rent-a-Car,** Hilton Air Terminal (☎ **01/714 65 65**), and **Hertz,** Kärntner-Ring 17 (☎ **01/512 86 77**). Prices vary according to day of the week and number of rental days, but expect to pay about 900 S ($85.70) per day for an Opel Corsa, including unlimited mileage and 20% tax. Keep in mind that weekend rates are usually lower than weekday rates, that there are almost always promotional bargains available, and that smaller independent companies may offer better deals than the larger international chains. At press time, for example, **Kalal,** Rennweg 73 (☎ **01/712 35 33**), offered a one-day rental of a Citröen for 640 S ($60.95), including unlimited mileage, tax, and insurance.

Keep in mind that parking, especially in or near the First Precinct, is practically nonexistent except for **parking garages.** Convenient garages in the First Precinct include Parkgarage Am Hof (☎ **01/533 55 71**), Parkgarage Freyung/Herrengasse (☎ **01/535 04 50**), and Tiefgarage Kärntner Strasse (☎ **01/587 17 97**). All are open 24 hours and charge 34 to 40 S ($3.25 to $3.80) per hour.

FAST FACTS: Vienna

Babysitters   For a babysitter in Vienna, call the Babysitting Service of the Austrian University Student Association (☎ **01/408 70 46-75** or 408 70 46-76), which takes calls Monday through Friday from 9am to 1pm. Note that reservations are required at least two days in advance.

Banks   The main banks of Vienna are open Monday through Friday from 8am to 12:30pm and 1:30 to 3pm (to 5:30pm on Thursday). Note that in Austria you cannot obtain cash from credit cards. If you need to exchange money outside bank hours, you can do so at **Intropa,** beside the Tourist Board office at the corner of Philharmoniker Strasse and Kärntner Strasse, open in summer daily from 9am to 5:30pm and in winter Monday through Friday from 9am to 5:30pm and Saturday from 9am to 1pm. In addition, there's a convenient automatic **money-exchange machine** in the heart of the city at Stephansplatz 2 (☎ **01/513 16 26**). Open 24 hours, it will change $20 bills into Austrian currency.

Finally, there are also money-exchange counters at the Westbahnhof, open daily from 7am to 10pm, and the Südbahnhof, open daily in summer from 6:30am to 10pm and in winter from 6:30am to 9pm.

An **American Express** office is at Kärntner Strasse 21–23 (☎ **01/51 540**), open Monday through Friday from 9am to 5:30pm and Saturday from 9am to noon.

Business Hours   Shop hours are generally Monday through Friday from 9am to 6pm and Saturday from 9am to noon or 1pm. Shops outside the city center may close for lunch from noon to 2 or 3pm. On the first Saturday of the month (called *langer Samstag*) shops are open longer, to 5pm.

Consulates   If you have questions or problems regarding American passports or visas, contact the Consulate of the **United States,** in the Marriott Hotel at Gartenbaupromenade 2 (☎ **01/313 39**), open Monday through Friday from 8:30 to 11am. The Consulate of **Australia** is at Mattiellistrasse 2–4 (☎ **01/ 512 85 80**), open Monday through Friday from 9am to 12:30pm for visa applications and also from 2 to 5pm for other matters such as lost passports. The Embassy of **Canada,** at Fleischmarkt 19 (☎ **01/531 38-0**), is open Monday through Friday 8:30am to 12:30pm and 1:30 to 3:30pm. The Consulate of the **United Kingdom,** Jauresgasse 10 (☎ **01/714 61 17**), is open Monday through Friday from 9:15 to noon and (for British passport holders) 2 to 4pm.

Currency   The Austrian currency is the **Schilling,** written ASch, AS, ÖS, or simply S (as I have). A Schilling is made up of 100 Groschen (which are seldom used). Coins are minted as 5, 10, and 50 Groschen, and 1, 5, 10, 20, 25, and 50 Schilling. Banknotes appear as 20, 50, 100, 500, 1,000, and 5,000 Schilling.

Dentists   For a list of English-speaking dentists in Vienna, contact one of the consulates above. If you need dental assistance on a weekend or during the night, telephone 01/512 20 78 for a recorded message of dentists with weekend or night emergency service.

Doctors   The consulates above have lists of English-speaking doctors in Vienna, or call the Doctors' Association at 1771 for a referral. If you need an emergency doctor during the night (daily from 7pm to 7am), call 141.

Emergencies   Dial 122 for the fire department, 133 for the police, 144 for an ambulance, and 1550 to find out which pharmacy has night hours. For medical emergencies, see "Dentists" or "Doctors," above, or "Hospitals," below.

Eyeglasses   For optical needs, a convenient shop in the heart of the city is Trude Kleemann Optik, Kärntner Strasse 37 (☎ **01/512 84 25**), open Monday through Friday from 9am to 6pm and Saturday from 9:30am to 12:30pm (to 5pm the first Saturday of the month).

Holidays   Vienna celebrates New Year's Day (Jan 1), Epiphany (Jan 6), Easter Monday, Labor Day (May 1), Ascension Day, Whit Monday, Corpus Christi, Assumption (Aug 15), National Holiday (Oct 26), All Saints Day (Nov 1), Feast of the Immaculate Conception (Dec 8), and Christmas (Dec 25–26).

Hospitals   There's a general hospital, the Neue Allgemeine Krankenhaus, at Währinger Gürtel 18–20 (☎ **01/40400-0**) and best reached by taking the U-bahn (U-6) to the Michelbeuern/Allgemeine Krankenhaus station. Otherwise, free first-aid treatment is available 24 hours at the Krankenhaus der Barmherzigen

Brüder, Grosse Mohren-Gasse 9 (☎ **01/21 12 10**). A hospital to serve primarily needy people, it also dispenses medications free of charge.

Information   See "Visitor Information" under "Vienna Specifics," earlier in this chapter, for addresses of the Vienna Tourist Board.

Laundry   Ask the proprietor of your hotel for directions to the nearest self-service laundry. Otherwise, a convenient coin laundry is the Münzwäscherei Margaretenstrasse, Margaretenstrasse 52 (☎ **01/587 04 73**), open Monday through Friday from 7am to 6pm and Saturday from 8 to 11am. It costs about 95 S ($9.05) to wash 6 kilos (13¹/₂ lb.) of laundry (including detergent), plus 25 S ($2.40) for drying.

Lost & Found   Vienna's lost-property office is at Wasagasse 22 (☎ **01/313 44-9211**), open Monday through Friday from 8am to noon. All found items end up here after a few days. First, however, they're turned in to the police. If you know approximately where you lost something, inquire first at the nearest police station.

Mail   Most post offices in Vienna are open Monday through Friday from 8am to noon and 2 to 6pm. The main post office (Hauptpostamt), open 24 hours daily for long-distance telephone calls, telegrams, and stamps, is located in the heart of the city inside the Ring at Fleischmarkt 19 (☎ **01/51 509**). If you don't know where you'll be staying in Vienna, you can have your mail sent here *Post Restante.* Occupying part of an older building that was recently renovated, the post office shares space with offices, boutiques, and restaurants. Other post offices with long hours are at the Westbahnhof, open 24 hours for stamps and telephone calls, and the Südbahnhof, open until midnight for telephone calls and 24 hours for stamps. Postcards to North America cost 8.50 S (80¢), while airmail letters cost 10 S (95¢), plus 1.50 S (14¢) for each 5 grams.

Newspapers   *USA Today,* the *Wall Street Journal,* and the *International Herald Tribune* are available at most international kiosk newspaper stands inside the Ring and at the larger hotels.

Photographic Needs   Niedermeyer, in the heart of the Altstadt just off Stephansplatz at Graben 11 (☎ **01/512 33 61**), is a convenient place for film. More shops are on Kärntner Strasse. Most are open Monday through Friday from 9am to 6pm and Saturday from 9am to 12:30pm (to 5pm the first Saturday of the month).

Police   The emergency number for the police is **133.**

Radio/TV   Tune in to 103.8 FM from 6am to 1am for "The Blue Danube," a radio program in English, German, and French with broadcasts of interest to tourists, including news and music, and the "What's On in Vienna" program daily at 1pm. Likewise, every Saturday at 12:30pm on ORF1, there's a television program called "Hello Austria, Hello Vienna" that also covers sightseeing and gives information about Vienna and Austria.

Shoe Repair   There are small neighborhood shoe-repair shops everywhere in the city, but one chain to look for is Mister Minit. You'll find a Mister Minit in department stores, including Gerngross at Mariahilfer Strasse 38–48 (☎ **01/52 180-0**) and Steffl at Kärntner Strasse 19 (☎ **01/514 31**).

Tax   Government tax and service charge is already included in restaurant and hotel bills. If you have purchased goods for more than 1,000 S ($95.25), you're entitled to a refund of part of the value-added tax (up to 32%). See "Shopping," later in this chapter, for more information.

Telephone   It costs 1 S (9¢) to make a one-minute local telephone call (insert several 1-Schilling coins to ensure against being cut off—unused coins will be returned at the end of the call). If you come across a telephone number with a dash at the end (such as 51553-0), it indicates an extension; treat it as you would any number and simply dial the whole number. Note that all telephone numbers in Vienna are gradually being changed to seven digits (a process that will take years). If you come across a number in this book that has been changed, call **information** (dial 1611) to inquire about the new number.

Because hotels add a surcharge on calls made from their rooms, you're best off going to a post office to make **long-distance telephone calls.** It costs 42 S ($4) to make a three-minute call to the United States. An alternative is to purchase a **telephone card,** available at any post office in values of 50 S ($4.75), 100 S ($9.50), and 200 S ($19.05), which can be used in special telephones found virtually everywhere (in fact, sometimes it's difficult to find a telephone that will accept coins, so popular are telephone cards).

The telephone **area/city code** for Vienna is 01 if you're calling from within Austria, 1 if you're calling from outside Austria.

Tipping   A 15% service charge is already included in restaurant bills, but it's customary to round off to the nearest 10 S (95¢) on bills under 100 S ($9.50). For more expensive meals, add 10%. The same rule applies to taxi drivers. Porters receive 20 S ($1.90) per bag.

4 Accommodations

The best budget accommodations are in the vicinity of the Westbahnhof train station and near the university along Alser Strasse. If you want to save money, take a room without private bath, but note that some establishments charge extra for showers in communal washrooms. Keep in mind that some rates include breakfast while others do not—the room-only rate may well end up being higher than rates that include free showers and breakfast. The most expensive accommodations are those inside the Ring in the old city center.

The recommendations below include rooms in private homes, pensions (usually cheaper than hotels and sometimes cheaper than private homes), and hotels. I've also listed a few university dormitories that take in tourists and boarders during summer. Note that floors are numbered according to the European system, starting with the ground floor and then going up to the first floor (the American second floor).

Incidentally, Vienna's telephone system is being computerized, which means that all households and businesses are gradually receiving new telephone numbers and the city code for Vienna changed from 0222 to 01 in 1994. Although I've made every effort to be as up-to-date as possible, some telephone numbers below may no longer be current when you arrive. Call the information operator (dial 1611) if you have any problems. And remember that if the suggested accommodations are full, the **Vienna Tourist Board** will book a room for a fee of 40 S ($3.80), including rooms in private homes.

Getting the Best Deal on Accommodations

- Accommodations that offer cooking facilities will help you save money on your dining bills.
- Take advantage of the winter discounts offered by some hotels and pensions.
- Inquire if there's an extra charge for taking a shower and if breakfast included in the room rate.
- Note if a surcharge is added on local and long-distance calls.

DOUBLES (IN PRIVATE HOMES) FOR LESS THAN 590 S ($56)
NEAR THE WESTBAHNHOF

If you're coming from the Südbahnhof, take tram no. 18 to the Westbahnhof. From Franz-Josefs-Bahnhof, take tram no. 5.

Frau Hedwig Gally

Arnsteingasse 25 (off Mariahilfer Strasse, a 10-minute walk southwest of the train station), Apt. 10, 1150 Wien. ☎ **01/892 90 73** or 893 10 28. Fax 01/893 10 28. 7 rms, 5 with shower only, 2 with shower and toilet; 5 apts. 250 S ($23.80) single without shower or toilet, 300 S ($28.55) single with shower only; 440–460 S ($41.90–$43.80) double without shower or toilet, 500 S ($47.60) double with shower only, 600 S ($57.15) double with shower and toilet; 600 S ($57.15) triple without shower or toilet, 690 S ($65.70) triple with shower only, 780 S ($74.30) triple with shower and toilet. Rates include showers. Breakfast 50 S ($4.75) extra. No credit cards. Free parking. Tram 52 or 58 from the Westbahnhof to Kranzgasse (two stops).

Frau Gally, who speaks good English, has a variety of clean rooms, including one single, doubles without and with shower, one double with shower and toilet, and even two large apartments, one with a kitchen, appropriate for families with children. Every room is equipped with a hotplate and utensils for cooking, as well as a sink with hot water. This place is good also for longer stays.

F. Kaled

Lindengasse 42 (a 10-minute walk from both the Westbahnhof and the Ring), 1070 Wien. ☎ **01/523 90 13.** Fax 01/526 25 13 or 523 90 13. 5 rms, 2 with shower and toilet. TV. 400 S ($38.10) single without shower or toilet; 550 S ($52.40) double without shower or toilet, 650 S ($61.90) double with shower and toilet; 800 S ($76.20) triple without shower or toilet. Rates include showers. Additional person 150 S ($14.30) extra; breakfast 75 S ($7.15) extra. No credit cards. U-Bahn U-3 to Neubaugasse. Tram 5 to Lindengasse. Bus 13A from the Südbahnhof to Mariahilfer Strasse.

Mr. Kaled, a Tunisian who speaks English, French, and German, offers spacious and spotless rooms, each with a radio/cassette player and cable TV with CNN broadcasts. His partner, Tina, speaks excellent English and is happy to give sightseeing tips. All rooms face a quiet inner courtyard. Highly recommended by many readers of this book.

Irmgard and Sandy Lauria

Kaiserstrasse 77 (about a 15-minute walk north of the Westbahnhof), 1070 Wien. ☎ **01/522 25 55.** 5 rms, 1 with shower. TV. 530 S ($50.45) double without shower, 700 S ($66.65) double with shower; 700 S ($66.65) triple without shower, 800 S ($76.20) triple with shower; 850 S ($80.95) quad without shower, 940 S ($89.50) quad with shower. Rates include showers. MC, V. U-Bahn U-6 from the Westbahnhof to Burggasse/Stadthalle (one stop); then a four-minute walk. Tram 5 from the Westbahnhof or Franz-Josefs-Bahnhof to

Burggasse. Bus 13A from the Südbahnhof to Kellermann Gasse, then 48A from Kellerman Gasse to Kaiserstrasse.

Independent backpackers who don't like the intimate quarters of living in someone's house might prefer staying here, since Frau Lauria lives in her own apartment in the same building. The atmosphere is laid-back and the rooms are cozy. Although breakfast is not served, the rooms have plates and flatware and a hot-water kettle; there's a communal fridge and toaster. The rooms are up on the second floor, Apartment 8—but be sure to call first.

NEAR THE SÜDBAHNHOF

Frank Heberling

Siccardsburggasse 42, Apt. 31, 1100 Wien. ☎ **01/607 21 17** or 604 02 29. 6 rms, 1 with shower. 450 S ($42.85) double; 120 S ($11.40) per person in the dormlike four-bed room. Rates include showers. Breakfast 35 S ($3.35) extra. No credit cards. Tram 6 from the Westbahnhof to Quellenplatz (fourth stop after the underpath), or O from the Südbahnhof to Quellenplatz; then a five-minute walk.

Be sure to call first, since the Heberlings are an older retired couple who live in a nearby building (in summer, however, Frau Heberling usually can be found at Apartment 31). The husband-and-wife team, who prefer guests who stay more than one night, speak very good English and are friendly, giving guests a local map with directions on how to reach the city center, where the closest laundry is, and the like. The building is 100 years old but is in excellent condition. The rooms are actually small apartments—with a front sitting room in addition to a bedroom—and are comfortable if a bit plain, each with a sink and its own heater. Breakfast is served in your room.

NEAR THE NASCHMARKT & KARLSPLATZ

Renate Gajdos

Pressgasse 28 (near the outdoor market and Karlsplatz, within a 10-minute walk of the Ring), 1040 Wien. ☎ **01/587 74 16.** 7 rms, none with bath. TV. 420 S (40) single; 580–600 S ($55.25–$57.15) double; 850 S ($80.95) triple. Rates include breakfast and showers. No credit cards. U-Bahn U-6 from the Westbahnhof to Längenfeldgasse, then U-4 from Längenfeldgasse to Kettenbrückengasse. Bus 13A from the Südbahnhof to Margaretenplatz, then 59A to Pressgasse.

One of the rooms here is a single and two others are joined, appropriate for families. The rooms are large, sunny, and well furnished, and the breakfast room is cheerful with lots of interesting knickknacks on the shelves, giving you something to look at as you eat Frau Gajdos's homemade marmalade along with yogurt, bread, and egg. She's been in business about 30 years. This private home is up on the first floor.

Frau Hilde Wolf

Schleifmühlgasse 7 (a few minutes' walk from the Staatsoper and Karlsplatz), 1040 Wien. ☎ **01/586 51 03.** 4 rms, none with bath. 395 S ($37.60) single; 540 S ($51.40) double; 790 S ($75.25) triple; 1,025 S ($97.60) quad. Breakfast 35 S ($3.35) extra; showers 20 S ($1.90) extra. No credit cards. Tram 6 from the Westbahnhof to Eichenstrasse (four stops), then 62 from Eichenstrasse to Paulanergasse; or D from the Südbahnhof or Franz-Josefs-Bahnhof to Oper, then 62 or 65 from Oper to Paulanergasse or bus no. 59A to Schleifmühlgasse.

Both Frau Wolf and her husband, Otto, speak English, and they offer large high-ceilinged rooms comfortably furnished with fin-de-siècle furniture. Frau Wolf, who loves children and welcomes families, serves a lavish breakfast and says that readers of this book can ask for second helpings of coffee, bread, butter, and marmalade. Her first-floor apartment is centrally located, near the outdoor market.

DOUBLES FOR LESS THAN 610 S ($58)
OFF MARIAHILFER STRASSE

Hotel Kugel

Siebensterngasse 43 / Neubaugasse 46 (on the corner of Neubaugasse and Siebensterngasse), 1070 Wien. ☎ **01/523 13 30** or 523 33 55. Fax 01/523 16 78. 38 rms, 17 with shower only, 17 with shower and toilet. 420 S ($40) single without shower or toilet, 500 S ($47.60) single with shower only, 600 S ($57.15) single with shower and toilet; 580 S ($49.15) double without shower or toilet, 760 S ($72.40) double with shower only, 940 S ($89.50) double with shower and toilet. Rates include breakfast and showers. No credit cards. Tram 18 from the Westbahnhof (going toward Burggasse/Stadthalle) one stop, then 49 to Neubaugasse/Siebensternqasse; or D from Franz-Josefs-Bahnhof to Westbahnstrasse/ Kaiserstrasse. Bus 13A from the Südbahnhof to Kirchengasse.

This century-old hotel has been owned by the same family from the beginning; it's now in its third generation. It shows its age, with small rooms and outdated wallpaper, but it has a good location and is adequate for the price. Only four rooms are without showers and/or toilets; showers were added as free-standing cabinets. Note that the cheapest doubles with and without shower are actually single rooms that have an extra bed.

Pension Lindenhof

Lindengasse 4 (behind the large Herzmansky department store), 1070 Wien. ☎ **01/ 523 04 98.** Fax 01/523 73 62. 19 rms, 10 with shower and toilet. 360 S ($34.30) single without shower or toilet, 460 S ($43.80) single with shower and toilet; 600 S ($57.15) double without shower or toilet, 820 S ($78.10) double with shower and toilet; 890 S ($84.75) triple without shower or toilet, 1,230 S ($117.15) triple with shower and toilet. Rates include breakfast. Showers 20 S ($1.90) extra. No credit cards. U-Bahn U-3 from the Westbahnhof to Neubaugasse. Bus 13A from the Südbahnhof to Kirchengasse.

Pension Lindenhof is owned by George Gebrael, an Armenian with Austrian citizenship who's married to a Bulgarian. Mr. Gebrael speaks seven languages, English among them, and both his daughter and his son go to an international school taught in English. The long corridor of the pension is filled with massive plants, and a few of the rooms even have balconies.

Pension Reimer

Kirchengasse 18, 1070 Wien. ☎ **01/523 61 62.** 14 rms, 5 with shower, 3 with shower and toilet. 375 S ($35.70) single without shower or toilet, 480 S ($45.70) single with shower only; 590 S ($56.20) double without shower or toilet, 700 S ($66.65) double with shower only, 820 S ($78.10) double with shower and toilet; 1,020 S ($97.15) triple with shower only, 1,140 S ($108.55) triple with shower and toilet. Rates include breakfast. V. U-Bahn U-3 from the Westbahnhof to Neubaugasse. Bus 13A from the Südbahnhof to Kirchengasse.

This second-floor pension, under proprietress Margarete Mattis, who speaks some English, offers sparsely decorated plain rooms, some rather small but others quite large. Those that face the back are quieter. The small breakfast room has a TV. There's an elevator, but guests must either use a 1-S (9¢) coin to operate it or ask for a key from Frau Mattis.

NEAR SCHOTTEN RING & THE UNIVERSITY

⑤ Pension Falstaff

Müllnergasse 5, 1090 Wien. ☎ **01/317 91 27.** Fax 01/317 91 864. 17 rms, 7 with shower only, 2 with shower and toilet. TEL. 360 S ($34.30) single without shower or toilet, 480 S

($45.70) single with shower only; 590 S ($56.20) double without shower or toilet, 720 S ($68.55) double with shower only, 820 ($78.10) double with shower and toilet. Rates include continental breakfast. Additional person 220 S ($20.95) extra; showers 30 S ($2.85) extra. V. U-Bahn U-3 from the Westbahnhof to Volkstheater, then tram D from Volkstheater to Schlichtgasse. Tram D from the Südbahnhof or Franz-Josefs-Bahnhof to Schlichtgasse.

This pension is one of the best finds in this price category, with simple but clean rooms—some of them enormous. There's a 40% discount for stays of a month or longer in winter. The reception is on floor "M," the mezzanine floor, and there's an elevator.

Pension Wild

Lange Gasse 10 (a 10-minute walk from the Ring), 1080 Wien. ☎ **01/406 51 74.** Fax 01/402 21 68. 16 rms, 2 with shower and toilet. 450 S ($42.85) single without shower or toilet; 590–690 S ($56.20–$65.70) double without or with shower and toilet; 870–970 S ($82.85–$92.40) triple without or with shower and toilet. Rates include breakfast and showers. AE, DC, MC, V. U-Bahn U-3 from the Westbahnhof to Volkstheater, then U-2 from Volkstheater to Lerchenfelderstrasse; then a two-minute walk. Tram D from Franz-Josefs-Bahnhof to Bellaria. Bus 13A from the Südbahnhof to Piaristengasse.

Run by friendly Frau Wild and her English-speaking son, Peter, this pension features refrigerators, cooking facilities, pots, pans, and utensils on every floor, making it popular with students and for longer stays (spaghetti, says Frau Wild, is the most frequently cooked dish). The place started out more than a quarter of a century ago with only one bed but now covers several floors, accessible by elevator. The rooms are clean, and multibed ones are available. There's even a fitness studio in the basement, with a sauna and steam bath that costs 50 S ($4.75) for guests. Unfortunately, the pension has a tendency to overbook, placing extra guests in nearby apartments at prices higher than those quoted in this book. Insist on a room in the pension when making your reservation.

DOUBLES (IN PRIVATE HOMES) FOR LESS THAN 810 S ($77)
INSIDE THE RING

Frau Adele Grün

Gonzagagasse 1 (just off Franz-Josefs-Kai), Apt. 19, 1010 Wien. ☎ **01/533 25 06.** 4 rms, none with bath. 400–450 S ($38.10–$42.85) single; 800–850 S ($76.20–$80.95) double; 1,000 S ($95.25) triple; 1,200 S ($114.30) quad. AE, DC, MC, V. Rates include showers. U-Bahn U-3 from the Westbahnhof to Stephansplatz, then U-1 from Stephansplatz to Schwedenplatz; then a one-minute walk. Tram D from the Südbahnhof to Oper, then 1 or 2 from Oper to Salztorbrücke; or D from Franz-Josefs-Bahnhof to Börserplatz, then 1 to Salztorbrücke.

In an elegant older building, up on the third floor (there's an elevator), the rooms here are pleasant and clean. There are two communal showers, one tub, and one toilet. Frau Grün, in her 70s, speaks English and is friendly. If no one answers the house phone, try her office number (☎ 01/533 62 73).

Frau Hoffmann

Annagasse 3A (just off Kärntner Strasse), 1010 Wien. ☎ **01/512 49 04.** 5 rms, 3 with shower. 700 S ($66.65) double without shower, 800 S ($76.20) double with shower. Rates include continental breakfast and showers. No credit cards. U-Bahn U-3 from the Westbahnhof to Stephansplatz; then a five-minute walk. Tram D from the Südbahnhof or Franz-Josefs-Bahnhof to Oper; then a three-minute walk.

Once a famous skater, Frau Hoffmann ran her establishment as a pension for more than 30 years but in 1988 changed to a private-room status. The rooms are enormous and the location can't be beat. Frau Hoffmann speaks English, serves big breakfasts, and gives advice on what to do in Vienna.

NEAR THE WESTBAHNHOF

Barbara Kolier

Schmalzhofgasse 11 (a 10-minute walk from the train station, near Mariahilfer Strasse in the direction of the Ring), 1060 Wien. ☎ **01/597 29 35.** 5 rms, all with shower and toilet. 360 S ($34.30) per person. Rates include continental breakfast. No credit cards. U-Bahn U-3 to Zieglergasse (take the Webgasse exit). Tram 18 from the Südbahnhof to the Westbahnhof.

This cheerful establishment has its own stairway up to the first floor—look for the iron gate. The rooms are large and spotless, with sturdy old-fashioned furniture. This private home wraps itself around an inner courtyard; next door is an Indian restaurant. Although the charges are a bit higher than the other private homes in this area, keep in mind that all rooms have baths and breakfast is included.

NEAR THE NASCHMARKT & KARLSPLATZ

Frau Renate Halper

Straussengasse 5 (less than a 15-minute walk from the city center), 1050 Wien. ☎ **01/587 12 78.** 3 rms and 1 apt, none with bath. 500 S ($47.60) single; 720 S ($68.55) double; 360 S ($34.30) per person in the apt. No credit cards. Rates include breakfast and showers. U-Bahn U-4 to Pilgramgasse; or U-3 from the Westbahnhof to Neubaugasse, then bus no. 13A (toward the Südbahnhof) to Ziegelofen Gasse. Bus 13A from the Südbahnhof to Ziegelofen Gasse.

Renate Halper is a young, outgoing, friendly woman who speaks English fluently. She has even prepared for her guests a small booklet in English with information regarding restaurants in the vicinity, how to get from her apartment to the various sights, explanations of Vienna's many kinds of coffee, and more. One room is outfitted with furniture that used to belong to Renate's grandmother. Another room has a balcony, and the apartment has its own kitchen and TV with cable and CNN broadcasts.

DOUBLES FOR LESS THAN 840 S ($80)

NEAR THE UNIVERSITY

Pension Adria

Wickenburggasse 23 (northwest of the Ring, a 20-minute walk from the old city center), 1080 Wien. ☎ **01/402 02 38** or 408 39 06. Fax 01/408 39 06. 14 rms, 3 with shower only, 11 with shower and toilet. TV TEL. 570 S ($54.30) single with shower only, 620 S ($59.05) single with shower and toilet; 840–950 S ($80–$90.45) double with shower and toilet; 1,100 S ($104.75) triple with shower and toilet. Winter discounts available. Rates include buffet breakfast and showers. MC. Tram D from the Südbahnhof to Schottentor, then a 10-minute walk; or 5 from the Westbahnhof or Franz-Josefs-Bahnhof to Langegasse.

This first-floor pension is simple and clean, good for people who are looking for a no-nonsense place to sleep. It's owned by English-speaking Mr. Hamde, a Jordanian who now has Austrian citizenship. All rooms have radios. The buffet breakfast is all-you-can-eat.

Pension Amon

Daungasse 1, 1080 Wien. ☎ **01/405 01 94.** 12 rms, all with shower. 530 S ($50.45) single; 750 S ($71.40) double; 1,000 S ($95.25) triple. Rates include continental breakfast. AE, DC, MC, V. Tram 5 from the Westbahnhof or Franz-Josefs-Bahnhof to Laudongasse. Bus 13A from the Südbahnhof to Skodagasse (the last stop).

English-speaking Herr Amon hunts for a hobby, as is apparent in the rows of ant-lers lining the corridor of his small pension. His cozy breakfast room, outfitted with a TV, is also decorated in the spirit of the hunt. The rooms are comfortable, if a bit old-fashioned, and Herr Amon will give sightseeing tips.

Pension Astra

Alserstrasse 32, 1090 Wien. ☎ **01/402 43 54** or 408 22 70. Fax 01/402 46 62. 17 rms, 2 with shower only, 15 with shower and toilet; 4 apts. TV TEL. 550 S ($52.40) single with shower only, 690 S ($65.70) single with shower and toilet; 760 S ($72.40) double with shower only, 990 S ($94.30) double with shower and toilet; 850 S ($80.95) apt for two, 1,200 S ($114.30) apt for three. No credit cards. Crib available. U-Bahn U-6 from the Westbahnhof to Alserstrasse. Tram 5 from Franz-Josefs-Bahnhof to Spittalgasse/Alserstrasse; then a five-minute walk. Bus 13A from the Südbahnhof to Skodagasse (the last stop).

Rooms in this first-floor pension are quiet and clean (all but one face off the street), managed by friendly English-speaking Gaby Brekoupil. Most of the room TVs have cable, and the apartments come with a small kitchenette and TV, making them especially good for families or for longer stays.

Pension Columbia

Kochgasse 9, 1080 Wien. ☎ **01/405 67 57.** Fax 01/405 67 57. 9 rms, 4 with shower. 490 S ($46.65) single without shower; 720–750 S ($68.55–$71.40) double without shower, 820–860 S ($78.10–$81.90) double with shower. Rates include buffet breakfast and showers. No credit cards. Tram 5 from the Westbahnhof to Kochgasse, or 5 from Franz-Josefs-Bahnhof to Lederergasse. Bus 13A from the Südbahnhof to Laudongasse.

The rooms here are literally large enough to dance in, with high ceilings typical of turn-of-the-century Viennese buildings, some with stucco. A pension for more than 40 years, it was acquired by Frau Nagel in 1994. The only drawback is that there's no elevator to the pension, located up two flights of stairs.

SUPER-BUDGET CHOICES
YOUTH HOSTELS

Believe-It-or-Not

Myrthengasse 10, Apt. 14, 1070 Wien. ☎ **01/526 46 58.** 10 beds. 110 S ($10.45) per per-son in winter (except Christmas and Easter), 160 S ($15.25) per person the rest of the year. Rates include sheets and showers. No credit cards. U-Bahn U-6 from the Westbahnhof to Burggasse/Stadthalle; then bus no. 48A from Gurggasse/Stadthalle to Neubaugasse/ Myrthengasse. Bus 13A from the Südbahnhof to Kellermanngasse.

This is a very small establishment, simply one room outfitted with bunk beds, available to both males and females. It's run by a charming young woman who speaks excellent English, and clean sheets are included in the price. No breakfast is served, but guests are welcome to make their own in a communal kitchen. You'll like this place.

Hostel Ruthensteiner

Robert-Hamerling-Gasse 24 (near the Westbahnhof), 1150 Wien. ☎ **01/893 42 02** or 893 27 96. 66 beds, no rooms with bath. 210 S ($20) single; 420 S ($40) double; 129–149 S ($12.30–$14.20) per person in multibed rooms. Rates include showers. Breakfast 25 S ($2.40) extra. No credit cards. Tram 18 from Südbahnhof or 5 from Franz-Josefs-Bahnhof to the Westbahnhof; then a five-minute walk.

This youth hostel run by Erin and Walter Ruthensteiner (Erin is American) requires a membership card (though nonmembers can stay by paying 40 S/$3.80 extra a night) and there's no age limit or curfew. Single, double, and dorm rooms are available, and all rooms have sinks. You can cook your own food in the kitchen, and even better is the brick patio where you can eat. Bikes are available for rent May through September for 78 S ($7.40) a day.

Jugendgästenhaus Brigittenau

Friedrich-Engels-Platz 24 (in the northern end of town, near the Danube), 1200 Wien. ☎ **01/332 82 94-0.** 282 beds. 150 S ($14.30) per person with youth-hostel membership card, 190 S ($18.10) per person without membership card. Rates include continental breakfast and showers. Lunch or dinner 60 S ($5.70) extra. No credit cards. U-Bahn: U-6 from the Westbahnhof to Nussdorfer Strasse; then bus no. 35A from Nussdorfer Strasse to Friedrich-Engels-Platz (the last stop). Tram 31 from Franz-Josefs-Bahnhof to Friedrich-Engels-Platz. S-Bahn (Schnellbahn, a commuter train): From the Südbahnhof to Traisengasse, then tram N from Traisengasse to Friedrich-Engels-Platz.

This modern youth hostel requires a membership card, but those who don't have one can stay by paying the 40 S ($3.35) extra per night.

Jugendgästenhaus Zöhrer

Skodagasse 26 (northwest of the city center, near the university district), 1080 Wien. ☎ **01/406 07 30.** Fax 01/408 04 09. 29 beds. 170 S ($13.30) per person. Rates include breakfast, sheets, and showers. No credit cards. Tram 5 from the Westbahnhof to Alserstrasse, or 5 from Franz-Josefs-Bahnhof to Skodagasse. Bus 13A from the Südbahnhof to Skodagasse (the last stop).

This casual small establishment offers eight dormitory-style rooms (most with their own shower) with bunk beds and lockers, plus a kitchen where you can cook your own meals, a TV lounge, and a laundry room. The atmosphere is friendly, the rooms are clean, and youth-hostel cards are not required. No age limit, no curfew.

Jugendherberge Wien

Myrthengasse 7 (☎ **01/523 63 16**) and Neustiftgasse 85 (☎ **01/523 74 62**), 1070 Wien. Fax (for both) 01/52 35 849. 245 beds. 150 S ($14.30) per person with youth-hostel membership card, 190 S ($18.10) per person without membership card. Rates include breakfast and showers. Lunch or dinner 60 S ($5.70) extra. No credit cards. U-Bahn U-6 from the Westbahnhof to Burggasse/Stadthalle; then tram no. 48A from Burggasse/Stadthalle to Neuburggasse. Tram D from Franz-Josefs-Bahnhof to Dr.-Karl-Ring, then 48A to Neubaugasse. Bus 13A from the Südbahnhof to Kellermanngasse.

There's no age limit and you don't have to have a youth-hostel card to stay here, though nonmembers pay more. The building was built in the Biedermeier style in 1828, but the renovated interior is modern and a new wing was recently added. Each room has three to six beds and its own shower; those in the new wing also have a toilet. Other facilities include a large dining room, TV room, laundry room, and table tennis and Foosball games. The front doors close at midnight.

Turmherberge Don Bosco

Lechnerstrasse 13, 1030 Wien. ☎ **01/713 14 94.** 50 beds. 60 S ($5.70) per person. Rates include showers. No credit cards. Closed Dec–Feb. Tram 18 from the Westbahnhof or Südbahnhof to Stadionbrücke; then a few minutes' walk.

This youth hostel is open from March to November. Its beds are divided into seven rooms on seven floors of a bell tower. A youth-hostel card is required.

CAMPING

Aktiv Camping Neue Donau

Am Kaisermühlendamm 119, 1220 Wien. ☎ **01/220 93 10.** 65 S ($6.20) per person per night, plus 61 S ($5.80) per night for the campsite. Closed mid-Sept to mid-May. U-Bahn U-3 to Schlachthausgasse; then bus no. 83A to the Campingplatz stop.

This would be my first choice in camping spots, since it's less than 3 miles from the city center and on the Donau, which offers swimming, sailing, and biking. Facilities at the camp itself include a communal kitchen, supermarket, and laundry room.

Camping Rodaun

An der Au 2, 1238 Wien-Rodaun. ☎ **01/888 41 54.** 60 S ($5.70) per person per night, plus 47 S ($4.50) per night for the campsite. Closed mid-Nov to mid-Mar. Tram 60.

Camping Rodaun is 6 miles from the city center and has a swimming pool and a restaurant.

Campingplatz Schloss Laxenburg

Münchendorferstrasse Laxenburg, 2361 Laxenburg. ☎ **02236/71 333.** 65 S ($6.20) per person per night, plus 61 S ($5.80) per night for the campsite. Closed from the end of Oct to Easter. Bus From the Vienna Centre bus station.

This campground is in Laxenburg, 9 miles from the city center. Facilities include a restaurant, a supermarket, a heated swimming pool, and a children's pool.

Campingplatz Wien West I

Hüttelbergstrasse 40, 1140 Wien. ☎ **01/94 14 49.** 65 S ($6.20) per person per night, plus 61 S ($5.80) per night for the campsite. Closed Feb. U-Bahn U-4 to Hütteldorf; then tram no. 152.

It's 4 miles from the city center. Facilities include a recreation room, kitchen with cooking facilities, laundry room, and supermarket.

Campingplatz Wien West II

Hüttelbergstrasse 80, 1140 Wien. ☎ **01/914 23 14.** 65 S ($6.20) per person per night, plus 61 S ($5.80) per night for the campsite. Closed Feb. U-Bahn: U-4 to Hütteldorf; then tram no. 152.

This campground 4 miles from the city center has a recreation room, laundry room, and store. There are also bungalows that sleep four renting for 410 S ($39.05), available April to October.

LONG-TERM STAYS

Both Frau Gally and Frau Halper and the Pension Astra and Pension Wild (all above) offer cooking facilities, making them ideal for longer stays. In addition, in the listings below under "Worth the Extra Money," Pension Aviano has a couple of rooms with cooking facilities and offers winter discounts. Pension Pertschy and Pension Edelweiss (below) have lower rates in winter.

WORTH THE EXTRA MONEY

Hotel-Pension Zipser

Langegasse 49 (about a five-minute walk behind the Rathaus and the Ring), 1080 Wien. ☎ **01/404 54-0.** Fax 01/408 52 66 13. Telex 115544. 50 rms, all with tub/shower and toilet. TV TEL. 760 S ($72.40) single; 1,290 S ($122.85) double without courtyard view, 1,320 S ($125.70) double with courtyard view. Rates include continental breakfast. Additional person 280 S ($26.65) extra. AE, DC, MC, V. Parking 180 S ($17.15). U-Bahn U-2 to Rathaus. Tram 5 from the Westbahnhof or Franz-Josefs-Bahnhof to Lederergasse. Bus 13A from the Südbahnhof to Theater in der Josefstadt.

The rooms here are comfortable, modern, and clean; some overlook a quiet inner courtyard with trees and have a balcony. All rooms have double doors (to seal out noise) as well as tile baths, cable TV with CNN, and radio. The pension has an elevator).

❂ Pension Aviano

Marco-d'Aviano-Gasse 1 (just off Kärntner Strasse), 1010 Wien. ☎ **01/512 83 30.** Fax 01/ 512 83 30-6. 17 rms, all with shower and toilet. MINIBAR TV TEL. Summer, 740 S ($70.50) single; 1,200 S ($114.30) double. Winter, 680–740 S ($64.75–$70.50) single; 1,080–1,200 S ($102.85–$114.30) double. Rates include buffet breakfast. MC, V. U-Bahn U-3 from the Westbahnhof to Stephansplatz. Tram 52 or 58 from the Westbahnhof to Burgring, or D from the Südbahnhof or Franz-Josefs-Bahnhof to Oper.

This centrally located, personable small pension offers rooms elegantly decorated in Old Vienna Biedermeier style, as well as such modern conveniences as radios and a private safe. A couple of rooms are equipped with hotplates, and some also face the famous shopping street, Kärntner Strasse (these have double-pane windows to keep them quiet). Reception is on the fourth floor.

Pension Baroness E

Langegasse 61, 1080 Wien. ☎ **01/405 10 61.** Fax 01/405 10 61-61. Telex 136375. 39 rms, all with tub/shower and toilet. MINIBAR TV TEL. Summer, 600–700 S ($57.15–$66.65) single; 880–1,020 S ($83.80–$97.15) double. Winter, 530–600 S ($50.50–$57.15) single; 800–920 S ($76.20–$87.60) double. Rates include buffet breakfast. DC, MC, V. Tram 5 from the Westbahnhof or Franz-Josefs-Bahnhof to Langegasse. Bus 13A from the Südbahnhof to Laudongasse.

Owned by the Pertschy family, which also runs the Pension Pertschy (below), this pleasant establishment has a friendly, competent English-speaking staff and newly refurbished Biedermeier-style or mahogany-furnished rooms with tiled baths and hairdryers. The breakfast room is especially cheerful.

Pension Nossek

Graben 17, 1010 Wien. ☎ **01/533 70 41.** Fax 01/535 36 46. 26 rms, 4 with shower only, 22 with tub/shower and toilet. TEL. 630 S ($60) single with shower only, 800 S ($76.20) single with tub/shower and toilet; 1,100 S ($104.75) double with tub/shower and toilet; 1,470 S ($140) triple with tub/shower and toilet. Rates include breakfast. No credit cards. U-Bahn: U-3 from the Westbahnhof to Herrengasse. Tram D from the Südbahnhof to Oper; then U-Bahn U-1 from the Südbahnhof to Stephansplatz (one stop). Bus 2A from Burgring to Graben-Petersplatz.

This pension has a great location, right on Graben Square in the heart of the city. It's managed by a two-sister team, Terika and Suzanne. An interesting feature is that Mozart lived in a third-floor apartment in this building from 1781 to 1782. (Mozart lived in many places in Vienna—moving when he couldn't pay the rent.) Singles have either a shower or shower and toilet; the doubles all have a shower or bathtub and toilet and are the same price whether they face the back or the more picturesque Graben. TVs are available on request. The people running this pension care about their guests and are happy to give advice and suggestions for sightseeing.

❂ Pension Pertschy

Habsburgergasse 5 (a few steps off the Graben, near Stephansplatz), 1010 Wien. ☎ **01/534 49.** Fax 01/534 49-49. Telex 136375. 43 rms, all with tub/shower and toilet. MINIBAR TV TEL. Summer, 770 S ($73.35) single; 1,130–1,300 S ($107.60–$123.80) double. Winter, 600– 680 S ($57.15–$64.75) single; 1,020–1,220 S ($97.15–$116.20) double. Rates include buffet breakfast. DC, MC, V. U-Bahn U-1 or U-3 to Stephansplatz. Tram D from the Südbahnhof to Oper; then bus no. 3A from Oper to Habsburgergasse.

This is a wonderful place for a splurge. It occupies the first several floors of an ancient "palais" built in 1725 and now an official historic landmark. The ceilings are high and vaulted, and the rooms are outfitted in Biedermeier style, complete with chandeliers. Three rooms even have tile heaters—one is 200 years old. To get from room to room, you walk along an enclosed catwalk on a balcony that traces around a courtyard. As for the Pertschys, they lived in Canada for 10 years and have run this pension for 30 years—the whole family speaks perfect English.

5 Dining

Because many shops and businesses are inside the Ring and along Mariahilfer Strasse, many of Vienna's best-known eateries are there as well. You don't have to spend a lot of money to eat well in Vienna, and there's enough variety to keep the palate interested.

But first you have to know what you're looking for. A *Billateria* (from the German word *billig,* meaning "cheap") is a self-service restaurant where you can create your own multicourse meal at very low prices. Along these same lines, but a bit more upscale, is a chain of cafeterias called Naschmarkt, all with very convenient locations. And finally, a *Beisl* is the Austrian word for pub or tavern, many of which serve hearty and inexpensive meals.

FAVORITE MEALS   Viennese cuisine is the culmination of various ethnic influences, including Bohemian, Hungarian, Croatian, Slovene, German, and Italian. At the top end of the price scale is wild game, followed by various fish, poultry, and beef dishes. Most restaurants serve complete meals—main dish and one or several side dishes. Prices listed for each restaurant below are usually for complete meals.

For starters, you might try a soup, such as *Griessnockerlsuppe* (clear soup with semolina dumplings), *Leberknödlsuppe* (soup with liver dumplings), *Rindsuppe* (beef broth), or *Gulaschsuppe* (Hungarian goulash).

For main courses, popular dishes include *Bauernschmaus* (a combination of many varied sausages and pork items with sauerkraut and dumplings), *Tafelspitz* (boiled beef with vegetables), *Wiener Schnitzel* (breaded veal cutlet), *Schweinebraten* (roast port), *Spanferkel* (suckling pig), *Backhendl* (fried and breaded chicken), and *Gulasch* (stew). *Nockerl* are little dumplings, usually served with sauce.

And, of course, there are desserts. Vienna's *Apfelstrudel* (apple strudel) is probably the best in the world. *Palatschinken* are light sugared pancakes; *Kaiserschmarren* is a diced omelet, served with jam and sprinkled with sugar. A *Sachertorte* is a sinfully rich chocolate cake.

And to top it all off you'll want coffee, of which there are at least 20 varieties. Introduced 300 years ago by the Turks during their unsuccessful attempt to conquer Vienna, coffee has become an art form, as served in Viennese coffeehouses. Among the many different kinds of coffee are the *kleiner Schwarzer,* a small cup without milk; the *kleiner Brauner,* small cup with a little milk; the *Melange,* a large cup with milk; *Mokka,* strong black Viennese coffee; *Melange mit Schlag,* same as Mokka but topped with whipped cream; *Einspänner,* a glass of coffee with whipped cream; and *Türkischer,* Turkish coffee boiled in a small copper pot and served in tiny cups. Coffee is always served with a glass of water.

Keep in mind that the opening hours given below are exactly that—the hours the doors remain open. Last orders are generally one hour before closing time.

LOCAL BUDGET BESTS

Mensa

Technische Universität Wien, Turm B, Wiedner Hauptstrasse 8–19. ☎ **01/586 65 02.** Fixed-price meals 31–43 S ($2.95–$4.10) for students, 35–47 S ($3.35–$4.50) for nonstudents. No

---

Getting the Best Deal on Dining

- Daily specials, often posted outside the door, are complete meals at discount prices.
- Stop at some of Vienna's many *Würstelstände,* food stalls selling sausages and beer.
- Take a few hearty meals in a *Beisl,* a typical Viennese tavern that also dishes out home-cooked food at low prices.
- Ask if there's an extra charge for each piece of bread consumed and if the main course comes with vegetables or a side dish.
- Note if there's a table charge (*Gedeck*).

---

credit cards. Mon–Fri 11am–2:30pm. Closed Christmas–Jan 7. U-Bahn U-1, U-2, or U-4 to Karlsplatz. AUSTRIAN.

Although technically for students, this student cafeteria (Mensa) also serves non-students for slightly more. It's up on the first floor of a modern light-green building not far from Karlsplatz. There are usually four platters available, from stews to grilled chicken or spaghetti. There are different counters for each, along with additional choices of soups and salad. Pay after choosing your food and be sure to clear your tray when you're finished. You'll also find an inexpensive snack bar here.

There's another Mensa, this one a student cafeteria of the Universität Wien, at Universitätstrasse 7, near Schottentor. It's open for lunch only, Monday through Friday from 11am to 2pm, and offers similar dishes at similar prices.

MEALS FOR LESS THAN 80 S ($7.60)
INSIDE THE RING

Bizi

Rotenturmstrasse 4 (on the corner of Wollzeile, just north of Stephansplatz). ☎ **01/513 37 05.** Pizza and pasta 65–80 S ($6.20–$7.60); meat courses 105–120 S ($10–$11.40). No credit cards. Daily 11am–11:30pm. U-Bahn U-1 or U-3 to Stephansplatz. ITALIAN.

This enormously popular self-service restaurant serves a variety of pizza and pasta, including ravioli, gnocchi, tagliatelle, and tortellini—with a choice of sauces. Pizza by the slice costs 27 S ($2.55), and there's also a salad bar—a large plate costs 50 S ($4.75). The decor is upbeat and pleasant, with modern art on the walls, and there's even a no-smoking section.

✪ Buffet Trzesniewski

Dorotheergasse 1 (just off Stephansplatz). ☎ **01/512 32 91.** Sandwiches 8 S (75¢) each. No credit cards. Mon–Fri 9am–7:30pm, Sat 9am–1pm (to 6pm on *langer Samstag*). U-Bahn U-1 or U-3 to Stephansplatz. SANDWICHES.

This is one of the most popular cafeterias in all of Vienna—and rightly so. It's a centrally located tiny shop, so small that the mealtime line often snakes through the entire store; it's best to come here during off-peak times. Trzesniewski is a buffet of small open-face finger sandwiches covered with such spreads as salami, egg salad, herring, tomatoes, or a couple dozen other selections. Four sandwiches are usually enough for me, along with a Pfiff, a very tiny beer (an eighth of a liter) for only 9 S (85¢). Very Viennese in atmosphere, this place is highly recommended.

Duran Superimbiss

Rotenturmstrasse 11 (just north of Stephansplatz). ☎ **01/533 71 15.** Sandwiches 7–12.50 S (65¢–$1.20); meals 25–40 S ($2.40–$3.80). No credit cards. Mon–Fri 9am–7pm, Sat 9am–1pm. U-Bahn U-1 or U-3 to Stephansplatz. SANDWICHES.

Duran Superimbiss is one of the most popular self-service chains in town, offering fast food to eat in its simple surroundings or to take out. This store sells about two dozen varieties of open-face finger sandwiches alone, as well as special platters that may include Schweinebraten, grilled sausage, pizza, or Schnitzel.

There are other branches at Alserstrasse 14 (☎ **01/42 67 25**); Mariahilfer Strasse 91 (☎ **01/596 23 73**); and Schwedenplatz 2 (☎ **01/533 68 33**) near the main post office.

Naschmarkt

Schottengasse 1. ☎ **01/533 51 86.** 55–110 S ($5.25–$10.50). No credit cards. Mon–Fri 10:30am–7:30pm, Sat–Sun and hols 10:30am–3pm. U-Bahn U-3 to Herrengasse or U-2 to Schottentor-Universität. Tram 1, 2, or D to Schottentor. AUSTRIAN.

Using the name of Vienna's popular outdoor market, Naschmarkt is a self-service cafeteria offering a variety of Austrian dishes, salads (including a salad bar), soups, beer, desserts, and other items at very reasonable prices. Especially good are the daily specials, which may include Schnitzel, Schweinebraten, chicken, stews, fish, or spaghetti, along with one or two side dishes. The interior is modern and pleasant. A good old standby.

Other convenient locations are Schwarzenbergplatz 16 (☎ **01/505 31 15**), open Monday through Friday from 6:30am to 10:30pm, and Saturday, Sunday, and holidays from 9am to 10:30m; and Mariahilfer Strasse 85–87 (☎ **01/ 587 63 06**), open daily from 7am to 10pm.

Nordsee

Kärntner Strasse 25 (between Stephansplatz and the Staatsoper). ☎ **01/512 73 54.** 65–115 S ($6.20–$10.95). No credit cards. Daily 9am–11pm. U-Bahn U-1 or U-3 to Stephansplatz, or U-1, U-2, or U-4 to Karlsplatz. FISH.

A simple seafood chain from northern Germany, Nordsee is a cafeteria with pictures on the wall of all the dishes available, making ordering a snap. There are fish sticks, fish soup, fish paella, herring, baked fish, salads, and fish sandwiches, and take-out service is available from its open-front streetside display counter. This cafeteria has an envied location right on Kärntner Strasse, and there's even outdoor dining.

There's another branch off the Graben in the center of town at Kohlmarkt 6 (☎ **01/533 59 66**), open Monday through Friday from 9am to 7pm and Saturday and Sunday from 10am to 7pm; and at Mariahilfer Strasse 34 (☎ **01/ 522 36 37**), open Monday through Friday from 9am to 7pm and Saturday from 9am to 2pm (to 6pm on *langer Samstag*).

Spaghetti & Co.

Stephansplatz 7. ☎ **01/512 14 44.** Pizza and pasta 55–110 S ($5.25–$10.50). No credit cards. Sun–Thurs 10:30am–midnight, Fri–Sat 10:30am–1am. U-Bahn U-1 or U-3 to Stephansplatz. PIZZA/PASTA.

With a convenient location just north of Vienna's best-known landmark, Stephansdom, this chain of spaghetti parlors offers more than a dozen kinds of spaghetti dishes, including one with chili sauce and one with salmon and mushrooms. It also offers half a dozen choices of lasagnes and gnocchi casseroles as well as pizza and salads. Good for a fast and inexpensive sit-down meal.

There's a second Spaghetti & Co. nearby at Petersplatz 1 (☎ **01/533 70 74**), just off the Graben, open the same hours.

OUTSIDE THE RING

Schnitzel-Imbiss

Webgasse 39 (just off Mariahilfer Strasse). ☎ **01/596 24 00**. 27–115 S ($2.55–$10.95). No credit cards. Mon–Fri 9am–10pm, Sat–Sun 10am–10pm. U-Bahn U-3 to Zieglergasse. AUSTRIAN.

Less than a five-minute walk east of the Westbahnhof, this simple cafeteria specializes in Vienna's most famous dish, the Schnitzel. A small Schnitzel served with either french fries or a salad costs only 41 S ($3.90); a huge one served with both french fries and a salad costs 82 S ($7.80). Other choices on the small menu include Cordon Bleu, turkey Schnitzel, and turkey and Schnitzel burgers.

✪ Schnitzelwirt

Neubaugasse 52 (near the corner of Siebensterngasse). ☎ **01/963 24 54**. 60–90 S ($5.70–$8.55). No credit cards. Mon–Sat 11am–10pm. Closed hols. U-Bahn U-3 to Neubaugasse; then a three-minute walk. Tram 49 from Dr.-Karl-Renner-Ring to Siebensterngasse. Bus 13A to Siebensterngasse. AUSTRIAN.

Known also as Gaststätte Helene Schmidt, this restaurant, specializing in variations of the Schnitzel, has been one of Vienna's leading budget restaurants for years, heavily patronized by students, shopkeepers, and employees working in the area. Little wonder—the Schnitzel are gigantic, covering the whole plate (if there are two of you, you might consider sharing one). Choices include Schnitzel Mexican style, Wiener Schnitzel, and garlic Schnitzel. It's a few blocks north of Vienna's popular shopping street, Mariahilfer Strasse. The place is often packed.

✪ Tunnel

Florianigasse 39 (behind the Rathaus). ☎ **01/405 34 65**. 40–120 S ($3.80–$11.40). No credit cards. Daily 9am–2am. U-Bahn U-2 to Rathaus; then a 10-minute walk. Tram 5. Bus 13A. INTERNATIONAL.

This informal establishment is actually a restaurant/bar, with a live-music house down in the basement. Catering to Vienna's large student population, it starts the day with huge breakfasts (including Arabian breakfast, granola, and omelets) and continues the day with sandwiches, salads, vegetarian dishes, pizza (big enough for two people to share), pasta, and Viennese pancakes. The menu is eclectic, with everything from hummus or gnocchi to moussaka or a dish of Asian vegetables. From 11:30am to 2:30pm there's a daily special for 45 S ($4.30); bread is free with your meal. You can stay as long as you wish, and you can come just for a drink. It's less than a 10-minute walk west of the Ring.

MEALS FOR LESS THAN 150 S ($14.30)

INSIDE THE RING

Bastei Beisl

Stubenbastei 10 (about a five-minute walk east of Stephansplatz). ☎ **01/512 43 19**. 100–200 S ($9.50–$19.05); fixed-price lunch 90 S ($8.55) and 110 S ($10.50). AE, DC, MC. Mon–Fri 9am–11:30pm, Sat 11am–3pm and 6–11:30pm. U-Bahn U-3 to Stubentor, or U-1 or U-3 to Stephansplatz. AUSTRIAN.

This family-style Beisl has a homey atmosphere with wooden booths and chairs. It offers a fixed-price lunch menu and a changing daily menu. Otherwise, perennial favorites include Wiener Tafelspitz, Beisl Gulasch, Wiener Schnitzel, Cordon

Bleu, Zwiebelrostbraten (roast beef with onion), fish, pork medallions, and pepper steak. There's a long wine list in addition to the usual beer.

✪ Dom Beisl

Schulerstrasse 4 (on the corner of Domgasse). ☎ **01/512 91 81.** 70–115 S ($6.65–$10.95). No credit cards. Mon–Thurs 7am–5pm, Fri 7am–3pm. U-Bahn U-1 or U-3 to Stephansplatz. AUSTRIAN.

A typical neighborhood Beisl, this simple eatery with its wooden floor and plain furniture is conveniently located directly behind St. Stephen's Cathedral. Maybe that's why it's a favorite eating place of the Fiaker, the famous Viennese horse-carriage drivers stationed around Stephansplatz. A family-run establishment (owner Alfred Massinger is almost always present), it posts its changing daily specials on a chalkboard hanging outside the front door. Otherwise, items on the regular menu include Schweinebraten with Knödel (dumplings), Bauernschmaus, Wiener Schnitzel, and Hühnerbrustfilet (chicken breast filet).

Figlmüller

Wollzeile 5. ☎ **01/512 61 77.** 85–175 S ($8.10–$16.65). No credit cards. Daily 11am–10:30pm. U-Bahn U-1 or U-3 to Stephansplatz. AUSTRIAN.

On a small alley just off Wollzeile, north of Stephansplatz, this cheerful restaurant with waiters in bow ties is famous for its huge Schnitzel and home-style Viennese specialties. The daily changing menu is written on a chalkboard (in German only) and may include such specialties as Tafelspitz or chicken breast in addition to its Schnitzel. It has a large selection of wines from its own vineyards.

Gösser Bierklinik

Steindelgasse 4 (just off the Graben). ☎ **01/535 68 97.** 85–185 S ($8.10–$17.60). AE, DC, MC, V. Mon–Sat 9am–11pm. Closed hols. U-Bahn: U-1 or U-3 to Stephansplatz; then a five-minute walk west. AUSTRIAN.

First mentioned in documents from 1406, this old building became a restaurant in the 17th century. Since 1924 it's been the property of Gösser Brewery, with dining spread among nine rooms on various floors. One room even displays a Turkish cannonball that hit the place 300 years ago when Vienna lay under siege. In this pleasantly decorated place, you can either splurge or eat for under $10. Hearty dishes on the English menu include fresh fish, homemade Gulasch, Bauernschmaus, grilled duck, Wiener Schnitzel, roast beef with onions, steak, and Tafelspitz. Gösser beer starts at 30 S ($2.85) for a *Seidel* (one-third liter).

Orpheus

Spiegelgasse 10 (parallel to Kärntner Strasse). ☎ **01/512 38 53.** 85–160 S ($8.10–$15.25). No credit cards. Sun–Thurs noon–midnight, Fri–Sat noon–1am. U-Bahn U-1 or U-3 to Stephansplatz. GREEK.

This popular Greek eatery is colorfully painted with blue and green walls, accentuated by black furniture. I recommend the Orpheus Plate, which comes with samplings of souvlaki, lamb cutlet, pork cutlet, and chicken breast. There's also the usual selection of moussaka, lamb, souvlaki, steaks, and fish selections, as well as daily lunch specials priced under 90 S ($8.55).

Pronto

Spiegelgasse 2. ☎ **01/512 29 58.** 80–110 S ($7.60–$10.50). No credit cards. Mon–Sat 11am–midnight. Closed hols. U-Bahn U-1 or U-3 to Stephansplatz. ITALIAN.

Pronto is a miniature casual eatery with genuine Italian cuisine, offering different dishes every day, from lasagne to minestrone or tortellini. There are only a dozen or so stools at its chest-high tables, and since it's extremely popular and packed during lunch and dinner with business types who work in the area, try to eat during off-hours.

○ Stadtbeisl

Naglergasse 21. ☎ **01/533 35 07.** 85–190 S ($8.10–$18.10). V. Daily 10am–11:30pm. U-Bahn U-1 or U-3 to Stephansplatz; then a five-minute walk west. AUSTRIAN.

A pleasant locale in the heart of Old Vienna, this Beisl has a history that stretches back to the early 1700s. Once under the ownership of a cloister that offered soup lines to the poor twice a week, the old building has a cellar three stories deep—part of which is old catacombs with underground passageways linked to Stephansdom and other parts of the inner city (you can visit the uppermost cellar with its arched ceilings and brick floor). At any rate, the building has been a restaurant since 1745, with rooms that resemble a hunting lodge. The front room is crowded with antiques, while antlers decorate the back room. Traditional tiled stoves (*Kachelofen*) heat the entire locale. The English menu offers such interesting choices as hazelnut steak with curry rice and Hungarian dishes, as well as such standbys as Wiener Schnitzel, fish, and spinach with fried eggs and potatoes.

Wienerwald

Annagasse 3 (just off Kärntner Strasse). ☎ **01/512 37 66.** 69–120 S ($6.55–$11.40). AE, DC, MC, V. Daily 11am–1am. U-Bahn U-1 or U-3 to Stephansplatz, or U-1, U-2, or U-4 to Karlsplatz. AUSTRIAN.

Wienerwald is a huge and successful chain of grilled-chicken restaurants found throughout Austria and Germany, with almost 20 locations in Vienna alone. The founder of the chain got the idea for his restaurant after visiting Munich's Oktoberfest after World War II and noticing the huge consumption of chicken. One of the best deals is the quarter grilled chicken, served with one side dish of your choice, for 69 S ($6.55). Other dishes on the English menu include soups and csseroles, salads (including a salad bar), turkey, rump steak, and club sandwich.

Other branches are at Freyung 6 (☎ **01/533 14 20**), Mariahilfer Strasse 156 (☎ **01/89 23 306**), and Goldschmiedgasse 6 (☎ **01/535 40 12**).

NEAR MARIAHILFER STRASSE & THE NASCHMARKT

Crêperie-Brasserie Spittelberg

Spittelberggasse 12 (north of Mariahilfer Strasse and west of the Natural History Museum). ☎ **01/526 15 70.** 90–200 S ($8.55–$19.05). AE, DC, MC, V. Daily 6–11:30pm. U-Bahn U-2 or U-3 to Volkstheater. Tram 49 from Dr.-Karl-Renner-Ring to Spittelberg. FRENCH.

In what used to be Vienna's red-light district but has since become a tiny enclave of trendy restaurants, this casual yet upscale French eatery has salads with a great selection of different dressings; galettes stuffed with such fillings as potatoes and leeks, spinach, or turkey; crêpes with sweet fillings; coq au vin; lamb ragoût; beef bourguignon; and vegetarian dishes. The restaurant itself is in a modernized old building, with hanging plants and lighting suspended from the super-tall ceiling. There's outdoor seating in the summer.

○ Gasthaus Witwe Bolte

Gutenberggasse 13. ☎ **01/93 14 50.** 80–210 S ($7.60–$20). No credit cards. Jan–Mar, daily noon–2:30pm and 5–11:30pm; Apr–Dec, daily noon–midnight. U-Bahn U-2 or U-3 to Volkstheater. Tram 49 from Dr.-Karl-Renner-Ring to Spittelberg. AUSTRIAN.

Its facade is fancy baroque, but the interior consists of several small and simple rooms, where the emphasis is on such hearty home-cooked meals as Tafelspitz,

Schnitzel, Schweinebraten, and Gulasch. There's also a wonderful outdoor dining area. The restaurant itself is near the Crêperie-Brasserie Spittelberg (above) on a narrow, lamp-lit cobblestone street that centuries ago used to be the center of Vienna's red-light district. Empress Maria Theresa, a staunch Catholic, tried to curb prostitution but had little success; according to local lore, her son, Josef II, fled through the door of this very house in 1778 disguised as a regular citizen.

Naschmarkt Beisl

Linke Wienzeile 14 (next to Vienna's outdoor market). ☎ **01/587 53 13.** 45–160 S ($4.30–$15.25). No credit cards. Mon–Sat 11am–2:30pm and 5–11pm. U-Bahn U-4 to Kettenbrückengasse, or U-1, U-2, or U-4 to Karlsplatz. LEBANESE.

This place is plain and cheap, good for a sit-down meal after you've strolled through the Naschmarkt. The menu lists tsatsiki, hummus, stuffed pepper, kebabs, pizza with meat and vegetables, a mixed-grill platter, and lamb, as well as Austrian dishes like Wiener Schnitzel and Gulasch. The owner, Hachem Safwan, speaks English and will be happy to translate the menu. Perhaps order the falafel for 45 S ($4.30) or one of the fixed-price meals for less than 60 S ($5.70).

Restaurant der Grieche

Barnabitengasse 5 (near Mariahilfer Strasse). ☎ **01/587 74 66.** 75–185 S ($7.15–$17.60); fixed-price lunch from 75 S ($7.15); *Gedeck* (table charge) 4 S (40¢) for lunch, 10 S (95¢) for dinner. No credit cards. Daily 11:30am–2:30pm and 6pm–11:30pm. U-Bahn U-3 to Neubaugasse. GREEK.

Just half a block from the Gerngross department store and behind the Mariahilfer Church, this modern restaurant has an outdoor garden for summer dining and a pleasant greenhouse for winter dining. Retsina and domestic Greek wines are, of course, available, as well as exochiko (lamb puff pastry), kleftiko (lamb cooked with cheese and garlic), moussaka, shrimp, fish, souvlaki, lamb chops, and Greek salad. There's an English menu.

Shalimar

Schmalzhofgasse 11 (just south of Mariahilfer Strasse). ☎ **01/596 43 17.** 85–190 S ($8.10–$18.10); fixed-price meals 175–210 S ($16.65–$20); *Gedeck* 22 S ($2.10) per person. AE, DC, MC, V. Daily 11am–2pm and 5:30–11pm. U-Bahn U-3 to Zieglergasse. INDIAN.

This brightly decorated Indian restaurant with outdoor seating offers tandoori chicken, curry dishes of chicken, pork, lamb, beef, and fish, and a variety of vegetarian dishes. Indian music plays softly in the background. There's a *Gedeck* (table charge) here, per person, but the food is good enough to warrant coming here.

COFFEEHOUSES INSIDE THE RING

Just as Paris has its sidewalk cafés, Vienna has its coffeehouses, which are institutions in themselves. There are literally dozens of ways to order coffee (refer to the beginning of the dining section, above). If all you're looking for is a cheap cup of coffee to give you fuel for the day, look for a chain called **Eduscho.** There's one at Graben 12 and another at Kärntner Strasse 12, where a cup of coffee or an espresso starts at 7 S (65¢). They're open Monday through Friday from 8am to 6pm and Saturday from 8am to 1pm (to 5pm the first Saturday of the month). There are chest-high tables where you can stand and sip your purchase.

Bräunerhof Cafe

Stallburggasse 2. ☎ **01/512 38 93.** U-Bahn: U-1 or U-3 to Stephansplatz.

On a tiny street that connects Dorotheergasse and Bräunergasse, this café falls somewhere between Demel and Hawelka as far as style and decoration go. Rather than the dark-paneled walls of many older coffeehouses, this one has a bright and simple interior with gracefully arching lamps by Hoffmann. There are several expensive antiques shops in the immediate area, and Saturday, Sunday, and holidays from 3 to 6pm a trio entertains customers. A Melange here costs 32 S ($3.05). Open Monday through Saturday from 7:30am to 8:30pm and Sunday and holidays from 10am to 6pm.

Cafe Hawelka

Dorotheergasse 6 (just off Stephansplatz). ☎ **01/512 82 30.** U-Bahn U-1 or U-3 to Stephansplatz.

Small and smoky, its walls covered with posters and placards, Cafe Hawelka attracts students, artists, writers, and other bohemian types. It's famous for its Buchtel, a pastry made fresh daily and available only after 10pm. I personally prefer this café to Demel, and its 36 S ($3.45) for a Melange is more acceptable. Open Monday and Wednesday through Saturday from 8am to 2am, Sunday and holidays from 4pm to 2am.

Demel

Kohlmarkt 14. ☎ **01/533 55 16** or 535 17 17. U-Bahn U-1 or U-3 to Stephansplatz.

Founded in 1785 by a pastry chef who later served as the pastry supplier to the royal family, Demel is the most expensive and most famous coffeehouse in Vienna. Its elegant interior looks like the private parlor of a count. A small pot of coffee here costs 45 S ($4.30), worth the cost just for the show of people and waitresses. Tortes and cakes start at 32 S ($3.05). And as though in admission of their high prices, Demel even accepts all major credit cards. Open daily from 10am to 7pm.

STREET EATS

The *Würstelstand* (frankfurter stand) is as much a part of the Viennese scene as its coffee shops. Situated throughout the city, they sell Bratwurst, Leberkäs, curry wurst, soft drinks, and beer, with most prices between 23 and 35 S ($2.20 and $3.35).

Conveniently located stands are those on Seilergasse (just off Stephansplatz), open Monday through Saturday from 7am to 1am and Sunday from 9am to 1am; on Kupferschmiedgasse (just off Kärntner Strasse), open Monday through Friday from 9am to 5pm; at the Gerngross department store at Mariahilfer Strasse 38–48, open 24 hours; at Schwarzenbergplatz, open 24 hours; and at the Naschmarkt (below).

PICNICKING

The best place for picnic supplies—and, indeed, one of Vienna's most colorful attractions—is the **Naschmarkt.** It's an open-air market a five-minute walk from Karlsplatz, with stalls selling fish, vegetables, fruit, meats, cheeses, Asian foodstuffs, Greek specialties, flowers, and tea. My Viennese friends say that this is the best place to shop because of the freshness of produce and variety of goods, including exotic items. In between the food stalls are a number of stand-up Imbisse, fast-food counters where you can buy sausages, sandwiches, döner kebabs, beer, grilled chicken, and other ready-made foods. The Naschmarkt is open Monday through Friday from 6am to 6:30pm and Saturday from 6am to 1pm or 3pm.

As for picnic settings, Vienna's most accessible parks are its **Stadtpark** and its **Volksgarten,** both on the Ring. In addition, both Schönbrunn and Belvedere Palaces have formal gardens. Keep in mind, however, that the Viennese are a bit stodgy and don't look kindly on people who wander off pathways and sprawl on the grass. Some of Vienna's younger generation have staged sit-ins in protest of the "Keep Off the Grass" rule, but things change slowly here. In any case, there are always lots of park benches. If you really want to get away from the city, take an excursion to the **Vienna Woods** or the Danube, both described under "Easy Excursions," at the end of this chapter.

WORTH THE EXTRA MONEY

In addition to the restaurants here, there are a number of wine cellars described under "Vienna After Dark" (later in this chapter) that offer meals at prices above our budget. Although you can experience these establishments for just the price of a drink, they're also great for a complete meal, which will cost about $15 and up.

Griechenbeisl

Fleischmarkt 11. ☎ **01/533 19 41** or 533 19 77. Main courses 160–250 S ($15.25–$23.80). AE, DC, MC, V. Daily 11:30am–11:30pm (last order). U-Bahn U-1 or U-3 to Stephansplatz, or U-1 or U-4 to Schwedenplatz. AUSTRIAN.

All Viennese know the Griechenbeisl and many of their ancestors have probably dined here as well, since it dates to the 15th century. Housed in an ancient-looking vine-covered building that's divided into several small rooms linked by narrow winding passageways, it offers a typical Viennese menu (available in English), including Wiener Schnitzel, Tafelspitz, Bauernschmaus, venison steak, and deer stew. It's a place with a lot of character, but if the menu is too expensive, you can always come after 11pm for just a drink (see "Vienna After Darke," later in this chapter, for more information).

✪ Restaurant Hauswirth

Otto Bauergasse 20. ☎ **01/587 12 61.** Main courses 180–270 S ($17.15–$25.70); fixed-price meals 235 S ($22.40) at lunch, 355 and 450 S ($33.80 and $42.85) at dinner. AE, DC, MC, V. Mon–Fri 11:30am–2:30pm and 6–11, Sat 6–11pm. Closed hols. U-Bahn U-3 to Zieglergasse. AUSTRIAN.

Come here for an elegant dining experience, complete with chandeliers, fresh flowers, and drawing room–like dining areas from the turn of the century. In summer there's also outdoor dining that still manages to maintain its high degree of elegance. The menu, featuring light, original cuisine, changes to complement each season, depending on what's available. Thus spring may feature fish; summer, mushrooms and asparagus; and autumn, wild game. The four-course lunches and three- and four-course dinners are especially recommended. There are 11,000 bottles of wine in the restaurant's own cellar, which you can visit on request.

Wiener Rathauskeller

Rathausplatz. ☎ **01/421 21 90.** Reservations recommended Tues–Sat for the fixed-price meal. Soups and appetizers 40–140 S ($3.80–$13.35); main courses 130–250 S ($12.40–$23.80). AE, DC, MC, V. Mon–Sat 11:30am–3pm and 6–11pm. U-Bahn U-2 to Rathaus. Tram 1, 2, or D to Burgtheater/Rathausplatz. AUSTRIAN.

A la carte dining is offered in the Rittersaal (Knights' Hall) in the cellar of Vienna's City Hall. It's a beautiful room, with medieval-style murals on the vaulted ceilings, pink tablecloths, beautiful lamps, and flowers on every table. In the evenings there's live classical music. Incidentally, farther down the hall is the Grinzinger Keller, where at 8pm Tuesday through Saturday nights in summer a fixed-price meal with traditional Viennese entertainment is offered for a package of 390 S ($37.15) per person. Call for reservations.

6 Attractions

SIGHTSEEING SUGGESTIONS

The Habsburgs, who ruled over a vast empire for 600 years, left behind a rich heritage, from palaces and churches to jeweled crowns and art masterpieces. With the score of museums and sights Vienna has to offer, it's advisable to plan your itinerary. Let the suggestions below be your guide.

If You Have 1 Day

Start the morning with a tour of Vienna's Altstadt (Old City), beginning at Stephansplatz. Here you'll find the towering St. Stephen's Cathedral, Vienna's most important gothic building and its best-known landmark. Constructed in the 12th century and then enlarged and reconstructed over the next eight centuries, it has a 450-foot-high south tower with 343 spiral steps—which you can climb round and round and be rewarded with a great view of the city (entrance is outside the church on its south side). If you don't like stairs, you can take an elevator to the top of the never-completed north tower, only about half as high as the south tower.

Radiating from Stephansplatz is the Altstadt. Of particular beauty are Schönlaterngasse and Annagasse, two lanes reminiscent of what Vienna used to look like, and Am Hof, Vienna's largest square. Have coffee at one of the famous coffeehouses, then stroll down the Kärntner Strasse pedestrian shopping street for a look at modern Vienna.

After you've seen the inner city, hightail it to the palace and gardens of Schönbrunn, Vienna's most famous attraction and once the summer home of the Habsburg dynasty. Finish the day with a performance at the opera or theater, followed by a drink in one of Vienna's historic wine cellars.

If You Have 2 Days

Spend your first day as outlined above. On the second, head toward the Hofburg, the official residence of the Habsburgs, which now contains the imperial rooms and a treasury with an astounding collection of riches. Nearby is the Kunsthistorisches Museum, a fine-arts museum with its great collection of old masters. If you have time, walk to the nearby Imperial Crypts, where the Habsburgs have been buried for the last 300 years. Spend the evening in Grinzing or one of Vienna's other wine districts.

If You Have 3 Days

In addition to the sights given above, try to schedule some activities that occur only on certain days of the week. Training sessions of the renowned Spanish Riding School, for example, take place Tuesday through Saturday from 10am to noon (except for the months of January, July, and August), and the Vienna Boys' Choir sings at masses on Sunday.

Other important sights you should include on a three-day stay are the open-air market at the Naschmarkt (on Saturday there's also a flea market) and Belvedere

Palace, where you'll find three art galleries. In the evening go to Prater, Vienna's old-fashioned amusement park.

If You Have 5 Days

Spend the first three days as outlined above. On the fourth day, explore your own special interests—visiting composers' homes, the Museum of Military History, the Museum of Applied Arts, the Clock Museum, or Vienna's Historical Museum. Architecture buffs should be sure to see the Hundertwasser Haus and KunstHausWien.

On your fifth day, take a trip to Vienna's countryside. Popular destinations include the famous Vienna Woods and the extensive park along the Danube (where you can even go swimming in summer).

TOP ATTRACTIONS

Remember to purchase a copy of "Vienna from A to Z" for an explanation of the city's many historically important buildings. In addition, the *Wien Monatsprogramm* lists all special exhibitions being held at museums and galleries in Vienna. Both are available at the Vienna Tourist Board.

Note that most museums are closed on January 1, Good Friday, Easter Sunday, May 1, Whitsunday, Corpus Christi, November 1–2, December 24–25, and for general elections. Exceptions are the Museum of Fine Arts, Schönbrunn Palace, the Hofburg, and the Imperial Burial Vault, which remain open on Easter Sunday/Monday and on Whitsunday/Monday.

If you're on a budget, keep in mind that all of Vienna's municipal museums are free on Friday until noon (excluding holidays), including all of the composer's homes, the Clock Museum, and the Vienna Historical Museum.

✪ Schönbrunn

Schönbrunner Schlossstrasse. ☎ **01/81113.** Schönbrunn tour, 95 S ($9.05) adults, 40 S ($3.80) children under 15; Wagenburg, 30 S ($2.85) adults, free for children 10 and under. Schönbrunn tours, Apr–Oct, daily 8:30am–5pm; Nov–Mar, daily 8:30am–4:30pm (closed Jan 1, Nov 1, Dec 25). Wagenburg, Apr–Oct, daily 9am–5:30pm; Nov–Mar, Tues–Sun 10am–3:30pm. U-Bahn U-4 to Schönbrunn or Hietzing. Tram 58 from anywhere along Mariahilfer Strasse to Schloss Schönbrunn.

A baroque palace with an astounding 1,441 rooms, the lovely summer palace of Schönbrunn was built between 1696 and 1730 in the midst of a glorious garden. Empress Maria Theresa left the greatest imprint on Schönbrunn: In the course of having 16 children (one of whom was Marie Antoinette), running the country, and fighting a war for her right to sit on the Austrian throne, she still found time to decorate and redesign Schönbrunn (1744–49), and it remains virtually as she left it. When the French besieged Vienna in the early 19th century, Napoléon I was so impressed with Schönbrunn that he occupied Maria Theresa's favorite rooms. Emperor Franz Josef I was born in the palace and lived here with his beautiful wife, Elisabeth. And it was here, too, that Charles I, Austria's last emperor, abdicated and renounced the Imperial Crown.

To see the inside of the predominantly white-and-gilt palace, you must join a 40-minute tour that visits 40 of its many rooms. Immediately upon arrival, check for the next English-language tour. If there's a wait, you can always take a walk through 500 acres of palace grounds, one of the most important baroque gardens in the French style. At the top of the hill opposite the palace is the **Gloriette,** a monument to soldiers. There's also the lovely Neptune Fountain, artificial Roman ruins, a zoo, a butterfly house, and the **Palmenhaus,** built in 1883 as the largest glasshouse in Europe. Be sure, too, to visit the **Wagenburg,** a museum with 36 carriages belonging to the imperial family.

As for the palace tour, among the rooms you'll visit are the exotic Chinese Rooms; the cheerful breakfast room decorated with appliqué work done by Maria Theresa's daughters; the Hall of Mirrors, where the six-year-old Mozart played for Maria Theresa; the Napoleon Room, where Napoleon lived and his only legitimate son died; and the Large Gallery, fashioned after a room in Versailles and used for imperial banquets. Most spectacular is perhaps the Millions Room, Maria Theresa's private salon, decorated with 260 precious parchment miniatures set under glass in the paneling and brought from Constantinople.

Hofburg (Imperial Palace)

Michaeler Platz 1, Burgring. ☎ **01/587 55 54.** Schauräume, 70 S ($6.65) adults, 35 S ($3.35) students and children; Weapons Collection or the Collection Ancient Musical Instruments, 30 S ($2.85) each for adults, 15 S ($1.45) students and children. Schauräume, daily 8:30am–4pm; Weapons Collection and Collection of Ancient Musical Instruments, Wed–Mon 10am–6pm. U-Bahn U-1 or U-3 to Stephansplatz. Tram 1, 2, 3, or J to Burgring.

The Hofburg was the Imperial Palace of the Habsburgs for more than six centuries, during which time changes and additions were made in every conceivable architectural style—gothic, Renaissance, baroque, rococo, and classical. The entire Hofburg occupies 47 acres, a virtual city within a city, with more than 2,600 rooms. Contained in the vast complex are the **Schauräume** (the former Imperial Rooms); the **Schatzkammer** (Treasury) with its magnificent imperial and religious treasures (described below); and the **Neue Hofburg,** with its collection of medieval armor and weapons and its museum of ancient musical instruments as well as instruments played by Brahms, Haydn, Schumann, and other composers. The Spanish Riding School and the Burgkapelle featuring Sunday masses with the Vienna Boys' Choir are also on the Hofburg grounds (also described below).

The Schauräume will seem a bit plain after the splendor of Schönbrunn, but what I like about it is that you can wander around on your own (guided tours are only in German most of the year). You'll see the apartments of Franz Josef and his wife, Elisabeth, and of Tsar Alexander I of Russia. There are several portraits of a young Elisabeth, a beautiful woman from the Wittelsbach family of Munich who was married to Franz Josef in 1854 to further German interests. Known as Sissi, she was talented, artistic, and vain—she would no longer sit for portraits after the age of 30. She was an excellent horsewoman, and in the Hofburg is her own small gymnasium where she kept in shape (much to the disgust of the court, which thought it improper for a lady). Crown Prince Rudolf, son of Elisabeth and Franz Josef and only male heir to the throne, committed suicide in a hunting lodge at Mayerling with his young mistress, Maria Vetsera. Elisabeth herself was assassinated in 1898 by an anarchist in Geneva.

You'll also see the royal dining room laid out with the imperial place setting—notice how the silverware is laid only on the right side and is turned down, according to Spanish court etiquette, which was the rage of the time. There are five wineglasses for each guest, and the napkins are 3.3 square feet each.

The Hofburg is inside the Ring, about a seven-minute walk from Stephansplatz.

Schatzkammer (Treasury)

Hofburg, Schweizerhof. ☎ **01/533 79 31.** Admission 60 S ($5.70) adults, 30 S ($2.85) senior citizens, students, and children. Wed and Fri–Mon 10am–6pm, Thurs 10am–9pm. U-Bahn U-1 or U-3 to Stephansplatz. Tram 1, 2, D, or J to Burgring.

Vienna

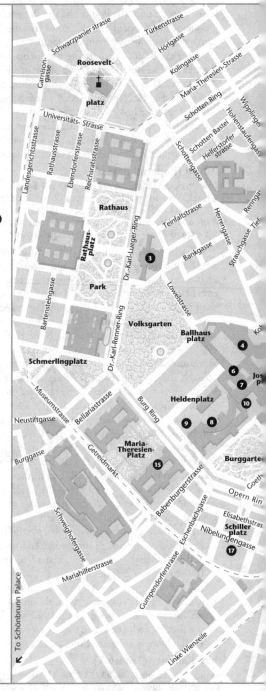

1094

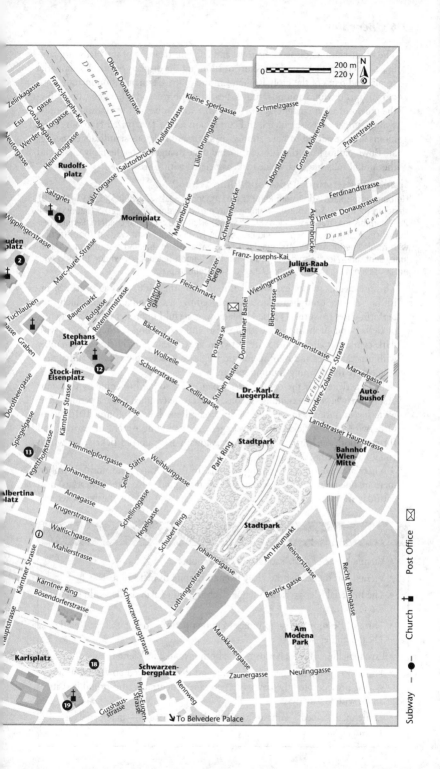

Subway – – –   Church ✝■   Post Office ☒

The Schatzkammer displays the royal and religious treasures of the Habsburg family, a collection that's nothing short of stunning. Its displays of priceless imperial regalia and relics of the Holy Roman Empire of the German nation include royal crowns inlaid with diamonds, rubies, pearls, sapphires, and other gems (including the crown of Charlemagne), as well as christening robes of the Habsburg family, swords, imperial crosses, altars, and coronation robes. Two prized Habsburg heirlooms are considered to have strange mystical and religious significance: the Agate Bowl, dating from the 4th century and once thought to be the Holy Grail; and the Ainkhörn, a huge narwhale tusk, associated with Christ.

Spanische Reitschule (Spanish Riding School)

Hofburg, Josefsplatz. Admission: Regular performances, seats 220–800 S ($20.95–$76.20), standing room 170 S ($16.20); "training with music" performances, 220 S ($20.95), plus 22% commission; training session, 80 S ($7.60) adults, 20 S ($1.90) children. Regular performances, Mar–June and Sept to mid-Dec, Sun at 10:45am and most Weds at 7pm; "training with music" performances, Apr–June and Sept, Sat at 10am; training sessions, mid-Mar to June, Sept, and Nov to mid-Dec, Tues–Sat 10am–noon (except Sat when "training with music" sessions are held). U-Bahn U-1 or U-3 to Stephansplatz.

This prestigious school has roots dating to more than 400 years ago when Spanish horses were brought to Austria for breeding; the baroque hall in which they perform dates from the 1730s. The famous graceful Lippizaner horses are a cross of Berber and Arabian stock with Spanish and Italian horses (they're born with dark coats that turn white only between ages 4 and 10). Their performances with intricate steps and movements are a sight to be seen, but cheaper and almost as good are the morning training sessions.

In fact, tickets for the regular performances are so hard to come by that your best bet may be for the training sessions. If you're determined to see a performance, write several months in advance to Spanische Reitschule, Hofburg, 1010 Wien. Otherwise, theater ticket and travel agencies (including American Express and Intropa, both on Kärntner Strasse) occasionally have unsold tickets, for which you'll pay an extra 22% commission.

There are two kinds of training sessions. In April, May, June, and September, there are one-hour "training with music" sessions (kind of like dress rehearsals) held Saturday morning at 10am, tickets for which are sold only at theater ticket and

❷ Did You Know?

- Vienna is one of three capitals on the Danube.
- Vienna was the seat of the Holy Roman Empire from 1558 to 1806.
- The Imperial Menagerie at Vienna's Schönbrunn Palace is the world's oldest zoo (1752).
- Three of Beethoven's symphonies were first performed in public at Vienna's Theater an der Wien.
- Psychoanalysis and Sachertorte were both invented in Vienna.
- The 1955 state treaty between Austria and the four Allied powers of World War II provided for the country's permanent neutrality and prohibited its union with Germany.
- Churchill described Vienna as "an elephant in a backyard"—an imperial capital in a small country.

travel agencies. There are also regular training sessions, held from about mid-March to the end of June, September, and November to mid-December, Tuesday through Saturday from 10am until noon (on Saturday in April, May, June, and September, only "training with music" sessions are held). If you decide to go to a regular training session, get there early and wait in line (Gate 2), since no reservations are accepted for these.

Wiener Sängerknaben (Vienna Boys' Choir)

Burgkapelle, Hofburg (entrance on Schweizerhof). Seats, 60–250 S ($5.70–$23.80); standing room, free. Mass said Sun and religious hols at 9:15am mid-Sept to June. Closed Jan 6, Ascension Day, Dec 8, and Dec 26. U-Bahn U-1 or U-3 to Stephansplatz.

The Vienna Boys' Choir was founded in 1498 to sing at church services for the Royal Chapel of the imperial palace. Both Joseph Haydn and Franz Schubert sang in the choir, which now actually consists of several choirs, two of which are usually on world tours. You can hear the Boys' Choir, accompanied by a full orchestra, every Sunday and religious holiday at 9:15am mass in the Burgkapelle of the Hofburg, from January to the end of June and from mid-September to Christmas. Seats should be ordered at least two months in advance by writing to Hofmusikkapelle, Hofburg, 1010 Wien. Don't enclose money or a check, but rather pick up your ticket at the Burgkapelle on the Friday preceding the performance between 11am and noon or on Sunday between 8:30 and 9am. Unsold tickets go on sale also at the Burgkapelle on Friday from 5pm (it's wise to get there by 4:30pm).

Note: Standing room for mass is free, but there's room for only 20 people on a first-come, first-served basis, so get there early if you're interested.

And if you're absolutely desperate to hear the Vienna Boys' Choir, you can also catch them at the Konzerthaus every Friday at 3:30pm in May, June, September, and October, but tickets start at a steep 350 S ($33.35) and can be obtained only at first-class hotels and Reisebüro Mondial, Faulmanngasse 4 (☎ 01/588 04-141).

✪ Kunsthistorisches Museum (Museum of Fine Arts)

Maria-Theresien-Platz. ☎ 01/521 77 301. Admission 45 S ($4.30) adults, 30 S ($2.85) senior citizens, students, and children; free for children 9 and under. Tues–Wed and Fri–Sun 10am–6pm, Thurs 10am–9pm. U-Bahn U-2 or U-3 to Volkstheater. Tram 1, 2, 52, 58, D, or J to Burgring.

This great museum owes its existence largely to the Habsburgs, who for centuries were patrons and collectors of art. There are several collections, of which the Egyptian-Oriental Collection and the Picture Gallery are the most outstanding. Other collections include coins and medals and sculpture and applied arts from the medieval, Renaissance, and baroque periods.

The Picture Gallery is up on the first floor, with paintings by Rubens, Rembrandt, Dürer, Memling, Titian, Giorgione, Tintoretto, Caravaggio, and Velázquez. The high point of the entire museum, however, is a room full of Brueghels, including the *Turmbau zu Babel* (Tower of Babel), *Die Jäger im Schnee* (The Hunters in the Snow—you can hardly believe it's not real), the *Kinderspiel* (in which children have taken over an entire town), and *Die Bauernhochzeit* (The Peasant Wedding—notice how the bride is isolated in front of the green cloth, barred by custom from eating or talking).

Belvedere

Prinz-Eugen-Strasse 27 (Oberes Belvedere) and Rennweg 6 (Unteres Belvedere). ☎ 01/798 4121-0. Admission (including all museums) 60 S ($5.70) adults, 30 S ($2.85) senior citizens, students, and children, free for children 9 and under. Tues–Sun 10am–5pm. Tram D to Schloss Belvedere (Oberes Belvedere); or 71 to Unteres Belvedere.

The Belvedere is a light, airy baroque palace built in the early 1700s as a summer residence for Austria's beloved Prince Eugene of Savoy, who protected Austria from Turkish invasion and was rewarded for his service by being made minister of war and later prime minister by Emperor Charles VI. He remained a bachelor his whole life, and when he died his estate fell to his heiress—"frightful Victoria," as the Viennese called her—who promptly sold the palace. The Imperial Court acquired the buildings and gardens in 1752, and it was here that Franz Ferdinand, heir to the throne, lived before taking his fateful trip to Sarajevo in 1914.

The Belvedere is actually two palaces, now containing some important galleries. The **Oberes Belvedere** (close to the Südbahnhof) is the more lavish of the two, situated up on a hill with a sweeping view of the city. It's now a gallery for 19th- and 20th-century Austrian art, including Biedermeier paintings by Amerling and Waldmüller. Be sure to go up to the top floor, where you'll find the works of Oskar Kokoschka and Egon Schiele, as well as of Gustav Klimt (1862–1918), considered the foremost representative of Viennese Jugendstil (art nouveau) painting. You'll see his famous *Der Kuss* (The Kiss) and *Judith* (the frame was made by his brother).

A walk through the beautiful landscaped gardens brings you to the **Unteres Belvedere,** now home of the Museum of Austrian Baroque with its works of the 17th and 18th centuries. And finally, in the **Orangerie** is the Museum of Medieval Austrian Art, which includes sculpture and panel paintings from the end of the 12th to the early 16th century.

Stephansdom (St. Stephen's Cathedral)

Stephansplatz. ☎ **01/515 52-563.** Cathedral, free; south tower, 20 S ($1.90) adults, 5 S (50¢) children; north tower elevator, 40 S ($3.80) adults, 15 S ($1.25) children; catacombs, 35 S ($3.35) adults, 15 S ($1.40) children; organ concerts, 80 S ($7.60). Cathedral, Mon–Sat 7am–7:30pm, Sun 7:30am–7:30pm. South tower, daily 9am–5:30pm. North tower, summer, daily 9am–5:30pm; winter, daily 8am–4:30pm. Catacombs, Mon–Sat 10–11:30am and 2–4:30pm, Sun and hols 2–4:30pm. U-Bahn U-1 or U-3 to Stephansplatz.

In the heart of Old Vienna, Stephansdom is the city's best-known landmark. Constructed in the 12th century and then enlarged and reconstructed for the next eight centuries, it remains Vienna's most important gothic structure. Its dimensions are huge—352 feet long with a nave 128 feet high. The highest part is its 450-foot-high south tower, completed in 1433, with 343 spiral steps. The south tower is open to the public (entrance is on the church's south side) and affords one of the best views of the city. If you don't like to climb stairs, you can take an elevator to the top of the north tower, which was never completed and is only about half as high as the south tower. Finally, the catacombs of the cathedral contain copper urns bearing the intestines of the Habsburg family (their bodies are in the Imperial Burial Vault, described below, while their hearts are in the Augustiner Church). From March through November there are organ concerts every Wednesday at 8pm.

MORE ATTRACTIONS

Heeresgeschichtliches Museum (Museum of Military History)

Arsenal. ☎ **01/79 561-0.** Admission 40 S ($3.80) adults, 20 S ($1.90) students, senior citizens, and children. Sat–Thurs 10am–4pm. Take U-Bahn U-1, tram D or 18, or bus no. 13A to the Südbahnhof; then it's a 10-minute walk, through the Schweizer Garten.

Special & Free Events

For information on Vienna's many musical festivals, refer to "Pretrip Preparations," earlier in this chapter. For free entertainment, don't forget that you can
hear the famous Vienna Boys' Choir absolutely free during Sunday mass if you're
willing to stand and you get there early (see "Top Attractions," above).

Housed in a Moorish-Byzantine–style building constructed in the 1850s as part
of the Vienna Arsenal, this museum has an admirable collection of weapons, uniforms, and memorabilia from the Thirty Years' War to the present. Included are
guns, sabers, planes, tanks, heavy artillery, and model ships. Most interesting, perhaps, is the room that commemorates the start of World War I, with displays of
the automobile Archduke Franz Ferdinand and his wife, Sophie, were riding in
when they were assassinated in Sarajevo and even the uniform the archduke was
wearing.

Historisches Museum der Stadt Wien (Vienna Historical Museum)
Karlsplatz 4. ☎ **01/505 87 47.** Admission 30 S ($2.85) adults, 15 S ($1.45) senior citizens,
10 S (95¢) students and children. Tues–Sun 9am–4:30pm. U-Bahn U-1, U-2, or U-4 to
Karlsplatz.

The Vienna Historical Museum is devoted to Vienna's 7,000 years of history, from
the Neolithic period and the time of the tribal migrations through the Middle Ages
to the blossoming of Biedermeier and Jugendstil. There's armor, booty from the
Turkish invasions, models of the city, furniture, glassware, and paintings by Klimt,
Waldmüller, and Schiele, among others. One room is the complete interior of poet
Franz Grillparzer's apartment; there's also the living room of architect Loos.

Kapuzinerkirche, with the Kaisergruft (Imperial Burial Vault)
Neuer Markt 1. ☎ **01/512 68 53.** Admission 30S ($2.85) adults, 20 S ($1.90) senior
citizens, students, and children. Daily 9:30am–4pm. U-Bahn U-1 or U-3 to Stephansplatz.

Most visitors to Vienna feel it their duty to make a pilgrimage to the Kapuziner
Church (inside the Ring, behind the Opera House on tiny Tegetthoffstrasse),
which contains the Imperial Burial Vault and the coffins of 136 Habsburg family members. Some of the coffins are very elaborate, made of pewter and adorned
with skulls, angels, and other harbingers of death; the biggest one belongs to Empress Maria Theresa and her husband, topped with their reclining statues. They're
surrounded by the coffins of their 16 children, many of whom died in infancy. The
only non-Habsburg to be buried here was the governess to Maria Theresa and her
children. Each coffin has two keys, which are kept at separate places to prevent foul
play. The coffins contain only the embalmed bodies; the intestines are kept in copper urns in the catacombs of Stephansdom, while the hearts are in the Augustiner
Church.

Kunsthalle Wien
Treitlstrasse 2, Karlsplatz. ☎ **01/586 97 76.** Admission 50 S ($4.75) adults, 30 S ($2.85)
senior citizens and students. Wed and Fri–Mon 10am–6pm, Thurs 10am–8pm. U-Bahn
U-1, U-2, or U-4 to Karlsplatz.

Opened in 1992, this is the newest addition to the Vienna art scene and is
dedicated to changing exhibitions of contemporary visual arts, including video

installations, experimental architecture, and modern art. Past shows have explored Austrian influence on modern American architecture, and displayed works by Oskar Schlemmer, Gary Hill, and Rebecca Horn.

KunstHausWien

Untere Weissgerberstrasse 13. ☎ **01/712 04 91.** Admission 70 S ($6.65) adults, 40 S ($3.80) senior citizens and students, free for children 11 and under; temporary exhibits cost extra. KunstHausWien, daily 10am–7pm. Kalke Village, winter, daily 10am–5pm; summer, daily 9am–7pm. Tram N or O to Radetzkyplatz.

One of the newer additions to Vienna's art scene, the KunstHausWien is the brainchild of Austrian painter and designer Friedensreich Hundertwasser, famous for his whimsical, fantastical, and thought-provoking paintings, prints, and architecture. Created from a former factory building of the Thonet Company (well known for its bentwood furniture), the museum houses approximately 300 works of Hundertwasser, including paintings, prints, tapestries, and architectural models. There are also temporary shows featuring the works of international artists. Typical of Hundertwasser, the building itself is one of the exhibits, a colorful protest against the mundane gray of modern cities.

There's a café that features 100 different Thonet chairs and an uneven, buckled floor, as well as a museum shop. Be sure, too, to see the **Hundertwasser Haus,** a nearby apartment complex Hundertwasser designed on the corner of Kegelgasse and Löwengasse in the mid-1980s (about a four-minute walk from the KunstHausWien). On Kegelgasse is also **Kalke Village,** another Hundertwasser architectural conversion, this time from a former stable and gas station into a small shopping complex housing boutiques and a café.

Museum Moderner Kunst (Museum of Modern Art)

Liechtenstein Palace, Fürstengasse 1. ☎ **01/317 69 00.** Admission 45 S ($4.30) adults, 25 S ($2.40) senior citizens and students, free for children. Tues–Sun 10am–6pm. Tram D to Fürstengasse.

Housed in a baroque building is the city's Museum of Modern Art, with international works of art from the 20th century. Included in the collection are works by Richard Estes, Malcolm Morley, Andy Warhol, Paul Klee, Wassily Kandinsky, and Austrians Kolo Moser, Max Oppenheimer, Oskar Kokoschka, and Egon Schiele. The emphasis of the museum is on Viennese works since 1900, "classical modern" art from cubism to abstraction, and abstract art since 1950. The permanent exhibitions are on the first and second floors. There are also temporary exhibitions both here and at a second location, Museum des 20. Jahrhunderts, in the Schweizer Garten.

○ Österreichisches Museum für Angewandte Kunst (Austrian Museum of Applied Arts)

Stubenring 5. ☎ **01/71136.** Admission 90 S ($8.55) adults, 45 S ($4.30) students, senior citizens, and children. Tues–Wed and Fri–Sun 10am–6pm, Thurs 10am–9pm. U-Bahn U-3 to Stubentor. Tram 1 or 2 to Dr.-Karl-Lueger-Platz.

Europe's oldest museum of applied arts, this is a fine collection of Austrian ceramics, furniture, silver, and jewelry, housed in a stately 19th-century building constructed in Florentine Renaissance style. Exhibits are arranged chronologically, from romanesque to 20th-century design. It contains a fascinating collection of Viennese chairs from the 1800s (including Thonet) as well as designs of the Wiener Werkstätte, a remarkable workshop founded at the turn of the century by Josef Hoffmann, Kolo Moser, and Fritz Waerndorfer. The museum's Jugendstil and art nouveau collections are particularly outstanding, with works from around Europe. There's also a room devoted to works from Asia, including lacquerware, porcelain, and Buddha statues, while another room shows the similarities between Eastern and Western art. There are also special exhibitions of experimental contemporary art from around the world, for which higher admission is charged. In short, it's a fascinating museum, and rarely crowded.

Prater

Hauptallee. ☎ **01/512 83 14.** Admission free; charges for amusement rides. Apr–Sept, daily 9am–11pm; Mar and Oct, daily 10am–10pm. Closed Nov–Feb. Take U-Bahn U-1 or the S-Bahn to Praterstern.

Prater is Vienna's amusement park, first opened to the general public in 1766 on the former grounds of Emperor Maximilian II's game preserve. Most notable is its giant Ferris wheel, built in 1896 (and then rebuilt after its destruction in World War II) and measuring 200 feet in diameter. There are also the usual shooting ranges, amusement rides, game arcades, and beer halls. This is a good place for a stroll on a warm summer's night.

Puppen & Spielzeug Museum (Doll and Toy Museum)

Schulhof 4. ☎ **01/535 68 60.** Admission 60 S ($5.70) adults, 30 S ($2.85) senior citizens, students, and children. Tues–Sun 10am–6pm. U-Bahn U-1 or U-3 to Stephansplatz, or U-3 to Herrengasse.

Right beside the Clock Museum is this museum dedicated to dolls and dollhouses. Most of the hundreds of dolls in the collection are German, dating from 1830 to 1930, but also included are dolls from France and other European countries. The displays are excellently laid out, and the museum itself is in a house centuries old. Most of the visitors, by the way, are adults.

Sigmund-Freud-Haus

Berggasse 19. ☎ **01/319 15 96.** Admission 60 S ($5.70) adults, 40 S ($3.80) senior citizens and students, 25 S ($2.40) children, free for children 11 and under. July–Sept, daily 9am–6pm; Oct–June, daily 9am–4pm. U-Bahn U-2 to Schottentor; then a 10-minute walk. Tram D to Schlickgasse.

Sigmund Freud lived and worked here from 1891 to 1938. This small museum documents his life, with photographs of him, his mother, his wife, and others who influenced his life. A notebook in English identifies everything in the museum, with translations of passages written by Freud. To enter the house, it's necessary to ring the doorbell and push the door at the same time.

Uhrenmuseum (Clock Museum)

Schulhof 2 (inside the Ring just off the northeast end of Am Hof square). ☎ **01/533 22 65.** Admission 30 S ($2.85) adults, 15 S ($1.40) senior citizens, 10 S (95¢) students and children. Tues–Sun 9am–4:30pm. U-Bahn U-1 or U-3 to Stephansplatz, or U-3 to Herrengasse.

More than 1,000 clocks from all over the world are on display in this delightful museum, including tower clocks (one is from Stephansdom), pocket watches, portable sun clocks, Japanese pillar clocks, and more. The oldest clock dates from the early 15th century (it still works).

PARKS & GARDENS

Just east of the gardens of Belvedere (see "Top Attractions," above), the **Botanischer Garten (Botanical Garden),** Mechelgasse 3 (☎ **01/79794-271**), was laid out in 1757 on the order of Empress Maria Theresa as a medicinal garden. Today it's known for its cacti, succulents, and orchids. Admission is free and it's open Easter to mid-October, Tuesday through Sunday from 9am to dusk. Take tram no. 71 to Unteres Belvedere or D to Schloss Belvedere.

Slightly smaller and also on the Ring, the **Burggarten,** Opernring-Burgring, is just south of the Hofburg. It came into being when Napoleon ordered the bastions of the Burg to be destroyed in 1809. Becoming a public park in 1919, it contains monuments to Mozart and Franz Josef I. Take tram no. 1, 2, 52, 58, D, or J to Burgring.

The 500 acres of **Schönbrunn Park,** Schönbrunner Schlossstrasse, are considered one of the most important baroque gardens laid out in the French style. It contains fountains, artificial Roman ruins, a large greenhouse, a butterfly house, a palm house, and a zoo. Take U-Bahn U-4 to Schönbrunn or Hietzing or tram no. 58 to Schloss Schönbrunn.

The **Stadtpark (City Park),** on Parkring, dates from the mid-1800s, covers about 22 acres, and is located in the center of town. At its western edge is the Kursalon, with classical music recitals every evening. Take U-Bahn U-4 to Stadtpark or tram no. 1, 2, J, or T to Stadtpark.

Even older than the Stadtpark is the **Volksgarten,** Dr.-Karl-Renner-Ring, which opened in 1820 on the site of fortifications blown up by the French. There's a memorial to Empress Elisabeth here, on the Ring just north of the Hofburg. Take U-Bahn U-2 or U-3 to Volkstheater or tram no. 1, 2, D, or J to Parliament.

SPECIAL-INTEREST SIGHTSEEING
FOR THE MUSIC LOVER

If you're a fan of Mozart, Schubert, Strauss, Haydn, or Beethoven, you've certainly come to the right city. Here you'll find the houses where they lived, the cemetery where most of them are buried, and statues of these musical giants everywhere (especially in the Stadtpark and the Burggarten).

In addition, you might also like to see the interior of the **Staatsoper,** Opernring 2 (☎ **01/514 44-2955**). Built in 1861–69 and rebuilt after World War II, it's considered one of the world's finest opera houses (see "Vienna After Dark," later in this chapter, for performance information). Unfortunately for opera lovers, there are no performances during the months of July and August, though other performances such as concerts are held here during this time, and tours of the Staatsoper are held throughout the year—check the board outside the entrance for times of the day's tours, usually twice a day in winter and as many as five times a day in summer, in both English and German. Tours cost 40 S ($3.80). The entryway for the tours is on the Kärntner Strasse side of the building.

You can also visit apartments where the composers lived. Set up as memorial rooms, they're all a bit plain and unadorned, something only devoted music fans might be interested in seeing. All the apartments are open the same hours for the same charge and are free on Friday morning (except holidays).

Beethoven-Gedenkstätte

In the Pasqualati House, Mölker Bastei 8. ☎ **01/535 89 05.** Admission 15 S ($1.40) adults, 5 S (50¢) students and children. Tues–Sun 9am–12:15pm and 1–4:30pm. U-Bahn U-2 to Schottentor. Tram 1, 2, or D to Schottentor.

Ludwig van Beethoven (1770–1827) came to Vienna from Germany when he was 22 and stayed here until his death. Moody and rebellious, Beethoven had habits so irregular (he sometimes played and composed in the middle of the night) that he was constantly being evicted from apartments all over Vienna. One landlord who loved him, however, was Mr. Pasqualati, who kept Beethoven's apartment free—no one else was allowed to live in it, even when the restless composer was not there. Beethoven lived here on and off from 1804 to 1815 and composed his Fourth, Fifth, and Seventh Symphonies here. Adjoining the Beethoven memorial rooms is the Adalbert Stifter Memorial, with paintings and drawings. (You can also visit other places he lived: at Probusgasse 6 and the Eroica House at Döblinger Hauptstrasse 92.)

Haydn-Wohnhaus mit Brahms-Gedenkraum

Haydngasse 19. ☎ **01/596 13 07.** Admission 15 S ($1.40) adults, 5 S (50¢) students and children. Tues–Sun 9am–12:15pm and 1–4:30pm. Tram 52 or 58.

Considered to have invented the symphony, Joseph Haydn (1732–1809) acquired this tiny house in 1793 and lived here until his death. In addition to his letters, manuscripts, and personal mementos are two pianos and his death mask. There's also a memorial room to Brahms.

Mozart's Figarohaus

Domgasse 5 (just off Stephansplatz). ☎ **01/513 62 94.** Admission 15 S ($1.40) adults, 5 S (50¢) students and children. Tues–Sun 9am–12:15pm and 1–4:30pm. U-Bahn U-1 or U-3 to Stephansplatz.

Born in Salzburg, Wolfgang Amadeus Mozart (1756–91) moved to Vienna in 1781 and lived here with his wife, Constanze, and son for three years, from 1784 to 1787. These were his happiest years—here he wrote *The Marriage of Figaro* and received visits from Haydn and a 16-year-old Beethoven. Set in what used to be a wealthy neighborhood, the Figarohaus was already 200 years old when Mozart lived here. His apartment is on the first floor, which you can reach by walking through a tiny courtyard and up some dark stairs. Mozart later lived in poverty and died a pauper.

Schubert's Birthplace

Nussdorfer Strasse 54. ☎ **01/345 99 24.** Admission 15 S ($1.40) adults, 5 S (50¢) students and children. Tues–Sun 9am–12:15pm and 1–4:30pm. U-Bahn U-6 to Nussdorfer Strasse. Tram D, 8, or 42.

This is the house where Franz Shubert was born in 1797. A versatile and prolific composer most famous for his songs but who also wrote symphonies and chamber music, Shubert died when he was only 31. In addition to his birthplace, you can also visit the place where he died, at Kettenbrückengasse 6.

Johann-Strauss-Wohnung

Praterstrasse 54. ☎ **01/214 01 21.** Admission 15 S ($1.40) adults, 5 S (50¢) for students and children. Tues–Sun 9am–12:15pm and 1–4:30pm. U-Bahn U-1 to Nestroyplatz.

This is where Strauss (1825–99) composed his famous "Blue Danube Waltz," which is probably better known than the Austrian national anthem. He lived here from 1863 to 1870.

Zentralfriedhof (Central Cemetery)

Simmeringer Hauptstrasse 234. ☎ **01/719 01-0.** Admission free. Summer, daily 7am–7pm; winter, daily 8am–5pm. Tram 71 from Schwarzenbergplatz to the next-to-the-last stop.

Austria's largest cemetery, it contains the graves of the Strausses (both father and son), Brahms, Schubert, Franz von Suppé, and Beethoven, as well as a commemorative grave for Mozart. To find the Graves of Honor, located near the Dr. Karl Lueger Church where you'll find all the composers buried within a few feet of one another, walk straight ahead from the main gate on the large pathway—the graves are to the left just before the path ends at the building.

FOR THE ARCHITECTURE BUFF

Vienna has a wealth of baroque palaces and fine buildings along and outside the Ring, including Schönbrunn, Belvedere, the Hofburg, and the Parliament. Other buildings of special interest to architects include the **Adolf Loos** building at Friedrichstrasse 6, constructed in 1899 and now a coffeehouse called Museum, and the Loos Building on Michaelerplatz, built in 1910 amid controversy because of its strict architectural style, void of any ornamentation. Loos also designed the public toilets on the Graben, which were recently renovated at a tremendous cost to the city—they may well be the most beautiful public toilets in the world. Lovers of art nouveau architecture should also check out the **Otto Wagner** U-Bahn station at Karlsplatz and his Postsparkasse bank at Georg-Coch-Platz 2. Both Loos and Wagner are Vienna's most important architects of the first part of this century.

Finally, the **Vienna Secession,** between the Opera and the Naschmarkt, is one of the city's most outstanding examples of turn-of-the-century architecture. Designed by art nouveau architect Joseph Maria Olbrich in 1898, the building takes its name from an association of artists founded by Gustav Klimt, Josef Hoffmann, and Kolo Moser, who used it as exhibition space. It contains a frieze by Klimt and still shows temporary exhibitions.

Of course, the Altstadt inside the Ring is a treasure trove of architectural styles, particularly patrician **houses built in the Middle Ages.** Am Hof, Annagasse, Bäckerstrasse, Fleischmarkt, and Schönlaterngasse are just some of the streets with famous houses. Information on individual houses, as well as Vienna's most famous buildings, is given in "Vienna from A to Z," available for 50 S ($4.75) from the Vienna Tourist Board.

In addition to Vienna's baroque palaces and its fine buildings inside the Ring, you might be interested in seeing the **Hundertwasser Haus,** on the corner of Löwengasse and Kegelgasse. It's an apartment house like none you've ever seen—irregularly shaped, turreted, and almost fluid. You can't visit the apartments inside, but there's a coffee shop up on the first floor. People flock here just to take a photograph of the exterior.

Across the street on Kegelgasse is **Kalke Village,** a shopping complex designed by Hundertwasser, and a four-minute walk away is the KunstHausWien, a museum designed by Hundertwasser to house his works (see "More Attractions," above).

ORGANIZED TOURS

WALKING TOURS   A number of walking tours are conducted in English. **Vienna Tourist Guides,** for example, offers guided walks through medieval Vienna, the old Jewish quarter, an art nouveau architectural tour, and other parts of Vienna. A tour costs 110 S ($10.50), excluding entrance fees, for adults; 60 S ($5.70) for children 17 and under.

Pick up a brochure, **"Walks in Vienna,"** detailing the various tours, times, and departure points from the Vienna Tourist Board, Kärntner Strasse 38. No reservations are necessary for the tours, which last about 1½ hours and are held regardless of the weather.

BUS TOURS   There are a number of tour companies offering general city tours of Vienna and specialized tours, which you can book at travel agencies and at top hotels throughout the city. The oldest tour company is **Vienna Sightseeing Tours,**

Stelzhamergasse 4 (☎ **01/712 46 83-0**), which offers various tours that include the Spanish Riding School, the Vienna Boys' Choir, the Vienna Woods, the Mayerling hunting lodge where Crown Prince Rudolph committed suicide, musicians' homes, Grinzing, Prater, Salzburg, and more. A three-hour city tour costs 320 S ($30.50). Departure for tours is at the Staatsoper or major hotels.

TRAM TOURS   From May through September, tours of Vienna via a 1929-vintage tram car are conducted on Wednesday and Saturday at 1:30pm and Sunday and holidays at 10pm and 1:30pm. Departure is from Karlsplatz; the cost is 200 S ($19.05) for adults and 70 S ($6.65) for children. For more information, contact the Vienna Tourist Board.

BOAT TOURS   Boats cruise the Danube April through October, departing from a pier next to the Schwedenbrücke (the U-Bahn station is Schwedenplatz), a five-minute walk from Stephansplatz, and including a stop at the KunstHausWien. Boats depart daily at 10:30am, 1pm, 2:30pm, and 4:30pm May through September; at 1pm in April and October. Tours last three hours and cost 220 S ($20.95) for adults, half price for children. For more information, call 727 50-0.

7 Shopping

Vienna is known for the excellent quality of its works, which of course do not come cheap. If money is no object, you may want to shop for petit-point items, hand-painted Augarten porcelain, gold jewelry, ceramics, enamel jewelry, and leather goods. Also popular is *Loden,* the boiled and rolled wool fabric fashioned into overcoats, suits, and hats, as well as knitted sweaters. If you're on a budget, Vienna's Saturday flea market is one of Europe's best.

Vienna's most famous **shopping streets** are in the city center, including the pedestrian Kärntner Strasse, the Graben, Kohlmarkt, and Rotenturmstrasse. Mariahilfer Strasse also has department stores and shops, including the Gerngross and Herzmansky department stores, and Generali-Center, a shopping mall.

If you make a purchase of more than 1,000 S ($95.25) at any store, you're entitled to a **refund of part of the value-added tax (VAT),** which is 20% to 32% on regular items (such as clothing) and 24% on luxury items (such as jewelry). Make sure to ask the store clerk for a U-34 tax-refund form, which you should present to Customs upon departing the last European Union country you visit before heading home. If you're leaving Europe from Vienna, you can obtain an immediate refund from the bank window at the airport (be sure you have your purchase with you and have your receipt stamped by a Customs official).

FLEA MARKETS   If you're in Vienna on a Saturday, head straight for the town's best-known flea market, held on **Linke Wienzeile** near the Kettenbrücken U-Bahn station. This is the most colorful place in town to look for curios, antiques, old books, and junk, evident from the hordes of people who descend upon the place. I've bought old coffee grinders here for almost everyone I know (although they aren't quite the bargain they were 15 years ago). Be sure to haggle. It's open Saturday from about 8am to 6pm.

If you're here only on a weekday, it's worth a trip to the adjoining **Naschmarkt,** Vienna's outdoor food and produce market (see "Dining," earlier in this chapter).

A market for **arts and crafts,** held only in summer from May through August, takes place Saturday from 2 to 6pm and Sunday from 10am to 6pm along the promenade of the Donaukanal at Franz-Joseph-Kai (near the Schwedenplatz U-Bahn station, north of Stephansplatz). From March to December, a small **antiques market** is held inside the Ring at Am Hof every Friday and Saturday, with about 40 vendors participating.

Finally, there's another wonderful market, the **Spittelberg Arts and Crafts Exhibition,** held daily in December until Christmas and on Saturday from April to October, with artists selling arts and crafts up and down the historic Spittelberg street, located outside the Ring just west of the Kunsthistorisches Museum.

DEPARTMENT STORES   Vienna's main department stores are all conveniently located: **Gerngross,** Mariahilfer Strasse 38–48 (☎ **01/521 80-0**); **Herzmansky,** Mariahilfer Strasse 26–30 (☎ **01/521 58-0**); **Stafa,** Mariahilfer Strasse 120 (☎ **01/523 86 21-0**); and **Steffl,** Kärntner Strasse 19 (☎ **01/514 31**).

8 Vienna After Dark

Everything in Vienna is somewhat theatrical, perhaps because of its majestic baroque backdrop. Small wonder that opera and theater reign supreme here. It would be a shame to come all this way without experiencing something that's very dear to the Viennese heart.

To find out what's being played on Vienna's many stages, pick up a copy of *Wien Monatsprogramm,* available free at the Vienna Tourist Board. In addition to monthly programs, it also lists places where you can purchase tickets in advance, thereby avoiding the 22% surcharge on tickets sold at travel agencies. If you're a student under 27 with a current valid ID from your college or university, you can purchase tickets for the Staatsoper, the Burgtheater, and Akademietheater for just 50 S ($4.75) on the night of the performance (an International Student Identity Card only will not be accepted as proof of student status; a current student card from your university is also required). Almost all other theaters also offer reduced rates for students, usually about 20% off the usual ticket price. Even if you're not a student, you can see the Burgtheater or Staatsoper (Austrian State Opera) for as little as 15 to 20 S ($1.50 to $1.90) for standing-room tickets.

THE PERFORMING ARTS

For advance sales of tickets for the Burgtheater, Akademietheater, Staatsoper, and Volksoper, go to the **Bundestheaterkassen,** Goethegasse 1 (☎ **01/514 44-2959**), just a minute's walk northwest of the Staatsoper. Tickets go on sale a week before each performance. The Bundestheaterkassen is open Monday through Friday from 8am to 6pm, Saturday from 9am to 2pm, and Sunday and holidays from 9am to noon. Tickets for all four stages are also available directly at each box office an hour before the performance, but only for that day's performance. Thus, if you're interested in seeing any production of the Burgtheater, Akademietheater, Staatsoper, or the Volksoper, this should be your first stop upon arrival in Vienna. Otherwise, you can also order tickets for these venues by credit/charge card by calling 01/513 15 13 Monday through Friday from 10am to 6pm, Saturday from 10am to 2pm, and Sunday and holidays from 10am to noon. Telephone sales begin six days before the day of performance and can be ordered by holders of American Express, Diners Club, MasterCard, and Visa. Note that standing-room tickets are not sold in advance but only on the night of the performance.

OPERA & BALLET

✪ Staatsoper

Opernring 2. ☎ **01/514 44-2959** or 514 44-2960. Seats, 100–2,300 S ($9.50–$219) for most productions; standing room, 20 S ($1.90) for the Galerie (upper balcony), 30 S ($2.85) for the slightly better Parterrestehplatz (ground floor); unsold tickets available to students with ID for 50 S ($4.75) on the performance night at the box office. U-Bahn U-1, U-2, or U-4 to Karlsplatz-Oper.

Considered one of the world's leading opera houses, the Staatsoper stages grand productions throughout the year, except during July and August. It's traditional to start off each new year with the production of Johann Strauss's operetta *Die Fledermaus* in January, followed by a repertoire of 40 operatic works each season. Opera or ballet is presented nightly during the season, accompanied by the Viennese Philharmonic orchestra. The Staatsoper employs 1,200 people, including the stage crew, singers, and production staff. The stage area is 5,300 square feet, one of the largest in Europe and much larger than the spectator floor of the opera house. The horseshoe-shaped theater has a red, ivory, and gold interior, and its walls are lined with box seats. It holds 2,200 people—1,700 in seats and 500 in the standing-room sections.

You can spend as much as $219 for a ticket, but the most economical way to see a performance is to purchase one of the 500 standing-room tickets available on the night of the performance. To do so, go to the Staatsoper at least three hours before the performance, stand in line, buy your ticket, and once inside, mark your "seat" by tying a scarf to the rail. You can then leave and come back just before the performance.

Performances are nightly, September to June. Incidentally, even though no operas or ballets are performed in July and August, other events take place, including concerts; check the *Monatsprogramm.*

Tours are given almost daily throughout the year, two to five times a day (check the board outside the entrance for the times of each day's tours); the cost is 40 S ($3.80).

Volksoper

Währinger Strasse 78. ☎ **01/514 44-3318.** Tickets: Seats, 60–850 S ($4.70–$80.95); standing room, 15 S ($1.45); student tickets 50 S ($4.75). U-Bahn U-6 to Währinger-Strasse–Volksoper. Tram 40, 41, or 42 to Währinger-Strasse–Volksoper.

Spectacular operettas and light operas are features here, from *Der Zigeunerbaron* by Johann Strauss to *Die Hochzeit des Figaro* by Mozart, as well as musicals performed in German. Standing-room tickets and discount tickets for students are sold on the night of the performance. Performances are nightly, September to June, usually at 7pm, and sometimes there are matinees Saturday and Sunday.

THEATER

Akademietheater

Lisztstrasse 1. ☎ **01/514 44-2959** or 514 44-2960. Seats, 50–450 S ($4.75–$42.85); standing room, 15 S ($1.45); student tickets, 50 S ($4.75). U-Bahn U-4 to Stadtpark. Tram 1, 2, 71, or D to Schwarzenbergplatz.

Another important theater, this one features performances of classic and modern playwrights, from Shakespeare to Bertolt Brecht. There are performances most evenings, September to June.

Burgtheater

Dr.-Karl-Lueger-Ring 2. ☎ **01/514 44-2959** or 514 44-2960. Seats, 50–450 S ($4.75–$42.85); standing room, 15 S ($1.45); student tickets, 50 S ($4.75). Tram 1, 2, or D to Burgtheater.

Under the direction of Claus Peymann, the Burgtheater stages the great German classics as well as modern plays, from Friedrich Schiller's *Wilhelm Tell* to Georg Büchner's *Woyzeck*. Actors and actresses consider an engagement here a highlight in their acting careers. Performances are given most evenings from September to June.

Theater an der Wien and the Raimundtheater

Linke Wienzeile 6 (Theater an der Wien) (☎ **01/588 30-265**) and Wallgasse 18–20 (Raimundtheater) (☎ **01/599 77 27**). Seat (for both theaters) 110–990 S ($10.50–$94.30); standing room, 25 S ($2.40). U-Bahn U-1, U-2, or U-4 to Karlsplatz-Oper (for Theater an der Wien); U-3 to Westbahnhof (for Raimund theater).

The Theater an der Wien, together with the Raimundtheater, stages musicals. Both are part of the Vereinigte Bühen (United Theaters) under the direction of Rudi Klausnitzer. Previous productions have included *Les Misérables*, *Phantom of the Opera*, *Freudiana*, *Kiss of the Spider Woman*, and *Cats*. Performances are given daily throughout the year. The theater box offices are open daily from 10am to 1pm and 2 to 6pm.

Incidentally, there's a small kiosk called **Wien Ticket** on Kärntner Strasse beside the Staatsoper that sells tickets for both the Theater an der Wien and Raimundtheater. It's open daily from 10am to 7pm, and after 2pm it offers unsold tickets for that evening's performances at half price.

International Theatre

Porzellangasse 8. ☎ **01/319 62 72**. Tickets 220–250 S ($20.95–$23.80), 130 S ($12.40) students and senior citizens. U-Bahn U-4 to Rossauer Lände.

In operation since 1974, this English-language theater stages American and British plays, usually offering four productions a year and an annual presentation of Charles Dickens's *A Christmas Carol*. Performances are given September to July, Tuesday through Saturday at 7:30pm.

Theater in der Josefstadt

Josefstädter Strasse 26. ☎ **01/402 51 27**. Tickets 50–500 S ($4.75–$47.60). U-Bahn U-2 to Rathaus. Tram J to Lederergasse. Bus 13A to Theater in der Josefstadt.

First opened in 1788, this is Vienna's oldest theater in continuous operation. Max Reinhardt (founder of the Salzburg Festival) brought fame here through renovations and with major productions in the 1920s. If you understand German, you'll like the intimate coziness of this theater with its performances of light drama and Viennese classics. Performances are given most nights at 7:30pm, plus Sunday matinees at 3 or 3:30pm.

Vienna's English Theater

Josefsgasse 12. ☎ **01/402 12 60**. Tickets 170–460 S ($16.20–$43.80). U-Bahn U-2 to Rathaus.

If you don't speak German, you might prefer a visit to this English-language theater, which presents highly professional productions of both classic and contemporary plays. Performances are usually Monday through Saturday at 7:30pm.

CLASSICAL MUSIC

Be sure to check the *Wien Monatsprogramm* for a current listing of concerts. From May through October, for example, the **Vienna Hofburg Orchestra** presents waltz and operetta concerts every Wednesday at 8:30pm at the Kozerthaus in the Hofburg for 400 S ($38.10) per person, while the **Vienna Mozart Orchestra,** dressed in period costumes, performs May to October, Wednesday, Friday, and Saturday at 8:15pm at various venues around town. Tickets for these start at 290 S ($27.60).

LIVE-MUSIC HOUSES

Metropol

Hernalser Hauptstrasse 55. ☎ **01/407 77 40.** Cover 170–500 S ($16.20–$47.60). Tram 43 from Schottentor.

The Metropol has served as a mecca of the Viennese youth scene for more than a decade, with productions ranging from rock, new wave, jazz, and reggae concerts to cabaret. Open Tuesday through Saturday from 7 or 8pm.

Papa's Tapas

Schwarzenbergplatz 10. ☎ **01/505 03 11.** Cover 30–80 S ($2.85–$7.60) for most bands. Tram 1, 2, 71, or D to Schwarzenbergplatz.

A couple of minutes' walk south of the Ring, this small basement establishment features blues, boogie woogie, country, and rock 'n' roll in a cozy and intimate setting. Open Monday through Thursday from 8pm to 2am and Friday and Saturday from 8pm to 4am; concerts begin around 9pm.

Next door and under the same management are Wurlitzer, a bar with a 1950s jukebox, and Atrium, Austria's oldest disco (see "Discos," below). You could easily spend the entire evening right here on Schwarzenbergplatz.

Rockhaus

Adalbert-Stifter-Strasse 73. ☎ **01/332 46 41.** Cover 80–150 S ($7.60–$14.30) for local bands, 150–300 S ($14.30–$28.55) for international bands. Tram 31, 32, or N. Bus 11A or 35A.

This is one of Vienna's best-known venues for live music, including blues, rock, reggae, new wave, and hard rock. International groups provide the main entertainment, while Austrian musicians are usually the warm-up band. Check the daily newspaper or *Wien Monatsprogramm* for current concerts. Open Tuesday through Sunday; the bar opens at 6pm and concerts begin around 8pm.

✪ Tunnel

Florianigasse 39 (behind the Rathaus near the university district). ☎ **01/405 34 65.** Cover 30–90 S ($2.85–$8.55) Tues–Sun (free after 11pm if there's room); Mon jam sessions free. U-Bahn U-2 to Rathaus; then a 10-minute walk. Tram 5. Bus 13A.

This basement establishment features live music nightly, from blues and rock to folk and jazz. Groups are mainly European, including bands from Eastern Europe. Monday nights feature jam sessions. If you're hungry, an inexpensive restaurant upstairs on the ground floor serves food until 1am. A *Seidel* (one-third liter) of beer begins at 26 S ($2.50); long drinks, at 36 S ($3.50). Open daily from 7pm to 2am (live music begins around 9pm); the café is open daily from 9am to 2am.

FILMS

A municipally run cinema, the **Stadtkino,** Schwarzenbergplatz 7 (☎ **01/712 62 76**), features unconventional films seldom shown in commercial theaters, including foreign films from all over the world in their original languages.

The **Burg Kino,** Opernring 19 (☎ **01/587 84 06**), shows films in their original languages.

With a comprehensive archive of rare copies and documents relating to film history, the cinema at the **Austrian Film Museum,** in the Albertina, Augustiner-strasse 1 (☎ **01/533 70 54**), shows films in their original languages, complete retrospectives, classics, and avant-garde and experimental films. Movies, presented Monday through Saturday at 6 and 8pm from October to May, often revolve around a special theme. The price here is 45 S ($4.30), plus a 45-S ($4.30) one-day membership.

THE BAR SCENE
HISTORIC WINE CELLARS

Since these wine cellars may be crowded during mealtimes, you might consider coming here for a drink later in the evening—unless, of course, you want to splurge on a meal that will cost $14 or more. They're all inside the Ring.

Augustiner Keller
Augustinerstrasse 1 (a minute's walk from the opera). ☎ **01/533 10 26** or 533 09 46. U-Bahn: Karlsplatz or Stephansplatz.

With a history stretching back several centuries, the Augustiner Keller does seem rather ancient, with its wooden floors, vaulted brick ceiling, and long, narrow room. There's traditional *Heurigenmusik* every evening starting at 6:30 (there's no cover charge, but drink prices are higher), and the menu here includes grilled chicken, grilled shank of pork, Tafelspitz, pork cutlet, and Apfelstrudel. A glass of wine begins at 26 S ($2.50) during the day, 30 S ($2.85) at night. Open daily from 11am to midnight.

Melkerstiftskeller
Schottengasse 3. ☎ **01/533 55 30.** U-BahnU-2 to Schottentor or U-3 to Herrengasse.

This *Heuriger* (Viennese wine tavern) features wine from its own vineyards, served in historic vaulted rooms. The menu features pork, chicken, veal, Bratwurst with Sauerkraut, and other typical Viennese cuisine. A glass of wine (a quarter liter) goes for 30 S ($2.85) and up. Open Monday through Saturday from 5pm to midnight.

✪ Urbanikeller
Am Hof 12. ☎ **01/533 91 02.** U-Bahn U-1 or U-3 to Stephansplatz, or U-3 to Herrengasse.

On one of Vienna's venerable old squares in the heart of the city, the Urbanikeller gets my vote as the city's most picturesque wine cellar. Founded in 1906, its dining room looks like the setting of some medieval movie, with its stone walls, arched ceiling, and heavy oak tables. There's live Viennese music from 7pm to midnight, making it a great place to stop off for a late-night drink. Wine is a bit more expensive here—a quarter-liter glass starts at 38 S ($3.60)—but it's worth it. Open daily from 6pm to 1am; closed mid-July to mid-Aug.

Zwölf Apostelkeller
Sonnenfelsgasse 3. ☎ **01/512 67 77.** U-Bahn U-1 to Stephansplatz.

This huge wine cellar is two levels deep. The vaulting of the upper cellar is mainly 15th-century gothic, while the lower cellar is early baroque. Unlike the places above, it offers only a limited menu, so it's perfectly acceptable to come here anytime just for drinks. A glass of wine (quarter liter) costs 25 S ($2.40) and up. Open daily from 4:30pm to midnight.

DRINKS IN VIENNA'S OLD QUARTER

✪ Griechenbeisl
Fleischmarkt 11. ☎ **01/533 19 41** or 533 19 77. U-Bahn U-1 or U-3 to Stephansplatz, or U-1 or U-4 to Schwedenplatz.

This historic inn is one of Vienna's most famous locales, dating back to the 15th century. Housed in an ancient-looking vine-covered building on one of the city's small crooked streets, the Griechenbeisl is fantastically picturesque, with lots of cozy little rooms linked by narrow winding passageways. One of the small rooms has signatures of famous personalities who have been here, including Beethoven, Wagner, Mark Twain, and Count Zeppelin. Since the Griechenbeisl is a restaurant (and too expensive for us), come after 11pm for a drink. Although there's no substantial proof, local legend says that it was in this inn that an anonymous ballad-singer wrote "Lieber Augustin" in 1679 while Vienna suffered from the plague. A half liter of beer costs 45 S ($4.30); a quarter liter begins at 44 S ($4.20). Open daily from 11am to 1am.

✪ Kaffee Alt Wien
Bäckerstrasse 9. ☎ **01/512 52 22.** U-Bahn U-1 or U-3 to Stephansplatz.

A dimly lit old coffeehouse in the heart of Old Vienna, this café/bar first opened in 1936 and is popular with students, artists, and writers. Its tired old walls are hidden beneath the barrage of posters announcing concerts and exhibitions. In the afternoon it's a good place to come to read the newspaper, study, write letters, and relax; late at night it can get so crowded that it's hard to get through the front door. A *Seidel* (one-third liter) of beer starts at 27 S ($2.55); a glass of wine (one-eighth liter), at 15 S ($1.45). Open daily from 10am to 4am.

Oswald & Kalb
Bäckerstrasse 14. ☎ **01/512 13 71** or 512 69 92. U-Bahn U-1 or U-3 to Stephansplatz.

This restaurant/bar caters to Vienna's young and upwardly mobile, including writers and artists. It's simple, with wooden floors and white tablecloths, and features a handwritten menu that changes daily. Main courses, running 95 to 180 S ($9.05 to $17.15), include fish, chicken, and pork dishes, but you may wish to come here just for a drink. A *Krügerl* (half liter) of beer goes for 36 S ($3.45). Open daily from 6pm to 1am.

Panigl
Schönlaterngasse 11. ☎ **01/513 17 16.** U-Bahn U-1 or U-3 to Stephansplatz, or U-3 to Stubentor.

Another trendy bar in Vienna's old quarter, this one also pulls in artists, journalists, and TV and film personalities. Although it's tiny, people pack in for the Italian antipasti, cheeses, and of course the Italian wines, a small glass of wine (one-eighth liter) for 26 S ($2.50). Open Monday through Friday from 4pm to 4am and Saturday, Sunday, and holidays from 8pm to 4am.

Schwimmende Pyramide
Seilerstätte 3A. ☎ **01/513 29 70.** U-Bahn U-1 or U-3 to Stephansplatz, or U-3 to Stubentor.

This interesting locale with avant-garde artwork on its front door and modern lamps inside offers more than 70 different kinds of beer; a half liter begins at

35 S ($3.35). It also has an extensive menu (food is served until 4am), featuring spareribs, fish, salads, omelets, Wiener Schnitzel, and Viennese specialties, with most main courses under 100 S ($9.55). Open Sunday through Thursday from 4pm to 4am and Friday and Saturday from 4pm to 5am.

Wunder Bar

Schönlaterngasse 8. ☎ **01/512 79 89.** U-Bahn U-1 or U-3 to Stephansplatz, or U-3 to Stubentor.

There's no sign outside to identify this place, apparently because everyone knows that it's here. A small locale with a ceiling that could be called a modern interpretation of gothic, it doesn't get crowded here until after 10pm. A glass of wine (one-eighth liter) begins at 20 S ($1.90); a *Seidel* (one-third liter) of beer, at 28 S ($2.65). Open daily from 4pm to 2am.

DRINKS IN RABENSTEIG

About a five-minute walk northeast of Stephansplatz brings you to Rabensteig, the old Jewish quarter of Vienna. Today it's one of Vienna's most popular nightspots, with several bars lining Rabensteig, Seitenstettengasse, and other small pedestrans-only streets, in an area popularly referred to as the Bermuda Triangle. These three are my favorites:

Cafe Billard Roter Engel

Rabensteig 5. ☎ **01/535 41 05.** Cover 40–70 S ($3.80–$6.65). U-Bahn U-1 or U-4 to Schwedenplatz.

This very popular place has live music in the evenings after 9pm, with everything from jazz to reggae. Upstairs are billiard tables, in case you're itching to shoot some pool. A *Seidel* (one-third liter) of beer runs 28 S ($2.65); a small glass of wine (one-eighth liter) begins at 20 S ($1.90). Open Monday through Saturday from 5pm to 4am and Sunday from 5pm to 2am. Live music starts at 9:30pm.

Casablanca

Rabensteig 8. ☎ **01/533 34 63.** Music charge 15 S ($1.45). U-Bahn U-1 or U-4 to Schwedenplatz.

Directly across from Roter Engel, this bar offers the usual wine and beer, along with live music provided by local bands and outdoor seating. A *Seidel* (one-third liter) of beer costs 28 S ($2.65). Open Tuesday through Saturday from 6pm to 4am and Sunday, Monday, and holidays from 6pm to 2am (in summer, if the weather's good, daily from 3pm). Live music begins at 8:30pm.

Krah Krah

Rabensteig 8. ☎ **01/533 81 93.** U-Bahn U-1 or U-4 to Schwedenplatz.

You can choose from among 40 kinds of beer. Incidentally, "Krah Krah" is the sound a raven makes, referring to the street Rabensteig, which means Ravens' Path. On Sunday from 11:30am to 3pm there's free jazz. A *Seidel* (one-third liter) of beer begins at 28 S ($2.65). Open Monday through Wednesday from 11am to 2am, Thursday through Saturday from 11am to 3am, and Sunday from 11am to 1am.

DISCOS

Atrium

Schwindgasse 1 (just off Schwarzenbergplatz). ☎ **01/505 35 94.** Cover 30 S ($2.85) Thurs–Fri and Sun, 40 S ($3.80) Sat; students pay 15 S ($1.45). Tram 1, 2, 71, or D to Schwarzenbergplatz.

The Atrium was Austria's first disco, opening in 1958 and still going strong. A cavernous underground club of various rooms, it attracts people in their 20s, due in part to a reduced student admission price and in part to promotions and weekly specials. On Thursday and Sunday, for example, admission is free if you come within the first hour of opening, which is worth it since all drinks are also half price during the same period. Friday features music of the 1960s. A half liter of beer costs 38 S ($3.60). Open Thursday through Sunday from 8:30pm to 3:30am.

Move

Daungasse 1. ☎ **01/406 32 78.** Cover 50 S ($4.75), 20 S ($1.90) of which goes toward the first drink; students free Mon and Wed, 20 S ($1.90) other days, 10 S (95¢) of which goes toward the first drink; women free Tues and Thurs. U-Bahn U-2 to Rathaus or U-6 to Josefstädter Strasse; then a 10-minute walk. Tram 43 or 44 to Skodagasse, or 5 or 31 to Laudongasse.

Stars come alive as soon as you descend into this basement establishment, with its black walls and thousands of orange and green neon dots. Holograms line the walls. Open daily from 9pm to 4am.

P1 Discothek

Rotgasse 9 (inside the Ring, not far from Stephansplatz). ☎ **01/535 99 95.** Cover 50 S ($4.75). U-Bahn U-1 to Stephansplatz.

This is probably Vienna's hottest disco at the moment, popular with people in their 20s. A former film studio, it's huge, with a large dance floor and enough room to accommodate 1,500 people throughout. It opened in 1988—and attained instant fame when Tina Turner came here at the start of her European tour. A *Seidel* (one-third liter) of beer costs 45 S ($4.30). Open Sunday through Thursday from 9pm to 4am and Friday and Saturday from 9pm to 6am.

Rock In

Kärntner Strasse 61 (just south of the Ring). ☎ **01/505 60 14.** Cover 50 S ($4.75) Fri–Sat, 10 S (95¢) of which goes toward your first drink; for live concerts, usually 60–120 S ($5.70–$11.45). U-Bahn U-1, U-2, or U-4 to Karlsplatz.

This is one of Vienna's better alternative establishments, drawing in a young clientele that wouldn't be caught dead in a slicker disco. It even publishes its own rock magazine, with information on who's playing where in Vienna and beyond. A combination bar/disco, it offers customers such diversions as dancing, drinking, eating, and shooting pool or playing Foosball or pinball. The disco, complete with five separate bars for drinks, is fashionably decorated in black and silver, while a bar upstairs offers food ranging from pasta and salads to pizza and Schnitzel, available until a late 4am. There's live music two or three times a month. A *Seidel* of beer goes for 41 S ($3.90). The bar is open Wednesday through Sunday from 9pm to 4am; the disco, Wednesday through Sunday from 10pm.

THE *HEURIGE*

Heurige are Viennese wine taverns featuring Viennese wines (called Heurige as well). Today there are about 400 families still cultivating vineyards in Vienna, spread over the wine-growing districts of Grinzing, Nussdorf, Stammersdorf, Heiligenstadt, Strebersdorf, Sievering, and Neustift, among others.

Of these, Grinzing is probably the best known, with about 20 Heurige clustered together. Most of them have wine gardens for summer drinking, but in the winter there's plenty of action indoors. Most also serve food, the favorites being sausage, potato salad, and Liptauer cheese spread. Look for the sprig of pine, usually hung above the entrance, and a small plaque with EIGENBAU written on it, which means that the grower serves his or her own wine. Grinzing is only 5 miles from the city center, and you can reach it by taking tram no. 38 from Schottentor. There's no cover charge; you can buy a quarter-liter mug of wine and linger as long as you wish. Otherwise, food and drink at a Heuriger will probably cost about $16 a person.

9 Easy Excursions

THE VIENNA WOODS   The Vienna Woods surround much of the city, offering mile upon mile of hiking trails, views, and solitude. One of the most popular destinations is **Kahlenberg,** which affords great views over the whole city. To reach Kahlenberg, take tram no. 38 to Grinzing and transfer there to bus no. 38A to Kahlenberg. If you're a hiker, you can also walk to Kahlenberg in about two hours by taking tram D to the last station and then striking out from there.

THE DONAUINSEL   How about a swim in the Danube? Actually, it's the Alte Donau (Old Danube), where you'll find beaches, restaurants, paddleboats, rental bikes, and other facilities. The largest and oldest beach is **Gänsehäufel,** a section of which is segregated for nudists. To reach the beach, take U-Bahn U-1 to either the Kaisermühlen or Alte Donau station. Nearby is also the 13-mile-long **Donauinsel,** sandwiched in between the Danube Canal and the New Danube, popular with joggers, cyclists, and strollers. It's the largest recreation area in Vienna's immediate vicinity and also offers bathing opportunities right off its bank. You can reach the Donauinsel by taking U-Bahn U-1 to the Donauinsel station or the S-Bahn to the Lobau station.

BOAT TRIPS ON THE DANUBE   From April to late October there are daily excursion trips from Vienna all the way to Lintz, Grein, even Budapest. A popular three-hour trip on the Danube departs daily from Schwedenplatz and costs 220 S ($20.95). For more information, contact the **Danube Steamship Company (DDSG)** (☎ 01/727 50-0) or pick up its brochure at the tourist office.

Appendix

Austrian National Tourist Office, 500 Fifth Ave., Suite 800, New York, NY 10110 (☎ 212/944-6880); 500 N. Michigan Ave., Suite 1950, Chicago, IL 60611 (☎ 312/644-8029); 11601 Wilshire Blvd., Suite 2480, Los Angeles, CA 90025 (☎ 310/477-3332).

Belgian Tourist Office, 745 Fifth Ave., New York, NY 10151 (☎ 212/758-8130).

British Tourist Authority, 551 Fifth Ave., New York, NY 10036 (☎ 212/986-2200); 625 N. Michigan Ave., Suite 1510, Chicago, IL 60611 (☎ 312/787-0464); 350 S. Figueroa St., Los Angeles, CA 90071 (☎ 213/628-5731).

Čedok (Czech Travel Bureau), 10 E. 40th St., Suite 1902, New York, NY 10016 (☎ 212/689-9720).

French Government Tourist Office, 444 Madison Ave., 16th Floor, New York, NY 10022 (☎ 212/838-7800); 676 N. Michigan Ave., Suite 3360, Chicago, IL 60611 (☎ 312/751-7800); 9454 Wilshire Blvd., Suite 303, Beverly Hills, CA 90212 (☎ 310/271-6665).

German National Tourist Office, 122 E. 42nd St., New York, NY 10168 (☎ 212/661-7200); 11766 Wilshire Blvd., Suite 750, Los Angeles, CA 90025 (☎ 310/575-9799).

Greek National Tourist Organization, 645 Fifth Ave., 5th Floor, New York, NY 10022 (☎ 212/421-5777); 168 N. Michigan Ave., Suite 600, Chicago, IL 60601 (☎ 312/782-1084); 611 W. 6th St., Suite 2198, Los Angeles, CA 90017 (☎ 213/626-6696).

IBUSZ Hungarian Travel Company, 250 W. 57th St., New York, NY 10107 (☎ 212/586-5230).

Irish Tourist Board, 345 Park Ave., New York, NY 10154 (☎ 212/418-0800).

Italian Government Travel Office, 630 Fifth Ave., New York, NY 10111 (☎ 212/245-4822); 401 N. Michigan Ave., Suite 3030, Chicago, IL 60611 (☎ 312/644-9448).

Netherlands Board of Tourism, 355 Lexington Ave., New York, NY 10017 (☎ 212/370-7360); 225 N. Michigan Ave., Suite 326, Chicago, IL 60601 (☎ 312/819-0300).

Portuguese National Tourist Office, 590 Fifth Ave., New York, NY 10036
(☎ 212/354-4403).

National Tourist Office of Spain, 665 Fifth Ave., New York, NY 10022
(☎ 212/759-8822); 845 N. Michigan Ave., Suite 915E, Chicago, IL 60611
(☎ 312/642-1992); 8383 Wilshire Blvd., Suite 960, Beverly Hills, CA 90211
(☎ 213/658-7188); 1221 Brickell Ave., Suite 1850, Miami, FL 33131
(☎ 305/358-1992).

Scandinavian Tourist Boards, 655 Third Ave., New York, NY 10017
(☎ 212/949-2333).

Swiss National Tourist Office, 605 Fifth Ave., New York, NY 10020
(☎ 212/757-5944); 150 N. Michigan Ave., Suite 2930, Chicago, IL 60601
(☎ 312/630-5840); 222 N. Sepulveda Blvd., Suite 1570, El Segundo, CA 90245
(☎ 310/335-5980).

B Train Fares & Schedules

FARES

The expected cost of one-way second-class tickets for trips between the major cities
of Europe for 1996 and 1997 are shown below.

AMSTERDAM   to: Paris, $71; Copenhagen, $137; London, $169 (via Brussels
and Eurotunnel), $94 (via Sealink); Vienna, $202; Brussels, $36; Frankfurt, $79;
Rome, $236; Venice, $209

LONDON   to: Brussels, $123 (via Eurotunnel), $100 (via Sealink); Edinburgh,
$102; Glasgow, $102; Dublin, $130; Paris, $1123 (via Eurotunnel); Amsterdam,
$169 (via Eurotunnel and Brussels), $94 (via Sealink)

PARIS   to: Brussels, $69; Amsterdam, $71; Madrid, $109; Copenhagen, $201;
Frankfurt, $82; Munich, $120; Zurich, $79; Rome, $125; Cannes, $83; Lourdes,
$95; Marseille, $66; Nice, $84; Strasbourg, $63

ROME   to: Florence, $28; Naples, $20; Genoa, $45; Venice, $48; Milan, $52;
Amsterdam, $236; Barcelona, $122; Brussels, $177; Frankfurt, $160; Geneva,
$103; London, $315 (via Eurotunnel), $264 (via Sealink); Madrid, $159; Munich,
$92; Paris, $125; Vienna, $105; Trieste, $59; Zurich, $102

MADRID   to: Barcelona, $45; Toledo, $9; Valencia, $31; Lisbon, $44; Paris,
$119; Rome, $159; Seville, $36

BARCELONA   to: Marseille, $54; Nice, $72; Paris, $93; Rome, $122;
Lourdes, $58

MUNICH   to: Amsterdam, $147; Brussels, $141; Copenhagen, $197;
Innsbruck, $31; Milan, $62; Naples, $104; Paris, $120; Rome, $92; Salzburg, $42;
Venice, $57; Vienna, $63; Zurich, $64

SCHEDULES

The rail schedules that follow show the trains that depart from major European
cities. With few exceptions, only the major international expresses are listed. But
not every international express is here, because many of these famous trains have
only first-class accommodations. You can be sure that if a train is mentioned in
Frommer's Europe from $50 a Day, it has second-class seats or couchettes.

These departure and arrival times are in effect between June 2 and September 28, 1996. The summer schedule for 1997 is in effect between June 1 and September 27.

Unless otherwise stated, these trains make their runs daily in all seasons. The abbreviation lv means "leaves"; ar indicates a train's arrival time. Usually, we'll give the train's departure time from all the cities in the country from which it sets out and provide its arrival in the various cities of the countries to which it goes.

EUROTUNNEL RAIL SERVICE

With the opening of the Eurotunnel/Channel Tunnel in 1995, one of the greatest engineering projects became a reality. Travel time on the Eurostar train between London and Paris was reduced to 3 hours, to Brussels 3 hours and 15 minutes. For fares and updated schedules for London, call 0233/617575 or fax 00441/233617998; for Paris, call 1/45-82-50-50 or fax 1/21-00-69-00; for Brussels, call 02/224-8856.

TRAINS LEAVING LONDON

London–Paris (via Eurostar and Eurotunnel)   10 daily departures weekdays, 8 on Sunday. Lv London (Waterloo) 6:57am, 8:23am, 9:23am, 10:23am, 11:57am, 12:53pm, 2:23pm, 4:23pm, 5:48pm, 6:53pm weekdays; 9:30am, 10:30am, 12:53pm, 3:10pm, 4:23pm, 4:57pm, 5:53pm, 6:53pm Sundays. Ar Paris (Gare du Nord) 3 hours later.

London–Brussels (via Eurostar and Eurotunnel)   6 daily departures weekdays, 5 on Sunday. Lv London (Waterloo) 7:23am, 10:27am, 12:27am, 4:27am, 5:15am, 5:27pm weekdays; 8:57am, 12:14pm, 2:14pm, 4:27pm, 5:27pm Sundays. Ar Brussels (Gare du Midi) 3 hours 15 minutes later.

London–Amsterdam (via Eurostar and Eurotunnel).   Same schedule as London–Brussels, with connecting train waiting in Brussels for Brussels–Amsterdam. Ar Amsterdam (Centraal) 6 hours 30 minutes later.

London–Copenhagen (via Eurotunnel, train change in Brussels)   Lv London (Waterloo) 12:27pm, Ar Brussels (Gare du Midi) 4:44pm; Lv Brussels (Gare du Midi) 6:47pm; Ar Copenhagen 8:30am.

London–Cologne–Vienna (via Eurotunnel, train change in Brusels)   Lv London (Waterloo Station) 4:27pm; Ar Brussels (Gare du Midi) 9:25pm; Ar Cologne 12:27 am, Ar Vienna (Westbanhhof) 10:58am.

London–Edinburgh   Lv London (King's Cross) Mon–Sat hourly from 6am to 7pm, Sun hourly from 9am to 6pm. Travel time is an average $4^1/_2$ hours.

TRAINS LEAVING PARIS

ORIENT EXPRESS   **Paris–Munich–Vienna–Budapest** Lv Paris (Gare de l'Est) 7:43pm; lv Strasbourg 11:50pm; ar Karlsruhe 0:58am; ar Munich 4:26am; ar Salzburg 5:53am; ar Vienna 9:25am; ar Budapest 1:08pm.

VIKING EXPRESS   **Paris–Hamburg–Copenhagen** Lv Paris (Gare du Nord) 6:33pm; lv Liège 10:54pm; ar Cologne 0:34am; ar Hamburg 4:43am; ar Puttgarden 6:41am; ar Copenhagen 10:25am.

Paris–Brussels–Amsterdam   Lv Paris (Gare du Nord) 7:52am, 10:25am, 2:45pm, 4:40pm, and 6:39pm; ar Brussels 10:49pm, 1:18pm, 5:42pm, 7:42pm, and 9:10pm; ar Amsterdam 2:02pm, 4:34pm, 9:02pm, 10:48pm, and 11:59pm.

Paris–London (via Eurotunnel) Lv Paris (Gare du Nord) 7:13am, 9:10am, 6:18pm, and 8:13pm; Ar London (Waterloo) 9:20am, 11:09am, 8:13pm and, 10:03pm.

Paris–Barcelona Lv Paris (Gare d'Austerlitz) 7:21am; ar Barcelona 10:10pm. Lv Paris (Gare d'Austerlitz) 9:31pm; ar Barcelona 11:28am.

Paris–Madrid Lv Paris (Gare d'Austerlitz) 6:05pm; ar Madrid 9:50am. Lv Paris (Gare d'Austerlitz) 8:00pm; ar Madrid 8:35am.

Paris–Luxembourg Lv Paris (Gare de l'Est) 8:54am; 10:53am, and 5:16pm; ar Luxembourg 12:31am, 2:36pm, and 8:48pm.

Paris–Rome Lv Paris (Gare de Lyon) 6:47pm; ar Torino 2:48am; ar Genoa 4:39am; ar Pisa 6:27am; ar Rome 9:45am (Termini).

Paris–Geneva Lv Paris (Gare de Lyon) 7:28am, 10:28am, 2:43pm, and 5:27pm; ar Geneva 10:57am, 2:01pm, 6:15pm, and 9:02pm. (This is the TGV train.)

TRAINS LEAVING BRUSSELS

OSTEND–VIENNA EXPRESS **Brussels–Cologne–Vienna** Lv Ostend 8:13pm; lv Brussels (Gare du Midi) 9:25pm; lv Liège 10:35pm; lv Aachen 11:32pm; ar Cologne 12:44am; ar Mainz 1:08am; ar Mannheim 3:19am; ar Würzburg 4:01am; ar Passau 7:29am; ar Vienna 10:58am.

Brussels–London Lv Brussels (Gare du Midi) 7:31am, 5:22pm, and 6:56pm; ar London (Waterloo) 9:43am, 7:39pm, and 9:09pm (all via Eurotunnel).

Brussels–Rotterdam–Amsterdam Lv Brussels (Gare du Midi) 6:10am; lv Antwerp 6:49am; ar Rotterdam 8:01am; ar The Hague 8:23am; ar Amsterdam 9:08am.

Brussels–Paris Lv Brussels (Gare du Midi) 7:04am, 8:00am, 2:13pm, and 6:32pm; ar Paris 9:38am, 11:15pm, 5:05pm, and 8:53pm.

Brussels–Luxembourg Lv Brussels (Gare du Midi) 5:21am, 6:21pm, 8:21pm, and 10:17pm; ar Luxembourg 8:15am, 9:15pm, 11:15pm, and 1:06pm (19 daily connections).

TRAINS LEAVING AMSTERDAM

NORTH-WEST EXPRESS **Amsterdam–Hamburg–Copenhagen–Stockholm** Lv Amsterdam 8:14pm; ar Hamburg 1:50am; ar Puttgarden 3:42am; ar Copenhagen 7:30am; ar Stockholm 3:40pm.

DONAUWALZER EXPRESS **Amsterdam–Cologne–Frankfurt–Nuremberg–Vienna** Lv Amsterdam 8:56pm; ar Cologne 11:30pm; ar Frankfurt 2am; ar Nuremberg 4:35am; ar Vienna 10:58am.

ERASMUS EXPRESS **Amsterdam–Cologne–Munich** Lv Amsterdam 8:56am; ar Cologne 12:22am; ar Munich 7:36am.

Amsterdam–London (via Eurotunnel) Lv Amsterdam 8:25am, ar Brussels (Gare du Midi) 11:30am; lv Brussels (Gare du Midi) 12:31pm; ar London (Liverpool) 2:43pm. Lv Amsterdam 3:25pm; ar Brussels (Gare du Midi) 6:30pm; lv Brussels (Gare du Midi) 6:56pm; ar London (Liverpool) 9:09pm.

Amsterdam–Brussels–Paris Lv Amsterdam 8:53am, 10:52am and 3:52pm, Ar Rotterdam 9:53am, 12:04am and 4:58pm, Ar Brussels 11:38am, 1:52pm and 6:51pm, Ar Paris 2:25pm, 5:05pm and 10:05pm.

TRAINS LEAVING COPENHAGEN

VIKING EXPRESS Copenhagen–Cologne–Paris Lv Copenhagen 9:05pm; ar Cologne 7:57am; ar Aachen 8:48am; ar Liège 9:49am; ar Paris 1:29pm.

NORTH-WEST EXPRESS Copenhagen–Hamburg–Bremen Amsterdam Lv Copenhagen 10:05pm; lv Puttgarden 1:35am; ar Hamburg 4:10am; lv Bremen 4:40am; ar Amsterdam 9:48am.

Copenhagen–Stockholm Lv Copenhagen 9:46am and 1:02pm; ar Stockholm 5:41pm and 9:41pm.

Copenhagen–Vienna Lv Copenhagen 10:05pm; ar Hamburg 4:10pm; ar Nuremberg 2:22am; ar Vienna 7:47am.

TRAINS LEAVING STOCKHOLM

Stockholm–Copenhagen Lv Stockholm 8:12am, 10:18am, and 10:30pm; ar Copenhagen 4:58pm, 6:58pm, and 7am.

TRAINS LEAVING MUNICH

GOTTFRIED KELLER EXPRESS Munich–Zurich Lv Munich 12:14pm; lv Lindau 2:22pm; ar Zurich 4:23pm.

MICHELANGELO EXPRESS Munich–Florence–Rome Lv Munich 9:30am; lv Innsbruck 11:22am; lv Verona 3:14pm; lv Florence 5:42pm; ar Rome 7:45pm.

SKANDIA EXPRESS Munich–Hamburg–Copenhagen Lv Munich 7:28pm; ar Hamburg 3:52am; ar Copenhagen 9:30pm (sleepers and couchettes only).

THE BAVARIA Munich–Zurich Lv Munich 6:14pm; lv Lindau 8:22pm; ar Zurich 10:23pm.

Munich–Innsbruck–Verona–Florence–Rome Lv Munich 8:30pm; lv Innsbruck 10:22pm; ar Verona 2:08am; ar Florence 5:34am; ar Rome 8:15am.

Munich–Venice Lv Munich 11:30am and 11:40pm (sleepers only); ar Venice 6:37pm, and 8:45am.

TRAINS LEAVING VIENNA

VIENNA–HOLLAND EXPRESS Vienna–Frankfurt–Brussels–London Lv Vienna (Westbahnhof) 6:44pm; ar Passau 10:04pm; ar Cologne 4:50am; ar Aachen 5:55am; ar Liège 6:47am; ar Brussels Midi 8:04am; lv Brussels Midi 10:28am; ar London Waterloo 12:39pm.

ORIENT EXPRESS Budapest–Vienna–Munich–Paris Lv Budapest 3:40pm; lv Vienna (Westbahnhof) 7:40pm; lv Salzburg 11:07pm; ar Munich 12:34am; ar Strasbourg 5:01am; ar Paris 9:34am.

THE MOZART Vienna–Paris Lv Vienna 9am; ar Paris 10:22pm (via Munich and Strasbourg).

THE ROSENKAVALIER Vienna–Paris Lv Vienna 7:40pm; ar Paris 9:34am (via Munich and Strasbourg).

Vienna–Venice The *Romulus Express* (lv Vienna 7:18am; ar Venice 3:27pm) is your best train for this trip, but three others that leave Vienna daily for Venice. All depart from the Südbahnhof. For instance, lv Vienna 1:22pm, ar Venice

10:22pm; lv Vienna 8:15pm, ar Venice 4:40am; lv Vienna 10:22pm, ar Venice 8:42am (the last two trains, sleepers only).

TRAINS LEAVING ROME

PALATINO EXPRESS **Rome–Torino–Paris** Lv Rome 7:22pm; lv Pisa 10:27pm; lv Torino 2:13am; ar Paris (Gare de Lyon) 10:16am (sleepers and couchettes only).

MICHELANGELO EXPRESS **Rome–Florence–Innsbruck–Munich** Lv Rome 8:15am; lv Florence 10:19am; lv Bologna 11:26am; lv Verona 1:00pm; ar Innsbruck 4:37pm; ar Munich 6:30pm.

SIMPLON EXPRESS **Rome–Florence–Venice–Trieste–Zagreb** Lv Rome 11:10pm; ar Florence 2:35am; ar Venice 6:28am; lv Trieste 9:15am; ar Ljubljana 1:15pm; ar Zagreb 3:04pm.

Rome–Florence Lv Rome 7:15am, ar Florence 9:10am; lv Rome 8:05am, ar Florence 9:59am; lv Rome 1:15pm, ar Florence 3:10pm; lv Rome 4:05pm, ar Florence 5:59pm; lv Rome 8:05pm; ar Florence 10:15pm (20 daily departures).

Rome–Milan Lv Rome 8:05am, ar Milan 1pm; lv Rome 1:45pm, ar Milan 6:05pm; lv Rome 3:05pm, ar Milan 8pm; lv Rome 5:45pm, ar Milan 10:05pm. (21 daily departures.)

Rome–Lausanne–Geneva Lv Rome Termini 8:05am; ar Florence 10:07am; ar Milano Centralo 1pm, lv Milano Centrale 2pm; ar Brig 4:13pm; ar Lausanne 5:40pm; ar Geneva 6:17pm. (Change trains in Milano.)

TRAINS LEAVING MADRID

PUERTA DEL SOL EXPRESS **Madrid–Bordeaux–Paris** Lv Madrid (Chamarti[ac]n) 6:15pm; ar Paris (Gare d'Austerlitz) 10:34am.

LUSITANIA EXPRESS **Madrid–Lisbon** Lv Madrid (Atocha) 10:30pm; ar Lisbon 8:30am.

TRAINS LEAVING BARCELONA

PAU CASALS EXPRESS **Barcelona–Geneva–Zurich** Lv Barcelona Franca 8:15pm; ar Geneva 5:52am; ar Zurich 9:15am.

C Menu Terms

CZECH

BASICS

snídaně breakfast
øbed lunch
večere dinner
chléba bread

cukr sugar
sul salt
voino wine

SOUP (POLÉVKA)

bramborová potato
čočková lentil
gulášová goulash

rajská tomato
slepičí chicken
zeleninová vegetable

EGGS (VEJCE)

míchaná vejce scrambled eggs
smažená vejce fried eggs
vařená vejce boiled eggs
vejce na měekko soft-boiled eggs

vejce se slaninou bacon and
eggs
vejce se šunkou ham and eggs

FISH (RYBA)

karp carp
kaviár caviar
rybí filé fish filet
sled herring

štika pike
treska cod
úhoř eel
ústřice oysters

MEAT (MASO)

biftek steak
guláš goulash
hovězi beef
játra liver
jehněčí lamb
kachna duck

klobása sausage
králík rabbit
skopové mutton
telecí veal
telecí kotleta veal cutlet
vepřové pork

VEGETABLES/SALADS (ZELENINA/SALÁT)

brambory potatoes
celer celery
chřest asparagus
cibule onions
fazolový salát bean salad
hlávkový salát mixed green salad
houby mushrooms

květák cauliflower
mrkev carrots
okurkový salát cucumber salad
paprika peppers
rajská jablíčka tomatoes
salát z červené řepy beet salad
zelí cabbage

FRUIT (OVOCE)

citrón lemon
hruška pears

jablko apple
švestky plums

DESSERT (MOUCNÍKY)

koláč cake
cukrovi cookies
čokoládová chocolate

jablkový závin apple strudel
palačinky pancakes
zmrzlina ice cream

BEVERAGES (NÁPOJE)

caj tea
káva coffee
mléko milk
víno wine

cervené red
bílé white
voda water

COOKING TERMS

smažený fried

pečený roasted

vařený boiled

grilovaný grilled

DANISH

BASICS

brod bread

ost cheese

salt salt

smor butter

SOUP

aspargessuppe asparagus soup

blomkalsuppe cauliflower soup

gule ærter pea soup

EGGS

æggekage omelet

blødkogt æg soft-boiled egg

hardkogt æg hard-boiled egg

roræg scrambled eggs

spejlæg fried egg

FISH

al eel

helleflynder halibut

hummer lobster

krabber crag

krebs crayfish

laks salmon

makrel mackerel

muslinger mussels

orred trout

pighvar turbot

rejer shrimp

rodspætte plaice

sild herring

torsk cod

MEAT

agerhons partridge

and duck

andesteg roast duck

bof steak

boller meatballs

due pigeon

oksesteg roast beef

dyr venison

fasan pheasant

gaas goose

hakkebof hamburger

kalkun turkey

kalve veal

kylling chicken

lam lamb

lever liver

leverpostej liver pâté

okse beef

flæskesteg roast pork

polser sausages

skinke ham

spegepolse salami

svin pork

tunge tongue

vildand wild duck

VEGETABLES

ærter peas

agurk cucumber

asparges asparagus

blomkaal cauliflower

bonner string beans

gulerodder carrots

hvidkal cabbage

kartofler potatoes

log onions

ris rice

rodkaal red cabbage

rosenkaal brussels sprouts

tomater tomatoes

FRUITS

æbler apples
ananas pineapple
appelsiner oranges
blommer plums

ferskner peaches
hindbær raspberries
jordbær strawberries
pærer pears

DESSERT

budding pudding
hindbær med
  flode raspberries with cream

kager pastry
is ice cream
kompot stewed fruit

BEVERAGES

æblemost apple juice
flode cream
kaffe coffee
mælk milk

ol beer
te tea
vand water
vin wine

COOKING TERMS

farseret stuffed
grilleret grilled
kogt boiled

ristet fried
stegt roast

DUTCH

BASICS

ontbijt breakfast
lunch lunch
diner dinner
boter butter
brood bread
honing honey

jam jam
kaas cheese
mosterd mustard
peper pepper
suiker sugar
zout salt

SOUP (SOEPEN)

aardappelsoep potato soup
bonensoep bean soup
erwtensoep pea soup
groentesoep vegetable soup

kippensoep chicken soup
soep soup
tomatensoep tomato soup
uiensoep onion soup

EGGS (EIER)

eieren eggs
hardgekookte eieren hard-
  boiled eggs
zachtgekookte eieren boiled
  eggs

roereieren scrambled eggs
spiegeleieren fried eggs

FISH (VIS)

forel trout
gerookte zalm smoked salmon
haring herring
kabeljauw haddock
kreeft lobster

makreel mackerel
mosselen mussels
oesters oysters
sardientjes sardines
zalm salmon

MEAT (VLEESWARER)

biefstuk steak
chateaubriand filet steak
eend duck
gans goose
kalkoen turkey
kip chicken
konin rabbit

koude schotel cold cuts
lamscotelet lamb chops
lever liver
ragout beef stew
runder bief beef
spek bacon
worst sausage

VEGETABLES/SALADS (GROENTE/SLA)

aardappelen potatoes
asperges asparagus
augurkjes pickles
bonen beans
bieten beets
erwtjes peas
groente vegetables
komkommersla cucumber salad
kool cabbage
patates frites french fried potatoes

prinsesseboontjes green beans
purée mashed potatoes
radijsjes radishes
rapen turnips
rijst rice
sla lettuce, salad
spinazie spinach
tomaten tomatoes
worteltjes carrots
zuurkool sauerkraut

FRUITS (VRUCHTEN)

appelen apples
bananen bananas
citroenen lemons
druiven grapes
frambozen raspberries

fruit fruit
kersen cherries
pruimen plums
sinaasappelen oranges
zwate bessen blackberries

DESSERT (DESSERTS)

ananas pineapple
cake cake
compôte stewed fruits

ijs ice cream
nagerecht dessert
omelette omelet

BEVERAGES (DRANKEN)

bier beer
cognac brandy
koffie coffee
melk milk

rode wijn red wine
thee tea
water water
witte wijn white wine

COOKING TERMS

gebakken fried
gekookt boiled
geroosterd broiled

goed doorgebakken well done
niet doorgebakken rare

FRENCH

BASICS

petit déjeuner breakfast
déjeuner lunch
dîner dinner
beurre butter

citron lemon
fromage cheese
moutarde mustard
pain bread

poivre pepper
sel salt

sucre sugar
vinaigre vinegar

SOUP (POTAGE)

bouillabaisse fish soup
consommé clear broth
potage à la reine cream of
chicken soup
potage de volaille chicken
soup

potage aux lentilles lentil
soup
potage portugais tomato soup
potage St-Germain pea soup
soupe à l'oignon onion soup

FISH (POISSON)

anguille eel
brochet pike
crevette shrimp
escargots snails
hareng herring
homard lobster

huîtres oysters
maquereau mackerel
moules mussels
saumon fumé smoked salmon
thon tuna
truite trout

MEAT (VIANDE)

agneau lamb
ailes chicken wings
aloyau sirloin
bifteck steak
boeuf beef
canard duck
caneton duckling
cervelles brains
charcuterie cold cuts
chauteaubriand filet steak
chevreuil venison
côtelette d'agneau lamb chop
dinde turkey
foie liver
foie gras goose liver

grenouille frog
jambon ham
lapin rabbit
mouton mutton
oie goose
pot au feu beef stew
poulet chicken
poussin squab
ris de veau sweetbreads
rognons kidneys
saucisse grillée fried sausage
tournedos small filet steaks
veau veal
viande en ragoût meat stew
volaille poultry

VEGETABLES/SALADS (LEGUMES/SALADE)

asperge asparagus
aubergine eggplant
choucroute sauerkraut
choux cabbage
cornichon pickle
crudités vegetable salad
épinards spinach
haricots verts green beans
navets turnips
petits pois green peas
pommes de terres potatoes

pommes frites french fried
potatoes
purée de pommes mashed
potatoes
radis radish
riz rice
**salade de
concombres** cucumber salad
salade de laitue lettuce salad
salade niçoise tuna salad

FRUIT (FRUIT)

ananas pineapple
fraises strawberries
framboises raspberries

oranges oranges
pamplemousse grapefruit
raisins grapes

DESSERT (DESSERT)

compôte de fruits stewed fruit
crème à la vanille vanilla
 custard
fromage à la crème cream
 cheese
fruits frais fresh fruit

gâteau cake
glace à la vanille vanilla ice
 cream
macedoine de fruits fruit
 salad
tartes pastries

BEVERAGES (BOISSON)

bière beer
café coffee
cognac brandy
crème cream
eau water

jus d'orange orange juice
lait milk
thé tea
vin blanc white wine
vin rouge red wine

COOKING TERMS

à point medium
bien cuit well done
farci stuffed
frit fried

meunière, au beurre buttered
rôti roast
saignant rare

GERMAN

BASICS

Frühstück breakfast
Mittagessen lunch
Abendessen dinner
Brot bread
Butter butter
Eis ice

Essig vinegar
Käse cheese
Salz salt
Senf mustard
Zitrone lemon
Zucker sugar

SOUP (SUPPEN)

Erbsensuppe pea soup
Gemüsesuppe vegetable soup
Hühnerbrühe chicken soup
Kartoffelsuppe potato soup
Linsensuppe lentil soup

Nudelsuppe noodle soup
Ochsenschwanzsuppe oxtail
 soup
Schildkrötensuppe turtle soup

EGGS (EIER)

Eier in Schale boiled eggs
Rühreier scrambled eggs

Spiegeleier fried eggs
Verlorene Eier poached eggs

FISH (FISCH)

Aal eel
Forelle trout

Hecht pike
Karpfen carp

Krebs crayfish
Lachs salmon
Makrele mackerel

Schellfisch haddock
Seezunge sole

MEAT (FLEISCH)

Aufschnitt cold cuts
Brathuhn roast chicken
Bratwurst grilled sausage
Deutsches
  Beefsteak hamburger steak
Eisbein pigs' knuckles
Ente duck
Gans goose
Geflügel chicken
Hammel mutton
Hirn brains
Kalb veal
Kaltes Geflügel cold poultry
Kassler Rippchen pork chops

Lamm lamb
Leber liver
Nieren kidneys
Ragout stew
Rinderbraten roast beef
Rindfleisch beef
Schinken ham
Schweinebraten roast pork
Speck bacon
Taube pigeon
Truthahn turkey
Wiener Schnitzel veal cutlet
Wurst sausage

VEGETABLES/SALADS (GEMÜSE/SALAT)

Artischocken artichokes
Blumenkohl cauliflower
Bohnen beans
Bratkartoffeln fried potatoes
Erbsen peas
Gemischter salat mixed salad
Grüne Bohnen string beans
Gurken cucumbers
Karotten carrots
Kartoffelbrei mashed potatoes
Kartoffelsalat potato salad
Knödel dumplings
Kohl cabbage

Kopfsalat lettuce salad
Reis rice
Rohkostplatte vegetable salad
Rote Rüben beets
Rotkraut red cabbage
Salat lettuce
Salzkartoffeln boiled potatoes
Sauerkraut sauerkraut
Spargel asparagus
Spinat spinach
Steinpilze boletus mushrooms
Tomaten tomatoes
Weisse Rüben turnips

FRUIT (OBST)

Ananas pineapples
Äpfel apples
Apfelsinen oranges
Bananen bananas
Birnen pears

Kirschen cherries
Pfirsiche peaches
Weintrauben grapes
Zitronen lemons

DESSERT (NACHTISCH)

Bratapfel baked apple
Kloss dumpling
Kompott stewed fruit
Obstkuchen fruit tart
Obstsalat fruit salad

Pfannkuchen sugared pancakes
Pflaumenkompott stewed
  plums
Torten pastries

Beverages (Getränke)

Bier   beer
Ein Dunkles   dark beer
Ein Helles   light beer
Eine Tasse Kaffee   cup of coffee
Eine Tasse Tee   cup of tea
Milch   milk

Rotwein   red wine
Sahne   cream
Schokolade   chocolate
Tomatensaft   tomato juice
Wasser   water
Weinbrand   brandy

Cooking Terms

Gebacken   baked
Gebraten   fried
Gefüllt   stuffed
Gekocht   boiled

Geröstet   broiled
Gut durchgebraten   well done
Nicht durchgebraten   rare
Paniert   breaded

GREEK

Basics

prono   breakfast
masimerianó   lunch
vradinó   dinner
aláti   salt
avgá   eggs

méli   honey
psomí   bread
soúpa   soup
tirí   cheese
yiaoúrti   yogurt

Fish (Psárl)

astakós (ladolémono)   lobster
(with oil and lemon sauce)
bakaliáro (skordaliá)   cod
(with garlic)
barboúnia (skáras)   red mullet
(grilled)
garídes   shrimp
glóssa (tiganití)
(skáras)   sole (grilled)

kalamarákia (tiganitá)   squid
(fried)
karavídes   crayfish
oktapódi   octopus
soupiés yemistés   stuffed
cuttlefish
taramosaláta   fish roe with
mayonnaise
tsipoúra   dorado

Meat (Kréas)

arní   avgolémono lamb with lemon
sauce
arní soúvlas   spit-roasted lamb
arní yiouvétsi   lamb with orzo
in tomato sauce
brizóla moscharísia   beef or
veal steak
brizóla chiriní   pork steak or
chop
dolmadakia   stuffed vine leaves
keftédes   meatballs
kotópoulo soúvlas   spit-roasted
chicken

kotópoulo yemistó   stuffed
chicken
loukánika   spiced sausages
moussaká   meat and eggplant
(or potato)
païdákia   lamb chops
piláfi rízi   rice pilaf
souvláki   lamb (sometimes veal)
on the skewer
youvarlákia   boiled meatballs
with rice

VEGETABLES (CHORTARLIKÁ)

angúria   cucumbers
bámies   okra
domátes   tomatoes
fassólia   green beans
karóta   carrots
kremída   onions
kritharáki   orzo

láchano   cabbage
maroúli   lettuce
melitzána   eggplant
patátes   potatoes
pipperiés   peppers
sélino   celery
spanáki   spinach

BEVERAGES (POTÁ)

bíra   beer
gála   milk
kafé(s)   coffee
krasí   wine
lemonáda   lemonade

neró   water
neró enfialoméno   mineral
water
tsáï   tea

HUNGARIAN

BASICS

reggeli   breakfast
ebéd   lunch
cukor   sugar
ecet   vinegar
kenyér   bread
méz   honey

mustár   mustard
olaj   oil
sajt   cheese
só   salt
vacsora   dinner
vaj   butter

SOUP (LEVESEK)

gulyasleves   goulash soup
gombaleves   mushroom soup
húsleves   bouillon

paradicsomleves   tomato soup
zöldborsóleves   pea soup
zöldségleves   vegetable soup

EGGS (TOJÁS)

kemény tojás   hard-boiled eggs
kolbásszal   eggs with sausage
lágy tojás   soft-boiled eggs
omlett   omelet

rántotta   scrambled eggs
sonkával   eggs with ham
szalonnával   eggs with bacon
túkörtojás   fried eggs

FISH (HALAK)

csuka   pike
csuka tejfölben   pike with
sour cream
fogas   pike-perch

halászlé   fish stew
pisztráng   trout
ponty   carp
tonhal   tuna

MEAT (HÚS)

barany   lamb
bécsi szelet   wienerschnitzel
borjúhús   veal
csirke   chicken
disznóhús   pork

kacsa   duck
kotlett   cutlet
liba   goose
malacsült   roast piglet
marhahús   beef

nyársonsùlt   shish kebab
paprikáscsirke   chicken paprika
pecsenye   roast

pörkölt   goulash
tokány   ragout

VEGETABLES/SALADS (FÖZELÉK/SALÁTÁK)

bab   beans
burgonya   potato
fejes saláta   green salad
gomba   mushrooms
káposzta   cabbage
paprikasaláta   pepper salad

paradicsom   tomato
rizs   rice
spenót   spinach
uborkasaláta   cucumber salad
vegyes saláta   mixed salad
zöldbab   green beans

FRUIT (GYŰMŐLCS)

barack   apricot
csereszyne   cherries
dinnye   melon

körte   pears
narancs   oranges
szőlő   grapes

DESSERT (TÉSZTÁK)

almás rétes   apple strudel
cseresznyes retes   cherry strudel
csokoládé torta   chocolate cake

fagylait   ice cream
túrós rétes   cheese strudel

BEVERAGES (ITALOK)

barna sör   dark beer
fehér bor   white wine
kakaó   cocoa
kávé   coffee
narancslé   orange juice

sör   beer
tea   tea
tej   milk
viz   water
vörös bor   red wine

COOKING TERMS

agyonsütve   well done
csipős   hot (peppery)
dinsztelve   braised
félig nyersen   rare
forró   hot (in temperature)
főzve   boiled
friss   fresh
fűszerezve   spicy

hideg   cold
közepesen kisütve   medium
nyers   raw
párolva   steamed
sós   salty
sütve   baked
töltve   stuffed
zsírban sütve   deep-fried

ITALIAN

BASICS

colazione   breakfast
pranzo   lunch
cena   dinner
aceto   vinegar
biscotti   crackers
burro   butter
formaggio   cheese
ghiaccio   ice

marmellata   jam
mostarda   mustard
olio   oil
pane   bread
pepe   pepper
sale   salt
sott'aceti   pickles
zucchero   sugar

SOUP (ZUPPA)

brodo consommé
minestra soup
minestrone vegetable soup
pastina in brodo noodle soup

riso in brodo rice soup
zuppa alla pavese egg soup
zuppa di fagioli bean soup
zuppa di pesce fish soup

EGGS (UOVA)

omelette, frittata omelette
pan dorato french-fried toast
uova a la coque boiled eggs
uova affogate poached eggs

uova fritte fried eggs
uova strapazzate scrambled eggs

FISH (PESCE)

acciughe anchovies
aragosta lobster
aringhe herring
filetto di sogliola filet of sole
frutta di mare assorted sea food
gamberi shrimp
merluzzo cold

ostriche oysters
sardine sardine
scampi fritti fried shrimp
sgombro mackerel
sogliola sole
tonno tuna fish
trota trout

MEAT (CARNE)

abbachio baby lamb
agnello lamb
anitra duck
bistecca steak
carne fredda assortita cold cuts
cervello brains
cotoletta alla milanese breaded veal cutlet
fagiano pheasant
fegatini chicken livers

fegato liver
lepre rabbit
lingua tongue
maiale pork
manzo lesso boiled beef
pancetta bacon
pollo chicken
prosciutto ham
reni kidney
rosbif roast beef

VEGETABLES/SALADS (VEGETALE/INSALATA)

antipasto hors d'oeuvres
asparagi asparagus
carciofi artichokes
carote carrots
cavolfiore cauliflower
cavolo cabbage
cetrioli cucumbers
cipolle onions
fagiolini string beans
fettuccine noodles
funghi mushrooms
insalata mista mixed salad
insalata verde lettuce salad
lattuga lettuce
melanzana eggplant
olive olives

patate potatoes
peperoni green, red, or yellow peppers
piselli peas
pomodori tomatoes
ravioli alla fiorentina cheese ravioli
ravioli alla vegetariana ravioli with tomato sauce
riso rice
risotto rice dish
sedano celery
spinaci spinach
zucchini squash
verdura vegetables

FRUIT (FRUTTA)

ananasso pineapple

aranci oranges

banane bananas

ciliegie cherries

frutta fruit

frutta cotta stewed fruit

limoni lemons

mele apples

pere pears

uva grape

DESSERT (DOLCI)

budino pudding

cassata ice cream with fruit

gelato ice cream

macedonia di frutta fruit salad

pasticceria pastry

pesca alla Melba peach Melba

torta cake

BEVERAGES (BIBITE)

acqua water

acqua minerale mineral water

aranciata orangeade

birra beer

caffè coffee

latte milk

limonata lemonade

thé tea

vino wine

COOKING TERMS

al sangue rare

arrosto roast

ben cotto well done

fritto fried

lesso, bollito boiled

PORTUGUESE

BASICS

pequeno almoço breakfast

almoço lunch

jantar dinner

açúcar sugar

alho garlic

azeite olive oil

caril curry

compota jam

manteiga butter

mostarda mustard

pão bread

pimenta pepper

queijo cheese

sal salt

SOUP (SOPA)

caldo verde potato-and-cabbage soup

canja de galinha chicken soup

creme de camarão cream of shrimp soup

creme de legumes cream of vegetable soup

sopa á Alentejano Alentejo soup

sopa de cebola onion soup

sopa de mariscos shellfish soup

sopa de queijo cheese soup

sopa de tomate tomato soup

EGGS (OVOS)

omeleta omelet

ovos com presunto ham and eggs

ovos cozidos hard-boiled eggs

ovos escalfados poached eggs

ovos estrelados fried eggs

ovos mexicos scrambled eggs

ovos quentes soft-boiled eggs

tortilha Spanish omelet

FISH (PEIXE)

ameijoas clams
atum tuna
bacalhau salted codfish
cherne turbot
camarãos shrimp
eiró eel
lagosta lobster
linguado sole
lulas squid

ostras oysters
peixe espada swordfish
percebes barnacles
pescada hake
robalo bass
salmonete red mullet
santola crab
sardinhas sardines

MEAT (CARNE)

bife steak
borracho pigeon
borrego lamb
cabrito kid
carneiro mutton
coelho rabbit
costeletas chops
dobrada tripe
frango chicken
galinha fowl
ganso goose

iscas liver
lingua tongue
perdiz partridge
perú duck
porco pork
presunto ham
rim kidney
salchicas sausages
vaca beef
vitela veal

VEGETABLES/SALADS (LEGUMES/SALADA)

agriãos watercress salad
aipo celery
alcachôfra artichoke
alface lettuce
arroz rice
azeitonas olives
batatas potatoes
berinjela eggplant
beterrabas beets
cebola onion
cenouras carrots
cogumelo mushroom

couve-flor cauliflower
couve cabbage
ervilhas peas
espargos asparagus
espinafres spinach
favas broad beans
feijão bean
nabo turnip
pepino cucumber
salada mista mixed salad
salada verde green salad
tomate tomato

FRUIT (FRUTAS)

abacate avocado
alperches apricots
ameixa plum
ananas pineapple
cerajas cherries
figos figs
framboesa raspberry
laranjas oranges
limão lemon
maçãs apples

melão melon
morangos strawberries
peras pears
pêssegos peaches
roma pomegranate
tâmara date
tâmara date
uvas grapes
toronja grapefruit

DESSERT (SOBREMESA)

arroz doce rice pudding
bolo cake
gelados diversos mixed ice creams
maçã assada baked apple
pastelaria pastry

pêssego Melba peach Melba
pudim flan egg custard
pudim de pão bread pudding
salada de frutas fruit salad
sorvetes sherbets
queijo cheese

BEVERAGES (BEBIDAS)

água water
água mineral mineral water
café coffee
chá tea
cerveja beer
com gelo with ice
laranjada orangeade

leite milk
sumo de fruta fruit juice
sumo de laranja orange juice
sumo de tomate tomato juice
vinho branco white wine
vinho tinto red wine

COOKING TERMS

assado no forno baked
cozdio boiled
estufada braised

frito fried
mal passado rare
bem passado well done

SPANISH

BASICS

desayuno breakfast
comida lunch
cena dinner
aceite oil
ajo garlic
azucar sugar
mantequilla butter

miel honey
mostaza mustard
pan bread
pimienta pepper
queso cheese
sal salt
vinagre vinegar

SOUP (SOPA)

caldo gallego Galician broth
caldo de gallina chicken soup
sopa de ajo garlic soup
sopa de cebolla onion soup
sopa clara consommé
sopa espesa thick soup
sopa de fideos noodle soup

sopa de guisantes pea soup
sopa de lentejas lentil soup
sopa de pescado fish soup
sopa de tomate tomato soup
sopa de verduras vegetable soup

EGGS (HUEVOS)

huevos escaltados poached eggs
huevos fritos fried eggs
huevos duros hard-boiled eggs

huevos revueltos scrambled eggs
huevos por agua soft-boiled eggs
tortilla omelet

FISH (PESCADO)

almejas clams
anchoas anchovies
anguilas eels
arenque herring
atún tuna
bacalao cod
calamares squid
cangrejo crab
caracoles snails
centollo sea urchin
chocos large squid
cigalas small lobsters
gambas shrimp
langosta lobster

langostinos prawns
lenguado sole
mejillones mussels
merluza hake
necoras spider crabs
ostras oysters
pescadilla whiting
pijotas small whiting
pulpo octopus
rodaballo turbot
salmonete mullet
sardinas sardines
trucha trout
vieiras scallops

MEAT (CARNE)

albondigas meatballs
bistec beefsteak
callos tripe
cerdo pork
chuleta cutlet
cocido stew
conejo rabbit
cordero lamb
costillas chops
gallina fowl
ganso goose
higado liver
jamón ham

lengua tongue
paloma pigeon
pato duck
pavo turkey
perdiz partridge
pollo chicken
riñón kidney
rosbif roast beef
solomillo loin
ternera veal
tocino bacon
vaca beef

VEGETABLES/SALADS (LEGUMBRES/ENSALADA)

aceitunas olives
alcachofa artichoke
arroz rice
berenjena eggplant
cebolla onion
col cabbage
coliflora cauliflower
ensalada mixta mixed salad
**ensalada de
  pepinos** cucumber salad
ensalada verde green salad

esparragos asparagus
espinacas spinach
guisantes peas
judías verdes string beans
lechuga lettuce
nabo turnip
patata potato
remolachas beets
setas mushrooms
tomate tomato
zanahorias carrots

FRUIT (FRUTA)

albaricoque apricot
aquacate avocado
cerezas cherries
ciruela plum

frambuesa raspberry
fresa strawberry
granada pomegranate
higo fig

limón lemon
manzana apple
melocotón peach
naranja orange
datil date

pera pear
piña pineapple
plátano banana
toronja grapefruit
uvas grapes

DESSERT (POSTRE)

buñuelos fritters
compota stewed fruit
flan caramel custard
fruta fruit

galletas tea cakes
helado ice cream
pasteles pastries
torta cake

BEVERAGES

agua water
agua mineral mineral water
café coffee
cerveza beer
ginebra gin
jerez sherry
leche milk
naranja zumo orange juice

sangría red wine, fruit juice, and soda
sidra cider
sifon soda
té tea
vino blanco white wine
vino tinto red wine

COOKING TERMS

asado roast
cocido broiled
empanado breaded
frito fried

muy hecho well done
poco hecho rare
tostado toasted

SWEDISH

BASICS

frukost breakfast
middag lunch
supén dinner
brod bread

salt salt
smör butter
socker sugar
vinäger vinegar

SOUP (SOPPA)

ärtsoppa pea soup
buljong broth

grönsakssoppa vegetable soup
kálsoppa cabbage soup

FISH (FISK)

anjovis anchovies
hummer lobster
kolja haddock
karp carp
makrill mackerel

ostron oyster
sill herring
stör sturgeon
torsk cod

MEAT (KÖTT)

anka duck
biffstek steak
fárkött mutton
fläsk pork

gás goose
kalv veal
korv sausage
kyckling chicken

lamm lamb
lever liver
oxe beef

renstek venison steak
rostbiff roast beef
skinka ham

VEGETABLES (GRÖNSAKS)

ärta pea
ärwskocka artichoke
blomkål cauliflower
bruna bönor kidney beans
gurka cucumber
kål cabbage

lök onion
makaroner macaroni
morot carrot
potatis potatoes
rödbeta beet
sparris asparagus

FRUIT

apelsiner oranges
avocado avocado
bläbär blueberries
hjortron cloudberries
körsbär cherry

päron pear
persika peach
plommon plum
smultron wild strawberries
vindruva grape

DESSERT

kakor pastry
russinkaka plumcake

sockerkaka cake
sm–bröd cookies

BEVERAGES

citronvatten lemonade
kaffe coffee
karnmjölk buttermilk
mineral vatten mineral water

mjölk milk
öl ale
te tea
vatten water

COOKING TERMS

kokt boiled
stert fried

ugnsbakat baked
ugnsstekt roasted

D Metric Conversions

Length

1 millimeter (mm)	=	.04 inches (or less than $1/16$ in.)
1 centimeter (cm)	=	.39 inches (or just under $1/2$ in.)
1 meter (m)	=	39 inches (or about 1.1 yards)
1 kilometer (km)	=	.62 miles (or about $2/3$ of a mile)

To convert kilometers to miles, multiply the number of kilometers by 0.62. Also use to convert speeds from kilometers per hour (kmph) to miles per hour (m.p.h.). **To convert miles to kilometers,** multiply the number of miles by 1.61. Also use to convert speeds from m.p.h. to kmph.

Capacity

1 liter (l) = 33.92 fluid ounces = 2.1 pints = 1.06 quarts = 0.26 U.S. gallons
1 Imperial gallon = 1.2 U.S. gallons

To convert liters to U.S. gallons, multiply the number of liters by 0.26.
To convert U.S. gallons to liters, multiply the number of gallons by 3.79.
To convert Imperial gallons to U.S. gallons, multiply Imperial gallons by 1.2.
To convert U.S. gallons to Imperial gallons, multiply U.S. gallons by 0.83.

Weight

1 gram (g)	=	0.04 ounces (or about a paperclip's weight)		
1 kilogram (kg)	=	35.2 ounces	=	2.2 pounds
1 metric ton	=	2,205 pounds	=	1.1 short ton

To convert kilograms to pounds, multiply the number of kilograms by 2.2.
To convert pounds to kilograms, multiply the number of pounds by 0.45.

Temperature

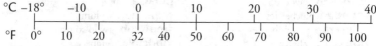

To convert degrees Celsius to degrees Fahrenheit, multiply °C by 9, divide by 5, then add 32.
To convert degrees Fahrenheit to degrees Celsius, subtract 32 from °F, then multiply by 5, then divide by 9.

Index

FREE Worldwide Upgrade

Terms and Conditions: Coupon valid for a one-time, one-car-group upgrade at participating Avis locations in the U.S., Canada, Europe, Africa and the Middle East. For legal reasons, this offer does not apply in Germany. In the U.S. and Canada, this offer is valid on an Intermediate (Group C) through a Full Size 4-door (Group E) car. Maximum upgrade to Premium (Group G). Elsewhere, valid on Group A through Group E. Maximum upgrade to Group F. **Offer valid on daily, weekend and weekly rates** only in the U.S. and Canada, and Standard, SuperValue or Discover Europe rates elsewhere. Offer not available during holiday and other blackout periods. If reservation is for a car with automatic transmission, upgrade car will be an automatic. If reservation is for a car with manual transmission, upgrade car will be a manual. Coupon is nontransferable and nonrefundable. Coupon must be surrendered at time of rental; one per rental. Cars and upgrades are subject to availability at time of rental. **An advance reservation with request for upgrade is required.** Renter must meet Avis age, driver and credit requirements. Minimum age is 25 but may vary by location. Offer expires 12/14/96.

Rental Sales Agent Instructions
Automated Locations In The U.S. And Canada. *At Checkout:* • Assign customer a car one group higher than car group reserved. Upgrade to no higher than Group G. Charge for car group reserved. • In CPN, enter **UULA008.** • Complete this information: RA #_____ Rental Location _____
• Attach to COUPON tape.

Manual Locations In Canada. *At Checkout:* • Assign customer a car one group higher than car group reserved. Upgrade to no higher than Group G. Charge for car group reserved. • Enter **UULA008** in box 15. • Complete this information: RA #_____Rental Location _____
• Submit COUPON to Marketing Department CHQ.

Automated And Manual Locations In Europe, Africa And The Middle East.
• Assign customer a car one group higher than car group reserved. Upgrade to no higher than Group F. Charge for car group reserved. • In AWD, enter **NO43003.** • Check in normally.

Country HQ Handling Instructions
• Submit COUPON to country Marketing Department. • Renting country must absorb cost of promotion. Chargebacks not allowed. • Complete this information: Rental Location_____
Rental Length _____ Days_____
• Car Group Reserved_____ Date_____

© 1995 Wizard Co., Inc. 5/95 DTPS

$15 Off A Weekly Rental Worldwide

Terms and Conditions: Coupon valid for $15 off Standard and SuperValue weekly rates at participating Avis locations in the U.S., Canada, Europe, Latin America and the Caribbean. For legal reasons, this offer does not apply in Germany. In the U.S. and Canada, this offer is valid on an Intermediate (Group C) through a Full Size 4-door (Group E) car for a minimum 5-day rental. Elsewhere, valid on Group B through Group E on Standard or SuperValue rates. May not be used in conjunction with any other coupon, promotion or offer. Offer not available during holiday and other blackout periods. Offer may not be available on all rates at all times. Coupon is nontransferable and nonrefundable. Coupon must be surrendered at time of rental; one per rental. Cars subject to availability at time of rental. **An advance reservation is required.** Taxes, local government surcharges and optional items, such as LDW, additional driver fee and refueling, are extra. Renter must meet Avis age, driver and credit requirements. Minimum age is 25 but may vary by location. Offer expires 12/14/96. Offer valid for $15 USD or equivalent in local currency at current Avis exchange rate at time of rental.

Rental Sales Agent Instructions
Automated Locations In The U.S., Canada, Latin America And The Caribbean. *At Checkout:* • In CPN, enter **MULA036.**
• Complete this information: RA #_____Rental Location _____
• Attach to COUPON tape.

Manual Locations In Canada, Latin America And The Caribbean. *At Checkout:* • Enter **MULA036** in box 15.
• Complete this information: RA #_____Rental Location _____
• At car return, enter amount to be deducted in box 36. Subtract this amount from the totals of boxes 30 through 35.
• Submit COUPON to Marketing Department CHQ.

Automated Locations In Europe. *At Checkout:* • In AWD, enter **NO43007.**
• Enter M, followed by monetary value of the coupon in local currency, in the ADJUSTMT field.
• Submit Certificate with copy 1 of RA to country HQ.

Manual Locations In Europe. *At Checkout:* • In AWD, enter **NO43007.**
• Enter M, followed by monetary value of the coupon in local currency, in the ADJUSTMT box (42).
• Submit Certificate with copy 1 of RA to country HQ.

Country HQ Handling Instructions
• Renting country must absorb the cost of this promotion. Chargebacks not allowed.

© 1995 Wizard Co., Inc. 5/95 DTPS

The Kemwel Group, Inc.
106 Calvert Street
Harrison, NY 10528-3199

FOR RESERVATIONS CALL:

Sleep	1-800-62-SLEEP
Comfort	1-800-228-5150
Quality	1-800-228-5151
Clarion	1-800-CLARION
Econo Lodge	1-800-55-ECONO
Friendship	1-800-453-4511
Rodeway	1-800-228-2000

Advance reservations through the toll free number required. Discounts are based on availability at
participating hotels and cannot be used in conjunction with other discounts or promotions.

Terms and Conditions:

1. Offer is available at participating locations in Europe.
2. Minimum rental period is three days.
3. Reservations must be made in the U.S. prior to departure on an Affordable Europe rate plan, using **PC #66920**. Advance reservation requirement is 8 hours before departure, or 14 days prior to departure for mailed vouchers.
4. Certificate may only be used as an allowance toward rental charges, including optional service charges, such as collision damage waiver, insurance services, refueling, luggage racks, baby seats, etc. paid at time of rental. Offer cannot be applied to charges prepaid before departure.
5. Certificate must be presented and surrendered at time of rental. It is valid one time for a value up to $10. U.S. dollar amount will be calculated in local currency at the exchange rate applicable at time of rental.
6. Certificate can neither be exchanged for cash nor negotiated.
7. Certificate may not be combined with any other offer, discount or promotion. Offer is not available on rentals reserved through tour operators, or on corporate/contract rates.
8. Standard Affordable Europe, intercity rules and restrictions apply.
9. Minimum rental age is 25. All renters must present a valid driver's license held for at least one year prior to rental.

Hertz®

Hertz rents Fords and other fine cars.

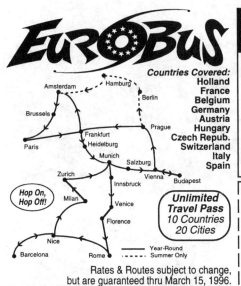

Terms & Conditions

1. Minimum rental is 7 days.
2. Reservations must be made and the rental must be fully prepaid in the U.S.
3. Certificate may be used to reduce DER Car's pre-paid rental rates on any basic or inclusive rental. Certificate must be mailed to DER after reservation is made by phone.
4. Certificate is valid one time only. It cannot be exchanged for cash or negotiated and may not be combined with any other offer, discount or promotion.
5. All DER Car terms and conditions in its car rental brochure apply, including minimum rental age of 25.

Mail to: DER Car   Expires 12/31/96
       9501 W. Devon Avenue
       Rosemont, IL 60018   DER Booking #_____

Name _____

Address _____

City _____ State_____

Zip _____ Phone (_____)_____

J & W NICHOLSON'S
-The Best In London Pubs-
Welcomes You To London

We operate a chain of traditional outlets in both the City and West End that offer an opportunity for you to sample the best in London pubs: traditional ales and lagers, interesting food for a good value, high quality surroundings and, of course..... the warmest of welcomes from all our staff.

In the 4 conveniently located pubs listed on the back of this coupon, we are pleased to offer you

*TWO MEALS FOR THE PRICE OF ONE!

Simply present the voucher with your purchase, sit back and enjoy the experience!

If you would like further information about the range of Nicholson's Houses available for you to visit, simply telephone us at one of the four locations listed on the back.

*You will be charged the price of the higher meal

Expires December 31, 1996

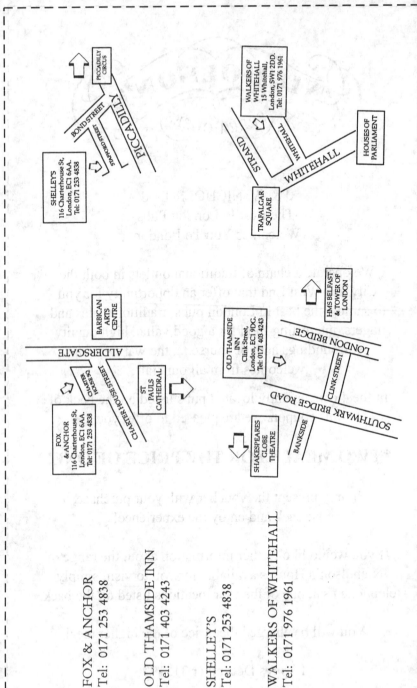

FOX & ANCHOR
Tel: 0171 253 4838

OLD THAMSIDE INN
Tel: 0171 403 4243

SHELLEY'S
Tel: 0171 253 4838

WALKERS OF WHITEHALL
Tel: 0171 976 1961

TRADITIONAL IRISH
MUSICAL PUB CRAWL

Experience Dublin's Famous Pubs & Musical Tradition

£1.00 OFF WITH THIS COUPON

Meet: *Oliver St John Gogarty's in Temple Bar.*
At: *7.30p.m. (every night except Fri).*

Duration: *2 ½ hrs. visiting Gogarty's, Mc Daids, The Clarendon and O'Donoghues.*

From May 2nd - October.

ADMISSION £6.00 INCLUDING FREE SONGBOOK

£5.00 WITH THIS COUPON

Group Bookings & Rates Tel: (01) 478 0191

---

simply the best

Vienna Sightseeing Tours
Wiener Rundfahrten

VOUCHER

-10% DISCOUNT

This voucher entitles the holder to 10% discount on any tour offered by Vienna Sightseeing Tours and can be redeemed only at our office which is located directly at the main departure point - bus terminal 'Wien Mitte' and will not be accepted at any travel agent or hotel concierge. Only one voucher per person can be accepted.
Valid until December 31, 1996.

VIENNA SIGHTSEEING TOURS
WIENER RUNDFAHRTEN

Stelzhamergasse 4, 1030 Vienna/Austria
Tel.:   0043/1/7124683

Now Save Money on All Your Travels by Joining

Frommer's
TRAVEL BOOK CLUB

The Advantages of Membership:

1. Your choice of any **TWO FREE BOOKS.**

2. Your own subscription to the **TRIPS & TRAVEL** quarterly newsletter, where you'll discover the best buys in travel, the hottest vacation spots, the latest travel trends, world-class events and festivals, and much more.

3. A **30% DISCOUNT** on any additional books you order through the club.

4. **DOMESTIC TRIP-ROUTING KITS** (available for a small additional fee). We'll send you a detailed map highlighting the most direct or scenic route to your destination, anywhere in North America.

Here's all you have to do to join:

Send in your annual membership fee of $25.00 ($35.00 Canada/Foreign) with your name, address, and selections on the form below. Or call 815/734-1104 to use your credit card.

Send all orders to:

FROMMER'S TRAVEL BOOK CLUB
P.O. Box 473 • Mt. Morris, IL 61054-0473 • ☎ 815/734-1104

YES! I want to take advantage of this opportunity to join Frommer's Travel Book Club.

[ ] My check for $25.00 ($35.00 for Canadian or foreign orders) is enclosed.
   All orders must be prepaid in U.S. funds only. Please make checks payable to Frommer's Travel Book Club.

[ ] Please charge my credit card: [ ] Visa or [ ] Mastercard

   Credit card number: _____

   Expiration date: ___ / ___ / ___

   Signature: _____

   Or call 815/734-1104 to use your credit card by phone.

Name: _____

Address: _____

City: _____ State: _____ Zip code: _____

Phone number (in case we have a question regarding your order): _____

Please indicate your choices for TWO FREE books (*see following pages*):

   Book 1 - Code: _____   Title: _____

   Book 2 - Code: _____   Title: _____

For information on ordering additional titles, see your first issue of the *Trips & Travel* newsletter.

Allow 4–6 weeks for delivery for all items. Prices of books, membership fee, and publication dates are subject to change without notice. All orders are subject to acceptance and availability.

AC1

The following Frommer's guides are available from your favorite bookstore, or you can use the order form on the preceding page to request them as part of your membership in Frommer's Travel Book Club.

FROMMER'S COMPLETE TRAVEL GUIDES

(Comprehensive guides to sightseeing, dining and accommodations, with selections in all price ranges—from deluxe to budget)

FROMMER'S $-A-DAY GUIDES

(Dream Vacations at Down-to-Earth Prices)

FROMMER'S COMPLETE CITY GUIDES

(Comprehensive guides to sightseeing, dining, and accommodations in all price ranges)

Amsterdam, 8th Ed.	S176	Minneapolis/St. Paul, 4th Ed.	S159
Athens, 10th Ed.	S174	Montréal/Québec City '95	S166
Atlanta & the Summer Olympic		Nashville/Memphis, 1st Ed.	S141
Games '96 (avail. 11/95)	S181	New Orleans '96 (avail. 10/95)	S182
Atlantic City/Cape May, 5th Ed.	S130	New York City '96 (avail. 11/95)	S183
Bangkok, 2nd Ed.	S147	Paris '96 (avail. 9/95)	S180
Barcelona '93-'94	S115	Philadelphia, 8th Ed.	S167
Berlin, 3rd Ed.	S162	Prague, 1st Ed.	S143
Boston '95	S160	Rome, 10th Ed.	S168
Budapest, 1st Ed.	S139	St. Louis/Kansas City, 2nd Ed.	S127
Chicago '95	S169	San Antonio/Austin, 1st Ed.	S177
Denver/Boulder/Colorado Springs,		San Diego '95	S158
3rd Ed.	S154	San Francisco '96 (avail. 10/95)	S184
Disney World/Orlando '96 (avail. 9/95)	S178	Santa Fe/Taos/Albuquerque '95	S172
Dublin, 2nd Ed.	S157	Seattle/Portland '94-'95	S137
Hong Kong '94-'95	S140	Sydney, 4th Ed.	S171
Las Vegas '95	S163	Tampa/St. Petersburg, 3rd Ed.	S146
London '96 (avail. 9/95)	S179	Tokyo '94-'95	S144
Los Angeles '95	S164	Toronto, 3rd Ed.	S173
Madrid/Costa del Sol, 2nd Ed.	S165	Vancouver/Victoria '94-'95	S142
Mexico City, 1st Ed.	S175	Washington, D.C. '95	S153
Miami '95-'96	S149		

FROMMER'S FAMILY GUIDES

(Guides to family-friendly hotels, restaurants, activities, and attractions)

California with Kids	F105	San Francisco with Kids	F104
Los Angeles with Kids	F103	Washington, D.C. with Kids	F102
New York City with Kids	F101		

FROMMER'S WALKING TOURS

*(Memorable strolls through colorful and historic neighborhoods,
accompanied by detailed directions and maps)*

Berlin	W100	Paris, 2nd Ed.	W112
Chicago	W107	San Francisco, 2nd Ed.	W115
England's Favorite Cities	W108	Spain's Favorite Cities (avail. 9/95)	W116
London, 2nd Ed.	W111	Tokyo	W109
Montréal/Québec City	W106	Venice	W110
New York, 2nd Ed.	W113	Washington, D.C., 2nd Ed.	W114

FROMMER'S AMERICA ON WHEELS

*(Guides for travelers who are exploring the U.S.A. by car, featuring a brand-new
rating system for accommodations and full-color road maps)*

Arizona/New Mexico	A100	Florida	A102
California/Nevada	A101	Mid-Atlantic	A103

FROMMER'S SPECIAL-INTEREST TITLES

FROMMER'S BEST BEACH VACATIONS

(The top places to sun, stroll, shop, stay, play, party, and swim—with each
beach rated for beauty, swimming, sand, and amenities)

FROMMER'S BED & BREAKFAST GUIDES

(Selective guides with four-color photos and full descriptions of
the best inns in each region)

FROMMER'S IRREVERENT GUIDES

(Wickedly honest guides for sophisticated travelers
and those who want to be)

FROMMER'S DRIVING TOURS

(Four-color photos and detailed maps outlining
spectacular scenic driving routes)

FROMMER'S BORN TO SHOP

(The ultimate travel guides for discriminating
shoppers—from cut-rate to couture)